lonely planet

P9-CEH-453

England

WITHDRAWN

David Else

Jolyon Attwooll, Charlotte Beech, Oliver Berry, Laetitia Clapton,
Fionn Davenport, Etain O'Carroll

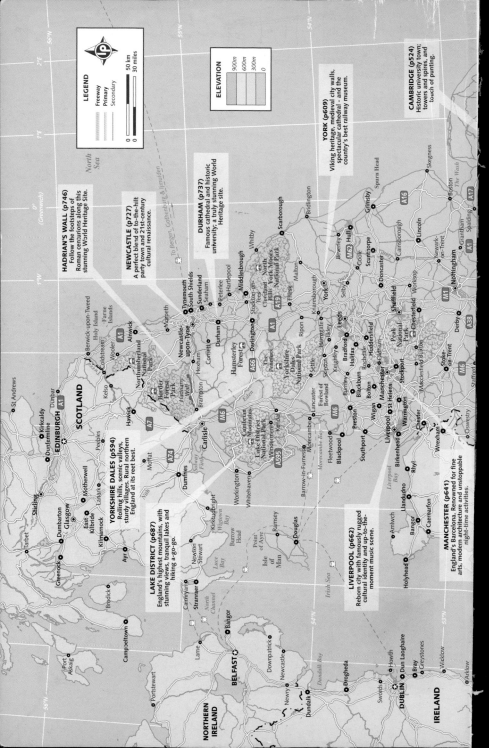

LEGEND

Freeway
Primary
Secondary

0 ———— 50 km
0 ———— 30 miles

ELEVATION

900m
600m
300m
0

CAMBRIDGE (p524)
Historic university town; towers and spires, and touch of punting.

YORK (p609)
Viking heritage, medieval city walls, spectacular cathedral - and the country's best railway museum.

DURHAM (p737)
Famous cathedral and historic university; a truly stunning World Heritage site.

NEWCASTLE (p727)
A perfect blend of to-the-hilt party town and 21st-century cultural renaissance.

HADRIAN'S WALL (p746)
Follow the footsteps of Roman centurions along this stunning World Heritage Site.

YORKSHIRE DALES (p594)
Rolling hills, scenic valleys, sturdy villages. Rural northern England at its reet best.

LAKE DISTRICT (p687)
England's highest mountains, with stunning views, tranquil lakes and hiking a-go-go.

LIVERPOOL (p662)
Reborn city with famously rugged cultural identity and up-to-the-moment music scene.

MANCHESTER (p641)
England's Barcelona. Renowned for fine arts, modern architecture and unstoppable night-time activities.

North Sea

To Bergen, Gothenburg & IJmuiden

SCOTLAND

EDINBURGH

NORTHERN IRELAND

BELFAST

IRELAND

DUBLIN

Irish Sea

North Channel

Isle of Man

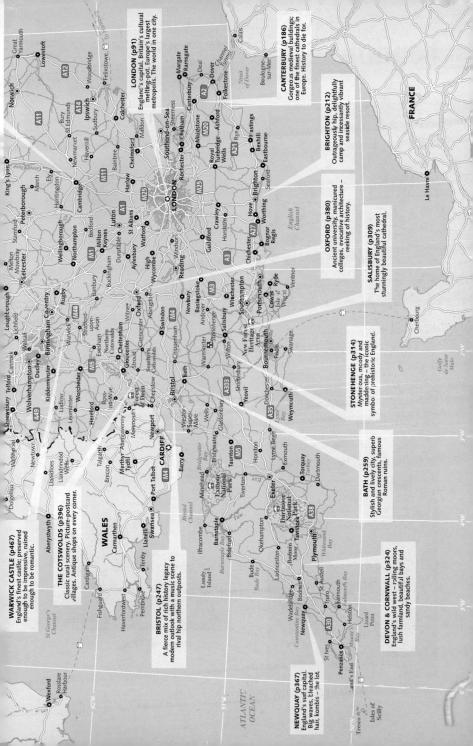

WARWICK CASTLE (p467)
England's finest castle; preserved enough to be impressive, ruined enough to be romantic.

THE COTSWOLDS (p396)
Classic rural scenery. Picture-postcard villages. Antique shops on every corner.

BRISTOL (p247)
A fierce mix of rich history legacy and modern outlook with a music scene to rival hip northern outposts.

NEWQUAY (p367)
England's surf capital. Big waves, bleached hair, kombis – the lot.

DEVON & CORNWALL (p324)
England's wild west – rolling moors, lush farmland, beautiful bays and sandy beaches.

BATH (p259)
Stylish and lively city, superb Georgian crescents, famous Roman ruins.

STONEHENGE (p314)
Mysterious, moody and maddening – the iconic symbol of prehistoric England.

SALISBURY (p309)
The home of England's most stunningly beautiful cathedral.

OXFORD (p380)
Ancient university, manicured colleges, evocative architecture – reeking of history.

BRIGHTON (p212)
Outrageously hip, delightfully camp and incessantly vibrant seaside resort.

CANTERBURY (p186)
Gorgeous medieval buildings; one of the finest cathedrals in Europe. History to die for.

LONDON (p91)
England's capital. Britain's cultural melting-pot, Europe's largest metropolis. The world in one city.

WALES

FRANCE

ATLANTIC OCEAN

London

NEIL SETCHFIELD

Take in the floral aromas at the Columbia Road Flower Market (p158)

GLENN BEANLAND

Wander the superb galleries at the British Museum (p119)

RICK GERHARTER

Rise high above the city on the London Eye (p124)

Southeast England

Visit the beautiful city of Oxford (p380) with its vibrant universities and stunning architecture

Join in the carnival atmosphere at seaside Brighton (p212)

Ramble around the majestic Leeds Castle (p202)

Southwest England

Experience the bracing winter chill in the small towns and villages of the Cotswolds (p396)

MANFRED GOTTSCHALK

Check out Salisbury Cathedral (p309), England's tallest

JON DAVISON

Wander through narrow lanes and past old fishing cottages in Polperro (p352)

CHRIS MELLC

Eastern England

Admire the stunning King's College Chapel (p520) in Cambridge

DAVID TOMLINSON

Fall in love with the exquisitely preserved buildings at Lavenham (p543)

GARETH MCCORMACK

Check out the neat row of beach huts in the getaway town of Southwold (p549)

ROD EDWARDS/ALAMY

The Midlands

Climb to the top of Froggatt 'edge' (p501) for breathtaking views of Peak District National Park

DAVID EL

JULIET COOMBE

Take in a performance at the grand old Swan Theatre (p472) in Stratford-upon-Avon

Admire the incredible interior of the stately old Chatsworth House (p513)

GLENN BEANLAN

Northwest England

Stroll along the dockland development at Manchester's Salford Quays (p647)

NEIL SETCHFIELD

GLENN BEANLAND

Admire the handsome Tudor buildings along the The Rows (p657) in Chester

Hike the 7.5 mile glassy arc of Lake Ullswater (p711)

DAVID ELSE

Yorkshire

Walk through the green pastures of the Yorkshire Dales near Kettlewell (p597)

GLENN VAN DER KNIJFF

CHRIS MELLOR

Be blown away by the awesome York Minster (p611), England's largest medieval cathedral

Pay your respects at the St Mary's Church (p635) cemetery in Whitby

TOM SMALLMAN

The Northeast

Overleaf:
Get out of town and escape the crowds
Chris Mellor

Follow the snaking wall (p749) near House-steads Roman Fort

Step back in time at the historical Bamburgh Castle (p754)

Paint the town red (or pink?) in the trendy bars of Newcastle-upon-Tyne (p727)

Contents

WITHDRAWN

Regional Map Contents

Northeast England p726

Cumbria & the Lakes p686

Yorkshire p576

Northwest England p640

The Midlands p452

Eastern England p515

The Marches p421

Oxfordshire, the Cotswolds & Gloucestershire p379

Home Counties p164

London p96

Wessex p246

The Southeast Coast p181

Devon & Cornwall p326

The Authors

DAVID ELSE
Coordinating Author

As a full-time professional travel writer, David has authored more than 20 guidebooks, including Lonely Planet's *Great Britain* and *Walking in Britain*. His knowledge of England comes from a lifetime of travel around the country – often on foot or by bike – a passion dating from university, when heading for the hills was more attractive than visiting the library. Originally from London, David slowly trekked northwards via Wiltshire, Bristol and Derbyshire (with exile in Wales and Africa) to his present base in Yorkshire. David is married with a baby daughter, who already finds herself tramping over mountains – in a backpack carried by her dad – whenever the sun shines.

My Favourite Trip

While researching this book, I revisited some of my favourite places in England: the Lake District, Yorkshire Dales and North York Moors, three of the country's finest national parks. I combined them into a coast-to-coast jaunt, and just for fun covered the entire distance (with a group of friends) by mountain bike, avoiding roads wherever possible. The route took us from St Bees Head, along the tranquil valley of Ennerdale, through Wordsworth's birthplace Grasmere, across the Pennine Hills via the lovely valley of Swaledale, round the edge of the Cleveland Hills escarpment and along sylvian Eskdale, to finish at Robin Hood's Bay. Great countryside, tough challenge, good company – all the ingredients for a favourite trip. We'll do it again next year.

St Bees Head ○   ○ Robin Hood's Bay

JOLYON ATTWOOLL
The Midlands

Jolyon's earliest childhood memory is of travelling in England as a toddler perched on the top floor of a Manchester double-decker bus. Although his primary school years in Melbourne, Australia, stifled a nascent northern accent, Jolyon's connection to the green and pleasant land had only just begun. Aged 11, he returned with his family to settle in the West Midlands metropolis of Coventry where he has remained on and off for more than two decades. Following stints as a bookseller, web and magazine editor, Jolyon now works as a full-time travel writer. He is most likely to be somewhere in Latin America when away from the Midlands.

LONELY PLANET AUTHORS

Why is our travel information the best in the world? It's simple: our authors are independent, dedicated travellers. They don't research using just the internet or phone, and they don't take freebies in exchange for positive coverage. They travel widely, to all the popular spots and off the beaten track. They personally visit thousands of hotels, restaurants, cafés, bars, galleries, palaces, museums and more – and they take pride in getting all the details right, and telling it how it is. For more, see the authors section on www.lonelyplanet.com.

LAETITIA CLAPTON
London; The Home Counties

Laetitia Clapton was born in London and after growing up in Canada, Cambridgeshire and Shropshire has spent the last ten years happily living in the capital. When she's not exploring the city's shops, galleries, markets and hidden corners, she escapes the smoke of the Big Smoke with weekend breaks in the lush and under-rated Home Counties or further afield. She has always been passionate about travel, studying French and German at Cambridge University, spending a year in Normandy teaching English to adolescents and generally trotting the globe at every available opportunity. These days she makes a living as a freelance writer and publishing consultant.

FIONN DAVENPORT
Yorkshire; Northwest England; Northeast England

Dublin-born and bred, Fionn has been traipsing about his favourite bits of England (north of the Watford gap) for nearly a decade, getting lost in Newcastle suburbs, snowed under in northern Lancashire and mobbed by pensioners in York. All the while he's learnt to love a country so near to his own yet so utterly unknown to most who assume that England is just one giant suburb dotted with roundabouts. His favourite place is the Northumberland coast, followed closely by the Trent House Soul Bar in Newcastle and his beloved Anfield in Liverpool.

ETAIN O'CARROLL
Oxfordshire, Gloucestershire & the Cotswalds

Coming from small-town Ireland, Etain found everything on childhood trips to England exotic: the motorway service stations serving gammon and pineapple; sparkly pens in swanky Woolworths; brightly-lit supermarkets with endless aisles and the cousins with funny accents. She barely registered the castles, abbeys and stately homes in between. Now living in Oxford, the childish awe has become an appreciation for the fine architecture, bucolic countryside and rich heritage of her adopted home. As a travel writer and photographer, Etain still gets her kicks from banal observations on life around the world, but cherished the opportunity to wax lyrical about her favourite spots in her own back yard.

CHARLOTTE BEECH
The Southeast Coast; The Marches; Southeast England

By happy coincidence, Charlotte found herself covering both the Marches region of her birth and her old university haunts in eastern England for this guide. And she was pleased to discover even with rose-tinted specs dutifully laid aside that they were still home to some of the loveliest gems in the country. Now a part-time Londoner and full-time travel writer, Charlotte has penned guidebooks from South America to Asia, but in taking on this book discovered that she relished writing in her own backyard as much as anywhere.

The Authors

OLIVER BERRY   Wessex; Devon & Cornwall; Cumbria & The Lakes

Oliver graduated from University College London with a degree in English and has been proud to call Kernow home for most of the last 28 years. He is always looking for excuses to wander the county's beaches and clifftops – writing a guidebook is the best one yet. For this book he also braved the perils of the traditional British beach holiday, ate cheddar in Cheddar, had a bath in Bath, went in search of Wordsworth & Co and met an unmistakably English assortment of white witches, latter-day druids, Morris dancers, bell ringers, mountain boarders and zorbing instructors on the way. Oliver has received several awards including *The Guardian* Young Travel Writer of the Year.

Destination England

A journey through England is a journey through history – from the ancient megaliths of Stonehenge to the space-age domes of the Eden Project. It's also a trip to the 21st-century: London is gearing up for the 2012 Olympics while cities like Manchester, Leeds and Newcastle revel in their heritage and confidently face the future, with industrial buildings revitalised as waterfront galleries or trendy apartments, flanked by tempting bars, shops, restaurants and some of the finest music venues in the world.

For visitors, the beauty of travel in England is the compact nature of the country. You spend less time going between places and more time *in* them. You get the chance to slow down and get off the beaten track. The chance to relax in a country pub, to enjoy a music festival or watch a cricket match. With time on your side, you'll get closer to understanding local sensibilities.

In the same way, you have time to immerse yourself in the scenery, instead of just breezing through. England is perfect for activity and adventure, whether you're strolling beside the River Thames, cycling in Norfolk, surfing off Newquay or rock-climbing in the Peak District.

The English themselves may take their country for granted, but whether you're from far-flung regions or just exploring your own backyard, this book is for you. We've handpicked the places we think are best, but there's loads more we couldn't fit in. So use this book as a guide – to steer you from place to place – and mix it with making your own discoveries. In England, you won't be disappointed.

Getting Started

Here's a handy slogan to remember while you're planning your trip: travel in England is easy. Granted, it may not be totally effortless, but it's a breeze compared to many parts of the world. In this compact country you're never far from the next town, the next pub, the next national park, or the next impressive castle on your hit list of highlights.

WHEN TO GO

Any visitor to England will soon sympathise with the locals' obsession with weather (see the boxed text Whither the Weather?, p51), but extremes of hot or cold are rare. The key word is *changeable:* the weather can be bad one minute, great the next. It wouldn't be unusual in April, for example, for the morning to be warm enough for T-shirts, lunchtime to be cloudy, a dash of rain and drop in temperature in the afternoon, polished off by a dump of snow in the evening.

Despite apparent randomness, there is a seasonal pattern. Rain falls less often in summer (June to August), and there's normally more sunshine, although there'll be cloudy days too. Conversely, winter (November to February) may enjoy fantastic clear spells between bouts of snow, while spring (March to May) or autumn (September to October) can sometimes produce the best weather of the year. There are also variations over distance: southern England might be chilly, while the north enjoys a heat wave. Or vice versa. Be prepared for anything and you won't get a surprise.

With all that in mind, May to September is undoubtedly the best period to travel in England. July and August are busiest (it's school holiday time), especially in coastal towns, national parks and historic cities like Oxford, Bath and York. In April and October you take a chance on the weather, but avoid crowds, although some hotels and attractions close mid-October to Easter and tourist offices have limited hours.

For winter visits, London and the big cities are an exception – they're busy all the time, with such a lot to see the weather is immaterial. Besides, you're almost as likely to have a damp day in June as you are in January…

For more weather facts and figures, see the climate charts on p768.

COSTS & MONEY

If you're a global traveller, whatever your budget, you'll know that England is expensive compared to many other countries. Don't let that put you off. If funds are tight you'll still have a great trip with some forward planning, a bit of shopping around and a modicum of common sense. A lot of stuff is cheap or good value, and some is completely free. The following gives some guidelines.

DON'T LEAVE HOME WITHOUT...

Travel in England is not like crossing the Sahara or exploring the Amazon. Anything can be bought as you go. Our advice is to take only what you absolutely need, which may include the following:

- rain jacket
- comfortable shoes
- small day-pack (for carrying that rain jacket when the sun shines)
- a taste for traditional English beer
- listening skills and a sense of humour

HALF-PRICE FOR KIDS

Taking your children into museums and historic sites can be absolutely free, half-price, or just a bit cheaper than the adult cost, so we've detailed kids' rates throughout this book (as well as adult prices). At campsites and self-catering hostels, children usually pay about 50% to 75% of the adult rate. At hotels, children between two and 12 years old usually get a 50% to 75% discount. Under this age is usually free of charge, while over-12s (or over-16s at some places) attract the full rate, on the assumption that growing children need a bed and will probably eat as much as their parents.

HOW MUCH?

B&B £20 per person

CD £12

The Times (newspaper) 50p

Restaurant meal £15 per person

Large latte £2

For midrange travellers, basic London hotels are about £50 to £80 per person. Very basic at the lower end of that bracket. Beyond £80, there's more choice, and around £100 gets you something pretty decent for the night, although you could easily spend more. When it comes to eating, a decent three-course meal with wine in a smart restaurant will set you back about £50 per person. Choose carefully and you can still get a great meal (with a glass or two of wine) for around £25. Of course, you can go wild at somewhere outrageously posh or trendy, and not get much change from £125.

Backpackers on a tight budget need £30 a day for bare survival in London, with dorm beds from £15, basic sustenance £10 and transport around £5 unless you prefer to hoof it.

Whatever your price bracket, extras in London might include clubbing (£5 to £10, up to £20 at weekends), a pint in a pub (£2.50 to £3) or admission to museums and galleries (£10 to £20 a day, though many places don't charge).

Out of London, costs drop. Shoestringers need around £25 per day for hostels and food. Midrangers will be fine on £50 to £75 per day, allowing £20 to £30 per person for B&B, £10 to £15 for lunch, snacks and drinks, £10 to £20 for an evening meal. Admission fees are the same for everyone – work on £10 per day.

Travel costs depend on transport choice. Trains can cost anything from £5 to £50 per 100 miles, depending on when you buy your ticket. Long-distance buses (called coaches in England) cost about half the train fare for an equivalent journey. Car drivers should allow £10 per 100 miles for fuel, plus around £5 per day for parking. Rental costs £20 to £50 per day, depending on model and duration.

TRAVEL LITERATURE

There's nothing like a decent travelogue to set the mood for your own trip. The choice of books about travel in England can be daunting, so here's a list of our favourites to add an extra dimension to your planning or help you dig under the English skin a little when you're on the road.

As I Walked Out One Midsummer Morning by Laurie Lee is a classic English travelogue. A young man literally walks out of the time-warped 1930s Cotswolds, then carves out a life in London – before heading off to Spain.

Notes from a Small Island by Bill Bryson, although based on travels in the 1970s, is still incisive. This American author really captures the spirit of England three decades ago. When he pokes fun, he's spot on, so the locals don't mind.

The Kingdom by the Sea by Paul Theroux provides keen observations from another cousin across the pond, although without Bryson's fondness. Published over 20 years ago (when Britain was at war with Argentina), but still worth a read.

TOP TENS

Must-see Movies

Predeparture planning is no chore if it includes a trip to the cinema or a night on the sofa with a DVD and a bowl of popcorn. Our parameters for an 'English' film? Anything about England. Anything which gives a taste of history, scenery or peculiar cultural traits. For reviews of these and other cinematic gems, see p60.

- *Brief Encounter* (1945)
  Director: David Lean

- *Passport to Pimlico* (1949)
  Director: Henry Cornelius

- *Sense & Sensibility* (1996)
  Director: Ang Lee

- *Brassed Off* (1996)
  Director: Mark Herman

- *The Full Monty* (1997)
  Director: Peter Cattaneo

- *Shakespeare in Love* (1999
  Director: John Madden

- *Billy Elliot* (2000)
  Director: Stephen Daldry

- *Bend it like Beckham* (2002)
  Director: Gurinda Chadha

- *Pride and Prejudice* (2005)
  Director: Joe Wright

- *Love + Hate* (2006)
  Director: Dominic Savage

Rave Reads

Travel broadens the mind. Especially if you read before you go. For a taste of life in England, try a few of these novels – from past classics to contemporary milestones. For more details on these and other great books, see p58.

- *Pride & Prejudice* (1813) Jane Austen
- *Oliver Twist* (1837) Charles Dickens
- *Wuthering Heights* (1847) Emily Brontë
- *The Trumpet Major* (1895) Thomas Hardy
- *The Rainbow* (1915) DH Lawrence

- *Waterland* (1983) Graham Swift
- *High Fidelity* (1995) Nick Hornby
- *Brick Lane* (2003) Monica Ali
- *Small Island* (2004) Andrea Levy
- *The Book of Dave* (2006) Will Self

Favourite Festivals

Serious opera, world music or dancing your head off in the rain – whatever you're into, there's a festival to weave your travels around. Here's a list of our favourites. For more details and inspiration see the individual town and city sections throughout this book, and the festivals list on p771.

- Bath International Music Festival (Bath)
  May – see p265

- Brighton Festival (Brighton)
  May – see p216

- Aldeburgh Festival (Suffolk)
  June – see p547

- Mela (Bradford, Yorkshire)
  mid-June – see p589

- Glastonbury Festival (Somerset)
  June -see p284

- Pride (London)
  June/July – see p133

- Womad (Reading, Berkshire)
  July – see p176

- Notting Hill Carnival (London)
  August – see p133

- Reading Festival (Reading)
  August – see p176

- The Big Chill (Herefordshire)
  August - see p436

Lights Out for the Territory by Iain Sinclair is a darkly humorous, entertaining and acerbic exploration of 1990s London, taking in – among other things – Jeffrey Archer's penthouse and an East End gangster funeral.

Park and Ride by Miranda Sawyer is a wry and minutely observed 2001 sojourn through English suburbia, the land of never-ending home improvements and keeping up appearances.

ENGLAND'S WORLD HERITAGE SITES

World Heritage Sites are places of great environmental or cultural significance. There are around 700 sites globally, of which about 25 are in the UK and British Overseas Territories. Those in England include:

Georgian city, Bath (p259)

Cathedral sites, Canterbury (p188)

Dorset and East Devon Coast (p293)

Maritime sites, Greenwich (p129)

Ironbridge Gorge (p441)

Maritime Mercantile City, Liverpool (p662)

Stonehenge & Avebury (p314 & p321)

Tower of London (p121)

Cornwall and West Devon's coastal mining landscape (p349)

Blenheim Palace (p392)

Derwent Valley Mills, Derbyshire (p498)

Castle & Cathedral, Durham (p737)

Hadrian's Wall (p746)

Royal Botanic Gardens, Kew (p131)

Saltaire (p589)

Fountains Abbey & Studley Royal Water Garden (p621)

Westminster Palace & Westminster Abbey (p114)

For more details on World Heritage Sites in the UK and globally, see:

www.icomos.org/uk

www.culture.gov.uk/historic_environment/World_Heritage.htm

http://www.cornish-mining.org.uk/

http://whc.unesco.org/en/list/1215

Two Degrees West by Nicholas Crane describes a walk in a perfectly straight line (two degrees west of the Greenwich meridian) across England, wading rivers, cutting through towns, sleeping in fields and meeting an astounding selection of real people along the way.

Slow Coast Home by Josie Drew describes the globe-trotting cyclist's 5000-mile tour of England and Wales; a cross between a journal of miscellany and a chatty letter to a friend back home.

England in Particular by Sue Clifford and Angela King of the campaign group Common Ground, is not actually a travelogue, but a beautiful and best-selling book described as a 'celebration of the commonplace, the local, the vernacular and the distinctive' and 'a living portrait of England here and now'.

INTERNET RESOURCES

The Internet is a wonderful planning tool for travellers, and there are millions of sites about England. Before plunging into the cyber-maze, try these for starters:

Able to Go (www.abletogo.com) Excellent listings for visitors with mobility difficulties.

Arts Festivals (www.artsfestivals.co.uk) Listing more than 100 festivals around the country; opera, theatre, literature, comedy, classical, folk, jazz and more.

Backpax (www.backpaxmag.com) Cheerful info on cheap travel, visas, activities and work.

BBC (www.bbc.co.uk) Immense and invaluable site from the world's best broadcaster.

eFestivals (www.efestivals.co.uk) News, confirmed (and rumoured) artists, tickets and updates from the lively world of rock, pop, dance and world music gatherings.

Enjoy England (www.enjoyengland.co.uk) The country's official tourism website; accommodation, attractions, events and much more.

i-UK (www.i-uk.com) Official site for all business, study and travel information.

Lonely Planet (www.lonelyplanet.com) Loads of travel news, a bit of merchandise, and the legendary Thorn Tree bulletin board.

UK Student Life (www.ukstudentlife.com) Language courses, and where to go outside study time.

Itineraries
CLASSIC ROUTES

HIGHLIGHTS LOOP
One to Two Weeks/London to Cambridge

Sure, some spots on this unashamed tour of England's top tourist attractions can get crowded, but it's for a reason – they're stunning, enticing or rich in history, so this itinerary is ideal for first-time trippers short on time.

Kick off in **London** (p91), the irrepressible capital brimming with spectacle, then go west to **Winchester** (p225) and **Salisbury** (p309), with their beautiful cathedrals. Next, to a site of older religion: prehistoric **Stonehenge** (p314), while nearby **Avebury Stone Circle** (p322) adds yet more mystic aura.

Carry on to **Bath** (p259), renowned for Roman remains and grand Georgian buildings, then cruise through quintessential English countryside in the **Cotswolds** (p396) to reach **Oxford** (p380), a city steeped in history with famously manicured colleges.

Onwards, ever onwards, to **Stratford-upon-Avon** (p470) Shakespeare's birthplace, then east to **Cambridge** (p517), another ancient university town, for more sightseeing and maybe a gentle punt on the river to recover from your whirlwind tour!

You could do this circuit in a couple of days. But with pauses to drink in the history (not to mention the occasional beer in a country pub), a week is better and two weeks ideal for the whole 400-mile (640km) loop.

ENGLAND'S GREEN & PLEASANT LAND

**Two to Four Weeks/
New Forest to Lake District**

'Did those feet in ancient times walk upon England's pastures green?' mused English poet William Blake. Who knows. But *your* feet certainly can stroll through the meadows or stride across the mountains in England's country-side today.

Start in the **New Forest** (p236), England's newest national park, for a spot of walking, cycling or horse-riding, or just simply relaxing in some country pub gardens. Then strike out west through the rural counties of Hampshire and Dorset to **Dartmoor** (p342) – the highest hills in southern England. Continue west to Cornwall, tempting the traveller with tranquil farmland and a beautiful coast of cliffs and sandy beaches, then north to the rolling landscape of **Exmoor** (p287).

Next stop, the **Cotswolds** (p396), a classic English vista of neat fields, clear rivers and pretty villages with honey-coloured cottages. Then to the **Marches** (p419), the often-overlooked rural landscape between Wales and the English Midlands, to reach the Pennine Hills, 'the backbone of England', and discover the limestone valleys of the **Peak District** (p500), the peaty moors around **Haworth** (p591), made famous by Brontë novels, and the delightful **Yorkshire Dales** (p594), home of Wensleydale cheese.

This itinerary ends on a high – in the glorious mountains of the **Lake District** (p687), home to Scaféll Pike (England's highest point), many other summits and valleys – a picturesque scenery immortalised by another English poet, William Wordsworth.

Free from urban life, this is a tour to replenish your soul and fill your lungs with fresh air. The whole 750 miles (1200km) could easily take a month. Do lots of walking or cycling, and it might be double that.

THE GRAND TOUR

**One to Two Months/
London to Cambridge (the Long Way)**

This is a tour for those who want everything. Begin in **London** (p91), England's lively capital, then head southeast to marvel at **Canterbury Cathedral** (p188). Travel through the chalky South Downs to hip-and-happening **Brighton** (p212) and along the coast to the **New Forest** (p236). Leave time for a ferry hop to the **Isle of Wight** (p240) then go north via the cathedral cities of **Winchester** (p225) and **Salisbury** (p309), and the menhirs at **Stonehenge** (p314), to reach the beautiful Georgian city of **Bath** (p259). Take a short loop to **Wells** (p278), or a longer jaunt into rural **Dorset** (p293) and **Devon** (p327).

Retrace to **Bristol** (p247), then travel through the scenic **Cotswolds** (p396) to historic **Oxford** (p380), spectacular **Warwick Castle** (p467) and Shakespeare's birthplace **Stratford-upon-Avon** (p470). Continue north to **Chester** (p656), **Liverpool** (p662) and **Manchester** (p641) – cities ancient and modern – followed by a change of scenery in the **Lake District** (p687) and a journey back in time along **Hadrian's Wall** (p746) to recently restyled **Newcastle-upon-Tyne** (p727).

Then head south, via the World Heritage-listed cathedral of **Durham** (p737) and the heather-clad **North York Moors** (p628), pausing for breath (or fish and chips) at the jolly resort of **Whitby** (p634) or the ancient Viking capital of **York** (p609). Maybe stop to sample the shopping in **Leeds** (p582) or the nightlife in **Nottingham** (p488) – and end your tour with a final flourish in beautiful **Cambridge** (p517).

This energetic pack-it-in loop is about 1240 miles (2000km) and takes four to eight weeks. If you're short of time, or don't want to rush, just leave out a few places.

ROADS LESS TRAVELLED

NEW ENGLAND   Seven to 12 days/Bristol to Newcastle

'I don't want to change the world, I'm not looking for a new England'. So sang urban troubadour Billy Bragg. Today's traveller can find a new England on this tour of the country's revitalised cities.

Start in **Bristol** (p247), once a poor cousin to grand neighbour Bath, but now a city with fierce pride, rich history and a music scene to rival top northern outposts. Next stop, **Birmingham** (p453), formerly famous for bland 1960s architecture, today oozing transformation with renovated waterside, energised museums and space-age shopping centre. Nearby is **Nottingham** (p488), formerly famous for men in tights, but renowned today for some very merry nightlife.

Then north to fashionable **Leeds** (p582), Yorkshire's shopping heaven, dubbed the Knightsbridge of the North, and voted UK favourite city by readers of *Conde Nast Traveller*. Retail not your thing? No problem. Head for **Manchester** (p641), England's second city and long-time hotbed of musical endeavour, with a thriving arts and club scene, galleries a-go-go, fine dining, dramatic new architecture and – oh yes – a rather famous football team. Nearby is **Liverpool** (p662); the Beatles may be done to death, but here's a rich and genuine musical heritage, not to mention another well-known football team.

And to finish, **Newcastle-upon-Tyne** (p727), now promoted to the outside world along with its neighbouring city as Newcastle-Gateshead – a perfect blend of to-the-hilt party-town and 21st-century cultural renaissance.

In theory you could do this 460-mile (750km) urban odyssey in a week, but England's cities may tempt you to linger longer. Better allow 10 days. Twelve would be even better. Don't say we didn't warn you...

HIDDEN ENGLAND   10 to 14 Days/Cambridge to Berwick-Upon-Tweed

England's best-known national parks and natural beauties are mentioned under Classic Routes (p25). This jaunt leads through less frequented (but no less scenic) countryside.

East of Cambridge lie the tranquil counties of **Suffolk** (p540) and **Norfolk** (p550): explore the coastline of shingle beaches, bird reserves, picturesque harbours and good old-fashioned seaside resorts. Inland you'll find rivers and lakes, pretty villages and endless miles of flat countryside – perfect for gentle cycling.

Then cruise across the even flatter fens of **Cambridgeshire** (p517) and **Lincolnshire** (p563) to reach **Beverley** (p607), a delightfully unassuming town with one of the finest cathedrals in the country, and gateway to the bumpy hills of the Yorkshire Wolds. The wolds meet the sea at **Bempton Cliffs** (p608), where massive flocks of nesting seabirds are one of England's top wildlife spectacles, well worth a stop even if ornithology isn't your thing.

From the coast, head inland, through the heather-covered hills of the **North York Moors** (p628), then north beyond **Hadrian's Wall** (p746) to **Northumberland National Park** (p758) where the Cheviot Hills' wild and empty big-sky landscapes give a taste of the Scottish mountains just over the border. Then go down to the sea again, to the **Northumberland coast** (p750) – famous for beaches and castles, not to mention delicious crab sandwiches – and end with a stroll on the dramatic ramparts of historic frontier-town **Berwick-upon-Tweed** (p755).

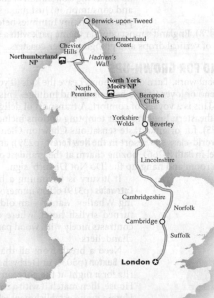

You could see these Cinderella places in seven days, covering about 620 miles (1000km). But allow two weeks if you want to wear your hiking boots, or relax over tea and cake, and catch a little local flavour off the beaten track.

TAILORED TRIPS

ENGLAND FOR KIDS

Are we nearly there yet? Travel through England with offspring in tow needn't be arduous. Certainly not if you visit some of these places.

London (p91) tops nearly every list, but justifiably so – the scope of kid-friendly attractions is mesmerising. Outside London, Bristol has **Explore** (p249) an interactive science museum bursting with hands-on exhibits and lots of action for inquisitive children. **Origins** (p552) is another great interactive museum with hands-on opportunities to flood the Fens.

Warwick Castle (p467) is preserved enough to be stunning, decaying just enough to be picturesque. Knights in armour? You bet. And those of a ghoulish disposition can creep around the dungeons. From here it's a short distance, but a leap across centuries, to the **National Space Centre** (p483) near Leicester, where highlights include interactive cosmic myths, interplanetary travel displays, zero-gravity toilets and germ-devouring underpants. We know why kids love it. And it *is* rocket science.

Hungry after crossing the galaxy? No problem. Head for **Cadbury World** (p458) in Birmingham, a lip-smacking exploration of chocolate production and consumption. Just make sure all those samples settle in tiny tummies before you reach **Alton Towers** (p478), England's most popular theme park with a stomach-churning selection of vertical drops and plunging roller coasters.

ENGLAND FOR GROWN-UPS

Forget about work. Turn off the phone. Leave the kids (if you have them), take a best friend or lover (if you have one), and indulge. This is not an arduous journey. This is a voyage of comfort. A transport of delight.

In southeastern England your tempting options include the Fat Duck at **Bray** (p175); for original taste sensations Chewton Glen Hotel & Country Club, a world-class spa resort in the **New Forest** (p239); and the Royal Crescent Hotel in **Bath** (p266), oozing charm at the grandest of grand addresses. Choose a room and hang up the 'Do Not Disturb' sign.

If luxury is becoming a bit of a habit, the **Cotswolds** (p319) offers numerous choices, including Whatley Manor – an old English mansion turned stylish hotel, where contemporary art contrasts nicely with wood panelling and crystal chandeliers.

Need a break from all that seclusion? Head for **Buxton** (p503), in Derbyshire, and put on the ritz for a night at the gorgeously restored Opera House, then match it with a room at the Old Hall Hotel a grand establishment whose former guests include Mary Queen of Scots.

For more regal flavours, the hotel at the 14th-century **Langley Castle** (p749), near Hadrian's Wall, offers four-poster beds and big sunken bathtubs.

SOUTHERN SEASIDES

Working west to east, here's some of our favourite beaches along the wonderfully varied coastline of southern England. (There are more great beaches in the north too, but no space to list them here!)

Beach-bums and surf addicts love the sandy sweep of **Gwithian** and **Godrevy Towans** (p365) and **Porranporth** (p367), while families and art fans dig **St Ives** (p363). Devon boasts surf-capital **Newquay** (p367) and swimmers' favourite **Croyde** (p341) – among others.

Dorset's coastline tempts with **Lulworth Cove** (p299), sheltered by a near-circle of cliffs, **Weymouth** (p302), a good old-fashioned family-focused resort, **Lyme Regis** (p304), a top spot for fossil hunting, and **Portland Harbour** (p304) for water sports, and the site for the 2012 Olympic sailing races. Yachties also enjoy the **Isle of Wight's** (p240) golden shores, along with the bucket-and-spade brigade.

Meanwhile, **Brighton** (p212) boasts hip beach-front bars alongside family-friendly paddling pools, and **Eastbourne** (p207) delivers mostly sedate silver-haired fun. **Ramsgate** (p195) has abundant maritime history and marina views, while little sis **Broadstairs** (p194) offers traditional Punch and Judy shows and a paddle. Round into the Thames Estuary, **Whit-stable** (p193) cures any cravings for seafood.

And finally, to Suffolk, where charming little **Al-deburgh** (p547) has shingly beaches, fine dining and coastal walks, while wonderfully quaint **Southwold** (p549) offers prom, pier, lighthouse on the High St, and some of the most expensive sheds (sorry, highly prized beach chalets) in the country.

NORTHERN EXPOSURE

Here's some ideas for grease monkeys and fans of large-scale machinery; top attractions from northern England's great industrial heritage.

Ironbridge Gorge (p441) was the crucible of the Industrial Revolution, the 18th century's Silicon Valley, today a World Heritage site boasting 10 fascinating museums. At **Stoke-on-Trent** (p477) the Wedgwood Story Visitor Centre displays space-age robots creating fine bone china, while the Royal Crown Derby factory in **Derby** (p495) provides more ceramic insights.

If china isn't your cup of tea, the Museum of Science & Industry in **Manchester** (p647) revels in the glory of the industrial age, with large-scale exhibitions including machinery from the cotton mills that made the city great.

Just over the Pennines, the prodigious industrial heritage of **Sheffield** (p577) is the subject of the excellent Kelham Island Museum, where highlights include a working steam engine the size of a house. Nearby, science adventure centre Magna celebrates heavy industry and hands-on high-technology, while the National Coal Mining Museum near **Leeds** (p590) offers a rare opportunity to go seriously underground. For another full day out, Beamish Open Air Museum near **Durham** (p741) is a highlight of a visit to Northeast England.

Last stop. All change please. The National Railway Museum in **York** (p614) is an award-winning mix of heritage, nostalgia and sheer gargantuan scale – the perfect place to go loco.

Snapshot

In mid-2006, as we were researching and writing this book, one topic of conversation dominated all others: England's performance in the World Cup. For some, this competition is known as the Football World Cup, or (worse) the Soccer World Cup. But in England it's simply the World Cup, for there is no other global sporting tournament that equals it in importance – especially when the national side does well enough to reach the finals, and *especially* when there's the chance of games against 'old enemies' Germany and Argentina.

As it turned out, the England football team's World Cup performance was less than enlightening, but still nothing unites the English more than sport – although it really helps if the English players are actually winning. Take England's 2005 victory over Australia (yet another 'old enemy') in a little cricket match called the Ashes. In the space of a week, everyone in England became a cricket fan. People who previously wouldn't know leg-before-wicket from silly-mid-off suddenly became experts. Star all-rounder Andrew 'Freddie' Flintoff became a national hero, feted by crowds in Trafalgar Square as the winners toured London by open-top bus. There was a surge of interest as children and adults across the country joined cricket clubs. And the name Freddie leapt up the favourite-name-for-boys charts overnight.

It's the same at Wimbledon in June each year. Everyone becomes a tennis fan, but then Tim Henman gets knocked out and half the country instantly loses interest. It may be the same when the Olympic Games come to London in 2012, although millions of pounds are being invested (or wasted, depending on your view) to ensure national success in the medals table.

But if it's not sport, what else do the English talk about? In the early years of the 21st century, what are the hot topics of conversation in the pubs, clubs and drawing rooms of England?

Top of the list on the political front is the performance of the incumbent Labour government, deep in its third term and facing increasing levels of public discontent as major reforms and increased expenditure in health and education has little impact. Performance-related 'league tables', a concept introduced by the Conservatives and continued by Labour, are a bone of contention. Politicians from both major parties believe competition forces schools and hospitals to excel, and claim their policies mean more choice. But they miss the point: the average patient doesn't want to choose between Hospital A and Hospital B. They just want to go to a place nearby, and they simply want it to be good.

Next on the list of concerns is crime. Although levels of certain crimes (such as violence resulting in injury) are actually going down, relatively low-level local stuff like graffiti, vandalism and nuisance behaviour caused by binge drinking remain serious problems. In response, some shopping centres have banned teenagers wearing 'hoodies' (hooded jackets) and in 2005 the government introduced antisocial behaviour orders (ASBOs), allowing police to restrict the movements of persistent offenders. Thus UK Prime Minister Tony Blair has kept to the first part of his promise to be 'tough on crime, tough on the causes of crime', but while policing expenditure has increased, government funding is in desperately short supply for youth clubs and other activities that might keep kids out of trouble in the first place.

On the up-side, ASBO swiftly entered the English language as a acronym ('I was caught with me spraycan, and had an asbo slapped on me') and has now become a byword for any control device. This, for example, from a

FAST FACTS

Population:
51 million

Size: 50,000 sq miles
(130,000 sq km)

Inflation: 2.5%

Unemployment: 5%

Number of monarchs
since William the
Conqueror: 40

Number of ships launched
by current Queen: 16

Per-person average
annual spend on alcohol:
£1300

Per-person average
annual spend on
takeaway food: £300

Per-person average
annual spend on fruit and
veg: £280

Proportion of people
overweight or obese:
60%

gushing motor journalist: 'a car is so powerful it doesn't just need good brakes, it needs an asbo'.

On more sobering matters, international issues through 2006 were dominated by the Iraq conflict. Reports of impending civil war and an ever-rising death-toll for military personnel plus countless (indeed, uncounted) innocent civilians fill the TV news, and feature regularly in all but the most banal and inward-looking newspapers. Across Britain, there's increasing resentment about the Labour government obediently backing the American-led war, especially as weapons of mass-destruction proved nonexistent and the lack of a post-invasion plan became apparent. There's discomfort too about Guantanamo Bay, where hundreds of prisoners (until recently including several British detainees) are still held in indefinite legal limbo.

In his defence, Tony Blair believes he's doing the right thing, and often echoes US President George W Bush, defending his actions in terms of his faith in God – an argument remarkably similar to Osama Bin Laden's. And while most English people might agree that Saddam Hussein was an evil dictator and a threat to world peace, if that's reason enough to go marching into counties and deposing their leaders, there's surely a long list of other candidates due the same treatment.

So has the 'war against terror' (the first time in history that hostilities have been declared on an abstract noun, as Monty Python comedian and columnist Terry Jones famously noted) made the world a safer place? It doesn't seem so – the bomb attack in London in July 2005 was just one example, giving England it's own 7/7, after America's 9/11, an event all the more shattering when it transpired the attackers were British. How bad have things got, asked the newspaper commentators, how big a rift has been created, when world events inspire disaffected young men to randomly attack hundreds of their fellow citizens?

So with the political scene at home and abroad not looking so rosy, a general air of disillusionment and disappointment prevails, and is perhaps why election turn-outs are so low. In the May 2006 council elections, for example, the average turn-out was around 40% with some areas managing only 25%. In reality, election turn-outs have been dropping since the 1960s (although a postal ballot in 2004 pushed figures up again), but it seems that the English are tired of politicians, or simply don't trust them – whatever their hue. It's a telling indictment that more people vote in TV talent shows than they do for their own political leaders.

That in turn is a symptom of England's ever-growing obsession with fame and celebrity. The popular newspapers carry endless articles about stars from the world of fashion, movies, TV soaps and sport, while celebrity magazines such as *Hello* and *Heat* sell half-a-million copies every week. And it seems the English lap up the stories of the famous-for-being-famous, and love to see pictures of these happy smiling people on the beach, leaving the gym, or – ideally – snorting cocaine, even though their 'celebrity' status is based on little more than the ability to scrub up well, sing a jolly tune or kick a ball in the right direction.

And that brings us nicely back to football. Putting aside politics and world events, the irrepressible English sports fans are already looking forward to 2010's World Cup. Let's hope the national team gets further than the quarter finals next time…

History

It may be a small country on the edge of Europe, but England was never on the sidelines of history. For thousands of years, invaders and incomers have arrived, settled, and made their mark. The result is England's fascinating mix of landscape, culture and language – a dynamic pattern that shaped the nation and continues to evolve today.

For many visitors, this rich historic legacy is England's main attraction – everything from Stonehenge and Hadrian's Wall to Canterbury Cathedral and the Tower of London, via hundreds of castles and an endless line of kings and queens – so this chapter concentrates on the high-profile events and the historic locations you'll see on your travels. Even if you're no fan of dates and dynasties, we hope this chapter will help you get the most from your trip.

The Isles: A History by Norman Davies provides much-acclaimed and highly readable coverage of the past 10,000 years in England within the broader history of the British Isles.

FIRST ARRIVALS

Stone tools discovered near the town of Lowestoft in Suffolk show that human habitation in England stretches back at least 700,000 years, although exact dates depend on your definition of 'human'. As the centuries rolled on, Ice Ages came and went, sea levels rose and fell, and the island now called Britain was frequently joined to the European mainland. Hunter-gatherers crossed the land-bridge, moving north as the ice melted and retreating to warmer climes when the glaciers advanced once again.

Around 4000 BC a group of migrants arrived from Europe that differed significantly from previous groups – instead of hunting and moving on, they settled in one place and started farming – most notably in open chalky hill areas like the South Downs and Salisbury Plain in southern England. Alongside the fields these early settlers built burial mounds (today called barrows), but perhaps their most enduring legacies are the great stone circles of Avebury (p321) and Stonehenge (p314), still clearly visible today.

Built around 3000 BC, Stonehenge is older than the famous Great Pyramids of Egypt.

IRON & CELTS

Move on a millennium or two, and it's the Iron Age. Better tools meant trees were felled and more land was turned to farming, laying down a patchwork pattern of fields and small villages that still exists in parts of rural England today.

ENGLAND? BRITAIN? WHAT'S IN A NAME?

The country of England, along with Wales and Scotland, is part of the state of Great Britain. Three countries in one might seem a strange set-up, and visitors are sometimes confused about the difference between England and Britain – as are a lot of English people. But getting a grip on this basic principle will ease your understanding of English history and culture, and make your travel more enjoyable too.

And just for the record, the United Kingdom (UK) consists of Great Britain and Northern Ireland. The island of Ireland consists of Northern Ireland and the Republic of Ireland (also called Eire). The British Isles is a geographical term for the whole group of islands that make up the UK, the Republic of Ireland and some autonomous or semiautonomous islands such as the Isle of Man. Got all that? Good. Now read on…

TIMELINE	**4000 BC**	**55 BC**
	Neolithic migrants arrive from Europe. Stonehenge built	Roman invaders under Julius Caesar make forays into southern England

As landscapes altered, this was also a time of cultural change. The Celts, a people who originally migrated from Central Europe, had settled across much of the island of Britain by around 500 BC, absorbing the indigenous people. A Celtic-British population then developed – sometimes known as 'ancient Britons' – divided into about 20 different tribes, including the Cantiaci (in today's county of Kent), the Iceni (today's Norfolk) and the Brigantes (northwest England). You noticed the Latin-sounding names? That's because the tribal tags were first handed out by the next arrivals on England's shores…

ENTER THE ROMANS

Think of the Romans, and you think of legions, centurions and aqueducts. They were all here, as Britain and much of Europe came under the power (or the yoke, for those on the receiving end) of the Classical Period's greatest military empire.

Julius Caesar, the emperor everyone remembers, made forays into England from what is now France in 55 BC. But the real Roman invasion happened a century later when Emperor Claudius led a ruthless campaign which resulted in the Romans controlling pretty much everywhere in southern England by AD 50. It wasn't all plain sailing though: some locals fought back. The most famous freedom fighter was warrior-queen Boudicca, who led an army as far as Londinium, the Roman port on the present site of London.

However, opposition was mostly sporadic and no real threat to the legions' military might. By around AD 80 the new province of Britannia (much of today's England and Wales) was firmly under Roman rule. And although it's tempting to imagine noble natives battling courageously against occupying forces, in reality Roman control and stability was probably welcomed by the general population, tired of feuding chiefs and insecure tribal territories.

A History of Britain by historian and TV star Simon Schama is an incisive and highly accessible three-volume set, putting events from 3000 BC to AD 2000 in a modern context.

HADRIAN DRAWS A LINE

North of the new province of Britannia was the land the Romans called Caledonia (one day to become Scotland). This proved a harder place to find a fan club, and in AD 122 Emperor Hadrian decided that rather than conquer the wild Caledonian tribes, he'd settle for keeping them at bay. So a barricade was built across northern England – between today's Carlisle and Newcastle. For nearly 300 years it marked the northernmost limit of the Roman Empire, and today a remarkably well-preserved section of Hadrian's Wall is one of England's best-known historic sites (see p746).

EXIT THE ROMANS

Settlement by the Romans in England lasted almost four centuries, and intermarriage was common between locals and incomers (many from other parts of the empire, including today's Belgium, Spain and Syria – rather than Rome itself) so that a Romano-British population evolved, particularly in the towns, while indigenous Celtic-British culture remained in rural areas.

The Year 1000 by Robert Lacey and Danny Danzinger looks hard and deep at English life a millennium ago. Apparently, it was cold and damp then too.

Along with stability and wealth, the Romans introduced another cultural facet – a new religion called Christianity, after it was recognised by Emperor Constantine in AD 313. But by this time, although Romano-British culture was thriving in what we now call England, back in its Mediterranean heartland the Empire was already in decline.

AD 43	AD 122
Full Roman invasion of Britain led by Emperor Claudius	Hadrian's Wall built

---

LEGACY OF THE LEGIONS

To control the territory they'd occupied, the Romans built castles and garrisons across England. Many of these developed into towns, later to be called 'chesters' and today remembered by names such as Winchester, Manchester, Cirencester and Chester (where the remains of Roman amphitheatres can still be visited). The Romans are also well known for the roads they built – initially so the legions could march quickly from place to place, and later so that trade could develop. Wherever possible the roads were built in straight lines (because it was efficient, not – as the old joke goes – to stop the ancient Britons hiding round corners), and included Ermine Street between London and York, Watling Street between London and Chester, and the Fosse Way between Exeter and Lincoln. As you travel around England today, you'll notice many ruler-straight Roman roads still followed by modern highways, and in a country better known for old lanes and turnpike routes winding through the landscape, they clearly stand out in the map.

It was an untidy finale. The Romans were not driven out by the ancient Britons (by this time, Romano-British culture was so established there was nowhere for the 'invaders' to go 'home' to). In reality, Britannia was simply dumped by the rulers in Rome, and the colony slowly fizzled out of existence. But historians are neat folk, and the end of Roman power in England is generally dated at AD 410.

'In reality, Britannia was simply dumped by the rulers in Rome, and the colony slowly fizzled out of existence'

THE EMERGENCE OF ENGLAND

When Roman power faded, the province of Britannia went downhill. Trade declined, Romano-British towns were abandoned, and rural areas became no-go zones as local warlords fought over fiefdoms. Not inappropriately, the next few centuries are called the Dark Ages.

The vacuum didn't go unnoticed and once again invaders crossed from the European mainland. Angles and Saxons – Teutonic tribes from the land we now call Germany – advanced across the former Roman turf. Historians disagree on exactly what happened next. Either the Anglo-Saxons largely overcame or absorbed the Romano-British and Celts, or the indigenous tribes simply adopted Anglo-Saxon language and culture. Either way, by the late 6th century much of the area we now call England was predominantly Anglo-Saxon, and divided into separate kingdoms dominated by Wessex (in today's southern England), Mercia (today's Midlands) and Northumbria (today's northern England).

Some areas remained unaffected by the incomers (records show that the Celtic language was still being spoken in parts of southern England when the Normans invaded 500 years later) but the overall impact was immense: today, the core of the English language is Anglo-Saxon in origin, many place names have Anglo-Saxon roots, and the very term 'Anglo-Saxon' has become a (much abused and factually incorrect) byword for 'pure English'.

On the religious front, the Anglo-Saxons were pagans, and their invasion forced the Christian religion to the edges of the British Isles – to Wales, Scotland and Ireland. The pope of the time, Gregory, decided this was a poor match, and in AD 597 sent missionaries to England to revive interest in the faith. One holy pioneer was St Augustine, who successfully converted Angles in Kent, and some good-looking specimens were sent to Rome as proof – giving rise to Pope Gregory's famous quip about Angles looking like angels.

597

Missionary St Augustine revives interest in Christianity among the Anglo-Saxons

850

Vikings occupy east and northeast England, making Yorvik (today's York) their capital

Meanwhile in northern England another missionary called St Aidan was even more successful. With admirable energy and fervour, he converted the entire populations of Mercia and Northumbria, and still had time to establish a monastery at Lindisfarne, a beautiful site on the coast which can still be visited today (see p755).

THE VIKING ERA

Just as Christianity was gaining a grip, England was yet again invaded by a bunch of pesky continentals. This time, Vikings appeared on the scene.

It's another classic historical image: blonde Scandinavians, horned helmets, big swords, square-sailed longboats, raping and pillaging. School history books give the impression that Vikings turned up, killed everyone, took everything, and left. There's *some* truth in that, but in reality many Vikings settled for good and their legacy is still evident in parts of northern England – in the form of local dialect, geographical terms such as 'fell' and 'dale' (from the old Norse 'fjell' and 'dalr'), and even the traces of Nordic DNA in some of today's inhabitants.

The main wave of Vikings came from today's Denmark, and conquered east and northeast England in AD 850. They established their capital at Yorvik (today's city of York, where many Viking remains can still be seen), then spread across central England.

Standing in their way were the Anglo-Saxon armies of Alfred the Great – the king of Wessex, and one of English history's best-known characters – and the fighting that followed was seminal to the foundation of the nation-state of England.

But the battles didn't all go Alfred's way. For a few months he was on the run, wading through swamps, hiding in peasant hovels, and famously burning cakes. It was the stuff of legend, which is just what you need when the chips are down. By AD 886, Alfred had garnered his forces and pushed the Vikings back to the north.

Thus England was divided in two: north and east was Viking 'Danelaw', while south and west was Anglo-Saxon territory. Alfred was hailed as king of the English – the first time the Anglo-Saxons regarded themselves as a truly united people.

Alfred's son and successor was Edward the Elder. After more battles, he gained control of the Danelaw, and thus the whole of England. His son, Athelstan, took the process a stage further and was specifically crowned King of England in AD 927. But it was hardly cause for celebration: the Vikings were still around, and later in the 10th century more raids from Scandinavia threatened the fledgling English unity. Over the following decades, control swung from Saxon (King Edgar), to Dane (King Knut), and back to Saxon again (King Edward the Confessor). As England came to the end of the first millennium AD, the future was anything but certain.

1066 & ALL THAT

When King Edward the Confessor died, the crown passed to Harold, his brother-in-law. That should've settled things, but Edward had a cousin in Normandy (the northern part of today's France) called William, who thought *he* should have succeeded to the throne of England.

The end result was the Battle of Hastings in 1066, the most memorable of dates for anyone who's studied English history – or for anyone who

> 'School history books give the impression that Vikings turned up, killed everyone, took everything, and left'

Athelstan, grandson of King Alfred the Great, crowned first King of England	Battle of Hastings – one in the eye for King Harold

hasn't. William sailed from Normandy with an army of Norman soldiers, the Saxons were defeated, and Harold was killed – according to tradition by an arrow in the eye.

William became king of England, earning himself the prestigious title William the Conqueror. It was no idle nickname. To control the Anglo-Saxons, the Norman invaders built numerous castles across their new-won territory, and by 1085–86 the Domesday Book provided a census of England's current stock and future potential.

The arrival in 1066 of William the Conqueror and the Norman army was the last serious land attack on England. To this day, no foreign power has successfully invaded.

William the Conqueror was followed by William II, but he was mysteriously assassinated during a hunting trip and succeeded by Henry I, another Norman ruler, and the first of a long line of kings called Henry.

In the years after the invasion, the French-speaking Normans and the English-speaking Anglo-Saxon inhabitants kept pretty much to themselves. A strict hierarchy of class developed, known as the feudal system. At the top was the monarch, below that the nobles (barons, bishops, dukes and earls), then knights and lords, and at the bottom were peasants or 'serfs', effectively slaves.

The feudal system may have established the basis of a class system which still exists in England to a certain extent, but intermarriage was not completely unknown. Henry himself married a Saxon princess. Nonetheless, such unifying moves stood for nothing after Henry's death: a bitter struggle for succession followed, finally won by Henry II who took the throne as the first king of the House – or dynasty – of Plantagenet.

ROYAL & HOLY SQUABBLING

The fight to follow Henry I continued the enduring English habit of competition for the throne, and introduced an equally enduring tendency of bickering between royalty and the church. Things came to a head in 1170 when Henry II had 'turbulent priest' Thomas Becket murdered in Canterbury Cathedral. (The stunning cathedral is still an important shrine and a major destination for visitors to England today. See p188).

Perhaps the next king, Richard I, wanted to make amends for his forebears' unholy sentiments by fighting against Muslim 'infidels' in the Holy Land (today's Middle East). Unfortunately, he was too busy crusading to bother about governing England – although his bravery earned him the Richard the Lionheart sobriquet – and the country fell into disarray. Richard was succeeded by his brother John, but things got even worse for the general population. According to legend, it was during this time that a nobleman called Robert of Loxley, better known as Robin Hood, hid in Sherwood Forest, and engaged in a spot of wealth redistribution.

RULING THE ROOST

A glance at the story of England's ruling dynasties clearly shows that life was never dull for the folk at the top. Despite immense power and privilege, the position of monarch (or, perhaps worse, *potential* monarch) probably ranks as one of history's least safe occupations. English kings have been killed in battle (Harold), beheaded (Charles I), assassinated (William II), murdered by a wicked uncle (Edward V), or knocked off by their queen and her lover (Edward II). As you visit the castles and battlefields of England, you may feel a touch of sympathy (but only a touch) for those all-powerful figures continually looking over their shoulder.

1337	1348
Start of the Hundred Years' War with France	Arrival of the Black Death – killing more than a third of the country's population

PLANTAGENETS PLOUGH ON

In 1215 the barons found King John's erratic rule increasingly hard to swallow, and forced him to sign a document called Magna Carta, limiting the monarch's power for the first time in English history. Although originally intended as a set of handy ground rules, Magna Carta was a fledgling bill of human rights which eventually led to the creation of parliament – a body to rule the country, independent of the throne. The signing took place at Runnymede, near Windsor, and you can still visit the site today (see p175).

The next king was Henry III, followed in 1272 by Edward I – a skilled ruler and ambitious general. During a busy 35-year reign, he expounded English nationalism and was unashamedly expansionist in his outlook, leading campaigns into Wales and Scotland, where his ruthless activities earned him the title 'hammer of the Scots'.

Edward I was succeeded by Edward II, but the new model lacked the military success of his forebear, and his favouring of personal friends over barons didn't help. Edward failed in the marriage department too, and his rule came to a grisly end when his wife, Isabella, and her lover, Roger Mortimer, had him murdered in Berkeley Castle.

Next in line was Edward III. Highlights – actually lowlights – of his reign include the start of the Hundred Years' War with France in 1337 and the arrival of a plague called the Black Death about a decade later, which eventually carried off 1.5 million people, more than a third of the country's population.

Another change of king didn't improve things either. Richard II had barely taken the throne when the Peasants' Revolt erupted in 1381. This attempt by commoners to overthrow the feudal system was brutally suppressed, further injuring an already deeply divided country.

HOUSES OF YORK & LANCASTER

The ineffectual Richard II was ousted in 1399 by a powerful baron called Henry Bolingbroke, who became Henry IV – the first monarch of the House of Lancaster.

Henry IV was followed, neatly, by Henry V, who decided it was time to stir up the dormant Hundred Years' War. He defeated France at the Battle of Agincourt and the patriotic tear-jerker speech he was given by Shakespeare ('cry God for Harry, England and St George') has ensured his pole position among the most famous English kings of all time.

Still keeping things neat, Henry V was followed by Henry VI. His main claim to fame was overseeing the building of great places of worship (King's College Chapel in Cambridge, Eton Chapel near Windsor – both architectural wonders can still be admired today, see p520 and p173), interspersed with great bouts of insanity.

When the Hundred Years' War finally ground to a halt in 1453, you'd have thought things would be calm for a while. But no. The English forces returning from France threw their energies into another battle – a civil conflict dubbed the Wars of the Roses.

Briefly it went like this: Henry VI of the House of Lancaster (whose emblem was a red rose) was challenged by Richard, Duke of York (proud holder of a white-rose flag). Henry was weak and it was almost a walkover for Richard, but Henry's wife, Margaret of Anjou, was made of sterner mettle and her

Shakespeare's *Henry V* was filmed most recently in 1989 – a superb modern epic, staring English cinema darling Kenneth Branagh as the eponymous king. An earlier film of the same name, staring Laurence Olivier and filmed in 1944 as a patriotic rallying cry, is also worth catching.

forces defeated the challenger. But it didn't rest there. Richard's son Edward entered with an army, turned the tables, drove out Henry, and became King Edward IV – the first monarch of the House of York. (For a slightly longer Wars of the Roses overview, see p642).

DARK DEEDS IN THE TOWER

Life was never easy for the guy at the top. Edward IV hardly had time to catch his breath before facing a challenger to his own throne. Enter scheming Richard Neville, Earl of Warwick, who liked to be billed as 'the kingmaker'. In 1470 he teamed up with the energetic Margaret of Anjou to shuttle Edward into exile and bring Henry VI to the throne. But a year later Edward IV came bouncing back; he killed Warwick, captured Margaret, and had Henry snuffed out in the Tower of London. Result.

Although Edward IV's position seemed secure, he ruled for only a decade before being succeeded by his 12-year-old son, now Edward V. But the boy-king's reign was even shorter than his dad's. In 1483 he was mysteriously murdered, along with his brother, and once again the Tower of London was the scene of the crime.

With the 'little princes' dispatched, this left the throne open for their dear old Uncle Richard. Whether he was the princes' killer is still the subject of debate, but his rule as Richard III was short-lived. Despite another famous Shakespearean soundbite ('A horse, a horse, my kingdom for a horse'), few tears were shed in 1485 when he was tumbled from the top job by Henry Tudor.

MOVES TOWARDS UNITY

The 1955 film version of Shakespeare's *Richard III*, staring Laurance Olivier and John Gielgud, is now available on DVD; a great choice for the award-winning drama of its time, and a view of this turbulent period in history.

There hadn't been a Henry on the throne for a while, and this new incumbent, Henry VII, harked back to the days of his namesakes with a skilful reign. After the York-vs-Lancaster Wars of the Roses, his Tudor family name was important. He also diligently mended fences with his northern neighbours by marrying off his daughter to James IV of Scotland, thereby linking the Tudor and Stewart lines.

Matrimony may have been more useful than warfare for Henry VII, but the multiple marriages of his successor, Henry VIII, were a very different story. Fathering a male heir was his problem – hence the famous six wives – but the pope's disapproval of divorce and remarriage led to a split with the Roman Catholic Church.

Henry became head of the Protestant Church of England and followed this up by 'dissolving' many monasteries – in reality more a blatant land takeover than a struggle between church and state. Authority was further exerted over Wales, effectively a colony since the days of Edward I, with the Acts of Union (1536–43) formally tying the two countries.

THE ELIZABETHAN AGE

Henry VIII died in 1547, succeeded by his son Edward VI, then by daughter Mary I, but their reigns were short. So, unexpectedly, the third child, Elizabeth, came to the throne.

As Elizabeth I, she inherited a nasty mess of religious strife and divided loyalties, but after an uncertain start she gained confidence and turned the country round. Refusing marriage, she borrowed biblical imagery and became known as the Virgin Queen – perhaps the first English monarch to create a

1509–47	1558
Rule of Henry VIII; marries six times, founds Church of England and dissolves monasteries	Elizabeth I comes to throne: enter stage right William Shakespeare and exit due west Walter Raleigh and Francis Drake

cult image. It paid off. Her 45-year reign was a period of boundless English optimism characterised by the defeat of the Spanish Armada, the expansion of trade, the writing of William Shakespeare and Christopher Marlowe, and the global explorations of English seafarers Walter Raleigh and Francis Drake.

Meanwhile, Elizabeth's cousin Mary (daughter of Scottish King James V, and a Catholic) had become known as Mary Queen of Scots. She'd spent her childhood in France and had married the French dauphin (crown prince), thereby becoming queen of France as well. Why stop at two? After her husband's death, Mary returned to Scotland, and from there ambitiously claimed the English throne as well – on the grounds that Elizabeth I was illegitimate. But Mary's plans failed; she was imprisoned and forced to abdicate in favour of her son (a Protestant, who became James VI of Scotland).

Mary escaped to England and appealed to Elizabeth for help. This could have been a rookie error, or she might have been advised by courtiers with their own agenda. Either way, it was a bad move. Mary was – not surprisingly – seen as a security risk and imprisoned once again. In an uncharacteristic display of indecision, before finally ordering her execution, Elizabeth held Mary under arrest for 19 years, moving her frequently from house to house, so that today England has many stately homes (and even a few pubs) claiming 'Mary Queen of Scots slept here'.

UNITED & DISUNITED BRITAIN

When Elizabeth died in 1603, despite a bountiful reign, one thing the Virgin Queen failed to provide was an heir. She was succeeded by her closest relative, James, the safely Protestant son of the murdered Mary. He became James I of England and VI of Scotland, the first English monarch of the House of Stuart (Mary's time in France had Gallicised the Stewart name). Most importantly, James united England, Wales and Scotland into one kingdom for the first time in history – another step towards British unity, at least on paper.

But James' attempts to smooth religious relations were set back by the anti-Catholic outcry that followed the infamous Guy Fawkes Gunpowder Plot, a terrorist attempt to blow up parliament in 1605. The event is still celebrated every 5 November, with fireworks, bonfires and burning effigies of Guy himself.

Alongside the Catholic-Protestant rift, the divide between king and parliament continued to smoulder. The power struggle worsened during the reign of the next king, Charles I, and eventually degenerated into the Civil War of 1644–49. The antiroyalist forces were led by Oliver Cromwell, a Puritan who preached against the excesses of the monarch and established church, and his army of parliamentarians (or Roundheads) was pitched against the king's forces (the Cavaliers) in a war that tore England apart – although fortunately for the last time in history. The war ended with victory for the Roundheads, the king executed, and England declared a republic – with Cromwell hailed as 'Protector'.

THE RETURN OF THE KING

By 1653 Cromwell was finding parliament too restricting and he assumed dictatorial powers, much to his supporters' dismay. On his death in 1658, he was followed half-heartedly by his son, but in 1660 parliament decided to re-establish the monarchy – as republican alternatives were proving far worse.

Elizabeth, directed by Shekhar Kapur (1998) and staring Cate Blanchett, covers the early years of the Virgin Queen's rule – as she graduates from novice princess to commanding monarch – a time of forbidden love, unwanted suitors, intrigue and death.

For chronological lists of English rulers, see the European history section of www.about. com or 'monarchs in the British Isles' at http:// en.wikipedia.org

Charles I wore two shirts on the day of his execution, to avoid shivering and being thought cowardly.

1642–49	1721–42
English Civil War between the king's Cavaliers and Oliver Cromwell's Roundheads	Robert Walpole becomes Britain's first prime minister

Charles II (the exiled son of Charles I) came to the throne, and his rule, known as 'the Restoration' – saw scientific and cultural activity bursting forth after the straitlaced ethics of Cromwell's time. Exploration and expansion was also on the agenda. Backed by the army and navy (modernised, ironically, by Cromwell), colonies stretched down the American coast, while the East India Company set up headquarters in Bombay, laying foundations for what was to become the British Empire.

The next king, James II, had a harder time. Attempts to ease restrictive laws on Catholics ended with his defeat at the Battle of the Boyne by William III, the Protestant king of Holland, better known as William of Orange. Ironically, William was married to James' own daughter Mary, but it didn't stop him doing the dirty on his father-in-law.

William and Mary both had equal rights to the throne and their joint accession in 1688 was known as the Glorious Revolution. Lucky they were married or there might have been another civil war.

For more details on England's rulers through history, see the monarchical website www.royal.gov.uk

UNITED COUNTRY, EXPANDING EMPIRE

In 1694 Mary died, leaving just William as monarch. He died a few years later and was followed by his sister-in-law Anne. During her reign, in 1707, the Act of Union was passed, finally linking the countries of England, Wales and Scotland under one parliament – based in London – for the first time in history.

Anne died without an heir in 1714, marking the end of the Stuart line. The throne passed to distant (but still safely Protestant) German relatives – the House of Hanover – but by this time, struggles for the throne seemed a thing of the past; Hanoverian kings increasingly relied on parliament to govern. As part of the process, from 1721 to 1742 a senior parliamentarian called Robert Walpole effectively became Britain's first prime minister.

A Brief History of British Kings & Queens by Mike Ashley provides a concise and comprehensive overview, with time-lines, biographies and family trees. Good for pub-quiz training too.

Meanwhile, the British Empire – which, despite its title, was predominantly an *English* entity – continued to grow in Asia and the Americas, while claims were made to Australia after James Cook's epic voyage, which began in 1768. The Empire's first major reverse was the American War of Independence (1776–83), forcing England to withdraw from the world stage for a while.

This gap was not missed by French ruler Napoleon; he threatened to invade England and hinder British power overseas, before his ambitions were curtailed by navy hero Nelson and military hero Wellington at the famous battles of Trafalgar (1805) and Waterloo (1815).

THE INDUSTRIAL AGE

While the Empire expanded abroad, at home Britain had become the crucible of the Industrial Revolution. Steam power (patented by James Watt in 1781) and steam trains (launched by George Stephenson in 1830) transformed methods of production and transport, and the towns of the English Midlands became the first industrial cities.

At the same time, medical advances allowed a sharp population increase, but the rapid change from rural to urban society caused great dislocation. For many ordinary people, the side-effects of Britain's economic blossoming were poverty and deprivation.

Nevertheless, by the time Queen Victoria took the throne in 1837, Britain's factories dominated world trade and Britain's fleets dominated the oceans.

1799–1815	1837
Napoleonic Wars; key battles: Trafalgar (1805) and Waterloo (1815)	Queen Victoria comes to the throne; rest of the 19th century seen as Britain's 'Golden Age'

The rest of the 19th century was seen as Britain's 'Golden Age' (for some people, it still is) – a period of confidence not seen since the days of the last great queen, Elizabeth I.

Victoria ruled a proud nation at home, and great swathes of territories abroad, from Canada through much of Africa and India to Australia and New Zealand – trumpeted as 'the Empire on which the sun never sets'. In a final move of PR genius, the queen's chief spin doctor and most effective prime minister, Benjamin Disraeli, had Victoria crowned Empress of India. She'd never even been to India, but the British people simply loved the idea.

The times were optimistic, but it wasn't all tub-thumping jingoism. Disraeli and his successor William Gladstone also introduced social reforms to address the worst excesses of the Industrial Revolution. Education became universal, trade unions were legalised and the right to vote was extended to commoners. Well, to male commoners. Women didn't get the vote for another few decades. Disraeli and Gladstone may have been enlightened gentlemen, but there *were* limits.

WORLD WAR I

Queen Victoria died in 1901 and ever-expanding Britain died with her. The new king, Edward VII, ushered in the relaxed new Edwardian era – and a long period of decline.

In continental Europe, four restless military powers (Russia, Austria-Hungary, Turkey and Germany) focussed their sabre-rattling on the Balkan states, and the assassination of Archduke Ferdinand at Sarajevo in 1914 finally sparked a clash which became the Great War we now call WWI. When German forces entered Belgium, on their way to invade France, soldiers from Britain and Allied countries were drawn into the war – a vicious conflict of stalemate and horrendous slaughter – most infamously on the killing fields of Flanders and the beaches of Gallipoli.

By the war's weary end in 1918 over a million Britons had died (not to mention millions more from many other countries) and there was hardly a street or village untouched by death, as the sobering lists of names on war memorials all over England still show. The conflict added 'trench warfare' to the dictionary, and further deepened the huge gulf that had existed between ruling and working classes since the days of the Norman feudal system.

For the soldiers who did return from WWI, disillusion led to a questioning of the social order. A new political force – the Labour Party, to represent the working class – upset the balance long enjoyed by the Liberal and Conservative parties, as the right to vote was extended to all men aged over 21 and women over 30.

The Labour Party was elected for the first time in 1923, in coalition with the Liberals, with James Ramsay MacDonald as prime minister. A year later the Conservatives were back in power, but the rankling 'them-and-us' mistrust, fuelled by soaring unemployment, led to the 1926 general strike. When 500,000 workers marched through the streets, the government's heavy-handed response included sending in the army – setting the stage for the style of industrial conflict that was to plague Britain for the next 50 years.

The unrest of the late-1920s worsened in the '30s as the world economy slumped and the Great Depression took hold, leading to a decade of misery

Birdsong by Sebastian Faulks is partly set in the trenches of WWI. Understated, perfectly paced and severely moving, it tells of love, passion, fear, waste, death, incompetent generals and the poor bloody infantry.

1914–18	1926
WWI; Britain at war with Germany	General Strike

and political upheaval. Even the royal family took a knock when Edward VIII abdicated in 1936 so he could marry a woman who was twice divorced and – horror of horrors – American. The ensuing scandal was good for newspaper sales and hinted at the prolonged 'trial by media' suffered by royals in more recent times.

The throne was taken by Edward's less-than-charismatic brother George VI and Britain dithered through the rest of the decade, with mediocre government failing to confront the country's problems.

WORLD WAR II

Meanwhile on mainland Europe, Germany saw the rise of Adolf Hitler, leader of the Nazi party. Many feared another Great War, but Prime Minister Neville Chamberlain met Hitler in 1938 and promised Britain 'peace in our time'. He was wrong. The following year Hitler invaded Poland. Two days later Britain was once again at war with Germany.

CHURCHILL

Ask any English person to name a 'great hero of English history' and Winston Churchill will be high on the list, along with King Arthur, Admiral Nelson and the Duke of Wellington – and quite possibly Margaret Thatcher and David Beckham. Sixty years after the end of WWII, Churchill's legacy is undeniable.

Although from an aristocratic family, Churchill's early years were not auspicious; he was famously a 'dunce' at school – an image he actively cultivated in later life. As a young man he joined the British Army, serving mainly in India, Sudan and South Africa, also acting as a war correspondent for various newspapers, and writing several books about his exploits.

In 1901, Churchill was elected to parliament as a Conservative MP, but in 1904 he defected to the Liberals, then the main opposition party. A year later, after a Liberal election victory, he became a government minister, then worked his way up through the ranks, including Minister of Munitions in WWI, before rejoining the Conservatives in 1922. Through the rest of the 1920s, Churchill held various ministerial positions. Highpoints of this period included alleged plans in 1926 to combat striking coal miners with machine-gun-wielding troops and calling Mussolini a 'genius', a sobriquet trumped in 1929 by his reference to Ghandi as 'a half-naked fakir'.

The 1930s were quiet on the political front for Churchill – apart from his criticism of Prime Minister Neville Chamberlain's 'appeasement' of Hitler and his call for British rearmament to face a growing German threat – so he concentrated on writing. His multivolume *History of the English-Speaking Peoples* was drafted during this period; although biased and flawed by modern standards, it remains his best-known work.

In 1939, Britain entered WWII and by 1940 Churchill was prime minister, taking additional responsibility as minister of defence. Hitler had expected an easy victory, but Churchill's extraordinary dedication (not to mention his radio speeches – most famously offering 'nothing but blood, toil, sweat and tears' and promising to 'fight on the beaches') inspired the British people to resist. Between July and October 1940 the Royal Air Force withstood Germany's aerial raids to win what became known as the Battle of Britain – a major turning point in the war, and a chance for land forces to rebuild their strength. It was an audacious strategy, but it paid off and Churchill became a national hero – a position he held to the end of the war, and still holds today.

It was an audacious strategy, but it paid off and Churchill was lauded as a national hero – praise that continued to the end of the war and until his death in 1965, and an honour he still holds today.

1939–45	1948
WWII; Britain at war with Germany – again	National Health Service founded

The German army moved with astonishing speed, swept west through France, and pushed back British forces to the beaches of Dunkirk in northern France in June 1940. An extraordinary flotilla of rescue vessels turned total disaster into a brave defeat – and Dunkirk Day is still remembered with pride and sadness in Britain every year.

By mid-1940 most of Europe was controlled by Germany. In Russia, Stalin had negotiated a peace agreement. The USA was neutral, leaving Britain virtually isolated. Neville Chamberlain, reviled for his earlier 'appeasement', stood aside to let a new prime minister – Winston Churchill – lead a coalition government. (See box for more Churchillian details.)

In 1941 the tide began to turn as the USA entered the war to support Britain, and Germany became bogged down on the eastern front fighting Russia. The following year, British forces were revitalised thanks to Churchill's focus on arms manufacturing, and the Germans were defeated in North Africa.

By 1944 Germany was in retreat. Britain and the USA controlled the skies, Russia's Red Army pushed back from the east, and the Allies were again on the beaches of France as the Normandy landings (D-Day, as it's better remembered) marked the start of the liberation of Europe from the west, and in Churchill's words, 'the beginning of the end of the war'. By 1945 Hitler was dead, and his country ruined. Two atomic bombs forced the surrender of Germany's allies Japan, and finally brought WWII to a dramatic and terrible close.

> The Normandy landings was the largest military armada in history; over 5000 ships were involved, with hundreds of thousands of troops landed in the space of about four days.

SWINGING & SLIDING

In Britain, despite the victory, there was an unexpected swing on the political front. An electorate tired of war and hungry for change tumbled Churchill's Conservatives, and voted in the Labour Party, led by Clement Attlee. This was the dawn of the 'welfare state'; key industries (such as steel, coal and railways) were nationalised, and the National Health Service was founded. But rebuilding Britain was a slow process, and the postwar 'baby boomers' experienced food rationing well into the 1950s.

The effects of depleted reserves were felt overseas too, as one by one the colonies became independent, including India and Pakistan in 1947, Malaya in 1957 and Kenya in 1963. People from these ex-colonies – and especially from the Caribbean – were drawn to the mother country through the 1960s. In many cases they were specifically invited, as additional labour was needed to help rebuild postwar Britain. In the 1970s many immigrants of Asian origin arrived, after being forced out of Uganda by dictator Idi Amin.

In the Empire the sun was setting, but Britain's royal family was still going strong. In 1952 George VI was succeeded by his daughter Elizabeth II, and following the trend set by earlier queens Elizabeth I and Victoria, she has remained on the throne for more than five decades, overseeing a period of massive social and economic change.

By the late 1950s, recovery was strong enough for Prime Minister Harold Macmillan to famously remind the British people they'd 'never had it so good'. Some saw this as a boast for a confident future, others as a warning about difficult times ahead, but most probably forgot all about it because by this time the 1960s had started and grey old England was suddenly more fun and lively than it had been for generations – especially if you were over 10 and under 30. There was the music of the Beatles, the Rolling Stones, Cliff

1952	1963
Queen Elizabeth II comes to the throne	The Beatles become household names. Outbreak of incurable Beatlemania

Richard and the Shadows, while cinema audiences flocked to see Michael Caine, Peter Sellers and Glenda Jackson.

Alongside the glamour, 1960s business seemed swinging too. But the 1970s brought inflation, the oil crisis and international competition – a deadly combination that revealed the weakness of Britain's economy, and a lot that was rotten in British society too. The ongoing struggle between disgruntled working classes and inept ruling classes was brought to the boil once again; the rest of the decade was marked by strikes, disputes and general all-round gloom – especially when the electricity was cut, as power stations went short of fuel or labour.

Neither the Conservatives under Edward Heath, nor Labour under Harold Wilson and Jim Callaghan, proved capable of controlling the strife. The British public had had enough, and the elections of 1979 returned the Conservatives led by a little-known politician named Margaret Thatcher.

THE THATCHER YEARS

Soon everyone had heard of Mrs Thatcher. Love her or hate her, no-one could argue that her methods weren't dramatic. British workers were Luddites? She fired them. Trade unions archaic? She smashed them. British industry inefficient? She shut it down. Nationalised companies a mistake? She sold them off – with a sense of purpose that made Henry VIII's dissolution of the monasteries seem like a Sunday-school picnic.

And just in case there was any doubt about Mrs Thatcher's patriotism, in 1982 she led Britain into war against Argentina in a dispute over the Falkland Islands, leading to a bout of public flag-waving which hadn't been seen since WWII, or probably since Agincourt.

By economic measures, Mrs Thatcher's policies were mostly successful, but by social measures they were a failure. The new, competitive Britain was also a greatly polarised Britain. Once again a trench formed, but not between the classes; this time it was between the people who gained from the prosperous wave of Thatcherism and those left drowning in its wake – not only jobless, but jobless in a harsh environment. Even Thatcher fans were unhappy about the brutal and uncompromising methods favoured by the 'iron lady', but by 1988 she was the longest-serving British prime minister of the 20th century, although her repeated electoral victories were helped considerably by the Labour Party's total incompetence and destructive internal struggles.

Things Can Only Get Better by John O'Farrell is a witty, self-deprecating tale of politics in the 1980s and early '90s – the era of Thatcher and Conservative domination – from a struggling Labour viewpoint.

STAND DOWN MARGARET, HELLO TONY

When any leader believes they're invincible, it's time to go. In 1990 Mrs Thatcher was finally dumped when her introduction of the hugely unpopular 'poll tax' breached even the Conservatives' limits of tolerance. The voters regarded Labour with even more suspicion, however, allowing new Conservative leader John Major to unexpectedly win the 1992 election.

Another half-decade of political stalemate followed, as the Conservatives imploded and Labour was rebuilt on the sidelines. It all came to a head in 1997 when 'New' Labour swept to power with a record parliamentary majority, under a fresh-faced new leader called Tony Blair. After nearly 18 years of Conservative rule, it really seemed that Labour's victory call ('things can only get better') was true – and some people literally danced in the street when the results were announced.

1979	1982
Margaret Thatcher elected prime minister	Britain at war with Argentina over the Falkland Islands

DRINKING IN HISTORY

As you travel around England, in between visits to castles and cathedrals, you'll probably visit a few pubs, where you can't fail to notice the splendid selection of pub names, often illustrated with attractive signboards. In days gone by, these signs were vital because most of the ale-swilling populace couldn't read. In our more literate era, pub signs are still a feature of the landscape, and remain as much a part of English history as medieval churches or fine stately homes.

Many pub names have connections to royalty. The most popular is the Red Lion, with over 500 pubs in England bearing this title. It dates from the early 17th century, when King James VI of Scotland became King James I of England. Lest the populace forget his origin, he ordered that the lion, his heraldic symbol, be displayed in public places.

The second-most popular pub name is The Crown, which has more obvious royal connections, while the third-most popular, the Royal Oak, recalls the days when King Charles II escaped Cromwell's republican army by hiding in a tree. (Look hard at most Royal Oak pub signs and you'll see his face peeping out from between the leaves.)

The King's Arms is another popular pub name with clear royal connections, as is the Queen's Head, the Prince of Wales and so on. Less obvious is the White Hart – the heraldic symbol of Richard II, who in 1393 decreed that every pub should display a sign to distinguish it from other buildings. The decree rounded off by saying anyone failing in this duty 'shall forfeit his ale', so many landlords chose the White Hart as a sign of allegiance, and an insurance against stock loss.

Another common pub name is the Rose and Crown. Again, the regal links are obvious, but look carefully at the colour of the rose painted on those signs, especially if you're in the north of England. West of the Pennine Hills it should be the red rose of the House of Lancaster; east of the Pennines it's the white rose depicting the House of York. Woe betide any pub sign that is sporting the wrong colour!

While some pub names crop up in their hundreds, others are far from common, although many still have links to history. Nottingham's most famous pub, Ye Olde Trip to Jerusalem, commemorates knights and soldiers departing for crusades in the Holy Land in the 12th century. Pub names such as the George and Dragon may date from the same era – as a story brought back from the east by returning crusaders. Move on several centuries and pub names such as the Spitfire, the Lancaster or the Churchill recall the days of WWII.

For a more local perspective, the Nobody Inn near Exeter in Devon is said to recall a mix-up over a coffin, a pub called the Hit or Miss near Chippenham in Wiltshire recalls a close-run game of village cricket, while the Quiet Woman near Buxton in Derbyshire, with a sign of a headless female, is a reminder of more chauvinistic times.

NEW LABOUR, NEW MILLENNIUM

Tony Blair enjoyed an extended honeymoon period, and the next election (in 2001) was another New Labour walkover. On the opposition benches the Conservatives replaced John Major with a succession of leaders – none of whom enjoyed enough support from their party or the British public to stay around for long – allowing Mr Blair to remain at the helm of government for another half-decade.

In the election of 2005, Labour won a historic third term, although with a reduced majority of around 350 seats in parliament (to 200 for the Conservatives, 60 for the Liberal Democrats, and around 30 for the other parties), and by 2006 Tony Blair was in his 12th year as party leader, ninth as prime minister, and the longest-serving prime minister from the Labour Party in British history. But the honeymoon years must have seemed a distant

1990	1997
Thatcher ousted as leader of the Conservative party	'New' Labour under Tony Blair wins general election, ending 18 years of Conservative rule

memory as Mr Blair and his ministers were forced to deal with a seemingly unending string of problems and controversies.

Top of the list was the on-going war in Iraq, the legal limbo of Guantanamo Bay (called a 'symbol of injustice' by Britain's own Attorney General) and the threat of international terrorism, brought so shockingly to the surface in England on 7 July 2005, when bombers attacked underground trains and a bus, killing 52 commuters. Other international issues include the expansion of the European Union to include the former Eastern-bloc countries, always linked in the public mind to the 'threat' of economic migrants and asylum seekers coming to England's shores. This overlapped into a controversy surrounding foreign criminals remaining in the country – rather than being repatriated – on release from prison, in turn leading to ministerial reshuffles and numerous knee-jerk reactions that failed to get to the root of the problem: ineffective long-term 'joined-up' government.

Also on the home front, the nation's education and health systems – despite billions of pounds of expenditure – appeared in constant crisis, while the controversy about the revival of Britain's nuclear power industry (promoted as a solution to the problem of global warming) gained increasing momentum. Meanwhile, revelations that civil honours, or even seats in the House of Lords, were being awarded to business leaders who just happened to be donors to the Labour party resurrected the 'Tony's cronies' debate, although delving by the media also revealed that the Conservatives were little different in their fund-raising tactics.

Windrush – The Irresistible Rise of Multi-Racial Britain by Mike and Trevor Phillips traces the history of Britain's West Indian immigrants – from the first arrivals in 1949 (on the merchant ship *Empire Windrush*) to their descendants living in our own time.

But by mid-2006 Tony Blair seemed determined to face the issues and work through to the end of his third term, with political commentators frequently citing the prime minister's desire to leave a 'legacy' on his departure – be it a peaceful Iraq, a re-energised National Health Service, or maybe the completion of his plans for 200 super-schools called City Academies to be built across the country.

Whatever his plans, Mr Blair has made it clear that he'll resign before the next election, so that a new leader can lead the battle to win a fourth term for Labour. Gordon Brown, the current Chancellor of the Exchequer (the British term for Minister of Finance) and so long the prime-minister-in-waiting, may finally get the top job, but his opportunity may have passed, as other young guns are waiting in the wings.

Outside of government, the Conservatives elected David Cameron as their party leader in December 2005, and Sir Menzies Campbell became leader of the Liberal Democrats in March 2006. This means all three major parties will enter the next election (expected in 2009, and due by 2010 at the latest) with new leaders.

It remains to be seen if the voters will award Labour with yet another term in office, or if the combination of terrible events overseas and mismanagement at home will mean the political pendulum finally swings back the other way.

2003	2005
Britain joins the US-led invasion of Iraq	Tony Blair and Labour re-elected for third term

The Culture

THE NATIONAL PSYCHE

It's difficult to generalise about an English national psyche or homogenous trait, as – perhaps unexpectedly – many English people have only started to consider an English (as opposed to British) national identity since Wales and Scotland achieved some political autonomy through the devolution process of the late-1990s. The writer Fay Weldon, for example, on realising that other nations in the British Isles were finding institutional identity, immediately joined the Church of England as a way to express her 'Englishness'.

Previously, English people often used the terms 'English' and 'British' interchangeably, and when English sports teams competed internationally it was as common to see the 'Union Jack' flag of Great Britain as it was the St George Cross flag of England. This patriotic faux pas is now seen less often, although a British (as opposed to English) national anthem – the turgid *God Save the Queen* – is still sung by players and crowd before the game.

The confusion is compounded because any 'Englishness' that does exist has developed through centuries of cultural cherry-picking from history's numerous invaders, and from neighbours in Wales, Scotland and Ireland, as well as from the numerous peoples – Russians, West Indians, Pakistanis, whoever – arriving in more recent times. Add the influence of other nations through the global speakeasy of TV and cinema, and it's undeniable – despite the claims of racial supremacists and some of the country's more excitable, and xenophobic, newspapers – the English are a mongrel race, and the national psyche is a real mixed bag.

That's why today many English people proudly honour traditions such as Christmas trees (introduced from Germany) and maypoles (Celtic), then wash down a chicken madras curry – the nation's most popular meal – with Fosters or Bud. Meanwhile, their kids mix distinctive regional accents with intonations apparently perfected in Queensland or California.

Nonetheless, despite this openness to foreign influences, many visitors to England hold a preconception that the English are reserved, inhibited and stiflingly polite. While this may indeed apply in some places, in general it simply doesn't. Anywhere in the country, if you visit a pub, a nightclub, a football match, a seaside resort, or simply go walking in city parks or on wild open hills, you'll soon come across other English characteristics – uninhibited, tolerant, exhibitionist, passionate, aggressive, sentimental, hospitable and friendly. It hits you like a breath of fresh air.

Then dig below the surface a little, and you'll find even more surprises. A major newspaper survey in mid-2006 revealed that 25% of the UK adult population (about nine million men and 1.4 million women) downloaded images from pornographic websites. Apparently, Britain is the fastest-growing market in the world for internet porn. But the old 'no sex, please, we're British' adage has not gone away either. Also in mid-2006 a 55-year-old woman discretely sunbathing naked in her own garden was taken to court by a neighbour and charged with 'grossly offensive' behaviour.

Alongside this surprising interest in virtual sex, the English are generous in other ways too: more than 80% donate to charity each year, and the annual income of the UK's charities totals almost £40 billion. There's inconsistency here as well though; people donate to Friends of the Earth but ignore their own bank's investments in the oil industry; they'll support Amnesty International but overlook their savings or pension fund's stake in arms companies supplying the world's most brutal regimes. Fortunately, awareness is growing in

The English by Jeremy Paxman is an incisive exploration of the English psyche, as befits one of the toughest interviewers on the airwaves.

QUEUING FOR ENGLAND

The English are notoriously addicted to queues – for buses, train tickets, or to pay at the supermarket. The order is sacrosanct and woe betide any foreigner who gets this wrong! Few things are more calculated to spark an outburst of tutting – about as publicly cross as most English get – than 'pushing in' at a queue.

The same applies to escalators – especially in London. If you want to stand still, keep to the right, so people can pass you on the left. There's a definite convention here and recalcitrants have been hung, drawn and quartered (well, at least provoked more tutting) for blocking the path of those in a hurry.

Britain, and about half a million people currently have accounts with 'ethical' banks or invest in socially responsible funds.

On a less profound level, a very notable feature of the English is their obsession with hobbies and pastimes. We're not talking about obvious things like football and cricket (although fanatical supporters number in their millions), but about bird-watchers, train-spotters, model-makers, home improvers, antique hoarders, pigeon fanciers, royal watchers, teapot collectors, steam engine renovators, ramblers, anglers, gardeners, caravanners and crossword fans. The list goes on, with many participants verging on the edge of complete madness. But it's all great, and England just wouldn't be the same without them.

LIFESTYLE

'An Englishman's home is his castle' runs an old saying from less emancipated times. This doesn't mean the people of England all live behind turreted battlements (although some would like to), but it does reflect the importance the English people place on owning a house. In other countries, it's perfectly acceptable to live in rented houses or apartments your whole life, but in England renting is seen as a temporary step for young folks, or a dead-end option for the poor. If you are 'still renting' or 'haven't got your own place' once you're past 30, you're regarded as a bit of a loser.

But buying can be outrageously expensive. The average price of a house is just under £200,000 nationally. In London, it's over £900,000 in the best areas, and in the heart of the capital it tops a cool £1.25 million. Compare this to average annual salaries of £22,000 nationwide and £31,000 in London. For many people, half their earnings go on rent or mortgage. In reality, the London picture is even worse, as hot-shots in The City (London's financial heart) earn big bucks and skew the averages, meaning key workers like nurses, teachers, ambulance drivers and rubbish collectors are earning only about £19,000 to £24,000 – simply not enough to buy something central, so many live in outer suburbs and add a long commute to their working day.

Workers in Southeast England commute for an average of 1.6 hours per day, a total of eight hours per week – a whole extra working day!

A benefit of living in London and the Southeast, however, is the work opportunities available. For example, the growth of high-tech companies along the 'M4 corridor' west of London make it England's answer to Silicon Valley, with under 1% unemployment. Around Cambridge in East Anglia (now dubbed Silicon Fen) it's the same story.

In sharp contrast, deserts of economic depression exist in the Midlands and north of England – an 'archipelago of deprivation' according to one report. Of course, the North-South divide is an oversimplified term that's been with us for years, and the situation is more mixed in reality, with pockets of affluence in poor areas, and 'sink estates' of council flats a few blocks away from Millionaires Row.

Wherever they live, when it comes to family life, many English people regard the 'Victorian values' of the late 19th century as an idyllic benchmark –

a time of perfect morals and harmonious nuclear families, a highpoint from which the country has been sliding ever since. As recently as the 1960s, only 2% of couples had 'lived in sin' under the same roof before getting married. Four decades later, it's perfectly acceptable in most circles for couples to live together, even if there's still no proper word for this status – other than 'cohabiting' (but what on earth are the married folk doing if they're not cohabiting too?) – although the term 'partner' is now widely used and accepted. Good job too; in 2006, about a third of all couples living together were unmarried, and around 60% of couples who got married were already living together – if they could afford a house of course.

In line with this trend, the number of nonmarried couples having children has also increased in the last 40 to 50 years. While illegitimate children were comparatively rare in the 1960s – and a social stigma that forced many unmarried mothers to give up their babies to adoption – today about 40% of births in the UK are to nonmarried couples. The 'pro-family' lobby argues that married couples provide more stability and a better environment for children. But a wedding apparently provides no guarantees: currently about one in three marriages ends in divorce.

All the above is about heterosexual marriages of course. It's only been legal for gay or lesbian couples to get hitched since the 2005 Civil Partnership Act came into force. This was a positive step, but there's still a way to go before total tolerance and full equality is reached.

Along with money and marriage, another major issue in England is health – with obesity a hot topic on everyone's lips. Currently, over 60% of the adult population is overweight, and almost 25% are clinically obese. In late 2005 the UK had the fastest growing rate of obesity of all developed nations.

So while the English pig out on junk food, at least they're not smoking so much. Tobacco has moved down to No 2 on the health-risk charts, and although it's still a major cause of disease, about 75% of the population does not smoke – the lowest figures since records began.

> Compared to the 1950s, there are now 25% fewer marriages per year, but five times as many divorces. For more fascinating figures see www.2-in-2-1.co uk/ukstats.

WHITHER THE WEATHER?

It was Dr Johnson who noted that 'when two Englishmen meet, their first talk is of the weather'. Two centuries later, little has changed: weather is without doubt a national obsession. According to the UK Meteorological Office – known to all as the Met Office (see www.metoffice.gov .uk) – weather reports are the third most watched television broadcasts, and when BBC Radio 4 proposed cutting the late-night shipping forecast ('warning of gales in North Atlantic; Viking, Forties, good' etc) there was a huge outcry from listeners – most of whom never went anywhere near the sea.

This fascination with the weather is part of a long tradition, and ancient folklore is rich in ideas for second-guessing the moods of the elements. Snow on St Dorothea's day (6 February) means no heavier snowfall that year, while rain on St Swithin's day (15 July) means it'll continue for the next 40 days. The slightest tinge of a pink cloud and the locals start to chant 'red sky at night, shepherd's delight' like a mantra.

But despite this obsession, the weather still manages to keep the English on their toes. A few weeks without rain and garden-hose bans are enacted; too much rain and low-lying houses are flooded – although those are symptoms of increased water use, and unsuitable building plots, as much as changing weather patterns. In the same way, a fall of snow often brings English cities and motorways to a halt (whereas the same amount in Germany or Switzerland would hardly be noticed). The poor old Met Office sometimes gets the blame, and so in response has now taken to issuing Severe Weather Warnings with increasing regularity, most recently in the winter of 2006 – when a mere 2cm of snow was expected.

POPULATION FIGURES

Throughout this book we give the population figures for towns and cities drawn from the 2001 national census. In some cases, the numbers may have changed by the time you read this, but you'll still know if a place is a tiny village or a major metropolis.

Time to celebrate? Oh yes – with a big drink. Across the country, alcohol consumption is on the rise, with the relatively new phenomenon of 'binge drinking' among young people a major concern for doctors, police and politicians. And it's not just the boys on the booze; thanks largely to a change in social attitudes (there's no more stigma attached to a woman getting drunk than there is to a man) and the invention of sweet but strong 'alcopops', around 70% of women are drinking more than the recommended amount – up from just 10% in the mid-1990s.

And alcohol isn't the only drug. A major survey in 2004 showed that about 20% of British people had used a recreational drug during their lifetime. More recent studies estimate that about 5% of young adults use cocaine, and about 5% of schoolchildren use ecstasy, while at any given time around 10% of the population regularly or occasionally use cannabis. It's too early to say if the highly controversial 2005 decriminalisation of cannabis use will have any impact on these figures.

POPULATION

England's population is just under 50.5 million (around 83% of the UK's total 59 million) and growth has been minimal (with numbers even reducing slightly) in recent years – if you don't count the annual influx of about 30 million tourists.

'The new country-dwellers seek a better standard of living, and many can work from home via phone and the internet'

The total numbers may be virtually static, but behind the headline figures England's population picture is remarkably fluid. For the last 100 years, there's been a gradual flow of people from the north, centre and west of England to London and the Southeast. And thanks to increased work opportunities in the London region and economic woes elsewhere in the country, the pattern continues, with people still inexorably drawn to the capital and its environs.

As the south of England runs out of places to build more houses, and the north cries out for employment, steps are being taken to reverse the flow. Since the 1980s, government departments and official bodies have been relocating from the south to the north (the BBC moved 1000 jobs from London to Manchester in 2004, for example) and private enterprise is being encouraged to do the same with offers of tax breaks or direct aid.

Meanwhile, a more-significant migration is under way. In the last decade, over one million people in England moved from urban to rural areas. A 2004 report from the Countryside Agency says this is four times more than the number moving north to south. The new country-dwellers seek a better standard of living, and many can work from home via phone and the internet, while others set up small businesses – especially valuable in rural areas where traditional jobs such as farming are on the wane. But there are downsides – notably the rise in rural house prices, which pushes property beyond the reach of locals and forces *them* to move to the towns which the incomers have vacated.

SPORT

The English invented many of the world's most popular spectator sports – or at least laid down the modern rules – including cricket, tennis, rugby and football. Trouble is, the national teams aren't always so good at playing them (as the newspapers continually like to remind us), although recent years have seen some notable success stories – most notably England winning the Rugby World Cup in 2004 and a cricketing victory over old rival Australia in the Ashes in 2005, success not quite repeated in 2006's football World Cup.

But even when England isn't winning, a poor result doesn't dull the enthusiasm of the fans. Every weekend, thousands of people turn out to cheer their favourite team, and sporting highlights such as the FA Cup, Wimbledon or the Derby keep the entire nation enthralled, while the biggest sporting event of all – the Olympic Games – is coming to London in 2012.

This section gives a brief overview of sports you might encounter as part of your travels around England; the regional chapters have more details on specific football stadiums, cricket grounds and so on. For information on participatory sports, see the Outdoor Activities chapter (p75).

> For dates and details of football, cricket, horse racing and other events in England tomorrow, next week or next month, start with the sports pages of www .whatsonwhen.com.

Cricket

The quintessentially English game of cricket has been played formally since the 18th century – although its roots are much older. It became an international game during Britain's colonial era, when it was exported to the countries of the Commonwealth, particularly in the Indian sub-continent, the West Indies and Australasia.

The rules and terminology may appear ridiculously arcane and confusing, and progress seems so *slow* (surely, say the unbelievers, this is the game for which TV highlights were invented), but for aficionados the game provides 'resolute and graceful confrontations within an intricate and psychologically thrilling framework'. OK, the quote is from a cricket fan. Nonetheless, at least one cricket match should feature in your travels around England. If you're patient and learn the intricacies, you could find cricket as enriching and enticing as all the Brits who remain glued to their radio or PC all summer, 'just to see how England's getting on'.

One-day games and five-day test matches are played against sides such as Australia and the West Indies at landmark grounds like Lords in London, Edgbaston in Birmingham and Headingley in Leeds. Test match tickets cost £25 to £100 and tend to sell fast. County championships usually charge £10 to £15, and rarely sell out. Watching a local game on the village green is free of charge.

Football (Soccer)

Despite what the fans may say in Madrid or Sao Paulo, the English football league has some of the finest teams and players in the world. They're the richest too, with multimillion-pound sponsorship deals regularly clinched by powerful agents.

At the top of the tree is the Premier League for the country's top 20 clubs, although the hegemony enjoyed by super-clubs Arsenal, Liverpool and globally renowned (and part US-owned) Manchester United has been challenged in recent years by former underdogs Chelsea, thanks to the seemingly bottomless budget of Russian owner Roman Abramovich.

Down from the Premiership, 72 other teams play in the divisions called the Championship, League One and League Two, and the football season lasts

---

SOCK IT TO ME

The word 'soccer' (the favoured term in countries where 'football' means another game) is reputedly derived from 'Association'. The sport is still officially called Association Football, to distinguish it from Rugby Football, Gaelic football, American Football, Aussie Rules Football and so on. Another source is the word 'sock'; in medieval times this was a tough leather foot-cover worn by peasants – ideal for kicking around a pig's bladder in the park on a Saturday afternoon.

THE SWEET FA CUP

The Football Association held its first interclub knockout tournament in 1871. Fifteen clubs took part, playing for a nice piece of silverware called the FA Cup – then worth about £20.

Nowadays, around 600 clubs compete for this legendary and priceless trophy. It differs from many other competitions in that every team – from the lowest-ranking part-timers to the stars of the Premier League – is in with a chance. The preliminary rounds begin in August, and the world-famous Cup Final is held in May. It's been staged at Wembley for decades, with a few years out at Cardiff's Millennium Stadium, while the national ground was rebuilt.

The team with the most FA Cup victories is Manchester United (a total of 10), but public attention – and affection – is invariably focussed on the 'giant-killers' – minor clubs that claw their way up through the rounds, unexpectedly beating higher-ranking competitors. The best-known giant-killing event occurred in 1992, when Wrexham, then ranked 24th in Division 3, famously beat league champions Arsenal. Other shocks include non-league Kidderminster Harriers' 1994 defeats of big boys Birmingham City and Preston North End, and Oldham Athletic beating the Premier League's Manchester City in 2005.

In recent years, the FA Cup has become one football competition among many. The Premier League and Champion's League (against European teams) have a higher profile, bigger kudos, and simply more money to play with. But – just as the country gets behind the English national side – nothing raises community spirit more than a town team doing better than expected. Gates are down, and perhaps the FA Cup will one day be consigned to history – but what a sweet and glorious history it's been!

from August to May, so seeing a match can easily be tied into most visitors' itineraries. But tickets are like gold-dust, and cost £20 to £50 even if you're lucky enough to find one. If you can't get in to see the big names, tickets for lower division games are cheaper and more easily available – either on the spot, ordered through a club website, or through a specialist such as www.ticketmaster.co.uk and www.myticketmarket.com.

Horse Racing

There's a horse race somewhere in England pretty much every day, but the top event in the calendar is Royal Ascot in mid-June, when even the Queen turns up to put a fiver each way on Lucky Boy in the 3.15. For details about Royal Ascot (www.royalascot.co.uk; see p174).

Other highlights include the Grand National steeplechase at Aintree in early April, and the Derby, run at Epsom on the first Saturday in June. The latter is especially popular with the masses so, unlike Ascot, you won't see morning suits and outrageous hats anywhere.

Rugby

A wit once said that football was a gentlemen's game played by hooligans, while rugby was the other way around. That may be true, but rugby is very popular, especially since England became world champions in 2004, and it's worth catching a game for the display of skill (OK, and brawn) and the fun atmosphere on the terraces. Tickets cost around £15 to £40 depending on the club's status and fortunes.

There are two versions of the game: rugby union is played more in southern England, Wales and Scotland, and is traditionally the game of the middle and upper classes, while rugby league is played predominantly in northern England, traditionally by the working classes – although these days there's a lot of cross-over.

Rugby traces its roots to a football match in 1823 at Rugby School, in Warwickshire. A player called William Ellis, frustrated at the limitations of mere

Queen Elizabeth II is a great horse-racing fan, with 19 Ascot winners to date from the royal stables. The 2005 Grand National clashed with Prince Charles' marriage; rumours abound that the start was delayed so the Queen could attend the nuptials *and* see the race.

SPORTING COVERAGE

Perhaps surprisingly, unlike many other countries, England has no dedicated sports newspaper. But read the hefty back pages of the *Daily Telegraph*, the *Times* and the *Guardian* and you'll see why. The tabloids also cover sport, especially if a famous personality has been caught with their pants down. Talking of which, despite the name, the *Daily Sport* is not a sports paper, unless photos of glamour models wearing only a pair of Arsenal socks counts as 'sport'.

---

kicking, reputedly picked up the ball and ran with it towards the opponents' goal. True to the sense of English fair play, rather than Ellis being dismissed from the game, a whole new sport was developed around his tactic, and the Rugby Football Union was formally inaugurated in 1871.

Today, leading rugby union clubs include Leicester, Bath and Gloucester, while London has a host of good-quality teams (including Wasps and Saracens). In rugby league, teams to watch include the Wigan Warriors, Bradford Bulls and Leeds Rhinos.

The international rugby union calendar is dominated by the annual Six Nations Championship between January and April, in which England does battle with neighbours Scotland, Wales, Ireland, France and Italy.

Tennis

Tennis is widely played at club and regional level, but the best known tournament is the All England Championships – known to all as Wimbledon – when tennis fever sweeps through England in the last week of June and first week of July. There's something quintessentially English about the combination of grass courts, polite applause and umpires in boaters, with strawberries and cream devoured by the ton. (That's 27 tonnes of strawberries and 7000L of cream annually, to be precise.) England's top player is Tim Henman, the cause of another disease – Henmania.

Demand for seats at Wimbledon always outstrips supply, but to give everyone an equal chance the tickets are sold (unusually) through a public ballot. You can also take your chance on the spot; about 6000 tickets are sold each day (but not the last four days) and queuing at dawn should get you into the ground. For details see www.wimbledon.org.

MULTICULTURALISM

England is home to many different races and cultures, as the country's colonial history, geographic position and economic strength has resulted in immigrants coming here for hundreds of years. Since the 1950s, large groups have arrived from Africa, the Caribbean and South Asia, while most recently (and controversially) many more have arrived from the countries of Eastern Europe.

While some immigrants may live in England for a few years, usually to work and get some money together before returning to their home country, others settle for good, take on British citizenship and have families, so that the second and third generations are no longer immigrants, but simply of 'immigrant origin' or an 'ethnic minority'.

In the census of 2001, around 8% of the UK's population identified themselves as 'ethnic minority', although the figure is probably higher given that not all immigrants fill in the census forms – especially those who are here illegally. The largest centres of immigrant population include the cities London and Birmingham. England's most multicultural city is Leicester, where around one-third of the population are from ethnic minorities.

Multiculturalism and immigration are major issues currently facing the British government, and much discussed in the media. Despite the benefits

'England's top player is Tim Henman, the cause of another disease – Henmania'

(if it wasn't for a ready and willing immigrant workforce, the National Health Service would be one of many employers finding it even harder to get the staff they need) immigration is often discussed in negative terms. This is not because the new arrivals may speak a different language or have dark skin – although for some people already in England, that can be a reason enough – but because they present an *economic* threat. The newcomers will often do the jobs that nobody else wants, and work harder for less money. The end result for the locals: salary levels go down. At the Trades Union Congress conference of 2006, delegates addressed this very issue: how to be good left-leaning fraternal internationalists, while at the same time protect incumbent workers from falling wage rates?

Despite the controversies surrounding new arrivals, general tolerance towards other cultures does prevail in most parts of England, with commercial organisations and official bodies such as the police trying hard to stamp out discrimination. But bigotry can still lurk close to the surface: far-right political parties won several seats in the local council elections of 2006, and it's not unusual to hear people openly discuss other races in quite unpleasant terms – in smart country pubs as much as rough city bars. And while it's no longer OK for comedians to tell racist jokes on prime-time TV (as it was until the 1980s), this type of humour still goes down well in some quarters.

The situation gets more complicated when the term 'immigrant' is used by the media as a catch-all phrase to also include asylum seekers and refugees. These are often a separate group of people, who have come here not to settle or work for a while (or even 'scrounge off the state', as some newspapers would have it), but because conditions at home got so bad they had nothing to lose by abandoning family and friends, handing over their life savings to a trafficker, risking death in leaky boat or travelling thousands of miles in the back of a lorry, to arrive with nothing in an unwelcoming land. That's not to say that the arrival of immigrants, refugees and asylum seekers in England isn't an issue to be discussed, but 'debates' rarely consider the reasons *why* these people leave their own country in the first place.

To end on a positive note, a benefit of the recent immigration from Eastern Europe is the large number of skilled manual workers available – notably plumbers. So now when you've got a burst pipe you can get someone around pretty quick, they don't suck their teeth as part of the estimate process, they do the job well, and you don't need to take out a second mortgage to pay the bill.

MEDIA
Newspapers

Breakfast need never be boring in England. For such a small country, there's an amazing range of daily newspapers to read over your cornflakes.

The bottom end of the market is occupied by easy-to-read tabloids, full of sensational 'exclusives' and simplistic political coverage. The *Sun* is a national institution with mean-spirited content and headlines based on outrageous puns – a good combination apparently, as it's Britain's biggest-selling paper, with a circulation of around three million, and a readership three times that. The *Mirror*, once the 'paper of the workers', tried to compete head-on with the *Sun* for a while, then rediscovered its left-of-centre, pro-Labour heritage. The *Sport* takes bad taste to the ultimate, with stories of aliens and celebrities (sometimes in the same report), and pictures of seminaked women of improbable proportions.

The *Daily Mail* and *Daily Express* bill themselves as middle-market, but are little different to the tabloids, both thunderously right-of-centre with a

'The bottom end of the market is occupied by easy-to-read tabloids, full of sensational 'exclusives' and simplistic political coverage'

NEWS DOWN THE LINE

Want to scan the papers online? Find them at:

Daily Express – www.express.co.uk   *Mirror* – www.mirror.co.uk
Daily Telegraph – www.telegraph.co.uk   *Sun* – www.the-sun.co.uk
Guardian – www.guardianunlimited.co.uk   *Times* – www.the-times.co.uk
Independent – www.independent.co.uk

---

steady stream of crime and scare stories about threatening immigrants and rampant homosexuals. Some may find this diet distasteful, but about eight million readers don't.

At the upper end of the market are the broadsheets: the *Daily Telegraph* is right-of-centre and easily outsells its rivals; the *Times* is conservative, Murdoch-owned, thorough and influential; the *Guardian* is left-of-centre and innovative; and the *Independent* lives up to its title. 'Tabloid' and 'broadsheet' have always referred more to substance than actual dimensions, but the distinction is now totally content-based as several serious papers are also issued in handy-to-carry sizes.

Most dailies have Sunday stablemates (the *Sunday Mirror*, *Sunday Express*, *Sunday Telegraph* and so on) and there's also the long-standing liberal-slanted *Observer*. The broadsheets are filled more with comment and analysis than hot news, and on their day of rest the English settle in armchairs to plough through endless supplements; the *Sunday Times* alone comes in 12 different parts, and must destroy a rainforest every issue.

TV & Radio

Alongside the wide range of newsprint stands an equally wide range of TV and radio. The BBC is the country's leading broadcaster and a venerable institution, with several channels of the world's best programming dominating national radio and free-to-air TV. Foreigners are frequently amazed that public service broadcasting can produce such a range of professional, innovative, up-to-date and stimulating programmes. All this – and without adverts too! – although ever-increasing competition from cable and satellite channels means some shows tend to be dumbed down as ratings are chased, especially as the majority of households now have digital receivers, in preparation for the analogue switch-off scheduled for 2012.

The main BBC TV stations are BBC One and BBC Two; others include BBC Three, BBC Four, News24 and some children's channels. Major commercial broadcasters include ITV and Channel 4 – both with several channels. Satellite broadcasting is heavily dominated by Sky, part of the gargantuan News International Corporation.

Turning to radio, the main BBC stations include Radio 1, playing everything from syrupy pop to underground garage, with a predominantly young audience and some truly inane presenters. When you get too old for this, tune into Radio 2, playing favourites from the 1960s to today, plus country, jazz and world music, with presenters who also got too old for Radio 1. Predominantly classical music is played on Radio 3, but this station also goes into roots and world, while media gem Radio 4 offers a mix of news, comment, current affairs, drama and humour. Other BBC stations include Radio 5 Live (a mix of sport and talk) and Radio 7 (drama and humour).

Alongside the BBC are many commercial radio broadcasters. Every city has at least one music station, while national stations include pop-orientated Virgin Radio and pleasantly nonhighbrow classical specialist Classic FM. To find the right spot on the dial, see p764.

'Foreigners are frequently amazed that public service broadcasting can produce such a range of professional, innovative, up-to-date and stimulating programmes'

RELIGION

The Church of England (or Anglican Church) was founded in the 16th century at the behest of Henry VIII, and today remains wealthy and influential – even in these increasingly secular times. Traditionally conservative, and predominantly Conservative (sometimes called 'the Tory Party at prayer'), it's only since 1994 that women have been ordained as priests. The debate has now moved on to the rights and wrongs of gay clergy.

In the 2001 national census, around 35 million people in England stated their religion as Christian, and although many English people write 'C of E' when filling in forms, only about a million attend Sunday services. Other Christian faiths in England include Roman Catholic (about 10% of the population), Methodists and Baptists, but attendances are down every year at mainstream churches, with evangelical and charismatic churches the only ones attracting growing congregations.

The 2001 census also showed that over 3% of the population of England are Muslims – a total of around 1.5 million in Britain. Other faiths include Hindus (1%), Sikhs (0.7%), Jews (0.5%) and Buddhists (0.3%). These numbers may appear small, but nowadays more non-Christians regularly visit their places of worship than do all the Anglicans, Catholics, Methodists and Baptists combined – especially if you include those druids at Stonehenge, and all those wags that amusingly wrote 'Jedi Knight' in the 'other' category.

ARTS
Literature

Modern English literature – poetry and prose – starts around 1387 (yes, that's modern in history-soaked England) with Geoffrey Chaucer's classic *The Canterbury Tales*, a collection of fables, stories and morality tales using travelling pilgrims – the Knight, the Wife of Bath, the Nun's Priest and so on – as a narrative hook. For more background, see the boxed text The Canterbury Tales, p189.

Two centuries later William Shakespeare entered the scene. Still England's best-known playwright (see p68), he was pretty good at poems too. The famous line 'Shall I compare thee to a summer's day?' comes from sonnet No 18. In all he penned more than 150.

Then came the metaphysical poets of the early 17th century. Their vivid imagery and far-fetched conceits or comparisons daringly pushed the boundaries. In *A Valediction: Forbidding Mourning*, for instance, John Donne compares two lovers with the points of a compass. Racy stuff in its day.

The stars of the 19th century were the Romantics: John Keats, Percy Bysshe Shelley and Lord Byron wrote with emotion, exulting the senses and power of the imagination, and were particularly passionate about nature. The best-known Romantic poet, William Wordsworth, lived in the Lake District, and his famous lines from *Daffodils*, 'I wandered lonely as a cloud', were inspired by a hike in the hills.

The Romantic movement produced a genre called 'literary Gothic', exemplified by Mary Shelley's *Frankenstein*, and satirised in *Northanger Abbey* by Jane Austen, still one of Britain's best-known and best-loved novelists; intrigues and passions boiling under the stilted preserve of provincial middle-class social convention are beautifully portrayed in *Emma* and *Pride & Prejudice*.

Next came the reign of Queen Victoria and the era of industrial expansion, so key novels of the time explored social and political issues. In *Oliver Twist*, Charles Dickens captures the lives of young thieves in the London slums, and in *Hard Times* he paints a brutal picture of capitalism's excesses. Meanwhile, Thomas Hardy's classic *Tess of the D'Urbervilles* deals with the peasantry's

For extra insight while travelling, the *Oxford Literary Guide to Great Britain and Ireland* gives details of towns, villages and countryside immortalised by writers.

decline, and *The Trumpet Major* paints a picture of idyllic English country life interrupted by war and encroaching modernity.

Other major figures from this era are the Brontë sisters. Charlotte Brontë's *Jane Eyre* and Anne Brontë's *The Tennant of Wildfell Hall* are classics of passion, mystery and love. Fans still flock to Haworth (p591), their former home, perched on the edge of the wild Pennine moors which inspired so many books.

In the 20th century, the pace of English writing increased. Inspired by the tragedy of WWI, poet Rupert Brooke's *The Soldier* is romantic and idealistic while Wilfred Owen's *Dulce et Decorum Est* is harshly cynical about the 'glory' of war.

Their contemporary, DH Lawrence picked up the theme of change and produced *Sons and Lovers* and *The Rainbow*, novels set in the English Midlands, following the lives and loves of generations, as the country changes from 19th-century idyll to the modern world we recognise today. In 1928, Lawrence further pushed his explorations of sexuality in *Lady Chatterley's Lover*, which was initially banned as pornographic. Torrid affairs are no great shakes today, but the quality of the writing still shines.

Other highlights of the interwar years included EM Forster's *A Passage to India*, about the hopelessness of British colonial rule, and Daphne du Maurier's romantic suspense novel *Rebecca*, set on the Cornish coast. In a different world entirely, JRR Tolkien published *The Hobbit*, trumping it some 20 years later with his awesome trilogy *The Lord of the Rings*.

After WWII, a new breed of writer emerged. George Orwell wrote *Animal Farm* and *Nineteen Eighty-Four*, his closely observed studies of totalitarian rule, while the Cold War inspired Graham Greene's *Our Man in Havana*, in which a secret agent studies the workings of a vacuum cleaner to inspire fictitious spying reports.

Another spook of that period was Ian Fleming's full-blooded hero James Bond – today better known as a movie franchise. He first appeared in 1953 in the book *Casino Royale*, then swashbuckled through numerous thrillers for another decade. Meanwhile, TH White's *The Once and Future King* covers battles of a different time – the magical world of King Arthur and the knights of the Round Table.

Alongside the novelists, the 20th century was a great time for poets. Big names include WH Auden's *Funeral Blues* (still his most popular work thanks to a role in *Four Weddings and a Funeral*) and TS Eliot's epic *The Wasteland*, although he is better known for *Old Possum's Book of Practical Cats* – turned into the musical *Cats* by Andrew Lloyd Webber. Different was the gritty verse of Ted Hughes, while fellow 1960s writer Roger McGough and friends determined to make art relevant to daily life and produced *The Mersey Sound* – landmark pop poetry for the streets.

Novelists breaking new ground in the 1970s included Martin Amis – just 24 when he wrote *The Rachel Papers*, a witty observation of sexual obsession in puberty. Since then Amis has published 15 books, the best-known including *The Information* and *London Fields*, mostly greeted with critical acclaim and high sales.

In contrast, authors Sebastian Faulks and Louis de Bernières struggled for recognition then hit the jackpot with later works. Their respective novels *Birdsong*, a perfect study of passion and the horrors of WWI, and *Captain Corelli's Mandolin*, a tale of love, war and life on a Greek island, were massive sellers in the 1990s.

Another notable work of the same era was *The Buddha of Suburbia* by Hanif Kureishi, about the hopes and fears of a group of suburban Anglo-Asians in London, and a forerunner of the many multicultural tales that dominate bestseller lists today.

Of the Brontë family's prodigious output, *Wuthering Heights* by Emily Brontë is the best known – an epic tale of obsession and revenge, where the dark and moody landscape plays as great a role as any human character.

As the Pennine moors haunt Brontë novels, so the marshy Cambridgeshire Fens dominate *Waterland* by Graham Swift – a tale of personal and national history, betrayal and compassion, and rated a landmark work of the 1980s.

As English literature entered the new millennium, two of the biggest-selling British authors were JK Rowling and Phillip Pulman; their *Harry Potter* and *His Dark Materials* series took children's literature to a level where they could be seriously enjoyed by adults too.

Back in the real world, Zadie Smith was only 25 when *White Teeth* became a major hit of 2000. She followed it with the equally hyped, and almost as good, *The Autograph Man* and *On Beauty,* the latter winning the prestigious Orange Prize for Fiction in 2006.

Other star novelists covering (loosely-defined) 'multicultural England' themes include Monica Ali, whose *Brick Lane* was shortlisted for the 2003 Man Booker Prize, and Hari Kunzru, who received one of the largest advances in publishing history in 2002 for his debut *The Impressionist.* His second novel *Transmission* was published in June 2004. The same year, *Small Island* by Andrea Levy won the Orange Prize for her novel about a Jamaican couple who settled in 1950s London. The author is of Jamaican origin, and draws on rich family memories of the time. Two years later, the book won the best-in-10-years 'Orange of Orange' award.

Also set in London are Alan Hollinghurst's 2004 Man Booker prize winner *The Line of Beauty* about high-society gays in the 1980s Thatcher era, and *The Book of Dave* by prolific novelist, journalist, broadcaster and social commentator Will Self, published in 2006. Although ostensibly fanciful (a new religion based on the rantings of a grumpy taxi driver), like many of Self's works, it's a wonderfully incisive satire on urban lifestyles in 21st-century Britain. An earlier collection of short stories, *Grey Area,* revels in more skewed and surreal aspects of the capital. Meanwhile, Martin Amis had produced the darkly stylised and frankly confusing *Yellow Dog* in 2002, while Nick Hornby left lad-lit behind and displayed a deeper maturity in the darkly comic *A Long Way Down.*

On the verse front, a highlight of 2006 was long-standing and prolific poet Fleur Adcock winning the Queen's Gold Medal for Poetry. Although she's published at least 10 books, press attention focussed on a single line in a single poem, about dreaming of *kissing John Prescott,* written *before* the Deputy Prime Minister's extra marital affair with an aide was made public. Spooky.

But perhaps the biggest literary highlight of the year was the record-breaking £5 million five-book publishing deal signed by footballer Wayne Rooney, star of Manchester United and England's 2006 World Cup campaign. As more than one wag has already noted, the signature is likely to be Rooney's only written contribution; in reality, the autobiography will be ghosted by an experienced sports columnist.

In a world of hype, the publishing of books these days may be as much about PR and marketing as it is about the quality of the writing, but the desire for big names and an eagerness to chase (or invent) new themes had undeniably revitalised the industry. It may turn out to be the literary equivalent of Putnam's famous, but sadly erroneous, 'the British are coming' speech, but for now the chairman of the 2004 Man Booker Prize judges seems correct in the assertion that 'our overall conclusion has been that contemporary English fiction is in robust health'.

Cinema

In the early years of the 20th century, silent movies from Britain gave the Americans a run for their money, and *Blackmail* by Alfred Hitchcock – still one of England's best-known film directors – launched the British film industry's era of sound production in 1929.

After a decline in film output during WWII, the English film recovery in the 1940s and '50s was led by Ealing Studios with a series of eccentric

> 'As English literature entered the new millennium, two of the biggest-selling British authors were JK Rowling and Phillip Pulman'

and 'very English' comedies such as *Kind Hearts and Coronets*, staring Alec Guinness. More serious box-office hits of the time included *Hamlet*, starring Laurence Olivier (the first British film to win an Oscar in the Best Picture category) and Carol Reed's *The Third Man*. An absolute classic of the era is *Brief Encounter*, directed by David Lean, who went on to make *Lawrence of Arabia* and *Doctor Zhivago*.

By the end of the 1960s, British film production had declined again and didn't really pick up until David Puttnam's *Chariots of Fire* won four Oscars in 1981. Perhaps inspired by this success, TV company Channel 4 began financing films for the large and small screen, one of the first being *My Beautiful Laundrette* – a story of multicultural life and love in Mrs Thatcher's England. The following year, Richard Attenborough's big-budget epic *Gandhi* carried off eight Oscars including best director and best picture, while another classic of the 1980s was *Withnail and I*, staring Richard E Grant and Paul McGann.

The 1990s saw another minor renaissance in British film-making, ushered in by *Four Weddings and a Funeral*, featuring US star Andie MacDowell, and introducing Hugh Grant as a likable and self-deprecating Englishman. This spearheaded a genre of 'Brit flicks', including *Secrets and Lies*, a Palme d'Or winner at Cannes, *Bhaji on the Beach*, a quirky East-meets-West-meets-Blackpool road movie, and *The Full Monty*, which in 1997 became England's most successful film ever.

More great films of the 1990s include *Lock, Stock and Two Smoking Barrels*, going on to spawn a host of gangster copycats, and *East is East*, a beautifully understated study of the clash between first- and second-generation Pakistanis in Manchester, and the Oscar-winning series of *Wallace and Gromit* animations. Also released was *Notting Hill*, set in a London bookshop in one of the most multicultural suburbs in the whole of Britain, staring Julia Roberts with Hugh Grant as, yes, a likable and self-deprecating Englishman, and possibly most famous for managing to include only Caucasian extras in the street scenes. Much more enjoyable was *Sense and Sensibility*, with English doyens Emma Thompson and Kate Winslet as the Dashwood sisters, and Hugh Grant as, you guessed it, a likable and self-deprecating Englishman.

A classic of the Brit-flick genre, and a great success of 2000, was *Billy Elliott*, yet another film with England's declining industry as backdrop, but also about people rising above it, particularly the son of a hardened

Passport to Pimlico is an Ealing Studios film classic, the story of a London suburb declaring independence from the rest of the country.

www.screenonline.org
.uk – the website of the British Film Institute – has complete coverage of Britain's film and TV industry.

REEL TO REAL

Still movie-hungry? Want to see actual sets? Here are some great recent films, with backdrops you can visit as you travel through England's towns and countryside:

The Full Monty (1997) A group of unemployed steelworkers become strippers, with all the action taking place in the city of Sheffield, Yorkshire.

Last Orders (2001) Four buddies take a trip down memory lane to scatter their friend's ashes, with scenes shot at Canterbury Cathedral, Eastbourne and Margate Pier.

Harry Potter and the Chamber of Secrets (2002) The schoolboy wizard works his magic in Gloucester Cathedral, Alnwick Castle and the steam railway at Goathland.

Calendar Girls (2003) Local ladies of the parish pose nude for a fund-raising calendar, while the villages and valleys of the Yorkshire Dales provide scenic background.

Pride and Prejudice (2005) Austen power comes to Derbyshire and Lincolnshire as Chatsworth and Burghley House play Darcy family abodes, while dramatic Peak District outcrops provide a perfect spot for the heroine's love-lost contemplation.

The Da Vinci Code (2006) Lincoln Cathedral stands in for Westminster, and doubles visitor numbers overnight.

coal-miner who strives to becomes a ballet dancer. In contrast, *About a Boy* was a feel-good movie about a dating ploy leading unexpectedly to fatherly responsibilities, staring the ever-popular Hugh Grant as (surprise, surprise) a likable and self-deprecating Englishman. Meanwhile, *Bend it like Beckham* addressed more fundamental themes: growing up, first love, sex, class, race – and football.

Despite the success stories of the 1990s, as we go through the first decade of the 21st century, the UK film industry has returned to its customary precarious financial state. Advocates call for more government funding, as in reality most UK-made and UK-set films are paid for with US money – epitomised perhaps by the globally-renowned series of Harry Potter adventures, starting with *Harry Potter and the Philosopher's Stone* in 2001, with roughly a movie per year as we follow the schoolboy wizard through at least six years of education.

Other notable British films of this decade (so far) include: *Shaun of the Dead*, a great low-budget horror spoof where the hero fails to notice the walking corpses because most of his neighbours are zombies at the best of times; *24 Hour Party People*, about the iconic Hacienda Club and all-round pop excess in 1980s Manchester; *Hitchhikers Guide to the Galaxy*, already a cult classic book and radio series; *Tristram Shandy: A Cock & Bull Story*, as the subtitle implies, an outrageously witty, deliberately meandering and multilayered film of the 'unfilmable' classic English novel, starring two of Britain's top comics; Tim Burton's *Corpse Bride*, offering animated necrophilia and Gothic fun for the whole family; *Wallace & Gromit: The Curse Of The Were-Rabbit*, another hand-crafted marvel from director Nick Park; *Confetti*, a 'mockumentry' charting three couples' attempts to win the title of 'Most Original Wedding of the Year'; *Pride and Prejudice*, another Jane Austen masterpiece skilfully adapted for the silver screen, filmed in Derbyshire and Lincolnshire, and staring Keira Knightly (following on from *Domino*, and a long way from *Bend it like Beckham*), along with fellow British stars Matthew MacFayden, Brenda Blethyn and the perennial Judi Dench; and finally *Love + Hate*, a classic in the Britflick genre, sharing some themes with *Pride and Prejudice*, but this time the forbidden passions run across race-lines instead of class-lines, and instead of the scenic Peak District the setting is the modern-day post-industrial landscape of northern England.

Music
POP & ROCK

Through the history of pop and rock music, England has been firmly on the main stage – with access all areas – since the dawn of the swinging '60s. Major early exports were the Beatles, the Rolling Stones, the Who and the Kinks, followed in the 1970s by stardust-speckled heroes like Marc Bolan and David Bowie. Other big-name artists of the time, still remembered today – or in some cases even still performing – include Cream (featuring Eric Clapton), Genesis (initially fronted by Peter Gabriel and later by Phil Collins), and Roxy Music (featuring for a while the highly influential Brian Eno), plus Pink Floyd, Deep Purple, Led Zeppelin, Queen and Elton John –

A film about love, betrayal, brass bands, coal-mine closures and the breakdown of society in 1980s England, *Brassed Off* makes you laugh, then cry, and shouldn't be missed.

THERE'S MORE

This section concentrates on pop and rock. Of course, England enjoys many other rich and diverse musical genres – jazz, folk, roots, fusion, banghra, R&B, drum'n'bass, dance, techno, chill-out, dub, gospel, urban, hip-hop and so on – but we simply haven't got space to cover them here.

ACE CLUBS

If dance music and clubbing floats your boat, the major cities of England have some of the best clubs and late bars in the world, with DJs and theme nights that bring in eager punters from miles around. London is indisputably the top spot, but Brighton, Bristol, Nottingham, Manchester, Sheffield, Leeds and Liverpool all have large and ecstatic club scenes. Whatever your taste when it comes to clubs (or any other kind of entertainment), the best way to find out who's who and what's hot is to check out posters, pick up flyers, or scan the local listing magazines. Then go out and enjoy!

all very different, but all globally renowned, and some, such as Bowie, still producing decent material today.

In the late 1970s and early '80s self-indulgent 'prog rock' of the 'dinosaur bands' was replaced by punk music. It was energetic, anarchic ('here's three chords, now form a band' ran a famous quote in a fanzine) and frequently tuneless, but punk was enormous fun and returned pop to grassroots level – at least for a while. The infamous Sex Pistols produced one album and a clutch of (mostly banned) singles, while more prolific were the Clash, the Damned, the Buzzcocks, the Stranglers and the UK Subs (still touring today).

Punk begat 'New Wave' (ie everything that was a bit punky), with leading exponents including the Jam and Elvis Costello. This briefly merged with the short-lived ska revival of the 1980s, led by the Specials, which influenced bands such as Madness and the Beat, while a punk-and-reggae-influenced trio called the Police – fronted by bassist Sting – became one of the biggest names of the decade, and gothic lost boys the Cure carved their own existential post-punk path.

Around the same time, heavy metal enjoyed an upsurge, with bands like Black Sabbath (featuring once-again-famous Ozzy Osbourne) and Judas Priest exporting soulful melodies and intriguing interpretations of established religion to concert halls worldwide.

The ever-changing 1980s also saw a surge of electronica with the likes of Depeche Mode, Cabaret Voltaire and Human League, and the rise of New Romantic bands such as Spandau Ballet, Duran Duran, and Culture Club – all frills and fringes, and a definite swing of pop's pendulum away from untidy punks. More hits and highlights were supplied by Wham! – a two-piece boy band headed by a bright young fellow called George Michael.

Meanwhile, a whole new sound was emerging in northwestern England; the pioneering Joy Division (later evolving into New Order), the Stone Roses and Happy Mondays epitomising the late '80s/early '90s Madchester Sound and the painfully morose but curiously engaging Smiths, fronted by Morrissey (also currently enjoying a comeback). On the other side of the Pennines, Leeds-based the Wedding Present championed guitar- and frustration-driven melodies that still influence many bands today.

By the cusp of the millennium, Cool Britannia's shine had predictably faded, but a host of bands from that era, such as Coldplay, spawned a wave of imitators. The Libertines similarly influenced music and fashion, although ex-frontman Pete Doherty is now more famous for drug-and-supermodel scandals than his subsequent band Babyshambles.

As we complete research on this book, halfway through the first decade of the 21st century, English pop and rock breaks down into a host of genres mixing a wide range of influences including glam, punk, electronica and folk (while English folk itself, thanks largely to the rise of world music, enjoys its biggest revival since the 1960s). Worth a listen are atmospheric and eclectic British Sea Power, the energetic and nostalgic Go! Team, internet-download

'More hits and highlights were supplied by Wham! – a two-piece boy band headed by a bright young fellow called George Michael'

LIVE AND KICKING

In England you're never short of choice in live music. London and several other cities have stadiums and world-class concert halls for major pop, rock, jazz and classical events, and across the country there's a massive choice of smaller venues where the less-well-known do their thing. Bands large and small are pretty much guaranteed to play in London, but often tour extensively so a weekend break in Blackpool, Sheffield or Bristol could include seeing a band at the Tower Ballroom, the legendary Leadmill or longstanding Bierkeller. Down the scale again, you can hear great sounds (and some really dire stuff) in pubs and small clubs everywhere. As well as checking local listings, country-wide agencies such as See (www.seetickets.com) are useful planning tools, while the Indie Travel Guide (www.indietravelguide.com) features local bands, venues and clubs across Britain (and beyond). Options are of course more restricted in the countryside – but then you're in the wrong place for bright lights and decibels anyway.

---

phenomenon Arctic Monkeys, the Guillemots, Editors, Kaiser Chiefs, Bloc Party, Interpol, Hard Fi, The Streets. The list goes on, and there will no doubt be more exciting names to add by the time you read this. If you get the chance to enjoy England's live music scene (see the boxed text Live & Kicking, above), you can feel smug about seeing unknown bands before they achieve world domination.

CLASSICAL MUSIC & OPERA

The country that gave you the Beatles and Oasis is also a hive of classical music, with several professional symphony orchestras, dozens of amateur orchestras, and an active National Association of Youth Orchestras. Such enthusiasm is all the more remarkable given England's small number of well-known classical composers, especially compared with Austria, Germany and Italy.

Key figures include: Henry Purcell, who flourished in the Restoration period, but is still regarded as one of the finest English composers; Thomas Arne, best known for the patriotic anthem 'Rule Britannia'; Edward Elgar, famous for his 'Enigma Variations'; Gustav Holst, from Cheltenham, who wrote 'The Planets' (everyone knows the Mars, Bringer of War bit); Vaughan Williams, whose London Symphony ends with chimes from Big Ben; and Benjamin Britten, perhaps the finest English composer of the last century, best known for the 'Young Person's Guide to the Orchestra' and the opera *Peter Grimes*. More recently, the works of Sir Michael Tippett, Peter Maxwell Davies, John Tavener and Harrison Birtwhistle have found international fame, while the music of composer William Lloyd Webber has been brought to public attention by his sons Julian and Andrew.

See www.bbc.co.uk /proms for full details of dates, tickets and when to sing 'Land of Hope and Glory'.

Best-known of all English classical music concert programmes is The Proms (short for 'promenade' – because people used to walk about, or stand, while they listened) – one of the world's greatest music festivals, held from mid-July to mid-September each year at the Royal Albert Hall in London and widely broadcast on radio and TV.

Architecture

One of the many good reasons to visit England is to savour its rich architectural heritage – everything from 5000-year-old Bronze Age burial mounds to the stunning steel-and-glass constructions of the early 21st centuries. Among the highlights for most visitors are the mysterious megaliths of Stonehenge (p314), and from the Roman era, the ramparts of Hadrian's Wall (p746) and the well-preserved swimming pools and saunas that gave the city of Bath (p259) its name.

SOUNDS OF SUMMER

If you're a fan of the performing arts, some fine productions are staged outdoors from May to September, in castle grounds (where plays like Macbeth at dusk are pure magic) or purpose-built venues such as Regent's Park Theatre (p127) in London and cliff-edge Minack Theatre (p362) in Cornwall. The best-known open-air music event is Glyndebourne (p212) – a programme of world-class opera in the spectacular setting of a country-house garden.

Summertime also inspires villages, towns and cities across the country to stage arts and music festivals – everything from small-scale weekend shows to massive spectaculars like the Bath International Music Festival, via specialist events like Buxton Opera Festival, Whitby Folk Festival, Cheltenham Jazz Festival and the Three Choirs Festival (held once every three years at the cathedrals of Gloucester, Hereford or Worcester).

And finally there's the open-air long-weekend pop and rock extravaganzas, such as the Big Chill (in the genteel grounds of Eastnor castle), the endearing and increasingly popular Truck (near Abingdon), the colourful Womad global music gathering in Reading and, of course, the daddy of them all, Glastonbury (p284). For more festival ideas see our Top Ten on p23 and for more information see p771 or www.efestivals.co.uk.

Bath is also top of the hit-lists for most visitors thanks to architecture from a later time – the 18th and early 19th century Georgian period – which produced the grand houses, squares, parades and the famous Royal Crescent, but if we turn the clock back it's clear that for much of the preceding 800 years or so English architecture was dominated by two aspects: worship and defence. This gave us the incredibly diverse and truly magnificent collection of cathedrals, minsters, abbeys and monasteries dotted across the country, and an equally diverse collection of forts and castles – from evocative ruins such as Dunstanburgh Castle (p753) and Richmond Castle (p601) through finely maintained classics like Leeds Castle (p202) and Windsor Castle (p170), to the iconic Tower of London (p121) itself, with walls and moats, battlements and ramparts from every century since the Norman Conquest.

As well as the grand cathedrals, England has over 12,000 parish churches – many packed with historical or architectural significance.

Castles were good for keeping out the enemy, but there were few other benefits of living in a large damp pile of stones, and as times grew more peaceful in England from around the 16th century, the landed gentry started to build fine residences – known simply as 'country houses'. There was a particular boom in the 18th century, and one of the most distinctive features of the English countryside today is the sheer number (not to mention the sheer size) of these grand and beautiful structures.

But it's not all about big houses. Alongside the stately homes, ordinary domestic architecture from the 16th century onwards can also still be seen in rural areas: black-and-white 'half-timbered' houses still characterise counties such as Worcestershire, brick-and-flint cottages pepper Suffolk and Sussex, and hardy centuries-old farms built with slate or local gritstone are a feature of areas such as Derbyshire and the Lake District.

In our own era, the rebuilding that followed WWII showed scant regard for the aesthetics of cities, or for the lives of the people who lived in them, as 'back-to-back' terraces of slum houses were demolished and replaced by tower-blocks (simply transposing horizontal rows of deprivation with vertical, according to some critics). Public buildings of the 1960s were often little better; heavy concrete 'brutalism' was much beloved by architects of the time – a style epitomised by London's South Bank Centre (p124), although even this monstrosity has its fans today.

Perhaps the insensitivity of the 1960s and '70s is why, on the whole, the English are conservative in their architectural tastes, and often resent ambitious or experimental designs, especially when they're applied to public

BUILDING ON SUCCESS

Two men have dominated modern English architecture for the last 30 years: Sir Norman Foster and Lord Richard Rogers. Both have designed numerous landmark buildings in England, and around the globe – they will each be designing towers to replace the World Trade Centre in New York – although their styles are quite distinct.

Foster favours clean designs with flowing lines. Key works in London include the conical Swiss Re building (known universally as The Gherkin), winner of the prestigious Stirling prize, the sensuous Great Court glass roof at the British Museum, and the sinuous Millennium Bridge between St Paul's and the Tate Modern. Other splendid recent examples of his work include the Imperial War Museum North in Manchester, and The Sage concert hall in Newcastle-Gateshead.

In contrast, the work of Rogers is technical and intricate. Perhaps his best-known work was the Millennium Dome (p130), a tent-like structure with vast curving white fields held aloft by cables and spindly yellow towers. A more recent work is the massive Paddington Basin complex, near the London train station of the same name. Rogers has also worked for Ken Livingstone, Mayor of London, on 20,000 new homes.

Meanwhile, Foster's project for Mayor Ken was City Hall (properly known as the Greater London Authority Building), which opened in July 2002. It looks like a tilted beehive, and the glass walls mean you can see everyone inside, hard at work – a deliberate symbol of local government transparency – while at the top there's the spectacular Londoner's Lounge where you can admire the panoramic views and buy a traditional English cappuccino.

buildings, or when form appears more important than function. But a familiar pattern often unfolds: after a few years of resentment, first comes a nickname (in London, the bulging cone of the Swiss Re building was dubbed 'the gherkin', and the near-spherical City Hall was called 'Livingstone's Ball' by some, a reference to London's high-profile mayor), then comes grudging acceptance, and finally – once the locals have got used to it – comes pride and affection for the new building. The English just don't like to be rushed, that's all.

With this attitude in mind, over the last 15 years or so English architecture has started to redeem itself, and many big cities now have contemporary buildings their residents can enjoy and admire. Outside of London, contemporary architecture is epitomised by Manchester's theatrical Imperial War Museum North (p647), the soaring wood and glass arcs of Sheffield's Winter Gardens (p579), Birmingham's chic new Bullring (p463), The Deep aquarium in Hull (p604), and The Sage Gateshead concert hall of Newcastle-Gateshead (p735). At the same time, architecture continues to be more internationalised as English architects design airports in Germany or Southeast Asia, while Spanish architects design offices in Britain.

To unravel the wonders of English architecture, handy books include *English Castles* by Adrian Pettifer, *The English Church* and *The English Cathedral* both by Tim Tatton-Brown, *The English Country House* by Peter Brimacombe and *Houses & Cottages of Britain* by RW Brunskill.

Painting & Sculpture

For centuries, English art was influenced by the great European movements, and in the days before cameras, portrait-painting was a reliable if unadventurous mainstay for most working artists. Top names include Sir Joshua Reynolds, whose portraits in the 'grand style' include *Lady Anstruther* (which you can see today in London's Tate Britain gallery, p115) and his rival, Thomas Gainsborough, who produced informal works with subjects at ease in a landscape, such as *Mr & Mrs Andrews* (National Portrait Gallery, p114).

In the 18th century William Hogarth was a breakaway figure from the comfortable world of portraits, producing a series of paintings which satirised social abuses. His most celebrated work is *A Rake's Progress*, displayed today at Sir John Soane's Museum (p119), London.

Two other key figures of the 18th-century English art scene were Joseph Wright, whose interest in science inspired the oddly titled but beautifully executed *An Experiment on a Bird in the Air Pump*, and George Stubbs, whose passion for animal anatomy, particularly horses, is evident in many works at Tate Britain, and in countless prints on countless country pub walls.

Gainsborough's English landscape tradition was continued by John Constable who painted mainly in Suffolk (still billed as 'Constable Country' by the local tourist board). His most famous work is *The Haywain* (National Gallery, p113) – an idyllic rural scene.

Constable's contemporaries include poet, painter and visionary William Blake, and JMW Turner, whose works increasingly subordinated picture details to the effects of light and colour. By the 1840s, Turner's compositions became almost entirely abstract and were widely vilified. Both artists have rooms dedicated to their work at Tate Britain (p115), and the Turner collection at Petworth House (p225) in West Sussex is exquisite.

In the 20th century, the place of English art in the international arena was ensured by Henry Moore's and Barbara Hepworth's monumental sculptures, Francis Bacon's contorted paintings, and David Hockney's highly representational images of – among other things – dachshunds and swimming pools. Much of Hockney's work can be seen at Salt's Mill gallery in his home town of Bradford (p589), some of Moore's work can be seen at the Yorkshire Sculpture Park (p590), between Sheffield and Leeds, while Hepworth is forever associated with St Ives (p365) in Cornwall.

After WWII, Howard Hodgkin and Patrick Heron developed an English version of American abstract expressionism. At the same time, but in great contrast, Manchester artist LS Lowry was painting his much-loved 'matchstick men' figures set in an urban landscape of narrow streets and smoky factories. A good place to see his work is in The Lowry (p648), Manchester.

In 1956 a young artist called Richard Hamilton created a photomontage called *Just what is it that makes today's homes so different, so appealing?* as a poster for the Whitechapel Art Gallery in London. It launched the pop-art movement in England, and the style was loved by millions when Peter Blake designed the record covers for the Beatles' seminal album *Sergeant Pepper's Lonely Hearts Club Band*.

The Whitechapel Art Gallery also helped launch the career of sculptor Anthony Caro, with a groundbreaking exhibition in 1963. Creating large abstract works primarily in steel and bronze, Caro has become a highly influential figure, considered by many to be England's greatest living sculptor. For more heavy metal see www.anthonycaro.org.

Moving towards our own era, the British art scene of the 1990s was dominated by a group of young artists championed by advertising tycoon Charles Saatchi, and displayed at his eponymous gallery (see www.saatchi-gallery.co.uk). As 'Britpop' developed in the music industry, so the paintings, sculptures and installations of these artists became known as 'Britart'. As notorious as they were talented – some would say more of the former, less of the latter – the group included Damien Hirst, infamous for his use of animals, alive and dead, Tracey Emin, most famous for *My Bed*, a combination of soiled sheets and 'sluttish detritus' (according to one review), and Rachel Whiteread, initially best-known for her resin casts of commonplace objects.

The early years of the 21st century have, inevitably, been dubbed the 'post-Britart' era, and although a generation of less obviously shocking artists is emerging, none have yet become a household name. Of the previous generation, Whiteread is still a major figure on the art scene today: in 2006 she created a massive labyrinthine installation called *Embankment* for the equally

Click on www.tate.org.uk for details of exhibitions at the Tate family of galleries, or www.saatchi-gallery.co.uk for a look at some of London's high-profile contemporary art.

Angel of the North is one of the most viewed works of art in the world. It stands beside the busy A1 highway and millions of drivers each year can't help but see this huge sculpture. See www.gateshead.gov.uk/angel.

gigantic Turbine Hall at the Tate Modern in London, a fitting work for one of the world's most impressive galleries. For more see www.tate.org.uk.

Other key artists of today include the sculptor Antony Gormley, whose *Angel Of The North* overlooks the city of Gateshead near Newcastle. A massive steel construction of a human figure with outstretched wings, more fitting on a 747 than a heavenly being, it was initially derided by the locals, but it is now a proud symbol of Northeast England.

Theatre

However you budget your time and money, make sure that you see some English theatre as part of your travels. It easily lives up to its reputation as the finest in the world, and London's West End is the international centre for theatrical arts – whatever New Yorkers say.

But first, let's set the stage with some history. England's best-known theatrical name is of course William Shakespeare, whose plays were first performed in the 16th century at the Globe Theatre. His brilliant plots and sharp prose, and the sheer size of his canon of work (including classics such as *Hamlet* and *Romeo and Juliet*), have turned him into a national icon (see p470). The Globe has now been rebuilt (see p123), so you can see the Bard's plays performed in Elizabethan style – in the round, with 'groundlings' in the audience heckling the actors and joining in the bits they know.

England's theatres were firmly closed as dens of iniquity in Oliver Cromwell's day, but when Charles II returned from exile in 1660 he opened the doors again, and encouraged radical practices such as actresses (female roles had previously been played by boys) – an innovation loved by London audiences, along with humorous plays known as Restoration comedies, delighting in bawdy wordplay and mockery of the upper classes. The leading lady of the day was Nell Gwyn, who also became Charles II's mistress.

In the 18th century, theatres were built in the larger English cities. The Bristol Old Vic and The Grand in Lancaster date from this time, along with plays such as Oliver Goldsmith's uproarious *She Stoops to Conquer*. Top of the bill was actor David Garrick, who later gave his name to one of London's leading theatres.

The 1950s also marked the emergence of new playwrights with new freedoms, such as John Osborne, whose best-known work is *Look Back in Anger*. A contemporary was Harold Pinter, who developed a new dramatic style and perfectly captured the stuttering illogical diction of real-life conversation.

> England's first theatre was built in 1576 on the northern outskirts of London and was called – rather unimaginatively– 'The Theatre'. Shakespeare's famous Globe Theatre came a little later.

IT'S ALL A BIT OF A PANTOMIME

If any British tradition seems specially designed to bemuse outsiders, it has to be pantomime, performed in theatres all over the country, usually in January and February. Essentially a pantomime is a comedy play or review, with dialogue, routines, songs, dances and lots of custard-pie humour (and – despite the name – no mime) loosely based on stories such as *Cinderella* or *Jack and the Beanstalk*.

Pantomime's roots go back to Celtic legends, medieval morality plays and the art of mumming, but the modern version is a post-Christmas ritual, with people packing out theatres to see old favourite 'pantos' updated to touch on recent political scandals or celebrity gossip, and always featuring a star from a TV soap or game-show, or from the world of pop or sport. Pantos also feature routines that everyone knows and joins in ('Where's that dragon/wizard/pirate/lion?' – 'He's behind you!') and tradition dictates that the leading 'boy' is played by a woman, and the leading lady, or 'dame', played by a man. It may be bizarre, but for kids and families it's a great evening out. Oh no it isn't. Oh yes it is. Oh no it isn't.

In the 1960s and 1970s, plays by Tom Stoppard *(Rosencrantz and Guildenstern are Dead)*, Peter Shaffer *(Amadeus)*, Michael Frayn *(Noises Off)* and Alan Ayckbourn *(The Norman Conquests)* took the country by storm – and famous English actors such as Helen Mirren, Glenda Jackson, Judi Dench and Tom Courtenay did justice to them on stage.

In the 1990s and first decade of the 21st century, big names in English theatre include Brenda Blethyn, Charles Dance, Judi Dench (still!), Ian McKellen, Anthony Sher, Simon Callow, Toby Stephens, Jane Horrocks and Ralph Fiennes – although most perform in stage productions only once or twice a year, combining this with more lucrative appearances on the small or silver screen.

Shakespeare in Love is an unashamedly romantic, undoubtedly modern and unrepentantly funny movie: providing a great insight on backstage Elizabethan London.

In London, other stars of the stage these days are the directors, especially Nicholas Hytner at the National Theatre, whose 2006 successes included *The History Boys* by the perennially dour English playwright Alan Bennet. After winning numerous accolades in Britain, the play transferred to Broadway – where it charmed the notoriously tough New York critics, and eventually scooped six Tony awards (the most for any production since Arthur Miller's *Death of a Salesman* in 1949). Another hit of 2006 was *Rock 'n' Roll*, a multi-themed play by Tom Stoppard about the fall of Communism in Czechoslovakia, directed by award-winning Trevor Nunn at London's Royal Court Theatre. As the title suggests, rock music also features in the play, and Mick Jagger has reportedly already bought the film rights.

It's thanks to the quality and success of English drama that native actors are frequently joined by colleagues from over the Pond, as the likes of Madonna, Nicole Kidman, Gwyneth Paltrow, Matthew Perry, Macaulay Culkin, Christian Slater, Kim Cattrall, Gael Garcia Bernal, David Schwimmer and Kevin Spacey have performed in London productions in recent years, exchanging Hollywood glamour for pay-cuts and the genuine cred that only treading West End boards can bestow. (For more cues on the capital's current drama scene see p151).

And while there's often an urge among producers to stick with the big names and safe (and profitable) productions, the risk and innovation normally more associated with fringe events does sometimes filter through too, making London's theatre arguably more innovative and exciting than it's been since the Restoration, and certainly – according to some critics – since the angry postwar era of Osborne and co. Only London could produce an entirely new genre by turning a TV talk-show for losers, misfits, weirdos and gender-benders into the wonderfully perverse, and highly controversial, *Jerry Springer – the Opera*.

Harold Pinter wrote numerous plays, but is probably still best known for his landmark work *The Birthday Party* – a study of sinister figures and shady untold pasts.

Alongside the frivolity, perhaps the most notable and possibly the most predictable trend in recent times has been the upsurge in political theatre in the wake of the Iraq war. The satire and analysis spread all the way from the fringe – where plays such as *Justifying War*, *The Madness of George Dubya* and *A Weapons Inspector Calls* were on show – to the West End, where political drama *Guantanamo* deeply moved and impressed audiences, although it has to be said that in many cases there was an element of preaching to the converted.

Despite the vital message of *Guantanamo* and *Jerry*'s much-deserved success, for many visitors to London the theatres of the West End mean one thing: musicals, from *Jesus Christ Superstar* in the 1970s, to *Cats*, *Les Mis*, *Chicago*, *Phantom* and all the rest. Many of today's shows are based on the pop lexicon, with singalongs from *Mamma Mia* to *Fame*, proving that – just like in Shakespeare's day – all we want to do really is join in.

Environment

England is the largest of the three nations on the island of Britain, with Scotland to the north and Wales to the west. Further west lies the island of Ireland. Looking south, France is just 20 miles away across the stretch of water known to the French as La Manche (the sleeve) and to the English – with their usual sense of humility – as the English Channel.

THE LAND

Wild Britain: A Traveller's Guide by Douglas Botting has excellent advice for escaping the crowds and exploring England's outback.

Geologically at least, England is part of Europe, on the edge of the Eurasian landmass, separated from the mother continent by the shallow English Channel. When sea levels were lower, England was *physically* part of Europe, and today – despite some misgivings on the part of anti-Europeans – the Channel Tunnel means the island is linked to the Continental mainland once again.

England is not a place of geographical extremes. There are no Himalayas or Lake Baikals here. But there's plenty to keep visitors enthralled, and even a relatively short journey can take you through a surprising mix of landscapes.

Southern England is covered in a mix of towns, cities and gently undulating countryside. East Anglia is almost entirely low and flat, while the Southwest Peninsula has granite outcrops, wild moors and rich pastures – hence Devon's world-famous cream – with a rugged coast and sheltered beaches that make it a favourite holiday destination.

Perhaps surprisingly, the most wooded county in England is Surrey, despite its proximity to London. The soil is too poor for agriculture, and while woodland in other parts of England has been cleared, especially since the 1950s, many of Surrey's trees got a stay of execution.

In the north of England, farmland remains interspersed with towns and cities, but the landscape is noticeably bumpier. A line of large hills called the Pennines (fondly tagged 'the backbone of England') runs from Derbyshire to the Scottish border, and includes the peaty plateaus of the Peak District, the wild moors around Haworth (immortalised in Brontë novels), the delightful valleys of the Yorkshire Dales and the frequently windswept but ruggedly beautiful hills of Northumberland.

Perhaps England's best-known landscape is the Lake District, a small but spectacular cluster of hills and mountains in the northwest, where Scaféll Pike (a towering 978m) is England's highest peak.

WILDLIFE

For a small country, England has a diverse range of plants and animals. Many native species are hidden away, but there are some undoubted gems – from lowland woods carpeted in shimmering bluebells to stately herds of deer on the high moors – and taking the time to have a closer look will enhance your trip enormously.

COMPARING COVERAGE

Statistics can be boring, but these essential measurements may be handy for planning or perspective as you travel around:

England: 50,000 sq miles
Britain: 88,500 sq miles
UK: 95,000 sq miles
British Isles: 123,000 sq miles

If you want some comparisons, France is about 212,000 sq miles, Texas 266,000 sq miles, Australia 2.7 million sq miles and the USA about 3.5 million sq miles.

SEA LIFE

Two seal species frequent English coasts: the larger grey seal, which is more often seen, and the misnamed common seal. Dolphins, porpoises, minke whales and basking sharks can also be seen off the western coasts, especially from about May to September when viewing conditions are better – although you may need to go with someone who knows where to look!

Animals

In farmland and woodland areas, a favourite English mammal is the black-and-white striped badger, while on riverbanks the once-rare otter is slowly making a comeback. Common birds include the robin, with its red breast and cheerful whistle. In open fields, the warbling cry of a skylark is a classic, but now threatened, sound of the English countryside.

Also in the fields, be on the look out for brown hares, an increasingly rare species, related to rabbits but much larger, with longer legs and ears. Males who battle for territory in early spring are, of course, as 'mad as a March hare'.

Other woodland mammals include the small white-spotted fallow deer and the even smaller roe deer. If you hear rustling among the fallen leaves it might be a hedgehog – a cute-looking, spiny-backed insect-eater – but it's an increasingly rare sound these days; conservationists say that hedgehogs will be extinct in Britain by 2025, possibly thanks to increased building in rural areas, the use of insecticides in farming, and the changing nature of both the countryside and the city parks and gardens that once made up the hedgehog's traditional habitat.

In contrast, foxes are very widespread and have adapted well to a scavenging life in country towns, and even in city suburbs. A controversial law banning the hunting of foxes with dogs was introduced in 2005, but it's too early to see what impact this has had on population numbers. Grey squirrels (introduced from North America) have also proved very adaptable, to the extent that native red squirrels are severely endangered because the greys eat all the food.

Perhaps unexpectedly, England is also home to a pocket of wild goats, near Lynmouth in Devon, where herds have been for almost 1000 years. (Wild goats can also be seen on the Great Orme Peninsula in Wales, but these are new kids on the block, having been introduced only a century ago.)

If you're hiking in the moors, birds you might see include the red grouse and the curlew, with its elegant curved bill. Golden plovers are beautifully camouflaged, while lapwings are just show-offs with spectacular aerial displays.

One of England's finest wildlife spectacles occurs on the coastal cliffs in early summer, particularly in Cornwall or Yorkshire; countless thousands of guillemots, razorbills, kittiwakes and other breeding sea birds fight for space on crowded rock ledges, and the air is thick with their sound.

For more in-depth information on the nation's flora and fauna, www .wildaboutbritain.co.uk is an award-winning site that's comprehensive, accessible and interactive.

Plants

In the chalky hill country of southern England and the limestone areas further north (such as the Peak District and Yorkshire Dales), the best place to see wild flowers are the fields that evade large-scale farming – many erupt with great profusions of cowslips and primroses in April and May.

Other flowers prefer woodland, and the best time to visit is also April and May, before the leaf canopy is fully developed so sunlight can break through to encourage plants such as bluebells – a beautiful and internationally rare species.

Another classic English plant is gorse: you can't miss the swaths of this spiky bush in heath areas, most notably the New Forest in southern England. Legend says that it's the season for kissing when gorse blooms. Luckily its vivid yellow flowers show year-round.

In contrast, the blooming season for heather is quite short, but no less dramatic; through August and September areas such as the North York Moors and Dartmoor are covered in a riot of purple.

NATIONAL PARKS

Way back in 1810, poet and outdoors-lover William Wordsworth suggested that the Lake District should be 'a sort of national property, in which every man has a right'. More than a century later it became a national park (although quite different from Wordsworth's vision), along with Dartmoor, Exmoor, the New Forest, Norfolk and Suffolk Broads, Northumberland, the North York Moors, the Peak District and the Yorkshire Dales. A new park, the South Downs, is in the process of being created.

It's an impressive total, but the term 'national park' can cause confusion. First, they are not state-owned: nearly all land is private, belonging to farmers, companies, private estates and conservation organisations. Second, they are not areas of total wilderness, as in many other countries. In England's national parks you'll see roads, railways, villages and even towns.

Despite these apparent anomalies, national parks still contain vast tracts of mountain and moorland, with rolling downs, river valleys and other areas of quiet countryside, all ideal for long walks, easy rambles, cycle rides, sightseeing or just lounging around. To help you get the best from the parks, they all have information centres, and various recreational facilities (trails, car parking, campsites etc) are provided for visitors. The table opposite outlines the highlights and the best time to visit.

ENVIRONMENTAL ISSUES

With England's long history of human occupation, it's not surprising that the country's appearance is almost totally the result of people's interaction with the environment. The most dramatic changes in rural areas came after WWII, when a drive to be self-reliant in food and timber meant new farming methods, changing the landscape from a patchwork of small fields to a scene of vast prairies, as walls were demolished, trees felled, ponds filled, wetlands drained and – most notably – hedgerows ripped out.

In most cases the hedgerows were a few metres wide, lines of dense bushes, shrubs and trees forming a network that stretched across the countryside, protecting fields from erosion, supporting a varied range of flowers and providing shelter for numerous insects, birds and small mammals. But in the rush to improve farm yields, thousands of miles of hedgerows have been destroyed since 1950, and since 1984 another 25% have disappeared, although in recent years the destruction has abated, partly because the farmers don't need to remove any more and partly because they're encouraged to maintain and 'set aside' such areas as wildlife havens.

Of course, environmental issues are not exclusive to rural areas. In England's towns and cities, topics such as air and light pollution, levels of car use, road building, airport construction, public-transport provision and household-waste recycling are never far from the political agenda, although some might say they're not near enough to the top of the list. Over the past decade, the main political parties have lacked engagement, although in 2006 the new leader of the opposition Conservatives, David Cameron, declared that sustainability would henceforth be a major tenet of his party, and his PR staff made a big deal of him cycling to work, which looked good (and would

Britain's new 'hedgerows' are the long strips of grass and bushes alongside motorways and major roads. Totalling almost 115 sq miles, they support rare flowers, thousands of insect species and populations of mice, shrews and other small mammals, so kestrels are often seen hovering nearby.

National Park	Features	Activities	Best Time to Visit	Page
Dartmoor	wild heath, marshy moorland: Dartmoor ponies, deer, otter, badger, rabbit, buzzard, peregrine falcon, sheep	hiking, horse riding	May-Jun (wild flowers in bloom)	p342
Exmoor	craggy sea cliffs, sweeping moors: native, wild red deer, Exmoor pony, horned sheep	horse riding, hiking	Sep (heather in bloom)	p287
Lake District	majestic fells, rugged mountains, osprey, red squirrel, waterfowl, sparrowhawk, sheep, England's only golden eagles, shimmering glassy lakes	water sports, hiking, cycling,	Sep-Oct (summer crowds have left and) autumn colours abound)	p687
New Forest	woodlands and heath: wild pony, otter, owl, Dartford warbler, southern damselfly	walking, cycling, horse riding	Apr-Sep (wild ponies are grazing)	p236
Norfolk & Suffolk Broads	expansive shallow lakes and marshlands: water lily, wildfowl, otter	walking, boating	Apr-May (birds most active)	p556
Northumberland	wild rolling moors of autumn-coloured heather and gorse: black grouse, red squirrel and sheep; Hadrian's Wall	walking, climbing, cycling	spring (lambs) & Sep (flowering of the heather)	p758
North York Moors	heather-clad hills and deep-green valleys punctuated by lonely farms and isolated villages: packed with moorland birds, such as curlew, golden plover and merlin	cycling, on and off-road	Aug-Sep (purple heather in bloom)	p628
Peak District	high moors, tranquil dales, limestone caves: jackdaw, kestrel, grouse, rabbit, fox, badger and, of course, sheep	walking, cycling, hang-gliding, climbing	Apr-May (newborn lambs everywhere)	p500
Yorkshire Dales	rugged hills and lush valleys crossed by rugged stone walls and spotted with extravagant houses and the faded, spectral grandeur of monastic ruins	walking, cycling	Apr-May (when lambs just about outnumber visitors)	p594

have been fine if they'd emphasised the health benefits of cycling) until it was realised his chauffer still drove his official car to Parliament, carrying a huge stack of paperwork and a change of clothes. But political point-scoring aside, when it comes to real issues apathy still abounds in most areas; for example, the Green Party enjoyed only modest support in the 2006 council elections – an increase of 20 councillors nationally, compared to a 300 swing from Labour to the Tories.

Meanwhile, back in the country, in addition to hedgerow clearance, other farming techniques remain hot environmental issues: the use of pesticides, monocropping, intensive irrigation, and the 'battery' rearing of cows, sheep and other stock. The results of these unsustainable methods, say environmentalists, are rivers running dry, fish poisoned by runoff, and fields with one type of grass and not another plant to be seen. These 'green deserts'

WILD READING

To further your enjoyment of wildlife-watching, here are some useful guidebooks:

- *Complete Guide to British Wildlife* by Arlott, Fitter & Fitter is a highly recommended single portable volume covering mammals, birds, fish, plants, snakes, insects and even fungi.
- *British Isles: Wildlife of Coastal Waters* by world-famous film-maker Tony Soper beautifully covers the birds, mammals and jelly fish you'll see from beach, boat and clifftop.
- *Birds*, *Trees*, *Fish* and *Wild Flowers* are part of the Gem series of books. They fit in your pocket, cost about £5 and are often sold at tourist offices.
- *Complete British Birds* by Paul Sterry is full of excellent photographs and handy notes, ideal for identifying anything feathered you may see on your travels.
- *Where to Watch Birds in Britain* by Simon Harrop & Nigel Redman is ideal if you need more detail about specific destinations.
- *Wildlife Walks* edited by Malcolm Tait (with a foreword by the nation's favourite ecologist, David Bellamy) suggests days out in over 500 wildlife reserves across the country.

support no insects, so in turn some wild bird populations have dropped by an incredible 70%. This is not a case of wizened old peasants recalling the idyllic days of their forbears; you only have to be over about 30 in England to remember a countryside where birds such as skylarks or lapwings were visibly much more numerous.

But all is not lost. In the face of apparently overwhelming odds, England still boasts great biodiversity, and some of the best wildlife habitats are protected (to a greater or lesser extent) by the creation of national parks and similar areas, or private reserves owned by conservation campaign groups such as the **Wildlife Trusts** (www.wildlifetrusts.org), **Woodland Trust** (www.woodland-trust .org), **National Trust** (www.nationaltrust.org.uk) and the **Royal Society for the Protection of Birds** (www.rspb.org.uk). Many of these areas are open to the public – ideal spots for walking, bird-watching or simply enjoying the peace and beauty of the countryside.

England buries most of its rubbish in 'landfill sites'. By 2015, say environmental campaigners, these will all be full. Options will then be more recycling, or more controversial methods such as incineration

Outdoor Activities

What's the best way to get beyond the beaten track as you travel around England? Simple: enjoy some outdoor activity. Fresh air is good for your body and soul, of course, and becoming *actively* involved in the country's way of life is much more rewarding than staring at it through a camera lens or car window.

Walking and cycling are the most popular and accessible of all outdoor activities, and open up some beautiful corners of the country. You can enjoy short rambles or work up a sweat on long tours, conquer mountains or cruise across plains. There's something for young and old, and these activities are often perfect for families. Whatever your budget, it's a wonderful opportunity to get out and explore, and a walk or ride through the English countryside could be a highlight of your trip.

Information

Throughout this book, the start of each regional chapter gives an overview of the best opportunities for outdoor activities in that area. For more ideas and inspiration, your first stop should always be a tourist office, where you can pick up free leaflets on local walks and rides, or places to climb, fish, surf, ride or play golf in the surrounding region. Tourist-office staff can also tell you where to hire bikes or surf gear, find local guided walks or riding stables, or join organised groups for activities like caving. For walkers and cyclists, tourist offices also sell booklets (for a nominal fee) plus detailed guidebooks and maps (around £4 to £8 each) describing everything from half-hour strolls to week-long expeditions. In rural areas, books and maps are also available in local newsagents and outdoor-gear shops.

The list of activities below starts with walking and cycling – stuff you can do virtually on a whim – then covers other activities that are a bit more structured or need some advance preparation.

WALKING

Perhaps because England is such a crowded place, open areas are highly valued, and every weekend millions of English people get their boots on and take to the countryside. You could do a lot worse than join them!

Every village and town is surrounded by a web of footpaths, while most patches of open country are crossed by paths and tracks, so the options are limitless. You can walk from place to place in true backpacking style, or base yourself in an interesting spot for a week or so and go out on day walks to explore the surrounding countryside.

Access & Rules

The joy of walking in England is due in no small part to the 'right of way' network – public paths and tracks across private property. Nearly all land (including in national parks) in England is privately owned, but if there's a right of way, you can follow it through fields, woods, even farmhouse yards, as long as you keep to the route and do no damage.

The main types of rights of way for walkers are footpaths and bridleways (the latter open to horse riders and mountain bikers too). You'll also see 'byways', which, due to a quirk of history, are open to *all* traffic, so don't be surprised if you have to wade through mud churned up by chunky tyres, or if you're disturbed by the antics of off-road driving fanatics as you're quietly strolling along enjoying the countryside.

The Ramblers' Association (☎ 020-7339 8500; www.ramblers.org.uk) is the country's leading walking organisation. The invaluable, annually updated *Walk Britain* handbook lists routes and walker-friendly accommodation.

Many long-distance routes are served by baggage-carrying services. For about £5 to £10 per day, your gear will be delivered to your next B&B while you walk or ride unencumbered. See www.carrylite.com, www.cumbria.com/pack horse, www.sherpavan .com and www.pikedaw .freeserve.co.uk/walks.

Thanks to the landmark Countryside Act of 2004, walkers (not bikes or other vehicles) can now move freely *beyond* rights of way in some mountain and moorland areas, but not in enclosed fields or cultivated areas. Where this is permitted it's clearly shown on maps and by 'Access Land' or 'Open Access' notices on gates and signposts. The land is still privately owned, and occasionally Access Land is closed, for example if wild birds are nesting or if the farmer is rounding up sheep, but the so-called 'right to roam' or 'freedom to roam' legislation opens up thousands of square miles of landscape previously off-limits to walkers – a milestone ruling resulting after more than 70 years of campaigning by the Ramblers Association and other groups. For more information see www.countrysideaccess.gov.uk.

Where to Walk

For comprehensive coverage of a selection of long and short walking routes, we recommend Lonely Planet's very own *Walking in Britain*, which also covers access, getting there, and places to stay and eat along the way.

Here's a quick rundown of some great walking areas in England, with everything from gentle hills to high summits to tempt you, whether you're a casual rambler or an energetic peak-bagger. With a map and a sense of adventure, the rest is up to you!

NORTHERN ENGLAND

In the northwest of the country, the Lake District (p687) is the heart and soul of walking in England – a wonderful area of soaring peaks, endless views, deep valleys and, of course, beautiful lakes. There's a great selection of country hotels, B&Bs and camp sites too. Good bases include the towns of Ambleside and Keswick, and the lakeside village of Patterdale.

Further north, keen walkers love the starkly beautiful hills of Northumberland National Park (p758), while the coast is less daunting but just as dramatic. In the park, good bases include Wooler and Bellingham. On the coast, head for Alnmouth or to Bamburgh, near a spectacular castle.

For something a little gentler, the valleys and rolling hills of the Yorkshire Dales (p594) make it one of the most popular walking areas in England. Good bases include the villages of Grassington and Malham. Further north, the dramatic valleys of Wensleydale and Swaledale give more options.

CENTRAL ENGLAND

The gem of central England is the Cotswold Hills (p396). This is classic English countryside, with gentle paths through neat fields and mature woodland, or pretty villages with churches, farms and cottages of honey-coloured stone. The marvellously named towns of Moreton-in-Marsh, Stow-on-the-Wold and Bourton-on-the-Water all make ideal bases.

SOUTHERN ENGLAND

What's the emptiest, highest and wildest area in southern England? It's Dartmoor (p342), where the rounded hills are dotted with granite outcrops called 'tors' – looking for all the world like abstract sculptures – and the valleys are full of Bronze Age sites and other ancient remains. Good places to base yourself for day walks include Buckfastleigh on the south side of Dartmoor, or Sticklepath on the north side.

Also in the southwest, Exmoor (p287) has grassy, heather-covered hills cut by deep valleys and edged by spectacular cliffs, great beaches, quiet villages and busy seaside resorts. The walking opportunities are immense. Good bases include Exford and Simonsbath, while on the coast you can head for Lynton and Lynmouth.

In the deep south lies the New Forest (p236). Visitors to England love this name, as the area is more than 1000 years old and there aren't *that* many trees – it's mainly conifer plantations and great open areas of gorse and heath. But

---

THERE'S COLD IN THEM THERE HILLS

The English countryside can appear gentle and welcoming, and often is, but sometimes the weather can turn nasty. At any time of year, if you're walking on the high hills or open moors, it's vital to be well equipped. You should carry warm and waterproof clothing (even in summer), good maps and a compass, some drink, food and high-energy stuff like chocolate. If you're really going off the beaten track, leave details of your route with someone. It may sound a bit extreme, but carrying a whistle and torch – in case of an emergency – is no bad thing either.

---

apart from these minor details, it's a wonderful place for easy strolls, and the towns of Lyndhurst or Lymington make good bases.

And just over the water is the Isle of Wight (p240). If you're new to walking in Britain, or simply not looking for high peaks and wilderness, this is a good first choice. The local authorities have put a lot of effort into footpaths and signposted routes; most are linear and can be done in a day, and you can always get back to your starting point using the island's excellent bus service.

Long-Distance Walks

Many walkers savour the chance of completing one of England's famous long-distance routes. There are hundreds, including several official national trails with better signposting and maintenance than many other long routes, making them ideal for beginners or visitors. You don't have to walk these routes end-to-end; you can walk just a section for a day or two, or use the route as a basis for loops exploring the surrounding area.

Here's a short list of our favourites to get you started:

Coast to Coast Walk (190 miles) The number-one favourite. A top-quality hike across northern England, through three national parks and spectacular scenery of valleys, plains, mountains, dales and moors.

Cotswold Way (102 miles) A fascinating walk through classic picture-postcard countryside with smatterings of English history.

Cumbria Way (68 miles) A fine hike through Lake District valleys, with breathtaking mountain views.

Hadrian's Wall (84 miles) In the footsteps of the legions, an epic stride across northern England.

Pennine Way (256 miles) The granddaddy of them all, along the mountainous spine of northern England.

South West Coast Path (610 miles) A roller-coaster romp round the southwest tip of England, past beaches, bays, shipwrecks, seaside resorts, fishing villages and cliff-top castles.

Thames Path (173 miles) A journey of contrasts beside England's best-known river, from rural Gloucestershire to the heart of London.

For more details on England's national trail options, stroll on over to www .nationaltrail.co.uk.

CYCLING

A bike is the perfect mode of transport for exploring back-road England. Once you escape the busy main highways, there's a vast network of quiet country lanes leading through fields and peaceful villages, ideal for touring on a road or mountain bike. Off-road riders can go further into the wilds on the many tracks and bridleways that cross England's farmlands, forests and high moors.

The opportunities are endless. Depending on your energy and enthusiasm you can amble along flat lanes, taking it easy and stopping for cream teas, or thrash all day through hilly areas, revelling in steep ascents and swooping

The Cyclists' Touring Club (☎ 0870 873 0060; www.ctc.org.uk), the UK's leading recreational cycling and campaigning body, has a comprehensive website with a cycle-hire directory and mail-order service for maps and books.

THE NATIONAL CYCLE NETWORK

Anyone riding a bike through England will almost certainly come across the National Cycle Network, a UK-wide 10,000-mile web of roads and traffic-free tracks. Strands of the network in busy cities are aimed at commuters or school kids (where the network follows city streets, cyclists normally have their own lane, separate from motor traffic), while other sections follow the most remote roads in the country and are perfect for touring.

The whole scheme is the brainchild of Sustrans (derived from 'sustainable transport'), a campaign group barely taken seriously way back in 1978 when the network idea was first announced. But the growth of cycling, coupled with near-terminal car congestion, has earned the scheme lots of attention – not to mention many millions of pounds from national government and regional authorities.

Several long-distance touring routes use the most scenic sections of the National Cycle Network, and a few less-than-scenic urban sections, it has to be said. Other features include a great selection of artworks to admire along the way. In fact, the network is billed as the country's largest outdoor-sculpture gallery. The whole scheme is a resounding success and a credit to the visionaries who persevered against inertia all those years ago. For more details see www.sustrans.org.uk.

downhill sections. You can cycle from place to place, camping or staying in B&Bs (many of which are cyclist friendly), or you can base yourself in one place for a few days and go out on rides in different directions.

Access & Rules

Bikes aren't allowed on motorways, but you can cycle on all other public roads, although main roads (A-roads) tend to be busy and should be avoided. Many B-roads suffer heavy motor traffic too, so the best places for cycling are the small C-roads and unclassified roads ('lanes') that cover rural England, especially in lowland areas, meandering through quiet countryside and linking small, picturesque villages.

Cycling is *not* allowed on footpaths, but mountain bikers can ride on unmade roads or bridleways that are a public right of way. For mountain biking it's often worth seeking out forestry areas; among the vast plantations, signposted routes of varying difficulty have been opened up for single-track fans.

Cycling in the UK is an excellent handbook, coving over 40 day-rides and a range of longer 'holiday routes'. For off-roading, the best book is *Where to Mountain Bike in Britain*, or see www.wheretomtb.com.

Where to Cycle

While you can cycle anywhere in England, some places are better than others. In popular spots, car traffic can be a problem on summer weekends, and if you're not a regular cyclist the hills in some areas can be daunting. This section gives a brief overview, but (just as with walking) all you need is a map and a sense of adventure, and the highways and byways of England are yours for the taking.

NORTHERN ENGLAND

It's no accident that many of England's top racing cyclists come from northern England – the mountain roads make an excellent training ground. The North York Moors offer exhilarating off-road rides, while the Yorkshire Dales are great for cycle touring. These areas are hilly and some routes can be strenuous, but the scenery is superb and it's all well worth the effort.

Derbyshire's Peak District is a very popular area for mountain biking and road cycling, although the hills are also quite steep in places. More leisurely options are excellent cycle routes cutting through the landscape along disused railways – dramatic and effortless at the same time.

CENTRAL ENGLAND
The Cotswolds offer good cycling options, with lanes through farmland and quaint villages. From the western side of the hills you get fantastic views over the Severn Valley, but you wouldn't want to go up and down this escarpment too often! The Marches area, where England borders Wales, is another rural delight, with good quiet lanes and some off-road options in the hills.

EASTERN ENGLAND
The counties of Norfolk and Suffolk are generally low-lying and flat, with quiet lanes winding through farmland and picturesque villages, past rivers, lakes and welcoming country pubs – great for easy pedalling.

SOUTHERN ENGLAND
Down at the southwestern tip of the country, Cornwall and Devon are beautiful and enjoy the best of the English climate, but the rugged landscape makes for tough days in the saddle. Somerset, Dorset and Wiltshire have more gentle hills (plus a few steep valleys to keep you on your toes) and a beautiful network of quiet lanes, making the area perfect for leisurely cycle touring. In Hampshire, the ancient woodland and open heath of the New Forest is especially good for on- and off-road rides, while in Sussex the South Downs offer numerous mountain-bike options.

OTHER ACTIVITIES
Coasteering
If a simple walk along the clifftops admiring the view just doesn't cut the mustard, and you'd like to combine elements of rock climbing with the element of water, then the whacky activity of coasteering might appeal. It's like mountaineering, but instead of going up a mountain, you go along the coast – a steep rocky coast, often with waves breaking around your feet. And if the rock gets too steep, it's simple – you jump in and start swimming. You need a wetsuit, an old pair of shoes, buoyancy aid, a helmet – and a sense of adventure. Cornwall and Devon are the main areas where coasteering is gaining popularity, although it's not something you should go off and do on your own. Ask at tourist offices about specialist local operators.

> 'And if the rock gets too steep, it's simple – you jump in and start swimming'

Fishing
Fishing is enormously popular in England, but in many areas it's highly regulated, with prime stretches of river privately owned and angling rights fiercely

---

WATERWAY TRAVEL

England's inland waterways consist of rivers and lakes plus a surprisingly extensive canal network. Built in the early Industrial Revolution, canals were the country's main form of transport until railways boomed in the 19th century. Today, canals are alive again, part of a booming leisure-boat industry, dubbed the 'New Canal Age'. Mile-for-mile, canals are being restored and reopened at the same rate they were built in their 1790s heyday.

Travel by boat reveals a hidden side of England, as canals lead past idyllic villages, pretty countryside and colourful waterside pubs. They also offer an unexpected view of cities like London and Birmingham. With well over 1000 miles of navigable canals and rivers in England, there's plenty to explore.

Across the waterway network, boats are easily hired (for a few hours, a day or a week, or longer - no special skills are needed), and exploring England this way can be immensely rewarding. For families or groups it's a fascinating, fun and economical combination of transport and accommodation. For more information see www.britishwaterways.co.uk and www.waterscape.com.

protected. There's a fishing club on the trout-filled River Itchen in Hampshire where it's rumoured even Prince Charles had to join the waiting list.

Fly fishers in Britain mainly catch salmon, brown trout and rainbow trout, while coarse fishing is principally for perch, carp, bream and the occasional oversize pike. There are plenty of well-stocked rivers and reservoirs, as well as stretches of wild waterway, but wherever you angle, you'll need to obtain a licence – available from post offices (from £3 per day to £60 for the season) or from the website of the **Environment Agency** (www.environment-agency.gov.uk).

If you want to try your luck, tourist-office staff can direct you to local clubs or places offering a day or two's fishing, such as stocked reservoirs that allow public access or smart hotels with private lakes or stretches of river.

On the sea, it's a different story. At resort towns around the coast of England, you can easily find skippered boats offering angling trips, usually with tackle, bait (and lunch) included in the fee. Details are given in the individual town sections.

Golf

'Golf may be 'a good walk spoilt', but a few rounds on a scenic course is a fine way to see the English countryside'

Golf may be 'a good walk spoilt', but a few rounds on a scenic course is a fine way to see the English countryside. Golf courses fall into two main categories: private and public. Some exclusive private clubs admit only golfers who have a handicap certificate from their own club, but most welcome visitors. Public courses run by town or city councils are open to anyone.

A round on a public course will cost around £10 (more at weekends). Private courses average around £40. Top-end hotels may have arrangements with nearby courses which will get you reduced fees or guaranteed tee-off times. If you need to hire, a set of golf clubs costs from £10 per round.

A very good starting point for golfers from overseas is the **Golf Club of Great Britain** (☎ 020-8390 3113; www.golfclubgb.co.uk); this friendly organisation can advise on where to play and arranges regular tournaments.

Horse Riding & Pony Trekking

There's a theory that humans are genetically programmed to absorb the world at a horse's walking pace. It's all to do with our nomadic ancestors, apparently. Add the extra height, and seeing England from horseback is a highly recommended way to go.

Across England, especially in rural areas and national parks such as Dartmoor and Northumberland, riding centres cater to all levels of proficiency. Generally, pony trekking is aimed at novice riders. If you're more experienced in equestrian matters, most centres have horses available.

Many riding centres advertise in national-park newspapers (available free from hotels, tourist offices and local shops). A half-day pony trek costs around £15, a full day £20 to £30. Serious riders pay higher rates for superior mounts. The website of the **British Horse Society** (☎ 0870 120 2244; www.bhs.org.uk) lists approved riding centres and – if you fancy a few days in the saddle – outfits offering riding holidays.

Kitesurfing & Kiteboarding,

If regular surfing just doesn't offer enough airtime, here's an easy solution: strap yourself to a board and an enormous parachute, and let the wind do the work. It's called kitesurfing, and combines elements of windsurfing, wakeboarding, surfing and kite flying. It's also one of the fastest-growing water sports in the world. Brisk winds, decent waves and great beaches make Cornwall a favourite spot, but kitesurfing is possible on beaches all round the English coastline. There are several schools that can show you the ropes. Contact the **British Kite Surfing Association** (☎ 01509 856500; www.kitesurfing.org) for more information.

Kitebuggying & Land-Yachting

If you like the idea of kites but don't fancy getting wet, you can experience wind-fuelled thrills on dry land too. Instead of balancing on a surfboard, you can pick up serious speed standing on an oversize skateboard or sitting on a specially built kite buggy. Also known as para-kiting, it's similar to land-yachting, but with a parachute instead of a sail. Both land-yachting and kite-buggying are usually available on the beaches where surfers lurk, and on any other big stretch of flat sand, notably near Burnham Deepdale (p559) in Norfolk, a great backpacker-friendly base for other activities too.

Mountain Boarding

Imagine hurtling down a rough, grassy hillside at horrendous speeds on a gigantic skateboard equipped with four oversize wheels, and you've pretty much got mountain boarding. This exhilarating activity combines elements of surfing, snowboarding and mountain biking, and is rapidly picking up momentum across the country since it's relatively simple to get started – all you really need is a board, a few hills and some sympathetic friends who can drive you to hospital once your ride is over. There are mountain-boarding centres in Yorkshire, Derbyshire, Shropshire and Cornwall (among other places), but you can do it practically anywhere where there's a grassy slope – as long as you've got the landowner's permission of course.

Rock Climbing & Mountaineering

There are indoor climbing competitions at various venues, but for the outdoor noncompetitive side of things, England's main centre for long multi-pitch routes (as well as some fine short routes) is the Lake District. Other popular climbing areas are the Peak District and Yorkshire Dales. England also offers the exhilaration of sea-cliff climbing, most notably in Cornwall. Nothing makes you concentrate more on finding the next hold than waves crashing 30m below!

The website of the **British Mountaineering Council** (☎ 0870 010 4878; www.thebmc .co.uk) covers indoor climbing walls, access rules (don't forget, all mountains and outcrops are privately owned), competitions and so on.

UK climbing grades are different from those in the USA and Continental Europe; there's a handy conversion table at www.rockfax.com/publica tions/grades.html.

Sailing & Windsurfing

England has a nautical heritage and sailing is a very popular pastime, in everything from tiny dinghies to ocean-going yachts. In recent years there's been a massive surge in windsurfing too. Places to sail in England include the coasts of Norfolk and Suffolk, southeast England (eg Brighton, Eastbourne and Dover), Devon, Cornwall, and the Solent (the stretch of water between the Isle of Wight and the south coast – and one of the most popular sailing areas in Britain). There are also many inland lakes and reservoirs, ideal for training, racing or just pottering.

Your first port of call for any sailing or windsurfing matter should be the **Royal Yachting Association** (☎ 0845 345 0400; www.rya.org.uk). This organisation can provide all the details you need about training centres where you can learn the ropes, improve your skills or simply charter a boat for pleasure.

Surfing

If you've come from the other side of the world, you'll be delighted to learn that summer water temperatures in England are roughly equivalent to winter temperatures in southern Australia (approximately 13°C). But as long as

'Imagine hurtling down a rough, grassy hillside at horrendous speeds on a gigantic skateboard equipped with four oversize wheels'

you've got a wetsuit, there are many excellent surf opportunities. England's huge tidal range means there's often a completely different set of breaks at low and high tides.

The best places to start are Cornwall and Devon, where the west coast is exposed to the Atlantic; from Land's End to Ilfracombe there's a string of surf spots. Newquay is the English surf capital, with all the trappings from Kombi vans to bleached hair. In 2006 a national newspaper carried a story about two guys from Hawaii who spent a year in Cornwall because the surf was more intriguing and challenging. Away from the southwest hotspots, there are smaller surf scenes in Norfolk and in Yorkshire on the east coast of England.

The main national organisation is the **British Surfing Association** (☎ 01637 876474; www.britsurf.co.uk); its website has news on approved instruction centres, courses, competitions and so on. Another good site is www.a1surf.com, with comprehensive links and weather forecasts. Combine these sites with *Surf UK* by Wayne Alderson, a comprehensive guidebook covering almost 400 breaks, and you're sorted.

Food & Drink

England once boasted a cuisine so undesirable that there's still no English equivalent for the phrase *bon appétit*. But these days the tide has turned; in 2005, food bible *Gourmet* magazine singled out London as having the best collection of restaurants in the world, and it's easy to find decent food in other cities, not to mention well-to-do market towns and country areas.

Having said that, Britain's culinary heritage of ready-sliced white bread, fatty meats and vegetables boiled to death, all washed down by tea with four sugars, remains firmly in place in many parts of the country. And that's before we get on to treats like pork scratchings and deep-fried Mars bars. But wherever you travel, for each greasy spoon or fast-food joint, there's a local pub or restaurant serving up enticing home-grown specialities. Epicures can splash out big bucks on fine dining, while for even the most budget-conscious of visitors, tasty eating in England definitely won't break the bank.

The infamous outbreaks of 'mad cow' disease in the late 1990s and foot-and-mouth disease in 2001 are history now, and British beef is once again exported to the world. An upside of the bad press was a massive surge in demand for organic food, and there's now a plethora of natural, unadulterated, chemical-free products available from producers or in shops, markets, cafés and restaurants across the country.

For locals and visitors, organic food usually means better food, but there are anomalies: it seems impossible to buy English apples in some supermarkets during the autumn cropping season, although you can chose between 10 different varieties imported from New Zealand, Chile or South Africa.

Alongside the greater awareness of food's quality and provenance, there have been other changes to English food thanks to outside influences. For decades most towns have boasted Chinese and Indian restaurants, so a vindaloo or a chow mein, while often very tasty, is no longer considered 'exotic'. It's quite usual for British people – even students – to cook a curry at home, whatever their racial heritage. And out on the street, curry is the most popular takeaway food in Britain, outstripping even fish and chips.

As well as the food available in 'Indian' restaurants (which in many cases are owned, run and staffed by people from Pakistan or Bangladesh), dishes from Japan, Korea, Thailand and other countries east of Suez have become

Rick Stein is a TV chef, energetic restaurateur and real-food evangelist. His book *Food Heroes* extols small-scale producers and top-notch local food, from organic veg to sausages made from free-roaming wild boars.

According to leading organic-food campaign group the Soil Association (www.soilassociation .org), three out of four households in Britain buy organic food.

WHERE THERE'S SMOKE

For years, the regulations concerning smoking in restaurants in England have been vague or nonexistent. Some places provide nonsmoking areas (often fairly half-hearted), while others don't bother at all – meaning the smokers at the next table won't hesitate in sparking up even if you're halfway through your meal. 'It's my right to smoke' they bleat if you should be so rude as to ask them to desist, and then look hurt if you reply, 'It's my right not to breathe your filthy smoke, go home smelling like an ashtray and give myself cancer'. In the face of such arrogance and selfishness, a new Health Act will come into force in summer 2007, banning smoking in 'all enclosed public places apart from licensed premises that do not serve or prepare food' throughout England (and Wales), replicating a similar law already in force in Scotland and Ireland. In short, this means all restaurants will be completely nonsmoking, as will pubs serving food. Pubs that make most of their money from beer, as opposed to food, will probably stop offering dodgy pies and cheese rolls, and allow smoking to continue. Through 2006, a fascinating debate raged through England: does a packet of peanuts count as 'food'? And what about pickled eggs? By the time you read this book, we'll know.

VEGETARIANS

It's official – vegetarians are no longer weird. Many restaurants and pubs in England have at least a token vegetarian dish (another meat-free lasagne, anyone?), but better places offer much more imaginative choices. Vegans will find the going more tricky, except of course at dedicated veggie/vegan restaurants – and where possible we recommend good options throughout this book. For more ideas see www.happycow.com.

available in more recent times too. From the other side of the world, there's been a growth in restaurants specialising in South American, African or Caribbean cuisine. Closer to home, pasta, pizza and a wide range of Mediterranean specialities – from countries as diverse as Morocco and Greece – are commonplace not only in decent restaurants, but also in everyday pubs and cafés.

The overall effect of these foreign influences has been the introduction to 'traditional' English restaurants of new techniques (like steaming), new condiments (like chilli or soy sauce), new implements (like woks) and even revolutionary ingredients (like crisp fresh vegetables). We've also seen the creation of 'modern British cuisine', where even humble bangers and mash rise to new heights when handmade thyme-flavoured sausages are paired with lightly chopped fennel and new potatoes.

London leads the way of course, whether you want indigenous classics, a taste of the world, or – most popular – a fusion of the two. And as trailblazing restaurants progressively raised the standard, so the others followed. Fresh, free-range, organic produce replaced processed ingredients, staff were drilled into professional service and designers created some of the world's coolest and most aesthetically pleasing eating spaces, so that eating out in the capital can be as diverse, stylish and satisfying as anywhere else on the planet.

But beware the hype. While some restaurants – in London and elsewhere – are undeniably excellent, others are not. Only a few months after *Gourmet* magazine called the capital 'the best place in the world to eat right now', one of the country's most respected food critics, the *Evening Standard*'s Fay Maschler, decried the domination of style over substance, and accused several top places of offering poor value for money. As any food-fan will tell you, rather than forking out £30 in a restaurant for a 'modern European' concoction that tastes like it came from a can, you're often better off spending £5 on a top-notch curry in Bradford or a homemade steak-and-ale-pie in a Devon country pub.

A pub? Yes. Many foreign visitors to England are surprised to learn that perhaps the biggest change in recent years has been to the quality of food in pubs. Not so many years ago your choice would be a ham or cheese roll, with pickled onions if you were lucky. These days, pubs are a good-value option whether you want a toasted sandwich or a three-course meal. Some pubs specialise in excellent food, but still maintain a relaxed informal atmosphere where you'll find mismatched cutlery, no tablecloths, waiters in T-shirts and you order and pay at the bar along with your drinks – bingo – we get to enjoy gastro-pubs. But nothing beats the luxury of a wholesome shepherd's pie washed down with a decent ale without the worry of guessing which fork to use.

Of course, there's more to food than eating out. The lavishly illustrated food sections in weekend newspapers and the bookshop shelves groaning under the weight of countless new cookery books all indicate that food is now officially fashionable. Many English people are being more adventurous in their own kitchens and more discerning when they shop. Feeding on this is the current phenomenon of so-called 'celebrity chefs', including Hugh Fernley-Whittingstall, who famously scored a £2 million deal with his publishers in early 2006, and Gordon Ramsay who featured in a list of Britain's richest

Like the taste of meat, but don't like the idea of battery pens? Click on www.farmgatedirect.com – a list of lamb, beef, chicken and salmon producers approved by the RSPCA.

For tasty details on the whereabouts of farmers markets see www.farmersmarkets.net.

self-made entrepreneurs a few months later. They are not alone; every night, on a TV channel near you, a star of the kitchen demonstrates imaginative and simple techniques for producing stylish, tasty and healthy food.

There's change afoot in the shops too. Supermarkets still dominate – four companies (Asda-Walmart, Morrison, Sainsbury, Tesco) accounted for around 80% of all grocery shopping in 2006 – squeezing suppliers to sell at ever-lower prices, while forcing out old-fashioned butchers and bakers from high streets and neighbourhoods – but they're selling more organic food than ever before, and new labels show just how much fat, salt and sugar foodstuffs contain. Alongside these changes runs an increase in the number of independent stores selling high-quality food, while the relatively new phenomenon of farmers markets create an opportunity for food producers to sell high-quality, locally sourced meat, veg, fruit, eggs, honey and so on direct to the public. And not just in country towns where you might expect to see them, but in cities too; there's around 20 farmers markets in London alone.

But behind the scenes, and despite the growing availability of good food in shops, markets, pubs and restaurants, the English still have an odd attitude to eating at home. In reality the whole thing is a sham. The people of England love to sit on the sofa and *watch* TV food shows. Inspired, they rush out and buy all the TV-tie-in recipe books. Then on the way back, they pop into the supermarket and buy a stack of ready-made meals. Homemade food sounds great in theory, but in reality the recipe for dinner is more likely to be something like this: open freezer, take out package, bung in microwave, ping, eat.

In fact, more junk food and ready-made meals are consumed in the UK than in the rest of Europe. So it's no surprise that the English are getting increasingly heavy, with over 60% of the adult population overweight, and almost 25% obese. But despite the vast intakes, average nutrition rates are lower now than they were during 1950s post-war rationing. Yes, you can find great food in England. It's just that not all the English seem to like eating it.

In Yorkshire, the eponymous pudding is traditionally eaten *before* the main meal, usually with gravy. This harks back to days of yore when food was scarce. The pudding was a stomach-filler, so you didn't worry so much about the tiny piece of meat on your platter.

STAPLES & SPECIALITIES

For generations, a typical English staple has been roast beef (that's why the French call the English 'les rosbif'), although meat consumption – and British farming – took a nose-dive in 2000 and 2001 following the outbreak of 'mad cow' and foot-and-mouth disease. These events were still most notoriously recalled in 2005 by France's President Jacques Chirac; joking with fellow leaders at an international conference, he quipped about the British, 'The only thing they have done for European agriculture is mad cow', and then went on to say 'You can't trust people who cook as badly as that … it's the country with the worst food'. But despite Mr Chirac's derogatory comments (about, we assume, meals he'd been served at state banquets rather than a steak pie at the pub), good-quality roasts from well-reared cattle now grace menus once again.

NAME THAT PASTY

A favourite in southwest England is the Cornish pasty – originally a mix of cooked vegetables wrapped in pastry – now available everywhere in England, and often including meat varieties (much to the chagrin of the Cornish people). Invented long before Tupperware, the pasty was an all-in-one-lunch-pack that tin miners carried underground and left on a ledge ready for mealtime. So pasties weren't mixed up, they were marked with owners' initials – always at one end, so the miner could eat half and safely leave the rest to snack on later without it mistakenly disappearing into the mouth of a workmate. And before going back to the surface, the miners traditionally left the last corner of the pasty as a gift for the spirits of the mine known as 'knockers', to ensure a safe shift the next day.

And with the beef comes Yorkshire pudding. It's simply roast batter, but very tasty when properly cooked. In pubs and cafés, especially in northern England, you can buy a big bowl-shaped Yorkshire pudding, filled with meat stew, beans, vegetables or curry – a favourite multicultural crossover that might possibly even epitomise British society today.

Another local speciality in northern England is Cumberland sausage – a tasty mix of minced meat and herbs so large it has to be spiralled to fit on your plate. Bring sausage and Yorkshire pud together and you have another classic dish: toad-in-the-hole.

But perhaps the best-known classic English staple is fish and chips, often bought from the 'chippie' as a takeaway wrapped in paper to enjoy at home, or 'open' to eat immediately as you walk back from a late night at the pub. Sometimes the fish can be greasy and tasteless (especially once you get far from the sea), but in towns with salt in the air this deep-fried delight is always worth trying. Yorkshire's coastal resorts are particularly famous for huge servings of cod – despite it becoming an endangered species, thanks to overfishing – while restaurants in Devon and Cornwall regularly conjure up prawns, lobster, oysters, mussels and scallops. Elsewhere on your travels, seafood specialities you may try include Norfolk crab, Northumberland kippers, and jellied eels in London.

> 'A legal victory in 2005 ensured that only pies made in the eponymous Midlands town could carry the Melton Mowbray moniker'

Other English specialities include Melton Mowbray pork pies (motto: 'gracious goodness for over 100 years') – cooked ham compressed in a casing of pastry and always eaten cold, ideally with pickle. A legal victory in 2005 ensured that only pies made in the eponymous Midlands town could carry the Melton Mowbray moniker – in the same way that fizzy wine from other regions can't be called Champagne.

Then there's rhubarb, the juicy stem of a large-leafed garden plant, best eaten in a 'crumble' – a topping of mixed flour, butter and sugar – topped with custard or ice cream. For much of the 20th century, rhubarb was a very popular food, with overnight trains dubbed the 'rhubarb express' bringing tons of the stuff to London and the cities of the south from the main growing area in Yorkshire, between the towns of Leeds, Wakefield and Morely, known – inevitably – as the 'rhubarb triangle'. It fell out of fashion around the 1980s but is currently enjoying a renaissance in gourmet restaurants as well as humble kitchens.

Perhaps less appealing, another English speciality is black pudding, effectively a large sausage made from ground meat, offal, fat and blood, and traditionally served for breakfast. It's known in other countries as 'blood sausage', but the English version has a high content of oatmeal so doesn't fall apart in the pan when fried.

Moving onto an altogether sweeter pudding, Bakewell pudding is an English speciality that blundered into the recipe books around 1860 when a cook at the Rutland Arms Hotel in the Derbyshire town of Bakewell was making a strawberry tart, but mistakenly (some stories say drunkenly) spread the egg mixture on top of the jam instead of stirring it into the pastry. Especially in northern England, the Bakewell pudding (pudding, mark you, not 'Bakewell tart' as it's sometimes erroneously called) features regularly on local dessert menus and is certainly worth sampling.

Also in the pudding club is plum pudding, a dome-shaped cake with fruit, nuts, and brandy or rum, traditionally eaten at Christmas, when it's called – surprise, surprise – Christmas pudding. The pudding is steamed rather than baked, cut into slices, and served with brandy butter. It's eaten after the traditional Christmas lunch of turkey and Brussels sprout, and shortly before the traditional sleep on the sofa when the Queen's speech is on TV. Watch out for the coins inserted in the pudding by superstitious cooks – if you bite one it means good luck for the next year, but it may play havoc with your fillings.

Staying with the sweet stuff, the international favourite banoffee pie (a desert made from bananas and toffee) is also an English invention, first developed in a pub in Sussex in southern England in the early 1970s. A plaque on the wall commemorates this landmark culinary event.

Back to the savoury stuff, and there's Marmite, a dark and pungent yeast extract, usually spread on toast, that generations of English kids have loved or hated. Either way, it's a passion that continues through adulthood. In 2006, when the manufacturer of Marmite moved from selling the stuff in a near-sperical glass jar to a (much more practical) plastic tube, much was the consternation across the land. Similar to the Australian favourite, Vegemite (but not the same – oh no, sir!), it's popular at breakfast and especially great for late-night munchies.

And finally, an English speciality that perhaps epitomises English food more than any other – especially in pubs – is the ploughman's lunch. Although hearty yokels almost certainly did carry a lump of cheese and a lump of bread to the fields (just as probably wrapped in a red spotted handkerchief) over many centuries, the meal is actually a modern phenomenon. It was invented in the 1960s by the marketing chief of the national cheese-makers' organisation as a way to boost consumption, neatly cashing in on public nostalgia and fondness for tradition – even if it was fake.

You can still find a basic ploughman's lunch offered in some pubs – and it undeniably goes well with a pint or two of local ale at lunchtime – but these days the meal has usually been smarted up to include butter, salad, pickle, pickled onion and dressings. At some pubs you get a selection of cheeses. You'll also find other variations, such as farmer's lunch (bread and chicken), stockman's lunch (bread and ham), Frenchman's lunch (brie and baguette) and fisherman's lunch (you guessed it, with fish).

DRINKS

In England, a drink means any ingestible liquid, so if you're from overseas and a local asks 'would you like a drink?', don't automatically expect a gin and tonic. They may well mean a 'cuppa' – a cup of tea – England's best-known beverage, sometimes billed as the national drink, although coffee is equally popular these days; the Brits consume 165 million cups a day and the British coffee market is worth almost £700 million a year – but with the prices some coffee shops charge, maybe that's not surprising.

Among alcoholic drinks, England is probably best known for its beer. Typical British beer is technically called ale, ranging from dark brown to brick red in colour, and generally served at room temperature. It's more commonly called 'bitter'. This is to distinguish it from lager – the drink that most of the rest of the word calls 'beer' – generally yellow and served cold. (Ale is also a synonym

Since the major coffee-shop chains arrived in Britain in the 1990s, around 80% of local cafés have closed. And a word of warning: if you're asked 'white or black?' don't be shocked: it's just English for 'do you take milk in your coffee?'.

The Campaign for Real Ale (www.camra.org.uk) promotes the understanding of traditional British beer – and recommends good pubs that serve it. Look for endorsement stickers on pub windows.

CLASSIC BREWS

For fans or students of real ale, classic brewery names to look out for (and their beers to sample) as you travel around England include Adnams (eastern England), Arkells (south, southwest), Black Sheep (north), Fullers (southeast), Greene King (eastern, central, south), Hardys & Hansons (central), Hook Norton (south, midlands), Jennings (northwest), Marstons (south, central, north), St Austel (west), Shepherd Neam (southeast), Timothy Taylor (north) and Wadworth (west). For more ideas, tipplers' favourite tomes include the annual *Good Beer Guide to Great Britain*, produced by the Campaign for Real Ale, which steers you to the best beers and the pubs that serve them, and the *Good Pub Guide*, which details thousands of fine establishments across the country. Look out too for the wonderful *300 Beers to Try Before you Die* by Roger Protz; unashamedly jumping on the current trend for lists, this homage to British beers (and a few from other countries) is educational and jolly good fun.

for beer or drinking – whatever alcoholic beverage is consumed in reality, so on your travels you might hear phrases such as 'We're going for a few ales' or 'There was a lot of ale talking last night and some big promises made'.)

The well-known international brands like Fosters, Carling and Budweiser are all available in England, but as you travel around the country, you should definitely try some traditional beer, also known as real ale. But be ready! If you're used to the 'amber nectar' or 'king of beers', a local English brew may come as a shock – a warm, flat and expensive shock. This is partly to do with England's climate, and partly to do with the beer being served by hand pump rather than gas pressure. Most important, though, is the integral flavour: traditional English beer doesn't *need* to be chilled or fizzed. Drink a cheap lager that's sat in its glass for an hour and you'll see it has very little taste.

'Most important, though, is the integral flavour: traditional English beer doesn't *need* to be chilled or fizzed'

Another key feature is that real ale must be looked after, usually meaning a willingness on the part of the landlord to put in extra effort (often translating into extra effort on food, atmosphere, cleanliness and so on), but is also why many pubs don't serve it, so beware of places where the staff gives the barrels as much care as the condom machine in the toilets. There's honestly nothing worse than a bad pint of real ale.

If beer doesn't tickle your palate, try cider – available in sweet and dry varieties. In western parts of England, notably Herefordshire and the counties of the Southwest Peninsula, you could try 'scrumpy', a very strong dry cider traditionally made from local apples. Many pubs serve it straight from the barrel.

On hot summer days, you could go for shandy – beer (lager or bitter) and lemonade mixed in equal quantities – an astonishing combination for some, but refreshing and of course not very strong. Another hybrid is 'snakebite' – an equal mix of cider and lager, favoured by students, as it reputedly gets you drunk quickly – thanks to the lager's bubbles and the cider's strength.

Back to more sensible tipples, many visitors are surprised to learn that wine is produced in England, and has been since the time of the Romans. Perhaps the country's best-known vineyard is **Denbies** (www.denbiesvineyard.co.uk), in southern England, established on the same strata of chalky soil that dips under the English Channel and comes to the surface in France's Champagne region – just one of the reasons the wine is so good. Denbies' wines are found in top restaurants and specialist stores across England, with savvy mail-order customers snapping up each year's production by the case-load, rarely leaving much for everyday shops and supermarkets.

WHERE TO EAT & DRINK

There's a huge choice of places to eat in England, and this section outlines just some of your options. For details on opening times, see p767. The tricky issue of tipping is covered on p774, while some pointers on restaurants' attitudes to kids are on p768.

For picnics or self-catering, markets can be a great place for bargains – everything from dented tins of tomatoes for 1p to home-baked cakes and organic goat's cheese. Farmers markets, mentioned earlier in this section, are always worth a browse; they're a great way for producers to sell good food direct to consumers, with both sides avoiding the grip of the supermarkets.

EATING INTO THE FINANCES

Most of the Eating sections in the chapters throughout this book are divided into three price bands: budget (under £10 per person), midrange (£10 to £20) and top end (over £20). In London the breakdown is: budget – under £15; midrange – £15 to £40; top end – over £40. For more guidance, see the Costs section on p21.

Cafés & Teashops

The traditional English café is nothing like its Continental European namesake. For a start, asking for a brandy with your coffee may cause confusion, as most British cafés don't serve alcohol. Most cafés are simply basic places serving basic food. And it's often pronounced 'caffy', or shortened to 'caff'. Meals like meat pie or omelette with chips cost around £3. Sandwiches, cakes and other snacks are £1 to £2.

Some cafés definitely earn their 'greasy spoon' handle, while others are neat and friendly. Smarter cafés are called teashops, and you might pay a bit extra for extras like twee décor and table service. In teashops, you can usually buy 'cream tea' – a plate of scones, clotted cream and jam, served with a pot of tea. This is known as a Devonshire tea in some other English-speaking countries, but not in England (except of course in the county of Devon, where it's still a Devonshire cream tea).

In country areas, many villages have cafés catering for tourists, walkers, cyclists and other outdoor types, and in summer they're open every day. Like good B&Bs, good cafés are a wonderful institution and always worth a stop during your travels.

As well as the traditional establishments, in most cities and towns you'll also find American-flavoured coffee shops – there seems to be a Starbucks on every corner – and Euro-style café-bars, serving decent lattes and espressos, and offering bagels or ciabattas rather than beans on toast (you'll probably be able to get that brandy, too). Some of these modern places even have outdoor chairs and tables – rather brave considering the narrow pavements and inclement weather much of England enjoys.

Restaurants

London has scores of excellent restaurants that could hold their own in major cities worldwide, while places in Bath, Leeds and Manchester can give the capital a fair run for its money (often for rather less money). We've taken great pleasure in seeking out some of the best and best-value restaurants in England, and have recommended a small selection throughout this book.

Prices vary considerably across the country, with a main course in a straightforward restaurant costing around £7 to £10 and rising to £15 or £20 at good-quality places. Utterly excellent food, service and surroundings can be enjoyed for £30 to £50 per person – although in London you can, if you want, pay double this.

Pubs & Bars

The difference between pubs and bars is sometimes vague, but generally bars are smarter, larger and louder than pubs, with a younger crowd. Drinks are more expensive too, unless there's a gallon-of-vodka-and-Red-Bull-for-a-fiver promotion – which there often is.

Eggs, Bacon, Chips & Beans by Russell Davies showcases 50 of the UK's best places to enjoy a traditional fry-up.

EARLY DOORS, LATE NIGHTS

Pubs in towns and country areas usually open daily, from 11am to 11pm Sunday to Thursday, sometimes to midnight or 1am Friday and Saturday. Most open all day, although some may shut from 3pm to 6pm. Throughout this book, we don't list pub opening and closing times unless they vary significantly from these hours.

In cities, some pubs open until midnight or later, but it's mostly bars and clubs that take advantage of new licensing laws ('the provision of late-night refreshment', as it's officially and charmingly called) to stay open to 1am, 2am or later. As every place is different, we list opening hours for bars and clubs.

THE OLDEST PUB IN ENGLAND?

Studious drinkers are often surprised to learn that the word 'pub', although apparently steeped in history, dates only from the 19th century. But places selling beer have been around for much longer, and the 'oldest pub in England' is a hotly contested title.

One of the country's oldest pubs, with the paperwork to prove it, is Ye Olde Trip to Jerusalem (p492) in Nottingham, which was serving ale to departing crusaders in the 12th century. Other contenders sniff at this newcomer: a fine old hotel called the Eagle & Child (p390) in Stow-on-the-Wold (Gloucestershire) claims to have been selling beer since around AD 950, and Ye Olde Fighting Cocks (p166) in St Albans apparently dates back to the 8th century – although the 13th is more likely.

But then back comes Ye Trip with a counter-claim: one of its bars is a cave hollowed out of living rock, and that's more than a million years old.

As well as beer, cider, wine and the other drinks mentioned earlier in this chapter, pubs and bars offer the usual choice of spirits, often drunk with a mixer, producing English favourites such as gin and tonic, rum and coke, and vodka and lime. These drinks are served in measures called singles and doubles. A single is 35ml – just over one US fluid ounce. A double is of course 70ml – still disappointingly small when compared to measures in other countries. To add further to your disappointment, the vast array of cocktail options, as found in America, is generally restricted to more upmarket city bars in England.

And while we're serving out warnings, here are two more: first, if you see a pub calling itself a 'free house', it's simply a place that doesn't belong to a brewery or pub company, and thus is 'free' to sell any brewer's beer. Unfortunately, it doesn't mean the beer is free of charge. Second, please remember that drinks in English pubs are ordered and paid for at the bar. If the pub serves food, that's usually ordered and paid for at the bar as well. You can always spot the out-of-towners – they're the ones sitting forlornly at their drinkless table for a good 15 minutes waiting for a waiter to appear before they realise they need to go to the bar and catch the barman or barstaff's attention.

'When it comes to gratuities, it's not usual to tip pub and bar staff, as it is, say, in America'

When it comes to gratuities, it's not usual to tip pub and bar staff, as it is, say, in America. However, if you're ordering a large round, or the service has been good all evening, you can say to the person behind the bar 'and one for yourself'. They may not have a drink, but they'll add the monetary equivalent to the total you pay, and keep it as a tip.

Apart from good service, what makes a good pub? It's often surprisingly hard to pin down, but in our opinion, the best pubs follow a remarkably simple formula: they offer a welcoming atmosphere, pleasant surroundings, and in villages where pubs have been the centre of the community for centuries, they often offer a sense of history too. (See the boxed text Drinking in History, p47.) The best pubs also offer a good range of hand-pulled beer and a good menu of snacks and meals, cooked on the premises, not shipped in by the truck-full and defrosted in the microwave by untrained staff. After months of painstaking research, this is the type of pub that we recommend throughout this book, but of course there are many more pubs in England than even we could sample, and nothing beats the fun of doing your own investigating, so armed with the advice in this chapter, we urge you to get out there and tipple your taste buds.

London

London has a buzz unlike any other European city. It's fashion forward, ethnically diverse and artistically pioneering while its unique geographical position between Continental Europe and the USA gives it the best of both cultural worlds. Hollywood stars are queuing up to tread the West End boards yet cheap flights link the capital easily to European cities and beer still runs on tap. Londoners are a proud lot, and rightly so.

With gastropubs, dim-sum joints and gourmet-burger places continuing to propagate, a multitude of cuisines on your plate and a raft of celebrity chefs dishing up, the restaurant scene is five-star. For night owls there's excellent comedy, theatre, superclubs, DJ bars, and a growing number of 'activity venues' where you can bowl, skate or sing while you drink. Shopaholics can get their fix here with internationally respected home-grown designers, affordable catwalk copies, tantalising food halls and Aladdin's Cave markets. The museums are first-rate, with vast, fascinating galleries you could lose yourself in and world-class exhibitions. Glittering modern architecture continues to enhance the skyline with the Swiss Re building (the Gherkin) and City Hall.

Yes, the city is eye-bogglingly huge and teeming with people but its vibrant multiculturalism is a vital part of London's identity. With so many different communities and neighbourhoods, as comic Jimmy Carr says 'even a local can feel like a tourist'.

Having won the 2012 Olympics bid and largely survived acts of terrorism, London is sailing high on a wave of determination, optimism and glee. Lucky you – coming along for the ride.

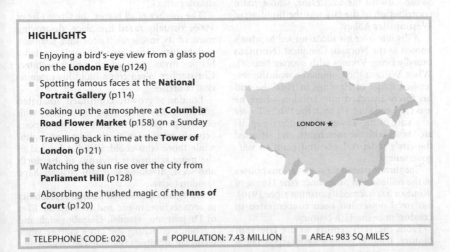

HIGHLIGHTS

- Enjoying a bird's-eye view from a glass pod on the **London Eye** (p124)
- Spotting famous faces at the **National Portrait Gallery** (p114)
- Soaking up the atmosphere at **Columbia Road Flower Market** (p158) on a Sunday
- Travelling back in time at the **Tower of London** (p121)
- Watching the sun rise over the city from **Parliament Hill** (p128)
- Absorbing the hushed magic of the **Inns of Court** (p120)

LONDON ★

| TELEPHONE CODE: 020 | POPULATION: 7.43 MILLION | AREA: 983 SQ MILES |

HISTORY

Celts first established themselves around a ford across the River Thames. However, it was the Romans who developed the 'square mile' now known as the City of London (which lies within today's Greater London city – note the small 'c') with a crossing, near today's London Bridge, that served as the hub of their road system. By the end of the 3rd century AD 'Londinium' was almost as multicultural as it is today with 30,000 people of various ethnic groups (albeit all Roman citizens, of course) and temples dedicated to a large number of cults. Parts of London like Aldgate and Ludgate get their names from the gates of the original city walls built by the Romans. Internal strife and relentless barbarian attacks took their toll on the Romans, who abandoned Britain in the 5th century, reducing the conurbation to a sparsely populated backwater.

The Saxons then moved in to the area, establishing farmsteads and villages, and their 'Lundenwic' prospered, becoming a large, well-organised town divided into 20 different wards. As the city grew in importance, it caught the eye of Danish Vikings who launched many invasions and razed the city in the 9th century. The Saxons held on until, finally beaten down in 1016, they were forced to accept the Danish leader Knut (Canute) as King of England, after which London replaced Winchester as its capital. In 1042 the throne reverted to the Saxon Edward the Confessor, whose main contribution to the city was the building of Westminster Abbey.

A dispute over his successor led to what's known as the Norman Conquest (Normans broadly being Vikings with shorter beards). When William the Conqueror won the watershed Battle of Hastings in 1066, he and his forces marched into London where he was crowned king. He built the White Tower (the core of the Tower of London), negotiated taxes with the merchants, and affirmed the city's independence and right to self-government.

The throne passed through various houses in the millennium or so since (the House of Windsor has warmed its cushion since 1910), but royal power has been concentrated in London since the 12th century.

From the 12th century to the late 15th century, London politics were largely taken up by a three-way power struggle between the monarchy, the church and city guilds.

The greatest threat to the burgeoning city was that of disease caused by unsanitary living conditions and impure drinking water. In 1348 rats on ships from Europe brought the bubonic plague, which wiped out a third of London's population of 100,000 over the following year.

Violence became commonplace in the hard times that followed. In 1381, miscalculating or just disregarding the mood of the nation, the king tried to impose a poll tax on everyone in the realm. Tens of thousands of peasants marched on London. Several ministers were murdered and many buildings razed before the so-called Peasants' Revolt ran its course. The ringleaders were executed, but there was no more mention of a poll tax (until Margaret Thatcher, not heeding the lessons of history, tried to introduce it in the 1980s).

Despite these setbacks, London was consolidated as the seat of law and government in the kingdom during the 14th century. An uneasy political compromise was reached between the factions, and the city expanded rapidly under the House of Tudor. The first recorded map of London was published in 1558, and John Stow produced the first comprehensive history of the capital in 1598.

The Great Plague struck in 1665 and 100,000 Londoners perished by the time the winter cold arrested the epidemic. Just as the population considered a sigh of relief, another disaster struck.

The mother of all blazes, the Great Fire of 1666, virtually razed the place, destroying most of its medieval, Tudor and Jacobean architecture. One plus was that it created a blank canvas upon which master architect Christopher Wren could build his magnificent churches.

London's growth continued unabated and by 1700 it was Europe's largest city with 600,000 people. An influx of foreign workers brought expansion to the east and south, while those who could afford it headed to the more salubrious environs of the north and west, divisions that still largely shape London today.

Georgian London saw a surge in creativity in architecture, music and art with the likes of Dr Johnson, Handel, Gainsborough and Reynolds enriching the city's culture while Georgian architects fashioned an elegant new

LONDON IN...

Two Days

Start off in **Trafalgar Square** (p113) with a visit to the **National Gallery** (p113) and/or **National Portrait Gallery** (p114). Follow the Mall to the **Institute for Contemporary Arts** (p116), where art goes 20th century and you can refuel. Next stop is a photo or tour of **Buckingham Palace** (p116), Wander through **Green Park** (p117) for tea at the **Ritz** (p135) and a **West End show** (p151). On day two, delve into history at the **Tower of London** (p121) then meander over **Tower Bridge** (p122) for lunch riverside. Finish with **Shakespeare's Globe Theatre** (p123) and the **Tate Modern** (p124) before a dusk turn on the **London Eye** (p124) and dinner at the **Oxo Tower** (p143).

Four Days

Expand your mind at the **Victoria & Albert** (p125), **Science** (p125) and **Natural History Museums** (p125) and contract your wallet at **Harrods** (p155). Take in the **British Museum** (p119), nose around **Covent Garden** (p117) and **Soho** (p117) then hit the high notes at **Lucky Voice** (p154). Taste political might in **Westminster** (p114) before relaxing in **Hyde Park** (p126), boating on the Serpentine and dining in **Notting Hill** (p144). Head east to the **Geffrye Museum** (p129), grab an open-air bite in **Hoxton Square** (p142) then dance off your dinner at the **clubs** (p151) nearby.

One Week

A week gives you a great chance to explore the capital. Spend a Sunday in the East End with brunch at **Canteen** (p142) and a rifle through **Spitalfields Market** (p158), **Sunday (Up)market** (p158) and **Brick Lane Market** (p158). Visit the **Imperial War Museum** (p125) then follow the river to the **South Bank** (p124), **HMS Belfast** (p123), **Borough Market** (p158), **London Dungeon** (p123) and **City Hall** (p123). Spend an evening in **Bermondsey St** (p149) and a night out in **Hoxton** and **Shoreditch** (p149). Head to Westminster for the **Houses of Parliament** (p115) and **Westminster Abbey** (p114) then explore the **City** (p120) and **St Paul's Cathedral** (p120). Take a boat to **Greenwich** (p129) for maritime history and time travel. Make the journey north for a tour around **Highgate Cemetery** (p128) and the welcome fresh air of **Hampstead Heath** (p128).

metropolis. At the same time the gap between the rich and poor grew ever wider, and lawlessness was rife.

In 1837 the 18-year-old Victoria ascended the throne. During her long reign (1837–1901), London became the fulcrum of the expanding British Empire, which covered a quarter of the earth's surface. The Industrial Revolution saw the building of new docks and railways (including the first underground line in 1863), while the Great Exhibition of 1851 showcased London to the world. The city's population mushroomed from just over two million to 6.6 million during Victoria's reign.

Road transport was revolutionised in the early 20th century when the first motor buses were introduced and replaced the horse-drawn versions that had trotted their trade since 1829.

Although London suffered relatively minor damage during WWI, it was devastated by the Luftwaffe in WWII when huge swathes of the centre and East End were totally flattened and 32,000 people were killed. Ugly housing and low-cost developments were hastily erected in postwar London, and immigrants from around the world flocked to the city and changed its character forever.

The latest major disaster to beset the capital was the Great Smog on 6 December 1952, when a lethal combination of fog, smoke and pollution descended on the city and killed some 4000 people.

Prosperity gradually returned, and the creative energy that had been bottled up in the postwar years was suddenly unleashed. London became the capital of cool in fashion and music in the 'swinging '60s'.

The party didn't last long, however, and London returned to the doldrums in the harsh economic climate of the 1970s. Recovery began – for the business community at least –

under the iron fist of Margaret Thatcher, elected Britain's first woman prime minister in 1979. Her monetarist policy and determination to crush socialism sent unemployment skyrocketing and her term was marked by civil unrest.

London got its first true mayor in 2000 when feisty 'Red' Ken Livingstone swept to victory. In a bid to improve transport, he introduced the controversial (but ultimately successful) congestion charge, and got the buses running on time. His axing of the much-loved Routemaster buses in 2005 has remained a much less popular move.

July 2005 was a roller-coaster month for London. Snatching victory from the jaws of Paris (the favourites), the city won their bid to host the 2012 Olympics and celebrated with a frenzy of parties and flag-waving. The following day, joy turned to horror as suicide bombers struck on the tube and a bus, killing 56 people. Only two weeks later a second terrorist attack was thankfully foiled. But Londoners are not easily beaten and they immediately returned to the tube, defiant. As ever, the city now has its face firmly turned towards the future.

ORIENTATION

The city's main geographical feature is the murky Thames, a river that was sufficiently deep (for anchorage) and narrow (for bridging) to attract the Romans here in the first place. It divides the city roughly into north and south.

The 'square mile' of the City of London – the capital's financial district – is counted as one of London's 33 council-run boroughs and is referred to simply as the City (look for the capital 'C'). The M25 ring road encompasses the 1572 sq km that is broadly regarded as Greater London.

London's Underground railway (the tube) makes this enormous city relatively accessible. Most of the important sights, theatres and restaurants lie within the tube's Circle Line (colour-coded yellow), which encircles central London just north of the river.

Londoners commonly refer to areas by their postcode. The letters correspond to compass directions from the centre of London, approximately St Paul's Cathedral. EC means East Central, W means West and so on. The numbering system after the letters is less helpful.

Maps

The *London A–Z* series is a range of excellent maps and hand-held street atlases. Lonely Planet also publishes an excellent *London City Map*.

INFORMATION
Bookshops

Books for Cooks (Map pp100-1; ☎ 7221 1992; 4 Blenheim Cres W11; ✆ Ladbroke Grove) Does what it says on the tin.

Borders (Map pp110-11; ☎ 7292 1600; 203 Oxford St W1; ✆ Oxford Circus) Flagship of the huge nonunionising chain.

Forbidden Planet (Map pp110-11; ☎ 7836 4179; 179 Shaftesbury Ave; ✆ Leicester Sq or Covent Garden) A trove of comics, sci-fi, horror and fantasy literature.

Foyle's (Map pp110-11; ☎ 7437 5660; 113-119 Charing Cross Rd WC2; ✆ Tottenham Court Rd) Venerable and respected independent store with a broad range, including Silver Moon, the women's literature specialist, and Ray's Jazz café.

Gay's the Word (Map pp98-9; ☎ 7278 7654; 66 Marchmont St WC1; ✆ Russell Sq) Everything from advice on coming out, to gay and lesbian literature.

Grant & Cutler (Map pp110-11; ☎ 7734 2012; 55-57 Great Marlborough St W1; ✆ Oxford Circus) The best foreign-language store in town.

Helter Skelter (Map pp110-11; ☎ 7836 1151; 4 Denmark St WC2; ✆ Oxford Circus) Biographies, fanzines and rock literature.

Stanfords (Map pp110-11; ☎ 7836 1321; 12-14 Long Acre W C2; ✆ Covent Garden) The granddaddy of travel bookstores.

Travel Bookshop (Map pp100-1; ☎ 7229 5260; 13 Blenheim Cres W11; ✆ Ladbroke Grove) The latest guidebooks, travel literature and antiquarian gems.

Waterstone's (Map pp110-11; ☎ 7851 2400; 203-206 Piccadilly W1; ✆ Piccadilly Circus) The best of this book-purveying giant with 5th View bar on the 5th floor (obviously).

Cultural Centres

Alliance Française (Map pp100-1; ☎ 7723 6439; 1 Dorset Sq NW1; ✆ Marylebone) Organises French-language classes, and social and cultural events.

British Council (Map pp110-11; ☎ 7930 8466; 10 Spring Gardens, SW1; ✆ Charing Cross) Can advise foreign students on educational opportunities in Britain.

Emergency

Police/Fire/Ambulance (☎ 999)

Rape & Sexual Abuse Support Centre (☎ 8683 3300)

Samaritans (☎ 08457 909 090)

Internet Access

Cyberia (Map pp102-3; ☎ 7209 0984; 39 Whitfield St W1; ✪ Goodge St)

easyInternetcafé (Map pp110-11; www.easy.com; 9-16 Tottenham Court Rd; ✪ Tottenham Court Rd) Branches throughout central London.

Internet Lounge (Map pp106-7; ☎ 7370 1734; 24A Earl's Court Gardens SW5; ✪ Earl's Court) Also in Hammersmith and Tottenham Court Rd.

Internet Resources

The Lonely Planet website (www.lonelyplanet .com) has speedy links to many of London's websites. You can also try the following:

BBC London (www.bbc.co.uk/London/whereyoulive)

Evening Standard (www.thisislondon.co.uk)

Time Out (www.timeout.com)

View London (www.viewlondon.co.uk)

Media

London's only real paper, the tabloid *Evening Standard* comes out in early and late editions throughout the day. *Metro* is a morning freebie from the same stable, while *Time Out* (£2.50) is the local listing guide *par excellence*, published every Tuesday.

Medical Services

To find a local doctor or hospital, consult the local telephone directory or call ☎ 100 (toll free). There is always one local chemist that opens 24 hours (see local newspapers or notices in chemist windows).

Hospitals with 24-hour accident and emergency units include:

Guy's Hospital (Map p105; ☎ 7188 7188; St Thomas St SE1; ✪ London Bridge). There's also a dental A&E located here.

Royal Free Hospital (Map pp96-7; ☎ 7794 0500; Pond St NW3; ✪ Belsize Park)

University College Hospital (Map pp98-9; ☎ 0845 155 5000; Grafton Way WC1; ✪ Euston Sq)

Money

Banks and ATMs are two-a-penny in central London. You can change cash easily at banks, bureaux de change and travel agents. If you use bureaux de change, check commission rates *and* exchange rates; some can be extortionate.

There are 24-hour bureaux in Heathrow Terminals 1, 3 and 4 (the one in Terminal 2 opens 6am to 11pm), in Gatwick's South and North Terminals, and at Stansted. The airport bureaux are good value, charging about 1.5% of the transaction value, with a £3 minimum.

The following are reliable bureaux (both have many outlets):

American Express (AmEx; Map pp110-11; ☎ 7484 9610; 30-31 Haymarket SW1; currency exchange ⏲ 9am-6pm Mon-Sat, 10am-5pm Sun; ✪ Piccadilly Circus)

Thomas Cook (Map pp110-11; ☎ 7853 6400; 30 St James's St SW1; ⏲ 9am-5.30pm Mon, Tue, Thu & Fri, 10am-5.30pm Wed; ✪ Green Park)

Post

London post offices usually open from 8.30am or 9am to 5pm or 5.30pm Monday to Friday. Some main ones also open 9am to noon or 1pm on Saturdays. The **Trafalgar Square post office** (Map pp110-11; GPO/Poste Restante), actually on William IV St, opens 8.30am to 6.30pm Monday to Friday, and 9am to 5.30pm Saturday.

Telephone

Call centres offer booths where you can dial internationally for less than the standard British Telecom (BT) rate. These can be found on most high streets. If you've brought your mobile, it's a good idea to buy a local SIM card. The **Link** (☎ 0870 154 5540; www.thelink.co.uk) and **Carphone Warehouse** (☎ 0870 168 2002; www .carphone-warehouse.com) have branches all over the city. If you'd rather rent a mobile try:

Cellhire (☎ 0870 561 0610; www.cellhire.com; delivery £18)

Mobell (☎ 0800 243 524; www.mobell.com; delivery free)

Tourist Information

For a list of all tourist information centres in London and around Britain see www.visit map.info/tic.

Britain & London Visitor Centre (Map pp110-11; www. visitbritain.com; 1 Regent St SW1; ⏲ 9.30am-6.30pm Mon, 9am-6.30pm Tue-Fri, 10am-4pm Sat & Sun; ✪ Piccadilly Circus) Walk-in inquiries only. A comprehensive information centre which can book accommodation, theatre and transport tickets, and offers a bureau de change, international telephones and computer terminals for accessing tourist information on the web. It's open longer hours (9am-5pm) on Saturday from June to September.

Corporation of London information centre (☎ 7332 1456; www.cityoflondon.gov.uk; ⏲ 9.30am-5pm daily Apr-Sep, 9.30am-5pm Mon-Fri, 9.30am-noon Sat rest of year; ✪ St Paul's) In St Paul's Churchyard EC4, opposite St Paul's Cathedral.

London Line (☎ 09068 663344; per min 60p) A telephone service that will give you the lowdown on events and attractions.

(Continued on page 113)

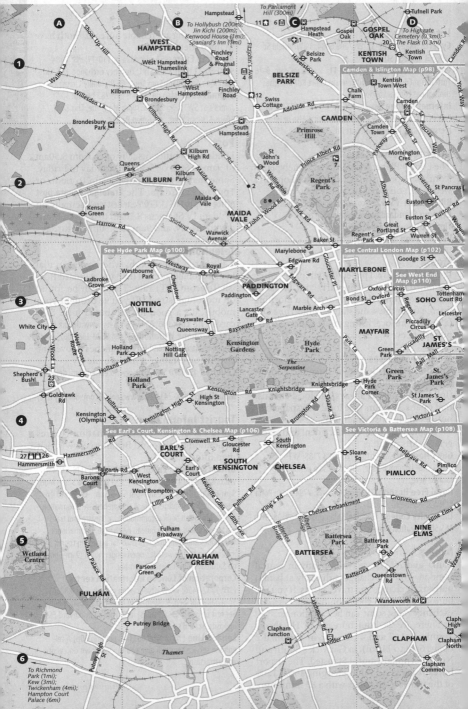

EATING (pp139–147)
Blueprint Café.................(see 3)
Delfina...........................14 F4

DRINKING (pp147–151)
Garrison Public House........15 F4
Village East.....................16 F4

ENTERTAINMENT (pp151–155)
Battersea Arts Centre........17 C6
Brit Oval........................18 E5
Brixton Academy...............19 E6
Forum............................20 D1
Hackney Ocean.................21 G1
Lord's Cricket Ground........(see 8)
Ministry of Sound.............22 E4
Shepherd's Bush Empire......23 A4

INFORMATION
Royal Free Hospital...........1 C1

SIGHTS & ACTIVITIES (pp113–133)
Abbey Rd Zebra Crossing......2 C2
Design Museum..................3 F4
Freud Museum...................4 C1
Geffrye Museum.................5 F2
Keat's House....................6 C1
London Zoo.....................7 C2
Lord's Cricket Ground.........8 C2
Tate Britain....................9 D4

SLEEPING (pp133–139)
Dover Castle Hostel...........10 F4
Hampstead Village Guesthouse..11 C1
Palmers Lodge...................12 C1
Rotherhithe YHA................13 G3

SHOPPING (pp155–158)
Bermondsey Market.............24 F4
Brixton Market.................25 E6
Primark.........................26 A4
TK Maxx.........................27 A4

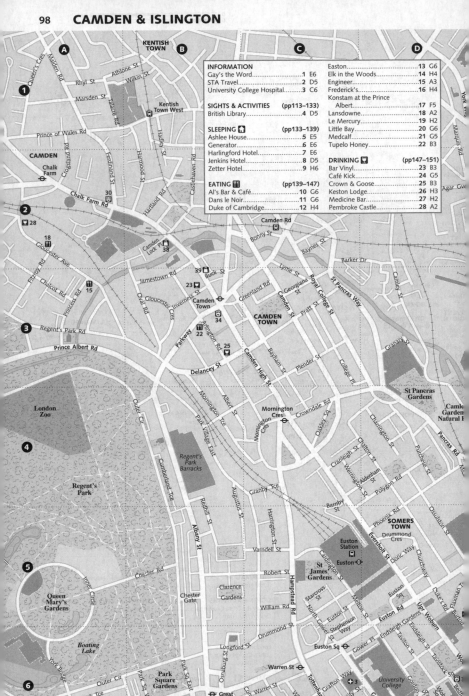

INFORMATION
Gay's the Word...........................1 E6
STA Travel..................................2 D5
University College Hospital.......3 C6

SIGHTS & ACTIVITIES (pp113–133)
British Library.............................4 D5

SLEEPING 🏠 (pp133–139)
Ashlee House..............................5 E5
Generator.....................................6 E6
Harlingford Hotel.......................7 E6
Jenkins Hotel..............................8 D5
Zetter Hotel.................................9 H6

EATING 🍴 (pp139–147)
Al's Bar & Café..........................10 G6
Dans le Noir..............................11 G6
Duke of Cambridge..................12 H4

Easton...13 G6
Elk in the Woods......................14 H4
Engineer.....................................15 A3
Frederick's.................................16 H4
Konstam at the Prince
  Albert.......................................17 F5
Lansdowne.................................18 A2
Le Mercury................................19 H2
Little Bay....................................20 G6
Medcalf......................................21 G5
Tupelo Honey...........................22 B3

DRINKING 🍷 (pp147–151)
Bar Vinyl....................................23 B3
Café Kick....................................24 G5
Crown & Goose........................25 B3
Keston Lodge.............................26 H3
Medicine Bar.............................27 H2
Pembroke Castle.......................28 A2

0 ———— 500 m
0 ———— 0.25 miles

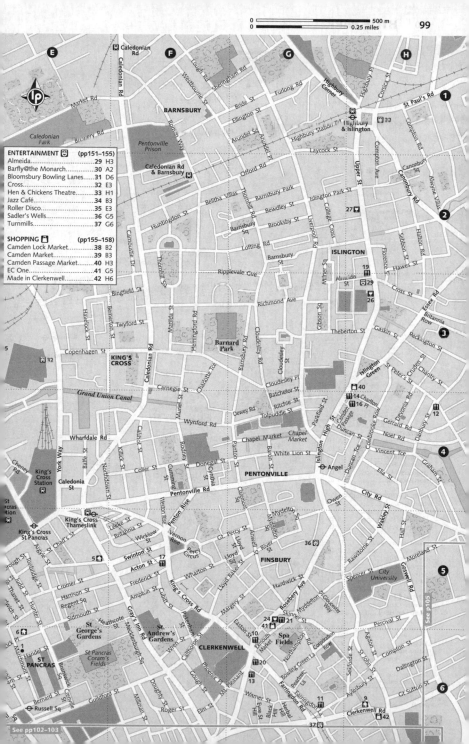

ENTERTAINMENT (pp151–155)

SHOPPING (pp155–158)

See pp102–103
See p105

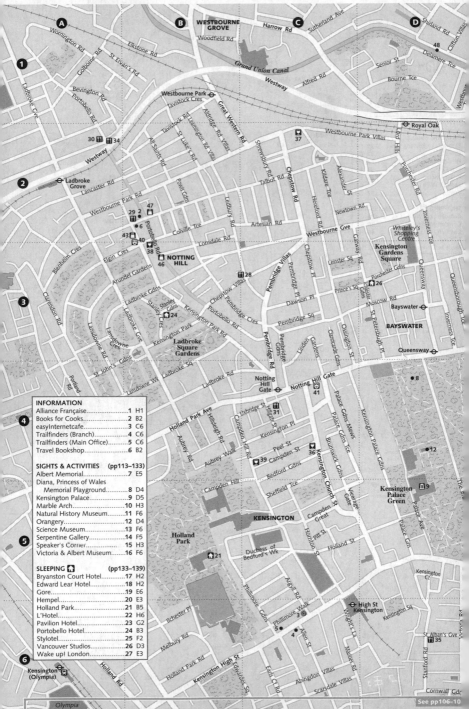

See pp106–10

Olympia

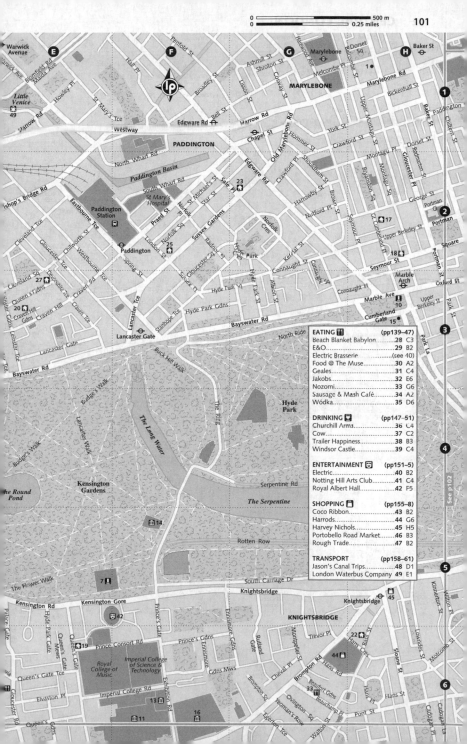

0 500 m
0 0.25 miles

EATING 🍴 (pp139–47)
Beach Blanket Babylon....................28 C3
E&O...29 B2
Electric Brasserie.........................(see 40)
Food @ The Muse..........................30 A2
Geales...31 C4
Jakobs...32 E6
Nozomi..33 G6
Sausage & Mash Café....................34 A2
Wódka...35 D6

DRINKING 🍷 (pp147–51)
Churchill Arms.............................36 C4
Cow..37 C2
Trailer Happiness..........................38 B3
Windsor Castle.............................39 C4

ENTERTAINMENT 🎭 (pp151–5)
Electric.......................................40 B2
Notting Hill Arts Club....................41 C4
Royal Albert Hall..........................42 F5

SHOPPING 🛍 (pp155–8)
Coco Ribbon................................43 B2
Harrods.......................................44 G6
Harvey Nichols............................45 H5
Portobello Road Market.................46 B3
Rough Trade................................47 B2

TRANSPORT (pp158–61)
Jason's Canal Trips.......................48 D1
London Waterbus Company............49 E1

See p102

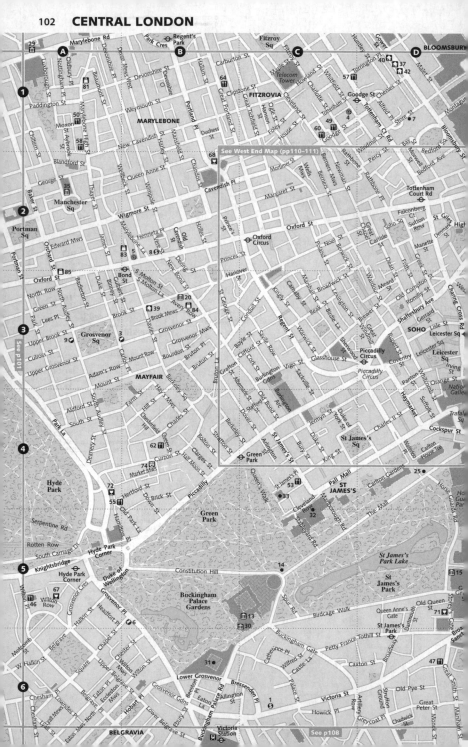

Marylebone Rd
Park Cres
Regent's Park
Fitzroy Sq

A   **B**   **C**   **D**

Paddington St

MARYLEBONE

FITZROVIA

Telecom Tower

Goodge St

Tottenham Court Rd

See West End Map (pp110–111)

Cavendish Pl

Oxford St

Oxford Circus

Hanover

SOHO

Leicester Sq

Manchester Sq

Portman Sq

Wigmore St

Oxford St

Bond St

Piccadilly Circus
Piccadilly Circus

Grosvenor Sq

MAYFAIR

Green Park

St James's Sq

Hyde Park

Piccadilly

Green Park

ST JAMES'S

Pall Mall

The Mall

Hyde Park Corner

Knightsbridge
Hyde Park Corner

Serpentine Rd
Rotten Row
South Carriage Dr

Duke of Wellington

Constitution Hill

Buckingham Palace Gardens

Green Park

St James's Park Lake

St James's Park

Birdcage Walk

St James's Park

Queen Anne's Gate
Old Queen St

BELGRAVIA

Buckingham Gate
Petty France
Tothill St

Victoria St

Victoria Station

See p108

CITY & AROUND (p105)

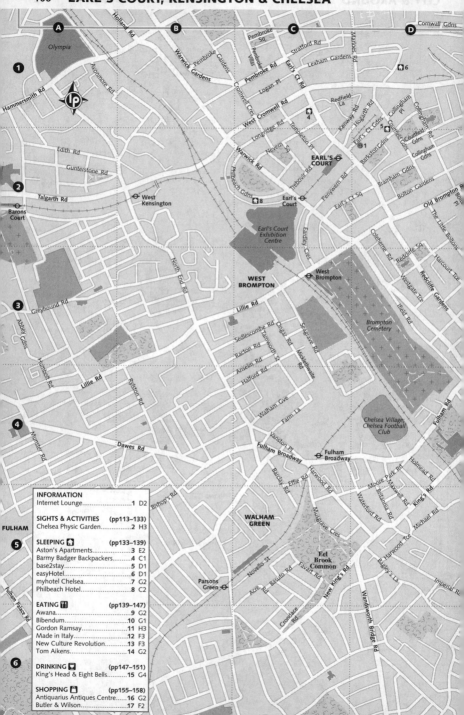

0 — 500 m
0 — 0.25 miles

See pp100–101

Victoria & Albert Museum

Natural History Museum

Queen's Gdns

Gloucester Rd

Cromwell Rd

Thurloe Pl

Thurloe St

South Kensington

South Terrace

Pelham St

SOUTH KENSINGTON

Harrington Rd

Pont St

Cadogan Pl

Sloane St

Pavilion Rd

Cadogan Gdns

Ellis St

Sloane Tce

Sloane Sq

Lower Sloane St

CHELSEA

Draycott Ave

Sloane Ave

Elystan St

Pelham St

King's Rd

Chelsea Embankment

Cheyne Walk

Albert Bridge

Battersea Bridge

Thames

Chelsea Creek

Battersea Park

Children's Zoo

Boating Lake

BATTERSEA

Prince of Wales Dr

Warriner Gardens

Battersea Park Rd

Ranelagh Gardens

Burton's Court

Great Hall

Royal Hospital Rd

See p108

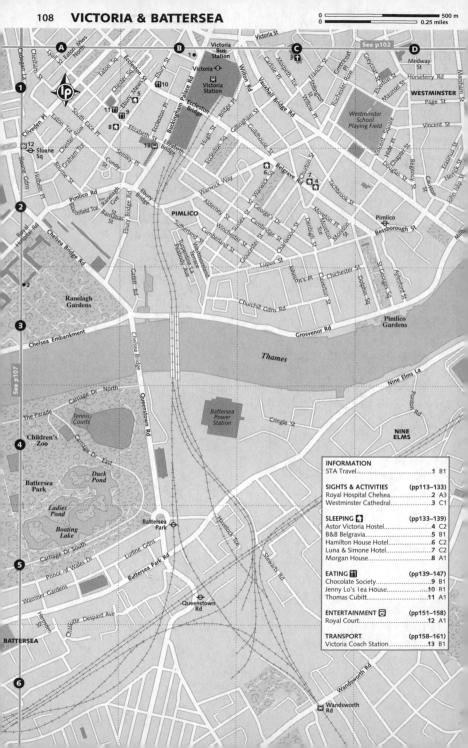

0 ———————— 500 m
0 ———————— 0.25 miles

See p102

INFORMATION
STA Travel.................................**1** B1

SIGHTS & ACTIVITIES   (pp113–133)
Royal Hospital Chelsea.....................**2** A3
Westminster Cathedral.....................**3** C1

SLEEPING   (pp133–139)
Astor Victoria Hostel.......................**4** C2
B&B Belgravia................................**5** B1
Hamilton House Hotel.....................**6** C2
Luna & Simone Hotel.....................**7** C2
Morgan House................................**8** A1

EATING   (pp139–147)
Chocolate Society..........................**9** B1
Jenny Lo's Tea House....................**10** B1
Thomas Cubitt.............................**11** A1

ENTERTAINMENT   (pp151–158)
Royal Court................................**12** A1

TRANSPORT   (pp158–161)
Victoria Coach Station..................**13** B1

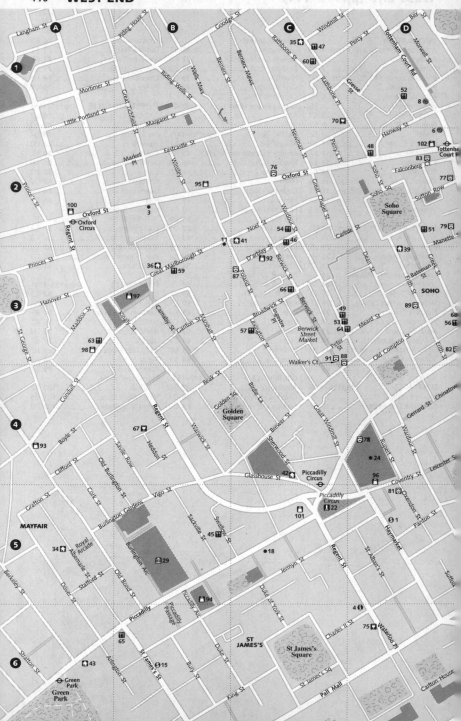

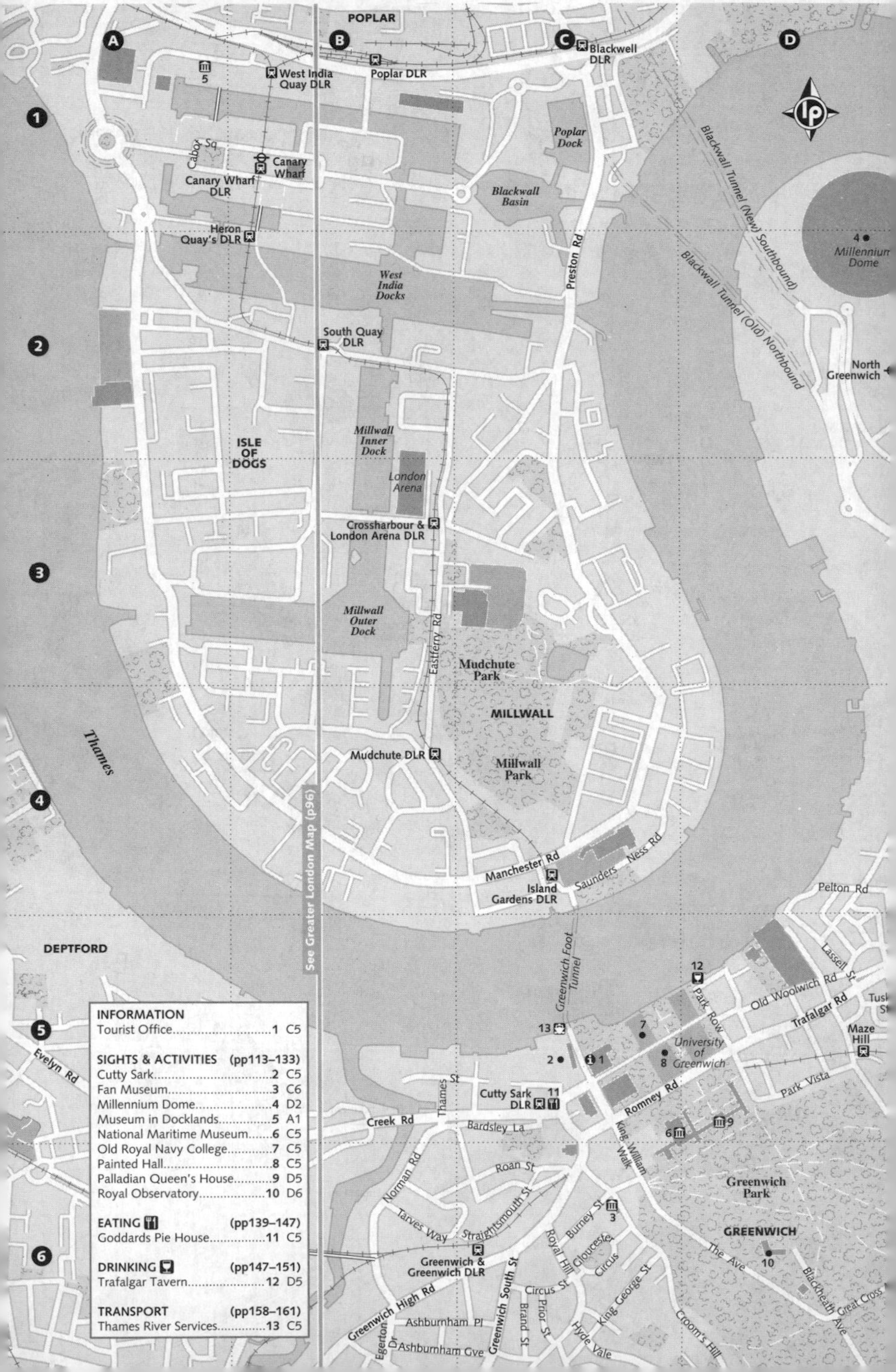

0   500 m
0   0.25 miles

POPLAR

A   **B**   **C** Blackwell
                           DLR
                      D

West India Poplar DLR
Quay DLR

1
                    Poplar
                    Dock
Cabot Sq
Canary Wharf   Canary   Blackwall
DLR   Wharf   Basin

Heron
Quay's DLR   Preston Rd

West
India
Docks

2   South Quay
         DLR   Millennium
                                          Dome

ISLE   North
OF   Millwall   Greenwich
DOGS   Inner
         Dock
         London
         Arena
Crossharbour &
London Arena DLR

3   Millwall
         Outer   Eastferry Rd
         Dock
                    Mudchute
                    Park

                    MILLWALL
Thames
Mudchute DLR   Millwall
                    Park

4
                    Manchester Rd
                              Saunders Ness Rd
         Island   Pelton Rd
         Gardens DLR
DEPTFORD
                    Greenwich Foot
                    Tunnel   Old Woolwich Rd Lassell
                              Park Row   Trafalgar Rd Maze
                    12   Hill
5   University
         13   of
Evelyn Rd 2   1   8 Greenwich Park Vista
                    7
                    Romney Rd
Cutty Sark
DLR 11   6   9
Creek Rd
         Thames Bardsley La
                              King William Walk
                                      Greenwich
Norman Rd   Park

                              Burney St 3   GREENWICH
6   Royal Hill
         Roan St   10
                    Straightsmouth St   The Ave Blackheath
Tarves Way   Great Cross
         Greenwich &   King George St
         Greenwich DLR   Croom's Hill
Greenwich High Rd Circus   Hyde Vale
Ashburnham Pl
Ashburnham Gve

See Greater London Map (p96)

(Continued from page 95)

Travel Agencies

STA Travel (☎ 0870-160 6070; www.statravelco.uk)
Victoria (Map p108; ☎ 0870-166 2642; 52 Grosvenor
Gardens SW1W; ⊗ 9.30am-7pm Mon-Thu, 10am-6pm
Fri, 11am-6pm Sat, noon-5pm Sun; ⊖ Victoria); Euston
Rd (Map pp98-9; ☎ 0870 166 2603; 117 Euston Rd NW1;
⊖ Euston) Long-standing and reliable with several
branches in London.

Trailfinders (Map pp100-1; worldwide travel ☎ 0845
058 5858, 1st & business class ☎ 0845 054 6666; www
.trailfinders.com; 194 & 215 Kensington High St W8;
⊗ 9am-7pm Mon-Fri, 9am-6pm Sat, 10am-6pm Sun;
⊖ High St Kensington) A visa and passport service
(☎ 0845 05 05 905), immunisation centre (☎ 7938
3999) and information centre (☎ 7938 3303). Branches in
Covent Garden, Piccadilly, the City and Canary Wharf.

DANGERS & ANNOYANCES

Considering its size and the disparities in
wealth, London is remarkably safe. That said,
keep your wits about you and don't flash your
cash unnecessarily.

Take care at night. When travelling by tube,
choose a carriage with other people in it and
avoid deserted suburban stations. Following
reports of sexual attacks, solo women travellers should avoid unlicensed minicabs.

Scams

Unfortunately tourists are always a target for
scamsters. At the time of research, card-clon-
ing through tampered ATMs was a concern.
So guard your PIN details carefully and don't
use an ATM that looks unusual.

Hotel and hostel touts descend on backpackers at popular tube and main-line stations. Only accept a lift if you know exactly
where you're headed.

Some Soho strip clubs and hostess bars are
dodgy, and people should be especially wary
of those that tout for business on the street.

SIGHTS

London is big and attacking the sights is best
done by area. Start in the tourist heart, the
West End, with Soho, Covent Garden and
Bloomsbury. Here are many of London's finest
galleries and museums, its mainstream entertainment and funkiest shopping. West of here
you enter old-money London, incorporating
the frightfully well-heeled neighbourhoods
of Mayfair, St James's and Kensington –
home to royalty, the wealthy and some great

museums. To the north, Marylebone and
Notting Hill are groovier while southwards
lie Westminster, Whitehall and the cradle of
British democracy.

Across the river from the West End, the
regenerated South Bank is home to some of
London's most popular attractions, including the London Eye and the Tate Modern.
Heading anticlockwise over the river again is
Britain's financial cockpit, the City – St Paul's
Cathedral is the main draw here. Continuing
the loop you'll hit Hoxton and Shoreditch,
new centres of London cool, and then Camden and Islington, the ones they replaced.

Trafalgar Square

Trafalgar Sq is the public heart of London,
hosting great rallies, marches and feverish New
Year's festivities. Londoners congregate here to
celebrate anything from football victories to the
ousting of political leaders. Formerly ringed
by gnarling traffic, the square's been tidied up
and is now one of the world's grandest public
places. Don't miss Marc Quinn's beautiful Car-
rara marble statue **Alison Lapper Pregnant** (2005)
in the northeast corner until April 2007.

The square is flanked by splendid buildings:
the National Gallery, the National Portrait
Gallery and the church of St Martin-in-the-
Fields. The ceremonial **Pall Mall** runs southwest
from the top of the square. Further south
stands **Admiralty Arch** (Map pp110–11; built in
honour of Queen Victoria in 1910), beyond
which the mall leads to Buckingham Palace.
Nelson surveys his fleet from the 43.5m-high
Nelson's Column (Map pp110–11), erected in
1843 to commemorate Nelson's 1805 victory
over Napoleon off Cape Trafalgar in Spain.

NATIONAL GALLERY

Following a two-year building project the
fantastic **National Gallery** (Map pp110-11; ☎ 7747
2885; www.nationalgallery.org.uk; Trafalgar Sq WC2; admission
free, temporary exhibition prices vary; ⊗ 10am-6pm Thu-Tue,
to 9pm Wed; ⊖ Charing Cross) is looking better than
ever, with bright spaces, a cleaned-up entrance
complete with beautiful dome, a highlights
gallery and the **National Dining Rooms** restaurant. And there are still the 2300-plus Western
European paintings spanning 1250 to 1900 to
draw the four million annual visitors.

Highlights include Turner's *The Fighting
Temeraire* (voted the nation's favourite paint-
ing in 2005), Botticelli's *Venus and Mars* and
Van Gogh's *Sunflowers* but audio tours cover

the lot. Free one-hour guided tours leave at 11.30am and 2.30pm on weekdays and at 11.30am, 12.30pm, 2.30pm and 3.30pm on Saturday (additional tours at 6pm and 6.30pm on Wednesday). If you prefer, you can devise and print off your own tour with the flashy computer screens of **Art Start**.

Visit on Wednesday evenings for live music, licensed bar and free talks.

NATIONAL PORTRAIT GALLERY

This **gallery** (Map pp110-11; ☎ 7306 0055; www.npg .org.uk; St Martin's Cres WC2; admission free; ☽ 10am-6pm Sat-Wed, to 9pm Thu-Fri; ⊖ Charing Cross) is so much better than the rather dry name suggests. Founded in 1856, the permanent collection (around 10,000 works) displays famous people from the 15th century right through to the present day, starting with the early Tudors on the top floor and descending to contemporary figures on the ground floor.

An audio guide for £2 will lead you through the gallery's most famous pictures. Look out for the temporary exhibitions – June to September hosts the prestigious National Portrait Award.

Whitehall

Whitehall is the administrative heart of the country and is best explored on foot (see the Whitehall Walking Tour p131).

BANQUETING HOUSE

The beautiful, classical design of the **Banqueting House** (Map pp102-3; ☎ 7930 4179; www.hrp.org .uk; Whitehall; adult/child £4.50/3; ☽ 10am-5pm Mon-Sat; ⊖ Charing Cross) was daringly conceived by Inigo Jones for James I in 1622. It's the only surviving part of the palace after the Tudor bit burnt down in 1698. The key attraction is the Main Hall's ceiling, painted by Rubens in 1635 at the behest of Charles I. Sadly he didn't get to enjoy it for long as in 1649 he was frogmarched out of the 1st-floor balcony to lose his head for treason. A bust outside commemorates the king. Audio guides are available for £4.50 per adult.

CHURCHILL MUSEUM & CABINET WAR ROOMS

The **Cabinet War Rooms** (Map pp102-3; ☎ 7930 6961; www.iwm.org.uk; King Charles St; adult/child under 16yr £11/free; ☽ 9.30am-6pm, last entry 5pm; ⊖ Westminster) were Churchill's underground military HQ during WWII. Now a wonderfully evoca-

tive and atmospheric museum, the restored and preserved rooms (including Churchill's bedroom) capture the drama of the time. The new **Churchill Museum** is the first national museum dedicated to the Prime Minister and an intriguing exposé of the public and private faces of the man.

Westminster & Pimlico

Westminster has been the centre of political power for over a millennium and most of its interesting places are linked with the monarchy, parliament or the Church of England. The area is a remarkable spectacle, a picture of rare architectural cohesion and an awesome display of power, gravitas and historical import. Pimlico, by contrast is pretty mind-numbing except for the Tate Britain.

WESTMINSTER ABBEY

One of the most sacred and symbolic sites in England is **Westminster Abbey** (Map pp102-3; ☎ 7654 4900; www.westminster-abbey.org; Dean's Yard SW1; adult/child £10/6; ☽ 9.30am-3.45pm Mon, Tue, Thu & Fri, 9.30am-6pm Wed, 9am-1.45pm Sat; ⊖ Westminster). With the exception of Edward V and Edward VIII, every sovereign has been crowned here since William the Conqueror, and most of the monarchs from Henry III (died 1272) to George II (1760) are also buried here.

The abbey is a magnificent and arresting sight. Though a mixture of architectural styles, it is considered the finest example of Early English Gothic (1180–1280) in existence. The original church was built in the 11th century, during the Dark Ages, by the King (later St) Edward the Confessor, who is buried in the chapel behind the main altar. Henry III (r 1216–72) began work on the new building but didn't complete it; the French Gothic nave was finished in 1388. Henry VII's huge and magnificent chapel was consecrated in 1519 after 16 years of construction. Unlike St Paul's, Westminster Abbey has never been a cathedral. It is what is called a 'royal peculiar' and is administered directly by the Crown.

The interior is less impressive than the exterior but there are many highlights, including the incongruously ordinary-looking **Coronation Chair**, the late perpendicular-style **Henry VII Chapel**, the **Royal Air Force (RAF) Chapel**, the octagonal **Chapter House** (admission with abbey ticket or separately for a donation; closes 1 hour before the abbey), the **Pyx Chamber** (admission as Chapter House) and the **Abbey Museum** with death masks of generations of royalty.

Free concerts are held from 12.30pm to 2pm once a week from the end of July through August in the 900-year-old **College Garden** (10am-6pm Tue-Thu Apr-Sep, to 4pm Tue-Thu Oct-Mar).

Sign up for a guided tour (£4) at the information desk or take an audio tour (£3). Evensong is at 6.30pm weekdays, 3pm weekends; Sunday Eucharist is at 11.15am.

Next door to the abbey is the smaller **St Margaret's Church** (admission free), the House of Commons' place of worship since 1614. There are windows commemorating churchgoers Caxton and Milton, and Sir Walter Raleigh is buried by the altar.

HOUSES OF PARLIAMENT

Comprising the House of Commons (where members of parliament discuss legislation) and the House of Lords (home of the peers), the **Houses of Parliament** (Map pp102-3; 7219 4272; www.parliament.uk; Parliament Sq SW1; Westminster) are in the Palace of Westminster, built by Sir Charles Barry and Augustus Pugin in 1840 when neogothic style was in vogue.

The most famous feature is the clock tower **Big Ben** (Map pp102-3). Ben is actually the 13-ton bell, named after Benjamin Hall, who was commissioner of works when the tower was completed in 1858. The best view of the whole complex is from the eastern side of Lambeth Bridge.

When Parliament is in session, visitors are admitted to the **House of Commons Visitors' Gallery**. Expect to queue for at least an hour if you haven't already organised a ticket through your local British embassy. Note that parliamentary recesses (ie holidays) last for three

months over the summer, and a couple of weeks over Easter and Christmas. The **House of Lords Visitors' Gallery** (7219 3107; admission free; from 2.30pm Mon-Tue, from 3pm Wed-Thu, from 11am some Fridays) is also open to outsiders.

The roof of **Westminster Hall**, added between 1394 and 1401, is the earliest known example of a hammer-beam roof and has been described as 'the greatest surviving achievement of medieval English carpentry'.

When parliament is in recess, there are guided **summer tours** (0870 906 3773; www.parliament.uk; from St Stephen's Entrance, St Margaret St; 75min tours £7/5; telephone for times) of both chambers and other historic buildings.

WESTMINSTER CATHEDRAL

Completed in 1903, **Westminster Cathedral** (Map p108; 7798 9064; Victoria St SW1; admission free; 7am-7pm; Victoria) is the headquarters of the Roman Catholic Church in Britain and the only good example of neo-Byzantine architecture in London. Its distinctive candy-striped redbrick and white-stone tower features prominently on the west London skyline.

The interior is part splendid marble and mosaic and part bare brick due to lack of funds. It features the highly regarded stone carvings of the 14 **Stations of the Cross** (1918) by Eric Gill. For £3 you can take a lift up to the 83m tower of the **Campanile Bell** for splendid views of London, or call to book a tour (£2.50).

TATE BRITAIN

The place to see, appreciate and interpret British art from the 16th century to the present, **Tate Britain** (Map pp96-7; 7887 8008; www.tate.org .uk; Millbank SW1; admission free; 10am-5.50pm; Pimlico) features works by notables such as William Blake, the Hogarths, Gainsborough, Whistler and Spencer, as well as the controversial annual Turner Prize. The quirky **Clore Gallery** holds the bulk of JMW Turner's paintings.

There are free one-hour guided tours running from 11am to 3pm. The immensely popular **Tate Restaurant** (7887 8825; mains £14.95), with an impressive Rex Whistler mural, is open for lunch and afternoon tea.

St James's & Mayfair

Monopoly wasn't lying – high-society Mayfair is the most expensive place in London. St James's is a mixture of exclusive gentlemen's clubs, historic shops and elegant buildings;

indeed, there are some 150 historically noteworthy buildings within its 36 hectares.

INSTITUTE FOR CONTEMPORARY ARTS

A one-stop contemporary art bonanza, the exciting programme at the **Institute for Contemporary Arts** (ICA; Map pp102-3; ☎ 7930 3647; www.ica .org.uk; The Mall SW1; admission varies; ☿ noon-11pm Mon, to 1am Tue-Sat, to 10.30pm Sun; ❷ Charing Cross) includes film, photography, theatre, installations, talks, performance art, DJs, digital art and book readings. Stroll around the galleries, watch a film, browse the bookshop then head to the bar for a late beer (open till 1am).

ST JAMES'S PARK & ST JAMES'S PALACE

The neatest of London's royal parks, **St James's Park** (Map pp102-3; The Mall SW1; ❷ St James's Park) has the best view, spanning Westminster, Buckingham Palace and St James's Palace. The flowerbeds are spectacular, but it's the lake and waterfowl that really pop.

The striking Tudor gatehouse of St James's Palace, initiated by the palace-mad Henry VIII in 1530, is best approached from St James's St to the north of the park. This was the residence of Prince Charles and his sons until they shifted next door to the former residence of the Queen Mother **Clarence House** (1828) after she died in 2002 (and the future king spent £4.6 million reshaping the house to his own design).

SPENCER HOUSE

The ancestral home of Princess Diana's family, **Spencer House** (Map pp102-3; ☎ 7499 8620; www .spencerhouse.co.uk; 27 St James's Pl SW1; adult/child £9/7; ☿ 10.30am-5.30pm Sun Feb-Jul & Sep-Dec; ❷ Green Park) was built in the Palladian style between 1756 and 1766. Although the Spencers moved out in 1927 and the house became offices, an £18 million restoration project returned it to its former glory in the 1980s. Visits through eight state rooms of the house are by guided tour only (last tour 4.45pm). The restored gardens (£3.50) are opened just a few days each summer.

BUCKINGHAM PALACE

The official residence of Queen Elizabeth II, **Buckingham Palace** (Map pp102-3; ☎ 7830 4832; adult/ child £14/8; ☿ 9.45am-3.45pm 26 July-24 Sep; ❷ St James's Park) is at the southwestern end of the Mall.

Built in 1803 for the Duke of Buckingham, it replaced St James's Palace as the royal family's London home in 1837. Nineteen lavishly furnished staterooms, used by the royals to meet and greet, are open to visitors when HRH takes her holidays in Scotland. The tour includes **Queen Victoria's Picture Gallery** (76.5m long, with works by Rembrandt, Van Dyck, Canaletto, Poussin and Vermeer) and the **Throne Room**, with his-and-hers pink chairs initialled 'ER' and 'P'.

Changing of the Guard

London's quintessential tourist attraction takes place when the old guard (Foot Guards of the Household Regiment) comes off duty to be replaced by the new guard in the forecourt of Buckingham Palace. If you arrive early, you can gape at the soldiers' bright-red uniforms and bearskin hats as they shout and march in one of the world's most famous displays of pageantry. Otherwise, the backs of heads will be your view. The **ceremony** takes place at 11.30am daily from April until the end of July and on alternate days for the rest of the year, weather permitting.

Queen's Gallery

This **gallery** (Map pp102-3; adult/child £7.50/4; ☿ 10am-5.30pm) houses displays from the extensive Royal Collection of art and treasures. Originally designed by John Nash as a conservatory, it was smashed up by the Luftwaffe in 1940 before being reopened as a gallery in 1962. Following a £20 million renovation and expansion, it reopened for the Queen's Golden Jubilee in 2002.

Royal Mews

Sheltering immaculately groomed royal horses, the **Royal Mews** (Map pp102-3; Buckingham Palace Rd SW1; adult/child £6.50/4; ☿ 10am-5pm 25 Jul-24 Sep, 11am-4pm 25 Mar-24 Jul & 25 Sep-29 Oct; ❷ Victoria) also houses opulent royal vehicles, including the stunning gold coach of 1762, which has been used for every coronation since George III, and the royal weddings' 1910 Glass Coach.

HANDEL HOUSE MUSEUM

George Frideric Handel's pad from 1723 to his death in 1759 is now a **museum** (Map pp102-3; ☎ 7399 1953; www.handelhouse.org; 25 Brook St W1K; adult/ child £5/2; ☿ 10am-6pm Tue-Wed, Fri & Sat, 10am-8pm Thu, noon-6pm Sun; ❷ Bond St) dedicated to his life and 18th-century culture. He wrote some of his greatest works, including *Messiah*, here and music still fills the house at live recitals (see the website for details).

Many years and genres later, Jimi Hendrix lived at number 23 so there's also a small collection of photographs taken in his flat.

GREEN PARK
Green Park is less manicured than the adjoining St James's Park. It was once a duelling ground and served as a vegetable garden during WWII.

West End – Soho to the Strand
The West End is more a cultural term than a geographical one, but it basically takes in Piccadilly Circus and Trafalgar Sq to the south, Oxford St and Tottenham Court Rd to the north, Regent St to the west and Covent Garden and the Strand to the east. A heady mixture of consumerism and culture, the West End is where outstanding museums, galleries, historic buildings and entertainment venues jostle with tacky tourist traps.

PICCADILLY CIRCUS
Named after the stiff collars (picadils) that were the sartorial staple of a 17th-century tailor who lived nearby, Piccadilly Circus is home to the popular landmark the **Eros statue** (Map pp110–11). It's a thronging hub charged with neon and choking fumes and reliable Virgin Megastore (p157).

London Trocadero
The green flags of the **Trocadero** (Map pp110–11; ☎ 0906 888 1100; www.troc.co.uk; 1 Piccadilly Circus W1; ⓨ 10am-midnight Sun-Thu, to 1am Fri & Sat; ⊖ Piccadilly Circus) will try and lure you into this supposed pleasure park of cinema, virtual reality rides, dodgems etc. But once you're inside this tortuous temple to tack you'll be screaming to be released.

PICCADILLY
Piccadilly is home to classic London icons the Ritz hotel and Fortnum & Mason department store.

Royal Academy of Arts
Britain's first art school, the wonderful **Royal Academy of Arts** (Map pp110–11; ☎ 7300 8000; www.royalacademy .org.uk; Burlington House, Piccadilly W1; admission varies; ⓨ 10am-6pm Sat-Thu, to 10pm Fri; ⊖ Green Park) has created a storm in recent years, with well-pitched shows ranging from China: the Three Emperors to its popular Summer Exhibitions showing the work of contemporary British artists.

Burlington Arcade
The well-to-do **Burlington Arcade** (Map pp110-11; 51 Piccadilly W1; ⊖ Green Park), built in 1819, is most famous for the Burlington Berties, uniformed guards who patrol the area keeping an eye out for punishable offences such as running, chewing gum or whatever else might lower the shopping arcade's tone.

REGENT STREET
Distinguished by elegant shop fronts, Regent St is home to Hamley's, London's premier toy and game store, and the upmarket department store Liberty (p155).

OXFORD STREET
Oxford St is the zenith of High St shopping, a must or a miss depending on your retail persuasion. West towards Marble Arch, you'll find many famous department stores including the stupendous Selfridges (p155).

SOHO
A decade ago this lively area was known mostly for strip clubs and peepshows. The sleaze is still there but these days it blends with some of London's trendiest clubs, bars and restaurants. West of Soho proper is **Carnaby St**, the epicentre of London's 'swinging '60s', whose tourist tack is getting trendy neighbours.

LEICESTER SQUARE
Pedestrianised Leicester (les-ter) Sq is usually heaving with tourists – and inevitably buskers. Dominated by large cinemas, it often hosts star-studded premieres.

CHINATOWN
Lisle and Gerrard Sts form the heart of Chinatown (Map pp110–11), which is full of verve and unfairly hip Japanese youngsters. Street signs are bilingual and the streets themselves are lined with Asian restaurants. If you're in town in late January or early February, don't miss the sparkles and crackles of Chinese New Year.

COVENT GARDEN
This elegant **piazza** (Map pp110-11; ⊖ Covent Garden), London's first planned square, is a tourist mecca where chain restaurants, souvenir shops, balconied bars and street entertainers vie for the punters' pound. It positively heaves in summer, especially weekends.

LONDON FOR FREE

Tell your bank manager to back off. Many of London's sights are absolutely free (hurrah) including the following: the British Museum, National Gallery, National Portrait Gallery, Photographers' Gallery, Guildhall, Museum of London, Tate Modern, Bank of England Museum, Imperial War Museum, Victoria & Albert (V&A) Museum, National History Museum, Science Museum and the Wallace Collection.

In the 1630s Inigo Jones converted the former vegetable field into a graceful square that at first housed the fruit and vegetable market immortalised in the film *My Fair Lady*. The area slumped and became home to brothels and coffee houses, but the market was shifted in the 1980s and Covent Garden was transformed into one of the city's grooviest hubs.

Photographers' Gallery
For photography fans, this small **gallery** (Map pp110-11; ☎ 7831 1772; www.photonet.org.uk; 5 & 8 Great Newport St WC2H; admission free; ☿ 11am-6pm Mon-Sat except Thu 11am-8pm, noon-6pm Sun; ☻ Leicester Sq) showcasing UK and international talent is worth a peep. At number 8 are the exhibition space and bookshop while at number 5 there's a café and print sales gallery.

London Transport Museum
At the time of writing, this excellent **museum** (Map pp110-11; ☎ 7379 6344; www.ltmuseum.co.uk; Covent Garden Piazza WC2; ☻ Covent Garden) was closed for an £18.6-million refurbishment. When it reopens (spring 2007) it promises even better displays on the city's transport in the past, present and future (spaceships in the capital? Flying cars?).

Theatre Museum
This **museum** (Map pp110-11; ☎ 7943 4700; Russell St WC2; admission free; ☿ 10am-6pm Tue-Sun; ☻ Covent Garden) is a branch of the Victoria & Albert Museum and has costumes, artefacts and curiosities relating to the history of British theatre.

THE STRAND
Described by Benjamin Disraeli in the 19th century as Europe's finest street, this 'beach' of the Thames – which was built to connect Westminster (the seat of political power) and the City (the commercial centre) – still boasts a few classy hotels but has lost much of its lustre.

Somerset House
The first Tudor **Somerset House** (Map pp110-11; www.somerset-house.org.uk; Strand WC2; ☻ Temple) was built for the Duke of Somerset in 1551. For two centuries it played host to wild masked balls, peace treaties, the Parliamentary army during the Civil War, Oliver Cromwell's wake, royals and foreign diplomats. Having fallen into disrepair it was pulled down in 1775 and rebuilt to designs by William Chambers. It went on to house, among other weighty organisations, the Royal Academy of the Arts, the Society of Antiquaries, the Navy Board and that most popular of institutions the Inland Revenue.

It's now home to three fascinating galleries surrounding a fantastic courtyard of dancing fountains with summer open-air events and a winter ice-rink. Out the back there's a wonderful terrace, restaurant and café overlooking the Thames.

The **Courtauld Gallery** (Map pp110-11; ☎ 7848 2526; adult/child £5/free; admission free 10am-2pm Mon; ☿ 10am-6pm) displays a wealth of 14th- to 20th-century works, including a roomful of Rubens and impressionist and postimpressionist works by Van Gogh, Renoir and Toulouse-Lautrec.

The **Gilbert Collection** (Map pp102-3; ☎ 7420 9400; adult/child £5/free; ☿ 10am-6pm) includes such treasures as European silverware, gold snuffboxes and Italian mosaics bequeathed to the nation by London-born American businessman Arthur Gilbert.

The **Hermitage Rooms** (Map pp102-3; ☎ 7845 4630; adult/child £6/free; ☿ 10am-6pm) display diverse and rotating exhibitions from St Petersburg's renowned (and underfunded) State Hermitage Museum, to which goes a slice of your admission fee.

Bloomsbury
Bloomsbury is a genteel blend of the University of London, beautiful Georgian squares, the British Museum and literary history. **Russell Square**, its very heart, was laid out in 1800 and is London's largest.

Between the world wars these pleasant streets were colonised by a group of artists and intellectuals known collectively as the Bloomsbury Group, which included the novelists Virginia Woolf and EM Forster, and the economist John Maynard Keynes.

BRITISH MUSEUM

London's most visited attraction, the **British Museum** (Map pp102-3; ☎ 7636 1555; www.thebritishmuseum .ac.uk; Great Russell St WC1; admission free; ☒ 10am-5.30pm Mon-Wed & Sat-Sun, to 8.30pm Thu & Fri; ☻ Tottenham Court Rd or Russell Sq) is the largest in the country and one of the oldest and finest in the world, boasting vast Egyptian, Etruscan, Greek, Oriental and Roman galleries among many others.

Before you get to the galleries, you'll be blown away by the **Great Court**, which was restored and augmented by Norman Foster in 2000. The courtyard now boasts a spectacular glass-and-steel roof and somehow manages to be more luminous than outside – it's one of the most impressive architectural spaces in the capital. In the centre is the **Reading Room**, with stunning blue and gold domed ceiling where Karl Marx wrote *The Communist Manifesto*. Off to the right is the **Enlightenment Gallery**, the oldest and grandest gallery in the museum, the first section of the redesigned museum to be built in 1823.

The enthralling exhibits began in 1753 with a 'cabinet of curiosities' bequeathed by Sir Hans Sloane to the nation on his death; this has mushroomed over the years partly through the plundering of the empire (see boxed text, below).

Among the must-sees are the **Rosetta Stone**, discovered in 1799 and the key to deciphering Egyptian hieroglyphics; the controversial **Parthenon Sculptures**, which once adorned the walls of the Parthenon in Athens; the stunning **Oxus Treasure** of 7th- to 4th-century BC Persian gold; and the Anglo-Saxon **Sutton Hoo**

Ship Burial site. Along with the Great Court, the most recent additions to the museum are the **Sainsbury African Galleries**, the restored **King's Library** and the new **Wellcome Gallery of Ethnography**.

You'll need multiple visits to savour even the highlights here; happily there are nine 50-minute free 'eye opener' tours, at 11am to 3.30pm daily except Friday (till 3pm), focussing on different world cultures. Other tours include the 90-minute highlights tour, at 10.30am, 1pm and 3pm daily (adult/child £8/5), and a range of audio guides (£3.50). Given the museum's mind-boggling size and scope, an initial tour is highly recommended.

Holborn & Clerkenwell

Holborn's most distinctive features are the wonderful Sir John Soane's Museum and the atmospheric Inns of Court, built here to symbolise the law's role as mediator in the traditional power struggle between Westminster and the City. The little pocket of Clerkenwell was for most of the 19th and 20th centuries a dilapidated, working-class area of no interest to anyone but its inhabitants. In the 1980s property developers moved in and Clerkenwell has been transformed into an appealing and trendy corner of the capital, replete with new pubs, restaurants and clubs.

SIR JOHN SOANE'S MUSEUM

One of the most charming London sights, this tragically undervisited **museum** (Map pp110-11; ☎ 7405 2107; www.soane.org; 13 Lincoln's Inn Fields WC2; admission free, tour 2.30pm Sat £3; ☒ 10am-5pm Tue-Sat, 6-9pm 1st Tue of month; ☻ Holborn) represents the taste of celebrated architect and collector extraordinaire Sir John Soane (1753–1837).

BRITAIN & GREECE SQUABBLE OVER MARBLES

Wonderful though it is, the British Museum can sometimes feel like one vast repository for stolen booty. Much of what's on display wasn't just 'picked up' along the way by Victorian travellers and explorers, but stolen, or purchased under dubious circumstances.

Restive foreign governments occasionally pop their heads over the parapet to demand the return of their property. The British Museum says 'no' and the problem goes away until the next time. Not the Greeks, however. They have been kicking up a stink demanding the return of the so-called Elgin Marbles, the ancient marble sculptures that once adorned the Parthenon. The British Museum, and successive British governments, steadfastly refuse to hand over the priceless works that were removed from the Parthenon and shipped to England by the British ambassador to the Ottoman Empire, the Lord Elgin, between 1801 and 1805. (When Elgin blew all his dough, he sold the marbles to the government.) The diplomatic spat continues. Only time will tell who blinks first.

The house is largely as it was when Sir John was taken out in a box. Among his eclectic acquisitions are an Egyptian sarcophagus, ancient vases and works of art, and the original *Rake's Progress,* William Hogarth's set of cartoon caricatures of late-18th-century London lowlife.

INNS OF COURT

Clustered around Holborn to the south of Fleet St are the Inns of Court (Map pp102–3), the alleys, atmosphere and open spaces of which provide an urban oasis. All London barristers work from within one of the four Inns, and a roll call of former members would include the likes of Oliver Cromwell and Charles Dickens to Mahatma Gandhi and Margaret Thatcher. It would take a lifetime working here to grasp all the intricacies of the arcane protocols of the Inns – they're similar to the Freemasons, and both are 13th-century creations. It's best just to soak up the dreamy atmosphere, relax, and thank your lucky stars you're not one of the bewigged and deadly serious barristers scurrying about.

Lincoln's Inn (☎ 7405 1393; Lincoln's Inn Fields WC2; ☽ grounds 9am-6pm Mon-Fri, chapel 12-2.30pm Mon-Fri; ✆ Holborn), largely intact with several original 15th-century buildings, is the most attractive of the bunch with a chapel and pretty landscaped gardens. **Gray's Inn** (☎ 7458 7800; Gray's Inn Rd WC1; ☽ grounds 10am-4pm Mon-Fri, chapel 10am-6pm Mon-Fri; ✆ Chancery Lane) was largely rebuilt after the Luftwaffe levelled it. **Middle Temple** (☎ 7427 4800; Middle Temple Lane EC4; ☽ 10-11.30am & 3-4pm Mon-Fri; ✆ Temple) and **Inner Temple** (☎ 7797 8250; King's Bench Walk EC4; ☽ 10am-4pm Mon-Fri; ✆ Temple) both sit between Fleet St and Victoria Embankment – the former is the best preserved while the latter is home to the Da Vinci Code's Temple Church.

The City

The City of London, the commercial heart of the capital, is the 'square mile' on the northern bank of the Thames where the Romans first built their walled community two millennia ago. Its boundaries have changed little since, and you can always tell when you're within them because the Corporation of London's coat of arms appears on the street signs. As well as atmospheric winding alleyways, St Paul's Cathedral and the Tower of London attract visitors.

Less than 10,000 people actually live here, although some 300,000 descend on it each weekday, where they generate almost three-quarters of Britain's entire GDP before heading home.

FLEET ST

As 20th-century London's 'Street of Shame', **Fleet St** (Map pp102-3; ✆ Blackfriars) was synonymous with the UK's scurrilous tabloids until the mid-1980s when the press barons embraced computer technology, ditched a load of staff and largely relocated to the Docklands.

DR JOHNSON'S HOUSE

Where Samuel Johnson and his assistants compiled the first English dictionary between 1748 and 1759, **Dr Johnson's House** (Map pp102-3; ☎ 7353 3745; www.drjohnsonshouse.org; 17 Gough Sq EC4; admission £4.50; ☽ 11am-5.30pm Mon-Sat May-Sep, to 5pm Mon-Sat Oct-Apr; ✆ Chancery Lane) is a well-preserved Georgian building. It's full of prints and portraits of friends and intimates, including Johnson's Jamaican servant, to whom he bequeathed the house in his will.

ST PAUL'S CATHEDRAL

Dominating the City with a dome second in size only to St Peter's in Rome, **St Paul's Cathedral** (Map p105; ☎ 7236 4128; www.stpauls.co.uk; adult/child £9.50/3.50; ☽ 8.30am-4pm; ✆ St Paul's) was built between 1675 and 1710 by Sir Christopher Wren after the Great Fire of 1666. Four other cathedrals preceded it on this site, the first dating from 604.

The dome is renowned for somehow dodging the bombs during the Blitz of WWII and became an icon of the resilience shown in the capital during the crisis. Outside the cathedral, to the north, is a **monument to the people of London**, a simple and elegant memorial to the 32,000 Londoners who weren't so lucky.

Inside, some 30m above the main paved area, is the first of three domes (actually a dome inside a cone, inside a dome) supported by eight huge columns. The walkway round its base is called the **Whispering Gallery**, because if you talk close to the wall your words will carry to the opposite side 32m away.

This, the **Stone Gallery** and the **Golden Gallery** can be reached by a staircase on the western side of the southern transept. It is 530 lung-busting steps to the Golden Gallery at the very top, and an unforgettable view of London. If that's too much, you still get terrific vistas from the lower galleries.

The **Crypt** has memorials to up to 300 military demigods, including Wellington, Kitchener and Nelson, whose body lies below the dome. But the most poignant memorial is to Sir Christopher Wren himself. On a simple slab bearing his name a Latin inscription translates as: 'If you seek his memorial, look about you'.

Audio tours lasting 45 minutes are available for £3.50. Guided tours (adult/child £3/1) leave the tour desk at 11am, 11.30am, 1.30pm and 2pm (90 minutes). There are organ concerts at St Paul's at 5pm most Sundays. Evensong takes place at 5pm most weekdays and at 3.15pm on Sunday.

GUILDHALL

Plum in the middle of the 'square mile', the **Guildhall** (Map p105; ☎ 7606 3030; Basinghall St EC2; admission free; ☯ 10am-5pm Mon-Sun May-Sep, 10am-5pm Mon-Sat Oct-Apr; ☻ Bank) has been the seat of the City's local government for eight centuries. The present building dates from the early 15th century.

Visitors can see the **Great Hall** where the mayor is 'sworn in' and where important chaps like the Czar of Russia and the Prince Regent celebrated beating Napoleon. It's a vast impressive space with the shields and banners of London's 12 principal livery companies; carved galleries, the west of which is protected by slightly disturbing statues of giants Gog and Magog; and a beautiful oak-panelled roof. Beneath it is London's largest **medieval crypt** (☎ 7606 3030, ext 1463; visited by free guided tour only) with 19 stained-glass windows showing the livery companies' coats of arms.

The **Guildhall Clock Museum** (admission free; ☯ 9.30am-4.45pm Mon-Fri) charts 500 years of timekeeping with over 700 ticking exhibits and the **Guildhall Art Gallery** (☎ 7332 3700; admission £2.50) displays around 250 artworks, the most significant of which is John Singleton Copley's masterpiece *The Defeat of the Floating Batteries at Gibraltar; September 1782.*

BARBICAN

Like Marmite, you either love or hate the concrete **Barbican** (Map p105; ☎ 7638 4141; Silk St EC2; ☻ Barbican or Moorgate). It's true that it is extraordinarily ugly in many ways, with forbidding high-rise tower blocks (romantically named Shakespeare, Cromwell and Lauderdale), gloomy raised walkways and tunnels, and apartment blocks that valiant window boxes attempt to prettify. But at the time, this vast complex of offices and residences with an arts centre at its heart was revolutionary, designed to fill the WWII bomb-splattered space with democratic modern housing by disciples of Le Corbusier, Chamberlain, Powell and Bon. Sadly this democratic dream never really materialised, and today around 80% of the flats are privately owned. It's been fashionable to loath the Barbican in the past, but in 2001 the complex became listed, so its detractors will just have to live with it.

The Barbican Centre (p153) is the home of the London Symphony Orchestra. It also houses the Museum of London and the wonderful **Barbican Art Gallery** (☎ 7638 8891; admission £8.50; ☯ 11am-8pm Mon, Wed, Fri-Sun, to 6pm Tue & Thu) on Level 3, with some of the best photographic exhibits in London. The programmes are generally first-rate, as long as you can find them. There's also a free gallery on Level 0 called the **Curve Gallery**.

MUSEUM OF LONDON

Explore the tunnels of the Barbican heading for gate 7 to reach the fascinating **Museum of London** (Map p105; ☎ 0870 444 3851; www .museumoflondon.org.uk; London Wall EC2; admission free; ☯ 10am-5.50pm Mon-Sat, noon-5.50pm Sun; ☻ Barbican) and a journey through London's history from the big bang to broadband. Its ever-expanding exhibitions include the new Medieval Galleries and a life-size slightly pongy Anglo-Saxon long house – for health and safety reasons they had to use fermented straw instead of dung to get an authentic whiffyness. The downstairs will be undergoing a complete redesign between 2007 and 2009 but the Roman, Medieval and prehistoric collections will remain open.

TOWER OF LONDON

One of the most essential sights to see in London, the **Tower of London** (Map p105; ☎ 7680 9004; www.hrp.org.uk; Tower Hill EC3; adult/child £15/9.50; ☯ 10am-5pm Mon, 9am-5pm Tue-Sat, 10am-5pm Sun; ☻ Tower Hill) is a window into a gruesome, fascinating history. It is also one of the city's three World Heritage Sites (joining Westminster Abbey and Maritime Greenwich).

To help get your bearings, take the hugely entertaining and free guided tour with any of the Tudor-garbed Beefeaters. Hour-long tours leave every 30 minutes from the Middle Tower between 9am and 3pm Monday to Saturday and from 10am Sunday.

In 1078 William the Conqueror laid the first stone of the White Tower to replace the timber-and-earth castle he'd already built here. By 1285 two walls with towers and a moat were built around it and the medieval defences have barely been altered since. A former royal residence, treasury, mint and arsenal, it became most famous as a prison when Henry VIII moved to Whitehall Palace in 1529 and started dishing out his preferred brand of punishment.

The most striking building is the huge **White Tower**, with its solid Romanesque architecture and four turrets, which today houses a collection from the Royal Armouries. On the 2nd floor is the **Chapel of St John the Evangelist**, dating from 1080 and therefore the oldest church in London.

On the small green in front of the church stood Henry VIII's **scaffold**, where seven people were beheaded, including Anne Boleyn and her cousin Catherine Howard (his second and fifth wives).

To the north is the **Waterloo Barracks**, which now contains the Crown Jewels. On the far side of the White Tower is the **Bloody Tower**, where the 12-year-old Edward V and his little brother were held 'for their own safety' and later murdered, probably by their uncle, the future Richard III. Sir Walter Raleigh did a 13-year stretch here, when he wrote his *History of the World*, a copy of which is on display.

On the patch of green between the Wakefield and White Towers you'll find the latest in the tower's long line of famous ravens, which legend says could cause the White Tower to collapse should they leave. Their wings are clipped in case they get any ideas.

TOWER BRIDGE

London was still a thriving port in 1894, when Tower Bridge was designed to rise and allow ships to pass through. It is raised electronically these days but you can still see the original steam engines. There are excellent views from the walkways.

For the **Tower Bridge Experience** (Map p105; ☎ 7940 3984; www.towerbridge.org.uk; adult/child £5.50/3; 🕑 10am-5.30pm Apr-Sep, 9.30am-5pm Oct-Mar; ⊖ Tower Hill), a lift takes you up from the modern visitors' facility in the northern tower where the story of its building is recounted with videos and animatronics. If you're coming from the Tower you'll pass through Dead Man's Hole where corpses were retrieved from the Thames after they'd been chucked from the prison.

ST KATHARINE DOCKS

A centre of trade and commerce for 1000 years, **St Katharine Docks** (Map p105) is now a buzzing waterside area of boats and eateries. **Ivory House** (built 1854) used to store ivory, perfume and other precious goods; the façade of **International House** (built 1983) is a replica of the original warehouse; **Dickins Inn** has its original 18th-century timber framework and is a popular boozer. There are free concerts on **Marble Quay** at lunchtimes or you can just mooch around looking at the historic vessels and snazzy yachts.

BANK OF ENGLAND MUSEUM

Guardian of the country's financial system, the Bank of England was established in 1694 when the government needed to raise some cash to support a war with France. It was moved here in 1734 and largely renovated by Sir John Soane. The **museum** (Map p105; ☎ 7601 5545; www.bankofengland.co.uk; Bartholomew Lane EC2; admission free; 🕑 10am-5pm Mon-Fri; ⊖ Bank) traces the history of the bank and banknotes with various interactive technology, and isn't quite as dry as it sounds.

THE MONUMENT

Designed by Christopher Wren to commemorate the Great Fire of 1666, the **Monument** (Map p105; ☎ 7626 2717; Monument St; adult/child £2/1; 🕑 9.30am-5pm; ⊖ Monument) is 60.6m high, the exact distance from its base to the bakery on Pudding Lane where the blaze began. Climb the 311 tight spiral steps (not advised for claustrophobics) for an eye-watering view from beneath the symbolic vase of flames.

South of the Thames

The southern part of central London used to be the city's forgotten underside – run-down and offering little for foreign visitors. But there are now pockets of refurbishment and revitalisation, as exemplified by the Design Museum, up-and-coming Bermondsey St and enticing Bermondsey Market (see To Market, To Market p158).

BERMONDSEY

Design Museum

The whiter than white **Design Museum** (Map pp96-7; ☎ 0870 833 9955; www.designmuseum.org; 28 Shad Thames SE1; adult £7; 🕑 10am-5.45pm; ♿; ⊖ Tower Hill) is a must for anyone interested in the evolution of design and all its applications.

The permanent collection Designing Modern Britain has varying displays and there are a number of temporary exhibitions including Designer of the Year for which the prize is an impressive £25,000. Feeling inspired?

SOUTHWARK

An important thoroughfare during the Middle Ages, Southwark (suth-erk)has almost lost its working-class gritty edge in the wake of sights and attractions such as the magnificent Tate Modern, and the modern More London site, home to offices, open-air exhibitions and dazzling City Hall.

City Hall

The Norman Foster–designed wonky-egg-shaped **City Hall** (Map p105; ☎ 7983 4000; www.london .gov.uk; The Queen's Walk SE1; admission free; ☻ 9am-6pm) is an architectural feast of glass, and home to the mayor, the London Assembly and the Greater London Assembly (GLA). Visitors can see the mayor's meeting **chamber** and attend **debates** (see website for timings). On one Saturday a month the 9th floor is opened for an even better view, accessed via a glass winding ramp similar to the one in Berlin's Reichstag.

HMS Belfast

Launched in 1938, the **HMS Belfast** (Map p105; ☎ 7407 6328; Morgan's Lane, Tooley St SE1; adult/child £8.50/ free; ☻ 10am-6pm Mar-Oct, to 5pm Nov-Feb; ⊖ London Bridge) took part in the D-day landings and saw action in Korea. Explore the nine decks and see the engine room, gun decks, galley, chapel, punishment cells, canteen and dental surgery.

London Dungeon

Kids love the **London Dungeon** (Map p105; ☎ 7403 7221; www.thedungeons.com; 28-34 Tooley St SE1; adult/ child £14.95/11; ☻ 9.30/10/10.30am-5/5.30pm depending on school holidays; ⊖ London Bridge) It's all spooky music, ghostly boat-ride, fake blood and actors dressed up as gory criminals or torturers – beware the interactive bits.

Britain at War Experience

You can pop down to the London Underground air raid shelter, look at gas masks and ration books, stroll around Southwark during the blitz and learn about the battle on the Home Front at the **Britain at War Experience** (Map p105; ☎ 7403 3171; www.britainatwar.co.uk; 64-66 Tooley St SE1; adult/child £9.50/4.85; ☻ 10am-5.30pm Apr-Sep, to 4.30pm Oct-Mar). This place is crammed

with fascinating memorabilia from London during WWII.

Old Operating Theatre Museum & Herb Garret

One of London's most genuinely gruesome attractions is the **Old Operating Theatre Museum** (Map p105; ☎ 7955 4791; www.thegarret.org.uk; 9A St Thomas St SE1; adult/child £4.95/2.95; ☻ 10.30am-4.45pm; ⊖ London Bridge). The primitive surgical tools of the 19th century are terrifying. Check out the recently added animal medicine section.

There's also an apothecary where medicinal herbs were stored; it now houses a medical museum hung with bunches of herbs.

Southwark Cathedral

Although the central tower dates from 1520 and the choir from the 13th century, **Southwark Cathedral** (Map p105; ☎ 7367 6722; Montague Close SE1; admission by donation; ☻ 8am-6pm; ⊖ London Bridge) is largely Victorian. It's been scrubbed up in recent years and has a new visitor centre. Inside are monuments and details galore, including a Shakespeare Memorial, and it's worth picking up one of the small guides. Catch Evensong at 5.30pm on Tuesday and Friday, 4pm on Saturday and 3pm on Sunday.

Shakespeare's Globe & Exhibition

Originally built in 1599, **Shakespeare's Globe** (Map p105; ☎ 7401 9919; www.shakespeares-globe .org; 21 New Globe Walk SE1; adult/child £9/5.50; ☻ 10am-6.30pm (last entry 5pm), 10am-5pm Oct-Apr; ⊖ London Bridge) burned down in 1613 and was immediately rebuilt. The Puritans, who regarded theatres as dreadful dens of iniquity, eventually closed it in 1642. American actor and director Sam Wanamaker fought to rebuild it last century, sadly dying before the opening night in 1997.

The visit includes a tour of the theatre, where you learn interesting snippets like where the audience used to go to the loo in the absence of lavatories (take a wild guess) and what theatre was like in Shakespeare's time, plus a fascinating exhibition on Elizabethan London and the rebuilding of the theatre.

Plays are still performed in this faithful replica with thatched open roof, and actors wear traditional costumes (made by painstaking traditional methods). See the website for upcoming performances. During summer matinee performances the guided tour visits the nearby site of Rose, Bankside's first theatre.

Tate Modern

This former power station is home to the tremendous **Tate Modern** (Map p105; information ☎ 7887 8008; www.tate.org.uk; Queen's Walk SE1; admission free; ☻ 10am-6pm Sun-Thu, to 10pm Fri & Sat; ☒ ; ⊖ Southwark), Europe's most successful contemporary art gallery and one of the South Bank's most exciting attractions.

Following the Tate's first re-hang since opening in 2000, the permanent collection is now organised by period so you can stroll through cubism, futurism and vorticism; surrealism and surrealist tendencies; abstract expressionism and European informal art; and minimalism. The vast Turbine Hall is as dramatic as it's always been and a real highlight of any visit; and the temporary exhibitions are still enticing.

Another attraction is the view from the top-floor restaurant and café. The audio guides (£2) are worthwhile for their descriptions of selected works. There are free daily guided tours of the collection's highlights at 11am and 3pm (meet on Level 3).

SOUTH BANK

The 20th-century South Bank may not be blessed with good looks, but new glass extensions are giving the cultural and arts venues – the Royal National Theatre and the National Film Theatre – a makeover, and the London Eye remains a popular sight.

Hayward Gallery

No permanent exhibition here, but the **Hayward Gallery** (Map pp102-3; ☎ 7921 0813; www.hayward -gallery.org.uk; Belvedere Rd SE1; admission prices vary; ⊖ Waterloo) showcases leading names in modern art through their video, installations, photography, collage, painting etc.

London Eye

Perched on the bank of the Thames, the British Airways' **London Eye** (Map pp102-3; ☎ 0870 5000 600; www.ba-londoneye.com; adult/child £13/6.50, discover flight £15/7.50; ☻ 10am-8pm Jan-May & Oct-Dec, to 9pm Jun-Sep; ⊖ Waterloo) is the world's largest sightseeing wheel. (For all sorts of technical reasons it can't be called a Ferris wheel.) Originally destined to be a temporary structure, Londoners took the wheel to their hearts and it's now a permanent addition to the cityscape.

The 135m-tall wheel takes 30 minutes to rotate completely and it's best experienced at dusk. Discovery flights include a guide who

---

TATE-A-TATE

To get between London's Tate galleries in style, the **Tate-to-Tate ferries** – one of which sports a Damien Hirst dot painting – will whisk you from the Millennium Pier at Tate Britain to the Bankside Pier at Tate Modern, stopping en route at the London Eye. Services run 10am to 6pm daily at 40-minute intervals. A River Roamer hop-on hop-off ticket (purchased on board) costs £7.30 (discounts available).

---

can point out the points of interest on the 25-mile view.

This attraction is so popular that it's advisable to book your ticket online to beat the queues (you also get a 10% discount).

The London Eye also runs a 40-minute **River Cruise** (adult/child £10/5) which takes in sights like the Houses of Parliament, Tower of London and St Paul's Cathedral and has multilingual commentary. Joint tickets for the London Eye and cruise are available.

London Aquarium

One of the largest in Europe, the **London Aquarium** (Map pp102-3; ☎ 7967 8000; www.london aquarium.co.uk; County Hall, Westminster Bridge Rd SE1; adult/child £11.75/8.25; ☻ 10am-6pm; ⊖ Westminster or Waterloo) has three levels of fish organised by geographical origin, but you may be peering over schoolchildren's excited heads in school holidays. Check the website for shark feeding times.

Dalí Universe

Europe's largest collection of famous artworks by the surrealist master, **Dalí Universe** (Map pp102-3; ☎ 0870 744 7485; www.daliuniverse.com; County Hall Gallery SE1; adult/child £11/6.50; ☻ 10am-5.30pm; ☒ ; ⊖ Westminster or Waterloo) takes you through his work by theme: Sensuality & Feminity, Religion & Mythology, Dreams & Fantasy. **Picasso: Art of a Genius** featuring 100 rare or unseen works is on show here too. Tickets get you into both exhibitions.

LAMBETH

Lambeth is the district just south of Westminster Bridge, home to a few interesting museums and Lambeth Palace, the official residence to successive archbishops of Canterbury since the 12th century.

Imperial War Museum

You don't have to be a little boy to appreciate the **Imperial War Museum** (Map pp96-7; ☎ 7416 5000; www.iwm.org.uk; Lambeth Rd SE1; admission free; ☯ 10am-6pm; ➋ Lambeth North) and its spectacular atrium with spitfires hanging from the ceiling, rockets (including the massive German V2), field-guns, missiles, submarines, tanks, torpedoes and other military hardware. Providing a telling lesson in modern history, highlights include a re-created WWI trench and WWII bomb shelter as well as a **Holocaust Exhibition**.

Florence Nightingale Museum

The thoughtful **Florence Nightingale Museum** (Map pp96-7; ☎ 7620 0374; www.florence-nightingale.co.uk; 2 Lambeth Palace Rd SE1; adult/child £5.80/4.80; ☯ 10am-5pm Mon-Fri, to 4.30pm Sat & Sun, last admission 1hr before closing; ☒ ; ➋ Westminster or Waterloo) recounts the story of 'the lady with the lamp' who led a team of nurses during the Crimean War, and who established a training school for nurses at St Thomas' hospital in 1859.

Chelsea, South Kensington & Earl's Court

The residents of Kensington and Chelsea have the highest incomes of any London borough (shops and restaurants will presume you do too) and the area, like the Chelsea football team, is thoroughly cosmopolitan chic. Thanks to the 1851 Great Exhibition, South Kensington is first and foremost museum land, boasting the Natural History, Science and Victoria & Albert Museums all on one road.

Further west, Earl's Court is lively and cosmopolitan, although less prosperous. It's particularly popular with travelling Antipodeans and was once known as Kangaroo Valley.

VICTORIA & ALBERT MUSEUM

A vast, rambling and wonderful museum of decorative art and design, the **Victoria & Albert (V&A) Museum** (Map pp100-1; ☎ 7942 2000; www.vam.ac.uk; Cromwell Rd SW7; admission free; ☯ 10am-5.45pm Thu-Tue, to 10pm Wed; ➋ South Kensington) is part of Prince Albert's legacy to Londoners in the wake of the successful Great Exhibition of 1851.

It's a bit like the nation's attic, comprising four million objects collected over the years from Britain and around the globe. Spread over nearly 150 galleries, it houses the world's greatest collection of decorative arts, including

ancient Chinese ceramics, modernist architectural drawings, Korean bronze and Japanese swords, samples from William Morris' 19th-century Arts and Crafts movement, cartoons by Raphael, spellbinding Asian and Islamic art, Rodin sculptures, Elizabethan gowns and dresses straight from this year's Paris fashion shows, ancient jewellery, a 1930s' wireless set, an all-wooden Frank Lloyd Wright study, and a pair of Doc Martens. Yes, you'll need to plan.

NATURAL HISTORY MUSEUM

Kids – and most adults – will lose their minds at the **Natural History Museum** (Map pp100-1; ☎ 7942 5725; www.nhm.ac.uk; Cromwell Rd SW7; admission free; ☯ 10am-5.50pm Mon-Sat, 11am-5.50pm Sun; ➋ South Kensington), where the main collections are divided between adjoining Life and Earth Galleries. Where once the former was full of dusty glass cases of butterflies and stick insects, there are now wonderful interactive displays on themes such as Human Biology and Creepy Crawlies. Plus there's the crowd pulling exhibition on mammals and dinosaurs, which includes animatronic movers and shakers such as the 4m-high Tyrannosaurus Rex. The Earth Galleries are equally impressive. An escalator slithers up and into a hollowed-out globe where two main exhibits – Earthquake and the Restless Surface – explain how wind, water, ice, gravity and life itself impact on the earth.

The **Darwin Centre**, a vast education centre, houses some 22 million zoological exhibits, which can be visited by tour.

SCIENCE MUSEUM

With seven floors of interactive and educational exhibits, the **Science Museum** (Map pp100-1; ☎ 7942 4455; www.sciencemuseum.org.uk; Exhibition Rd SW7; admission free; ☯ 10am-6pm; ➋ South Kensington) helps you discover everything from the history of the Industrial Revolution to the exploration of space. There is something for all ages, from vintage cars, old trains and antique aeroplanes to labour-saving devices for the home, a wind tunnel and flight simulator. The even more hi-tech extension, the **Wellcome Wing**, focuses on contemporary science and makes presentations on recent breakthroughs. There's also a 450-seat **IMAX cinema**.

CHELSEA PHYSIC GARDEN

Established in 1673 to provide a means for students to study medicinal plants and healing, this peaceful **garden** (Map pp106-7; ☎ 7352 5646; www.chelseaphysicgarden.co.uk; 66 Royal Hospital Rd SW3; admission £5; ☺ noon-5pm Wed & Sun Apr-Oct, noon-5pm Tue & Thur Jul-Sep; ☻ Sloane Sq) is one of the oldest botanical gardens in Europe and contains many rare trees and plants.

ROYAL HOSPITAL CHELSEA

Designed by Christopher Wren, the **Royal Hospital Chelsea** (Map p108; ☎ 7881 5204; Royal Hospital Rd SW3; admission free; ☺ 10am-noon & 2-4pm Mon-Sat, 2-4pm Sun; ☻ Sloane Sq) was built in 1692 to provide shelter for ex-servicemen. Today it houses hundreds of war veterans known as Chelsea Pensioners, who are fondly regarded as a national treasure. As you wander around the grounds or inspect the elegant chapel you may see them in their winter blue coats or summer reds. The Chelsea Flower Show takes place in the hospital grounds in May.

Knightsbridge & Kensington

These are among London's poshest precincts and of particular interest to shoppers. Knightsbridge is where you'll find some of London's best-known department stores, including Harrods and Harvey Nichols, while Kensington High St has a lively mix of chains and boutiques.

KENSINGTON PALACE

Dating from 1605, **Kensington Palace** (Map pp100-1; ☎ 0870 751 5170; www.hrp.org.uk; Kensington Gardens W8; adult/child £11.50/7.50; ☺ 10am-6pm Mar-Oct, to 5pm Nov-Feb; ☻ High St Kensington) was the birthplace of Queen Victoria in 1819 but is best known today as the last home of Princess Diana. Hour-long tours take you around the surprisingly small **Staterooms**. A collection of Princess Di's dresses is on permanent display along with frocks and ceremonial gowns from HRH and her predecessors. There's an audio tour, included in the entry fee, if you want to explore on your own.

KENSINGTON GARDENS

Blending in with Hyde Park, these **royal gardens** (Map pp100-1; ☺ dawn-dusk) are part of Kensington Palace. There's a splendid, contemporary art space, the **Serpentine Gallery** (Map pp100-1; ☎ 7402 6075; www.serpentinegallery.org; admission free; ☺ 10am-6pm; ☻ Knightsbridge or Lancaster Gate), south of the lake. The **Sunken Garden**, near the palace, is at its prettiest in summer, while tea in the **Orangery** (Map pp100-1)

is a treat. For canine lovers there's a **Dog's Cemetery** tucked away.

On the southern edge of the gardens, opposite the Royal Albert Hall, is the restored **Albert Memorial** (Map pp100-1; ☻ South Kensington or Gloucester Rd), as over-the-top as the subject, Queen Victoria's German husband Albert (1819–61), was purportedly humble. It was designed by George Gilbert Scott in 1872.

On the far side of the gardens is **Diana, Princess of Wales Memorial Playground** (Map pp100–1) for kids.

Notting Hill

The status of the Notting Hill Carnival (in late August) reflects the multicultural appeal of this part of West London, into which West Indian immigrants moved in the 1950s. After decades of exploitation and strife, the community took off in the 1980s and the area is now a thriving, vibrant corner of central London that is retaining its charm despite steady gentrification.

Bayswater, to the east, was neglected for centuries, but is now mainly a fairly well-to-do residential area with Queensway as its main thoroughfare.

Hyde Park

At 145 hectares, **Hyde Park** (Map pp100-1; ☺ 5.30am-midnight) is central London's largest open space. Henry VIII expropriated it from the Church in 1536, when it became a hunting ground and later a venue for duels, executions and horse-racing. The 1851 Great Exhibition was held here and during WWII the park became an enormous potato field. These days, it serves as an occasional concert venue and a full-time green space for fun and frolics. There's boating on the Serpentine for the physically energetic or, near Marble Arch, there's **Speaker's Corner** (Map pp100–1) for oratorical acrobats. These days, it's largely total nutters and religious fanatics who maintain the tradition begun in 1872 as a response to rioting.

A plaque on the traffic island at Marble Arch indicates the spot where the infamous Tyburn Tree, a three-legged gallows, once stood. It is estimated that up to 50,000 people were executed here between 1300 and 1783, many having been dragged from the Tower of London.

A more soothing structure, in memory of Princess Diana – a meandering stream that splits at the top, flows gently downhill and reassembles in a pool at the bottom – was unveiled here in mid-2004 with inevitable debate over matters of taste and gravitas.

MARBLE ARCH
London's grandest bedsit – with a one-room flat inside – **Marble Arch** (Map pp100–1; ⊖ Marble Arch) was designed by John Nash in 1827 as the entrance to Buckingham Palace. It was moved here in 1851.

Marylebone
Increasingly hip Marylebone is home to several attractions, from London's primo tourist haunt Madame Tussauds to the oft-overlooked artistic treasure Wallace Collection.

WALLACE COLLECTION
Housed in a beautiful, opulent Italianate mansion the **Wallace Collection** (Map pp102–3; ☎ 7563 9500; www.wallacecollection.org; Hertford House, Manchester Sq W1; admission free, audio guide £3; ✆ 10am-5pm; ⊖ Bond St) is a treasure-trove of exquisite 18th-century French furniture, Sèvres porcelain, arms, armour and art by masters such as Rubens, Titian, Rembrandt and Gainsborough. The lovely glassed-in courtyard restaurant is popular with an older crowd. Past temporary exhibitions have included Great British Watercolours; check the website for the current schedule.

MADAME TUSSAUDS
You'll probably have to queue for **Madame Tussauds** (Map pp102–3; ☎ 0870 999 0046; www.madame-tussauds.com; Marylebone Rd NW1; prices vary according to time of year & entry, admission including Chamber Live adult/child £24/20; ✆ 9.30am-5.30pm Mon-Fri, 9am-6pm Sat & Sun; ⊖ Baker St), you'll pay through the nose and really, just how interesting is looking at celebrities made out of wax, taking part in a wax X-factor or hanging out with wax serial killers? Kids do seem to like it though, so if they insist on going, drop them off and then go for a mosey down Marylebone High St.

LONDON PLANETARIUM
Attached to Madame Tussauds (and included in the admission charge), the **London Planetarium** (Map pp102–3; www.london-planetarium.com; admission £3; ✆ 9.30am-5.30pm Mon-Fri, 9am-6pm Sat & Sun) presents a 15-minute star show projected onto the dome ceiling.

> **TOP FIVE PLACES TO POTTER**
>
> ■ Portobello Rd (Map pp100–1)
>
> ■ Marylebone High St (Map pp102–3)
>
> ■ Brick Lane (Map p105)
>
> ■ Exmouth Market (Map pp98–9)
>
> ■ Hampstead (Map pp96–7)

Regent's Park
A former royal hunting ground, **Regent's Park** (Map pp98–9; ⊖ Baker St or Regent's Park) was designed by John Nash early in the 19th century, although what was actually laid out is only a fraction of the celebrated architect's grand plan. Nevertheless, it's a lovely space in the middle of the city – at once lively and serene, cosmopolitan and local – with football pitches, tennis courts and a boating lake. **Queen Mary's Gardens**, towards the south of the park, are the prettiest part of the gardens with spectacular roses in summer when the **open-air theatre** (☎ 7486 7905) hosts performances of Shakespeare.

LONDON ZOO
Established in 1828 and one of the world's oldest, **London Zoo** (Map pp98–9; ☎ 7722 3333; www.londonzoo.co.uk; Regent's Park NW1; adult/child £14.50/11.50; ✆ 10am-5.30pm Mar-Oct, to 4pm Nov-Feb; ⊖ Camden Town) got into hot water because its historical buildings weren't conducive to animal comforts. Smarting from the criticism, the zoo embarked on a 10-year, £21-million project focusing on conservation, education and breeding programmes. All the same, you'll find this zoo as thrilling or upsetting as any other. Feeding times, reptile handling and the petting zoo are always popular.

North London
The northern reaches of central London stretch in a broad arc from St John's Wood in the west to Islington in the east. Camden Market and Hampstead Heath are among North London's most popular attractions, while Islington is awash with lively pubs and eateries, and Upper St, in particular, is worth a wander.

EUSTON & KING'S CROSS
These aren't especially inviting areas and will be most familiar to users of the tube and any-

one taking a train to the north of England. The area around King's Cross is a bit of a building site as the new Eurostar terminal and surrounding entertainment and residential complexes take shape.

British Library

Colin St John's new **British Library** (Map pp98-9; ☎ 7412 7332; www.bl.uk; 96 Euston Rd NW1; admission free; 🕙 9.30am-6pm Mon & Wed-Fri, 9.30am-8pm Tue, 9.30am-5pm Sat, 11am-5pm Sun; ⊖ King's Cross St Pancras), which opened in 1998, has copped some flak for its red-brick façade, but the interior is superb. You need to be a 'reader' (ie member) to use the collection of every British publication in print, but historical documents, including the Magna Carta, are on public display.

ST JOHN'S WOOD

Posh St John's Wood is where you'll find Lord's, the home of world cricket; and 3 Abbey Rd, where the Beatles recorded most of their albums, including *Abbey Road* (1969) itself, with its cover shot taken on the **zebra crossing** (Map pp96–7) outside.

MCC Museum & Lord's Tour

The next best thing to watching a test at **Lord's Cricket Ground** (Map pp96-7; ☎ 7616 8595; www.lords .org; St John's Wood Rd NW8; adult/child £8/5; tours 10am, noon & 2pm Apr-Sep, noon & 2pm Oct-Mar when there's no play; ⊖ St John's Wood) is the absorbingly anecdotal 90-minute tour of the ground and facilities, which takes in the famous (members only) Long Room and a museum featuring evocative memorabilia.

CAMDEN

Technicolour hairstyles, facial furniture, heavy tattoos and ambitious platform shoes are the look du jour in Camden, the popularity of which is largely fuelled by Camden Market (see boxed text, p158), London's most popular 'unticketed' tourist attraction with an estimated 10 million visitors a year. This was a working-class Irish and Greek enclave just two decades ago but has been largely gentrified since.

HAMPSTEAD & HIGHGATE

These quaint and well-heeled villages, perched on hills above central London, are home to an inordinate number of celebrities and intelligentsia. The villages are largely as they were

---

TOP FIVE GREEN SPACES

- Hyde Park (p126)
- St James's Park (p116)
- Hampstead Heath (below)
- Regent's Park (p127)
- Kew Gardens (p131)

---

laid out in the 18th century and boast close proximity to the vast Hampstead Heath.

Hampstead Heath

With its rolling woodlands and meadows, **Hampstead Heath** (Map pp96-7; ⊖ Hampstead, Gospel Oak or Hampstead Heath mainline station) is a million miles away – well approximately four – from central London. A walk up **Parliament Hill** affords one of the most spectacular views of the city.

Kenwood House (Map pp96-7; ☎ 8348 1286; Hampstead Lane NW3; admission free; 🕙 11am-5pm Apr-end Oct, 11am-4pm rest of year; ⊖ Archway or Golders Green) is a magnificent neoclassical mansion on the northern side of the heath, and houses a small collection of paintings by European masters. From the station catch bus No 210.

The Heath also has several swimming ponds – for the strong and hardy – with separate ponds for single-sex and mixed bathing. Once you've worked up a thirst, that's *after* your swim, there are good pubs nearby (p151).

Highgate Cemetery

The Victorian symbols – shrouded urns, obelisks, upturned torches (life extinguished) and broken columns (life cut short) – along with the eerily overgrown graves and the twisting paths of the western side of **Highgate Cemetery** (Map pp96-7; ☎ 8340 1834; Swain's Lane N6; ⊖ Archway) weave a creepy kind of magic. From Archway station walk up Highgate Hill till you reach Waterlow Park on the left. Go through the park; the cemetery gates are opposite the exit.

Admission to the western side of the cemetery is by tour only (adult/child £3/1; 2pm Monday to Friday, on the hour 11am to 4pm Saturday and Sunday). On the other, less atmospheric eastern side you can visit other graves (admission £2; 10am to 4.30pm Monday to Friday, 11am to 4.30pm Saturday and Sunday April to October, to 3.30pm rest of the year), including those of Karl Marx and George Eliot.

Keats House

This elegant Regency **house** (Map pp96-7; ☎ 7435 2062; Wentworth Pl, Keats Grove NW3; adult/child £3.50/free; ⏰ 1-5pm Tue-Sun; ⊖ Hampstead) was Keats' home from 1818 to 1820, until he left for sunnier Rome to help his tuberculosis. Here he wrote *Ode to a Nightingale* and fell in love with his neighbour Fanny Brawne. Among the personal mementos are Fanny's engagement ring, love letters and old manuscripts.

Freud Museum

After fleeing Nazi-occupied Vienna in 1938, Sigmund Freud came to this house where he lived the last 18 months of his life. The **Freud Museum** (Map pp96-7; ☎ 7435 2002; www.freud.org.uk; 20 Maresfield Gardens NW3; adult £5; ⏰ noon-5pm Wed-Sun) contains the psychoanalyst's original couch, his books and his Greek and Asian artefacts.

East London

The eastern reaches of central London are taken up by the East End – the London of Christmas pantomimes and old Hollywood films – and the sprawl of the Docklands, where the brand new sits alongside the old and decaying.

EAST END

The East End districts of Shoreditch, Hoxton, Spitalfields and Whitechapel were traditionally working-class London, settled by waves of immigrants all of whom have left their mark. Run-down and neglected by the 1980s, pockets of it are now highly cool. There are no major attractions here, but it's a good place to experience modern, multicultural London.

Geffrye Museum

The only museum in the UK to specialise in historic domestic interiors, the **Geffrye Museum** (Map pp96-7; ☎ 7739 9893; www.geffrye-museum.org.uk; 136 Kingsland Rd E2; admission free; ⏰ 10am-5pm Tue-Sat, noon-5pm Sun; ⊖ Old St, then bus No 243) is a lot more interesting than it sounds, and if you like poking around other people's houses it's positively orgasmic. You'll see oriental-inspired wallpaper and tiles in the Aesthetic style room; bright colours and carved side chairs in the Victorian room; exotic woods, brass mounts and inlays in the Regency room; Arts and Crafts–style furniture in the Edwardian room; the gramophone and Moderne style of the 1930s; an early '60s living room complete with sideboard that looks suspiciously like ones

you can buy in Habitat on Tottenham Court Rd; and the rather boring-looking style of the 1990s IKEA generation. And on top of all that interiors porn, there's a lovely walled herb garden, a design centre, shop and restaurant,

White Cube

Set in an industrial building with impressive glazed roof extension **White Cube** (Map p105; ☎ 7930 5373; www.whitecube.com; 48 Hoxton Sq N1; admission free; ⏰ 10am-6pm Tue-Sat; ⊖ Old St) has an appealing programme of contemporary-art exhibitions from sculptures to video, installations and painting.

DOCKLANDS

The Port of London was once the world's greatest port, the hub of the British Empire and its enormous global trade. Since being pummelled by the Luftwaffe in WWII its fortunes have been topsy-turvy, but new development and infrastructure have seen people and tenants return in recent years.

The **Museum in Docklands** (Map p112; ☎ 7515 1162; www.museumindocklands.org.uk; Hertsmere Rd, West India Quay E17; adult/child £5/free; ⏰ 10am-5.50pm Mon-Sat, noon-5.50pm Sun; ⊖ Canary Wharf), housed in a heritage-listed warehouse, uses artefacts and multimedia to chart the history of the Docklands from Roman trading to its renewal in the twilight of the 20th century. It's a fascinating look through the Docklands' window into Britain's past.

South London

Glamorous Greenwich is the main attraction south of London's centre but you will also have fun exploring Brixton's colourful market or visiting the excellent Horniman Museum in Forest Hill.

GREENWICH

Quaint and villagelike, Greenwich (*gren-itch*) is a delightful place with a recharging sense of space, splendid architecture and strong connections with the sea, science, sovereigns and time. It has earned its place on Unesco's list of World Heritage Sites and you should allow a full day to do it justice. All the great architects of the Enlightenment made their mark here, largely due to royal patronage, and there's an extraordinary cluster of classical buildings.

The **tourist office** (Map p112; ☎ 0870 608 2000; fax 8853 4607; 2 Cutty Sark Gardens SE10; ⏰ 10am-5pm; Docklands Light Rail [DLR] Cutty Sark) has all the information you need on the area.

LONDON

Cutty Sark

A famous Greenwich landmark, this **clipper** (Map p112; ☎ 8858 3445; www.cuttysark.org.uk; King William Walk; admission £5; ☺ 10am-5pm) was the fastest ship in the world when it was launched in 1869. It's now undergoing major restoration work (till April 2009) but you can book a hard-hat tour to meet the architects and learn about the project.

Old Royal Naval College

Walk south along King William Walk and you'll see the **Old Royal Naval College** (Map p112; ☎ 8269 4747; www.greenwichfoundation.org.uk), designed by Wren and a magnificent example of monumental classical architecture. Now used by the University of Greenwich, you can still view the **chapel** and the stunning **Painted Hall** (adult/child £5/free; ☺ 10am-5pm Mon-Sat), which took artist Sir James Thornhill 19 years of hard graft to complete.

National Maritime Museum

Further south along King William Walk, you'll come to the **National Maritime Museum** (Map p112; ☎ 8312 6565; www.nmm.ac.uk; Romney Rd SE10; admission free; ☺ 10am-6pm), a magnificent neoclassical building by Inigo Jones, which houses a massive collection of marine paraphernalia recounting Britain's seafaring history. Exhibits range from interactive displays to old-fashioned humdingers like Nelson's tunic complete with a hole from the bullet that killed him.

Queen's House

Attached to the National Maritime Museum on its eastern side, the **Palladian Queen's House** (Map p112; ☎ 8858 4422; admission free; ☺ 10am-5pm) has been restored to something like Inigo Jones' intention when he designed this place in 1616. It is a stunning exhibition venue, focusing on illustrious seafarers and historic Greenwich.

Royal Observatory

Charles II had the **Royal Observatory** (Map p112; ☎ 8858 4422; www.rog.nmm.ac.uk; Greenwich Park; admission free; ☺ 10am-6pm) built here in 1675 to help solve the riddle of longitude. Success was confirmed in 1884 when Greenwich was designated as the prime meridian of the world, and Greenwich Mean Time (GMT) became the universal measurement of standard time. On this spot you can stand with your feet straddling the western and eastern hemispheres.

If you arrive just before lunchtime, you will see a bright-red ball climb the observatory's northeast turret at 12.58pm and drop at 1pm – as it has every day since 1833, when it was introduced to allow the ships on the Thames to set their clocks. If you arrive just *after* lunchtime, you can console yourself with superb views across London or a visit to the atmospheric preserved rooms containing the actual timepieces described in Dava Sobel's *Longitude*, the bestselling book about the fascinating quest to measure longitude.

Fan Museum

Greenwich also provides the engaging **Fan Museum** (Map p112; ☎ 8305 1441; www.fan-museum.org; 12 Croom's Hill SE10; admission £3.50; ☺ 11am-5pm Tue-Sat, noon-5pm Sun; DLR Greenwich), housed in an 18th-century Georgian house and one of only two of its kind in the world. A fraction of the hand-held folding fans, collected from around the world and dating back to the 17th century, are on display at any one time.

Getting There & Away

Greenwich is easily reached on the Docklands Light Railway (DLR, p160); Cutty Sark is the station closest to the tourist office and most of the sights. There are fast, cheap trains from Charing Cross to Greenwich station (preferably Maze Hill) about every 15 minutes.

Alternatively come by boat. **Thames River Services** (☎ 7930 4097; www.westminsterpier.co.uk) departs half-hourly from both Westminster Pier (Map pp102–3) and Greenwich, and the trip takes approximately an hour (return £9).

AROUND GREENWICH

Millennium Dome

The public never took to the famously costly **dome** (Map p112), the centrepiece of Britain's millennium celebrations. However, it is now being transformed into a 20,000-seater sports and entertainment arena surrounded by shops, restaurants and affordable housing. The new complex formed part of the Olympics bid, and is due to be completed by the time you read this. Maybe Londoners will like it more in its new incarnation.

FOREST HILL

Horniman Museum

Set in an Art Nouveau building with a clock tower and mosaics, **Horniman Museum** (☎ 8699 1872; www.horniman.ac.uk; 100 London Rd SE23; admission free; ⊗ 10.30am-5.30pm; ⊖ Forest Hill) has a collection of African art and sculpture, including Africa's largest mask and a fab collection of musical instruments, which were collected by the Victorian tea-merchant Frederick John Horniman.

Turn left out of Forest Hill station along Devonshire Rd, then right along London Rd, and you'll see the Horniman on your right.

West London
KEW GARDENS

In 1759 botanists began rummaging around the world's gardens for specimens they could plant in the 3-hectare plot known as the **Royal Botanic Gardens at Kew** (☎ 8332 5655; www.rbgkew .org.uk; Kew Rd, Kew; adult/child £11.75/free; ⊗ 9.30am-6pm Mon-Fri, 9.30am-7pm Sat & Sun, earlier closing in winter; ⊖ Kew Gardens). They never stopped collecting, and the gardens, which have bloomed to 120 hectares, provide the most comprehensive botanical collection on earth (including the world's largest collection of orchids) as well as a delightful pleasure garden.

First-time visitors should board the **Kew Explorer** (adult/child £3.50/1), a hop-on hop-off road train that leaves from Victoria Gate – where you will enter from if you get the tube – and takes you around the gardens' main sights.

Kew has all sorts of charms within its borders. Highlights include the enormous **Palm House**, a hothouse of metal and curved sheets of glass; the stunning **Princess of Wales Conservatory**; the red-brick, 1631 **Kew Palace** (adult/child £5/3.50; ⊗ 10am-6pm 27 Apr-30 Sep), formerly King George III's country retreat and now open following a £6.6-million restoration project; the celebrated **Great Pagoda** designed by William Chambers in 1762; and the **Temperate House**, which is the world's largest ornamental glasshouse and home to its biggest indoor plant, the 18m Chilean Wine Palmand.

The gardens are easily reached by tube but you might prefer to cadge a lift on a river boat from the **Westminster Passenger Services Association** (☎ 7930 2062; www.wpsa.co.uk), which runs boats several times daily departing from Westminster Pier from April to September (return adult/child £16.50/5.25).

HAMPTON COURT PALACE

Built by Cardinal Thomas Wolsey in 1514, but coaxed out of him by Henry VIII just before the chancellor fell from favour, **Hampton Court Palace** (☎ 8781 9500; www.hrp.org.uk; adult/ child £12.30/8; ⊗ 10am-6pm mid-Mar–Oct, 10am-4.30pm Nov–mid-Mar; Hampton Court station) is the largest and grandest Tudor structure in England. It was already one of the most sophisticated palaces in Europe when, in the 17th century, Christopher Wren was commissioned to build an extension. The result is a beautiful blend of Tudor and 'restrained baroque' architecture.

Take a themed tour led by costumed historians, or if you're in a rush visit the highlights: **Henry VIII's State Apartments**, including the Great Hall with its spectacular hammer-beamed roof; the **Tudor Kitchens**, staffed by 'servants'; and the **Renaissance Picture Gallery**. Spend some time in the 60 acres of riverside gardens and get lost in the 300-year-old **maze**.

Hampton Court Palace is 13 miles southwest of central London and is easily reached by train from Waterloo station via Hampton Court station. Alternatively, you can take the 3½-hour riverboat journey from Westminster Pier (see left).

RICHMOND PARK

London's wildest park spans more than 1000 hectares and is home to all sorts of wildlife, most notably herds of red and fallow deer. It's a terrific place for bird-watching, rambling and cycling.

To get there from the Richmond tube station, turn left along George St, then left at the fork that leads up Richmond Hill until you come to the main entrance of Richmond Gate.

WHITEHALL WALKING TOUR

Lined with government buildings, statues, monuments and other historical sights, Whitehall (⊖ Charing Cross or Westminster), and its extension, Parliament St, is the wide avenue that links Trafalgar Sq with Parliament Sq. Whitehall was once the administrative heart of the British Empire and is still the focal point for British government.

The best way to take it all in is with the following short and leisurely stroll.

Start at the statue of King Charles, on a traffic island at the southern end of Trafalgar Sq. Right in front of you, you can see the Houses of Parliament at the end of Whitehall and to your right you'll see 1910 **Admiralty Arch (1**; p113).

Walk south down Whitehall and you'll see the **Old Admiralty (2)** on your right. Further along on the left is the **Ministry of Defence (3)**, on the far side of which you'll find the **Banqueting House (4**; p114).

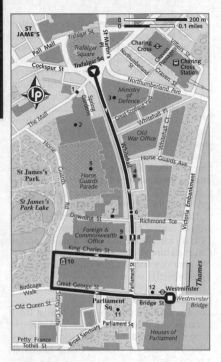

Walk Facts

Start: King Charles statue,
Trafalgar Square
Finish: New Parliament Building
Distance: 0.5 miles
Duration: 40 minutes

On the other side of Whitehall is **Horse Guards Parade (5**; ☺ parades 11am Mon-Sat, 10am Sun), where the mounted troopers of the Queens Life Guard are changed in a ceremony you'll find more accessible than the one outside Buckingham Palace. The guards have been here for 200 years. Have your picture taken next to one, but don't expect them to smile, they're on duty.

Carrying on, you'll soon see the bold **Women of World War II (6)** sculpture in the middle of the road. Unveiled on 9 July 2005 by the Queen, it commemorates the work of over seven million women in World War II. Further down on your right is **Downing St (7)**, site of the British prime minister's official residence since 1732, when George II presented No 10 to Robert

Walpole. Tony Blair and his family actually live in the larger apartments at No 11.

Whitehall becomes Parliament St and, on your left, you'll see the **Cenotaph (8)** – Greek for 'empty tomb' – a memorial to Commonwealth citizens killed during the two world wars.

On your right is the **Foreign & Commonwealth Office (9)**, built in 1872 and restored by Sir George Gilbert Scott and Matthew Digby Wyatt. A right turn down King Charles St will bring you to the **Churchill Museum & Cabinet War Rooms (10**; p114).

Whitehall ends at **Parliament Square (11)**, watched over by statues of past prime ministers. Left along Bridge St is the ultramodern **New Parliament Building (12)**.

LONDON FOR CHILDREN

London has tons for youngsters. Apart from the obvious destinations like London Dungeon (p123), London Zoo (p127), Madame Tussauds (p127), the Science Museum (p125), Tower of London (p121), the aquarium (p124) and the London Eye (p124), there are many playgrounds throughout the centre, a number of city farms (see www.london-footprints.co.uk/visitfarms.htm) and children are widely welcomed everywhere except pubs.

All top-range hotels offer in-house babysitting service. Prices vary enormously from hotel to hotel, so ask the concierge about hourly rates. Alternatively try www.babysitter.co.uk; membership costs £12.75 for three months, then sitters cost as little as £5.50 per hour.

TOURS

If you're short on time and big on company, the **Original London Sightseeing Tour** (☎ 8877 1722) and the **Big Bus Company** (☎ 7233 9533) offer tours of the main sights on hop-on hop-off, double-decker buses, which you'll see trundling through town. They cost adult/child £20/10 for the day, but are only worth getting if you're in town for a short stopover.

Citisights (☎ 8806 3742; www.chr.org.uk/cswalks.htm), **Historical Tours** (☎ 8668 4019), **London Walks** (☎ 7624 3978; www.walks.com) and **Mystery Tours** (☎ 07957 388280; mysterywalks@hotmail.com) offer a variety of themed walking tours.

More imaginative and rewarding tours include the following:
Black Taxi Tours of London (☎ 7935 9363; www.blacktaxitours.co.uk; 8am-6pm £80, 6pm-midnight £85)
Takes you on a two-hour spin past the major sights with a chatty cabbie as your guide.

Cabair Helicopters (☎ 8236 2400; www.cabair.com; Elstree Aerodrome, Borehamwood, Herts; tours £149) Offers 30-minute helicopter 'flight-seeing' tours over London every Sunday.

City Cruises (☎ 7740 0400; www.citycruises.com; Westminster Pier SW1; cruises £9.50; ⏰ 10am-4.30pm, later Jun-Aug, fewer sailings Nov-Mar) Operates a year-round ferry service from Westminster Pier to Tower Pier and Tower Pier to Greenwich in a continuous loop that allows passengers to jump on and off at various stops.

London Bicycle Tour Company (☎ 7928 6838; www .londonbicycle.com; 1A Gabriel's Wharf, 56 Upper Ground SE1; tour incl bike £16.95) Offers themed cycle tours of the 'East' and 'Royal West'.

London Duck Tours (Map pp102-3; ☎ 7928 3132; www.londonducktours.co.uk; departing from County Hall; adult/child £17.50/12; ⏰ 10am-6pm) Uses the same sort of amphibious landing craft used on D-Day in WWII. You cruise the streets of central London before making a dramatic plunge into the Thames.

FESTIVALS & EVENTS

Although not renowned as a festival city, London has a few events that might influence your plans.

London Art Fair (www.londonartfair.co.uk; ☎ 0870 7399500 for tickets; Business Design Centre, Islington; unlimited access £12.50) Held in January, this fair sees over 100 major galleries participating in what is now one of the largest contemporary art fairs in Europe.

Chinese New Year (www.chinatown-online.co.uk; Chinatown) Late January or early February sees Chinatown snap, crackle and pop with a colourful street parade and eating aplenty.

Chelsea Flower Show (www.rhs.org.uk; Royal Hospital Chelsea) Held in May, this is the world's most renowned horticultural show and attracts green fingers from near and far.

Royal Academy Summer Exhibition (www.royal academy.org.uk; Royal Academy of Arts) Beginning in June and running through August, this is an annual showcase of works submitted by artists from all over Britain, mercifully distilled to a thousand or so pieces.

Wimbledon Lawn Tennis Championships Held at the end of June, the world's most splendid tennis event is as much about strawberries, cream and tradition as smashing balls.

Pride (www.pridelondon.org) Concerts and parties rock the capital's popular gay and lesbian festival, culminating in a technicolour parade and rally in June/July.

Notting Hill Carnival (www.thecarnival.tv) Held in August, this is Europe's largest and London's most vibrant outdoor carnival, which celebrates its Caribbean community with music, dancing, costumes over the summer bank holiday weekend.

SLEEPING

Accommodation in London can put a serious dent in your budget. Anything below £80 for a double is pretty much 'budget' in London. Earl's Court and Victoria are best for cheaper beds while Bloomsbury has some good midrange deals. The West End has a predictable number of top-end places, and some seriously deluxe options. Most hotels now have internet access and many have rooms equipped for disabled guests.

If you're visiting in July and August consider booking at least a couple of nights in advance.

West End – Soho to the Strand

You can't get more central than this so, naturally, accommodation here comes at a price. It specialises in deluxe hotels, many of which are tourist attractions in their own right.

BUDGET

Oxford St YHA (Map pp110-11; ☎ 0870 770 5984; oxfordst@yha.org.uk; 14 Noel St W1; 3- or 4-bed dm £22.60, tw per person £24.60; 💻 ; ⊖ Oxford Circus) It's a good idea to book this popular, supercentral hostel two weeks before arriving. There's a kitchen, TV room, balcony, laundry and PC. Since the 76 beds (31 rooms of two, three or four beds) are spread over the 4th and 5th floors of this building the views are pretty good – you can even see the London Eye from some back rooms.

MIDRANGE

Regent Palace Hotel (Map pp110-11; ☎ 0870 400 8703; fax 7734 6435; Piccadilly Circus, cnr Glasshouse St W1; s without bathroom/d with bathroom from £69/120; ⊖ Piccadilly). This is a practical rather than personal choice. The sights are on your doorstep but then so are an uninspiring café, Irish bar and souvenir shop in the lobby – ignore these and enjoy the delights of Soho.

Fielding Hotel (Map pp110-11; ☎ 7836 8305; www .the-fielding-hotel.co.uk; 4 Broad Ct, Bow St WC2; s/d from £80/100; ⊖ Covent Garden) On a quiet pedestrianised street a block away from the Royal Opera House. Space is at a premium and the décor is shop-bought but the central location is a winner.

TOP END

Hazlitt's (Map pp110-11; ☎ 7434 1771; www.hazlittshotel .com; 6 Frith St W1; d from £205, ste £300; 💻 ; ⊖ Tottenham Court Rd) Staying in this charming Georgian house, the former abode of author William

---

BOOKING SERVICES

It's possible to make same-day accommodation bookings for free at most tourist offices, and **Visit London** (☎ 08456 443 010; www.visitlondonoffers.com) also has good deals.

At Home in London (☎ 8748 1943; www.athomeinlondon.co.uk) Can arrange B&B accommodation and charges percentage booking fees.

British Hotel Reservation Centre (☎ 7340 1616; www.bhrconline.com; free online booking)

Lastminute (www.lastminute.com) There are kiosks at the Britain & London Visitor Centre and Victoria station.

London Homestead Services (☎ 7286 5115; www.lhslondon.com) Charges 5% booking fee.

Uptown Reservations (☎ 7937 2001; www.uptownres.co.uk) Has centrally located self-catering apartments and B&Bs on its books.

Youth Hostels Association (YHA; ☎ 0870 870 8808; lonres@yha.org.uk) Operates its own central reservations service provided you can give them at least two weeks' notice.

Hazlitt, is a trip back in time. Each of the 23 rooms is packed with antiques and named after a personage connected with the house. There's no bar and only a small sitting room containing books signed by famous guests. Truly special.

Covent Garden Hotel (Map pp110-11; ☎ 7806 1000; www.coventgardenhotel.co.uk; 10 Monmouth St WC2; d/ste £220/350; ☐ wi-fi; ⊖ Covent Garden) Think antiques successfully mixed with vibrant reds, pinks and leopard print and you'll have a vision of this welcoming hotel. The colourful but cosy 1st-floor library with honesty bar is perfect for a pause and the individually designed bedrooms and marble bathrooms offer respite from busy Covent Garden. Very friendly staff too.

Courthouse Hotel Kempinski (Map pp110-11; ☎ 7297 5555; www.courthouse-hotel.com; 19-21 Great Marlborough St; r from £270; ☐ wi-fi; ⊖ Leicester Sq) This is a unique opportunity to stay in an Old Magistrates Court. In the bar you can sip your G&T in a holding cell, and the Silk Thai/Indian fusion restaurant still has the witness box and judge's bench, although a Buddha now presides instead of a be-wigged old fellow. The rooms boast Italian bathrooms and comfortable fittings (and no bars on the windows). The health spa has a pool, gym and treatments.

Westminster & Victoria

Victoria may not be particularly attractive but there's a good pick of budget accommodation and the transport links are handy.

BUDGET

Astor Victoria Hostel (Map p108; ☎ 7834 3077; 71 Belgrave Rd SW1; dm from £16.50, d £25; ☐ ; ⊖ Victoria) This cheap and cheerful hostel has 20 mixed dorms (four- to eight-bed), eight women-only dorms (four- and six-bed), one twin room with bunk beds and only one double room so book early if you want privacy en couple. There are two comfortable lounges with PCs, a fully equipped kitchen and weekly dinners where you can meet other travellers over grub.

Luna & Simone Hotel (Map p108; ☎ 7834 5897; www.lunasimonehotel.com; 47-49 Belgrave Rd SW1; s/d incl breakfast from £35/70; ☐ wi-fi; ⊖ Victoria) The hotel ensign of Luna (the moon) and Simone (the owner) is etched into the glass porch and this personal touch continues inside with the friendly service. The blue and yellow rooms are clean and calming; the ones at the back are quieter. There's a full English breakfast and there are free storage facilities if you want to leave bags while travelling.

Hamilton House Hotel (Map p108; ☎ 7821 7113; www.hamiltonhousehotel.com; 60 Warwick Way SW1; s/d £50/60; ☐ wi-fi; ⊖ Victoria) Following a major refurbishment, everything in this hotel is shiny and new. The bathrooms feature lovely large showers and the compact rooms (all en suite) are nicely decorated and contain 51cm LCD tellies. Basement rooms are a little dark.

Morgan House (Map p108; ☎ 7730 2384; www.morganhouse.co.uk; 120 Ebury St SW1; s/d/t with bathroom £82/92/110, without bathroom 52/72/92, all incl breakfast; ⊖ Victoria) From the minute you enter this Georgian house you feel at home. Romantic iron beds, chandeliers, period fireplaces, a sunny little garden, sparkling bathrooms and a full English breakfast top it off.

MIDRANGE

B&B Belgravia (Map p108; ☎ 7259 8570; www.bb-belgravia.com; 64-66 Ebury St SW1; s/d from £94/99; ☐ ☐ ; ⊖ Victoria) This small hotel's unassuming façade

---

SWANK IT UP

Brown's Hotel (Map pp110-11; ☎ 7493 6020; www.roccofortehotels.com; 30 Albemarle St W1; d from £295; 🖳 wi-fi; ⊖ Green Park) Following an 18-month refit, Brown's Hotel has a chic new look. Stay here and you're in good company – Rudyard Kipling penned many of his works here, and Kate Moss has been known to pop into the spa.

One Aldwych (Map pp110-11; ☎ 7300 1000; www.onealdwych.com; 1 Aldwych WC2; d/ste from £345/550; 🖳 wi-fi; ⊖ Covent Garden) Granite bathrooms, long swimming pool with underwater music, US and UK electricity sockets, majestic bar and restaurant, modern art, and a lift that changes colour to literally lift your mood – this hotel has all luxuries and services covered.

Claridges (Map pp102-3; ☎ 7629 8860; www.savoy-group.co.uk/claridges; Brook St W1; d from £370; 🖳 wi-fi; ⊖ Bond St) One of the greatest of London's five-star hotels and a leftover from a bygone era with original Art Deco features.

Ritz (Map pp110-11; ☎ 7493 8181; www.theritzlondon.com; 150 Piccadilly W1; d/ste from £400/600; 🖳 ; ⊖ Green Park) London's most celebrated hotel, with opulent rooms that are popular with royalty and the cultural elite.

---

belies a chic, contemporary interior comprising fireplace with flaming pebbles, chandelier with flying light bulbs, white Formica chairs and tables in an eat-in kitchen connected to the lounge via a glass bridge, innovative bathroom design, floor-to-ceiling dark wood cupboards etc. The only design blip is the EasyJet-style orange staff uniform. Outside, the pretty courtyard garden is a suntrap.

Bloomsbury & Fitzrovia

Bloomsbury and Fitzrovia are very convenient, especially for the West End and the British Museum. Tucked away in Georgian crescent Cartwright Gardens to the north of Russell Sq, you'll find some of London's best-value hotels.

BUDGET

Generator (Map pp98-9; ☎ 7388 7666; www.the-generator.co.uk; Compton Pl, 37 Tavistock Pl WC1; dm £12.50-17, s £35, all incl breakfast; 🖳 🛝 ; ⊖ Russell Sq) Imagine lashings of primary colours and shiny metal and you'll get an idea of this futuristic but fun hostel designed to resemble a generator. This former police barracks has long corridors housing 850 beds; a bar that stays open until 2am and hosts quizzes, pool competitions, karaoke and DJs; 24-hour Internet access; safe-deposit boxes; and a large eating area but no kitchen.

Ashlee House (Map pp98-9; ☎ 7833 9400; www.ashleehouse.co.uk; 261-265 Grays Inn Rd; dm from £14, s £35-37, tw £23-25; ⊖ Kings Cross) This hostel is a cheery surprise in a rather gritty but central location. There's a large tube map and sheepskin bench in reception, green dice tables in the small lounge, purple paint on the walls of the compact rooms, and stripy duvets on the blue bunk beds. Nearby, its sister hostel in a converted courthouse (complete with cells) was a building site at the time of writing but should be open by the time you read this; call Ashlee House if you fancy a turn behind bars.

Arran House Hotel (Map pp102-3; ☎ 7636 2186; www.arranhotel-london.com; 77-79 Gower St WC1; dm from £18.50, s/d from £45/72; 🖳 wi-fi; ⊖ Goodge St) Period features such as cornicing and fireplaces, a pretty pergola-decked back garden and a comfy lounge with PCs and TV lift this hotel from the average to the attractive. Slightly squashed en suite bathrooms are small letdown (literally).

Hotel Cavendish (Map pp102-3; ☎ 7636 9079; www.hotelcavendish.com; 75 Gower St WC1; s/d from £50/65; 🖳 wi-fi; ⊖ Goodge St) Following a complete refurbishment in 2006, bedrooms have a contemporary look with flat-screen LCD TVs, and all are equipped with compact en suite shower rooms (some have pretty mosaic tiles and bumper mirrors). The breakfast room is relieved of basement dinginess by a bright white lick of paint. The two gardens at the back seem to have missed out on the refurb, but are still a good place to catch some rays.

Ridgemount Hotel (Map pp102-3; ☎ 7636 1141; www.ridgemounthotel.co.uk; 65-67 Gower St WC1; d with/without bathroom from £68/52; ⊖ Goodge St) This old-fashioned, slightly chintzy place has been in the same family for 40 years and has a comfortable, welcoming feel.

MIDRANGE

Jenkins Hotel (Map pp98-9; ☎ 7387 2067; www.jenkinshotel.demon.co.uk; 45 Cartwright Gardens WC1; s £52, s/d with bathroom from £72/85; ⊖ Russell Sq) This attractive hotel has featured in the TV series of Agatha Christie's *Poirot*. Rooms are on the small side but the hotel has charm.

St Margaret's Hotel (Map pp98-9; ☎ 7636 4277; www .stmargaretshotel.co.uk; 26 Bedford Pl WC1; d with/without bathroom £97/67.50; ☐ wi-fi; ✈ Russell Sq) This light and airy hotel comprises four conjoined Georgian town houses; with four staircases it's easy to get lost, so keep your bearings. Many rooms used to be piano rooms and have lovely high ceilings (for better acoustics). The décor wouldn't look out of place in your granny's house, but the natural light and space are big pluses and the family who own it are welcoming.

Harlingford Hotel (Map pp98-9; ☎ 7387 1551; www .harlingfordhotel.com; 61-63 Cartwright Gardens WC1; d from £99, f £115; ☐ wi-fi; ✈ Russel Sq) This family-run hotel sports refreshing, upbeat décor: – bright-green mosaic-tiled bathrooms (with trendy bowl sinks), fuchsia bedspreads and colourful paintings. With lots of stairs and no lift, consider requesting a 1st-floor room.

TOP END

Charlotte Street Hotel (Map pp110-11; ☎ 7806 2000; www.firmdale.com; 15 Charlotte St W1; d from £230; ☐ wi-fi; ✈ Goodge St) A favourite with media types, this place, designed with a 'Bloomsbury Set' theme, comes up with the goods: great service, stylish quarters, relaxing lounge with honesty bar, popular bar and restaurant, small gym and screening room showing Sunday-night movies.

Clerkenwell

The availability of accommodation hasn't kept pace with Clerkenwell's revival but this is still a great area to stay in.

MIDRANGE

Zetter Hotel (Map pp98-9; ☎ 7324 4455; www.thezet ter.com; 86-88 Clerkenwell Rd EC1; d from £140; ☐ wi-fi; ✈ Farringdon) A slick 21st-century conversion of a Victorian warehouse. The furnishings are an enticing blend of old and new, and the facilities cutting edge – you can even choose the colour of your room's lighting, how about pink this evening?

Malmaison (Map pp102-3; ☎ 7012 3700; www.mal maison.com; 18-21 Charterhouse Sq EC1; d from £195, weekend rates from £125; ☐ wi-fi; ✈ Farringdon) The *Alice in Wonderland* lobby of chessboard carpet, black seats that look like pawns, endless Veuve Cliquot and supersized chairs is a quirky surprise.

Once in the rooms, the look is more classic with contemporary fittings in neutral shades, flat-screen TVs, DVD and CD players etc. The aubergine walls are designed to quieten guests in the halls (more wonderland magic), but they look good too. A well-located hotel with a touch of pizzazz.

TOP END

Rookery (Map pp102-3; ☎ 7336 0931; www.rookery hotel.com; Peter's Lane, Cowcross St EC1; s/d from £215/245; ☐ wi-fi; ✈ Farringdon) Smithfield used to be an inner-city slum reportedly home to the original Fagin and Bill Sykes as well as hookers banned from the City. These seedy spots were known as rookeries, and although signs of the past remain with the butcher's name above the windows and period features inside, this discreet luxury hotel made up of six 18th- to 19th-century houses has come a long way from those smutty times. For a bird's-eye view of St Paul's and the Old Bailey book the Rook's Nest.

The City

The centrally located City is schizophrenic: manic during the week and deathly quiet at weekends, when you can often pick up good deals.

BUDGET

City of London YHA (Map pp102-3; ☎ 7236 4965; city@yha .org.uk; 36 Carter Lane EC4; ☐ wi-fi; dm £17.20-32; ✈ St Paul's) This former St Paul's Cathedral Choir Boys School is located in a lovely building just notes away from the cathedral itself. An excellent facility with 190 beds in three- to 15-bed dorms, there's a licensed cafeteria but no kitchen.

Barbican YMCA (Map p105; ☎ 7628 0697; city. reception@cityymca.org; 2 Fann St EC2Y; s/d £33.95/31.95; ✈ Barbican) No bar, no dorms, no internet but there is a gym, the rooms are mega cheap and you get to stay in a classic Barbican tower block – yes, its appeal is more architectural than aesthetic.

TOP END

Threadneedles (Map p105; ☎ 7657 8080; www .theetoncollection.com; 5 Threadneedle St EC2R; d from £260 weekdays, from £110 weekends; ☐ wi-fi; ✈ Liverpool St) The incredible stained-glass dome in the lobby points to its former status as the City Bank HQ. Today the bar and restaurant are still popular with suits, but the atmosphere is chic. At weekends this top-end spot is an absolute bargain.

Borough & Southwark

Just south of the river is good if you want to immerse yourself in workaday London, still be central and get a reasonably priced hotel.

BUDGET

Dover Castle Hostel (Map pp96-7; ☎ 7403 7773; www .dovercastlehostel.com; 6a Great Dover St; dm £10-16; ☐ wi-fi; ⊖ Borough) This is a fairly standard hostel with kitchen, lockers (downstairs rather than in the dorm) and TV room, but it does have its own pub with a pool table and DJs till 3am and the dorms have lots of natural light.

St Christopher's Village (Map p105; ☎ 7407 1856; www.st-christophers.co.uk; 163 Borough High St SE1; dm £16-24; ☐ ; ⊖ Borough) This bright and breezy hostel has a club that opens till 4am on Friday and Saturday (with karaoke, comedy and cheap drinks), a slightly dark chill-out room with big screen, table football and PCs, Belushi's restaurant and bar next door, and 172 beds, but the *pièce de résistance* is undoubtedly the roof terrace with BBQ, sauna and hot tub. Twin rooms are available. The chain has two other hostels on this street and in Camden, Shepherd's Bush and Greenwich.

MIDRANGE

Southwark Rose Hotel (Map p105; ☎ 7015 1480; www .southwarkrosehotel.co.uk; 47 Southwark Bridge Rd SE1; d weekdays £125, weekends £75, ste £190; ☐ wi-fi; ⊖ Borough) Popular with business travellers and with great rates for weekenders, this hotel manages to be minimalist and colourful. Neutral en suite shower rooms and metallic beds are given a boost of colour with mauve leather headboards and chairs. The suites with double room plus sofa-bed and kitchenette are a good family option. Concealed lighting in the rooms and photographs by Mayumi add a touch of style.

Chelsea, South Kensington & Knightsbridge

Classy Chelsea and 'South Ken' offer easy access to the museums and fashion retailers. The prices are reasonable for the neighbourhood and there's a relaxing villagey vibe.

BUDGET

Holland Park (Map pp100-1; ☎ 0870 770 5866; hollandpark@yha.org.uk; Holland Walk W8; dm incl breakfast £17.20; ☐ ; ⊖ High St Kensington) With 200 beds, it's built into the Jacobean wing of Holland House and overlooks Holland Park. Though large, very busy and rather institutional, the position can't be beaten. There's a café and kitchen.

MIDRANGE

L'Hotel (Map pp100-1; ☎ 7589 6286; www.lhotel .co.uk; 28 Basil St SW3; d from £155; ☐ wi-fi; ⊖ Knightsbridge) Given its enviable proximity to Harrods and Harvey Nichols (p155) it's no wonder that this boutique hotel is a hit with the ladies, although the mainly female staff can take some credit too. There are 12 rooms including three deluxe and one suite, and guests can use the health spa of Carlton Towers next door – if you prefer to exercise outdoors a jogging partner will drag you around Hyde Park. Le Metro brasserie serves breakfast, lunch, tea and dinner.

TOP END

Gore (Map pp100-1; ☎ 7584 6601; www.gorehotel.com; 189 Queen's Gate SW7; s/d from £130/190; ☐ wi-fi; ⊖ High St Kensington or Gloucester Rd) Features include lots of polished mahogany, Turkish carpets, antique-style bathrooms, aspidistras, thousands of portraits and prints, and a great bar.

myhotel Chelsea (Map pp106-7; ☎ 7225 7500; www .myhotels.com; 35 Ixworth Pl SW3; d from £206; ☐ wi-fi; ⊖ South Kensington) Just around the corner from Bibendum and the shops of Fulham Rd, this hotel's location is as fabulous as its purple bar with funky chairs and bright and airy library/conservatory. The rooms sit lower down the fabulousness scale but the soft pink and grey décor is attractive and the en suite bathrooms are spacious. There's also a small gym and treatment room. If you like shopping, check out the dress agencies (see p156) on Elystan St.

Earl's Court

Earl's Court is not awash with sights but it does have inexpensive digs and an infectious holiday atmosphere.

BUDGET

Barmy Badger Backpackers (Map pp106-7; ☎ 7370 5213; www.barmybadger.com; 17 Longridge Rd SW5; dm incl breakfast from £16; ⊖ Earl's Court) A basic hostel with dorm beds. There's a big kitchen and safe-deposit boxes. (There's also a YHA hostel nearby.)

easyHotel (Map pp106-7; www.easyHotel.com; 14 Lexham Gardens W8; d from £30; ⊖ Earl's Court) Much like the airline, this orange hotel operates on a no-frills basis and you have to book your room online. The rooms (all with double beds) are very compact and the en suites are only about twice as big as a plane loo, but there is a flat-screen TV. As you'd expect, there's no lounge, bar or kitchen.

MIDRANGE

Philbeach Hotel (Map pp106-7; ☎ 7373 1244; www.philbeachhotel.co.uk; 30-31 Philbeach Gardens; s/d £58.50/81; 🖳 wi-fi; ⊖ Earl's Court) In a pleasant, quiet side street, this is one of London's few gay hotels, and its interiors are predictably stylish and unique. The Thai restaurant and bar are both popular with the local gay crowd and there's a lovely garden.

base2stay (Map pp106-7; ☎ 0845 262 8000; www.base2stay.com; 25 Courtfield Gardens SW5; s/d £80/99; 🖳 wi-fi 🅰; ⊖ Earl's Court) This boutique hotel is excellent value. With smart décor of chocolate-brown carpets, light olive walls, oak wardrobes and limestone bathrooms, as well as power showers, flat-screen TV with internet access and artfully concealed kitchenettes, it feels like a four-star hotel at two-star prices.

Notting Hill, Bayswater & Paddington

Bayswater is an extremely convenient location but parts west of Queensway are shady. Scruffy Paddington has lots of cheap hotels and is a handy transit point. Notting Hill is expensive in comparison, but has lots of good bars and restaurants.

BUDGET

Wake up! London (Map pp100-1; ☎ 7262 4471; www.wakeuplondon.co.uk; 1 Queen's Gardens W; dm with/without bathroom £16/15, s £25/22.50, d £35/30; 🖳 ; ⊖ Paddington) This Australian hostel has an obsession with exclamation marks preceded by the word up; the facilities are described as cook up! (kitchen), wash up! (laundry), hook up! (24-hour internet), call up! (phones), lock up! (lockers) etc. The hiccup! bar is a little on the small side considering how spacious the other communal areas are, but if the punctuation doesn't give you a headache this is a good budget option.

Stylotel (Map pp100-1; ☎ 7723 1026; www.stylotel.com; 160-162 Sussex Gardens; s/d incl breakfast £50/72; 🖳 wi-fi; ⊖ Paddington) If you don't like modern design, look away now. Rooms feature glass and steel

illuminated furniture, floor-to-ceiling mirrors and walls clad in aluminium. The breakfast area (full English breakfast) is a jagged comb of booths while the lounge has bright-blue sofas. You get lots of design-bang for your buck here as well as a practical location round the corner from Paddington station.

MIDRANGE

Pavilion Hotel (Map pp100-1; ☎ 7262 0905; www.msi.com.mt/pavilion; 34-36 Sussex Gardens W2; d from £100; ⊖ Paddington) This hotel is so cluttered with animal-print chairs, velvet drapes, portraits and knick-knacks that it's amazing to think there are 30 rooms inside. Each one is themed: Casablanca Nights has a leopard-print bedspread, red Moroccan chairs and golden lanterns. It's a lot of fun if you overlook the diminutive en suite bathrooms.

TOP END

Portobello Hotel (Map pp100-1; ☎ 7727 2777; www.portobello-hotel.co.uk; 22 Stanley Gardens W11; d from £180; 🖳 wi-fi; ⊖ Notting Hill Gate) Imagine a wealthy aunt has invited you to stay in her London town house stuffed with antique furniture and a 24-hour bar. Other guests might include movie or music stars who love the homely but luxurious rooms and their gorgeous four-poster beds, large TVs, vintage clawfoot baths and sumptuous fabrics. If it's available, request number 16, whose round bed with fairytale canopy has seen action from the likes of Johnny Depp and Kate Moss.

Hempel (Map pp100-1; ☎ 7298 9000; www.the-hempel.co.uk; 31-35 Craven Hill Gardens; d from £275; 🖳 wi-fi; ⊖ Bayswater) As soon as you enter the expansive all-white lobby with sunken seating areas, supermodern fireplaces, and dramatic pole and orchid ceiling-grazing flower arrangement, you know you're in for something special. Created by Anouska Hempel, every detail is a feat of superb design, from the Zen garden to the minimalist but luxurious rooms and the suite with suspended caged bed.

Marylebone

Increasingly hip Marylebone has graceful Georgian squares and bustling High Sts. It's within walking distance of Hyde Park and staggering distance of West End nightlife.

MIDRANGE

Edward Lear Hotel (Map pp100-1; ☎ 7402 5401; www .edlear.com; 28-30 Seymour St W1; d with/without bathroom from £89/66.50; ☐ ; ✆ Marble Arch) This former home of Edward Lear has a fantastic location mere winking distance from Oxford St. The décor is a little uninspired but welcoming enough, and the staff are smiley.

Bryanston Court Hotel (Map pp100-1; ☎ 7262 3141; www.bryanstonhotel.com; 56-60 Great Cumberland Pl W1; d from £99; ✆ Marble Arch) Open fireplaces, leather armchairs, creaky floors and oil paintings give it a hushed and traditional English atmosphere. There are 60 pleasantly furnished rooms, although the ones at the back are quieter and brighter. If this hotel is full, you'll sleep in the Concorde Hotel next door.

Outside Central London

Staying outside the centre and commuting can be a drag, but these places are handy for great attractions on the outskirts.

BUDGET

Palmers Lodge (Map pp96-7; ☎ 7483 8470; www .palmerslodge.co.uk; 40 College Cres NW3; dm from £14, d & tw with/without bathroom £48/44, all incl breakfast; ☐ wi-fi ⓖ ; ✆ Swiss Cottage) Reminiscent of a period murder mystery (in a good way), this former nursing home has bags of character. Listed by English Heritage, who even chose the plants that flank the drive, it's stuffed with cornicing, moulded ceilings, original fireplaces and imposing wooden panelling. Ceilings are high, rooms are spacious, there's a chapel bar with pews, a kitchen with continental breakfast and a roomy lounge with flat-screen telly and free internet access.

Rotherhithe YHA (Map pp96-7; ☎ 0870 770 6010; rotherhithe@yha.org.uk; 20 Salter Rd SE16; dm/tw incl breakfast £15/55; ☐ ⓖ ; ✆ Rotherhithe) YHA's flagship London hostel is right by the River Thames and the perfect choice for anyone who's keen on Greenwich and doesn't mind being a little isolated. There are 320 rooms including 22 en suite doubles (four of them adapted for disa-

bled visitors). There's a bar and restaurant, as well as kitchen facilities and a laundry.

MIDRANGE

Hampstead Village Guesthouse (☎ 7435 8679; www .hampsteadguesthouse.com; 2 Kemplay Rd NW3; s/d with bathroom £70/90, without £60/75; ✆ Hampstead) Only 20 minutes by tube to the centre of London, it has rustic, antique décor and furnishings, comfy beds and a delightful back garden in which you can enjoy a cooked breakfast (if you pay the extra £7). There's also a studio flat, which can accommodate up to five people.

EATING

Dining out in London has become so fashionable that you can hardly open a menu without banging into some celebrity chef or restaurateur. Unfortunately, this doesn't automatically guarantee quality – food can be hit-and-miss regardless of price tag. In this section, we steer you towards restaurants and cafés distinguished by their location, value for money, unique features, original settings and, of course, good food.

Opening hours vary. Many restaurants in Soho close Sunday, those in the City for the whole weekend. We've tried to note where places stray from the standard 'open daily for lunch and dinner' (standard business hours are outlined on p767), but it's always safest to call and check.

Vegetarians needn't worry. London has a host of dedicated meat-free joints, while most other restaurants offer vegetarian options.

West End – Soho to the Strand

Soho is the gastronomic heart of London, with stacks of restaurants and cuisines to choose from. The liveliest streets tend to be Greek, Frith, Old Compton and Dean Sts. Gerrard and Lisle Sts are chock-a-block with Chinese eateries.

BUDGET

Breakfast Club Café (Map pp110-11; ☎ 7434 2571; 33 D'Arblay St W1F; toasties/jacket potatoes from £1.95/3.50, healthy brekkie £4.95; ☐ ; ✆ Oxford Circus) Fans of the film will immediately clock this place, and if the name doesn't jog your memory the bright-yellow façade will get your attention. It's much less confronting inside with distressed floorboards, newspapers, computers with free internet access and battered signs on the walls – a chilled-out spot for a Fair Trade coffee or a snack.

LONDON

MEAL COSTS

Our pricing categories for London are per person for a two-course dinner and a drink. You'll pay much less for lunch.

- Budget – under £15
- Midrange – £15 to £40
- Top end – over £40

Hummus Bros (Map pp110–11; ☎ 7734 1311; 88 Wardour St W1F; 🖳 wi-fi; meals £2.50-6 ⊖ Leicester Sq) This relaxed café is hummus heaven. The scrummy stuff comes in small or regular bowls with a choice of meat and veggie toppings and a side of pitta bread. You can read about the founder's hummus obsession in the loo.

Food for Thought (Map pp110–11; ☎ 7836 0239; 31 Neal St WC2; mains from £3.20; ⊖ Covent Garden) A classic old vegetarian joint that's big on sociability and flavour but small on price and space. Food ranges from soups to traditional Indian *thalis* (all-you-can-eat mixed plates).

Neals Yard Salad Bar (Map pp110–11; ☎ 7836 3233; Neal's Yard WC2; salads £3.50-4; ⊖ Covent Garden) Occupying both sides of the courtyard, this bright-orange salad bar serves fresh leafy meals and moist cakes.

Café in the Crypt (Map pp110–11; ☎ 7839 8362; St Martin-in-the-Fields, Duncannon St WC2; mains £5.95-7.50; 🕑 closed Sun; ⊖ Charing Cross) An atmospheric crypt complete with tombstones underfoot and top nosh on your plate. Lunchtime is frantic.

Abeno Too (Map pp110–11; ☎ 7379 1160; 47 Great Newport St WC2H; okonomi-yaki £6.95; ⊖ Leicester Sq) Specialists in *okonomi-yaki* (Japanese-style pancakes), which is cooked in front of you on a hotplate and looks a bit like omelette. Sit at the bar or by the window and feast. Japanese noodle dishes are also available.

MIDRANGE

Yauatcha (Map pp110–11; ☎ 7494 8888; 15 Broadwick St; dim sum £3.00-24; ⊖ Oxford Circus or Piccadilly Circus) Restaurants don't come much cooler than this. The glass-fronted exterior has just enough transparent sections to tempt you in without revealing anything. With a starlight ceiling, multicoloured tea-lights in the brick-lined walls, low green seating and the out-of-this-world fish-tank bar you could be forgiven for mistaking the dim-sum restaurant downstairs for a Tokyo nightclub. The menu is fantastic –

try the *cheung fun* (type of sim sum). Upstairs the chilled-out teahouse serves pretty cakes.

Imli (Map pp110–11; ☎ 7287 4243; 167-169 Wardour St W1F; dishes £3.95-5.25; ⊖ Oxford Circus) This baby of Mayfair's Tamarind does a good job of Asian street food. The helpful staff recommends you order two or three dishes each to have a full meal. There's a lot of orange going on in the décor but it works.

Mildreds (Map pp110–11; ☎ 7494 1634; 45 Lexington St W1; mains £5.50-7.50; ⊖ Piccadilly Circus) Even dedicated carnivores will love the wholesome vegetarian fare served up here. You can't book, so turn up early and don't be afraid to share a table.

Sarastro (Map pp110–11; ☎ 7836 0101; 126 Drury Lane WC2B; mains £7.50-15.50; ⊖ Covent Garden) This Mediterranean restaurant is gaudy and kitsch and loads of fun. The opera theme – with gold everywhere (even the ceiling), crushed velvet and myriad lamps – is totally over the top but the balcony tables are a scream. Good for pre- and post-theatre meals.

Wolseley (Map pp110–11; ☎ 7499 6996; 160 Piccadilly W1; mains £7.50-18.50; ⊖ Piccadilly) Most customers here are checking to see if their co-diners are as impressive as the building. And the grade-II listed former showroom for Wolseley cars is certainly stunning but the food and service do not always live up to their price-tag. We advise coming for a drink and light bite, to soak up the ambience and pose.

Kettners (Map pp110–11; ☎ 7734 6112; 29 Romilly St W1; mains £8.25-19.50; ⊖ Leicester Sq) A gem, serving mouth-watering pizzas and burgers, which you can wash down with champagne while soaking in the gently fading grandeur and tinkling piano.

Spiga (Map pp110–11; ☎ 7734 3444; 84-86 Wardour St W1; mains from £8.50, set menu 2/3 courses £15.50/19.50; ⊖ Tottenham Court Rd) With Italian movie posters on the walls, warm, colourful décor and a tasty menu of pastas, pizzas, fish and meat dishes, this popular restaurant is a winner.

Ping Pong (Map pp110–11; ☎ 7851 6969; 45 Great Marlborough St W1F; mains £8.50-15.50; ⊖ Covent Garden) Prepare to queue at this chic but cheery dim-sum joint (you can't book). Grab a table or perch at the semicircular bars and mark up your menu (a novel but effective ordering approach). It's all good but the *char sui bun* (roast pork buns) and the *har gau* (shrimp dumplings) are tasty and the jasmine tea has an exploding flower. The loos take the sleek look to a new level with a touch-in touch-out system.

Joe Allen (Map pp110-11; ☎ 7836 0651; 13 Exeter St W1B; mains £8.50-15.50; ✆ Covent Garden) This favourite with theatregoers and thespians has a daily menu of modern American dishes, photos of performers plastering the brick-lined walls, a piano-player in the evenings, jazz on Sunday and buckets of atmosphere. Burgers aren't on the menu but they serve them if you ask.

Gay Hussar (Map pp110-11; ☎ 7437 0973; 2 Greek St W1; mains £9.50-16.50; ✆ Tottenham Court Rd) Founded in 1953 and looking pretty much as it did then, this old-style Hungarian eatery is a Soho institution. It's popular with politicians, and the walls are covered with cartoons of famous bods who've dined here. The rich, authentic, meaty dishes are colossal. Try the veal goulash or the crispy roast duck.

TOP END

Bentley's Oyster Bar & Grill (Map pp110-11; ☎ 7734 4756; 11-15 Swallow St W1B; oysters £9.50-26, mains £13.50-29.50; ✆ Leicester Sq) Bentley's has been here since 1916 but the new owner, award-winning chef Richard Corrigan, has gutted and refurbished it to give it a new lease of life. The oyster bar's look is classic with a modern twist: wood panelling is painted charcoal grey, punters perch on high red leather chairs by the marble-topped bar, and stripy seats cluster around low wood tables. It's fun and inviting. There's a more formal dining room upstairs.

Sketch (Map pp110-11; ☎ 0870 777 4488; 9 Conduit St W1; Gallery mains from £12, Lecture Room mains £50-75; ✆ Oxford Circus) A design enthusiast's wet dream, with shimmering white rooms, designer Louis XIV chairs and toilet cubicles shaped like eggs. And that's just the downstairs video art gallery, which becomes a buzzy restaurant at night, then a funky club after midnight. There's also the Glade daytime restaurant, a ground-floor Parlour tea room and the Lecture Room upstairs which has a six-course tasting menu for £90.

Floridita (Map pp110-11; ☎ 7314 4000; 100 Wardour St W1F; mains £13.50-27.50; ✆ Leicester Sq) Cuban cuisine, Latin beats, sexy black mirrored walls, cream leather seating, cigar girls… Floridita brings a glossy Havana to Soho. If the Cuban bands and DJs don't make you hit the dance floor, the cocktails will. For those who just want to salsa, entry is free before 10pm. Cuban lobster (flown over in blocks of ice to be kept alive but sleepy) is the restaurant's signature dish.

Rules (Map pp110-11; ☎ 7836 5314; 35 Maiden Lane; mains £15.95-19.95; ✆ Covent Garden) Established in

1798, this is London's oldest restaurant and specialises in classic game cookery, serving some 18,000 birds a year. Despite the history, it's not a museum piece and its sustained vitality attracts locals as well as the tourist masses.

Westminster, Pimlico & St James's

There's very little action around these parts at night, although the following restaurants are worth a short detour in themselves.

BUDGET

Chocolate Society (Map p108; ☎ 7259 9222; 36 Elizabeth St SW1; mains £5-7; ✆ Victoria) Now we're not suggesting woman (or man) can survive on chocolate alone, but this supercharming Parisian-style café tests the theory with mounds of the stuff in glass jars, ribbon-tied bags and cute tins. A hot chocolate will set you back £3.50 but knowing they support traditional production methods and ethical farming makes it taste all the sweeter.

Jenny Lo's Tea House (Map p108; ☎ 7259 0399; 14 Eccleston St SW1; noodle dishes £6.50-7.95; ✆ Victoria) A simple, popular Asian place that serves soups and rice dishes, but specialises in noodles and other wok-based specials.

MID RANGE

Thomas Cubitt (Map p108; ☎ 7730 6060; 44 Elizabeth St SW1W; bar meals £6-12.50; ✆ Victoria) Named after the area's prolific architect Mr Cubitt, this boozer has gone posh in a delightfully unfussy way, with smart National Trust–type paint on the panelling and a beautiful glazed front which opens up in summer. Try the slow-cooked pork belly on toast. Upstairs the menu gets pricey.

TOP END

Tamarind (Map pp102-3; ☎ 7629 3561; 20 Queen St W1; mains £12.95-24, 2-/3-course set lunch £16.95/18.95; ✆ Green Park) London's only Michelin-starred Indian restaurant serves up mouth-watering spicy classics in a simple, chic dining room.

Luciano (Map pp102-3; ☎ 7408 1440; 72-73 St James's St SW1; mains £8-21.50; ✆ St James) On the site of Madame Prunier's early-20th-century fashionable fish restaurant, Marco Pierre White goes back to his roots with classic Italian dishes at this spacious dining room with Art Deco touches. The portions are as generous as the space, so it's probably best to skip breakfast (and lunch if you're coming in the evening).

TOP FIVE BRUNCH SPOTS

- Hoxton Square Bar & Kitchen (right)
- Canteen (right)
- Providores (p144)
- Wolseley (p140)
- Al's Bar & Café (p145)

Cinnamon Club (Map pp102-3; ☎ 7222 2555; Old Westminster Library, 30 Great Smith St W1; mains from £20; ⊖ St James's Park) The domed skylights, high ceilings, parquet flooring and book-lined mezzanine evoke the Westminster Library this restaurant used to be. Head downstairs and the vibe is altogether funkier, with rubber floor, leather chairs and Indian films projected on the walls. Enjoy a drink before dining on elegant Indian cuisine.

Hoxton, Shoreditch & the City

From the hit-and-miss Indian and Bangladeshi restaurants of Brick Lane to the trendy eateries of Hoxton and Shoreditch, the East End has finally made it onto London's culinary map. City restaurants that stay open late are harder to find.

BUDGET

Brick Lane Beigel Bake (Map pp96-7; ☎ 7729 0616; 159 Brick Lane E2; most bagels less than £1; ⏱ 24hr; ⊖ Liverpool St) A relic of London's Jewish East End, it's more of a takeaway than a café and sells the cheapest bagels anywhere in London. You only get what you pay for, but they're a good snack on a bellyful of booze.

Leon (Map pp102-3; ☎ 7489 1580; Ludgate Circus EC4; big dishes £4.90-5.70; 🖳 wi-fi; ⊖ St Pauls) Voted best new restaurant, takeaway and bar by the *Observer* panel which included culinary kings Gordon Ramsey and Rick Stein, this self-proclaimed natural fast-food joint serves delights from the Med such as Moorish Vegetable Tagine. Choose between red metal chairs, sink-in-me sofas or silver bar stools and dig into your cardboard box...

Story Deli (Map p105; ☎ 7247 3137; 3 Dray Walk; pizzas £6.50-9; ⊖ Liverpool St) This organic café with mismatched cutlery poking out of jam jars, vintage mirrors leaning haphazardly against walls, high ceilings and solid wooden furniture (mismatched of course) is justifiably popular with the trendy workers of the Truman Brewery. The salmon and mascarpone pizza is to

die for. It also serves burgers, sandwiches, pies and puddings.

Le Taj (Map p105; ☎ 7247 4210; 134 Brick Lane E1; mains £6.50-9.50; ⊖ Liverpool St) Among the hordes of curry houses on Brick Lane, this purple-fronted Bangladeshi restaurant is a good choice. The three-course lunch for £6.95 is an absolute bargain.

MIDRANGE

Real Greek (Map p105; ☎ 7739 8212; 14-15 Hoxton Market N1; mezedes £1.75-6.25, mains £14.50-16.55; ⊖ Old St) Set in Hoxton Market, this popular restaurant is split into Mezedopolio – whose memorial tablets on the wall reveal its previous life as a mission, and which serves *mezedes* (small meze) – and a restaurant specialising in innovative Greek cuisine. Go for Hellenic Happy Hour between 3pm and 6pm and bag an outdoor table. If the place looks familiar, you're thinking of the fight scene from the film *Bridget Jones's Diary*.

Canteen (Map p105; ☎ 0845 686 1122; 2 Crispin Pl E1; mains £7-12.50; ⊖ Liverpool St) This hip new joint by Spitalfields market has a modern British seasonal menu with additive-free meat, fresh fish and lip-smacking pies, modernist wooden tables and benches (as the name suggests), a charmingly effervescent manager, perfect people-watching windows and outdoor tables. Try the eggs Benedict – it's divine.

Hoxton Apprentice (Map p105; ☎ 7749 2828; 16 Hoxton Sq N1; mains £7-17, set lunch 1/2 courses £6.99/9.99; ⊖ Old St) Set up by charity Training for Life to give unemployed people a vocation, this restaurant in a Victorian Grade-II listed former primary school is staffed by professionals and apprentices. The delicious modern fusion dishes, devised by Prue Leith, are served in a stylish dining room overlooked by a glassed-in mezzanine. Outdoor tables make prime people-spotting territory.

Hoxton Square Bar & Kitchen (Map p105; ☎ 7613 0709; 2/4 Hoxton Sq N1; mains £7.50-14; ⊖ Old St) The grey concrete interior gives this place a cool, chilled-out vibe and the outdoor tables are fab year-round thanks to the heaters. While it's happening in the evening, with people coming for bevvies, a bite or a gig, this is a top brunch spot too.

TOP END

Fifteen (Map p105; ☎ 0871 330 1515; 15 Westland Pl N1; mains £11-26; ⏱ booking line 9.30am-9pm Mon-Sun; ⊖ Old St) It can only be a matter of time before

Jamie becomes Sir Jamie, and Fifteen was where all his culinary philanthropy started. Set up to give unemployed young people a shot at a career, disadvantaged kids are trained on the job and all profits go to the Fifteen foundation. Book a table and if he's not cooking for an A-list friend in Hollywood, you may even catch a glimpse the cheeky chappy himself.

Southwark, Bermondsey & Lambeth

This part of south London has a surprising number of good-value eateries.

BUDGET

Mesón Don Felipe (Map pp102-3; ☎ 7928 3237; 53 The Cut SE1; tapas £1.95-5.25; ⊖ Waterloo) Tops for tapas and authentic Spanish atmosphere, helped along by classical Spanish guitar in the evenings. There are about half a dozen vegetarian options, more than you would get in Spain.

Stoney Street Café (Map p105; ☎ 7407 6221; 8 Stoney St SE1; most dishes around £4; ⊖ London Bridge) This quirky café in a converted garage opposite Borough Market serves up fresh comfort food such as fish finger in a roll, burgers, soup, salad and heaps of different sausages. You can also buy homemade pickles and preserves from Scotland and a book by the scriptwriter for radio classic The Archers.

Konditor & Cook (Map p105; ☎ 7407 5100; 10 Stoney St SE1; most dishes around £5; ⊖ London Bridge) The original location of arguably the best bakery in London, it serves excellent hot and cold lunches. There's not much space but everything is yours to take away. There's a larger branch in the Curzon Soho (p154).

MIDRANGE

Tas (Map pp102-3; ☎ 7928 1444; 33 The Cut SE1; casseroles £8.75; ⊖ Southwark) This outstanding restaurant is an outstanding Turkish place with plush surroundings, tasty kebabs and an impressive range of vegetarian fare. Order a casserole and you'll see a *tas* first-hand – it's the Anatolian cooking pot used to stew this tasty dish.

Delfina (Map pp96-7; ☎ 7357 0244; 50 Bermondsey St SE1; mains £9.95-14.95; ✆ noon-3pm Mon-Fri; ⊖ London Bridge) This restaurant-cum-art-gallery in a converted Victorian chocolate factory serves delicious modern cuisine with an Asian twist, to a backdrop of contemporary canvases. Studios upstairs house artists, and there's an exhibition space downstairs showing more works.

> ### TOP FIVE ALMOST ALTRUISTIC EXPERIENCES
>
> - Fifteen (opposite)
> - Hoxton Apprentice (opposite)
> - Planet Organic (p145)
> - Made in Clerkenwell (p157)
> - Chocolate Society (p141)

Livebait (Map pp102-3; ☎ 7928 7211; 43 The Cut SE1; mains £9.95-21; ⊖ Southwark) The old fishmongers décor with brick tiles, wooden floors and dark wood tables sets an authentic, relaxed tone in this popular seafood bar and fish restaurant. You can get a special lunch for £7.75 and there's a pretheatre menu for £14.50 (two courses) or £18.50 (three courses). All the fishy dishes are yummy; for a good taster order the classic platter with crab, crevettes, prawns, oysters, cockles, whelks and mussels.

Blue Print Café (Map pp96-7; ☎ 7378 7031; Design Museum, Butlers Wharf, Shad Thames SE1; mains £12.50-21.50; ⊖ Tower Hill) With spectacular views of the river and an ever-changing menu of modern European cuisine, this restaurant by Sir Terence Conran is perfect for a bite before or after visiting the Design Museum.

TOP END

Oxo Tower Restaurant & Brasserie (Map pp102-3; ☎ 7803 3888; Barge House St SE1; mains £8.95-14.75; ⊖ Waterloo) Offers good grub – a bit Mediterranean, a bit French, some Pacific Rim – and is all about special-event dining. There are splendid views over the Thames and St Paul's Cathedral. This price guide is for the slightly cheaper brasserie. If you're not hungry but fancy checking out the view, head to the bar.

Chelsea, South Kensington & Knightsbridge

The menus tip towards the pricey end in these three gastronomic areas but you can find budget eats if you're not in the market for Michelin stars.

BUDGET

New Culture Revolution (Map pp106-1; ☎ 7352 9281; 305 King's Rd SW3; mains around £7; ⊖ Sloane Sq) A trendy, good-value dumpling and noodle bar.

Jakobs (Map pp100-1; ☎ 7581 9292; 20 Gloucester Rd SW7; meals around £10; ⊖ Gloucester Rd) A charismatic café/

delicatessen serving a mixture of Armenian, Persian and Mediterranean dishes, including salads, falafel and quiches, that treat your palate without upsetting your purse.

MIDRANGE

Nozomi (Map pp100-1; ☎ 7838 1500; 15 Beauchamp Pl SW3; yakitori £3.50-14.50, tempura £6.20-29; ♦ Knightsbridge) Located on the distinctly well-heeled Beauchamp Pl, Nozomi's visitors ascend marble steps under a black awning to enter this minimalist restaurant serving tasty Japanese cuisine.

Made in Italy (Map pp106-7; ☎ 7352 1880; 249 King's Rd SW3; pizzas £5.70-10.50; ♦ Sloane Sq) Family-run and convivial, with the best pizzas for miles, Made in Italy is as close as you'll get to southern Italy without needing your passport.

Wódka (Map pp100-1; ☎ 7937 6513; 12 St Alban's Grove W8; mains £12.50-15.50; ♦ High St Kensington) Authentic Polish and Eastern European cuisine in Kensington Palace's old dairy. The menu changes monthly and there are daily specials. In the winter try the warming Polish hunter's stew and wash it down with vodka (obviously) fresh from the deep freeze.

Boxwood Café (Map pp102-3; ☎ 7235 1010; Berkeley Hotel, Wilton Pl SW1; mains £13-18; ♦ Knightsbridge) A New York–style café set up by superchef Gordon Ramsay in a valiant attempt to kick back with young folk and make fine dining in London 'a little bit more relaxed'. The décor is a little dreary but the food first-rate.

TOP END

Nobu (Map pp102-3; ☎ 7447 4747; Metropolitan Hotel, 19 Old Park Lane W1; mains £5-28; ♦ Hyde Park Corner) Very popular with celebrities wearing black, this place feels like a London designer's idea of a Japanese restaurant. It's nonetheless a strong contender for the best Asian food in town. Comfortably minimalist, anonymously efficient and out of this world when it comes to exquisitely prepared and presented sushi and sashimi.

Bibendum (Map pp106-7; ☎ 7581 5817; 81 Fulham Rd SW3; mains £10.50-28.50; ♦ South Kensington) Another Sir Terence Conran establishment, it's in one of London's finest settings for a restaurant – the Art Nouveau Michelin House (1911). The popular Bibendum Oyster Bar (£9.50 to £10 for half a dozen) is on the ground floor at the heart of the architectural finery. Upstairs is lighter and brighter.

Awana (Map pp106-7; ☎ 7584 8880; 85 Sloane Ave SW3; mains £12.50-24.50; ♦ South Kensington) This wood-clad Malaysian restaurant has a small satay bar (£7 to £9.50), a varied menu offering grills, curries and stir-fries, and a cool bar area with marble tables and red leather stools.

Tom Aikens (Map pp106-7; ☎ 7584 2003; 43 Elystan St SW3; set lunch menu £29; à la carte without drinks £60; ♦ South Kensington) Tom Aikens is the name of the notorious kitchen firebrand who runs this wonderful modern European restaurant where the setting is handsome and the food delish.

Gordon Ramsay (Map pp106-7; ☎ 7352 4441; 68-69 Royal Hospital Rd SW3; set lunch/dinner £40/90; ♦ Sloane Sq) One of Britain's finest restaurants and the only one in the capital with three Michelin stars. The food is, of course, blissful and perfect for a luxurious treat. The only quibble is that you don't get time to linger. Bookings are made in specific eat-it-and-beat-it time slots and, if you've seen the chef on TV, you won't argue.

Notting Hill, Bayswater & Marylebone

Notting Hill teems with good places to eat, from cheap takeaways to atmospheric pubs and restaurants worthy of the fine-dining tag.

BUDGET

Sausage & Mash Café (Map pp100-1; ☎ 8968 8898; 268 Portobello Rd W10; mains £5.75-7.95; ♦ Ladbroke Grove) Takes the British favourite of bangers and mash to new levels. There is not just a choice of different sausages, as you'd expect, but also variations of creamy mounds of mash and even gravy in this S&M club that won't give your wallet a spanking.

Geales (Map pp100-1; ☎ 7727 7528; 2 Farmer St W8; fish & chips £10; ♦ Notting Hill Gate) A popular fish restaurant that's more expensive than your average chippy (prices vary according to weight and season), but worth every penny.

MIDRANGE

Providores (Map pp102-3; ☎ 7935 6175; 109 Marylebone High St W1; tapa room £2.80-13.60; ♦ Baker St or Bond St) Named after the ceremonial cloth hanging on the wall, the tapa room downstairs is a sociable place with leather bench seats and excellent coffee. Brunch on Sunday is great: try the French toast stuffed with banana and pecans with grilled smoked streaky bacon and vanilla verjus syrup. Upstairs the dining room serves exquisite treats from New Zealand at higher prices.

La Fromagerie Café (Map pp102-3; ☎ 7935 0341; 2-4 Moxon St W1; mains £6-12.40; ♦ Baker St) This place is just like food writer and owner Patricia

Michelson's own kitchen, with bowls of delectable salads, antipasto, peppers and beans scattered about the long communal table. Huge slabs of bread invite you to tuck in, and all the while the heavenly waft from the cheese room beckons. Sensational food, smiley service, sensible prices.

Electric Brasserie (Map pp100-1; ☎ 7908 9696; 191 Portobello Rd W11; mains £9-28; ● Notting Hill Gate) The leather and cream look is suitably cool for the brasserie that's attached to the Electric Cinema. And the food's very good too; head to the back area for a darker, moodier dinner.

Food @ the Muse (Map pp100-1; ☎ 7792 1111; 269 Portobello Rd W11; mains £12-15; ● Notting Hill Gate). Developed 'for artists by artists', this smart, small restaurant uses its bright, white walls as the perfect blank canvas for the art that graces them. Enjoy succulent dishes like soy and honey Barbary duck breast and wait for inspiration to strike.

Villandry (Map pp102-3; ☎ 7631 3131; 170 Great Portland St W1; mains £12.50-19.50; ● Great Portland St) Resist the foodstore's tempting cheese, ham, Spanish tortas, pickles and other goodies (for the moment anyway) and enter a simple, attractive dining room at the back with a tasty modern European menu that changes daily.

TOP END

E&O (Map pp100-1; ☎ 7229 5454; 14 Blenheim Cres W11; dim sum £3-8.50, mains £6-13.50; ● Notting Hill Gate or Ladbroke Grove) This Asian bar and restaurant is a Notting Hill favourite. The black of the façade continues inside with lots of dark wood and brown leather stools – it's sleek and stylish. Dim sum at the bar or dine in the white tableclothed dining room. Evenings get rammed.

Beach Blanket Babylon (Map pp100-1; ☎ 7229 2907; 45 Ledbury Rd W11; mains £14.50-25.50; ● Notting Hill Gate) BBB, with its French-chateau-meets-Gaudi décor of extravagant chandeliers, distressed bar, statues, bare brick walls, red velvet and gilt chairs, and huge gargoyle fireplace has been around for a while but it's still fabulous. Request a table in the chapel for a memorable dining experience.

Fitzrovia & Clerkenwell

Fitzrovia is a hidden gem of restaurants, while Clerkenwell has a happening dining scene.

BUDGET

Greenery (Map pp102-3; ☎ 7490 4870; 5 Cowcross St EC1; light meals from £1.50; ● Farringdon) A salt-of-

the-earth veggie café, offering such tantalizing juice cocktails as Beetroot Blast (carrot, beetroot, apple and ginger). There's always a lunchtime queue of workers needing their superfoods.

Planet Organic (Map pp102-3; ☎ 7436 1929; 22 Torrington Pl WC1; hot food & salads from £2.25; ● Goodge St) As the name suggests, everything in this café/supermarket is organic. Fresh veggies are sourced (where possible) directly from British farms. For healthy beauty ingest the skin tonic superjuice of wheatgrass, apple, celery, mixed greens and aloe vera or buy skin-care of the slap-it-on variety.

ICCo (Map pp102-3; ☎ 7580 9688; 46 Goodge St; pizzas from £3; ● Goodge St) The Italian Coffee Company does a great turn in cheap and tasty pizzas. It also offers a free croissant with every hot drink before midday, which makes good breakfast sense. It's the building on the corner decked out in the colours of the Italian flag.

Little Bay (Map pp98-9; ☎ 7278 1234; 171 Farringdon Rd EC1R; mains £5.95-7.95 ● Farringdon) The crushed-velvet ceiling, handmade twisted lamps that improve around the room (as the artist got better) and elaborately painted bar and tables showing nymphs frolicking is bonkers but fun. The tasty food is good value.

Al's Bar & Cafe (Map pp98-9; ☎ 7837 4821; 11-13 Exmouth Market EC1R; mains £5.95-8.00; ● Farringdon) Al's is a bit like a pair of novelty slippers but without the embarrassment – cheerful, comfortable and perfect for resting your feet. The café's red awnings are as chirpy as the staff and the food (try the goat's cheese bruschetta). Outdoor tables get busy in summer, especially during happy hour (4pm to 7pm).

St John (Map pp102-3; ☎ 7251 0848; 26 St John St EC1; mains £12.80-21.50; ● Farringdon) Bright whitewashed brick walls, high ceilings and simple wooden furniture keep diners free to concentrate on ye olde English staples such as offal, ox tongue and devilled kidneys. The bar menu includes oysters and Welsh rarebit (if the kidneys didn't do it for you).

MIDRANGE

dim t (Map pp110-11; ☎ 7637 1122; 32 Charlotte St W1; dim sum from £2.50, noodle bar £7.65; ● Goodge St) Follow the pink neon sign to this lip-smacking dim-sum and noodle restaurant. Choose your meat, fish or tofu, then your noodle type, and top if off with a sauce: spicy, Thai, Hong Kong, etc. If you're a low-carb customer, the Vietnamese duck and pomegranate salad is scrummy (and packed with antioxidants). And the dim sum are great too (yes, we really like it here).

Salt Yard (Map pp102-3; ☎ 7637 0657; 54 Goodge St W1T; tapas £2.75-8.50; ⊖ Goodge St) Named after the place where cold meats are cured, this buzzing local joint serves delicious Spanish and Italian tapas. The smart navy awning, low lighting, terracotta walls and intimate tables surrounded by happy eaters draw you in. Try the tiger prawns chargrilled with rosemary and chilli or flex your palate with fennel and parmesan gratin.

Eagle Bar Diner (Map pp110-11; ☎ 7637 1418; 3-5 Rathbone Pl W1T; mains £4-12.95; ♈ open till 1am Sat; ⊖ Tottenham Court Rd) The burgers here are sensational and with 15 speciality types as well as the classic (with a selection of cheeses of course), you're spoilt for choice. Cosy down in the leather booths, enjoy the DJ's funky electro jazz or house, and sip a peanut butter martini (the signature cocktail).

Smiths of Smithfield (Map pp102-3; ☎ 7251 7950; 67-77 Charterhouse St EC1; mains £5-58; ⊖ Farringdon) This converted meat-packing warehouse is one of our favourite spots out east. Hit the ground-floor café for brunch, follow the silver-clad pipe-work upstairs to find a sexy champagne and cocktail bar, or climb again for a brasserie and smarter dining room.

Rasa Samudra (Map pp110-11; ☎ 7637 0222; 5 Charlotte St W1; mains £6.25-12.95; ⊖ Goodge St) The hot-pink exterior of this restaurant specialising in seafood and vegetarian cuisine from Kerala sets an upbeat tone that continues inside. The goddess Parvati greets you, gold elephant furniture hangs on the walls, a purple sari adorns the ceiling and a lit lamp nods to the gods. Try the Kerala seafood feast for £30.

Bleeding Heart Restaurant & Bistro (Map pp102-3; ☎ 7242 8238; Bleeding Heart Yard; bistro mains £7.45-14.95, restaurant mains £11.95-21.50; ⊖ Farringdon) Locals have taken this place, tucked in the corner of Bleeding Heart Yard, to their hearts. Choose from formal dining in the downstairs restaurant or more relaxed meals in the buzzy bistro – wherever, the French food is divine.

Easton (Map pp98-9; ☎ 7278 7608; 22 Easton St; mains £8.95-12.95; ♈ until 1am Fri & Sat; ⊖ Farringdon) This comfortable, spacious gastropub serves up reliably good grub. There's a DJ on Friday nights when tapas replace the full menu. Staff get a bit twitchy with noisy leavers – and don't ever dance on the outside tables (they come from Bali apparently).

Medcalf (Map pp98-9; ☎ 7833 3533; 40 Exmouth Market EC1R; mains £10.50-16.50; ⊖ Farringdon) The façade tells you this used to be a butcher's but the meat hooks now sport large light bulbs and the walls are festooned with changing art exhibitions rather than beef. The meat market's loss is our gain – come here for delicious British fare, good wine and a chilled-out vibe.

Dans le Noir (Map pp98-9; ☎ 7253 1100; 30-31 Clerkenwell Green EC1R; surprise meal 2/3 courses £29/37; ⊖ Farringdon) If you've often felt in the dark about food, eating in the pitch black might suit you. A waiter guides you to your table, plate and cutlery. Then it's up to you to guess what you're eating and enjoy the anonymous conviviality of the dark…

TOP END

Hakkasan (Map pp110-11; ☎ 7907 1888; 8 Hanway P W1; mains £7.50-38; ⊖ Tottenham Court Rd) Hidden down a lane like all fashionable haunts need to be, the first Chinese restaurant to get a Michelin star combines celebrity status, a stunning design, persuasive cocktails and surprisingly sophisticated Chinese food. If you're feeling flash why not order the whole duck, 30g Royal Beluga caviar and baby cucumber (24 hours notice required) for a tidy £140.

Camden & Islington

There are plenty of decent places to eat on and around Camden High St and Upper St in Islington.

BUDGET

Le Mercury (Map pp98-9; ☎ 7354 4088; 140A Upper St N1; mains £5.95, specials £7-12; ⊖ Highbury or Islington) A cosy Gaelic haunt ideal for a romantic tête-à-tête. Sunday lunch by the open fire upstairs is a treat although you'll have to book.

Tupelo Honey (Map pp98-9; ☎ 7284 2989; 27 Parkway NW1; mains £7.95; ⊖ Camden Town) Toasted sandwiches, hot meals and salad are on offer in this sweet-like-honey café with old wooden furniture, squishy sofas upstairs and an inviting roof terrace.

MIDRANGE

Lansdowne (Map pp98-9; ☎ 7483 0409; 90 Gloucester Ave NW1; mains £5-16; ⊖ Chalk Farm) Very popular with locals (both celeb and nonceleb), this relaxed gastropub serves mean pizzas and a selection of tasty pub grub.

Duke of Cambridge (Map pp98-9; ☎ 7359 3066; 30 St Peter's St N1; mains £5-16; ⊖ Chalk Farm) Tucked away from busy Upper St, this organic gastropub is a feast of tasty but overpriced rustic British cuisine, real ale and gentrified boozing.

Konstam at the Prince Albert (Map pp98-9; ☎ 7833 5040; 2 Acton St WC1; mains £10.50-15.50; ✛ Kings Cross) How's this for a kooky idea? Chef Oliver Rowe sources all his ingredients from within the London tube map. He has to cheat on a few (tea, coffee, spices) but not enough to stop BBC2 crowning him 'The Urban Chef' in a TV series that got viewers even during the football World Cup (which in England is really saying something). Book a table below the draping metallic ceiling and watch your dish take shape in the open kitchen.

Elk in the Woods (Map pp98-9; ☎ 7226 3535; 39 Camden Passage N1; mains £11-15; ✛ Angel) This intriguing restaurant with brick tiles, a metal bar, eclectic mirrors and a stuffed elk's head dishes up lip-smacking stews, game and other warming plates.

Engineer (Map pp98-9; ☎ 7722 0950; 65 Gloucester Ave NW1; mains £11.75-16.75; ✛ Chalk Farm) One of London's original gastropubs serving up consistently good international cuisine to hip north Londoners. There's a good selection of wines and beers, and a splendid garden.

TOP-END

Frederick's (Map pp98-9; ☎ 7359 3902; Camden Passage N1; mains £11.50-19.50; ✛ Angel) Civilised and sophisticated with excellent European food, Frederick's has fine dining in the conservatory and a comprehensive drinks list in the bar, which spills outside in summer. Pretheatre and lunch menus are available.

Outside Central London

If you're visiting the sights in Greenwich, Hampstead or Kew, consider a meal at any of the following restaurants and save yourself having to bolt back to the centre of town.

GREENWICH

Goddards Pie House (Map p112; ☎ 8293 9313; 45 Greenwich Church St SE10; meals from £2.20; ✆ 10am-7pm) A real London caff, with wooden benches and meals such as steak and kidney pie with liquor and mash, and shepherd's pie with beans and a rich brown gravy.

HAMPSTEAD

Jin Kichi (Map pp96-7; ☎ 7794 6158; 73 Heath St NW3; mains £4.30-12.80; ✛ Hampstead) One of the best Japanese restaurants in North London. It's

small and slightly shabby but so popular with London's Japanese that you won't be able to enjoy its grilled meats and other Asian flavours unless you book.

KEW

Glasshouse (☎ 8940 6777; 14 Station Parade W9; set lunch/ dinner £23.50/35; ✛ Kew Gardens) Virtually next to the tube station, it specialises in modern British cuisine and is a pleasant way to round off a visit to the gardens. The menus are set but the choice is large.

DRINKING

The pub is the social focus of London life and savouring pub life is a pleasure of any visit. From ancient atmospheric taverns to slick DJ bars, London has a lot to offer the discerning tippler no matter how hard the themed and chain bars try to take over.

West End – Soho to the Strand

W Sens (Map pp110-11; 12 Waterloo Pl SW1; ✆ 11am-1am Mon-Sat, 5pm-midnight Sun; ✛ Piccadilly) London outpost of French Compagnie des Comptoirs bar/restaurant group, W Sens has a chilled, sophisticated vibe. The amber-lit bar hugged by chocolate snakeskin stools, matching silver-backed Louis XIV chairs, huge suspended spherical lamp and silver curtains was designed by Philippe Starck pupil Imad Ramouni. Jean-Marc Challe's (of Buddha Bar fame) brother DJs periodically; on other nights you'll hear similar Asian loungey sounds.

Absolut Ice Bar (Map pp110-11; 31-33 Heddon St W1B; ✆ 12.30-midnight; entry Thu, Fri & Sat evenings £15, lunchtimes & other evenings £12; ✛ Piccadilly) At -6°C this is literally the coolest bar in London. Entry is limited to 40 minutes in this bar made entirely of ice, and your ticket includes a vodka cocktail served in ice glasses imported from Sweden. The compulsory futuristic silver polyester cape is to protect the bar from your body heat not the other way around so wear warm togs. It's a gimmick, but it makes a fun change from the norm and is perfect if you need to chill (sorry).

Queen Mary (Map pp110-11; Waterloo Pier WC2R; ✛ Temple) Ignore the rather tacky signage outside and climb aboard this steamer for a welcoming publike bar with great views of the London Eye and the South Bank. In summer there's a fish shop on deck. On Fridays and Saturdays the Hornblowers Nightclub pumps with House and dance music.

TOP FIVE PLACES TO DRINK IN THE SUN

- George Inn (opposite)
- Flask (p151)
- Café Kick (right)
- Queen Mary (p147)
- Windsor Castle (p150)

Gordon's Wine Bar (Map pp110-11; 47 Villiers St WC2N; ⊖ Charing Cross) What's not to love about this cavernous wine cellar lit by candles and practically unchanged over the last 100 years? Choose between wines, sherries, ports and Madeiras accompanied by warming home-cooked grub. Duck your head to settle in.

Coach & Horses (Map pp110-11; 29 Greek St W1; ⊖ Leicester Sq) This Soho institution was made famous by writer and newspaper columnist Jeffrey Bernard who, more or less, drank himself to death here. It was also patronised by Sigmund Freud, Francis Bacon, Dylan Thomas, Peter Cooke and Peter O'Toole. At the time of writing the new owner was planning a 50-cover restaurant upstairs serving traditional English pies.

Heights (Map pp102-3; 15th fl, St George's Hotel, Langham Pl W1A; ⊖ Oxford St) Take the lift up to this understated bar with leather seats, contemporary lighting and huge windows: spot the BT Tower, the Gherkin (Swiss Re building), Canary Wharf and Battersea Power Station while you tuck into tapas and sip your cocktail.

Lamb & Flag (Map pp110-11; 33 Rose St WC2; ⊖ Covent Garden) A popular historic pub and everyone's Covent Garden 'find' so is often jammed. It was built in 1623 and was formerly called the 'Bucket of Blood'.

Westminster & Pimlico

Red Lion (Map pp102-3; 48 Parliament St SW1; ⊖ Westminster) This classic, late-19th-century pub with polished mahogany, etched glassware, dark-red curtains and carved ceiling has a cosy feel. Keep your eyes peeled for MPs popping out for a pint.

Westminster Arms (Map pp102-3; 9 Storey's Gate SW1; ⊖ Westminster) It's mainly standing room only on the ground floor of this pleasant pub but head downstairs to the wine bar and you can just imagine the politicians plotting in the discreet booths.

Bloomsbury, Fitzrovia, Holborn & Clerkenwell

Café Kick (Map pp98-9; ☎ 7739 8700; 43 Exmouth Market; ☾ to midnight Fri & Sat; ⊖ Farringdon) This former French bar has been happily overtaken by Latin flags, football scarves, Mediterranean food and mojitos. With an unusually high table-football-to-floor-space ratio, drinkers often spill out onto Exmouth Market. During happy hour (4pm to 7pm) cocktails are a tidy £4.

Cock Tavern (Map pp102-3; East Poultry Ave EC1; ⊖ Farringdon) This pub is legendary, despite its rather bland interior, for serving booze with breakfast from 6.30am; it's understandably popular with the workers from Smithfield Market who've done a day's work while most of us are still getting our beauty sleep.

Deux Beers (Map pp102-3; ☎ 7405 9777; 3 Hatton Wall EC1N; ☾ till midnight Fri & Sat; ⊖ Farringdon) Within twinkling distance of the diamond district (hence the name), this smallish bar has a wall-bound wheel of shots – a sort of tequila roulette. Too many of these and you'll be dancing on the bar (mind your head on the groovy tentacular chandeliers).

Jerusalem Tavern (Map pp102-3; ☎ 7490 4281; 55 Britton St; ⊖ Farringdon) Pick a wood-panelled cubbyhole to park your behind in at this gorgeous former 18th-century coffee shop-turned-inn, and choose from a selection of St Peter's beers such as cinnamon & apple, lemon & ginger, or good old-fashioned ale (if you're not feeling fruity).

Jerusalem (Map pp110-11; ☎ 7255 1120; 33/34 Rathbone Pl; ☾ to 1am Thu, Fri & Sat, till midnight Tue & Wed; ⊖ Tottenham Court Rd) This uncomplicated bar/restaurant has been drawing a media crowd for a decade and is still going strong. The chunky wooden tables shift for dancers moving to the DJ's pop, chart and House on Thursday, Friday and Saturday.

Princess Louise (Map pp110-11; ☎ 7405 8816; 208 High Holborn WC1; ⊖ Holborn) This late-19th-century Victorian boozer was voted London's most beautiful pub by *London Tonight* news programme and we have to agree – it's an absolute stunner. Spectacularly decorated with a riot of fine tiles, etched mirrors, plasterwork and a gorgeous central horseshoe bar, the pub gets packed with the after-work crowd so get there early if you want a seat.

Museum Tavern (Map pp110-11; 49 Great Russell St WC1; ⊖ Tottenham Court Rd) Where Karl Marx used to retire to for a sup after a hard day in the British Museum Reading Room. If it was good enough for him...

Hoxton, Shoreditch & the City

Bar Music Hall (Map p105; ☎ 7613 5951; 134 Curtain Rd EC2; ☷ 10am-midnight Mon-Thu, 11am-2am Fri & Sat, 11am-midnight Sun; ⊖ Old St) Keeping the old East End music-hall tradition alive but with a modern twist, this roomy space with central bar and bags of squishy seats amuses the friendly punters with DJs and live bands. Music runs the gamut from punk to jazz to rock and roll and disco.

Cantaloupe (Map p105; 35-43 Charlotte Rd EC2; ☷ 11am-midnight Mon-Fri, noon-midnight Sat, noon-11.30pm Sun; ⊖ Old St) This founding member of the Shoreditch warehouse conversion scene may not be as achingly trendy as the newer kids on the block but it's still a favourite.

Grapeshots (Map p105; 2/3 Artillery Passage E1; ⊖ Liverpool St) Half the fun of this wine bar is walking down the Dickensian passage, complete with old street-lamps, that leads to it. Once inside, it's the perfect spot for a glass of old-fashioned chilled vino.

Ten Bells (Map p105; cnr Commercial & Fournier Sts E1; ⊖ Liverpool St) The most famous Jack the Ripper pub, patronised by his victims before their grisly ends, and possibly the slayer himself. Admire the wonderful 18th-century tiles and ponder the past over a pint.

Loungelover (Map p105; ☎ 7012 1234; 1 Whitby St E1; ☷ 6pm-midnight Tue-Thu, 6pm-1am Fri, 4-10.30pm Sun; ⊖ Liverpool St) Book a table, check your coat and bag in at the door and feel like a movie star. This eclectically decorated lounge, loosely divided into different areas – red, the cage, baroque and the front – could almost be a film set, or the shoot of a supercool interiors magazine. Sip a cocktail and admire the Louis XIV chairs, the oversized wine glasses acting as vases, the huge hippo head, the cage-turned-living room, the neon twirling stools and the loopy chandeliers. Utterly fabulous.

T Bar (Map p105; ☎ 7729 2973; 56 Shoreditch High St; ☷ 9am-midnight Tue & Wed, 9am-1am Thu, 9am-2am Fri, 8pm-2am Sat, 5pm-midnight Sun; ⊖ Liverpool St) This student-union-style cavernous bar is very 'now'. DJs spin a range of sounds from hard House to old rock like Johnny Cash. An illuminated clock outside counts down the seconds to last orders so there's no excuse for wasting any (seconds or orders).

Drunken Monkey (Map p105; 222 Shoreditch High St E1; ☷ noon-midnight; ⊖ Liverpool St) This hip bar-cum-dim sum house is a nice surprise. Orange Chinese lanterns cast a warm glow over the red walls to a soundtrack of electro-funk and jazz, the bar has a friendly, buzzing vibe, and the food is tasty (particularly the crab & pork dumplings). During happy hour (5pm to 7pm weekdays, 6pm to 7.30pm on Saturday) cocktails slip down for £4.50 each.

Old Blue Last (Map p105; ☎ 7739 7033; 39 Great Eastern St; ☷ noon-midnight Mon-Wed, noon-1am Thu & Sun, noon-2am Fri & Sat; ⊖ Old St) A bright-pink neon sign saying VICE declares this grungy pub's owners (*Vice* magazine) and the crowd hugging the horseshoe bar certainly do get down to the rockin' tunes from DJs or the juke box.

Sosho (Map p105; ☎ 7920 0701; 2 Tabernacle St EC2; ☷ noon-10pm Mon, noon-midnight Tue, noon-1am Wed & Thu, noon-3am Fri, 7pm-4am Sat, 9pm-4am Sun; ⊖ Moorgate) Sexy, glamorous and off limits if you're not feeling either of the above, although the cocktails could soon get you in the mood.

Jamaica Wine House (Map p105; 12 St Michael's Alley EC3; ⊖ Bank) London's first coffee house is now a Victorian pub attractively divided into wood-panelled areas and popular with city-boys who work nearby.

Vertigo 42 (Map p105; Tower 42, Old Broad St; ⊖ Liverpool St) Book a two-hour slot at a table in this bar with expansive views that stretch across all of London. The views bounce off the mirrors as well as through the windows making it a truly vertiginous experience.

Ye Olde Cheshire Cheese (Map pp102-3; Wine Office Ct EC4; ⊖ Blackfriars) Rebuilt six years after the Great Fire, it was popular with Dr Johnson, Thackeray, Dickens and the visiting Mark Twain. Touristy but always atmospheric and enjoyable for a pub meal.

Borough, Southwark & Bermondsey

Anchor (Map p105; 34 Park St SE1; ⊖ London Bridge) An 18th-century boozer just east of the Globe Theatre, it has a terrace offering superb views over the Thames. Dr Johnson is said to have written some of his dictionary here.

George Inn (Map p105; Talbot Yard, 77 Borough High St SE1; ⊖ London Bridge or Borough) Tucked away in a cobbled courtyard near Borough Market is London's last surviving galleried coaching inn, dating from 1677 and now belonging to the National Trust. Charles Dickens and Shakespeare used to prop up the bar here (but not together obviously). There are great outdoor tables for sunny days.

Garrison Public House (Map pp96-7; 99-101 Bermondsey St; ✪ London Bridge) Stepping into this French country-kitchen style pub is like slipping on a cashmere sweater – you feel comforted and more attractive immediately. Choose between modern grey flannel seats, secluded booths and high window tables perching beneath the dried flowers and watched over by a stag's head. Settle in for breakfast (try French toast with banana, bacon and maple syrup), a gastro-meal or just a warming drink.

Village East (Map pp96-7; 171 Bermondsey St; ☺ noon-1.30am Thu, Fri & Sat, to 10.30pm Sun, to midnight Mon-Wed; ✪ London Bridge) Sitting with one half in a modern glass apartment block and the other in a converted, listed cloth factory doesn't seem to have given this bar schizophrenia. In fact the exposed brick goes very well with soft bespoke lights, dark wood, metal bar stools and retro furniture. There's a lounge bar, a cocktail bar and two dining rooms, one with visible kitchen.

Chelsea, South Kensington & Knightsbridge

Grenadier (Map pp102-3; 18 Wilton Row SW1; ✪ Hyde Park Corner) In summer, drinkers pile down the steps of this tiny pub, settling in the sentry box or standing outside. It's not easy to find, nestling down a pretty mews, but the welcoming, panelled interior is worth the journey.

King's Head & Eight Bells (Map pp106-7; 50 Cheyne Walk SW3; ✪ Sloane Sq) An attractive corner pub pleasantly hung with flower baskets in summer. It was a favourite of the painter Whistler and the writer Carlyle.

Notting Hill, Bayswater & Marylebone

Trailer Happiness (Map pp100-1; ☎ 7727 2700; 177 Portobello Rd W11; ✪ Notting Hill Gate) Think shag-pile carpets, '60s California kitsch and trashy trailer-park glamour. Try the genuine Tiki cocktails and share a flaming volcano bowl of Zombie with a friend to ensure your evening goes with a bang. If you get peckish there are reasonably priced snack platters like Dr Jay's Green Chilli Fireballs and Trailer Happiness Smokin' Sausage salsa. With a soundtrack that's as loungey as the ambience, a night at Trailer H is truly groovy.

Cow (Map pp100-1; ☎ 7221 5400; 89 Westbourne Park Rd W2; ✪ Westbourne Park or Royal Oak) A superb gastro-pub with outstanding food and a jovial pub-is-a-pub atmosphere. Seafood is a speciality and the staff are much friendlier than you'd expect from somewhere so perpetually hip.

Churchill Arms (Map pp100-1; 119 Kensington Church St W8; ✪ Notting Hill Gate) A lovely, traditional tavern with tankards and casks dangling from the ceiling, Winston memorabilia and bric-a-brac. There's an excellent Thai restaurant in the pleasant conservatory (mains £6) out the back.

Windsor Castle (Map pp100-1; 114 Campden Hill Rd W11; ✪ Notting Hill Gate) A memorable pub with oak partitions separating the original bars. The panels have tiny doors so big drinkers will have trouble getting past the front bar. It also has one of the loveliest walled gardens (with heaters in winter) of any pub in London.

Camden & Islington

Keston Lodge (Map pp98-9; 131 Upper St N1; ✪ Angel) A chilled-out, trendy-leather-sofa and distressed-wood type place with DJs on Friday and Saturday, good pies and table service.

Crown & Goose (Map pp98-9; 100 Arlington Rd NW1; ✪ Camden Town) One of our favourite London pubs. The square room has a central wooden bar between British Racing Green walls studded with gilt-framed mirrors and illuminated by big shuttered windows. More importantly, it combines a good-looking crowd, good beer, easy conviviality and top tucker.

Bar Vinyl (Map pp98-9; 6 Inverness St NW1; ✪ Camden Town) With loud music and groovy clientele, it's an earful of the Camden scene. There's a record shop in the basement.

Medicine Bar (Map pp98-9; 181 Upper St N1; ✪ Highbury or Islington) Coolly unpretentious, it plays good music from funk to disco and stays open until 2am at the weekend. It also has a sister bar in Shoreditch.

Pembroke Castle (Map pp98-9; 150 Gloucester Ave NW1; ✆ Chalk Farm) A light, airy retro place with beer garden, where you can feel just as comfortable supping wine as ale.

Outside Central London
GREENWICH
Trafalgar Tavern (Map p112; Park Row SE10; DLR Cutty Sark) A Regency-style pub that was built in 1837 and stands above the site of the old Placentia Palace where Henry VIII was born. It is the former drinking den of Dickens, Gladstone and Disraeli.

HAMPSTEAD & HIGHGATE
Hollybush (22 Holly Mount NW3; ✆ Hampstead) A truly beautiful pub that makes you envy the privileged residents of Hampstead. It has an antique Victorian interior, a lovely secluded hill-top location, open fires in winter and a knack for making you stay a bit longer than you had intended any time of the year. It's above Heath St, reached via the Holly Bush Steps.

Flask (77 Highgate West Hill N6; ✆ Highgate) Charming candlelit nooks and crannies, an old circular bar complete with pumps (don't knock yourself when you sit down) and a lovely beer garden make this the perfect place for a pint after visiting Highgate Cemetery (p128). If the bar queues are awful head into Highgate village for other pleasant pubs.

Spaniard's Inn (Spaniard's Rd NW3; ✆ Hampstead, then bus 21) A marvellous tavern that dates from 1585. Dick Turpin, the dandy highwayman, was born here and used it as a hang out in his later years, while more savoury sorts like Dickens, Shelley, Keats and Byron also availed themselves of its charms. There's a big, blissful garden and good food.

CROW'S NEST COCKTAILS
There's nothing like surveying the city with a drink in hand. Take the lift to some of these beauties:

- Vertigo 42 (p149)
- 5th View (see Waterstone's, p94)
- Heights (p148)
- Oxo Tower (p143)
- **Windows Restaurant & Bar** (Map pp102-3; ✆ 7493 8000; The Hilton, 22 Park Lane; ✆ Hyde Park Corner)

ENTERTAINMENT
You've done the sights and supped and drunk your fill – you're ready to take on London's thriving entertainment scene. From cutting-edge clubs and international bands to Hollywood stars doing theatre turns – you'd need a lifetime to exhaust the opportunities for fun. This list only scratches the surface; make sure to check the listings (see p95) for what's going on.

Theatre
London is a world capital for theatre and there's a lot more than mammoth musicals to tempt you into the West End. The term 'West End' – as with Broadway – generally refers to the big-money productions like musicals, but also includes such heavyweights as the **Royal Court** (Map p108; ✆ 7565 5000; Sloane Sq SW1; ✆ Sloane Sq), the patron of new British writing; the **Royal National Theatre** (Map pp102-3; ✆ 7452 3000; South Bank; ✆ Waterloo), which has three auditoriums and showcases classics and new plays from some of the world's best companies; and the **Royal Shakespeare Company** (RSC; ✆ 0870 609 1110), with productions of the Bard's classics and stuff he might have been interested in.

On performance days you can buy half-price tickets for West End productions (cash only) from the **Leicester Square Half-Price Ticket Booth** (Map pp110-11; ✆ noon-6.30pm; Leicester Sq; ✆ Leicester Sq), on the south side of Leicester Sq. The booth is the one with the clock tower – beware of touts selling dodgy tickets.

Off West End – where you'll generally find the most original works – includes venues such as the **Almeida** (Map pp98-9; ✆ 7359 4404; www .almeida.co.uk; Almeida St N1; ✆ Highbury & Islington), **Battersea Arts Centre** (Map pp96-7; Lavender Hill SW1; ✆ Chapham Junction) and the **Young Vic** (Map pp102-3; 66 The Cut, Waterloo Rd SE1; ✆ Waterloo). The next rung down is known as the Fringe and these shows take place anywhere there's a stage (and can be very good).

For a comprehensive look at what's being staged where, consult *Time Out* or visit www. officiallondontheatre.co.uk.

Nightclubs
If you like clubbing, you've come to the right place. From cabaret to superclub, the city has a mind-boggling number of venues pumping music from disco, to R&B, garage or house. Some clubs have several different rooms,

while others change the tempo according to the night. Admission prices vary from £3 to £10 Sunday to Thursday, but on Friday and Saturday can be as much as £20.

Astoria (Map pp110-11; ☎ 7434 9592; www.g-a-y .co.uk; 157-165 Charing Cross Rd WC2 ✪ Tottenham Court Rd) This dark, sweaty and atmospheric club has the famous G-A-Y night Saturday with live shows from stars like Madonna and Shayne Ward, a cheap Pink Pounder Monday, a disco-oriented Camp Attack Friday and other attractions such as Porn Idol, an amateur strip night. Popular with young out-of-towners.

Guanabara (Map pp110-11; ☎ 7242 8600; cnr Parker St & Drury Lane W1; admission £5-8; ✪ Covent Garden) Brazil comes to London in this hot club with live music seven nights a week. On Wednesdays enjoy an authentic Roda de Samba played by the sons of the founding fathers of samba. Tuck into Brazilian snacks and Caipirinha and shake your booty. Admission is free before 8.30pm.

Herbal (Map p105; ☎ 7613 4462; 14 Kingsland Rd E2; ☪ 9pm-2am Tue-Thu & Sun, 9pm-3am Fri & Sat; admission £3-10, free Tue-Thu; ✪ Old St) With two dance floors and a smashing roof terrace, it's no wonder Herbal remains popular. Music weaves through drum 'n' bass, disco, hip-hop, break beats, garage and house.

Fabric (Map pp102-3; ☎ 7336 8898; 77A Charterhouse St EC1; admission £10-15; ✪ Farringdon) Voted the world's best club by 600 international DJs in *DJ* magazine (March 2006), Fabric, with its three dance floors set in a converted meat cold-store is riding high. Fridays offer drum 'n' bass, break beats, hip-hop and live bands, Saturdays see house, techno and electro while Sunday holds gay night DTPM.

Ghetto (Map pp110-11; ☎ 7287 3726; 5-6 Falconce Ct W1; ✪ Tottenham Court Rd) Home to the celebrity-attended, mixed-evening Nag, Nag, Nag on Wednesday, and Friday's electro/pop the Cock, among others, this is London's friendliest and least pretentious gay club, with inexpensive drinks and alternative music. It's small and it can get a bit sweaty, but that's just all the more reason to take your shirt off, right?

Bar Rumba (Map pp110-11; ☎ 7287 2715; 36 Shaftesbury Ave W1; ✪ Piccadilly Circus) Along a Soho backstreet, it's a small club with a big reputation. There's a different style each night – from Latin and jazz to deep house and garage – but everyone's a winner.

Cargo (Map p105; ☎ 7739 3440; 83 Rivington St EC2; admission £5-10; ✪ Old St) A hugely popular club with local and international DJs and a courtyard where you can simultaneously enjoy big sounds and the great outdoors. The music policy is particularly innovative, but you can usually rely on Latin house, nu-jazz and rare grooves.

Cross (Map pp98-9; ☎ 7837 0828; Goods Way Depot, York Way N1; ✪ King's Cross St Pancras) A little out of the way, in the King's Cross wastelands, but it's one of London's leading clubs serving up a Continental-style beat to a convivial crowd.

Turnmills (Map pp98-9; ☎ 7250 3409; 638 Clerkenwell Rd; admission £12-15; ✪ Farringdon) House-music fans should head straight to this industrial-style club with wacky silver, red and yellow inflatable stars and myriad mirror balls. Fridays is progressive house and trance, Saturdays is funky house and the Sunday after-party offers more house, this time of the electro variety.

Heaven (Map pp110-11; ☎ 7930 2022; The Arches, Villiers St WC2; admission £5-15; ✪ Charing Cross) One of the world's best-known gay clubs. It has three rooms; some nights are mixed but it positively fizzes with party boys on Saturday night, while there are cheap drinks and no pretension at Monday's Popcorn.

Madame Jo Jo's (Map pp110-11; ☎ 7734 3040; 8 Brewer St W1; ✪ Piccadilly Circus) A renowned transvestite cabaret, which is sleazy, fun and kitsch. It gives way to a deep house/nu-jazz club night on Saturday and a 'Deep Funk' night on Friday.

Ministry of Sound (Map pp96-7; www.ministryof sound.co.uk; 103 Gaunt St SE1; admission £12-15; ☪ until 8am; ✪ Elephant & Castle) Where the global brand started. It lost a little of its edge over time, but sharpened up with a major refurbishment in late 2003. It's London's most famous club and still packs in a diverse crew with big local and international names.

Notting Hill Arts Club (Map pp100-1; ☎ 7460 4459, 21 Notting Hill Gate W11; admission £5-8; ☪ until 2am, 1am Sun; ✪ Notting Hill Gate) A laid-back, funky basement club that attracts an eclectic crowd and has art exhibitions plus music ranging from global music to hip-hop and jazz.

Too2Much (Map pp110-11; ☎ 7734 0377; Walker's Ct; ✪ Piccadilly Circus) Elton John and David Furnish held their stag party here, and the club with piano bar on one side, cabaret stage on the other (linked by a bridge over the alley) is a rampant riot of crushed velvet and retro styl-ing. Popular with the gay fash-pack.

333 (Map p105; ☎ 7739 5949; 333 Old St EC1; ☺ 10pm-5am Fri & Sat, to 4am Sun; ⊖ Old St) A Hoxton old-timer with three shambling levels of electro, indie, rock and live acts.

Live Music
ROCK & JAZZ
London's live music scene is fantastic, and any night of the week you can catch bands and performances that would be the envy of any other gig-goer around the world.

Barfly@the Monarch (Map pp98-9; ☎ 0870 907 0999; www.barflyclub.com; Monarch pub, 49 Chalk Farm Rd NW1; ⊖ Chalk Farm) Pleasantly grungy, and the place to see the best upcoming bands.

Borderline (Map pp110-11; ☎ 7734 5547; www.borderline.co.uk; Orange Yard W1; ⊖ Tottenham Court Rd) A small, relaxed venue, hosting bands on the verge of the mainstream. It's also your best bet to see big-name acts performing under pseudonyms.

Brixton Academy (Map pp96-7; ☎ 7771 3000; www.brixton-academy.co.uk; 211 Stockwell Rd SW9; ⊖ Brixton) This Grade-II listed Art Deco venue is always winning awards for 'best live venue' and has hosted top names like The Clash, Madonna and Bob Dylan.

Forum (Map pp96-7; ☎ 0870 154 40 40; 9-17 Highgate Rd NW5; ⊖ Kentish Town) A grand old theatre and one of London's best large venues.

Hackney Ocean (Map pp96-7; ☎ 8986 5336; 270 Mare St E8; ⊖ Bethnal Green) Has sensational acous-tics and hosts the usual headliners, but adds a strong line in world music, reflecting the multiculturalism of Hackney.

Jazz Café (Map pp98-9; ☎ 7534 6955; 5 Parkway NW1; ⊖ Camden Town) A rather swanky restaurant venue. While you don't have to eat, it's better to book a table for the big names.

Ronnie Scott's (Map pp110-11; ☎ 7439 0747; 47 Frith St W1; ⊖ Leicester Sq) Familiar to aficionados as the best jazz club in London. The food, atmos-phere and acts are always spot-on.

Shepherd's Bush Empire (Map pp96-7; ☎ 8354 3300; www.shepherds-bush-empire.co.uk; Shepherd's Bush Green W12; ⊖ Shepherd's Bush) A slightly dishevelled, midsize theatre that hosts some terrific bands watched by laid-back punters.

100 Club (Map pp110-11; ☎ 7636 0933; 100 Oxford St W1; ⊖ Oxford Circus) This legendary London venue once showcased the Stones and was at the centre of the punk revolution. It now divides its time between jazz, rock and even a little swing.

CLASSICAL
With four world-class symphony orchestras, two opera companies, various smaller ensem-bles, brilliant venues, reasonable prices and high standards of performance, London is a classical capital.

South Bank Centre (☎ 08703 800 400; South Bank; ⊖ Embankment) Home to the London Philhar-monic Orchestra and the Philharmonia Or-chestra, this centre has three premier venues in the Royal Festival Hall (Map pp102–3; under refurbishment until 2007) and the smaller Queen Elizabeth Hall (Map pp102–3) and Purcell Room (Map pp102–3), which host classical, opera, jazz and choral music. As part of an improvement plan to bring the centre into the 21st century, it has recently added an attractive riverside people-watching mecca of glassed-in shops and restaurants. Check out the free recitals in the foyer.

Barbican Centre (Map p105; ☎ 0845 120 7500; www.barbican.org.uk; Silk St EC2; ♿; ⊖ Barbican) At the time of writing, the centre was undergoing a much-needed refurbishment to make the rather ugly entrances more attractive. The hulking complex has a full programme of film, music, theatre, art and dance, including loads of concerts from the London Symphony Orchestra, which is based here.

Royal Albert Hall (Map pp100-1; ☎ 7589 8212; www.royalalberthall.com; Kensington Gore SW7; ⊖ South Ken-sington) A splendid Victorian arena that often hosts classical concerts, but is best known as the venue for the Proms.

Opera & Dance
Royal Opera House (Map pp110-11; ☎ 7304 4000; www.royaloperahouse.org; Royal Opera House, Bow St WC2; tickets £4-180; ⊖ Covent Garden) The once starchy and now gleaming Royal Opera House has been attract-ing a young, wealthy audience since its £213 million millennium redevelopment, which seems to have breathed new life into program-ming. The Royal Ballet, the best classical-ballet company in the land, is based here.

Sadler's Wells (Map pp98-9; ☎ 0870 737 7737; www.sadlers-wells.com; Rosebery Ave EC1; tickets £10-35; ⊖ An-gel) A glittering modern venue that was in fact first established in the 17th century. It has been given much credit for bringing modern dance to the mainstream. There are several in-dependent dance companies in London too.

Coliseum (Map pp110-11; ☎ 7632 8300; St Martin's Lane WC1; ⊖ Leicester Sq) The home of the progressive English National Opera.

NOVEL NIGHTS OUT

It seems some people have had enough of going clubbing, listening to a band or propping up a bar with a pint. To plant your finger on the party pulse, check out some of these activity-based night-haunts.

Bloomsbury Bowling Lanes (Map pp98-9; ☎ 7691 2652; cnr Bedford Way & Tavistock Sq; ✪ noon-2am Mon-Wed, to 3am Thu-Sat, to midnight Sun; ✪ Russell Sq) With eight 10-pin bowling lanes, a complete diner and details down to the carpet all dating from the 1950s and shipped in from America, this place is the real deal. And the fun doesn't stop with dubious footwear and a burger, there's also two private karaoke rooms, a cinema screening independent movies, DJs playing tunes from '50s rock to '60s anthems and the latest numbers, plus up-and-coming live bands. With beer a snip at £3, this car park-turned-retro fun-park equals a top night out. And you could be in celebrity company – if the curtain's drawn around lane number 8 Kevin Spacey might be playing...

Lucky Voice (Map pp110-11; ☎ 7439 3660; 52 Poland St W1F; ✪ 5.30pm-1am Mon-Fri, 3pm-1am Sat; booth per person per hr £5-10; ✪ Tottenham Court Rd) Moulded on the private karaoke bars of Tokyo, superstylish Lucky Voice is a low-lit maze of dark walls with hidden doors revealing snug leather-clad soundproofed booths for your secret sing-along. Select one of 50,000 songs from a touch screen to display the lyrics on a 32cm, pick up a microphone and choose your voice function: reverb, rapper, stadium feel, etc. In the Super Lucky rooms you've got wigs and blow-up guitars to enhance your performance. Drinks and bento boxes are ordered by the touch of a button and if you need Dutch courage to warm up, sip a delicious Lucky Destiny cocktail in the bar.

Roller Disco (Map pp98-9; ☎ 7630 6625; www.rollerdisco.info; Canvas, – Bagley's Studios, Kings Cross Freight Depot, York Way N1; ✪ 8pm-midnight Thu, to 2am Fri; admission incl skate hire £10; ✪ Kings Cross) Remember those adolescent roller discos you used to go to? Well, this is your chance to dust off your skating skills and roll around the three arenas to a changing soundtrack of disco, funk, House, garage and R&B. To get really into the spirit dress up in '70s or '80s gear. If you're lucky maybe you'll make out with that guy/babe you've been eyeing up for ages (oh sorry we're not actually back at school, are we?) This is a popular night, so book in advance.

Comedy

The thought of coming to London and not seeing some stand-up is laughable. With so many men and women tickling our funny bone, it's no wonder that there are numerous venues to choose from, and many pubs getting in on the act. As ever *Time Out* has more details but here are a couple to whet your appetite.

Comedy Store (Map pp110-11; ☎ 7344 4444; Haymarket House, 1a Oxendon St SW1; ✪ Piccadilly Circus) One of the first comedy clubs in London, featuring the capital's most famous improvisers, the Comedy Store Players, on Wednesday and Saturday.

Comedy Café (Map p105; ☎ 7739 5706; 66-68 Rivington St EC2; ✪ Old St) Have dinner and watch some comedy; take to the stage on Wednesday if you fancy a turn.

Cinemas

Glitzy British premieres usually take place in Leicester Sq at one of the mega multiplexes. You don't have to be a movie star to catch a flick here and they do show the blockbusters,

but for a more local experience try a **Curzon** (☎ 0870 756 4621; www.curzoncinemas.com; Mayfair Map pp102-3; 38 Curzon St; Soho Map pp110-11; 99 Shaftesbury Ave), which show less mainstream releases too. There are also a clutch of independent cinemas spread out over the capital which make the cinema experience a particular treat. Check listings in *Time Out* for details.

National Film Theatre (Map pp102-3; ☎ 7928 3232; South Bank Centre; ✪ Waterloo) A film-lover's dream, it screens some 2000 flicks a year, ranging from vintage classics to foreign art house. There's also an informal 'drop-in' cinema, viewing stations where you can select what you want to watch, a film shop and exhibition space.

Electric (Map pp100-1; ☎ 7908 9696; 191 Portobello Rd; www.the-electric.co.uk; ✪ Ladbroke Grove) Grab a glass of wine from the bar and wander inside to your leather sofa to snuggle down for a good movie, or a Sunday double-bill. Tickets are cheapest on Mondays. All cinemas should be like this.

London IMAX (Map pp102-3; ☎ 0870 787 2525; ; Waterloo; ✪ Waterloo) Watch 3-D movies and

---

BURLESQUE IS BACK

Basques, suspenders, cinched waists, circle skirts, tweed, top hats, trilbies, spats, feathers, fox-trot, lindy hop, divas, mime artists and of course cabaret – burlesque's retro sexy sophistication sizzles. Revived by Immodesty Blaize in Blighty and Dita von Teese stateside, there's no hotter trend for night owls. Here are the most decadently divine nights: don't forget to dress up and adopt an air of languid panache.

Baroness Ball (www.baronessaball.com/)
Flash Monkey (www.theflashmonkey.biz)
Immodesty Blaize (www.immodestyblaize.com)
Jack and Ginger (www.myspace.com/jack_and_ginger)
Jitterbugs (www.jitterbugs.co.uk/home.asp)
Lady Luck (www.ladyluckclub.co.uk)
Modern Times Club (www.themoderntimesclub.co.uk/)
Viva Cake (www.myspace.com/vivacakebitches)
Volupté (www.volupte-lounge.com/inside.php)
Whoopee (www.thewhoopeeclub.com)

---

cinema releases on the UK's biggest screen at 20m high (nearly five double decker buses) and 26m wide.

Sport

As the capital of a sports-mad nation, you can expect London to be brimming over with sporting spectacles throughout the year. As always, the entertainment weekly *Time Out* is the best source of information on fixtures, times, venues and ticket prices.

FOOTBALL

Tickets for Premier League football matches are ridiculously hard to come by for casual fans these days, and London's top-flight clubs play to full stadiums most weeks. But if you want to try your luck, the telephone numbers for some Premiership clubs are listed here:

Arsenal (☎ 7704 4040)
Charlton (☎ 0871 226 1905)
Chelsea (☎ 0870 300 2322)
Fulham (☎ 0870 442 1234)
Tottenham Hotspur (☎ 0870 420 5000)
West Ham United (☎ 0870-112 2700)

RUGBY

Twickenham (☎ 8892 2000; Rugby Rd, Twickenham; tickets around £40, more for internationals; ↔ Hounslow East, then bus 281 or Twickenham mainline station) is the home of English rugby union, but as with football, tickets for internationals are difficult to get unless you have contacts. The ground also boasts the state-of-the-art **Museum of Rugby** (☎ 0870 405 2001; admission incl stadium tour £9; ☑ 10am-5pm Tue-Sat, 11am-5pm Sun).

CRICKET

Cricket is as popular as ever in the land of its origin. Test matches take place at two venerable grounds: **Lord's Cricket Ground** (Map pp96-7; ☎ 7432 1066; St John's Wood Rd NW8; ↔ St John's Wood) and the **Brit Oval** (Map pp96-7; ☎ 7582 7764; Kennington Oval SE11; ↔ Oval), commonly known as The Oval. Tickets are from £15 to £50, but if you're a fan it's worth it.

SHOPPING

From world-famous department stores to quirky backstreet retail revelations, London is a mecca for shoppers with an eye for style and a card to exercise. If you're looking for something distinctly British, eschew the Union Jack–emblazoned kitsch of the tourist thoroughfares and fill your bags with Burberry accessories, Paul Smith shirts, Royal Doulton china and Marmite. Or you could just visit some of the stores listed here…

Department Stores

It's hard to resist the lure of London's famous department stores, even if you don't intend to spree.

   Harrods (Map pp100-1; ☎ 7730 1234; 87 Brompton Rd SW1; ↔ Knightsbridge) Like a theme park for fans of the British establishment, Harrods is always crowded with slow tourists.

   Harvey Nichols (Map pp100-1; ☎ 7235 5000; 109-125 Knightsbridge SW1; ↔ Knightsbridge) Harvey Nicks is London's temple of high fashion. The jewellery and perfume departments are divine.

   Fortnum & Mason (Map pp110-11; ☎ 7734 8040; 181 Piccadilly W1; ↔ Piccadilly Circus) The byword

JIMMY CARR'S LONDON

Award-winning stand-up comic, TV and radio presenter, star of the film Confetti, and author of The Naked Jape, Jimmy Carr has called North London's Islington home for the last four years. We met him to chat about this bustling, smoky city.

'London has the strongest stand-up comedy scene in the world. There are so many clubs and places to play and there's a real tradition for live acts, which probably goes back to the days of music hall.' Like a comic's version of a cabbie's 'Knowledge' (see p161), Jimmy can tell you the nearest restaurant, bar and bus/tube stop to pretty much every comedy venue in London. For those not blessed with his encyclopaedic knowledge he recommends www.chortle.co.uk for info on the comedy scene.

Despite finding his first gig 'petrifying' and believing 'there's something generally wrong with comics – they're the only people in the room facing the wrong way', he's continued to master his own brand of hilariously transgressive humour. We asked him what made the British sense of humour special and he explained 'word play is at the heart of it – because of the richness of the English language there's so much you can say', concluding 'everything that's British can be summed up in a neat little joke'. As he points out, the Brits take pride in laughing at themselves and 'to say that someone can't take a joke is very scathing'.

Jimmy loves London's 'variety – the little villages, communities and neighbourhoods that are all so different', and the fact that 'there's always so much going on and even a local can feel like a tourist, discovering new places'. He gets his inspiration 'from everyday life' and tests his material in small venues like the **Hen & Chickens Theatre** (Map pp98-9; ☎ 7704 2001; 109 St Paul's Rd N1; ✇ Highbury & Islington).

For Jimmy, London is ripe with potential gags. 'A shop has recently opened up round the corner from my house called the Duke of Yuke selling ukuleles only. It's common in London to find shops named after bad puns – I know a 'Lunatic Fringe' hairdressers too – and/or selling a highly specific (if not particularly useful) item. Every time I pass the Duke of Yuke on my way home, I phone my girlfriend to say 'I'm just by the Duke of Yuke, do you need anything?'. And that's what's so great about London.'

To check out Jimmy's next gig, see www.jimmycarr.com.

for quality and service from a bygone area, steeped as it is in 300 years of tradition. It is especially noted for its old-world ground-floor food hall where Britain's elite come for their cornflakes and bananas.

Selfridges (Map pp102-3; ☎ 0870 837 7377; 400 Oxford St W1; ✇ Bond St) The funkiest and most vital of London's one-stop shops where fashion runs the gamut from street to formal. The food hall is unparalleled and the cosmetics hall the largest in Europe.

Liberty (Map pp110-11; ☎ 7734 1234; 214-220 Regent St W1; ✇ Oxford Circus) An irresistible blend of contemporary styles in an old-fashioned atmosphere. And you can't leave London without some Liberty Florals (printed fabrics).

Fashion

If there's a label worth having, you'll find it in central London. Oxford St is the place for High St fashion, while the chains of Regent St crank it up a notch. Kensington High St has a nice mix of chains and boutiques, while the

Covent Garden area is crammed with groovy labels – try Monmouth St for vintage fashion and the risqué Coco de Mer. South Molton St is a must for shoes. Bond St has designers galore, while Knightsbridge draws the hordes with quintessentially English department stores. Savile Row has bespoke tailoring, and Jermyn St is the place for Mr to buy his smart togs (particularly shirts). Look out for dress agencies which sell second-hand designer clothes, bags and shoes – there are particularly rich pickings in the wealthier parts of town.

Burberry (Map pp110-11; ☎ ; 21-23 New Bond St W1S; ✇ Bond St) Friend of Kate Moss and Sienna Miller, British designer Christopher Bailey is making Burberry cool again.

Cath Kidston (Map pp102-3; ☎ 7935 6555; 51 Marylebone High St W1U; ✇ Baker St) A feast of vintage-style floral prints and polka dots on just about every kind of accessory.

Giles by Giles Deacon (Map pp102-3; ☎ 7629 1234; Selfridges, 400 Oxford St W1; ✇ Bond St) London's favourite designer dresses women in saucy but sophisticated style.

Paul Smith Sale Shop (Map pp102-3; ☎ 7493 1287; 23 Avery Row W1; ⊖ Bond St) Classic Paul Smith big-print shirts and other delights by London's most commercially successful designer, at a discounted price.

Mulberry (Map pp102-3; ☎ 7493 2546; 11-12 Gees Ct W1; ⊖ Oxford Circus) Spend your return air fare on the 'it' bag of the moment.

Coco Ribbon (Map pp100-1; ☎ 7730 8555; 21 Kensington Park Rd W11 2EU; ⊖ 7229 4904; ⊖ Ladbroke Grove) A shabby-chic emporium selling delicious girly loveliness like honeymoon bikinis proclaiming your new status, beauty books and feathery negligees.

Start (Map p105; ☎ 7629 1234; 42-44 Rivington St EC2A 3BN; ⊖ Old St) *The* place to purchase designer jeans.

Primark (Map pp96-7 ☎ 8748 7119; Kings Mall, King St W6; ⊖ Hammersmith) Also known as 'Primarni' by the fashion editors who shop here. It's brilliant for catwalk copies at a fraction of the price, but be prepared – you may have to fight for them.

TK Maxx (Map pp96-7; ☎ 8563 9200; 57 King St W6; ⊖ Hammersmith) Up to 60% off designer fashion labels.

Top Shop Oxford Circus (Map pp110-11; ☎ 7629 1234; 216 Oxford St W1; ⊖ Oxford Circus) Billed as the 'world's largest fashion store', Top Shop is a must for any budding fashionista. So hip it shows at London Fashion Week and the Parisians have been crying out for their own branch (they've now got one). Where London leads…

Butler & Wilson (Map pp106-7; ☎ 7352 8255; 189 Fulham Rd SW3; ⊖ South Kensington) Beautiful costume jewellery, antique baubles and vintage clothing.

EC One (Map pp98-9; ☎ 7713 6185; 41 Exmouth Market; ⊖ Farringdon) Husband-and-wife team Jos and

Alison Skeates sell beautiful contemporary collections by British and international jewellery designers.

Rigby & Peller (☎ 7491 2200; 22A Conduit St W1S 2XT; ⊖ Oxford Circus) Revamp your lingerie with a trip to the Queen's corsetière.

Antiques

Curios, baubles and period pieces abound along Camden Passage, Bermondsey Market, the Saturday market at Portobello and along Islington's Upper St from Angel towards Highbury Corner (see boxed text, p158 for market details).

Antiquarius Antiques Centre (Map pp106-7; ☎ 7969 1500; 131 King's Rd SW3; ⊖ Sloane Sq) Packed with 120 stalls and dealers selling everything from top hats and corkscrews to old luggage and jewellery.

London Silver Vaults (Map pp102-3; ☎ 7242 3844; 53-63 Chancery Lane WC2; ⊖ Chancery Lane) Has 72 subterranean shops forming the world's largest collection of silver under one roof.

Music

If it's been recorded, you can buy it in London. For the biggest general collections of CDs and tapes, take on the West End giants of **Virgin Megastore** (Map pp110-11; ☎ 7439 2500; 1 Piccadilly Circus W1; ⊙ until 11pm Mon-Sat; ⊖ Piccadilly Circus) and **HMV** (Map pp110-11; ☎ 7631 3423; 150 Oxford St W1; ⊙ until 8.30pm Mon-Sat, until 9pm Thu; ⊖ Oxford Circus), which both have many central branches.

For personality, visit the following:

Rough Trade Neal's Yard (Map pp110-11; ☎ 7240 0105; 16 Neal's Yard WC2; ⊖ Covent Garden); Talbot Rd (Map pp100-1; ☎ 7229 8541; 130 Talbot Rd W11; ⊖ Ladbroke Grove) In the basement of Slam City Skates, it's the most central outlet of this famous store that was at the forefront of the punk explosion in the 1970s. This – and its original store in Notting Hill – is the best place to come for

---

MADE IN CLERKENWELL

Support local craftspeople with a trip to **Made in Clerkenwell** (Map pp98-9; www.cga.org.uk; admission £2.50), run by The Clerkenwell Green Association charity (CGA).

Formed in 1970 to support traditional trades (including the famous clock-makers), which were in danger of being lost, the CGA opens its historic Pennybank Chambers and Cornwell House to the public every summer and winter (see website for dates) so visitors can meet the craftspeople and see them at work. Wandering through the maze of tiny studios meeting milliners, jewellery makers, silversmiths, ceramicists, bag-makers, artists, antiques restorers and musical instrument makers is a fascinating window into another world. And if you fancy a souvenir, you can often pick up unique hand-crafted pieces at a good price.

LONDON

TO MARKET, TO MARKET

London has more than 350 markets selling everything from antiques and curios to flowers and fish. Some, such as Camden and Portobello Rd, are well known to tourists, while others exist just for the locals and have everything from dinner to underwear for sale in the stalls. Here's a sample.

Bermondsey Market (Map pp96-7; Bermondsey Sq SE1; ⏱ 4am-3pm Fri; ⊖ Borough) The place to come if you're after old opera glasses, bowling balls, hatpins, costume jewellery, porcelain or other curios. The main market is outdoors on the square, although adjacent warehouses shelter the more vulnerable furnishings and bric-a-brac.

Borough Market (Map p105; cnr Borough High & Stoney Sts SE1; ⏱ noon-6pm Fri, 9am-4pm Sat; ⊖ London Bridge) A farmers market sometimes called London's Larder, it has been here in some form since the 13th century. It's a wonderfully atmospheric food market, where you'll find everything from organic falafel to a boar's head.

Brick Lane Market (Map p105; Brick Lane E1; ⏱ early-2pm Sun; ⊖ Aldgate East) This is an East End pearl, a sprawling bazaar featuring everything from fruit and veggies to paintings and bric-a-brac.

Brixton Market (Map pp96-7; Electric Ave & Granville Arcade; ⏱ 10am-dusk Mon-Sat, closes 1pm Wed; ⊖ Brixton) A cosmopolitan treat that mixes everything from the Body Shop and reggae to slick Muslim preachers, South American butcher shops and exotic fruits. On Electric Ave and in the covered Granville Arcade you can buy wigs, unusual foods and spices, and homeopathic root cures.

Camden Market (Map pp98-9; Camden High St NW1; ⏱ 9.30am-5.30pm; ⊖ Camden Town) One of London's most popular tourist attractions although it stopped being cutting edge a long time ago. It's positively mobbed at the weekend.

Camden Lock Market (Map pp98-9; Camden Lock Pl NW1; ⏱ 10am-6pm; ⊖ Camden Town) Jewellery, bags, holistic therapies, gifts, posters, fashion and cafés for a post-retail cuppa.

Camden Passage Market (Map pp98-9; Camden Passage N1; ⏱ 10am-2pm Wed, 10am-5pm Sat; ⊖ Angel) Get your fill of antiques and trinkets galore. Not in Camden (despite the name).

Columbia Road Flower Market (Map p105; Columbia Rd; ⏱ 8am-2pm Sun; ⊖ Old St) An unbeatably beguiling mix of East End barrow boys selling bouquets and locals scouring the surrounding antiques, jewellery, perfume and porcelain shops with their hands full of foliage.

Petticoat Lane Market (Map p105; Wentworth St & Middlesex St E1; ⏱ 9am-2pm Mon-Fri & Sun; ⊖ Aldgate, Aldgate East or Liverpool St) A cherished East End institution overflowing with cheap consumer durables of little interest to tourists (although you'll see a hell of a lot of them).

Portobello Rd Market (Map pp100-1; Portobello Rd W10; ⏱ 8am-6.30pm Mon-Sat, closes 1pm Thu; ⊖ Notting Hill Gate, Ladbroke Grove or Westbourne Park) One of London's most famous (and crowded) street markets. New and vintage clothes are its main attraction.

Spitalfields Market (Map p105; Commercial St E1; ⏱ 9.30am-5.30pm Sun, organic market 9.30am-5pm Fri; ⊖ Liverpool St) In a Victorian warehouse, with a great mix of arts and crafts, clothes, books, food and *fun*.

Sunday (Up)market (Map p105; The Old Truman Brewery, Brick Lane E1; ⏱ 10am-5pm Sun; ⊖ Liverpool St) A relatively recent addition to the East End market scene, Upmarket has handmade handbags, jewellery, new and vintage clothes and shoes, plus food if you need refuelling.

---

underground specials, vintage rarities and pretty much anything of an indie or alternative bent.

Ray's Jazz Shop (Map pp110-11; ☎ 7437 5660; Foyle's, 113-119 Charing Cross Rd WC2; ⊖ Tottenham Court Rd) Where aficionados will find those elusive back catalogues from their favourite jazz and blues artists.

BM Soho (Map pp110-11; ☎ 7437 0478; 25 D'Arblay St W1; ⊖ Oxford Circus) Your best bet for dance, and if they haven't got what you're after, they'll know who has.

GETTING THERE & AWAY

London is the major gateway to Britain, so further transport information can be found in the main Transport chapter.

Air

For information on flying to/from London see p778.

Bus

Most long-distance coaches leave London from **Victoria coach station** (Map p108; ☎ 7730 3466; 164 Buckingham Palace Rd SW1; ⊖ Victoria, then about a 10min walk), a lovely 1930s-style building. The arrivals terminal is in a separate building across Elizabeth St from the main coach station.

Car

See p782 for reservation numbers of the main car-hire firms, all of which have airport and various city locations.

Train

London has 10 main-line terminals, all linked by the tube and each serving a different geographical area of the UK.

Charing Cross (Map pp110-11) Southeast England.

Euston (Map pp98-9) Northern and northwest England, Scotland.

King's Cross (Map pp98-9) North London, Hertfordshire, Cambridgeshire, northern and northeast England, and Scotland.

Liverpool Street (Map p105) East and northeast London, Stansted airport, East Anglia.

London Bridge (Map p105) Southeast England.

Marylebone (Map pp100-1) Northwest London, the Chilterns.

Paddington (Map pp100-1) South Wales, western and southwest England, southern Midlands, Heathrow airport.

St Pancras (Map pp98-9) East Midlands, southern Yorkshire.

Victoria (Map p108) Southern and southeast England, Gatwick airport, Channel ferry ports.

Waterloo (Map pp102-3) Southwest London, southern and southwest England, St Pancras and Waterloo.

Most stations now have left-luggage facilities (around £4) and lockers, toilets (a 20p coin) with showers (around £3), newsstands and bookshops, and a range of eating and drinking outlets. Victoria and Liverpool St stations have shopping centres attached.

GETTING AROUND
To/From the Airports
HEATHROW

The airport is accessible by bus, the Underground (between 5am and 11pm), main-line train and taxi. The fastest way to and from central London is on the **Heathrow Express** (☎ 0845 600 1515; www.heathrowexpress.co.uk), an ultramodern train to and from Paddington station (one way £14.50, return £27, 15 minutes, every 15 minutes 5.10am to 11.30pm). You can purchase tickets on board (£2 extra), online or from self-service machines (cash and credit cards accepted) at both terminals.

The cheapest way between Heathrow and central London is on London Underground's Piccadilly line (£4, one hour, departing every five to 10 minutes 5.30am to 11.45pm), accessed from all terminals. Note that there are often vast queues at the Underground's ticket office. Get some £1 coins when you exchange money, and buy a ticket at the automatic machine instead.

A black cab to the centre of London will cost you around £50, a minicab around £30.

GATWICK

The **Gatwick Express train** (☎ 0845 748 4950; www.gatwickexpress.co.uk) runs nonstop between Victoria train station and the South Terminal (adult one way/return £14/25, 30 minutes, departing every 15 minutes 5.50am to 1.35am, with an earlier train at 5.20am). The normal train service is slower but cheaper. A black cab to/from central London costs around £80 to £85.

STANSTED

The **Stansted Express** (☎ 0845 748 4950; www.stanstedexpress.com) connects with Liverpool St station (one way/return £15/25, 45 minutes, departing every 15 minutes 6am to 12.30pm, otherwise every 30 minutes). The **Airbus A6** (☎ 0870 580 8080; www.nationalexpress.com) links with Victoria coach station (one way/return £10/16, departing every 20 minutes 5.30am to midnight). A black cab to/from central London costs about £100 to £105.

LONDON CITY

The Docklands Light Railway runs between City Airport and the following London stations: Bank (22 minutes), Canning Town (eight minutes), Canary Wharf (14 minutes). Tickets cost £3 one way. A black taxi costs around £25 to/from central London.

LUTON

First Capital Connect (☎ 0845 748 4950; www.firstcapitalconnect.co.uk) runs trains from King's Cross and other central London stations to Luton Airport Parkway station (adult/child one way £11.20/5.60, 35 minutes, departing every five to 15 minutes 7am to 10pm), from where a shuttle bus will get you to the airport within eight minutes. **easyBus** (www.easybus.co.uk) minibuses run between Luton Airport and central London (Gloucester Place, near Baker St) at tasty one-way prices that start from £2 (online advance bookings) or £8 (on-board fare). A black taxi costs around £95 to/from central London.

Car

Driving in London is not for the faint-hearted. Traffic is very heavy, parking is a nightmare and wheel-clampers keep busy. If you drive into central London from 7am to 6.30pm on a weekday, you'll need to pay an £8 per day congestion charge (visit www.cclondon.com to register) or face a hefty fine.

Public Transport

Transport for London (TfL; www.tfl.gov.uk) aims to integrate the entire London transport network. Its website has a handy journey planner and information on all transport in the capital.

Servicing a city this large is clearly a logistical nightmare for planners, who get plenty of criticism from locals. But amazingly, the system works pretty well, especially since Mayor Ken Livingstone has made it his cause célèbre. Trains, tube lines, day and night buses, cabs and even shuttle boats work in tandem to fill the gaps and make it possible to navigate the behemoth (unless you're trying to get out of Soho on a weekend night, of course).

A Travelcard (see right) can be used on all forms of public transport as can the pre-pay **Oystercard** (www.oystercard.com), which offers cheaper fares and is recommended for an extended stay.

BOAT

Myriad boats ply the Thames, with more services being announced all the time. Travelling by boat avoids traffic jams while affording great views. Travelcard holders get one-third off all fares.

City Cruises (☎ 7740 0400; www.citycruises.com) operates year-round from Westminster Pier (for more details see p133).

Westminster Passenger Services Association (☎ 7930 2062; www.wpsa.co.uk) is the only company that operates a scheduled service upriver from Westminster. It takes in Kew Gardens and Hampton Park (for prices see Kew Gardens p131).

London Waterbus Company (Map pp100-1; ☎ 7482 2660) runs trips between Camden Lock and Little Venice, or try **Jason's Canal Trips** (Map pp100-1; ☎ 7286 3428; www.jasons.co.uk) at Little Venice. London has some 40 miles of inner-city canals, mostly built in the 19th century and in the process of renewal.

BUS

Travelling round London by double-decker bus is an enjoyable (and often efficient) way to explore the city and get a feel for its districts and size. It can seem more difficult than the tube though so pick up a bus map from an underground station. A recommended 'scenic' route is number 24, which runs from Victoria to Hampstead Heath through the West End.

Buses run regularly between 7am and midnight. Single-journey bus tickets (valid for two hours) cost £1.50, day passes are £3.50. If you're planning to bus it a lot it's worth buying a book of six tickets for £6. Children ride for free. In central London, at stops with yellow signs you have to buy your ticket from the automatic machine *before* boarding.

Less-frequent night buses (prefixed with the letter 'N') wheel into action when the tube stops. They stop on request, so clearly signal the driver with an outstretched arm. Trafalgar Sq, Tottenham Court Rd and Oxford Circus are the main terminals for them.

Stationlink buses (☎ 7941 4600) have a driver-operated ramp for wheelchair access and follow a similar route to the Underground Circle Line, joining up all the main-line stations. From Paddington there are services clockwise (501) from 8.15am to 7.15pm, and anticlockwise (502) from 8.40am to 6.40pm.

DLR & TRAIN

The independent, driverless **Docklands Light Railway** (DLR; ☎ 7363 9700; www.dlr.co.uk) links the City at Bank and Tower Gateway with Canary Wharf, Greenwich and Stratford. It provides good views of development at this end of town. Fares operate in the same way as the tube.

Several rail companies also operate suburban rail services in and around London. These are especially important south of the river where there are few tube lines. Once again, fares operate in the same way as those on the tube.

LONDON UNDERGROUND

The 12 tube lines extend as far as Buckinghamshire, Essex and Heathrow. There are Underground travel information centres at all Heathrow terminals, a half-dozen major tube stations and at larger main-line train stations. Services run from 5.30am to roughly midnight (from 7am on Sunday).

The Underground is divided into six concentric zones. The basic fare for Zone 1 is adult/child £3/1.50; to cross all six zones (eg

THE KNOWLEDGE

Taking a black cab is a quintessential London experience. It's more expensive than a minicab, but significantly more comfortable and reliable. To get an all-London licence, cabbies must do 'The Knowledge', which tests them on up to 25,000 streets within a 6-mile radius of Charing Cross and all the points of interest from hotels to churches. If you see people on mopeds with clipboards, they are probably revising. It's a feat that can sometimes take years to achieve, and ensures, according to the Public Carriage Office, that only the most committed join the noble trade. It also ensures you get the most direct route to your destination.

to/from Heathrow) costs £4/2. Tickets can be bought from machines or counters at the entrance to each station.

If you're travelling through a couple of zones or several times in one day, consider a Travelcard. One-day Travelcards can be used on all transport: tubes, main-line trains, the DLR and buses (including night buses). Most visitors find a one-day Travelcard for Zones 1 and 2 (£4.90) is sufficient. Before 9.30am Monday to Friday, you need a Peak Travelcard (£6.20/3.10 for Zones 1 and 2). Three-day Travelcards cost £15.40/7.70. Children under 11 years old can travel for free with an adult anytime after 9.30am.

Note that taking the tube for the miniscule journey between Covent Garden and Leicester Sq (£3 for 250m) is more expensive than taking a stretch limo.

Taxi

Wonderfully reliable black cabs are available for hire when the yellow light above the windscreen is lit. Fares are metered, with flag fall at £2.20 and each successive kilometre costing 90p. To order a black cab by phone, try **Dial-a-Cab** (☎ 7253 5000); you must pay by credit card and will be charged a premium.

Licensed minicabs are a cheaper alternative to cabs. To find a local minicab firm visit www.tfl.gov.uk/pco/findaride or if you're out and about and you need a minicab right now, text HOME to 60835 to get the telephone numbers for your two nearest minicab firms.

Be aware that there have been many reports of assault by unlicensed minicab drivers. Female travellers should not jump into an unlicensed minicab alone.

The Home Counties

Fanning out from London, the Home Counties – Hertfordshire, Bedfordshire, Buckingham-shire, Berkshire and Surrey – are known to many as the capital's wealthy and well-spoken commuter belt. But here you'll find more than just suits and boots (of the Wellington variety). Quiet, sleepy villages, pretty and bustling market towns, stunning natural vistas, fabulous walking and cycling trails, stately homes and less sedate tourist attractions pepper the land-scape. And apart from Windsor Castle and Legoland, many of the area's charms escape the coach-bound hordes, so you'll be able to nose around at a blissfully tranquil pace. In fact some of these spots are so far off the beaten track that you can enjoy them even in the height of summer.

It's hard to believe there are rural escapes so near to the capital, but all of these towns and sights make the perfect day trip, so you can either tour the area or just pop in and out of London when you need some respite from city life. That's exactly what the Queen does, spending private weekends at her castellated pad – and if it's good enough for HRH…

HIGHLIGHTS

- Coming nose to nose with a tiger at **Woburn Safari Park** and then visiting the wonderful **Woburn Abbey** (p168)
- Pottering around the pretty town of **Farnham** (p176) and walking in the **Surrey Hills** (p177)
- Finding spiritual satisfaction at **St Albans Cathedral** (p165) followed by earthly pleasure at **Ye Olde Fighting Cocks** (p166) in St Albans
- Being queen (or king) for a day at **Windsor Castle** (p150)
- Walking your gladiator sandals back in time at **Verulamium Museum & Roman Ruins**(p165) in St Albans

- POPULATION: 3.1 MILLION
- AREA: 3174 SQ MILES

Information

In this little-visited region, it's no surprise that tourist offices are rather thin on the ground. St Albans and Windsor have good tourist offices, and information can always be found online (see www.visitsoutheast england.com and www.enjoyengland.com). The area's proximity to London means hotel rates can be high but weekends often bring better deals. Banks and ATMs are easy to find (because after all, many of London's bankers live here).

Activities

No-one goes to the Home Counties for extreme sports (it just wouldn't fit with the name) but there are plenty of pleasant walking and cycling options.

There's good hiking and mountain biking in Buckinghamshire's leafy Chiltern Hills, while the rolling mounds of Surrey's North Downs offer a gentler pace.

The latter's Box Hill and Devil's Punchbowl offer breathtaking views, sloping grasslands and romantic wooded areas. There are also bridleways just crying out for a mountain bike. On Box Hill is a shop and **tourist office** (☎ 01306-888793; 🕙 11am-dusk), which provides maps and information on guided and self-guided walks. It also has an ice-cream kiosk.

Several longer walks start in the Home Counties (or end, depending on which way you're facing) and wind up much further afield. Walking the full length would take some energy and stamina, but don't panic, it's perfectly possible to pick a section for a one- or two-day amble.

North Downs Way (153 miles) Starts in Farnham, takes in the Pilgrims' Way (trod by pilgrims on their way to worship at the shrine of St Thomas Becket in Canterbury) and ends in Dover.

Thames Path (184 miles; www.nationaltrail.co.uk/tha mespath) Winds along the River Thames from its source in the Cotswolds, in Oxfordshire, right to the Thames Barrier in London. Before it reaches the capital, it skirts Reading and Windsor in Berkshire.

Ridgeway national trail (87 miles) Begins near Avebury Stone Circles and runs through the Chilterns to Ivinghoe Beacon near Aylesbury in Buckinghamshire.

Getting There & Around

Regular trains and buses rumble in and out of London to the Home Counties but using public transport through this area is a bit

---

HOME FROM HOME

Sometimes a hotel just isn't as convenient or relaxing as a self-catering cottage. There aren't as many options here as in more touristy areas, but look and ye shall find. Remember to book quite far in advance for school holidays and public holidays. **English Country Cottages** (www.english -country-cottages.co.uk) has a good selection, as does **Rural Retreats** (www.ruralretreats .co.uk). If these fail to tick your boxes, visit the website of the tourist office for the entire southeast (www.visitsoutheastengland .com); search under Accommodation/Self Catering.

---

like making like a crab and moving sideways. Renting a car is ideal for touring, but beware the rush hours of 6am to 9.30am and 4pm to 7pm when commuter cars can snarl the traffic to a snail's pace. **Traveline** (☎ 0870 608 2 608 ext 820) provides timetable information on all public transport.

BUS

Explorer (tickets up to 2 adults and 2 children £14, adult £7) provides day-long unlimited travel on most buses throughout the region.

Stagecoach (☎ 0845 121 0180) and **Arriva** (☎ 08701 201088) offer a variety of day, weekly and monthly passes.

All tickets and passes can be purchased onboard the buses or at Pay Points in local newsagents.

TRAIN

For general rail information call **National Rail** (☎ 08457 48 49 50; www.nationalrail.co.uk).

BritRail SouthEast Pass (p784) allows unlimited rail travel for three or four days in eight, or seven days out of 15. Note that it must be purchased outside the UK.

Network Railcard (☎ 08457 48 49 50 for the phone number of your nearest station; www.railcard.co.uk; per yr £20) is a discount card for visitors travelling in London, the Home Counties and southern England. It costs £20 and entitles the card-holder plus three other adults to a 33% discount, and up to four children (five to 16 years) save 60%. There are some restrictions on its usage (see the website for details), and you can't travel before 10am Monday to Friday.

THE HOME COUNTIES

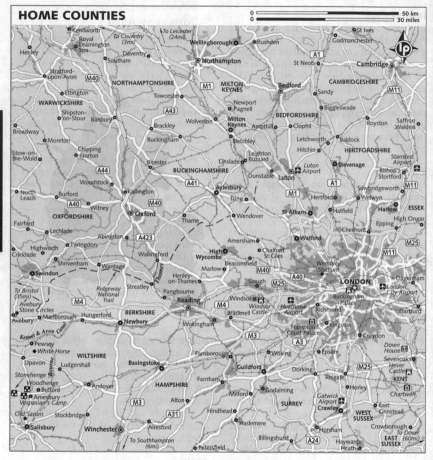

HOME COUNTIES

HERTFORDSHIRE

Hertfordshire is a small county of fast-disappearing though still pastoral farmland. But it's not all daisies and buttermilk here. Hertfordshire is also home to stunning St Albans, a predominantly Georgian town that dates back to Roman times, and Hatfield House, one of Britain's most important stately homes and the county's top attraction.

ST ALBANS

☎ 01727 / pop 114,710

A mere 25-minute train ride from London, St Albans is one of the most interesting and attractive spots in the Home Counties.

Founded as Verulamium after the Roman invasion of AD 43, St Albans was renamed in the 3rd century after a Roman soldier, Alban, lost his head (both literally and his detractors believed figuratively) in punishment for sheltering a Christian priest in AD 209. He became England's first Christian martyr, and the small city soon became a site of pilgrimage – visitors can still see the shrine in the majestic cathedral.

Other attractions include the excellent Roman museum, the Georgian and Tudor architectural eye-candy, the bustling market on Wednesday and Saturday, good shopping, even better pubs and the local fondness of beer (see the boxed text St Albans Beer Festival, p166).

Orientation & Information

St Peter's St, 10 minutes' walk west of the train station on Victoria St, is the focus of the town. East of St Peter's, St George St turns into Fishpool St, a charming lane that winds its way past old-world pubs to leafy Verulamium Park.

The **tourist office** (☎ 864511; tic@stalbans.gov .uk; Market Pl; ☺ 10am-5pm Mon-Sat, 10am-4pm every 2nd Sunday of the month & public holidays) is in the grand town hall in the marketplace. It has bags of literature on the town's attractions including the useful *Discover St Albans* town trail (95p) and the free *Visitors Guide*, which features a handy town map. If you like guided walks, a selection of themed options including 'Monks, Mysteries and Mischief' and the intriguing combination 'Pubs & Chapels' start from here – check times (tours are usually on Wednesday and Sunday but it varies) and buy your ticket (£2) at the tourist office.

All the major banks and ATMs are on St Peter's St, near the tourist office. The main **post office** (St Peter's St; ☺ 9.30am-5pm Mon-Sat) is also in the town centre. Internet access is free in the **library** (☎ 737333; Maltings Shopping Centre).

Paton Books (34 Holywell Hill) is a marvellous bookshop full of new and dusty old books (including hard-to-find titles) housed in an elegant 17th-century building.

There's a **laundrette** (13 Catherine St) off St Peter's St.

Sights

ST ALBANS CATHEDRAL

This magnificent **cathedral** (☎ 890200; ☺ 8am-5.45pm) started life in 793 as a Benedictine church, built by King Offa of Mercia around the tomb of St Alban. Between 1077 and 1115 the church was completely rebuilt using material from the old Roman town of Verulamium, and then in the 12th and 13th centuries Gothic extensions and decorations were added. The resulting mishmash reveals a host of interesting features, including semilost wall paintings, stunningly ornate ceilings (a surprise after the relatively plain nave), a 20th-century luminescent rose window unveiled by Princess Diana, the elaborate nave screen and of course the shrine of St Alban (which in many ways is less impressive than these other delights).

There are guided **tours** (☺ 11.30am & 2.30pm Mon-Fri, 11.30am & 2pm Sat, 2.30pm Sun) of the cathe-

dral and there's a café in the chapterhouse. Admission is by donation.

VERULAMIUM MUSEUM & ROMAN RUINS

Arrowheads, glassware, grave goods (items the dead take to the afterlife), interactive and audiovisual displays and recreated rooms make this **museum** (☎ 751810; St Michael's St; adult/ child £3.30/2; ☺ 10am-5.30pm Mon-Sat, 2-5.30pm Sun) a fantastic exposé of everyday life under the Romans. Most impressive is the Mosaic Room, where five outstanding floors, uncovered between 1930 and 1955, are laid out. Tickets allow you a return visit on the same day.

Adjacent **Verulamium Park** has remains of a basilica, bathhouse and parts of the city wall. A mobile-phone tour costing £2 (ask at the museum) will guide you by text message (just don't forget to look up in case you bump into a ruin).

Across the busy A4147 are the grassy foundations of a **Roman theatre** (☎ 835035; adult/child £2/1; ☺ 10am-5pm Mar-Oct, 10am-4pm Nov-Feb).

MUSEUM OF ST ALBANS

For an uncomplicated history of St Albans, this **museum** (☎ 819340; Hatfield Rd; admission free; ☺ 10.30am-5pm Mon-Sat, 2-5pm Sun) does a good job. Exhibits include tools used between 1700 and 1950 by English tradespeople, and artefacts dug up by archaeologists in the city.

CLOCK TOWER

The only medieval belfry in England stands on the High St. It was built around 1410 and 'Gabriel' (the original bell) is still there. Take a deep breath and climb the 93 steps of the **tower** (the High St; admission 30p; ☺ 10.30am-5pm Sat, Sun & bank holidays Apr-Oct) for great views over the town.

Sleeping

Mrs Thomas' (☎ 858939; 8 Hall Place Gardens; s/d £25/50) This well-kept, friendly B&B has a lovely single room with balcony and a spacious double, both of which share a bathroom.

White Hart (☎ 853624; 25 Holywell Hill; s & d £40, family r £75; ✗) A charming half-timbered hotel with exposed beams and creaky floors just a couple of minutes' walk from the centre. A full English breakfast is £5.50 extra.

ourpick St Michael's Manor (☎ 864444; Fishpool St; s/d from £145/180) Set in 7 acres of beautiful grounds complete with a lake, this traditionally decorated hotel makes a wonderful retreat on photogenic and historic Fishpool St.

THE HOME COUNTIES

ST ALBANS BEER FESTIVAL

Beer means business in England, and to prove it the South Hertfordshire branch of Campaign for Real Ale (Camra) puts on a four-day festival at the end of September to celebrate the sanctity of good beer and its key role in the national culture. There are many beer festivals in England worth checking out, and this one is no exception. Close to 5000 people converge on the Alban Arena off St Peter's St to sample and talk about hundreds of real ales from the UK and overseas. (For more information on real ales see p87.) There's food available, and on Friday and Saturday evenings there's music to keep everyone entertained. Depending on the day you go, tickets range from £2 to £3, which is a bit of a bargain. For more information see www.stalbansbeerfestival.info or www.hertsale.org.uk.

Eating

St Albans has plenty of restaurants, cuisines and good pub food vying for your appetite.

Waffle House (☎ 853502; St Michael's St; mains £4.95-6.95; 🕑 10am-6pm Mon-Sat, 10am-5pm Sun) Everything in this Saxon-era low-beamed snug comes with a Belgian waffle made with organic flour. Choose from savoury delights such as ham, cheese and mushroom, or satisfy your sweet tooth with a banoffee waffle. Yummy.

Thai Rack (☎ 850055; 13 George St; mains £5-10) This peaceful and small restaurant has a meditative outdoor patio and excellent curry.

our pick **Lussmanns Eatery** (☎ 851941; Waxhouse Gate; mains £6.20-16.45) This stylish three-floored Mediterranean restaurant off the High St, with oak, leather and metal décor and plenty of glass for natural light, is understandably popular with locals. Book in advance for Friday and Saturday nights.

Drinking

St Albans has one of the best collections of pubs in southern England.

our pick **Ye Olde Fighting Cocks** (☎ 865830; 16 Abbey Mill Lane) Reputedly the oldest pub in England (a former manager allegedly proved a pub stood here in AD 795!), this unusual octagonal-shaped inn has oodles of charm. Oliver Cromwell spent a night here, stabling his horses in what's now the bar; underground tunnels lead to the cathedral. Drink in this historic atmosphere while you nurse your pint.

Rose & Crown (☎ 851903; 10 St Michael's St) Another St Albans favourite, this 16th-century pub with beautiful beer garden features live music Mondays at 9pm and Irish music on Thursdays at 8pm.

Goat (☎ 833934; 37 Sopwell Lane) Tucked away on a residential lane, this delightful pub is a warren of little rooms including library and games room with Chesterfield sofas.

Also recommended:

Black Lion Inn (☎ 851786; 198 Fishpool St) Roman malting ovens were found here. Probably the least atmospheric of all St Albans pubs.

Lower Red Lion Freehouse (☎ 855669; 36 Fishpool St) Has regular beer festivals. A little rough around the edges, but there's a charming outdoor beer garden.

Six Bells (☎ 856945; 16-18 St Michael's St) Next door to the Rose & Crown, this popular, low-ceilinged spot has a cosy fireplace and good pub food.

Getting There & Away

Rail is the most direct way to get to St Albans, although if you are coming from Heathrow you can catch Green Line bus 724, which leaves hourly and takes an hour. St Albans station is on Victoria St, a 10-minute walk east of St Peter's St. Thameslink trains depart every 15 minutes from London King's Cross to St Albans station (£7.80, 23 minutes).

AROUND ST ALBANS
Hatfield House

England's most magnificent Jacobean mansion, **Hatfield House** (☎ 01707-287010; adult/child £8/4, park only £2; 🕑 noon-4pm Wed-Sun & public holidays, gardens 11am-5.30pm Easter-Sep) was built between 1607 and 1611 for Robert Cecil, first earl of Salisbury and secretary of state to both Elizabeth I and James I.

Inside, you'll find a grand marble hall, famous portraits and a magnificent oak staircase decorated with carved figures, including one of John Tradescant, the 17th-century botanist responsible for the gardens.

Four-course Elizabethan banquets, complete with minstrels and court jesters, are held in the great hall on Friday nights for around £40. Book on ☎ 01707-262055.

The house is opposite Hatfield train station, and there are numerous trains from London King's Cross station (£6.80, 25 minutes).

Regular bus services run between St Albans and Hatfield.

Shaw's Corner

George Bernard Shaw (1856–1950) spent the last 44 years of his life in this attractive **Arts & Crafts house** (☎ 01438-820307; Ayot St Lawrence; adult/child £4.20/2.10; ☉ 1-5pm Wed-Sun mid-Mar–Nov) and it has been preserved pretty much as he left it. In the garden is the writing hut (which revolves to catch the sun) where he penned several works including *Pygmalion,* the play on which the film *My Fair Lady* was based and which won him an Oscar.

Bus 304 from St Albans will drop you off at Gustard Wood, 1.5 miles from Ayot St Lawrence.

BEDFORDSHIRE

The main draws of this sleepy, rural county are the major town of Bedford and the majestic stately home at Woburn. The River Great Ouse winds across the fields to the north and through Bedford, creating several pristine nature reserves and some good woodland walks. It's also very accessible to London with the M1 motorway running across its semi-industrial south. For information on buses around the county, phone **Traveline** (☎ 0870 608 2 608) or check the website of **Stagecoach** (www .stagecoachbus.com/bedford), the main regional bus company, for its local timetable.

BEDFORD

☎ 01234 / pop 82,488

Bedford's claim to fame is its well-known previous resident, John Bunyan (1628–88). For literature students or fans of the 17th-century Nonconformist preacher and author of *The Pilgrim's Progress,* it's a must on any tour of the Home Counties. For everyone else, the riverside town makes a pleasant stop en route to the magnificent Woburn Abbey and Safari Park.

Located in the town hall, the **tourist office** (☎ 215226; touristinfo@bedford.gov.uk; 10 St Paul's Sq; ☉ 9am-4.30pm Mon-Sat & 10am-2pm Sun May-Aug, 9.30am-5pm Mon-Sat Sep-Apr) stocks the *Bedford What's On Guide* as well as a free guide to places with a Bunyan connection. In summer, free guided walks depart from the tourist office at 11am on Sundays and 7pm on Wednesdays.

Sights

The **Bunyan Meeting Free Church** (☎ 213722; Mill St; ☉ 10am-4pm Tue-Sat Mar-Oct) was built in 1849 on the site of the barn where Bunyan preached from 1671 to 1678. The church's bronze doors, inspired by Ghiberti's doors for the Baptistry in Florence, show 10 scenes from *The Pilgrim's Progress* and were a present from Hastings, the ninth duke of Bedford. The stained-glass windows also depict scenes from the tome.

Next door, the **John Bunyan Museum** (☎ 213722; admission free; ☉ 10am-3.45pm Tue-Sat Mar-Oct) has displays on the author's life including his time in prison, as well as 169 editions of *The Pilgrim's Progress* from around the world. There are recreated scenes from the period including a kitchen, and various artefacts such as a violin made by Bunyan, his prison door from the county jail, which was demolished in 1801, and his writing desk. Stewards will happily give you a tour in return for a donation and there are activity sheets for kids.

Cecil Higgins Art Gallery (☎ 211222; Castle Lane; ☉ 11am-5pm Tue-Sat, 2-5pm Sun) houses a splendid display of glass, porcelain and colourful Victorian furniture, plus an enviable collection of watercolours by Blake, Turner, Rossetti and Millais and prints by stars such as Picasso and Edvard Munch. The collection of watercolours and prints is in excess of 1000 but only a portion is on display at any one time. The **Bedford Museum** (☎ 353323; ☉ 11am-5pm Tue-Sat, 2-5pm Sun), with archaeological and historical exhibits telling Bedford's story, is next door. Admission to both is free.

Eating

Pizzeria Santaniello (☎ 353742; 9 Newnham St; pizzas £4.90-7.90) Bedford has quite a large Italian community, and this cheery pizza place serves up Italian favourites with a smile.

Bar Citrus (☎ 273843; 29 Harpur St; mains £5-7) A light, airy place with a relaxed atmosphere and daily specials. Food is served until 6pm.

Getting There & Away

Bedford is 50 miles north of London and 30 miles west of Cambridge.

National Express (☎ 08705 808080; www.national express.com) runs direct coaches to Cambridge (£9.90 economy return, one hour, three daily). The bus station is 800m west of the High St.

THE HOME COUNTIES

There are frequent trains from King's Cross with Thameslink (£16 cheap day return, approx one hour, every 15 minutes) to Bedford's Midland station, a well-signposted 500m walk west of the High St.

WOBURN ABBEY & SAFARI PARK

These two sights make a fabulous day out and are an absolute must on any Home Counties itinerary.

A Cistercian abbey before Henry VIII got dissolving and gave it to the earl of Bedford, **Woburn Abbey** (☎ 01525-290333; www.woburnabbey .co.uk; adult/child £10.50/6; ⏰ 11am-5.30pm Apr-Oct) is a wonderful stately home set in a deer park and stuffed with mainly 18th-century furniture, porcelain, silver and paintings. Highlights include Queen Victoria's bedroom where she slept with Prince Albert in a marvellous bed fit for – well – a queen; the beautiful wall hangings and cabinets of the Chinese Room; the inspiring and ultimately mysterious story of the Flying Duchess; the design of the Long Gallery, perfect for perambulating; and the dining room adorned with a collection of Canaletto paintings commissioned by the fourth duke of Bedford and enjoyed by the current duke (the 15th) when the family entertains.

Just a giraffe's neck away is **Woburn Safari Park** (☎ 01525-290407; www.woburnsafari.co.uk; adult/ child £15/11; ⏰ 10am-5pm daily Apr-Oct, 11am-3pm Sat & Sun Nov-Feb), the country's largest drive-through animal reserve. Your car will skirt rhinos, tigers, lions, zebras, bison, elephants, giraffes and a host of other animals you'd never expect to see so close up in Bedfordshire. Don't be surprised if a monkey climbs all over your car (no convertibles allowed) and chews your wing mirror. There's also a 'foot safari' area with sea lions, penguins, and lemurs, plus adventure playgrounds, a restaurant and bouncy funland for toddlers. Feeding times and demonstrations are scattered throughout the day.

If you visit the safari park first you'll be given a 50%-off voucher for the abbey and vice versa.

Although the abbey and safari park are easily accessible by car off the M1 motorway, trains from King's Cross with Thameslink only run to Flitwick, leaving you to take a taxi for the last 5 miles. If you have time, pop into the very pretty village of Woburn after your visit.

BUCKINGHAMSHIRE

With the chalky, forested Chiltern Hills and a history of polished country estates and famous residents, Buckinghamshire is one of the most attractive Home Counties. The county was known as Rothschildshire in the 19th century due to the beautiful houses built by the dynasty around Aylesbury. Buckinghamshire was also a favourite with the more poetic types: John Milton lived in Chalfont St Giles; Robert Frost spent time in Beaconsfield; and TS Eliot and Percy Bysshe Shelley both lived in Marlow, 100 years apart.

The Chilterns are famous for their beech woods, and the countryside is attractive in autumn. There are forest walks and mountain-bike trails (see the boxed text, opposite), plus footpaths along the Grand Union Canal, which cuts across the county's northeastern edge on its way from London to Birmingham.

AYLESBURY

☎ 01296 / pop 69,021

Affluent Aylesbury is a mixture of old and new, with 17th-century architecture, modern shopping precincts, a thriving market, which has been going since the 13th century, and the medieval St Mary's Church. The town was popular with Henry VIII when he was courting Anne Boleyn (apparently they had many dates in the King's Head pub), and Roald Dahl hung out here. Half-hourly trains run to and from London Marylebone (£10.80, 54 minutes). The **tourist office** (☎ 330559; 8 Bourbon St; ⏰ 9.30am-5pm Mon-Sat Apr-Oct, 10am-4.30pm Mon-Sat Nov-Mar) can provide general information on Buckinghamshire.

The **Buckinghamshire County Museum** (☎ 331441; Church Street; admission free; ⏰ 10am-5pm Mon-Sat, 2-5pm Sun) takes the visitor through different aspects of county life including Roman times and the lace industry. In the **Roald Dahl Children's Gallery** (admission £3.50) kids can step inside James' Giant Peach and explore Fantastic Mr Fox's tunnel, among other treats.

If the idea of grand living whets your appetite, spend the night at the **Five Arrows** (☎ 651727; the High St, Aylesbury; s/d from £70/85). This lavish 11-room Victorian hotel was built in 1887 by Baron Rothschild to house the architects and craftsmen who were working on his house, Waddesdon Manor. The five arrows refer to the Rothschild coat of arms and represent

---

WENDOVER WOODS

About a mile northeast of the town of Wendover (off the B4009) are the **Wendover Woods** (forest ranger ☎ 01296-625825), 325 hectares of beech and conifer forest lining the northern edge of the Chiltern Hills. There are a number of walks you can do, ranging from the half-mile walk to the top of Coombe Hill, the highest point in the Chilterns at 260m, to the 2-mile firecrest trail. There are cycling routes and bridleways, but if that sounds too much like hard work you can bring a hamper and hunker down for a picnic.

The **tourist office** (☎ 01296-696759; fax 622460; the High St; ☒ 10am-4pm) in the clocktower, Wendover, has information on the Chilterns, the Ridgeway national trail (p163) and the Wendover Woods. You can also pick up a walking map from the information stand at the woods themselves.

There are half-hourly train services to Wendover from London Marylebone (£8.50, 45 minutes). Aylesbury bus 54 goes to Wendover every half-hour (15 minutes).

---

the five sons of the dynasty's founder, Mayer Amschel Rothschild.

AROUND AYLESBURY
Waddesdon Manor
Baron Ferdinand de Rothschild was an avid collector of French decorative arts, which he liked to show off to guests at his glamorous house parties. And in what better place than this stunning Renaissance **chateau-style house** (☎ 01296-653226; adult/child house & gardens £12/8.50; ☒ 11am-4pm Wed-Sun 29 Mar-29 Oct, noon-4pm Wed-Fri & 11am-4pm Sat & Sun Nov-Dec), which was designed by French architect Destailleur and completed in 1889. Visitors today can see Rothschild's art collection, Sèvres porcelain and French furniture, as well as the family's extensive wine cellar (no sampling allowed). Before Christmas the house and gardens are bedecked with boughs of holly, and visitors can follow a festive trail through the East Wing and the Bachelors' Wing. Weekends get busy so book tickets in advance.

The beautiful **gardens** (admission to gardens only adult/child £5/2.50; ☒ 10am-5pm Wed-Sun 29 Mar-23 Dec) boast colourful flower beds, divine views and a Rococo-revival aviary and its breeds of exotic birds.

The chateau is 6 miles northwest of Aylesbury. From Aylesbury bus station, take bus 16 or 17. The trip takes 15 minutes. For information about bus timetables call **Travelink** (☎ 0870 608 2 608).

BUCKINGHAM
☎ 01280 / pop 12,512
This one-time county town (until the honour officially went to Aylesbury in the 18th century) has been largely overrun by suburban commuters, but it still remains a relatively

quiet sort of a place with a very pleasant main street, Market Hill. The town is serviced by hourly buses leaving from Aylesbury (45 minutes).

AROUND BUCKINGHAM
Stowe
About 3 miles west of town is Stowe, the sort of private school so exclusive that its drive way is half a mile long. The extraordinary Georgian **gardens** (☎ 01280-822850; adult/child £6/3; ☒ 10am-5.30pm Wed-Sun Mar-Oct, 10am-4pm Sat & Sun Nov-Feb) in the school grounds cover 400 hectares and were worked on by the greatest British landscape gardeners, including Charles Bridgeman, William Kent and Lancelot 'Capability' Brown.

The gardens are best known for their 32 temples, created in the 18th century by the wealthy owner Sir Richard Temple (no kidding), whose family motto was *Templa Quam Delecta* (How Delightful Are Your Temples). There are also arches, lakes and a Palladian bridge among other buildings.

Last admission is at 4pm. There are no buses that go past the gardens. It's a £8 taxi ride from Buckingham.

BERKSHIRE

Home to royals and prime ministers, posh and prosperous Berkshire is and has long been the home county of many of England's most important figures. The top toff of the lot, the Queen, regularly stops in to spend time at her favourite castle. But aside from the impressive fortress at Windsor, the county is full of exquisitely maintained villages and fabulous countryside.

SOMETHING FOR THE WEEKEND

Start the weekend in Windsor by checking into a Thames-front room at **Sir Christopher Wren's House Hotel** (p174) on Friday night. Stroll along the river and feed the swans before dining on exotic Moroccan fare at **Al Fassia** (p174). An after-dinner cocktail at the upscale bar/club **Mantra** (p174) should round off the evening. The next day, after a leisurely morning at the hotel, strap on some walking shoes for a wander through the magnificently royal rooms of **Windsor Castle** (p150). Enjoy a late lunch across the river in Eton at the stylish dark-wooded **Henry IV** pub (p174). Afterwards, hop on a late-afternoon **river-boat tour** (p173) up the Thames. Enjoy a special night out at the **House on the Bridge** (p174). Sunday morning, take a drive south through the countryside to the nearby Surrey Hills for a short walk through the **Devil's Punchbowl** (p178).

WINDSOR & ETON

☎ 01753 / pop 30,568

Windsor and the adjacent college town of Eton are two of the most visited destinations in the country, and with good reason. Windsor Castle, with its romantic architecture, superb state rooms and traditional changing of the guard, is an absolute must-see. It's so prominent, you'd be hard pressed to visit Windsor and avoid it.

Over the water, Eton is a quieter town with England's most famous public school and a clutch of endearing antique shops. Not forgetting the Thames itself, which flows attractively between the two towns and is just asking for a boat trip.

Orientation

The town of Windsor sits beside the River Thames, dwarfed by Windsor Castle. Skirting the castle are Thames St and Castle Hill, but the town's main drag is pedestrianised Peascod St. The village of Eton is on the far side of a small pedestrian bridge spanning the swan-filled Thames.

Information

The **Royal Windsor Information Centre** (☎ 743900; www.windsor.gov.uk; Old Booking Hall, Windsor Royal Shopping Arcade; ☒ 10am-5pm daily Apr-Sep [till 5.30pm Jul & Aug], 10am-4pm Mon-Fri & Sun, 10am-5pm Sat Oct-Mar) is an agent for the National Express bus service and sells tickets to some local attractions. It also offers an **accommodation booking service** (☎ 743907; £5).

Both the tourist office and post office have bureaux de change. There are plenty of ATMs along the High and Thames Sts.

The **post office** (☒ 9am-5.30pm Mon-Sat) is in Peascod St. High-speed internet is available in McDonald's easyInternetcafé on Thames St, and for books there's **Ottaker's** (20/21 Peascod St).

H Wilkins (67 Dedworth Rd; ☒ 8am-5.30pm Mon-Fri, 9am-5pm Sat) will take care of all your washing and dry-cleaning needs.

Sights
WINDSOR CASTLE

The largest and oldest occupied fortress in the world, **Windsor Castle** (☎ 020-7766 7304; adult/child £13.50/7.50; ☒ 9.45am-4pm Mar-Oct, 9.45am-3pm Nov-Feb) is a majestic and robust vision of battlements and towers, and the Queen's weekend retreat.

At 30 metres above the Thames, the only naturally defendable spot in the Thames valley was the perfect pitch for William the Conqueror to build a Norman motte and bailey in 1070 as part of his fortifications around London. And once he clocked the quality hunting nearby, the site got its second purpose – a royal residence. Successive monarchs have put their own stamp on the castle: Henry II replaced the wooden stockade in 1165 with a stone round tower and built the outer walls to the north, east and south; Charles II gave the state apartments a baroque makeover; George IV swept in with his preference for Gothic style; Queen Victoria left the beautiful Albert Memorial Chapel. The castle largely escaped the bombings of WWII, but in 1992 a shocking fire sparked in the Queen's private chapel and tore through the building destroying or damaging more than 100 rooms. Thankfully the rooms were being rewired at the time and most artistic treasures had been removed. The marvellous restoration took five years and that devastating night is now a mere memory.

Weather and other events permitting, the **changing of the guard** takes place at 11am Monday to Saturday April to June and on alternate days the rest of the year. In summer the crowd congregates by the gate but if you stay to the right you'll have a better

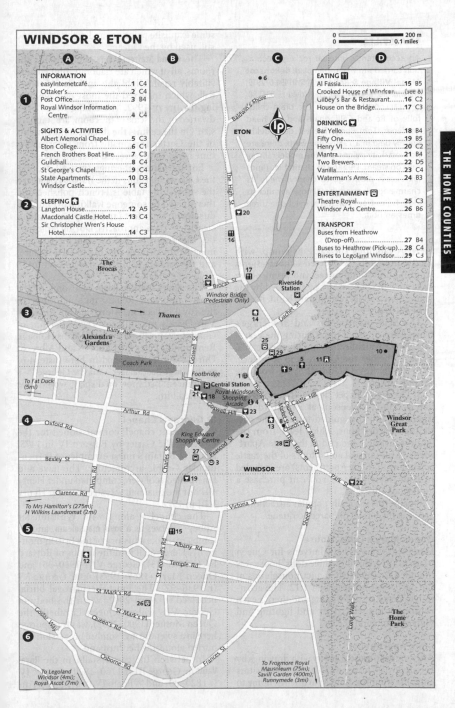

WINDSOR & ETON

0 — 200 m
0 — 0.1 miles

INFORMATION	
easyInternetcafé	1 C4
Ottaker's	2 C4
Post Office	3 B4
Royal Windsor Information Centre	4 C4

SIGHTS & ACTIVITIES	
Albert Memorial Chapel	5 C3
Eton College	6 C1
French Brothers Boat Hire	7 C3
Guildhall	8 C4
St George's Chapel	9 C4
State Apartments	10 D3
Windsor Castle	11 C3

SLEEPING	
Langton House	12 A5
Macdonald Castle Hotel	13 C4
Sir Christopher Wren's House Hotel	14 C3

EATING	
Al Fassia	15 B5
Crooked House of Windsor	(see 8)
Gilbey's Bar & Restaurant	16 C2
House on the Bridge	17 C3

DRINKING	
Bar Yello	18 B4
Fifty One	19 B5
Henry VI	20 C2
Mantra	21 B4
Two Brewers	22 D5
Vanilla	23 C4
Waterman's Arms	24 B3

ENTERTAINMENT	
Theatre Royal	25 C3
Windsor Arts Centre	26 B6

TRANSPORT	
Buses from Heathrow (Drop-off)	27 B4
Buses to Heathrow (Pick-up)	28 C4
Buses to Legoland Windsor	29 C3

ETON

The Brocas

Baldwin's Shore

The High St

Brocas St

Windsor Bridge (Pedestrian Only)

Thames

Riverside Station

Cachet St

Alexandra Gardens

Barry Ave

Coach Park

Footbridge

Central Station

Royal Windsor Shopping Arcade

Coswell St

Coswell Hill

Thames St

Castle Hill

Market St

Church St

St Albans St

The High St

Windsor Great Park

To Fat Duck (5mi)

Oxford Rd

Arthur Rd

Bexley St

Charles St

Alma Rd

King Edward Shopping Centre

Peascod St

WINDSOR

Clarence Rd

To Mrs Hamilton's (275m); H Wilkins Laundromat (2mi)

Victoria St

Park St

Sheet St

St Leonard's Rd

Albany Rd

Temple Rd

St Mark's Rd

St Mark's Pl

Queen's Rd

Costar Way

Osborne Rd

Frances St

Long Walk

The Home Park

To Legoland Windsor (4mi); Royal Ascot (7mi)

To Frogmore Royal Mausoleum (75m); Savill Garden (400m); Runnymede (3mi)

SMALLVILLE

An accountant's unusual rockery decoration turned utopian urban plan, **Bekonscot Model Village & Railway** (☎ 01494-672919; Warwick Rd, Beaconsfield; adult/child £5.90/3.80; ☺ 10am-5pm Feb-Oct) was the brain-child/ folly of Roland Callingham and his head gardener, Tom Berry. The village is deliberately held in a 1930s time warp: there are no electricity pylons and the model railway runs on steam. This and its charitable stance (all excess profits go to charity) mean its charm appeals to adults (almost) as much as kids. Trains from London Marylebone three times an hour.

view. A fabulous spectacle of pomp, with loud commands, whispered conversations, shuffling and stamping feet (no wonder they have such big boots), all accompanied by the triumphant tootles of a military band, it's not to be missed.

The State Apartments and St George's Chapel are closed at times during the year – see www.royalcollection.org.uk for details. To see whether the Queen is in residence, look for the Royal Standard flying from the Round Tower.

St George's Chapel closes on Sunday but you can attend Evensong at 5.15pm (daily). There are two free guided tours of the castle precinct per hour, which leave from the audio-tour shop and end at the State Apartments. Multilingual audio tours of the castle (including the State Apartments) are included in your ticket price or you can purchase a guidebook for £4.95.

Finally, this is a really popular attraction so arrive early and be prepared to queue.

Queen Mary's Dolls' House

Designed by Sir Edwin Lutyens for Queen Mary in 1924, this incredible dolls' house was intended to accurately depict households of the day, albeit on a scale of 1:12. The attention to detail is spellbinding and there's even running water, electricity and lighting and vintage wine in the cellar!

State Apartments

After the **dolls' house**, a **gallery** with drawings by Leonardo da Vinci and a **China Museum**, visitors enter the stunning State Apartments, home to some exquisite paintings and architecture and still used by the Queen.

The **Grand Staircase** sets the tone for the rooms, all of which are elaborate, opulent and suitably regal. Highlights include **St George's Hall**, which incurred the most damage during the fire of 1992. The dining chairs here, dwarfed by the scale of the room, are standard size. On the ceiling, the shields of the Knights of the Garter (originally from George IV's time here) were recreated after the fire.

For intimate gatherings (just 60 people), the Queen entertains in the **Waterloo Chamber** – the supershiny table is French-polished and then dusted by someone walking over it with dusters on their feet (an unconventional but clearly effective approach). During large parties this room is used for dancing (try and imagine the princes rocking to a DJ in here) and the table is tripled in size and set up in St George's Hall.

The **King's Dressing Room** has some of the most important Renaissance paintings in the royal collection. Alongside Sir Anthony Van Dyck's magnificent *Triple Portrait* of Charles I you will see works by Hans Holbein, Rembrandt, Peter Paul Rubens and Albrecht Dürer. Charles II kipped in here instead of in the **King's Bedchamber** – maybe George IV's magnificent bed (now on display) would have tempted him.

St George's Chapel

This elegant chapel, commissioned for the Order of the Garter by Edward IV in 1475, is one of Britain's finest examples of Perpendicular Gothic architecture. The nave and fan-vaulted roof were completed under Henry VII but the final nail was struck under Henry VIII in 1528.

The chapel – along with Westminster Abbey – serves as a **royal mausoleum**, and its tombs read like a history of the British monarchy. Here you'll find the tombs of Edward IV (r 1461–83), George V (r 1910–36) and Queen Mary (1867–1953), and George VI (r 1936–52). The most recent royal burial occurred in April 2002, when the body of George VI's widow, Queen Elizabeth, the Queen Mother (1900–2002), was transported here in a splendid and sombre procession and buried alongside her husband.

In between the garter stalls, in the **Royal Vault** lie George III (r 1760–1820), George IV (r 1820–30) and William IV (r 1830–37). Another vault contains Henry VIII (r 1509–47), his favourite wife (the third of six) Jane Seymour (1509–37), and Charles I (r 1625–49), reunited with his head after it was chopped off during the Civil War.

The gigantic **battle sword** of Edward III, founder of the Order of the Garter, is mounted on the wall near the tombs of Henry VI (r 1422–61 and 1470), and Edward VII (r 1901–10) and Queen Alexandra (1844–1925).

On 9 April 2005 Prince Charles and Camilla Parker-Bowles were blessed here following their civil marriage in the **Guildhall**. A full symphony orchestra and around 800 guests probably made up for the Queen's apparent refusal to hold the wedding due to both parties being previously divorced.

Albert Memorial Chapel

Originally built in 1240 and dedicated to Edward the Confessor, this small chapel was the place of worship for the Order of the Garter until St George's Chapel snatched that honour. After the death of Prince Albert at Windsor Castle in 1861 Queen Victoria ordered its elaborate redecoration as a tribute to her husband. A major feature of the restoration is the magnificent vaulted roof whose gold mosaic pieces were crafted in Venice. There's a monument to the prince, although he's actually buried with Queen Victoria in the Frogmore Royal Mausoleum in the castle grounds.

Windsor Great Park

Stretching behind Windsor Castle almost all the way to Ascot, Windsor Great Park covers about 40 sq miles. There is a lake, walking tracks, a bridleway and gardens. The **Savill Garden** (☎ 860222; ◷ 10am-6pm Mar-Oct, 10am-4pm Nov-Feb) is particularly lovely. Admission ranges from £4 to £5.50 (adult) and £2 to £2.75 (child) depending on the time of year.

The **Long Walk** is a three-mile walk along a tree-lined path from King George IV Gate to the Copper Horse statue (of George III) on Snow Hill, the highest point of the park. Locals have informed us that the Queen occasionally drives herself down the Long Walk, accompanied only by a bodyguard. The walk is signposted from the town centre.

ETON COLLEGE

Cross the Thames by the pedestrian-only Windsor Bridge to arrive at another enduring symbol of England's class system: **Eton College** (☎ 671177;

adult/child £4/3.25, tours £5/4.20; ◷ 10.30am-4.30pm Mar-Apr, Jul-Sep [school holidays], 2-4.30pm term-time, guided tours 2.15pm & 3.15pm), the largest and most famous public (meaning very private) school in England. It was founded by Henry VI in 1440–41 with a view towards educating 70 highly qualified boys awarded a scholarship from a fund endowed by the king. Every year since then, 70 King's Scholars have been chosen based on the results of a highly competitive exam for boys aged 12 to 14; these pupils are housed in separate quarters from the rest of the 1000 or so other students, who are known as Oppidans.

While the King's Scholars are chosen exclusively on the basis of exam results, Oppidans must be able to foot the bill for £23,000-per-annum fees as well as passing entrance exams. Its alumni count no fewer than 18 prime ministers, as well as a few royals, including hunky Prince William.

The college is open to visitors. Tours take in the **chapel** (which you can see from Windsor Castle), the **cloisters**, the **Museum of Eton Life**, **lower school** and the **school yard**.

LEGOLAND WINDSOR

Windsor's other great attraction – for those still in short trousers – **Legoland** (☎ 08705 040404; www.legoland.co.uk; adult/child 3-15 £30/23; ◷ 10am-5pm/6pm/7pm depending on day of the week, see website), is a crazy world of model masterpieces, live shows, 3-D cinema, white-knuckle rides and tamer activities (drive your own JCB digger anyone?). If you prebook online you save about £2 (but you need to be able to print out your ticket).

Buses run from Thames St to Legoland between 10am and 5.15pm.

Tours

Open-top double-decker bus tours of the town are run by **City Sightseeing Tours** (adult/child £7/3.50; ◷ every ½-hr daily Mar-Sep, Sat & Sun Nov & Dec) and leave from Castle Hill opposite Ye Harte & Garter Hotel. From Easter to October, **French Brothers Boat Hire** (☎ 851900; www.frenchbrothers .co.uk; Clewer Court Rd; ◷ 11am-5pm) runs a variety of boat trips to Runnymede, Maidenhead and around Windsor and Eton. The 45-minute round trip to Runnymede costs £4.50 for adults and £2.25 for children. Boats leave from just next to the Windsor Bridge. If you fancy doing the hop-on-hop-off bus plus a 35-minute boat trip, a combined boat and bus ticket costs £9.50/5.

THE HOME COUNTIES

Sleeping

Windsor has a good selection of quality hotels and B&Bs. Since the YHA hostel burned down in 2004 there are few budget options. A Travelodge (uninspiring but affordable) is due to open in summer 2007 on the corner of Goswell Hill and Goswell St (www.travelodge.co.uk).

Mrs Hamilton's (☎ 865775; 22 York Ave; s/d £35/58; P) Large bright rooms and very friendly service make this an extremely comfortable place to stay.

Langton House (☎ 858299; www.langtonhouse .com; 46 Alma Rd; s/d/tr £63/75/90; P ✗ ▣) The four elegant rooms here are superb (three are en suite, one has a private bathroom), and its friendly owners make sure they are always on hand to fill you in with local information, offer guided walks, provide tips on surviving Legoland etc.

Macdonald Castle Hotel (☎ 0870 400 8300; www .macdonaldhotels.co.uk/castle; 18 the High St; s/d weekdays £132/70, weekends £235/210; P ▣ wi-fi) This newly refurbished traditional-style hotel has a smashing location and large car park right in the centre of town. Guests can see weddings at the Guildhall opposite – recent celebrity ceremonies include Charles and Camilla, and Elton John and David Furnish – and the castle turrets from the 1st floor. Opt for a four-poster bed in the main building, a 500-year-old coaching inn with charming sloping floors and wooden beams.

our pick Sir Christopher Wren's House Hotel (☎ 861354; www.sirchristopherwren.co.uk; Thames St; s/d £165/220; P) For comfortable rooms, wonderful river views, a terrace overlooking Windsor Bridge and a pampering spa and gym, this luxurious 90-room hotel built by the man himself in 1676 fits the bill. Its 'sister' hotel the Christopher, across the way in Eton, is a delightful boutique hotel (but there's no spa).

Eating

There are plenty of eateries in Windsor and Eton: here's a selection.

our pick Crooked House of Windsor (☎ 857534; 52 the High St; mains £5.50-9; dinner Wed-Sat only; ✗) This little black-and-white house looks like it's had too much to drink. Enjoy a light lunch, a Royal cream tea (tea and scones with clotted cream and jam; £7–12) or dinner (bring your own wine). A member of the Slow Food movement, which advocates healthy eating,

this adorable restaurant sources its produce locally.

Al Fassia (☎ 855370; 27 St Leonard's Rd; mains £8.50-12.95; ✗) Situated away from the tourist hubbub, this Moroccan restaurant has a very good reputation. With its traditional wall hangings, mosaic tables, lanterns and other knick-knacks, it's a pleasant place for lunch or dinner.

Gilbey's Bar & Restaurant (☎ 854921; 82-83 the High St, Eton; mains £11-18.50) This attractive restaurant has a courtyard garden and good wines.

House on the Bridge (☎ 790197; 71A the High St, Windsor Bridge, Eton; mains £16.50-20.95) This formal, elegant restaurant overlooks the Thames and the castle.

Drinking

Windsor and Eton are packed with pubs, and a few trendy bars have sprung up.

Henry VI (☎ 866051; 37 the High St, Eton) A super-cool pub in which to sip an afternoon pint and discuss poetry. On Friday and Saturday evenings, rock out to live pop music.

our pick Two Brewers (☎ 855426; 34 Park St) A gorgeous 17th-century inn perched just near Windsor Great Park and the Long Walk.

Mantra (☎ 831331; 19-21 The Arches, Goswell Hill; £5 after 9pm; ☽ Fri & Sat, closed Mon) The chandeliers and exposed brickwork make this bar/club under the railway arches a chic evening option (no trainers) for the over-25 crowd.

Vanilla (☎ 831122; 15A Goswell Hill; £5 after 9pm Sat, prices vary Fri) This funky bar/club has a champagne-and-cocktail bar, dance floor, lounge area and a snappy dress code.

Also recommended:
Bar Yello (☎ 622667; Goswell Hill) Another boozing option under the railway arches.
Fifty One (☎ 755950; 51 Peascod St) Slightly lacking in atmosphere, this bar has live music on Wednesdays and theme nights such as Brazilian samba.
Waterman's Arms (☎ 861001; Brocas St, Eton) The place to meet rowers.

Entertainment

The **Windsor Arts Centre** (☎ 859336; cnr St Leonard's & St Mark's Rds) is a comedy, film, theatre, live music and dance venue with events for kids.

The **Theatre Royal** (☎ 853888; 32-34 Thames St) features a wide repertoire of theatre productions, from pantomime to first runs.

Getting There & Away

Windsor is 21 miles west of central London and only about 15 minutes by car from Heathrow airport.

BUS

Green Line bus 702 departs for Windsor and Legoland from London Victoria coach station hourly (about every two hours on Sunday, £7, 1¼ hours). Bus 77 connects Windsor with Heathrow airport. Buses depart from the High St, Windsor, opposite the Parish Church and head to Heathrow Central Station. For further details phone **Traveline** (☎ 0870 608 2 608).

TRAIN

There are two Windsor and Eton train stations – Central station on Thames St, opposite Windsor Castle, and Riverside station near the bridge to Eton.

From London Waterloo, trains run to Riverside station every half hour (hourly on Sunday). Some services from London Paddington to Central station require a change

at Slough, five minutes from Windsor, but take about the same time with a similar fare (£7, 50 minutes).

AROUND WINDSOR & ETON
Runnymede

In June 1215 King John met his barons and bishops in a large field 3 miles southeast of Windsor, and over the next few days they hammered out an agreement on a basic charter of rights guaranteeing the liberties of the king's subjects and restricting the monarch's absolute power. The document they signed was, of course, the Magna Carta, the world's first constitution. It formed the basis for statutes and charters throughout the world's democracies. (Both the national and state constitutions of the United States, drawn up more than 500 years later, paraphrase directly from this document.)

Runnymede – from the Anglo-Saxon words *ruinige* (take council) and *moed* (meadow) – was chosen because it was the largest piece of open land between the king's residence at Windsor and the bishop's palace at Staines. Today the field remains pretty much as it was, except now it features two **lodges** (1930) designed by Sir Edward Lutyens. In the woods behind the field are two **memorials**, the first to the Magna Carta designed by Sir Edward Maufe (1957). The second is to John F Kennedy, and was built by Geoffrey Jellicoe in 1965 on an acre of land granted in perpetuity to the US government following Kennedy's assassination in 1963.

Magna Carta Tea Rooms (☎ 01784-477110; Gate Lodge, Windsor Rd) is in one of Lutyens' lodges, and does a pretty good cream tea in the afternoons.

Bus 41 stops near here on the Windsor to Egham route.

WORTH THE TRIP

If you've ever fancied mixing sweet and savoury tastes, with dishes such as smoked-bacon-and-egg ice cream, sardine-on-toast sorbet or snail porridge, the **Fat Duck** (☎ 01628 580 333; the High St, Bray) is the place to visit. The menu may sound odd, but experimental and self-taught chef Heston Blumenthal was awarded an OBE by the Queen in January 2006 and the Fat Duck was voted the best restaurant in the world by 600 critics the year before – so he must be doing something right. This acclaimed gastronomic outing comes at a price – the Tasting Menu costs £90 per person including wine, while dining à la carte will set you back at least £80 – but it's a once-in-a-lifetime experience. (It could help you with future 'how can I combine the random leftovers in my fridge into a nice meal?' dilemmas too.) To get there by car take the A308 from Windsor then follow signs for Bray Village. Drive into the village and you'll see the Fat Duck on your right.

Reading

☎ 0118 / pop 232,662

This prosperous industrial town, only 12 miles southwest of Windsor but a world away in atmosphere, straddles the Thames on the Berkshire–Oxfordshire border. Once an important guarding post for London, there is now little to see in the town itself apart from the **abbey ruins**. What puts Reading on the map, however, is its flourishing arts scene, which culminates in the excellent **Reading Festival** (☎ 020-8963 0940; www .readingfestival.com), a three-day extravaganza during the third week in August that features top acts in pop, rock and dance music. Tickets will set you back £60 per day (not including camping or parking) or £135 for a three-day pass.

The festival is preceded (at the end of July) by the **World of Music, Arts & Dance Festival** (WOMAD; ☎ 939 0930; www.womad.org), founded by Peter Gabriel in 1982. Tickets cost from £10 to £110.

There are trains every 15 minutes from London Waterloo or Paddington stations to Reading (£12.20, 25 minutes).

SURREY

Surrey is *the* place for wealthy London commuters to choose when they sprog (reproduce), move out of the city and buy a country pad. As such there are two strands of residents – those who commute and earn fat bonuses and those who are local and don't – and some people mix better than others. Further away from the roaring motorways, the county reveals some inspiring landscapes made famous by authors Sir Arthur Conan Doyle, Sir Walter Scott and Jane Austen.

FARNHAM

☎ 01252 / pop 36,298

Farnham is Surrey's most attractive market town. It's practically empty during the week, which makes it a lovely and relaxing place to visit. The town's main enticements include admiring the exquisite Georgian homes, shopping in the independent boutiques (some of which are on the pricey side), walking and cycling in the surrounding countryside, visiting the charming museum and popping into one of Surrey's only intact castles.

Orientation & Information

The easiest and most pleasant way to explore Farnham is on foot. The most interesting part of town is its historical centre, where East, West, South and Castle Sts meet.

The Borough (the eastern end of West St) is the town's main shopping street. The train station is at the southern end of South St (Station Hill).

The **Waverley Locality Office** (☎ 712667; tourism@farnham.gov.uk; South St; ☼ 9am-noon Mon, 9.30am-5pm Tue-Fri, 9am-noon Sat) has free maps of the town and surrounding countryside, the free *Farnham Heritage Trail* and an updated list of accommodation in the area. It also offers free internet access.

You'll find an ATM on the Borough, near the corner of Castle St (where banks can be found). The main post office and a bureau de change are on West St, which is the continuation of The Borough.

Guided walks (☎ 718119; adult/child £3/1) of approximately 1½ hours run at 3pm on the first Sunday of every month between April and October. Meet at the entrance of the Wagon Yard car park at the southern end of Downing St.

Sights

FARNHAM CASTLE

The **castle keep** (☎ 252 2000; admission £2.80, free audio tour; ☼ noon-5pm Fri-Sun & public holidays Apr-Sep) was constructed in 1138 by Henry de Blois, the grandson of William the Conqueror. There's not much left except the beautiful old ramparts. Even if the keep is closed, it's worth walking around the outside (everyone seems to ignore the private signs) to drink in the lovely view.

A residential palace house, Farnham Castle was built in the 13th century for the bishops of Winchester as a stopover on London journeys. From 1926 to the 1950s it was taken over by the bishops of Guildford. It's now owned by the Farnham Castle International Briefing & Conference Centre but you can visit it on a guided **tour** (☼ 2-4pm Wed).

Farnham Castle is located up the old steps at the top of Castle St.

MUSEUM OF FARNHAM

This appealing **museum** (☎ 715094; 38 West St; admission free; ☼ 10am-5pm Tue-Sat) is located in the splendid Willmer House, a Georgian townhouse built for wealthy hop merchant and maltster John Thorne in 1718. Since it

---

STROLL THE SURREY HILLS

There are plenty of enchanting walks through the Surrey Hills. Find different routes on www.surreyhills.org or grab leaflets from the Waverley Locality Office. Frensham Ponds, Box Hill (p163) and Tilford are particularly scenic spots.

---

opened in 1962, the museum has won many awards, including the European Museum of the Year Award.

The museum traces the history of Farnham through themes such as 'country life', 'art and architecture', 'on the road' and 'town life'. Kids will envy the amazing 1780s **dolls' house**, modelled on the house next door and built for the Manwaring children.

Possibly the most precious exhibit is a morning cap that once belonged to Charles I. He stayed in the house that's now the Waverley Locality Office on his way to trial in Westminster Hall in 1648, and gave the cap to his host Sir Henry Vernon as a souvenir, perhaps mindful that he would no longer be needing it…

Sleeping
Accommodation in Farnham tends towards the midrange to top-end.

Sandiway (☎ 710721; 24 Shortheath Rd; s/d £30/50; P ☒) This spot is about a 15-minute walk from town in a 1920s house with a pleasant garden.

Exchange Hotel (☎ 726673; Station Hill; s/d £49.35/69.95; P ▣ wi-fi) After a full refurb there are nine attractive en-suite rooms with TV at a good price just by the station.

ourpick **Bush Hotel** (☎ 0870 400 8225; www.macdonald-hotels.co.uk/bush; The Borough; s/d Mon-Thu £168/178, Fri-Sun £117/130; ☒) Set back from the road, this central, charming 17th-century inn has 82 well-turned-out rooms, a cosy Coachman's Bar with suitably wonky beamed ceiling and a pleasant restaurant.

Eating & Entertainment
Farnham contains a good choice of tempting eateries.

ourpick **Nelson Arms** (☎ 716078; 50 Castle St; 2-course lunch £7.95, dinner £8.95-16.50) A superb mix of old-world charm and contemporary chic, this gastro pub is understandably popular with the locals. Try the delicious homemade burger.

Colony Restaurant (☎ 725108; 68 Castle St; dishes £3.50-7.50; ☺ dinner only Mon, closed Sun) Very tasty Peking cuisine on Farnham's attractive Castle St.

Coach Bar Restaurant (☎ 724520; Castle St; mains under £10) This blue-and-white-fronted tapas bar at the bottom of Castle St has a sleek metal bar, cool colour scheme, DJs, occasional salsa nights and great nosh. There are larger dishes if tapas won't sate your hunger.

Farnham Maltings (☎ 726234; Bridge Sq; www.farnhammaltings.com) This multipurpose venue has a riverside bar, live music, exhibitions, fairs, movies, workshops and comedy.

Getting There & Away
Half-hourly train services run from London Waterloo (50 minutes). From Winchester, trains depart every 45 minutes for Woking (30 minutes). Change there for half-hourly trains to Farnham (25 minutes). The train station is at the end of South St, on the other side of the A31 from the old town centre.

Stagecoach (☎ 01256-464501) bus X64 runs from Winchester to Farnham at 10 minutes past the hour (one hour and 10 minutes). The stop is on the Borough.

AROUND FARNHAM
Waverley Abbey
The inspiration for Sir Walter Scott's eponymous novel, the Waverley Abbey ruins sit almost forlornly on the banks of the River Wey about 2 miles southeast of Farnham.

This was the first Cistercian abbey built in England (construction began in 1128) and, like Beaulieu Abbey in the New Forest, was based on a parent abbey at Cîteaux in France.

Across the Wey is the impressive **Waverley Abbey House** (closed to the public), built in 1783 using bricks from the demolished abbey. In the 19th century it was owned by Florence Nightingale's brother-in-law, and the famous nurse was a regular visitor. Fittingly, the house was used as a military hospital in WWI. Since 1973, it has been the headquarters of the Crusade for World Revival (CWR), a Christian charity.

The abbey and house are off the B3001.

Hindhead
The tiny hamlet of Hindhead, 8 miles south of Farnham off the A287, lies in the middle of the largest area of open heath in Surrey.

During the 19th century a number of prominent Victorians bought up property in the area, including Sir Arthur Conan Doyle (1859–1930), creator of Sherlock Holmes. One of the three founders of the National Trust, Sir Robert Hunter, lived in nearby Haslemere, and today much of the area is administered by the foundation.

The most beautiful part of the area is to the northeast, where you'll find a natural depression known as the **Devil's Punchbowl**. There are a number of excellent trails and bridle paths

here. To get the best view, head for Gibbet Hill (280m), which was once an execution ground.

The **Hindhead YHA Hostel** (☎ 01428-604285; www.yha.org.uk; Devil's Punchbowl, Thursley; dm £11.95) is a completely secluded cottage run by the National Trust on the northern edge of the Punchbowl. It's perfect if you like walking – the nearest bus stop and car park are a half-mile away.

Bus 19 runs hourly to Hindhead from Farnham.

The Southeast Coast

China has its Great Wall, the US plans its Son of Star Wars and England has…the southeast Coast? These days it takes a leap of imagination but this has long been the nation's front line of defence: a reinforced shield fending off continental invasion. But like a veteran soldier who has been through the wars, the region is now fonder of its own age-old tales and mellow ales than maintaining its vigil.

With their softer underbelly exposed, the counties of Essex, Kent, East and West Sussex and Hampshire are some of England's most desirable places to live and visit. The formidable cliffs, castles and the fortified ports may remain, but these days they're invaded by holidaymakers armed with cameras and picnics. It's a middle-class stronghold of cosy home comforts, medieval villages and commuter-belt towns, all enfolded in a blanket of gentle agricultural fields, rolling chalk downs and manicured gardens.

A string of seaside resorts exploit the mild climate and fast links from London, fêting seedy casinos to silver-haired fun, nostalgic funfairs to fast-paced nightlife. Here too you'll find England's spiritual heart at Canterbury, the ancient seat of Saxon might at Winchester and the pleasure seekers Holy Grail at Brighton. You can soak up maritime history, dine out on seafood, and charge around battlegrounds, clifftops, palaces and Roman remains. And all the while you can revel in the knowledge that as a tourist you're part of the first successful invasion of these shores in almost 1000 years.

HIGHLIGHTS

- Partying the night away beside beautiful **Brighton Beach** (p212)
- Following in the footsteps of pilgrims to the enchanting cathedral city of **Canterbury** (p186)
- Roaming the cobbled backstreets of picturesque **Rye** (p203)
- Clambering aboard mighty warships in the historic naval dockyard of **Portsmouth** (p230)
- Surrendering to the romance of moated marvel **Leeds Castle** (p202)
- Delving through the part-sunken cathedral and ancient treasures of **Winchester** (p225)
- Bringing on the vertigo peering down the 150m chalk cliffs of **Beachy Head** (p209)

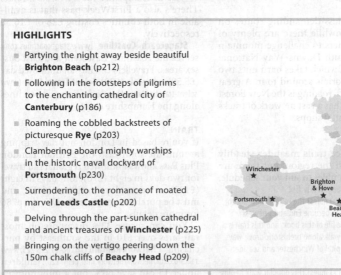

Winchester ★
Leeds Castle ★
Canterbury ★
Brighton & Hove ★
Rye ★
Portsmouth ★
Beachy Head ★

■ POPULATION: 6.2 MILLION | ■ AREA: 10,681 SQ MILES

Information

Tourism South East (www.visitsoutheastengland.com) is the official website for south and southeast England. Other helpful websites include:
Kent Attractions (www.kentattractions.co.uk)
Kent Tourism (www.kenttourism.co.uk)
Visit Hampshire (www.visit-hampshire.org.uk)
Visit Sussex (www.visitsussex.org)

Activities

The southeast of England may be Britain's most densely populated corner, but there are still plenty of off-the-beaten-track walking and cycling routes to enjoy here. We concentrate on the highlights here, but you'll find more information throughout the chapter and in the Outdoor Activities chapter. Regional tourist offices are also well stocked with leaflets, maps and guides to start you off walking, cycling, paragliding, sailing and more.

CYCLING

Finding quiet roads for cycle touring takes a little extra perseverance in southeast England, but the effort is richly rewarded. Long-distance burns that form part of the **National Cycle Network** (www.sustrans.org.uk) include:
Downs & Weald Cycle Route (150 miles) London to Brighton and on to Hastings.
Garden of England Cycle Route (165 miles) London to Dover and then Hastings.

You'll also find less-demanding routes on its website. Meanwhile there are plenty of uppers and downers to challenge mountain bikers on the South Downs Way National Trail (100 miles), which takes hard nuts two days but mere mortals around four. A great spot for gentler off-roading is the New Forest (see p236), which has a vast network of tracks and numerous rental shops.

WALKING

Two long-distance trails meander steadily westward through the region, but there are plenty of shorter ambles to suit your schedule, stamina and scenery wish list.
South Downs Way (100 miles) The rolling chalk South Downs are hotly tipped to become England's newest national park during the life of this book, and this trail is a beautiful roller-coaster walk along prehistoric drove ways between the ancient capital of Winchester and seaside resort Eastbourne.
North Downs Way (153 miles) This popular walk begins near Farnham in Surrey but one of its most beautiful sec-

tions runs from near Ashford to Dover in Kent, and there's also a loop that takes in Canterbury near its end.

Both long-distance routes have sections ideal for shorter walks. History buffs will revel in the 1066 Country Walk (p204), which connects with the South Downs Way. England's newest national park (at least for the moment), the New Forest (see p236) is also popular walking country. And the Isle of Wight (see p240) is crisscrossed by paths and has some fine coastal stretches to explore on foot.

Getting There & Around

The southeast is easily explored by train or bus, and many attractions can be visited in a day trip from London. Contact the **National Traveline** (☎ 0870 608 2608; www.travelinesoutheast.org .uk) for comprehensive information on public transport in the region.

BUS

Explorer tickets (adult/child £6.80/5.30) provide day-long unlimited travel on most buses throughout the region; buy them at bus stations or on your first bus.

First Group (www.firstgroup.com) offer a FirstDay Essex pass for a day's unlimited bus travel on its county services. It costs £6/4.40/12 per adult/child/family. It operates a similar service in Hampshire for £4.40/3.35/10.00. There's also a FirstWeek pass that is available in both counties costing £28 or £16.50 respectively.

Stagecoach Coastline (www.stagecoachbus.com) serves the coastline, East Kent and East Sussex areas. Travellers can buy an unlimited day (£5.50) or week (£20) **Solent Travel Card** (www .solent-travelcard.org.uk), good on major bus lines along the Hampshire coast.

TRAIN

If you're based in London but day-tripping around the southeast, the BritRail London Plus Pass allows unlimited regional rail travel for two days in eight (£70), four days in eight (£132), or seven days in fifteen (£176) and must be purchased outside the UK; see p786 for more details.

You can secure 33% discounts on most rail fares over £10 in the southeast by purchasing a **Network Railcard** (☎ 08457 225 225; www .railcard.co.uk/network/network.htm; per yr £20). Children under 15 can save 60%, but a minimum £1 fare applies.

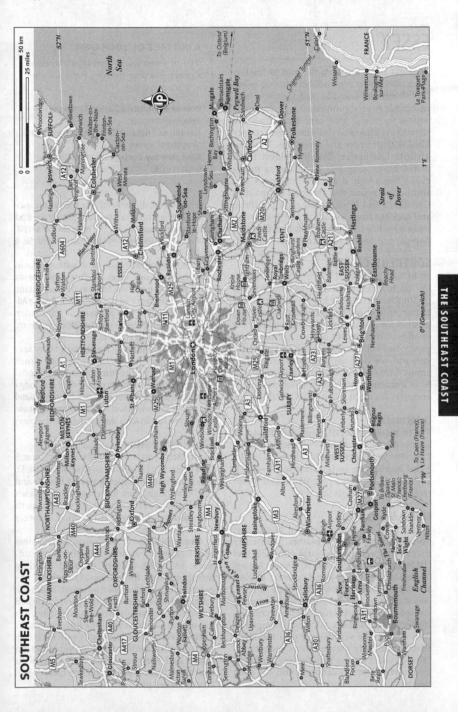

ESSEX

Poor old Essex has been the butt of English jokes and target for snobbery for decades. Its inhabitants are ridiculed for their bottle-blonde manes, promiscuous persuasions, witless ways and loud cars. But throw the stereotypes aside and you'll discover a county filled with diversity and diversions. Here lies historic Colchester, Britain's oldest town with a burgeoning arts scene. Sleepy medieval villages hide down winding lanes and amid countryside that inspired the painter Constable. But if you'd rather skip culture and seek out Essex's saucy stereotypical soul, make a beeline to Southend-on-Sea, the most popular fun-in-the-sun resort near London.

SOUTHEND-ON-SEA

☎ 01702 / pop 160,257

On the doorstep of London, the seaside resort of Southend certainly has its selling points to the capital's weekenders: sandy sprawling beaches for one and an absurdly long pier for another. However, it's also one of the more gaudy and belligerent of England's summer sun-and-sea destinations, thick with lurid amusements and seedy nightclubs. But if you have a craving for ice cream, fish and chips and salty sea air, it will be well satisfied here.

Information

The **tourist office** (☎ 215120; www.visitsouthend.co.uk; Southend Pier, Western Esplanade; ⏰ 8.15am-6pm Mon-Fri, 8.15am-8pm Sat & Sun Apr-May & Oct, 8.15am-9pm Mon-Fri, 8.15am-10pm Sat & Sun Jun-Sep, 8.15am-4pm Nov-Mar) is at the entrance to the pier. Banks and shops crowd along the High St.

Sights & Activities

Other than mile upon mile of tawny imported-sand and shingle **beaches**, Southend's main attraction is the world's longest **pier** (☎ 215620; www.southendpier.co.uk; admission Apr-Sep/Oct-Mar £2.50/50p; ⏰ 8am-10pm daily Apr-Oct, 8am-5pm Mon-Fri & 8am-7pm Sat & Sun Nov-Mar), built in 1830. At a staggering 1.33 miles long it's an impressive edifice and a magnet for boat crashes, storms and fires, the last of which ravaged its tip in 2005. The surprisingly peaceful stroll to its tip will help burn off those rock-candy calories, and a wheezy Pier Railway (included in admission price) can save you the long slog back.

A COTTAGE OF YOUR OWN

If you'd prefer a self-catering holiday using a cottage as your base, try these websites as a starting point:

Best of Brighton & Sussex Cottages (www .bestofbrighton.co.uk)
Garden of England Cottages (www.garden ofenglandcottages.co.uk)
Kent Holiday Cottages (www.kentholiday cottages.co.uk)

Afterwards, dip beneath the pier's entrance to explore an old 'toasts-rack' pier train and antique slot machines at the **museum** (☎ 611214; adult/under 12yr 60p/free; ⏰ 11am-5pm Tue-Wed, Sat & Sun May-Oct).

Kids can come nose to nose with sharks in glass tunnels and meet celebrity sea horses while parents grit their teeth at the saccharine seaside soundtrack in the good little **Sealife Adventure** (☎ 442211; www.sealifeadventure.co.uk; Eastern Esplanade; adult/child £6/4.50; ⏰ 10am-7pm) aquarium, half a mile east of the pier.

Or you can embrace Southend's tacky seaside soul, inhale Rossi's velvety ice cream, rock or candy-floss before jumping on head-spinning rides or ramming each other in dodgems at lurid amusement park **Adventure Island** (☎ 443400; www.adventureisland.co.uk; Western Esplanade; ⏰ daily Apr-Aug, Sat & Sun Sep-Mar), beside the pier.

Sleeping & Eating

Terrace Hotel (☎ 348143; www.theterracehotel.co.uk; 8 Royal Tce; s/d from £29.60/44.65, s/d with bathroom £40/57; ✗) Festooned in scarlet flowering baskets and filigree wrought iron, this charming Victorian row-house is very central and boasts superb pier and beach views. It has nine sprucely decorated rooms in warm colours.

Gleneagles Hotel (☎ 333635; www.thegleneagleshotel .co.uk; 5 Clifftown Pde; s/d/ste £32.50/55/80; ✗) A handsome mid-19th-century terraced building facing out into the estuary, Gleneagles has many of its Victorian features intact. It also has crisply maintained rooms with period style and thoughtful extras, an extra-special suite with panoramic windows and cute little patio café.

Pipe of Port (☎ 614606; 84 High St; mains £9-12) Day or night, this sawdust-scattered subterranean bistro and wine bar oozes crusty candlelit charm, and serves wonderful fish specials and freshly baked pies.

Fleur de Provence (☎ 352987; www.fleurdeprovence.co.uk; 54 Alexandra St; mains £16-18, set meal £15; ☺ lunch & dinner Mon-Fri, dinner Sat) For a glimpse of Southend's sophisticated side head away from the seafront to this chic Continental restaurant behind frosted-glass façade, with pastel blush walls, blonde-wood floors and romantic ambience.

Drinking

Clarence Yard (☎ 392153; 23-29 Clarence St; ☺ noon-11pm) An atmospheric 19th-century bakery and courtyard stables now houses this refined but relaxed wine bar, which capitalises on the cobbled floors, rough tiles and exposed brick with its own rustic-chic leather sofas and wickerwork.

Getting There & Around

The easiest way to arrive is by train. There are several services each hour from both London Liverpool St to Southend Victoria station or from London Fenchurch St to Southend Central station (£10.90, 55 minutes). The seafront is a 10- to 15-minute walk from either train station. For taxis, try **Southend Radio Cars** (☎ 345678).

COLCHESTER

☎ 01206 / pop 104,390

An easy day or weekend foray from London, Colchester is a charming place with a likable easygoing feel and a history that's hard to beat. It claims the title as Britain's oldest recorded city, with settlement noted here as early as the 5th century BC. Centuries later in AD 43, the Romans came, saw, conquered and constructed their northern capital Camulodunum here. So too, the invading Normans, who saw Colchester's potential and built a monstrous war machine of a castle on Roman foundations. But it's not all bygones and battlements here. By the end of 2007, Colchester will also be home to a spectacular new horseshoe-shaped gallery, Firstsite.

Orientation & Information

There are two train stations, but most services stop at North station, about half a mile north of the centre. The current bus station is off Queen St near the tourist office, but by 2010 will move to a new location on Vineyard St.

The **tourist office** (☎ 282920; www.visitcolchester.com; 1 Queen St; ☎ 9.30am-6pm Mon-Sat, 11am-4pm Sun) is opposite the castle. **Pulse** (☎ 570577; Centurion House, St John's St; per hr £2; ☺ 9am-10pm Mon-Fri, 10am-10pm Sat & Sun) has internet access. There are a couple of **post offices** (North Hill and Longe Wyre St) while banks with ATMs can be found on the High St.

Sights & Activities

England's largest surviving Norman keep, bigger even than that of the Tower of London and once a hair-raising symbol of foreign invasion, now slumbers innocently amid a sweet-smelling park across from the tourist office. **Colchester Castle** (☎ 282939; www.colchestermuseums.org.uk; adult/child £4.90/3.10; ☺ 10am-5pm Mon-Sat, 11am-4.30pm Sun) was begun in 1076, building upon the foundations of a Roman fort. The interactive castle museum is exceptional, with plenty of try-on togas and sound effects to keep young curiosity alive. There are also illuminating guided tours (adult/child £1.90/1) of the Roman vaults, Norman rooftop chapel and castle walls.

Beside the castle, a solid Georgian town house hosts the **Hollytrees Museum** (☎ 282940; admission free; High St; ☺ 10am-5pm Mon-Sat, 11am-5pm Sun), which trawls through 300 years of domestic life with quirky surprises that include a shipwright's boat-cum-pram and a make-your-own Victorian silhouette feature.

Tymperleys, a magnificent timber-framed 15th-century building 100m east of the High St, also houses the hypnotic **Clock Museum** (☎ 282939; admission free; ☺ 10am-1pm & 2-5pm Tue-Sat Apr-Oct), which echoes to the steady ticktocking of one of the largest clock collections in Britain.

A short stroll north of High St will bring you to the interesting **Dutch Quarter**, established in the 16th century by Protestant refugee weavers from Holland.

Sidestep the town's lacklustre natural-history museum in favour of the world-class naturalistic enclosures of **Colchester Zoo** (☎ 331292; www.colchester-zoo.co.uk; Maldon Rd, Stanway; adult/child £13.50/7.50; ☺ 9.30am-6pm Apr-Jun & Sep, 9.30am-6.30pm Jul & Aug, 9.30am-dusk Oct-Mar), 5 miles northeast of the castle, where you can get hands on with elephants and giraffes, and watch sea lions pirouette from underwater tunnels. Eastern National bus 75 stops at the zoo.

Tours

The tourist office has a variety of themed, guided **walking tours** (adult/child £3/2; ☺ Apr-Oct) of the town at 11.30am on weekends, and

THE SOUTHEAST COAST

Mondays July and August. Visit www.col chesterwhatson.co.uk or call ahead for details. The tourist office also sells tickets for **City Sightseeing** (www.citysightseeing.co.uk; adult/child £7.50/3; ☉ Apr-Sep) open-top bus tours.

Sleeping

Scheregate Hotel (☎ 573034; www.scheregatehotel .co.uk; 36 Osbourne St; s/d from £31/48; P) This faded but characterful hotel, with 27 spacious and well-worn-in rooms, a scattering of oak beams and that rare luxury, private parking, is in a terrific central location. A third of rooms are en suite but they book up the quickest.

Old Manse (☎ 545154; www.doveuk.com/oldmanse; 15 Roman Rd; s/d incl breakfast £35/60; ✗) A lovely Victorian home with a chunk of Roman wall in its garden, Old Manse is only a few minutes' walk from the centre and is run by a motherly hostess. Its three rooms are tastefully done and breakfast is a sociable communal affair.

Red Lion (☎ 577986; www.corushotels.com; High St; s/d from £75/85; P ✗ 🖳 wi-fi) This show-stealing oak-timbered hotel built in 1465 and over-hanging the High St doesn't disappoint inside either, especially not in the high-beamed ban-queting hall where guests can enjoy traditional English fare. A few of the shipshape rooms also boast exposed oak beams and wattle-and-daub walls.

Rose & Crown Hotel (☎ 866677; www.rose-and-crown .com; East St; s/d from £90/100; P ✗ 🔌 🖳) This en-dearingly lopsided 14th-century posting inn, with leaded windows, overhang and exposed timber frame, is the oldest hotel in town, but features a showroom-perfect modern wing. Its bar is the most atmospheric in Colchester, and its restaurant is renowned for its fusion of French and Indian flavours.

Eating

Garden Café @ the Minories Art Gallery (☎ 500169; 74 High St; mains £4-6; ☉ 10am-5pm Mon-Sat) An eccen-tric little neo-Gothic folly graces the sprawling garden behind this artsy café, housed in a town house art gallery of big repute. It dishes up generous daily specials until 3pm.

Lemon Tree (☎ 767337; 48 St John's St; mains £9-13.50; ☉ 10.30am-9.30pm Mon-Sat) This zesty little eatery is graced by a knobbly Roman wall and cavern in the corner and creative British and Conti-nental cuisine on the menu. Décor strikes a nice chic-to-rustic balance and there are tasty blackboard specials, frequent gourmet nights and occasional live jazz.

North Hill Exchange (☎ 769988; 19/20 North Hill; set lunch £7, mains £9-16; ☉ lunch & dinner Mon-Sat) This fine Georgian former ironmongers still retains its quirky kettle sign swinging outside, but inside it's minimalist Art Deco all the way with elegant iron chairs, mahogany floors and panelled bar. Its European-influenced menu is strong on fish.

Getting There & Around

Colchester is 62 miles from London. There are three daily National Express buses from London Victoria (£9.80, 2½ hours) and rail services every 15 to 20 minutes from London Liverpool St (£18.70, 55 minutes). For a cab, call **A1 Taxis** (☎ 544744).

AROUND COLCHESTER
Dedham Vale

'I love every stile and stump and lane…
these scenes made me a painter'
  John Constable (1776–1837)

Remember John Constable's canvas encap-sulation of English rural life in his famous painting *The Hay Wain*? It and many of the artist's other romantic visions of country lanes, springtime fields and babbling creeks were painted in this serene vale, which has hung onto its charm in the centuries that followed.

Now known as Constable country, Dedham Vale centres around the villages of Dedham, East Bergholt (where Constable was born) and Flatford. There's a **tourist office** (☎ 01206-299460; flatford@babergh.gov.uk; Flatford Lane; ☉ 10am-5pm mid-Mar–Oct, 10.30am-4pm Sat & Sun Nov-mid–Mar) beside the vale's top attraction, a riverside mill once owned by the artist's family. **Flatford Mill** now houses arts courses, and public access comes via group **tours** (☎ 01206-298283; adult £2.50).

Near the mill is thatched **Bridge Cottage** (NT; ☎ 01206-298260; Flatford Lane, East Bergholt; admission free; ☉ 10.30am-5.30pm daily May-Sep, 11am-4pm daily Oct, 11am-5pm Wed-Sun Mar-Apr, 11am-3.30pm Wed-Sun Nov-Dec, 11am-3.30pm Sat & Sun Jan-Feb), which has an exhibition on the artist, a tea garden and boat hire. When guided tours are not available audio tapes can be hired (£2).

The area is best explored by bike or in your own car, though there are bus and train services. Bus 93/4 from Colchester runs to East Bergholt, from where it's less than a mile to the mill. Or come by train to Manningtree (eight minutes), and you get a lovely 1¾-mile walk along pretty footpaths.

OAST HOUSES

While travelling through Kent you're bound to spy the jaunty conical tips of the county's distinctive oast houses peeking out from amid the trees. These giant kilns were used for drying hops, a key ingredient in beer, introduced to the region in the early 15th century. The odd cone-shaped roof was necessary to create a draught for the kiln fire, and the crooked nozzles sticking out from their tops could be moved to regulate the airflow to the fire.

If your curiosity is piqued, you can stick your nose into a few prime examples at the **Hop Farm Country Park** (☎ 01622-872068; www.thehopfarm.co.uk; Paddock Wood, Tonbridge; adult/child £7.50/6.50; ☒ 10am-5pm), which also re-creates the history of hop picking in Kent. It's signed off the A228 near Paddock Wood, southwest of Maidstone.

Many oast houses have been converted into homes and oast-house B&Bs are becoming more common throughout the county; check with the various tourist information centres for information on local possibilities.

SAFFRON WALDEN

☎ 01799 / pop 14,313

Saffron Walden is home to a delightful knot of gabled and timber-framed buildings peppered with picturesque pargeting and antique shops. It gets its curious title from the saffron crocus, which was cultivated in the surrounding fields from the 15th century right through to the first half of the 20th century.

The **tourist office** (☎ 510444; tourism@uttlesford .gov.uk; 1 Market Pl; ☒ 9.30am-5.30pm Mon-Sat Apr-Oct, 10am-5pm Mon-Sat Nov-Mar) sells a useful town trail leaflet for 25p. It will guide you to the stunning example of 17th-century pargeting on the **Sun Inn** (Church St), which is wreathed with the patterned plasterwork and a freeze-framed fight scene based on legend of the Wisbech Giant.

The offbeat little **museum** (☎ 510333; Museum St; adult/child £1/free; ☒ 10am-5pm Mon-Sat, 2-5pm Sun), itself dating from 1835, is worth a peek for its mixed bag of local-history exhibits and an Egyptian mummy. The bramble-covered ruins of **Walden Castle Keep**, built about 1125, lie alongside.

A symbol of the town's saffron-inspired golden age, the jumbo-sized 15th-century **Church of St Mary the Virgin** (Church St) is one of the largest in the county and sports some impressive Gothic arches and decorative wooden ceilings.

On the eastern side of the town is a tiny earthen **maze** thought to be 800 years old; a path circles for about 1500m and takes a bit of head-scratching to complete.

Sleeping & Eating

Most of the B&Bs are in tiny houses and have only one or two rooms.

YHA Hostel (☎ 0870 770 6014; saffron@yha.org.uk; 1 Myddylton Pl; dm member/nonmember £11.95/14.95; ☒ mid-Apr-Oct; ☒) This hostel's stunning medieval timber-framed building with its overhanging timber frame was once a malt house, and is Saffron Walden's oldest inhabited building. There are relatively basic facilities and no access is permitted between the hours of 10am and 5pm.

Archway Guesthouse (☎ 501500; archwayguesthouse@ntlworld.com; 11 Church St; s/d from £35/55; ☒) A quirky old toy and rock-and-roll memorabilia collection decorates this cosy familial guesthouse, which has brightly coloured en suite rooms with unfussy décor and a friendly welcome.

No 9 Market Place (☎ 525429; 9 Market Pl; 2-/3-course set meal £19.95/27.50; ☒ Tue-Sat) This 400-year-old farmhouse in the town's heart is decorated with parget swirls and houses a traditional country-style wine bar and restaurant, serving good solid English fare.

Drinking

Eight Bells (☎ 522790; 18 Bridge St) This famous old pub near the youth hostel dates from the 16th century and is rich in old-world atmosphere, with carved beams, and a pargeted overhanging façade hung with its trademark bells.

Getting There & Away

On weekdays, trains leave London Liverpool St twice hourly (£13.80, one hour) for Audley End station, 2½ miles west of town. Services run hourly on Sunday. Trains from Cambridge (18 minutes) run approximately every 20 minutes.

Buses 301 and 59 run from the station into Saffron Walden (six minutes) regularly on weekdays, less often on weekends.

AROUND SAFFRON WALDEN

Positively palatial in its scale, style and the all-too-apparent ambition of its creator, the first Earl of Suffolk, the fabulous early-Jacobean **Audley End House** (EH; ☎ 01799-522399; adult/child house & park £8.95/4.50, park £4.80/2.40; ☾ 11am-5pm Wed-Fri & Sun, 11am-3pm Sat Apr-Sep, 10am-4pm Sat & Sun Oct & Mar) eventually did become a royal palace when it was bought by Charles II in 1668.

Although hard to believe, the enormous building today is only one-third of its original size, but it's still magnificent. Its rooms glitter with silverware, priceless furniture and paintings, while Lancelot 'Capability' Brown's signature brand of dreamy landscaped **park** (☾ 11am-6pm Wed-Sun) surrounds the house.

Audley End House is one mile west of Saffron Walden on the B1383. Audley End train station is 1¼ miles from the house. Taxis will ferry you here from the town marketplace for around £3.50.

KENT

Sitting demurely in London's backyard, Kent is justly described the garden of England. This neatly manicured landscape of lush farmland, cultivated country estates, fruitful orchards, and carefully nurtured tourist attractions seems to mirror its own glorious public gardens on a grand scale. It's also the beer garden of England, producing the world-renowned Kent hops and some of the country's finest ales. Here too are long coastal stretches dotted with old-fashioned beach resorts, spellbinding Canterbury crowned by its fascinating cathedral, and the port of Dover which is close enough to France to smell the garlic or hop over on a day trip to taste it.

CANTERBURY

☎ 01227 / pop 43,552

With history along every lane, an old alehouse on every corner and a captivating World Heritage–listed cathedral plump in its heart, Canterbury is one of southern England's top attractions. Its narrow medieval alleyways and precarious timber-beamed buildings are a joy to explore, as are its riverside gardens and ancient city walls. Yet Canterbury is no mere showpiece to times past, but a spirited and lively place with a large student contingent and a wide choice of contemporary bars, restaurants and arts. But book ahead for the best hotels and eateries: pilgrims may no longer flock here in their thousands but there's a year-round flood of tourists to replace them.

History

Canterbury's past is as rich as it comes. From AD 200 there was a Roman town here, which later became the capital of the Saxon kingdom of Kent. When St Augustine arrived in England in 597 to carry the Christian message to the pagan hordes, he chose Canterbury as his *cathedra* (primary see) and set about building an abbey on the outskirts of town. Following the martyrdom of Thomas Becket (see boxed text, below), Canterbury became northern Europe's most important centre of pilgrimage, which in turn led to Geoffrey Chaucer's *The Canterbury Tales*, one of the most outstanding poetic works in English literature (see boxed text, p189).

Blasphemous murders and rampant tourism thrown aside, the city of Canterbury still

---

KEEP YOUR ENEMIES CLOSE...

In 1162 King Henry II did what every good monarch should do. He appointed his good mate Thomas Becket to the highest clerical office in the land in the hope that a friendly archbishop could force the increasingly vocal religious lobby to toe the royal line. But Henry didn't count on Thomas taking his job as seriously as he did, and by 1170 Henry had become exasperated with his former favourite's penchant for disagreeing with virtually everything the king said or did. He sulked and raged for a while, then late in the year 'suggested' to four of his knights that Thomas was a little too much to bear. The dirty deed was done on December 29. Becket's martyrdom – and canonisation in double-quick time (1173) – catapulted the cathedral to the top spot in northern Europe's top 10 pilgrimage sites. Mindful of the growing opprobrium at his role in Becket's murder, Henry arrived here in 1174 for a dramatic *mea culpa,* and after allowing himself to be whipped and scolded was granted absolution.

remains the primary see for the Church of England.

Orientation

The Old Town is enclosed by a bulky medieval city wall that makes a wonderful walk. The Unesco World Heritage Site encompasses the cathedral, St Augustine's Abbey and St Martin's Church. Much of the centre is pedestrianised, but there is parking inside the wall.

Information

BOOKSHOPS

Chaucer Bookshop (☎ 453912; 6-7 Beer Cart Lane) Antiquarian and used-books.

Waterstones (☎ 456343; 20-21 St Margaret's St)

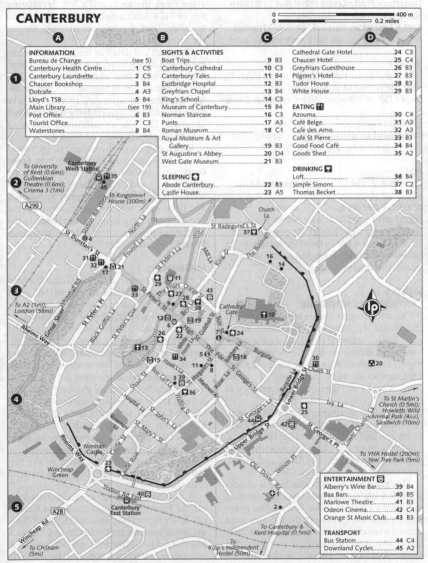

CANTERBURY

| 0 | 400 m |
| 0 | 0.2 miles |

INFORMATION
Bureau de Change	(see 5)
Canterbury Health Centre	1 C5
Canterbury Laundrette	2 C5
Chaucer Bookshop	3 B4
Dotcafe	4 A3
Lloyd's TSB	5 B4
Main Library	(see 19)
Post Office	6 B3
Tourist Office	7 C3
Waterstones	8 B4

SIGHTS & ACTIVITIES
Boat Trips	9 B3
Canterbury Cathedral	10 C3
Canterbury Tales	11 B4
Eastbridge Hospital	12 B3
Greyfriars Chapel	13 B4
King's School	14 C3
Museum of Canterbury	15 B4
Norman Staircase	16 C3
Punts	17 A3
Roman Museum	18 C4
Royal Museum & Art Gallery	19 B3
St Augustine's Abbey	20 D4
West Gate Museum	21 B3

SLEEPING
Abode Canterbury	22 B3
Castle House	23 A5

EATING
Azouma	30 C4
Café Belge	31 A3
Café des Amis	32 A3
Café St Pierre	33 B3
Good Food Café	34 B4
Goods Shed	35 A2

DRINKING
Loft	36 B4
Simple Simons	37 C2
Thomas Becket	38 B3

Cathedral Gate Hotel	24 C3
Chaucer Hotel	25 C4
Greyfriars Guesthouse	26 B3
Pilgrim's Hotel	27 B3
Tudor House	28 B3
White House	29 B3

ENTERTAINMENT
Alberry's Wine Bar	39 B4
Baa Bars	40 B5
Marlowe Theatre	41 B3
Odeon Cinema	42 C4
Orange St Music Club	43 B3

TRANSPORT
Bus Station	44 C4
Downland Cycles	45 A2

THE SOUTHEAST COAST

INTERNET ACCESS

Dotcafe (☎ 478778; 19-21 St Dunstan's St; per hr £3; ⏰ 10am-7pm) Large cyber café near the railway station.

Main library (☎ 463608; 18 High St; ⏰ 9.30am-6pm Mon-Sat) Free internet access in the same building as the Royal Museum & Art Gallery.

MEDICAL SERVICES

Canterbury Health Centre (☎ 452444; 26 Old Dover Rd) For general medical consultations.

Kent & Canterbury Hospital (☎ 766877; Etherbert Rd) Has an emergency room and is a mile from the centre.

MONEY

ATMs and other major banks are on High St, near the corner of St Margaret's St.

Lloyd's TSB (28 St Margaret's St) Has a bureau de change.

LAUNDRY

Canterbury Laundrette (☎ 452211; Nunnery Fields; ⏰ 9am-6pm Mon-Fri, to 4pm Sat, to 3pm Sun)

POST

Post office (29 High St; ⏰ 9am-5.30pm Mon-Sat)

TOURIST OFFICES

Tourist office (☎ 378100; www.canterbury.co.uk; 12 Sun St; ⏰ 9.30am-5pm Mon-Sat, 10am-4pm Sun Easter-Oct, 10am-4pm Mon-Sat Nov-Easter) Situated opposite the cathedral gate; the staff can help book accommodation, excursions and theatre tickets.

Sights

CANTERBURY CATHEDRAL

It's hard to imagine a more imposing mother church for Anglicanism than this majestic early Gothic **cathedral** (☎ 762862; www.canterbury -cathedral.org; adult/concession £5/4; ⏰ 9am-6pm Mon-Sat May-Aug, 9am-4.30pm Mon-Sat Sep-Apr, plus 12.30-2.30pm & 4.30-5.30pm Sun year-round), the centrepiece of the city's World Heritage Site and repository of over 1400 years of Christian history.

It's an overwhelming edifice filled with enthralling stories, striking architecture and a very real and enduring sense of spirituality. Though visitors can't help but pick up on the ominous undertones of violence and blood-shed that whisper from its walls.

This great antique war machine is chock-a-block with monuments commemorating the nation's battles. Also here is the grave and heraldic tunic of one of the nation's most famous warmongers, Edward the Black Prince (1330–76). And of course, it was here that saintly Archbishop Thomas Becket met his

grisly end at the altar (see the boxed text, p186). You'll find the very spot that has drawn pilgrims for over 800 years in the northwest transept, marked by a lit candle and striking modern altar.

The doorway to the crypt is beside the altar. This cavernous space is the cathedral's highlight, an entrancing 11th-century survivor from the cathedral's last devastating fire in 1174, which destroyed the rest of the building. Look for original carvings among the forest of pillars.

The wealth of detail in the cathedral is immense and unrelenting, so it's well worth joining a one-hour **tour** (adult/child £4/2; ⏰ 10.30am, noon & 2.30pm Mon-Fri, 10.30am, noon & 1.30pm Sat Apr-Sep, noon & 2pm Mon-Sat Oct-Mar), or you can take a 30-minute self-guided **audio tour** (adult/child £2.95/1.95). There is an additional charge to take photographs.

When you leave the cathedral, go round the eastern end and turn right into **Green Court**, surrounded on the eastern side by the Deanery and the northern side (straight ahead) by the early-14th-century Brewhouse and Bakehouse, which now house part of the very exclusive prep school, **King's School**. In the northwestern corner (far left) is the famous **Norman Staircase** (1151).

MUSEUMS

If you're in the mood for museums the Museum Passport (adult/child £6/3.60) will grant you free admission to all the following. Individual charges are given with each listing.

A fine 14th-century building, once the Poor Priests' Hospital, now houses the absorbing **Museum of Canterbury** (☎ 475202; www .canterbury-museums.co.uk; Stour St; adult/child £3.30/2.20; ⏰ 10.30am-5pm Mon-Sat year-round, plus 1.30-5pm Sun Jun-Sep), which has varied exhibits from pre-Roman times to the assassination of Becket, Joseph Conrad to locally born celebs. The kids' room is excellent, with a memorable glimpse of real medieval poo among other fun activities. There's also a fun Rupert Bear Museum (Mary Tourtel, creator of the yel-low-chequered trousered bear, was born in Canterbury).

A fascinating subterranean archaeological site forms the basis of the **Roman Museum** (☎ 785575; Butchery Lane; adult/child £3/1.85; ⏰ 10am-5pm Mon-Sat year-round, plus 1.30-5pm Sun Jun-Oct), which lets you get hands on with artefacts and walk around reconstructed rooms. The museum

---

THE CANTERBURY TALES

If English literature has a father figure, then it is Geoffrey Chaucer (1342/3–1400). Chaucer was the first English writer to introduce characters – rather than 'types' – into fiction, and he did so to greatest effect in his most popular work, *The Canterbury Tales*.

Written between 1387 and his death, the *Tales* is an unfinished series of 24 vivid stories as told by a party of pilgrims on their journey from London to Canterbury and back. Chaucer successfully created the illusion that the pilgrims, not Chaucer (though he appears in the tales as himself), are telling the stories, which allowed him unprecedented freedom as an author.

Chaucer's achievement remains a high point of European literature, but it was also the first time that English came to match Latin (the language of the Church) and French (spoken by the Norman court) as a language of high literature. *The Canterbury Tales* remains one of the pillars of the literary canon, but more than that it's a collection of rollicking good yarns of adultery, debauchery, crime and edgy romance, and filled with Chaucer's witty observances of human nature. That said, contemporary modern readers tend to make more sense of modern transliterations than the often obscure original Old English version.

---

culminates with the original mosaic floors, which despite dim lighting and awkward display, are impressive.

The city's only remaining medieval gateway, a brawny 14th-century bulk with murder holes pointing over the passing cars below, is home to the small **West Gate Museum** (☎ 789576; St Peter's St; adult/concession £1.20/75p; ﹆ 11am-12.30pm & 1.30-3.30pm Mon-Sat) of arms and armour. The rooftop views are worth squeezing up the spiral staircase for.

The mock-Tudor façade of the **Royal Museum & Art Gallery** (☎ 452747; High St; admission free; ﹆ 10am-5pm Mon-Sat) is a splendid display of Victorian foppery, with intricate carving and big wooden gables. The interior houses mostly ho-hum art and military memorabilia, but has a few surprises from the likes of Pissaro, Henri Moore and Van Dyke.

THE CANTERBURY TALES

Aiming to resurrect Chaucer's classic characters in all their respective smutty, bawdy, conniving and holier-than-thou technicolour, the ambitious **Canterbury Tales** (☎ 479227; www.canterburytales.org.uk; St Margaret's St; adult/child £7.25/5.25; ﹆ 10am-5pm Mar-Jun, 9.30am-5pm Jul-Aug, 10am-5pm Sep-Oct, 10am-4.30pm Nov-Feb) certainly makes for an entertaining 45 minutes trailing through a series of reconstructed scenes from the book. While the jerky animatronics could never do full justice to the classic tales, it's a lively introduction for the young or uninitiated.

ST AUGUSTINE'S ABBEY

An integral but oft-overlooked part of the Canterbury World Heritage Site, **St Augustine's**

Abbey (EH; ☎ 767345; adult/child £3.90/2; ﹆ 10am-6pm Apr-Sep, 10am-4pm Wed-Sun Oct-Mar) was founded in AD 597, marking the rebirth of Christianity in southern England. Later requisitioned as a royal palace, it was to fall into disrepair and now only stumpy foundations remain. A small museum and a worthwhile audio tour do their best to underline the site's importance and put flesh back on its now humble bones.

ST MARTIN'S CHURCH

This stumpy little **church** (☎ 768072; North Holmes Rd; admission free; ﹆ 11am-4pm Tue, Thu & Sat Apr-Sep, to 3pm Oct-Mar) is thought to be England's oldest parish in continuous use, and where Queen Bertha (wife of the Saxon King Ethelbert) welcomed Augustine upon his arrival in the 6th century. The original Saxon church has been swallowed by a medieval refurbishment, but it's still worth the 900m walk east of the abbey.

EASTBRIDGE HOSPITAL & GREYFRIARS CHAPEL

A 'place of hospitality' for poor pilgrims, soldiers and the elderly since its foundation in 1180, the Hospital of St Thomas the Martyr **Eastbridge** (☎ 471688; www.eastbridgehospital.org.uk; 25 High St; adult/under 5yr/5-16yr/senior £1/free/50p/75p; ﹆ 10am-5pm Mon-Sat) is worth a visit for the Gothic-arched undercroft and historic chapel. Its 16th-century almshouses are still in use today.

In serene riverside gardens behind the hospital you'll find **Greyfriars Chapel** (admission free; ﹆ 2-4pm Mon-Sat Easter-Sep), the first English monastery built by Franciscan monks in 1267.

Tours

Canterbury Walks (☎ 459779; www.canterbury
-walks.co.uk; adult/under 12yr/senior & student
£4.25/3/3.75; ☼ 2pm daily Apr-Oct, plus 11.30am Mon-
Sat Jul–mid-Sep) Chaperoned walking tours; leave from
the tourist office.

Canterbury Historic River Tours (☎ 07790 534744;
www.canterburyrivertours.co.uk; adult/child £5.50/4;
☼ 10am-5pm Apr-Sep) Will take you on a rowing-boat
tour including (prebooked) candlelit tours, from behind
The Old Weaver's House on St Peter's St.

Canterbury River Navigation Company (☎ 07816
760869; www.crnc.co.uk; Westgate Gardens; adult/child
£7/4; ☼ Apr-Sep) Relaxing punt trips.

Ghost Tours (☎ 07779 575831; adult/child £5/4)
Depart from outside Alberrys wine bar in St Margaret's St
at 8pm year-round every Friday and Saturday. Only groups
need book.

Festivals & Events

Myriad musicians, comedians, theatre groups
and other artists from around the world come
to the party for two weeks in mid-October,
during the **Canterbury Festival** (☎ 452853; www
.canterburyfestival.co.uk).

Sleeping
BUDGET

Yew Tree Park (☎ 700306; www.yewtreepark.com; Stone
St, Petham; tent & 2 adults £11-15; ☼ Apr-Sep; Ⓟ 🖳 wi-
fi 🖳) This lovely family-run camp site set in
gently undulating countryside, 5 miles south
of Canterbury, has plenty of soft grass to pitch
a tent on. Call for directions and transportation information.

Kipp's Independent Hostel (☎ 786121; www.kipps
-hostel.com; 40 Nunnery Fields; dm/s/d £14/18.50/32; ✗ 🖳)
This gabled town house impresses with its relaxed, just-like-home atmosphere with friendly
folk and long-term residents, lots of communal
areas, clean though cramped dorms, bike hire,
space for a few tents in the garden and an adorable pet Labrador. It's just south of the centre.

YHA Hostel (☎ 462911, canterbury@yha.org.uk; 54 New
Dover Rd; dm £16.95; Ⓟ ✗ 🖳) Further out but
worth it, this grand Victorian Gothic-style villa
is spacious and organised, with a garden and
cheaper prepared tent accommodation. It's a
great deal, and has single rooms and a bureau
de change. It's 1¼ miles southeast of the centre,
and open year-round by advanced booking.

MIDRANGE

Tudor House (☎ 765650; 6 Best Lane, s £25-35, d £48-55;
✗) Three overlapping storeys decorated by

whitewashed shingles introduce this historic
guesthouse, which sits beside the river near
the High St. While the interior underplays
its period features, it has a cheerful and personable atmosphere, seven clean rooms with
downmarket but cosy décor, sloping floors
and the odd exposed beam.

Cathedral Gate Hotel (☎ 464381; cgate@cgate.dem
on.co.uk; 36 Burgate; s/d without bathroom from £35/50,
with bathroom from £60/90; ✗) Canterbury's most-
photographed hotel adjoins the spectacular
cathedral's gate, which it predates: a fact increasingly believable upon exploring its labyrinthine passageways where few rooms escape
an angled floor, low door or wonky walls.
Rooms are simple, but barring camping on
the cathedral's stone porch you simply can't
get a better position.

Castle House (☎ 761897; www.castlehousehotel.co.uk;
28 Castle St; s/d/f from £45/65/85; Ⓟ ✗ 🖳) Sitting opposite the ruins of Canterbury's Norman castle,
and incorporating part of the old city walls,
this tastefully decorated early-18th-century
guesthouse has an amiable welcome and seven
classic high-ceilinged rooms. Families are very
welcome.

White House (☎ 761836; www.canterburybreaks
.co.uk; 6 St Peter's Lane; s/d/f £50/70/80; 🖳 ✗) This
exceedingly handsome Regency town house,
supposedly once home to Queen Victoria's
head coachman, has a friendly welcome, nine
spick-and-span rooms with delicate floral patterns, period features and a few unexpected
frills like tasselled light switches and classical
music over breakfast.

Pilgrim's Hotel (☎ 464531; www.pilgrimshotel.com;
18 The Friars; s/d/f £55/75/99; Ⓟ ✗) Exit stage left
from the Marlowe Theatre and you'll stumble
upon this 16th-century hotel, the chintzy tra-
ditionalist interior of which is appointed with
a few country-style antiques and 15 pleasantly
comfortable rooms. There's a two-night minimum at weekends.

Other options:

Greyfriars Guesthouse (☎ 456255; www.greyfriars
-house.co.uk; 6 Stour St; s/d/f from £35/55/75; Ⓟ ✗)
Former church-dormitory with décor your aunt would pick.

Kingsmead House (☎ 760132; john.clark52@
btopenworld.com; 68 St Stephens Rd; s/d £35/60; ✗)
Timber-framed 17th-century house north of the centre.

TOP END

Chaucer Hotel (☎ 464427; www.swallowhotels.com;
63 Ivy Lane; s/d from £93/115; Ⓟ ✗) Just outside
the old city walls, this once elegant red-brick

Georgian house now has the aura of a chain hotel: plush but more than a little bland. The position makes up for its lack of personality, however.

Abode Canterbury (☎ 766266; www.abodehotels.co.uk; 30 High St) Right in the very heart of the city on a busy shopping street opposite the striking Royal Museum & Art Gallery, Canterbury's most central top ender was set to reopen after a thorough revamp and ownership change at the time of writing. Check the website for details.

Eating

Café St Pierre (☎ 456791; 40 St Peter's St; snacks £2-3.50; ☒ 8am-6pm Mon-Sat, 9am-5.30pm Sun) A bona fide little French coffee shop with melt-in-the-mouth pastries and bistro-style specials, St Pierre's offers people-watching to the front or on a tranquil little garden at the back.

Good Food Café (☎ 456654; 1 Jewry Lane; soups £3.95, specials £6.95; ☒ 11am-3pm Tue-Fri, 10am-4pm Sat) They aren't kidding. The vegetarian food at this simple but elegant café above a health-food store is more than good. Plates overflow with locally sourced, organic and biodynamically grown veggies and daily specials such as tortillas and lasagne.

Café des Amis (☎ 464390; 95 St Dunstan's St; mains £7-13; ☒ lunch & dinner) This fun Mexican restaurant is well loved for its all-afternoon lunch, great food in enormous portions and a lively colourful atmosphere augmented by Latin music, entertaining artwork, beautiful staff and chilled margaritas.

Goods Shed (☎ 459153; Station Rd West; lunch £8-12, dinner £10-16; ☒ market 10am-7pm Tue-Sat & 10am-4pm Sun, restaurant lunch & dinner Tue-Sun) Farmers market, food hall and fabulous restaurant all rolled into one, this converted station warehouse by the railway is a hit with everyone from self-caterers to sit-down gourmets. The chunky wooden tables sit slightly above the market hubbub but in full view of its appetite-whetting stalls, and country-style daily specials exploit the freshest farm goodies available.

Café Belge (☎ 768222; 89-90 St Dunstans St; mains £8.95-16; ☒ lunch & dinner) Think Belgian meal times and mussels, *frites* and beer spring to mind, but this award-winning restaurant will astonish with its variety. Its '50 ways to eat a mussel' leaves diners drooling, and the list of beers tops a hundred. The cosy dining area is decorated with images of Tin Tin and pop art.

Azouma (☎ 760076; 4 Church St; mains £10-14; ☒ lunch & dinner) Behind a timber-framed façade

WORTH THE TRIP

Housed in a splendid Georgian mansion in large elegant grounds, **Read's Restaurant with Rooms** (☎ 01795-535344; www.reads .com; Macknade Manor, Canterbury Rd, Faversham; lunch/dinner £21/48; (P) (X)) sets out to be a quintessentially English venue, and pulls its off with the highest class. Its Michelin-starred chef has a menu firmly grounded in garden herbs, local produce and classic combinations. There are also six enormous rooms (double £155 to £185) decorated in equally traditional fashion. To cap it off Read's has impeccable service and is only a short drive to Canterbury.

lies this sumptuous North African, Arabian and Mediterranean spot, which serves up rich mezzes and roasted couscous amid vivid Moroccan finery. There's belly dancing on Thursdays, and hubbly bubbly hookah pipes to finish.

Drinking

Simple Simons (☎ 762355; 3-9 Church Lane) If you've come to England on a real-ale pilgrimage, this is one stop you shouldn't miss. A medley of local beers, guest ales, stouts, porters and scrumpy line the bar in this atmospheric 15th-century pub, which has heavy-beamed ceiling, roaring fire and a rhododendron-dotted rear garden.

Thomas Beckett (☎ 464384; 21 Best Lane) Another classic English pub with a garden's worth of hops hanging from its timber frame, several quality ales to sample and a traditional décor of copper pots, comfy seating and a fireplace to cosy up to on winter nights. It also serves decent pub grub (mains £6 to £9).

Loft (☎ 456515; 516 St Margaret's St) A world away from Canterbury's quaint alehouses, this slick Londonesque bar plays chilled electronic beats in a retro-edged setting with one extremely long couch, a black granite bar and DJs spinning at the weekend. It draws a youthful crowd and serves a medley of multicoloured cocktails.

Entertainment

NIGHTCLUBS

Alberry's Wine Bar (☎ 452378; St Margaret's St) Every night is different at this hip after-hours music bar, which puts on everything from smooth

THE SOUTHEAST COAST

live jazz to DJ-led drum and bass to commercial pop. It's a two-level place where you can relax over a French Kiss (cocktail or otherwise) above, before partying in the basement bar below.

Baa Bars (☎ 462520; 15 Station Rd East; admission £3) There are three floors of different DJs, dance floors and bars at this edgy, almost industrial-looking, nightclub beside the train station.

Orange St Music Club (☎ 760801; www.orangestreet music.com; 15 Orange St; ☯ Tue-Sat) This Bohemian music and cultural whatnot venue in a 19th-century hall puts on a medley of jazz, salsa, folk, DJ competitions, hip-hop and even poetry.

CINEMAS
Odeon Cinema (☎ 0871 224 4007; cnr Upper Bridge St & St George's Pl) Catch the latest movies here.

Cinema 3 (☎ 769075; University of Kent) Part of the Gulbenkian Theatre complex. Shows a mix of mainstream and arty films and old classics.

THEATRE
Marlowe Theatre (☎ 787787; www.marlowetheatre .com; The Friars) Canterbury's central venue for performing arts brings in some wonderful touring plays, dances, concerts and musicals year-round.

Gulbenkian Theatre (☎ 769075; www.kent.ac.uk /gulbenkian; University of Kent) Out on the university campus, this large long-time venue puts on plenty of contemporary plays, modern dance and great live music.

Getting There & Away
Canterbury is 58 miles (93km) from London and 15 miles from Margate and Dover.

BUS
The bus station is just within the city walls off High St. There are frequent buses to London Victoria (£11.40, two hours, hourly), and services to Dover (35 minutes) hourly. Around three buses per hour run to Margate (53 minutes), and twice hourly to Broadstairs (one hour) and Ramsgate (one hour 20 minutes). Services to Whitstable leave every 15 minutes (30 minutes).

TRAIN
There are two train stations: Canterbury East (for the YHA hostel), accessible from London Victoria; and Canterbury West, accessible from London's Charing Cross, Victoria and Waterloo stations.

London-bound trains leave frequently (£18.70, 1½ hours, two to three hourly), as do Canterbury East to Dover Priory trains (£5.20, 16 to 28 minutes, every 30 minutes).

Getting Around
Canterbury's centre is mostly pedestrianised. Car parks are dotted along and just within the walls. Central parking vouchers cost from £6 to £10 for 24 hours or £1 to £1.60 per daytime hour. Daytrippers may prefer to use one of the city's three park and ride sites, which cost £2 per day and are connected to the centre by buses every 10 minutes from 7am to 7.30pm Monday to Saturday, or 10am to 6pm Sunday.

Taxi companies include **Cathedral Cars** (☎ 451000) and **Cabwise** (☎ 712929). **Downland Cycles** (☎ 479643; www.downlandcycles.co.uk; ☯ 10am-6pm Tue-Sat, 11am-5pm Sun) rents bikes from the London-bound platform at Canterbury West station. Bikes cost £12 per day with helmet.

AROUND CANTERBURY
Howlett's Wild Animal Park
You can trade grins and glowers with the world's largest captive breeding collection of lowland gorillas at this 28-hectare **park** (☎ 01227-721286; www.totallywild.net; Bekesbourne; adult/ under 4yr/4-16yr £13.95/free/10.95; ☯ 10am-6pm Apr-Sep, to 5pm Oct-Mar). Rather than simply keeping the animals in captivity, the park funds projects to reintroduce these rare and endangered animals back to their natural habitat. You'll also see tigers, African elephants, monkeys, giant anteaters, rhinos and more.

The park is 4 miles east of Canterbury. By car, take the A257 and turn right at the sign for Bekesbourne, then follow the signs. Several regular buses run from Canterbury bus station to Littlebourne, from where it's about a mile's walk.

Chilham
Compact little Chilham is a near-perfect example of a medieval 'one master and his serfs' kind of town, five miles southwest of Canterbury on the A252. Clustered in typical feudal fashion around a square beside the 12th-century castle, the village consists of a 13th-century church and Tudor and Jacobean timber-framed houses.

The town makes a lovely day's walking destination from Canterbury via the North Downs Way (see p180). Hourly trains also run from Canterbury (nine minutes). The centre is a half-mile walk from the station.

WHITSTABLE
☎ 01227 / pop 30,159
Famous for its succulent oysters, which have been harvested off these warm shores since Roman times, Whitstable has an unspoiled charm far removed from other regional resorts. Still a humble fishing village at heart, its streets sport names like Squeeze Gut Alley and Skinner's Alley, and a host of venerable old seafood restaurants. The shingle beach is barbed with rows of groins, but is a pretty stretch nonetheless, dotted with multicoloured beach huts and overlooked by sharp cliffs east of town. And from atop the grass-topped Tankerton Slopes you can spy the Street, a narrow shingle ridge stretching half a mile out to sea but only exposed at low tide.

The **tourist office** (☎ 275482; www.visitwhitstable .co.uk; 7 Oxford St; ☼ 10am-5pm Mon-Sat Jul & Aug, to 4pm Mon-Sat Sep-Jun) can help you find and book accommodation, while the nearby **library** (☎ 273309; 31-33 Oxford St; ☼ 9.30am-6pm Mon, Tue, Thu & Fri, to 1pm Wed, to 4pm Sat) can make you a temporary member to use its internet terminals.

The modest **Whitstable Museum & Gallery** (☎ 276998; www.whitstable-museum.co.uk; 8 Oxford St; admission free; ☼ 10am-4pm Mon-Sat year-round, plus 1-4pm Sun Jul & Aug) has good exhibits on Whitstable's oyster and fishing industry.

Festivals & Events
For a week at the end of July, the town hosts seafood, arts and music extravaganza, the **Whitstable Oyster Festival** (www.whitstableoysterfes tival.co.uk), which not only gives you double the excuse to wash down juicy oysters with Guinness or champagne but offers a packed schedule of events, from the traditional 'blessing of the waters' to samba and jazz bands, oyster-eating competitions to a beer festival.

Sleeping
Alliston (☎ 779066; bobgough57@aol.com; 1 Joy Lane; s/d £40/60; P ✗) A 10-minute walk from the centre, this delightful B&B is run by a charming double act of Ernie Wise and Albert Finney lookalikes. It has just three spacious, pristine rooms with plenty of daylight, and breakfast is served looking out over the pretty garden.

Hotel Continental (☎ 280280; www.hotelcontinental .co.uk; 29 Beach Walk; s/d/huts from £55/60/100, d with sea view & balcony £100; P ✗) This elegant three-storey Art Deco building by the waterfront has cheerfully decorated if somewhat overpriced rooms as well a row of charmingly converted fisherman's huts on the beach. Room rates increase by £35 to £45 at weekends, and in July and August.

Eating
Whitstable's famous oysters are harvested between April and September.

Wheeler's Oyster Bar (☎ 273311; 8 High St; mains £13-19; ☼ lunch & dinner Thu-Tue) This adorable little spot has served oysters since 1856, and continues to peddle the freshest catch as passionately as ever. It also has a tiny Victorian parlour, filled with seafaring gear and old photos, for a dignified sit-down meal.

Whitstable Oyster Fishery Co Restaurant (☎ 276856; www.oysterfishery.co.uk; The Horsebridge; mains £13-25; ☼ lunch & dinner Tue-Sun) The most famous seafood restaurant in the region sits right beside the water and serves a variety of simply cooked, fresh-from-the-nets treats from sea bass to cockles.

Getting There & Away
Buses 4 and 6 go to Canterbury (30 minutes) every 15 minutes.

AROUND WHITSTABLE
Herne Bay
A host of waterborne tours run from the jetty at nearby Herne Bay, the best of which is on the **Wildlife** (☎ 01227-366712; www.wildlifesailing.com; 8 Western Esplanade; ☼ Apr-Oct), a traditionally styled boat with a knowledgeable skipper that sails to an offshore sandbank packed with seals. Trips last five hours and prices depend on group size but start from £16 each. Another company to try is **Bayblast Tours** (☎ 373372; www .bayblast.co.uk; 3hr seal trip £32; ☼ Apr-Oct).

There's an enjoyable coastline walk two miles east from Herne Bay into **Reculver Country Park** (admission free), where you'll find the remains of a Roman fort built in AD 280 and the 7th-century Saxon Church of St Mary. The church collapsed in 1809 due to coastal erosion, but the distinctive 12th-century twin towers have been rebuilt. It's an atmospheric if melancholic site that dominates the flat scenery around it.

Buses run from Whitstable to Herne Bay (20 minutes, every 15 minutes). Stagecoach buses 7 and 36 also go from Herne Bay train station to Reculver Park.

THE SOUTHEAST COAST

ISLE OF THANET

You won't need a ferry or a wetsuit to reach this island, which was swallowed by the mainland during the first millennium as the Watsun Channel dried up. It now forms a perky peninsula jutting out to sea at the far eastern tip of the country. But in its island days, Thanet was the springboard to several epoch-making episodes of English history. It was here that the Romans kicked off their invasion in the first century AD, and where Augustine landed in AD 597 to begin his conversion of the pagans. These days, Thanet's pretty coastline is home to a string of Victorian resorts that are only invaded by the summer bathing-suit brigade. Walkers can also look to conquer the **Thanet Coastal Path**, a 20-mile trail that hugs the shore from Margate to Pegwell Bay via Broadstairs and Ramsgate.

Margate

☎ 01843 / pop 57,000

A popular seaside resort for over 250 years thanks to its fine-sand beaches, Margate still strives to recapture its Victorian heyday of candy-striped beach huts, donkey rides and Punch and Judy puppet shows. But these days it's more about amusements and chippies, and outside summer has the melancholy air of a town past its prime.

Visit the **tourist office** (☎ 292019; www.tourism .thanet.gov.uk; 12-13 The Parade; ◷ 9.15am-4.15pm Mon-Fri, 10am-4pm Sat) for maps and information.

SIGHTS

Margate's unique attraction is the mystifying subterranean **Shell Grotto** (☎ 220008; www.shell grotto.co.uk; Grotto Hill; adult/child £2.50/1.50; ◷ 10am-5pm daily Easter-Oct, 11am-4pm Sat & Sun Nov-April), a snug set of passageways discovered in 1835 and plastered with several million shells arranged in symbol-rich mosaics. It has inspired feverish speculation over the years but presents few answers; some think a 2000-year-old pagan temple, others an elaborate 19th-century hoax. Either way it's an exquisite place worth seeing.

A new **Turner Contemporary** (☎ 294208; www .turnercontemporary.org) gallery – a key part of Margate's plans for turnaround – is planned for the next few years to highlight the town's links with JMW Turner, although its location had not been decided at the time of writing.

SLEEPING & EATING

YHA Hostel (☎ 0870 770 5956; margate@yha.org.uk; The Beachcomber, 3-4 Royal Esplanade; dm member/nonmember £10.95/13.95; ✗) This faintly hotel-like hostel sits mere paces from a sandy Blue Flag beach and about half a mile west from the tourist office. It caters especially well to families. Book 48 hours in advance.

Elonville Hotel B&B (☎ 298635; www.elonvillehotel .com; 70-72 Harold Rd, Cliftonville; s/d with breakfast £30/60, without £25/50; P ✗ ☐ wi-fi) You may feel you've slid back in time to the 1980s at this friendly guesthouse, with hopeful palm-tree motifs and dated but cosy style. Rooms are simple but the lively hostess goes out of her way to serve.

Walpole Bay Hotel (☎ 221703; www.walpolebayhotel .co.uk; 5th Ave, Cliftonville; s/d from £50/70; ✗) For a dose of good ol' English eccentricity look no further than this musty part-hotel, part-museum of Victorian life. The pink flouncy rooms are furnished with antiques while public spaces are filled by glass-cased displays of 19th-century memorabilia. The hotel is a mile from central Margate, in Cliftonville.

Newbys Wine Bar & Brasserie (☎ 292888; 1 Market St; mains £8-13; ◷ dinner Thu, lunch & dinner Fri & Sat) In a town not blessed by good eateries, this is the best place for fine wines, country-fresh food and bubbly French atmosphere. It serves seasonal menus with good local seafood.

GETTING THERE & AWAY

Buses to Margate leave from London Victoria (£11.50, 2½ hours, five daily). From Canterbury take bus 8 (41 minutes, three hourly).

Trains run twice hourly from London Victoria and less frequently from Charing Cross (£21.60, 1¾ hours).

Broadstairs

☎ 01843 / pop 24,370

Unlike its bigger, brasher neighbours, the pretty little resort village of Broadstairs revels in its quaintness, plays the Victorian nostalgia card at every opportunity and names every second business after the works of its most famous holidaymaker, Charles Dickens. Behind the neatly manicured gardens, the cute little orange-sand bay and its wistful Punch and Judy shows, however, is a far grittier history of smuggling and shipbuilding.

The **tourist office** (☎ 861232; 2 Victoria Pde, Dickens House Museum; ◷ 10am-4pm Mon-Sat) has details of the annual, week-long **Dickens Festival** in mid-June which culminates in a banquet-cum-ball in Victorian dress (£15). It's located in the quaint **Dickens House Museum** (☎ 861232; www .dickenshouse.co.uk; 2 Victoria Pde; adult/child £2.30/1.20; ❂ 10am-4pm Apr-Oct), which was actually the home of Mary Pearson Strong, inspiration for the character of Betsey Trotwood in *David Copperfield*. Diverse Dickensiana on display includes letters from the author.

Dickens wrote parts of *Bleak House* and *David Copperfield* in the handsome if slightly worse-for-wear clifftop house above the pier between 1837 and 1859. Now private property, it suffered severe fire damage in 2006.

SLEEPING & EATING

Hanson Hotel (☎ 868936; hotelhanson@aol.com; 41 Belvedere Rd; s/d £28/50, d with bathroom £54) Smothered from top to toe in creeping vines that change colour with the seasons, this small eight-room hotel is on a quiet residential street near the waterfront and has a jumble of old and new furnishings.

Victoria (☎ 871010; www.thevictoriabroadstairs.co.uk; 23 Victoria Pde; s from £52-117, d £88-129; ✗) A refined spot with service to match, this Victorian house has plentiful period style and features six spotlessly maintained bedrooms. And if that doesn't convince you, it's a mere stone's throw from the beach.

Thai Four Two (☎ 862925; 42 York St; mains £4.50-7; ❂ 6-9pm Mon-Thu, 6-11pm Fri & Sat) This restful little nook with trickling fountains, lush greenery and bamboo chairs serves wonderful homestyle Thai food, most of which can be adapted for vegetarians.

GETTING THERE & AWAY

The Thanet Loop bus runs every 15 minutes through the day to Ramsgate (20 minutes) and Margate (20 minutes).

Buses 8 and 9 also run twice hourly to Canterbury (1½ hours) via Margate, Broadstairs and Ramsgate. National Express buses leave High St for London Victoria (£11.50, three hours, five daily).

Trains to London Victoria (£22.50, 1¾ to 2¼ hours) leave twice hourly and there are less frequent services to London Bridge and Charing Cross. You may have to change at Ramsgate.

Ramsgate

☎ 01843 / pop 38,200

More welcoming than jaded big sis Margate and livelier than twee little neighbour Broad-

stairs, Ramsgate is the kind of varied and often quirky resort town that can appeal to all ages. While families and surfers still splash about along the Blue Flag beach, cosmopolitan bars and easygoing street cafés line the marina and seafront promenade, and a different breed of cultural visitor is drawn to the town's rich maritime history and neo-Gothic architecture. And picturesquely sheltered below the town's handsomely arched harbour walls is a forest of rigging that creaks and whistles in the sea breeze.

On a small alleyway off Leopold St, the **tourist office** (☎ 583333; www.tourism.thanet.gov.uk; 17 Albert Ct; ❂ 9.15am-4.15pm Mon-Fri) has information and a self-guided walking map of the areas smugglers' caves.

SIGHTS & ACTIVITIES

When the sun shines, rollerbladers, coffee quaffers, surfers and sunbathers all make a beeline to Ramsgate's reddish-sand and shingle beach and pleasant promenade, to the east of the main harbour under an imposing cliff.

At least 620 hapless ships have been wrecked in the notorious Goodwin Sands off this stretch of coast, and an intriguing assortment of loot from their barnacled carcasses can be found in the **Ramsgate Maritime Museum** (☎ 290399; www.ekmt.co.uk; The Clock House, Royal Harbour; adult/child £1.50/75p; ❂ 10am-5pm Tue-Sun Easter-Sep, 11am-4.30pm Thu-Sun Oct-Easter), inside the town's 19th-century clocktower near the harbour. Here too is a line marking Ramsgate's own meridian (the town has its own Ramsgate Mean Time).

SLEEPING

Crescent (☎ 591419; www.ramsgate-uk.com; 19 Wellington Cres; s/d from £25/50) This guesthouse is the prettiest building in a row of curvaceous three-storey Georgian homes on a seafront clifftop. It's run by very affable DIYers who keep its dozen rooms in good order. There are a few en suites for £10 more.

Royal Harbour Hotel (☎ 591514; www.royalharbourhotel.co.uk; Nelson Crescent; s/d from £65/85, superior £100-215; ✗ ⬜) Occupying a parallel seafront crescent to the west, this boutique hotel exudes an infectious enthusiasm. Books, paintings and newspapers lie everywhere and the 'cabins' have squeaky clean blue-and-white wood-panelled décor and postcard views over the forest of masts below.

EATING

Peter's Fish Factory (97 Harbour St; fish & chips from £2.95; 🕑 11.30am-11.30pm) Follow the tangy smells of salt and vinegar to this classic fish-and-chip shop (built in the shape of a giant sandcastle) with cheap, sinful and salty treats that can be devoured on outside seating.

Surin Restaurant (☎ 592001; www.surinrestaurant .co.uk; 30 Harbour St; mains £6-13; 🕑 lunch & dinner Tue-Sun) Ramsgate is an unlikely spot to eat some of the best Thai, Cambodian and Laotian food this side of the Hindu Kush, but sure enough, this darling little restaurant delivers. The restaurant is a dumpling's throw from the seafront and even serves its own label of microbrewed beers.

DRINKING

Ramsgate Brew House (☎ 594758; 98 Harbour Pde) Revelling in its own eccentricity, this part bakery, part brewery, part nuthouse on the harbourfront thumbs its nose at tradition. You're equally likely to see elderly bow-tied gents tinkering on the piano as ale-swilling holidaymakers, and civilised townfolk partaking of tea and pastries. Choose between outdoor tables or a vast sawdusty interior with ale-making paraphernalia and quirky nude statues.

Jazz Room (☎ 595459; 88 Harbour Pde; 🕑 1-11pm) Just steps away from the Ramsgate Brew House, this sophisticated Continental-flavour café-cocktail bar is a world away in ambience. It has high ceilings and soccer-goal-sized windows that it often throws open, an over-25s clientele and live jazz and funk on weeknights.

GETTING THERE & AWAY

National Express bus 22 runs to London Victoria (£11.50, three hours, five daily) via Margate and Broadstairs. There are also local buses to Canterbury, Broadstairs and Ramsgate. Trains run twice hourly to London Victoria and Charing Cross (£22.50, two hours).

TOP FIVE CASTLES

- Leeds Castle (Kent Weald; p202)
- Dover Castle (Dover; p198)
- Arundel Castle (Arundel; p221)
- Hever Castle (Kent Weald; p202)
- Bodiam Castle (Around Battle; p206)

There's also a ferry service to Ostend in Belgium run by **Transeuropa Ferries** (☎ 595522; www.transeuropaferries.com; 3 per day) from Ramsgate New Port just west of the centre (five hours, £39 per passenger with car).

SANDWICH

☎ 01304 / pop 4398

With a top slice of ancient churches, gables and peg-tiled roofs, a juicy filling of medieval streets and timber-framed houses, and a wholesome bottom slice of riverside strolls and superb golf links, Sandwich makes a very tasty morsel for passing travellers. Today it's a sleepy little inland settlement, but the town retains a certain salty tang from its days as an important Cinque Port before the coastline shifted and its harbour silted up in the 17th century.

Inside the Elizabethan Guildhall, the **tourist office** (☎ 613565; www.open-sandwich.co.uk; New St; 🕑 9.30am-4pm Apr-Oct) has information packs on short and long walks in the area. Guided tours of town can be arranged by contacting the **Sandwich Local History Society** (☎ 613476; £2; evenings only).

Sights & Activities

Sandwich's haphazard tangle of medieval and Elizabethan streets invites visitors to wander at will, and preferably get pleasurably lost amid them. **Strand St** in particular has one of the highest concentrations of half-timbered buildings in the country. Stepped gables betray the strong influence of Protestant Flemish refugees who settled in the town in the 16th century.

A dear little flint-chequered **Barbican** tollgate, also dating from this period, snares up traffic on the waterfront.

Architecture buffs should also track down the **Church of St Clement**, which has a superb Norman tower. Sandwich's earliest church, now retired, is **St Peter's** (King St). It's a real mishmash of styles and eras: its tower collapsed in dramatic fashion in 1661 and was rebuilt with a bulbous cupola. It houses sparse displays on the often scandalous earls of Sandwich, the fourth of which is credited with inventing the sandwich as a quick snack to eat whilst engrossed in gambling.

The historic Guildhall hosts a small but thorough **museum** (☎ 617197; adult/child £1/50p; 🕑 10.30am-12.30pm & 2-4pm Tue-Sat, 2-4pm Sun) on Sandwich's rich past as a Cinque Port.

THE SOUTHEAST COAST

CINQUE PORTS

Due to their proximity to Europe, the coastal towns of southeast England were the front line against raids and invasion during Anglo-Saxon times. In the absence of a professional army and navy, these towns were frequently called upon to defend themselves, and the kingdom, at land and sea.

In 1278 King Edward I formalised this already ancient arrangement by legally defining the Confederation of Cinque (pronounced 'sink', meaning five) Ports. The five head ports – Sandwich, Dover, Hythe, Romney and Hastings – were granted numerous perks and privileges in exchange for providing the king with ships and men. At their peak, the ports were deemed England's most powerful institution after Crown and Church.

Even after shifting coastlines silted up several Cinque Port harbours, a professional navy was based at Portsmouth and the ports' real importance evaporated, the pomp and ceremony remains. The Lord Warden of the Cinque Ports is a prestigious post now given to faithful servants of the crown. The most recent warden was the Queen Mother, while previous incumbents included the Duke of Wellington and Sir Winston Churchill.

On fair-weather days, hop aboard the **Sandwich River Bus** (☎ 07958 376 183; www.sandwichriverbus .co.uk; adult/child 30min trip £5/3, 1 hour £8/5; ⊗ every 30-60min 11am-6pm Thu-Sun Apr-Sep, Sun only Oct-Mar) beside the toll bridge for a quick river jaunt or out to Richborough (right).

Sandwich is also home to **Royal St Georges** (☎ 613090; www.royalstgeorges.com), one of the most challenging golf links in England.

Sleeping & Eating

King's Arms Hotel (☎ 617330; Strand St; s/d £40/75; P ⊗) Cosiness prevails in this eight-room 15th-century inn near the water, rumoured to have once put up Elizabeth I herself. The tastefully decorated rooms are spacious and well polished, and there's an atmospheric hops-decorated and low-beamed bar serving good food (mains £8 to £17) below.

Fisherman's Wharf (☎ 613636; The Quay; mains £8-17; ⊗ lunch & dinner) Lifebelts, nets and vines decorate the cute courtyard area at this waterside restaurant hidden around the corner from the old tollgate. You can enjoy its seafood-dominated menu outside on ironwork chairs, inside on chequered tablecloths or in the more formal upstairs dining area. Children are welcome.

Getting There & Away

National Express runs two daily buses from London Victoria to Deal (£11.50, 3¼ hours), from where a local bus takes you to Sandwich (25 minutes).

Trains run half-hourly from Dover Priory (23 minutes) or from London's Charing Cross or London Bridge (£22.50, 2¼ hours) to Sandwich.

Buses also go to Ramsgate (25 minutes, hourly), Dover (50 minutes, hourly) and Canterbury (40 minutes, hourly).

AROUND SANDWICH
Richborough

Roman Britain began right here amid the windswept ruins of **Richborough Roman Fort** (☎ 01304-612013; adult/under 5yr/5-15yr £3.90/free/2; ⊗ 10am-6pm Apr-Sep), just 2 miles north of Sandwich. This is the spot from which the successful AD 43 invasion of Britain was launched, then being a handy island base to muster forces. To celebrate their victory a colossal triumphal arch was planted here, the base of which remains. The fort's clearest features today – high walls and scores of deep defensive ditches that give it the appearance of a vast jelly mould – came later as the Romans were forced to stave off increasingly vicious seaborne attacks.

There's a small onsite museum and an audio tour to steer you through the rise and fall of Roman Richborough. To arrive as the Romans did, by boat, take the Sandwich River Bus (see left) from Sandwich. Return passengers pay an extra £2, but get a 25% discount for fort admission.

Deal

This peaceful little town's shingle beach was where Julius Caesar and his armies arrived for their first exploratory dip into Britain in 55 BC. Today there's a gorgeous little 16th-century **castle** (EH; ☎ 01304-372762, Victoria Rd; adult/under 5yr/5-15yr £3.90/free/2; ⊗ 10am-6pm Apr-Sep) with curvaceous bastions that form petals in a Tudor rose shape. Far from delicate, however, it's the largest and most complete of Henry VIII's chain of defence on the south coast.

And hardly a mile south is another link in the 16th-century coastal defences, **Walmer Castle** (EH; ☎ 01304-364288; Kingsdown Rd; adult/under 5yr/5-15yr £6.20/free/3.10; ⏰ 10am-6pm Apr-Sep, 10am-4pm Mar, 10am-4pm Wed-Sun Oct), the much-altered and really rather lavish official residence of the warden of the Cinque Ports (see boxed text, p197). English hero, the Duke of Wellington died here.

DOVER
☎ 01304 / pop 39,078

Dreary Dover is the kind of ugly port town that you either visit to pile on and off its ponderous cross-channel ferries steering the narrow 20-mile stretch to France, or else to make a dash for its premier attractions and move quickly on. That said, as attractions go it has several humdingers. The port's vital strategic position so close to the Continent gave rise to a vast and unusual hilltop castle with around 2000 years of history under its belt. Also here are the spectacular white cliffs that are as much a symbol of English wartime resilience as Winston Churchill or the Battle of Britain. However, the town itself has an embattled aura, with run-down postwar architecture and often palpable tensions between asylum seekers and long-term residents.

Orientation

Dover Castle dominates the town from a high promontory east of town, above the white cliffs. Ferry departures are from the Eastern Docks southeast of the castle. Dover Priory train station is a short walk west of the centre. The bus station is on Pencester Rd.

Information

Banks and ATMs are located on Market Sq.
Internet Café (☎ 242474; 21 High St; per hr £3; ⏰ 9am-10pm)
Mangle laundrette (Worthington St; per load £3; ⏰ 8am-8pm)
Post office (Pencester Rd; ⏰ 9am-5.30pm Mon-Sat)
White Cliffs Medical Centre (☎ 201705; 143 Folkestone Rd)
Tourist Office (☎ 205108; www.whitecliffscountry.org.uk; Biggin St; ⏰ 9am-5.30pm Mon-Fri, 10am-4pm Sat & Sun) Located in the Old Town Gaol and has accommodation- and ferry-booking services (both free).

Sights & Activities
DOVER CASTLE

Top contender for England's most formidable fortress, the gargantuan **Dover Castle** (EH; ☎ 211067; adult/under 5yr/5-15yr £9.50/free/4.80; ⏰ 10am-6pm Apr-Sep, 10am-5pm Oct, 10am-4pm Thu-Mon Nov-Jan, 10am-4pm Feb-Mar; P) was built to bolster the country's weakest point at this, the shortest sea-crossing to the Continent. It commandeers the sprawling hilltop over the city and commands a superb view of the English Channel as far as the French coastline.

The site has been in use for as many as 2000 years. On the vast grounds are the remains of a **Roman lighthouse**, which dates from AD 50 and may be the oldest standing building in Britain. Beside it lies a restored **Saxon church**.

The robust 12th-century **keep**, with walls up to 7m thick, is filled with reconstructed scenes of Henry VIII's visit, and its base shelters a sound-and-light re-creation of a brutal 13th-century siege. However, the castle's biggest attraction is the warren of claustrophobic **secret wartime tunnels** that honeycomb the cliffside. Excellent 50-minute tours delve into the hillside passageways, which were first excavated during the Napoleonic Wars and then expanded to house a command post and hospital in WWII. They now house reconstructed scenes of their wartime use, complete with sounds, smells and erratic lighting. One of Britain's most famous wartime operations, code-named Dynamo, was directed from here in 1940. It saw the evacuation of hundreds of thousands troops from the French beaches of Dunkirk.

Buses 90c and 111 run from Dover Priory station to the castle.

ROMAN PAINTED HOUSE

Some of the most extensive if stunted Roman wall paintings north of the Alps are on show at the **Roman Painted House** (☎ 203279; New St; adult/child £2/80p; ⏰ 10am-5pm Tue-Sun Apr-Sep), although they're housed in an amateurish museum. Several scenes depict Bacchus (the god of wine and revelry), which makes perfect sense as this large villa was built around AD 200 as a *mansio* (hotel) for travellers in need of a little lubrication to unwind. Some things never change.

OTHER SIGHTS & ACTIVITIES

By far the most enthralling exhibit in the three-storey **Dover Museum** (☎ 201066; www.dover museum.co.uk; Market Sq; adult/child £2.50/1.50; ⏰ 10am-

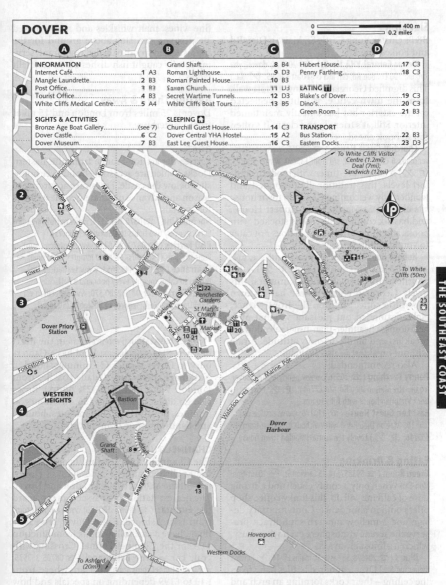

DOVER

0 ———— 400 m
0 ———— 0.2 miles

THE SOUTHEAST COAST

5.30pm Mon-Sat year-round & noon-5pm Sun Apr-Sep) is that of an astonishing 3600-year-old Bronze Age boat discovered here in 1992. Vaunted as the world's oldest-known seagoing vessel, it measures a thumping great 9.5m by 2.4m. Kids will love the touchy-feely activities, white coats and microscopes that accompany the exhibit.

The easily dizzied may prefer to avoid the **Grand Shaft** (admission £1; Snargate St; 2-5pm Tue-Sun Jul & Aug), which is a unique 43m triple staircase cut into the chalky white cliffs as a short cut for troops during the Napoleonic Wars. Make sure you phone the tourist office before arriving as it doesn't open every year.

Sleeping

B&Bs cluster along Castle St, Maison Dieu Rd and Folkestone Rd.

Dover Central YHA Hostel (☎ 201314; dover@yha .org.uk; 306 London Rd; dm incl breakfast £16.95; ☒ ▣) This dignified Georgian building, a short walk from the town centre, is a little neglected on the exterior but has a neatly maintained interior. Still, it's friendly and clean. It's often full so book ahead.

Churchill Guest House (☎ 208365; www.toastofdo ver.co.uk; 6 Castle Hill Rd; s/d from £35/50, winter £30/45; ℗ ☒) A stately old-timer with modern comfort levels, this traditionally decorated and wonderfully welcoming Georgian town house sits close to St Martin's and Hubert House, and has six comfortable rooms stocked with books and thoughtful extras. It does not cater to young children.

Hubert House (☎ 202253; www.huberthouse.co.uk; 9 Castle Hill Rd; s/d incl breakfast £40/50; ℗ ☒) A favourite with cross-channel swimmers, this lovely Georgian corner house has its own twee little coffee shop on the front terrace, eight outmoded but pleasant virginal-pink bedrooms, a healthier-than-usual selection for breakfast and family-friendly attitude. A rate without breakfast is also available.

Also recommended:

Penny Farthing (☎ 205563; www.pennyfarthingdover .co.uk; 109 Maison Dieu Rd; s/d £27/44; ℗ ☒) Greybrick Victorian house with frilly rooms.

East Lee Guest House (☎ 210176; www.eastlee.co .uk; 108 Maison Dieu Rd; d with/without breakfast from £52/46; ℗ ☒) Lovely terracotta-shingled town house.

Eating & Drinking

Green Room (☎ 593857; 14-15 Cannon St; ☯ 10am-6pm Mon-Sat) When only a comfy couch and a strong dose of caffeine will do, this funky coffee shop offers both in abundance. Contemporary design and a mellow modern soundtrack preserve the serene atmosphere even when busy, which it almost always is.

Dino's (☎ 204678; 58 Castle St; mains £7-14; ☯ lunch & dinner Tue-Sun) Over a hundred bottles hang from the ceiling – their corks forming an arch and decorating the front desk – of this wonderfully authentic family-run Italian restaurant. What it lacks in natural light, it makes up for with delicious freshly made pasta.

Blake's of Dover (☎ 202194; www.blakesofdover .com; 52 Castle St; mains £10-18; ☯ noon-3pm & 6-11.30pm Mon-Fri, lunch only Sat) This snug but stylish English restaurant has an intimate cellar bar with

fine wines, malt whiskies and microbrewed ales, or you can stay above ground for the sophisticated wood-panelled restaurant, serving locally caught fish dishes all on candlelit tables.

Getting There & Away

Dover is 75 miles from London and 15 miles from Canterbury.

BOAT

Ferries depart for France from the Eastern Docks (which are accessible by bus; see opposite) below the castle. Fares vary according to season and advance purchase. See the websites for specials.

Norfolk Line (☎ 0870 164 2114; www.norfolkline.com) Services every two hours to Dunkirk (1¾ hours).

P&O Ferries (☎ 0870 598 0333; www.poferries.com) Runs to Calais (1¼ hours) every 40 minutes to an hour.

Seafrance (☎ 0870 443 1653; www.seafrance.com) Ferries to Calais roughly every hour and a half.

SpeedFerries (☎ 0870 2200 570; www.speedferries. com) Up to five daily services to Boulogne (50 mins).

BUS

Dover's **bus station** (Pencester Rd) is in the heart of town. Stagecoach East Kent has a Canterbury to Dover service (35 minutes, hourly). National Express run 20 daily coaches from London Victoria (£11.50, 2¾ hours). Buses also go direct to Hastings (£6, two hours 50 minutes, hourly), Deal (45 minutes, hourly) and Sandwich (one hour, hourly).

CHANNEL TUNNEL

The Channel Tunnel begins its descent into the English Channel 9 miles west of Dover, just off the M20 between London and Dover. The nearest station foot passengers can board the **Eurostar** (☎ 08705 186186; www.eurostar.com) train is at Ashford. From Dover, it's easier if you have a car: follow signs from junction 11A for the Channel Tunnel. Crossing with your car via the **Eurotunnel** (☎ 08705 353535; www.eurotunnel.com) can cost anywhere from £49 to £199 depending on specials and how far ahead you book. For more information, see p781.

TRAIN

There are more than 40 trains daily from London Victoria and Charing Cross stations to Dover Priory via Ashford and Sevenoaks (£22.50, two hours).

Getting Around

The ferry companies run regular shuttle buses between the docks and the train station (five minutes) as they're a long walk apart.

Heritage (☎ 204420) and **Star Taxis** (☎ 228822) have 24-hour services. A one-way trip to Deal costs £12; to Sandwich it's £17.

AROUND DOVER
The White Cliffs

Immortalised in song, film and literature, these iconic cliffs are more than just precipices of 100m-high white chalk extending for 10 miles on either side of Dover and visible from France. They are a part of the national psyche, acting as a big white welcome-home sign to generations of travellers and soldiers.

It is the 6-mile stretch east of town – properly known as the Langdon Cliffs – that particularly captivates visitors' imaginations. The chalk here is about 250m deep, and the cliffs themselves are about half a million years old, formed when the melting icecaps of northern Europe were gouging a channel between France and England.

The Langdon Cliffs are managed by the National Trust, which has a **visitor centre** (☎ 01304-202756; admission free; ☾ 10am-5pm Mar-Oct, 11am-4pm Nov-Feb) and **car park** (£2.50 for nonmembers) 2 miles east of Dover.

From the visitor centre, a stony path snakes its way further east along the clifftops for a bracing 2-mile walk to the stout Victorian **South Foreland Lighthouse** (NT; ☎ 01304-202756; adult/child £3.60/1.80; ☾ guided tours 11am-5pm Fri-Mon late Apr-Oct). This was the first lighthouse to be powered by electricity, and site of the first international radio transmissions in 1898.

The cliffs are 2 miles east of Dover along Castle Hill Rd and the A258 road to Deal or off the A2 past the Eastern Docks. Buses Nos 113 and 90/1 from Dover stop near the main entrance.

To see them in all their full-frontal glory, **White Cliffs Boat Tours** (☎ 01303-271388; www.white cliffsboattours.co.uk; adult/child £6/3; ☾ daily Jul-Aug, Sat & Sun Apr-Jun & Sep-Oct) runs 40-minute water tours at 10am, noon, 2pm and 4pm from the Western Docks.

Romney Marsh

This eerie landscape of flat reed beds, sparsely populated and echoing with the whistling wind and lonely squawks of sea birds, was once a favourite haunt of smugglers and wreckers.

It's now home to kids' favourite and adults' worst sardine nightmare, the world's smallest-gauge public railway. Opened in 1927, the pocket-sized **Romney, Hythe & Dymchurch Railway** (☎ 01797-362353; www.rhdr.org.uk; adult/child £10.90/5.45; ☾ daily Apr-Sep, Sat & Sun Oct-Mar) trains trundle and toot their way 13.5 miles from Hythe to Dungeness lighthouse and back (roughly an hour each way). Cute, undoubtedly. But prone to cramped leg space and sore heads? You better believe it.

Dungeness

Jutting out from the lonely western edge of Romney Marsh is a low shingle spit overshadowed by a brooding nuclear power station. Despite the *Mad Max*–like desolation, this spot hosts an important nature reserve home to the largest sea-bird colony in the southeast. The **Royal Society for the Protection of Birds (RSPB) Nature Reserve** (☎ 01797-320588; www .rspb.org.uk; Dungeness Rd; adult/child £3/1; ☾ 9am-9pm or sunset, visitor centre ☾ 10am-5pm Mar-Oct, 10am-4pm Nov-Feb) has displays, binocular hire, explorer backpacks for kids, and information on bird-watching hides.

THE KENT WEALD

Known simply as the Weald by locals, this gently rolling stretch of Kent and East Sussex gets its name from an Old German world *wald*, meaning 'forest'. But today the timber is long-since harvested and replaced by lush fields, sleepy villages and neatly trimmed gardens, including the green-fingered triumph at Sissinghurst Castle. The region also hosts a huddle of extraordinary castles and manor houses.

Sevenoaks
☎ 01732 / pop 26,699

A pleasant commutersville just off the M25, Sevenoaks is home to one of the country's most celebrated country estates. The gates to glorious **Knole House** (NT; ☎ 450608; adult/child £7.50/3.75; ☾ noon-4pm Wed-Sun Apr-Oct) sit on the southern High St, and from there it's a beautiful winding walk or drive through a rolling medieval park dotted with bold deer. The 12th-century estate was snapped up in 1456 by Archbishop of Canterbury Thomas Bouchier, who was far from frugal in his religious outlook. He set about building a vast and lavish house 'fit for the Princes of the Church'. Its curious calendar design encompasses 365 rooms, 52 staircases and seven courtyards. The house was later home to Vita Sackville-West, whose love affair with Virginia Woolf spawned the novel *Orlando*, set at Knole.

The house is 1.5 miles southeast of Sevenoaks **train station** (London Rd). Trains leave every 15 minutes from London Charing Cross station (£7.30, 35 minutes) and three per hour continue to Tunbridge Wells (20 minutes) and Hastings (£13, 1¼ hours).

Chartwell

A breathtakingly intimate insight into the life of Sir Winston Churchill (see boxed text, p44), England's famous cigar-chomping bombast, can be found at **Chartwell** (☎ 01732-868381; Westerham; adult/child £10/5, garden & studio only £5/2.50; ☿ 11am-5pm Wed-Sun Apr-Jun & Sep-Oct, 11am-5pm Tue-Sun Jul & Aug), 6 miles east of Sevenoaks. This 19th-century house was his home from 1924 until his death in 1965.

The house and its lake-speckled grounds have been preserved much as Winnie left them, and you can almost picture him pacing about his study with a furrowed brow (he would often work standing up, saying he found it easier to think). Churchill was also a prolific painter and his daubings are scattered throughout the house and fill the garden studio.

Transport options are limited without a car. Coaches run from Sevenoaks train station (30 minutes) every two hours on Wednesdays from May to mid-September. Metrobus 401 runs on Sundays only.

Hever Castle

A few miles west of Tonbridge, this too-cute-to-be-true **castle** (☎ 01732-865224; www.hevercastle.co.uk; adult/5-14yr £9.80/5.30, gardens only £7.80/5; ☿ noon-6pm Mar-Oct, to 4pm Nov) sits amid a narrow duck-trailed moat, in family-friendly grounds with kooky topiary of woodland creatures in its outer courtyard, and no less than three mazes scattered about.

The castle is famous for being the childhood home of Anne Boleyn, mistress to Henry VIII and then his doomed queen. It dates from 1270, with a Tudor house added in 1505 by the Bullen (Boleyn) family. The castle later fell into disrepair until 1903, when it was bought by the American multimillionaire William Waldorf Astor, who poured obscene amounts of money into a massive refurbishment. The exterior is unchanged from Tudor

times, but the interior is thick with Edwardian panelling.

From London Victoria trains go to Hever (£7.70, 50 minutes, hourly; change at Hurst Green), a poorly signposted 1-mile walk from the castle. Alternatively, you could take a direct train from London Bridge to Edenbridge (£7.70, 37 to 50 minutes), from where it's a 4-mile taxi or bike ride.

Penshurst

Timber-framed Tudor houses and a fanciful four-spired church adorn the pretty village of Penshurst, 6 miles west of Tonbridge on the B2176, but most people come for majestic medieval manor house **Penshurst Place** (☎ 01892-870307; www.penshurstplace.com; adult/under 5yr/5-16yr £7.50/free/5; ☿ noon-4pm Apr-Oct). Its showpiece is the splendid **Baron's Hall**, built in 1341. It has a stunning 18m-high chestnut roof studded with satirical carved characters thought to be of workers in the estate. Just outside the main house is a vintage-toy museum with enough empty-eyed dolls to give even adults nightmares.

Outside, Penshurst's famous **walled gardens** (☿ 10.30am-6pm Apr-Oct) were designed in 1346 and remain virtually unchanged since Elizabethan times. There are also lovely riverside walks in the grounds.

From Edenbridge, buses 231 and 233 leave for Tunbridge Wells via Penshurst every hour (27 minutes).

Leeds Castle

This immense moated pile is for many the world's most romantic **castle** (☎ 01622-765400; www.leeds-castle.com; adult/4-15yr/senior & student £13.50/8/11; ☿ 10am-5pm Apr-Oct, to 3.30pm Nov-Mar), and it's certainly one of the most visited in Britain. While it looks formidable enough from the outside – a hefty structure balancing on two islands amid a large lake and sprawling estate – it actually has the reputation as something of a 'ladies castle'. This stems from the fact that in its over 1000 years of history, it has been home to a who's who of medieval queens, most famously Henry VIII's first wife, Catherine of Aragon.

The castle was transformed from fortress to lavish palace over the centuries, and its last owner, the high-society hostess Lady Baillie, used it as a princely family home and party pad to invite the likes of Errol Flynn, Douglas Fairbanks and JFK.

THE SOUTHEAST COAST

The castle's vast estate offers enough attractions of its own to justify a day trip: there are peaceful walks, a duckery, aviary and falconry demonstrations. You'll also find a quirky dog-collar museum and a hedge maze, overseen by a grassy bank where fellow travellers can shout encouragement or misdirections.

Since Lady Baillie's death in 1974, a private trust has managed the property. This means that some parts of the castle are periodically closed for private events.

Leeds Castle is just east of Maidstone. National Express runs one direct bus daily from London Victoria coach station, leaving at 9am and returning at 4.40pm (£10.80, 1½ hours). It must be prebooked. There is a combined entrance and bus-fare ticket that costs £18.

Southeastern Trains also offer an 'All-In-One' ticket combining travel from London Victoria to Bearsted Station (£25.50, one hour), a connecting coach service to and from Leeds Castle and castle admission.

Sissinghurst Castle Garden

The stunning gardens of **Sissinghurst** (NT; ☎ 01580-710700; Sissinghurst; adult/child £7.80/3.50; ☷ 11am-6.30pm Fri-Tue mid-Mar–Oct) are some of the nation's best loved, and a romantic artist-gardener's vision of beauty. Though the castle dates to the 12th century, the delightful gardens were crafted by writer Vita Sackville-West after she bought the estate in 1930. Highlights include the exuberant rose garden and the virginal snowy-bloomed White Garden. Sissinghurst is 2 miles northeast of Cranbrook and one mile east of Sissinghurst village off the A262.

EAST SUSSEX

East Sussex is a richly varied county that absorbs armies of weekending Londoners whenever the weather is fine. Some come for the scintillating nightlife and shingly shores of Brighton, others to explore the white cliffs and civilised seaside charms of Eastbourne. Many more opt for romance amid the medieval streets of Rye or historic Battle, where William the Conqueror first engaged the Saxons in 1066. But you needn't chase the Chelsea tractors to enjoy East Sussex. It's just as rewarding to get off the beaten track and explore its lush countryside, linger along its winding country lanes and stretch your legs across the rolling South Downs.

RYE

☎ 01797 / pop 4195

Seemingly pickled, put on a shelf and promptly forgotten about by old Father Time, Rye is one of England's most beautiful medieval villages. You can't help but fall under its spell as you slip and wobble through the cobbled lanes, past mysterious passageways and crooked timber-beamed buildings. Romantics can lap up the townsfolk's tales of resident smugglers, ghosts, writers and artists, and even the most hardened cynic will be seduced by a slew of exquisite accommodations in its heart.

Once a coastal Cinque Port but long since abandoned by the shifting coastline, the town sits prettily atop a rocky outcrop, and sheep graze where the waters once lapped. If you do visit – and you absolutely should – try to avoid summer weekends when hoards of day-trippers dilute the town's time-warp effect.

Information

The **tourist office** (☎ 226696; www.visitrye.co.uk; Strand Quay; ☷ 9.30am-5pm Mar-Oct, 10am-4pm Nov-Feb) runs a town model audiovisual history for £3. More fun is the freaky collection of penny-in-the-slot novelty machines upstairs. The tourist office also sells a *Rye Town Walk* map for £1, and rents out multilingual audio tours costing £3/1 per adult/child.

You can get online at **PC Hut** (☎ 224367; 46 Ferry Rd; per min 5p; ☷ 10am-6pm Mon-Tue & Thu-Sat). The **post office** (☷ 8.30am-5.30pm Mon-Fri, 8.30am-1pm Sat) is on Cinque Ports St.

Sights

From the tourist office, turn away from the water and go through Strand Quay, and clamber up the famous cobbled **Mermaid St**, thick with 15th-century timber-framed houses with quirky house names such as 'The House with Two Front Doors', 'The House Opposite' and more.

Turn right at the T-junction for the Georgian **Lamb House** (NT; ☎ 229542; West St; adult/child £3/1.50; ☷ 2-6pm Thu & Sat late Mar-Oct), a handsome house supposedly home to several ghosts, but not that of its most famous resident, American writer Henry James, who lived here from 1898 to 1916; James wrote *The Wings of the Dove* here.

Continue around the dogleg into cobbled Church Sq, ringed by historic houses, including the **Friars of the Sack**, which was once part of a 13th-century Augustinian friary

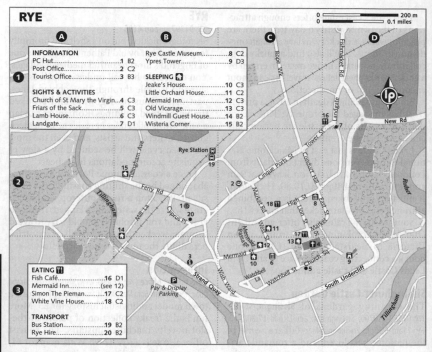

RYE

but is now a private home. The pretty **Church of St Mary the Virgin** (9am-6pm Apr-Sep, to 4pm Oct-Mar) is a mishmash of medieval and later styles and its turret clock is the oldest in England (1561) still working with its original pendulum mechanism. There are great views from its **tower** (adult/child £2/free), weather permitting.

Turn right at the square's east corner for the sandcastle-archetype **Ypres Tower** (tower & museum adult/child £2.90/1.50, tower only adult/child £1.90/1; 10.30am-1pm & 2-5pm Thu-Mon Apr-Oct, 10.30am-3.30pm Sat & Sun Nov-Mar), pronounced 'wipers'. This 13th-century building has great views over Romney Marsh and Rye Bay, and houses one part of Rye Castle Museum. It's overseen by a friendly warden fit to bust with colourful tales from the tower's long history as fort, prison, mortuary and museum (the last two at overlapping times).

The other branch of the **museum** (226728; www.ryemuseum.co.uk; 3 East St; adult/child £1.90/1; 10.30am-1pm & 2-5pm Thu-Mon Apr-Oct), a short stroll away on East St, is home to a 1745 fire engine made of leather and wood and other intriguing loot.

At the northeastern edge of the village, the thickset pale-stone **Landgate** dates back from 1329, and is the only remaining gate out of four.

Activities

To combine history and a hearty hike, the well-signposted 31-mile **1066 Country Walk** meanders from Rye to Battle and Pevensey where it connects with the South Downs Way.

Festivals & Events

Rye wholeheartedly celebrates its maritime heritage with a two-day festival in August, and in September it gets arty for the two-week **Festival of Music and the Arts** (224442; www.ryefestival.co.uk).

Sleeping

Rye boasts an exceptional choice of unique historic accommodations.

Windmill Guest House (224027; www.ryewindmill.co.uk; Mill Lane; s/d from £30/58;) It's not every night that you sleep beneath the arms of a windmill, this one rebuilt in 1932 and a working bakery until 1976. This riverside mill-turned-guesthouse sits a short hop from

---

SOMETHING FOR THE WEEKEND

Start on a high by checking into the excessively atmospheric **Mermaid Inn** (below) at Rye. Learn some of its ghost stories over dinner then put your best black cloak on to roam the cobbled medieval streets after dark. After a night untroubled by spirits (unless they come in a glass), set out to explore the town's beauty by daylight. Navigate your way through narrow country lanes to picture-perfect **Bodiam Castle** (p206). Take a ramble around its ramparts then picnic in its pretty parkland. In the afternoon drive on to historic site of the 1066 Battle of Hastings at **Battle** (p206), and see the spot where King Harold was shot in the eye. Have dinner at the stunning **Pilgrim's Restaurant** (p206) and then settle in at the **Powdermills** (p206) country hotel. On Sunday, skip over to the beautiful coastline at **Beachy Head** (p209) and embark on a windswept walk along its chalky clifftops. Reward yourself with a hearty pub lunch at the **Thatched Bar** (p209) before heading back rosy cheeked and refreshed to face the week ahead.

---

town and its eight en suite bedrooms (one with private bathroom) are simply decorated and trimmed with wood. It's located off Ferry Rd.

Old Vicarage (☎ 222119; www.oldvicaragerye.co.uk; 66 Church Sq; s/d £50/78; **P** ✗) This fairy-pink former vicarage is tucked discretely away on a cobbled lane. It wins intense loyalty from guests with its pretty walled garden, four prim rooms with sherry and biscuits, and superb breakfasts of homemade bread, jams and a complimentary newspaper. Children over five only.

Jeake's House (☎ 222828; www.jeakeshouse.com; Mermaid St; d from £88; ✗) A cosy 17th-century town house on cobbled Mermaid St, Jeake's was once home to US poet Conrad Aitken. Fast forward to today and it's an exquisitely appointed 11-room guesthouse. You can literally take a pew in the snug book-lined bar, furnished with old chapel seats, and continuing the theme, breakfast is served in an 18th-century former chapel.

Mermaid Inn (☎ 223065; www.mermaidinn.com; Mermaid St; d £160-220; **P** ✗) Few inns can claim to be as atmospheric as this ancient hostelry, dating from 1420. Every room is different – but each is thick with dark beams, lit by leaded windows and some graced by secret passageways that now act as fire escapes. Small wonder it's a favourite spot for celebs, royals and honeymooners. Mind out for the resident ghost though.

More great choices:

Wisteria Corner (☎ 225011; mmpartridge@lineone .net; 47 Ferry Rd; s/d £25/50; **P** ✗) Less glitzy, but homely and affordable B&B.

Little Orchard House (☎ 223831; www.littleorchard house.com; West St; s/d £50/80) Two-room B&B with bucketloads of character.

Eating & Drinking

Simon the Pieman (☎ 222207; 3 Lion St; snacks £1.50-3.50; ☺ 9.30am-5pm Mon-Sat, 1.30-5.30pm Sun) Ever-so-English Rye seems to have a pretty tea shop for every occasion. This is one of the more traditional spots with calorific cream teas of freshly baked scones and simple lunches.

White Vine House (☎ 224748; www.whitevinehouse .co.uk; 24 High St; mains £7.50-11) Fine dining in a fine setting can be had at this elegant vine-covered Tudor building, with an exquisitely painted dining room and a reputation for cooking the freshest local produce. It also has pristine rooms (singles/doubles from £70/115).

Fish Café (☎ 222226; www.thefishcafe.com; 17 Tower St; mains £10-23; ☺ lunch & dinner) A contemporary renovation of an old antiques warehouse, furnished in calm shades with chocolate high-back chairs, this restaurant focuses on modern local seafood, cooked simply but to perfection.

Mermaid Inn (☎ 223065; Mermaid St; mains £19-36, set lunch/dinner £18.50/37.50; ☺ lunch & dinner) The special-night-out restaurant at this excessively atmospheric medieval inn more than lives up to its location. It complements Anglo-French delights such as roast grouse with antique silverware and pristine white linen.

Getting There & Away

Bus 711 runs twice hourly between Dover (two hours) and Hastings (30 minutes) via Rye. Trains run three times hourly to London Charing Cross (£20.40, two hours), but you must change either in Hastings or Ashford.

Getting Around

You can rent all-terrain bikes from £12/8 per day/four hours from **Rye Hire** (☎ 223033; ryehire@tiscali.co.uk; 1 Cyprus Pl; ☺ 8am-5pm Mon-Fri). Call ahead for weekend hire.

BATTLE

☎ 01424 / pop 5190

A small but attractive village with a monumental place in British history, Battle grew up around the point where invading French duke William of Normandy, aka William the Conqueror, scored a decisive victory over local King Harold in 1066, so beginning Norman rule and changing the face of the country for good.

Orientation & Information

The train station is a short walk from High St, and is well signposted. The **tourist office** (☎ 773721; www.battletown.co.uk; High St; ☯ 10am-6pm Apr-Sep, to 4pm Oct-Mar) should be operating from a spanking new visitor centre alongside the site entrance by the time you read this. The post office, banks and ATMs are also on High St.

Sights

Another day, another photogenic ruin? Hardly. On this spot raged *the* pivotal battle in the last successful invasion of England in 1066: an event with unparalleled impact on the country's subsequent social structure, architecture and well…pretty much everything. Just four years afterwards, the conquering Normans began work on **Battle Abbey** (EH; ☎ 773792; adult/child £6.30/3.20; ☯ 10am-6pm Apr-Sep, to 4pm Oct-Mar), smack in the middle of the battlefield: a penance ordered by the Pope for the loss of life incurred here.

Only the foundations of the original church remain, the altar's position marked by a plaque – also supposedly the spot England's King Harold famously took an arrow in his eye. But other impressive monastic buildings survive and make for atmospheric explorations.

The battlefield's innocently rolling lush hillsides do little to evoke the ferocity of the event, but high-tech interactive presentations and blow-by-blow audio tours do their utmost to bring the battle to life.

Sleeping & Eating

Tollgate Farmhouse (☎ 777436; www.tollgatefarmhouse .co.uk; 59 North Trade Rd; d £60-70; ℗ ✗ ☒) A homely atmosphere can be found a 10-minute walk from the centre of Battle at this large domestic residence with a handful of florid en suite rooms dotted with embroidery and fake flowers, and several extra surprises tucked up its sleeve: Jacuzzi, sauna and outdoor pool among them.

Powdermills (☎ 775511; www.powdermillshotel.com; Powdermill Lane; s/d £95/120; ℗ ✗ ☒) Rebuilt in the 18th century after a Napoleonic gunpowder works dispatched the previous manor with a bang, this well-heeled country-house hotel revels in 200-acre grounds of tranquil lakes and woodland that adjoin Battle Abbey's grounds. It has classic four-postered rooms and a wonderful orangery restaurant.

Pilgrim's Restaurant (☎ 772314; 1 High St; mains £11-22; ☯ lunch & dinner Mon-Sat, lunch Sun) Misshapen beams crisscross rough-plastered walls in this spectacular 15th-century pilgrim's lodging, now housing the finest and funkiest place to dine in Battle. Committed to using local produce, it's also open for afternoon tea and evening cocktails and there's a children's menu available.

Getting There & Away

National Express bus 023 from London (£10.80, 2¼ hours) to Hastings passes through Battle daily. Bus 4/5 runs every hour to Hastings (26 minutes). Trains also run to London Charing Cross every half-hour (£18, 1½ hours), via Hastings (16 minutes).

AROUND BATTLE
Bodiam Castle

Seemingly an escapee from a bedtime storybook of medieval knights and feisty princesses, this archetypal four-towered **castle** (NT; ☎ 01580-830436; adult/child £4.60/2.30; ☯ 10am-6pm mid-Feb–Oct, 10am-4pm Sat & Sun Nov-early Feb) is surrounded by a square moat teeming with oversized goldfish. It is the legacy of 14th-century soldier of fortune (the polite term for knights that slaughtered and pillaged their way around France) Sir Edward Dalyngrigge, who married the local heiress and set about building a castle to make everybody damn sure who was the new boss.

TOP FIVE PAMPERED GETAWAYS

■ Chewton Glen Hotel & Country Club (New Forest; p239)

■ Amberley Castle Hotel (Around Arundel; p221)

■ Mermaid Inn (Rye; p205)

■ Hotel du Vin (Winchester; p228)

■ Drakes (Brighton; p217)

THE LAST INVASION OF ENGLAND

The most famous battle in the history of England took place in 1066: a date seared into every English schoolchild's brain. The Battle of Hastings began when Harold's army arrived on the scene on October 14th and created a three-ring defence consisting of archers, then cavalry, with massed infantry at the rear. William marched north from Hastings and took up a position about 400m south of Harold and his troops. He tried repeatedly to break the English cordon, but Harold's men held fast. William's knights then feigned retreat, drawing some of Harold's troops after them. It was a fatal mistake. Seeing the gap in the English wall, William ordered his remaining troops to charge through, and the battle was as good as won. Among the English casualties was King Harold who, as graphically depicted in the Bayeux Tapestry, was hit in the eye by an arrow. While he tried to pull the arrow out he was struck down by Norman knights. At news of his death the last English resistance collapsed.

In their wonderfully irreverent *1066 And All That* (1930), WC Sellar and RJ Yeatman suggest that 'the Norman conquest was a Good Thing, as from this time onward England stopped being conquered and thus was able to become top nation...' When you consider that England hasn't been successfully invaded since, it's hard to disagree.

Parliamentarian forces left the castle in ruins during the English Civil War, but in 1917 Lord Curzon, former viceroy of India, bought it and restored the exterior. Much of the interior remains unrestored, but it's possible to climb to the battlements for some sweeping views.

You'll most likely hear the tooting of the nearby **Kent & East Sussex steam railway** (☎ 0870 600 6074; www.kesr.org.uk; adult/3-15yr £10.50/5.50), which runs from Tenterden in Kent through 11 miles of gentle hills and woods to Bodiam village, from where a bus takes you to the castle. It operates three to five services on most days from May to September and at the weekend and school holidays in October, December and February. It's closed November, January and most of March.

The castle is 9 miles northeast of Battle. Arriva Bus 254 stops at Bodiam from Hastings (38 minutes) hourly during the day Monday to Saturday.

Bateman's

It was love at first sight when Rudyard Kipling, author of *The Jungle Book*, set eyes on **Bateman's** (NT; ☎ 01435-882302; adult/child £6.20/2.60; 🕑 11am-5pm Sat-Wed mid-Mar–Oct), the glorious little 1634 Jacobean mansion he would call home for the last 34 years of his life, and where he would draw inspiration for *The Just So Stories* and other vivid tales.

Even today, the house is pervaded with a sense of Kipling's cosy contentment here. Everything is pretty much just as the writer left it after his death in 1936, down to the blotting paper on his study desk. Furnishings often reflect his fascination with the East, with many oriental rugs and Indian artefacts adding colour.

The house is surrounded by lovely gardens and a small path leads down to a water mill that grinds corn on Wednesdays and Saturdays at 2pm.

Bateman's is about half a mile south of the town of Burwash along the A259.

EASTBOURNE

☎ 01323 / pop 106,562

A classic golden-oldie seaside resort that has long brought to mind images of octogenarians dozing in deck chairs or tapping their feet to brassy tunes on the 1930s bandstand, elegant Eastbourne nonetheless likes to promote its many charms to sprightlier generations. There's certainly no doubting the appeal of its pebbly beaches, scrupulously snipped seaside gardens and picturesque arcade-free promenade, but if you're looking for cosmopolitan buzz, grab your chocolate-flake ice cream and head for Brighton.

The **tourist office** (☎ 0906 7112212; www.visiteast bourne.com; Cornfield Rd; 🕑 9.30am-5.30pm Mon-Fri, to 5pm Sat Apr-Sep) can fix you up with accommodation for £3. Email can be found at **Coffee Republic** (☎ 438576; 69 Terminus Rd; per 20 min/hr £1/3; 🕑 7am-6pm), near the tourist office.

Sights & Activities

A lovely vantage point for the sunset, Eastbourne's pretty filigree-trimmed pier also has a curious Victorian **Camera Obscura** (adult/child

BIZARRE ENGLAND

A few oddball regional events include the **World Marbles Championship** on Tinsley Green, near Crawley, in mid-April, when teams compete to knock each other's balls out of action. Another event some may put down to lost marbles is the Isle of Wight's late August **Newchurch Garlic Festival**, where visitors can achieve new heights of bad breath trying garlic ice cream, jelly beans, beer and more bulb-inspired products. And what could be more English than October's almighty shouting match the **National Town Criers Championship** in Hastings. These iconic newspapers-on-legs once roamed the streets with a bell and throaty 'Oyez, Oyez, Oyez...' from as early as 1066 right up to the 19th century.

£2/1; ◷ noon-5pm Apr-Sep) that projects images of the outside world into a dish within a darkened room. In July daredevils in feathery frocks hurl themselves from the pier in the annual birdman competition.

Eastbourne's two quirky little museums are devoted purely to nostalgia. The **Museum of Shops** (☎ 737143; www.how-we-lived-then.co.uk; 20 Cornfield Tce; adult/child £4/3; ◷ 10am-5pm) is swamped by an obsessive collection of how-we-once-lived memorabilia, while **Eastbourne Heritage Centre** (☎ 411189; www.eastbourneheritage centre.co.uk; 2 Carlisle Rd; adult/child £1/50p; ◷ 2-5pm Apr-early Oct) perks up exhibits on the town's development with eccentric asides, such as on Donald McGill, the pioneer of the 'naughty postcard.'

As part of Eastbourne's drive to attract younger visitors, water sports are increasingly popular. **Spray Water Sports Centre** (☎ 417023; Royal Pde) offers courses in sailing, windsurfing, kayaking and power boating.

Tours

City Sightseeing (☎ 0871 666 0000; www.city-sightsee ing.co.uk; adult/child £7/3.50; ◷ tours every 30 min 10am-4.30pm Apr-Sep) runs buses around local sights, including Beachy Head cliffs.

Sleeping

Ebor Lodge (☎ 640792; beryl@mnewson.freeserve.co.uk; 71 Royal Pde; s/d from £25/50) A motherly welcome sweeps you into this homey, well-maintained B&B five minutes' walk west of the centre

along the seafront. It's a great deal with en suite rooms decorated by a feminine eye for frills, and about a 10-second run from the seashore.

Devonshire Park Hotel (☎ 728144; www.devonshire -park-hotel.co.uk; Carlisle Rd; s/d from £40/70; Ⓟ ⊠ ▣) There are rooms the size of footy pitches, elegantly trimmed with decorated plaster ceilings and kitted out with DVD players, fresh afternoon coffee and a personal welcome from the owners at this old-school hotel. It caters mostly to an elderly clientele, and only welcomes children over 14.

Albert & Victoria (☎ 730948; www.albertandvictoria .com; 19 St Aubyns Rd; s/d 45/70; ⊠) Book ahead to stay at this delightful Victorian terraced house with opulent rooms, canopied beds, crystal chandeliers and bay windows, mere paces from the seafront promenade.

Eating

Eastbourne's 'restaurant row' can be found on the seafront end of Terminus Rd.

Ye Old Fashioned Humbugge Shoppe (☎ 721295; 250 Terminus Rd; ◷ 10am-5pm Mon-Sat) Willy Wonka wouldn't look out of place in this classic rock-candy and sweets shop complete with chequered floors, twinkly-eyed counter lady and salivating children.

Lamb (☎ 720545; cnr High St & Ocklynge Rd; mains £5-8) About 1km inland, this atmospheric old pub is worth the walk for its creaky old dining room with a giant stone fireplace, laid-back service, low ceiling and lack of loud music.

Café Belge (☎ 729967; www.cafebelge.co.uk; 11/23 Grand Pde; mains £9-16; ◷ lunch & dinner) A fabulous position near the pier with large windows facing the seafront, a ridiculous choice of seafood dishes with an emphasis on mussels, and three-score choices of Belgian beer make this a hard restaurant to resist.

Getting There & Around

National Express operates two daily buses to London Victoria (£11.40, 2¾ hours) and to Brighton (55 minutes). The slower bus 12 runs three times an hour (twice hourly on Sunday) to Brighton (one hour and 20 minutes).

Trains for London Victoria (£19.60, 1½ hours) and Brighton (£7.90, 30 to 40 minutes) leave every half hour.

Wheely Good Fun (☎ 479077; www.onelifegroup.co .uk) hire skates and bikes from Fisherman's Green on Royal Pde.

AROUND EASTBOURNE

Pevensey Castle

Now picturesquely dissolving into its own moat, **Pevensey Castle** (EH; ☎ 01323-762604; adult/child £3.90/2; ⏰ 10am-6pm Apr-Oct, 10am-4pm Sat & Sun Nov-Mar) marks the point where William the Conqueror landed in 1066, just two weeks before the Battle of Hastings. And shortly afterwards, Old Bill wasted no time in building upon sturdy Roman walls to create his first stronghold here. Five miles east of Eastbourne, off the A259, the castle was used time and again through the centuries, right up to WWII. You can roam about its decaying husk with an enlightening audio guide, free with entry.

Across the road, the creaky mid-14th-century **Mint House** (☎ 01323-762337; admission £1) is worth visiting for its wacky collection of antiques and knick-knacks.

Regular train services between London Victoria and Hastings via Eastbourne (10 minutes) stop at Westham, half a mile from Pevensey.

Beachy Head

The famous chalk cliffs of Beachy Head are the highest point of a string of milky-white rock faces that slice across this rugged stretch of coast at the southern end of the South Downs. It's a spot of thrilling beauty, at least until some fool guidebook spoils it all by mentioning that this is also one of England's top suicide spots.

From Beachy Head, the famous Seven Sisters Cliffs rollercoaster their way west. Along the way, you'll stumble upon tiny seaside hamlet Birling Gap. Stop at the unthatched but still wood-beamed and log-fire-warmed **Thatched Bar** (☎ 01323-423197; mains £4.50-7; ⏰ 11am-11pm Mon-Sat, noon-11pm Sun), beside the Birling Gap Hotel, for decent pub grub, real ale or ice cream. One you're fortified, you might want to descend the metal cliffside steps to the grey shingly beach and make the bracing several-mile walk back to the lighthouse. Just keep a wary eye on the tide.

Beachy Head is off the B2103, from the A259 between Eastbourne and Newhaven. Eastbourne's City Sightseeing tour bus (see p216) stops at the clifftop.

The Long Man

If you're travelling along the A27 between Eastbourne and Lewes, be sure to look southwards, just east of the town of Wilmington, to see the spindly stick-figure-like **Long Man of Wilmington**. No-one really knows how this leggy 70m-high man – now marked out with white concrete – arrived here or what he represents.

There is a turn-off for the Long Man at the town of Wilmington, 7 miles west of Eastbourne, from where you can get a better view. If you're walking this section of the South Downs you will pass him and get a close-up view

Charleston Farmhouse

The former inhabitant's passion for work and life is palpable in the Bloomsbury Group's Bohemian country getaway, **Charleston Farmhouse** (☎ 01323-811265; www.charleston.org.uk; Firle, off A27; adult/child £6.50/4.50; ⏰ 2-6pm Thu, Fri & Sun, 11.30am-6pm Wed & Sat Apr-Oct). Even now that the joyous frescoes and vivid furniture have begun to fade, and the last of its pioneering occupants and visitors long since passed away, it's still a tangible example of the rich intellectual and aesthetic life that they came to represent (see boxed text, p211).

In 1916 Virginia Woolf's sister, painter Vanessa Bell, moved here with her lover Duncan Grant and they set about redecorating with abandon in a style that owed much to the influence of the post-impressionists. Hardly a wall, door or piece of furniture was left untouched, and the walls featured paintings by Picasso, Derain, Delacroix and others. There's also a striking garden, planted with a painter's eye, and a medieval dovecote.

Charleston is 5 miles west of Eastbourne. Visits are by guided tour only except on Sunday and bank holiday Mondays. The nearest train station is at Berwick, on the Brighton to Eastbourne line, a 2-mile walk from the farmhouse.

LEWES

☎ 01273 / pop 15,988

A charming hillside town with a turbulent past and fiery traditions (see boxed text, p212), Lewes is strung out along a lengthy High St flanked by elegant Georgian buildings, a part-ruined castle and a traditional brewery just across the River Ouse. Off the main drag, however, there's a more intimate atmosphere as the surviving medieval street plan twists and turns through narrow streets called twittens.

THE SOUTHEAST COAST

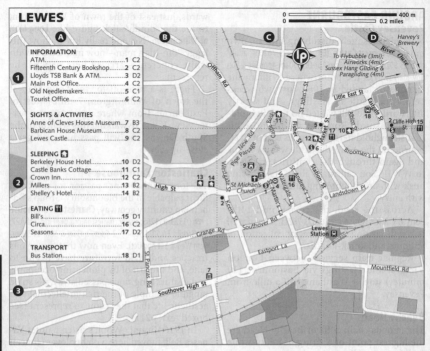

LEWES

0 ——— 400 m
0 ——— 0.2 miles

Harvey's Brewery

To Flybubble (3mi);
Airworks (4mi);
Sussex Hang Gliding &
Paragliding (4mi)

INFORMATION	
ATM.................................1	C2
Fifteenth Century Bookshop........2	C2
Lloyds TSB Bank & ATM...........3	D2
Main Post Office....................4	C2
Old Needlemakers..................5	C1
Tourist Office.......................6	C2

SIGHTS & ACTIVITIES	
Anne of Cleves House Museum...7	B3
Barbican House Museum............8	C2
Lewes Castle.......................9	C2

SLEEPING	
Berkeley House Hotel...............10	D2
Castle Banks Cottage..............11	C1
Crown Inn..........................12	C2
Millers.............................13	B2
Shelley's Hotel....................14	B2

EATING	
Bill's...............................15	D1
Circa..............................16	C2
Seasons...........................17	D2

TRANSPORT	
Bus Station........................18	D1

Orientation & Information

The town occupies a steep ridge between the river and the castle ruins, with High St climbing the spine and the twittens running off it.

You'll find the **tourist office** (☎ 483448; lewes .tic@lewes.gov.uk; 187 High St; ⊗ 9am-5pm Mon-Fri, 9.30am-5.30pm Sat & 10am-2pm Sun Apr-Sep, 9am-5pm Mon-Fri, 10am-2pm Sat Oct-Mar) at the top of the hill, and the **main post office** (High St) is a short walk west.

Lloyds TSB (Cliff High St) has ATMs at either end of the centre. While you're here it's worth browsing the quaint craft shops of the **Old Needlemakers** (West St) and rummaging through the dusty tomes and not-so-antiquarian treasures of the half-timbered **Fifteenth Century Bookshop** (☎ 474160; 99 High St).

Sights

LEWES CASTLE & MUSEUM

Built shortly after the Norman invasion of 1066, this unusual twin-motte **castle** (☎ 486290; www.sussexpast.co.uk; 169 High St; adult/child £4.50/2.25; ⊗ 10am-5.30pm Tue-Sat, 11am-5.30pm Sun-Mon) never saw warfare, unless you count the riotous celebrations following the Navy's victory over the Spanish Armada in 1588, when happy citizens blew great chunks out of the castle's walls! They left enough standing for it to remain an impressive sight, however, and its windy top affords excellent views over the town. The castle grounds also host summertime concerts.

The neighbouring **Barbican House Museum** has a good collection of prehistoric flint axeheads, Anglo-Saxon jewellery and medieval long swords.

Admission to the Lewes Castle and the Anne of Cleves House can be purchased together for £6.40/3.20 per adult/child.

ANNE OF CLEVES HOUSE MUSEUM

This endearingly skew-whiff timber-framed **house** (☎ 474610; 52 Southover High St; adult/child £3.10/1.55; ⊗ 10am-5pm Tue-Sat year-round, plus 11am-5pm Sun & Mon Mar-Oct), with creak-and-groan floors and a spider's web of a wooden roof, was given to Henry VIII's ex-wife Anne of Cleves, later dubbed the Flanders Mare, as part of her 1541 divorce settlement, although the one-time queen never actually moved in.

THE SOUTHEAST COAST

Today it houses an idiosyncratic folk museum, with everything from a donkey-sized bed-warming contraption to a witch's effigy complete with pins.

Activities

Paragliders can get one step closer to heaven in the South Downs near Lewes, an excellent spot for the sport. A half-hour tandem flight costs around £80, and a day's tuition from £125. Local companies include:

Airworks (☎ 858108; www.airworks.co.uk; Glynde)
Flybubble (☎ 812442; www.flybubble.co.uk; Ringmer)
Sussex Hang Gliding & Paragliding (☎ 858170; www.flysussex.co.uk; Tollgate)

Sleeping

Castle Banks Cottage (☎ 476291; aswigglesworth@aol.com; 4 Castle Banks; s/d £27.50/55; ✗) Hidden away on a quiet lane near the High St, this tiny two-guestroom period cottage has an easy-going atmosphere and a multilingual owner well versed in the area's history. Breakfast is served in the pretty garden in summer

Berkeley House Hotel (☎ 476057; www.berkeley houselewes.co.uk; 2 Albion St; s from £60, d £70-85; ✗) This bright and uncluttered Georgian terraced town house has lovely extras like a front balcony and roof terrace with view to the Downs, as well as carefully furnished rooms and courteous service.

Shelley's Hotel (☎ 472361; www.shelleys-hotel.com; High St; s/d from £120/165; P ✗) Get a buzz from staying in a 16th-century manor house once home to the Earl of Dorset and even pad to the poet Shelley. The classiest hotel in Lewes, it overflows with country charm and has a good restaurant overlooking the garden.

Other options:

Crown Inn (☎ 480670; www.crowninn-lewes.co.uk; 191 High St; s/d from £40/60) Attractive 17th-century inn.
Millers (☎ 475631; www.hometown.aol.com/millers /134; 134 High St; s/d £68/75; ✗) Chivalrous service in 16th-century town house.

Eating

Bill's (☎ 476918; 56 Cliffe High St; snacks £2.50-5, specials £5-10; ☾ lunch) There's something doubly delicious about a forkful of fresh food when its ingredients are piled all around you. Part grocers, part delicatessen, part rustic-styled café, Bill's envelopes customers in its colours and smells then dishes up melt-in-the-mouth tartlets, gourmet pizzas, salads, deserts and other artisan snacks.

Seasons (☎ 473968; High St; mains £4-6.50; ☾ lunch Tue-Sat) One of the town's cosiest spots, this family-run vegetarian café and takeaway is tucked away in a subterranean nook down narrow steps, easily missed despite its position on High St.

Circa (☎ 471777; Pelham House Hotel, St Andrew's Lane; 2-course set lunch/dinner £11.75/24.50; ☾ lunch & dinner) Lewes most renowned restaurant is peacefully housed in an elegant hotel, with lovely countryside views. It revels in borrowing flavours from around the world and giving them its own adventurous spins.

THE SOUTHEAST COAST

THE BLOOMSBURY GROUP

Britain's most influential artistic and intellectual circle to arise from the first half of the 20th century, the Bloomsbury Group, was a set of Cambridge graduates, artists and scholars that all gravitated to the Bloomsbury area of London around the same pre-WWI period. Its most famous members included Virginia Woolf, Maynard Keynes, Vanessa Bell, Duncan Grant, Lytton Strachey, TS Elliot and EM Forster.

The outspokenly pacifist group gained notoriety for stunts that embarrassed the military forces during WWI, and scandalised London society with their intergroup relationships and, in several cases, bisexuality. Their tastes in post-impressionist art and avant-garde literature were ahead of their time, and were often savaged by critics only to be later hailed as masterpieces. Woolf of course was winning herself acclaim as a novelist, and with her husband Leonard founded the Hogarth Press. Her artist sister Vanessa and lover Duncan Grant were two of several group members to make a name through the modernist design firm Omega Workshops. Keyes meanwhile became one of the foremost economic theorists of the day, and Strachey had several uncompromising biographies under his belt.

Though the group gradually drifted apart after the war and Woolf committed suicide in 1941, their once controversial views were steadily accepted into the mainstream and their work has continued to influence generations of new writers, poets, artists and musicians.

THE SOUTHEAST COAST

BIZARRE ENGLAND

The English enjoy an evening of frenzied pyromania nationwide on **Bonfire Night** (5th November) in memory of a plot to blow up the Houses of Parliament in 1605. But unassuming little Lewes has double the reason to host one of the craziest fireworks celebrations you're ever likely to see.

In 1555, at the height of Mary Tudor's Catholic revival, 17 protestant martyrs were burned at the stake in the town's High St. Lewes has not forgotten, and every 5 November tens of thousands of people gather for the famous fireworks display, in which effigies of the pope are burnt in memory of the martyrs. These days he's often joined by modern-day figures, prime ministers, presidents and terrorists among them. Locals parade the streets in outlandish medieval garb with flaming crosses, and send barrels filled with bangers to crack and fizzle their way down to the river, chased by local youth.

Though not shy of controversy, there's no sectarian fervour these days and it's one of the most enjoyable nights on the southeastern calendar.

Getting There & Away

Lewes is 9 miles northeast of Brighton and 16 miles northwest of Eastbourne.

The bus station is north of the town centre off Eastgate St. Buses 28 and 29 run to Brighton (30 minutes) every 15 minutes on weekdays and hourly Sundays. The 29 bus continues north to Tunbridge Wells (one hour).

Lewes is on the main train line between London Victoria and Eastbourne and the coastal link between Eastbourne and Brighton. Trains leave every 10 to 20 minutes from London Victoria (£18.30, 1¼ hours) and Brighton (15 minutes) and four times an hour from Eastbourne (£5.70, 20 minutes).

AROUND LEWES

In 1934 science teacher John Christie and his opera-singer wife decided to build a 1200-seat opera house in the middle of nowhere. It seemed a magnificent folly at the time. But now, **Glyndebourne** (☎ 01273-812321; www .glyndebourne.com) is one of England's best places to enjoy the lyric arts, with a season that runs from late May to the end of August. Tickets can be gold dust so book well ahead. And bring your glad rags: dress code is strictly black tie and evening dress. Glyndebourne is 4 miles east of Lewes off the B2192.

BRIGHTON & HOVE

☎ 01273 / pop 206,648

Brighton, Brighton, Brighton. Where to start? This is the most vibrant seaside resort in England and a high point in any visit to the region. In summer its pebbled shoreline throngs with sunbathers and beachside bars fizzle with energy and music. A multitude of trendy restaurants, slick boutique hotels and shops catering to every taste jam the streets leading back from the sea. The city's nightlife is legendary and more concentrated than its rivals in London and Manchester. Family fun, high-brow culture, an exuberant gay population and cutting-edge club scene all mingle into one good-time getaway not to miss.

Don't listen to the folk that call Brighton little London-on-the-Sea. However cosmopolitan it has become, this is a place with a character and quirkiness all its own. It has embraced the outlandish ever since the Prince Regent built his party palace here in the 19th century. And these days anyone can join in the fun. Celebrities rub shoulders with dread-locked hippies, drag queens party next to designer-clad urbanites, couples stroll past fishermen and kids toddle around the tables of coffee-quaffing media types. It's a city with a devil-may-care attitude: from its edgy cool underbelly to its hedonistic highs, its chic gloss to its seedy Soho glam, its candy floss frolics to its Bohemian detachment. Mix all its flavours together to get one heady cocktail, and a place for everyone in the shaker.

Orientation

Brighton Town merged with its western neighbour Hove in 2000. The train station is half a mile north of the beach, while the tiny bus station is tucked away in Poole Valley close to Brighton Pier. Old Steine (pronounced 'steen') is the major thoroughfare linking pier and centre. To the west lies a tangle of pedestrian alleyways known as the Lanes, packed with pubs, restaurants and trendy boutiques. A short walk north is the North Laine, full of quirky stores and Bohemian cafés. The city's effervescent gay scene

TOP FIVE BEACH TOWNS

- Brighton & Hove (p212)
- Broadstairs (p194)
- Eastbourne (p207)
- Ramsgate (p195)
- Whitstable (p193)

---

flourishes in Kemptown, east of Old Steine along St James' St. Brighton's burgeoning marina, east of town, is also a vibrant waterside shopping, dining, drinking and watersports centre.

Information

BOOKSHOPS

Borders Books (☎ 731122; Churchill Square Shopping Centre; 🕓 9am-10pm Mon-Sat, 11am-5pm Sun)
Brighton Books (☎ 693845; 18 Kensington Gardens; 🕓 10am-6pm Mon-Sat) Second-hand bookshop.

INTERNET ACCESS

Internet Junction (☎ 607650; 109 Western Rd; per hr £2.50)
Netpama (☎ 227188; 37 Preston St; per 30 min £50p)
Jubilee Library (☎ 296961; Jubilee St; 🕓 10am-7pm Mon-Tue, to 5pm Wed & Fri, to 8pm Thu, to 4pm Sat) Bring ID and sign up to use machines for free.

INTERNET RESOURCES

Brighton City Guide (www.brighton.co.uk)
Insight City News (www.theinsight.co.uk)
visitbrighton.com (www.visitbrighton.com)

LAUNDRY

Preston Street Laundrette (☎ 738556; 75 Preston St; 🕓 8am-9pm Mon-Sat, 9am-7pm Sun)

MEDICAL SERVICES

Royal Sussex County Hospital (☎ 696955; Eastern Rd) Has an accident and emergency department 2 miles east of the centre.
Wistons Clinic (☎ 506263; 138 Dyke Rd) For general medical consultations; under a mile from the centre.

MONEY

American Express (☎ 712906; 82 North St) Has bureau de change.
NatWest (Castle Sq) Bank with ATM.

POST

Main post office (Ship St; 🕓 9.30am-5.30pm Mon-Sat)

TOURIST INFORMATION

Tourist office (☎ 0906 711 2255; www.visitbrighton .com; 10 Bartholomew Sq; 🕓 10am-5pm Mon-Sat, 10am-4pm Sun Easter-Sep, 10am-5pm Mon-Sat Sep-Easter) Overworked staff and a 50p-per-minute telephone line provide local information. You may find the website and on-site 24-hour accessible computer more helpful.

Sights

ROYAL PAVILION

If you thought the current batch of British royals was an eccentric bunch, just wait until you see Brighton's outlandish crowning jewel, the **Royal Pavilion** (☎ 290900; www .royalpavilion.org.uk; adult/under 15yr £7.50/5; 🕓 10am-4.30pm Oct-Mar, 9.30am-5pm Apr-Sep). The dazzlingly exotic palace-cum-playpad of Prince George (see boxed text The Prince, the Palace & the Piss-Up, opposite), later Prince Regent then King George IV, is easily one of the most self-indulgently decadent buildings in England and an apt symbol of Brighton's reputation for hedonism. Even the forest of Indian-style domes and minarets outside is only a prelude to the palace's lavish oriental-themed interior, where no colour is deemed too strong, dragons swoop and snarl from gilt-smothered ceilings, gem-encrusted snakes slither down pillars, and crystal chandeliers seem ordered by the tonne. While gawping is the main activity, you can pick up an audio tour (included in the admission price) to learn more about the palace, room by room.

BRIGHTON MUSEUM & ART GALLERY

Set in the Royal Pavilion's renovated stable block, this **museum and art gallery** (☎ 290900; Royal Pavilion Gardens; admission free; 🕓 10am-7pm Tue, 10am-5pm Wed-Sat, 2-5pm Sun) has a glittering collection of 20th-century art and design, including a crimson Salvador Dali sofa modelled on Mae West's lips. There's also an enthralling gallery of world art, and a multimedia exhibit on Brighton's history where you can listen in on stories told by older and past generations.

BRIGHTON PIER

This grand old centenarian **pier** (Palace Pier; www .brightonpier.co.uk; admission free) is Brighton beach's centrepiece and the place to shake off the city's cosmopolitan gloss and embrace its tackier seaside soul. Start by dizzying yourself on a few stomach-churning fairground rides, whiz around the Helter Skelter made famous by the Beatles song, buy a few souvenir sticks of

---

THE PRINCE, THE PALACE & THE PISS-UP

It's widely known that England's George III was periodically, to be polite, off his rocker. But you'd be forgiven for thinking that 'Mad King George's' eldest son Prince George (1762–1830) was the eccentric in the family upon visiting his princely pavilion at Brighton. The young prince began drinking with abandon and enjoying the pleasures of women while still a teenager. And to daddy's displeasure he soon started hanging out with his dissolute uncle the Duke of Cumberland, who was enjoying himself royally by the sea in Brighton.

In 1787 George commissioned Henry Holland to design a neoclassical villa as his personal pleasure palace. While he waited to accede to the throne (when his father was declared officially insane in 1810 he was sworn in as Prince Regent), George whiled away the years with extravagant piss-ups for himself, his mistresses and his aristocratic mates.

Ever conscious of what was trendy, George decided in 1815 to convert the Marine Pavilion to reflect the current fascination with all things Eastern. He engaged the services of John Nash, who laboured for eight years to create a Mogul Indian–style palace, complete with the most lavish Chinese interior imaginable. George finally had a palace suited to his outlandish tastes, and to boot he was now the king.

His brother and successor, William IV (1765–1837), also used the pavilion as a royal residence, as did William's niece Victoria (1819–1901). But the conservative queen never really took to the place and in 1850 sold it to the town, but not before stripping it of every piece of furniture – 143 wagons were needed to transport the contents. Thankfully, many original items were later returned and the palace is restored to its former glory.

Brighton Rock, then flop into a candy-striped deck chair and scoff candy floss to your heart's content.

Look west to see its sad skeletal twin **West Pier** (www.westpier.co.uk), a ghostly iron hulk that attracts flocks of birds at sunset. It's a sad end for a Victorian marvel upon which the likes of Charlie Chaplin and Stan Laurel once performed. There are now plans afoot to replace it with a *Jetsons*-esque Brighton i-360 observation mast.

BOOTH MUSEUM OF NATURAL HISTORY

With a vast collection that ranges from bugs to dinosaur bones, this Victorian dead-zoo **museum** (☎ 292777; 194 Dyke Rd; admission free; ☼ 10am-5pm Mon-Wed & Fri-Sat, 2-5pm Sun) has a particularly creepy bird room, especially if you've seen the Hitchcock movie. The museum is about half a mile north of the train station. Buses 27 and 27A stop nearby on Dyke Rd.

HOVE MUSEUM & ART GALLERY

Hove can justifiably claim to be the birthplace of British cinema, with the first short film shot here in 1898. You can see it alongside other fascinating films at this attractive Victorian **villa** (☎ 290200; 19 New Church Rd; admission free; ☼ 10am-5pm Tue-Sat, 2-5pm Sun). Another highlight is the kids' room, which resounds to the snores of a wizard and the whirr of an un-

derfloor train. Exhibits include old zoetropes, a magic lantern and a small cupboard with a periscope inside. From central Brighton take buses 1, 1A, 6 or 6B.

BRIGHTON SEA LIFE CENTRE

This grand old Victorian **aquarium** (☎ 604234; www.sealifeeurope.com; Marine Pde; adult/child £9.95/7.50; ☼ 10am-5pm) is the world's oldest operational sea-life centre, and makes for a fun hour or two pressing your nose up again glass and making fishy faces at seahorses, rays, sea turtles and other inhabitants.

Activities

Brighton has activities for one and all from beach volleyball to skateboarding, paragliding to paddling, dance classes to yoga, and of course myriad water sports: ask the tourist office for details. **Lagoon Watersports** (☎ 684260; www.lagoon.co.uk; West Jetty, Brighton Marina) can help you onto the waves, whether in a dinghy, windsurfer, powerboat or yacht.

Tours

The tourist office can organise a range of guided tours, including:
Brighton Walks (☎ 888596; www.brightonwalks.com; adult/child £6/3.50) Offers a huge variety of standard and offbeat themes including Gay's The Word and Ghost Walk. Show up for prescheduled walks or contact to book.

City Sightseeing (www.city-sightseeing.co.uk; adult/child £6.50/2.50; ⏰ tours every 30 min mid-Jun–Aug) Has open-top hop-on hop-off bus tours that leave from Grand Junction Rd near Brighton Pier and take you around the main sights.

Tourist Tracks (www.tourist-tracks.com) Has MP3-format audio guides downloadable from their website (£5) or you can hire them on a preloaded MP3 player at the tourist office for £6 per half-day.

Festivals & Events

From Gay Pride to sand sculpture, there's always something fun going on in Brighton, but the showpiece is May's three-week-long **Brighton Festival** (☎ 709709; www.brighton-festival .org.uk), the biggest arts festival in Britain after Edinburgh. A packed programme of theatre, dance, music and comedy features performers from all over the world.

Sleeping

Despite a glut of hotels in Brighton, prices are relatively high and you'd be wise to book well ahead for summer weekends and the Brighton Festival in May.

BUDGET

Brighton's hostels are a varied bunch – several catering to raucous stag and hen nights, while others are more traditional and homely. Choose wisely!

Baggies Backpackers (☎ 733740; 33 Oriental Pl; dm/d £13/35) A warm familial atmosphere, worn-in charm and motherly onsite owner, as well as clean, snug dorms have made this long-established hostel something of an institution. It's also blessed with a homely kitchen, an all-too-comfy basement music room thick with cassettes, and TV room piled high with videos.

Grapevine (☎ 703985; www.grapevinewebsite.co.uk; 75-76 Middle St; per person Sun-Thu £13-18, Fri & Sat £22-30; 🖳) This ex-hostel's rooms still have the aura of a hospital ward but now boast more privacy, better cleanliness and generally quieter nights. It's run by a young crowd and has a great central location. Weekend rates include breakfast.

St Christopher's (☎ 202035; www.palacebrighton .co.uk; Palace Hotel, 10/12 Grand Junction Rd; dm £16-19.50, s/d £25/50; 🖳) Party people gravitate to this no-frills hostel on the seafront. While quiet is a rare luxury, it boasts sea views and a spot near Brighton Pier and clubbing hot spots. Price includes breakfast and linen, but bring a lock for the under-bed cage. There's no kitchen.

Brighton YHA (☎ 556196; brighton@yha.org.uk; Patcham Pl, London Rd; dm £16.95) One for walkers and cyclists: this character-rich hostel is in a 16th-century mansion three miles inland and on the doorstep of the South Downs. Spacious if well-broken-in dorms, stained-glass windows and a grand staircase add atmosphere.

MIDRANGE

Brighton is blessed with a wide selection of midrange accommodations.

Oriental Hotel (☎ 205050; www.orientalhotel.co.uk; 9 Oriental Pl; s without bathroom £35-40, d with bathroom Sun-Thu £60-100, Fri & Sat £80-125; ✗ 🖳 wi-fi) Once home to a famously Bohemian nightclub, this stylishly renovated boutique hotel now houses sleek modern rooms in shades of coffee and mint, with fresh flowers, aromatherapy lights, and CD and DVD players. Downstairs there's a cosy candlelit bar with mosaic-tiled tables. The breakfast is organic.

Brighton House Hotel (☎ 323282; www.brighton househotel.co.uk; 52 Regency Sq; s £35-80, d £55-140; ✗ 🖳 wi-fi) A traditionally styled Regency hotel with immaculate rooms, welcoming proprietors and refreshingly healthy breakfasts with organic ingredients and fish or vegetarian options. Children are not catered to here. There's discounted parking in an underground lot next to the hotel.

Lichfield House (☎ 777740; www.lichfieldhouse.free serve.co.uk; 30 Waterloo St; s/d £40/60; ✗) You'll get honest value and a warm welcome at this unpretentious Regency town house B&B in Hove. Its seven rooms are vividly painted and decorated with polished-wood floors and furniture, and some period features. Families welcome.

Seaspray (☎ 680332; www.seaspraybrighton.co.uk; 25 New Steine; s/d incl breakfast from £40/95) This mildly insane little guesthouse in Kemptown has a fun selection of themed rooms. Feathers adorn the pink-and-scarlet Boudoir suite, the pint-sized Warhol room has soup-can tables and the Dali room has spongy red lips as a headboard and a lobster-topped telephone.

Genevieve Hotel (☎ 681653; www.genevievehotel .co.uk; 18 Madeira Pl; s/d from £49/79; ✗ 🖳 wi-fi) Central, simple rooms in a Regency town house. There is a minimum two-night stay at weekends.

Amsterdam (☎ 688825; www.amsterdam.uk.com; 11-12 Marine Pde; d with bathroom £55-70, without bathroom from £50) Popular gay-run hotel – that also welcomes tolerant straights – with tastefully decorated, spacious, bright rooms and wonderful sea views. It sits above one of Brighton's best gay bars and saunas, which guests use half price. Request a room on higher floors if you're a light sleeper.

Neo Hotel (☎ 711104; www.neohotel.com; 19 Oriental Pl; Fri-Sun s £60, d £100-150, Mon-Thu s £55, d £95-135; ✗ ☐ wi-fi) No surprise that the owner of this gorgeous designer-chic hotel is an interiors stylist. The nine rooms could belong in a showroom, each finished in rich colours and tactile fabrics, with bold floral and Asian motifs. Kick back in satin kimono robes, and watch a DVD on your flat-screen TV or indulge in massage and beauty treatments. One for couples, but not the kids.

TOP END
Drakes (☎ 696934; www.drakesofbrighton.com; 43-44 Marine Pde; s £95-125, d £115-165, ste £145-295) Drakes oozes understated class: a stylish, minimalist boutique hotel that eschews the need to shout its existence from the rooftops. Feature rooms have giant free-standing tubs set in front of full-length bay windows with stunning views out to sea. It also has a restaurant, Gingerman.

Hotel du Vin (☎ 718588; www.hotelduvin.com; Ship St; d from £135; ✗) This endearing jumble of Gothic-styled buildings near the seafront has been gifted with a new gloss of sophistication to become one of Brighton's foremost boutique hotels. Fronted by young, sparky staff and boasting three-dozen elegant rooms with Egyptian linen and irreproachable bathrooms, the hotel's trump card is its wonderful bistro with a wine list to impress savvy connoisseurs. Breakfast is extra.

De Vere Grand Hotel (☎ 224300; www.devere.co.uk; King's Rd; s/d incl breakfast from £140/220; ℗ ✗ ☐ ⌨) Attracting the gentry since 1864, this five-star institution overlooks the seafront. Trimmed by confectionlike filigree wrought iron outside, its palatial interior is dotted with top-hatted bellboys and dignitaries. Luxurious rooms boast superb views and some Lilliputian balconies.

Eating
Brighton has the biggest and best choice of eateries on the south coast, with cafés, diners and restaurants to fulfil every whim.

BUDGET
Brighton is one of the UK's best destinations for vegetarians, and its innovative meat-free menus are also terrific value for anyone on a tight budget.

Cherry Tree (☎ 698684; 107 St James' St; ☽ 9am-6pm Mon-Sat, 10am-5pm Sun) Pick a patch of beach, snag a deck chair and unpack your picnic from this rustic Mediterranean deli that stocks delicious cold sandwiches, salads, ambrosial cakes and Italian ice creams to go. And if you're missing anything, there's a big Somerfield supermarket a short hop away.

Pokeno Pies (☎ 684921; 52 Gardner St; pies £3.85; ☽ 10am-6pm) Bang goes the greasy image of the great British pie shop: this is guilt-free comfort food at its best. The slick glass-fronted café-takeaway has cornered the local market in affordable and surprisingly healthy gourmet pies. There are over a dozen fillings, from richly flavoured Mediterranean lamb to Moroccan aubergine and feta.

Wai Kika Moo Kau (☎ 671117; 11a Kensington Gdns; mains £5-8; ☽ 9am-6pm) Say its daft name fast and you'll get a clue to the ethos of this primarily veggie-vegan café. It spills onto the pedestrian street outside so you can sip your soyachino or tuck into meat-free specials as the shoppers pass by.

Food For Friends (☎ 202310; 17a Prince Albert St; mains £6-10; ☽ lunch & dinner) This airy glass-sided restaurant attracts the attention of passersby as much as it does the loyalty of its customers with an ever-inventive choice of vegetarian and vegan food. Children are also catered to.

Other worthy contenders:

Picasso's (☎ 321233; 24 Ship St; mains £3.50-7; ☽ lunch & dinner) Cheap pizza served at breakneck speed and garnished with well-placed Italian cheek.

Red Veg (☎ 679910; 21 Gardner St; mains £4-6; ☽ 11am-10pm) Vegetarian fast-food classics from blueberry pancakes to burgers.

MIDRANGE
Nia Café (☎ 671371; 87-88 Trafalgar St; mains £8-13; ☽ 9am-11pm Mon-Sat, to 6pm Sun) There's a very organic, textured feel about this simple rustic-chic café furnished with rough-cut wooden tables, pitted floor and exposed brick. It's a popular spot to chew the fat over a cappuccino or glass of organic wine, or to tuck into daily specials.

Terre á Terre (☎ 729051; 71 East St; mains £10-15; ☽ lunch & dinner Wed-Sun, dinner Tue) Herbivores have never had it so good. Terre á Terre offers cultured vegetarian dining in a blissful air-con environment with simple wood furniture, elegant stemware and striking citrus art. The inventive dishes, full of rich robust flavours, are exhaustively explained in the menu.

Seven Dials (☎ 885555; 1-3 Buckingham Pl; set lunch/dinner from £10/26.50; ☺ lunch & dinner Tue-Sun) Housed in an imposing former bank, this formal and crisply set-out restaurant is praised for excellent seasonal fish dishes. It's almost a mile from the seafront but worth the walk or taxi fare for a special occasion or well-deserved splurge.

Due South (☎ 821218; 139 Kings Rd Arches; mains £11-15; ☺ lunch & dinner Mon-Sat, lunch Sun) Sheltered under a cavernous Victorian arch on the seafront with a curvaceous front window and small bamboo-screened terrace on the promenade, this refined yet relaxed restaurant specialises in dishes cooked with local, environmentally sustainable and seasonal ingredients.

English's Oyster Bar (☎ 327980; 29-31 East St; mains £11-25; ☺ lunch & dinner) A 60-year institution, this Brightonian seafood paradise dishes up everything from oysters to traditional scampi to lavish lobster thermidor. It's converted from fishermen's cottages, with echoes of the elegant Edwardian era inside and buzzing alfresco dining on the pedestrian square outside.

De Vere Grand Hotel (☎ 224300; King's Rd; afternoon tea £14; ☺ 3-6pm) The place for that most English of English traditions, afternoon tea. Take a table in the conservatory and nibble on cucumber sandwiches with tea while live piano music tinkles in the background.

Gingerman (☎ 696934; Drake's Hotel, Marine Pde, Hove; 2/3 courses £25/30) Chic and minimalist, this well-loved eatery has a modish menu bolstered by classical French influence. It's set in an exclusive hotel and occupies a curvaceous room, with red blinds and soft jazz. It also has an equally good but more informal venue on Norfolk Sq.

Also try:

Saint (☎ 607835; 22 St James' St; 2-course set lunch/dinner £12/16, 3-course £16/19; ☺ lunch & dinner Tue-Sun) Beloved Italian and Spanish bistro.

Moshi Moshi (☎ 719195; Bartholomew Sq; dishes £1.75-3, bento box £14.50; ☺ noon-10.30pm Tue-Sun) Ultramodern Japanese in frosted-glass fish tank.

Drinking

Brighton's nightlife is second only to London's, and has its own unique cocktail mix of clubs and bars along the seafront. For more ideas, visit www.drinkinbrighton.com.

Evening Star (☎ 328931; www.eveningstarbrighton.co.uk; 55 Surrey St) Hopheads heap praise on this beer-drinkers paradise; a snug unpretentious pub with a conveniently short stagger to the station after a send-off from its wonderful selection of award-winning real ales, Belgian beers, organic lagers and real ciders.

Beach (☎ 722272; 171 Kings Rd Arches) On a summer's day, there's nowhere better to sit and watch the world go by than at this popular beach bar and club. It has a funky brick-vaulted interior, and a wide terrace spilling onto the promenade within earshot of the surf and sight of the talent dipping into it.

Koba (☎ 720059; www.kobauk.com; 135 Western Rd; ☺ 5pm-late) This übercool cocktail bar oozes it-crowd extravagance and exclusivity. It's technically a member's club but the sumptuous velvet-draped front bar opens to the hoi polloi until 11pm, just enough time to ingratiate yourself with a member to be invited back into the private 'Champagne Bar' or 'The Gods' with high ceiling and altar-style bar.

Dorset (☎ 605423; www.thedorset.co.uk; 28 North Rd) There's a laid-back Parisian street-café feel to this gastropub and Brighton institution, which throws open its doors and windows in fine weather and spills tables onto the pavement. You'll be just as welcome for a morning coffee as for an evening pint here, and if you decide not to leave between the two, there's always its decent menu too.

Riki Tik (☎ 683844; 18a Bond St; ☺ 4pm-late) This try-hard-cool bar is a popular preclub venue pumping out kaleidoscopic cocktails and thumping beats. Its décor is as varied as its booze with hypnotic oil-lamp projections, and even a pair of whimsical swings beneath an oversized moon.

Entertainment

Brighton offers the best entertainment line-up on the south coast, with clubs to rival London and Manchester for cool. Keep tabs on what's hot and what's not by searching out publications such as the *List* or the *Source* and *What's On*.

NIGHTCLUBS

When Britain's top DJs aren't plying their trade in London, Ibiza or Aya Napia, chances are you'll spy them here. All Brighton's clubs open until 2am, and many as late as 5am.

Honey Club (☎ 202807; www.thehoneyclub.co.uk; 214 Kings Rd Arches; admission £5-12) A cavernous seafront

GAY & LESBIAN BRIGHTON

Perhaps it's Brighton's long-time association with the theatre, but for more than 100 years the city has been a gay haven. Gay icons Noel Coward and Ivor Novello were regular visitors, but in those days the scene was furtive and separate. From the 1960s onwards, the scene really began to open up, especially in the Kemptown area and around Old Steine. Today, with more than 25,000 gay men and 10,000 to 15,000 lesbians living in the city, it is the most vibrant queer community in the country outside London.

Kemptown (aka Camptown), on and off St James' St, is where it's all at. In recent years the old Brunswick Town area of Hove has emerged as a quieter alternative to the traditionally cruisy (and sometimes seedy) Kemptown, but the community here has responded by branching out from the usual pubs that served as nightly pick-up joints. Now you will find a rank of gay-owned businesses, from cafés and hotels to bookshops as well as the more obvious bars, clubs and saunas. There's even a Gay's The Word walking tour (see Brighton Walks, p215).

For up-to-date information on what's going on in gay Brighton, check out the websites www.gay.brighton.co.uk and www.realbrighton.com or pick up the free monthly magazine **Gscene** (www.gscene.com) from various venues or the tourist office.

For drinking...

Café 22 (☎ 626682; 129 St James' St; ☯ 8am-6pm Mon-Fri, 10am-6pm Sat & Sun) This cool coffee shop hangout and internet café is *the* place to get word on everything going on in town. It has snacks for £2 to £3.
Amsterdam (☎ 688825; www.amsterdam.uk.com; 11-12 Marine Pde; ☯ noon-2am) Hotel, sauna, restaurant and extremely hip bar above the pier; its sun terrace is a particular hit.
Candy Bar (☎ 622424; www.thecandybar.co.uk; 129 St James' St; ☯ 9pm-2am) Slick café-bar-club venue for the girls, with pink-lit arches, curvaceous bar, pool table and dance floor
Queen's Arms (☎ 696873; www.queensarmsbrighton.com; 7 George St; ☯ 3pm-late) Plenty of camp in the cabaret and karaoke acts at this pub make it a definite stop on the Brighton gay trail.

For dancing...

Bars and pubs may be fun, but the real action takes place on and off the dance floor.

Revenge (☎ 608133; www.revenge.co.uk; 7 Marine Pde; ☯ 10.30pm-3am) Nightly disco, occasional cabaret and a dash of drag.
Club Envy (8-9 Marine Pde; ☯ 9am-2am) Stylish, chic but claustrophobic club where every night is different.

club that jumps from strength to strength, almost as popular with DJs as it is with the weekly queues of clubbers that pile into its glittering depths. Dress up, party hard, then cool off your aching feet in the sea.

Audio (☎ 606906; www.audiobrighton.com; 10 Marine Pde; admission £3-8) Some of the city's top club nights can be found at this ear-numbing venue, where the music's top priority, cheap-drink offers roll and the dress-down rule of thumb deters designer dollies. Every night is different.

Funky Buddha (☎ 725541; www.funkybuddhabrighton.co.uk; Kings Rd Arches; admission £2-8) Lotus flower lamps and stylish chandeliers illuminate the twin arches of this sexy little subterranean seafront club, which dips into everything from acid house to disco.

Concorde 2 (☎ 673311; www.concorde2.co.uk; Madeira Dr, Kemptown; admission £7.50-16) Brighton's best-known and best-loved club is a disarmingly unpretentious den where DJ Fatboy Slim pioneered the Big Beat Boutique and still occasionally graces the decks.

Ocean Rooms (☎ 699069; www.oceanrooms.co.uk; 1 Morley St; admission £3-10) This enduring favourite crams in three floors of dance variety, from don't-touch-me minimalist chic to velveteen cabaret bar, and the down-to-business dance floor where you can lap up the efforts of top DJs.

CINEMAS

Odeon Cinema (☎ 08/1 22 44 007; cnr King's Rd & West St) Check out this seafront cinema for mainstream movies.

THE SOUTHEAST COAST

Duke of York (☎ 602503; Preston Circus) About a mile north of North Rd; shows more art-house films and old classics.

THEATRE

Brighton Dome (☎ 709709; www.brighton-dome.org.uk; 29 New Rd) Once the stables and exercise yard of King George IV, this Art Deco complex houses three theatre venues within the Royal Pavilion estate. The box office is on New Rd.

Theatre Royal (☎ 328488; New St) Built by decree of the Prince of Wales in 1806, this venue hosts plays, musicals and operas.

Komedia Theatre (☎ 467100; www.komedia.co.uk; Gardner St, North Laine) This former billiards hall and supermarket is now a stylish comedy, theatre and cabaret venue.

Shopping

An atmospheric jigsaw of narrow lanes and tiny alleyways that was once a fishing village, the **Lanes** is Brighton's most popular shopping district. Its every twist and turn is jam-packed with jewellers and gift shops, coffee shops and boutiques selling everything from antique firearms to the latest foot fashions. There's another, less claustrophobic shopping district in **North Laine**, a series of streets northwest of the Lanes, including Bond, Gardner, Kensington and Sydney Sts, that are full of retro-cool boutiques, music stalls and craft outlets.

Getting There & Away

Brighton is 53 miles from London and transport is fast and frequent.

BUS

Coaches leave hourly to London Victoria (£10, two hours 20 minutes) and twice hourly to Lewes (50 minutes) and Eastbourne (one hour 30 minutes). They also go twice daily to Chichester (2¼ hours) and Arundel (two hours). **National Express** (☎ 08705 808080; www.nationalexpress .com) has coach links to all London airports.

TRAIN

There are four hourly services to London Victoria and King's Cross stations (£17.70, 1¼ hours). For £2 on top of the rail fare you can get a PlusBus ticket that gives unlimited travel on Brighton & Hove buses for the day. There are three services per hour to Portsmouth (£13.80, 1½ hours), twice-hourly services to Chichester, Eastbourne and Hastings, and links to Canterbury and Dover.

Getting Around

Brighton is a sizable place but you'll be able to cover most of it on foot. Alternatively you can buy a day ticket (£2.80) from the driver to scoot back and forth on Brighton & Hove buses.

Parking can be expensive. To park in any central street space you will need a voucher. They can be purchased from various garages and shops around town and cost £1.50 per half-hour in the centre, or per hour further out. Alternatively, there's a park and ride outside town with connecting buses, and pay-and-display parking on the Kingsway in Hove.

Cab companies include **Brighton Streamline Taxis** (☎ 747474) and **City Cabs** (☎ 205205) and there's a taxi rank on the junction of East St with Market St.

You can rent bikes from **Planet Cycle Hire** (☎ 748881; West Pier Promenade; ⏰ 10am-6pm Thu-Tue May-Sep, 10am-4pm Fri-Mon Oct-Apr), next to West Pier, for £8/12 per half day/day. Deposit and ID required.

WEST SUSSEX

Serene West Sussex comes as a little light relief after the faster-paced adventures of Brighton and East Sussex. The tumbling hills and valleys of the South Downs dominate the countryside. And both dreamy Arundel and dignified big sister Chichester make good bases from which to explore the county's winding country lanes and scout out its remarkable Roman ruins.

ARUNDEL

☎ 01903 / pop 3297

There's something irresistibly romantic about Arundel: this attractive little town with its vast fairy-tale castle and steep hillside streets lined by excellent restaurants and antique stores makes a great weekend break or stopover. While much of the town appears medieval – especially the whimsical castle that has been home to the dukes of Norfolk for centuries – most of it dates to Victorian times.

Information

The **tourist office** (☎ 882268; www.sussexbythesea.com; 61 High St; ⏰ 10.30am-4pm Mon-Sat, 2-4pm Sun Easter-Oct, 10am-3pm daily Nov-Easter) has maps and an accommodation-booking service for £1.50. Here too is a small **museum** (☎ 885708; www.arundelmuseum .org; adult/child £2/1) on Arundel's history.

THE SOUTHEAST COAST

WORTH THE TRIP

After cooing over majestic Arundel Castle, you might find yourself fancying a piece of that princely lifestyle pie for yourself. And hidden away in the countryside near the pretty village of Amberley, about 5 miles north of Arundel, **Amberley Castle Hotel** (☎ 831992; www.amberleycastle.co.uk; Amberley; d £165-780; P ✕) lets you convert your daydreaming into reality. Set in a 900-year-old castle complete with moat and two-tonne oak portcullis that is lowered every night, this luxurious hotel feels anything but embattled. Rather, its 19 sumptuous rooms, Jacuzzi bathrooms, landscaped gardens complete with tennis, croquet, golf, thatched treehouse and traditional British dining will leave you feeling utterly at peace. At least until you get the credit card bill.

Sights & Activities

The 18th- and 19th-century English gentry were famously fond of a good folly, but you'll see few more elaborate than **Arundel Castle** (☎ 883136; www.arundelcastle.org; adult/under 16yr/student & senior £12/7.50/9.50; ⏰ 11am-5pm Sun-Fri Apr-Oct), which builds upon the altogether more modest remains of an 11th-century keep in its heart. The original castle was largely razed during the English Civil War, but it was enthusiastically reconstructed to heroic proportions by the eighth, 11th and 15th dukes of Norfolk between 1718 and 1900. The castle is still home to the current duke. Highlights include the atmospheric keep, the massive Great Hall and the library, which has paintings by Gainsborough and Holbein.

While you're here, take a quick tour of Arundel's ostentatious 19th-century **cathedral** (☎ 882297; www.arundelcathedral.org; ⏰ 9am-6pm summer, to dusk winter), built in the French Gothic style by the 15th duke. It houses the remains of his ancestor, St Philip Howard, now a canonised Catholic martyr who was caught praying for a Spanish victory against the English in 1588.

Kids meanwhile, will most likely opt for the **Arundel Ghost Experience** (☎ 889821; High St; adult/child £4/3; ⏰ 10am-6pm), where they'll hear hair-raising ghost stories and see old prison cells that are supposedly haunted themselves.

Bird fanciers will be rewarded by a trip to the 4-hectare **Wildfowl & Wetlands Centre** (☎ 883355; www.wwt.org.uk; Mill Rd; adult/child £6.95/3.75; ⏰ 9.30am-5pm Apr-Sep, to 4.30pm Oct-Mar), a mile east of the centre as the duck flies.

At the foot of High St is the Town Quay, from where you can hire your own boat or hop on a **cruise** (adult/child £6/4) of the River Arun.

Sleeping

Arundel YHA (☎ 0870 770 5676; arundel@yha.org.uk; Warningcamp; dm £15; P ✕ 🖥) Muddy boots and young families are welcome at this excellent hostel, housed in a Georgian mansion and principally catering to South Downs walkers. It's in sprawling grassy grounds on a charming country lane a 20- to 30-minute walk from town off the A27 (call for directions).

Town House (☎ 883847; www.thetownhouse.co.uk; 65 High St; s/d from £65/75; ✕) This gem of a boutique hotel has five wonderful Regency-style rooms, variously furnished with white four-poster beds, filmy fabrics and panelled walls. The charming service and period décor are accompanied by the requisite mod-cons, including DVD players.

Norfolk Arms (☎ 882101; www.forestdale.com; High St; s/d from £75/125; P ✕) A rambling old Georgian coaching inn built by the 10th duke, the Norfolk Arms has a comfortable old feel that resists any hint of modern pizzazz but has beautifully kept country-style rooms and a family of plastic ducks to accompany you at bathtime.

Also worth a look:

Arden Guest House (☎ 882544; 4 Queen's Lane; s/d £35/54; P ✕) Victorian house B&B by the river.

Arundel House (☎ 882136; www.arundelhouseonline .co.uk; 11 High St; d Mon-Thu from £60, Fri-Sun from £100; ✕) Stunning contemporary rooms and restaurant.

Eating

Pallant of Arundel (☎ 882288; www.pallantofarundel; The Square; ⏰ 9am-6pm Mon-Sat) Fancy a riverside picnic in true English style? Take your pick of local cheese, freshly baked bread, pâté, wine and more sinful treats from this irresistible delicatessen.

Tudor Rose (☎ 883813; 49 High St; mains £5-8; ⏰ 9am-6pm) There's a likeably kitsch spirit to this bustling family-run tearoom, with shades of pub-décor and walls cluttered with everything from faux armour to brollies, ship wheels to a portrait of the Queen. The staff is uncommonly welcoming and efficient.

Lezinc (☎ 884500; www.lezinc.co.uk; 51 High St; mains £6-10; ☺ 9.30am-7pm Fri-Wed, to 10pm Thu) Slick modern designware and silver-grey rattan furniture combine with low ceilings and oak beams of an old town house at this chic Parisian-style bistro, where it's all too easy to linger over fine wines by the glass, great coffees or light bites including *pain Poîlane* (an unusual French bread with a slightly sour flavour) and gourmet tarts.

Town House (☎ 883847; 65 High St; 2-/3-course set lunch £12.50-16, set dinner £22/25; ☺ Wed-Sat) The only thing that rivals the stunning 16th-century Florentine gilded walnut ceiling at this elegant eatery is the acclaimed Mediterranean-influenced cuisine, and sparkling atmosphere. Book ahead.

Getting There & Away
Trains are the way to go. They run to London Victoria (£19.70, 1½ hours, twice hourly), and to Chichester (20 minutes, twice hourly). There are also links to Brighton (£7.30, 1¼ hours, twice hourly).

AROUND ARUNDEL
At **Bignor Roman Villa** (☎ 869259; adult/child £4.35/1.85; ☺ 10am-6pm Jun-Sep, 10am-5pm May & Oct, 10am-5pm Tue-Sun Mar-Apr) you can discover an astonishingly fine collection of mosaics preserved within an atmospheric thatched complex that's historic in its own right. Happened upon by a farmer in 1811, the villa was built around AD 190. The wonderful mosaic floors include vivid scenes of chunky-thighed gladiators, a beautiful Venus whose eyes seem to follow you about the room, and an impressive 24m-long gallery design.

While Bignor is well worth the trip, it's a devil of a place to reach without your own wheels. It's located 6 miles north of Arundel off the A29.

CHICHESTER
☎ 01243 / pop 27,477
Compact Chichester is a well-to-do Georgian market town that manages to straddle the divide between countryside charm and cosmopolitan culture. On the one hand, it's home to an array of traditional tea-and-crumpet shops, well-mannered townsfolk, a fine cathedral and streets of handsome 18th-century town houses. While on the other, Chichester boasts a famous theatre and arts festival and a superb modern-art

gallery. Also the administrative capital of West Sussex, the town is within easy striking distance of some fascinating Roman remains that recall its days as a sprawling port garrison shortly after the invasion of AD 43.

Orientation & Information
The centre of town is marked by a striking crown-shaped Market Cross, built in 1501. The streets around it are pedestrianised and everything you'd want to see is within walking distance. There is a **tourist office** (☎ 775888; www.visitchichester.org; 29a South St; ☺ 9.15am-5.15pm Mon-Sat year-round, plus 11am-3.30pm Sun Apr-Sep) and a **post office** (cnr Chapel & West Sts) in town. **Internet Junction** (☎ 776644; 2 Southdown Building, Southgate; per hr £1; ☺ 9am-8pm Mon-Fri, 11am-8pm Sat & Sun) has double-quick internet access.

Sights
CHICHESTER CATHEDRAL
A vision in clean-cut elegance, this **cathedral** (☎ 782595; www.chichestercathedral.org.uk; West St; requested donation £5; ☺ 7.15am-7pm Jun-Aug, to 6pm Sep-May) was begun in 1075 and largely rebuilt in the 13th century. Three storeys of beautiful arches sweep upwards, and Romanesque carvings are dotted around. The freestanding church tower was built in the 15th century, and the spire is 19th century. There are also a few bold modern flourishes, including an entrancing stained-glass window by Marc Chagall and the not-so-pretty disembodied likenesses of the Queen and Prince Phillip outside the main entrance.

Guided tours operate at 11.15am and 2.30pm Monday to Saturday, Easter to October, and the excellent cathedral choir are guaranteed to give you goose bumps during the daily **Evensong** (☺ 5.30pm Mon-Sat, 3.30pm Sun).

PALLANT HOUSE GALLERY
Based in a wonderful Queen Anne town house once owned by a wealthy wine merchant, **Pallant House** (☎ 774557; www.pallant .org.uk; 9 North Pallant; adult/child/student £6.50/2/3.50; ☺ 10am-5pm Tue-Sat, 12.30-5pm Sun) is now an outstanding art gallery. Reopened with a swish new wing in 2006, it houses a superb collection of 20th-century British art, with names such as Caulfield, Freud, Sutherland and Moore represented. There are also historic works from British and international artists, from Picasso to Cézanne, Gainsborough to Rembrandt.

CHURCH OF THE GREYFRIARS

If you fancy a stroll in the park, it's worth a peek at the remains of this Franciscan **church** (☎ 784683; Priory Park; admission free; ☒ noon-4pm Sat Jun–mid-Sep), built in the northeastern corner of the town in 1269. After dissolution in 1536 the structure became the guildhall and later a court of law, where William Blake was tried for sedition in 1804.

Festivals & Events

Running for over 30 years, the annual **Chichester Festivities** (☎ 785718; www.chifest.org.uk) squeezes a wealth of terrific theatre, art, remarkably highbrow and fun low-brow speakers, fireworks and performances of every musical genre it can into three weeks in June and July.

Sleeping

Most accommodation in Chichester is midrange, with little for budget travellers.

University College Chichester (☎ 816071; College Lane; rooms from £27; ☒ Jun-Aug) Functional students' rooms are for rent during summer months.

Litten House (☎ 774503; www.littenho.demon.co.uk; 148 St Pancras St; s/d from £30/44; ☒) Freshly home-baked bread and jams are served up for breakfast in the garden or conservatory at this disarming central Georgian town house, which has three spacious and gracious old-style rooms. Request room No 2 for an idyllic little balcony that overlooks the garden. Ther's a car park that lies across the way in New St.

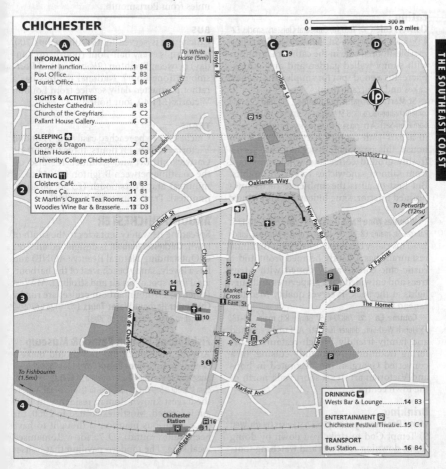

CHICHESTER

George & Dragon (☎ 785660; www.georgeanddrag oninn.co.uk; 51 North St; s/d £55/85; ☒) Bedding down in a barn has never been so comfortable. Located behind a pleasant old pub, this converted building now houses 10 modern en suite rooms with chunky wooden beds, sunny colours and touches of metal tracery.

White Horse (☎ 535219; www.whitehorsechilgrove .co.uk; Chilgrove; s/d Mon-Thu £65/95, Fri-Sun £95/120; ℗ ☒) For those with their own wheels, this beautiful whitewashed 18th-century coaching inn covered in wisteria is well worth the 6-mile drive north of Chichester. It has a first-rate restaurant (with a renowned 600-strong wine list) and nine polished contemporary rooms with king-sized beds, bathrobes and CD players.

Eating

Cloisters Café (☎ 783718; Cathedral Cloisters; snacks £2-4; ☺ 8.30am-5.30pm Mon-Sat, 10am-4pm Sun) Sparkling marble-floored café in the cathedral grounds with sunny walled garden and airy atmosphere. It's a good spot for simple sandwiches, cakes and fair trade drinks.

St Martin's Organic Tea Rooms (☎ 786715; www .organictearooms.co.uk; 3 St Martins St; snacks £3-5; ☺ 9am-6pm Mon-Sat) An oasis of quirky English calm in a part-18th-century part-medieval town house, this passionately organic café serves freshly ground coffee and wholesome fare from salmon sandwiches to Welsh rarebits. But best of all is the ambience of its low-beamed interior, snug hideaways and winter fire.

Woodies Wine Bar & Brasserie (☎ 779895; 10-13 St Pancras St; mains £8-12; ☺ lunch & dinner Mon-Sat, lunch Sun) This classy but relaxed, lively but romantic restaurant has a darkly beamed front and a rustic-chic conservatory dotted with citrus trees and entwined with grapevines and fairy lights at the back. It serves quality Mediterranean food.

Comme Ça (☎ 788724; 67 Broyle Rd; mains £8-13; ☺ lunch Wed-Sun, dinner Tue-Sat) A family-owned and family-friendly French restaurant, offering traditional Normandy cuisine, in a converted Georgian inn decorated in hops and Victorian art. It's a short walk north of the town centre.

Drinking

West's Bar & Lounge (☎ 539637; St Peters Church, West St) Tempt God to strike you down by doing shots, downing cocktails and watching football in this converted Gothic church opposite the cathedral. Its soaring arches, dark wooden ceiling and candlelit tables add weight and atmosphere to what's basically just a trendy wine bar.

Entertainment

Chichester Festival Theatre (☎ 781312; www.cft.org.uk; Oakland's Park) This modern playhouse was built in 1962 and has a long and distinguished history. Sir Laurence Olivier was the theatre's first director and Ingrid Bergman, Sir John Gielgud and Sir Anthony Hopkins are a few of the other famous names to have played here.

Getting There & Away

Chichester is 60 miles from London and 18 miles from Portsmouth.

BUS

Chichester is served by Coastliner bus 700, which runs every half-hour (hourly on Sunday) between Brighton (2¼ hours) and Portsmouth (one hour). National Express has a rather protracted daily service from London Victoria (£11.40, four hours).

TRAIN

Chichester can be reached easily from London Victoria (£18.50, 1¾ hours, three hourly) via Gatwick airport and Arundel. It's also on the coastline between Brighton (£9, 44 to 58 minutes) and Portsmouth (£5.30, 30 to 40 minutes). Trains run twice hourly.

AROUND CHICHESTER

Spreading its watery tentacles to the south of town, **Chichester Harbour** is designated an Area of Outstanding Natural Beauty (AONB) and has a lovely, sandy beach west of the harbour, ideal for a spot of sea air and strolling. At West Itchenor, 1½-hour harbour cruises are run by **Chichester Harbour Water Tours** (☎ 01243-670504; www.chwt.co.uk; adult/child £6.50/3).

Fishbourne Roman Palace & Museum

Anyone mad about mosaics should make a beeline to **Fishbourne Palace** (☎ 01243-785859; www .sussexpast.co.uk; Salthill Rd; adult/child £6.50/3.40; ☺ 10am-5pm Mar-Jul & Sep-Oct, to 6pm Aug, to 4pm Nov-Feb), where the largest known Roman residence in Britain is located. Mostly excavated in 1960, the once-luxurious mansion is thought to have been built around AD 75 for a Romanised local king. The modern pavilion that houses its foundations, hypocaust and painstakingly re-laid mosaics give the site a rather sterile atmosphere but the mosaics are enthralling enough to propel the visitor back in time. The centrepiece is a spectacular floor depicting cupid riding a dolphin flanked by sea horses and panthers. There's a fascinating little museum and replanted Roman gardens.

Fishbourne Palace is 1½ miles west of Chichester, just off the A259. Buses 11 and 700 leave hourly from Monday to Saturday (bus 56 on Sunday) from outside Chichester Cathedral and stop at the bottom of Salthill Rd (five minutes' walk away). The museum is a 10-minute stroll from Fishbourne train station.

Petworth

The high-and-mighty 17th-century stately home **Petworth House** (NT; ☎ 01798 342207; adult/ child £8/4; ☻ 11am-5pm Sat-Wed Apr-Oct) is found on the outskirts of its namesake village, 12 miles northeast of Chichester. It's home to an extraordinary art collection. JMW Turner was a regular visitor and the house is still home to the largest collection (20) of his paintings outside London's Tate Gallery. There are also many paintings by Van Dyck, Reynolds, Gainsborough, Titian, Bosch and William Blake. Other highlights are the fabulously theatrical grand staircase, and the exquisite Carved Room, which ripples with wooden reliefs by master-chiseller Gibbons.

But best of all is the surrounding **Petworth Park** (adult/child £3/1.50; ☻ 8am-sunset), the supreme realisation of Capability Brown's romantic natural landscape theory. It's home to herds of deer, and is the site of open-air concerts in summer.

Petworth is 5 miles from the train station at Pulborough, from where bus 1 runs hourly to Petworth Sq (15 minutes, Monday to Saturday).

HAMPSHIRE

Think of Hampshire and images of petticoated heroines, stiff-backed gentlemen and rolling rural landscapes of novelist Jane Austin (1775–1817) may spring to mind. But while still blessed with those undulating chalk downs and fertile agricultural valleys, this is a remarkably varied county. Winchester, once capital of the powerful Kingdom of Wessex that extended into Wiltshire and Dorset, delights with its fascinating cathedral and beautiful setting. The coastline too is rich in maritime history, not least at Portsmouth, home of the once-mighty Royal Navy. And Hampshire's southwestern corner also claims the lovely open heath and woodlands of the New Forest.

WINCHESTER

☎ 01962 / pop 41,420

The ancient, wistful and often eye-wateringly lovely cathedral city of Winchester is a must for all visitors to the region. A capital of Saxon kings and power-base of bishops, the city's rich history is reflected in heroic statues, handsome Elizabethan and Regency buildings, narrow winding streets and above all, the wondrous cathedral that marks its centre. Thanks to its moist location, nestled in a valley of the River Itchen, there are also charming waterside trails to explore, and as walkers will be well aware, the city marks the beginning of the beautiful South Downs Way (see p180).

History

The Romans first put their feet under the table here, but Winchester really took off when the powerful West Saxon bishops moved their Episcopal see here in AD 670. Thereafter, Winchester was the most important town in the powerful kingdom of Wessex. King Alfred the Great (r 871–99) made it his capital, and it remained so under Knut (r 1016–35) and the Danish kings. After the Norman invasion of 1066, William the Conqueror arrived here to claim the throne of England, and in 1086 he commissioned local monks to write the all-important *Domesday Book*, an administrative survey of the entire country and the most important clerical accomplishment of the Middle Ages. Winchester thrived right until the 12th century, when a fire gutted most of the city, after which London took its crown. A long slump lasted until the 18th century, when the town revived as a market town.

Orientation

The city centre is compact and easily managed on foot. Partly pedestrianised High St runs from west to east through the town. The bus station is smack in the middle of town opposite the Guildhall and tourist office, while the train station is five minutes' walk northwest. Jewry St borders the western centre and was once part of the Jewish quarter.

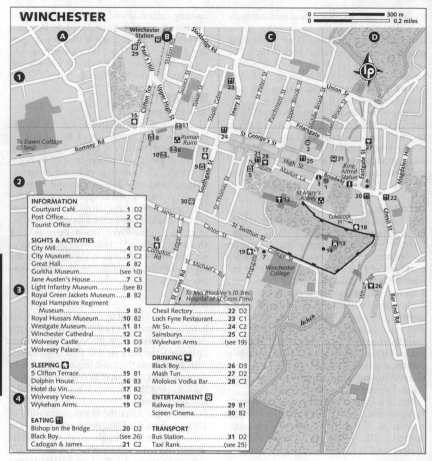

WINCHESTER

INFORMATION
Courtyard Café	1	D2
Post Office	2	C2
Tourist Office	3	C2

SIGHTS & ACTIVITIES
City Mill	4	D2
City Museum	5	C2
Great Hall	6	B2
Gurkha Museum	(see 10)	
Jane Austen's House	7	C3
Light Infantry Museum	(see 8)	
Royal Green Jackets Museum	8	B2
Royal Hampshire Regiment Museum	9	B2
Royal Hussars Museum	10	B2
Westgate Museum	11	B1
Winchester Cathedral	12	C2
Wolvesey Castle	13	D3
Wolvesey Palace	14	D3

SLEEPING
5 Clifton Terrace	15	B1
Dolphin House	16	B3
Hotel du Vin	17	B2
Wolvesey View	18	D2
Wykeham Arms	19	C3

EATING
Bishop on the Bridge	20	D2
Black Boy	(see 26)	
Cadogan & James	21	C2

Chesil Rectory	22	D2
Loch Fyne Restaurant	23	C1
Mr So	24	C2
Sainsburys	25	C2
Wykeham Arms	(see 19)	

DRINKING
Black Boy	26	D3
Mash Tun	27	D2
Molokos Vodka Bar	28	C2

ENTERTAINMENT
Railway Inn	29	B1
Screen Cinema	30	B2

TRANSPORT
Bus Station	31	D2
Taxi Rank	(see 25)	

Information

The **tourist office** (☎ 840500; www.visitwinchester
.co.uk; Broadway; ✆ 9.30am-5.30pm Mon-Sat, 11am-4pm
Sun May-Sep, 10am-5pm Mon-Sat Oct-Apr), in the pompous Gothic Revival Guildhall, has information
and an accommodation booking service. The
Courtyard Café (☎ 840820; per 30 min £2), also in the
Guildhall, has internet access. There's a **post office** (✆ 9.30am-6pm Mon-Sat) on Middle Brook St,
and plenty of banks and ATMs on High St.

Sights
WINCHESTER CATHEDRAL

Almost a thousand years of history is crammed
into Winchester's superb **cathedral** (☎ 857200;
www.winchester-cathedral.org.uk; adult/under 16yr/student £4/
free/2; ✆ 8.30am-6pm), which is not only the city's

star attraction but one of southern England's
most inspirational buildings. Admittedly it
makes an unusual picture from outside, with
a squat, almost half-hearted tower, a slightly
sunken rear and a fine Gothic façade. But once
inside you'll be struck by the one of the longest
medieval naves (164m) in Europe, and a fascinating jumble of features from all eras.

The cathedral sits beside foundations marking the town's original minster church built
in 643. It was begun in 1070 and completed
in 1093, and subsequently entrusted with the
bones of its patron saint, St Swithin (bishop
of Winchester from 852 to 862), who is best
known for the proverb that if it rains on St
Swithin's day, 15 July, it will rain for a further
40 days and 40 nights.

Soggy ground and poor workmanship did not augur well for the early church; the original tower collapsed in 1107 and major restructuring continued until the mid-15th century. At the cathedral's rear you'll spy a monument to diver William Walker, who is celebrated as having saved the cathedral from collapse by delving repeatedly into its waterlogged underbelly from 1906 to 1912 to bolster rotting wooden foundations with vast quantities of concrete and brick.

Advancing down the south side of the nave, it's worth being sidetracked by the **Cathedral Library & Triforium Gallery** (adult/senior & under 16yr £1/free; ☽ 11am-4pm Tue-Sat, 1-4pm Mon Apr-Oct), which affords a fine elevated view of the cathedral body and an up-close view of the dazzling illuminated pages of the 12th-century *Winchester Bible* – its colours as bright as if they were painted yesterday.

There's also the opportunity to walk over the bones of one of England's best loved authors, Jane Austen, whose grave is near the entrance in the northern aisle. Austen died a stone's throw from the cathedral in 1817 at **Jane Austen's House** (College St), where she spent her last six weeks; it's now a private residence.

The transepts are the most original parts of the cathedral, and the intricately carved medieval choir stalls are another must-see, sporting everything from mythical beasts to a mischievous green man.

Flooding often prevents **crypt tours** (free; ☽ tours 10.30am, 12.30pm & 2.30pm Mon-Sat) from going ahead, but you may still be able to peek inside to see the poignant solitary sculpture by Anthony Gormley called *Sound 2*.

Cathedral body **tours** (free; ☽ tours every hr 10am-3pm Mon-Sat) are run by enthusiastic volunteers and last one hour. There are also **tower and roof tours** (£4; ☽ tours 2.15pm Mon-Tue & Thu-Sat, plus 11.30am Sat Oct-May, 2.15pm Mon-Sat, plus 11.30am Sat Jun-Sep) up narrow stairwells and with views as far as Portsmouth. Sunday services take place at 8am, 10am and 11.15am, with Evensong at 3.30pm. Evensong is also held at 5.30pm Monday to Saturday.

THE GREAT HALL

Winchester's other showpiece is at the cavernous **Great Hall** (☎ 846476; admission free; ☽ 10am-5pm), the only part of 11th-century Winchester Castle that Oliver Cromwell spared from destruction. It's just south off Romsey Rd. Crowning the wall like a giant-sized dartboard

of green and cream spokes is what centuries of mythology have called **King Arthur's Round Table**. Before you get too excited, it's a 700-year-old fake, but a fascinating one nonetheless. It's thought to have been constructed in the late 13th century and later painted in the reign of Henry VIII (King Arthur's image is strangely reminiscent of Henry's youthful face).

This hall was also the stage for several dramatic English courtroom dramas, including the trial of adventurer Sir Walter Raleigh in 1603, who was sentenced to death but reprieved at the last minute.

Outside, near the hall's entrance, there's also a section of the old Roman wall, built around AD 200.

MUSEUMS

City Museum (☎ 863064; www.winchester.gov.uk/heritage; The Square; admission free; ☽ 10am-5pm Mon-Sat, noon-5pm Sun Apr-Oct, 10am-4pm Tue-Sat, noon-4pm Sun Nov-Mar) whizzes through Winchester's fascinating Roman and Saxon history, lingers on its Anglo-Norman golden age, pays homage to Jane Austen, and reconstructs several early-20th-century Winchester shops.

Fitting snugly into one of Winchester's two surviving medieval gateways, **Westgate Museum** (☎ 848269; High St; admission free; ☽ 10am-5pm Mon-Sat, noon-5pm Sun Apr-Oct, 10am-4pm Tue-Sat, noon-4pm Sun Feb & Mar) is a one-time debtors' prison with a macabre set of gibbeting irons last used to display an executed criminal's body in 1777. Scrawled crudely all over the interior walls is the 17th-century graffiti of prisoners.

For the military-minded, there's a clutch of army museums dotted around the Peninsula Barracks on Romsey Rd. The pick of the bunch is probably the **Royal Green Jackets Museum** (☎ 828549; www.winchestermilitarymuseums.co.uk; adult/child £2/1; ☽ 10am-5pm Mon-Sat, noon-4pm Sun Mar–mid-Nov), which has a mini rifle-shooting range, a room of 6000 medals and an impressive blow-by-blow diorama of Napoleon's downfall, the Battle of Waterloo.

And if that's your cup of tea, you may also enjoy the **Gurkha Museum** (☎ 842832; www.thegurkhamuseum.co.uk; adult/child/senior £2/free/1; ☽ 10am-5pm Mon-Sat, noon-4pm Sun), the **Light Infantry Museum** (☎ 828550; admission free; ☽ 10am-4pm Mon-Sat, noon-4pm Sun), the **Royal Hampshire Regiment Museum** (☎ 863658; Southgate St; admission free; ☽ 10am-12.30pm & 2-4pm Mon-Fri year-round, plus noon-4pm Sat & Sun Apr-Oct) and the **Royal Hussars Museum** (☎ 828541; admission free; ☽ 10am-4pm Tue-Fri, noon-4pm Sat & Sun).

THE SOUTHEAST COAST

WOLVESEY CASTLE & PALACE

The crumbling remains of early-12th-century **Wolvesey Castle** (EH; ☎ 023-9237 8291; admission free; ☷ 10am-5pm Apr-Sep) still sulk in the protective embrace of the city's walls, despite the building having been largely demolished in the 1680s. According to legend, its odd name comes from a Saxon king's demand for an annual payment of 300 wolves' heads. It was completed by Henry de Blois, and it served as the bishop of Winchester's residence throughout the medieval era. Queen Mary I and Philip II of Spain celebrated their wedding feast here in 1554. Today the bishop lives in the adjacent Wolvesey Palace.

CITY MILL

This 18th-century water-powered **mill** (NT; ☎ 870057; Bridge St; adult/child £3.20/1.60; ☷ 11am-5pm Wed-Sun Apr-Dec, also Mon & Tue Jun-Dec) straddles the river with an island garden. It's now a working water mill once again, and you can see the grinding process in action.

HOSPITAL OF ST CROSS

Monk, bishop, knight, politician and grandson of William the Conqueror, Henry de Blois was a busy man. But somewhere along the way he found time to found this still-impressive **hospital** (☎ 851375; www.stcrosshospital.co.uk; St Cross Rd; adult/child/senior £2.50/50p/£2; ☷ 9.30am-5pm Mon-Sat, 1-5pm Sun Apr-Oct, 10.30am-3.30pm Mon-Sat Nov-Mar) in 1132. As well as treating the ill and housing the needy, the hospital was built to feed and bed pilgrims and crusaders en route to the Holy Land. It's the oldest charitable institution in the country, and is a delightfully traditional place, still wandered by 25 elderly black- or red-gowned brothers in pie-shaped trencher hats, who continue to dole out alms. Take a peek into the stumpy church, the brethren hall, kitchen and the peaceful gardens. The best way to arrive is via the 1-mile Water Meadows Walk (below). Upon entering, claim the centuries-old traditional Wayfarer's Dole, a crust of bread and horn of ale (now a small swig of beer) from the Porter's Gate.

Activities

There are several options for a quiet amble through surrounding countryside, lanes or riverside parks. The **Water Meadows Walk** can be picked up near the entrance to Wolvesey Castle and goes for a mile to the St Cross Hospital. The tranquil **Riverside Walk** trails a

short distance from the castle along the bank of the River Itchen to High St. The stiffer walk up to **St Giles' Hill** rewards with fine city views. It's at the top of East Hill, half a mile from the castle, and is signposted.

Tours

A wide variety of 1½-hour **guided walks** (£3, under 16yr free; ☷ tours 11am & 2.30pm Mon-Sat Apr-Oct, 2.30pm Sun Jun-Sep, 11am Sat Nov-Mar) are organised through the tourist office. From May to September, evening walks also leave every Tuesday at 6.30pm (adult/child £4/1), and encompass subjects as diverse as Jane Austen's Winchester and a spooky 'Bring Out Your Dead' plague tour.

Sleeping

Budget accommodation is hard to come by. The tourist office's booking service costs £5, but can arrange some great deals.

Wolvesey View (☎ 852082; www.wintonian.com; 10 Colebrook Pl; s/d £44/58; P ☒) Squirreled away in a quiet cul de sac in the middle of town, this family home is easy strolling distance from cathedral and Wolvesey Castle, which its Yellow Room overlooks. The three simple rooms share a bathroom, and its owners are extremely knowledgeable about the city.

5 Clifton Terrace (☎ 890053; chrissiejohnston@hotmail .com; 5 Clifton Tce; s/d/f £55/65/80; ☒) This polished two-room B&B has a pleasant mix of new and antique furnishings, and a charming proprietor. It sits amid an elegant row of Georgian terraced town houses that rises to the west of town, a short walk from the train station.

Wykeham Arms (☎ 853834; www.accommodating -inns.co.uk; 75 Kingsgate St; r without bathroom £57, s/d £85/95; ☒) A Winchester institution, as much for its quirky bar and food (see p229) as its accommodation, this 18th-century inn also has 14 lovely, traditionally styled rooms above the pub and in the charming converted post office across the road. This place is highly recommended.

Dawn Cottage (☎ 869956; dawncottage@hotmail.com; 99 Romsey Rd; d £68; P ☒) Worth the mile-long hike outside town, this utterly charming vine-covered property offers a particularly tranquil stay and friendly welcome, with lovely views, a sun deck and pretty gardens, and just three tastefully decorated rooms.

Hotel du Vin (☎ 841414; www.hotelduvin.com; Southgate St; r £120-175; P ☒ ☐ wi-fi) Simple yet sophisticated, this fashionable boutique hotel will not only impress the wine-savvy clientele. Set in a handsome Georgian building from 1715, it offers 23 deeply comfortable rooms with organic, textured fabrics and plenty of mod cons. The bistro's famous in its own right. Breakfast is extra.

Also recommended:

Mrs Blockley's (☎ 852073; martinblockley@uwclub .net; 54 St Cross Rd; s/d £32/52; P ✗) Edwardian-house B&B on town's outskirts. Families, walkers and cyclists welcome.

Dolphin House (☎ 853284; www.dolphinhousestudios .co.uk; 3 Compton Rd; s/d £50/65; P ✗) Gorgeous town house with two garden-facing rooms.

Eating

Sainsburys (☎ 861792; Middle Brook St) For everyday supplies try this supermarket.

Cadogan & James (☎ 840805; 31a The Square; 🕙 9.30am-5.30pm Mon-Sat) Self-caterers will need dragging out of this delightful delicatessen, full of the smells of freshly baked breads, herbs and spices, and gourmet goodies.

Bishop on the Bridge (☎ 855111; 1 High St; mains £6.50-9; 🕙 noon-11pm) The good bar food and beers at this contemporary riverside watering hole taste even better when enjoyed on the secluded outdoor seating area overlooking the rushing water below.

Loch Fyne Restaurant (☎ 872930; 18 Jewry St; mains £9-15; 🕙 lunch & dinner) Winchester's branch of this quality seafood and fish chain is housed in a stunning Tudor jailhouse, full of twisted beams, wooden galleries and beautiful fireplaces. Depending on which section you're in, the atmosphere can be both lively and romantic.

Wykeham Arms (☎ 853834; 75 Kingsgate St; mains £9-13.50; 🕙 lunch & dinner) You might face each other across graffiti-dotted old school desks in this character-packed pub-restaurant, but the mood is far more mischievous than studious. Walking canes and tankards hang from the ceiling and open fires warm clients in winter. The food is sublime, the sausages (flavoured with local bitter) are famous, and the sticky-toffee pudding addictive.

Chesil Rectory (☎ 851555; 1 Chesil St; 2-/3-course lunch £19/23, 3-course dinner £45; 🕙 lunch & dinner Tue-Sat) Duck through the hobbit-size door of this gorgeous 15th-century half-timbered building, Winchester's oldest house, to enjoy a romantic and refined setting in oak-beamed rooms. Its modern Continental cuisine is perfect for a special night out.

Also recommended:

Mr So (☎ 861234; 3 Jewry St; mains £6-9; 🕙 lunch & dinner Mon-Sat) Winchester's favourite Chinese restaurant.

Black Boy (☎ 861754; 1 Wharf Hill; mains £8-10; 🕙 lunch & dinner) Serves decent pub qrub in a doolally environment.

Drinking

Black Boy (☎ 861754; 1 Wharf Hill; 🕙 11am-11pm) A celebration of English eccentricity, this adorable old pub is filled with obsessive and sometimes freaky collections, from pocket watches to wax facial features, bear traps, sawn paperbacks and tobacco pipes. Even the women's toilets cheekily sport gynaecological clamps and fish murals.

Molokos Vodka Bar (☎ 849236; 31b The Square; 🕙 noon-midnight, to 2am Fri) One of the city's slicker contemporary venues, Molokos lures in the youth of Winchester with just about every flavour of vodka under the sun, touts an R & B soundtrack and buzzing ambience. It graduates into a club on weekend nights.

Mash Tun (☎ 861440; 60 Eastgate St; 🕙 11am-midnight) Totally free from pretension or glitz, this small riverside pub is just a snug tranquil place to hang out with a glass of ale by the water, play pool, board games or tuck into Tex-Mex food in the low-lit modern bar. Families welcome during the day.

Entertainment

Winchester isn't a town for late-night revelry, though the students head for cheap pubs along Jewry St. Pick up the free *What's On in Winchester* from the tourist office for listings.

Railway Inn (☎ 867795; www.liveattherailway.co.uk; 3 St Paul's Hill; 🕙 noon-2.30pm & 5-11pm) Catch live bands from 8pm at this grungy place behind the station.

Screen Cinema (☎ 877007; www.screencinemas.co.uk; Southgate St; adult/under 15yr £5/4) Watch movies in a converted 19th-century military chapel.

Getting There & Away

Winchester is 65 miles from London and 15 miles from Southampton.

BUS

National Express has several direct buses to London Victoria Bus Station (£12.60, 2¼ hours). Buses also run to Southampton (30 minutes). **Wilts & Dorset** (adult/child £6.50/3.25) explorer tickets let you roam the region to the west, including the New Forest.

THE SOUTHEAST COAST

TRAIN

Train is often the more direct option. Trains leave every 20 minutes from London Waterloo (£22, one hour) and Southampton (15 to 23 minutes) and hourly from Portsmouth (£7.90, one hour). There are also fast links to the Midlands.

Getting Around

Your feet are the best form of transport. There's plenty of day parking within five minutes' walk of the centre or you can use the park-and-ride service for £2 per day. If you're staying for longer, consider joining the **Bikeabout** (☎ 847474; www.winchestermiracles .org; membership £15) scheme, which lets over-18s borrow bikes free for up to 24 hours at a time, as often as you like. Bikes can be picked up and dropped off at the tourist office, railway station and St Catherine's park-and-ride.

For a taxi try the rank outside Sainsbury's on Middle Brook St or phone **Wintax Taxis** (☎ 878727).

PORTSMOUTH

☎ 023 / pop 187,056

Be sure to swash those buckles and practice your salty sea-dog arrrs before arriving at this brawny harbour city. For Portsmouth is the principal port of Britain's Royal Navy, and its historic dockyard ranks alongside Greenwich as England's most fascinating centre of maritime history. Here you can jump aboard Lord Nelson's glorious warship HMS *Victory*, which led the charge at Trafalgar in 1805, and glimpse the timber-shivering remains of Henry VIII's 16th-century flagship, the *Mary Rose*.

Regeneration at the nearby Gunwharf Quays has added new glitz to its scurvy-riddled waterfront. A spectacular millennium-inspired structure, the Spinnaker Tower – keelhauled by the British media for its delays and spiralling costs – finally opened here in 2005, with views to knock the wind from its critics' sails.

However, Portsmouth is by no means a city noted for its beauty; it was heavily bombed during WWII and a combination of soulless postwar architecture and surprisingly deserted waterfront promenades can leave a melancholy impression. An array of museums justify an overnight stay for naval nuts, however, and the suburb of Southsea boasts some fair beaches, bars and good restaurants.

Orientation

The central quay known as The Hard is where you'll find the Historic Dockyard, tourist office, train station, Spinnaker Tower and the passenger-ferry terminal for the Isle of Wight. Another hop east is Old Portsmouth and The Point, a cluster of sea-worn, atmospheric buildings around the old harbour. Southsea is about 2 miles south.

Information

There are plenty of ATMs to be found on Osbourne Rd.

Laundry Care (☎ 9282 6245; 59 Osborne Rd; ⏰ 8am-6pm).

Library (☎ 9281 9311; Guildhall Sq; ⏰ 9.30am-7pm Mon-Fri, to 4pm Sat) Free internet access.

Online Café (☎ 9283 1106; 163 Elm Grove, Southsea; per 10 min/hr 50p/£2.60; ⏰ 9am-10pm)

Post office (Palmerston Rd) In Southsea.

Tourist office (☎ 9282 6722; www.visitportsmouth .co.uk; The Hard; ⏰ 9.30am-5.45pm Apr-Sep, to 5.15pm Oct-Mar) Can arrange walking tours and an accommodation service (for £2).

Tourist office branch (☎ 9282 6722; Clarence Esplanade; ⏰ 9.30am-5.45pm Jun-Sep, to 5.15pm Mar-May, to 4pm Oct-Feb); Next to the Blue Reef Aquarium in Southsea, this branch gives discounts to several attractions for tickets bought in advance.

Sights & Activities

SPINNAKER TOWER

Spiking the sky 170m above Gunwharf Quays is Portsmouth's unmistakeable new seamark and symbol of the city's newfound razzle-dazzle, the **Spinnaker Tower** (☎ 857520; www.spin nakertower.co.uk; Gunwharf Quays; adult/child £5.95/4.80; ⏰ 10am-10pm Jun-Aug, 10am-5pm Sun-Thu, 10am-10pm Fri & Sat Apr-May & Sep-Oct, 10am-5pm Sun-Fri, 10am-10pm Sat Nov-Mar). Opened in late 2005, an impressive *five years* later than originally planned, and vastly over budget at £36 million, the construction is the tallest publicly accessible structure in the UK.

Its two sweeping white arcs resemble a billowing sail from certain angles, and a sharp skeletal ribcage from others. There are some truly extraordinary views from its three observation decks (not to mention the hair-raising view through a glass floor). Below, the glitzy mall, wide people-watching patios and promenade dotted with palm trees complete the designers' vision of Portsmouth in the new millennium – give or take a few years.

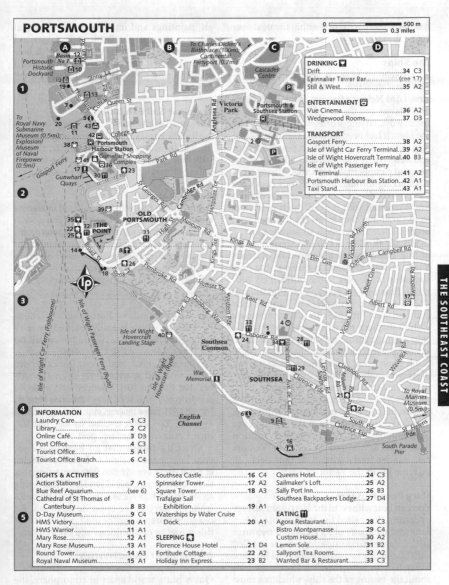

PORTSMOUTH

0   500 m
0   0.3 miles

THE SOUTHEAST COAST

PORTSMOUTH HISTORIC DOCKYARD

Portsmouth's biggest attraction, the **Historic Dockyard** (☎ 9286 1512; www.historicdockyard.co.uk; adult/child single-attraction ticket £10/8, all-inclusive ticket £16/13, season ticket £30/25; ⏰ 10am-6pm Apr-Oct, 10am-5.30pm Nov-Mar, last admission 1½ hours before closing) is a real bobby-dazzler. Set in the heart of the country's most important naval port, it comprises three stunning ships and a clutch of museums that pay homage to the historical might of the Royal Navy. Together they make for a full day's outing, though you may spend much of your time swimming through a tide of school children. The all-inclusive ticket lets you scramble about all the ships and museums and if you miss anything on your first visit, you can return within the next year to see the rest.

The Ships

As resplendent as she is venerable, the dockyard's star attraction is **HMS Victory** (www.hms-victory .com), Lord Nelson's flagship at the 1805 Battle of Trafalgar and the site of his infamous 'Kiss me Hardy...' dying words when victory over the French had been secured. This remarkable ship is topped by a forest of ropes and masts, and weighted by a swollen belly filled with cannon and paraphernalia for an 850-strong crew. Clambering through its numerous decks is a stirring experience, though these days cannon fire is replaced with the dull thuds of visitors so in thrall that they forget the low overhead beams. There are excellent 40-minute tours.

Equally thrilling are the adjacent remains of 16th-century warship and darling of Henry VIII, the **Mary Rose** (www.maryrose.org), the only such ship on display in the world. This 700-tonne floating fortress sank off Portsmouth after a mysterious incident of 'human folly and bad luck' in 1545. In an astoundingly ambitious piece of marine archaeology, the ship was raised from its watery grave in 1982. It now presents a ghostly image that could teach Hollywood a few tricks, its vast flank preserved in dim lighting, dripping and glistening in a constant mist of sea water.

Anywhere else the magnificent warship **HMS Warrior**, built in 1860, would grab centre stage. This handsome fella was at the cutting edge of technology in its day, riding the transition from wood to iron and sail to steam. Visitors can wander freely around its four decks to imagine life in the Victorian navy.

Mary Rose Museum

You can bear witness to the Herculean salvage operation that raised the 16th-century *Mary Rose* and see many of its recovered treasures at this fascinating museum, which is filled with fascinating facts and audiovisual insights. Every half an hour there's a 15-minute film about the raising of the ship, which is a must for all who didn't see coverage of the astonishing event in 1982. Purchasing a single-attraction ticket to this museum includes admission to the ship itself (see above).

Royal Naval Museum

This huge museum has five galleries of naval history, ship models, battle dioramas, medals, paintings and much more. Audiovisual displays re-create the Battle of Trafalgar and one even lets you take command of a battleship – see if you can cure the scurvy and avoid mutiny. One gallery is entirely devoted to Lord Nelson.

Trafalgar Sail Exhibition

This small **exhibition** (10am-5pm Apr-Oct, to 4pm Nov-Mar) showcases HMS *Victory*'s only remaining sail from the Battle of Trafalgar, riddled with holes made by Napoleonic cannon and a telling illustration of the battle's ferocity.

Action Stations!

Stumble into this warehouse-based **interactive experience** (www.actionstations.org) and you'll soon be controlling a replica Merlin helicopter, commanding a warship, upping periscope or jumping aboard a jerky simulator. The whole setup is a thinly disguised recruitment drive for the modern navy, but a fun one nonetheless.

GOSPORT

On the other side of Portsmouth Harbour is Gosport, which is easily reached by ferry from The Hard, and taxis and buses wait on the other side to whisk you around.

You can climb aboard a bona fide ex-service submarine and spare a thought for the sailors that lived in such cramped and odorous conditions at the **Royal Navy Submarine Museum** (9252 9217; www.rnsubmus.co.uk; adult/child £6.50/5; 10am-5.30pm Apr-Oct, to 4.30pm Nov-Mar), just less than a mile from the ferry port.

Or if it's things that go bang that float your boat, head straight to **Explosion! Museum of Naval Firepower** (9250 5600; www.explosion.org. uk; Priddy's Hard; adult/child £5.50/3.50; 10am-5.30pm Apr-Oct, 10am-4.30pm Thu, Sat & Sun Nov-Mar), 1.5 miles from the ferry in the opposite direction. An old gunpowder magazine built in 1771 houses this museum of munitions and ordinance.

OTHER SIGHTS & ACTIVITIES

A short hop over the water from Gunwharf Quays but a world apart in atmosphere, the **Point** is home to the characterful cobbled streets of Old Portsmouth, populated by salty-dog pubs with outdoor seating ideally positioned to watch the passing stream of ferries and navy ships, and to ponder the Spinnaker Tower from a new angle.

Just off The Point you can mount the **Round Tower** (originally built by Henry V), the **Square**

Tower of 1494 and take a stroll along the old fort walls. A short walk back from the water, the airy **Cathedral of St Thomas of Canterbury** (☎ 9282 3300; www.portsmouthcathedral.org.uk; High St; ☺ 9am-5pm) retains fragments of its 12th- and 17th-century incarnations, but has undergone a striking modern makeover that includes some quirky little statuettes by Peter Eugene Ball; look for Thomas Becket with a sword through his mitred head.

There's a cluster of attractions on Clarence Esplanade at the Southsea end of the waterfront. The unusually hands-on **Blue Reef Aquarium** (☎ 9287 5222; www.bluereefaquarium.co.uk; adult/child £7.50/5; ☺ 10am-5pm Mar-Oct, to 4pm Nov-Feb) has open-top tanks and huge underwater walkways and is a sure hit with kids. Another short stroll away is the bunkerlike **D-Day Museum** (☎ 9282 7261; www.ddaymuseum.co.uk; Clarence Esplanade; adult/child £6/3.60; ☺ 10am-5.30pm Apr-Sep, to 5pm Oct-Mar), which recounts Portsmouth's important role as departure point for the Allied D Day forces in 1944.

Then right next door by the water is ugly grey **Southsea Castle** (☎ 9282 7261; www.southseacastle .co.uk; adult/child £3/1.80; ☺ 10am-5.30pm Apr-Oct), built by Henry VIII, and by all accounts from where he would have watched his beloved *Mary Rose* sink. The castle was much altered in the early 19th century and there's now a lighthouse plonked on its top.

Further south, the **Royal Marines Museum** (☎ 9281 9385; www.royalmarinesmuseum.co.uk; Barracks Rd; admission £4.75; ☺ 10am-5pm Jun-Aug, to 4.30pm Sep-May) tells the story of the navy's elite force, and has a jungle warfare display complete with live snake and scorpions.

You can also poke your nose into **Charles Dickens' Birthplace** (☎ 9282 7261; www.charlesdickens birthplace.co.uk; 393 Old Commercial Rd; adult/child £3/1.80; ☺ 10am-5.30pm Apr-Oct) to see where the hard-hitting author drew his first breath in 1812 and to ponder the very couch upon which he breathed his last in 1870.

Tours
Local Haunts Bus Tours (☎ 0800 389 6897; www.loc alhaunts.com; adult/child/student £6.50/2.50/4.50; ☺ Mar-Oct) Runs 1½-hour sightseeing tours on old Routemaster buses from the bus station.
Walking tours (adult/child £3/free; ☺ tours 2.30pm) A wide range of themed tours is operated through the tourist office, which also rents out self-guided audio tours for £5.
Waterbus (☎ 07746 628169; Gunwharf Quays; complete circuit adult/child £5/3, one stop only £1/50p)

Runs circular harbour tours on the water, dropping off passengers between attractions in the process. The whole circuit takes 60 minutes.

Sleeping
Most B&Bs are in Southsea. Centrally located spots fill up quickly so book ahead.

Southsea Backpackers Lodge (☎ 9283 2495; www .portsmouthbackpackers.co.uk; 4 Florence Rd, Southsea; dm/d £13/30; ℗ 🖥) This grungy but friendly hostel with no-frills rooms packs three score beds into four- to eight-bed dorms, and has plenty of extras facilities like lockers, pool table and garden. Bike storage is available.

Fortitude Cottage (☎ 9282 3748; www.fortitudecot tage.co.uk; 51 Broad St, The Point; s from £35, d £60-75) With interesting if industrial views of the ferry port, this three-storey building is decorated in fresh light colours, has a lovely bow-windowed breakfast area, and has three decades experience of making travellers comfortable.

Sally Port Inn (☎ 9282 1860; High St, Old Portsmouth; s/d/f £45/65/75; ✗) If history makes you happy, and you don't mind a few shared facilities or mildly musty rooms, this creaky 16th-century inn has slanting floors, beams scavenged from ships and a Georgian cantilever staircase built with a ship's mast. The comfortable bar below serves food and there's a pay-and-display car park close by.

Holiday Inn Express (☎ 0870 417 6161; www.hiex press.com; The Plaza, Gunwharf Quays; r Mon-Thu/Fri-Sun £60/99; ℗ ✗ 🖥 ⅙) The location has it. Part of Gunwharf Quays shopping city, within stumbling distance of restaurants and bars, and spitting distance from the Spinnaker Tower, this spotlessly bland chain cuts a few corners (no cooked breakfasts or restaurant here) but still wins hands down for convenience.

Florence House Hotel (☎ 9275 1666; www.floren cehousehotel.co.uk; 2 Malvern Rd, Southsea; d £70-90; ℗ ✗ 🖥 wi-fi) One of the city's most stylish boutique hotels is in this lovingly restored Edwardian house, studded with original features that sit comfortably amid contemporary décor. Bedrooms vary from chaste Victorian to ultramodern, and feature designer bathrooms with blissful power shower.

Also recommended:
Sailmaker's Loft (☎ 9282 3045; sailmakersloft@aol .com; 5 Bath Sq, The Point; s/d £25/55) Unbeatable views across the water but off-site owners.
Queens Hotel (☎ 9282 2466; www.bw-queenshotel .co.uk; Clarence Pde, Southsea; s/d from £55/80; ℗ ✗ 🖥) Pompous neoclassical pile with Solent views.

THE SOUTHEAST COAST

Eating

Southsea has the best eating options.

Sallyport Tea Rooms (☎ 9281 6265; 35 Broad St, The Point; breakfasts £3.75-5.25, lunches £3-5; ☺ 10am-5pm) Just as a traditional teashop should be: homely, civilised, filled with fussy collectibles and serving up loose-leaf speciality teas and other old-fashioned tearoom delights to the strains of 1940s jazz.

Custom House (☎ 9283 2333; Gunwharf Quays; meals £6-9) The best of Gunwharf Quays numerous swanky eateries is in the 1790 Vernon Building, recently repurposed as a traditional-style pub with better than average bar food.

Wanted Bar & Restaurant (☎ 9282 6858; 39 Osborne Rd, Southsea; mains £6-10, 3-course set meal £21.95; ☺ 11am-11pm) This swish restaurant-bar boasts an inventive menu and a sleek minimalist vibe, featuring an illuminated wall of bottle bases and a light soundtrack of chill-out acoustics.

Agora Restaurant (☎ 9282 2617; 9 Clarendon Rd, Southsea; mains £8.50-10.50; ☺ lunch & dinner) This familial little Turkish hookah bar is tucked into an old beamed building and serves up tasty Greek and Turkish food, washed down with Ouzo and Raki. It's a favourite place to take the kids, and there's a children's menu at the ready.

Lemon Sole (☎ 9281 1303; 123 High St, Old Portsmouth; mains £9.50-18; ☺ lunch & dinner) A colourful little pick-your-own seafood restaurant, Lemon Sole lets you size up freshly netted critters at a counter, then choose how you want it cooked. It's in an attractive period building near The Point and has a cellar bar below.

Bistro Montparnasse (☎ 9281 6754; 103 Palmerston Rd, Southsea; 2-/3-course lunch £14.50/17.50, dinner £22.50/27.50; ☺ lunch & dinner Tue-Sat) This classy but cosy bistro serves zesty French dishes with an English twist amid chic décor and polished wood floors.

Drinking

For a taste of modern Portsmouth, pick your way through the rows of bars and trendy terraced and balconied eateries that line the Gunwharf Quays.

Still & West (☎ 9282 1567; 2 Bath Sq) This relaxed salty-dogs pub on The Point has served many a sailor and smuggler in its day, and is still great for a drink on its waterside terrace, watching the passing yachts and ferries and looking back toward the Spinnaker Tower.

Drift (☎ 9277 9839; www.driftbar.com; 78 Palmerston Rd; ☺ 9pm-3am) This hip London-style bar lan-guishes behind whirlpool frosted glass and pebble-dashed front, has a slick chrome and wood interior, and lounge showcasing DJs on the weekends. Be sure to visit the quirky ultracool bathrooms.

Spinnaker Tower Bar (☎ 9285 7520; Gunwharf Quays; ☺ 10am-11pm) OK it's the most touristy café-bar in Portsmouth, but you'll find no better coffee-sipping and wine-supping vantage point to watch the boats slosh past than this glass-sided café below its namesake edifice.

Entertainment

Southsea is thick with nightclubs and live-music venues.

Wedgewood Rooms (☎ 9286 3911; www.wedgewood-rooms.co.uk; Albert Rd) One of Portsmouth's best live-music venues, also hosting DJs and co-medians.

For cinema, head to **Vue Cinema** (www.myvue.com; Gunwharf Quays).

Getting There & Away

Portsmouth is situated 75 miles southwest of London.

BOAT

There are several ways to reach the Isle of Wight from Portsmouth (see p241 for details).

P&O Ferries (☎ 0870 598 0333; www.poferries.com) sails twice a week to Bilbao (10 hours) in Spain. **Brittany Ferries** (☎ 0870 366 5333; www.brittanyferries.co.uk) has overnight services to St Malo (10¾ hours), Caen (5½ hours) and Cherbourg (three hours) in France. **Acciona Transmediterranea** (☎ 0871 720 6445; www.trasmediterranea.es) sails to Bilbao several times weekly, and **LD Lines** (☎ 0870 428 4335; www.ldlines.co.uk) has daily overnight ferries to Le Havre (8½ hours) in France. **Condor Ferries** (☎ 0870 243 5140; www.condorferries.co.uk) runs a weekly car-and-passenger service to Cherbourg (5½ hours).

For prices and more information, check the websites. The Continental Ferryport is north of the Historic Dockyard.

BUS

There are 15 National Express buses from London (£13.90, 2½ hours) daily, some via Heathrow airport (£13.90, 2¾ hours) and continuing to Southampton (50 minutes). Bus 700 runs to Chichester (one hour) and to Brighton (3½ hours) half-hourly Monday to Saturday, hourly on Sunday.

TRAIN

There are trains every 10 minutes or so from London Victoria (£23, two hours 20 minutes) and Waterloo stations (£23, one hour 40 minutes). Trains also go to Southampton (£7.10, 40 to 55 minutes), Brighton (£13.80, one hour 40 minutes, hourly), Winchester (£7.90, one hour, hourly) and Chichester (£5.30, 30 to 46 minutes, two hourly).

For the Historic Dockyard get off at the final stop, Portsmouth Harbour.

Getting Around

Bus 6 operates between the Portsmouth Harbour bus station and South Parade Pier in Southsea via Old Portsmouth.

The **Gosport Ferry** (☎ 9252 4551; www.gosportferry .co.uk; £1.80 return, bicycles travel free) shuttles back and forth between The Hard and Gosport every 10 to 15 minutes.

For a taxi try **Aquacars** (☎ 9261 1111 or 9278 7666) in Southsea. There's also a taxi stand near the bus station.

Waterbus (p233) boats will drop you between Gunwharf Quays and Old Portsmouth for £1/50p per adult/child.

SOUTHAMPTON

☎ 023 / pop 234,224

This down-to-business port city and gateway to the Isle of Wight has a long and eventful past thanks to its position on the Solent, an 8-mile inlet into which flow the Itchen and Test rivers. However, Southampton's history does not always make happy reading. While the city was once a flourishing medieval trading centre, its centre was gutted by merciless bombing in WWII and consequently there's little left of its early heritage. The city's gritty waterfront is also the point from which the *Titanic* set sail on its ill-fated voyage in 1912, and larger-than-life ocean liners such as the *QEII* still dock on the waterfront.

The **tourist office** (☎ 8083 3333; www.visit-south ampton.co.uk; 9 Civic Centre Rd; ☼ 9.30am-5pm Mon-Sat, plus 10.30am-4pm Sun Apr-Sep) has details of free 90-minute guided walks – at 10.30am Sunday and bank holidays year-round, 10.30am daily July to September, plus 2.30pm daily August – which meet at the Bargate on High St.

Sights & Activities

The city's top attraction is **Southampton Art Gallery** (☎ 8083 2277; www.southampton.gov.uk/art; admission free; Commercial Rd; ☼ 10am-5pm Tue-Sat, 1-4pm

Sun), in the colossal Civic Centre opposite the tourist office. The collection is spaced through airy surrounds and features the best of 20th-century British art, including work by Spencer, Turner and Gainsborough.

A boxy little 14th-century warehouse on the waterfront now houses the **Maritime Museum** (☎ 8022 3941; The Wool House, Town Quay; admission free; ☼ 10am-4pm Tue-Sat, to 4pm Sun Apr-Oct), which tells the tragic story of the *Titanic*, as well as running through Southampton's port history since 1838. The building was once used as a prison, and has an impressive timber roof upon which inmates carved their names.

For a glimpse of Southampton's medieval heyday, visit the nearby **Medieval Merchant's House** (EH; ☎ 8022 1503; 58 French St; adult/child £3.50/1.80; ☼ 10am-5pm), which dates back to 1290. Entrance includes an audio guide.

Getting There & Away

AIR

Southampton International Airport (☎ 0870 040 0009; www.southamptonairport.com) has flights to around 40 destinations in the UK and Europe, including Amsterdam, Paris, Dublin and holiday resorts in Spain. There are five trains hourly between the airport and the main train station (seven minutes).

BOAT

Red Funnel (☎ 0870 444 8898; www.redfunnel.co.uk) runs regular passenger and car ferries to the Isle of Wight and there is a ferry service to Hythe in the New Forest

BUS

National Express coaches run to London and Heathrow 16 times per day (£13.40, 2½ hours). It also runs a 6.50pm bus to Lymington (40 minutes) via Lyndhurst (20 minutes) in the New Forest.

Bus M4 runs to Portsmouth three times daily (40 minutes). Bus 32 runs to Winchester (30 minutes) roughly hourly with reduced services on Sunday. Bus 56/56A goes to all the main towns in the New Forest hourly (every two hours on Sunday). When boarding, ask about the good-value Explorer tickets valid on these route.

TRAIN

Trains to Portsmouth run twice hourly (£7.10, 46 to 59 minutes) and to Winchester (15 to 23 minutes) every 20 minutes.

NEW FOREST

The only thing new about this ancient swathe of wild heath and woodland is its status of national park, finalised in 2005. It's a unique place, with an even more singular history and archaic traditions that date back almost 1000 years (see the boxed text, below), but more than that it's a joy to explore. Wild ponies mooch around its picturesque scrubland, paying no attention to the walkers and cyclists that pant past. Deer flicker in the distance and rare birds flit among the foliage. A scattering of genteel villages dot the landscape and a web of walking and cycling trails connects them.

The park is also a hugely popular destination for campers, and Lyndhurst's tourist office has a free brochure detailing its many designated camping areas. For more information, go to www.thenewforest.co.uk.

Activities

CYCLING

This is an ideal spot for two-wheel explorations and there are several rental shops. You will need to pay a deposit (usually £20) and provide identification.

AA Bike Hire (☎ 023-8028 3349; www.aabikehirenew forest.co.uk; Fern Glen, Gosport Lane, Lyndhurst; adult/child per day £10/5)

Country Lanes (☎ 01590-622627; www.countrylanes .co.uk; Railway Station, Brockenhurst; bike/tandem per day £14/25; ☽ Easter-Oct)

Cyclexperience (☎ 01590-624204; www.cyclex.co.uk; Brookley Rd, Brockenhurst; per half/full day from £6.50/11)

Forest Leisure Cycling (☎ 01425-403584; www. forestleisurecycling.co.uk; The Cross, Village Centre, Burley; per day from £11)

HORSE RIDING

No, we're *not* talking about saddling up one of the wild ponies. But nonetheless riding is a wonderful way to roam the New Forest. The following stables can arrange rides, and welcome beginners:

Arniss Equestrian Centre (☎ 01425-654114; Godshill, Fordingbridge)

Burley-Villa (Western Riding; ☎ 01425-610278) It's off the B3058, just south of New Milton.

OTHER ACTIVITIES

There are regular guided walks with park staff called **Rambles with a Ranger** (☎ 023-8028 6840; walks £2); the tourist office has details. Canoeing is also possible with **Liquid Logistics** (☎ 01590-624730; www.liquidlogistics.co.uk; 2hr session £20), which has several locations around the forest.

Getting There & Around

Southampton and Bournemouth bracket the New Forest and there are regular bus services from both. Trains run every half-hour to Brockenhurst from London Waterloo station (£29.50, 1½ hours) via Winchester (£8, 31 minutes) and on to Bournemouth (£5, 15 to 27 minutes). Local trains also link Brockenhurst with Lymington, see above.

VERDERERS, AGISTERS & PONIES

The New Forest is the only area of England to remain relatively untouched since Norman times, thanks in large part to its unsuitability as agricultural land. If the presence of so much unfenced territory is remarkable enough, what is fascinating about the New Forest is that it still retains a code of law handed down during the reign of William the Conqueror.

William officially declared the whole area a royal hunting preserve in 1079, thereby protecting it from development. The crown still owns 260 sq km of the New Forest, though the Forestry Commission has maintained it since 1924.

The remaining 130 sq km are owned by verderers, or commoners, who in the pre-automobile age reared the ponies as work horses. Today they are either reared as riding ponies or left to graze the land at will. The verderers' status is protected by the Commoners' Charter, first laid down in 1077, which guaranteed them six basic rights, the most important of which is the right to pasture. Every year, the 300-odd verderers gather to elect five agisters, who are responsible for the daily management of the 3000 ponies, 1800 cattle and smaller numbers of donkeys, pigs and sheep in the New Forest.

You can wander freely throughout the forest, but don't feed or touch the wild ponies. To protect ponies, cyclists and walkers, there is a 40mph speed limit. If you find an injured pony phone Lyndhurst Police on ☎ 0845 045 45 45.

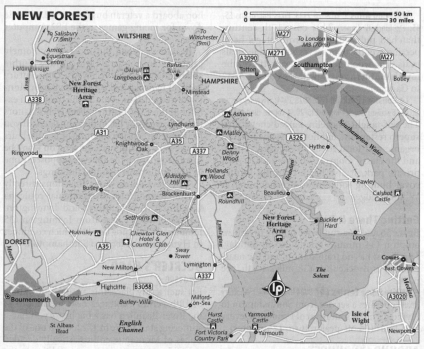

NEW FOREST

The **New Forest Tour Bus** (www.city-sightseeing .co.uk; adult/child £9/4.50; ☺ tours hourly 10am-4pm Jun-Aug) runs two-hour hop-on hop-off bus tours that pass through Lyndhurst main car park, Brockenhurst Station, Lymington and Beaulieu; they also have a cycle trailer to rest tired legs.

Busabout tickets offer unlimited travel on main bus lines in the region for seven days and cost £25/16 per adult/child; details are on www.wdbus.co.uk, along with local timetables.

LYNDHURST
☎ 023 / pop 2281

A good base from which to explore the national park or simply stop off for a pint, a cuppa or a map, the quaint little country village of Lyndhurst is one of the larger settlements in the area and has an excellent information centre, good facilities and several cosy pubs and restaurants.

The **tourist office** (☎ 8028 2269; www.thenewforest .co.uk; High St; ☺ 10am-5pm) sells a wide variety of information on the New Forest, including cycling maps, a map showing walking tracks,

and a free camping and caravanning guide. It also sells the Ordnance Survey (OS) map (No 22, £7.49), which covers the area in greatest detail. In the same building, the informative **New Forest Museum** (☎ 8028 3444; www.newforest museum.org.uk; adult £3) runs through the unique ecology and social history of the region.

Just across the car park, the **library** (☎ 8028 2675; ☺ 10am-1pm Fri & Sat, 10am-1pm & 4-7pm Tue, 3-5pm Wed) has free internet access.

Sleeping & Eating

Forest Cottage (☎ 8028 3461; www.forestcottage.co.uk; High St; s/d £28/50; P ✗) A cosy little 300-year-old cottage perched at the far end of High St, but just a two-minute walk from the centre, this wholesome B&B lets you relax into the country mind-set with inviting rooms, a library of natural history and pretty garden.

Crown Hotel (☎ 8028 2922; www.crownhotel-lynd hurst.co.uk; High St; s/d £87.50/145; P ✗ ▣) An old English country house with mullioned windows and creaky staircases now hosts this reliable hotel, with pleasant enough if slightly fuddy-duddy décor, teddy bears on the beds and pleasant professional service.

Waterloo Arms (☎ 8028 2113; Pikes Hill; mains £5-15; ☽ lunch & dinner) This cosy 17th-century thatched pub with ponderous stag's head peering over the door serves good-value meals in its snug wood-beamed interior. It's on the town's northern edge, signposted off the A337 to Cadnam.

Le Poussin@Parkhill (☎ 8028 2944; www.lepoussin .co.uk; Beaulieu Rd; set lunch £15-20, 4-course dinner £35) The self-taught Michelin-starred chef at this superb restaurant and hotel uses the freshest organic and local foods to orgasmic effect, and the classy rooms (£70) overlook its own private park. It also has a beautiful former royal hunting lodge near Brockenhurst at Whitley Ridge.

Getting There & Away

Buses 56 and 56a run twice hourly to Southampton (34 minutes) daily except Sunday. Lyndhurst has no train station, and the nearest stop is Brockenhurst, 8 miles south, see p236.

White Horse Ferries (☎ 8084 0722; www.hytheferry .co.uk) operates a service from Southampton to Hythe, 13 miles southwest of Lyndhurst, every half-hour (£4 off-peak return, 12 minutes).

AROUND LYNDHURST

Rev-heads, historians and ghost-hunters all gravitate to **Beaulieu** (☎ 01590-612345; www.beau lieu.co.uk; adult/child £15/7.75; ☽ 10am-6pm May-Sep, to 5pm Oct-Apr), pronounced bewley, a tourist complex based around the site of what was once England's most important 13th-century Cistercian monastery. Following Henry VIII's monastic land-grab of 1536, the abbey fell to the ancestors of current proprietors, the Montague family.

Moto-maniacs will be in clover at Lord Montague's **National Motor Museum**, but you don't need to be one to enjoy the comedy or sheer glossy splendour of its vehicles, which come in every shape and size. Some will even leave you wondering if they are really are a car, or strange hybrid planes, boats or metal bubbles with wheels. It's hard to resist the romance of the early classics, or the oomph of winning F1 cars. Here too are several jet-powered land-speed record breakers including *Bluebird*, which famously broke the record (403mph, or 649km/h) in 1964. There is even a large collection of celebrity bangers such as Mr Bean's Austin Mini and James Bond's whizz-bang speed machines. Outside you can

hop aboard a veteran bus from 1912, or settle down for racing games in the PS2 computer area.

Beaulieu's grand but indefinably homely **palace** began life as a 14th-century Gothic abbey gatehouse, but received a 19th-century Scottish Baronial makeover from Baron Montague in the 1860s. Around the corner, an exhibit in the 13th-century **abbey** walks visitors through everyday life in the monastery. If you hear eerie Gregorian chanting or feel the hairs on the back of your neck quiver, you won't be surprised to learn the abbey is supposedly one of England's most haunted buildings.

The New Forest Tour Bus stops directly outside the complex on its circular route via Lyndhurst, Brockenhurst and Lymington. You can also get here from Lymington (35 minutes) by catching bus 112 which continues to Hythe and the ferry to Southampton.

BUCKLER'S HARD
☎ 01590

For such a tiny place, this picturesque huddle of 18th-century cottages near the mouth of the River Beaulieu has a big history. It had a stuttering start to life in 1722, when one of the dukes of Montague enthusiastically decided to build a port to finance an expedition to the West Indies. His dream was never realised, but then came the war with France, and the embryonic village with its sheltered gravel waterfront became the ideal location to secretly build several of Nelson's triumphant warships. Then again in the 20th century it played its part in the secret wartime manoeuvrings that preceded the D-Day landings.

Fast forward to today, and the hamlet has been converted into a fascinating heritage centre, the **Buckler's Hard Story** (☎ 616203; www .bucklershard.co.uk; adult/child £5.50/4; ☽ 10am-5pm Mar-Oct, to 4.30pm Nov-Feb). You can traipse through several immaculately preserved 18th-century labourer's cottages, and stop by for a lengthy perusal of the maritime museum, which charts the history of several great ships built here, especially for Nelson's navy and the Battle of Trafalgar. And as little light relief, seek out the heroic Nelson's baby clothes. There's also a film explaining the river's role in WWII.

Also part of the complex are altogether more luxurious digs in the **Master Builders House** (☎ 616253; www.themasterbuilders.co.uk; s/d from £134/180; ℗ ☒), which was just that in its former life. Now it's a higgledy-piggledy

---

WORTH THE TRIP

Unquestionably one of the top hotel-spas in Britain, some say Europe or even the world, five-star **Chewton Glen Hotel & Country Club** (☎ 01425-275341; www.chewtonglen.com; r from £290; P ⊠ ⌘ ⛶ ☎) lives up to every one of its rave reviews. A country house in sprawling grounds, with a croquet lawn and golf course that seem snipped by nail scissors, the building itself is filled with character and antiques. The staff is programmed to anticipate every need before you've even realised them, the sophisticated rooms and facilities astound and the superb Marryat restaurant has won many a plaudit on its own merits. Enough superlatives already? Well we've one more reserved for the hotel spa, which is the absolute epitome of luxury.

Chewton is situated 1 mile north of New Milton village, in the southern reaches of the New Forest.

---

luxury hotel with 25 chintz rooms decorated by salty-dog maritime pictures. It's also home to an acclaimed restaurant (mains £10 to £18) overlooking the river; there's also the Yachtsman's Bar, which serves pub grub from £4.

Swiftsure boats operate 30-minute **river cruises** from the waterfront between Easter and October.

Buckler's Hard is 2 miles downstream from Beaulieu, and there's a lovely riverside walking trail that links the two.

LYMINGTON

☎ 01590 / pop 14,227

The bustling little harbour town of Lymington has several strings to its tourism bow, being not only a popular yachting base with two marinas freckled with fibreglass floaters, but also a handy base for the New Forest and a jumping-off point to the Isle of Wight. It's a pleasing Georgian town with a few cobbled streets and a range of quirky bookshops, inns and nautical stores.

Information

Free internet can be arranged at Lymington's main **library** (☎ 673050; North Close; 9.30am-7pm Mon-Tue & Thu-Fri, 9.30am-1pm Wed, 9.30am-5pm Sat), a few blocks from Lymington Town train station.

Lymington Laundrette (☎ 672898; 11 New St; 8am-6pm Mon-Fri, to 1pm Sat) is on hand to make hiking gear smell sweet again; it's next door to the tourist office.

ATMs, banks and shops line the Georgian and Victorian High St. There's a post office at the end of the High St near St Thomas Church.

The **tourist office** (☎ 689000; www.thenewforest .co.uk; New St; 10am-5pm Mon-Sat), a block off the High St next to the museum, sells walking tours of town and will help you find accommodation.

Sights

Lymington was once known as a contrabandist port, and you can learn all about the local smugglers, salt makers and yachties in the **St Barbe Museum** (☎ 676969; www.stbarbe -museum.org.uk; New St; adult/child £3/2; 10am-4pm Mon-Sat).

Sleeping & Eating

Angel Inn (☎ 672050; www.roomattheinn.co.uk; 108 High St; r Mon-Thu/Fri-Sun £44.95/79.95; P ⊠) Striking a fair balance between traditional and modern, this boutique hotel in a renovated Georgian coaching inn features clean, warmly decorated and woody rooms and a cosily lit and imaginative bistro downstairs.

Wistaria (☎ 688090; www.wistaria.org.uk; St Thomas St; mains £11-20; breakfast, lunch & dinner) Festooned with flowering wisteria, this elegantly converted Georgian town house was formerly a doctor's surgery, and is now an airily elegant eatery with fawning service and exquisite seasonal food. It also offers three sumptuously decorated top-end rooms (single/double £95/120). It's 200m up the High St from The Angel Inn.

Getting There & Away

The bus station is just off High St. Lymington has two train stations: Lymington Town and Lymington Pier, which is where the Isle of Wight ferry drops off and picks up. Trains to Southampton (£7.80, 45 minutes) via Brockenhurst leave every half-hour.

Wightlink Ferries (☎ 0870 582 7744; www.wightlink .co.uk) cross to Yarmouth on the Isle of Wight every half-hour costing £10/45.60 return for foot passenger/cars (30 minutes).

ISLE OF WIGHT

This lovely island, just a few miles off the Hampshire coast, does its utmost to bottle traditional childhood-holiday nostalgia and sell it. A popular escape for yachties, cyclists, walkers and the bucket-and-spade brigade since Victorian times, it alternates between chocolate-box quaint and crazy-golf kitsch, rosy-cheeked activity and rural respite. But the last few years have also seen a fresh youthful buzz injecting life into its southern resort towns, attracting a new generation of urbanites and romantic weekenders with gastropubs, slick hotels and big music festivals. Still, the island's principal appeal is its surprisingly mild climate, its myriad outdoorsy activities and its lush green hills that roll gently down to 25 miles of clean, unspoilt beaches.

For good online information, check out www.islandbreaks.co.uk.

Activities

CYCLING

Cyclists will be in clover here. There is a 62-mile cycleway, and the island has its very own **Cycling Festival** (☎ 01983-203891; www.sun seaandcycling.com) held every September. You can pick up exhaustive information and buy trail guides from the tourist offices and at sports shops such as **Offshore Sports** (www.off shore-sports.co.uk; Shanklin ☎ 01983-866269; 8 Atherley Rd Shanklin; Cowes ☎ 01983-290514; 2-4 Birmingham Rd, Cowes).

Bike rentals are available all over the island for around £10 to £15 per day or £45 per week. Companies include:

Extreme Cycles (☎ 01983-852232; www.extremecy cles.co.uk; Church St, Ventnor)

Island Pedal Power (☎ 01983-292665; www.island pedalpower.co.uk; 5-7 York St, Cowes) There's also an outlet at Brading Railway Station.

Tavcycles (☎ 01983-812989; www.tavcycles.co.uk; 140 High St, Ryde)

Wavells (☎ 01983-760738; The Square, Yarmouth)

Wight Cycle Hire (☎ 01983-731888; www.wightcycle hire.co.uk; Calbourne) Offers delivery and collection across the island.

WALKING

This is one of the best spots in southern England for gentle rambling. Walkers can pick and choose their way via 500 miles of well-marked walking paths through green landscapes and coastal routes. The island's **Walking Festival** (☎ 813818; www.isleofwightwalkingfestival .co.uk & www.walkthewight.org.uk) is fêted as the largest in the UK, and is held over two weeks in May. Tourist offices have trail pamphlets from £3.

OTHER ACTIVITIES

Water sports are a serious business on Wight's northern shores, especially sailing but also windsurfing, kayaking, surfing and numerous other forms of water-bound fun. For just as much splash but less sweat, powerboat trips also run out to the Needles (p243). Or for something more unusual, Wight also offers **gliding** lessons, **falconry** and even **llama trekking**. Tourist offices can help fix you up with all of these.

WIGHT'S OWN WOODSTOCK

The tranquil Isle of Wight is commonly described as 'England, only a few decades ago', making reference to its genteel traditions and largely unspoilt charm. But the last few years have seen an altogether different revival of past decades. For this island was the once setting for a series of infamous rock festivals that burned short but bright from 1968 to 1970.

The final festival is the stuff of rock legend: an incredible 600,000 doped-up hippies gathered here to see the likes of the Doors, the Who, Joni Mitchell and – most famously – the last performance of rock icon Jimi Hendrix. He was to die less than three weeks later, aged just 27. The festival also bit the dust in the same year after a bunch of the so-called love children ran amok; the incident led to an Isle of Wight Act being passed in parliament, and all gatherings of over 10,000 people were henceforth banned.

But the noughties have recently seen a rekindling of the island's revolutionary festivals, which are fast growing into some of England's top music events. The new generation of **Isle of Wight Festivals** (www.isleofwightfestival.com), held in mid-June, has already been headlined by the likes of REM and Coldplay, while dance-oriented newborn **Bestival** (www.bestival.net), in mid-September, has seen the Pet Shop Boys, Scissor Sisters and more.

ISLE OF WIGHT

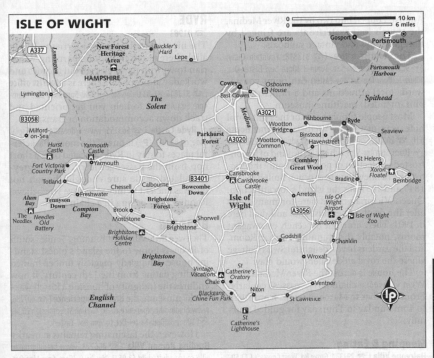

THE SOUTHEAST COAST

Getting There & Away

Wightlink (☎ 0870 5827744; www.wightlink.co.uk) operates a passenger ferry from The Hard in Portsmouth to Ryde pier (15 minutes) and a car-and-passenger ferry (35 minutes) to Fishbourne. They run about every half-hour (£11 day return). Car fares start at £47 for a short break return.

The Wightlink car ferry between Lymington and Yarmouth costs £10 day return for passengers and from £45.60 for cars (30 minutes, every half-hour). Children travel for half price.

Hovertravel (☎ 01983-811000; www.hovertravel .co.uk) hovercrafts zoom back and forth between Southsea (near Portsmouth) and Ryde (£10.70 day return, 10 minutes).

Red Funnel (☎ 0870 444 8898; www.redfunnel.co.uk) operates car ferries between Southampton and East Cowes (£10.50 return, from £40 with car, 55 minutes) and high-speed passenger ferries between Southampton and West Cowes (£10/12.60 one way/return, 22 minutes). It also runs combined deals including admission to island attractions: see the website for details.

Getting Around

Southern Vectis (☎ 532373; www.islandbuses.info) runs relatively comprehensive bus services around the island. Only the remote southwest side between Blackgang Chine and Brook does not receive regular services. Buses run between the eastern towns about every 30 minutes. **Stagecoach Island Line** (www.island-line.com) run trains twice hourly from Ryde to Shanklin (25 minutes) and the **Isle of Wight Steam Railway** (☎ 884343; www.iwsteamrailway.co.uk; ☒ May-Sep) branches off from this line at Smallbrook Junction and goes to Wootton (adult/child £8.50/5.50, first class £12.50/8.50).

Rover Tickets give you unlimited use of buses and trains for £9 for a day, £16 for two days and £35 for a week.

COWES
☎ 01983

This hilly Georgian harbour town on the island's northern tip is famous for **Cowes Week** (www.skandiacowesweek.co.uk), one of the longest-running and biggest annual sailing regattas in the world. Started in 1826, the regatta still sails with more gusto than ever in late July or early

August. Lopped into two by the River Medina, the town's long waterfronts are fringed by fibreglass toys and vintage sailboats.

The **tourist office** (☎ 813818; Fountain Quay; ☺ 9.30am-5pm Mon-Sat, 10am-3.30pm Sun Easter-Oct, 10am-3.30pm Tue-Sat Nov-Easter) can point you towards local attractions and a rather dry (no pun intended) maritime museum.

Most people simply head for the right-royal hideaway of Queen Victoria, **Osborne House** (EH; ☎ 200022, 281784; East Cowes; adult/child £9.50/4.80; ☺ 10am-6pm Apr-Sep), which is the kind of lemon-frosted confection of pomp that only the Victorian era knew how to execute. Built between 1845 and 1851, it's the island's top attraction. Queen Victoria grieved here for many years after the death of her husband, and died here in 1901. There are some obscenely extravagant rooms, notably the stunning Durbar Room, and the gardens have a delightful Swiss Cottage where the royal ankle biters would play.

The house is across the River Medina from West Cowes; a chain ferry crosses regularly. From October to March, it opens from 10am to 4pm Sunday to Thursday for guided tours only.

Sleeping & Eating

Halcyone Villa (☎ 291334; Grove Rd, West Cowes; s £22.50-40, d £45-70; P ⊠) You'll be made to feel right at home in this family-run B&B a short walk from the centre of town. It's an unpretentious but very clean spot with shared bathroom but in-room sink.

Fountain (☎ 292397; www.fountaininn-cowes.com; High St, West Cowes; s/d £65/90) This classic old pub has a handful of neatly kept rooms with modern amenities, CD players and en suite, and serves enormous portions of food (mains £6.50 to £9) as well as a good pint in its downstairs bar.

NEWPORT & AROUND

The capital of the Isle of Wight, rambling Newport has little for holidaymakers except for nearby **Carisbrooke Castle** (EH; ☎ 522107; adult/child £5.50/2.80; ☺ 10am-5pm Apr-Sep, to 4pm Oct-Mar). An oft-repeated local saying states that whoever controlled this castle also controlled the island. As you scramble around the sturdy ramparts of this medieval castle, spare a thought for the unfortunate Charles I, who was imprisoned here before his execution in 1649. Kids adore the Carisbrook donkeys, which still draw water from a well using a treadmill.

RYDE
☎ 01983

The nippiest foot-passenger ferries to Wight alight here in this none-too-charming Victorian town with its tacky seafront arcades and workaday atmosphere. There is a **tourist office** (☎ 813818; 81-83 Union St; ☺ 9.30-5pm Mon-Sat, 10am-4pm Sun Apr-Oct) to help you get oriented and track down accommodation or transport.

Ryde Castle (☎ 563755; www.rydecastle.com; Esplanade; d £85-100; P) is one of the more characterful places to stay in Ryde. Located only a short hop from the passenger ferry, this is a grey-crenulated castle sure enough, though not quite as ancient as they may have you believe. Rooms could belong in a chain hotel.

BRADING

The twee little village of Brading, 4 miles south of Ryde, is home to the island's oldest standing house. A higgledy-piggledy timber-framed building dating from the 13th century, it now endures the indignity of housing a kitsch waxworks museum, the **Brading Experience** (☎ 407286; www.bradingtheexperience.co.uk; 46 High St; admission £6.50; ☺ 10am-5.30pm Easter-Oct, to 5pm Nov-Easter).

However, the fascinating remains at nearby **Brading Roman Villa** (☎ 406223; www.bradingroman villa.co.uk; adult/child £3.95/1.95; ☺ 9.30am-6pm Mar-Oct, 10am-4pm Nov-Feb) have escaped with pride intact. Located just south of the village, this archaeological site boasts some exquisitely preserved mosaics, including a famous cockerel-headed man and various other images that illustrate the owner's notoriously bacchanalian pursuit of pleasure.

About 8 miles east of Brading on the coast is **Xoron Floatel** (☎ 874596; www.xoronfloatel.co.uk; Embankment Rd; d £58). It doesn't look especially menacing now, draped in flowers and bunting, but it's an ex-WWII gunboat converted into a houseboat B&B, with reasonably roomy en suite cabins.

Trains (11 minutes) and bus 3 (16 minutes) go run regularly from Ryde to Brading.

SANDOWN & SHANKLIN
☎ 01983

The island's southeast coast is home to some of its best-known beaches, and families wielding buckets, spades and blow-up dinghies descend in their droves to the twin resort towns of Sandown and Shanklin. Once you've had your fill of candy floss, beachside frolics and funfair rides you can also go and growl at Britain's largest collection of tigers in the sprawling **Isle of Wight**

THE SOUTHEAST COAST

Zoo (☎ 405562; Sandown; adult/child £5.95/4.95; ✆ 10am-6pm Apr-Sep, 10am-4pm Feb-Mar & Oct).

VENTNOR
☎ 01983

The Victorian town of Ventnor slaloms steeply down along the island's southern coast, and these days it's the island's creative epicentre, brimming with a new wave of quirky boutiques, musicians and artists.

Perched right on the seafront esplanade, the **Spy Glass Inn** (☎ 855338; www.thespyglass.com; The Esplanade; 2-person flats from £60) has several self-contained flats with fuddy-duddy décor but sea views; no kids allowed. The lively pub below is festooned with nautical knick-knacks.

Or for a taste of new Wight and a spot of pampering in the process, book yourself in at chintz-free boutique hotel the **Hambrough** (☎ 856333; www.thehambrough.com; d with sea view £160-200; P ✗), where great views, chic décor, lots of natural light and sea views seal the deal. Room six even has a sea-view bath for two.

SOUTH WIGHT

The southernmost point of the island is marked by sturdy mid-19th-century **St Catherine's Lighthouse**. Far more exciting for visitors, however, is the stone rocket-ship lookalike, **St Catherine's Oratory**. This odd construction is a lighthouse dating from 1314 and marks the highest point on the island.

You'll find something for the kids a couple of miles further west at **Blackgang Chine Fun Park** (☎ 01983-730052; www.blackgangchine.com; 4yr & up £8.50; ✆ 10am-10pm mid-Jul–Aug, 10am-5pm Apr-early Jul & Sep-Oct), a Victorian landscaped garden-turned-theme park with water gardens, animated shows and a hedge maze.

Slightly further west, a dairy farm hosts the glorious hippy-throwback **Vintage Vacations** (☎ 07802-758113; www.vintagevacations.co.uk; Chale; 4-person caravans per weekend £135-165, per week £315-425; P ✗), renting out four 1960s dazzling-aluminium Airstream trailers from California, and lovingly refitted with retro furnishings. Flower-power two-man tents can also be hired for £20 per night. Camping has never been so cool.

WEST WIGHT

The island's southwestern corner is its most remote, with bumpy scenic drives past sheep and cattle farms, thatched farmhouses and secluded beaches. But the most stunning stretch of cliffs is on its western tip, also home to the most famous chunks of chalk in the region: the **Needles**. These jagged white rocks rise shardlike out of the sea, forming a perfect line like the backbone of a prehistoric sea monster.

Here too you'll find the military **Needles Old Battery** (NT; ☎ 01983-754772; admission £3.90; ✆ 10.30am-5pm daily Jul & Aug, 10.30am-5pm Sun-Thu Apr-Jun, Sep & Oct), a fort established in 1862 and used as an observation post during WWII. There's a 60m tunnel through the cliff to a searchlight lookout.

You can get to the point by a 1-mile clifftop walk from Alum Bay or hold out for one of the tourist buses that run between bay and battery hourly, or twice hourly in July and August.

In Alum Bay you'll also find the happy hullabaloo of kiddies rides, boat trips and souvenir shops at the **Needles Park** (☎ 0870-458 0022; www.theneedles.co.uk; admission free; ✆ 10am-dusk Apr-Nov), which also has a chairlift down to the beach and a sweet factory with demonstrations of how its teeth-rotting treats are made. There are fireworks nightly in August.

Moving on round the northwestern coast, **Fort Victoria Country Park** (☎ 01983-760283; www.fortvictoria.co.uk), off the A3054, marks the shortest crossing to the mainland and has accumulated an odd mix of attractions including an aquarium, marine museum, planetarium, model railway and Sunken History Exhibition.

Just beyond the park, Yarmouth is home to Henry VIII's last great fortress, **Yarmouth Castle** (EH; ☎ 01983-760678; Quay St; adult/child £2.80/1.40; ✆ 11am-4pm Sun-Thu Apr-Oct), with new-fangled arrowhead artillery bastions. Its façade, which is all that's left of it now, dates from 1547.

Sleeping
Totland Bay YHA (☎ 0870 770 6070; totland@yha.org.uk; Hirst Hill, Totland; dm £10.95; P ✗) A large, marvellous Victorian house overlooking the water, with mostly family-oriented dorms and a maximum of eight beds per room.

Brighstone Holiday Centre (☎ 01983-740244; www.brighstone-holidays.co.uk; tents 2/4 persons £12/18, caravans from £16, B&B adult/child £25/13, 2-person cabins per week from £230; P ✗) Long-time family favourite, this self-contained caravan and self-catering cabins park and B&B perches atop cliffs overlooking a stunning stretch of coastline. It's located on the A3055, 6 miles east of Freshwater.

Wessex

The ancient land of Wessex is best known as the setting for the tales of Thomas Hardy, but its history stretches much further back than the novels of the 19th century. In fact, the realm of Wessex is older than England itself; it was one of the seven Anglo-Saxon kingdoms that sprang up in ancient Britain after the end of Roman rule, and although Wessex officially ceased to exist after the foundation of the English state in the 9th century, its spirit lives on in the modern-day counties of Somerset, Dorset and Wiltshire.

It's a place where history and myth often seem to go hand in hand: eerie stone circles, Iron Age forts and crumbling medieval castles litter the rolling landscape, and a day's drive can carry you from the legendary Isle of Avalon to the pleasure baths of ancient Rome and the country retreats of England's Victorian gentry. Stately cathedrals pierce the skyline, cob cottages huddle in the shadow of knotted hills, and chalk-white horses gallop across the grassy hilltops. But Wessex is more than just a living museum piece; over the last decade the old industrial centre of Bristol has reinvented itself as one of Britain's most vibrant and progressive cities, and the regal streets of Bath are home to a clutch of clubs, cafés and glitzy bars that would put most Soho streets to shame. One thing's for certain – whether you're hunting for fossils along the Jurassic Coast, hiking the hilltops of rural Exmoor, or watching the sun sink over the majestic stones of Avebury, this is one area of Britain you'll need plenty of time to explore.

HIGHLIGHTS

- Standing on the deck of the **SS Great Britain** (p251) in Bristol's refurbished dockside
- Strolling the streets, admiring the architecture and playing the dandy in **Bath** (p259)
- Walking the processional avenue to Britain's largest stone circle, **Avebury** (p322)
- Exploring the ancient hilltop forts of **Maiden Castle** (p301) and **Old Sarum** (p313)
- Digging up some prehistoric fossils on the rust-red **Jurassic Coast** (p304)
- Savouring the silence at two of England's finest cathedrals, **Wells** (p278) and **Salisbury** (p309)

★ Bristol ★ Avebury
Bath ★
Wells ★
Salisbury ★
★ Dorchester
Jurassic Coast ★

■ POPULATION: 1.3 MILLION   ■ AREA: 3570 SQ MILES

History

The first modern humans arrived in Wessex during the Stone Age – one of the oldest skeletons ever discovered in the area was found at Cheddar Gorge (p280), and dates back at least 9000 years. By 3000 BC a complex tribal society had developed in this part of Britain, with clearly defined social hierarchies and shared religious beliefs; this so-called Wessex culture was responsible for the construction of the magnificent stone circles of Avebury (p322) and Stonehenge (p314), as well as the many barrows and processional avenues scattered across the region. Later, Iron Age settlers constructed some defensive forts at Maiden Castle (p301), Badbury Rings (p297) and Old Sarum (p313), and the area was subsequently conquered by the Romans, who then established several major settlements including Aquae Sulis, which is now known as Bath (p259).

The kingdom of Wessex was founded in the 6th century by the Saxon Cerdic, and by the 9th century Wessex was the only sizable part of the Anglo-Saxon lands not overrun by the Danes. King Alfred (r 849–99) was its leader and, effectively, the first king of England. At its peak, Wessex stretched west to Cornwall and east to Kent and Essex, and was officially incorporated into the kingdom of England in the mid-9th century; although the old title of Earl of Wessex, last used in the 11th century, has recently been revived and presently belongs to HRH Prince Edward.

Orientation & Information

The three counties of Wessex are similar in size. Dorset runs along the south coast, Somerset the north, and Wiltshire sits slightly inland. Bristol is the main transport and industrial hub, and is the only big city. The national park of Exmoor sits along the northern coastline and spills over the border into Devon, while Salisbury Plain stretches across much of the northern part of Wiltshire.

The most useful regional website is www .visitsouthwest.com, which has ideas for accommodation, activities and themed holidays across the southwest. County-specific sites are listed throughout this chapter.

Activities

CYCLING

Gentle gradients and quiet country lanes make Wessex ideal cycling country. Wiltshire

---

A COTTAGE OF YOUR OWN

After a rural bolt hole far from the madding crowd? Then check out these companies for self-catering cottages:

Cottages Direct (☎ 0870 197 69 64; www .cottagesdirect.com)

Dorset Coastal Cottages (☎ 0800 980 4070; www.dorsetcoastalcottages.com)

Dream Cottages (☎ 01305 789000; www .dream-cottages.co.uk)

Farm & Cottage Holidays (☎ 01237 479146; www.holidaycottages.co.uk)

Hideaways (☎ 01747 828170; www.hideaways .co.uk)

---

is particularly good and the 160-mile circular **Wiltshire Cycleway** makes a good basis for longer or shorter rides.

Of the long-distance cycle routes in this region, the **West Country Way** is one of the most popular, a fabulously varied 250-mile jaunt from Bristol to Padstow in Devon.

For off-road riding, good areas include the **North Wessex Downs** and **Exmoor** (p287).

As always the best places to go for leaflets and guides on cycling in Wessex are local tourist offices or the Visit Wiltshire website (www.visitwiltshire.co.uk). **Sustrans** (☎ 0845 113 00 65; www.sustrans.org.uk), the government's new sustainable transport body, has information on all the major cycling routes throughout the area – you can order route maps by telephone or you can download them from the website.

WALKING

This is a fantastic region for hitting the trail. Top spots include **Exmoor** (p287), the **Mendips** (p281) and the **Quantock Hills** (p285). The **South West Coast Path** runs along both the northern and southern coastlines of the region, cutting through some of the main coastal towns en route.

In northeast Wiltshire, the **Ridgeway national trail** starts near Avebury and winds 44 miles through chalk hills to meet the River Thames at Goring in Oxfordshire. The trail then continues another 41 miles (another three days' walk) through the Chiltern Hills.

OTHER ACTIVITIES

Water sports are popular along the south coast, especially around Weymouth (p303)

WESSEX

WESSEX

and Poole (p296), where you can try your hand at everything from kitesurfing to powerboating. Horse riding, fishing and falcony are available on Exmoor, and fossil-hunting is a favourite pastime on the Jurassic Coast around Lyme Regis (p304); but for something really different, how about a spot of zorbing (p300)?

Getting Around

BUS

Local bus services are fairly comprehensive, but it pays to have your own wheels to reach the more remote spots. Route maps and timetables are available online and at tourist offices. See p264 for details of Bath-based bus tours of the region.

First Travel (www.firstgroup.com) The region's largest bus company. The FirstDay Southwest ticket (adult/child £7/5) is valid for one day on all First buses.

Plusbus (www.plusbus.info) This scheme allows you to add local bus travel to your train ticket; participating cities include Bath, Bristol, Taunton and Weymouth. Tickets cost from £2 to £3 per day and can be bought at railway stations.

Wilts & Dorset (☎ 01202-673555; www.wdbus.co.uk) One-day Explorer tickets (£6.99) cover transport on most Wilts & Dorset buses and some other companies.

CAR

There are plenty of car-hire companies in the region, often concentrated around the airports and main-line train stations. Rates are similar to elsewhere in the UK, starting

at around £35 per day for a small hatchback (see p782).

TRAIN

The main railway hub is Bristol, which has links to London and the southwest along the old Great Western Railway line, and also has services north to Scotland via Birmingham. For more information contact **National Rail Enquiries** (☎ 0845 748 4950; www.nationalrail.co.uk) or **Traveline** (☎ 0870 608 2 608; www.traveline.org.uk).

The **Freedom of the SouthWest Rover pass** allows unlimited train travel in an area west of Salisbury, Bath, Bristol and Weymouth. It's available in two versions, allowing either three days' travel in one week (£70) or eight days' travel in 15 days (£95).

BRISTOL

☎ 0117 / pop 393,300

For years gritty, grimy old Bristol has been the ugly sister of Britain's cities, outclassed by Bath, outsmarted by London and upstaged by the rejuvenated cities of Newcastle and Manchester to the north. But the fortunes of this old industrial city have changed dramatically in recent years, and the transformation that's taken place over the last decade is pretty astonishing. There's a new sense of swagger and self-belief around Bristol these days; while the once-great trades of shipbuilding, manufacturing and the railways have long since sailed upriver, the city has steadily reclaimed its rightful place as an economic powerhouse, gastronomic centre and a cultural force to be reckoned with. The crumbling docks have been prettified and polished up; the streets are packed with cutting-edge restaurants, designer bars and world-class museums; and the city's music, media and nightlife scenes are all showing the rest of the country how things should be done. It's real, raw and just a little rough around the edges, but if you really want to know exactly where Britain's at right now, then Bristol is hard to beat.

HISTORY

A small Saxon village at the confluence of the Rivers Frome and Avon became the thriving medieval Brigstow (later Bristol) as the city began to develop its trade in cloth and wine with mainland Europe. Religious houses were established on high ground (now Temple) above the marshes and it was from here that celebrated 'local hero' John Cabot (actually a Genoese sailor called Giovanni Caboto) sailed to discover Newfoundland in 1497. Over the following centuries, Bristol became one of Britain's major transatlantic ports, and grew wealthy on the lucrative trade of cocoa, sugar, tobacco – as well as slaves – from Africa to the New World.

By the 18th century the city was suffering from competition, from Liverpool in particular, and with large ships having difficulty reaching the city-centre docks, trade moved to new ports at Avonmouth and Portishead instead. To compensate for the disappearing maritime trade, the city repositioned itself as an industrial centre; Bristol became

WESSEX

BRISTOL IN TWO DAYS

Start off with a tour around Bristol's historic dockside, allowing a few hours to explore the cutting-edge **Arnolfini** (opposite) and the attractions at **@tBristol** (opposite). Grab some food at **Severnshed** (p255) before cruising down the river aboard the Bristol **ferryboat** (p254) to the **SS Great Britain** (p251). Check into the **Brigstow Hotel** (p254), dine out in style at the **Glassboat** (p255) and catch an evening film at the **Watershed** (p258) if there's time.

On day two catch a bus over to Clifton, stopping at the **Georgian House** (opposite) and the **city museum and art gallery** (opposite) en route, before taking a wander around Clifton's many shops, boutiques and cafés. Take an afternoon stroll across the marvellous **suspension bridge** (p251) and around the **Downs** (p251) nearby, and finish up with a slap-up supper at **Quartier Vert** (p255) on Whiteladies Rd.

---

an important hub for shipbuilding, as well as the terminus for the pioneering Great Western Railway line from London to the southwest. Unfortunately, the city became a target for German bombing during WWII; much of the city centre had been levelled by the time peace was declared in 1945. The postwar rush for reconstruction left Bristol with plenty of concrete carbuncles, but over the last decade or so the city has undergone extensive redevelopment, especially around the dockside.

ORIENTATION

The city centre, north of the river, is easy to get around on foot but very hilly. The central area revolves around the narrow streets by the markets and Corn Exchange and around the newly developed docklands. Park St is lined with trendy shops and cafés, while a strip of Whiteladies Rd is the hub of bar and restaurant life. The genteel suburb of Clifton, with its Georgian terraces and boutique shops, is on the hilltop west of the centre.

As in any big city, it pays to keep your wits about you after dark, especially around the suburb of St Paul's, just northeast of the centre. It's still a run-down area with a heavy drug scene, and is best not visited alone at night.

The main train station is Bristol Temple Meads, a mile southeast of the centre. Some trains use Bristol Parkway, 5 miles to the north. The bus station is on Marlborough St, northeast of the city centre.

INFORMATION
Bookshops

Blackwell's/George's (☎ 927 6602; 89 Park St) This vast bookshop sells both secondhand and new titles.

Waterstones (☎ 925 2274; The Galleries, Broadmead) General bookshop in the Galleries shopping centre.

Emergency

Police (☎ 927 7777; Nelson St)

Internet Access

LAN Rooms (☎ 973 3886; 6 Cotham Hill; per hr £2.50; ⏲ 10am-11pm Mon-Thu, 10am-10pm Fri, 10am-9pm Sat & Sun)

Internet Resources

This is Bristol (www.thisisbristol.com) Web edition of the *Bristol Evening Post*.

Venue (www.venue.co.uk) Online version of Bristol's listings guide, with reviews of clubs, bars and restaurants.

Visit Bristol (www.visitbristol.co.uk) Official tourism website with info on events, accommodation, transport and exploring the city.

What's On Bristol (www.whatsonbristol.co.uk) Useful online city guide with comprehensive listings.

Laundry

Alma Laundrette (☎ 973 4121; 78 Alma Rd; ⏲ 7am-9pm)

Redland (☎ 970 6537; Chandos Rd; ⏲ 8am-8pm)

Medical Services

Bristol Royal Infirmary (☎ 923 0000; 2 Marlborough St)

Money

You'll find all the main banks along Corn St, including Barclays at No 40, Lloyds at No 55, and NatWest at No 32.

Post

Post office (Upr Maudlin St & The Galleries, Broadmead)

Tourist Information

i-plus points Free touch-screen kiosks around the city providing tourist information.

Tourist office (☎ 0906 711 2191; www.visitbristol .co.uk; The Annexe, Wildscreen Walk, Harbourside;

WESSEX

🕙 10am-6pm Mar-Oct; 10am-5pm Mon-Sat, 11am-4pm Sun Nov-Feb) Well stocked with leaflets, transport maps and local info, and books rooms for £3.

Travel Agencies
STA Travel (☎ 929 4399, 43 Queens Rd)
Trailfinders (☎ 929 9000; 48 Corn St; 🕙 9am-6pm)

SIGHTS
@tBristol
Just off the harbourfront on Millennium Sq, **@tBristol** (☎ 0845 345 1235; www.at-bristol.org.uk; Harbourside; combined tickets Explore & Wildwalk adult/child £15/11, Explore & IMAX £14/10.50, Wildwalk & IMAX £13/10, all three £20/15; 🕙 10am-5pm Mon-Fri, 10am-6pm weekends) houses three fantastic attractions under one roof.

Explore (adult/child £9/6.50) is Bristol's impressive science museum, with several zones spanning space, technology and the human brain, as well as the Curiosity Zone, where you can walk through a tornado, spin on a human gyroscope and strum the strings of a virtual harp. Rotating exhibitions are held in the Live Science Zone on the 1st floor. It's fun, imaginative and highly interactive, and should keep kids of all ages enthralled for a few hours.

The natural world takes centre stage at **Wildwalk** (adult/child £8/6). Highlights include the steamy Botanical House, which re-creates the rainforest in the heart of Bristol (complete with butterflies and Touraco birds) and contains a living replica of a coral reef. There's also an exhibit exploring the world's ecosystems, where you can calculate your own eco-footprint.

The **IMAX** (adult/child £7/5.50) shows several jaw-dropping 3-D films: subjects range from the moon landings to an African safari, and there's a terrifying sharks documentary that'll put you off taking a bath for a week.

One of Bristol's most famous sons was Cary Grant (aka Archibald Leach), who was born here in 1804; look out for his statue on Millennium Sq.

Museums
The city's municipal **museums** (www.bristol-city .gov.uk/museums) are free, and are open 10am to 5pm Saturday to Wednesday unless otherwise stated.

The **City Museum & Art Gallery** (☎ 922 3571; Queen's Rd; 🕙 10am-5pm) is housed in a stunning Edwardian baroque building split into several floors. There's an excellent collection of British and French art on the first floor, along with galleries dedicated to ceramics and decorative arts. On the ground floor you'll find the archaeological, geological and natural history wings, as well as the museum's best known resident, Alfred the Gorilla.

Outside, the steam-powered **Bristol Harbour Railway** (single/return £1/60p; 🕙 weekends Mar-Oct) runs along the dock to SS *Great Britain* (p251).

The 18th-century **Georgian House** (☎ 921 1362; 7 Great George St) is an atmospheric illustration of aristocratic life in Bristol during the Georgian era. The six-storeyed house was home to the West India merchant John Pinney, along with his slave Pero (after whom Pero's Bridge across the harbour is named), and is still decorated throughout in period style; the huge kitchen (complete with cast-iron roasting spit) and the grand drawing rooms are particularly impressive.

The Elizabethan **Red Lodge** (☎ 921 1360; Park Row) was built in 1590 but was much remodelled in 1730, and its architecture reflects both periods. The highlight is the Elizabethan Oak Room, which still features its original oak panelling, plasterwork ceiling and carved chimneypiece.

In the northern suburb of Henbury lies **Blaise Castle House Museum** (☎ 950 6789; Henbury Rd), a late-18th-century house and social history museum. Displays include vintage toys, costumes and other Victorian ephemera. Across the road is **Blaise Hamlet**, a cluster of picturesque thatched cottages designed for estate servants by John Nash in 1811.

Bus 43 (45 minutes, every 15 minutes) passes the castle from Colston Ave; bus 1 (20 minutes, every 10 minutes) from St Augustine's Pde doesn't stop quite as close, but is quicker and more frequent.

Arnolfini Arts Centre (☎ 929 9191; www.arnolfini .org.uk; 16 Narrow Quay) This massive avant-garde arts venue has had an impressive facelift, and remains the top venue in town for dance, photography and art exhibitions.

British Empire & Commonwealth Museum
Isambard Brunel's marvellous old train station at Temple Meads houses the **British Empire & Commonwealth Museum** (☎ 925 9480; www.empiremuseum.co.uk; Clock Tower Yard; adult/child £6.95/3.95; 🕙 10am-5pm), which tells the story of 500 years of British exploration, trade

BRISTOL

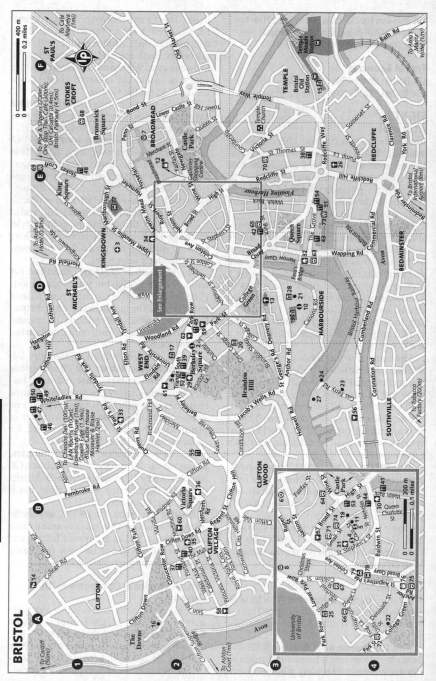

WESSEX

and conquest. There's everything here from flickering old films to Inuit whalebone sunglasses and a Hawaiian feather cape, and the museum doesn't skimp on confronting the more gruesome facts of Empire – particularly the issues of slavery and indigenous exploitation. A series of fascinating oral histories from across the globe and from Bristol's own multiracial population helps put everything in context.

SS Great Britain

In 1843 Brunel designed the mighty **SS Great Britain** (☎ 929 1843; www.ssgreatbritain.org; adult/child £8.95/4.95; ☼ 10am-5.30pm Apr-Oct, 10am-4.30pm Nov-Mar), the first transatlantic steamship to be driven by a screw propeller. For 43 years the ship served as a luxury ocean-going liner and cargo vessel, carrying passengers as far as Australia, before being damaged in 1886 near the Falkland Islands. The cost of repairs proved uneconomic and the ship's owners sold her off as a coal hulk, an ignominious fate for such a grand vessel; by 1937 she was no longer watertight and was abandoned near Port Stanley in the Falklands. There she remained, forgotten and rusted, before finally being towed back to Bristol in 1970.

Since then a massive 30-year programme of restoration costing £11.3m has allowed the ship to rediscover her former splendour. The ship's rooms have been refurbished in impeccable detail, including the ship's galley, surgeon's quarters, mess hall, and the great engine room; but the highlight is the amazing 'glass sea' on which the ship sits, enclosing an airtight dry dock which preserves the delicate hull and allows visitors to see the ground-breaking screw propeller up close. Moored nearby is a replica of John Cabot's ship *Matthew*, which sailed from Bristol to Newfoundland in 1497.

The informative **Maritime Heritage Centre** (☎ 927 9856; Great Western Dockyard, Gas Ferry Rd; admission £6.75; ☼ 10am-5.30pm Apr-Oct, 10am-4.30pm Nov-Mar), is also part of the site, and houses temporary exhibitions relating to the ship and her illustrious history.

Clifton & the Suspension Bridge

Bristol grew rich on the proceeds of the transatlantic trade, and during the 18th and 19th centuries the former spa resort of Clifton was transformed into an elegant suburb of Georgian townhouses and porticoed mansions, where the city's well-heeled businessmen

WESSEX

BRISTOL & BRUNEL

The year 2006 saw the 200th anniversary of the birth of one of Bristol's towering figures, the extravagantly named **Isambard Kingdom Brunel** (1806–59) – industrial genius, pioneering engineer, and general all-round renaissance man. The early 19th century was an era of incredible industrial advances, but even in an age brimming over with brilliant minds, Brunel's achievements stand head and shoulders above the crowd.

The precocious young Isambard was picked out for greatness at an early age. Educated at the Lycée Henri-IV in Paris and the University of Caen in Normandy, Brunel was barely 20 years old when he was appointed chief engineer of the pioneering Thames Tunnel between Rotherhithe and Wapping in London, designed by his father Marc. The project was fraught with technical difficulties and considerable danger; foul-smelling river water and explosive gases were a constant threat, and the tunnel was breached twice by serious floods in 1827 and 1828. Brunel was almost drowned during the second flood while trying to rescue trapped workers; while recovering, he entered a competition to design a bridge over the Avon at Clifton. His first submission was rejected along with all the other entries, but the competition was run again in 1831 and this time Brunel's design was awarded first prize. The foundation stone was laid in June of the same year, but sadly Brunel died before his first major commission was completed.

Thankfully he had plenty of opportunity to bask in the glory of his other achievements. During his 30-year career Brunel was responsible for many of the landmark projects of Victorian engineering, including the construction of the first rail bridge over the River Tamar, the foundation of the Great Western Railway line from London to the southwest, and the design of three of the greatest ships the world has ever seen: the ground-breaking transatlantic vessels *Great Western* and *Great Eastern*, as well as the first iron-hulled, screw-propeller steamship, *Great Britain* (p251). He also built more than 1000 miles of railway lines, modernised the docks at Bristol, Plymouth and Cardiff, designed the first prefabricated field hospital for use during the Crimean War, and worked on railway projects everywhere from India to Italy.

Despite surviving on a diet of four hours' sleep and 40 cigars a day, and suffering from numerous bouts of ill health, Brunel's closest shave came when he nearly choked to death having accidentally swallowed a coin while performing a conjuring trick for his children. His eventual end was rather more prosaic; he suffered a stroke in 1859, just before the *Great Eastern* made its first voyage to New York, and died 10 days later at the age of 53.

were able to live far from the squalor of the city's docks. Clifton sits on a curved hilltop above the city overlooking the Avon Gorge, stretching from Whiteladies Rd to the river; the further west you go, the posher the houses become, especially around **Cornwallis Cres** and **Royal York Cres**. These days Clifton is still the poshest postcode in Bristol, with a wealth of streetside cafés, upmarket boutiques and designer shops, and a villagey atmosphere that's far removed from the rest of the city.

Clifton's most famous (and photographed) landmark is another Brunel masterpiece, the 76m-high **Clifton Suspension Bridge** (www.clifton -suspension-bridge.org.uk), which spans the Avon Gorge from Clifton over to Leigh Woods in northern Somerset. It's a beautiful, graceful sight, and undoubtedly one of Britain's most elegant bridges. Though initial construction work began in 1836, sadly Brunel died before the bridge's completion in 1864. It was mainly

designed to carry light horse-drawn traffic and foot passengers, but these days around 12,000 motor vehicles cross it every day – testament to the quality of the bridge's construction and the vision of Brunel's design. It has also become a magnet for stunt artists and suicides; in 1885 Sarah Ann Hedley jumped from the bridge after a lovers' tiff, but her voluminous petticoats parachuted her safely to earth and she lived to be 85.

There's a small **visitor information point** (☎ 974 4665; visitinfo@clifton-suspension-bridge.org; ✆ 10am-5pm) in the timber-clad building close to the tower on the Leigh Woods side; guided tours (£2.50) are available by arrangement.

The grassy parks of **Clifton Down** and **Durdham Down** (often referred to as just The Downs) beside the bridge make a fine spot for a picnic. Nearby, a tatty observatory houses Britain's only **camera obscura** (☎ 974 1242; admission £1; ✆ from 12.30pm Mon-Fri, 10.30am Sat & Sun), which offers incredible views of the suspension bridge. Opening hours vary depending on the weather.

Bristol Zoo (☎ 973 8951; www.bristolzoo.org.uk; Clifton; adult/child £10/6; ☺ 9am-5.30pm summer, 9am-5pm winter) is renowned as much for its conservation work as for its exotic residents. Attractions include a group of West African gorillas, underwater walkways for viewing seals and penguins, and a Brazilian rainforest section where you can get up close and personal with agouti, capybara and golden lion tamarins.

See p259 for details of buses to Clifton and the zoo.

Bristol Cathedral

Originally founded as the church of an Augustinian monastery in 1140, **Bristol Cathedral** (☎ 926 4879; www.bristol-cathedral.co.uk; College Green; ☺ 8am-6pm) has a remarkably fine Norman chapter house and gate, while the attractive chapels have eccentric carvings and fine heraldic glass. Although much of the nave and the west towers date from the 19th century, the 14th-century choir has fascinating misericords depicting apes in hell, quarrelling couples and dancing bears. The south transept shelters a rare Saxon carving of the 'Harrowing of Hell', discovered under the chapter-house floor after a 19th-century fire.

St Mary Redcliffe

Described as 'the fairest, goodliest and most famous parish church in England' by Queen Elizabeth I, **St Mary Redcliffe** (☎ 929 1487; www.stmaryredcliffe.co.uk; Redcliffe Way; ☺ 8.30am-5pm Mon-Sat summer, 9am-4pm Mon-Sat winter, 8am-7.30pm Sun year-

round) boasts a soaring, 89m-high spire, a grand hexagonal porch and a vaulted ceiling decorated with fine gilt bosses. At the entrance to the America Chapel is a whale rib presented to the church by John Cabot as a souvenir of his trip to Newfoundland in 1497.

Lord Mayor's Chapel

Once the chapel of St Mark's Hospital, the **Lord Mayor's Chapel** (☎ 929 4350; Park St; ☺ 10am-noon & 1-4pm Tue-Sun) is a medieval gem packed with 16th-century, stained-glass windows, medieval monuments and ancient tiles. The church-loving poet John Betjeman dubbed it 'for its size one of the very best churches in England'.

BRISTOL FOR CHILDREN

There's no shortage of things to keep kids happy in Bristol, with loads of hands-on activities and interesting events. Most hotels and some B&Bs can rustle up a baby cot or heat up a bottle; confirm that when you book. Baby-changing facilities are available in most supermarkets, department stores, shopping centres and major attractions.

First port of call has to be the brilliant **Bristol Zoo** (p251), where there are enough hairy apes and even hairier spiders to keep the young whippersnappers entertained for hours. If you still haven't had your fill of bugs and beasties, head over to **Wildwalk** at **@tBristol** (p249), where you'll also find lots of interactive exhibits at the **Explore** science museum. Then you could join a detective trail in search of the missing ship's cat, Sinbad, at the **SS Great Britain** (p251), chug along the dockside on the **Harbour Railway** (p249), or take a river cruise aboard the **Bristol**

WESSEX

CLIFTON'S FORGOTTEN FUNICULAR

Hidden away inside the cliffs of the Avon Gorge is one of the city's great architectural secrets. From 1893 to 1934, the **Clifton Rocks Railway** ferried passengers via a 500-foot long tunnel from the top of Sion Hill, near the suspension bridge, down to the quay at Hotwells, from where pleasure steamers sailed on to Avonmouth and the Bristol Channel. It was an expensive and technologically challenging enterprise; the gradient of the climb is 1 in 2.2, and due to the unstable nature of the limestone cliffs, the tunnel had to be brick-lined to a width of 2 feet for its entire length. It was hailed as a triumph of Victorian engineering when it finally opened to the public in 1893, but barely 40 years later the tunnel was forced to close due to dwindling trade and the economic pressures of the Great Depression. It was later used as a secret radio station during WWII, but fell into disrepair during the postwar years and has lain almost forgotten for the last half-century. Since May 2005 a dedicated team of enthusiasts and historians have set about trying to raise funds to restore the funicular to full working order – you can follow their progress at www.cliftonrocksrailway.org.uk.

Packet (below), before joining an early evening pirate walk (below). The **Bristol Children's Festival** kicks off at the beginning of August on The Downs, with four days of puppetry, circus skills, magic and children's theatre, and there are also annual festivals for **hot-air balloons** and **kite-flying** (below).

For babysitters try:
Park Lane Nannies (☎ 373 0003; www.parklanenan nies.com)
Tinies (☎ 3005630; bristol@tinieschildcare.co.uk)

TOURS

Bristol Highlights Walk (☎ 968 4638; studytours@aol .com; £3.50; ✆ 11am & 2pm Sat Apr-Sep) is a regular tour of the old town, city centre and harbourside, run every Saturday by Bristol's Blue Badge guides; there's no need to book, just turn up outside the tourist office. Themed tours exploring Clifton, Brunel and the history of Bristol's many trades are run by request.

Visit Eastside (www.visiteastside.co.uk) offers two free downloadable tours of the multicultural districts of St Paul's and Easton.

City Sightseeing (☎ 926 0767; www.bristolvisitor .co.uk; adult/child £8.50/4; ✆ 10am-4pm Easter-Sep) has an open-top hop-on, hop-off bus visiting all the major attractions. Buses leave St Augustine's Pde hourly (every 30 minutes July to September).

Bristol Packet Boat Trips (☎ 926 8157; www.bristol packet.co.uk; adult/child £4.25/2.75; ✆ Mar-Oct) offers cruises around the harbour area, as well as weekend day trips to Avon Gorge (adult/child £11.50/8.50, July to October) and Bath (adult/child £20/15, July to September).

Pirate Walk (☎ 07950 566483; adult/child £3.50/2.50; 6.15pm Tue, Thu & Sat Apr-Sep) is a swashbuckling two-hour trail of pirates, smugglers and other ne'er-do-wells, aimed at kids.

FESTIVALS & EVENTS

Bristol has an ever-expanding programme of annual events. Things kick off in April with **bristolive** (www.bristolive.co.uk), a festival for amateur orchestral groups. The **St Paul's Carnival** (☎ 944 4176) is on the first Saturday of July, swiftly followed by the **Bristol Harbour Festival** (☎ 922 3148), the city's biggest waterside event, and the **Ashton Court Festival** (www .ashtoncourtfestival.co.uk), an outdoor extravaganza of bands, theatre and performing arts held on the Ashton Court estate. Ashton Court is also the venue for the **International Balloon**

Fiesta (☎ 953 5884; www.bristolfiesta.co.uk), and the **International Kite Festival** (☎ 977 2002; www.kite -festival.org), in September. Bristol's biggest film festival is the **Encounters Festival** (☎ 929 9188; www .encounters-festival.org.uk), held at the Watershed every November, and there's a **Christmas market** held on various nights in late November and December.

SLEEPING

Bristol is a bit of a mixed bag when it comes to finding a place to stay. There's a great riverside hostel and a couple of stunning places at the top end, but most of the city centre business is hoovered up by the bland chain hotels along the river. Pick up the free *Bristol* guide for accommodation listings and a foldout map.

Budget

Bristol Backpackers (☎ 925 7900; www.bristolback packers.co.uk; 17 St Stephen's St; dm/tw £14/36; ✖ 🖳) Plump in the heart of town, this ecofriendly independent hostel is another decent budget option, although the private rooms are cramped and the grungy dorms sometimes get very busy in summer. There's cheap internet access (£2 for three hours) and no curfew, so expect some noise on weekends.

Bristol YHA Hostel (☎ 0870 770 5726; bristol@yha.org. uk; Hayman House, 14 Narrow Quay; dm £19.95, s incl breakfast £25-35, d incl breakfast £40-45; ✖ 🖳) In a wonderful spot beside the river, this smartly converted brick warehouse makes a fantastic base, and offers much better value than many of the city's midrange hotels. The modern dorms and doubles are spread over several floors, and the facilities include internet access and the excellent Grainshed coffee lounge.

Midrange

Downlands House (☎ 962 1639; www.downlands house.com; 33 Henleaze Gardens; s £38-52, d £55-75; ✖ 🖳 ♿ 🖳) Pleasant, uncomplicated bedrooms are scattered around this 19th-century gabled house, perched on the edge of Dirdham Downs. Pretty curtains, plush carpets and framed watercolour prints (as well as the odd china figurine) characterise the interior décor, and there's free wi-fi throughout.

Downs Edge (☎ 968 3264; www.downsedge.com; Saville Rd; s £48-57, d £71-78; ✖) This quiet, countrified B&B would be more at home in the Cotswolds than central Bristol. In a fine spot on the edge of the Bristol Downs, overlooking private gardens, the double-gabled house offers a choice of fresh, light-filled rooms filled with antique furniture and frippy furnishings.

Victoria Square Hotel (☎ 973 9058; www.vicsquare.com; Victoria Sq; s £59-89, d £79-99; P ✕) Despite being owned by the Best Western behemoth, this brick-built pile is the pick of the hotels in Clifton village. It's kitted out with more character than you'd normally expect from a chain-run hotel, with large pocket-sprung beds, pine furniture and lovely views across the wooded square, and all the Clifton nightspots are within easy reach.

Arno's Manor (☎ 971 1461; arnos.manor@forestdale.com; 470 Bath Rd; s/d from £60/75; P ✕ ▢) This crenellated chateau is a couple of miles from the city centre, but it's easy to reach by bus or cab, and more interesting than most of the bland multinationals in the heart of town. The rooms are spacious and comfortable, if a little corporate; the highlight of the building is the grand vaulted lounge and glass-roofed restaurant, which is handy if you don't feel like making the trek into town.

Rodney Hotel (☎ 973 5422; rodney@cliftonhotels.com; 4 Rodney Pl; s £64-87, d £79-92; P) Shabby chic sums up this venerable hotel, which stands in a glorious terrace of Georgian townhouses in the heart of Clifton. A couple of the rooms are really rather grand, with smart furnishings and tasteful pastel fabrics, but most tend towards the scruffy side. The main draw here is the fantastic location, with some of the city's best cafés and brasseries galore right on your doorstep.

Arches Hotel (☎ 924 7398; www.arches-hotel.com; 132 Cotham Brow; s £28.50-45, d £50.50-58.50; ✕) Great value eco-conscious guesthouse with huge veggie-only breakfasts.

Clifton Hotel (☎ 973 6882; clifton@cliftonhotels.com; St Paul's Rd; s £64-74, d £79-84; ✕) Decent hotel in the B&B-heavy area around St Paul's Rd, though the rooms are looking tired.

Top End

our pick **Hotel du Vin** (☎ 925 5577; www.hotelduvin.com; Narrow Lewins Mead; d £130-160, ste £185-205; P ✕) Manhattan comes to Bristol at the swish, sumptuous and downright sexy Hotel du Vin, housed in six converted warehouses near the city centre. Much of the building's industrial character has been incorporated into the stripped-back rooms: hefty wooden beams and iron pillars sit stylishly alongside the huge futon beds and bespoke furniture. The rooms

are named after vintage wines, and all boast plenty of indulgent touches – clawfoot baths, walk-in showers, hi-fis and Egyptian cotton bathrobes – and if you can afford them, the split-level loft suites are absolutely out of this world.

Brigstow Hotel (☎ 929 1030; www.brigstowhotel.com; Welsh Back; r midweek £149-250, weekend £99-250; ✕ ▢) The concrete-and-glass exterior of this riverside hotel has all the appeal of a municipal car park, but don't be put off by appearances – inside you'll discover one of Bristol's funkiest, freshest places to stay. The plate glass windows and gleaming wood floors of the lobby set the designer tone, and the same sleek aesthetic is carried into the bedrooms, which boast trendy floating beds, curved wood-panel walls and tiny TVs set into the bathroom tiles. Make sure you bag one with a river view.

Berkeley Square Hotel (☎ 925 4000; berkeley@cliftonhotels.com; 15 Berkeley Sq; s £79-129, d £115-139; P ✕ ▢) Beautifully situated on a leafy Georgian square, this hip hotel brings baroque imagination to a traditional Bristol town house. Puce and purple sofas and gilt mirrors are dotted around the ice-white lobby and downstairs restaurant. While the bedrooms aren't quite as whacky, they're still luxurious and beautifully appointed, with widescreen TVs, fresh fruit and complimentary sherry. Guests also have access to a private members club, The Square, which keeps the cocktails flowing until the wee small hours.

EATING

Eating out in Bristol is a real highlight – the city is jammed with restaurants of every description, ranging from classic British caffs to designer dining emporiums.

Budget
RESTAURANTS

Obento (☎ 929 7392; 69 Baldwin St; mains £4-9; ✹ lunch & dinner Tue-Sun) The city has a growing number of Oriental eateries, but this is one of the newest and most exciting. Yakitori chicken, fresh sushi and hot noodles are served up in the stark minimalist dining room, as well as authentic bento boxes – a Japanese three-course lunch box that's practically a work of art in itself.

One Stop Thali Café (☎ 942 6687; 12A York Rd; set meal £6.95; ✹ lunch) For an introduction to Bristol's spicier side, look no further than this wonderful little Indian place in the heart of Montpelier.

Students and neighbourhood diners cram into the tiny dining room for the hectic street-market vibe and the fantastic-value set menu, which costs just £6.95 for six courses.

Planet Pizza (☎ 907 7112; 83 Whiteladies Rd; pizzas from £8.95; ☺ daily) Top option for huge, freshly made pizzas, with a vivid technicoloured interior and a huge choice of 12-inch specials, all named after astronomical bodies and big enough to share.

CAFÉS & QUICK EATS

York Café (☎ 923 9656; 1 York Pl; breakfast £1-5; ☺ breakfast & lunch) A British greasy spoon from the old school, famous across the city for its huge, heart-stopping all-day fry-up. The tea's served in solid china mugs, the menus are printed on Day-Glo sheets and there's brown sauce and ketchup on every table – what more could you possibly ask for?

Oppo} Music Coffee House (☎ 929 1166; 72 Park St; breakfast £1.50-5, lunch £3-6; ☺ breakfast & lunch) This excellent little place turns into Bristol's only haiku-café on Thursday and Friday lunchtimes, but it's popular throughout the week for rich Lavazza coffee and herbal teas, as well as a lunchtime menu of Thai fishcakes and hefty sandwiches.

Pieminister (☎ 942 9500; 24 Stokes Croft; pies £3; ☺ lunch) The great British pie is alive and well at this yummy little eatery, but there's more on offer than just the traditional steak and kidney. All the pies are handmade on the spot and drowned in lashings of mash, gravy and mushy peas – try the creamy Chicken of Aragon or the award-winning Mr Porky Pie.

Rocotillo's (☎ 929 7207; 1 Queens Row; mains from £4; ☺ breakfast & lunch) Bristol's version of a traditional American diner, complete with bar stools, leather booths and an open grill kitchen, serving gourmet burgers and the best milkshakes in town (including unusual concoctions such as crunchie and mint choc chip).

Bar Chocolat (☎ 974 7000; 19 The Mall; ☺ 9am-6pm Mon-Sat, 11am-5pm Sun) If there is such a thing as death by chocolate, then this holy temple to the cocoa bean is where you'll find it. There's everything from hot chocolates and chocolate-flavoured coffees to chocolate-chip muffins and chocolate with a Fairtrade conscience – and remember to leave room for some handmade chocolates before you leave.

Midrange

Oh! Calcutta! Indian Kitchen (☎ 924 0458; 216 Cheltenham Rd; mains £8-12; ☺ dinner) The best of the cluster of Indian restaurants strung along Cheltenham Rd. Stone-topped tables and back-lit chrome benches fill the vibrant dining room, and the menu is filled with all the usual Indian standards as well as a range of intriguing blackboard specials.

Clifton Sausage (☎ 973 11192; 7-9 Portland St; mains £8.50-14; ☺ lunch & dinner) Despite the name, this Clifton classic isn't just about bangers (although there are eight different varieties, from reindeer and cranberry to traditional toad-in-the-hole). In fact, it's one of Bristol's smartest British gastropubs, with a refined ambience and a menu that takes in everything from Cornish fish to fillet steak and apple crumble.

Picture House (☎ 973 9302; 44 Whiteladies Rd; mains £11-16; ☺ lunch & dinner) Movies have given way to Mediterranean-British cooking inside this former cinema, now one of the best midrange options on Whiteladies Rd. Light pours in through the large picture windows into an airy dining room decked out in chocolate-coloured leather and blonde-wood floors. Dishes revolve around locally sourced ingredients and organic veg, with an imaginative tapas selection and mains including roast guinea fowl and wild black bream.

Severnshed (☎ 925 1212; The Grove; mains from £12; ☺ lunch & dinner) Another stunning, sophisticated restaurant along the old quay, inside a renovated goods shed designed by Brunel. It's a stylish mix of designer bar, modern bistro and waterside café, mixing industrial trappings with contemporary chrome and a floating bar; the 977 menu (served before 7pm) features two courses for £9.77.

our pick riverstation (☎ 914 4434; The Grove; mains £14; ☺ lunch & dinner) Housed in a dramatic dockside building with an amazing barrelled roof, this swish restaurant has been a favourite with Bristol's fooderati since its opening nine years ago, and has recently been refurbished with vibrant colours and an all-new bar. The food's as good as ever; light lunches, coffee and crumbly pastries define the downstairs café, while up on the first floor it's all effortless elegance and European cuisine.

Cafe Maitreya (☎ 951 0100; 89 St Marks Rd; 3 courses £20.95; ☺ dinner Tue-Sat) Voted the UK's top vegetarian restaurant two years running, the Maitreya has firmly established itself as one of the city's most inventive eateries. It's a long way from the world of veggie hotpots and bean casseroles: the seasonal menu is renowned for its culinary creativity, and dabbles in everything from red onion *tartelette* to cashew nut roulade.

Mud Dock (☎ 934 9734; 40 The Grove; mains £8-16; ❤ daily) Über-trendy combo of bar, bistro and bike shop, in a brick warehouse by the harbour.

La Taverna Dell'Artista (☎ 929 7712; 33 King St; mains £12-25; ❤ dinner Tue-Sat) This chaotic, cramped Italian is an old fave with the post-theatre crowd.

Top End

Glassboat (☎ 929 0704; Welsh Back; lunch mains £7-8, dinner mains £14-21; ❤ closed Sun) This double-decked barge is the city's most romantic place to eat, with a fine wood-panelled interior lit by soft globe lanterns, an extensive menu stuffed with British and French country dishes, and dreamy views across the water.

Quartier Vert (☎ 973 4482; 84 Whiteladies Rd; mains £11.50-18.50; ❤ lunch & dinner) Consistently featuring in all the major food guides for the last 20-odd years, the split-level QV remains a Bristol big-hitter, with a lovely front patio, a fine ground-floor café and a smart European bistro upstairs. A second branch is due to open up by the harbour in late 2006, housing a deli, bakery and the restaurant's much-respected cookery school.

Byzantium (☎ 922 1883; 2 Portwall Lane; mains £17-20; ❤ dinner Mon-Sat) With a main dining room that looks like it's been plucked straight out of Kubla Khan's pleasure dome, this outlandishly extravagant restaurant is definitely the place to head if you're after a cinematic supper. The décor's a cross between Middle Eastern mosque and North African bazaar, but the cooking is quintessentially French.

Self-Catering

Papadeli (☎ 973 6569; 84 Alma Rd) A delectable Italian deli stocked with the kind of zesty flavours and sweet treats you'd normally only find in a Tuscan street market. Fresh pasta salads, salami sandwiches and goat's cheese tarts are served in the main café, or you can load up with picnic supplies and Italian cakes at the deli counter.

Chandos Deli (☎ 970 6565; 121 Whiteladies Rd & 6 Princess Victoria St) Gourmet sandwiches, handmade tapas and great takeaway coffee make this a favourite lunch stop for many Bristolians.

St Nicholas Market (Corn St; ❤ 9.30am-5pm Mon-Sat) The city's lively street market has a bevy of food stalls selling everything from artisan bread to cheese toasties; the best sarnies come from **Royce Rolls**, while Gallic crêpes are made in the time-honoured fashion at **Crêperie**.

DRINKING

The fortnightly listings magazine **Venue** (www .venue.co.uk; £1.20) contains the latest info on what's hot and what's not in Bristol and Bath. The freebie mag *Folio* is published monthly.

Elbow Room (☎ 930 0242; 64 Park St) Part dimly lit bar, part hustler's pool hall, this is a favourite hang-out for Bristol's style-conscious crowd. Rack up the balls and knock back the bourbons to a soundtrack of jazz, funk and whatever else is on the playlist. For budding Fast Eddies, there's a pool competition every Monday.

Woods (☎ 925 0890; 1 Park St Ave; ❤ 4pm-2am Sun-Thu, 4pm-4am Fri, 4pm-6am Sat) Run by the same chaps behind the Elbow Room, this high-class drinking hole is split into a main bar, mezzanine and a patio garden dotted with plants and chrome outdoor heaters.

Arc (☎ 922 6546; 27 Broad St; ❤ noon-2am Tue-Fri, 7pm-2am Sat, 6pm-12.30am Sun) Arguably Bristol's hippest bar, mixing industrial styling and an underground vibe with plenty of hip-hop and electronic beats.

Park (☎ 37 Triangle St West; ❤ 4.30pm-1am Sun-Wed, 4.30pm-2am Thu, 4.30pm-4am Fri & Sat) This place has got the metropolitan bar aesthetic nailed – stripped wood, banquette seats and moody lighting abound, and designer drinks are mixed behind the wood-panelled bar. Funk and hip-hop on Wednesday and Thursday give way to classic beats on weekends.

Avon Gorge Hotel (☎ 973 8955; Sion Hill; www.avon gorge-hotel-bristol.com) The golden age of this huge Victorian hotel has long since passed, but its panoramic drinks terrace is still the top place to watch the sun set over the Avon Gorge.

MBargo (☎ 925 3256; 38-40 Triangle St West; ❤ noon-2am) New incarnation of an old bar next door to the Park, with a totally overhauled interior heavy on the marble and leather, a huge cocktail list and a selection of weekend DJs.

Hop Pole (☎ 446327; 7 Albion Bldgs) This old-fashioned boozer in Clifton makes a fine stop for a pint of ale, with a mismatched interior filled with eclectic furniture, a huge ticking clock and a reassuringly local crowd.

Pipe & Slippers (☎ 942 7711; 118 Cheltenham Rd) Bath Ales on tap and a menu of Picminister pies make this unpretentious pub a reliable bet for late-night drinking, as well as Sunday lunch.

Albion (☎ 975 3522; Boyces Ave) Another venerable pub packed with evening drinkers from Clifton's well-heeled streets.

ENTERTAINMENT
Cinemas
Watershed (☎ 927 5100; www.watershed.co.uk; 1 Canon's Rd) The city's leading arthouse cinema and digital media centre, specialising in new indie releases and the occasional silver screen classic.

Nightclubs
The Bristol club scene moves fast, so check the latest listings to see where the big nights are happening.

Timbuk2 (22 Small St; ☽ 9am-2pm; admission £5-10) The city's current club tip is this underground venue crammed into a labyrinth of caverns and arches just off Corn St. The regular breaks, house and drum and bass nights usually get the seal of approval.

Native (☎ 930 4217; www.nativebristol.co.uk; 15 Small St; admission £5-8) Jointly run by a trio of Bristol trendsetters, this tiny 200-cover club is making waves on the Bristol circuit, with drum and bass on Tuesday, Latin and soul during the week, and resident DJs on weekends, including Bristol-based names Ben Dubuisson and Boca45.

Thekla (☎ 929 3301; www.thekla.co.uk; The Grove; admission £5-7) Longstanding two-floored club in a converted ship by the harbour, with DJs and dance floor downstairs, and a chill-out zone on the upper level. The house night on Friday and the Espionage night on Saturday are always crammed.

Nocturne (☎ 929 2555; 1 Unity St) A hyper-exclusive members club part owned by Massive Attack, with a decadent designer vibe and notoriously fussy bouncers, so smarten up your act and start queuing early.

Carling Academy (☎ 0870 711 2000; Frogmore St; £6-10) Bristol's original superclub can hold a 2000-strong crowd on its biggest nights, but it's practically never that busy. There's indie and R&B during the week and big house nights on weekends.

Cosies (☎ 942 4110; www.cosies.co.uk; 34 Portland Sq; admission £2 after 9pm) This diminutive club is a real gem, especially if you're sick of the big beats and designer attitude of some of Bristol's larger venues. Upstairs there's a bistro and wine bar, but it's the weekend reggae nights that draw in the crowds.

Theatre
Bristol Old Vic (☎ 987 7877; www.bristol-old-vic.co.uk; King St) The city's oldest theatre stages big touring productions, with occasional forays into comedy and dance.

Tobacco Factory (☎ 902 0344; www.tobaccofactory. com; Raleigh Rd) This small-scale theatre venue stages cutting-edge drama and dance. Catch bus 24 or 25 from Broadmead to the Raleigh Rd stop.

Live Music
Big names tend to play at the **Carling Academy** (see left), while a host of smaller venues feature emerging acts.

Fleece & Firkin (☎ 945 0996; www.fleecegigs.co.uk; St Thomas St) A small, intimate venue, much favoured by indie artists and breaking names on the local scene.

Colston Hall (☎ 922 3686; www.colstonhall.org; Colston St) The biggest concert hall in Brizzle, hosting everything from big-name comedy to touring bands.

Croft (☎ 987 4144; www.the-croft.com; 117-119 Stokes Croft) Chilled venue with a policy of supporting new names and Bristol-based artists. There's usually no cover charge if you arrive by 10pm Sunday to Thursday.

Bierkeller (☎ 926 8514; www.bristolbierkeller.co.uk; All Saints St) A legendary place that has played host to plenty of rock stars down the years, and still gets packed out on weekends.

GETTING THERE & AWAY
Air
Bristol International Airport (☎ 0870 121 2747; www.bristolairport.co.uk) is 8 miles southwest of town. Most flights are holiday charters but there are also scheduled flights to European destinations.

Air Southwest (☎ 0870 241 6830; www.airsouthwest.com) Several UK destinations including Newquay, Plymouth and Jersey.

Easy Jet (☎ 0870 600 0000; www.easyjet.com) Budget flights to UK destinations including Edinburgh, Glasgow, Newcastle, Inverness and Belfast, as well as several European cities.

British Airways (☎ 0845 773 3377; www.ba.com) Flies to Edinburgh, Glasgow and Paris.

Bus
National Express coaches go to Birmingham (£16.60, two hours, eight daily), London (£16.50, 2½ hours, at least hourly), Cardiff (£6.50, 1¼ hours, two daily) and Exeter

WORTH THE TRIP

Tyntesfield (NT; ☎ 01275 461900; Wraxall; adult £9; ⏱ 11am-5pm Sat, Sun, Mon & Wed) Formerly the aristocratic home of the Gibbs family, this ornate Victorian pile has recently been acquired by the National Trust (NT). Prickling with spiky turrets and towers, the house was built in grand Gothic Revival style by the architect John Norton, and is crammed with Victorian decorative arts, a working kitchen garden and a magnificent private chapel. The house is currently undergoing extensive renovation, so it's still a work in progress – call ahead for the latest updates.

(£11.60, two hours, four daily). There's also a direct daily bus to Nottingham (£24.50, 4¾ hours) and Oxford (£13, three hours).

Bus X39 (one hour, several per hour) and 332 (50 minutes, hourly, seven on Sunday) run to Bath. Bus 375/376 goes to Wells (one hour) and Glastonbury (1¼ hours) every half-hour during the week and hourly on Sunday. There are buses to most destinations around Somerset and Wiltshire from Bath and Wells.

Train
Bristol is an important rail hub, with regular connections to London (£58, 1¼ hours) and the southwest, including Exeter (£17.60, 1¼ hours), Plymouth (£44, 2½ hours) and Penzance (£73, four hours). Virgin Trains travel north to Glasgow (£97, 5¾ hours, five direct daily) via Birmingham (£29.50, 1½ hours, eight direct daily). Most main line trains arrive at Bristol Temple Meads.

Bath makes an easy day trip (single £5.20, 11 minutes, four per hour).

GETTING AROUND
To/From the Airport
Bristol International Flyer runs buses (single/return £5/7, 30 minutes, half-hourly 5am to 11pm) to the airport from Marlborough St bus station and Temple Meads train station. A taxi to the airport costs around £25.

Bicycle
Hilly as Bristol is, masochists might want to hire bikes at **Blackboy Hill Cycles** (☎ 973 1420; 180 Whiteladies Rd; per day £10; ⏱ 9am-5.30pm Mon-Sat).

Boat
The nicest way to commute around the city is with the **Bristol Ferry Boat Co** (☎ 927 3416; www.bristolferryboat.co.uk), which runs two routes: one from the city centre to Temple Meads (one hour, six to 10 daily April to October, weekends only November to March), stopping at Bristol Bridge and Castle Park; and one from the city centre to Hotwells (40 minutes, 12 to 16 daily year-round), stopping at Mardyke and the SS *Great Britain*. A single fare is £1.50, or you can pay £6 for a day's unlimited travel.

Bus
Buses run from Parkway Station to the centre every 15 minutes (30 minutes). Buses 8 and 9 run every 15 minutes to Clifton (10 minutes), Whiteladies Rd and Bristol Zoo from St Augustine's Pde; add another 10 minutes from Temple Meads.

FirstDay tickets (adult/child £4.40/2.70) are valid on all buses for one day in the Greater Bristol area. The **FirstFamily ticket** (£7) buys one day's travel for two adults and three children, but is only valid after 9am Monday to Friday.

Car & Motorcycle
Bristol's traffic can be a real headache, and the city has a seriously confusing one-way system – you'd be better off avoiding driving altogether or using the **park-and-ride** (☎ 922 2910; return £3 Mon-Fri before 10am, £2.50 after 10am Mon-Fri, £2 Sat; every 10 mins Mon-Sat), which operates from Portway, Bath Rd and Long Ashton. They're well signed on routes into the city.

Taxi
The taxi rank on St Augustine's Pde is a central but rowdy place on weekend nights. There are plenty of companies; try **Bristol Hackney Cabs** (☎ 953 8638).

BATH

☎ 01225 / pop 90,144
Ask any visitor for their ideal image of an English city, and chances are they'll come up with something pretty close to Bath – an architectural icon, cultural trendsetter and fashionable haunt for the cream of British society for the last 300 years. With its grand Georgian terraces, Palladian parades and lofty townhouses of honey-coloured stone, it's certainly one of Britain's most attractive cities, and still exudes

an air of gentility and chi-chi sophistication – in fact, Bath boasts more listed buildings than almost anywhere else in the country, and houses here change hands for truly eye-popping sums. The whole city has been named a World Heritage Site by Unesco, and it's blessed with a wealth of architectural wonders, including the glorious Royal Cres and one of the world's finest Roman spas. But it's not without its problems: the hills are knackering, the bars are snooty, the hotels are expensive, and the rush hour traffic will have you weeping into your steering wheel, but despite all the niggles, it's impossible not to fall in love with this finely wrought jewel in England's crown.

HISTORY

Prehistoric peoples probably knew about the hot springs, and legend has it that King Bladud, a Trojan refugee and father of King Lear, founded the town some 2800 years ago. He was supposedly cured of leprosy by a bath in the muddy swamps. The Romans established the town of Aquae Sulis in AD 44 and built the extensive baths complex and a temple to the goddess Sulis-Minerva.

Long after the Romans had departed, the Anglo-Saxons arrived and in 944 a monastery was founded on the site of the present abbey. Throughout the Middle Ages, Bath was an ecclesiastical centre and a wool-trading town and it wasn't until the early 18th century that Ralph Allen and Richard 'Beau' Nash (see the boxed text, p264) made Bath the centre of fashionable society. Allen developed the quarries at Coombe Down, constructed Prior Park (p277) and employed the two John Woods (father and son) to create the glorious buildings you see today.

As the 18th century wore on, Beau Nash lost his influence and sea bathing started to draw visitors away from Bath; by the mid-19th century the city was thoroughly out of fashion. Fortunately, most of Bath's grand architecture has been preserved.

ORIENTATION

Like Rome, Bath is famed for its seven hills, and although the city centre is compact it will test your legs. Most street signs are carved into the golden stone of the buildings.

The train and bus stations are both south of the tourist office at the end of Manvers St. The most obvious landmark is the abbey, across from the Roman Baths and Pump Room.

INFORMATION

Bath Quarterly (www.bathquarterly.com) Guide to sights, accommodation, restaurants and events.
Click (☎ 481008; 13A Manvers St; ✆ 10am-10pm; internet per 20 min £1)
i-plus points Free touch-screen kiosks providing tourist information, scattered around the city.
Laundrette (4 St Margarets Bldgs; per load £2; ✆ 6am-9pm)
Main post office (☎ 0845 722 3344; 25 New Bond St)
Retailer Internet (☎ 443181; 12 Manvers St; ✆ 9am-9pm Mon-Sat, 3-9pm Sun; per 20 min £1)
Royal United Hospital (☎ 428331; Combe Park)
Tourist office (☎ 0906 711 2000 (per min 50p); www. visitbath.co.uk; Abbey Churchyard; ✆ 9.30am-6pm Mon-Sat, 10am-4pm Sun)
What's On (www.whatsonbath.co.uk) Up-to-date listing of the city's events and nightlife.

SIGHTS
Baths

Ever since the Romans arrived in Bath, life in the city has revolved around the three natural springs that bubble up near the abbey. In typically ostentatious style, the Romans constructed a glorious complex of bathhouses above the springs to take advantage of their natural hot water, which emerges from the ground at a constant temperature of 46°C. The buildings were left to decay after the Romans departed and, apart from a few leprous souls who came looking for a cure in the Middle Ages, it wasn't until the end of the 17th century that Bath's restorative waters again became fashionable.

The site now forms one of the best-preserved ancient Roman spas in the world (and one of the city's most popular tourist attractions). The **Roman Baths Museum** (☎ 477785; www.romanbaths .co.uk; Abbey Churchyard; adult/child £10/6, incl Museum of Costume £13/7.60; ✆ 9am-6pm Mar-Jun & Sep-Oct, 9am-10pm Jul & Aug, 9.30am-5.30pm Nov-Feb) gets very, very busy in summer; you can usually avoid the worst crowds by visiting early on a midweek morning, or by visiting outside July and August. An audio guide (read by the bestselling author Bill Bryson) is included in the admission price.

The first sight inside the complex is the **Great Bath**. Head down to water level and along the raised walkway to see the Roman paving and lead base. A series of excavated passages and chambers beneath street level lead off in several directions and let you inspect the remains of other smaller baths and hypocaust (heating) systems.

SOMETHING FOR THE WEEKEND

Kick your trip off in glorious, Georgian Bath. Check into one of the city's excellent hotels – try **Paradise House** (p266) for city views, or the **Queensberry** (p266) for pure pampering – and then set out to explore the city's many attractions: Royal Cres, the Roman Baths and Bath Abbey are all essential stops. Indulge in a memorable meal at **Onefishtwofish** (p267) or the **Olive Tree** (p268), and catch a late-night gig over at **Moles** (p268), the city's top music venue.

On Sunday head east from Bath to **Bradford-on-Avon** (p317), famous for its 14th-century tithe barn, and **Lacock** (p319) with its beautiful medieval abbey. Grab a delicious country lunch at the **Sign of the Angel** (p319) before heading on to **Avebury** (p321), Britain's largest and argu-ably most spectacular stone circle, best seen in the light of late afternoon. And for the ultimate weekend getaway, round your trip off at **Whatley Manor** (see boxed text, p319) – possibly the most luxurious night's sleep anywhere in Britain.

One of the most picturesque corners of the complex is the 12th-century **King's Bath**, built around the original sacred spring; 1.5 million litres of hot water still pour into the pool every day. You can see the ruins of the vast 2000-year-old **Temple of Sulis-Minerva** under the Pump Room, and recent excavations of the **East Baths** give an insight into its 4th-century form.

Head outside to Bath St and note the colon-naded arcade, constructed so bathers could walk between the town's three main baths without getting wet. At the end of Bath St stands the **Cross Bath**, where Mary of Modena, wife of James II, erected a cross in gratitude for her pregnancy in 1688. Opposite is the **Hot Bath**, the third bath built over Bath's hot springs. These two historic sites have been restored and, together with the Hetling Pump Room, now form part of the **Thermae Bath Spa** (☎ 331234; www.thermaebathspa.com; Hot Bath St), a steel-and-glass complex that's ruffled many local feathers thanks to its super-modern design. The privately-owned enterprise was originally due to open in 2002, but has been beset by countless legal problems and a spiralling construction budget. It finally opened its doors to the general public in the summer of 2006.

Bath Abbey

Edgar, the first king of united England, was crowned in a church in Abbey Courtyard in 973, but the present **Bath Abbey** (☎ 422462; www.bathabbey.org; requested donation £2.50; ⏰ 9am-6pm Mon-Sat Easter-Oct, 9am-4.30pm Nov-Easter, afternoons only Sun) was built between 1499 and 1616, mak-ing it the last great medieval church raised in England. The nave's wonderful fan vaulting was erected in the 19th century.

The most striking feature of the abbey's exterior is the west façade, where angels climb up and down stone ladders, commemorating a dream of the founder, Bishop Oliver King. The abbey boasts the second-largest collection of wall monuments after Westminster Abbey. Among those buried here are Sir Isaac Pitman, who devised the Pitman method of shorthand, and Beau Nash.

On the abbey's southern side, steps lead down to the small **Heritage Vaults Museum** (⏰ 10am-4pm Mon-Sat), which explores the ab-bey's history and its links with the nearby baths. It also contains fine stone bosses, ar-chaeological artefacts and a weird model of the 10th-century monk Aelfric, dressed in his traditional black Benedictine habit.

Royal Crescent & The Circus

The crowning glory of Georgian Bath and the city's most prestigious address is Royal Cres, a semicircular terrace of majestic houses over-looking a private lawn and the green sweep of Royal Victoria Park. Designed by John Wood the Younger (1728–82) and built between 1767 and 1775, the houses would have origi-nally been rented by the season by wealthy socialites. These days flats on the crescent are still keenly sought after, and entire houses almost never come up for sale.

For a glimpse into the splendour and razzle-dazzle of Georgian life, head for **No 1 Royal Crescent** (☎ 428126; www.bath-preservation -trust.org.uk; adult/child £5/2.50; ⏰ 10.30am-5pm Tue-Sun Feb-Oct, 10.30am-4pm Nov), which has been restored with painstaking detail and an astonishing amount of period furniture. Only materials available during the 18th century were used during its refurbishment, so it's about as au-thentically Georgian as you can get; sadly, the

WESSEX

WESSEX

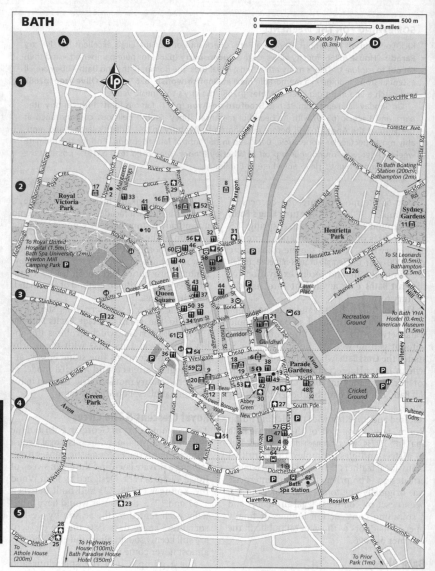

same can't be said for the endearingly hammy staff dressed in period costume.

A walk along Brock St leads to the **Circus**, a magnificent circle of 30 houses. Plaques on the houses commemorate famous residents such as Thomas Gainsborough, Clive of India and David Livingstone. To the south is the restored 18th-century **Georgian Garden**, where gravel replaces grass to protect women's long dresses from unsightly stains.

Assembly Rooms & Museum of Costume

Opened in 1771, the city's glorious **Assembly Rooms** (☎ 477785; www.museumofcostume.co.uk; Bennett St; ⏰ 11am-6pm Mar-Oct, 11am-5pm Nov-Feb) were where fashionable Bath socialites once gathered to waltz, play cards and listen to the latest chamber music. You're free to wander around the rooms as long as they haven't been reserved for a special function; highlights include the card room, tea-room and the truly splendid ball room, all of which are lit by their original 18th-century chandeliers.

In the basement is the **Museum of Costume** (adult/child £6.50/4.50, incl Roman Baths Museum £13/7.60), displaying costumes worn from the 16th to late 20th centuries, including some alarming crinolines that would have forced women to approach doorways side on. There's an audio guide to talk you through the fickle vagaries of fashion.

Jane Austen Centre

Bath is perhaps best known as the location for the novels of Jane Austen, who visited the city many times throughout her life, and lived here from 1801 to 1806 (a plaque marks one of her former houses at No 4 Sydney Pl, opposite the Holburne Museum). *Persuasion* and *Northanger Abbey* were both largely set in Bath, and the **Jane Austen Centre** (☎ 443000; www.janeausten.co.uk; 40 Gay St; admission £4.45; ☾ 10am-5.30pm Mon-Sat, 10.30am-5.30pm Sun) explores the author's connections with the city. Its displays include period costume, contemporary prints of Bath and lots of exhibits relating to the author's life.

Other Museums

The fine 18th-century **Holburne Museum** (☎ 466669; Great Pulteney St; admission £5.50; ☾ 10am-5pm Tue-Sat, 11am-5pm Sun) houses the booty of Sir William Holburne, a 19th-century Bath resident who brought together an outstanding collection of porcelain, antiques, and paintings by great 18th-century artists such as Gainsborough, Turner and Guardi.

Housed in an 18th-century Gothic chapel, the **Building of Bath Museum** (☎ 333895; www.bath-preservation-trust.org.uk; The Vineyards; admission £4; ☾ 10.30am-5pm Tue-Sun mid-Feb–Nov) details how Bath's Georgian splendour came into being, tracing the city's evolution from a sleepy spa town to one of the centres of Georgian society. There are some intriguing displays on contemporary construction methods, and the museum also explores the way in which social class and interior décor were intimately linked during the Georgian era; heaven forbid you should use a wallpaper that outstripped your station!

In 1781 the astronomer William Herschel discovered Uranus from the garden of his home, which now houses the **William Herschel Museum** (☎ 311342; 19 New King St; admission £3.50; ☾ 1-5pm Mon-Tue & Thu-Fri, 11am-5pm weekends Feb-Nov). The house is decorated as it would have been in the 18th century; an astrolabe in the garden marks where Herschel would probably have placed his telescope.

WESSEX

BEAU NASH: PRINCE REGENCY

If Ralph Allen, John Wood the Elder and John Wood the Younger were responsible for the physical construction of Georgian Bath, Richard 'Beau' Nash was the force that shaped high society in its heyday. A contradictory character, Nash was a dandy, gambler and womaniser, yet he was also purportedly charming, friendly, witty, influential and (at least to some degree) philanthropic.

Born in Wales in 1674, Richard Nash was an Oxford scholar and ex-soldier who was appointed Master of Ceremonies in Bath in 1705. By revitalising spa culture and providing entertainment for the rich, Nash effectively created a prestigious social milieu over which he would rule, imposing strict regulations on behaviour and dress, for almost 50 years.

Quite how he wielded such power is something of a mystery. He wasn't a public leader or employee, and he derived his income from a proportion of gambling-house profits. In any case, by the 1750s his influence was waning and he died in poverty in 1761. However, there's no doubt that Bath was changed irrevocably by his presence and simply wouldn't be what it is without his legacy.

The **Victoria Art Gallery** (☎ 477233; www.victoria gal.org.uk; Pulteney Bridge; admission free; ✆ 10am-5pm Tue-Sat, 1.30-5pm Sun) houses the city's main arts collection, mainly dating from the 15th to 20th centuries. There are some particularly fine canvases by Gainsborough, Turner and Sickert, as well as a wonderful series of Georgian caricatures from the wicked pens of artists such as James Gillray and Thomas Rowlandson.

The **Museum of East Asian Art** (☎ 464640; www .meaa.org.uk; 12 Bennett St; admission £4; ✆ 10am-5pm Tue-Sat, noon-5pm Sun) contains more than 500 jade, bamboo, porcelain and bronze objects from Cambodia, Korea and Thailand, and substantial Chinese and Japanese carvings, ceramics and lacquerware.

The **American Museum** (☎ 460503; www.american museum.org; Claverton Manor; ✆ noon-5pm Tue-Sun mid-Mar–Oct) houses a collection of Stateside artefacts, memorabilia and furniture dating from the 17th century to the English Civil War. There are 15 individually decorated rooms scattered around the manor house, including a suitably sparse Shaker Room and a New Orleans room, decked out in the lavish style of a plantation villa. Even the trees and plants in the surrounding grounds have a Yankee provenence. The museum is 2 miles southeast of the city centre; bus No 18 and several other buses to the university stop nearby.

TOURS
GUIDED TOURS
The best all-round introduction is provided by the free two-hour **Mayor's Guide walking tours** (☎ 477411; www.thecityofbath.co.uk), which leave from outside the Pump Room at 10.30am and 2pm Sunday to Friday, 10.30am on Saturday. From May to September there are additional tours at 7pm on Tuesday, Friday and Saturday.

For something less reverential, try **Bizarre Bath Comedy Walks** (☎ 335124; www.bizarrebath.co.uk; adult/child £7/5; ✆ 8pm Mar-Sep), a chaotic and frequently hilarious blend of street theatre, live performance and guided tour. Wallflowers be warned – you'll probably find yourself being roped into the act whether you like it or not. Tours leave from outside the Huntsman Inn on North Pde Passage and last about 1½ hours.

Jane Austen's Bath (☎ 443000; adult/child £4.50/3.50), as you'd probably expect, focuses mainly on the Georgian city and various sites associated with the author, with plenty of history and cultural context thrown in. Tours leave from the Abbey Churchyard at 11am on Saturday, Sunday and bank holidays.

Tourist Tracks (www.tourist-tracks.com/tours/bath) offers a couple of self-guided MP3 tours you can download (£5) or hire from the tourist office (half-/full day £6/10).

Bath Bus Company (☎ 01225 330444; www.bath buscompany.com) provides a hop-on hop-off **city tour** (adult/child £9.50/5; ✆ 9.30-5pm, later in summer) with commentary in seven languages. Buses stop every 20 minutes or so at various points around town. There's also a second route, the **Skyline tour**, that travels out to Prior Park (p277); the same tickets are valid on both routes.

The **Heritage Hopper Tour** (☎ 01225 838621; £19.95 incl 4 children; ✆ spring-autumn) includes bus travel and admission to the Holburne Museum, American Museum and Prior Park.

WESSEX

There are also minibus tours to some of the surrounding attractions around Bath:

Mad Max Tours (☎ 325900; www.madmaxtours.com) One-day tours to Stonehenge, Avebury, Lacock and Castle Combe (£22.50), half-day to Stonehenge and Lacock (£12.50).

Scarper Tours (☎ 0773 9644155) Twice-daily tour to Stonehenge (£12.50), full-day tour to Wells and Glastonbury on Wednesday and Saturday.

BOAT TRIPS

Various cruise operators offer boat trips up and down the River Avon; try **Bath City Boat Trips** (☎ 07974 560197; www.bathcityboattrips.com) or **Avon Cruising** (☎ 0779 1910650; pulteneyprincess@tiscali .co.uk), which both operate from Pulteney Weir. For cruises to Bristol, see p254.

FESTIVALS & EVENTS

The annual events calendar in Bath would keep even the most demanding Georgian socialite busy, with a varied programme of music, arts and theatre throughout the year.

The annual **Bath Literature Festival** (☎ 463362; www.bathlitfest.org.uk) takes place in early March, and attracts bookworms and big-name authors alike.

From mid-May to early June the **Bath International Music Festival** (www.bathmusicfest.org.uk) takes over the city, with a main programme of classical music and opera, as well as jazz, world and folk gigs in the city's smaller venues. The **Bath Fringe Festival** (www.bathfringe.co.uk) hits town around the same time; it's the biggest fringe festival in Britain after Edinburgh, with all kinds of theatre shows and street acts dotted around town.

The highlight of the **Jane Austen Festival** (www .janeaustenfestival.co.uk) in September is a grand Georgian costumed parade through the city's streets all the way to Royal Cres. The city's **film festival** (www.bathfilmfestival.org.uk) takes place in the last two weeks in September, followed by the annual **Mozartfest** (www.bathmozartfest.org .uk) in mid-October.

Bookings for all events are handled by the **Bath Festivals box office** (☎ 463362; www.bathfestivals .org.uk; 2 Church St; ⏰ 9.30am-5.30pm Mon-Sat).

SLEEPING

Bath features on practically everyone's tourist itinerary, and finding a bed during busy periods can be challenging. The tourist office will book rooms for a £3 fee, and sells an excellent

brochure, *Bath & Beyond* (£1), available free through the website.

BUDGET

Bath Backpackers' Hostel (☎ 446787; bath@hostels .co.uk; 13 Pierrepont St; dm £12-13; 🖥) The city's only independent hostel is a typically chaotic affair, with bunk beds crammed into the smallish dorms, and a rather modest kitchen. The run-down décor is livened up by the odd wall mural and funky feature, and there's a party 'dungeon' in the cellar – but as ever the lack of any curfew can mean late-night noise is a problem.

Bath YHA Hostel (☎ 465674; bath@yha.org.uk; dm £12.50, d from £35; 🅿 ⊠ 🖥) Hostels don't come much grander than this wonderful Italianate mansion, a steep climb uphill (or a short hop on bus 18) from the city centre. Despite the period exterior, the refurbished rooms are surprisingly modern and many look out across the private tree-lined gardens; book early if you're after a double.

YMCA (☎ 325900; www.bathymca.co.uk; International House, Broad St Pl; dm £13-18, d & tw from £36) Brilliantly located hostel in the heart of Bath, with lots of rooms and excellent facilities including a health suite, internet access and an onsite café. The functional décor is a bit bland, but you can't beat the price or the location.

Henry (☎ 424052; 6 Henry St; www.thehenry.com; s £35, d £60-65; ⊠) Run by the same people who own Three Abbey Green, this excellent budget option shows the same attention to detail and personable service but at a knock-down price. The furniture's a tad generic and the street noise is a headache, but you won't find many hotels this near the centre of town for the money.

MIDRANGE

There's quite a wide range of hotels in this price bracket; generally you'll get much better value for money the further you head from the city centre.

Three Abbey Green (☎ 428558; www.threeabbey green.com; 3 Abbey Green; d £85-100; ⊠) On a secluded terrace just steps from Bath Abbey, this fine B&B is a fantastic trade-off between location and price. The rooms are plain, smart and plushly finished with muted colours, huge beds and sparkling white linen; pick of the bunch is the Lord Nelson suite, which has a private sitting area and gas fire, as well as a regal four-poster bed. Quite a find.

Bath Paradise House Hotel (☎ 317723; www.para dise-house.co.uk; 86-88 Holloway; d £65-110; P ⊗) It's a long trek from the heart of Bath, but this fabulous chimney-topped villa enjoys one of the most breathtaking hilltop locations in the whole city. It's tucked away in private walled gardens and decorated in charmingly old-world style, with a surfeit of frills, antiques and gleaming en suite bathrooms (some with super-posh Jacuzzis). Rooms 4 and 5 have the best views, and are unsurprisingly more expensive.

Oldfields (☎ 317984; www.oldfields.co.uk; 102 Wells Rd; s £45-69, d £65-99; P ⊗) For the money, this has to be one of the best deals in Bath. The huge lemon-stone Victorian house commands sweeping views across the city, and offers lots of spacious, heritage-style rooms decked out in Laura Ashley fabrics and patterned wallpaper, with the odd oil painting and half-tester bed thrown in for good measure.

Dorian House (☎ 426336; www.dorianhouse.co.uk; 1 Upper Oldfield Park; s £65-78, d £65-140; P ⊗) It's pricey, but this three-storey late Victorian mansion is worth the extra cash. The rooms are all named after famous composers, and feature a mix of turn-of-the-century grandeur and French Riviera chic; some opt for almond-coloured carpets, gingham checks and leather bedbacks, while others go the full Victorian hog, with four-poster beds and varnished dressing tables.

Athole House (☎ 320009; www.atholehouse.co.uk; 33 Upper Oldfield Park; s £52-62, d £72-82; P ⊡) This cosy guesthouse swaps showiness for superb value, with a selection of modernised rooms furnished in plain pine, pastel colours and simple furniture. Owner Wolfgang is a mine of local information and cooks up a mean brekkie of buttermilk pancakes, Swiss muesli and home-baked bread.

St Leonards (☎ 442800; www.stleonardsbath.co.uk; Warminster Rd; s £40-75, d £65-90; P ⊗) Another hilltop gem with a glorious outlook across the valley and canal. The bedrooms are a little austere, and a few have peculiar layouts thanks to the odd shape of the 19th-century house, but they're all comfy, clean and well appointed, with en suite shower rooms and some pleasant period furniture.

Other recommended options:

Abbey Rise (☎ 316177; www.abbeyrise.co.uk; 97 Wells Rd; s £38-48, d £45-68; P ⊗) Attractively refurbished, contemporary B&B whose owner trained as a housekeeper at Buckingham Palace.

Highways House (☎ 421238; www.highwayshouse .co.uk; 143 Wells Rd; d £69-75; P ⊗ ⊡ ⊛) Family-run guesthouse with pastel-flavoured rooms and wi-fi.

TOP END

Queensberry Hotel (☎ 447928; www.thequeensberry .co.uk; Russell St; s £105-145, d £105-205; P ⊗) A favourite haunt for fashionistas and the national style mags, the Queensberry comprises four Georgian townhouses that have been combined into one of the city's top boutique hotels. Modern fabrics, period architecture and a muted colour palette make for a supremely chic sleep.

Dukes (☎ 787960; www.dukesbath.co.uk; Great Pulteney St; s £115, d £155-215; P) The rooms at this Grade I–listed Palladian pile are some of the most extravagant you'll find in Bath, harking back to the splendour of a bygone age. There's a choice of themes – Oriental finery, Italianate splendour, English botanica or French baroque – and all of the bedrooms are crammed with original cornicing and carved plasterwork.

Royal Crescent Hotel (☎ 823333; www.royalcrescent. co.uk; 16 Royal Cres; d £290-390, suites £530-850; P ⊗ ⊛) The original luxury hotel in Bath is still leading the way in terms of pomp and pageantry. This is about as close as you'll get to staying in a royal palace; the rooms are furnished with the same ornaments and antiques that would have welcomed guests in the 18th century, from the original oil paintings to the chandeliers and upholstered chaise longues, and there's a swooningly romantic secret garden that could have fallen straight from the pages of Jane Austen.

EATING
Budget
RESTAURANTS

Number 8 Manvers St (☎ 331888; lunch £4-8, dinner mains £7-12; 8 Manvers St; ☾ Mon-Sat) Light white interiors, stripped wood and local artwork define the tasteful dining room of this new café-brasserie, which is rapidly gaining a reputation for its pan-global menus, where wild mushroom risotto sits alongside ribeye steak and Thai curry broth.

Sally Lunn's (☎ 461634; 4 North Pde Passage; lunch £5-6, dinner mains from £8) There are some things you just *have* to do when you come to Bath, and one of them is to have afternoon tea at Sally Lunn's. There's been a tearoom and bakery on this site since the 18th century; the atmosphere is as frilly and English as ever, but it's the trademark Sally Lunn's bun that's still packing in the crowds.

Walrus & the Carpenter (☎ 314864; 28 Barton St; mains £7-15; ☺ lunch & dinner) The food's far from *haute cuisine* at this time-honoured restaurant, but that's all part of its considerable charm. The tables are packed in tight around its warren of candlelit rooms, and the menu is divided into 'befores' and 'afters'. The huge burgers and kebabs are always popular, and there's a good selection of veggie mains too.

CAFÉS

Café Réné (☎ 447147; Shires Yard; ☺ breakfast & lunch) This delightful café has an air of Paris' Left Bank thanks to its lovely courtyard terrace and an authentic menu of baguettes, croissants, *croques-monsieurs* (toasted cheese-and-ham sandwich) and *moules marinières* (mussels cooked in white wine).

Adventure Café (☎ 462038; 5 Princes Bldgs; mains £3-6) Big city style in little city Bath. Huge plate glass windows, dark-wood floors and laid-back tunes conjure a sophisticated metropolitan atmosphere at this trendy café-bar, which is as popular for a lunchtime ciabatta as for a late-night Bud.

Café Retro (☎ 339347; 18 York St; mains £5-11) Retro by name, retro by nature, this popular boho hang-out is the perfect venue for a light lunch or an extended coffee break. If you don't feel like sitting in, grab a sandwich and a takeaway coffee from Retro2Go and head over for a picnic in the Parade Gardens nearby.

QUICK EATS

Boston Tea Party (☎ 313901; 19 Kingsmead Sq; ☺ Mon-Sat) With a lovely outside terrace spilling onto Kingsmead Sq, the Bath outpost of this small southwest franchise is always full to bursting at lunchtime thanks to its prodigious selection of sandwiches, homemade soups and sweet treats.

Café Fromage (☎ 313525; 1 John St; ploughman's from £4.95; ☺ Mon-Sat) Cheese in all its wonderful, whiffy forms underpins practically every dish at this first-floor café, perched above the city's top *fromagerie*. The ploughman's (complete with homemade chutney) is the favourite choice, but the Welsh rarebit and cheese soufflé are worth trying too.

SELF-CATERING

Self-caterers should head for the covered **Guildhall Market**, where you'll find crêpes and other takeaway food. The major supermarket chains are all represented in the city.

Blackstones (☎ 338803; 10 Queen St; mains £2-7; ☺ Mon-Sat) This fantastic gourmet takeaway is such good value you might never need to pick up a pan again. Delicious dishes such as rich cottage pie, Italian casserole and Chinese noodles are made on the premises every day, and served either in the small café or packed up for the ultimate take-home meal. The owners have recently also opened a sit-down restaurant right across the street from the kitchens (mains £7 to £13).

Paxton & Whitfield (☎ 01225 466403; 1 John St; ☺ Mon-Sat) Underneath the Café Fromage, this upmarket cheese shop specialises in local brands, and stocks more varieties of cheddar than you would have thought possible.

Chandos Deli (☎ 314418; George St; ☺ Mon-Sat) Gourmet sarnies, fresh pasta and Italian cakes are the mainstays at this excellent deli, perfect for stocking up on picnic supplies.

Midrange

Circus (☎ 318918; 34 Brock St; set menu £19.95; ☺ Tue-Sun) The razor-edge tablecloths and blindingly bright cutlery should tell you all you need to know about this swish Anglo-French restaurant. It's undoubtedly one of the city's top tables, with a complex menu that mixes Gallic flavours with local produce, and an atmosphere that's starchier than a matron's apron.

FishWorks (☎ 448707; 6 Green St; mains from £13; ☺ lunch & dinner) This wonderful place combines a fishmonger, cookery school and seafood restaurant into one piscatorially perfect bundle. Choose your fish from the ice-packed trays downstairs, or select something fresh from the chalkboard menu, and sit back and enjoy the flavours of the sea.

Onefishtwofish (☎ 330236; 10A North Pde; mains £13-18; ☺ dinner Tue-Sun) More top-class seafood is on offer at this new restaurant by the weirside, housed in an extraordinary barrel-vaulted cellar built from rough brick and flagstone tiles. The menu changes according to the daily catch; if it's available, plump for the sumptuous Marseillaise bouillabaisse, which offers a true taste of the Côte d'Azur.

Firehouse Rotisserie (☎ 482070; 2 John St; mains £11-15; ☺ lunch & dinner Mon-Sat) Stateside flavours and a Californian vibe characterise this excellent American restaurant, run by a couple of ex-LA chefs. The menu takes its cue from Mexico and the deep South, with signature dishes including rotisserie chicken, Louisiana catfish and Texan steak, as well as huge brick-fired pizzas.

Demuth's (☎ 446059; 2 North Pde Passage; mains £11.50-12.50; ☽ lunch) This much-admired vegetarian restaurant is renowned for its inventive cooking and dedication to seasonal produce. The intimate townhouse dining room is finished with lustrous wood and abstract art, and the mood is buzzy and informal. If you fancy learning some of its culinary secrets, book a place at www.vegetariancookeryschool.com.

Bistro Papillon (☎ 310064; 2 Margarets Bldgs; 2-course lunch £8.50, mains £11-15; ☽ Tue-Sat) Ooh la la – a little piece of *la belle France* comes to Bath at this quintessentially Gallic bistro near Royal Cres. Rustic Mediterranean dishes are matched by a thoroughly French ambience, complete with checked tablecloths, clattering pans, sunbaked colours and a streetside terrace.

Top End

Olive Tree Restaurant (☎ 447928; Russell St; 2-/3-course lunch £14.50/16.50, dinner mains £15-23; ☽ lunch Tues-Sun, dinner Mon-Sun) If you're after a special supper, look no further than the inhouse restaurant at the Queensberry Hotel, which boasts a new Michelin-starred chef and a fresh minimalist look. The cooking is straight from the top drawer, and specialises in creative takes on local meat, seafood and game.

Hole In The Wall (☎ 425242; 16 George St; ☽ lunch & dinner Mon-Sat) Back in the '60s, the venerable Hole In The Wall was one of the restaurants that heralded the rebirth of British cuisine, and though it's changed hands many times since then, it's still a beacon for innovative cooking. Fusion flavours and a modern country-tinged interior have given a new lease of life to this old fave.

DRINKING

Common Room (☎ 425550; 2 Saville Row) Next door to an anarchic antiques shop, this tiny little bar is a favourite with Bath's beautiful people. It's got all the designer credentials – exposed brickwork, blonde-wood floors, black leather sofas – and a more chilled atmosphere than the drinking dens on George St.

Revolution (☎ 336168; George St) Swish and ever-so-slightly snooty Manhattan-style bar, with the standard-issue blend of retro lamps and chrome fixtures, and a selection of cocktails served by the jug.

Sub 13 (☎ 466667; 4 Edgar Bldgs, George St; ☽ closed Sun) This hip new hang-out has established itself as a smooth-operating alternative to Bath's bigger, brasher joints. Iced beers, bespoke cocktails and an intimate vibe are the order of the day.

Delfter Krug (☎ 443352; Sawclose) A sprawling café-pub that covers practically every eventuality, with a large outside terrace, a mix-and-match interior bar and busy club nights on weekends.

Porter (☎ 424104; George St) Bath's only veggie pub is a rustic, spit-and-sawdust affair run by the folk behind Moles nightclub. Regular bands play in the downstairs cellar, and it's usually jammed to the rafters on Friday and Saturday night.

Bath Tap (☎ 404344; 19-20 St James Pde; ☽ to 2am Thu-Sat) The classic pub hang out for Bath's gay community, with a late weekend licence and a fun range of theme nights ranging from drag to cabaret.

Crystal Palace (☎ 482666; Abbey Green) You couldn't ask for a nicer location for this popular pub, nestled in the shadow of the abbey on a tree-shaded green. Local beers and a gorgeous patio garden make this a top spot for a quiet pint.

ENTERTAINMENT

Venue magazine (www.venue.co.uk; £1.20) has comprehensive listings with details of theatre, music, gigs – the works, basically – for Bristol and Bath. Pick up a copy at any newsagency.

Nightclubs

Moles (☎ 404445; www.moles.co.uk; 14 George St; admission £5-7) The best venue in town continues to go from strength to strength, hosting a regular line-up of cutting-edge new acts and breaking bands, as well as occasional club nights. There's also live music in the cellar bar of Porter across the road.

Babylon (☎ 465002; Kingston Rd; admission £3-5; ☽ Thu-Sat) This is Bath's big night out, at least if you're a student; drum and bass, house, funk, breaks and indie all feature on the revolving programme of events, but seasoned clubbers tend to head over to Bristol instead.

Cadillacs (☎ 464241; 90B Walcot St; £4-6) A venerable old club that's been around for donkey's years and is starting to show its age; still, its worth a look for a late-night drink and the occasional decent night.

(Continued on page 277)

WESSEX

History

Iron bridge, Ironbridge Gorge (p441), Shropshire

Statue, Winchester Cathedral (p226), Hampshire

Stonehenge (p314), Wiltshire

TOM SMALLM

Castle Howard (p620), Yorkshire

Warwick Castle (p467), Warwick

TONY WHEELER

Rievaulx Abbey (p631), Yorkshire

GRANT DIXON

STAEVEN VALLAK

Roman Baths Museum (p260), Bath

Annual procession, Windsor Castle (p170), Berkshire

ADINA TOVY AMSEL

Culture

Old Trafford (p648), Manchester

DAVID TOMLINSON

Baltic – the Centre for Contemporary Art (p731),
Gateshead

DOUG MCKINLAY

Dummies, Glastonbury Festival (p284)

GUY MOBERLY

BBC Proms concert, Royal Albert Hall (p153), London

ELLIOT DANIEL

Cricket, Warkworth Castle (p752), Northumberland

Minack Theatre (p362), Cornwall

Clubbing (p151), London

Food & Drink

Traditional English 'real ale' (p87)

NEIL SETCHFIELD

Curry Mile (p651), Wilmslow Rd, Manchester

MARK DAI

ADAM WOOLFITT/CORBIS

A classic roast beef meal (p85)

DAVID ELSE

Old Sun Inn (p505), Buxton

DAVID TOMLINSON

Strawberries and cream,
Wimbledon Lawn Tennis
Championships (p133)

NEIL SETCHFIELD

Fish and chips (p86)

Architecture

Angel of the North (p736), Gateshead

St Paul's Cathedral (p120), London

Blenheim Palace (p392), Oxfordshire

(Continued from page 268)

Theatre & Cinemas

Theatre Royal (☎ 448844; www.theatreroyal.org.uk; Saw-close) This seriously posh provincial theatre features comedy, drama, opera, ballet, and world music in the main auditorium, and more experimental productions at its smaller Ustinov Studio.

Rondo Theatre (☎ 463362; www.rondotheatre.co.uk; St Saviours Rd, Larkhall) This small but adventurous rep theatre mixes up professional, amateur and community work through a varied programme of comedy, music, dance and drama.

Little Theatre (☎ 466822; St Michael's Pl) Bath's arthouse cinema, screening mostly fringe and foreign-language films.

GETTING THERE & AWAY

Bus

National Express coaches run to London (£16.50, 3½ hours, 10 daily) via Heathrow (£16.50, 23/4 hours), and to Bristol (45 minutes, two daily) for buses to the north. Services to most other cities require a change at Bristol or Heathrow.

Buses X39/339 (55 minutes, several per hour) and 332 (50 minutes, hourly, seven on Sunday) run to Bath. Other useful services include buses X4/X5 to Bradford-on-Avon (30 minutes, half-hourly), X71/X72 to Devizes (one hour, hourly Monday to Saturday, six on Sunday) and 173/773 to Wells (1¼ hours, hourly Monday to Saturday, seven on Sunday).

Map-timetables for individual routes are available from the **bus station office** (☎ 464446; Manvers St; ☼ 8am-5.30pm Mon-Sat).

Train

There are half-hourly trains to London Paddington (£56, 1½ hours) and Cardiff (£12.90, 1¼ hours), and several each hour to Bristol (£5.20, 11 minutes), where you can connect with the main line trains to northern England.

Trains travel to Oxford approximately hourly (£17.20, 1½ hours, change at Didcot Parkway); Weymouth (£11.60, 2¼ hours) every two hours via Bradford-on-Avon (15 minutes) and Dorchester West (£11.30, two hours); and to Portsmouth (£24.10, 2½ hours) hourly via Salisbury (£11.20, one hour).

GETTING AROUND

Bicycle

Hire bikes from **Avon Valley Cycles** (☎ 461880; www.bikeshop.uk.com; Arch 37; half-/full day £10/15; ☼ 9.30-5pm Mon-Sat, till 8pm Thu) near the train station.

The 13-mile **Bristol and Bath Railway Path** (www.bristolbathrailwaypath.org.uk) runs along the disused track of the old Midland Railway, decommissioned in the late 1960s.

Bus

Bus 18 runs from the bus station, High St and Great Pulteney St up Bathwick Hill past the YHA to the university every 10 minutes. Bus 4 runs every 20 minutes to Bathampton from the same places. A FirstDay Pass for unlimited bus travel in the city costs adult/child £4/2.60.

Car

Bath has a serious traffic problem (especially at rush hour) and an infuriating one-way system. **Park-and-ride services** (☎ 464446; return £1.70, 10 min to centre, every 10-15 min; ☼ 6.15am-7.30pm) operate at Lansdown to the north, Newbridge to the west and Odd Down to the south.

AROUND BATH

Prior Park

The celebrated landscape gardener Capability Brown and the satirical poet Alexander Pope both had a hand in the creation of **Prior Park** (NT; ☎ 833 422; admission £4.50; Ralph Allen Dr; ☼ 11am-5.30pm Wed-Mon Feb-Nov, 11am-dusk Fri-Sun Dec & Jan), an 18th-century ornamental garden dreamt up by the local entrepreneur Ralph Allen. Cascading lakes, a Gothic temple and a famous Palladian bridge can be found around the garden's winding walks, and the sweeping views over the Bath skyline are something to behold.

Prior Park is 1 mile south of the centre; it can be reached on foot or by bus (2 or 4, every 10 minutes), as well as the City Skyline tour (p264).

SOMERSET

With its landscape of knotted hedgerows, hummocked hills and russet-coloured fields, sleepy Somerset is the very picture of the rural English countryside, and makes the perfect escape from the tourist hordes of Bath and the big city hustle of Bristol. The county's agricultural image and distinctive Somerset burr have long made it the butt of yokel jokes,

WESSEX

and while things certainly move at a drowsier pace around these parts, that's all part of what makes this charming county tick. From the elegant streets of the cathedral city of Wells to the hippie chic of Glastonbury and the open fields of Exmoor, this is a place to wander, ponder and drink in the sights at your own laid-back pace.

Orientation & Information

Somerset nestles around the crook in the elbow of the Bristol Channel. The Mendip Hills (the Mendips) follow a line below Bristol, just north of Wells and Cheddar, while the Quantock Hills (the Quantocks) sit just east of Exmoor. Most places of interest are in northern Somerset. Bath or Wells make good bases to the east, as do Lynton and Lynmouth to the west.

Most towns have tourist offices and there's a central **Somerset Visitor Centre** (☎ 01934-750833; somersetvisitorcentre@somerset.gov.uk; Sedgemoor Services M5 South, Axbridge, Somerset BS26 2UF) for general information. The new website at www.somerset. net is a useful source of info.

Getting Around

Most buses in Somerset are operated by **First** (☎ 0845 606 4446; www.firstgroup.com), supplemented by a few smaller operators and coach companies. For timetables and general travel information, visit the First website, contact **Traveline** (☎ 0870 608 2 608; www.traveline.org.uk) or contact **Somerset County Council's transport department** (☎ 0845 345 9155; transport@somerset.gov.uk). Area timetables are available at bus stations and tourist offices.

WELLS
☎ 01749 / pop 10,406

Tiny Wells is England's smallest city, and only qualifies for the title of 'city' thanks to its magnificent medieval cathedral, which sits in the heart of town beside the grand Bishop's Palace – the main seat of ecclesiastical power in this part of Britain since the 12th century, and still the official residence of the Bishop of Bath and Wells. Medieval buildings and cobbled streets radiate out from the cathedral green to the main marketplace, which has been the bustling heart of Wells for some nine centuries. These days Wells is a quiet provincial city, with some good restaurants and busy shops, and makes a good launch pad for exploring the Mendips and northern Somerset.

Information

The **tourist office** (☎ 672552; www.wells.gov.uk; Market Pl; ⊙ 9.30am-5.30pm Apr-Oct, 10am-4pm Nov-Mar) stocks the *Wells City Trail* leaflet (30p) and sells discount tickets to the nearby attractions of Wookey Hole, Cheddar Gorge and Longleat. Wednesday and Saturday are market days.

Wells Laundrette (☎ 01458 830409; 39 St Cuthbert St; ⊙ 8am-8pm) is opposite St Cuthbert's Church.

Sights
WELLS CATHEDRAL

Set in a marvellous medieval close, the **Cathedral Church of St Andrew** (☎ 674483; www.wellscathedral.org .uk; Chain Gate, Cathedral Green; requested donation adult/child £5/2; ⊙ 7am-7pm Apr-Sep, 7am-6pm Oct-Mar) was built in stages between 1180 and 1508. The building incorporates several Gothic styles, but its most famous asset is the wonderful **west front**, an immense sculpture gallery decorated with more than 300 figures, built in the 13th century and restored to its original splendour in 1986. The façade would once have been painted in vivid colours, but has long since reverted to its original sandy hue. Apart from the figure of Christ, installed in 1985 in the uppermost niche, all the figures are original.

Inside, the most striking feature is the pair of **scissor arches** separating the nave from the choir, designed to counter the subsidence of the central tower. High up in the north transept is a wonderful **mechanical clock** dating from 1392 – the second-oldest surviving in England after the one in Salisbury Cathedral (p309). The clock shows the position of the planets and the phases of the moon.

Other highlights are the elegant **lady chapel** (1326) at the eastern end and the seven **effigies** of Anglo-Saxon bishops ringing the choir. The 15th-century **chained library** houses books and manuscripts dating back to 1472. It's only open at certain times during the year or by prior arrangement.

From the north transept follow the worn steps to the glorious **Chapter House** (1306), with its delicate ceiling ribs sprouting like a palm from a central column. Externally, look out for the **Chain Bridge** built from the northern side of the cathedral to Vicars' Close to enable clerics to reach the cathedral without getting their robes wet. The **cloisters** on the southern side surround a pretty courtyard.

Guided tours (⊙ Mon-Sat) of the cathedral are free, and usually take place every hour.

Regular **concerts** (☎ 832201) and cathedral choir **recitals** (☎ 674483) are held in the cathedral throughout the year. If you want to take pictures, you'll need to buy a permit (£2) from the cathedral shop.

CATHEDRAL CLOSE
Wells Cathedral forms the centrepiece of a cluster of ecclesiastical buildings dating back to the Middle Ages and beyond. Facing the west front, on the left are the 15th-century **Old Deanery** and the **Wells Museum** (☎ 673477; 8 Cathedral Green; www.wellsmuseum.org.uk; admission £3; ☯ 10am-5.30pm Mon-Sat, 11am-4pm Sun Easter-Oct, 11am-4pm Nov-Easter), with exhibits on local life, cathedral architecture and the infamous Witch of Wookey Hole.

Further along on the left, **Vicars' Close** is a stunning cobbled street of uniform houses dating back to the 14th century, with a chapel at the end; members of the cathedral choir still live here. It is thought to be the oldest complete medieval street in Europe. Passing under the Chain Bridge, inspect the outside of the lady chapel and a lovely medieval house called The Rib, before emerging at a main road called The Liberty.

Penniless Porch, a corner gate leading onto Market Sq and built by Bishop Bekynton around 1450, is so called because beggars asked for alms here.

BISHOP'S PALACE
Beyond the cathedral is the moated 13th-century **Bishop's Palace** (☎ 678691; www.bishopspalacewells.co.uk; adult/child £5/1; ☯ 10.30am-6pm Mon-Fri, noon-6pm Sun Apr-Oct), purportedly the oldest inhabited building in England. Surrounded by a huge fortified wall, the palace complex contains several fine Italian Gothic state rooms, an imposing Great Hall and beautiful tree-shaded gardens. The natural wells that gave the city its name bubble up in the palace's grounds, feeding the moat and the fountain in the market square. The swans in the moat have been trained to ring a bell outside one of the windows when they want to be fed.

Sleeping
Infield House (☎ 670989; www.infieldhouse.co.uk; 36 Portway; s/d £28/54; P ✗) The best (and cheapest) of several B&Bs scattered along the busy Portway road, offering simple, spacious B&B rooms in a Victorian townhouse. There are no real surprises, but the buffet breakfast is generous and the town centre is a short walk away.

Islington Farm (☎ 673445; www.islingtonfarmatwells.co.uk; s/d £45/60; P ✗) A lovely ivy-covered farmhouse on the edge of the city, with idyllic views across the surrounding farmland. As you'd expect from such an old building, some of the pastel-themed, fluffy-pillowed rooms are a little cramped, jammed into the rafters of the 17th-century house; for a bit more space, ask for the converted cottage behind the main house.

Beryl (☎ 678738; www.beryl-wells.co.uk; Hawkers Lane; s £60-75, d £75-115; P ✗ ☖) A mile from the city centre, this stately gabled Victorian mansion is set in 13 acres of private parkland and boasts the kind of luxurious accommodation you'd normally find at double (or triple) the price. The richly furnished rooms have bags of country character, with swags, frills and elegant drapes and a smattering of veneered antiques. The heated outdoor swimming pool is the icing on the cake.

Ancient Gate House Hotel (☎ 672029; www.ancientgatehouse.co.uk; Browne's Gate; s £76, d £91-97.50; ✗) You can't get much more central than this 15th-century inn, which actually forms part of the Great West Gate of Cathedral Close. The wood beams, wonky walls and slightly musty atmosphere have been faithfully preserved, and there are a couple of rooms with carved wooden four-poster and half-tester beds.

Old Farmhouse (☎ 675058; www.plus44.com/oldfarmhouse; r from £60; P ✗) Fine 17th-century farmhouse with its own walled garden and comfy if unspectacular rooms.

Swan Hotel (☎ 836300; www.bhere.co.uk; Sadler St; d from £90; ✗) Elegant 15th-century coaching room with large period-themed rooms.

Eating
Café Romna (☎ 670240; 13 Sadler St; mains £10-15; ☯ lunch & dinner Mon-Sat) A stylish Bangladeshi fusion restaurant, decked out with hot colours, low lighting and black banquette sofas, and an intriguing menu of unusual dishes such as *zingha bhajee* (Bangladeshi vegetable curry) and *chingri palack* (tiger prawns cooked with garlic and spinach).

Goodfellows (☎ 673866; 5 Sadler St; mains £13-22, set menu £29; ☯ lunch & dinner Tues-Sat) This sophisticated restaurant has scooped several awards for its creative blend of Somerset produce and French-inspired cuisine. During the day it's a relaxed café-cum-artisan baker, with designer

---

WORTH THE TRIP

Glencot House (☎ 677160; www.glencothouse.co.uk; Wookey Hole; s/d £74/97, 4-poster-bed rooms £130; P ⊠) If you're after the ultimate country getaway, look no further than this breathtaking 19th-century manor house, built in opulent Jacobean style and surrounded by 18 acres of private woods and riverside grounds (as well as its own cricket pitch). Walnut panelling, carved ceilings and dazzling chandeliers decorate the public rooms, and there are 13 graceful rooms spread out around the house's meandering corridors, all individually finished with a selection of chaise longues, country prints and antique dressers. Downstairs there's a well-stocked library, a firelit drawing room, and a wood-beamed dining hall that could have fallen straight from the pages of *The Remains of the Day*.

---

sandwiches, crumbly pastries and traditional breads, as well as a selection of fresh fish; for something more complex head for the formal dining room, where you'll find classy multi-course menus for lunch and dinner.

Rugantino (☎ 672029; Browne's Gate; 3-course menu £18.90; ☽ dinner) Practically every Italian dish you could possibly think of is served up at this rustic restaurant, situated on the ground floor of the Ancient Gate House Hotel. All the pasta and pizza classics are present and correct, as well as more esoteric fare such as bread-crumbed pork and chicken in pancetta.

Getting There & Around

National Express runs direct to London once a day (£18, 4½ hours), although it's usually more convenient to travel to Bristol and catch a local bus.

Bus 173 runs from Bath to Wells (1¼ hours, hourly, seven on Sunday). Bus 375/376 travels to Wells from Bristol (one hour, hourly) before continuing on to Glastonbury (15 minutes) and Street (25 minutes). Bus 29 travels to Taunton (1¼ hours, seven daily Monday to Friday, five or six on weekends) via Glastonbury. Bus 126 runs to Cheddar (25 minutes) hourly Monday to Saturday and every two hours on Sunday. There's no train station in Wells.

Bike City (☎ 671711; 31 Broad St; ☽ 9am-5.30pm Mon-Sat) charges £15 per day for bike hire.

WOOKEY HOLE

On the southern edge of the Mendips, the River Axe has carved out a series of deep caverns collectively known as **Wookey Hole** (☎ 01749-672243; www.wookey.co.uk; adult/child £10.90/8.50; ☽ 10am-5pm Apr-Oct, 10.30am-4pm Nov-Mar). The caves are littered with dramatic natural features, including a subterranean lake and some fascinating stalagmites and stalactites

(one of which is supposedly the legendary Witch of Wookey Hole, who was turned to stone by a local priest). The caves were inhabited by prehistoric people for some 50,000 years, but these days the deep pools and underground rivers are more often frequented by cave divers – the deepest subterranean dive ever recorded in Britain was made here in September 2004, when divers reached a depth of more than 149 feet.

Admission to the caves is by guided tour. The rest of the complex is taken up by a motley assortment of plastic dinosaurs, mirror mazes and an Edwardian penny arcade, as well as a working paper mill. There are a few prehistoric finds displayed at the onsite museum, but most are on display at the Wells City Museum (p278).

Bus 670 runs from Wells (10 minutes, nine daily, four on Sunday).

CHEDDAR GORGE
☎ 01934

If Wookey Hole is a little too touristy for your tastes, then you'd better be prepared for **Cheddar Caves** (☎ 742343; www.cheddarcaves.co.uk; Explorer Ticket adult/child £11.50/8.50; ☽ 10am-5.30pm Jul & Aug, 10.30am-5pm Sep-Jun), a spectacular series of limestone caverns that's always jammed with visitors throughout the summer months.

Despite the tourist throng, it's hard not to be impressed by the natural wonders on display. Although the network of caves extends deep into the surrounding rock, only a few are open to the public; the most impressive are Cox's Cave and Gough's Cave, both decorated by an amazing gallery of stalactites and stalagmites, and subtly lit to bring out the spectrum of colours in the limestone rock. After the end of the last Ice Age, the caves were inhabited by prehistoric people; a 9000-year-old skeleton (imaginatively named 'Cheddar Man') was discovered here in 1903, and genetic tests have revealed that some of his descendants are still living in the surrounding area.

Outside the caves, the 274 steps of **Jacob's Ladder** lead up to an impressive panorama of the surrounding countryside; on a clear day you can see all the way to Glastonbury Tor and Exmoor.

Nearby, a signposted 3-mile-round walk follows the cliffs along the most spectacular parts of **Cheddar Gorge**, which cuts a mile-long swathe through the southern side of the Mendip Hills. At some points the cliff walls tower 138m above the winding narrow road that lies at its base. Most visitors only explore the first section of the path, and you can usually escape the crowds by venturing further up the valley.

The **tourist office** (☎ 744071; cheddar.tic@sedgemoor. gov.uk; ☺ 10am-5pm Easter-Sep, 10.30am-4.30pm Oct, 11am-4pm Sun Nov-Easter) is at the southern end of the gorge, and has some useful information on local walks and caving trips.

A mile southwest of the caves on the western side of Cheddar village is the **Cheddar YHA Hostel** (☎ 0870 770 5760; cheddar@yha.org.uk; Hillfield; dm £13.95).

Bus 126 runs to Wells (25 minutes) hourly Monday to Saturday and every two hours on Sunday.

MENDIP HILLS

The Mendip Hills are a ridge of limestone hills stretching from the coast near Weston-Super-Mare to Frome in eastern Somerset. Their highest point is Black Down (326m) to the northwest – but because they rise sharply,

---

GOING UNDERGROUND

If a visit to the Cheddar caves piques your interest in the strange subterranean world beneath the gorge, then you might like to take a **caving trip** to explore the area a little further. **Rocksport** (☎ 01934-742343; caves@visitcheddar.co.uk; trips £16-30) offers 1½-hour introductory caving sessions into the dark, dank caves around the gorge, as well as adventurous subterranean trips into the more remote caverns. Needless to say, you'll get wet and muddy, and you'll need to be up to the physical challenges of underground caving – and if you're even vaguely claustrophobic, don't even think about it.

---

there are panoramic views towards Exmoor and across northwest Wiltshire.

Historically, the area has seen its share of action, and Neolithic earthworks, Bronze Age barrows and Iron Age forts can be found scattered over the hills. More recently, lead and coal mining have left their mark, with remains of mines dotting the area around Radstock and Midsomer Norton. Quarrying for stone is an important (and controversial) industry to this day.

Until the Middle Ages, large tracts of land lay beneath swampy meadows, and the remaining wetlands provide an important habitat for wildlife and flora. The marshland hid relics too, including a lake village excavated at the turn of the 20th century (see p283).

The landscape is dotted with pretty villages and isolated pubs that once served the thirsty miners. The villages are home to some delightful timbered houses, and several have fine perpendicular church towers. The one at **Chewton Mendip** (off the A37 between Bristol and Wells) is especially impressive and has a nice medieval churchyard cross. Further west, the village of **Priddy**, the highest in the Mendips, has a massive sheep fair on the green in mid-August, while the village of **Compton Martin** has a Norman church with a 15th-century tower. A mile to the east, **West Harptree** is prettier, with two 17th-century former manor houses. Near **East Harptree** are the remains of Norman Richmont Castle. Local tourist offices stock leaflets with information on walking and cycling in the area.

The A371 skirts the southern side of the Mendip Hills, and any of the towns along it make good touring bases, though Wells has the best range of facilities.

GLASTONBURY

☎ 01458 / pop 8429

If you suddenly feel the need to get your third eye cleansed or your chakras realigned, then there's really only one place in England that fits the bill: good old Glastonbury, a bohemian haven and centre for New Age culture since the days of the Summer of Love, and still a favourite hang out for hippies, mystics and counter-cultural types of all descriptions. The main street is more Haight Ashbury than Somerset hamlet, thronged with a bewildering assortment of crystal sellers, veggie cafés, mystical bookshops and bong emporiums,

WESSEX

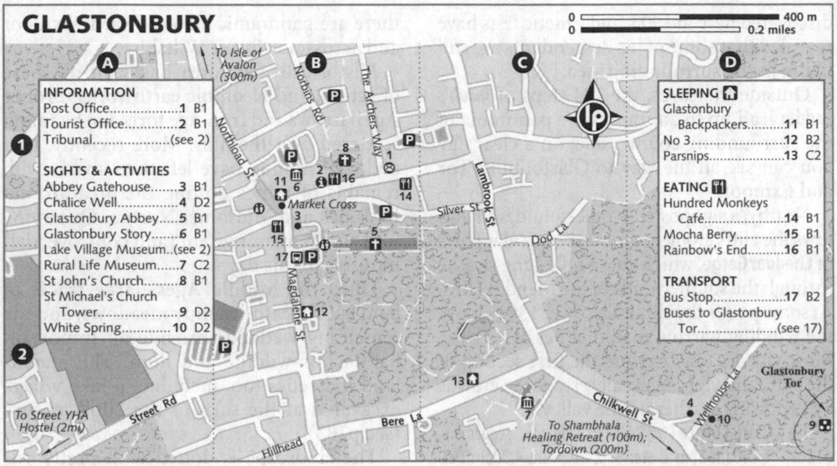
GLASTONBURY
0 400 m
0 0.2 miles
INFORMATION
Post Office....1 B1
Tourist Office....2 B1
Tribunal....(see 2)
SIGHTS & ACTIVITIES
Abbey Gatehouse....3 B1
Chalice Well....4 D2
Glastonbury Abbey....5 B1
Glastonbury Story....6 B1
Lake Village Museum..(see 2)
Rural Life Museum....7 C2
St John's Church....8 B1
St Michael's Church Tower....9 D2
White Spring....10 D2
SLEEPING
Glastonbury Backpackers....11 B1
No 3....12 B2
Parsnips....13 C2
EATING
Hundred Monkeys Café....14 B1
Mocha Berry....15 B1
Rainbow's End....16 B1
TRANSPORT
Bus Stop....17 B2
Buses to Glastonbury Tor....(see 17)
To Isle of Avalon (300m)
Northload St
Norbins Rd
The Archers Way
Lambrook St
Silver St
Market Cross
Magdalene St
Dod La
Street Rd
Bere La
Hillhead
Chilkwell St
Wellhouse La
Glastonbury Tor
To Street YHA Hostel (2mi)
To Shambhala Healing Retreat (100m); Tordown (200m)

but Glastonbury has been a spiritual centre since long before the weekend Buddhists and white witches arrived. It's supposedly the birthplace of Christianity in England, and several of Britain's most important ley lines are said to converge on nearby Glastonbury Tor. Whether you find spiritual enlightenment or just a solid veggie meal in Glastonbury, one thing's for certain: it's not a bad place to stock up on joss sticks.

Information

Glastonbury's **tourist office** (☎ 832954; www.glastonburytic.co.uk; The Tribunal, 9 High St; 10am-5pm Apr-Sep, 10am-4pm Oct-Mar) stocks free maps and accommodation lists, and sells leaflets describing local walks and the *Glastonbury Millennium Trail* (60p).

Sights

GLASTONBURY ABBEY

Legend has it that Joseph of Arimathea, great-uncle of Jesus, owned mines in this area and returned here with the Holy Grail (the chalice from the Last Supper) after the death of Christ. Joseph supposedly founded England's first church on the site, now occupied by the ruined **abbey** (☎ 832267; www.glastonburyabbey.com; Magdalene St; admission £4; 9.30am-6pm Jun-Aug, 9.30am-6pm Apr-May & Sep, 9.30am-5pm Mar & Oct, 9.30am-4.30pm Nov, 10am-4.30pm Dec), but the earliest proven Christian connection dates from the 7th century, when King Ine gave a charter to a monastery in Glastonbury. In 1184 the church was destroyed by fire and reconstruction began in the reign of Henry II.

In 1191, monks claimed to have had visions confirming hints in old manuscripts that the 6th-century warrior-king Arthur and his wife Guinevere were buried in the abbey grounds. Excavations uncovered a tomb containing a skeletal couple, who were reinterred in front of the high altar of the new church in 1278. The tomb survived until 1539, when Henry VIII dissolved the monasteries and had the last abbot hung, drawn and quartered on the tor.

The remaining ruins at Glastonbury mainly date from the church built after the 1184 fire. It's still possible to make out some of the nave walls, the ruins of the St Mary's chapel, and the remains of the crossing arches, which may have been scissor-shaped like those in Wells Cathedral (p278). The site of the supposed tomb of Arthur and Guinevere is marked in the grass. The grounds also contain a small museum, cider orchard and herb garden, as well as the **Holy Thorn** tree, which supposedly sprung from Joseph's staff and mysteriously blooms twice a year, at Christmas and Easter.

GLASTONBURY TOR

There are all kinds of myths swirling around the grassy mound of Glastonbury Tor, a 160m-high hill just outside town that commands glorious views over the surrounding countryside. According to some it's the home of a faery king, while an old Celtic legend

---

A CHEESY STORY

As well as its spectacular cave system, cheddar is also famous as the spiritual home of the nation's favourite cheese. Cheddar's strong, crumbly, tangy cheese is the essential ingredient in any self-respecting ploughman's sandwich, and has been produced in the area since at least the 12th century; Henry II boldly proclaimed cheddar to be 'the best cheese in Britain', and the king's accounts from 1170 record that he purchased 10,240lbs (around 3650kg) of the stuff. In the days before refrigeration, the Cheddar caves made the ideal cool store for the cheese, with a constant temperature of around 7°C, but the powerful smell attracted rats and the practice was eventually abandoned.

These days most cheddar cheese is made far from the village, but if you're interested in seeing how the genuine article is made, head for the **Cheddar Gorge Cheese Company** (☎ 01934-742810; www.cheddargorgecheeseco.co.uk; admission £1.85; ☼ 10am-5.30pm). You can take a guided tour of the factory from April to October, and pick up some cheesy souvenirs at the onsite shop.

---

identifies it as the stronghold of Gwyn ap Nudd (ruler of Annwyn, the Underworld); but the most famous legend identifies the tor as the mythic Isle of Avalon, where King Arthur was taken after being mortally wounded in battle by his nephew Mordred, and where Britain's 'once and future king' sleeps until his country calls again.

Whatever the truth of the legends, the tor has been a site of pilgrimage for many years, and was once topped by the medieval church of St Michael, although today only the tower remains. On the way up to the tour look out for **Gog** and **Magog**, two gnarled oak trees believed to be the last remains of an ancient processional avenue.

It takes 45 minutes to walk up and down the tor. Parking is not permitted nearby, so take the Tor Bus (£1) from Dunstan's car park near the abbey. The bus runs to the tor and back every 30 minutes from 10am to 7.30pm April to September, and from 10am to 3.30pm from October to April. It also stops at Chalice Well and the Rural Life Museum.

CHALICE WELL & GARDENS

Shaded by knotted yew trees and surrounded by peaceful paths, the **Chalice Well & Gardens** (☎ 831154; www.chalicewell.org.uk; admission £3; ☼ 10am-5.30pm Apr-Oct, 10am-4pm Nov-Mar) has been a site of pilgrimage since the days of the Celts. The iron-red waters from the 800-year-old well are rumoured to have healing properties, good for everything from eczema to smelly feet; some legends also identify the well as the hiding place of the Holy Grail. You can drink the water from a lion's-head spout, or rest your feet in basins surrounded by flowers.

The Chalice Well is also known as the 'Red Spring' or 'Blood Spring'; its sister, **White Spring**, surfaces across Wellhouse Lane. Spigots from both springs empty into the street, where there's often a queue to fill containers.

RURAL LIFE MUSEUM

Somerset's agricultural heritage is explored at the **Rural Life Museum** (☎ 831197; Abbey Farm, Chilkwell St; admission free; ☼ 10am-5pm Tue-Fri, 2-6pm Sat & Sun Apr-Oct, 10am-5pm Tue-Sat Nov-Mar), which contains a varied collection of artefacts relating to traditional trades such as willow growing, peat-digging, cider-making and cheese-making. There are often live displays of local skills, so if you fancy trying your hand at beekeeping, lacemaking and spinning, this is the place to do it. The late-14th-century tithe barn has fine carvings on the gables and porch, and an impressive timber roof; it now houses a collection of vintage agricultural machinery.

GLASTONBURY STORY

The tale of King Arthur's grave and many other Glastonbury legends is explored at the **Glastonbury Story** (☎ 831666; www.glastonburystory .org.uk; St John's Sq; admission £3; ☼ 11am-5pm late-Mar–Oct). It's a little low-budget, but the exhibition is a decent introduction to the various legends that swirl around the town and its famous tor.

LAKE VILLAGE MUSEUM

Upstairs from Glastonbury's tourist office, in the medieval courthouse, the **Lake Village Museum** (EH; admission £2) displays finds from a prehistoric bog village discovered nearby.

THE OTHER GLASTONBURY

To many people, the village of Glastonbury is practically synonymous with the **Glastonbury Festival of Contemporary Performing Arts** (www.glastonburyfestivals.co.uk), an annual extravaganza of music, street theatre, dance, cabaret, carnival, ecology, spirituality and general all-round weirdness that's been held on and off on Piltdown Farm, near Glastonbury, for the last 30 years. The first event was held in 1970, when the young dairy farmer Michael Eavis invited some bands to play on makeshift stages in his field; 30 years later, the festival has become the longest-running performing arts festival in the world, attracting some of the world's biggest acts and an annual crowd of more than 120,000 festival-goers. Glastonbury is more a way of life than a music festival, and it's a rite of passage for every self-respecting British teenager; it's also the subject of a new feature-length documentary by filmmaker Julian Temple.

Tours

There are lots of companies offering guided tours of Glastonbury's main sights.

Mystical Tours of Glastonbury (☎ 831453; www .gothicimagetours.co.uk; 7 High St; per person £60) Based at the Gothic Image bookshop on the High St, this company offers guided tours to the Wearyall Hill, Gog and Magog and Glastonbury Tor itself, as well as day tours to Stonehenge and Avebury.

Goddess Tours (☎ 275084; kathy.jones@ukonline.co.uk) Guided tours run by the mystical Priestesses of Avalon, who are members of the matriarchal 'Goddess' religious order.

Secret Landscape Tours (☎ 07854-316754; www. secretlandscapetours.com) offers guided trips to sacred sites throughout the southwest, including to Glastonbury Tor and Stonehenge.

Sleeping

If you're a fan of wind chimes, organic brekkies and homemade muesli, then Glastonbury's B&Bs won't disappoint.

Glastonbury Backpackers (☎ 833353; www.glastonburybackpackers.com; 4 Market Pl; dm/tw/d £14/35/40; P ▯) As you might expect, the town's only hostel is a really friendly, welcoming affair, decked out in jazzy colours with some lovely double rooms and small dorms, as well as a TV lounge and kitchen. You can get online and grab a sandwich at the café-bar downstairs.

Tordown (☎ 832287; www.tordown.com; 5 Ashwell Lane; s/d £28/54-62; P ✄) This red-brick townhouse is half ecofriendly B&B, half religious retreat. If all you're after is a peaceful sleep and a massive veggie breakfast, then all well and good; but for the more enlightened there's a range of courses on offer, including cellular healing, 'higher self sessions' and Egyptian ear coning (don't ask).

Shambhala Healing Retreat (☎ 831797; www.shambhala.co.uk; Coursing Batch, s/d £36/92) Another spiritual sanctuary offering several bright 'clear energy' rooms furnished in a choice of Tibetan and Egyptian themes, and a meditation tent on the top floor. Reiki massage, DNA activation and colonic hydrotherapy are all offered onsite, and you can even meet your guardian angel here.

No 3 (☎ 832129; www.numberthree.co.uk; 3 Magdalene St; s £75-85, d £100-110; P ✄) This luxurious Georgian-style B&B is the poshest place to stay in Glastonbury, with five classy bedrooms all named after English trees, overlooking a beautiful walled garden filled with silver birch and weeping willow trees.

Other possibilities:

Street YHA Hostel (☎ 0870 770 6056; www.yha.org .uk; The Chalet, Ivythorn Hill; dm £11.95; P ✄) A simple Swiss-style chalet hostel about 4 miles south of town. Take hourly bus 376 (15 minutes).

Parsnips (☎ 835599; www.parsnips-glastonbury.co.uk; 99 Bere Lane; s/d £40/60; P ✄ ▯) A smart, modern B&B with refurbished rooms and a refreshing lack of spiritual guidance.

Eating

Rainbow's End (☎ 833896; 17A High St; mains £4-7; ✆ 10am-4pm) The classic Glastonbury wholefood café, with a down-to-earth dining room plastered with potted plants and wooden tables, and a rotating menu of organic meals including veggie moussaka, sweet potato flan and fiery chilli. Needless to say, the carrot cake is divine.

Hundred Monkeys Café (☎ 833386; 52 High St; mains £4-10; ✆ lunch & dinner Mon-Sat) This smart café is a welcome alternative to Glastonbury's more rustic eateries, with a light dining area filled with leather sofas, pine tables and complementary newspapers, and a huge blackboard of fresh pastas, salads, baguettes and mains.

Mocha Berry (☎ 832149; 14 Market Pl; mains £5-8; ☺ Sun-Wed) This ever-popular café is the top spot in Glastonbury for a frothy latte, a fresh milkshake or a stack of breakfast pancakes.

Getting There & Away

There's one early-morning National Express service to Bath (£5.70, 1¼ hours) and on to London (£18, 4¼ hours).

Bus 29 travels to Glastonbury from Taunton (1½ hours, seven daily Monday to Friday, five or six on weekends). Bus 375/376 travels to Wells (30 minutes, half-hourly, hourly on Sunday) and Bristol (1¼ hours), and to Street (15 minutes), Yeovil (30 minutes) and Bridgwater (one hour) in the opposite direction. There is no train station.

QUANTOCK HILLS

Officially designated an AONB (Area of Outstanding Natural Beauty), this ridge of red sandstone hills runs for 12 miles down to the sea at Quantoxhead in western Somerset. They're only 3 miles wide and just 385m at their highest point, which makes them popular with weekend walkers – Samuel Taylor Coleridge was partial to wandering around the Quantocks during his six-year sojourn in Nether Stowey. Their name comes from the Celtic word *cantuc*, meaning 'rim' or 'circle'.

Some of the most attractive country is owned by the National Trust (NT), including the Beacon and Bicknoller Hills, which offer views of the Bristol Channel and Exmoor to the northwest. In 1861, red deer were introduced to these hills from Exmoor and there's a local tradition of stag-hunting.

The **AONB Service** (☎ 01278-732845; www.quantockhills.com; Castle St, Nether Stowey), in the library at Nether Stowey, organises guided walks.

Nether Stowey & Holford

The rural village of Nether Stowey is best known for its association with Samuel Taylor Coleridge, who moved to the village in 1796 with his wife Sara and son Hartley. They lived at **Coleridge Cottage** (NT; ☎ 01278-732662; admission £3.20; ☺ 2-5pm Thu-Sun Apr-Sep), where the poet composed some of his great early work, including *The Rime of the Ancient Mariner*. Wordsworth and his sister Dorothy spent 1797 at nearby Alfoxden House in **Holford**; during that year they worked on the poems for *Lyrical Ballads* (1798), a short booklet that heralded the beginning of the British Romantic movement.

The best-value accommodation in town is the **Old Cider House** (☎ 01278-732228; www.oldciderhouse.co.uk; 25 Castle St, Nether Stowey; s £42-55, d £60-80; Ⓟ ✗), a smart Edwardian red-brick house offering simple, subtly shaded rooms filled with pine furniture and a homely atmosphere, as well as home-cooked meals (2/3 courses £13.50/17.50). For a little more luxury, head half a mile out of town to the **Castle of Comfort** (☎ 741264; www.castle-of-comfort.co.uk; s £38-84, d £95-129; pns), a Grade II–listed manor set in rolling fields on the northern slopes of the Quantock Hills.

The small **Quantock Hills YHA Hostel** (☎ 01278 741224; reservations@yha.org.uk; Sevenacres; dm £11.95; Ⓟ ✗) is 1½ miles west of Holford. There are only three dorms and a couple of private rooms, so book ahead.

Tucked away in a wooded valley is **Combe House** (☎ 01278-741382; www.combehouse.co.uk; Holford Combe; s/d £65/115; Ⓟ ✗ Ⓑ), one of the best-known country retreats in the Quantocks. It certainly isn't shy about pampering its guests; the best rooms boast huge four-poster beds and views over the private wooded gardens, and there's a gorgeous heated indoor swimming pool, a private sauna and a fine country restaurant finished in gleaming Cornish oak.

Crowcombe

One of the prettiest Quantock villages, Crowcombe still has cottages made of stone and cob (a mixture of mud and straw), many with thatched roofs. The ancient **Church of the Holy Ghost** has wonderful carved 16th-century bench ends with surprisingly pagan themes (the Green Man is common). Part of its spire still stands in the churchyard where it fell when lightning struck in 1725.

Crowcombe is a little short on places to stay and eat – the best option is the village inn, the **Carew Arms** (☎ 618631; www.thecarewarms.co.uk; mains £11-16; s/d £49/79; Ⓟ ✗), which has six newly refurbished upstairs rooms and serves up great pub grub including Brixham scallops and four varieties of steak.

There's also a good camp site, the **Quantock Orchard Caravan Park** (☎ 01984-618618; www.quantockorchard.co.uk; Flaxpool; tent or caravan £11-18).

GETTING THERE & AWAY

Bus services around the Quantocks are very limited. Bus 14 travels from Bridgwater to Nether Stowey (40 minutes, four daily Monday to Saturday) en route to Williton. Bus 23

WESSEX

travels from Taunton to Nether Stowey (30 minutes, one daily) en route to Bridgwater, but the service only runs during term time.

Half-hourly bus 28 runs from Taunton to Minehead but only stops at Crowcombe (30 minutes) once daily.

TAUNTON
☎ 01823 / pop 58,241

Somerset's main county town and administrative capital is an underwhelming place. There's not much to see, but it's a useful transport hub and is the main gateway to the Quantocks.

The **tourist office** (☎ 336344; tauntontic@taunt ondeane.gov.uk; Paul St; ✆ 9.30am-5.30pm Mon-Sat) is in the library and has some useful leaflets on exploring the Quantocks and northern Somerset.

The 12th-century **Taunton Castle** is home to the **Somerset County & Military Museum** (☎ 320201; Castle Green; admission free; ✆ 10am-5pm Tue-Sat), which houses the county's main collection of archaeological artefacts, including an icthyosaur skeleton and the Shapwick coin hoard, the largest collection of Roman *denarii* ever discovered in Britain.

Taunton's other famous landmark is the **Church of St Mary Magdalene** (✆ 10am-4pm Mon-Fri, 10am-1pm Sat), with its 50m-high tower carved from red Quantock rock.

SLEEPING
Elm Villa (☎ 336165; ferguson@elmvilla10.freeserve .co.uk; s £32-35, d £50; P ✗) Another good option within walking distance of the town centre, with several comfy if unremarkable rooms dotted around a pale-cream Victorian villa. The best rooms have (distant) views to the Blackdown Hills.

Salisbury House Hotel (☎ 272083; 14 Billetfield; s/d from £45/66; P ✗) Probably the most comfortable place to stay in town, this large detached townhouse near Vivary Park has large heritage-style bedrooms, equipped with pocket-sprung beds, thick carpets and small sitting areas.

GETTING THERE & AWAY
National Express coaches run to London (£16, four hours, six daily), Bristol (£6.20, 1½ hours, four daily) and Exeter (£5.70, 50 minutes, six daily).

Bus 28 (hourly Monday to Saturday, nine on Sunday) crosses the Quantocks to Minehead (1¼ hours). Bus 29 travels to Wells (1¼ hours, seven daily Monday to Friday, five or six on weekends) via Glastonbury.

Trains run to London (£37.50, two hours, every two hours), to Exeter (£8.50, 30 minutes, half-hourly) and to Plymouth (£22.50, 1½ hours, half-hourly).

AROUND TAUNTON
Montacute House
This extraordinary Elizabethan **Montacute House** (NT; ☎ 01935-823289; montacute@nationaltrust. org.uk; admission house £8, garden only £4.50; ✆ house 11am-5pm Wed-Mon mid-Mar–Oct, garden 11am-6pm Wed-Mon mid-Mar–Oct, 11am-4pm Wed-Sun Nov-Mar) was built in the 1590s for Sir Edward Phelips, a Speaker of the House of Commons, and contains some of the finest 16th- and 17th-century interiors in the country. The house is particularly renowned for its remarkable plasterwork, fine chimneypieces and magnificent tapestries, but the highlight is the Long Gallery, decorated with Elizabethan-era portraits borrowed from the National Portrait Gallery (p114) in London.

Bus 681 from Yeovil (20 minutes, hourly Monday to Saturday) to South Petherton passes close by.

Haynes Motor Museum
The 300-strong car collection at **Haynes Motor Museum** (☎ 01963-440804; www.haynesmotormuseum .com; Sparkford; admission £7.50; ✆ 9.30am-5.30pm Apr-Oct, 10am-4.30pm Nov-Mar) includes an array of the outstanding, the old and the merely odd – Aston Martins and Ferraris rub shoulders with Bentleys and, well, the Sinclair C5. And yes, it's *that* Haynes, of the ubiquitous car repair manuals that you'll find in charity shops throughout the country. The museum is on the A359 off the A303 near Yeovil.

West Somerset Steam Railway
Steam enthusiasts will be in seventh heaven aboard the **West Somerset Steam Railway** (24-hr talking timetable ☎ 01643-707650, other information ☎ 01643-704996; www.west-somerset-railway.co.uk), Britain's longest privately run railway, which chugs through the Somerset countryside from Bishops Lydeard to Minehead, 20 miles away (£12.40 return, 1¼ hours), with stops at Dunster and other stations depending on the time of year. Trains run daily from mid-March to October, otherwise occasional days only.

Bus 28A runs to Bishops Lydeard from Taunton (15 minutes, 11 daily Monday to Saturday).

WESSEX

EXMOOR NATIONAL PARK

Running along the northwestern coastline of Somerset into Devon, this tiny national park is a hiker's haven and a twitcher's dream come true. With its idyllic landscape of emerald-green meadows, wooded combes and crumbling cliffs, Exmoor is a more pastoral place than its sister national park on the opposite coast, Dartmoor (p342). It's also home to some of Britain's oldest agricultural land; some of its farms date back to the Domesday Book and beyond, and ancient herds of horned sheep, Exmoor ponies and wild red deer roam its fields and bridleways.

Most of the park's main towns are dotted along the coastline, which stretches from the coastal resorts of Lynton and Lynmouth in the far west, along to the pretty harbour of Porlock and the medieval town of Dunster, with its brooding red-brick castle, all the way to the family-fun resort of Minehead in the east. Inland, Exmoor is dotted with small hamlets and sleepy villages that make ideal getaways from the coastal crowds.

Orientation

The park is only about 21 miles wide from west to east and just 12 miles from north to south. Waymarked paths crisscross the park and a dramatic section of the South West Coast Path runs from Minehead, just outside the park, to Padstow in Cornwall.

Information

There are five **National Park Authority (NPA) visitor centres** (☼ 10am to 5pm Easter-October, limited hrs Nov-Easter):

Blackmoor Gate (☎ 01598-763466; NPCBlackmoorGate@exmoor-nationalpark.gov.uk)

Combe Martin (☎ 01271-883319; NPCCombeMartin@exmoor-nationalpark.gov.uk; Cross St)

County Gate (☎ 01598-741321; NPCCountyGate@exmoor-nationalpark.gov.uk; A39 Countisbury)

Dulverton (☎ 01398-323841; NPCDulverton@exmoor -nationalpark.gov.uk; 7-9 Fore St)

Dunster (☎ 01643-821835; NPCDunster@exmoor -nationalpark.gov.uk; Dunster Steep)

The **Exmoor NPA Administrative Offices** (☎ 01398-323665; www.exmoor-nationalpark.gov.uk; Exmoor House, Dulverton) is a good point of contact for general information before you arrive. It also publishes the free *Exmoor Visitor* newspaper, which contains accommodation lists, timetables of organised activities and a handy map.

There are three comprehensive websites covering Exmoor:

Exmoor National Park (www.exmoor-nationalpark.gov .uk) The official NPA site.

Exmoor Tourist Association (www.exmoor.com) The Exmoor Tourist Association site listing details on accommodation and activities.

Visit Exmoor (www.visit-exmoor.info) Excellent information site with advice on activities, events, accommodation and eating out.

What's On Exmoor (www.whatsonexmoor.com) Local listings and information.

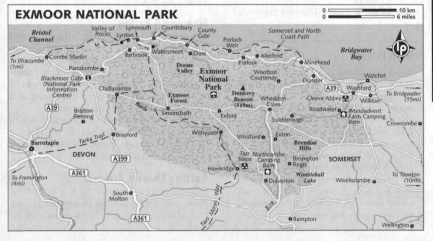

EXMOOR NATIONAL PARK

WESSEX

Activities

ADVENTURE SPORTS

You can sail, surf and kayak at **Wimbleball Lake Watersports Centre** (☎ 01398-371460), while **Exmoor Adventure** (☎ 01271-830628; www.exmooradventure.co.uk) can arrange rock climbing and abseiling.

CYCLING

The network of bridleways and quiet lanes makes Exmoor great cycling country, but let's be honest – you're not going to get away without tackling a few hills. NPA centres have leaflets on specific routes around the park; popular trails travel through the Brendon Hills, the Crown Estate woodland and along the old Barnstaple railway line.

Several sections of the National Cycle Network (NCN) cross the park, including the **West Country Way** (NCN Rte 3) from Bristol to Padstow, and the **Devon Coast to Coast Cycle Route** (NCN Rte 27) between Exmoor and Dartmoor.

MOORLAND SAFARIS

Several companies offer 4WD 'safari' trips across the moor, which stop at all the main beauty spots and provide lots of useful background. If you're a nature lover or a keen photographer, bird-watching and deer-watching safaris can be arranged. Half-day trips start at around £20.

Barle Valley Safaris (☎ 01643-851386; www.exmoor-barlevalley-safaris.co.uk; Dulverton & Minehead)

Discovery Safaris (☎ 01643-863080; www.discovery safaris.com; Porlock)

Exmoor Safari (☎ 01643-831229; www.exmoorsafari .co.uk; Exford)

HIGH FLIERS

Bored with hiking and biking? Then how about trying the ancient sport of falconry? **Exmoor Falconry** (☎ 862816; www.exmoor falconry.co.uk; Allerford, nr Porlock) conduct half- and full-day falconry activities with various birds, including a bateleur eagle, a tawny eagle and a harris hawk. Alternatively, you can just visit the **falconry centre** (adult/child £7/5; ❂ 10.30am-5pm Apr-Oct), which houses an amazing collection of parrots, swans, owls and birds of prey, as well as a small animal farm complete with Exmoor ponies, pigs and even a few meerkats.

PONY TREKKING & HORSE RIDING

Exmoor is popular riding country. There are lots of stables offering pony and horse treks for around £15 per hour – see the *Exmoor Visitor* for full details.

Brendon Manor Riding Stables (☎ 01598-741246; nr Lynton)

Burrowhayes Farm (☎ 01643-862463; www.burrow hayes.co.uk; Porlock)

Outovercott Stables (☎ 01598-753341; www.outover cott.co.uk; Lynton)

WALKING

The open fields and many marked bridleways make Exmoor an excellent area for hiking. The best-known routes are the **Somerset and North Devon Coast Path** (part of the South West Coast Path) and the Exmoor section of the **Two Moors Way**, which starts in Lynmouth and travels south to Dartmoor.

Part of the 180-mile **Tarka Trail** (based on the countryside that inspired Henry Williamson's *Tarka the Otter*) is in the park. Join it in Combe Martin and walk to Lynton/Lynmouth, then inland to Brayford and Barnstaple.

The **Coleridge Way** winds for 36 miles through Exmoor, the Brendon Hills and the Quantocks, taking in Coleridge's home at Nether Stowey and the village of Porlock, where he's said to have written *Kubla Khan*.

Organised walks run by the NPA are held throughout the year – contact one of the NPA centres, visit www.exmoor-national park.gov.uk, or see the listings in the *Exmoor Visitor* for details. Short walks cost £3, longer walks £5.

Sleeping & Eating

There are YHA hostels in Minehead and Ilfracombe (outside the park), and Lynton and Exford in the park. There are organised camping grounds along the coast and **camping barns** (☎ 01200-420102 for bookings; per person £6) at Woodadvent Farm near Roadwater and Northcombe, 1 mile from Dulverton.

There's no shortage of B&Bs and hotels in the park, and plenty of places to eat. If you'd like to hire a cottage, **Exmoor Holiday Group** (www .exmoor-holidays.co.uk) is a good bet.

Getting There & Around

Getting around Exmoor by bus is tricky – there are only a couple of regular routes, and practically none to the west side of the park.

WESSEX

BICYCLE

Several places around the park hire mountain bikes.

Fremington Quay (☎ 01271-372586; www.biketrail.co.uk; Fremington; per day £6.50-24) Delivers bikes to your door.

Tarka Trail (☎ 01271-324202; Train Station, Barnstaple; per day £7-10)

BUS

National Express runs from London to Barnstaple (£27.50, 5½ hours, four daily) and Ilfracombe (£27.50, 6½ hours, two daily), and from Bristol to Barnstaple (£17.80, three hours, one daily).

The *Taunton & West Somerset Public Transport Guide*, free from tourist offices, contains timetables for all the main bus routes.

DULVERTON

☎ 01398

The southern gateway to Exmoor is Dulverton, which sits at the base of the Barle Valley near the confluence of the region's two main rivers, the Exe and Barle. It's a solid, no-nonsense sort of country town, home to a collection of gun sellers, fishing tackle stores, clothing boutiques and gift shops, as well as the main **NPA Visitor Centre** (☎ 01398-323841; dulvertonvc@exmoor-nationalpark.gov.uk; 7-9 Fore St; ◔ 10am-5pm Easter-Oct).

Walking

There's a stunning 12-mile circular walk along the river from Dulverton to Tarr Steps – an ancient stone clapper bridge haphazardly placed across the River Barle and shaded by gnarled old trees. The bridge was supposedly built by the devil for sunbathing. It's a four- to five-hour trek for the average walker. You can add another three or four hours to the walk by continuing from Tarr Steps up Winsford Hill for distant views over Devon.

Sleeping & Eating

Town Mills (☎ 323124; www.townmillsdulverton .co.uk; High St; s incl breakfast £32-46, d incl breakfast £54-60; ✗) For something more central, try this old whitewashed millhouse in the middle of Dulverton, with five snug rooms brimming over with flowery furnishings and puffy duvets, as well as the occasional original fireplace.

Three Acres (☎ 323730; www.threeacrescountryhouse .co.uk; Brushford; s £50-65, d £75-100; Ⓟ ✗) Practically hidden by a blanket of trees, this fine country retreat makes a wonderful base from which

to explore the southern moor. The house is old-fashioned, elegant and unfussy, with a licensed bar decked out in British racing green and a firelit lounge. Upstairs you'll find a clutch of bedrooms finished with bold colours and crisp linen, and a few with freestanding baths and moor views.

Tarr Farm (☎ 01643-851507; www.tarrfarm.co.uk; s/d £65/130; Ⓟ ✗) This old Exmoor farm near Tarr Steps, 7 miles from Dulverton, has long since given up the agricultural racket and now markets itself as a supremely comfortable rural getaway. The beautiful stone farmhouse contains several bedrooms finished in a surprisingly contemporary style, all topped off with thoughtful extras such as private fridges and homemade cookies. The excellent restaurant specialises in local flavours – think Exmoor lamb, Devon beef and ham hock with piccalilli.

Lewis' Tea Rooms (☎ 323850; 13 High St; ◔ breakfast & lunch Mon-Sat, dinner Thu-Sat) Pastel prints, ticking clocks and pine floors characterise the sunny dining room of this tiny restaurant and tearoom, where you can tuck into a hearty ploughman's lunch, followed by homemade scones for tea and an upmarket country menu by night.

Northcombe Camping Barn (☎ 01200-420102; per person £6) A converted watermill about 1 mile from town.

Springfield Farm (☎ 323722; www.springfieldfarms .co.uk; Ashwick Lane; s £30, d £55-57; Ⓟ ✗) Traditional Exmoor farmhouse offering basic, good-value rooms.

Getting There & Away

Bus 398 stops at Dulverton six times daily on its way from Minehead (50 minutes) and Dunster (40 minutes) to Tiverton.

EXFORD

☎ 01643

Nestled on the banks of the River Exe near the heart of the moor, Exford is a delightful muddle of cottages and slate-roofed houses collected around a village green. The village is well known as a centre for hunting, fishing and horse riding, as well as a local hiking base – Exmoor's highest point is 4 miles northeast of the village at Dunkery Beacon (519m), and the village is surrounded by secluded hills and quiet bridleways.

Sleeping & Eating

Exford YHA Hostel (☎ 0870 770 5828; exford@yha.org .uk; Exe Mead; dm £12.95; Ⓟ ✗) This brick Victorian house makes an excellent budget base in

Exford; it's just a short walk from the village centre and is well set up for cyclists, hikers and outdoorsy types. The dorm rooms are small and a smidgen institutional, but most people don't seem too bothered, as it's still the best-placed hostel on Exmoor.

Exmoor House (☎ 841432; www.exmoorhouse.com; Wheddon Cross; s/d £35/70; P ⊠) If you're after something a little less countrified, head a few miles west to this contemporary hotel-restaurant in Wheddon Cross, where the bedrooms are all about stark simplicity, quirky furniture and upbeat colours. All the food comes from local suppliers, so Yeo Valley yogurts, farm-reared bacon and Dartmouth kippers all find their way onto the breakfast table.

Edgcott House (☎ 831495; www.edgcotthouse.co.uk; s £40-42.50, d £70-75; P ⊠) A beautiful 17th-century house set in private riverside gardens and packed with period features, including a terracotta-tiled hallway and an amazing 15m 'Long Room' decorated with hand-painted murals. The bedrooms, like the rest of the house, make a virtue of their venerable character, so don't expect too many flat-screen TVs or designer flourishes.

Crown Hotel (☎ 831554; www.crownhotelexmoor .co.uk; Chapel St; s/d £55/95; P ⊠) Exford's old coaching inn is still the best place to sleep in town. The rooms combine traditional rural character with a bright, light palette, offset by the occasional swag-draped bed and sporting print. The hotel's well used to catering for country pursuits, with its own stables and a stretch of private salmon river.

Getting There & Away

Over the moor, it's a 7-mile walk to Exford from Porlock, 10 miles from Minehead YHA Hostel, 12 miles from Dunster and 15 miles from Lynton.

The 398 bus from Tiverton to Minehead stops at Exford once daily Monday to Saturday. The circular bus 400 from Minehead stops at Dunster, Exford and Porlock twice daily on Tuesday and Thursday.

LYNTON & LYNMOUTH
☎ 01598

The attractive harbour of Lynmouth is rooted at the base of a steep, tree-lined valley, where the West Lyn River empties into the sea along Exmoor's northern coastline. Its similarity to the harbour at Boscastle (p372) is striking, and in fact the twin harbours share more than just a

common geography; like Boscastle, Lynmouth is famous as the location of a devastating flash flood that swept through the village in 1952. Sadly, Lynmouth paid a much heavier price than its Cornish cousin; 34 people lost their lives in the flood, and memory of the disaster remains strong in the village to this day.

These days Lynmouth is a busy tourist harbour town lined with pleasant pubs, souvenir sellers and fudge shops. Up on the rocky cliffs above the harbour is the more genteel Victorian resort of Lynton, which can be reached via an amazing water-operated railway or an arduous climb up the clifftop path.

The **tourist office** (☎ 0845 660 3232; info@lyntourism .co.uk; Lynton Town Hall, Lee Rd; ⏰ 10am-4pm Mon-Sat, 10am-2pm Sun) provides the **Lynton & Lynmouth Scene** (www.lyntonandlynmouthscene.co.uk), which is a free newspaper with accommodation, eating and activities listings.

There's a small **NPA visitor centre** (☎ 752509; The Esplanade; ⏰ 10am-5pm Apr-Oct, 10am-9pm Jul & Aug) near Lynmouth harbour.

Sights

The history of the flood is explored at the **Lyn & Exmoor Museum** (☎ 752317; St Vincent's Cottage, Market St, Lynton; adult/child £1/20p; ⏰ 10am-12.30pm & 2-5pm Mon-Fri, 2-5pm Sun), which also houses some interesting archaeological finds and a collection of tools, paintings and period photos.

The **Cliff Railway** (☎ 753486; www.cliffrailwaylynton .co.uk; single/return £1.75/2.75; ⏰ 8.45am-7pm Easter-Nov) is an amazing piece of Victorian engineering designed by George Marks, believed to be a pupil of Brunel. Two cars linked by a steel cable descend or ascend the slope according to the amount of water in their tanks. It's been running like clockwork since 1890, and it's still the best way to commute between the two villages. The views aren't bad, either.

From the Lynmouth crossroads follow signs 200m to **Glen Lyn Gorge** (☎ 753207; adult/child £4/3; ⏰ Easter-Oct), the steepest of the two valleys into Lynmouth. There are several lovely gorge walks and a small **exhibition centre** devoted to hydroelectric power.

Walking

There are some beautiful short walks in and around the two villages, as well as access to some longer routes; the South West Coast Path, the Coleridge Way and the Tarka Trail all pass through there, and Lynmouth is the official starting point of the Two Moors Way.

The most popular walk is to the dramatic **Valley of the Rocks**, described by the poet laureate Robert Southey as 'rock reeling upon rock, stone piled upon stone, a huge terrifying reeling mass'. It's just over a mile west of Lynton, and is believed to mark the original course of the River Lyn. Many of the tortuous rock formations have been named over the years – look out for the Devil's Cheesewring and Ragged Jack – and the valley is also home to a population of feral goats.

There are also popular trails to the lighthouse at **Foreland Point** east of Lynmouth, and to **Watersmeet**, 2 miles upriver from Lynmouth, where there's a handily placed National Trust teashop housed in a Victorian fishing lodge.

Sleeping

There are plenty of mid-price B&Bs dotted along Lee Rd in Lynton.

Lynton YHA Hostel (☎ 0870 770 5942; www.yha.org.uk; Lynbridge; dm £11.95; P ✗) A decent walkers' lodge in a large Victorian house, about a 500m steep walk uphill from town. The accommodation is a little cramped, but there are three square meals served up daily, and hikers' picnics are available too.

Sea View Villa (☎ 753460; www.seaviewvilla.co.uk; 6 Summer House Path; s £40, d £50-90; ✗) Down by the harbour, this 18th-century Georgian villa is a cut above most of the region's B&Bs, and worth splashing out on if you're into some seaside pampering. Indian silk fabrics, shag-pile carpets and designer stripes characterise the super-swanky rooms, all carefully finished in coordinated shades of 'champagne', 'ginger' and 'vanilla' (not just your average yellow, brown and cream). And the breakfast is as good as any you'll find in Exmoor – forget your greasy fry-up, here it's all eggs benedict, smoked salmon and cafetière coffee.

Victoria Lodge (☎ 753203; www.victorialodge.co.uk; Lee Rd; r £60-90; ✗) This ostentatious gem is the pick of the places along Lee Rd, and boasts a bevy of truly over-the-top bedrooms, all stuffed with heritage fabrics, burnished furniture and poshly pelmeted beds, and each aptly named after a royal princess.

St Vincent Lodge (☎ 752244; www.st-vincent-hotel.co.uk; Castle Hill; d £65; P ✗) Run by an Anglo-Belgian couple and named Hotel of the Year by Les Routiers, no less, this elegant guesthouse brings a bit of class to the quiet streets of Lynton. The hotel once belonged to a comrade of Nelson's, and all the delightful, pared-back rooms are named after battleships from Horatio's fleet. But the real treat is the downstairs restaurant, where Belgian dishes meet Mediterranean spice and Exmoor game.

Eating

Eat Moor (☎ 752424; 3 Watersmeet Rd, Lynmouth; mains from £8) This fresh, fiery new restaurant specialises in traditional dishes with a pan-global twist, so it's equally just as good for roast local lamb as for Moroccan tagine or authentic Spanish tapas. The décor's hot and sultry, the vibe is buzzy and the cooking's top-notch, so you might have to book on weekends.

Mad Hatters Bistro (☎ 753614; Church Steps, Lynton; mains £12-17; ✧ dinner Mon-Sat) Another reliable bistro with a strong focus on local produce, serving mainly modern British and Mediterranean-influenced cuisine in a quirky cellar dining room, just off the main road through Lynton.

Getting There & Away

Bus 39/300 runs from Lynmouth to Minehead (70 minutes) via Porlock (50 minutes) four times daily Monday to Saturday.

The most scenic route to Porlock is the steep, twisting road that hugs the coast all the way from Lynmouth. The stunning scenery is worth the £2 toll, and you get to avoid the notoriously steep descent via Porlock Hill.

PORLOCK & AROUND
☎ 01643

The small village of Porlock is one of the prettiest on the north Exmoor coast, with a huddle of thatched cottages running along its main street all the way to the picturesque breakwater of Porlock Weir, 2 miles to the west. Coleridge's famous poem *Kubla Khan* was written during a brief sojourn in Porlock (helped along by a healthy slug of laudanum and a vicious head cold), and the village is still a popular stop-off for summertime tourists, as well as walkers on the Coleridge Way and the South West Coast Path.

The village of **Selworthy**, 2½ miles east of Porlock, forms part of the 12,500-acre Holnicote Estate, the largest NT-owned area of land on Exmoor. Though its cob-and-thatch cottages look ancient, in fact the village was almost entirely rebuilt in the 19th century by the local philanthropist and landowner Thomas Acland to provide accommodation for elderly workers on his estate.

WESSEX

SOMETHING SPECIAL

Andrews on the Weir (☎ 863300; www.andrewsontheweir.co.uk; Porlock Weir; d £100-180; 2-/3-course menu £31.50/38.50; ☺ lunch & dinner Wed-Sun) Every meal becomes an 'experience' at this outlandishly fine restaurant-with-rooms, hovering beside the lapping waves on Porlock Weir. Local contacts (including Porlock fishermen, Exmoor farmers and a sympathetic park ranger) help the chefs source the very best produce, from farm-reared meat to sea-fresh fish; the cuisine is classic British with a soupçon of Gallic panache, the atmosphere is all effortless elegance, and the tablecloths are sharp enough to enough to cut your finger on. Classy with a capital 'C'.

Porlock's **visitor centre** (☎ 863150; www.porlock. co.uk; West End, High St; ☺ 10am-5pm Mon-Sat, 10am-1pm Sun Mar-Nov; 10.30am-1pm Tue-Fri, 10am-2pm Sat Nov-Mar) is a mine of local knowledge, and is also the point of contact for info on the Coleridge Way.

The tiny **Dovery Manor Museum** (High St; admission free; ☺ 10am-1pm & 2-5pm Mon-Fri, 10am-noon & 2.30-4.30pm Sat May-Oct) is housed in a pretty, 15th-century building, and exhibits artefacts and interesting photos of the village.

Sleeping & Eating

Rose Bank Guesthouse (☎ 862728; www.rosebankguesthouse.co.uk; High St; s £30, d £50-60; ☒ ▣) This grand half-timbered house stands right in the centre of the village. The plainly furnished rooms are nothing to write home about, but it's good value and in a handy location for the village pubs.

Ship Inn (☎ 862507; www.shipinnporlock.co.uk; High St; s/d £30/70; ℗) If history's your thing, then head straight for this 13th-century thatched inn, once a haven for local smugglers and a favoured haunt of Coleridge and his chum Robert Southey. Wicker, pine and cream characterises the 10 plain upstairs rooms, and the hugger-mugger pub bar is an excellent spot for a Devon stew and a pint of local ale.

Porlock Vale House (☎ 862338; www.porlockvale. co.uk; West Porlock; s/d from £70/110; ℗ ☒) This ravishing Edwardian manor house is a real treat, mixing grand period features (think oak panelling, popping log fires, Persian rugs and mounted stags' horns) with a refreshingly unstuffy atmosphere. The rooms are a little flouncy, with flowery pelmets and bedspreads to match, but they're cushy and comfortable nonetheless. The owners can organise horse-riding trips if you fancy a day in the saddle.

Getting There & Away

Bus 39/300 runs from Lynmouth to Porlock (50 minutes, four daily Monday to Saturday) and on to Minehead.

DUNSTER

☎ 01643

Dominated by a striking russet-red castle and centred around a cobbled market square, the village of Dunster is an undeniably attractive place and also boasts some unusual architectural features, including a medieval packhorse bridge, a 16th-century stone dovecote and a curious octagonal yarn market. Unfortunately, it's also a favourite on the coach tour trail, and in high summer the main street is thronged with a constant stream of honking motors and scarlet-faced day-trippers; if you're arriving in July or August, you'll be better off hightailing it straight for the castle, which sits on a hilltop above the village, or just steering clear altogether.

The beautiful **St George's Church** dates mostly from the 15th century and boasts a wonderfully carved fan-vaulted rood screen. Further down the road is the **watermill** (☎ 821759; Mill Lane; admission £2.60; ☺ 11am-4.45pm Jul-Sep, 11am-4.45pm Sat-Thurs Apr-Jun & Oct-Nov), a working 18th-century mill that's been turning since the Domesday Book.

The **NPA visitor centre** (☎ 821835; Dunster Steep; ☺ 10am-5pm Easter-Oct) is in the main car park.

Dunster Castle

Dunster Castle (NT; ☎ 821314; admission castle £6.80, garden & park only £3.70; ☺ 11am-5pm Sat-Wed Mar-Oct, 11am-4pm Sat-Wed Nov) has served as a fortress for around a thousand years, but the present-day castle bears little resemblance to the original Norman stronghold. The 13th-century gateway is probably the only original part of the castle; the turrets, battlements and towers were all added later during an overly romantic remodelling at the hands of Victorian architects. Despite its 19th-century makeover, the castle is still an impressive sight, decorated with Tudor furnishings, stunning 17th-century plasterwork and ancestral portraits of the Luttrell family. The terraced gardens are also worth exploring, with fine views across Exmoor and the coastline, and an important national collection of strawberry trees.

Sleeping & Eating

Yarn Market Hotel (☎ 821425; www.yarnmarkethotel .co.uk; s £40, d £60-80; P ☒) If the best rooms at the Luttrell are gone, then head across to this small hotel just beside the Yarn Market. There are plenty of pleasant, well-proportioned rooms to choose from, though there are few surprises; floral fabrics, identikit furniture and cream-coloured walls are about as adventurous as things get.

Spears Cross (☎ 821439; www.spearscross.co.uk; 1 West St; s £42, d £55-65; ☒) Cake and tea greets you as you step through the door of this peach-coloured cottage near the heart of the village, and you'll be well looked after throughout your stay. Several rustic rooms are tucked around the creaky corridors of the 15th-century house, and most boast their own eccentric features, from wonky ceilings to wood-panelled walls.

Luttrell Arms (☎ 821555; www.luttrellarms.co.uk; d from £100; P ☒) This glorious old coaching inn has been welcoming weary travellers through its doors for centuries, and it's still the loveliest place to stay in the village. It's crammed with offbeat touches and period character; huge flagstones, heavy armchairs and faded tapestries are dotted all around the lounge and downstairs bar, and a few of the lavish four-poster-bed rooms upstairs would put most royal retreats to shame. If you can, bag the master suite with its rib-vaulted ceiling, sunken fireplace and oak-wood bed.

Cobblestones Café (☎ 821595; lunches £5-10; ☿ breakfast & lunch Mon-Fri, dinner Sat) This dinky little café makes the perfect spot for a light lunch or a sticky tea-time cake. Baguettes, patés, salads and homemade pies dominate the lunchtime menu, and it's open on Saturday night for a set three-course supper.

Getting There & Away

Bus 28 runs from Minehead to Taunton via Dunster hourly Monday to Saturday, and nine times on Sunday. Bus 398 travels from Dunster to Exford (30 minutes, once daily except Sunday) and Dulverton (40 minutes, six daily except Sunday), and to Minehead (50 minutes, six daily except Sunday) in the opposite direction.

The West Somerset Steam Railway (p286) stops at Dunster during the summer.

DORSET

For many people the bustling market towns, babbling brooks and thatch-roofed cottages of rural Dorset are inextricably bound up with one name – Thomas Hardy, the 19th-century novelist, who lived most of his life in Dorset and used it as the setting for some of his most famous tales. But the county is more than just a literary landmark, it's a historical one too – Iron Age remains, tumbledown abbeys and medieval towns are dotted all over the Dorset landscape, and the glorious stretch of crumbling coastline along the county's southern edge – the Jurassic Coast – is where many of Britain's most important fossils have been discovered. The centre for budding ammonite-hunters is Lyme Regis, but for a taste of the classic British seaside, head west to the popular coastal resorts of Weymouth and Bournemouth, where day-trippers have been strolling along the promenades since the days when crinoline and whalebone corsets were in vogue.

Orientation & Information

Dorset stretches along the south coast from Lyme Regis on the western (Devon) border, to Christchurch abutting Hampshire on the east. Dorchester, the county town, sits in between and is the most central base for exploring, but Lyme Regis or Weymouth will suit those who prefer the coast.

Dorset has several useful regional websites, including:

Dorset County Council (www.dorset-cc.gov.uk)
Rural Dorset (www.ruraldorset.com)
West Dorset (www.westdorset.com)

Getting Around

One of the reasons for Dorset's backwater status is that few major transport routes cross it. There are two slow railway lines, running from Bristol and Bath through Dorchester West to Weymouth, and from London and Southampton to Bournemouth and Poole.

The main operator in east and central Dorset is **Wilts & Dorset** (☎ 01202-673555; Poole; www.wdbus.co.uk). For western Dorset and on to Devon and southern Somerset, **First** (☎ 01305-783645; www.firstgroup.com) is the main operator.

WESSEX

Regional timetables are available free from tourist offices or bus stations, or by download from the companies' websites. Otherwise call **Traveline** (☎ 0870 608 2608; www.traveline.org.uk).

BOURNEMOUTH

☎ 01202 / pop 167,527

Sprawling for seven miles along the southern Dorset coastline, Bournemouth is one of the largest seaside resorts in Britain, famous for its grand seafront and broad sandy beaches. It's a place with a rather strange split personality; part faded Victorian resort, part corporate anytown and part mass-market tourist holiday park, where wrinkly day-trippers and holidaying coach parties rub shoulders with stag parties, boozed-up clubbers and conference delegates. Still, it's an atmospheric introduction to the befuddling world of the British beach holiday, and there are plenty of things to keep you occupied: sunbathing, shopping and water sports by day, and a wealth of bars, clubs and dodgy variety shows to explore by night.

Orientation & Information

Bournemouth straggles all the way along the coast towards Poole to the west and Christchurch to the east. The pier marks the central seafront area, and northeast from there is the town centre and train station.

Bournemouth Library (☎ 454848; 22 The Triangle; ☯ 10am-7pm Mon, 9.30am-7pm Tue, Thu & Fri, 9.30am-5pm Wed, 10am-4pm Sat) Internet access.

Cyber Place (☎ 290099; 25 St Peter's Rd; per hr £2; ☯ 10am-11pm)

Tourist office (☎ 451700; www.bournemouth.co.uk; Westover Rd; ☯ 9.30am-5.30pm Mon-Sat, 10.30am-4.30pm Sun) Beside the Winter Gardens.

Sights & Activities

The first holiday home was established in Bournemouth in 1811 by the local landowner Louis Tregonwell, and during the 19th century the town quickly grew into one of the largest Victorian resorts in Britain. The ornamental **Pleasure Gardens** in the heart of town are the most obvious reminder of the town's genteel golden age, but sadly most of Bournemouth's Victorian architecture has been smothered by a modern mass of retail shops and conference centres. The Bournemouth area is particularly noted for its chines (sharp-sided valleys), most of which are lined with holiday villas.

An ostentatious mix of Italianate villa and Scottish baronial pile, the **Russell-Cotes Art Gallery & Museum** (☎ 451800; www.russell-cotes.bournemouth.gov.uk; Russell-Cotes Rd; admission free; ☯ 10am-5pm Tue-Sun) is set in landscaped grounds including a formal Japanese garden with views across Poole Bay. It's had a recent £3m overhaul designed to spruce up the historic building and the clifftop garden, and is particularly renowned for its galleries of Victorian art and sculpture, as well as a fine Japanese collection gathered by the museum's benefactors, Sir Merton and Lady Russell-Cotes, during a visit to Japan in 1885.

Right next to Bournemouth Pier, **Oceanarium** (☎ 311933; www.oceanarium.co.uk; admission £7.50; ☯ 10am-6pm) is a great aquarium re-creating various marine habitats from around the world, including the Great Barrier Reef, the Amazon River and the inky depths of the deep sea. Underwater inhabitants of practically every shape and size are on display, from guitarfish and flesh-eating piranhas to giant sea turtles.

The tethered hot-air balloon hovering above the city is the **Bournemouth Eye** (☎ 314539; www.bournemouthbaloon.com; Lower Gardens; admission £10; ☯ 7.20am-11pm Apr-Sep). Ascents last about 15 minutes and reach around 500ft, and, unsurprisingly, the views are great.

Construction on Bournemouth's long-awaited **artificial reef** – the only one of its kind in Europe – was due to start in late 2006, and should be finished by the summer of 2007.

Dorset Belle Cruises (☎ 558550; www.dorsetbelles.co.uk) operate ferry trips to Swanage, Poole and Brownsea Island from Bournemouth Pier.

Sleeping

Bournemouth is absolutely chock-a-block with B&Bs, but none of them are going to win any awards for design or originality (or even simple good taste, for that matter).

Bournemouth Backpackers (☎ 299491; www.bournemouthbackpackers.co.uk; 3 Frances Rd; dm £12-15) This small 20-bed hostel is inside a rather plain suburban house near the bus and train stations. The dorms are small and basic, with aluminium bunk beds and the bare minimum of facilities, but it's cheap and friendly. Reception is only open from 5pm to 6pm on weekdays, and closed all weekend, so book ahead.

Tudor Grange (☎ 291472; www.tudorgrangehotel.co.uk; 31 Gervis Rd; s £45-52, d £60-70; **P**) Escape

Bournemouth's suburban drudgery at this smart half-timbered house, which stands in private grounds and offers much more character than most of the hotels around town. The oak-panelled, armchair-ridden public rooms set the tone for the rest of the hotel; antiquated, frill-heavy and rather faded, with soft mattresses, battered furniture and ancient television sets.

Balincourt Hotel (☎ 552962; 58 Christchurch Rd; www
.balincourt.co.uk; s/d from £45/60; P ☒) In a town of decidedly average B&Bs, this is a surprisingly comfortable choice, with a mixed bag of rooms ranging from tiny austere singles to spacious superior rooms with small sitting areas, oodles of chintz and the odd cast-iron fireplace.

Langtry Manor (☎ 553887; www.langtrymanor.com; Derby Rd, East Cliff; s/d £70/140; P ☒) For something with considerably more style, seek out this gabled mansion built by Edward VII for his mistress, Lilly Langtry. It's by far the best place to stay in Bournemouth, brimming over with original furniture, patterned carpets, potted plants and Edwardian prints; the pick of the rooms are the Langtry Suite (complete with heart-shaped spa bath) and the opulent King's Suite (with inglenook fireplace, gold-tapped bath and Jacobean four-poster bed).

Eating

Indian Ocean (☎ 311222; 4 West Cliff Rd; mains £8-11; ☽ lunch & dinner) Standard Indian dishes are supplemented by intriguing Korai and Bangladeshi specials at this snazzy Indian place, with a modern, funkily lit interior hidden away behind a rather tacky glass frontage.

Ciao (☎ 555657; 144 Old Christchurch Rd; mains £8-14; ☽ lunch & dinner) This small contemporary café-bar is a great option for pizza, pasta and gourmet panini, with sliding doors opening onto the street and a plain, minimalist theme of white walls, pine tables and starchy tablecloths.

West Beach (☎ 587785; Pier Approach; mains £12-20; ☽ daily) Bournemouth's best beachfront location and finest food go hand in hand at this excellent seafood brasserie, with a clean, chic interior, a fantastic alfresco deck with views across to Bournemouth Pier, and a menu stuffed with oven-roasted cod, line-caught sea bass and pan-seared tuna.

Basilica (☎ 757722; 73 Seamoor Rd; 3-course menu £13.95; ☽ Mon-Sat) On a sunny summer's day,

you could almost convince yourself you were on the Côte d'Azur at this buzzy restaurant a mile from the town centre. Farm-fresh ingredients, crunchy salads and a daily fishboard are all laced with a punchy Mediterranean tang, and it makes a great place to pick up supplies for a beach picnic.

Entertainment

The traditional Bournemouth boozer gave up the ghost long ago in the city centre, and these days chain pubs and cheesy clubs rule the roost. Most of the main venues are clustered around Firvale Rd, St Peter's Rd and Old Christchurch Rd.

Alcatraz (☎ 554566; 24-26 Holdenhurst Rd) Shamelessly cheesy club with a populist playlist firmly aimed at pleasing the crowds.

Elements (☎ 311178; www.elements-nightclub.co.uk; Firvale Rd) Massive queues and club anthems are the mainstays at Bournemouth's biggest club.

K-bar/K1 (☎ 317818; 4 Terrace Rd) Former casino with a varied programme of comedy, DJ sets and club nights; there's usually no entry fee for the pre-club K-bar.

Opera House (☎ 399922; www.operahouse.co.uk; 570 Christchurch Rd) Bournemouth's answer to the superclub, housed in an amazing converted 19th-century theatre.

Getting There & Away

National Express runs from London (£17.60, 2½ hours, hourly), Bristol (£14.60, one daily) and Oxford (£17.80, three hours, two daily).

Bus X3 runs half-hourly from Salisbury (1¼ hours) and on to Poole (20 minutes) every hour, while the X34/35 comes from Southampton (one hour, five daily Monday to Saturday). There's a multitude of buses between Bournemouth and Poole (15 minutes).

Trains run every half-hour from London Waterloo (£34.50, two hours); half of these continue on to Poole (£2.70, 10 minutes), Dorchester South (£8.30, 45 minutes) and Weymouth (£10.50, one hour).

POOLE

☎ 01202 / pop 144,800
Exactly where Poole begins and Bournemouth ends is hard to tell, as the towns' outskirts simply merge together as you move west along the coastline; but it doesn't take long to realise Poole is an altogether more attractive place than its brash, busy sister just along the bay. The town has grown up around its pretty old harbour, which was once busy with fishing

WESSEX

boats and trading vessels, and now bustles with designer yachts and cruise boats heading to the offshore islands around the bay. The quay area is dotted with restaurants and salty old pubs, and the Sandbanks area has an excellent beach and is a popular centre for water sports.

The **tourist office** (☎ 253253; www.pooletourism .com; Poole Quay; ✆ 9.15am-6pm Jul-Aug, 10am-5pm Apr-Jun & Sep-Oct, 10am-4pm Mon-Sat Nov-Mar) is on the quay.

Sights & Activities
BROWNSEA ISLAND
This small wooded **island** (NT; ☎ 707744; www.nation altrust.org.uk/brownsea; admission £4.40; ✆ 10am-6pm mid-Jul–Sep, 10am-5pm Mar–mid-Jul & Sep, 10am-4pm Oct) in Poole Bay is now a nature reserve and wildlife haven run by the National Trust. There are several tranquil walks around the island, which is home to a population of deer, peacocks and rare red squirrels, as well as terns, gulls and wading birds.

To get to the island you'll need to catch a ferry from Poole Quay; there are several operators, but the most experienced is **Brownsea Island Ferries** (☎ 01929-462383; www.brownseaisland ferries.com; to Brownsea adult/child £6.50/4.50), which also offers cruises to Sandbanks (adult/child £4.50/3.50) and the other bay islands, as well as a daily trip to Wareham (adult/child £8.50/5). Look out for the Old Harry Rocks along the coastline, a set of limestone stacks that have been separated from each other by sea erosion.

POOLE OLD TOWN & HARBOUR
Poole Old Town has attractive 18th-century buildings, including a wonderful Customs House and Guildhall. The **Scaplen's Court Museum** (☎ 633558; Old High St) is housed in the town's most complete medieval building, and is open to the public in August, when it hosts displays on domestic life in Poole throughout the ages.

The Waterfront Museum is currently undergoing a major programme of refurbishment, but the **Local History Centre** (☎ 262621; ✆ 10am-3pm) next door is still open, with some small displays exploring Poole's history.

WATER SPORTS
Poole has a growing reputation as a centre for water sports. There are loads of operators offering everything from wakeboarding to powerboating, mostly based around the Sand-

banks area. Try **H2O Sports** (☎ 733744; www.h2o -sports.co.uk) or **FC Watersports Academy** (☎ 708283; www.fcwatersports.co.uk) for windsurfing, kayaking and kitesurfing. The wakeboarding specialists are **Poole Wakeboarding** (☎ 07799-878734; www .poolewakeboarding.co.uk).

For something more adrenaline-fuelled, **Shockwave** (☎ 558850; www.parkstonebay.com) offers 10-minute speedboat trips around the bay, and you can try powerboating and sailing with **Rockley Watersports** (☎ 0870-7770541), or jetskiing with **Absolute Aqua** (☎ 666118; www .absoluteaqua.co.uk).

POOLE LIGHTHOUSE
This cutting-edge **arts centre** (☎ 685222; www .lighthousepoole.co.uk; 21 Kingland Rd) hosts a lively events calendar including live music, theatre, film and exhibitions.

Sleeping & Eating
Milsoms Hotel (☎ 609000; www.milsomshotel.co.uk; 47 Haven Rd; d £75; ✗) A beautifully appointed semi-boutique hotel decked out in achingly tasteful tones of mauve and cream, and finished with thoughtful extras such as cafetières and Molton Brown bath products. Breakfast is served in the excellent Loch Fyne restaurant, which is also one of the top places in town for seafood.

Mansion House (☎ 685666; www.themansionhouse .co.uk; Thames St; s £90, d £140-160; P ✗) Poole's *belle addresse* is this beautiful brick mansion just off the harbourfront, which is almost as renowned for its lavish bedrooms as for its glamorous fine-dining restaurant. Indian, Oriental and cottage themes distinguish the upmarket décor, and all the rooms are littered with individual touches (from brass beds to antique suites), but it's the downstairs dining room that really deserves the accolades.

Custom House (☎ 676767; Poole Quay; mains from £12; ✆ lunch & dinner) This exciting continental-style brasserie is housed, as its name suggests, in Poole's refurbished customs house. Downstairs there's a funky coffee-bar furnished with chrome seats and technicolour walls, which majors in pastries, cakes and quick lunches; upstairs the smart Georgian-style dining room specialises in seafood and steak, and is reached by an impressive exterior staircase.

Other options:
Saltings (☎ 707349; saltings_poole@yahoo.co.uk; 5 Salterns Way; d from £60; ✗ 🖵) Unusual marine-themed B&B in a great location just off Poole Quay.

BH13 (☎ 701101; 37 Haven Rd; mains £10-15; ☯ lunch & dinner Mon-Sat, lunch Sun) Glossy British-Asian fusion restaurant in Canford Cliffs.

Storm (☎ 674970; 16 High St; mains £13-18; ☯ dinner) Another excellent seafood restaurant along the High St.

Getting There & Away
Countless buses cover the 20-minute trip to Bournemouth. National Express runs hourly to London (£17.60, three hours). Train connections are as for Bournemouth, just 13 minutes closer to London Waterloo (£36.10).

You can hire bikes from **Cycle Paths** (☎ 680123; www.cycle-paths.co.uk; Dolphin Shopping Centre) for around £15 per day.

Sandbanks Ferry (☎ 01929-450203; www.sandbanksferry.co.uk; pedestrian/car 90p/£2.80) shuttles across to Studland every 20 minutes. This is a short cut from Poole to Swanage, Wareham and the west Dorset coast, but summer queues can be horrendous.

Bus 152 goes from Poole to Sandbanks (15 minutes, hourly).

WIMBORNE
☎ 01202 / pop 14,844
The quiet town of Wimborne was once home to both Thomas Hardy and the infamous smuggler Isaac Gulliver, who conducted a lucrative racket smuggling gin, silk, lace and tea along the south Dorset coastline; but the town's most prominent feature is its historic minster and its extraordinary chained library. Wimborne makes a peaceful day trip from the glitzy seaside resorts to the south, except during June, when the town holds its annual **folk festival**.

The helpful **tourist office** (☎ 886116; wimborne.tic@eastdorset.gov.uk; 29 High St; ☯ 9.30am-5.30pm Mon-Sat Apr-Sep, 9.30am-4.30pm Oct-Mar) is situated near the minster and the **Priest's House Museum** (☎ 882533; 23-27 High St; adult/child £3/1; ☯ 10am-4.30pm Mon-Sat Apr-Oct), an interesting local-history museum with a reconstructed Victorian kitchen, Georgian parlour and village school room.

Wimborne Minster
St Cuthburga founded a monastery in Wimborne in around 705, but most of the present-day **Wimborne Minster** (☎ 884753; ☯ 9.30am-5.30pm) was built by the Normans between 1120 to 1180, with a few extra additions dating from the 14th century. As well as the impressive perpendicular tower and its odd 'Quarterjack',

who strikes the quarter-hour, the minster also houses a remarkable 14th-century astronomical clock. In **Holy Trinity Chapel** is the tomb of Ettricke, the 'man in the wall', a local eccentric who refused to be buried in the church or village and was interred in the church wall.

Above the choir vestry is the famous **chained library** (☯ 10.30am-12.30pm & 2-4pm Mon-Fri Easter-Oct), established in 1686, and filled with some of the country's oldest medieval books and manuscripts – the chains seem to have done a decent job of deterring any unauthorised borrowing.

Kingston Lacy
When the aristocratic Bankes family was evicted from Corfe Castle (p298) by the Roundheads, its members established a new home at **Kingston Lacy** (NT; ☎ 01202-883402; admission house £9, grounds only £4.50; ☯ house 11am-5pm Wed-Sun Mar-Oct), 2 miles west of Wimborne. The house was later clad in stone by Charles Barry, architect of the Houses of Parliament (p115), but it's best known for its wonderfully preserved 17th-century interior and its Spanish Room, hung with gilded leather and other continental souvenirs brought back by the inveterate 19th-century traveller William Bankes. Sir William also had a collector's eye for artwork – paintings by Titian, Brueghel and Van Dyck are scattered around the corridors of the mansion's corridors. Outside, the extensive landscaped gardens encompass the Iron Age hill fort of Badbury Rings.

Sleeping & Eating
Old Merchant's House (☎ 841955; 44 West Borough; s/d £45/65; Ⓟ ☒) A Grade II–listed house set around a delightful walled garden, offering exactly what you'd expect from a rural British B&B – clean, well-appointed rooms, a hearty cooked breakfast and just the occasional touch of floral frippery.

Old George (☎ 888510; 2 Corn Market; d £50-60; Ⓟ ☒) Right in the centre of Wimborne, on a quiet square just a short stroll from the minster, this grey stone Georgian townhouse is an excellent (if slightly outdated) place to stay, with spacious rooms decorated with original cornicing and characterful furniture.

Getting There & Away
Bus 3 (the 'Wimborne Flyer') travels from Wimborne to Poole (40 minutes, four per hour). Bus 13 travels from Wimborne to

Bournemouth (50 minutes, hourly Monday to Saturday, six on Sunday).

SOUTHEAST DORSET

Dorset's most beautiful stretch of coastline runs along its southeastern edge, dotted with glittering bays and crumbling cliffs, as well as the romantic ruins of Corfe Castle and the remote Isle of Purbeck (actually a peninsula).

Wareham & Around

☎ 01929 / pop 2568

Saxons established the sturdy settlement of Wareham on the banks of the River Frome in around the 10th century, and the remains of their defensive walls can still be seen encircling the town. St Martin's Church dates from around the same period, and is one of the last remaining Saxon churches in Dorset. The town is also well known for its connections to the enigmatic figure of TE Lawrence, immortalised in David Lean's epic *Lawrence of Arabia.*

Purbeck tourist office (☎ 552740; www.purbeck.gov .uk; Holy Trinity Church, South St; ☺ 9.30am-5pm Mon-Sat & 10am-1pm & 1.45-4pm Sun Apr-Sep, 10am-3pm Mon-Sat Oct-Mar) is opposite the library.

SIGHTS

The bijou **Wareham Museum** (☎ 553448; East St; admission free; ☺ 10am-4pm Easter-Oct) has a Lawrence of Arabia collection supplementing the usual local items with relics of early settlers from the Iron Age and Roman occupation.

Standing on the wall beside North St is the tiny but delightful Saxon **St Martin's Church**, which dates from about 1020. Although the porch and bell tower are later additions, the basic structure is unchanged. Inside there's a 12th-century fresco on the northern wall and a marble effigy of Lawrence of Arabia.

The tiny cottage of **Clouds Hill** (NT; ☎ 405616; admission £3.10; ☺ noon-5pm Thu-Sun Apr-Oct) was TE Lawrence's rural retreat, and remains largely unchanged since his death in 1935. There's a small exhibition exploring Lawrence's incredible life and his achievements during WWI; there are also a few relics that hint at his enduring fascination with the art and culture of the Middle East.

Lawrence was stationed at Bovington Camp, now an interesting **Tank Museum** (☎ 405096; www.tankmuseum.org; adult/child £10/7; ☺ 10am-5pm), 6 miles from Wareham. He died at Bovington Military Hospital six days after a motorcycle

accident nearby. The museum has a collection of more than 300 armoured vehicles, from the earliest WWI prototypes to remnants from the first Gulf War.

Nearby is **Monkey World** (☎ 462537; www.mon keyworld.co.uk; Longthorns; adult/child £9/6.50; ☺ 10am-5pm Sep-Jun, 10am-6pm Jul & Aug), a sanctuary for rescued chimpanzees, orangutans, gibbons, marmosets and some ridiculously cute ring-tailed lemurs.

SLEEPING & EATING

Gold Court House (☎ 553320; www.goldcourthouse.co.uk; St John's Hill; s/d £40/60; ✗) Set on a small square near the centre of town, this sweet little 18th-century house jettisons the normal chintzy décor in favour of a refined, pared-back look. There are a couple of rooms tucked in around the house's attic beams, characterised by clean white walls, blonde pine and the odd mahogany dresser.

Old Granary (☎ 552010; The Quay; d £70-95) This village pub-cum-hotel is perched in an idyllic spot right beside the riverbanks. The downstairs bar is littered with all kinds of trinkets, rustic knick-knacks and mismatched furniture, and the cluttered country theme continues into the upstairs rooms, reached via a little 'Alice door' carved into the wood-panelled walls. It's a little on the pricey side, but you couldn't ask for a better location.

GETTING THERE & AWAY

Buses 142, 143 and 144 run between Poole (35 minutes) and Wareham hourly (every two hours on Sunday). Bus 142/143 stops at Wareham hourly on its way from Poole (40 minutes) to Swanage (30 minutes).

Corfe Castle

☎ 01929

The fractured ruins of **Corfe Castle** (NT; ☎ 01929-481294; admission £5; ☺ 10am-6pm Apr-Oct, 10am-5pm Mar, 10am-4pm Nov-Feb) are evocatively perched on a grassy hilltop with commanding views along the southern Dorset coastline. The castle was the ancestral home of Sir John Bankes, right-hand man and attorney general to Charles I, and was besieged by Cromwellian forces during the Civil War; following a six-week defence directed by the plucky Lady Bankes, the castle was eventually betrayed from within and reduced to rubble by the Roundheads' cannons. The Bankes family established its new family seat at Kingston Lacy (p297);

guided tours of the castle are usually available during opening hours.

Buses 142/143 run hourly from Poole (50 minutes) through Wareham (15 minutes) to Swanage (20 minutes) via Corfe Castle.

The **Swanage Steam Railway** (☎ 475800; www. swanagerailway.co.uk; adult day rover £8.50) runs between Swanage and Norden and stops at Corfe Castle. Joint tickets to the castle and railway are available, and there are discounts if you arrive by public transport.

The Blue Pool

Once used as a claypit, and opened to the public in 1935, the amazing **Blue Pool** (☎ 01929-551408; www.bluepooluk.com; Furzebrook; admission £4.40; 9.30am-5pm Mar-Nov) has an extraordinary tendency to change colour according to the time of day and the intensity of sunlight striking the water's surface. The lake's colour-shifting abilities are due to minute particles of clay defracting light through the water; in a matter of seconds the lake can change from deep aquamarine to pale blue to turquoise-green. Designated a Site of Special Scientific Interest (SSSI), the lakeshore is also home to rare wildlife including green sand lizards and Dartford warblers. The pool is signposted from the A351; buses 142/143 from Wareham (10 minutes) stop nearby.

Lulworth Cove & the Coast

☎ 01929

West of Swanage the Isle of Purbeck gives way to a stunning stretch of coastline, pockmarked by shimmering bays, towering cliffs and tiny beaches. The coast's best-known features are the natural rock arch at **Durdle Door** and the almost perfectly circular bay at **Lulworth Cove**, but the clifftop walks around St Aldhem's Head and the nature reserve at Kimmeridge Bay are also worth exploring.

With its box-shaped centre flanked by four corner turrets, **Lulworth Castle** (☎ 400352; www. lulworth.com; East Lulworth; admission £7; 10.30am-6pm Apr-Oct, 10.30am-4pm Nov-Mar) looks more like a French chateau than a traditional English castle. Built in 1608 as a hunting lodge, the castle has endured several centuries of ups and downs – including several extravagant owners, some extensive remodelling and a disastrous fire in 1929 – but it's now been thoroughly refurbished by English Heritage. The grounds also contain St Mary's Chapel, with its richly decorated 18th-cen-

tury interior, and host everything from blues concerts to jousting tournaments during the summer.

There are plenty of places to stay around Lulworth. The best option is the **Lulworth Beach Hotel** (☎ 400404; www.lulworthbeachhotel.com; Lulworth Cove; d £80-95), a modern, bright and airy place with several uncluttered rooms sprinkled with wicker furniture and colourful prints. The best have French doors leading onto small balconies with top-drawer views over Lulworth Cove.

Alternatively, try **Cove House** (☎ 400137; West Lulworth; d £75; ✗), a double-gabled Victorian villa with a brace of solid, cosy B&B rooms, finished in plain pine and typically generic shades of cream and magnolia, with the occasional framed print or book-lined shelf to liven things up.

There's also a basic single-storey **YHA Hostel** (☎ 0870 770 5940; School Lane; dm £11.80; Mar-Oct), in West Lulworth, and a great clifftop campsite at **Durdle Door Holiday Park** (☎ 400200; durdle .door@lulworth.com; tents £14-18; Mar-Oct).

DORCHESTER

☎ 01305 / pop 16,171

Thomas Hardy connections abound around Dorchester, which doubles in his novels as the market town of Casterbridge. Hardy was born just outside Dorchester in the village of Higher Bockhampton, and the author lived here for much of his life; its solid red-brick streets, stately Georgian townhouses and agricultural heritage seem to have held an enduring fascination for him, and the place certainly seems immediately familiar if you've ever read any of his novels. Hardy's memory lingers on at two of his former homes; for something less literary there are some good restaurants scattered around towns, as well as some odd museums dedicated to dinosaurs, teddy bears, Tutankhamen and the Terracotta Warriors.

Orientation & Information

Most of Dorchester's action takes place along South St, which runs north into pedestrianised Cornhill and then emerges in High St.

The **tourist office** (☎ 267992; dorchester .tic@westdorset-dc.gov.uk; Antelope Walk; 9am-5pm Mon-Sat, 10am-5pm Sun Apr-Nov; 10am-4pm Mon-Sat Nov-Mar) is brimming over with Hardy information, and sells several town walks and 'location' guides to the main places featured in his novels.

WESSEX

Sights

Dorchester was once a thriving Roman settlement, and excavations have uncovered the foundations of a 1st-century **Roman villa** behind the town hall on Northern Hay. The layout of the house is clearly visible and the remains of the main building, housed within a glass structure, boast remarkable mosaic floors.

The main gallery of the **Dorset County Museum** (☎ 262735; www.dorsetcountymuseum.org; High West St; admission £6; ☿ 10am-5pm Jul-Sep, 10am-5pm Mon-Sat Oct-Jun) is housed inside the 19th-century Victorian Hall, inspired by the Great Exhibition of 1851 and dominated by a fine rose window. The varied collection includes archaeological finds from Maiden Castle, canvases by Gainsborough and Alfred Wallis and stunning fossils from the Jurassic Coast, but the highlight is the museum's extensive Hardy collection – the largest in the world – donated by the author's second wife, Florence. Many of Hardy's manuscripts, diaries and notebooks are on display, and there's a reconstruction of his study at Max Gate.

Rather less educational are the tacky displays at the **Dinosaur Museum** (☎ 269880; www .dinosaur-museum.org.uk; Icen Way; adult/child £6.50/4.75; ☿ 9.30am-5.30pm), where most of the skeletons are plastic mock-ups. The **Tutankhamun Exhibition** (☎ 269571; www.tutankhamun-exhibition.co.uk; High West St; adult/child £6.50/4.75; ☿ 9.30am-5.30pm) and the **Terracotta Warriors Museum** (☎ 266040; www .terracottawarriors.co.uk; East High St; admission £5; ☿ 10am-5.30pm) are slightly better, with atmospheric reconstructions of the pharoah's tomb and the X'in warriors. There's also a **Teddy Bear Museum** (☎ 263200; Antelope Walk; ☿ 9.30am-5pm Sun 10am-4pm), populated by various historical and famous bears, as well as a rather disturbing family of life-sized teddies.

If you still haven't had your museum fix, head for the **Keep Military Museum** (☎ 264066; www.keepmilitarymuseum.org; Bridport Rd; adult/child £4/3; ☿ 9.30am-5pm Mon-Sat Apr-Sep, Tue-Sat Oct-Mar), which traces the story of the historic Devon and Dorset regiments with plenty of regimental uniforms, vintage muskets and mean-looking cannons.

On the northern side of town is **Poundbury**, a cod-Georgian town dreamt up by Prince Charles as a model housing development for the 21st century.

THOMAS HARDY SITES

Hardy's early career was as an apprentice architect, and he was responsible for the design of **Max Gate** (NT; ☎ 262538; Alington Ave; admission £2.60; ☿ 2-5pm Mon, Wed & Sun Apr-Sep), where he lived from 1885 until his death in 1928. *Tess of the D'Urbervilles* and *Jude the Obscure* were both written here, and the house contains several pieces of original furniture, but otherwise it's a little slim on sights. The house is a mile east of Dorchester on the A352.

The small cob-and-thatch **Hardy's Cottage** (NT; ☎ 01305-262366; admission £3; ☿ 11am-5pm Thu-Mon Apr-Oct), where the author was born, is a bit short on attractions, but it makes an evocative stop for Hardy completists. It's in Higher Bockhampton, 3 miles northeast of Dorchester.

Look out for Hardy's statue at the top of High West St.

Sleeping

Casterbridge Hotel (☎ 264043; www.casterbridge hotel.co.uk; 49 High East St; r £45-75) This exquisite guesthouse lives up to the town's heritage atmosphere, with a choice of rooms: some are classically countrified, with florid wallpaper, stylish table lamps and feathery duvets, while

---

ZORBING

If hurtling down a steep incline trapped inside a giant plastic ball sounds like fun rather than borderline insanity, then the zany sport of zorbing could be for you. Unsurprisingly, this bizarre pastime was invented in the world's capital of life-endangering adventure sports, New Zealand, and was apparently inspired by Leonardo da Vinci's 'anatomy of man' drawings. The zorb itself is a 3.2m inflatable ball with around 1000 internal ties that serve as shock absorbers, with an inner cockpit that can take up to three 'zorbonauts'. Once you're inside and strapped in, the zorb's let loose and you speed down the hill at around 50mph, protected by a cushion of bouncy air. At least, that's the theory.

Zorb South (☎ 01929-426595; www.zorbsouth.co.uk), based in Dorchester, is one of the UK's only licensed operators. Prices start at £35 for a single zorb ride.

SOMETHING SPECIAL

Morton's House Hotel (☎ 1929 480 988; www.mortonshouse.co.uk; East St, Corfe Castle; r £129-230; Ⓟ ☒)
This heart-meltingly beautiful 16th-century manor was built in the shape of an 'E' in honour of
Queen Elizabeth, and it certainly makes an impressive tribute. Built from solid grey Purbeck stone
overlooking beautiful private gardens, the house is crammed with Elizabethan and Jacobean
character; stone fireplaces and wood-panelled friezes adorn the downstairs drawing room, and
the luxuriant heritage feel runs into the upstairs bedrooms, especially in the 'character' rooms
and more expensive suites (get the Elizabethan-themed suite if you can). It's a place to languish
in front of a crackling fire or stuff yourself silly with a rich Sunday roast – traditional, classic and
very, very English.

---

others are more contemporary. Breakfast is
served in a lovely conservatory overlooking
the rear garden.

Little Court (☎ 261576; www.littlecourt.net; Charmin-
ster; r from £69; Ⓟ ☒) Surrounded by renowned
landscaped gardens just a mile from Dorchester, this Lutyens-style manor house makes
for a lavish night's sleep, with huge, luxurious bedrooms equipped with CD players and
complementary umbrellas, and a gourmet
breakfast made with produce from the hotel's
walled garden.

Yalbury Cottage (☎ 262382; www.yalburycottage
.com; Lower Bockhampton; s/d £70/100; Ⓟ ☒) Just
a short stroll from Hardy's birthplace, this
chocolate-box thatched house looks appropriately rustic from the outside, and the excellent country restaurant boasts plenty of
rural trappings (inglenook fireplaces, oak
beams, exposed brick); but all of the eight
bedrooms are in the modern annexe, so
they're comfortable and current, if a little
short on period features.

Beggars Knap (☎ 268191; beggarsknap@hotmail.co
.uk; 2 Weymouth Ave; s £28-35, d £55; Ⓟ ☒) Solid
Victorian house with smart rooms, some with private bay
windows.

Higher Came Farmhouse (☎ 268908; www.higher
came.co.uk; d £58; Ⓟ ☒) Fine farmhouse B&B with
snug, homey rooms and a great farm-fresh brekkie.

Eating

Prezzo (☎ 259678; 6 High West St; pizza £7-9; ☖ daily)
A typically reliable outpost of this Italian
chain, with a baroque interior filled with
black-leather sofas and twisted willow, and
top-notch pizzas and pastas.

Sienna (☎ 250022; 36 High West St; 2-course set lunch/
dinner £13/24; ☖ Tue-Sat) Don't be fooled by the
simplicity of this miniature restaurant on the
High St – the stripped-down décor might be
austere, but the food is colourful and complex,

mixing modern British cooking with Spanish,
Italian and southern French flavours. Zesty.

Getting There & Around

There's a daily National Express coach to
London (£19.20, four hours).

The hourly bus 31 travels from Dorchester
to Weymouth (30 minutes) and to Lyme Regis
(1¾ hours). Bus 10 also travels to Weymouth
(35 minutes, three per hour). Bus 188 goes
to Poole (one hour, three daily Monday to
Saturday).

There are two train stations, Dorchester
South and Dorchester West, both southwest
of the town centre. Trains run at least hourly
from Weymouth (£2.90, 11 minutes) to London (£37.80, 2½ hours) via Dorchester South,
Bournemouth (£8.30, 45 minutes) and Southampton (£17, 1¼ hours).

Dorchester West has connections with Bath
(£11.30, 1¾ hours) and Bristol (£12.40, two
hours).

Dorchester Cycles (☎ 268787; 31 Great Western Rd;
per day £15) hires bikes.

AROUND DORCHESTER
Maiden Castle

The massive earthwork ramparts of Maiden
Castle, Europe's largest and finest Iron Age
hill fort, stretch for 3 miles and enclose nearly
20 hectares. The site has been inhabited since
Neolithic times but the first fort was built here
around 800 BC. It was then abandoned and
rebuilt. Later the earth walls were extended
and enlarged. Despite the addition of more
defences, the Romans captured it in AD 43,
finally abandoning it in the 4th century. The
sheer size of the walls and ditches is stunning,
and there are wonderful views. Finds from the
site are displayed at Dorset County Museum
(opposite). Maiden Castle is 1½ miles southwest of Dorchester.

Cerne Abbas & the Cerne Giant

With its quiet lanes, sleepy pubs and picturesque cottages, the little village of Cerne Abbas is a typically attractive Dorset hamlet, home to the ruins of an old **abbey** (adult/child £1/20p) and a pretty 14th-century **church**. But one particular resident completely overshadows the rest of the village: the notoriously well-endowed **Cerne Giant**, who stands to attention on a hilltop above the village. Opinions vary regarding the age of the 55m-high giant – some believe him to be a pre-Roman fertility symbol, although no official record exists of the giant until the 17th century – but one thing's for certain: this old man is certainly not shy about showing off his vital assets. Predictably enough, the Victorians found the whole thing deeply embarrassing and allowed grass to grow over the giant's most outstanding feature, but thankfully, he's since been allowed to rediscover his manhood.

There are several pleasant places to stay and eat around the village: for rooms try the **New Inn** (☎ 01300-341274; thenewinncerneabbas .co.uk; 14 Long St; d from £55; P ✂), a great country coaching inn with simple rustic rooms and an excellent menu of pub grub, and for food head for the thatched **Royal Oak** (☎ 01300-341797; Long St; mains £5-8; ☽ lunch & dinner), an ivy-clad pub renowned for its hearty Dorset dishes and traditional ales.

Dorchester, 8 miles to the south, is reached on bus 216 (20 minutes, four times Monday to Saturday).

TOP FIVE ANCIENT SITES

- **Stonehenge** (p314) The world's most famous stone circle; shame no-one's got a clue what it was for.

- **Avebury** (p321) Much bigger, and arguably more impressive than Stonehenge, this huge ring of stones is part of an amazing network of ancient sites.

- **Maiden Castle** (p301) The biggest Iron Age Fort anywhere in Europe.

- **Glastonbury Tor** (p282) The Isle of Avalon, gateway to the underworld, or a fairy king's palace? Who cares – it's still a breathtaking sight.

- **Old Sarum** (p313) Another stunning Iron Age stronghold on Salisbury Plain.

WEYMOUTH

☎ 01305 / pop 48,279

Stripey deckchairs, candy-floss stalls, rickety windbreaks and Punch & Judy booths line the beachfront at the well-worn seaside town of Weymouth, once a favoured holiday haunt of the English gentry, and now more popular with bawling nippers, family day-trippers and members of the blue rinse brigade. Depending on your point of view, it's either a glorious example of British kitsch or a soulless summation of everything that's wrong with the domestic seaside experience. Whatever you make of the present-day town, Weymouth looks set for a massive transformation over the next five years, having been chosen as the sailing centre for the 2012 Olympics.

Orientation & Information

Central Weymouth is strung along the seafront, which stretches west to the old harbour with its cluster of pubs, fishermen's cottages and seafood restaurants.

The **tourist office** (☎ 785747; tic@weymouth.gov.uk; The Esplanade; ☽ 9.30am-5pm Apr-Oct, 10am-4pm Nov-Mar) sells discounted tickets to many local attractions and can help arrange local accommodation for a fee.

Sights & Activities

Weymouth has been a popular seaside spot since King George III (the mad one) took an impromptu dip here in 1789. People are still flocking to the seafront some two and a half centuries later, and during the summer holidays the beach is usually packed with nose-to-tail sunbathers. There are lots of places along the seafront to hire deckchairs and arm yourself with that all-important bucket and spade; you can also rent pedalos for £5 per hour. For sailing and windsurfing lessons, see p304.

Over in the old part of town, Brewer's Quay has a shopping centre and plentiful attractions, including **Timewalk** (☎ 777622; Hope Sq; adult/child £4.50/3.25; ☽ 10am-5.30pm), which explores various key events in Weymouth's history, including the Black Death, the Spanish Armada and the town's transition from fishing harbour to tourist resort.

Also in Brewer's Quay is the **Weymouth Museum** (admission free; ☽ 10am-5pm), uncovering the town's maritime heritage with displays on smuggling, paddle steamers and shipwrecks. Nearby, the **Tudor House** (☎ 812341; 3 Trinity St; adult/

WESSEX

child £2.50/1; 1-3.45pm Tue-Fri Jun-Sep, 2-4pm 1st Sun of the month Oct-May) is one of the few 17th-century buildings left in Weymouth and is furnished in period style.

The **Deep Sea Adventure** (0871 222 5760; www .deepsea-adventure.co.uk; 9 Custom House Quay; adult/child £4/3; 9.30am-7pm Sep-Jun, 9.30am-8pm Jul & Aug) looks depressingly tacky, but it actually offers a decent look at the history of diving, with exhibits on local shipwrecks and the *Titanic*. If the kids get bored, there are lots of play areas and a laser shootout zone.

More aquatic exhibits are on offer at **Sea Life** (788255; www.sealife.co.uk; Lodmoor Country Park; adult/child £11.50/8; 10am-5pm), which offers seal, otter and penguin enclosures, a shark nursery and a new green turtle sanctuary.

Perched on the end of the promontory, 19th-century **Nothe Fort** (766465; www.fortress weymouth.co.uk; Barrack Rd; adult/child £5/1; 10.30am-5.30pm May-Sep, 2.30pm-4.30pm Sun Oct-Apr) is currently undergoing refurbishment, but its collection of weapons and military memorabilia is still on display while the work is being carried out.

WATER SPORTS

With so many wrecks dotted along the coastline, Weymouth and Portland are popular dive centres; try **Dive Dorset** (860269; www.dive dorset.com; 15 Castletown) on Portland, or the **Old Harbour Dive Centre** (760888; oldharbourdive@aol .com; 11 Nothe Pde) in Weymouth. Day trips start at around £85 per day including equipment.

Windsurfing is also excellent along the Weymouth coastline; **Second Wind** (01305 835301; www.second-wind.co.uk; Overcombe Beach) and **Windtek** (787900; www.windtek.co.uk; 109 Portland Rd) both offer lessons (£90 per day) and hire gear (£15 to £30 per day).

Weymouth & Portland Sailing Academy (860101; www.wpnsa.org.uk; Osprey Quay) runs two-day sailing courses for £155.

Sleeping

Weymouth is practically wall-to-wall B&Bs, but you'll need to discover your inner fondness for net curtains and doily-covered tablecloths. There are plenty of camp sites near Chesil Beach and Weymouth Bay.

Chatsworth (785012; www.thechatsworth.co.uk; 14 The Esplanade; d £30-100; P) Nicely positioned near the Old Harbour, this smart guesthouse offers much more up-to-date accommodation

---

---

than most of Weymouth's B&Bs. The nicest room has French doors that lead to a private balcony overlooking the harbour, and there are a couple more with beautiful bay windows; there's also an excellent inhouse brasserie and also a rather pleasant harbourside breakfast terrace.

Seaham (782010; www.theseaham.co.uk; 3 Waterloo Pl; d £56-60;) The best of the cluster of B&Bs along Victoria Rd, with five well-kept rooms finished in pastel fabrics, prefab furniture and faintly nautical colours. The rooms at the front just about have sea views, but traffic noise on the main seafront road can be a headache.

Eating

You couldn't come to Weymouth and not try the local staple of fish and chips. The top chippy in town is **King Edward's** (786924; 100 The Esplanade); for the full seaside experience, chase down the chips with a classic 99 from **Rossi's** (785557; 92 The Esplanade), which has been serving up ice creams on the Weymouth seafront since the 1930s.

Perry's (785799; 4 Trinity Rd; mains £12-17; lunch Tue-Fri, dinner Tues-Sat) Right on the quayside, this relaxed bistro specialises in seafood straight off the Weymouth fishing boats – crab soup, lobster bisque and roast sea bass are served up in the light, cheery dining room, dotted with local paintings and dried flowers.

Isobar (750666; 19 Trinity Rd; mains £12.95-15.50; dinner Tues-Sat) For a quirkier vibe head along the quay to this baroque-styled gastropub, where rough wood floors meet gilt-framed pictures, hot-pink walls and upholstered chairs. There's a great chalkboard menu ranging from Thai fish cakes to wholetail scampi, and plenty of bottled beers and world wines behind the bar.

Getting There & Away

BUS
There's one daily National Express coach to London (£19.20, 4¼ hours).

Bus 10 is the quickest to Dorchester (30 minutes, three per hour). The hourly bus 31 also stops in Dorchester en route to Lyme Regis (two hours) and Axminster, while the X53 travels from Weymouth to Wareham (50 minutes, six daily, four on Sunday) and Bournemouth (two hours), and to Abbotsbury (35 minutes), Lyme Regis (90 minutes) and Exeter (three hours) in the opposite direction. Bus 1 travels regularly over to Portland (30 minutes).

TRAIN
Trains run hourly to London (£63, 2¾ hours) via Dorchester South (11 minutes) and Bournemouth (£10.50, one hour), and every two hours to Dorchester West, Bath (£11.60, two hours) and Bristol (£13, 2¼ hours).

AROUND WEYMOUTH
Portland
Portland is essentially a craggy island joined to the mainland by the long sweep of Chesil Beach. It's a proud, sturdy kind of place, where the traditional quarrying industry is still the main employer; Portland's unique white limestone has been quarried here for centuries and has found its way into many of the world's finest buildings (including the British Museum, St Paul's Cathedral and the United Nations headquarters in New York). The sea views from Portland's rugged clifftops are breathtaking, especially around the **lighthouse** (☎ 01305-861233; ⏰ 11am-5pm Apr-Sep) on Portland Bill, where there's also a summer-only **tourist office** (☎ 01305-861233). It costs adult/child £2.50/1.50 to climb the 41m-high tower. Look out for the treacherous stretch of water known as The Race, which is just beyond the lighthouse.

Sturdy **Portland Castle** (EH; ☎ 820539; admission £3.50; ⏰ 10am-6pm Jul-Aug, to 5pm Apr-Jun & Sep, to 4pm Oct) is one of the finest examples of the defensive castles constructed during Henry VIII's castle-building spree. You can try on period

armour and get great views over Portland harbour.

The first curator of the **Portland Museum** (☎ 821804; 217 Wakeham St; adult/child £2.50/free; ⏰ 10.30am-5pm Fri-Tue Easter-Oct) was Dr Marie Stopes, who went on to pioneer the birth-control pill. Housed in two thatched cottages overlooking Church Ope Cove, the museum has some varied displays exploring Portland's history, especially its reputation for smuggling and shipwrecks; there are also some huge fossils and ammonites collected along the Jurassic Coast nearby.

Bus 1 runs to Portland from Weymouth every half-hour.

Chesil Beach
A massive expanse of pebbles stretches along the coast for 10 miles between Portland and Abbotsbury, at times reaching up to 15m high. It's an incredible sight and encloses Fleet Lagoon, a haven for water birds.

The stones vary from pebble size at Abbotsbury in the west to around 15cm in diameter at Portland. Local fishers can supposedly tell their position along the bank by gauging the size of the stones.

Chesil Beach Centre (☎ 01305-760579; Ferrybridge; ⏰ 11am-6pm Apr-Sep, 11am-4pm Oct-Mar) provides information, and organises talks and guided walks.

LYME REGIS
☎ 01297 / pop 4406
Nestled at the edge of the Jurassic Coast, the genteel resort of Lyme Regis is famous for two things: fossils and *The French Lieutenant's Woman*. John Fowles' classic tale of a seaside love triangle was set in Lyme Regis and the Hollywood film starring Richard Gere was later filmed here, providing a briefly lived boost to both the town's tourist industry and the local housing market. But the town is perhaps better known for its archaeological attractions; some of the first dinosaur skeletons ever discovered in Britain were found here during the 19th century, and the town has been a magnet for fossil-hunters ever since.

Information
Lyme Regis' **tourist office** (☎ 442138; lyme .tic@westdorset-dc.gov.uk; Guildhall Cottage, Church St; ⏰ 10am-5pm Mon-Sat & 10am-4pm Sun Apr-Oct, 10am-3pm Mon-Sat Nov-Mar) is on the corner of Church and Bridge Sts.

WORTH THE TRIP

Abbotsbury Swannery (☎ 871858; New Barn Rd; admission £7.50; ☒ 10am-6pm mid-Mar–Oct) was founded by the monks of Abbotsbury's monastery about 600 years ago. Every May the colony of mute swans makes its nests at the swannery, protected by the pebble banks of Chesil Beach; the cygnets usually hatch out in late June. Feathers from the Abbotsbury swans are still used in the helmets of the Gentlemen At Arms, the Queen's official bodyguard, and by calligraphers at the historic insurance broker Lloyd's of London.

Sights

One of the 19th century's most famous fossil collectors was Mary Anning (1799–1847), who was born in a seafront cottage on a site now occupied by the excellent **Lyme Regis Philpot Museum** (☎ 443 370; www.lymeregismuseum.co.uk; Bridge St; adult/child £2.20/1.60; ☒ 10am-5pm Mon-Sat, 11am-5pm Sun Apr-Oct, Sat & Sun Nov-Mar). Mary Anning found the first icthyosaur skeleton near Lyme Regis in 1812, and did much to pioneer the science of modern-day palaeontology; the museum traces her story, and also exhibits many spectacular fossils and other prehistoric finds.

The **Dinosaurland Fossil Museum** (☎ 443541; www.dinosaurland.co.uk; Coombe St; adult/child £5/4; ☒ 10am-5pm) has lots of excellent fossil displays and also organises fossil-hunting trips; if your own expeditions prove unsuccessful, you can always pick up an ammonite at the museum shop.

The **Cobb**, Lyme's famous 183m-long jetty-cum-breakwater, was constructed in the 13th century to protect the town from sea surges. Though it's been patched up and improved many times over the last 700 years, it still fails to protect the town from occasional flooding; consequently a massive sea protection programme is currently under way along the town's seafront, and you might well find the town beach is closed when you're there.

There's a low-budget **Marine Aquarium** (☎ 443678; admission £2.50; ☒ 10am-5pm Apr-Oct, extended hr peak season) near the Cobb.

Sleeping

Old Lyme Guest House (☎ 442929; www.oldlymeguesthouse.co.uk; 29 Coombe St; s £35, d £60-65; ⓟ ☒) Once home to Lyme's old post office, this stone-fronted house is now an award-winning B&B, with several feminine rooms finished in pale creams and soft hues, topped off by patterned curtains and china trinkets.

Hotel Alexandra (☎ 442010, www.hotelalexandra.co.uk; Pound St; s £60, d £100-140; ⓟ ☒) Built in 1735 for a dowager countess and run for the last 25 years by a local family, this delightful small hotel feels like a relic from another age. There are 26 quietly classy rooms, 16 of which have views across the neatly tended lawns to Lyme Bay; there's also a refined restaurant (complete with tinkling pianist) and a garden conservatory tailor-made for afternoon tea.

Fairwater Head Hotel (☎ 678349; Hawkchurch; www.fairwaterheadhotel.co.uk; d £140-190; ⓟ ☒) A couple of miles north of Lyme Regis in the 'village of roses', this excellent country retreat brings an unmistakably Gallic accent to its rural English setting. The plush en suite bedrooms overlook private gardens and are divided between the main house and a newer annexe.

Eating

Cobb Arms (☎ 443242; Marine Pde; mains £5-10; ⓟ ☒) This salty old harbourfront pub pulls the best pint in Lyme and also serves up plates of battered cod, scampi and chips, and club sandwiches.

Jurassic Seafood (☎ 444345; 47 Silver St; mains £9-15; ☒ lunch & dinner) Seafood, steak and stir-fried veg underpin the menu of this upbeat, contemporary café-bistro. The décor is fun and fresh, with blazing-orange walls, an open-plan chrome kitchen and the odd dino mural, and the food takes in everything from spicy crab cakes to lamb kebabs and scallop brochettes.

Broad St Restaurant (☎ 445792; 57-58 Broad St; lunch £9-13, 3-course dinner £25; hdinner weekdays, lunch & dinner weekends) This spanking-new restaurant on the main street has quickly built up a reputation as one of the finest restaurants on the south Dorset coast. Blindingly white tablecloths, flagstone floors and sparkling wine glasses set the upmarket mood, and the menu dazzles with its dishes of local Dorset produce and Lyme Bay fish.

Getting There & Away

Bus 31 runs to Dorchester (1¼ hours) and Weymouth (1¾ hours) hourly (every two hours on Sunday). Bus X53 goes west to Exeter (1¾ hours) and east to Weymouth (1½ hours. six daily, four on Sunday).

AROUND LYME REGIS

Forde Abbey

Originally a Cistercian monastery constructed in the 12th century, **Forde Abbey** (☎ 01460-221290; www.fordeabbey.co.uk; abbey adult/child £7.70/free, gardens £5.60/free; ☼ abbey noon-4pm Tue-Fri & Sun Apr-Oct, gardens 10am-4.30pm) was updated in the 17th century and has been a private home since 1649. The building boasts magnificent plasterwork ceilings and fine tapestries but it's the outstanding gardens that are the main attraction: 12 hectares of lawns, ponds, shrubberies and flowerbeds with many rare and beautiful species. It's 10 miles north of Lyme Regis; public transport is a non-starter.

SHERBORNE

☎ 01935 / pop 9350

All streets in the honey-stoned town of Sherborne lead to its majestic abbey, set at the centre of a grassy green and once the most important church in Wessex; both of Alfred the Great's elder brothers, Ethelred and Ethelbert, are buried beneath the abbey's flagstones. Sherborne was the capital of Wessex until the end of the 11th century, when the bishopric moved to Old Sarum (p313), but continued to be a town of strategic and religious importance throughout the Middle Ages. These days it's a quiet and attractive market town, filled with antique shops, haberdashers and estate agents; reminders of its former status remain in its twin castles, which stand on either side of the silvery sheen of Sherborne Lake.

Sherborne's **tourist office** (☎ 815341; sherborne .tic@westdorset-dc.gov.uk; Digby Rd; ☼ 9am-5pm Mon-Sat Apr-Oct) stocks the free *All About Sherborne* leaflet with a map and town trail. **Walking tours** (£3; ☼ 11am Fri May-Sep) depart from the tourist office and last 1½ hours.

Sherborne Museum (☎ 812252; www.sherbornemu seum.co.uk; Church Lane; adult/child £1/free; ☼ 10.30am-4.30pm Tue-Sat, 2.30pm-4.30pm Sun Apr-Oct) explores the town's history through costumes, period photos and some fascinating illustrations, but the museum's most prized possession is a digital version of the *Sherborne Missal*, the most exquisite illuminated manuscript to survive from the Middle Ages. The original is held in the British Library (p128).

Sights

SHERBORNE ABBEY

Established early in the 8th century, the **Abbey Church of St Mary the Virgin** (☎ 812452; suggested

---

FOSSIL FEVER

The Jurassic Coast is one of the most unstable areas of Britain's seashore, and there are regular landslips all along the coastline. This instability is a real bonus for fossil-hunters, however, as it exposes fossils and prehistoric remains that would normally be locked into the rock. **Fossil-hunting trips** frequently run from Lyme Regis, and collectors say that once you've caught the bug it's hard to stop – ammonites, belemnites and fossilised bone are all regular finds, but you might have to put in a few hours if you're after a full-sized icthyosaur. Contact the tourist office for tour details, or visit www .jurassiccoast.com.

---

donation £2; ☼ 8.30am-6pm late-Mar–late Oct, 8.30am-4pm Nov–mid-Mar) became a Benedictine abbey in 998 and functioned as a cathedral until 1075. The church boasts the oldest fan vaulting in the country, and there are several intriguing tombs – look out for the elaborate marble effigy marking the one belonging to John Lord Digby, Earl of Bristol, flanked by his two wives. Ethelred and Ethelbert are buried in the corner of the abbey.

The abbey also has some notable architectural features: solid Saxon-Norman piers support the central tower and the main entrance has a Norman porch built in 1180. On the edge of the abbey close are the **St Johns' Almshouses** (admission £1.50; ☼ 2-4pm Tue & Thu-Sat May-Sep), constructed in the 15th century.

OLD CASTLE

East of the town centre stand the ruins of the **Old Castle** (EH; ☎ 812730; admission £2.40; ☼ 10am-6pm Jul-Aug, 10am-5pm Apr-Jun & Sep, 10am-4pm Oct), constructed from 1107 by Roger, Bishop of Salisbury. Sir Walter Raleigh acquired it (with the help of Elizabeth I) in the late 16th century, and spent large sums of money modernising the castle before deciding it wasn't worth the effort and moving across the River Yeo to start work on his new castle. It became a Royalist stronghold during the English Civil War, but Cromwell reduced the 'malicious and mischievous castle' to rubble after a 16-day siege in 1645.

SHERBORNE CASTLE

Sir Walter Raleigh began building **New Castle** (☎ 813182; www.sherbornecastle.com; house adult/child

WESSEX

£8/free, gardens only £4/free; ⏰ 11am-4.30pm Tue-Thu & weekends Apr-Oct) – really a splendid manor house – in 1594. However, by 1608 he was back in prison, this time at the hands of James I, who eventually sold the castle to Sir John Digby, the Earl of Bristol, in 1617. It's been the Digby family residence ever since, and contains fine collections of art, furniture and porcelain, as well as grounds landscaped by Capability Brown.

Sleeping & Eating

Eastbury Hotel (☎ 813131; www.theeastburyhotel .co.uk; Long St; s/d from £49/90; Ⓟ ⊠) The rooms might be named after flowers at this fine red-brick house, but they're refreshingly light on floral patterns; the atmosphere is closer to a Georgian country residence, with plenty of upholstered armchairs, rich wallpapers and wooden furniture, as well as a sweet conservatory restaurant and a walled garden (complete with croquet lawn).

Old Vicarage (☎ 251117; www.milborneport.freeserve .co.uk, s £63-84, d £79-112; Ⓟ ⊠) The vicar obviously wasn't short of a few bob when he built this fantastic neo-Tudor mansion on the edge of the village. The gabled, double-chimneyed frontage is impressive enough, but the interior rooms are even smarter, melding country clutter and Victorian bric-a-brac with a vaguely Oriental ambience.

Alders (☎ 220666; www.thealdersbb.com; Sandford Orcas; d £48-60; Ⓟ ⊠) Traditional rooms in a modernised stone house 3 miles' drive from Sherborne.

Stoneleigh Barn (☎ 815964; www.stoneleighbarn. com; North Wootton; d £55-80; Ⓟ ⊠ 🐾) Elegantly converted stone barn with four-poster-bed rooms, 2 miles from town.

Eating

Pear Tree Deli (☎ 812828; Half Moon St; mains £4-8; ⏰ lunch) This delectable deli is an ideal place to stock up on a gourmet sandwich or some lunchtime picnic supplies. Homemade pies, soup specials and Greek cheeseburgers are chalked up above the counter, and the shelves are stacked with a mouthwatering array of chutneys, jams, bikkies and cakes.

Half Moon Inn (☎ 812017; Half Moon St; mains £5-12; ⏰ lunch & dinner) The town's liveliest pub specialises in hot food platters and local brews, best appreciated on the streetside terrace as the sun sets over the abbey nearby.

Paprika (☎ 816429; Half Moon St; mains £7-12; ⏰ lunch & dinner) Laminate floors, scarlet-leather chairs

and big glass windows characterise the interior of this thoroughly modern Indian place, where the menu also contains a few surprises – try the vegetarian curry with cashew nuts or chicken curry with pineapple and coconuts.

Getting There & Away

Bus 57 runs from Yeovil (30 minutes, half-hourly Monday to Saturday, six on Sunday), as does the quicker 58 (15 minutes, every two hours Monday to Saturday), which sometimes continues to Shaftesbury (1½ hours).

Hourly trains run to Exeter (£13.20, 1¼ hours), London (£35.10, 2½ hours) and Salisbury (£9.20, 45 minutes).

SHAFTESBURY & AROUND

☎ 01747 / pop 6665

Perched on an idyllic hilltop overlooking a panorama of pastoral meadows and hog-backed hills, the village of Shaftesbury was home to the largest community of nuns in England until 1539, when Henry VIII came knocking during the Dissolution. These days its attractions are rather more prosaic; the town's best-known landmark is Gold Hill, a cobbled slope lined by chocolate-box cottages and thatched houses that graces many a local postcard, and which also starred in a famous telly advert for Hovis bread.

The **tourist office** (☎ 853514; www.shaftesburydorset .com; 8 Bell St; ⏰ 10am-5pm Apr-Sep, 10am-3pm Mon-Sat Oct-Mar) is by the Bleke St car park.

Sights

Sitting on a flat rise with sweeping views across the hills, **Shaftesbury Abbey** (☎ 852910; www.shaftesburyabbey.co.uk; Park Walk; admission £2.50; ⏰ 10am-5pm Apr-Oct) was at one time England's largest and richest nunnery. It was founded in 888 by Alfred the Great, the first religious house in Britain built solely for women; Alfred's daughter, Aethelgifu, was its first abbess. St Edward is thought to have been buried here, and King Knut died at the abbey in 1035. Most of the buildings were dismantled by Henry VIII and his cronies, but you can still wander around its foundations with a well-devised audio guide, and visit the intriguing museum.

The small **Shaftesbury Museum** (☎ 852157; Sun & Moon Cottage, Gold Hill; adult/child £1.50/free; ⏰ 10.30am-4.30pm Thu-Tue) is worth visiting for its local-interest exhibits, including an 18th-century fire engine, a collection of Dorset decorative buttons, and the ornamental Byzant, used during the town's ancient water ceremony.

Old Wardour Castle

The six-sided **Old Wardour Castle** (EH; ☎ 01747-870487; admission £3.20; ☺ 10am-6pm Jul-Aug, 10am-5pm Apr-Jun & Sep, 10am-4pm Oct, 10am-4pm weekends Nov-Mar) was built around 1393 and suffered severe damage during the English Civil War, leaving the magnificent remains you see today. It's an ideal spot for a picnic and there are fantastic views from the upper levels. Bus 26 runs from Shaftesbury (four Monday to Friday), 4 miles west.

Sleeping & Eating

Retreat (☎ 850372; www.the-retreat.org.uk; 47 Bell St; s/d £35/70; **P** ✗) This period townhouse on one of Shaftesbury's quiet backstreets makes an excellent base for exploring the town, though the rooms might be a little sparse; white walls, plain chairs and the occasional framed print are about as decorative as things get.

Cobwebbs (☎ 853505; www.cobwebbs.me.uk; 14 Gold Hill; s/d £35/70; ✗) If it's a picturesque setting that you're after, then look no further than this miniature whitewashed cottage halfway up Gold Hill. Unsurprisingly, the rooms are on the snug side, but very cosy; the nicest is the garden room, with a king-sized brass bed and patio doors onto the delightful rear terrace.

3 Ivy Cross (☎ 853857; www.3ivycross.co.uk; 3 Ivy Cross; d £50-55; **P** ✗) Three colour-coordinated rooms are available at this brick-fronted house a couple of minutes' walk from the town centre – choose from pale pink, duck egg blue or sunny yellow, and expect the usual puffy pillows, thick duvets and off-the-shelf furniture.

Mitre Inn (☎ 852549; 23 The High St; mains £6-10) A heart-warming country pub that still boasts an authentic Dorset atmosphere, as well as quality beers, homecooked food and a wooden-decked terrace with fabulous hill views.

Getting There & Away

Bus 182/183 runs to Blandford (40 minutes, eight Monday to Saturday, three on Sunday); seven daily go on to Bournemouth (two hours). Buses 26/27 run from Salisbury (1¼ hours, five Monday to Saturday).

WILTSHIRE

Britain's ancient history comes to life around the fields, plateaus and plains of rural Wiltshire. It's a place that teases and tantalises the imagination, littered with more ancient barrows, processional avenues and mysterious stone rings than anywhere else in Britain; the stunning prehistoric sites of Avebury and Stonehenge understandably receive the most visitors, but there are plenty of lesser-known sites to explore too, including Woodhenge, Silbury Hill and the Iron Age fort at Old Sarum. Wiltshire is also home to the stately homes of Longleat and Stourhead and the delightful villages of Castle Combe and Lacock, as well as the magnificent cathedral city of Salisbury.

Information

The **Visit Wiltshire** (☎ 0870 240 5599; www.visitwilt shire.co.uk) website is the best source for pre-planning info, and you can pick up the usual range of brochures and leaflets from local tourist offices.

Activities
WALKING

Wiltshire is great walking country, with mostly flat countryside and stunning views, as well as a wealth of ancient monuments to seek out. The long-distance Ridgeway national trail starts near Avebury (p321), but there are plenty of shorter walks, including several trails around Stonehenge (p314), Old Sarum (p313) and the Stourhead Estate (p316).

The *Walking in Wiltshire* booklet (£3) details 10 easy walks around the region, while the *White Horse Trail* leaflet (£6) covers a 90-mile route taking in all of Wiltshire's eight chalk horses. Both leaflets are available from tourist offices or the Visit Wiltshire website (http://www.visitwilt shire.co.uk/pages/walks.asp). There are some useful downloadable walking maps available from the Visit Wiltshire website.

Foot Trails (☎ 01747-861851; www.foottrails.co.uk) leads guided walks and can help you plan your own self-guided route.

WESSEX

CYCLING

Cyclists should pick up the *Wiltshire Cycleway* leaflet (£3) in tourist offices, which includes a detailed route guide and lists handy cycle shops. *Off-Road Cycling in Wiltshire* (£6) is a waterproof guide with trail maps for mountain-bikers.

CANAL TRIPS

The 87-mile-long **Kennet & Avon Canal** runs all the way from Bristol to Reading. If you fancy getting out on the water, contact **Sally Boats** (☎ 01225-864923; www.sallyboats.ltd.uk; Bradford-on-Avon) or **Foxhangers** (☎ 828795; www.foxhangers .co.uk), which both have narrowboats for hire: weekly rates start at around £600 for four people in winter, rising to about £1600 for a 10-berth boat in high summer.

Dedicated cycling tours are offered by several operators including **History on Your Handlebars** (☎ 01249 730013; www.historyonyourhandlebars .co.uk; Lacock).

Getting Around
BUS

The bus coverage in northwest Wiltshire still leaves a lot to be desired, especially in the northwest of the county. The two main operators are:

First (☎ 0845 606-4446; www.firstgroup.com) Serves the far west of the county.
Wilts & Dorset Buses (☎ 01722 336855; www.wdbus .co.uk) Covers most destinations.

For general bus info contact the **Wiltshire Bus Line** (☎ 0845 709 0899). The Wiltshire Day Rover (adult/child £6.50/4.50) is valid with most operators and can be bought from bus drivers.

TRAIN

Rail lines run from London to Salisbury and beyond to Exeter and Plymouth, branching off north to Bradford-on-Avon, Bath and Bristol, but most of the smaller towns and villages aren't served by trains.

SALISBURY

☎ 01722 / pop 43,335

Centred around a majestic cathedral topped by a soaring central spire – the tallest in England – the gracious city of Salisbury makes a charming place from which to explore the rest of Wiltshire. It's been an important provincial city for more than a thousand years, and its streets are dusted with buildings from almost every period in Britain's architectural history – medieval walls, half-timbered Tudor townhouses, Georgian mansions and Victorian villas – but Salisbury is a modern, lively place, with plenty of bars, restaurants and terraced cafés, as well as a concentrated cluster of excellent museums.

Orientation

Salisbury's compact town centre revolves around Market Sq, which is dominated by its impressive guildhall. The train station is a 10-minute walk to the west, while the bus station is just 100 yards north up Endless St.

Information

Library (☎ 324145; Market Pl; ⏱ 10am-7pm Mon, 9am-5pm Tue-Fri, 9am-1pm Sat)

Post office (cnr Castle St & Chipper Lane)
Salisbury Online (☎ 421328; ⏱ 10am-8pm Mon-Sat, 10am-5pm Sun)
Tourist office (☎ 334956; www.visitsalisburyuk.com; Fish Row; ⏱ 9.30am-6pm Mon-Sat, 10.30am-4.30pm Sun Jun-Sep; 9.30am-5pm Mon-Sat, 10.30am 4pm Sun May; 9.30am-5pm Mon-Sat Oct-Apr)
Washing Well Laundrette (☎ 421874; 28 Chipper Lane; ⏱ 8am-9pm)

Sights
SALISBURY CATHEDRAL

Britain is a nation blessed with countless stunning churches, but few can match the grandeur and sheer spectacle of **Salisbury Cathedral** (☎ 555100; www.salisburycathedral.org.uk; requested donation adult/child £4/2; ⏱ 7.15am-6.15pm Sep-May, 7.15am-7.15pm Jun-Aug). Built between 1220 and 1258, the cathedral bears all the hallmarks of the early English Gothic style, with an elaborate exterior decorated with pointed arches and flying buttresses, and a sombre, austere interior designed to keep its congregation suitably pious.

Beyond the highly decorative **West Front**, a small passageway leads into the 70m-long nave, lined with handsome pillars of Purbeck stone. Look out for a fascinating old **clock** from 1386 in the north aisle, probably the oldest working clock in the world. At the eastern end of the ambulatory the glorious **Prisoners of Conscience** stained-glass window (1980) hovers above the ornate tomb of Edward Seymour (1539–1621) and Lady Catherine Grey. Other monuments and tombs line the sides of the nave, including that of **William Longespée**, son of

WESSEX

Henry II and half-brother of King John. When the tomb was excavated a well-preserved rat was found inside Longespée's skull.

The splendid **spire** was added in the mid-14th century. At 123m, it's the highest in Britain, and represented an enormous technical challenge for its medieval builders; it weighs around 6500 tons and required an elaborate system of cross-bracing, scissor arches and supporting buttresses to keep it upright. Look closely and you'll see that the additional weight has buckled the four central piers of the nave.

Sir Christopher Wren surveyed the cathedral in 1668 and calculated that the spire was leaning by 75cm. A **brass plate** in the floor of the nave is used to measure any shift, but no further lean was recorded in 1951 or 1970. Despite this, reinforcement on the notoriously 'wonky spire' continues to this day.

There are 1½-hour tower **tours** (adult/child £4/3; 11.15am & 2.15pm Mar & Oct, 11.15am, 2.15pm & 3.15pm Apr-Sep, plus 5pm Mon-Sat Jun-Aug), which climb up 332 vertigo-inducing steps to the base of the spire, from where there are jaw-dropping views across the city and the surrounding countryside.

One of the four surviving copies of the **Magna Carta**, the historic agreement made between King John and his barons in 1215, is kept in the cathedral's **Chapter House** (9.30am-6.45pm Jun-Aug, 9.30am-5.30pm Mar-Jun & Sep-Oct, 10am-4.30pm Nov-Feb).

CATHEDRAL CLOSE

The cathedral is surrounded by one of the country's most beautiful medieval **closes**. Many of the houses date from the same period as the cathedral, although the area was heavily restored during an 18th-century clean-up by James Wyatt. The close is encircled by a sturdy outer wall, constructed in 1333; the stout gates leading into the complex are still locked every night.

The highlight at the **Salisbury & South Wiltshire Museum** (332151; www.salisburymuseum.org.uk; 65 The Close; admission £4; 10am-5pm Mon-Sat, plus 2-5pm Sun Jul & Aug), in the King's House, is the interactive Stonehenge gallery, but there are also some interesting artefacts recovered from Old Sarum and lots of ceramics, historical artefacts and paintings, including a dreamy watercolour of Stonehenge by JMW Turner.

Military buffs will enjoy the **Wardrobe** (414536; www.thewardrobe.org.uk; 58 The Close; adult/child £2.75/75p; 10am-5pm Apr-Oct, 10am-5pm Tue-Sun Feb-Nov), home to the official museum of the

Royal Gloucestershire, Berkshire and Wiltshire Regiment.

Built in 1701, **Mompesson House** (NT; 335 659; The Close; admission £4.40; 11am-5pm Sat-Wed Mar-Oct) is a fine Queen Anne house with magnificent plasterwork ceilings, exceptional period furnishings and a wonderful carved staircase, which made it the perfect location for the 1995 film of *Sense and Sensibility*.

With a façade by Wren, **Malmesbury House** (327027; The Close) was a canonry in the 13th century and later the residence of the earls of Malmesbury, visited by notables including Charles II and Handel. It's still a private residence, but can be visited on pre-booked tours from April to October.

Just inside narrow High St Gate is the **College of Matrons**, founded in 1682 for widows and unmarried daughters of clergymen. South of the cathedral is the **Bishop's Palace**, now the Cathedral School, parts of which date back to 1220.

ST THOMAS'S CHURCH

This elegant church was built for cathedral workmen in 1219 and named after St Thomas Becket, although it was modified in the 15th century. Its most famous feature is the amazing **doom painting** above the chancel arch, painted in 1475. It depicts Christ on the day of judgment, sitting astride a rainbow flanked by visions of heaven and hell; on the hell side, look out for two naked kings and a nude bishop, a miser with his moneybags, and a female alehouse owner, the only person allowed to hang on to her clothes.

MARKET SQUARE

Markets were first held here in 1219, and the square still bustles with traders every Tuesday and Saturday. The narrow lanes that surround the square reveal their medieval specialities (Oatmeal Row, Fish Row, Silver St) but today the action is confined to the square, where you can pick up anything from fresh fish to dodgy digital watches. The 15th-century **Poultry Cross** is the last of four market crosses that once stood on the square.

Tours

Salisbury City Guides (320349; www.salisburycity guides.co.uk) leads 1½-hour tours (adult/child £3.50/1.50) from the tourist office at 11am from April to October, Saturday and Sunday only November to March. There are also

SALISBURY

themed walks at 2.30pm on Saturday and an 8pm ghost walk on Friday night from May to September.

Festivals & Events

The **Salisbury Festival** (☎ 320333; www.salisburyfestival.co.uk) is a prestigious, wide-ranging arts event encompassing classical, world and pop music, theatre, literature, art and puppetry. It runs over three weeks from late May to early June.

Sleeping

BUDGET

Salisbury YHA Hostel (☎ 0870 770 6018; salisbury@yha .org.uk; Milford Hill; dm £17.50; P ☒) This great hostel has a wide choice of rooms, ranging from smallish doubles to big, cheap bunk dorms, and a lovely location with private gardens surrounding the listed 19th-century house.

MIDRANGE

Rokeby Guesthouse (☎ 329800; www.rokebyguesthouse .co.uk; 3 Wain-a-long Rd; s/d from £45/55; P ☒ ▢) This grand red-brick house is the pick of the midrange B&Bs in town. It's an elegant Edwardian affair, distinguished by its above-average bedrooms (the best of which have half-tester beds and freestanding enamel baths) and a cute breakfast conservatory, reached by a winding iron staircase.

Wyndham Park Lodge (☎ 416517; www.wyndham parklodge.co.uk; 51 Wyndham Rd; s £38-42, d £50-55; ☒ P ▢ Ꮪ) This old-school B&B is a touch more traditional, but still very comfortable. The top rooms are the huge family suite on the first floor, and the stylish garden double with doors onto a private patio; little extras such as complementary fruit teas and wi-fi are very welcome.

Old Rectory (☎ 502702; www.theoldrectory-bb.co.uk; 75 Belle Vue Rd; d £50-70; P 🞪)Another old clergyman's residence that's been reworked into a decent B&B, with straightforward rooms decked out in standby shades of cream and pale yellow, as well as a charming walled garden with views across to St Edmund's Church. Some of the en suite bathrooms are tiny, though.

Websters (☎ 339779; www.websters-bed-breakfast .com; 11 Hartington Rd; s £40-44, d £50-54; P 🞪 🖳) A choice of checks, stripes or floral wallpapers greets you at this much-recommended B&B, which is decorated to a high standard throughout and bends over backwards to make sure you're happy. Some of the colour schemes are a little lurid, but extra treats such as hot chocolate, free broadband and a varied tea tray more than make up for that.

Farthings (☎ 330749; www.farthingsbandb.co.uk; 9 Swaynes Close; s/d £25/50; P 🞪) Victorian-era B&B with quilted beds and a pleasant garden; the cheaper rooms share facilities.

Malvern Guesthouse (☎ 327995; www.malvern guesthouse.com; 31 Hulse Rd; d from £50; P 🞪) Family-run guesthouse with pretty pastel rooms and homemade marmalade.

TOP END

White Hart Hotel (☎ 327476; St John St; whitehartsa lisbury@macdonald-hotels.co.uk; P) This big, central hotel – part of the Macdonald Hotels group – is a great option if you're up for a bit of pomp and pampering. The imposing porticoed frontage stands right opposite the cathedral close, and offers exactly the kind of swish rooms and attentive service you'd expect – as always, you get what you pay for, and the four-poster-bed rooms are worth the premium.

Eating
BUDGET

Square (☎ 331136; Market Sq; mains from £5; 🕑 daily) The kind of urban-style café you might not expect to find in provincial Salisbury, with the requisite clean lines and cream-and-chocolate tones, and a menu of paninis, pasta bakes and designer breakfasts.

Salisbury Chocolate Bar (☎ 327422; 33 High St; 🕑 9.30-5pm Mon-Sat, 2-5pm Sun) Handmade chocolates, continental pastries and super-sticky cakes make this the venue of choice for Salisbury choc-jocks.

Prezzo (☎ 341333; 52-54 High St; mains £7-9; 🕑 lunch & dinner) Housed in a decidedly wonky half-timbered house, this sleek Italian does all the standard pizza, pasta and Italian dishes fantastically well, supplemented by some unusual choices including Sicilian chicken and a delicious red pesto burger.

Lemon Tree (☎ 333471; 92 Crane St; mains £7-12; 🕑 lunch & dinner Mon-Sat) Packed with character but short on space, this tiny bistro crams the tables into a conservatory dining room; for more space head outside to the patio garden. Expect light, modern British food with a quirky twist – 'tipsy' chicken, perhaps, or pork pan-fried with apricots.

MIDRANGE

Mojito (☎ 417999; 2-4 Salt Lane; tapas £2-6, mains from £8; 🕑 lunch & dinner) Authentic tapas and an unmistakably Spanish atmosphere characterise this sassy restaurant, which has a couple of dining areas split over twin floors, and plenty of Iberian attitude. There's an open-plan kitchen where you can see the dishes being put together – our top tip is the fantastic paella, which also comes in a veggie version.

Café Med (☎ 328402; 68 Castle St; mains £9-20; 🕑 lunch & dinner) This breezy brasserie brings some Mediterranean vim to Salisbury's streets, and it's a popular spot for an early-evening meal. The menu offers British classics shot through with sun-kissed flavours – think sirloin steak with grilled vine tomatoes, or roast cod with pancetta.

Marrakech (☎ 411112; 129-133 South Western Rd; 🕑 lunch Tues-Sun, dinner daily) This great little restaurant is the nearest you'll get to North Africa in Wiltshire, serving tangy tagines and bona fide Moroccan couscous in a terracotta-coloured dining room full of earthenware pots and tiled tables. There's even a small souk where you can buy Moroccan handicrafts, and with luck you might even get a spot of Middle Eastern dancing thrown in for free.

Après LXIX (☎ 340000; 67-69 New St; mains £10-18; 🕑 lunch & dinner Tue-Sat) This achingly trendy bistro feels closer to Soho than Salisbury, with an artfully understated dining room filled with exposed brickwork and designer spotlights, and an imaginative menu with a magpie eye –

Italian, French and Oriental flavours find their way into many dishes, all based around a solid reliance on good old British produce.

Drinking

Moloko (☎ 507050; 5 Bridge St) This curious bar seems to take its visual cue from Stalinist Russia – black paint, stark interiors and red stars abound – and you'll need the constitution of a Tartar to stomach the flavoured vodkas.

Escoba (☎ 329608; 5-7 Winchester St) Orange walls, Dali-esque paintings and a hot and sultry atmosphere make this Spanish-style bar a popular drinking den. Cool Sol beers and jugs of margarita are the tipple of choice, accompanied by plates of fresh tapas.

Spirit (☎ 338387; 46 Catherine St) This hip hangout is always packed with a young and beautiful crowd on weekends, with banging tunes on the decks and a choice of technicolour cocktails.

Level 2 (☎ 330053; 48 Catherine St) Salisbury's newest club, Level 2 has guest DJs on Friday and a 'champagne and house' night on Saturday.

Salisbury has plenty of decent pubs: try the medieval **Haunch of Venison** (☎ 322024; 1-5 Minster St) for a choice of more than 50 malt whiskies, or the **Ox Row Inn** (☎ 424921; 10-11 Ox Row) for local ales.

Entertainment

Salisbury Arts Centre (☎ 321744; www.salisburyartscentre.co.uk; Bedwin St) Housed in the converted St Edmund's church, this exciting arts centre has a reputation for staging cutting-edge theatre, dance and live gigs; photography and arts exhibitions are often held in the foyer.

Salisbury Playhouse (☎ 320333; www.salisburyplayhouse.com; Malthouse Lane) is the town's big arts venue, and hosts top touring shows, musicals and new plays.

The **Odeon Cinema** (☎ 0870 505 0007; New Canal) is quite possibly the only cinema in the world with a medieval foyer.

Getting There & Away

BUS
Three National Express coaches run daily to London via Heathrow (£14, 3½ hours), and there's a daily coach to Bath (£8.30, 1½ hours) and Bristol (£8.30, two hours).

Salisbury is the main bus hub in Wiltshire. The X4/X5 travels direct to Bath (two hours, hourly, five on Sunday) via Bradford-on-

Avon (1½ hours), and there are regular local buses to Lacock (p319), Castle Combe (p318), Shaftesbury (p307), Devizes (p320), Avebury (p321) and Stonehenge (p314).

TRAIN
Trains run half-hourly from London Waterloo station (£25.20, 1½ hours) and hourly on to Exeter (£22.70, 1¾ hours) and the southwest. Another line runs from Portsmouth (£12.50, 1½ hours, hourly) via Southampton (£7.10, 45 minutes), with connections to Bradford-on-Avon (£8.10, 40 minutes, hourly), Bath (£11.20, one hour, half-hourly) and Bristol (£13.60, 1¼ hours, half-hourly).

AROUND SALISBURY
Old Sarum
The abandoned settlement of **Old Sarum** (☎ 01722-335398; admission £2.50; ☾ 9am-6pm Jul-Aug, 10am-5pm Apr-Jun & Sep, 10am-4pm Oct, 11am-3pm Nov-Mar) sits on a grassy rise about 2 miles from Salisbury. It began life as a huge hill fort during the Iron Age, and was later occupied by both the Romans and the Saxons. By the mid-11th century, the town had grown into one of the most important in the west of England; William the Conqueror convened one of his earliest councils here, and the first cathedral was built here in 1092, snatching the bishopric from nearby Sherborne Abbey. But Old Sarum was never a comfortable place to live: it was short on water and exposed to the elements, and in 1219 the bishop was given permission to move the cathedral to a new location beside the River Avon, founding the modern-day city of Salisbury. By 1331 the cathedral had been demolished for building material and Old Sarum had been practically abandoned; a scale model in Salisbury Cathedral illustrates how the site once looked.

There are free guided tours at 3pm in July and August, and medieval tournaments, open-air plays and mock battles on selected days.

Buses 3, 5, 6 and 8 all run at least hourly to Old Sarum throughout the week.

Wilton House
For an insight into how England's aristocracy once lived, **Wilton House** (☎ 01722-746729; www.wiltonhouse.com; adult/child house £9.75/5.50, gardens only £4.50/3.50; ☾ 10.30am-5.30pm Sun-Fri Apr-Oct) is hard to top. It's quite simply one of the finest stately homes in the country, home to

WESSEX

the Earls of Pembroke since 1542, and expanded, improved and embellished by successive generations since a devastating fire in 1647. The result is quite staggering, providing a whistlestop tour through all the great periods of English art and architecture: the house is dotted with magnificent period furniture, stately rooms, frescoed ceilings and elaborate plasterwork, as well as paintings by Van Dyck, Rembrandt, Brueghel and Joshua Reynolds; and the landscaped grounds were largely laid out by Capability Brown. Most spectacular of all are the Single and Double Cube Rooms, designed by the pioneering 17th-century architect Inigo Jones.

With so much architectural eye candy on display, it's hardly surprising that the house is a favourite location for filmmakers: *The Madness of King George, Sense and Sensibility* and the most recent version of *Pride and Prejudice* were all shot here. But Wilton was serving as a haven for the arts long before the cinema – the house's famous guests include Ben Jonson, Edmund Spenser, Kit Marlowe and John Donne, and Shakespeare's *As You Like It* was performed here in 1603.

Wilton House is 2½ miles west of Salisbury; buses 60, 60A and 61 run from Salisbury (10 minutes, every 15 minutes).

STONEHENGE

Arguably one of the world's most important prehistoric sites, and certainly one of Britain's biggest tourist attractions, the ancient ring of monolithic stones at **Stonehenge** (EH/NT; ☎ 01980-624715; admission £5.90; ☼ 9am-7pm Jul-Aug, 9.30am-6pm mid-Mar–May & Sep–mid-Oct, 9.30am-4pm Oct-Mar) has been attracting a steady stream of pilgrims, poets and philosophers for the last 5000 years. Despite the constant flow of traffic from the main road beside the monument, and the huge numbers of visitors who traipse around the stones on a daily basis, Stonehenge still manages to be a mystical, ethereal place – a haunting echo from Britain's forgotten past, and a reminder of a lost civilisation who once walked the many ceremonial avenues across Salisbury Plain. Even more intriguingly, it's still one of Britain's great archaeological mysteries: although there are countless theories about what the site was used for, ranging from a sacrificial centre to a celestial timepiece, in truth no-one really knows what drove prehistoric Britons to expend so much time and effort on its construction.

The Site

The first phase of construction at Stonehenge started around 3000 BC, when the outer circular bank and ditch were erected. A thousand years later an inner circle of granite stones, known as bluestones, was added. It's thought that these mammoth four-ton blocks were hauled from the Preseli Mountains in South Wales, some 250 miles away – an almost inexplicable feat for Stone Age builders equipped with only the simplest of tools. Although no-one is entirely sure how the builders transported the stones so far, it's thought that they probably used a system of ropes, sledges and rollers fashioned from tree trunks – not entirely impossible given that Salisbury Plain was still covered

THE STONEHENGE PROJECT

For such a celebrated site, Stonehenge has seen a surprising amount of upheaval over recent years. The tense stand-offs between solstice-goers and police that marked the late '80s and early '90s have been replaced by a fresh controversy over the alleged mismanagement of the World Heritage Site. It's certainly far from perfect: hemmed in by busy roads and wire barricades, jammed with visitors throughout the summer, and underscored by a cacophony of roaring traffic, it's a long way from the haven of peace and spiritual tranquillity most visitors expect to find, and was even described by one government department as a 'national disgrace'.

Thankfully, plans are afoot to reinvent the Stonehenge experience. Over the next decade the main A303 road will be tunnelled underneath the monument, the arable fields around Stonehenge will be turned back into chalk downland, and a new visitor centre will be built 2 miles from the site, with regular connecting buses to the stones. Despite the obvious good sense of the plan, progress has been predictably slow; planning applications for the new visitor centre have still not been approved and the rerouting of the road is a long way off. Keep up to speed with developments at www.thestonehengeproject.org.

by forest during the time of Stonehenge's construction.

Around 1500 BC, Stonehenge's main stones were dragged to the site, erected in a circle and topped by massive lintels to make the trilithons (two vertical stones topped by a horizontal one). The sarsen (sandstone) stones were cut from an extremely hard rock found on the Marlborough Downs 20 miles from the site. It's estimated that dragging one of these 50-ton stones across the countryside to Stonehenge would require about 600 people.

Also around this time, the bluestones from 500 years earlier were rearranged as an **inner horseshoe** with an **altar stone** at the centre. Outside this a second horseshoe of five trilithons was erected. Three of these are intact; the other two have just a single upright. Then came the major circle of 30 massive vertical stones, of which 17 uprights and six lintels remain.

Further out, another circle is delineated by the 58 **Aubrey Holes**, named after John Aubrey, who discovered them in the 1600s. Just inside this circle are the **South and North Barrows**, each originally topped by a stone. Like many stone circles in Britain (including Avebury), the inner horseshoes are aligned to coincide with sunrise at the midsummer solstice, which seems to support the theory that the site was some kind of astronomical calendar.

Prehistoric pilgrims would have entered the site via the **Avenue**, whose entrance to the

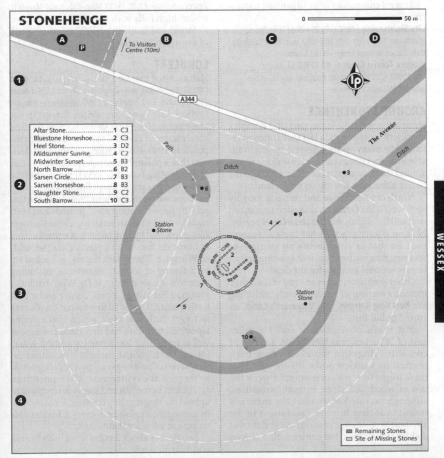

STONEHENGE

0 — 50 m

Altar Stone	1	C3
Bluestone Horseshoe	2	C3
Heel Stone	3	D2
Midsummer Sunrise	4	C2
Midwinter Sunset	5	B3
North Barrow	6	B2
Sarsen Circle	7	B3
Sarsen Horseshoe	8	B3
Slaughter Stone	9	C2
South Barrow	10	C3

To Visitors Centre (10m)

A344

Path

The Avenue

Ditch

Ditch

Station Stone

Station Stone

■ Remaining Stones
□ Site of Missing Stones

circle is marked by the **Slaughter Stone** and the **Heel Stone**, located slightly further out on one side.

A marked pathway leads around the site, and although you're not permitted to walk into the circle itself, it's still possible to see the stones fairly close up. An audio guide is included in the admission price.

Private tours into the circle can be arranged outside normal opening hours by calling ☎ 01722-343834, but you'll need to book well in advance.

Getting There & Away

Bus 3 connects Salisbury bus station with Stonehenge (40 minutes, nine daily, eight on Sunday) via Old Sarum.

Several companies offer organised tours – try:

City Sightseeing (☎ 01789-294466; £16 including admission; 3 daily Apr-Oct) Two-hour tours from Salisbury train station to Stonehenge via Old Sarum.

Wessex Tourist Guides (☎ 01980-623463 or ☎ 01980-620596) Specialist local tour guides recommended by English Heritage.

AROUND STONEHENGE

Stonehenge actually forms part of a complex of ancient monuments, a fact that's often overlooked by many visitors. Several leaflets available from the visitor centre detail walking routes around the main sites; most are accessible to the public although a few are on public land.

North of Stonehenge and running roughly east–west is the **Cursus**, an elongated embanked oval and the slightly smaller **Lesser Cursus** nearby. No-one is sure exactly what these sites were used for, but as usual there's no shortage of theories, ranging from ancient sporting arenas to processional avenues for the dead.

Other prehistoric sites around Stonehenge include a number of burial mounds, including the **New King Barrows**, and **Vespasian's Camp**, an Iron Age hill fort.

Just north of Amesbury and 1½ miles east of Stonehenge is **Woodhenge**, a series of concentric rings that would once have been marked by wooden posts. It's thought that there might be some correlation between the use of wood and stone in both structures, although no-one knows what the materials meant to ancient Britons. Excavations in the 1970s at Woodhenge revealed the skeleton of a child buried near the centre with a cloven skull.

STOURHEAD

Inspired by classical Italy, **Stourhead** (NT; ☎ 01747-841152; Stourton; admission garden or house £6.20, house & garden £10.40; ☉ house 11am-5pm Fri-Tue mid-Mar–Oct, garden 9am-7pm or sunset year-round) is landscape gardening at its finest. The Palladian house has some fine Chippendale furniture and paintings by Claude and Gaspard Poussin, but for most visitors it's the sideshow to the magnificent 18th-century gardens, which spread out across the valley and feature stunning vistas, rare plants, magnificent trees and ornate temples. A lovely 2-mile circuit takes you past the most ornate follies, around the lake and to the **Temple of Apollo**. If you're feeling energetic, from near the **Pantheon**, a 3½-mile side trip can be made to **King Alfred's Tower** (admission £2.30; ☉ 11.30am-4.30pm mid-Mar–Oct), a 50m-high folly with wonderful views.

Stourhead is off the B3092, 8 miles south of Frome in Somerset.

LONGLEAT

Half ancestral mansion, half safari park, **Longleat** (☎ 01985-844400; www.longleat.co.uk; adult/child house £10/7, grounds £3/2, safari park £10/7, all-inclusive passport £19/15; ☉ house 10am-5.30pm, safari park 10am-4pm Apr-Nov, other attractions 11am-5.30pm Apr-Nov) became the first stately home in England to open its doors to the public in 1946. It was more a commercial decision than a philanthropic enterprise; heavy taxes and mounting bills after WWII meant that the house had to earn its keep. Britain's first safari park opened on the estate in 1966, and soon Capability Brown's landscaped grounds had been transformed into an amazing drive-through zoo, populated by a menagerie of animals more at home on the African plains than the fields of Wiltshire. These days the zoo is backed up by a throng of touristy attractions, including a narrow-gauge railway, a Dr Who exhibit, a Postman Pat village, a pets' corner and a butterfly garden. Under all this tourist tat it's easy to forget the house itself, which contains fine tapestries, furniture and decorated ceilings, as well as seven libraries containing around 40,000 tomes. The highlight, though, is an extraordinary series of paintings and psychedelic murals by the present-day Marquess, who trained as an art student in the '60s and seems determined to uphold the longstanding tradition for eccentricity among the English aristocracy. Check out his website at www.lordbath.co.uk.

Longleat is about 3 miles from both Frome and Warminster.

BRADFORD-ON-AVON

☎ 01225 / pop 8800

Tumbling down the slopes of a wooded hillside to the banks of the River Avon, the beautiful amber-coloured town of Bradford is one of Wiltshire's prettiest – a handsome jumble of Georgian townhouses and riverside buildings that makes a pleasant day trip from Bath, just 8 miles away.

The **tourist office** (☎ 865797; www.bradfordonavon .co.uk; ☼ 10am-5pm Apr-Oct, 10am-4pm Mon-Sat, 11am-3pm Sun Nov-Mar) stocks leaflets on guided rambles around the town and can help with accommodation.

Sights & Activities

Bradford grew rich in the 17th and 18th centuries as a thriving centre for the weaving industry, and the town's elegant architecture serves as a reminder of its former wealth. There are some glorious houses scattered around the town, best seen along **Middle Rank** and **Tory**; but the town's most important building is much older, dating back to some time in the early 11th century. The tiny church of **St Laurence** is one of the last surviving Saxon

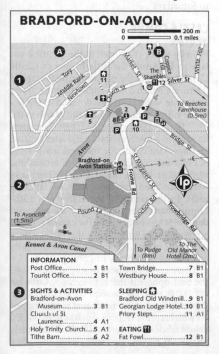

BRADFORD-ON-AVON

0 _____ 200 m
0 _____ 0.1 miles

INFORMATION		
Post Office	1	B1
Tourist Office	2	B1

SIGHTS & ACTIVITIES		
Bradford-on-Avon		
Museum	3	B1
Church of St		
Laurence	4	A1
Holy Trinity Church	5	A1
Tithe Barn	6	A2

Town Bridge	7	B1
Westbury House	8	B1

SLEEPING		
Bradford Old Windmill	9	B1
Georgian Lodge Hotel	10	B1
Priory Steps	11	A1

EATING		
Fat Fowl	12	B1

churches in Britain, and is particularly noted for the twin angels carved above the chancel arch, discovered in 1856.

Near the river is **Westbury House**, where a riot against the introduction of factory machinery in 1791 led to three deaths. The machinery in question was subsequently burned on **Town Bridge**. The unusual room jutting out from the bridge was originally a chapel but was later used as a jail.

Across the river a riverside path leads to the 14th-century **Tithe Barn** (EH; admission free; ☼ 10.30am-4pm) on the bank of the Kennet and Avon Canal. The barn originally belonged to monks from nearby Shaftesbury Abbey, and was used to store tithes (a one-tenth tax made on local landowners) during the Middle Ages. It's worth visiting for its wood-vaulted interior and stone-tiled roof.

The tiny **Bradford-on-Avon Museum** (☎ 863280; Bridge St; admission free; ☼ 10.30am-12.30pm & 2-4pm Wed-Sat, 2-4pm Sun Easter-Oct) is above the library.

Sleeping & Eating

Georgian Lodge Hotel (☎ 862268; www.georgian lodgehotel.com; mains £10-18; s/d £40/80; ☼ lunch & dinner daily) This old coaching hotel sits in the centre of Bradford near the town bridge. The classic British menu serves up generous portions of rib-eye beef and roast monkfish in a bright, understated dining room, and the upstairs rooms are fresh and simple. Only the front rooms have views, but the back ones are usually quieter.

Priory Steps (☎ 862230; www.priorysteps.co.uk; Newtown; s/d £68/82-90) Six weavers' cottages have been knocked into one to form this smart and very contemporary B&B, with five stark, minimalist bedrooms, a lovely library crammed with leather armchairs and old books, and a great silver service restaurant. There's also an open-plan cottage available, but you'll need to book for at least three days.

Bradford Old Windmill (☎ 866842; www.bradfordold windmill.co.uk; 4 Masons Lane; r £79-109; P ✗) This quirky B&B is housed in Bradford's former windmill, and offers a choice of oddly shaped rooms full of character – the top-floor Damsel room has a giant waterbed, whirlpool bath and circular wood-beamed ceiling, while the Fantail room boasts a wrought-iron bed, private sitting room and views across the Bradford countryside.

Fat Fowl (☎ 863111; Silver St; mains from £8; ☼ daily) Bradford's top table is this truly outstanding

---

WORTH THE TRIP

Woolley Grange (☎ 864705; www.woolleygrangehotel.co.uk; Woolley Green; r £145-335; Ⓟ ☒ ☜) This fabulous country house mixes boutique style with a refreshing family-friendly attitude to create one of the most welcoming hotels in Wiltshire. With its designer bedrooms, laid-back attitude and quietly impressive service, it's a place whose *raison d'être* seems to be keeping everyone in a state of mild euphoria throughout their stay; while the little 'uns are kept lavishly entertained with everything from giant trampolines to PlayStation 2s at the Woolley Bear Den, mum and dad can relax with a truly indulgent range of spa treatments, aromatherapy massages, gourmet meals and champagne cocktails by the heated outdoor pool. Rooms are all individually styled, with a smattering of patchwork quilts, shiny antiques and funky fixtures. Pricey, but worth every penny.

French-inspired bistro near the river. Coffees and freshly baked pastries are served on the front terrace, while finer food is dished up in the conservatory dining room or the light-filled restaurant on the 1st floor.

Other options:

Beeches Farmhouse (☎ 865170; www.beeches -farmhouse.co.uk; Holt Rd; s £45-80, d £70-85; Ⓟ ☒) Smartly converted farmhouse mixing rustic touches with en suite luxury.

Old Manor Hotel (☎ 777393; Trowle Common; s £70-90, d £90-130; Ⓟ ☒) Rambling, regal rooms at a beautifully renovated manor house just outside town.

Getting There & Away

Bus X5 travels from Bath to Bradford-on-Avon (30 minutes, hourly, eight on Sunday) en route to Warminster. The X4 travels the same route but continues on to Salisbury (1¾ hours, hourly Monday to Saturday). Trains go roughly hourly from Bath (£3, 15 minutes).

MALMESBURY ABBEY

A wonderful blend of ruin and living church, **Malmesbury Abbey** (☎ 826666; donation requested; ☻ 10am-5pm Mon-Sat mid-Mar–Oct, 10am-4pm Mon-Sat Nov–mid-Mar) has had a somewhat turbulent history. It began life as a 7th-century monastery, which was later replaced by a Norman church. By the mid-15th century the abbey had been embellished with a spire and twin towers; but in 1479 a storm toppled the east tower and spire, destroying the eastern end of the church, and the west tower followed suit in 1662, destroying much of the nave. The present-day church is about a third of its original size, and is flanked by ruins at either end. Notable features include the Norman doorway decorated with biblical carvings, the Romanesque **Apostle** carvings and a four-volume, illuminated bible dating from

1407. A window at the western end of the church depicts Elmer the Flying Monk, who in 1010 strapped on wings and jumped from the tower. Although he broke both legs, he survived and became a local hero.

Just below the abbey are the **Abbey House Gardens** (☎ 822212; www.abbeyhousegardens.co.uk; admission £5.50; ☻ 11am-5.30pm mid-Mar–mid-Oct) with a herb garden, river, waterfall and five acres of colourful blooms.

Bus 31 runs to Swindon (45 minutes, hourly Monday to Saturday), while 92 heads to Chippenham (35 minutes, hourly Monday to Saturday).

CASTLE COMBE
☎ 01249

Proudly trumpeting itself as the 'prettiest village in England', the little hamlet of Castle Combe presents the picture-perfect image of the rural English countryside – its quiet streets and stone-walled cottages doubled as the fictional village of Puddleby-on-the-Marsh in the 1967 film of *Doctor Dolittle*. The village grew up around a medieval castle and later became an important centre for the local wool trade: old weavers' cottages are huddled around the medieval packhorse bridge, and the riverbanks were once lined with more than 20 clattering mills. In the centre of the village is a 13th-century **market cross**, and nearby, the medieval **church of St Andrew** contains the carved tomb of Sir Walter de Dunstanville, the 13th-century lord of the manor, who fought in the Crusades and was killed in battle in 1270.

There are a few places to stay in the village: the best option is the 12th-century **Castle Inn** (☎ 783030; www.castle-inn.info; s £75.50-95, d £100-165; ☒), offering smartly renovated rooms topped off with luxurious touches such as free cookies, deluxe fabrics and whirlpool baths. The homely restaurant serves up classic dishes including tenderloin of pork and rack of lamb (£11 to £18), as well as a rather special Sunday lunch.

Alternatively, try the **White Hart** (☎ 782295; mains £6-12) for warm beer, cheap eats and country atmosphere.

Between them buses 35, 635 and 75 run to Chippenham bus station (30 minutes) six times daily Monday to Friday and four times on Saturday. There's also a direct bus to Bath on Wednesday (one hour).

LACOCK
☎ 01249

With its geranium-covered cottages, higgledy-piggledy rooftops and idyllic location next to a rushing brook, the medieval village of Lacock seems to have been preserved in aspic since the mid-19th century. The village has been in the hands of the National Trust since 1944, and is almost entirely untouched by modern development – there are no telephone poles or electric streetlights, and it's kept largely free of traffic thanks to the main visitor car park on the outskirts of the village. Unsurprisingly, it's also a popular location for costume dramas and feature films – parts of the *Harry Potter* films, as well as BBC adaptations of *Moll Flanders* and *Pride and Prejudice*, were all filmed here.

Lacock Abbey

Lacock Abbey (NT; ☎ 730227; admission abbey, museum, cloisters & grounds £7.80, abbey, cloisters & grounds only £6.30; ☉ abbey 1-5.30pm Wed-Mon Mar-Oct, gardens 11am-5.30pm Feb-Oct) was founded as an Augustinian nunnery in 1232 by Ela, Countess of Salisbury. After the Dissolution the abbey was sold to Sir William Sharington in 1539, who converted the nunnery into a home, demolished the church, tacked a tower onto the corner of the abbey and added a brewery. The wonderful Gothic entrance hall is lined with bizarre terracotta figures; spot the scapegoat with a lump of sugar on its nose. Some of the original 13th-century structure is evident in the cloisters and there are traces of medieval wall paintings. The recently restored botanic garden is also worth a visit.

In the early 19th century, William Henry Fox Talbot (1800–77), a prolific inventor, developed the photographic negative while working at the abbey: the **Fox Talbot Museum of Photography** (☎ 730459; admission museum, cloisters & grounds only £4.80; ☉ 11am-5.30pm Mar-Oct, 11am-4pm weekends Nov-Feb) details his ground-breaking work and displays a fine collection of his photographs.

Sleeping & Eating

King John's Hunting Lodge (☎ 730313; kingjohns@ amserve.com; 21 Church St; s/d £55/95; tearooms ☉ 11am-5.30pm) This tearoom-cum-B&B is a local landmark in more ways than one – it's housed in Lacock's oldest building and run by one of the village's biggest characters, an ex-shepherdess, nurse and celebrity chef. Local specialities such as 'priddy oggies' (a cheese pastry with pork, bacon and stilton), cheese muffins and homemade elderflower cordial all find their way onto the eclectic menu, and upstairs you'll find snug, old-fashioned rooms crammed with quirky furniture and Tudor touches.

our pick **Sign of the Angel** (☎ 730230; www.lacock .co.uk; 6 Church St; s £75, d £105-155; **P**) This charmingly eccentric country restaurant and hotel makes a memorable place for an overnight stay. Rough wooden benches, rustic beams and old washpresses are scattered around the twin dining rooms, each of which boasts a crackling log-fire, and the same old-world

WESSEX

WORTH THE TRIP

Whatley Manor (☎ 01666-822888; www.whatleymanor.com; Easton Grey; d £280-480, suites £605-805; **P** ☒ ☲) If you happen to be a holidaying film star or celebrity supermodel, then it's time to whip out your platinum card and book your suite at this jaw-dropping hotel, which takes louche luxury and designer pampering to a whole new level. Housed in a stunningly restored Cotswold manor house in the village of Easton Grey, 3 miles west of Malmesbury, it's quite simply one of the poshest, plushest hotels in Britain, blending period architecture and a glorious country setting with a razor-sharp eye for interior design. Underfloor heating, Bang & Olufsen stereos, presidential beds and massive bathroom suites distinguish every room; there are also two award-winning restaurants, 12 acres of landscaped gardens and a futuristic spa that's been voted the best in Europe. Oh, and there's a private cinema too, just in case you need somewhere to screen your dailies.

feel is carried through into the upstairs rooms, where you'll find antique beds and burnished chests crammed in under the low ceilings. The restaurant specialises in traditional, old-fashioned English cooking – our tip is the 'angel plate' of cold meats and bubble and squeak, followed by treacle tart with clotted cream.

Other options:

George Inn (☎ 730263; 4 West St; mains from £8) A dinky 13th-century pub on the edge of the village, dispensing local ales and pub food.

Old Rectory (☎ 730335; www.oldrectorylacock.co.uk; s £35-50, d £60-75; P ✗) Elegant Victorian-style rooms in a Grade II–listed house dotted with stained glass windows and patterned rugs.

Getting There & Away

Bus 234 runs hourly from Chippenham (Monday to Saturday, 20 minutes).

AROUND LACOCK
Corsham Court

Two miles northwest of Lacock, the Elizabethan mansion of **Corsham Court** (☎ 01249-701610; www.corsham-court.co.uk; admission £6.50; ⏱ 2-5.30pm Tue-Thu & weekends Mar-Sep, 2-4.30pm weekends Oct–late-Mar) dates from 1582, although the house and grounds were later improved by John Nash and Capability Brown. The house is renowned for its superb art collection, which features works by Reynolds, Caravaggio, Rubens and Van Dyck, and for its formal gardens, which contain some stunning ornamental box hedges and a Gothic bathhouse.

DEVIZES

☎ 01380 / pop 14,379

The busy market town of Devizes is famous for its grand semicircular marketplace – the largest anywhere in England – but apart from some intriguing Georgian architecture and two fine churches, there's not a great deal to keep you entertained. Nevertheless, the town makes a handy base for exploring southern Wiltshire and nearby Avebury.

The **tourist office** (☎ 729408; kennet@kennet.gov.uk; Cromwell House, Market Pl; ⏱ 9.30am-5pm Mon-Sat) has a couple of useful walking leaflets around town and can help with local accommodation.

Sights

Between St John's St and High St, **St John's Alley** has a wonderful collection of Elizabethan houses, their upper storeys cantilevered over the street. **St John's Church**, on Market Pl, dis-

plays elements of its original Norman construction, particularly in the solid crossing tower. Other interesting buildings include the **Corn Exchange**, topped by a figure of Ceres, goddess of agriculture, and the **Old Town Hall** of 1750–52.

The **Wiltshire Heritage Museum & Gallery** (☎ 727369; www.wiltshireheritage.org.uk; 41 Long St; adult/under 16yrs £4/free, free Sun & Mon; ⏱ 10am-5pm Mon-Sat, noon-4pm Sun) is worth a look for its collection of artefacts from Avebury, Stonehenge and other burial barrows across Wiltshire.

The **Kennet & Avon Canal Museum** (☎ 729489; The Wharf; adult/child £1.75/50p; ⏱ 10am-5pm Easter-Sep, 10am-4pm Oct-Easter) explores the history of this historic canal. On the western outskirts of Devizes are the 29 successive locks at **Caen Hill**, which raise the water level 72m in just 2½ miles.

Sleeping & Eating

Eastleigh House (☎ 726918; www.eastleighhouse .co.uk; 3 Eastleigh Rd; s/d £34/55; P ✗) A reliable and welcoming B&B in a modern red-brick townhouse, with several pleasant if unremarkable rooms, swapping the usual chintz and prints for simple colours and plain fabrics.

Blounts Court Farm (☎ 727180; www.blountscourtfarm .co.uk; s/d £34/56; P ✗) Surrounded by 150 acres of working arable land, this lovely farmhouse B&B offers a selection of pleasant ground-floor rooms in a converted barn. Pine doors, country ornaments and flowery duvets feature in every room, and a couple have pretty four-poster beds.

Rosemundy Cottage (☎ 727122; www.rosemundy cottage.co.uk; London Rd; s/d £32/55; ▢ wi-fi) Modern B&B with welcome extras including wi-fi and digital TV.

Bear Hotel (☎ 0845 456 5334; www.thebearhotel.net; Market Pl; s/d £70/95; P ✗) Rambling old coaching inn with 25 recently refurbished rooms and a decent restaurant.

Getting There & Away

Bus 49/X49 serves Avebury (25 minutes, hourly Monday to Saturday, five on Sunday), while bus 2 runs from Salisbury (1¼ hours, hourly Monday to Saturday).

AROUND DEVIZES
Bowood House

The stately **Bowood House** (☎ 01249-812102; www .bowood.org; adult/child £7.50/5; ⏱ 11am-5.30pm Apr-Oct) was first built around 1725 and has been home to the successive earls of Shelburne (now the Marquess of Lansdowne) since 1754. The house has an impressive picture gallery and a fine sculpture gallery, as well as the laboratory where Dr Joseph Priestly discovered oxygen in 1774. The gardens, designed by Capability Brown, are an attraction in themselves and Include a terraced rose garden.

Bowood is 3 miles southeast of Chippenham and 6 miles northwest of Devizes.

AVEBURY
☎ 01672

While the tour buses and snap-happy tourists make a beeline for Stonehenge, prehistoric purists head for the massive ring of stones at **Avebury** instead. Though it lacks the huge stones and dramatic trilothons of its sister site across the plain, Avebury is arguably a much more rewarding place to visit: it's bigger, older and much quieter than Stonehenge, and judging by its huge scale, and its location at the centre of a complex of barrows, burial chambers and processional avenues, it may also have been a more Important ceremonial site to its ancient builders.

Orientation & Information

The village itself is entirely encircled by the stones and neatly bissected by two main roads, but it's much easier to take advantage of the National Trust car park on the A4361, just a short walk from the village. The **tourist office** (☎ 539425; all.tic@kennet.gov.uk; Chapel Centre, Green St; ☺ 9.30am-5pm Tue-Sun) is housed in a converted chapel near the centre of the village.

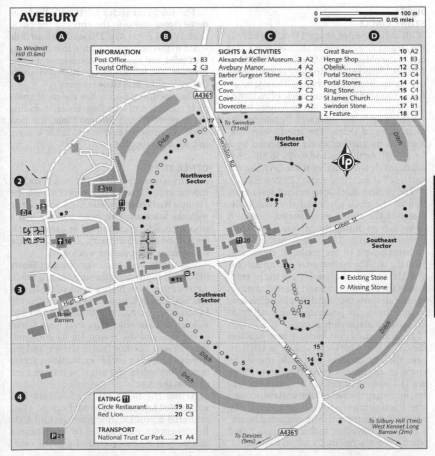

AVEBURY

0 ――――― 100 m
0 ――――― 0.05 miles

INFORMATION
Post Office...................1 B3
Tourist Office................2 C3

SIGHTS & ACTIVITIES
Alexander Keiller Museum...3 A2
Avebury Manor...............4 A2
Barber Surgeon Stone.......5 C4
Cove........................6 C2
Cove........................7 C2
Cove........................8 C2
Dovecote....................9 A2
Great Barn.................10 A2
Henge Shop.................11 B3
Obelisk....................12 C3
Portal Stones..............13 C4
Portal Stones..............14 C4
Ring Stone.................15 C4
St James Church............16 A3
Swindon Stone..............17 B1
Z Feature..................18 C3

EATING 🍴
Circle Restaurant..........19 B2
Red Lion...................20 C3

TRANSPORT
National Trust Car Park....21 A4

● Existing Stone
○ Missing Stone

WESSEX

CROP CIRCLE CENTRAL

Wiltshire is famous across the world for its astonishing **crop circles**. These strange symmetrical patterns regularly appear in farmers' fields and areas of grassland across the county, and can range from basic circles to mind-boggling complex fractal designs. An entire industry has sprung up around the circles; scientists have sampled the molecular structure and chemical composition of the affected areas, conspiracy theorists have posted countless blogs, and a bewildering number of books have been published claiming to explain the secrets of the circles. Some people believe they're caused by extra-terrestrial life-forms or freak weather patterns, while others are convinced they're simply the work of practical jokers with a penchant for high-school geometry. Check out www.cropcircleconnector.com, which has regular updates on new circles, or www.circlemakers .org, which claims to spill the beans on how the mysterious rings are made.

If you fancy spotting a circle for yourself, the best areas to see them are around the Marlborough Downs and Pewsey Vale; you can usually pick up tips at the **Barge Inn** (☎ 01672-851705) in Honeystreet, 5 miles east of Devizes, where the pool room has been devoted to detailing all the latest finds.

Sights

STONE CIRCLE

With a diameter of about 348m, Avebury is the largest stone circle in the world. It's also one of the oldest, dating from around 2500 to 2200 BC, between the first and second phase of construction at Stonehenge. The site originally consisted of an outer circle of 98 standing stones from 3m to 6m in length, many weighing up to 20 tons, carefully selected for their size and shape. The stones were surrounded by another circle delineated by a 5½m-high earth bank and a 6m- to 9m-deep ditch. Inside were smaller stone circles to the north (27 stones) and south (29 stones).

The present-day site represents just a fraction of the circle's original size; tragically, many of the stones were buried, removed or broken up during the Middle Ages, when Britain's pagan past became something of an embarrassment to the medieval church. In 1934 the wealthy businessman and archaeologist Alexander Keiller supervised the re-erection of the buried stones and planted markers to indicate those that had disappeared; he later bought the site for posterity using funds from his family's marmalade fortune.

Modern roads into Avebury neatly dissect the circle into four sectors. Start at High St, near the Henge Shop, and walk round the circle in an anticlockwise direction. There are 11 standing stones in the southwest sector, including the **Barber Surgeon Stone**, named after the skeleton of a man found under it. The equipment buried with him suggested he was a medieval travelling barber-surgeon, killed when a stone accidentally fell on him.

The southeast sector starts with the huge **portal stones** marking the entry to the circle from West Kennet Ave. The **southern inner circle** stood in this sector and within this circle was the **Obelisk** and a group of stones known as the **Z Feature**. Just outside this smaller circle, only the base of the **Ring Stone** remains.

The northwest sector has the most complete collection of standing stones, including the massive 65-ton **Swindon Stone**, the first stone encountered and one of the few never to have been toppled.

OTHER SITES

Avebury is surrounded by a network of ancient monuments. Lined by 100 pairs of stones, the 1½-mile **West Kennet Ave** links the Avebury circle with the **Sanctuary**. Post holes indicate that a wooden building surrounded by a stone circle once stood at the Sanctuary, although no-one knows quite what the site was for.

Just to the west, the huge dome of **Silbury Hill** rises abruptly from the surrounding fields. At more than 40m high, it's one of the largest artificial hills in Europe, and was constructed in stages from around 2500 BC, but no significant ancient relics have ever been found at the site, and the reason for its construction remains unclear. Due to erosion and the damage caused by earlier excavations, access is now forbidden; you can view it from a car park on the A4.

Across the fields south of Silbury Hill stands **West Kennet Long Barrow**, England's finest burial mound, dating from around 3500 BC. Its entrance is guarded by huge sarsens and its roof is constructed of gigantic overlapping capstones. About 50 skeletons were found when it was excavated and finds are on display at the Wiltshire Heritage Museum & Gallery in Devizes (p320).

Northwest of the Avebury circle you'll find **Windmill Hill**, a Neolithic enclosure or 'camp' dating from about 3700 BC, the earliest site in the area.

The **Ridgeway national trail** starts near Avebury and runs westwards across **Fyfield Down**, where many of the sarsen stones at Avebury (and Stonehenge) were collected.

AVEBURY MANOR

Avebury Manor (NT; ☎ 539250; admission manor £3.80, garden only £2.90; ☽ manor 2-4.40pm Sun-Tue, gardens 11am-5pm Fri-Tue) dates back to the 16th century but was later modified during the Edwardian era. Keiller bought the manor in 1939 and spent much of his later life here; now owned by the National Trust, the house is still used as a private residence, but it's a little scant on attractions. Entry is by timed ticket.

Housed in the old stables of Avebury Manor, the **Alexander Keiller Museum** (NT; ☎ 539250; admission £4.20; ☽ 10am-6pm Apr-Oct, 10am-4pm Nov-Mar) explores the archaeological history of the circle and traces the story of the man who dedicated his life to unlocking the secret of the stones.

Sleeping & Eating

Red Lion (☎ 539266; redlion.avebury@whitbread.com; d from £60; mains from £10; **P** ✗) There's not much accommodation in the village itself, although if you get stuck this thatched pub has a few basic upstairs rooms. Sensitive types might choose to stay elsewhere, however – the pub is notoriously haunted by the ghost of Flori, a woman who was supposedly murdered here by her jealous husband during the English Civil War. The medieval well she was supposedly thrown down now forms the centrepiece of the rustic dining room.

Circle Restaurant (☎ 539514; mains from £6; ☽ lunch) This lovely veggie/wholefood café beside the Great Barn serves delicious sandwiches, cakes and afternoon teas.

Getting There & Away

Bus 5 runs to Avebury from Salisbury (1½ hours, four or five Monday to Saturday). Bus 49/X49 serves Swindon (30 minutes) and Devizes (25 minutes, hourly Monday to Saturday, five on Sunday).

WESSEX

Devon & Cornwall

Jutting out into the grey Atlantic Ocean on a narrow sliver of land, the neighbouring counties of Devon and Cornwall collectively make up an area known as the Westcountry – a rural landscape of quiet hamlets, jewel-green meadows and winding backcountry lanes, ringed by the most breathtaking coastline anywhere in Britain. Unsurprisingly, it's one of Britain's top holiday spots, and every year millions of visitors flock to the region's shores to feel the sand between their toes – but there's much more to this fascinating region than just candy-floss and clifftop views.

Though Devon and Cornwall have long been relegated to the realms of coach tours and bucket-and-spade holidays, things are really starting to change out west. Gastropubs, designer bars and boutique hotels are opening up practically everywhere you look. Old fishing harbours, derelict mining towns and faded seaside resorts are reinventing themselves for the 21st century as cultural centres, artistic havens and gastronomic hubs. Giant greenhouses are springing up in abandoned clay pits, forgotten gardens are emerging from the undergrowth and celebrity chefs are setting up shop by the seaside in their droves. After decades of economic underinvestment, industrial decline, and downright metropolitan snobbery, it seems everybody wants a slice of the Westcountry lifestyle these days – whether it's weekend surfers looking for an offshore break, urban warriors in search of the great outdoors or city slickers looking to escape the hustle and hum of the modern world.

HIGHLIGHTS

- Visiting the towering Gothic cathedral in **Exeter** (p329)
- Exploring the secluded beaches and clifftops around the **Lizard** (p356) and Cornwall's **north coast** (p367)
- Taking to the trail around the tors and hills of **Dartmoor** (p342)
- Sampling the world-class cuisine at the restaurants around **Padstow** (p371) and **Dartmouth** (p335)
- Exploring the beautiful landscaped gardens of **Trebah** (p357), **Glendurgan** (p357) and **Heligan** (p354)
- Marvelling at the world's most extravagant greenhouses at the **Eden Project** (p353)

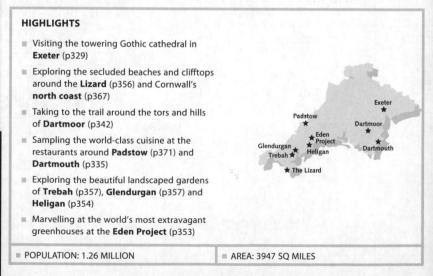

- POPULATION: 1.26 MILLION
- AREA: 3947 SQ MILES

Orientation & Information

Imagine this region as the leg of England. Devon is the thigh, Cornwall the calf and foot; Plymouth sits at the back of the knee, while the Isles of Scilly hover above the toe of Land's End. With the exception of Dartmoor, most of the region's attractions line the coast.

The **South West Tourist Board** (www.visitsouthwest.com) covers a huge area from Gloucester and Dorset down to the Isles of Scilly, and has links to several themed subsites exploring nature, adventure, family and heritage holidays around the region.

Stranger Magazine (www.stranger-mag.com) is a new publication that keeps its finger firmly on the region's pulse – you can pick it up for £1.50 from bookshops, cafés and surf shops all over Cornwall, Devon and Bristol.

The free monthly listings magazine **twenty4-seven** (www.twenty4-seven.co.uk) covers all the latest bars, gigs and clubs, and is available from tourist offices, bars and restaurants around the region.

Activities

With some of the most beautiful countryside anywhere in Britain, Devon and Cornwall are perfect for all kinds of outdoor activities. Tourist offices can provide information on most outdoor sports, and for more adventurous pastimes there are some excellent outdoor centres dotted around the region.

CYCLING

Devon and Cornwall are becoming increasingly popular with cyclists. Several sections of the National Cycle Network (NCN) cross the region, including the **West Country Way** (NCN Route 3), a 250-mile jaunt from Bristol to Padstow via Glastonbury, Taunton and Barnstaple, and the **Devon Coast to Coast Cycle Route** (NCN Route 27), which travels for 102 miles between Exmoor and Dartmoor.

Many cycle trails trace the routes of old railway lines, including the 11-mile **Granite Way**, which travels along a disused line between Okehampton and Lydford, passing across the Meldon Viaduct en route; and the popular **Camel Trail** (p370) linking Padstow with Wadebridge. Bikes can be hired in most large towns, including Plymouth, Penzance, Exeter and Padstow.

SURFING

Cornwall is Britain's surfing mecca, with breaks running all the way from Porthleven (near Helston) in Cornwall, west around Land's End and along the north coast. Popular spots include Newquay, Perranporth, St Agnes and Bude in Cornwall, and Croyde in north Devon. The latest surf updates can be found online at www.a1surf.com.

WALKING

At 610 miles the **South West Coast Path** is Britain's longest national trail. You can pick it up at many points along the coast for a short (and spectacular) day's stroll, or tackle longer stretches between the main coastal towns. The South West Coast Path Association (www.swcp.org.uk) publishes an annual guide.

Dartmoor is another favourite location for walkers, with some of the highest hills and best hiking trails in southern England. The park is crisscrossed by several walking routes – see the boxed text Dartmoor Hikes, p345.

OTHER ACTIVITIES

Devon and Cornwall's more esoteric pursuits include horse riding on Exmoor and Dartmoor, rock climbing on the cliffs of Cornwall, windsurfing, kitesurfing and kiteboarding on the region's beaches and scuba diving around Cornwall's shipwrecks. The adrenaline-fuelled thrills don't stop there, though – caving, coasteering, mountainboarding, wakesurfing and kitebuggying are all popular pastimes in these parts. Check out www.adventuresw.co.uk for info on just about every adventure sport you could think of.

Getting Around

Local tourist offices are trying hard to promote ways to get around the counties without resorting to the good old automobile, but the reality is to reach the more out of the way spots you'll need your own wheels. But if you're just sticking to the main towns and sights, it's quite possible to get around by bus and train. Timetables and transport maps are available from stations and tourist offices, and the handy *Car-Free Days Out* (www.carfreedaysout.com) booklet has comprehensive public-transport listings.

BUS

The region's main cities are served by regular National Express coaches, which are usually much quicker (and more reliable) than local buses. Transport routes become patchy the further you move away from the main

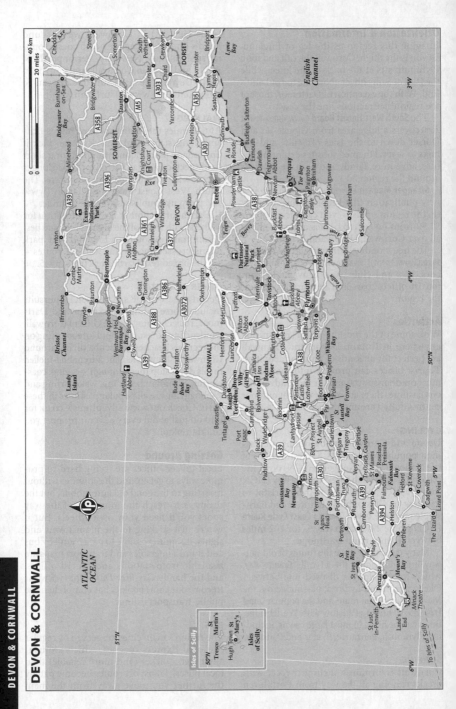

DEVON & CORNWALL

towns; Dartmoor and west Cornwall are particularly tricky to negotiate. For regional timetables, call ☎ 01392-382800 in Devon, or ☎ 01872-322142 in Cornwall or contact **Traveline** (☎ 0870 608 2608; www.travelinesw.com).

The **First group** (☎ 0845 600 1420; www.firstgroup .com) provides the majority of the region's bus services. The First Bus & Rail Card (one/seven days £11/44) allows unlimited travel for one day on First Great Western trains and most First buses in Cornwall and Devon. The pass can be bought from bus drivers and main train stations. The Firstday Southwest (adult £7) is valid on First buses in Devon and Cornwall, as well as Bristol, Somerset, Gloucestershire and Dorset.

The PlusBus scheme allows you to add on bus travel around many main towns (including Plymouth, Exeter, Truro, Falmouth, Penzance and Bodmin) to your train ticket from around £2 per day – ask at any train station or consult www.plusbus.info.

TRAIN

Train services are mostly limited to the south coast. Beyond Exeter, a single line follows the coast as far as Penzance, with spurs to Barnstaple, Paignton, Gunnislake, Looe, Falmouth, St Ives and Newquay. The line from Exeter to Penzance is one of England's most scenic routes.

Several regional rail passes are available from train stations, including the Freedom of the SouthWest Rover pass (adult £61), which allows eight days' unlimited travel over 15 days in an area west of (and including) Salisbury, Bath, Bristol and Weymouth.

The Devon and Cornwall Rover ticket allows unlimited travel across the train network throughout Devon and Cornwall. It's available either for three day's travel in one week (£40), or eight day's travel in 15 (£60); it can be bought at most main train stations.

DEVON

Picture-perfect Devon has long been one of the country's favourite holiday destinations, and with such a smorgasbord of natural wonders, it's not hard to see what keeps the holidaymakers coming back. Blanketed with patchwork pastures, dotted with rural villages, and bordered by some of the country's most stunning coastline, it's a county with

---

> **CAMPER CAPERS**
>
> Want to tour the southwest in style? Then you'll need your own vintage VW campervan, complete with grill, fridge, crockery, cutlery, four bunk beds and the kitchen sink. Contact **O'Connor's Campers** (☎ 01837-659599; www.oconnorscampers .co.uk) in Okehampton or **Kernow Kampers** (☎ 01637-830027; www.kernowkampers.co.uk) near Newquay. Prices start from around £375 per week; surfboards and sunglasses not included.

something to offer everyone: a place to walk the hills, roam the fields and bike the bridleways before stuffing yourself with some hearty Devonian cooking in a backcountry inn. If it's the quintessentially kitsch British seaside you're after, then head for the chintzy seaside resorts of Torquay, Paignton and Ilfracombe, and for a bit more class, the ancient Roman city of Exeter has some of the best preserved medieval architecture in the southwest, not to mention one of its most impressive cathedrals. And if you're really looking to get away from it all, the wild expanse of Dartmoor makes the perfect place to escape the summertime crowds.

Orientation & Information

Devon is bounded to the east by Somerset and Dorset, the border skirting the southern edge of Exmoor and hitting the coast west of Lyme Regis. The border with Cornwall follows the River Tamar from its source near the north Devon coast to the estuary at Plymouth. Dartmoor claims much of the inland area between Plymouth and Exeter in the east.

The Discover Devon website (www.discov erdevon.com) has plenty of useful information to get you started.

Getting Around

Contact the **Devon County Public Transport Help Line** (☎ 01392-382800; www.devon.gov.uk/devonbus; ⏱ 9am-5pm Mon-Fri) for information and timetables. It also provides the invaluable *Devon Public Transport Map* and the *Discovery Guide to Dartmoor*.

First Western National (☎ 01271-376524; www .firstgroup.com) serves most of north Devon and much of the south and east, including most Dartmoor services.

Stagecoach Devon (☎ 01392-427711; www.stage coachbus.com) operates mostly local services and buses from Plymouth to Exeter or Totnes. Timetables are available to download from the website. The Day Explorer (adult £5) allows one day's travel on Stagecoach Devon buses, while the Goldrider pass (one week £18) is valid for a week.

Devon's rail network skirts along the south coast through Exeter and Plymouth to Cornwall. There are picturesque stretches where the line hugs the seashore. Two branch lines run north: the 39-mile Tarka Line from Exeter to Barnstaple and the 15-mile Tamar Valley Line from Plymouth to Gunnislake. The Devon Day Ranger (£10) allows a day's unlimited travel on Devon trains including Plymouth and the Tamar Valley line.

EXETER

☎ 01392 / pop 116,393

Though it's often eclipsed by the better-known cities of Bristol and Bath, Exeter is well worth visiting in its own right, with a thriving nightlife, a lively cultural scene and a rich history stretching back 2000 years. Founded by Celts and expanded by the Romans, Exeter grew rich as a trading port during the early Middle Ages, and the city's fortunes were demonstrated by the completion of its glorious Gothic cathedral in the early 15th century. Exeter suffered heavily during the Luftwaffe raids of WWII, although the cathedral close survived relatively intact, and still boasts some fine medieval architecture. It might be old, but Exeter's kept young at heart thanks to a large student crowd and plenty of bars, cafés and clubs, especially around the revitalised dock area.

History

Archaeological digs have revealed evidence of a Celtic settlement on the banks of the River Exe, but the modern-day city was built on the foundations laid by the Romans, who established Exeter as the administrative capital for the Dumnonii of Devon and Cornwall around AD50. The Romans built a fortified wall around the city, which was later improved by Alfred the Great as protection against Danish raids; parts of both the Roman and Saxon walls can still be seen at various points around the modern city. William the Conqueror laid siege to the city in 1067 and took 18 days to break through the walls. He appointed a Norman *seigneur* (feudal lord) to construct a castle, the ruins of which can still be seen in Rougemont and Northernhay Gardens.

Exeter was a major trading port until a weir was built across the river in 1290, halting river traffic. It wasn't until 1563, when the first ship canal in Britain was dug to bypass the weir, that the city began to re-establish itself, especially through the cloth and wool trade.

Orientation

South of the ruined castle, the city centre radiates out from the leafy square around the cathedral; the redeveloped quay is 500m south. There are two main train stations, Central and St David's; most long-distance trains use St David's, a mile northwest of the centre.

Information

BOOKSHOPS

Waterstone's (☎ 218392; 48-49 High St; ☯ 9am-5.30pm Mon-Fri, 9am-6pm Sat, 10am-4.30pm Sun) Main branch of this large chain bookshop.

EMERGENCY

Police station (☎ 08452 777444; Heavitree Rd; ☯ 24hr)
Royal Devon & Exeter Hospital (☎ 411611; Barrack Rd)

INTERNET ACCESS

Exeter Library (☎ 384201; Castle St; per hr £3; ☯ 9.30am-7pm Mon, Tue, Thu & Fri, 10am-5pm Wed, 9.30am-4pm Sat, 11am-2.30pm Sun)

LAUNDRY

Silverspin (12 Blackboy Rd; ☯ 8am-10pm)
Soaps (Isambard Pde; ☯ 8.15am-7.45pm Mon-Sat, 9.15am-5.45pm Sun; per load £3.50-6) Beside St David's train station.

MEDIA

The List is a free magazine detailing events, listings and bars and restaurants in the Exeter area.

POST

Main branch (☎ 223344; Bedford Rd; ☯ 9am-5.30pm Mon-Sat)

TOURIST INFORMATION

Quay House Interpretation & Visitor Centre (☎ 265213; The Quay; ☯ 10am-5pm Easter-Oct, 11am-4pm weekends only Nov-Easter) Offers tourist information and displays on the quay's history.
Tourist office (☎ 265700; tic@exeter.gov.uk; Paris St; ☯ 9am-5pm Mon-Sat, 10am-4pm Sun Jul & Aug)

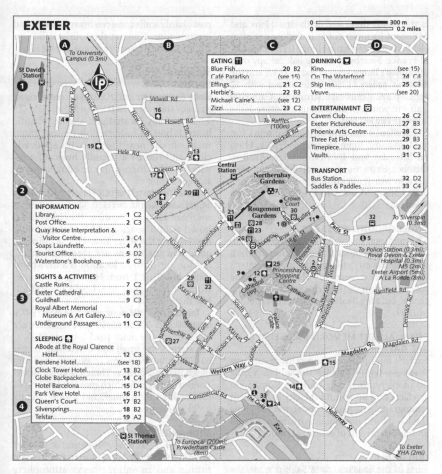

EXETER

EATING 🍴
Blue Fish...................20 B2
Café Paradiso.............(see 15)
Effings........................21 C2
Herbie's.....................22 B3
Michael Caine's..........(see 12)
Zizzi...........................23 C2

DRINKING 🍷
Kino...........................(see 15)
On The Waterfront......24 C4
Ship Inn.....................25 C3
Veuve........................(see 20)

ENTERTAINMENT 🎭
Cavern Club................26 C2
Exeter Picturehouse....27 B3
Phoenix Arts Centre....28 C2
Three Fat Fish.............29 B3
Timepiece..................30 C2
Vaults.......................31 C3

TRANSPORT
Bus Station................32 D2
Saddles & Paddles.......33 C4

INFORMATION
Library.........................1 C2
Post Office...................2 C3
Quay House Interpretation &
    Visitor Centre............3 C4
Soaps Laundrette..........4 A1
Tourist Office................5 D2
Waterstone's Bookshop...6 C3

SIGHTS & ACTIVITIES
Castle Ruins.................7 C2
Exeter Cathedral..........8 C3
Guildhall.....................9 C3
Royal Albert Memorial
    Museum & Art Gallery..10 C2
Underground Passages..11 C2

SLEEPING 🛏
ABode at the Royal Clarence
    Hotel.......................12 C3
Bendene Hotel...........(see 18)
Clock Tower Hotel........13 B2
Globe Backpackers.......14 C4
Hotel Barcelona...........15 D4
Park View Hotel...........16 B1
Queen's Court.............17 B2
Silversprings...............18 B2
Telstar.......................19 A2

Sights

EXETER CATHEDRAL

At the heart of the city is the magnificent **Cathedral Church of St Peter** (☎ 255573; www.exeter-cathedral.org.uk; The Close; suggested donation £3; ⏰ 7.30am-6.30pm Mon-Fri, 11.30am-5pm Sat, 8am-7.30pm Sun), which has stood largely unchanged for the last 600 years, despite some WWII bomb damage. Built within a fairly short time span, it's one of the most graceful of England's cathedrals, with celebrated features including the 14th-century stained glass of the East Window, the West Window and the largest section of Gothic rib-vaulting in the world.

There's been a church on this spot since 932; in 1050 the Saxon church was granted cathedral status, and between 1112 and 1133 a

Norman cathedral replaced the original building. In 1270 Bishop Bronescombe instigated the remodelling of the whole building, a process that took about 90 years and resulted in a mix of Early English and Decorated Gothic styles.

You enter through the impressive Great West Front, which boasts the largest collection of 14th-century sculpture in England. The niches around the three doorways are decorated with weatherworn statues of Christ and the Apostles surrounded by saints, angels, and kings (including King Knut and King Alfred).

Inside, the carved **Pulpitum Screen**, completed in 1325, features some marvellous 17th-century ecclesiastical paintings. Behind is the choir, decorated with fine 13th- and 14th-century misericords, including one of an elephant given to King Henry III by Louis IX of France. Nearby, the huge oak canopy over the **Bishop's Throne** was carved in 1312, and the **minstrels' gallery** (1350) is decorated with 12 angels playing musical instruments. Cathedral staff will point out the famous sculpture of the **lady with two left feet**.

Excellent 45-minute free guided tours run at 11am and 2.30pm Monday to Friday, 11am on Saturday and 4pm on Sunday, April to October. Extra tours are available in summer. It's also worth attending a service: evensong is at 5.30pm Monday to Friday and 3pm on Sunday.

UNDERGROUND PASSAGES

The medieval maintenance passages built to house the lead pipes that once brought fresh water to the city still survive under Exeter's streets. They're currently closed due to the redevelopment of the Princesshay shopping centre, but are scheduled to reopen sometime in 2007.

ROYAL ALBERT MEMORIAL MUSEUM & ART GALLERY

Exeter's multipurpose **museum** (☎ 665858; Queen St; admission free; ⏰ 10am-5pm Mon-Sat) has a little bit of everything, ranging from Roman-era artefacts dug up around the city to excellent ethnographic displays from across the globe (look out for some spooky African masks and an impressive suit of samurai armour).

GUILDHALL

Parts of the **Guildhall** (☎ 665500; High St; admission free) date from 1160, making it the oldest municipal building in the country still in use. It was mainly built in the 14th century and the impressive portico was added at the end of the 16th century. Inside, the city's silver and regalia are on display. Opening hours vary, depending on civic functions, so call ahead for times.

Tours

The best introduction to the city's history is provided by volunteer Exeter 'Redcoats', who provide free guided tours leaving from the Royal Clarence Hotel or Quay House Visitor Centre several times daily. The tours are organised along various themes, ranging from the city's Roman architecture to its 'forgotten

past'; hardy souls can even brave a ghosts and legends tour. Contact the tourist office on ☎ 265203 or tic@exeter.gov.uk for details.

Sleeping
BUDGET

Globe Backpackers (☎ 215521; www.exeterbackpack ers.co.uk; 71 Holloway St; dm £14, 7th night free, d £35; ⌨) This centrally located and slightly chaotic hostel is housed inside a 17th-century grand manor house near the quay. It's spotlessly clean and run by a friendly husband-and-wife team, but there's only one double room, so plan ahead.

Exeter YHA Hostel (☎ 0870 770 5826; exeter@yha.org .uk; 47 Countess Wear Rd; dm £15.50; ⌨) Some 2 miles southeast towards Topsham, the city's official hostel is in a spacious 17th-century house overlooking the River Exe. The facilities are good and the dorms are reasonably sized, but the out-of-town location is a drawback. Catch bus K or T from High St, or 57 or 85 from the bus station to School Lane and follow the signs.

Telstar (☎ 272466; www.telstar-hotel.co.uk; 75-77 St David's Hill; s £25-45, d £45-65; ✗) In a small terrace of B&Bs on the main road towards St David's station, the small and welcoming Telstar has 20 attractive rooms in varying shades of magnolia and cream. There's a small brick-floored courtyard, which makes a lovely spot for breakfast in summer, and a wide-ranging brekkie menu.

MIDRANGE

Raffles (☎ 270200; www.raffles-exeter.co.uk; 11 Blackall Rd; s/d from £38/60; Ⓟ ✗) Victorian fixtures and fittings and an antique-heavy atmosphere make this classically English B&B one of the top B&B options in the city. All the rooms are spacious and pleasantly furnished with framed prints and flowery bedspreads; the best have their own bay windows.

Clock Tower Hotel (☎ 424545; www.clocktowerhotel .co.uk; 16 New North Rd; s £45, d £50-70; Ⓟ ✗) This excellent value city-style B&B makes a good midrange base, though the rooms are a little on the anonymous side, and there are several flights of stairs to negotiate if you're on the upper floors.

Silversprings (☎ 494040; www.silversprings.co.uk; 12 Richmond Rd; s £45, d £70-75, ste £100; ✗) Styling itself as a Georgian townhouse hotel, this is really just a plush B&B in disguise. The 10 rooms are comfortable if a little heavy on the floral décor, and all have spacious en suite bathrooms; little touches like fluffy bathrobes and complementary herbal teas are very welcome. There's also a self-contained cottage suite with its own kitchen and lounge.

Queen's Court (☎ 272709; www.queenscourt-hotel .co.uk; 6-8 Bystock Tce; s £77-87, d £93-103; ✕) This large gabled hotel on a quiet terrace off the main road offers a selection of contemporary-styled bedrooms with large bedbacks, multicoloured furniture, and Roberts radios and power showers in every room.

Other recommendations:

Bendene Hotel (☎ 213526; www.bendene.co.uk; 15-16 Richmond Rd; s £25-34, d £48-65; ✕ 🐾) Reliable B&B with comfy rooms, welcoming service and a garden swimming pool.

Park View Hotel (☎ 271772; www.parkviewhotel.free serve.co.uk; 8 Howell Rd; s £26-40, d £48-60; P ✕) Grade-II listed Georgian house decked out in heritage style.

TOP END

our pick **Hotel Barcelona** (☎ 281000; barcelona@alias hotels.com; Magdalen St; s £90, d £105-125; P ✕) Ever fancied staying inside a movie set? Then the delightfully decadent Barcelona is for you. The city's former Eye Infirmary has been renovated with enormous imagination and a playful retro aesthetic. You'll find cinematic prints, '60s furniture and reclaimed wheelchairs dotted around the foyer and downstairs lounge, and the bedrooms are kitted out with an eclectic mishmash of gilt mirrors, wonky wardrobes and Cubist bedspreads. It's fresh, funky and great fun – the kind of place that turns an overnight stay into an event in itself.

ABode at the Royal Clarence Hotel (☎ 319955; www.abodehotels.co.uk/exeter; Cathedral Yard; r £125-225) Keen not to be outdone by the Alias crowd, Exeter's oldest hotel has recently reinvented itself as a boutique beauty. The old-fashioned rooms have been transformed into four categories of varying luxury, ranging from 'comfortable' to 'fabulous'; flat-screen TVs, sleek furniture and huge beds are standard throughout, but it's worth splashing out on the lovely cathedral view rooms if you can.

Eating

Café Paradiso (☎ 281000; barcelona@aliashotels.com; Magdalen St; lunch £5-8, dinner mains from £12; 🕑 lunch & dinner) Sheltered under a soaring canopy, the in-house restaurant at Hotel Barcelona is furnished in typically unusual style, with an all-white interior offset by technicoloured panels and painted bicycles. Café food and gourmet sandwiches are served by day, followed by a sophisticated brasserie menu by night.

Herbies (☎ 258473; 15 North St; mains £5-8; 🕑 lunch Mon-Sat, dinner Tue-Sat) A longstanding favourite with Exeter's veggie crowd, serving up homemade cashew nut loaf, butternut squash risotto and huge curries in a homely, sun-filled dining room.

Zizzi (☎ 274737; 21/22 Gandy St; mains £6-10; 🕑 lunch & dinner) This excellent Italian-influenced brasserie is fantastic value, serving up huge pizzas and pasta dishes in the swish, high-ceilinged dining room or a suntrap garden terrace.

Blue Fish (☎ 493581; 44 Queen St; mains £12-20; 🕑 lunch & dinner Mon-Sat) Look no further for fresh seafood than the Blue Fish, the newly-opened Exeter outpost of an original restaurant in St Ives. Expect the same top quality fish dishes and a similarly laid-back, quasi-continental atmosphere. For a post-dinner tipple, try the chic Veuve cellar bar downstairs.

Michael Caine's (☎ 310031; www.michaelcaines.com; Cathedral Yard; mains from £18.50-25) Exeter's resident celebrity chef continues to work wonders at his flagship restaurant, recently given a thorough makeover as part of the refurbishment of the Royal Clarence Hotel. The décor's all gleaming mirrors, crisp tablecloths and

---

SOMETHING FOR THE WEEKEND

Start your weekend by checking into the fabulous **Hotel Barcelona** (above), stopping for a cocktail at the Med-themed **Café Paradiso** downstairs. Then it's time for a slap-up meal at **Michael Caine's Restaurant** (above) before checking out Exeter's nightspots, including the **Cavern Club** (p332) and the **Phoenix Arts Centre** (p332). Day two is set aside for exploring the villages and tors of wild **Dartmoor** (p342), with a hearty pub lunch in **Chagford** (p347) or **Widecombe** (p346), and a luxurious night's sleep at the lavish **Holne Chase Hotel** (p347). On Sunday take a leisurely drive down to designer **Dartmouth** (p335), allowing time for a visit to the castle and a light lunch at **Café Alf Resco** (p335), followed by a relaxing cruise along the River Dart to **Totnes** (p336).

smoke-coloured seats, and the cooking is as creative as ever.

Effings (☎ 211888; 74 Queen St; 🕑 9am-6pm Mon-Sat, dinner from 7pm Fri & Sat) This new delicatessen is an Aladdin's cave for picnickers, with a mouthwatering selection of Italian meats, local cheeses, freshly-made quiches and sticky tarts; there's also a pleasant café that opens on Friday and Saturday for regionally themed dinners.

Drinking

Ship Inn (☎ 272040; Martin's Lane) Tucked away along a side street off the main cathedral square, this cramped old tavern is said to have been Francis Drake's favourite boozer, and it's still popular with Exeter's ale-drinking crowd.

Kino (Magdalen St; members & guests only after 10pm) This cinematic cellar bar would be more at home on New York's Lower East Side than central Exeter. Expect handmade cocktails, a Chinese-baroque ambience and regular comedy and club nights.

On The Waterfront (☎ 210590; The Quay) An excellent waterfront pub with tables that spill out onto the quayside on hot days.

Entertainment
NIGHTCLUBS

Three Fat Fish (☎ 424628; www.threefatfish.co.uk; 1 Mary Arches St) A popular bar and late-night venue, hosting a mix of gigs, comedians, music nights and DJs.

Cavern Club (☎ 495370; www.cavernclub.co.uk; 83-84 Queen St) The top venue for live gigs in Exeter, attracting big-name DJs and breaking acts from the indie and underground scene.

Timepiece (☎ 493096; www.timepiecenightclub.co.uk; Lt Castle St) Arguably the best club in town, with a revolving programme of urban, garage, drum and bass and indie nights.

Exeter's other clubs include the **Vaults** (☎ 203939; 8 Gandy St), a lively basement bar along Gandy St, and a knot of cheesy nightclubs across the river from the quayside.

THEATRES & CINEMAS

Phoenix Arts Centre (☎ 667080; www.exeterphoenix.org.uk; Gandy St) An excellent arts complex hosting dance, theatre, films, DJs and live music. The café-bar's pretty hip, too.

Exeter Picturehouse (☎ 435522; Bartholomew St West) Screens a mix of mainstream and art-house flicks.

Getting There & Away
AIR

Scheduled services connect **Exeter International Airport** (☎ 367433; www.exeter-airport.co.uk) with several UK cities including Glasgow, Manchester and Newcastle, as well as the Channel Islands and the Isles of Scilly. There are also regular flights to various European destinations. The budget carrier **FlyBe** (www.flybe.com) operates many of the most popular routes.

BUS

The most useful local bus is the X38, which runs to Plymouth (1¼ hours, hourly Monday to Sunday). The X9 runs to Bude (three hours, eight daily, two on Sunday) via Okehampton; for most other destinations the train is faster and more reliable.

TRAIN

The fastest trains between London and Exeter St David's use Paddington station and take around 2½ hours (£45.40, hourly). There are also half-hourly connections with Bristol (£17.60, 1¼ hours) and Penzance (£28.40, three hours).

The picturesque Tarka Line between Exeter Central and Barnstaple (£10.80, 1¼ hours, every hour Monday to Friday, four to six on Sunday) follows the valleys of the Rivers Yeo and Taw and gives good country views.

Getting Around
TO/FROM THE AIRPORT

The airport is 5 miles east of the centre, off the A30. Buses 56 and 379 run to the airport from the bus station (20 minutes, hourly Monday to Saturday).

BICYCLES & CANOES

Saddles & Paddles (☎ 424241; www.sadpad.com; 4 Kings Wharf, The Quay) on the quayside rents out bikes (adult per day £14) and canoes (single kayaks per hour/day £7/18).

BUS

Exeter is well served by public transport. The one-day Dayrider pass (£4) gives unlimited transport on Stagecoach's Exeter buses. Bus N links St David's and Central train stations and passes near the bus station.

CAR

The tourist office provides a list of car-hire offices; try **Europcar** (☎ 275398; Water Lane).

There are several large city centre car parks, but if you'd rather not drive into the city, there are park and ride schemes from car parks at Sowton (Bus PR4), Matford (Bus PR5), Digby Rd (Bus PR3) and Honiton Rd (PR2). Connecting buses go to the city every 10 minutes.

TAXI
There are taxi ranks outside the train stations. Alternatively, try **A1 Cars** (☎ 218888) or **Capital Taxis** (☎ 433433).

AROUND EXETER
Powderham Castle
Powderham (☎ 01626-890243; www.powderham.co.uk; admission £7.95; ⏱ 10am-5.30pm Apr-Oct) has been the ancestral home of the Courtenay family for over 600 years. Built in 1391, and extensively modified following damage caused during the English Civil War, the castle has some of the best preserved Stuart and Regency furniture of any of Britain's stately homes, as well as some impressive state rooms and a fine wood-panelled Great Hall.

Powderham is on the River Exe in Kenton, 8 miles south of Exeter. Bus 85A runs from Exeter (20 minutes, every 15 minutes Monday to Saturday, every 30 minutes Sunday).

À la Ronde
Having returned from their European Grand Tour, sisters Jane and Mary Parminter planned to combine the magnificence of the Church of San Vitale, which they'd visited in Ravenna, with the homeliness of a country cottage. The result, completed around 1796, is an intriguing 16-sided National Trust (NT) **house** (☎ 01395-265514; Summer Lane, Exmouth; admission £5; ⏱ 11am-5.30pm Sun-Thu Mar-Oct) with bizarre interior décor that includes a shell-encrusted room, a frieze of feathers, and sand and sea-weed collages.

It's 2 miles north of Exmouth on the A376; Stagecoach Devon bus 57 runs close by en route to Exeter (30 minutes, at least every 30 minutes).

SOUTH DEVON COAST
Torquay & Paignton
☎ 01803 / pop 110,370
If you thought the British seaside holiday was dead, then think again; it's alive and well along the stretch of coastline between Torquay, Paignton and Brixham collectively known as the English Riviera. Despite the name (and the

best efforts of the South Devon Tourist Board to convince us otherwise), this is a long way from St Tropez, but the region does have its peculiar charms – especially if you've got a soft spot for amusement arcades, deckchairs and good old-fashioned fish and chips. Queen of the coastline is grand old Torquay, where the Victorian villas and chintzy hotels are stacked up like dominoes above the bay. Just to the west of Torquay is Paignton, the picture of an English seaside resort, complete with a seafront promenade, multicoloured beach-huts and a faded 19th-century pier.

The **tourist office** (☎ 0870 70 70 010; torbay.tic@ torbay.gov.uk; Vaughan Pde; ⏱ 9.30am-5pm Mon-Sat & 10am-4.30pm Sun May-Sep, 9.30am-5pm Mon-Sat Oct-Apr) sells discounted tickets to local attractions.

SIGHTS & ACTIVITIES
Torquay has two famous residents: Agatha Christie, who was born in Torquay in 1890 and lived for many years at the manor house of Greenaway, just outside town; and Basil Fawlty, the deranged Torquay hotelier memorably played by John Cleese in the classic British comedy *Fawlty Towers*.

Torquay Museum (☎ 293975; 529 Babbacombe Rd; admission £3; ⏱ 10am-5pm Mon-Sat & 1.30-5pm Sun Oct-Apr, 10am-5pm Mon-Fri, 1.30-4pm Sat May-Sep) has an intriguing selection of Agatha Christie memorabilia, including family photos, first edition novels and a couple of display cases devoted to her famous detectives Hercule Poirot and Miss Marple.

Regular boat trips sail along the coastline from Torquay to Dartmouth (£14) and Brixham (£5). Contact **Torbay Belle Cruises** (☎ 528555) or **Western Lady Cruises** (☎ 842424) or just pitch up on the pier.

Torquay is surrounded by pleasant beaches, the best of which is family-friendly **Babba-combe**, about 2 miles north of the centre, which still has a working **funicular** (☎ 328750; ⏱ 9.30am-6pm) connecting the beach to the clifftop.

SLEEPING
You won't have any trouble finding somewhere to sleep in Torquay – the town is practically wall-to-wall B&Bs and hotels, with a concentrated cluster around Avenue Rd and Bridge Rd.

Torquay International Backpackers (☎ 299924; jane@torquaybackpackers.co.uk; 119 Abbey Rd; dm/d £10/12 in winter, £12/14 in summer) This small hostel is in the middle of a row of Victorian terraced houses, and makes a friendly base in Torquay. The owner, Jane, is full of useful local info and often organises summer barbecues, beach trips and local pub tours.

Norwood Hotel (☎ 294236; www.norwoodhoteltorquay.co.uk; 60 Belgrave Rd; d £44-50; ✗) In the heart of Torquay's B&B ghetto, the Norwood stands head and shoulders above its neighbours. The frill-heavy, Victoriana bedrooms might not be to everyone's taste, but they're fantastic value and handily placed for exploring the rest of Torquay.

English House (☎ 328760; Teignmouth Rd, Maidencombe; d £70-90) This is another surprisingly stylish B&B-cum-restaurant in the suburb of Maidencombe, with delightful upstairs rooms decorated in warm tones and gingham checks. The breakfast menu includes Luscombe sausages, grapefruit and toasted muffins.

Hillcroft (☎ 297247; www.thehillcroft.co.uk; 9 St Lukes Rd; d £75-130) Not what you'd expect to find in Torquay – a semiboutique hotel kitted out with Indonesian furniture, Balinese furnishings and Tuscan tiling, with individually-styled rooms ranging from a four-poster Indian suite to a chic Provençal penthouse.

Other recommendations:

Haven Hotel (☎ 293390; www.havenhotel.biz; 11 Scarborough Rd; s £30-40, d £25-65) Lemon-coloured townhouse with three well-appointed rooms.

Everglades Hotel (☎ 295389; www.evergladeshotel.co.uk; 32 St Marychurch Rd; d £54-56; **P** ✗) Detached hotel with an elevated sundeck and modern sea-view rooms.

EATING & DRINKING

Terrace Restaurant (☎ 211801; lunch £3-9; ☾ breakfast & lunch) On the top floor of the old Pavilion, this quintessentially English café serves light lunches, jacket potatoes and cream teas, best appreciated from the outside terrace with its original Victorian gazebos and wrought-iron railings.

Pier Point (☎ 299935; mains £5-20; ☾ lunch & dinner) In a lovely seafront location next to the Princess Theatre, this breezy bistro-bar is the best bet for lunch or a light supper in Torquay, with crispy pizzas, fresh salads and seafood and an extensive selection of wines, cocktails and cold beers.

English House (☎ 328760; Teignmouth Rd, Maidencombe; 2/3 courses £26/30; ☾ dinner) Locally-sourced Devonian ingredients underpin the monthly-changing menu at this award-winning restau-

rant, from Brixham mussels and monkfish to slow-roasted Devon lamb and asparagus.

GETTING THERE & AWAY

The X80 travels every half hour from Torquay to Paignton (20 minutes), Totnes (one hour) and Plymouth (two hours 10 minutes). Bus 111 travels to Dartmouth (1¾ hours, hourly, Monday to Saturday) via Totnes.

A branch train line runs from Exeter via Torquay (45 minutes) to Paignton (50 minutes). The **Paignton & Dartmouth Steam Railway** (☎ 555872; www.paignton-steamrailway.co.uk) runs from Paignton on the scenic 7-mile trip to Kingswear on the River Dart, linked by ferry (six minutes) to Dartmouth; a combined ticket costs £9 return per adult. You can add on a river cruise (£14) or a Round Robin boat trip to Totnes and back to Paignton by bus (£14.50).

Brixham

☎ 01803 / pop 17,460

On the opposite side of the bay from Torquay, the old fishing town of Brixham has built its fortunes on the fruits of the sea, and remains one of the country's busiest harbours. A ring of pastel-shaded fishermen's cottages and old warehouses surround the harbourside and spill over onto the nearby cliffs, but this is far from a neatly-packaged tourist resort; Brixham has a rough, gritty charm entirely absent from the other Torbay towns, and offers a more authentic glimpse of life along the southwest coastline.

The **tourist office** (☎ 0906-680126; brixham.tic@torbay.org.uk; Old Market House, The Quay; ☾ 9.30am-6pm Mon-Sat Jun-Sep, 9.30am-5pm Mon-Fri Oct-May) is right beside the harbour.

Brixham Heritage Museum (☎ 856267; www.brixhamheritage.org.uk; Bolton Cross; admission £1.50; ☾ 10am-5pm Mon-Fri, 10am-1pm Sat) has a range of displays exploring the town's history and its connection to the sea, with exhibits on smuggling, the Brixham lifeboat and some unusual items dragged up by local fishing trawlers.

Anchored in the harbour is a replica of the **Golden Hind** (☎ 856223; admission £3; ☾ 9am-5.30pm Mar-Sep), Drake's surprisingly small globe-circling ship.

There are plenty of chippies scattered around the quay, but for a real taste of the British seaside, you can't beat a pot of prawns or fresh crab from one of the seafood booths on the harbourside; the best is **Browse Seafoods** (☎ 882484), next to the tourist office.

Bus 22 runs along the coast to Kingswear (30 minutes, half-hourly Monday to Saturday), from where you can catch buses to Torquay or the river ferry over to Dartmouth.

Dartmouth
☎ 01803 / pop 5693

The pretty riverside town of Dartmouth has long been known as the location for Britain's largest naval college, but in recent years it's also established itself as a favourite seaside escape for city types fleeing from the rat race. There are some surprisingly chic shops and boutiques dotted around town, not to mention an astonishing concentration of upmarket restaurants – in high summer it's all a bit Knightsbridge by the sea, with posh yachts jostling for space in the small riverside harbour and plenty of impeccably-coiffured ladies doing lunch at one of the town's street-side cafés.

The **tourist office** (☎ 834224; www.discoverdartmouth.com; Mayor's Ave; 🕑 9.30am-5pm Mon-Sat year-round, plus 10am-2pm Sun Apr-Oct) houses the Newcomen Engine, an early (1712) steam engine.

Perched on a promontory at the entrance to the Dart Estuary, the English Heritage (EH) **Dartmouth Castle** (☎ 833588; admission £3.70; 🕑 10am-6pm Jul & Aug, 10am-5pm Apr-Jun & Sep, 10am-4pm Oct, 10am-4pm Sat & Sun Nov-Mar) was built to protect the harbour from seaborne raids in conjunction with its companion castle at Kingswear. There's a ferry along the estuary to the castle, three-quarters of a mile outside town, from South Embankment every 15 minutes from 10am to 4.45pm (adult one-way £1.20).

The **Dartmouth Museum** (☎ 832923; Duke St; admission £1.50; 🕑 10am-4pm Mon-Sat Apr-Oct, 11am-3pm Mon-Sat Nov-Mar) displays a jumbled collection of costumes, swords, ships-in-bottles and vintage toys. The museum stands at the end of the **Butterwalk**, a row of super-wonky timber-framed houses that look as though they could collapse at any moment; incredibly, they've somehow managed to remain standing since the late 17th century.

Dartmouth is justifiably proud of its spanking new arts centre, the **Flavel** (☎ 839530; www.theflavel.org.uk), which hosts small-scale theatre and dance, as well as live music and films.

SLEEPING
Hill View House (☎ 839372; www.hillviewdartmouth.co.uk; 76 Victoria Rd; d £56-82; 🕱) A short walk uphill from the harbour, this tasteful B&B wears its environmental credentials on its sleeve: eco-friendly toiletries, long-life light bulbs and organic breakfasts are all *de rigueur*, and though some of the rooms are on the small side, you couldn't ask for a friendlier night's sleep.

our pick **Brown's Hotel** (☎ 832572; www.brownshoteldartmouth.co.uk; 29 Victoria Rd; s £60, d £80-165; 🕱) This effortlessly elegant hotel has built up a reputation as one of the top seaside retreats in Devon, and it certainly brings a touch of Chelsea class to Dartmouth's streets. The contemporary rooms are decorated in pale tones of chocolate and cappuccino, offset by the odd zebra print or piece of designer furniture. Downstairs there's a top-notch British restaurant serving Devon lamb and local shellfish, and to top it off you can kick back in the super-sleek bar next door, complete with comfy sofas, board games and an imaginative tapas menu.

Orleans Guest House (☎ 835450; www.orleans-guesthouse-dartmouth.co.uk; 24 South Town; d £80-85, ste £150; 🕱) Another beautifully designed B&B in a 17th-century Georgian townhouse, with three rooms finished in varying shades of red, gold or mauve, with Egyptian cotton bedspreads and DVD players in every room.

EATING & DRINKING
Café Alf Resco (☎ 835880; Lower St; mains from £6; 🕑 lunch & dinner Wed-Sun) Despite its notoriously erratic opening hours, this wonderful little bistro blends the best elements of a Tuscan trattoria with a Parisian street-side café. Rickety wooden chairs and old street signs are scattered around the front terrace, which makes a great place for a frothy latte or a ciabatta sandwich.

Station Restaurant (☎ 832125; South Embankment; mains £7-10; 🕑 lunch and dinner) If you're on a budget, this homey restaurant in Dartmouth's old station-house is your best bet, with stodgy standards such as pie and mash, tikka curry and Lancashire hotpot.

RB's Diner (☎ 832882; 33 Lower St; mains £15-18; 🕑 dinner) Padded chairs, stripped pine floors and gleaming wine glasses tell you all you need to know about this refined restaurant, where the food is more South Kensington than south Devon – tenderloin of pork, beef fillet and lemon mousse with raspberries are some of the treats in store.

New Angel (☎ 839425; 2 South Embankment; mains £18-23; 🕑 breakfast, lunch & dinner Tue-Sat, breakfast & lunch Sun) Run by celebrity TV chef John Burton

DEVON & CORNWALL

Race, this modern British bistro is the proud owner of a Michelin star, so you'll have to book well ahead for a table; but the top-level cooking is more than worth the effort.

GETTING THERE & AWAY

Bus 93 runs to Plymouth (two hours, hourly, four on Sunday) and bus 111 runs to Torquay (1¾ hours, hourly Monday to Saturday) via Totnes. There are regular ferries across the river from Kingswear (car/pedestrian £3.30/1) every six minutes.

River Link (☎ 834488; www.riverlink.co.uk; return £8.50; ☻ Apr-Oct) operates cruises along the River Dart from Totnes.

For details of the popular Paignton & Dartmouth Steam Railway, see p334.

Totnes

☎ 01803 / pop 8194

The delightful little town of Totnes has been something of a hippy haven since the 1960s, and its artistic connections continue thanks to the nearby Dartington College of Arts, a couple of miles up the road from the town. But the history of Totnes stretches back much further than the summer of love; a well-preserved Norman keep stands guard on a hilltop above town, and the main street is lined with elegant Tudor and Elizabethan buildings that hint at Totnes' history as a mercantile town. In fact, tiny Totnes has a higher percentage of listed buildings than anywhere in Britain.

The tourist office (☎ 863168; www.totnesinformation.co.uk; Coronation Rd; ☻ 9.30am-5pm Mon-Sat) is in the town's old mill.

SIGHTS

Totnes Elizabethan Museum (☎ 863821; 70 Fore St; admission £1.50; ☻ 10.30am-5pm Mon-Fri Apr-Oct) is in a house dating from 1575 and still retains many Tudor and Elizabethan features. Its displays explore the history of Totnes, and there's a room dedicated to the mathematician Charles Babbage, father of the modern computer.

The Devonshire Collection of Period Costume (☎ 863168; High St; admission £2; ☻ 11am-5pm Mon-Fri May-Sep) features annually changing selections from the extensive costume collection, one of the finest in Britain.

Totnes Castle (EH; ☎ 864406; admission £2.40; ☻ 10am-6pm Jul & Aug, 10am-5pm Apr-Sep, 10am-4pm Oct) occupies a commanding position on a grassy hilltop above town. Little remains of the original Norman motte-and-bailey for-

tress, but the outer keep is still standing, and the views of the town and surrounding fields are fantastic.

SLEEPING

Dartington YHA Hostel (☎ 0870 770 5788; dm £11.95; ☻ mid-Apr-Oct) This small hostel is located inside a 16th-century riverside cottage, complete with original features including a log-burning stove. It's 2 miles northwest of Totnes off the A385; bus X80 stops nearby at Shinners Bridge half a mile away.

Old Forge (☎ 862174; www.oldforgetotnes.com; Seymour Pl; s £46-55, d £60-71; P ☒) As its name suggests, this lovely B&B once housed workshops for the nearby castle of Berry Pomeroy, but it's now been converted to provide delightful country rooms equipped with huge, soft beds and plush pillows. There's a peaceful garden beside the breakfast room, and an original lock-up once used to incarcerate local miscreants.

Steam Packet Inn (☎ 863880; www.steampacketinn.co.uk; St Peters Quay; d £79.50; P ☒) A historic pub a little way along the river from town, with four pleasant bedrooms equipped with understated furniture, flat-screen TVs and tranquil river views.

EATING

Willow Vegetarian Restaurant (☎ 862605; 87 High St; mains £4-5.50; ☻ lunch Mon-Sat, dinner Wed, Fri & Sat) The hang-out of choice for Totnes' new agers, this rustic wholefood café does a nice line in couscous, quiches, hotpots and homemade cakes during the day, all served in a sunny dining room packed with pine tables, potted plants and free newspapers. Dinner is served three nights a week and there's live music at weekends.

Wills (☎ 0800 056 3006; 3 The Plains; ☻ lunch daily, dinner Tue-Sat) Posh nosh served in a two-floored restaurant at the bottom of Fore St. Illy coffee, sticky tarts and light lunches are served in the downstairs café; upstairs the atmosphere is more refined, with elegant Regency style furniture and food to match.

Rumours (☎ 864682; 30 Fore St; mains £10.50-14; ☻ 10am-11pm Mon-Sat, 6-10.30pm Sun) This venerable restaurant is so friendly it's almost like eating out in a friend's front room. Photographs and artwork cover the walls, and the menu's stuffed with everything from pizzas to pan-fried sea trout and Salcombe ice cream.

GETTING THERE & AWAY

Bus X64 runs to Exeter (one hour, six daily Monday to Saturday, two Sunday) and bus X80 goes to Plymouth (1¼ hours, hourly). Bus 200 also travels to Paignton (hourly, 30 minutes) and Torquay (50 minutes).

Frequent trains run to Exeter (£7.80, 45 minutes) and Plymouth (£5.70, 30 minutes, hourly). The train station is half a mile from the centre.

A short walk from Totnes main-line train station, steam trains of the private **South Devon Railway** (☎ 0845 345 1420; www.southdevonrailway.org) run to Buckfastleigh (adult return £8.80, four or five daily Easter to October) on the edge of Dartmoor.

There are cruises on the river with frequent departures to Dartmouth from April to October (opposite).

PLYMOUTH

☎ 01752 / pop 256,633

Britain is historically a nation of seafarers, and nowhere is this maritime heritage more obvious than at the port of Plymouth, from where the Pilgrim Fathers set sail for the New World and Sir Francis Drake allegedly eyed up the Spanish Armada while indulging in a spot of bowls. The best place to view old Plymouth is the much-restored Barbican area, where half-timbered houses and Tudor buildings look out across a harbour filled with fishing trawlers and upmarket yachts; sadly the rest of Plymouth was practically levelled by bombing raids during WWII, and was largely rebuilt in functional concrete after the war. But the city's slowly smartening up its act, with a new shopping development in the city centre, a growing selection of bars and restaurants around the Barbican, and the reopening of one of the city's best-loved landmarks, the Tinside Lido, in 2003.

History

The city's position at the mouth of the Plym and Tamar estuaries and its proximity to the deepwater harbour of Plymouth Sound made it an ideal location for a naval base. During the 15th and 16th centuries, most of the British naval fleet was stationed here; the royal dockyard was established at Devonport beside the River Tamar in 1690 and remains an important naval base.

The globetrotting hero Sir Francis Drake sailed from Plymouth in 1577 aboard the *Golden Hind*, returning three years later having become the first man to circumnavigate the globe. Eleven years later, Drake played a major part in the defeat of the Spanish Armada, chasing the Spanish fleet all the way to Calais and then attacking them with fire ships. Many of the Spanish vessels escaped but were wrecked off the Scottish coast. Total losses: England nil, Spain 51.

Orientation

Plymouth has three main sections. The pedestrianised centre is south of the train station, and contains the city's main shopping streets. Further south is the headland Hoe area, packed with guesthouses and B&Bs, and east of the Hoe is the regenerated Barbican area, where you'll find the best places to eat and drink.

Information

Hoegate Laundromat (☎ 223031; 55 Notte St; ☉ 8am-6pm Mon-Fri, 9am-5pm Sat)

Plymouth Internet Café (☎ 221777; 32 Frankfort Gate; per hr £5; ☉ 9am-5pm Mon-Sat)

Police station (Charles Cross; ☉ 24hr)

Tourist office (☎ 306330; www.visitplymouth.co.uk; 3-5 The Barbican; ☉ 9am-5pm Mon-Sat, 10am-4pm Sun May-Sep, 10am-4pm Mon-Sat Oct-Apr) Housed inside the Plymouth Mayflower building.

University Bookseller (☎ 660428; 42 Drake Circus; ☉ 9am-5.30pm Mon-Sat)

West Hoe Laundrette (☎ 667373; 1 Pier St; ☉ 9.15am-8pm Mon-Fri, 9am-6pm Sat, 10am-5pm Sun)

Sights & Activities

PLYMOUTH HOE

Francis Drake supposedly spied the Spanish fleet from this grassy headland overlooking Plymouth Sound; the fabled bowling green on which he finished his game was probably where his statue now stands. Later the Hoe became a favoured holiday spot for the Victorian aristocracy, and the headland is backed by an impressive array of multistoreyed villas and once-grand hotels.

The red-and-white-striped lighthouse of **Smeaton's Tower** (The Hoe; admission £2.25; ☉ 10am-4pm daily Apr-Oct, Tue-Sat Nov-Mar) was built on the Eddystone Rocks in 1759, then rebuilt on the Hoe in 1882 when it was replaced by a larger lighthouse. You can climb the 93 steps for great views and an insight into the history of the Eddystone lighthouses.

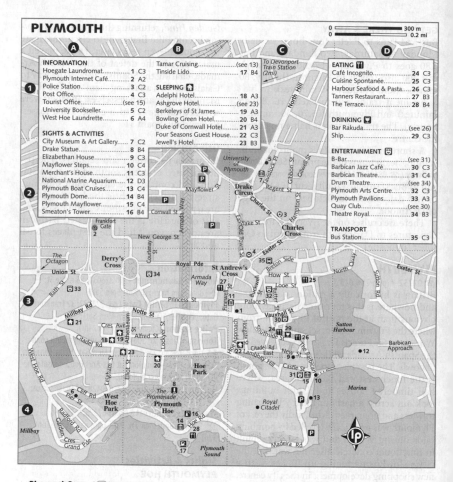

PLYMOUTH

INFORMATION	
Hoegate Laundromat............... **1** C3	
Plymouth Internet Café............ **2** A2	
Police Station........................ **3** C2	
Post Office............................ **4** C3	
Tourist Office.................(see 15)	
University Bookseller............... **5** C2	
West Hoe Laundrette............... **6** A4	
SIGHTS & ACTIVITIES	
City Museum & Art Gallery...... **7** C2	
Drake Statue.......................... **8** B4	
Elizabethan House.................. **9** C3	
Mayflower Steps.................... **10** C4	
Merchant's House.................. **11** C3	
National Marine Aquarium...... **12** D3	
Plymouth Boat Cruises........... **13** C4	
Plymouth Dome..................... **14** B4	
Plymouth Mayflower.............. **15** C4	
Smeaton's Tower................... **16** B4	

Tamar Cruising...................(see 13)
Tinside Lido......................... **17** B4
SLEEPING
Adelphi Hotel....................... **18** A3
Ashgrove Hotel................(see 23)
Berkeleys of St James........... **19** A3
Bowling Green Hotel............. **20** B4
Duke of Cornwall Hotel......... **21** A3
Four Seasons Guest House...... **22** C3
Jewell's Hotel....................... **23** B3

EATING
Café Incognito...................... **24** C3
Cuisine Spontanée................ **25** C3
Harbour Seafood & Pasta...... **26** C3
Tanners Restaurant............... **27** B3
The Terrace.......................... **28** B4
DRINKING
Bar Rakuda.....................(see 26)
Ship................................... **29** C3
ENTERTAINMENT
B-Bar.............................(see 31)
Barbican Jazz Café................ **30** C3
Barbican Theatre................... **31** C4
Drum Theatre..................(see 34)
Plymouth Arts Centre............ **32** C3
Plymouth Pavilions................ **33** A3
Quay Club......................(see 30)
Theatre Royal...................... **34** B3
TRANSPORT
Bus Station.......................... **35** C3

Plymouth Dome (☎ 603300; The Hoe; admission £4.75; ◷ 10am-5pm Easter-Oct, 10am-4pm Oct-Easter) provides an entertaining romp through Plymouth's history, using models and audiovisual shows to explore subjects including Elizabethan life in Plymouth, the Luftwaffe raids and the construction of the Eddystone lighthouses.

BARBICAN

To get an idea of what old Plymouth was like before the Luftwaffe redesigned it, head for the Barbican, with its many Tudor and Jacobean buildings (now converted into galleries, craft shops and restaurants).

The Pilgrim Fathers' *Mayflower* set sail for America from the Barbican on 16 September 1620. At the **Mayflower Steps** a plaque lists the passengers and marks the point of departure. Another famous voyage was led by Captain James Cook, who set out from the Barbican in 1768 in search of a southern continent.

Plymouth Mayflower (☎ 306330; 3-5 The Barbican; admission £4; ◷ 10am-6pm Apr-Oct, 10am-5pm Nov-Mar) is another hi-tech rundown through Plymouth's nautical heritage, providing the background to the Pilgrim Fathers' trip with plenty of interactive gizmos and multisensory displays.

The **Elizabethan House** (☎ 304774; 32 New St; admission £1.25; ◷ 10am-5pm Tue-Sat Apr-Nov) is the former residence of an Elizabethan sea captain, housing 16th-century furniture and other period artefacts.

Across the harbour from the Barbican and over a footbridge, the **National Marine**

DEVON & CORNWALL

SWIMMING IN STYLE

Downhill from the Hoe is the **Tinside Lido** (☎ 0870 300 0042; ☽ noon-6pm during school holidays, 10am-6pm May-Sep), an outdoor saltwater pool built in classic Art-Deco style, first opened to the public in 1935. During the Lido's heyday in the '40s and '50s, thousands of Plymouthians flocked to the pool on summer days (backed by the soothing strains of a string orchestra), and during the war it made the perfect place to cool off after cleaning up the rubble from the city's bomb-ravaged streets. On one memorable occasion, some 3000 people took to the water in a very un-British display of high spirits. Sadly, package holidays took their toll on the Lido in the '70s and '80s, and the pool fell into disrepair, finally closing in 1992. It's since been restored to its former glory thanks to a hefty £3.4m investment by the city council and local benefactors, and it's packed throughout summer with school kids and sun-worshippers; sadly, though, there's no sign of the string orchestra returning just yet.

Aquarium (☎ 220084; The Barbican; www.national-aquarium.co.uk; admission £8.75; ☽ 10am-6pm Apr-Oct, 10am-5pm Nov-Mar) is one of the country's top aquariums. The various tanks recreate marine life in a variety of habitats, including coral seas, an Atlantic reef and the deep ocean.

MERCHANT'S HOUSE

Between the Barbican and the centre is the 17th-century **Merchant's House** (☎ 304774; 33 St Andrews St; admission £1.25; ☽ 10am-5.30pm Tue-Fri & 10am-5pm Sat year-round, closed 1-2pm Apr-Oct), a Jacobean building with models, pictures, local curiosities (including manacles and truncheons) and a replica of a Victorian school room.

CITY MUSEUM & ART GALLERY

Near the university is the **City Museum & Art Gallery** (☎ 304774; Drake Circus; admission free; ☽ 10am-5.30pm Mon-Fri, 10am-5pm Sat) hosting collections of local history, porcelain and naval art. The Cottonian Collection includes some significant paintings, prints and etchings by artists including Joshua Reynolds.

BOAT TRIPS

Several boat operators offer cruises from the Barbican to the dockyards and warships (adult return £5), and four-hour cruises up the River Tamar (adult return £7.50) to Calstock. Contact **Plymouth Boat Cruises** (☎ 822797) or **Tamar Cruising** (☎ 822105), both on Phoenix Wharf.

Sleeping

Most of Plymouth's B&Bs are concentrated around the Hoe, especially along Citadel Rd.

BUDGET & MIDRANGE

Jewell's Hotel (☎ 254760; 220 Citadel Rd; s £25, d £35-55; ☒) This excellent B&B just off the Hoe has a number of tastefully-finished rooms spread out over several floors, including some with original Victorian fireplaces and cast-iron beds.

Ashgrove Hotel (☎ 664046; www.ashgrovehotel-plymouth.co.uk; 218 Citadel Rd; s/d £30/40) A simpler option next door to Jewell's, with interior décor that's taken straight from the pages of the British B&B catalogue (think lacy beds, flowery curtains and pine furniture).

Four Seasons Guest House (☎ 223591; www.fourseasonsguesthouse.co.uk; 207 Citadel Rd East; s £30-45, d £45-60; ☒) Slightly further down the hill towards the Barbican, in a small terrace of Victorian houses, this lovely B&B has standard and deluxe rooms all decorated in relaxing shades of mustard and cream, but the highlight is the fantastic breakfast, which includes scotch pancakes, organic yoghurt and local bacon.

Bowling Green Hotel (☎ 209090; www.bowlinggreenhotel.co.uk; 9-10 Osborne Pl; d from £60; Ⓟ ☒) Ignore the unedifying pebble-dash front – the bedrooms at this five-diamond B&B are some of the nicest in the Hoe, with a welcome absence of floral prints and views right across Francis' famous bowling green.

Other recommendations:

Berkeleys of St James (☎ 221654; www.onthehoe.co.uk; 4 St James Pl East; s £35, d £50-55; ☒) Reliable B&B distinguished by its organic breakfasts.

Adelphi Hotel (☎ 225520; 59 Citadel Rd; s/d £40/50; Ⓟ ☒) Old sea-captain's residence with a guest lounge and bog-standard B&B rooms.

TOP END

Duke of Cornwall Hotel (☎ 275850; www.thedukeofcornwallhotel.com; Millbay Rd; s £94, d £104-160) With one of the most striking edifices in Plymouth, a grand turret-topped pile dotted with balconies and Gothic gables, this is undoubtedly the most luxurious place to stay in town. The rooms are massive, if a touch old-fashioned; if you can afford it the four-poster suite, complete with champagne and complimentary fruit basket, is definitely the one to choose.

Eating
CAFÉS

Terrace (☎ 603533; Madeira Rd; lunch £3-6; ☷ breakfast & lunch) Tucked away beside the Tinside Lido, this bright and breezy café has the best location of any eatery in town, with sweeping views across Plymouth Sound and a selection of sandwiches, coffees and generous jacket potatoes.

Café Incognito (☎ 265999; 92 North Hill; lunch £3-6; ☷ 8am-8pm) If you're after a light bite or an all-day brekkie, head for the sunny Incognito, with a showcase of local art on the walls and all the café classics – baguettes, tortilla wraps and paninis.

RESTAURANTS

Harbour Seafood & Pasta (☎ 260717; 10 Quay Rd; mains £8-16; ☷ lunch & dinner) A cosy pasta and fish joint with tables out on the quayside or in the small dining room, serving sumptuous pasta and probably the best seafood in the Barbican.

Cuisine Spontanée (☎ 673757; Century Quay; mains £9.95-17.95; ☷ lunch & dinner Mon-Sat) The gastronomic equivalent of a mix-and-match sweet-shop – choose your ingredients (meat, fish or veg) and an accompanying sauce (Thai, Chinese, Mexican) and watch the chef put them together at your table. The menu prices are on a sliding scale throughout the week, with the weekends being the most expensive.

Tanners Restaurant (☎ 252001; www.tannersrestaurant.com; Finewell St; 2-/3-course dinner £24/30; ☷ lunch & dinner Tue-Sat) Housed in the city's oldest building, a merchant's mansion built in 1498, Plymouth's most renowned fine-dining restaurant is run by the Tanner brothers, who've made a name for themselves reinventing classic British and French dishes with their own individual twist.

Drinking
Plymouth has a buzzing nightlife, but the main club strip, Union St, has a reputation for trouble at kicking-out time. The area around the Barbican is wall-to-wall pubs and bars.

Bar Rakuda (☎ 221155; 11 Quay Rd; ☷ 9am-11pm) One of the best quayside bars, ideal for a morning latté, a lunchtime mocha or a cocktail jug when the sun goes down.

Ship (☎ 667604; Quay Rd) Just along the quay, this historical tavern is another popular boozer in the Barbican, with plenty of real ales and pub grub.

Entertainment
BARS & NIGHTCLUBS

Barbican Jazz Café (☎ 672127; 11 The Parade; admission Fri & Sat £2; ☷ noon-2am Mon-Sat, noon-midnight Sun) Nightly jazz and guest DJs keep the crowd happy at this barrel-vaulted club.

Quay Club (☎ 224144; 11 The Parade; ☷ 10am-2pm) Next to Jazz Café, this cavernous club is a favourite with Plymouth's night owls, with drum and bass on Monday, jazz and soul on Wednesday and cheese and chart (top 40s, pop, soft rock or dance classics) on Friday and Saturday.

B-Bar (☎ 242021; Castle St) The in-house café-bar of the Barbican Theatre, B-Bar hosts live music, DJs, cabaret and comedy.

THEATRES & CINEMAS

Theatre Royal (☎ 267222; www.theatreroyal.com; Royal Pde) Plymouth's main theatre puts on large-scale touring productions, while its **Drum Theatre** stages fringe plays.

Plymouth Pavilions (☎ 229922; www.plymouthpavilions.com; Millbay Rd) Plymouth's main venue for theatre and comedy, hosting everything from the League of Gentlemen to the Flaming Lips.

Barbican Theatre (☎ 267131; www.barbicantheatre.co.uk; Castle St) An innovative arts theatre with regular dance and theatre, and photographic exhibitions in the downstairs café.

Plymouth Arts Centre (☎ 206114; www.plymouthac.org.uk; 38 Looe St) An excellent indie cinema and gallery, with a recently overhauled veggie restaurant and bar.

Getting There & Away
BUS

Bus X38 runs to Exeter (1¼ hours, hourly Monday to Sunday); bus 82 runs twice daily at weekends to Plymouth via Moretonhampstead, Postbridge and Princetown on Dartmoor. Bus X80 runs every half hour to Torquay (1¾ hours) via Totnes (one hour 10 minutes) from Monday to Saturday, and hourly on Sunday.

National Express runs regular coaches to Birmingham (£41, 5½ hours, four daily), Bristol (£24.50, three hours, four daily), London (£27.50, five to six hours, eight daily) and Penzance (£6.50, 3¼ hours, seven daily).

TRAIN

Services run to London (£63, 3½ hours, half-hourly), Bristol (£44, two hours, two or three per hour), Exeter (£11.60, one hour, two or three per hour) and Penzance (£11.60, two hours, half-hourly).

AROUND PLYMOUTH
Buckland Abbey

Originally a Cistercian monastery and 13th-century abbey church, **Buckland Abbey** (NT; ☎ 01822-853607; Yelverton; admission £7; ☿ 10.30am-5.30pm Fri-Wed mid-Mar–Oct, 2-5pm Sat & Sun Nov–mid-Mar) was transformed into a family residence by Sir Richard Grenville and purchased in 1581 by his cousin and nautical rival Sir Francis Drake. Exhibitions on its history feature Drake's Drum, said to beat by itself when Britain is ever in danger of being invaded. There's also a very fine Elizabethan garden.

Buckland is 11 miles north of Plymouth. Take buses 83, 84 or 86 (40 minutes, every 30 minutes) to Yelverton, then bus 55 (10 minutes, hourly) to Buckland Abbey.

NORTH DEVON

The north Devon coastline is markedly different to its southern cousin; altogether more rugged and rather less touristy, with some great beaches, pretty seaside towns and excellent surf breaks.

Braunton & Croyde
☎ 01271 / pop 8319

Croyde Bay and the nearby beach at Saunton Sands are Devon's most popular surfing spots, with a clutch of good camp sites, B&Bs and pubs. Check out the Croyde Surf Club website (www.croydesurfclub.com) for webcam shots from all the area's main breaks.

Braunton is the centre for surf shops and board hire. The **tourist office** (☎ 816400; brauntontic@visit.org.uk; The Bakehouse Centre; ☿ 10am-4pm Mon-Sat) provides information and also houses a small local museum.

Croyde has numerous surf-hire shops, charging around £15 per day for board and wet suit: try **Le Sport** (☎ 890147; Hobbs Hill; ☿ 9am-9pm Apr-Sep) or **Redwood Surfhire** (☎ 890999; Down End car park). For lessons, contact **Surfing Croyde Bay** (☎ 891200; www.surfingcroydebay.co.uk) or **Surf South West** (☎ 890400; www.surfsouthwest.com; per half/full day £25/45), both accredited by the BSA.

SLEEPING & EATING

Camp sites are plentiful but you should still book ahead.

Bay View Farm (☎ 890501; www.bayviewfarm.co.uk; sites from £15) On the road from Braunton, this is one of the area's best camp sites, with laundry and showers onsite.

Mitchum's Campsites (☎ 890233; www.croydebay .co.uk) There are two locations, one in Croyde village and one by the beach, but they're only open on certain weekends in summer, so phone ahead.

Chapel Farm (☎ 890429; www.chapelfarmcroyde.co.uk; Hobbs Hill; r £44-56; P ✗) A lovely old thatched farmhouse with beamed rooms, rustic furniture and an inglenook fireplace; there's also self-catering in the old smithy behind the house.

Thatch (☎ 890349; www.thethatch.com; 14 Hobbs Hill; d £50-60) Legendary among surfers for its great pub atmosphere and hearty food; the upstairs rooms are fine, but the nightlife can get a little rowdy.

Billy Budd's (☎ 890606; Hobbs Hill; mains £4-10) Another popular surfer's hang-out, serving jacket potatoes, chilli, nachos and huge sandwiches, as well as more substantial main meals and local ales.

Getting There & Away

Bus 308 runs from Barnstaple (40 minutes, hourly Monday to Saturday, five on Sunday).

Ilfracombe
☎ 01271 / pop 12,430

Strung out along a grand seafront promenade backed by a string of Edwardian villas and budget B&Bs, the coastal town of Ilfracombe has been attracting tourists since before Queen Victoria was on the throne, and it's still a favourite destination for holidaying Brits looking for a spot of bracing sea air and summer sunshine. Chic it certainly isn't, but Ilfracombe makes an attractive spot to sample the peculiar charms of the British seaside – candy-floss, cloudy days, chip wrappers and all. There are small beaches beyond the grassy headland of Hillsborough, but the best sand is 5 miles west at Woolacombe; the little cove of Lee Bay around the headland is also worth seeking out.

The **tourist office** (☎ 863001; www.ilfracombe -tourism.co.uk; The Landmark, The Seafront; ☿ 10am-5pm Mon-Sat, longer hours in summer) is housed inside the twin-towered **Landmark Theatre**.

DEVON & CORNWALL

SLEEPING

Ocean Backpackers (☎ 867835; www.oceanbackpackers .co.uk; 29 St James Pl; dm £9-12) A well-run backpackers in a large house near the seafront, with smallish dorms and a chaotic kitchen; the owners can help organise local activities including surfing, kayaking and even archery.

Norbury House Hotel (☎ 863888; Torrs Park; d £60-78; P ⊠) For something altogether more up-to-date, head for this delightful townhouse hotel, where contemporary styling (low-level beds, abstract art and bathroom murals) meets the venerable architecture of a former Victorian gentleman's residence.

Beechwood Hotel (☎ 863800; www.beechwoodhotel .co.uk; Torrs Park; d £76-90; P ⊠) Another handsome detached house with lovely private gardens filled with tall trees and rhododendrons, offering pleasant if slightly sparse rooms, some of which overlook the town and seashore.

Elmfield Hotel (☎ 863377; Torrs Park; www.elmfield hotelilfracombe.co.uk; d from £84; P ⚒) The pick of Ilfracombe's hotels is this elegant detached pile, set in an acre of private grounds, and decorated in endearingly old-fashioned style with lots of polished wood and well-worn furniture. The indoor heated swimming pool justifies staying here even if the rooms aren't quite to your taste.

GETTING THERE & AWAY

Buses 3 and 30 (40 minutes, every half-hour Monday to Friday, hourly Sunday) run to Barnstaple. Bus 300 heads to Lynton (one hour) and Minehead (two hours) three times daily.

Knightshayes Court

This Victorian fantasy **manor house** (NT; ☎ 01884-254665; Bolham; admission £7; ⊙ 11am-5.30pm Sat-Thu Apr-Sep, to 4pm Oct) was designed by the eccentric architect William Burges for the Tiverton MP John Heathcoat Mallory. Judging by the mix-and-match style of its construction, evidently they never quite managed to agree on the eventual style of the house. Burges' obsession with the Middle Ages resulted in a plethora of stone curlicues, ornate mantles and carved figurines, but Mallory preferred austere Victorian grandeur, best seen in the billiard room and his ornate boudoir. The extensive gardens feature a waterlily pool and wonderful topiary.

Bus 398 runs from Tiverton to Bolham (10 minutes, six to eight daily Monday to Saturday), three-quarters of a mile away.

Clovelly

☎ 01237 / pop 452

Clifftop villages don't come more picturesque than Clovelly, which seems to have been stuck in a time warp since the middle of the 19th century. A tangle of cob cottages and slate roofs tumbling down the side of a practically sheer cliff, Clovelly was once one of the busiest fishing harbours on the north Devon coast. The cobbled main street leads all the way uphill from the quay, and once clattered with the sound of donkeys drawing sledges filled with the daily catch. Charles Kingsley, author of the children's classic *The Water Babies*, spent much of his early life in Clovelly (his father was parish rector from 1830 to 1836), and it's still possible to visit his former house, as well as an old fisherman's cottage and the village's twin chapels.

Entry to the privately owned village is via the **visitor centre** (☎ 431781; admission £4.75), where there's a short film about the history of the village and a tearoom and shops. From Easter to October, Land Rovers regularly ferry visitors up and down the slope for £2 between 10am and 5.45pm.

Bus 319 runs five times daily to Bideford (40 minutes) and Barnstaple (one hour).

Hartland Abbey

This 12th-century **monastery-turned-stately-home** (☎ 01237-441264; www.hartlandabbey.com; admission £7; ⊙ 2-5.30pm Wed, Thu & Sun Apr-Oct, plus Tue Jul & Aug) was another post-dissolution handout, given to the sergeant of Henry VIII's wine cellar in 1539. It boasts some fascinating murals, ancient documents, paintings by English masters, Victorian photos, as well as marvellous gardens.

Hartland Abbey is 15 miles west of Bideford, off the A39 between Hartland and Hartland Quay.

DARTMOOR NATIONAL PARK

After spending a few days exploring the gentle coastline of south Devon, Dartmoor comes as something of a shock to the senses. The largest stretch of open moorland in the southwest, Dartmoor covers an area of 365 sq miles between Plymouth and Exeter, stretching for around 22 miles between Yelverton in the east and Dunsford in the west. It's a stark, wild and bleakly beautiful place, dotted with granite-topped hills, marshy bogs and patches of purple heather, as well as many weirdly shaped tors – rock pillars sculpted into strange forms by the wind and weather.

Dartmoor is named after the River Dart, which has its source here; the West and East Dart merge at Dartmeet. Most of the park is around 600m high – the highest spot is High Willhays (621m) near Okehampton. About 40% of Dartmoor is common land but 15% (the northwestern section, including High Willhays and Yes Tor) is leased to the Ministry of Defence and is closed for firing practice for part of the year.

Dartmoor encloses some of the wildest, bleakest country in England: suitable terrain for *The Hound of the Baskervilles* (one of Sherlock Holmes' more notorious foes). The landscape and weather can make this an extremely eerie place; try not to think of *An American Werewolf in London* on a dark, foggy night. With its forbidding landscape and scattered prehistoric remains, it's magnificent walking country, but bring a good map: it's easy to get lost, particularly when the mist rolls in.

Orientation

Dartmoor is 6 miles from Exeter and 7 miles from Plymouth. The B3212 cuts right across the centre of the moor, passing through the tiny villages of Two Bridges, Postbridge and Moretonhampstead. A number of small market towns and villages, including Ashburton, Buckfastleigh, Tavistock and Okehampton, ring the outer edge of the moor. Most of the

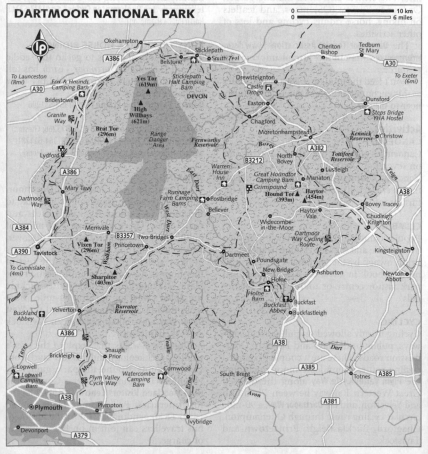

DARTMOOR NATIONAL PARK

villages and sights are on the eastern side; the western part is mainly frequented by serious walkers (and MOD artillery).

Information

There's plenty of info on getting out and about on the moor available from tourist offices in Exeter, Plymouth and most other local towns. The **National Park Authority** (NPA; www.dart moor-npa.gov.uk) runs the main High Moorland Visitors Centre in Princetown (opposite), and smaller visitor centres at **Haytor** (☎ 01364-661520), **Postbridge** (☎ 01822-880272) and **Newbridge** (☎ 01364-631303). They're generally open from 10am to 5pm daily, April to October.

The free *Dartmoor Visitor* newspaper is published annually and is packed with useful info. The centres also stock walking guides, Ordnance Survey (OS) maps, and leaflets on hiking, horse riding, cycling and lots of other activities.

The **Dartmoor Tourist Association** (www.discov erdartmoor.co.uk) is another useful information resource.

Don't feed the miniature Dartmoor ponies as this encourages them to move dangerously near to the roads.

Activities

CANOEING

Canoeing is possible during the winter months on several of Dartmoor's rivers. The British Canoeing Union operates a permit system for the River Dart; visit www.dartaccess.co.uk for further information.

CLIMBING

Popular climbing areas are at Haytor, owned by the NPA, and the Dewerstone near Shaugh Prior, owned by the National Trust. Groups need to book in advance. Ask at a national park visitor centre or tourist office for details.

CYCLING

Cycling is only allowed on public roads, byways, public bridleways and Forestry Commission roads. There are a couple of marked cycling routes around the moor, including the **Plym Valley Cycle Way** along the disused Great Western Railway between Plymouth and Yelverton, and the **Dartmoor Way**, a 90-mile circular cycling route through Okehampton, Chagford, Buckfastleigh, Princetown and Tavistock.

> **WARNING**
>
> Much of the northwest corner of Dartmoor is owned by the Ministry of Defence (MOD), and is regularly used for artillery practise. The areas are marked by red-and-white posts and notice boards at the main approaches; red flags (red lights at night) denote live firing is in progress. Firing schedules are available from the **MOD** (☎ 0800 458 4868), the National Park Authority and tourist offices.

The best place for bike hire is **Devon Cycle Hire** (☎ 01837-861141; www.devoncyclehire.co.uk; Sourton Down, nr Okehampton; bikes per day £12), which is handily situated along the Granite Way. Alternatively try **Okehampton Cycles** (☎ 01837-53248; North Rd, Okehampton).

PONY TREKKING & HORSE RIDING

There are lots of places to get in the saddle around Dartmoor. *Dartmoor Visitor* has full details. Prices start at around £18 per hour for half-day rides.

Babeny Farm Riding Stable (☎ 01364-631296; Poundsgate)

Dartmoor Riding Centre (☎ 01364-73266; Cheston)

Shilstone Rocks Riding Centre (☎ 01364-621281; www.dartmoor-riding.com; Widecombe-in-the-Moor).

WALKING

Walking is the main activity on Dartmoor, and every year thousands of people take to the moor to explore its open heaths and rocky tors. There are some 730 miles of public footpaths and bridleways to discover, and following the Countryside and Rights of Way Act in 2005, much of the rest of the moor is now open to enthusiastic ramblers. Waymarked walking routes include the **Abbot's Way**, an ancient 14-mile route from Buckfast to Princetown, and the **West Devon Way** a 14-mile hike between Tavistock and Okehampton.

Organised walks that explore the area's wildlife, archaeology and folklore start from various points around the park, guided by volunteer Dartmoor rangers. Contact the **High Moorland Visitors Centre** (☎ 01822-890414) for itineraries. Prices range from around £4 to £8 depending on the route although bus travellers can join in on the walks free of charge.

Sleeping & Eating

Camping rough on Dartmoor is generally allowed, but it's better for the park if you stick to designated camp sites. Many farms and hostels provide space for campers. There also several camping barns around the park, including six run by the YHA. Cooking and shower facilities and a wood burner are provided, but only a few barns have bunk beds. For bookings, phone ☎ 01200-420102, or visit www.yha.org.uk.

For a little more comfort, there are excellent YHA hostels at Postbridge (Bellever) and Steps Bridge, as well as Okehampton, Exeter and Dartington. B&Bs and country hotels are dotted around most towns and villages around the moor.

The **Dartmoor Tourist Association** (☎ 01822-890567; www.discoverdartmoor.com; High Moor Visitors Centre, Princetown) produces an annual *Dartmoor Guide* with full accommodation listings.

Getting There & Around

The *Discovery Guide to Dartmoor*, free from most Devon tourist offices and NPA offices, has full details of bus and train services around the park. There are scheduled buses to various points around the park from Totnes, Exeter, Plymouth and Okehampton. The most useful bus is 82, the Transmoor Link, running between Exeter and Plymouth via Moretonhampstead, Warren House Inn, Postbridge, Princetown and Yelverton (three daily Monday to Saturday, five Sunday).

The Dartmoor Sunday Rover ticket (adult £5, June to September) entitles you to unlimited travel on most bus routes, and to train travel on the Tamar Valley line from Plymouth to Gunnislake. Buy your ticket from bus drivers or at Plymouth train station.

The only main-line train station within easy reach of the park is Okehampton; see p348 for train details.

Princetown
☎ 01822

Perched on a bleak rise of moorland 8 miles east of Tavistock, Princetown is England's highest town, but it's best known as the location of one of Britain's most infamous high-security prisons. The gloomy granite form of **Dartmoor Prison**, built in 1809 to house French and American prisoners of war, looms ominously over the northern edge of town. It's far from the most beautiful spot on Dartmoor, but Princetown's central location makes it a good base for walking.

If you're after an unusual souvenir, the **Dartmoor Prison Museum** (☎ 890305; www.dartmoor -prison.co.uk; admission £2; 9.30am-4.30pm Tue-Sat) sells craftwork (mainly benches and garden gnomes) whittled into shape by current prisoners. The museum itself offers an insight into the gaol's early days.

The **High Moorland Visitors Centre** (☎ 890414; hmvc@dartmoor-npa.gov.uk; Old Duchy Hotel; 10am-5pm) has displays on Dartmoor and an information centre that stocks maps, guides and books. The visitor centre started life as Princetown's main hotel, where Arthur Conan Doyle began his classic Dartmoor tale *The Hound of the Baskervilles*.

There's no great reason to stay in Princetown, but there are a couple of pleasant inns

---

DARTMOOR HIKES

The **Templer Way** is an 18-mile hike from Teignmouth to Haytor, following the route originally used to transport Dartmoor granite down to the docks.

The **Two Moors Way** is a longer option, running from Ivybridge, on the southern edge of Dartmoor, 103 miles across Dartmoor and Exmoor to Lynmouth on the north Devon coast.

The **Dartmoor Way** is a 90-mile circular route, stretching from Buckfastleigh in the south, through Moretonhampstead, northwest to Okehampton and south through Lydford to Tavistock. The *Dartmoor Way* pack (£7.95) includes a book and 1:25,000 scale map, and is available from tourist offices and NPA centres. For further information, call ☎ 0870 241 1817 or check www .dartmoorway.org.uk.

The **Tarka Trail** circles north Devon and links with Dartmoor, south of Okehampton; *The Tarka Trail: A Walkers' Guide* can be purchased for £6.45.

It's always wise to carry a map, compass and rain gear since the weather can change very quickly and not all walks are waymarked. OS Explorer Map No 28 (1:50,000; £6.99) is the most comprehensive map, showing the park boundaries and MOD firing-range areas.

serving stout pub grub; try the **Railway Inn** (☎ 890232; Two Bridges Rd) or the **Plume of Feathers** (☎ 890240; The Square), which also has a camping barn and a few unspectacular rooms.

GETTING THERE & AWAY

Bus 82 (the Transmoor Link) runs to Princetown from Exeter (one hour, 40 minutes) and Plymouth (50 minutes).

Postbridge

☎ 01822

There's not much to the tiny village of Postbridge apart from a couple of shops, pubs and whitewashed houses. It's best known for its 13th-century **clapper bridge** across the East Dart, made of large granite slabs supported by stone pillars.

From April to October, there's an **NPA centre** (☎ 01822-880272) in the car park. There's also a **post office** and **shop** in the village.

SLEEPING & EATING

Runnage Farm (☎ 880222; www.runnagecampingbarns .com; camping from £5, bunk-beds £6.50-10) This farm has two YHA camping barns, space for camping, and mountain bike hire. Take the small road off the B3212 towards Moretonhampstead just after Postbridge.

Bellever YHA Hostel (☎ 0870 770 5692; bellever@yha .org.uk; dm £13.95; ✹ Mar-Oct) Formerly part of a Duchy farm, this cosy walker's hostel is a mile south of Postbridge, with dorm-only rooms and a small restaurant. Bus 98 runs from Tavistock (40 minutes, daily Monday to Saturday) and Princetown (20 minutes).

Two Bridges Hotel (☎ 892309; www.twobridges.co.uk; r £65-90; P ✗) A few miles west in the hamlet of Two Bridges, this venerable country hotel offers three categories of accommodation, ranging from standard en suites to premier bedrooms complete with four-poster beds, spa baths and burnished wood furniture. For something extra special, ask for Vivien Leigh's favourite suite.

Warren House Inn (☎ 880208; mains £6-12) Championing itself as Dartmoor's remotest pub, this isolated inn certainly feels a long way from the outside world, surrounded by rolling moorland and warmed by a fire that's allegedly been burning since 1845.

GETTING THERE & AWAY

Bus 82 runs through Postbridge between Plymouth (one hour) and Exeter (1½ hours).

Widecombe-in-the-Moor

☎ 01364

One of the prettiest villages on the moor is Widecombe, centred around a charming green shaded by majestic oaks and a 14th-century granite church (known as the Cathedral in the Moor). The village is commemorated in the traditional English folksong of Widdicombe Fair; the fair still takes place here on the second Tuesday of September.

There's a **visitor information point** at Sexton's Cottage, adjacent to the Church House. Built in 1537 as a brew house, the Church House is now the village hall.

SLEEPING & EATING

Cockingford Farm Campsite (☎ 621258; sites £3-8; ✹ mid-Mar–Nov) This camp site is around 1½ miles south of Widecombe.

Dartmoor Expedition Centre (☎ 621249; www .dartmoorbase.co.uk; bunkhouse £9.50, loft r £11.50) This outdoor activities centre offers bunk beds in a comfortable converted barn, and organises orienteering, canoeing, walking and climbing trips.

Lower Blackaton (☎ 621369; www.lowerblackaton .co.uk; d from £40; P ✗) This traditional 17th-century granite longhouse is 3 miles from Widecombe in a commanding position overlooking wild moorland. The five bedrooms have been carefully converted to preserve the house's traditional character, and there's an Aga-equipped kitchen and a well-stocked library.

Higher Venton Farm (☎ 621235; www.ventonfarm .com; tw/d £44/48; ✗) Half a mile from the village centre, this delightful 15th-century thatched farmhouse sits at the centre of 45 acres of working farmland, and offers three rustic, oak-beamed bedrooms; as you'd expect, the home-cooked breakfasts are superb.

Rugglestone Inn (☎ 621327; mains from £5) Just downhill from the village centre, this flower-covered pub has a homely main bar and an outside terrace peacefully placed beside a rushing brook.

Old Inn (☎ 621207; mains £5-12) The heart of village life for three centuries and still going strong, this fine old country inn serves hearty meals and great beer.

GETTING THERE & AWAY

Bus 272 stops at Widecombe from Tavistock (one hour 20 minutes, two daily) travelling via Princetown and Two Bridges en route. The

---

WORTH THE TRIP

Holne Chase Hotel (☎ 01364-631471; www.holne-chase.co.uk; Tavistock Rd; d £160-180, ste £200-210; dinner £35; P ✗) Hidden away in a beautiful wooded valley above the River Dart, this is arguably the finest of the country house hotels on Dartmoor. Built as a hunting lodge for nearby Buckfast Abbey, the grand gabled house commands sweeping views across private parkland, and is decorated with the style and sophistication you'd expect from a top-notch hotel; antique furniture, opulent fireplaces and effortlessly chic furnishings are dotted throughout the bedrooms and public lounges, and there are several 'stable suites' housed in a cluster of detached cottages beside the main hotel. The in-house restaurant is renowned for miles around for its inventive country-inspired cuisine, and the hotel even provides a luxury weekend getaway for visitors of the canine kind. One to remember.

---

afternoon bus continues to Totnes. Bus 274 travels from Okehampton (1¾ hours, three on Sunday) via Moretonhampstead. Several other buses stop at Widecombe on Sunday only as part of the Sunday Rover scheme.

Moretonhampstead
☎ 01647

The small market town of Moretonhampstead stands at an old crossroads where two of the main routes across Dartmoor meet, and makes a handy base for exploring the eastern moor.

EATING & SLEEPING

Steps Bridge YHA Hostel (☎ 0870 770 6048; dm adult £10.95; ☾ Apr-Sep) A typically efficient chalet-style YHA hostel, about 4½ miles east of Moretonhampstead along the B3212. Buses 82 and 359 run to Moretonhampstead (15 minutes) and Exeter (40 minutes).

Sparrowhawk Backpackers (☎ 440318; www.sparrowhawkbackpackers.co.uk; 45 Ford St; dm £13, r £30) This welcoming, environmentally-friendly backpacker's offers dorm beds in a smartly converted stone stable, solar-heated showers and an excellent veggie kitchen – you can even order your organic veg supplies in advance.

Moorcote Guest House (☎ 440966; www.moorcotehouse.co.uk; s £38, d £48; P ✗) This elegant double-gabled Victorian house is surrounded by grassy gardens, set back slightly from the main road. The rooms are plain and pleasant, though not all are en suite.

White Hart Hotel (☎ 441340; The Square; mains £8-16; s £60-70, d £99-120; P ✗) Owned by local entrepreneur Peter de Savary, who also runs a super-exclusive country house hotel nearby, this old Dartmoor pub has been renovated in a mix of traditional and modern styles – the restaurant and bar have bags of rough-stoned,

wood-beamed charm, while the upstairs rooms are thoroughly up-to-date, with flat-screen TVs, big beds and all the mod-cons.

GETTING THERE & AWAY

Bus 82 runs twice daily in summer from Moretonhampstead to Princetown (40 minutes), Plymouth (1½ hours) and Exeter (one hour). Bus 359 also goes to Exeter (seven daily Monday to Saturday).

Chagford
☎ 01647

Centred around a peaceful square with an unusual octagonal market house, Chagford seems to have been preserved in amber since the mid-'50s. Many of the shops still bear their old-fashioned shop signs, and the streets are lined with charming cottages, country food shops and a couple of excellent rural pubs. In the 14th century Chagford was a Stannary town, where local tin was weighed and checked, and was briefly famous as the first town west of London to be equipped with electric street lights.

EATING & SLEEPING

Easton Court (☎ 433469; www.easton.co.uk; Easton Cross; d £60 72; P ✗) A fabulous B&B housed inside an ivy-covered Edwardian long house. Pretty checks, cast-iron beds and William Morris fabrics add lots of character to the charming rooms.

Three Crowns Hotel (☎ 433444; www.chagford-accom.co.uk; High St; d £80) This 13th-century thatched inn is one of Dartmoor's spookiest spots – the corridors are said to be haunted by the spirit of Sydney Godolphin, a young Cavalier who died in the inn's doorway during the Civil War. The rooms still have an air of antiquated grandeur, with dark furniture and hefty four-poster beds,

DEVON & CORNWALL

PREHISTORIC DARTMOOR

The first settlers arrived on Dartmoor somewhere around 12,000 years ago, after the end of the last ice age. The moor looked very different then; it was almost entirely covered by trees, providing a rich source of food, fuel and natural shelter. Evidence of these early settlers is dotted all over Dartmoor; over 1500 cairns and burial chambers have been discovered and the area has more ceremonial rows and stone circles than anywhere else in Britain. The **Grey Wethers** stone circles stand side by side on a stretch of open moor halfway between Chagford and Postbridge, about half a kilometre from another stone circle near **Fernworthy**. **Scorhill** stone circle, near Gidleigh, is sometimes called the Stonehenge of Dartmoor, although only half of the original stones remain. Another intriguing site is at **Merrivale**, on the main road from Princetown to Tavistock, where you'll find several stone rows and standing stones, as well as a small ceremonial circle and the remains of several stone huts. But the most impressive site is the Bronze Age village of **Grimspound**, just off the B3212, where you can still see the remains of the circular stone wall that once surrounded the village, and the ruins of several granite round houses.

---

and the restaurant serves up generous portions of Brixham plaice, pollock fillet and fish pie (mains £9 to £15).

Courtyard (☎ 432571; 76 The Square; mains £4-9) A popular organic café inside a wholefood shop, always packed at lunch for its doorstep sandwiches, homemade pies and chunky cakes.

Ring O'Bells (☎ 432466; 44 The Square; mains £9-12) A wood-panelled pub with wholesome food and a beer garden.

GETTING THERE & AWAY

Bus 179 runs to Okehampton (one hour, two daily). Bus 173 travels from Moretonhampstead to Exeter via Chagford twice daily.

Okehampton

☎ 01837 / pop 7029

Just outside the national park on the main A30 road, Okehampton is the largest town within easy reach of Dartmoor, and makes an ideal base for exploring the northern part of the moor.

The **tourist office** (☎ 53020; oketic@visit.org.uk; Museum Courtyard, 3 West St; ☼ 10am-5pm Mon-Sat Easter-Oct) can help with local accommodation and walks.

SIGHTS & ACTIVITIES

A Norman motte and ruined keep is all that remains of Devon's largest **castle** (EH; ☎ 52844; admission £3; ☼ 10am-5pm Apr-Jun & Sep, 10am-6pm Jul & Aug); a free audio guide fills in the missing parts.

It's a pleasant three- to four-hour walk along the Tarka Trail from Okehampton to Sticklepath, where the **Finch Foundry** (NT; ☎ 840046; admission £3.70; ☼ 11am-5.30pm Wed-Mon Apr-Oct) has three working water wheels.

SLEEPING

Okehampton YHA Hostel (☎ 0870 770 5978; okehampton-yha.co.uk; Klondyke Rd; dm £15.50; ☼ Feb-Nov; P ☒) The YHA's flagship Dartmoor hostel stands on the site of the old Okehampton station, and doubles as an outdoor activities centre, complete with its own climbing wall and regular organised adventure trips.

Knole Farm (☎ 861241; www.knolefarm-dartmoor-holidays.co.uk; Bridestowe; d £46-50; P ☒) A fine country B&B inside an imposing stone farmhouse 10 miles west of Okehampton, with three floral rooms named after local landmarks and breathtaking views across the moor from the front garden.

Collaven Manor (☎ 861522; www.collavenmanor.co.uk; Sourton; s £61, d £98-120; P ☒) Nine cosy rooms are squeezed in among the roof beams and solid stone walls of this elegant manor house in the hamlet of Sourton, 5 miles west of Okehampton.

GETTING THERE & AWAY

Lots of local buses run through Okehampton. Bus X9 runs from Exeter (50 minutes, hourly Monday to Saturday, two on Sunday) via Okehampton to Bude. Bus 179 runs two or three times daily to Chagford (30 minutes) and Moretonhampstead (50 minutes). Extra buses run across the moor on summer Sundays.

The steam **Dartmoor Railway** (☎ 55637; www.dartmoorrailway.co.uk) runs between Okehampton and Meldon (£3.50 single, 10 minutes, two on Tuesday, five to seven on weekends April to October), with extra trains to Sampford Courtenay (£3 single) on some Saturdays. Timetables change regularly; phone for details or check the website.

Connecting trains to Okehampton from Exeter run on certain Sundays in summer.

CORNWALL

You can't get much further west than the ancient kingdom of Cornwall (or Kernow, as it's often referred to around these parts). With the longest stretch of continuous coastline in Britain, this is a land whose history is intricately bound up with the sea, and all around the county's shores you'll discover remnants of its maritime heritage. There are tiny fishing ports, old smuggler's inns and sturdy granite breakwaters, not to mention countless beaches and sweeping bays once filled with pilchard boats, gill netters and seagoing schooners. Although fishing is still an important industry, these days tourism is by far the biggest trade, and it's not hard to see what keeps the visitors coming back year after year. From the secluded coves and tree-clad creeks along the county's southern coast to the wild grandeur of the north coast cliffs, Cornwall is one of Britain's most breathtakingly beautiful counties. It's also an intriguing mix of old and new, where futuristic greenhouses and world-class galleries meet crumbling mines and ancient market towns. Although many of the old industries may be gone, there's a real buzz in the Cornish air these days – after years of economic hardship, this is definitely a county on the up.

Orientation & Information

Cornwall is just over 50 miles wide at its broadest, near the Devon border, and it's only 77 miles from Penzance to Plymouth, just across the Tamar from Cornwall, so you're never far from the coast and the main attractions.

WORTH THE TRIP

Lydford is best known for the 1½-mile **Lydford Gorge** (NT; ☎ 820320; admission £5; ☒ 10am-5.30pm Apr-Sep, 10am-4pm Oct, 10.30am-3pm Nov-Mar). An attractive but strenuous riverside walk leads to the 28m-high White Lady waterfall past a series of bubbling whirlpools, including the Devil's Cauldron. Alternatively, you can drive to the car park at the other end of the track, near the waterfall itself.

The county is divided into several districts, most of which publish handy brochures with accommodation listings. **Visit Cornwall** (☎ 01872-322900; www.visitcornwall.co.uk), otherwise known as the Cornwall Tourist Board, is the main point of contact, and can provide you with information on subjects ranging from Cornish cuisine to cycling trails and adventure sports.

For the low-down on all the latest events and arts exhibitions, check out the comprehensive listings at www.seencornwall.com.

Getting Around

Most of Cornwall's main bus, train and ferry timetables are collected into one handy brochure (available free from bus stations and tourist offices).

BUS

The main bus operator in Cornwall is **First** (☎ 0845 600 1420; www.firstgroup.com). The FirstDay ticket (£6) offers unlimited travel on its bus networks for 24 hours, it's also available in weekly (£28) and monthly (£80) versions.

Two of the smaller companies, **Truronian** (☎ 01872-273453; www.truronian.com) and **Western Greyhound** (☎ 01637-871871; www.westerngreyhound .com), also offer handy Day Rover tickets (£5). Many tourist attractions (including the Eden Project) offer discounts if you arrive by bus.

For the latest timetables, call ☎ 01872-322003 or visit www.cornwall.gov.uk/buses.

TRAIN

If you're taking the train, phone **National Rail Enquiries** (☎ 08457 484950) for the latest timetables and fares. The main route from London passes through Bristol, Exeter, Plymouth, Liskeard, Truro and Camborne en route to Penzance; there are also branch lines to St Ives, Falmouth, Newquay and Looe.

The Cornish Day Ranger (£10) ticket allows one day's travel on trains after 9.30am Monday to Friday and all weekend. There are also Branch Rover tickets valid on one of the county's spur lines. The Cornish Railcard (£10 per year) entitles you to 33% off most train fares in Cornwall.

TRURO

☎ 01872 / pop 17,431

Cornwall's capital city has been at the centre of the county's fortunes for over eight centuries. Truro grew up around a hilltop castle (no longer standing) built by Richard

Lucy, a minister of Henry II's, but it was the town's position at the confluence of the Rivers Allen, Kenwyn and Truro that sealed its fortunes (the town's name is thought to derive from the Cornish word *tri-veru*, meaning three rivers). Throughout the Middle Ages, Truro was one of five Stannary towns in Cornwall, where the county's tin and copper was assayed and stamped. During the 18th and 19th centuries, it became one of the southwest's most important industrial towns, attracting an influx of wealthy merchants and the construction of a swathe of elegant townhouses, best seen along Lemon St and Falmouth Rd. Truro was granted its own bishop in 1877, and the city's three-spired **cathedral** followed soon after – finally completed in 1910, it was the first new cathedral in England since St Paul's. Today, little evidence remains of Truro's industrial heyday, but the city still makes a good base, with a selection of shops, galleries and restaurants and Cornwall's main museum.

Information

Library (☎ 279205; Union Pl; ☺ 9am-6pm Mon-Fri, 9am-4pm Sat) Net access costs £3 per hour.
Post office (High Cross; ☺ 9am-5.30pm Mon-Sat).
Tourist office (☎ 274555; tic@truro.gov.uk; Boscawen St; ☺ 9am-5.30pm Mon-Fri, 9am-5pm Sat).

Sights

The **Royal Cornwall Museum** (☎ 272205; www.royal cornwallmuseum.org.uk; River St; admission free; ☺ 10am-5pm Mon-Sat) is the county's oldest museum and has some excellent displays exploring the county's industrial and archaeological past. There are also temporary exhibitions of art, photography and local craft.

Built on the site of a 16th-century parish church in soaring Gothic Revival style, **Truro Cathedral** (☎ 276782; www.trurocathedral.org.uk; High Cross; suggested donation £4) contains an impressive high-vaulted nave, some fine Victorian stained glass and the world-famous Father Willis Organ.

The **Lemon Street Market** (Lemon St) houses craft shops, cafés, delicatessens and an upstairs art gallery. There are several excellent art galleries around town, including the upmarket **Lemon St Gallery** (☎ 275757; 13 Lemon St; ☺ 10.30am-5.30pm Mon-Sat).

Guided tours (☎ 271257; blue.badge@kernow.net; adult/child £3/1.50) of the town depart from the tourist office at 11am every Wednesday.

Sleeping

Carlton Hotel (☎ 223938; www.carltonhotel.co.uk; 49 Falmouth Rd; s £40-47.50, d £57.50-65; Ⓟ ✗) This excellent-value B&B just up the main hill from the city centre makes a great base for exploring Truro and further afield, with a range of simply-finished rooms inside the gabled townhouse. Little luxuries include a sauna, Jacuzzi and cycle storage.

Royal Hotel (☎ 270345; www.royalhotelcornwall.co.uk; Lemon St; s £69, d £90-115; Ⓟ ✗ ▯) In the heart of the city, the Georgian-fronted Royal Hotel is the top place to stay in the city, with 35 bold, bright bedrooms, each with a slightly different character (the best is the loft-style room £39). For something even more stylish, check out the super-sleek 'aparthotels' just behind the main building, which come with dishwashers, galley kitchens and contemporary workspaces.

Alverton Manor (☎ 276633; reception@alvertonmanor .co.uk; Tregolls Rd; s £80, d £95-180; Ⓟ ✗) Just outside the town centre, this grand hotel, housed in a former convent and surrounded by landscaped grounds, makes a luxurious place to stay. There's a selection of country-style rooms, ranging from standard singles to spacious suites – make sure you bag one with a garden view.

Other recommendations:
Fieldings (☎ 262783; www.fieldingsintruro.com; 35 Treyew Rd; s/d £18/32) Pleasant Edwardian house run by a local couple, with great city views.
Townhouse (☎ 277374; www.trurotownhouse.com; 20 Falmouth Rd; s £45, d £65-75; Ⓟ ✗) City-style B&B with pleasant rooms, guest kitchen and a buffet breakfast.

Eating

Xen Noodle Bar (☎ 222998; 47-49 Calenick St; mains £4-8; ☺ lunch & dinner) Truro's Oriental love affair continues at this reliable noodle bar, which brings out the best from Chinese standards without overdosing on the MSG.

Saffron (☎ 263771; Quay St; mains £8-15; ☺ dinner Tue-Sat) For something more intimate, you can't do better than this tiny backstreet brasserie – local produce and fish dishes always feature heavily on the ever-changing menu.

Mannings Restaurant (☎ 247900; www.trurores taurants.co.uk; mains £11.95-18.95; ☺ lunch and dinner) The restaurant at the Royal Hotel is one of the town's busiest eating places. Cocktails and beers are served in the foyer bar, and the main restaurant menu takes in everything from fresh fish to blackened chicken and Mexican fajitas.

Tabbs (☎ 262110; 85 Kenwyn St; mains £12.50-19; ☺ lunch & dinner) This renowned restaurant has upped sticks from Portreath and set up shop in a refurbished pub in the centre of Truro. The stylish interior, all dark slate floors, pale tones and futuristic fireplaces, is matched by the sophisticated menu, especially strong on fresh seafood and local meat.

Stingi Lulu's (☎ 262300; River St; mains £13.95-18.95; ☺ lunch & dinner) A funky, buzzy restaurant next door to the museum, with an eclectic Eastern-themed décor and a menu that ranges through Thai, Japanese and Indonesian flavours.

Drinking

Indaba (☎ 274700; Tabernacle St) If you like plate glass and chrome pipes with your pints, then head for this award-winning industrial-style café just off Lemon Quay.

Kasbah (☎ 272276; 3 Quay St) This vaguely Eastern wine bar is always stuffed to the gunnels with 30-something boozers at the weekend, so it's hardly surprising that it's expanded into the old teashop next door.

MI Bar (☎ 277214; Lemon Quay) Next to the Hall for Cornwall, this metropolitan-style bar boasts a modern ambience and guest DJs on weekends.

Old Ale House (☎ 271122; Quay St) There are plenty of pubs around town, but this old-fashioned ale den is the best of the bunch – pick your poison from the daily ale blackboard, find a handy nook, and settle in for the night.

Heron (☎ 272773; Malpas; ☺ 11am-3pm & 6-11pm Mon-Sat, 7-10.30pm Sun) Two miles from the city along the river estuary, in the tiny village of Malpas, this creekside pub serves good beer and excellent pub grub.

Entertainment

Hall for Cornwall (☎ 262466; www.hallforcornwall .co.uk; Lemon Quay) The county's main venue for touring theatre and music, housed in Truro's former town hall on Lemon Quay.

Plaza Cinema (☎ 272894; www.wtwcinemas.co.uk; Lemon St) A four-screen cinema showing mainly mainstream releases.

Getting There & Away

BUS

There are direct National Express coaches to London Victoria (£35.50, 7½ hours, four

daily), and local buses to destinations across the county. Bus 18 (1½ hours, hourly) travels to Penzance via Camborne and Redruth, and bus 14 (1½ hours, hourly) travels to St Ives; lots of services travel to Falmouth and Newquay. Buses leave from the bus station just off Lemon Quay.

TRAIN

Truro is on the main line between London Paddington (£102.50, 4½ to five hours, hourly) and Penzance (£7.10, 45 minutes, hourly). There's a branch line to Falmouth (£3, 20 minutes, hourly Monday to Saturday).

SOUTHEAST CORNWALL

Dotted with picturesque fishing villages and patchwork fields, southeast Cornwall offers a much gentler side to the county than the stark, sea-pounded granite cliffs along the northern coast. Carpeted with wildflowers and crisscrossed by hedgerows, this is still working dairy country, where much of Cornwall's famously rich milk and clotted cream is produced.

Looe

☎ 01503 / pop 5280

The twin villages of East and West Looe stand on opposite sides of a broad river estuary, linked by a seven-arched Victorian footbridge, and there's long been a sense of friendly rivalry between the two communities. In previous centuries Looe was a thriving shipyard and fishing port, but these days tourism has taken over as the town's biggest industry. Victorian bathing machines rolled up to the water's edge off **Banjo Pier** throughout the 19th century, and the small beach in East Looe is still a popular spot for sandcastle-building and sunbathing, although the town itself is almost invisible beneath a jumble of pubs, tearooms and bucket-and-spade shops.

The **tourist office** (☎ 262072; www.southeastcorn wall.co.uk; Fore St; ☺ 10am-5pm Easter-Oct, noon-5pm Mon-Fri & 10am-5pm Sat & Sun Oct-Easter) is in the Guildhall.

The **Monkey Sanctuary** (☎ 262532; www.monkey sanctuary.org; St Martins; admission £5; ☺ 11am-4.30pm Sun-Thu Easter-Sep), a popular attraction half a mile west of Looe, is home to some unfeasibly cute woolly monkeys and a colony of horseshoe bats.

A mile offshore from Hannafore Point is tiny Looe Island, a 22-acre nature reserve

established by sisters Babs and Evelyn At-
kins, who jointly bought the island in 1965
and lived and worked there for most of their
lives. The island is now administered by the
Cornwall Wildlife Trust; occasional boat
trips travel there in summer from the quay
in East Looe. Ask at the tourist office for
details.

SLEEPING

Barclay House (☎ 262929; www.barclayhouse.co.uk; St
Martins Rd; d £70-90; P ⊠ ✕) This gorgeous detached Victorian villa in 6 acres of private gardens has the best bedrooms in Looe, decorated
in graceful shades of peach, pistachio and
aquamarine, and some of the most glorious
river views you could possibly wish for.

Trehaven Manor Hotel (☎ 262028; www.trehavenho
tel.co.uk; Station Rd; d £80-110; P ✕) A grand 19th-
century manor house that's been lovingly
converted to provide several delightful rooms,
all with their own unique touches – some have
rolltop baths and cast-iron bedframes, others
have small sitting areas and estuary views.

Other recommendations:

Tresco (☎ 265981; www.trescolooe.co.uk; Dawn Rd;
r £64-76; P ✕) Plush B&B with balcony bedrooms
overlooking Hannafore Point.

Beach House (☎ 262598; www.thebeachhouselooe
.com; Hannafore Point; d £80-110; P ✕) Stunningly
situated, contemporary B&B, with rooms named after
Cornish beaches.

GETTING THERE & AWAY

Trains travel the scenic Looe Valley Line
from Liskeard (£2.50, 30 minutes, 11 daily
Monday to Saturday, eight on Sunday), on
the London–Penzance line.

WORTH THE TRIP

At the head of the Fal estuary, 4 miles south
of Truro, **Trelissick Garden** (NT; ☎ 01872-
862090; Feock; admission £5.50; ⏰ 10.30am-
5.30pm Feb-Oct, 11am-4pm Nov-Dec) is one of
Cornwall's most beautiful landscaped gardens, with several tiered terraces covered
in magnolias, rhododendrons and hydran-
geas. A lovely walk runs all the way from the
main garden along the river to the estate's
private beach.

The Truronian T16 bus runs from Truro
(20 minutes, six daily) from Monday to
Saturday.

Bus 80A or 81A (four daily, two on Sunday)
and bus 72 (two daily Monday to Saturday)
from Polperro both stop at Looe en route to
Plymouth. Bus 573 from Looe only stops at
Polperro on Sunday.

Polperro

Polperro is another ancient fishing village, a
picturesque muddle of narrow lanes and fishing cottages set around a tiny harbour, best
approached along the coastal path from Looe
or Talland. It's always jammed with day-trippers and coach tours in summer, so arrive in
the evening or out of season if possible.

Polperro was once heavily involved in pilchard fishing by day and smuggling by night;
the small **Heritage Museum** (☎ 01503-272423; The
Warren; admission £1; ⏰ 10am-6pm Easter-Oct) features
some fascinating smuggling memorabilia and
tells some interesting tales.

For buses to Polperro see left.

Fowey

☎ 01726 / pop 2273
Nestled on the steep tree-covered hillside
overlooking the River Fowey, opposite the
old fishing harbour of Polruan, Fowey (pronounced Foy) is a pretty tangle of pale-shaded
houses and snaking lanes. It has a long maritime history, and in the 14th century raids
on French and Spanish coastal towns were
conducted from here. To defend the town
against Spanish raids, Henry VIII constructed
St Catherine's Castle (EH; admission free), above Read-
ymoney Beach, south of town. The town later
prospered by shipping china clay, quarried at
the clay pits around St Austell, but the industrial trade has long disappeared and Fowey
has now reinvented itself for summertime
tourists and second homeowners.

The **tourist office** (☎ 833616; www.fowey.co.uk; 5
South St; ⏰ 9am-5.30pm Mon-Sat, 10am-5pm Sun) shares
a building, phone and opening hours with
a literary centre devoted to Fowey's most
famous resident, the British thriller writer
Daphne du Maurier (1907–89), who lived
most of her life in a house at nearby Polrid-
mouth Cove. Every May Fowey hosts the
Daphne du Maurier Literary Festival (www.dumaurier
.org) in her honour.

Fowey is at the southern end of the Saints'
Way, a 26-mile waymarked trail running to
Padstow on the northern coast. **Ferries** (car/pe-
destrian £2.30/90p; ⏰ in summer last ferry 8.50pm) cross
the river to Bodinnick. The 4-mile Hall Walk

leads along the river to Polruan, from where you can catch a return ferry to Fowey.

SLEEPING & EATING

Golant YHA Hostel (☎ 0870 770 5832; golant@yha.org.uk; Penquite House; dm £15.50; ☐) This imposing whitewashed Georgian manor house makes a fantastic base in Fowey, with views across the estuary and helpful staff who can organise walking trips and other local activities.

Globe Posting House Hotel (☎ 833322; www.globepostinghouse.co.uk; 19 Fore St; s £22.50, d £45-55; ✗) For much better value and an equally central location, this snug little hotel has a clutch of cosy rooms tucked away along its higgledy-piggledy corridors, all with the requisite low ceilings and sturdy walls, and decorated in relaxing shades of white and blue. The refurbished restaurant has been turned into a light, modern place to eat, with light pine furniture and a seasonally-inspired menu.

Marina Hotel (☎ 833315; www.themarinahotel.co.uk; The Esplanade; d £108-152) Another boutique-styled gem slightly out of the town centre, with an elegant staircase leading to a confection of plush, expensive bedrooms. Some are exceedingly pokey for the money – hold out for a back room on the upper floors if you can, most of which have private patios and lovely river views.

Old Quay House (☎ 833302; 28 Fore St; www.theoldquayhouse.com; d £160-210; ✗) This beautifully appointed luxury hotel is right in the heart of Fowey, and offers some really lavish rooms, decorated with natural fabrics, rattan chairs and achingly tasteful tones; seven rooms have private balconies above the estuary.

King of Prussia (☎ 627208; www.kingofprussia.co.uk; Town Quay) The king of Fowey's many pubs takes its name from the local 'free trader' John Carter, and makes a lovely spot for a quayside pint or a quick lunchtime sandwich.

Food For Thought (☎ 832221; 4 Town Quay; menu £19.95; ✆ lunch & dinner) There's a touch of the French Riviera to this smart restaurant on the corner of Town Quay, with an excellent fixed-price menu filled with fishy treats and a pleasant outside terrace shaded by navy blue awnings.

GETTING THERE & AWAY

Bus 25 from St Austell (55 minutes, half-hourly) runs to Fowey via Par, the closest train station.

Lanhydrock House

Set in 900 acres of sweeping grounds above the River Fowey, the 16th-century manor house of **Lanhydrock** (NT; ☎ 01208-73320; house & gardens £9, gardens only £5; ✆ house 11am-5.30pm Tue-Sun Mar-Sep, 11am-5pm Tue-Sun Oct, gardens 10am-6pm year-round) was devastated by fire in 1881, but was later rebuilt in lavish style. The house offers a fascinating insight into *Upstairs Downstairs* life in Victorian England: highlights include the gentlemen's smoking room (complete with old Etonian photos, moose heads and tiger-skin rugs), the children's toy-strewn nursery, and the huge original kitchens. There's also a fabulous plaster ceiling in the Long Gallery, which somehow escaped the fire.

Lanhydrock is 2½ miles southeast of Bodmin. Bus 554 runs from Bodmin Parkway train station three times daily.

Restormel Castle

Built sometime in the 13th century, the ruined castle at **Restormel** (☎ 01208-872687; admission £2.40; ✆ 10am-6pm Jul & Aug, 10am-5pm Apr-Jun & Sep, 10am-4pm Oct) has one of the best-preserved circular keeps in the country, affording fine views across the surrounding fields from its crenellated battlements. Edward, the Black Prince, is thought to have stayed there twice during his reign. The castle is reached via a steep lane just above Lostwithiel, 6 miles from St Austell. Western Greyhound Bus No 536 (20 minutes, three daily Monday to Friday) and 554 travels to Lostwithiel from St Austell.

The Eden Project

The giant biomes of the **Eden Project** (☎ 01726-811911; www.edenproject.com; Bodelva; admission £13.80; ✆ 10am-6pm Apr-Oct, 10am-4.30pm Nov-Mar) – the largest greenhouses in the world – have become one of Cornwall's most celebrated landmarks since being raised from the dust of an abandoned china clay pit near St Austell in 2000. Tropical, temperate and desert environments have been recreated inside the biomes, so a single visit can carry you from the steaming rainforests of South America to the dry deserts of Northern Africa.

The Core, a newly-built education centre (constructed according to the Fibonacci sequence, one of nature's most fundamental building blocks) was opened in 2006. In summer the biomes become a spectacular backdrop to a series of gigs known as the **Eden Sessions** (recent artists include José Gonzalez,

Goldfrapp and The Magic Numbers) and from November to February Eden transforms itself into a winter wonderland for the **Time of Gifts** festival, complete with a full-size ice-rink.

It's impressive and immensely popular: crowds (and queues) can be large, so avoid peak times if possible, especially during summer. Eden is about 3 miles northeast of St Austell. **Truronian** (☎ 01872-273453) runs shuttle buses from St Austell, Newquay, Helston, Falmouth and Truro; combined bus and admission tickets are available onboard. Alternatively, if you arrive by bike, you'll get £3 off the admission price.

The Lost Gardens of Heligan
Before he dreamt up the futuristic phenomenon known as the Eden Project, ex-record producer Tim Smit was best known for rediscovering the lost gardens of **Heligan** (☎ 01726-845100; www.heligan.com; Pentewan; admission £7.50; ☯ 10am-6pm Mar-Oct, 10am-5pm Nov to Feb). Heligan was the former home of the Tremayne family, and during the 19th century was renowned as one of Britain's finest landscaped gardens; but the gardens fell into disrepair following WWI (where most of its staff were killed), and are only now regaining their former glory thanks to a dedicated team of gardeners and volunteers. Formal terraces, flower gardens, a working kitchen garden and a spectacular jungle walk through the 'Lost Valley' are just some of Heligan's secrets.

The Lost Gardens of Heligan are 1½ miles from Mevagissey and 7 miles from St Austell. Bus 25 leaves from St Austell station (30 minutes, nine daily), or you can catch bus 526 (six daily, two on Sunday), which travels from Newquay via St Austell station.

Cotehele
Dating from Tudor times, the manor house at **Cotehele** (NT; ☎ 01579-351346; St Dominick; admission £8, garden & mill only £4.80; ☯ 11am-4.30pm Sat-Thu Apr-Oct) served as the family seat of the aristocratic Edgecumbe dynasty for 400 years. It's stocked with some of Britain's finest Tudor interiors, best seen in the great hall, and dotted throughout with impressive tapestries and suits of armour. It's also notoriously haunted – several ghostly figures are said to wander through the house, accompanied by music and a peculiar herbal smell.

Outside, the lovely terraced gardens include a Victorian summerhouse and a medieval

---

TOP FIVE GARDENS

- Glendurgan – The Helford (p357)
- Heligan – near Mevagissey (left)
- Lanhydrock – St Austell (p353)
- Trebah – The Helford (p357)
- Trelissick – near Falmouth (p352)
- Check out www.gardensofcornwall.com for further tips.

---

dovecote. **Cotehele Quay** is part of the National Maritime Museum and has a small museum with displays on local boat-building and river trade, while the restored **Cotehele Mill** is a 15-minute walk away.

Cotehele is 7 miles southwest of Tavistock on the western bank of the Tamar. Bus 190 travels to Cotehele from Gunnislake station via Callington (40 minutes) four times daily on Sunday.

Roseland Peninsula
South of Truro, this beautiful rural peninsula gets its name not from flowers but from the Cornish word *ros*, meaning promontory. Highlights include the coastal villages of **Portloe**, a wreckers' hangout on the South West Coast Path, and **Veryan**, awash with daffodils in spring and entered between two thatched roundhouses. Nearby are the beaches of **Carne** and **Pendower**, which join at low tide to form one of the best stretches of sand on Cornwall's south coast.

St Mawes has an unusual clover-leaf **castle** (EH; ☎ 01326-270526; admission £3.60; ☯ 10am-6pm Jul & Aug, 10am-5pm Apr-Jun & Sep, 10am-4pm Oct, 10am-4pm Fri-Mon Nov-Mar), designed as the sister fortress to Pendennis (opposite) across the estuary.

St-Just-in-Roseland boasts one of the most beautiful churchyards in the country, full of flowers and tumbling down to a creek with boats and wading birds.

SOUTHWEST CORNWALL
Cornwall's southwest coastline, dotted with inlets, estuaries and wooded creeks, has long been one of the county's main maritime areas. The deepwater port at Falmouth – the third-largest natural harbour in the world – is still a busy seafaring town, and the remote area further to the west around the Lizard was once notorious as a haven for smugglers and wreck-

ers. These days, history and natural scenery are the main attractions, with long stretches of protected coastline, fine beaches and some of Cornwall's most impressive subtropical gardens all within easy reach of Falmouth.

Falmouth

☎ 01326 / pop 20775

The maritime port of Falmouth sits on the county's south coast at the end of the Carrick Roads, a huge river estuary that empties out into the third deepest natural harbour in the world. Falmouth's fortunes were made during the 18th and 19th centuries, when clippers, trading vessels and mail packets from across the world stopped off to unload their cargoes in the town, and Falmouth remains an important centre for shipbuilding and repairs. These days, however, it's better known for its lively nightlife and the newly-built campus of the CUC (Combined Universities of Cornwall), a few miles up the road in Penryn; although salty seadogs can still get a taste of the town's nautical heritage at the stunning National Maritime Museum beside the harbour.

The **tourist office** (☎ 312300; falmouthtic@yahoo .co.uk; 28 Killigrew St; ⏰ 9.30am-5.15pm Mon-Sat Apr-Sep, Mon-Fri Oct-Mar, plus 10am-2pm Sun Jul & Aug) is opposite the bus terminal.

SIGHTS & ACTIVITIES
Pendennis Castle

Falmouth's deepwater harbour has been a vital strategic asset throughout the town's history, a fact acknowledged by Henry VIII, who constructed Cornwall's largest fortress out on Pendennis Point. **Pendennis Castle** (EH; ☎ 316594; adult £4.80; ⏰ 10am-6pm Jul-Aug, 10am-5pm Apr-Sep, 10am-4pm Oct-Mar) was designed to defend the entrance to the Carrick Roads in tandem with its sister fortress to St Mawes (opposite), on the opposite side of the estuary, although neither fortress was ever engaged in battle.

The recently-refurbished visitor centre includes an education suite and an interactive exhibition, which aims to bring the history of the castle to life using reconstructions, artefacts and a hands-on scale model of the castle.

National Maritime Museum

The **National Maritime Museum** (☎ 313388; www .nmmc.co.uk; Discovery Quay; adult £7.00; ⏰ 10am-5pm), housed in an award-winning building by Falmouth Docks, contains vessels and exhibitions

exploring Britain's seafaring heritage through the ages. The Flotilla Gallery houses more than 40 boats from the national collection.

Boat Trips

In summer, boat trips set out from the Prince of Wales pier to the Helford River and Frenchman's Creek (£8 return), a 500-year-old smuggler's cottage upriver (£6.50 return), and Truro (£8 return, one hour). The pier is lined with boat companies' booths; try **Enterprise Boats** (☎ 374241) or **Cornish Belle** (☎ 01872-580309).

Passenger ferries cross to St Mawes and Flushing from the pier every hour in summer.

Beaches

The nearest beach to town is busy **Gyllyngvase**, a short walk from the town centre, where you'll find plenty of flat sand and a decent beach café. Further along the headland, **Swanpool** and **Maenporth** are usually quieter.

SLEEPING

Falmouth is crammed with B&Bs and hotels, especially along Melvill Rd and Avenue Rd.

Grove Hotel (☎ 319577; www.thegrovehotel.net; Grove Pl; s £30-45, d £60-65; 🅿 ✕) This Georgian residence, formerly the home of a 19th-century sea captain, has had a thorough facelift and now offers plain, great-value rooms in a handy location for the centre of Falmouth and the Maritime Museum.

WORTH THE TRIP

Lugger Hotel (☎ 01872-501322; www.lugger hotel.co.uk; Portloe; depending on season r £160-180) Teetering over the harbour's edge in the beautiful old fishing town of Portloe, this supremely indulgent boutique hotel makes the consummate place for a romantic getaway. A range of higgledy-piggledy rooms are dotted around the old smuggler's inn and a couple of adjoining fishermen's cottages, making for some imaginative layouts and a charming mix of rough oak beams, clean, contemporary furnishings and huge, decadent beds. Downstairs the elegant restaurant serves fishy treats straight off the boats, and the panoramic portside terrace makes the ideal place for watching the sun go down. When did the British seaside get this sexy?

DEVON & CORNWALL

Dolvean Hotel (☎ 313658; www.dolvean.co.uk; 50 Melvill Rd; s £40-46, d £76-96; **P** **☒**) If you're looking for clean lines and contemporary style, then you'd be sensible to look elsewhere, but it's lashings of lace and frilly drapes you're after, then this homely B&B will fit the bill.

St Michael's Hotel (☎ 312707; www.stmichaels-hotel .co.uk; s £49-69, d £69-126, ste £90-145; **P** **♨** **☒**) A programme of refurbishment has turned this venerable hotel into one of Falmouth's most stylish sleeping spots, with a selection of light, unfussy bedrooms decked out with nautical touches, and a beautiful spa and seafood restaurant.

Greenbank Hotel (☎ 312440; www.greenbank-hotel .com; Harbourside; harbour view d £125-215, nonharbour view d £105-150; **P** **☒**) A little way out of town along the harbourfront, the Greenbank is the grand old dame of Falmouth hotels, with a huge old-fashioned coffee lounge with panoramic views, and plenty of comfy, country-style rooms.

Other recommendations:

Chelsea House (☎ 212300; www.chelseahousehotel .com; 2 Elmslie Rd; s £35, d £42-70; **P** **☒**)

Rosemullion Hotel (☎ 314690; gail@rosemullionhotel .demon.co.uk; Gyllyngvase Hill; d £45-55; **P** **☒**) Mock-Tudor hotel split over three floors, uphill from Gyllyngvase Beach.

EATING & DRINKING

Boathouse (☎ 315425; Trevethan Hill; mains £6-10; 🕑 lunch & dinner) This fantastic gastropub is so laid-back it's almost horizontal. It's especially popular with Falmouth's creative crowd, who come for the generous plates of food, cold beer and chilled-out vibe.

Three Mackerel (☎ 311886; Swanpool Beach; mains £11-20 🕑 lunch & dinner) Perched on the cliff above Swanpool Beach, a mile or so from Falmouth

---

WORTH THE TRIP

Ferryboat Inn (☎ 01326-250625; Helford Passage; mains £5-15) Tucked away along the beautiful Helford Estuary, this riverfront pub is an old favourite with locals and visiting yachties alike. On summer nights the creekside patio is packed with a lively crowd tucking into huge plates of beer-battered fish or triple-decker club sandwiches, and in winter it becomes the quintessential smuggler's pub, perfect for Sunday lunch in front of a roaring log fire.

---

town, this light, bright bistro makes the perfect place to watch the sun go down over a plate of tapas and a cold beer. For something more sophisticated, head inside for imaginative seafood and steaming hot mussels.

Hunky Dory (☎ 212997; 46 Arwenack St; mains £12.25-24.95; 🕑 dinner) This stylish seafood restaurant at the end of Arwenack St has fast gained a reputation as one of the top tables in town. The décor's clean and minimal, with plain wooden tables, muted lighting and terracotta floors, and the menu's stuffed to the gills with local produce, from pan-fried seabass to baked Newlyn cod.

There are plenty of pubs around town, ranging from the **Quayside** (☎ 312113; Arwenack St), with outside seating on the harbour, and the nautically-themed **Chain Locker** (☎ 311685; Quay St).

ENTERTAINMENT

Falmouth Arts Centre (☎ 314566; www.falmoutharts.org; Church St) A good arts venue with programmes of theatre, music and independent cinema.

GETTING THERE & AWAY

Falmouth is at the end of the branch train line from Truro (£2.30 single, 20 minutes, every two hours Monday to Saturday).

Bus 7 runs to Penzance (1¼ hours, six daily Monday to Saturday). Bus 88 offers the most frequent service to Truro (1¼ hours, half-hourly Monday to Saturday, six on Sunday).

The Lizard

☎ 01326

For a glimpse of Cornwall's stormier side, the ink-black cliffs, rugged coves and open heaths of the Lizard Peninsula are hard to beat. This is England's most southerly point, and on a wind-lashed winter's day, it certainly feels a long way from the outside world; but in high summer the clifftops burst into life with wildflowers and butterflies, and the remote coves make the perfect place for a spot of secluded swimming. In past centuries the Lizard was at the centre of Cornwall's smuggling industry, and the area is crammed with tales of Cornish 'free-traders' sneaking barrels of liquor and contraband goods under the noses of government Preventive boats. Some smugglers even became local legends – the most notorious was John Carter, the so-called King of Prussia, after whom Prussia Cove near Marazion is named.

CORNWALL'S FURRY FLING

Helston, the only real town on the Lizard, is famous for its annual **Flora Day**, held every year on 8 May. Believed to be the last remnant of an old pagan celebration marking the coming of spring, this ancient festival is a peculiar mixture of street dance, musical parade and floral pageant. Local residents dress up in traditional finery and the town is covered in blossoms collected from the surrounding countryside. The day itself is marked by several stately dances; the first is at 7am, followed by the lively Hal-An-Tow pageant and a children's dance. The main highlight of the day is the Furry Dance, which kicks off at noon and proceeds around the town's streets; participants take part by invitation only, and the dance is always led by a local couple. The final dance of the day is at 5pm, before the entire town descends on the local pubs for a hard-earned pint or six. Unsurprisingly, the Victorians took a dim view of the proceedings, and the festival was banned in the 19th century for promoting 'drunken revelry'.

For more information visit www.lizard-peninsula.co.uk.

GOONHILLY EARTH STATION

The last thing you'd expect to find in the middle of the Lizard is a radio station, but in fact the vast dishes of the **Goonhilly Earth Station** (☎ 0800-679593; www.goonhilly.bt.com; admission £6.50; ☻ 10am-6pm late May-Sep, 10am-5pm Apr–late May & Oct, 11am-4pm Tue-Sat Nov, Dec & mid-Feb–Mar) make up the largest satellite station on earth. The multimedia visitor centre has lots of interactive exhibits and romps through the last 200 years of telecommunications.

RIVER HELFORD

Across the north of the Lizard flows the **River Helford**, lined with overhanging oaks and hidden inlets: the perfect smugglers' hideaway. **Frenchman's Creek**, the inspiration for Daphne du Maurier's novel of the same name, can be reached on foot from the car park in **Helford** village.

On the northern bank of the river is **Trebah** (☎ 250448; www.trebahgarden.co.uk; admission Mar-Oct £5.80, Nov-Feb £3; ☻ 10.30am-6.30pm, last entry 5pm), touted as Cornwall's 'Garden of Dreams'. First planted in 1840, it's one of Cornwall's finest subtropical gardens, dramatically situated in a steep ravine filled with giant rhododendrons, huge Brazilian rhubarb plants and jungle ferns.

Located just to the east are the gardens of **Glendurgan** (☎ 250906; glendurgan@nationaltrust .org.uk; admission £5; ☻ 10.30am-5.30pm Tue-Sat Feb-Oct), established in the 18th century by the Fox family, who made their fortune importing exotic plants from the New World. There are stunning views of the River Helford, and there's also a 19th-century maze and a secluded beach near Durgan village.

Near Gweek, 6 miles from Helston at the western end of the river, is the **National Seal Sanctuary** (☎ 221361; www.sealsanctuary.co.uk; adult/child £11/8; ☻ 10am-5pm May-Sep, 9am-4pm Oct-Apr), which cares for sick and orphaned seals washed up along the Cornish coastline before returning them to the wild.

LIZARD POINT & AROUND

Three miles west of Helston is **Porthleven**, another quaint fishing port with excellent beaches nearby. **Cadgwith** is the quintessential Cornish fishing village, with thatched, whitewashed cottages and a small harbour. **Lizard Point** is a 3½-mile walk along the South West Coast Path.

At the peninsula's tip is the **Lizard Lighthouse** (☎ 290065), built in 1751 and now entirely automated. Lizard Point is one of the most treacherous coastal areas in Cornwall; hundreds of ships have foundered on the peninsula's rocky shores and cliffs over the years. Below the lighthouse, a rough track leads down to the disused lifeboat station and a shingle cove. The views from the surrounding cliff tops are some of the most dramatic in all of Cornwall.

A mile west is the beautiful National Trust beach of **Kynance Cove**, overlooked by towering cliffs and flower-covered headland. Much of the red-green serpentine rock fashionable during the Victorian era was mined here.

SLEEPING

Lizard YHA Hostel (☎ 0870 770 5780; lizard@yha.org .uk; dm £15.50; ☻ Apr-Oct) Few top-end hotels can boast the kind of spectacular sea view enjoyed by this gloriously situated hostel, in a renovated Victorian hotel right below the lighthouse on Lizard Point.

FESTIVAL FEVER

Cornwall has much more going on than just sand, sea and spectacular views. The county's calendar is packed with festivals and events – here's a whistle-stop guide to the main attractions.

■ Helston Flora Day – (see the boxed text Cornwall's Furry Fling, p357) This spring festival has been bursting into life every May for as long as anyone can remember, with street dancing, traditional music and a lively community atmosphere.

■ Padstow Obby Oss – (see the boxed text My Kingdom for an Oss, p372) Cornwall's oldest, and quite possibly weirdest, pagan festival – expect people-packed streets, two profoundly disturbing manmade 'osses and enough booze to make your liver quiver.

■ Golowan Arts Festival – (www.golowan.com) Lively arts and music festival held around Penzance in June.

■ Port Eliot Litfest – (www.porteliot.com) Cult literary festival held on the St Germans estate, near Saltash, every July.

■ Fowey Regatta Week – (www.fowey.co.uk) Yachts and yachties converge on Fowey for this annual sailing festival, held in August.

■ Eden Sessions – (www.edenproject.com) The Eden Project's biomes are transformed into the county's most spectacular live venue over four nights in July and August.

■ Falmouth Oyster Festival – (www.falmouthoysterfestival.co.uk) Three days of oyster-themed feasting on the Falmouth quayside every October.

■ St Ives September Festival – (www.stivesseptemberfestival.co.uk) A long-running creative arts festival in St Ives, with an extensive programme of exhibitions, gigs, readings and workshops.

■ Cornwall Film Festival – (www.cornwallfilmfestival.com) Every November, Cornwall's film festival screens all the latest work from the county's film scene in Falmouth.

■ City Of Lights – Withy lanterns and giant paper puppets take to Truro's streets for this Christmassy spectacle in December.

Coverack YHA Hostel (☎ 0870 770 5780; coverack@yha .org.uk; Coverack; dm £15.50; ⊗ Mar-Oct) Tucked away above the pretty harbour of Coverack, this is another good hostel, with spacious dorms arranged over several floors in an old gentleman's townhouse.

Housel Bay Hotel (☎ 290417; www.houselbay.com; The Lizard; d £64-136; ⓟ ⊠) By far the most impressive hotel on Lizard Point, this grand gabled manor was constructed by a group of Victorian entrepreneurs to offer its discerning guests the sort of stirring views and luxurious rooms they'd expect from a Cornish country house. A century later it's still a gorgeous place to stay, with plenty of antiques, period rugs and a charming old-world atmosphere.

GETTING THERE & AWAY

The Lizard's transportation hub is Helston, served by **Truronian** (☎ 01872-273453; www.truronian .co.uk). Bus T1 runs from Truro to Helston (50 minutes, 16 to 20 Monday to Saturday, five on Sunday); for onward connections to the

Lizard village, catch bus T34 from the Tesco car park in Helston.

Bus T2 runs from Helston to Goonhilly (20 minutes), Coverack (25 minutes) and St Keverne (40 minutes, 15 daily Monday to Saturday).

A Day Rover ticket valid on all Truronian buses costs £5.

St Michael's Mount

Before the domes of the Eden Project appeared on the scene, Cornwall's best-known landmark was undoubtedly **St Michael's Mount** (NT; ☎ 01736-710507; admission £6; ⊗ 10.30am-5.30pm Mar-Oct, phone ahead at other times; last admission 4.45pm), an island abbey connected to the mainland at Marazion by a cobbled causeway, and completely cut off at high tide.

The first church was believed to have been founded on the island in the 5th century, although most of the present-day abbey derives from a 12th-century chapel constructed by the same Benedictine monks who built Mont St Michel off the Normandy coast. The mount became an important place of pilgrimage throughout the Middle Ages, and briefly served as a fortress during the Civil War. Since 1659 the mount has been the home of the St Aubyn family, and has been open to the public since 1954 under the stewardship the National Trust.

Highlights include the rococo Gothic drawing room, the original armoury and the 14th-century priory church, but the island is perhaps most famous for its subtropical **gardens** (admission £3), teetering dramatically above the sea.

It's possible to walk across the causeway at low tide, or you can catch a ferry at high tide in summer.

Bus 2 passes Marazion as it travels from Penzance to Falmouth.

Penzance
☎ 01736 / pop 21,168
Perched dramatically above the glittering sweep of Mounts Bay, Penzance has been the last stop on the main line from London since the days of the Great Western Railway, and the town still feels one step removed from the rest of the county. With its hotchpotch of winding streets, old shopping arcades and grand seafront promenade, it feels much more authentic than the polished-up, prettified towns of Padstow and St Ives, and makes an excellent base for exploring the rest of west Cornwall and Land's End.

INFORMATION
Library (☎ 363954; internet access per hr £3; Morrab Rd)
Polyclean Laundrette (☎ 364815; 4 East Tce; 7.30am-7.30pm; per load £3.50)
Tourist office (☎ 362207; pztic@penwith.gov.uk; Station Approach; 9am-5pm Mon-Sat, 10am-1pm Sun) Next to the bus station.
www.penzance.co.uk Useful local guide to Penzance and the surrounding area.

SIGHTS & ACTIVITIES
Despite what you may have heard from Messrs Gilbert and Sullivan, Penzance was never renowned for its pirate population – it was much better known for its exports of tin, grain and pilchards (one of Cornwall's signature dishes was 'stargazey pie', so called because the fishes' heads were left gazing through the pie's crust). Like Truro and Falmouth, Penzance grew rich on the export trade, and the old town is littered with elegant Georgian and Regency houses,

especially around Chapel St. Perhaps the most outlandish example is the 19th-century **Egyptian House**, which looks like a bizarre cross between a Georgian townhouse and an Egyptian sarcophagus.

Penlee House Gallery & Museum (☎ 363625; www.penleehouseorg.uk; Morrab Rd; admission £2, free on Sat; 10am-5pm Mon-Sat May-Sep, 10.30am-4.30pm Mon-Sat Oct-Apr) displays a fine range of paintings by artists of the Newlyn School (including Stanhope Forbes) and hosts regular exhibitions exploring the history of art in Cornwall.

The **Trinity House National Lighthouse Centre** (☎ 360077; Wharf Rd; admission £3; 11am-5pm Apr-Oct) relates the history of the lighthouses that have helped keep ships from harm along the treacherous Cornish coastline.

The busy fishing harbour of **Newlyn**, on the western edge of Penzance, was the centre of the Newlyn School of artists in the late 19th century; the cutting-edge **Newlyn Art Gallery** (☎ 363715; www.newlynartgallery.co.uk) is currently undergoing extensive refurbishment and is set to reopen in 2007.

SLEEPING
Budget
Penzance has lots of low-price B&Bs, especially along Alexandra Rd and Morrab Rd.

Penzance Backpackers (☎ 363836; www.pzbackpack.com; Alexandra Rd; per person dm/d £13/14;) Penzance's only independent hostel is a cheery, welcoming affair, with a few dorms and private rooms squeezed into a converted townhouse, and a decent-sized lounge and kitchen.

Penzance YHA Hostel (☎ 0870 770 5992; penzance@yha.org.uk; Castle Horneck, Alverton; dm £15.50;) The official YHA hostel in Penzance is housed inside an 18th-century Georgian manor on the outskirts of town, with an onsite café and mostly four- to 10-bed dorms. Buses 5 and 6 run from the bus station to Alverton; it's a 500m walk from the bus stop.

Glencree House (☎ 362026; www.glencreehouse.co.uk; 2 Mennaye Rd; r £32-50 depending on season) Fantastic value B&B just a short stroll from the town centre with eight old-fashioned rooms, including a couple with sea views; the huge breakfast includes a choice of smoked butterfly kippers, croissants and fresh fruit.

Midrange & Top End
Blue Seas Hotel (☎ 364744; www.bluehayeshotel-penzance.co.uk; 13 Regent Tce; s £30-35, d £60-80;) One of several posh B&Bs along Regent's

DEVON & CORNWALL

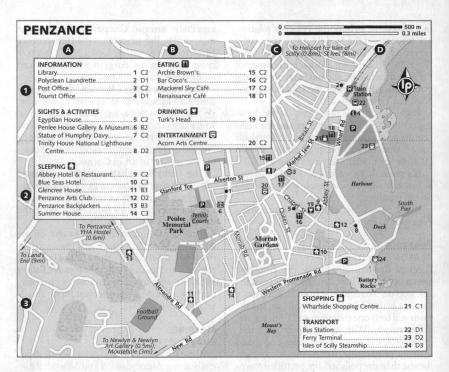

PENZANCE

0 — 500 m
0 — 0.3 miles

INFORMATION	
Library....................................	1 C2
Polyclean Laundrette.................	2 D1
Post Office...............................	3 C2
Tourist Office...........................	4 D1

SIGHTS & ACTIVITIES	
Egyptian House.........................	5 C2
Penlee House Gallery & Museum..	6 B2
Statue of Humphry Davy............	7 C2
Trinity House National Lighthouse	
Centre..................................	8 D2

SLEEPING	
Abbey Hotel & Restaurant..........	9 C2
Blue Seas Hotel........................	10 C3
Glencree House.........................	11 B3
Penzance Arts Club....................	12 D2
Penzance Backpackers...............	13 B3
Summer House..........................	14 C3

EATING	
Archie Brown's.........................	15 C2
Bar Coco's...............................	16 C2
Mackerel Sky Café....................	17 C2
Renaissance Café......................	18 D1

DRINKING	
Turk's Head..............................	19 C2

ENTERTAINMENT	
Acorn Arts Centre.....................	20 C2

SHOPPING	
Wharfside Shopping Centre.............	21 C1

TRANSPORT	
Bus Station...............................	22 D1
Ferry Terminal..........................	23 D2
Isles of Scilly Steamship...............	24 D3

Tce, with plain, pale-toned rooms and a spacious lounge and reading room downstairs. The top-notch breakfast features homemade kedgeree and smoked salmon scrambled eggs.

Penzance Arts Club (☎ 363761; www.penzanceartsclub.co.uk; Chapel St; s £55-70, d £80-100) Penzance's funkiest place to stay is this fabulous cross between an arts club and boutique B&B. The colour-coded rooms are simple, comfortable and unfussy, but the centre of the action is the downstairs lounge, decked out like a Victorian gentleman's residence, where there are regular gigs, poetry readings, salsa nights and residential arts courses.

Summer House (☎ 363744; www.summerhouse-cornwall.com; Cornwall Tce; s £70, d £75-95; ☒ closed Nov-Mar; P ☒) If you're looking to stay in style in Penzance, the super-swish Summer House is tough to top. The grand, Grade-II listed Regency house offers a patchwork of rooms decorated in checks, pinstripes and sunny tones, with tons of original features and carefully chosen furniture; downstairs there's a Mediterranean-themed restaurant and a garden perfect for summer barbecues.

Abbey Hotel (☎ 366906; www.theabbeyonline.co.uk; Abbey St; r £130-190) The excellent Abbey Hotel is run by the same husband-and-wife team who own the Abbey Restaurant next door (see opposite). The sky-blue 17th-century townhouse has been refurbished with taste, grace and plenty of period furniture, but it's the very opposite of an anonymous style hotel – quirky antiques and topsy-turvy layouts are the order of the day.

EATING
Bar Coco's (☎ 350222; 13 Chapel St; tapas £2-6; ☒ closed Sun) The Mediterranean hits Penzance at this laid-back restaurant and tapas bar, where you can tuck into Provençal fish soup and seared tuna or just sit back with an ice-cold Sol and a bowl of marinated olives.

Archie Brown's (☎ 362828; Bread St; mains £3-6; ☒ 9.30am-5pm Mon-Sat) This much-loved veggie/vegan café is on the first floor above a health-food shop, and serves up hearty portions of old veggie faves including homity pie, hot chilli and crumbly carrot cake.

Renaissance Café (☎ 366277; 6 Wharfside Shopping Centre; mains £5-12; ☒ lunch & dinner) A continental-style café-bar, tucked away in the Wharfside shopping centre, with an excellent menu packed with club sandwiches, burgers and seafood specials, and fine views across Mount's Bay.

Mackerel Sky Café (☎ 366866; 45 New St; mains £7-10; ⏲ lunch Tue-Sat) Next door to the upmarket Harris' restaurant, this new café is a cosy spot for a huge open sandwich or a gourmet burger, but also serves up fresh fish dishes and quite possibly the frothiest cappuccinos in Penzance.

Abbey Restaurant (☎ 330680; Abbey St; 2/3 courses £18/23; ⏲ lunch Fri-Sun, dinner Tue-Sat Jun-Sep, phone ahead at other times) One of Cornwall's most acclaimed restaurants, run by the renowned chef Ben Tunnicliffe. Upstairs the restaurant serves cutting-edge British cuisine in a contemporary dining room; downstairs the boldly-coloured cellar bar serves all the aperitifs and digestifs you could wish for.

DRINKING & ENTERTAINMENT

Turk's Head (☎ 363093; Chapel St) Purportedly the oldest pub in Penzance, with a rabbit's warren of rooms and bars perfect for a pint of real ale and a plate of sausage and mash. Rumour has it there used to be a smuggler's tunnel from the pub all the way to the harbour.

Acorn Arts Centre (☎ 363545; www.acorn-theatre.co.uk; Parade St) An excellent independent arts centre, with regular programmes of film, theatre and live music, in an intriguing two-tiered auditorium.

GETTING THERE & AWAY

Bus

National Express coaches travel to London (£35.50, nine hours, eight daily) via Exeter (£22, five hours, two daily), sometimes changing at Plymouth (£6.50, 3½ hours, seven daily). For buses to Land's End, see p362.

Train

There are regular services to Penzance from London Paddington (£108, six hours, eight daily) via Truro. There are frequent trains from Penzance to St Ives (£4.40, 20 minutes, hourly), with connections at St Erth.

WEST CORNWALL

West Cornwall contains some of the county's wildest scenery, a classic landscape of sea-battered cliffs, churning surf, crumbling mine-workings and wheeling gulls. The West Penwith area was one of the oldest Celtic settlements in Cornwall, and the area is littered with prehistoric sites.

Mousehole

☎ 01736

The compact harbour Mousehole was once at the heart of Cornwall's thriving pilchard industry, but these days it's best known for its colourful Christmas lights, and as the location for a much-loved local children's story called *The Mousehole Cat*.

Old Coastguard (☎ 731222; www.oldcoastguardhotel.co.uk; depending on season r £80-160) is a swish, modernised hotel decorated with a healthy dose of designer flair. Deep sofas, smart pine floors and neutral colours characterise the rooms, half of which are in a detached lodge by the harbour; the sunlit restaurant has beautiful bay views and specialises, as you might expect, in fantastic seafood.

Bus 6 runs the 20-minute journey to Penzance half-hourly.

ANCIENT CORNWALL

Like many other areas of Celtic Britain, Cornwall is strewn with reminders of its ancient past. The area between St Just and St Ives is dotted with dolmens, menhirs and mysterious stone circles – if prehistory is your thing, track down **Lanyon Quoit** (a table-shaped dolmen between Madron and Morvah), the **Mên-an-Tol stone** (a ring-shaped stone near Madron), the **Merry Maidens** (Cornwall's most complete stone circle, near Trewoofe) and **Chysauster Iron Age Village** (☎ 07831-757934; adult £2.40; ⏲ 10-6pm Jul-Aug, 10am-5pm Apr-Jun & Sep, 10am-4pm Oct), the most complete prehistoric settlement in Cornwall.

Perhaps the most impressive ancient monument in Cornwall is the **Hurlers**, a series of stone circles near the village of Minions on Bodmin Moor. Legend has it that the stones were once local men who were turned to stone for playing the local game of hurling on the Sabbath. Around 1.5 km across the moor is the **Cheesewring**, a 20-foot stack of stones balanced on top of each other. Although it looks like it's been manmade, in fact it's an entirely natural formation that's been weathered down by the elements over several million years.

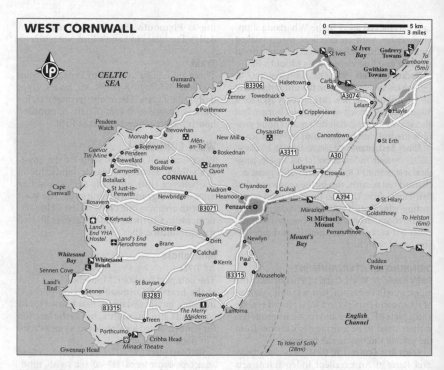

WEST CORNWALL

Minack Theatre

Surely the world's most spectacularly located theatre, the **Minack** (☎ 01736-810181; www.minack.com; tickets from £7.50) is carved into the cliffs overlooking Porthcurno Bay. The **visitor centre** (admission £3; 🕙 9.30am-5.30pm Apr-Sep, 10am-4pm Oct-Mar) recounts the story of Rowena Cade, the indomitable local woman who originally conceived the theatre and oversaw it until her death in 1983. From the original production in 1929, the Minack has grown into a full-blown theatrical venue, with a 17-week season running from mid-May to mid-September – though aficionados always bring umbrellas and blankets in case the British weather should take centre stage. The centre is closed when there's a matinée.

The Minack is above the beautiful beach of Porthcurno, 3 miles from Land's End and 9 miles from Penzance. Bus 345 from Penzance to Land's End stops at Porthcurno, Monday to Friday.

Land's End

Last stop on the journey from John O' Groats is Land's End, where the crumbling granite cliffs of west Cornwall tumble into the booming Atlantic surf. It's one of Britain's most dramatic and unforgettable locations, which makes the decision to build the monumentally tacky **Legendary Land's End** (☎ 0870 458 0099; www.landsend-landmark.co.uk; admission £10; 🕙 10am-5pm summer, 10am-3pm winter) theme park all the more inexplicable. Take our advice – skip the ragtag collection of fibreglass models and half-hearted multimedia shows and take an exhilarating clifftop stroll along the headland instead. On a clear day, it's possible to see all the way to the Scilly Isles, 28 miles out to sea.

Land's End is 9 miles from Penzance and 886 miles from John O'Groats. Bus 1 runs around the coast to St Ives (1½ hours) and Penzance (2½ hours, five daily) – for some reason it becomes bus 300 in the opposite direction. The twice daily bus 345 offers a quicker service straight to Penzance.

St Just-in-Penwith

☎ 01736 / pop 1890

There's not much to see around the grey-granite settlement of St Just, 6 miles north of Land's End, but a century or so ago this

---

WHEN DID CORNISH DIE?

A Celtic language akin to Welsh, Cornish (Kernewek) was spoken west of the Tamar until the 19th century. Written evidence indicates that it was still widely spoken at the time of the Reformation, but suppressed after a Cornish uprising in 1548. By the 17th century only a few people in the far-west of Cornwall still claimed it as their mother tongue.

Towards the end of the 18th century linguistic scholars foresaw the death of Cornish and scoured the peninsula for people who still spoke it. One such scholar, Daines Barrington, visited Mousehole in 1768 and recorded an elderly woman called Dolly Pentreath abusing him in Cornish for presuming she couldn't speak her own language.

Dolly died in 1769 and has gone down in history as the last native speaker of Cornish. However, Barrington knew of other people who continued to speak it into the 1790s, and an 1891 tombstone in Zennor commemorates John Davey as 'the last man to possess any considerable knowledge of the Cornish language'.

Recently efforts have been made to revive the language – unfortunately there are now three conflicting varieties of 'Cornish' (unified, phonemic and traditional), so reintroduction could prove tricky. You can find out more on www.cornish-language.org.

---

was a hub of activity for the local tin and copper mining industry. The old **Geevor Tin Mine** (☎ 788662; www.geevor.com; admission £7.50; ⊙ 9am-5pm Sun-Fri Easter-Oct, to 4pm Nov-Mar) at Pendeen, north of St Just, finally closed in 1990, and now offers tours of the underground shafts every hour in summer, offering an amazing insight into the dark and dangerous conditions in which Cornwall's miners once worked.

St Just is also the site of the **Plen-an-gwary**, an open-air auditorium, which was once used to stage outdoor theatre and Cornish mystery plays.

Land's End YHA Hostel (☎ 0870 770 5906; Letcha Vean; dm £13.95; ⊙ Easter-Oct) is in an isolated spot half a mile south of the village, and makes an ideal spot for keen bird-watchers and walkers on the coast path. It's definitely a no-frills hostel, with smallish dorms and a basic kitchen, but it's ideal if you're after some peace and quiet.

Bus 17 travels from St Ives via Penzance every half hour Monday to Saturday.

Zennor
☎ 01736 / pop 217

A stunning 6-mile stretch of the South West Coast Path runs from St Ives to the windswept village of Zennor, where DH Lawrence wrote much of *Women in Love*. **St Senara's Church** dates from at least 1150. Look for the carved Mermaid Chair; legend tells of a beautiful, mysterious woman who lured a chorister into the sea at Mermaid's Cove, where you can still hear them singing.

The extraordinary **Wayside Folk Museum** (☎ 796945; admission £3; ⊙ 10.30am-5pm Sun-Fri May-Sep, 11am-5pm Sun-Fri Apr & Oct) started out as a private collection of local artefacts gathered by Colonel 'Freddie' Hirst in the 1930s, and over the last 60 years has grown into the country's most fascinating folk museum. The treasure trove of exhibits includes original equipment belonging to local blacksmiths, miners and cobblers, an 18th-century kitchen, two reclaimed watermills and an extensive photographic archive of the local area – it really has to be seen to be believed.

The only place to stay locally is the **Old Chapel Backpackers Hostel** (☎ 798307; dm/d £12/40; P), handily placed along the coast path. Inside it's smart, modern and efficient, with dorm rooms and a great value café downstairs.

DH Lawrence's favourite local while he lived on the Zennor coastline was the **Tinner's Arms** (☎ 792697; lunch from £7-10) a classic Cornish inn with a rambling, atmospheric main bar sheltering under a slate roof. Pub lunches and local ale are served either inside or on the sea-view patio.

From St Ives, catch bus 300 (20 minutes, five daily) or bus 343 (20 minutes, four daily Monday to Saturday).

St Ives
☎ 01736 / pop 9870

Tucked into the coastline of a glittering arc-shaped bay, St Ives was once one of the county's busiest pilchard-fishing harbours, but it's better known these days for its longstanding reputation as the centre of the Cornish arts

DEVON & CORNWALL

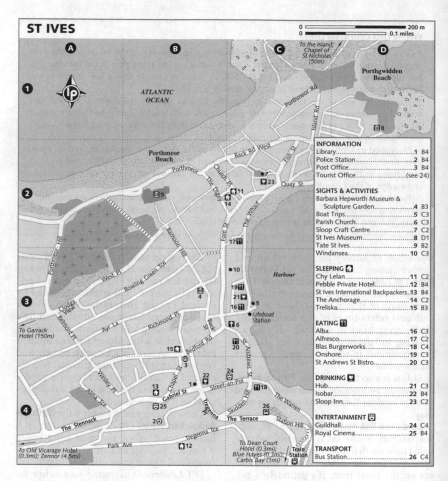

ST IVES

scene. From the old harbour, cobbled alleyways and switchback lanes lead uphill into a jumble of buzzy galleries, cafés and brasseries, catering for the thousands of summertime visitors who arrive every year to sample the artistic atmosphere for themselves. It makes for an intriguing mix, where boutique chic meets the old-fashioned British seaside, and while the high-season traffic can certainly take the shine off things, St Ives is still an essential stop on any Cornish grand tour.

INFORMATION
Library (☎ 795377; 1 Gabriel St; internet access per hr £3)
Post office (☎ 795004; Tregenna Pl; 9am-5.30pm Mon-Fri, 9am-12.30pm Sat)

stives-cornwall.co.uk Official town website with accommodation and activity guides.
Tourist office (☎ 796297; ivtic@penwith.gov.uk; Street-an-Pol; 9am-5.30pm Mon-Fri, 9am-5pm Sat, 10am-4pm Sun) Inside the Guildhall.

SIGHTS & ACTIVITIES
Tate St Ives
The artwork almost takes second place to the surroundings at the stunning **Tate St Ives** (☎ 796226; www.tate.org.uk/stives; Porthmeor Beach; admission £5.75, joint ticket with Barbara Hepworth museum £8.75; 10am-5pm Mar-Oct, 10am-4pm Tue-Sun Nov-Feb), which hovers like a white concrete curl above Porthmeor Beach. Built in 1993, the gallery contains work by celebrated local artists, including Terry Frost, Patrick Heron and

ST IVES & THE ARTS

Ever since Turner sketched the town in 1811, St Ives has been a focal point for British art. During the 19th century, St Ives was linked with the Newlyn School, a group of figurative painters headed by Stanhope Forbes, who found ideal subjects among the rustic characters and landscapes of Cornwall. Whistler and Sickert made regular visits, and by the beginning of the 20th century, there were scores of artists working in and around St Ives. In the 1930s and '40s, the work of abstract painters like Peter Lanyon, Henry Moore and Ben Nicholson, and his wife, the sculptor Barbara Hepworth, led to the formation of the Penwith Society of Artists in 1949. Their avant-garde techniques inspired a third wave of St Ives artists in the 1960s and '70s, including Terry Frost, Patrick Heron and Roger Hilton. Today, St Ives continues to hold an enduring fascination – the Penwith area supports more working artists than almost anywhere else in Britain.

Barbara Hepworth, and hosts regular special exhibitions. On the top floor there's a stylish café-bar with the best sea views in town.

There are plenty more art galleries to discover around town – perhaps the most interesting is the **Sloop Craft Centre**, just off the harbour, where you'll find a treasure trove of tiny artist's studios selling everything from handmade jewellery to driftwood furniture.

Barbara Hepworth Museum & Sculpture Garden

Barbara Hepworth was one of the leading abstract sculptors of the 20th century, and a key figure in the St Ives art scene, so it seems fitting that her former studio has been transformed into a moving archive and **museum** (☎ 796226; www.tate.org.uk/stives; Barnoon Hill; admission £4.75, joint ticket with Tate St Ives £8.75; ⊙ 10am-5.30pm Mar-Oct, 10am-4.30pm Tue-Sun Nov-Feb). The studio itself has remained almost untouched since her death in a fire in 1975, and the adjoining garden contains some of her most famous sculptures. Hepworth's work is scattered throughout St Ives; look for her sculptures outside the Guildhall and inside the 15th-century parish church of St Ia.

St Ives Museum

Housed in a pier-side building variously used as a pilchard-packing factory, laundry, cinema, sailor's mission and copper mine, the **heritage museum** (☎ 796005; admission £1.50; ⊙ 10am-5pm Mon-Fri & 10am-4pm Sat Mar-Oct) contains local artefacts relating to blacksmithery, fishing and shipwrecks.

Beaches

The largest town beaches are **Porthmeor** and **Porthminster**, but the tiny cove of **Porthgwidden** is also popular. Nearby, the pre-14th-century **Chapel of St Nicholas**, patron saint of children and sailors, is the oldest (and smallest) church in St Ives. **Carbis Bay**, to the southeast, is popular with families and sun-seekers.

On the opposite side of the bay from St Ives, the receding tide reveals over 3 miles of golden beach at **Gwithian** and **Godrevy Towans**, both popular spots for kiteboarders and surfers. The lighthouse just offshore at Godrevy was the inspiration for Virginia Woolf's classic stream-of-consciousness novel *To The Lighthouse*.

Several places on Porthmeor Beach and Fore St rent wet suits and surfboards; try **Windansea** (☎ 794830; 25 Fore St).

Boat Trips

Sea-fishing trips and coastal cruises to the grey-seal colony on Seal Island (£8) are run by the **St Ives Pleasure Boat Association** (☎ 01736-796080, 07712-386162) and several other operators on the harbour.

SLEEPING

Budget

St Ives International Backpackers (☎ 799444; www.backpackers.co.uk/st-ives; The Stennack; depending on season dm £10.95-16.95; ⬜) This grungy old hostel, housed in an old chapel school, could do with some serious spring cleaning, but if you don't mind cramped rooms and the odd spot of peeling paintwork, it makes a good budget base for exploring the town.

Chy Lelan (☎ 797560; Bunkers Hill; www.chylelan.co.uk; d £50-60; ✗) Just up the hill from the Anchorage, two old fishermen's cottages now provide simple, plain B&B rooms, with views onto the street or across the town's slate-covered rooftops.

Anchorage (☎ 797135; 5 Bunkers Hill; info@theanchoragebandb.co.uk; s £30-35, d £60-70; ✗) This 18th-century cob cottage just off the main street is packed with old-world atmosphere – think oak beams, rough stone walls and a maze of snug, tiny rooms leading off the low-ceilinged corridors.

Midrange

Pebble Private Hotel (☎ 794168; www.pebble-hotel .co.uk; 4 Park Ave; s £30-42, d £60-88; ✕) Up on the steep hillside above town, this gorgeous and very contemporary B&B comes as a breath of fresh air, with a choice of imaginatively decorated rooms kitted out in technicolour tones, funky patterns and crazy-shaped mirrors.

Treliska (☎ 797678; treliska@connexions.co.uk; 3 Bedford Rd; ✕) Another beautifully finished B&B that's a world away from chintzy curtains and flock wallpaper – here it's all clean lines, chrome bath-taps and elegantly understated pine furniture.

Old Vicarage Hotel (☎ 796124; www.oldvicarage hotel.com; Parc-an-Creet; s/d £51/68; P ✕) A former rectory in lovely landscaped gardens, set back from the tourist-thronged streets of the town centre, and decorated throughout in mock-Victorian style. Most impressive is the mahogany and red velvet lounge-bar, although the bedrooms themselves aren't quite as striking.

Dean Court Hotel (☎ 796023; www.deancourthotel .com; Trelyon Ave; d £80-104; P) A short walk uphill from the town centre, this upmarket six-room hotel in a double-fronted Victorian townhouse commands panoramic views across the bay. All the bedrooms are smartly furnished with fluffy beds and sitting areas, but the seaview ones are the pick of the bunch.

Top End

Blue Hayes (☎ 797129; www.blue-hayes.co.uk; Trelyon Ave; r £140-170; P ✕) There are a couple of seriously grand country hotels around town, but for something less ostentatious try this boutique beauty, where you'll find five luxurious cream-coloured suites (including one with its own private roof patio) and a balustraded breakfast terrace overlooking the bay.

EATING

St Ives has almost as many restaurants and brasseries as Padstow. Most are dotted along the harbourfront, but the back lanes can turn up some surprising treats too.

Blas Burgerworks (☎ 797272; The Warren; burgers £4-8; ✕ lunch) The humble burger suddenly becomes a work of art at this fantastic new diner, where the gourmet creations range from beetburgers in sunflower baps to black bean burgers livened up with lashings of chilli sauce.

Onshore (☎ 796000; The Wharf; pizzas £7-16; ✕ lunch & dinner) Gourmet pizzas cooked to perfection in a wood-fired oven are the mainstay at this lively chrome-and-glass pizzeria, next door to the Hub.

our pick St Andrews St Bistro (☎ 797074; 16 Andrews St; mains £9-15; ✕ lunch on Sun, dinner Wed-Sun) The latest entry on the St Ives eating scene is this eclectic new bistro, serving up British classics fused with north African flavours in a boho dining room filled with Moroccan rugs, murals and *objets d'art*.

Alfresco (☎ 793737; The Wharf; mains £10-18; ✕ lunch & dinner) On a fine summer's day this tiny wharfside bistro is the only place to be, with sliding doors that open onto the harbour and a blackboard menu that takes its cue from the daily catch.

Alba (☎ 797222; Old Lifeboat House; mains £14-18; ✕ lunch & dinner) The award-winning Alba is still one of the top places for seafood on the harbourfront, with a split-level dining room and sumptuous seafood such as pan-fried seabass and fillet of john dory with spring vegetables.

DRINKING

Hub (☎ 799099; The Wharf; ✕ 10am-late) This harbourfront café-bar opens late into the night, but makes a good spot for morning coffee too, with a trendy chocolate-coloured interior and a fine sea-view aspect.

Isobar (☎ 796042; Tregenna Pl; ✕ to 2am) St Ives's main nightspot boasts a pared-back bar on the ground floor and a hot-and-sweaty club upstairs, with regular funk, house and techno nights, and the odd cheesy disc thrown in for good measure.

Sloop Inn (☎ 796584; The Wharf) A classic old fishermen's boozer, complete with low ceilings, tankards behind the bar and a comprehensive selection of Cornish ales.

ENTERTAINMENT

Royal Cinema (☎ 796843; www.merlincinemas.co.uk; The Stennack) Shows new films and often has cheap matinées.

Guildhall (☎ 796888; 1 Street-An-Pol) Regular programmes of music and theatre, especially during the St Ives September Festival.

GETTING THERE & AWAY
National Express operates coaches to London (£35.50, nine hours, four daily), Plymouth (£6.50, three hours, four daily) and most local towns.

Local First buses 16, 17/17A/17B regularly connect St Ives with Penzance; the circular bus 300 travels to Land's End en route.

St Ives is on a scenic branch train line from St Erth (£2.20, 20 minutes, hourly), on the main London–Penzance line via Truro.

NORTH CORNWALL
The north Cornish coast is where the rolling grey Atlantic smacks hard into the county's granite cliffs, and for many people it's the quintessential Cornish landscape – a wild mix of grassy headlands, craggy bluffs and pounding surf. It's also where you'll find the county's best beaches and biggest waves, so in summer the winding clifftop roads are often jammed with tourists; but visit in the off-season when the weather's cooler and the holidaymakers have left for home, and you might have some of Cornwall's finest sand all to yourself.

Porthtowan & St Agnes
The secluded beaches and reliable swells around the coastal towns of St Agnes and Porthtowan are popular with surfers and holidaymakers alike. The tiny National Trust cove of **Chapel Porth**, tucked away at the bottom of a beautiful river valley, is a particularly fine spot; a dramatic coast path travels along the clifftops to the abandoned mine at **Wheal Coates** and breathtaking views at **Tubby's Head**.

The best place to stay around St Agnes is the **Rose-in-Vale Hotel** (☎ 01872-552202; www.rose-in-vale-hotel.co.uk; Mithian; d from £130; P ✗ ☒), a lovely grand country-house hotel set in flower-filled grounds 2 miles from St Agnes, with 18 tasteful rooms and a smart restaurant.

Alternatively, the **Driftwood Spars** (☎ 01872-552428; www.driftwoodspars.com; d £82-94; P ✗), a lively beachside pub at Trevaunance Cove near St Agnes, has 15 delightful upstairs rooms, many of which have sea views and attractive nautical touches.

Over at Porthtowan, the **Blue Bar** (☎ 01209-890329; www.blue-bar.co.uk; Porthtowan; ☽ lunch & dinner Thu-Sun) is one of the favourite hangouts for Cornwall's beach crowd, with a bright surf-style interior and a sea-view patio. Burgers, sandwiches and salads are on the menu, and there's live music and DJs at weekends.

TOP FIVE BEACHES
- For safe swimming: Perran Sands, Perranporth (below)
- For scenic views: Bedruthan Steps, near Padstow (below)
- For peaceful strolling: Gwithian and Godrevy Towans, near St Ives (p365)
- For family fun: Holywell Bay, near Newquay (p368)
- For learning to surf: Fistral or Crantock, both near Newquay (p369)

GETTING THERE & AWAY
Bus 557 travels along the north coast from Newquay to St Ives once in each direction Sunday to Friday, stopping at St Agnes and Perranporth en route. Bus T1 travels from Truro (40 minutes, hourly) to St Agnes, but only a few daily buses travel on to Perranporth (15 minutes, five daily Monday to Saturday).

Perranporth
North of St Agnes is the busy beach town of Perranporth, packed to bursting with scarlet-faced holidaymakers in summer and all but deserted in the winter months. Life revolves around the beach in Perranporth, and it's one of the best places on the north coast for hitting the surf or just kicking back on the sand.

Most of the hotels in Perranporth are pretty substandard, but there are some decent camp sites nearby including **Perran Sands Holiday Park** (☎ 01872-573511; ☽ Easter-Oct) and **Tollgate Farm Touring Park** (☎ 01872-572130; Budnick; sites £6-12; ☽ Easter-Oct), about a mile inland from the beach.

Watering Hole (☎ 01872-572888; Perranporth Beach) is one of the liveliest beach bars on the north coast, with outside tables on the sand, regular bands and a buzzy surf-shack vibe.

GETTING THERE & AWAY
For buses see above.

Newquay
☎ 01637 / pop 19,423
If Padstow is Cornwall's Cannes, then Newquay is its Costa del Sol. Perched on the cliffs above a cluster of white-sand beaches, and packed with enough pubs, bars and dodgy clubs to give Ibiza a run for its money, it's

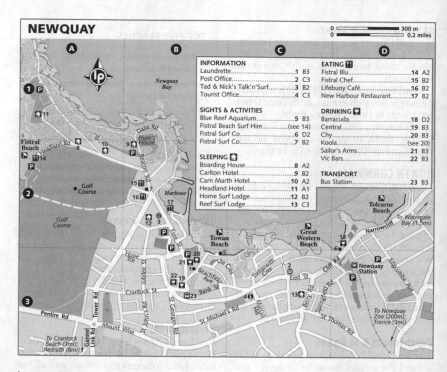

NEWQUAY

INFORMATION		
Laundrette..............................1	B3
Post Office..............................2	C3
Tad & Nick's Talk'n'Surf..............3	B2
Tourist Office..........................4	C3

SIGHTS & ACTIVITIES		
Blue Reef Aquarium....................5	B3
Fistral Beach Surf Hire.........(see 14)	
Fistral Surf Co...........................6	D2
Fistral Surf Co...........................7	B2

SLEEPING		
Boarding House.........................8	A2
Carlton Hotel............................9	B2
Carn Marth Hotel.....................10	A2
Headland Hotel.........................11	A1
Home Surf Lodge......................12	B2
Reef Surf Lodge.......................13	C3

EATING		
Fistral Blu...............................14	A2
Fistral Chef.............................15	B2
Lifebuoy Café..........................16	B2
New Harbour Restaurant............17	B2

DRINKING		
Barracuda...............................18	D2
Central..................................19	B3
Chy.......................................20	B3
Koola...............................(see 20)	
Sailor's Arms..........................21	B3
Vic Bars.................................22	B3

TRANSPORT		
Bus Station.............................23	B3

become the summer venue of choice for beer boys, beach bums and surf addicts alike, all of whom descend on the town in droves. It's also the unofficial capital of Cornish surfing, and if you're looking to learn how to brave the waves, this is the place to do it.

INFORMATION

Laundrette (☎ 875901; 1 Beach Pde, Beach Rd)

Tad & Nick's Talk'n'Surf (☎ 874868; 72 Fore St; internet access per hr £3; ⏰ 10am-6pm)

Tourist office (☎ 854020; www.newquay.co.uk; Marcus Hill; ⏰ 9.30am-5.30pm Mon-Sat, 9.30am-12.30pm Sun)

SIGHTS & ACTIVITIES

Newquay's trump card is its spectacular location near some of the best beaches on the north coast. **Fistral**, west of Towan Head, is England's best-known surfing beach, and the venue for the annual Boardmasters surfing festival. Below town are **Great Western** and **Towan**, and a little further up the coast you'll find Tolcarne, Lusty Glaze and Porth. All the beaches are good for swimming and supervised by lifeguards in summer.

Blue Reef Aquarium (☎ 878134; www.bluereefaquar ium.co.uk; Towan Promenade; admission £5.95; ⏰ 10am-5pm) on Towan Beach has a selection of weird and wonderful underwater characters, including jellyfish, seahorses, octopi and rays; several of the tanks have open tops allowing you to touch the fish.

There are lots more beautiful beaches to discover around Newquay. Three miles to the southwest is **Crantock**, sandwiched between the twin headlands of East and West Pentire, and a little further west is family-friendly **Holywell Bay**. Just east of Newquay is **Watergate Bay**, where you'll find a glorious sandy beach and an excellent outdoor activities centre (see opposite). The stately rock towers of **Bedruthan Steps**, are a few miles further east towards Padstow.

Most of Newquay is relentlessly modern, but on the cliff above Towan Beach stands the 14th-century **Huer's House**, a lookout for approaching pilchard shoals. Until they were fished out early in the 20th century, these shoals were enormous: one catch of 1868 netted a record 16.5 million fish. Many Cornish fishing villages once had a watchtower.

SLEEPING

Budget

There are plenty of surf lodges in Newquay – the best ones have secure board storage and links with local surf schools.

Reef Surf Lodge (☎ 879058; www.reefsurflodge.info; 10-12 Berry Rd; dm £15-29.50; ☐) This place is a quantum leap away from your average surf lodge – forget saggy beds and overcrowded dorms, here it's all plasma screen TVs, cappuccino machines and groovy modern furniture. There's a great onsite bar, and surfing courses are provided by the in-house Reef Surf School (www.reefsurfschool.com).

Home Surf Lodge (☎ 873387; www.homesurflodge .co.uk; 18 Tower Rd; dm £16-20; ☐) Another popular lodge near the town centre, with basic dorm rooms, free internet access and a pleasant DVD lounge and licensed bar.

Boarding House (☎ 873258; www.theboardinghouse .co.uk; 32 Headland Rd; dm £18-25; ☐) This stylish surf lodge is in a fantastic location near Fistral Beach. Rooms are clean and modern; downstairs there's a lively bar decorated with potted plants and Indonesian furniture, and a fantastic wooden-decked terrace overlooking the golf course and Trevose Head.

Midrange & Top End

Carlton Hotel (☎ 872658; www.carltonhotelnewquay .co.uk; 6 Dane Rd; d £60-70; P ✗) This sumptuous B&B offers nine cream-themed bedrooms, complete with huge, plush beds, country prints and DVD players in every room.

Carnmarth Hotel (☎ 872519; www.carnmarth.com; Headland Rd; depending on season d £65-100) This old package-holiday hotel is in the midst of transforming itself into Newquay's first boutique hotel. The rooms themselves are still on the tired side, although most have decent sea views – at the moment the highlight is the fantastic steel-and-glass bar and panoramic drinks terrace. One to watch.

Headland Hotel (☎ 872211; www.headlandhotel.co.uk; Fistral Beach; d £80-302; P ✗ ☐ ☎) The grand old lady of Newquay hotels is this fabulous red-brick pile perched above Fistral Beach. The impeccable rooms range from budget singles to ornate sea-view suites, and facilities include a brace of swimming pools, tennis courts and a nine-hole golf course.

EATING

Lifebuoy Café (☎ 878076; Lower Tower Rd; mains £4.50-12) This reliable old café is an excellent spot for breakfast smoothies and coffee, baguettes, burgers and fresh salads at lunch time.

Fistral Chef (☎ 850718; 2 Beacon Rd; breakfasts £2-6, mains £6-10; ✗ breakfast daily, dinner in summer) This popular new café champions all-day breakfast as the best in town, and judging by the crowds, they can't be far wrong. On summer nights there's also a Thai-themed evening menu, with a BYO wine policy.

Fistral Blu (☎ 879444; www.fistral-blu.co.uk; Fistral Beach; mains £7-19; ✗ lunch & dinner) Housed in the retail complex just behind Fistral Beach, this impressive glass-fronted restaurant experiments with Thai and Mediterranean flavours, as well as Cornish standards such as fish pie and local scallops. The beachfront terrace makes a glorious place for a twilight supper, and for something more relaxed, you can grab sandwiches and burgers at the informal café downstairs.

SURF'S UP

With such a wealth of beaches at its disposal, Newquay is one of the country's top places for learning to **surf**. The town is literally brimming over with surf schools, offering everything from half-day taster lessons (£25 to £30) to full-blown multiday 'surfaris' (from £130). Reputable operators include the **British Surfing Association** (Fistral Beach ☎ 850737, Tolcarne Beach ☎ 851487; www .nationalsurfingcentre.com), **Reef Surf School** (☎ 879059; Great Western Beach; www.reefsurfschool.com) and the **Extreme Academy** (☎ 860840; Watergate Bay; www.extremeacademy.co.uk) on Watergate Bay, who also offers lessons in kitebuggying, mountainboarding and waveskiing. If you choose another school, make sure the instructors are certified by the BSA.

Lots of surf shops around Newquay hire out equipment, including boards (£10/25/45 for one/three/seven days) and wet suits (£5/12/25 for one/three/seven days). Try **Fistral Surf Co** (Cliff Rd ☎ 850808; 19 Cliff Rd; ✗ 9am-6pm; Beacon Rd ☎ 850520; Beacon Rd; ✗ 9.30am-5.30pm) or **Fistral Beach Surf Hire** (☎ 850584; Fistral Beach).

And for seasoned surfers looking for a few more thrills and spills, how about a spot of kitesurfing? Contact **Mobius Kite School** (☎ 831383; Cubert; www.mobiusonline.co.uk).

DEVON & CORNWALL

New Harbour Restaurant (☎ 874062; South Quay Hill; mains £10-15; ☿ lunch & dinner) In a lovely spot beside the old harbour, this relaxed restaurant is a fine place to escape the crowds along Newquay's main drag. Fish and seafood are the menu's mainstays – think crab claws, homemade fishcakes and skate wing.

DRINKING & ENTERTAINMENT

Chy (☎ 873415; www.the-chy.co.uk; 12 Beach Rd) This sophisticated café-bar is a world away from most of the dodgy clubs and pubs around Newquay, with plenty of stripped wood, chrome fixtures and plush sofas, not to mention a fantastic panoramic terrace.

Koola (☎ 873415; www.thekoola.com; 12 Beach Rd) Underneath the Chy, the Koola is the venue of choice for connoisseur clubbers, with regular house, latin, and drum and bass nights, and a regular slot for local DJs Jelly Jazz.

Central (☎ 878310; 11 Central Sq) As its name suggests, this popular pre-club pub is right in the heart of town, and the outside patio is always overflowing on warm summer nights.

Vic Bars (☎ 872671; King St) Cavernous pub with regular bands on Friday and Saturday night.

Barracuda (☎ 875800; 27-29 Cliff Rd) One of the largest clubs in town, with big-name DJs on weekends.

Sailor's Arms (☎ 872838; Fore St) Pub-club playing cheesy house and chunky choons.

GETTING THERE & AWAY

National Express has direct buses to London (£35.50, seven hours, five daily), Plymouth (£5.70, 1½ hours, four daily) and Penzance (£5, 1¾ hours, two daily).

There are trains every couple of hours between Newquay and Par (£4.80 single, 45 minutes), on the main London–Penzance line.

Trerice

Built in 1751, the charming Elizabethan manor of **Trerice** (NT; ☎ 01637-875404; admission £6; ☿ 11am-5pm Sun-Fri Mar-Oct, gardens from 10.30am) is famous for the elaborate barrel-roofed ceiling of the Great Chamber, but has plenty of other intriguing features, including ornate fireplaces, original plasterwork and a fine collection of period furniture. There's also an amusing lawnmower museum in the barn, with over 100 grass-cutters going back over a century.

Trerice is 3 miles southeast of Newquay. Bus 526 runs from Newquay to Kestle Mill, about a mile from the manor house.

Padstow

☎ 01841 / pop 3162

Wind the clock back a decade or two and Padstow was just another quiet fishing village along Cornwall's north coast, but over recent years this little harbour has been transformed into the capital of Cornish cuisine, with some of the poshest restaurants and swishest boutiques this side of the Tamar. The transformation is almost entirely due to the efforts of one man, celebrity chef Rick Stein, who opened his first seafood restaurant on the harbourside back in the mid-'70s and has since expanded his property portfolio with a second café, a couple of hotels, a seafood school, a delicatessen and even a fish and chip shop. Hardly surprising, then, that the locals often wryly refer to the town as 'Pad-stein' – but despite its chichi provenance, it's still a pretty place to visit, with a cluster of cafés and fishermen's cottages nestled around its old harbour.

The **tourist office** (☎ 533449; www.padstowlive .com; North Quay; ☿ 10am-5pm Mon-Sat) charges £3 to book accommodation.

Much favoured by directors of costume dramas, the stately manor house of **Prideaux Place** (☎ 532411; admission £6; ☿ 12.30-4pm Sun-Thu Easter Sun–mid-Apr & mid-May–Oct) above the village was built by the Prideaux-Brune family (who still reside here), purportedly descendants of William the Conqueror.

The disused Padstow to Bodmin railway line now forms the **Camel Trail**, one of Cornwall's most popular cycling tracks. The trail starts in Padstow and runs east through Wadebridge (5¾ miles), Bodmin (11 miles) and beyond. Bikes can be hired from **Padstow Cycle Hire** (☎ 533533; www.padstowcyclehire.com; South Quay; ☿ 9am-5pm) and **Brinhams** (☎ 532594; South Quay; ☿ 9am-5pm) for something like £10 to £15 per day.

The **Jubilee Queen** (☎ 521093) offers boat trips (adults £6) around the bay and offshore islands, leaving from the harbourside.

Padstow is surrounded by some excellent beaches, including the ones at **Polzeath** and **Treyarnon Bay**.

SLEEPING

Treyarnon Bay YHA Hostel (☎ 0870 770 6076; Tregonnan; dm £15.50; P ☒ ▣) Possibly one of the best-situated hostels in Cornwall, in a fantastic headland position above Treyarnon Bay, 4½ miles west of Padstow. There's a café, kitchen and barbecue area and the beach is just a stone's throw away. Bus 556 from Padstow stops at nearby Constantine several times daily.

Althea Library (☎ 532717; www.althealibrary.co.uk; 27 High St; d £78-110; P ⊠) One of the nicest B&Bs in central Padstow, with a couple of cosy, tasteful rooms tucked away on the first floor of the listed cottage, and a more expensive 'nook suite'. Guests have use of a pretty little A-frame lounge, complete with CD player and board games, and the Aga-cooked breakfasts will keep you going for hours.

Cross House Hotel (☎ 532391; Church St; d £90-125; P ⊠) A short stroll uphill from the harbour brings you to this imposing Georgian townhouse, with a range of traditionally-styled bedrooms decorated with rich bedspreads and heavy curtains – the more expensive even have plasma TVs and the odd piece of antique furniture.

St Ervan Manor (☎ 540255; www.stervanmanor. co.uk; St Ervan; r £140-245; P ⊠) This award-winning B&B is really a country-house hotel in disguise, with five beautifully-appointed bedrooms decorated in sumptuous shades and polished furniture, and a truly palatial garden cottage complete with a regal lounge and private patioed garden.

EATING

Rojano's (☎ 532796; 9 Mill Sq; pizzas £4-8, pasta £6-10; ⊗ lunch & dinner Tue-Sun) This bright, buzzy Italian joint turns out excellent pizza and pasta, served either in the snug, sunlit dining room or the tiny front terrace.

Rick Stein's Café (☎ 532700; Middle St; mains £8.50-15; ⊗ closed Sun) For something rather less exclusive, head for this relaxed bistro along the backstreet behind the harbour, which offers a straightforward, daily-changing menu of seafood specials and a laid-back continental vibe.

Pescadou (☎ 532359; South Quay; mains £14-18; ⊗ lunch & dinner) Mr Stein isn't the only one around town who can turn out top-notch seafood, as this pleasant restaurant next to the Old Custom House pub proves. Our tip? Try the rosemary-roasted turbot.

Seafood Restaurant (☎ 532700; www.rickstein.com; Riverside; mains £17.50-45; ⊗ lunch & dinner) The restaurant that started the Stein empire, and still one of the county's most celebrated eateries. As you'd expect, the fish and seafood is of the highest calibre, but you'll need to plan your visit with military precision to bag a table.

WORTH THE TRIP

Fifteen Cornwall (☎ 01637-861000; www.fifteencornwall.com; Watergate Bay; 6-course dinner menu £50; ⊗ breakfast, lunch & dinner) Fresh from his campaign to change the stomach-churning eating habits of Britain's school kids, everyone's favourite mockney chef Jamie Oliver opened the second UK branch of his Fifteen restaurant in 2006 in a stunning location on Watergate Bay. Designed to give underprivileged Cornish youngsters an opportunity to work and train in a professional restaurant environment while turning out top-quality cooking, Fifteen is currently the hottest ticket in the county – if you manage to bag a table, the beach views, electric atmosphere and contemporary cooking won't disappoint.

GETTING THERE & AWAY

Bus 555 goes to Bodmin Parkway (50 minutes, hourly, six on Sunday) via Wadebridge. Bus 595 travels to Truro (1¾ hours, once or twice daily), while bus 556 serves Newquay (1¼ hours, seven daily Monday to Saturday, five Sunday).

Tintagel

☎ 01840 / pop 1822

The spectre of King Arthur looms large over the village of Tintagel and its spectacular clifftop **castle** (EH; ☎ 770328; admission £4.30; ⊗ 10am-6pm Apr-Sep, 10am-5pm Oct, 10am-4pm Nov-Mar). Though the present-day ruins mostly date from the 13th century, archaeological digs have revealed the foundations of a much earlier fortress, fuelling speculation that the legendary king may indeed have been born at the castle as local legend claims. Part of the crumbling stronghold stands on a rock tower cut off from the mainland, accessed via a bridge and steep steps, and it's still possible to make out several sturdy walls and much of the castle's interior layout.

The village is awash with touristy shops and tearooms making the most of the King Arthur connection, but there's not much to keep you entertained for long. The **Old Post Office** (NT; ☎ 770024; Fore St; admission £2.60; ⊗ 11am-5.30pm daily Jul-Aug, 11am-5.30pm Sun-Fri Mar-Jul & Sep, 11am-4pm Sun-Fri Oct) is a beautiful example of a traditional Cornish longhouse and mostly dates from the 1500s; it was used as the village's post office during the 19th century.

DEVON & CORNWALL

The **tourist office** (☎ 779084; tintagelvc@btconnect .com; Bossiney Rd; ☯ 10am-5pm Mar-Oct, 10.30am-4pm Nov-Feb) has a few exhibits exploring local history and the Arthur legend.

GETTING THERE & AWAY

Bus 594 runs from Truro via Wadebridge (1¼ hours, six daily Monday to Friday); the more frequent bus 524 runs from Wadebridge only. Both buses go on to Boscastle (10 minutes).

Boscastle

☎ 01840

A few years ago Boscastle was just another pretty village on the north Cornish coast, renowned for its beautiful harbour and picturesque valley setting. But on 16 August 2004, the village hit the headlines thanks to a devastating flash flood, the worst in Britain since the deluge at Lynmouth in 1952. Some 440 million gallons of water tore through the heart of the village in just a few hours, carrying away cars, trees and the Boscastle visitor centre, and causing devastating damage to many of village's oldest buildings. Fifty-eight properties were flooded, over a hundred cars were swept out to sea and most of the village was evacuated by helicopter – but miraculously not a single person lost their lives.

Residents have spent the last two years piecing Boscastle back together, and though many properties have been completely refurbished, rebuilding work is still going on by the harbour. The **visitor centre** (☎ 250010; visitorcentre@boscastle.demon.co.uk; ☯ 10am-5pm Mar-Oct) is currently housed in a Portakabin opposite the Cobweb Inn, although plans are afoot to move it into a building near the harbour sometime in 2006.

The much-loved **Museum of Witchcraft** (☎ 250111; The Harbour; admission £2.50; ☯ 10.30am-6pm Mon-Sat, 11.30am-6pm Sun) has been thoroughly renovated since the flood, and its eclectic collection of witch-related memorabilia (the world's largest, apparently) is back on display. Artefacts include some spooky wooden poppets (a kind of voodoo doll), lots of witchy implements, and a hideous cast-iron 'witch's bridle' designed to extract confessions from suspected hags.

SLEEPING & EATING

Riverside Hotel (☎ 250216; www.hotelriverside.co.uk; s/d £30/60; ✗) A lovely B&B housed in one of the village's oldest buildings, with pleasant pastel-coloured rooms and a new restaurant serving open sandwiches and cream teas on a delightful riverside terrace.

Old Rectory (☎ 250225; www.stjuliot.com; St Juliot; d from £52; P ✗ ; ☯ Mar-Nov) Formerly the home of the vicar of St Juliot, this opulent B&B is famous as the house where Thomas Hardy fell in love with his future wife, Emma Lavinia Gifford (the rector's sister-in-law). Period antiques, Victorian knick-knacks and heavy drapes recreate the Hardy-era atmosphere; bookworms can stroll through the woods to St Juliot Church, which features in the pages of Hardy's novel *A Pair Of Blue Eyes*.

Wellington Hotel (☎ 250202; www.boscastle-wellington.com; The Harbour; d £76-140; P ✗) The grand old Welly Hotel, complete with its own crenellated turret, is the poshest place to stay in the village, with 15 old-fashioned country rooms dotted with antique clocks, polished dressers and thick floral carpets. The ground-floor bar is one of the village's main meeting spots and makes a great place for Sunday lunch.

Other recommendations:

Old Coach House (☎ 250398; www.old-coach.co.uk; Tintagel Rd; d £40-48; P ✗) Chintzy rooms inside a 200-year-old coaching house above the village.

Bottreaux Hotel (☎ 250231; www.boscastlecornwall .co.uk; d £65-100; P ✗) Fine, understated rooms inside an end-of-terrace townhouse, including one with a regal four-poster bed.

GETTING THERE & AWAY

For buses see left

MY KINGDOM FOR AN OSS

Padstow's raucous May Day fertility rite, featuring the fabled Obby Oss (hobby horse), is believed to be the oldest such event in the country. The ritual begins just before midnight on 30 April, as villagers sing to the innkeeper at the Golden Lion with the news that summer is 'a-come'. Then, at 10am the next morning the Blue Ribbon Oss – a man garbed in a huge hooped sailcloth dress and wild-looking horse headdress – dances around the town, grabbing any woman close enough and daubing her with coal (or, often, pinching her – it's believed to aid child-bearing!). He's followed at 11am by the Old Original (or Red) Oss and the madness continues until late.

Bude

☎ 01288 / pop 9242

The last town of any note on the north Cornish coast, Bude is a busy seaside resort and another popular surfing hang-out, thanks to several great beaches all within easy reach. Summerleaze beach is closest to town and a favourite with picnicking families; the surfer's choice is Crooklets, just to the north. Widemouth Bay and Sandymouth are also worth a look, while the cove at Duckpool is often quieter than its neighbours.

Bude Visitor Centre (☎ 354240; www.visitbude.info; The Crescent; ☺ 10am-5pm Mon-Sat, plus 10am-4pm Sun summer) is south of the town centre.

Camelot Hotel (☎ 0800 781 2536; www.camelot-hotel .co.uk; Downs View; s/d £49/98; P ☒ ☐) The pick of the B&Bs in Bude, with plenty of plain and comfortable rooms dotted around the rambling house and views across the fairways of the nearby golf course.

Life's a Beach (☎ 355222; Summerleaze Beach; mains £11-16; ☺ Mon-Sat) A beachside café, which transforms from a lunch-time bistro to a snazzy candlelit restaurant by night, specialising in seafood and fantastic fish dishes.

Bus 594 travels from Truro (three hours, four daily Monday to Saturday) via Wadebridge, Boscastle and Tintagel.

Bodmin Moor

Cornwall's 'roof' is a high heath pockmarked with bogs and granite hills, including Rough Tor (pronounced *row-tor*, 400m) and Brown Willy (419m), Cornwall's highest point. It's a desolate place that works on the imagination; the Beast of Bodmin, a large black catlike creature, has been seen regularly for many years, although no-one's ever managed to snap a decent picture.

Bodmin tourist office (☎ 01208-76616; www.bod minlive.com; Mount Folly; ☺ 10am-5pm Mon-Sat) can help with information on exploring the moor. The small **Town Museum** (☎ 01208-77067; Mount Folly; admission free; ☺ 10.30am-4.30pm Mon-Sat Apr-Sep) is opposite.

The A30 cuts across the centre of the moor from **Launceston**, which has a ruined 11th-century **castle** (EH; ☎ 01566-772365; admission £2; ☺ 10am-6pm Jul-Aug, 10am-5pm Apr-Jun & Sep, 10am-4pm Oct), and an interesting granite **church**.

Jamaica Inn (☎ 01566-86250; www.jamaicainn.co.uk; s £65, d £70-100; P ☒), out on the desolate moor near Bolventor, was made famous by Daphne du Maurier's novel. On a misty winter's night

the place still feels hugely atmospheric; the inn also contains a small smuggling museum and a room devoted to du Maurier.

About a mile south is **Dozmary Pool**, said to have been where Arthur's sword, Excalibur, was thrown after his death. It's a 4-mile walk northwest of Jamaica Inn to Brown Willy.

The **Bodmin & Wenford Railway** (☎ 0845-125-9678; www.bodminandwenfordrailway.co.uk; return ticket £7.50) is the last standard-gauge railway in Cornwall plied by steam locomotives. The old-fashioned steam trains are still decked out with their original 1950s livery, and chug from Bodmin Parkway and Bodmin General station to Boscarne Junction, where you can join up with the Camel Trail cycle route (p370). There are two to four return trips daily depending on season.

GETTING THERE & AWAY

Bodmin has bus connections with St Austell (bus 529, one hour, hourly Monday to Saturday), as well as Bodmin Parkway (bus 555, 15 minutes, hourly Monday to Saturday), on the London to Penzance train line.

ISLES OF SCILLY

☎ 01720

It's not quite true to say that Land's End is the most westerly point of the British Isles; that claim truly belongs to the tiny Isles of Scilly, 28 miles southwest of mainland Cornwall. Over 140 islands make up this miniature archipelago, but only five are inhabited; St Mary's is the largest and busiest island, closely followed by Tresco, while only a few hardy souls remain on Bryher, St Martin's and St Agnes. Nurtured by the Gulf Stream and blessed with a balmy subtropical climate, the Scillys have long survived on the traditional industries of farming, fishing and flower-growing, but these days tourism is by far the biggest money-spinner. With a laid-back island lifestyle, a strong community spirit and some of the most glorious beaches anywhere in England, it's hardly surprising that many visitors find themselves drawn back to the Scillys year after year. While life moves on at breakneck speed in the outside world, time in the Scillys just seems happy to stand still.

Information

The **Isles of Scilly Tourist Board** (☎ 422536; tic@scilly .gov.uk; Hugh Town, St Mary's; ☺ 8.30am-6pm Mon-Fri, 9am-5pm Sat, 9am-2pm Sun May-Sep, shorter hours in winter) is on St Mary's.

DEVON & CORNWALL

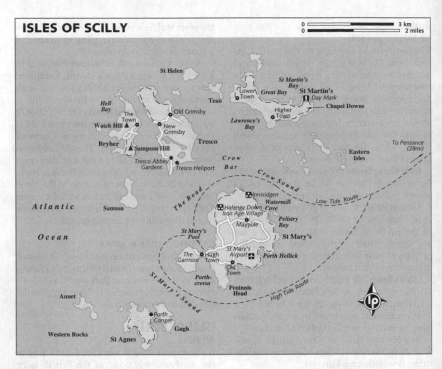

ISLES OF SCILLY

There are several good resources available online, including the locally run website www.scillyonline.co.uk and the tourist office's website (www.simplyscilly.co.uk), which has full accommodation listings.

The island gets extremely busy in summer, and many businesses shut down completely in winter, so make sure you plan ahead accordingly. All of the islands, except Tresco, have a simple camp site, but many visitors choose to stay in self-catering accommodation – check out **Island Properties** (☎ 422082; St Mary's) or **Sibley's Island Homes** (☎ 422431; sibleys@scilly.fsnet.co.uk).

St Mary's
The largest and busiest island in the Scillys is St Mary's, and by local standards it's a bustling metropolis, with most of the islands' big hotels, B&Bs, restaurants and shops, and the vast majority of the summertime visitors. The Scillonian ferry and all flights from the mainland arrive on St Mary's, but the other main islands are easily reached via the inter-island launches that leave from the harbour every morning.

About a mile south of the airport is the main settlement of **Hugh Town**, where you'll find most of the island's hotels and guesthouses, and the **Isles of Scilly Museum** (☎ 422337; Church St; adult/child £2/50p; ☻ 10am-4.30pm in summer, 10am-noon Mon-Sat in winter, or by arrangement), which has some fantastically atmospheric exhibits, including lots of archive photos of the islands, various artefacts recovered from shipwrecks (including muskets, a cannon and a ship's bell) and a fully rigged pilot gig dating from 1877.

The island even has its very own **perfumery** (☎ 423304; Porthloo; ☻ 9am-5pm Mon-Sat), which sells handmade soaps, pot pourri and perfumes scented with the essence of Scilly flowers.

A little way south of Hugh Town is **Old Town**, once the island's main harbour, but now home to a few small cafés, a village pub and a pleasant beach. Look out for the minuscule Old Town Church, where the services are still conducted by candlelight – the graveyard contains a memorial to Augustus Smith, founder of the Abbey Garden, as well as the grave of former prime minister Harold Wilson.

DEVON & CORNWALL

There are lots of small inlets scattered around the island's coastline, best reached on foot or by bike: Porth Hellick, Watermill Cove and the relatively remote Pelistry Bay are worth seeking out. St Mary's also has some unique ancient sites, notably the Iron Age village at Halangy Down, a mile north of Hugh Town, and the barrows at Bant's Carn and Innisidgen.

Scilly Walks (☎ 423326; www.scillywalks.co.uk) leads three-hour archaeological and historical tours, costing £5/2.50 per adult/child, as well as visits to other offshore islands. Twitchers should get in touch with **Will Wagstaff** (☎ 422212), who runs regular bird-watching tours.

For diving on St Mary's, contact **Island Sea Safaris** (☎ 422732), who also offers white-knuckle speedboat rides (£18 to £25) around the islands and snorkelling trips to the local seal colonies (£36).

The traditional sport of pilot gig racing is still popular in the Scillys. These six-oared wooden boats were originally used to race out to rescue foundering ships, but these days gig racing is a highly competitive sport. Races are held most weekends, and every May St Mary's hosts the World Pilot Gig Championships, which attracts teams from as far away as Holland and the USA.

SLEEPING

Camp site (☎ 422670; tedmoulson@aol.com; Tower Cottage, Garrison; tent sites per person £6-8) This popular, well-run camp site is tucked away in the dunes just behind Middle Town beach. The facilities are a little basic, but still a cut above most other camp sites on the Scillys. There's a laundry and a toilet block equipped with coin-operated showers, kitchen sinks and hot and cold water, and the beach is just steps away.

Evergreen Cottage (☎ 422711; www.evergreencottageguesthouse.co.uk; The Parade; d £58-69) This tiny little whitewashed cob cottage has unsurprisingly mini-sized rooms, but its sturdy walls mean it stays cool even in the height of summer.

Wheelhouse (☎ 422719; Porthcressa Beach; d £60-90) This lovely modern B&B has perhaps the best position of any on St Mary's, right above Porthcressa Beach, with a small outside terrace where you can soak up the sunshine while tucking into a hearty home-cooked breakfast.

Crebinick Guest House (☎ 422968; www.crebinick.co.uk; Church St; d £66-80; ☒) Small, sweet rooms

in a solid 18th-century terraced house, carefully renovated and efficiently run by its local owners.

Star Castle Hotel (☎ 422317; www.star-castle.co.uk; The Garrison; depending on season r £110 140, ste £166-296; ☒ ☙) This strangely-shaped hotel was originally part of a 16th-century fort, which explains its peculiar layout in the form of an eight-pointed star. These days it's a supremely comfortable island hotel, boasting lovely maritime-themed rooms and a brace of restaurants where the seafood is out of this world.

St Mary's Hall Hotel (☎ 422316; www.stmaryshallhotel.co.uk; r £160-240; ☒) This beautifully renovated mansion was built for the Italian nobleman, Leon de Ferrari in 1938, and it's still an upper-class place to stay, with a choice of flowery Count Leon rooms or lavish designer suites, complete with LCD TVs and Chinese rugs.

Tresco

Once owned by Tavistock Abbey, Tresco is the second largest island, and the second-most visited after St Mary's. The main attraction is the **Abbey Garden** (☎ 424105; www.tresco.co.uk /the_abbey_garden; admission £8.50; ☉ 9.30am-4pm), first laid out in 1834 on the site of a 10th-century Benedictine abbey. The terraced gardens feature more than 5000 subtropical plants, including species from Brazil, New Zealand and South Africa, and the intriguing Valhalla collection, made up of figureheads and name-plates salvaged from the many ships that have foundered off Tresco's shores.

There are only two places to stay on the island, apart from self-catering cottages.

New Inn (☎ 422844; newinn@tresco.co.uk; depending on season d £77-110; mains £5-18; ☒) This old stone inn has been whetting Scillonian whistles for several centuries, and is still the hub of island life. The upstairs rooms are smartly-finished with subtle colours and all the mod-cons, and a few boast views over the channel to Bryher.

Island Hotel (☎ 422883; islandhotel@tresco.co.uk; r £150-440; ☒ ☒ ☙) For something altogether more upmarket, this eye-poppingly expensive hotel has bedrooms spread across several wings, with a choice of either private garden patios or glorious sea-view balconies. The décor throughout is elegance personified, ranging from gingham-checked bedrooms to luxurious suites decked out in gold and navy blue.

Bryher & Samson

Home to approximately 70 people, Bryher is the smallest and wildest inhabited island in the Scillys. Much of the landscape is covered by rough bracken and heather, and the coast often takes the full force of the Atlantic weather; Hell Bay in a winter gale is a powerful sight. There are good views over the islands from the top of Watch Hill, and Rushy Bay is one of the finest beaches in the Scillys. From the quay, occasional boats visit local seal and bird colonies and deserted Samson Island, where abandoned settlers' cottages tell a story of hard subsistence living.

The **camp site** (☎ 422886; sites £7.50) is near the quay.

Hell Bay Hotel (☎ 422947; hellbay@aol.com; d £135-420; ✗ ☎) is a beautiful hotel that consists entirely of upmarket, impeccably finished suites, most of which boast sleek, contemporary décor, en suites, sitting rooms and private balconies.

St Martin's

The most northerly of the main islands, St Martin's is renowned for its beautiful beaches. The largest settlement is **Higher Town**, where you'll find a small village shop and the **Scilly Diving** (☎ 422848; www.scillydiving.com; Higher Town; dives from £36.50). A short way to the west is **Lower Town**, home to a cluster of tightly huddled cottages and the island's only hotel.

There are several small art galleries scattered across the island, as well as a tiny vineyard and a flower farm.

On the island's southern shore is Lawrence's Bay, which reveals a broad sweep of sandy flats at low tide. Along the northern side is Great Bay, arguably the finest beach in the Scillys; from the western end, you can cross to White Island at low tide. If you walk east along the windswept northern cliffs you'll find the Day Mark, a red-and-white candy-striped landmark that was built back in 1687, and the secluded cove of Perpitch.

The **camp site** (☎ 422888; chris@stmartinscampsite .freeserve.co.uk; Middle Town; tent sites £6-8) is near Lawrence's Bay at the western end of the island.

Polreath (☎ 422046; Higher Town; s £35-50, d £70-100; ✗) is a traditional cottage and one of the few B&Bs on the island. Rooms are snug and cosy, and it's handy for the island bakery and post office.

St Martin's on the Isle (☎ 422090; www.stmartinsho tel.co.uk; d £230-550; ✗ ☎) is the only hotel on St Martin's, and arguably one of the best in the Scillys, with landscaped grounds, an indoor swimming pool and a private quay. The 30 bedrooms have a choice of sea or garden views, and there are several upmarket suites with private sitting rooms. The in-house restaurant is renowned throughout the islands.

St Agnes

England's most southerly community somehow transcends even the tranquillity of the other islands in the Isles of Scilly; it's an ideal spot to stroll, unwind and reflect, with lots of cloistered coves, coastal walks and even a scattering of prehistoric sites. Visitors disembark at **Porth Conger**, near the decommissioned **Old Lighthouse**, which is indeed one of the oldest lighthouses in the country. Other points of interest include the tiny **Troy Town Maze**, and the historic inlets of Periglis Cove and St Warna's Cove (dedicated to the patron saint of shipwrecks). At low tide you can cross over to the island of **Gugh**, where you'll find some intriguing Bronze Age remains as well as standing stones.

The **camp site** (☎ 422360; Troy Town Farm; tent sites £5.75-8) is at the southwestern corner of the island.

The little stone-walled **Covean Cottage** (☎ 422620; d £56-68) is the perfect location for getting away from the crowds; it offers four pleasant, good-value rooms and serves excellent cream teas, light meals and sticky treats during the day.

The most southwesterly pub in all of Britain, the **Turk's Head** (☎ 422434; mains £6-10) is a real treat, with fine views, excellent beers, good pub grub and a hearty island atmosphere.

Getting There & Away

There's no transport to or from the islands on a Sunday.

AIR

The **Isles of Scilly Skybus** (☎ 0845 710 5555; www.ios -travel.co.uk) flies between St Mary's and Land's End (£119, 15 minutes) and Newquay (£138, 30 minutes) several times daily year-round. Cheaper saver fares are available for flights leaving Land's End after 2pm, or leaving St Mary's before noon. There's also at least one daily flight to Exeter (£221, 50 minutes) and Bristol (£266, 70 minutes). All prices are return fares.

British International (☎ 01736-363871; www.islesof scillyhelicopter.com) helicopters fly to St Mary's (20 minutes, nine to 11 daily Monday to Friday, 15 to 17 on Saturday March to September; seven daily Monday to Friday, 13 on Saturday in September) and Tresco (20 minutes, four to six daily Monday to Saturday April to October, four daily November to March) from Penzance heliport.

Adult return fares are £142 including taxes and fuel surcharges; a cheap day-return costs £98. Parking at the heliport costs £6 per day.

BOAT

The *Scillonian* ferry (☎ 0845 710 5555; www.ios -travel.co.uk) sails between Penzance and St Mary's (£89 return, two hours 40 minutes, daily Monday to Saturday). The crossing can be notoriously rough – landlubbers might be better off taking the chopper.

Getting Around

Regular inter-island launches sail from St Mary's harbour daily in summer to the other main islands. The boats usually leave in the early morning and return in late afternoon, although there are several daily boats over to Tresco. A return trip to most offshore islands costs £6.80, although there are lots of operators and off-island trips available – ask around at the harbour to see what's on offer.

If you're travelling between the islands, make sure you pack your luggage well and label it clearly with your name and the island you're going to, as the inter-island boat-trips can be a little rough and ready. Luggage rarely gets totally lost, but in the busy summer season bags sometimes end up on the wrong island and might not turn up till the next trip.

The airport bus service (single/return £2.50/4.50) departs from the strand in Hugh Town approximately 40 minutes before each flight. A circular bus service runs around St Mary's several times daily in summer (£1 to all destinations).

There's a twice-daily trip around St Mary's on a vintage open-top bus known as the Island Rover (www.islandrover.co.uk, £6), leaving at 10.15am and 1.30pm from the park. Ferry passengers can buy bus tickets on board the boat.

Bikes are available from **Buccaboo Hire** (☎ 422289; Porthcressa, Hugh Town) from around £6 per day.

For taxis, try **Island Taxis** (☎ 422126) or **Scilly Cabs** (☎ 422901).

Oxfordshire, the Cotswolds & Gloucestershire

A landscape of lush rolling hills, thatched roofs and absurdly pretty villages makes up the counties of Oxfordshire and Gloucestershire, home to the honey-coloured stone and gentle charm of the Cotswold Hills. The spoils of the prosperous medieval wool trade litter the area, from lofty church steeples and grandiose manors to crushingly quaint almshouses and cosy, fire-lit inns. It's the stuff that jigsaws are made of, and as close to the misty-eyed English idyll as you'll get.

Beyond the rural Arcady, this region boasts the legendary city of Oxford, an academic powerhouse and bastion of classical English architecture. Riddled with elegant college buildings, world-class museums and top-notch bookshops, it makes a good base for exploring the area. Just north of here is the stunning Churchill pile of Blenheim Palace, while to the west you'll find the genteel charms of Regency Cheltenham and the graceful lines of the magnificent Gothic cathedral in Gloucester.

However, the glut of attractions and beauty of the hills and villages means that this is prime tourist territory. In summer the area can be swamped with visitors and the narrow roads get choked with monstrous 4WDs and tourist coaches. At this time it's best to visit the most popular villages early in the morning or late in the evening, spending your day getting lost on the countless back roads and walking or cycling trails that crisscross the region. One of the greatest joys of travelling in the Cotswolds lies in discovering your own bucolic village seemingly undisturbed since medieval times.

HIGHLIGHTS

- Soaking up the studious calm and weight of academic achievement at **Oxford University** (p383)

- Wandering the sumptuous rooms and gardens of **Blenheim Palace** (p392)

- Hanging out at one of the many festivals in graceful **Cheltenham** (p416)

- Marvelling at the magnificent cloisters of **Gloucester Cathedral** (p410)

- Getting lost on the winding roads of the **Cotswolds** (p396)

- Going medieval with a tankard of ale at the **Falkland Arms** in Great Tew (p399)

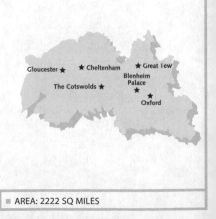

Gloucester ★   ★ Cheltenham   ★ Great Tew

The Cotswolds ★   Blenheim Palace ★

★ Oxford

■ POPULATION: 3.1 MILLION   ■ AREA: 2222 SQ MILES

OXFORDSHIRE & GLOUCESTERSHIRE

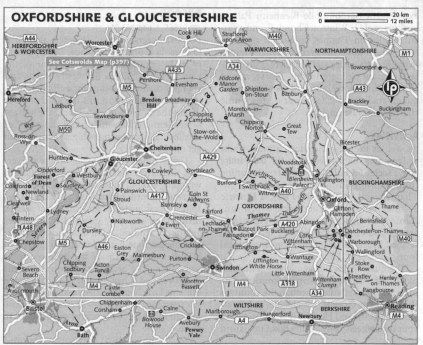

Activities

Walking or cycling through the Cotswolds is an ideal way to get away from the crowds and discover some of the lesser-known vistas and villages of the region. For more information, see the Outdoor Activities chapter (p75) or specific suggestions for walks and rides throughout this chapter.

CYCLING

Gentle gradients and scenic vistas make the Cotswolds ideal for cycling, with only the steep western escarpment offering a challenge to the legs. Plenty of quiet country lanes and gated roads crisscross the region or follow the way-marked **Thames Valley Cycle Way**, part of the National Cycle Network (see boxed text, p78).

Mountain bikers can use a variety of bridleways in the **Cotswolds** and **Chilterns** and in the west of the region, the **Forest of Dean** has many dirt-track options, and some dedicated mountain bike trails.

WALKING

The **Cotswold Hills** offer endless opportunities for day hikes, but if you're looking for something more ambitious, the **Cotswold Way** (www.cotswold-way.co.uk) is an absolute classic. The route covers 102 miles from Bath to Chipping Campden and takes about a week to walk.

Alternatively, the **Thames Path** (www.thames-path.co.uk) follows the river downstream from its source near Cirencester to London. It takes about two weeks to complete the 173-mile route, but there's a very enjoyable five-day section from near Cirencester to Oxford.

OXFORDSHIRE

A region of old money, scholarly pursuits, thatched roofs and undulating hills, Oxfordshire is a well-bred, well-preened kind of place with plenty of rustic charm and headline attractions.

The county is dominated by its world-renowned university town, a genteel city soaked in history and full of august buildings, gowned cyclists, ivy-clad quads and dusty academics. Yet Oxfordshire is so much more than its university suggests. It is also home to the extravagant Baroque pile Blenheim Palace, birthplace of Sir Winston Churchill, and affluent Henley-on-Thames, an elegant riverside town which hosts the ever-so-stylish Henley Royal Regatta each year. Near here is the mysterious giant Uffington White Horse, carved from the limestone hills, and a smattering of quaint traditional villages oozing the gentle charm of middle England.

Activities

As well as the long-distance national trails, walkers may be interested in the **Oxfordshire Way**, a scenic 65-mile waymarked trail running from Bourton-on-the-Water to Henley-on-Thames, and the **Wychwood Way**, a historic 37-mile route from Woodstock, which runs through an ancient royal forest. The routes are divided up into manageable sections described in leaflets available from most local tourist offices and libraries.

The quiet roads and gentle gradients also make Oxfordshire good cycling country. The main waymarked route through the county is the **Oxfordshire Cycleway**, which takes in Woodstock, Burford and Henley. If you don't have your own wheels you can hire bikes in Oxford (p392).

You'll find information about all walking and cycling routes in the county at www .oxfordshire.gov.uk/countryside.

Getting Around

You can pick up bus and train timetables for most routes at local tourist offices. The main train stations are in Oxford and Banbury and have frequent connections to London Paddington and Euston, Hereford, Birmingham, Bristol and Scotland.

The main bus operators are the **Oxford Bus Company** (☎ 01865-785400; www.oxfordbus.co.uk) and **Stagecoach** (☎ 01865-772250; www.stagecoachbus.com /oxfordshire). If you plan to do a lot of travelling by bus, Stagecoach offers 1-/7-/14-day bus passes for unlimited use of its services in southern Britain (excluding London) for £6/18/34.

Alternatively, **Cotswold Roaming** (☎ 01865-308300; www.cotswold-roaming.co.uk) runs guided bus tours from Oxford between April and October. Half-day tours run to Blenheim Palace (adult/under 15 years £16/10) and the Cotswolds (adult/under 15 years £19/11), while full-day tours (£30/18) go to Bath and Castle Combe, and the Cotswolds.

OXFORD

☎ 01865 / pop 143,016

Bookish, conservative, closeted and elite, Oxford is a privileged place, highly aware of its international standing as one of the world's most famous university towns and yet remarkably restrained for a city driven by its student population. It's the kind of place where the pursuit of excellence, the weight of academic achievement and the whiff of intellectual ideals is palpable as soon as you get off the bus.

Thirty-nine colleges make up the university, their elegant honey-coloured buildings wrapping around winding cobbled streets and attracting hoards of tourists each year. Yet despite the rushing traffic and throngs of people, inside their jealously guarded quadrangles an aura of studious calm descends. The oldest colleges date back almost 750 years and little has changed inside the hallowed walls since then. The archaic traditions, customs and dress codes live on and the architecture remains largely untouched, allowing visitors to experience the colleges as countless prime ministers, poets, writers and scientists have done.

Yet, the university is only part of Oxford's story; long before Mensa was ever born the Morris motor car was rolling off production lines in Cowley, and today the university's academic elite are still far outnumbered by the real-world majority. Butting up against all that fine architecture, the celebrated libraries, world-class museums and historic pubs is an increasingly urbane city flush with chic restaurants, trendy bars and exclusive shops.

History

Strategically placed at the confluence of the River Cherwell and the Thames (called the Isis here, from the Latin *Tamesis*), Oxford was a key Saxon town heavily fortified by Alfred the Great during the war against the Danes.

By the 11th century the Augustinian abbey in Oxford had begun training clerics, and when Henry II banned Anglo-Norman students from attending the Sorbonne in 1167, the abbey began to attract students in droves. Whether bored by the lack of distractions in the tiny town or revolted by the ignorance of the country folk we'll never know, but the new students managed to create a lasting enmity with the local townspeople, culminating in the St Scholastica's Day Massacre in 1355

ST SCHOLASTICA'S DAY MASSACRE

The first real wave of students arrived in Oxford in the 12th century and right from the start an uneasy relationship grew between the townspeople and the bookish blow-ins. Name calling and drunken brawls escalated into full-scale riots in 1209 and 1330 when browbeaten scholars abandoned Oxford to establish new universities in Cambridge and Stamford respectively. The riots of 10 and 11 February 1355, changed everything however, and left a bitter scar on relations for hundreds of years.

It all began when celebrations for St Scholastica's Day grew out of hand and a drunken scuffle spilled into the street. Years of simmering discontent and frustrations let loose and soon students and townspeople took to each other's throats. The chancellor ordered the pealing of the university bells and every student who heard it rushed to join the brawl. By the end of the day the students had claimed victory and an uneasy truce was called.

The next morning, however, the furious townspeople returned with the help of local villagers armed with pickaxes, shovels and pikes. By sundown 63 students and 30 townspeople were dead. King Edward III sent troops to quell the rioting and eventually decided to bring the town under the control of the university.

To prove its authority, the university ordered the mayor and burgesses (citizens) to attend a service and pay a penny for every student killed on the anniversary of the riot each year. For 470 years the vengeful practice continued, until one mayor flatly refused to pay the fine. His successors all followed suit but it took until 1955, 600 years after the original event, for the university to extend the olive branch and award a Doctorate of Civil Law to Mayor William Richard Gowers, MA, Oriel.

(see boxed text, above). Thereafter, the king ordered that the university be broken up into colleges, each of which then developed its own traditions.

The first colleges, Balliol, Merton and University, were built in the 13th century, with at least three more being added in each of the following three centuries. Newer colleges, such as Keble, were added in the 19th and 20th centuries to cater for an ever-expanding student population. Old habits die hard at Oxford however, and it was 1877 before lecturers were allowed to marry, and another year before female students were admitted. Even then, it still took another 42 years before women would be granted a degree for their four years of hard work. Today, there are 39 colleges that cater for about 16,500 students, and in 2006 the last all-female college, St Hilda's, historically voted to allow male students and academics onto its grounds.

Meanwhile, the arrival of the canal system in 1790 had a profound effect on the rest of Oxford. By creating a link with the Midlands' industrial centres, work and trade suddenly expanded beyond the academic core. However, the city's real industrial boom came when William Morris began producing cars here in 1913. With the success of his Bullnose Morris and Morris Minor his Cowley factory went on to become one of the largest motor plants in the world. Although the works have been scaled down since their heyday, new Minis still run off BMW's Cowley production line today.

Orientation

Oxford is fairly compact and can easily be covered on foot. Carfax Tower makes a good central landmark and is a short walk from the bus and train stations, which are conveniently located close to the centre of town.

The university buildings are scattered throughout the city, with the most important and architecturally significant in the centre. Jericho, in the northwest, is the trendy, artsy end of town, with slick bars and restaurants and an arthouse cinema, while Cowley Rd, southeast of Carfax, is the edgy student and immigrant area packed with cheap places to eat and drink.

Information
BOOKSHOPS

Blackwell (☎ 792792; www.blackwell.co.uk; 48-51 Broad St) 'The Knowledge Retailer' stocks any book you could ever need.

Little Bookshop (☎ 559176; Ave 2, Covered Market) Tiny shop bursting with first editions and rare books.

OXFORDSHIRE, THE COTSWOLDS & GLOUCESTERSHIRE

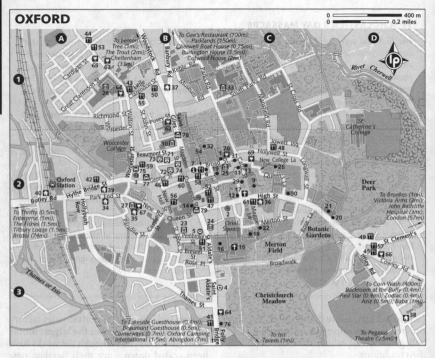

OXFORD

QI (Quite Interesting; ☎ 261507; www.qi.com; 16 Turl St) 'Ridiculously well-read and over-educated' staff to help you trawl through specially chosen titles.

EMERGENCY
Police (☎ 0845 8 505 505)

INTERNET ACCESS
Mices (☎ 726364; 118 High St; per 20min £1; ✆ 9am-11pm Mon-Sat, 10am-11pm Sun) There's another branch on Gloucester Green.

Virgin (☎ 723906; 18-20 Cornmarket St; per 20min £1; ✆ 9am-6.30pm Mon-Sat, 11am-5pm Sun)

INTERNET RESOURCES
Daily Info (www.dailyinfo.co.uk) Daily listings for events, gigs, performances, accommodation and jobs.

Oxford City (www.oxfordcity.co.uk) Accommodation and restaurant listings as well as entertainment, activities and shopping.

Oxford Online (www.visitoxford.org) Oxford's official tourism website.

LAUNDRY
Coin Wash (127 Cowley Rd; per load £3; ✆ 9am-9pm Mon-Sat)

MEDICAL SERVICES
John Radcliffe Hospital (☎ 741166; Headley Way, Headington) Three miles east of the city centre.

MONEY
Every major bank and ATM is represented on or near Cornmarket St.

POST
Post office (☎ 223344; 102 St Aldate's; ✆ 9am-5.30pm Mon-Sat)

TOURIST INFORMATION
Tourist office (☎ 726871; www.visitoxford.org; 15-16 Broad St; ✆ 9.30am-5pm Mon-Sat, 10am-4pm Sun) Stocks a *Welcome to Oxford* (£1) brochure, with a walking tour with college opening times, as well as the *University of Oxford* leaflet and *Oxford Accessible Guide* for travellers with disabilities. Look out for *In Oxford*, a free publication listing events, museums, restaurants and accommodation. It can book accommodation for a £4 fee plus a 10% deposit.

UNIVERSITIES
Oxford Brookes (☎ 741111; www.brookes.ac.uk; Gipsy Lane) Oxford's lesser-known university.

Oxford University (☎ 270000; www.ox.ac.uk)

INFORMATION

- Blackwell......1 C2
- Mices......2 C2
- Mices......3 B2
- Police Station......4 C3
- Post Office......5 B2
- QI......6 D2
- Tourist Office......7 B2
- Virgin......8 B2

SIGHTS & ACTIVITIES

- All Souls College......9 C2
- Ashmolean Museum......10 B2
- Bodleian Library......11 C2
- Brasenose College......12 C2
- Bridge of Sighs......13 C2
- Carfax Tower......14 B2
- Christ Church Cathedral......15 C3
- Christ Church College......16 C3
- Church of St Mary the Virgin......17 C2
- Corpus Christi College......18 C2
- Exeter College......19 B2
- Howard C & Sons Punts......20 D2
- Magdalen College......21 D2
- Merton College......22 C2
- Modern Art Oxford......23 B2
- Museum of Oxford......24 B2
- Museum of the History of Science......25 C2
- New College......26 C2
- Oxford Castle......27 B2
- Oxford University Press Museum......28 A1
- Radcliffe Camera......29 C2
- St Edmund Hall......30 C2
- Sheldonian Theatre......31 C2
- Trinity College......32 B2
- University & Pitt Rivers Museums......33 C1

SLEEPING

- Central Backpackers......34 A2
- Malmaison......35 B2
- Old Bank Hotel......36 C2
- Old Parsonage Hotel......37 B1
- Orchard House......38 D3
- Oxford Backpackers......39 A2
- YHA Oxford......40 A2

EATING

- Aziz......41 B3
- Bangkok House......42 A2
- Big Bang......43 B1
- Branca......44 A1
- Café Coco......45 D3
- Chutneys......46 B2
- Covered Market......47 B2
- Edamame......48 C2
- Fishers......49 D3
- G&D's......50 B1
- G&D's......51 B3
- Georgina's......52 B2
- Jericho Café......53 A1
- Mortons......54 B2
- Mortons......55 B1
- Mortons......(see 47)
- Mortons......56 B2
- Moya......57 D3
- News Café......58 B2
- Noodle Bar......59 B2
- Nosebag......60 B2
- Quod......61 C2

DRINKING

- Eagle & Child......62 B1
- Frevd......63 A1
- Head of the River......64 C3
- Jericho Tavern......65 A1
- Kazbar......66 D3
- Living Room......67 B2
- Raoul's......68 B1
- Turf Tavern......69 C2
- White Horse......70 C2

ENTERTAINMENT

- Burton Taylor Theatre......71 B2
- New Theatre......72 B2
- Oxford Playhouse......73 B2
- Po Na Na......74 B2

TRANSPORT

- Gloucester Green Bus/Coach Station......75 B2
- Salter Bros......76 C3
- Taxi Rank......77 B2
- Taxi Rank......78 B2
- Taxi Rank......79 B2

Sights

UNIVERSITY BUILDINGS & COLLEGES

Christ Church College

The largest and grandest of all of Oxford's colleges, **Christ Church** (☎ 276492; www.visitchristchurch.net; St Aldate's; adult/under 16yr £4.70/3.70; 🕑 9am-5pm Mon-Sat, 1-5pm Sun) is also its most popular. The magnificent buildings, illustrious history and latter-day fame as a location for the Harry Potter films has tourists coming in droves.

The college was founded in 1525 by Cardinal Thomas Wolsey – who suppressed 22 monasteries to acquire the funds for his lavish building project – and over the years numerous luminaries have been educated here. Albert Einstein, philosopher John Locke, poet WH Auden and Charles Dodgson (Lewis Carroll) all studied here, as did 13 British prime ministers.

The main entrance is below imposing **Tom Tower**, the upper part of which was designed by former student Sir Christopher Wren. Great Tom, the 7-ton tower bell, still chimes 101 times each evening at 9.05pm (Oxford is five minutes west of Greenwich), to sound the curfew imposed on the original 101 students.

Mere visitors, however, are not allowed to enter the college this way and must go further down St Aldate's to the side entrance. Immediately on entering is the 15th-century cloister, a relic of the ancient Priory of St Frideswide, whose shrine was a focus of pilgrimage. From here you go up to the **Great Hall**, the college's magnificent dining room, with its hammer-beam roof and imposing portraits of past scholars.

Coming down the grand staircase you'll enter **Tom Quad**, Oxford's largest quadrangle, which was used as a cattle pen by Royalist forces during the Civil War. From the quad you enter **Christ Church Cathedral**, the smallest cathedral in the country. Inside, brawny Norman columns are topped by elegant vaulting, while beautiful, stained-glass windows adorn the walls. Look out for a rare depiction of the murder of Thomas Becket.

You can also explore another two quads and the **Picture Gallery**, with its modest collection of Renaissance art. To the south of the college is **Christ Church Meadow**, a leafy expanse bordered by the Isis and Cherwell rivers and ideal for leisurely walking.

Magdalen College

Set amid a hundred acres of lawns, woodlands, river walks and deer park, **Magdalen** (mawd-len;

☎ 276000; www.magd.ox.ac.uk; High St; adult/under 16yr £3/2; ☺ noon-6pm Jul-Sep, 1pm-dusk Oct-Jun) is one of the wealthiest and most beautiful of Oxford's colleges.

An elegant Victorian gateway leads into a medieval chapel with its glorious 15th-century tower, and on to the remarkable cloisters, some of the finest in Oxford. The strange gargoyles and carved figures here are said to have inspired CS Lewis' stone statues in *The Chronicles of Narnia*. Behind the cloisters the lovely Addison's Walk leads through the grounds and along the banks of the River Cherwell for just under a mile.

Magdalen has a reputation as an artistic college and some of its most famous students and fellows have included Oscar Wilde, poet laureate Sir John Betjeman and Nobel Laureate Seamus Heaney.

The college also boasts a fine choir that sings *Hymnus Eucharisticus* at 6am on May Day (1 May) from the top of the 42m-bell tower. The event now marks the culmination of a solid night of drinking for most students as they gather in their glad rags on Magdalen Bridge to listen to the dawn chorus.

Opposite the college and sweeping along the banks of the River Cherwell are the beautiful and excellently labelled **Botanic Gardens** (☎ 286690; www.botanic-garden.ox.ac.uk; adult/under 16yr £2.60/free; ☺ 9am-6pm May-Aug, 9am-4.30pm Oct-Apr). The gardens are the oldest in Britain and were founded in 1621 for the study of medicinal plants.

Sheldonian Theatre

The monumental **Sheldonian Theatre** (☎ 277299; www.sheldon.ox.ac.uk; 15-16 Broad St; adult/under 16yr £2/1; ☺ 10am-12.30pm & 2-4.30pm Mon-Sat Mar-Oct, 10am-12.30pm & 2-3.30pm Mon-Sat Nov-Feb) was the first major work of Christopher Wren, at that time a University Professor of Astronomy. Inspired by the classical Theatre of Marcellus in Rome, it has a rectangular front end and a semicircular back, while inside, the ceiling of the main hall is blanketed by a fine 17th-century painting of the triumph of truth over ignorance. The Sheldonian is now used for college ceremonies and public concerts but you can climb to the cupola for good views of the surrounding buildings.

Bodleian Library & Radcliffe Camera

Oxford's **Bodleian Library** (☎ 277224; www.bodley .ox.ac.uk; cnr Broad St & Parks Rd) is one of the old-est public libraries in the world, and one of England's three copyright libraries. It holds more than seven million items on 118 miles of shelving and has seating space for up to 2500 readers.

The oldest part of the library surrounds the stunning Jacobean-Gothic **Old Schools Quadrangle**, which dates from the early 17th century. On the eastern side of the quad is the **Tower of Five Orders**, an ornate building depicting the five classical orders of architecture. On the west side is the **Divinity School** (admission £2; ☺ 9am-5pm Mon-Fri, 9am-4.30pm Sat), the university's first examination room. It is renowned as a masterpiece of 15th-century English Gothic architecture and has a superb fan-vaulted ceiling. A self-guided audio tour (£2.50) to these areas is available.

Most of the rest of the library is closed to visitors, but **library tours** (admission £6; ☺ tours 10.30am, 11.30am, 2pm & 3pm Apr-Oct, 11am, 2pm & 3pm Nov-Mar) allow access to the medieval Duke Humfrey's library, where the library proudly boasts, no less than five kings, 40 Nobel Prize winners, 25 British prime ministers and writers such as Oscar Wilde, CS Lewis and JRR Tolkien studied. You'll also get to see 17th-century **Convocation House and Court**, where parliament was held during the Civil War. The tour takes about an hour and is not suitable for children less than 11 years old.

Just south of the library is the **Radcliffe Camera** (Radcliffe Sq; ☺ no public access), the quintessential Oxford landmark and one of the city's most photographed buildings. The spectacular circular library was built between 1737 and 1749 in grand Palladian style, and boasts Britain's third-largest dome.

For excellent views of the Radcliffe Camera and surrounding buildings, climb the 14th-century tower in the beautiful **Church of Saint Mary the Virgin** (☎ 279111; www.university-church .ox.ac.uk; cnr High & Catte Sts; tower admission £2.50/1.50; ☺ 9am-6pm Jul-Aug, 9am-5pm Sep-Jun). On Sunday the tower does not open until about noon, after the morning services.

New College

From the Bodleian stroll under the **Bridge of Sighs**, a 1914 copy of the famous bridge in Venice, to **New College** (☎ 279 555; www.new.ox.ac .uk; cnr Holywell St & New College Lane; admission £2 Easter-Sep, free Oct-Easter; ☺ 11am-5pm Easter-Sep, 2-4pm Oct-Easter). This 14th-century college was the first in Oxford to accept undergraduates and is a fine example of the glorious perpendicular style. The chapel here is full of treasures including superb stained glass, much of it original, and Sir Jacob Epstein's disturbing statue of Lazarus. During term time visitors may attend the beautiful Evensong, a choral church service, held nightly at 6pm.

William Spooner was once a college warden here and his habit of transposing the first consonants of words gave rise to the term 'spoonerism'. Local lore suggests that he once reprimanded a student by saying, 'You have deliberately tasted two worms and can leave Oxford by the town drain'.

Merton College

From the High St follow the wonderfully named Logic Lane to **Merton College** (☎ 276310; www.merton.ox.ac.uk; Merton St; admission free; ☒ 2-4pm Mon-Fri, 10am-4pm Sat & Sun), one of Oxford's original three colleges. Founded in 1264, Merton was the first to adopt collegiate planning, bringing scholars and tutors together into a formal community and providing a planned residence for them. The charming 14th-century **Mob Quad** here was the first of the college quads.

Just off the quad is a 13th-century **chapel** and the **Old Library** (admission by guided tour only; admission £2), the oldest medieval library in use. It is said that Professor JRR Tolkien spent many hours here while writing *The Lord of the Rings*. Other literary giants associated with the college include TS Eliot and Louis MacNeice.

If you're visiting in summer, look out for posters advertising candlelit concerts in the chapel.

All Souls College

One of the wealthiest of Oxford's colleges and unique in not accepting any undergraduate students, **All Souls** (☎ 279379; www.all-souls.ox.ac.uk; High St; admission free; ☒ 2-4pm Mon-Fri) is primarily an academic research institution. It was founded in 1438 as a centre of prayer and learning, and today fellowship of the college is one of the highest academic honours in the country. Each year the university's top finalists are invited to sit an exam for fellowship of the college, with an average of only two making the grade annually.

Much of the college façade dates from the 1440s and unlike other older colleges, the front quad is largely unchanged in five centuries. It also contains a beautiful 17th-century sundial

designed by Christopher Wren. Most obvious, though, are the twin mock-Gothic towers on the north quad. Designed by Nicholas Hawksmoor in 1710, they were lambasted for ruining the Oxford skyline when erected.

Other Colleges

Much of the centre of Oxford is taken up by graceful university buildings and elegant colleges, each one individual in its appearance and academic specialities. However, not all are open to the public. You'll find details of visiting hours and admission at www.ox.ac.uk/colleges.

Set back off Broad St, **Trinity College** (☎ 279900; www.trinity.ox.ac.uk; Broad St; adult/under 16yr £1/50p; ☒ 10.30am-noon & 2-4.30pm Mon-Fri, 2-4pm Sat & Sun) is worth a visit for the exquisite carvings in its chapel and Wren's beautiful Garden Quad.

Nearby **Exeter College** (☎ 279600; www.exeter.ox.ac.uk; Turl St; admission free; ☒ 2-5pm) is known for its elaborate 17th-century dining hall and ornate Victorian Gothic chapel that houses *The Adoration of the Magi*, a William Morris tapestry.

Small and select **Brasenose College** (☎ 277830; www.bnc.ox.ac.uk; admission £1; ☒ 2-5pm) is an elegant 16th-century place with more charm than many of the larger colleges. Look out for the doorknocker hanging above the high table in the dining hall – it has a fascinating history.

The sole survivor of the original halls, the teaching institutions that preceded colleges in Oxford, medieval **St Edmund Hall** (☎ 279000; www.seh.ox.ac.uk; Queen's Lane; admission free; ☒ sunrise-sunset) is worth a visit to see its small chapel decorated by William Morris and Edward Burne-Jones.

Sandwiched between Christ Church and Merton you'll find the small and beautiful **Corpus Christi College** (☎ 276700; www.ccc.ox.ac.uk; Merton St; admission free; ☒ 1.30-4.30pm). Look out for the pelican sundial in the middle of the front quad.

ASHMOLEAN MUSEUM

A vast, rambling collection of art and antiquities is on display at the mammoth **Ashmolean** (☎ 278000; www.ashmol.ox.ac.uk; Beaumont St; admission free; ☒ 10am-5pm Tue-Sat, noon-5pm Sun), Britain's oldest public museum. Established in 1683, it is based on the extensive collection of the remarkably well-travelled John Tradescant, gardener to Charles I, and housed in one of

THE BRAINS BEHIND THE OED

In 1879 the Oxford University Press began work on an ambitious project: a complete re-examination of the English language since the 12th century. The four-volume work was expected to take 10 years to complete. Recognising the mammoth task ahead, editor James Murray issued a circular appealing for volunteers to pore over their books and make precise notes on word usage. Their contributions were invaluable but after five years, Murray and his team had still only reached the word 'ant'.

Of the thousands of volunteers who helped out, the most prolific of all was Dr WC Minor, a US Civil War surgeon. Over the next 20 years, he became Murray's most valued contributor, providing tens of thousands of illustrative quotations and notes on word origins and usage. Murray received all of the doctor's contributions by post from Broadmoor, a hospital for the criminally insane. When he decided to visit the doctor in 1891 however, he discovered that Minor was not an employee but the asylum's longest-serving inmate, a schizophrenic committed in 1872 for a motiveless murder. Despite this, Murray was deeply taken by Minor's devotion to his dictionary project and continued to work with him, a story told in full in Simon Winchester's book *The Surgeon of Crowthorne*.

Neither Murray nor Minor lived to see the eventual publication of *A New English Dictionary on Historical Principles* in 1928. Almost 40 years behind schedule and 10 volumes long, it was the most comprehensive lexicographical project ever undertaken, and a full second edition did not appear until 1989.

Today, the updating of such a major work is no easier and the public were again asked for help in 2006. This time the BBC ran a TV programme, *Balderdash and Piffle*, encouraging viewers to get in contact with early printed evidence of word use, new definitions and brand new entries for the dictionary.

For a full history of the dictionary and the development of printing you can visit the **Oxford University Press Museum** (☎ 353527; Great Clarendon St; admission free; ☒ by appointment only).

Britain's best examples of neo-Grecian architecture.

Bursting with Egyptian, Islamic and Chinese art; rare porcelain, tapestries and silverware; priceless musical instruments; and extensive displays of European art (including works by Raphael and Michelangelo), it's impossible to take it all in at once. However, the Ashmolean is undergoing a substantial redevelopment phase, and as some galleries are closed a 'Treasures of the Ashmolean Museum' exhibition offers a cross section of highlights from the vast collection. The exhibition runs until December 2008. Otherwise, study the floor plan well and choose a manageable route through the sumptuous rooms and hallways.

UNIVERSITY & PITT RIVERS MUSEUMS

Housed in a glorious Victorian Gothic building with slender, cast-iron columns, ornate capitals and a soaring glass roof, the **University Museum** (☎ 272950; www.oum.ox.ac.uk; Parks Rd; admission free; ☒ noon-5pm) is worth a visit for its architecture alone. However, the real draw is the mammoth natural history collection of more than five million exhibits ranging from exotic insects and fossils to a towering T-Rex skeleton.

Hidden away through a door at the back of the main exhibition hall, the **Pitt Rivers Museum** (☎ 270927; www.prm.ox.ac.uk; admission free; ☒ noon-4.30pm) is a treasure-trove of weird and wonderful displays to satisfy every armchair adventurer's wildest dreams. In the half-light inside are glass cases and mysterious drawers stuffed with Victorian explorers' prized trophies. Feathered cloaks, necklaces of teeth, blowpipes, magic charms, Noh masks, totem poles, fur parkas, musical instruments and shrunken heads lurk here, making it a fascinating place for adults and children. The museum also runs an excellent series of children's workshops (usually the first Saturday of the month).

OXFORD CASTLE

Newly opened in 2006, **Oxford Castle Unlocked** (☎ 260666; www.oxfordcastleunlocked.co.uk; 44-46 Oxford Castle; adult/under 15yr £6.95/5.25; ☒ 10am-5pm) explores the 1000-year history of Oxford's castle and prison. You can explore the remains of the medieval motte and bailey and see the 11th-century Crypt of St George's Chapel, possibly the first formal teaching venue in Oxford. Two wings of the Victorian prison are also open and tell tales of the inmates' grisly lives, daring escapes and cruel punishments. Visitors can also see the Debtors' Tower and the Saxon St George's Tower, which has excellent views of the city.

OTHER ATTRACTIONS

Far removed from Oxford's musty hallways of history, **Modern Art Oxford** (☎ 722733; www .modernartoxford.org.uk; 30 Pembroke St; admission free; ☺ 10am-5pm Tue-Sat, noon-5pm Sun) is one of the best contemporary art museums outside London, with a wonderful gallery space and plenty of activities for children.

Nearby, the **Museum of Oxford** (☎ 252761; www.museumofoxford.org.uk; St Aldate's; admission free; ☺ 10am-4.30pm Tue-Fri, 10am-5pm Sat, noon-4pm Sun) is dedicated to the history of the city and its university, and explores everything from Oxford's prehistoric mammoths to its history of car manufacturing.

Science, art, celebrity and nostalgia come together at the **Museum of the History of Science** (☎ 277280; www.mhs.ox.ac.uk Broad St; admission free; ☺ noon-4pm Tue-Sat, 2-5pm Sun), where the exhibits include a blackboard used by Einstein, as well as a significant collection of historic scientific instruments.

Oxford's central landmark, **Carfax Tower** (☎ 792653; adult/under 15yr £1.90/95p; ☺ 10am-5.30pm Apr-Sep, 10am-4.30pm Mar & Oct, 10am-3.30pm Nov-Feb), is the sole reminder of medieval St Martin's Church and offers good views over the city centre.

A haven of traditional butchers, fishmongers, cobblers and barbers, Oxford's **covered market** (☺ 8.30am-5.30pm Mon-Sat) is the place to go for Sicilian sausage, handmade chocolates, traditional pies, funky T-shirts and expensive brogues. It's a fascinating place to explore and, if you're in Oxford at Christmas, a must for its traditional displays of freshly hung deer, wild boar, ostrich and turkey.

Activities

PUNTING

Apart from visiting the colleges and museums, the quintessential Oxford experience includes an afternoon punting on the river, quaffing Pimms as you watch the dreaming spires float by. In reality, punting can be quite difficult and you may spend much of your time struggling to get out of a tangle of low branches or avoiding the path of an oncoming eight.

Either way, punting is one of the best ways to soak up the Oxford atmosphere, and with a little practice you'll be gliding gracefully through the water (see boxed text, p524). Punts are available from mid-March to mid-October, 10am to dusk, and hold five people including the punter. They cost £10 per hour weekdays and £12 per hour on weekends.

The most central location to rent punts is at Magdalen Bridge, from **Howard C & Sons** (☎ 202643; High St; deposit £30). From here you can punt downstream around the Botanic Gardens and Christ Church Meadow or upstream around Magdalen Deer Park. Alternatively, head for the **Cherwell Boat House** (☎ 515978; www .cherwellboathouse.co.uk; Bardwell Rd; deposit £60) for a countryside amble where the destination of choice is the busy boozer the **Victoria Arms** (☎ 241382; Mill Lane). To get to the boathouse take bus 2 or 7 from Magdalen St to Bardwell Rd and follow the signposts.

Tours

Blackwell (☎ 333606; oxford@blackwell.co.uk; 48-51 Broad St; adult/child £7/6.50; ☺ May-Oct) Runs 1½-hour tours including a literary tour (2pm Tuesday, 11am Thursday), an 'Inklings' tour (11.45am Wednesday) and a historic Oxford tour (2pm Friday).

City Sightseeing (☎ 790522; www.citysightseeingox ford.com; adult/under 16yr £9.50/4.50; ☺ every 10-15 min 9.30am-6pm Apr-Oct) Runs hop-on hop-off bus tours from the bus or train stations or any of the 20 stops around town.

Oxford Information Centre (☎ 726871; www .visitoxford.org; 15-16 Broad St; ☺ 9.30am-5pm Mon-Sat, 10am-4pm Sun) Runs 1½-hour tours of Oxford city and colleges (adult/under 16yr £6.50/3; ☺ tours 11am & 2pm Sun-Fri, 10.30am, 11am, 1pm & 2pm Sat); Inspector Morse tours (£7/3; ☺ tours 1.30pm Sat); ghost tours (£5/3; ☺ tours 7.45pm Fri & Sat Jun-Oct); family walking tours (£5/3; ☺ tours 1.30pm school hol); and pub tours (adults only £6.50; ☺ tours 7pm Wed).

Salter Bros (☎ 243421; www.salterssteamers.co.uk; Folly Bridge; boat trips £8.60; ☺ mid-May–mid-Sep) offers boat trips along the Isis to Abingdon.

Sleeping

Accommodation in Oxford is often overpriced and underwhelming, and in the midrange bracket in particular, suffocating floral patterns are the norm. Between May and September beds fill up quickly in all price ranges, so book in advance or join the queue at the tourist office and pay for help.

If you're stuck, you'll find a selection of B&Bs along the Iffley, Abingdon, Banbury and Headington roads.

BUDGET

Oxford Camping International (☎ 244088; 426 Abingdon Rd; sites per person £6.90) Conveniently located for easy access to the city centre but consequently lacking in character and suffering from noise, this well-maintained camp site is popular, especially on weekends, so book in advance.

Central Backpackers (☎ 242288; www.centralbackpackers.co.uk; 13 Park End St; dm £14-18; ✕ ☐) Oxford's newest backpacker accommodation offers good-quality dorms right in the centre of town. The basic but bright and simple rooms sleep up to 12 people, the beds and duvets are new, there's a decent lounge with satellite TV, a rooftop terrace, and free internet and luggage storage.

Oxford Backpackers (☎ 721761; www.hostels.co.uk; 9 Hythe Bridge St; dm £14-18; ✕ ☐) Championing the laid-back, party-central attitude of student halls, this slightly scruffy place is brightly painted with cartoon-like murals and has a lounge full of picnic tables and battered sofas. It has a licensed bar, dorms sleeping up to 18 and tiny bathrooms for the number of beds.

YHA Oxford (☎ 727275; oxford@yha.org.uk; 2A Botley Rd; dm/d £20.95/55; ✕ ☐ ⑤) By far the best budget option in town, the YHA offers top-notch dorm accommodation, private rooms and loads of facilities including a restaurant, library, garden, laundry and a choice of lounges. All rooms have en suite and are bright and cheery, if a little functional – well worth considering over the city's cheapest B&Bs.

MIDRANGE

Lakeside Guesthouse (☎ 244725; www.lakeside-guesthouse.co.uk; 118 Abingdon Rd; s £45, d with/without bathroom £70/56; ⓟ ✕) This Victorian guesthouse near the river offers good-value rooms close to the city centre. Although heavily patterned carpets leach up the stairs, the rooms are calmer, with stripped wood, silky bedspreads, and a cream-and-gold colour scheme.

Burlington House (☎ 513513; www.burlington-house.co.uk; 374 Banbury Rd; s £45-60, d £85-90; ⓟ ✕) Everything in this Victorian merchant house is

immaculately kept and elegantly decorated, and although a long way from the centre, it's well worth the trip. The big, bright rooms are loaded with period character but decked out in contemporary style with pale neutral colours, silky bedspreads and plenty of cushions.

Cornerways (☎ 240135; jeakings@btopenworld.com; 282 Abingdon Rd; s/d £45/64; ⓟ ✕) A thoroughly modern interior awaits at this friendly guesthouse set in lovingly tended gardens. The rooms are big and bright with pale cream and deep red furnishings, all have en suite and there's a lovely bright conservatory and patio garden for breakfast.

Tilbury Lodge (☎ 862138; www.tilburylodge.com; 5 Tilbury Lane; s £50-60, £d £70-80; ⓟ ✕ ☐) Although a little out of the centre, Tilbury Lodge is well worth the effort for its spacious top-of-the-line rooms with plush, contemporary décor and excellent bathrooms. Giant pillows in funky fabrics adorn the big beds, light streams through the large windows, and downstairs there's a conservatory for guest use.

Beaumont (☎ 241767; www.oxfordcity.co.uk/accom/beaumont; 234 Abingdon Rd; s £50-72, d £ 58-72; ✕) Newly redecorated and sparkling clean, the Beaumont offers four excellent-value rooms with simple but elegant décor. With crisp white linen, pale and trendy flock wallpaper, mosaic bathrooms and beautiful furniture, it's all a class above most B&Bs of this price.

Orchard House (☎ 249200; www.theorchardhouseoxford.co.uk; 225 Iffley Rd; s £60-85, d £80-90; ⓟ ✕) This lovely arts-and-crafts-style house is set in beautiful secluded gardens and makes a wonderful retreat from the city. The sleek and stylish extra-large bedrooms each have their own sofa and breakfast table, elegant but luxurious modern décor and limestone bathrooms.

TOP END

our pick Malmaison (☎ 268400; www.malmaison-oxford.com; 3 Oxford Castle; d £140-150, ste £195-350; ✕ ☐ ⑤) Oxford's newest hotel is spectacularly set in a former Victorian prison with sleek and slinky rooms created out of the vaulted cells. The wow factor is matched by the plush interiors, sultry lighting, dark woods and giant beds. If you're planning a real bender, go for the Governor's Suite, complete with four-poster bed and mini cinema.

Old Parsonage Hotel (☎ 310210; www.oldparsonage-hotel.co.uk; 1 Banbury Rd; r £155-195; ⓟ ✕ ☐) Dripping with character and skilfully blending just

---

SOMETHING SPECIAL

Trout at Tadpole Bridge (☎ 01367-870382; www.troutinn.co.uk; Buckland Marsh; s/d £55/80; **P**) Set on the banks of the Thames, this 17th-century stone inn is all mismatched furniture, old flagstones, log fires and cosy atmosphere. It's renowned for its divine food (mains £12 to £15) made from locally sourced ingredients. Go for pan-fried scallops, with chorizo and lamb sweetbreads, or duck breast with vanilla mash and lime sauce. There are real ales on tap, a gorgeous riverside garden and six guest bedrooms tastefully decked out in white linens.

The Trout is just off the A420 east of Faringdon.

---

the right mix of period charm and modern luxury, this 17th-century boutique hotel is a wonderfully quirky place to stay. An eclectic art collection, a buzzing bar-restaurant and oddly mismatched furniture make the public areas, while the chic bedrooms have handmade beds, marble bathrooms and flat-screen TVs.

Old Bank Hotel (☎ 799599; www.oldbank-hotel.co.uk; 92 High St; r £165-240; **P** ⊠ ⊒) Sleek rooms with stunning views of Oxford's dreaming spires are on offer at the Old Bank, a contemporary hotel in the centre of town. Slick furnishings, modern artworks, marble bathrooms and a buzzing restaurant make it a popular spot, but it lacks some of the inherent character of other top-end options.

Eating

There's plenty of choice for food in Oxford, but a glut of predictable chain restaurants in the centre of town. The new castle complex has a lovely pedestrianised square for alfresco dining but few original options. Head to Jericho or Cowley for a more quirky selection.

BUDGET

Jericho Café (☎ 310840; 112 Walton St; mains £5-7; ⊙ lunch & dinner) Relaxed meals over the newspaper, long coffees with a crossword, and a choice of delectable meals with vaguely healthy ingredients make the quirky Jericho a favourite hang-out. Go for Moroccan lamb, fish pie, falafel, or wholesome salads; choose from the range of vegetarian dishes; or simply give in to those luscious cakes.

Georgina's (☎ 249527; Ave 3, Covered Market; mains £5-8; ⊙ 8.30am-5pm Mon-Sat) Hidden up a scruffy staircase in the covered market and plastered with old cinema posters, this funky little café serves up a bumper crop of bulging salads, hearty soups, doorsteps of bread and such goodies as goats cheese quesadillas and scrumptious cakes.

our pick Edamame (☎ 246916; 15 Holywell St; mains £6-8; ⊙ Tue & Wed 11.30am-2.30pm, Thu-Sat 11.30am-2.30pm & 5-8.30pm, Sun noon-3.30pm & 5-8.30pm) Small, simple and intimate, this tiny Japanese restaurant places a firm emphasis on the food rather than the fanfare and dishes up the best noodles, rice dishes and sushi (Thursday night only) in town. Don't let the queue put you off – it's well worth the wait.

Nosebag (☎ 721033; 6-9 St Michael's St; mains £6-8; ⊙ lunch & dinner) Hearty and wholesome meals lure students to this popular café, where the queues can be just as impressive as the food. The giant portions mean that the colourful salads, casseroles, stir-fries and curries are great value, and there's a decent choice of goodies for vegetarians.

Aziz (☎ 794945; 228 Cowley Rd & Folly Bridge; mains £7-8; ⊙ lunch & dinner) Feted as Oxford's best curry house, this award-winning restaurant attracts vegans, vegetarians and curry lovers in hoards. There's an extensive menu, chilled surroundings and portions generous enough to ensure you'll be rolling out the door.

Quick Eats

For a quick bite en route between colleges, look out for the ever-popular **Mortons** (☎ 200867; baguettes £2.30-2.80) Covered Market (103 Covered Market); Broad St (22 Broad St); Little Clarendon St (36 Little Clarendon St); New Inn Hall St (22 New Inn Hall St) for its fine selection of innovatively filled baguettes.

For more hearty fare try the **Noodle Bar** (☎ 201400; 100 Gloucester Green; mains £5-5.50; ⊙ lunch & dinner) for bowls of steaming noodles and generous rice dishes, or **Red Star** (☎ 251248; 187 Cowley Rd; mains £5.50-7; ⊙ lunch & dinner) for pan-Asian dishes and giant bento boxes.

Another popular haunt is the busy **News Café** (☎ 242317; 1 Ship St; mains £5.50-9; ⊙ 9am-10pm), where you can read international papers and magazines while waiting.

At all other times head for funky **G&D's** (☎ 516652; ⊙ 8am-midnight) Little Clarendon St (55 Little Clarendon St); St Aldate's (94 St Aldate's), for the best ice cream, brownies and desserts in town. You'll also get copies of the *Beano and Dandy* and regular silly hat, cow-dunking and most-authentic-mooing competitions.

MIDRANGE

our pick Bangkok House (☎ 200705; 42A Hythe Bridge St; mains £5.50-9.25; ☾ lunch & dinner) The food's delicious, the service impeccable, the prices affordable, and unsurprisingly, this little slice of Thailand is always packed. Elaborately carved tables, massive chairs and ornate wall hangings set the scene for the wonderfully aromatic Thai curries, sizzling meat dishes and delicately prepared dumplings.

Café Coco (☎ 200232; 23 Cowley Rd; mains £7-14; ☾ lunch & dinner) Chilled out, clued-in and serving a superb selection of Mediterranean food, Café Coco is a Cowley Rd institution, as popular for Sunday brunch as late-night cocktails. It's a sort of hip, bohemian hangout, with classic posters on the walls and a bald clown in an ice-bath.

Big Bang (☎ 511441; 124 Walton St; mains £8-12; ☾ lunch & dinner) It's small, not much to look at and has a very simple menu, but deciding between the tasty sausages, choosing a speciality mash and selecting just the right gravy can be very difficult indeed. Come on a Wednesday and you'll even get live jazz thrown in.

Branca (☎ 556111; 111 Walton St; mains £9-14; ☾ lunch & dinner) Floor-to-ceiling glass, dark woods, moody lighting and exposed pipework set the scene at this slick Italian restaurant in Jericho. The food is rustic, though, with stone-baked pizzas, simple pastas and hearty meats pulling in the crowds every night of the week.

Fishers (☎ 243003; St Clements; mains £9-15; ☾ lunch & dinner) Nautically themed and generally buzzing, Oxford's finest seafood restaurant serves up simple but heavenly plates of everything from traditional haddock and chips to Shetland mussels, yellow fin tuna and New England lobster.

Other options:

Chutneys (☎ 724241; 36 St Michael's St; mains £8-11; ☾ lunch & dinner) Top-notch Indian with consistently great food and chilled atmosphere.

Moya (☎ 200111; 97 St Clements; mains £9-11; ☾ lunch & dinner) Sleek Slovak restaurant and cocktail bar with unusual dishes and killer cocktails.

TOP END

Quod (☎ 202505; 92 High St; mains £9-17; ☾ lunch & dinner) Bright, buzzing and decked out with modern art and beautiful people, this designer joint dishes up Mediterranean brasserie-style food to the masses. It doesn't take reservations, is always heaving and at worst will tempt you to chill by the bar with a cocktail while you wait for a table.

Lemon Tree (☎ 311936; 268 Woodstock Rd; mains £9-19; ☾ lunch & dinner Wed-Sun, dinner Mon & Tue) Slightly out of town but worth the trip, the Lemon Tree is a smart but unpretentious restaurant set in a North Oxford villa. The food is loosely Mediterranean and ranges from such delicacies as spiced butternut squash and chickpea tagine to pork belly with honey-glazed parsnips and curly kale.

Drinking

Oxford has plenty of choice when it comes to drinking venues, so there's no excuse for ending up in the chain pubs and bars in the centre of town.

PUBS

Turf Tavern (☎ 243235; 4 Bath Pl; ☾ 11am-11pm Mon-Sat, noon-10.30pm Sun) Hidden away down narrow alleyways, this tiny medieval pub is one of the best loved in town. Packed with a mix of students, professionals and the lucky tourists who manage to find it, its low-ceilinged bar and outdoor courtyards host regular poker nights, pub quizzes and acoustic sets.

Eagle & Child (☎ 302925; 49 St Giles'; ☾ noon-11pm Mon-Sat, noon-10.30pm Sun) Affectionately known as the 'Bird & Baby', this atmospheric place has been a pub since 1650 and is still a hotchpotch of nooks and crannies. It was once the favourite haunt of JRR Tolkien, CS Lewis and their literary friends and still attracts a mellow crowd.

White Horse (☎ 728318; 52 Broad St; ☾ 11am-11pm Mon-Sat, noon-10.30pm Sun) More a large cupboard than an actual pub, this tiny olde-worlde place was a favourite retreat for TV detective Inspector Morse. It gets pretty crowded in the evening, but is good for a quiet afternoon pint and intellectual conversation.

Oxford has some wonderful riverside pubs worth checking out, most of which can be reached by a stroll along the towpaths:

Head of the River (☎ 721600; Folly Bridge; ☾ 11.30am-11pm Mon-Sat, noon-10.30pm Sun) Right in the centre of town and a great place to watch struggling punters go by.

Fishes (☎ 249796; North Hinksey; mains £9-15; ☾ noon-11pm Mon-Sat, noon-10.30pm Sun) Old and quaint on the outside but sleek and modern inside, this popular summer haunt does excellent modern food.

Trout (☎ 302071; 195 Godstow Rd; mains £8-14; ◷ 11am-11pm Mon-Sat, 11am-10.30pm Sun) Charming old-world pub with lovely garden and roaming peacocks but extra-long queues on weekends.

BARS

Raoul's (☎ 553732; 32 Walton St) Packed to the gills on weekends and serving some of the best cocktails in town, this trendy retro-look bar is one of Jericho's finest. Guest DJs play chilled funky jazz as effortlessly cool punters try hard not to look impressed by the pestle-wielding bar staff.

Kazbar (☎ 202920; 25-27 Cowley Rd; ◷ 11am-11pm Mon-Sat, noon-10.30pm Sun) This funky Moroccan-themed bar has giant windows, low lighting, warm colours and a cool vibe. It's buzzing most nights with hip young things sipping cocktails and filling up on the Spanish and North African tapas (£3 to £5).

Jericho Tavern (☎ 311775; 56 Walton St; ◷ noon-midnight Mon-Sat, noon-11pm Sun) Chilled out and super cool with big leather sofas, tasselled standard lamps and boldly patterned wallpaper, this hip bar also has a live music venue upstairs. Adorned with giant portraits of John Peel, Supergrass and Radiohead, it's supposedly where the Abingdon boys played their first gig.

Frevd (☎ 311171; 119 Walton St; ◷ 11am-midnight Mon-Tue, 11am-1am Wed, 11am-2am Thu-Sat, 11am-10.30pm Sun) Once a neoclassical church, now a happening bar, Frevd's is a cavernous place with soaring ceilings, distressed walls, quirky artwork and a mixed bag of punters. It's popular with a young style-conscious clientele and cocktail-sipping luvvies by night.

Living Room (☎ 260210; Oxford Castle; ◷ 10am-midnight Sun-Wed, 10am-1am Thu, 10am-2pm Fri-Sat) The best of the new set of chain pubs that have blown in to the castle development, this one is all neutral tones, deep leather sofas, low lighting and lads on the pull. There's live blues on the baby grand from Tuesday to Saturday nights, a lengthy cocktail menu and the best outdoor seating in Oxford.

Entertainment
NIGHTCLUBS

Despite a large student population, Oxford's club scene is fairly limited, with several cattle-mart clubs in the centre of town and a lot of middle-of-the-road music. Try the suggestions here for something a little more adventurous.

Zodiac (☎ 420042; 190 Cowley Rd; club admission up to £6; ◷ 7pm-2am Mon-Thu, 7pm-3am Fri & Sat, 7-10.30pm Sun) Oxford's best live music venue is a wonderfully grubby place that attracts an eclectic crowd with its proudly indie vibe and unpretentious attitude. Live gigs upstairs feature anything from singer-songwriters to guitar-thrashing rockers, while the club downstairs plays anything from funk, soul and disco to reggae, glam rock and punk.

Po Na Na (☎ 249171; 13-15 Magdalen St; admission up to £6; ◷ 10pm-2am Tue-Thu, 10pm-3am Fri & Sat) Still one of the best bets in town for a night out, Po Na Na is a small cave-like place with plenty of Moroccan lanterns, drapes and candles, a hip crowd and in between the regular club nights, some big-name DJs and live events. Expect funk, indie, Old Skool, house and reggae.

Backroom at the Bully (☎ 244516; 162 Cowley Rd; admission up to £5; ◷ noon-midnight Mon-Wed, noon-2am Thu-Sat, noon-10.30pm Sun) Drinks promos, a relaxed attitude and bare basic décor make this pub's backroom a favourite student haunt. Music ranges from live jazz to cheesy disco, drum 'n' bass, funk and dance.

THEATRE

The city's main stage for quality drama is the **Oxford Playhouse** (☎ 305305; www.oxfordplayhouse.com; Beaumont St), which also hosts an impressive selection of touring productions of theatre, music and dance. Just around the corner, the **Burton Taylor Theatre** (☎ 798600; Gloucester St) hosts quirky student shows, while the **Pegasus Theatre** (☎ 722851; www.pegasustheatre.org.uk; Magdalen Rd) hosts alternative independent productions. For ageing pop stars, comedians and plenty of fanfare, the **New Theatre** (☎ 0870 606 3500; www.getlive.co.uk/oxford; George St) is the place to go.

Performing in a variety of non-traditional venues, including city parks, the BMW plant and Oxford Castle, **Creation Theatre** (☎ 761393; www.creationtheatre.co.uk) produces highly original, mostly Shakespearean, shows featuring plenty of magic and special effects. If you're in town when a performance is running, don't miss it.

CLASSICAL MUSIC

With a host of spectacular buildings with great acoustics and two orchestras, Oxford is an excellent place to attend a classical concert. You'll find the widest range of events at www.musicatoxford.com or www.oxfordtickets.com. Alternatively, watch out for posters around town or contact one of these groups:

City of Oxford Orchestra (☎ 744457; www.cityofoxfordorchestra.co.uk)

Oxford Contemporary Music (☎ 488369; www.ocmevents.org)

Oxford Philomusica (☎ 0870 6060804; www.oxfordphil.com)

Getting There & Away

BUS

Competition on the Oxford–London route is fierce, with three companies offering cheap and cheaper services at all hours of the day and night.

Oxford Espress (☎ 785400; www.oxfordbus.co.uk) Runs up to every 15 minutes to Victoria coach station (return £13, 1½ hours).

Megabus (www.megabus.com) Coaches run every half-hour to Buckingham Palace Rd (one way from £1, 1¾ hours).

Oxford Tube (☎ 772250; www.oxfordtube.com) Runs every 10 minutes to Buckingham Palace Rd (return £13, 1½ hours).

The Heathrow Express (£19, 70 minutes) runs half-hourly 4am to 10pm, hourly midnight to 4am, while the Gatwick Express (£27, two hours) runs hourly 5.15am to 8.15pm and every two hours 10pm to 4am.

National Express has five direct buses to Birmingham (£10.20, two hours), and one service to Bath (£8.90, two hours) and Bristol (£12, 2¾ hours).

Stagecoach serves most of the small towns in Oxfordshire and runs the X5 service to Cambridge (£7, 3½ hours) roughly every half-hour. If you're planning a lot of bus journeys it's worth buying a Goldrider pass (£18), which allows unlimited bus travel in Oxfordshire for seven days.

CAR & MOTORCYCLE

Thanks to a complicated one-way system and a shortage of parking spaces, driving and parking in Oxford is a nightmare. Drivers are strongly advised to use the five park-and-ride car parks on major routes leading in to town. Three car parks are free to use, the others cost 60p. The return bus journey to town (10 to 15 minutes, every 10 minutes) costs £2.

TRAIN

There are half-hourly services to London Paddington (£18.80, one hour); and roughly hourly trains to Birmingham (£20, 1¼ hours), Worcester (£16.40, 1½ hours) and Hereford (£14.70, two hours). Hourly services also run to Bath (£17.20, 1¼ hours) and Bristol (£18.70, 1½ hours) but require a change at Didcot Parkway.

Getting Around

BICYCLE

The *Cycle into Oxford* map, available from the tourist office, shows all local cycle routes. You can hire bikes from **Cyclo Analysts** (☎ 424444; 150 Cowley Rd; per day/week £10/27).

BUS

If sightseeing has worn you out buses 1 and 5 go to Cowley Rd from Carfax, 2 and 7 go along Banbury Rd from Magdalen St, and 16 and 35 run along Abingdon Rd from St Aldate's.

A multi-operator Plus Pass (per day/week/month £5/16/44) allows unlimited travel on Oxford's bus system.

TAXI

There are taxi ranks at the train station and bus station, as well as on St Giles and at Carfax. Be prepared to join a long queue after closing time.

WOODSTOCK

☎ 01993 / pop 2389

Conveniently close to Oxford, yet a quintessential rural retreat, the charming village of Woodstock makes a wonderful day trip from the city. The big draw here is Blenheim Palace, the opulent country pile of the Churchill family, but the village itself is full of picturesque creeper-clad cottages and elegant town houses.

The hub of the village is the imposing **town hall**, built at the Duke of Marlborough's expense in 1766. Nearby, the **Church of St Mary Magdalene** had a 19th-century makeover but retains its Norman doorway, early English windows and a musical clock.

Opposite the church, the **Oxfordshire Museum** (☎ 811456; Park St; admission free; ⏱ 10am-5pm Tue-Sat, 2-5pm Sun) has displays on local history, art, archaeology and wildlife. It also houses the **tourist office** (☎ 813276).

Blenheim Palace

One of England's greatest stately homes, **Blenheim Palace** (☎ 08700 602080; www.blenheimpalace.com; adult/under 16yr £14/8.50, park & garden only £9/4.50; ⏱ 10.30am-5.30pm mid-Feb–Oct, Wed-Sun Nov–mid-Dec, park open year-round) is a monumental Baroque fantasy designed by Sir John Vanbrugh and Nicholas Hawksmoor between 1705 and 1722. The land and funds to build the house were granted to John Churchill, Duke of Marlborough, by a grateful Queen Anne after his decisive victory at the Battle of Blenheim. Now a Unesco World Heritage Site, Blenheim (pronounced *blen*-num) is home to the 11th duke and duchess.

Inside, the house is stuffed with statues, tapestries, ostentatious furniture and giant oil paintings in elaborate gilt frames. You enter through the **Great Hall**, a vast space topped by 20m-high ceilings adorned with images of the first duke in battle. From here you proceed to the opulent **Saloon**, the grandest and most important public room, and on to the three **state rooms** with their plush décor and priceless **china cabinets**. Further on, the magnificent 55m **Long Library** was originally intended as a picture gallery but now houses a significant collection of books, a Willis organ and marble sculptures of Marlborough and Queen Anne.

From the library you can access the **Churchill Exhibition**, which is dedicated to the life, work and writings of Sir Winston, who was born at Blenheim in 1874 (see boxed text, p44). Churchill and his wife, Lady Clementine Spencer-Churchill, are buried in nearby Bladon Church.

If the crowds in the house become too oppressive, retire to the lavish gardens and vast parklands, parts of which were landscaped by Lancelot 'Capability' Brown. To the front, an artificial lake sports a beautiful bridge by Vanbrugh, while a mini train is needed to take visitors to a maze, adventure playground and butterfly house. For a quieter and longer stroll, glorious walks lead to an arboretum, cascade and temple.

Sleeping & Eating

Woodstock has a good choice of accommodation, but it's not cheap. Plan a day trip from Oxford if you're travelling on a budget.

Townhouse B&B (☎ 810843; info@woodstock-townhouse.com; 15 High St; s £45-65, d £70-100; ✗) This lovely 18th-century stone town house offers a selection of en suite rooms right in the centre of town. There's plenty of period character but no lack of modern style, and facilities include TVs with DVD player.

Kings Arms Hotel (☎ 813636; www.kings-hotel-woodstock.co.uk; 19 Market St; s/d £70/130; ✗ 🖳) Set in a lovely Georgian town house, the rooms here are sleek and stylish yet manage to retain much of their period charm. Downstairs there's a bright bistro serving modern British fare (mains £9 to £14) and a good bar with leather sofas and cheaper snacks.

Bear Hotel (☎ 0870 400 8202; www.macdonaldhotels.co.uk/bear; Park St; d £144-184; 🅿 ✗ 🖳) One of England's oldest hotels, the lavish Bear has long been a hideaway for romantic couples. The 13th-century coaching inn has recently been refurbished and along with the open fireplaces, stone walls and exposed beams you'll get the height of modern luxury.

Brotherton's Brasserie (☎ 811114; 1 High St; mains £8-15; ☽ lunch & dinner, closed Tue) Set in an atmospheric 17th-century stone house and lit with the warm glow of gaslight, this popular brasserie is one of the best spots in town. The rustic interior provides an informal ambience for the competent menu, which features everything from pasta to wild boar casserole.

Hampers (☎ 811535; 31-33 Oxford St; ☽ lunch) On a fine day you couldn't do better than a picnic in the grounds of the palace and this deli provides all the essential ingredients: fine cheeses, olives, cold meats, Cotswold smoked salmon and delicious cakes.

Getting There & Away

Stagecoach bus 20 runs every half-hour (hourly on Sunday) from Oxford bus station (20 minutes). **Cotswold Roaming** (☎ 308300; www.cotswold-roaming.co.uk) offers half-day tours (adult/under 15 years £18/11) to Blenheim from Oxford. The cost includes admission to the palace.

DORCHESTER & THE WITTENHAMS

A sleepy, winding street flanked on either side by old coaching inns, quaint cottages and timber-framed buildings flows through **Dorchester-on-Thames**, a little-visited gem just south of Oxford. The town's main draw, however, is the magnificent medieval church of **SS Peter & Paul** (www.dorchester-abbey.org.uk; admission free; ☽ 8am-6pm). Dorchester Abbey, as it is more commonly known, is a beautiful space, built on the site of a Saxon cathedral and home to a wonderful Jesse window, a rare Norman font and, in the Cloister Gallery, a collection of medieval decorated stones explaining the evolution of architectural styles. There's also a small **museum** (admission free; ⊗ 2-5pm Apr-Sep) in the grounds.

From the village you can take a pleasant 3-mile walk to **Wittenham Clumps**, two ancient tree-topped hills offering wonderful views of the surrounding area. For centuries the hills held an important defensive position overlooking the Thames, and Castle Hill shows the clear remains of an Iron Age hill fort.

At the bottom of the hills lies the village of **Little Wittenham**, a rustic idyll. Known for its beautiful cottages and the imposing **St Peter's Church**, it has made its mark on the international sporting calendar by hosting the **Pooh Sticks World Championships** in March each year. Teams from all over the world compete by dropping sticks into the river and watching them 'race' to the finish line.

Two miles by road from Little Wittenham is the village of **Long Wittenham**, where more thatched cottages line the road. There's also a 12th-century church that contains a 900-year-old lead font. Just north of here on the banks of the river is stunning **Clifton Hampden**, where thatched cottages face the bridge across the river to the 15th-century **Barley Mow Inn** (☎ 01865-407847). Jerome K Jerome wrote most of his timeless classic *Three Men in a Boat* here and described the pub as 'without exception the quaintest most old-world inn up the river'.

Bus 107 connects Long Wittenham with Oxford (25 minutes, hourly Monday to Saturday), while buses 105 and 106 connect Dorchester with Oxford (15 minutes, hourly Monday to Saturday) but require a change in Berinsfield outside peak hours.

WARBOROUGH

Idyllic thatched cottages, black-and-white timber-framed buildings and lovely town houses make up the picturesque village of Warborough, a sleepy kind of place with no specific attractions but a wonderful languid charm. The village green is surrounded by beautiful buildings and is generally home to a hotly contested cricket game. Stop for lunch or a pint at the gorgeous thatched **Six Bells on the Green** (☎ 01865-858265; mains £8-15), an old-world pub featured in the TV series *Midsomer Murders*. Its low ceilings, open fires, real ales and hearty home-cooked food draw the crowds on weekends.

The only public transport to Warborough is the Friday shoppers' bus to Wallingford

(nine minutes). Bus 105 (one hour) runs between Oxford and Wallingford hourly.

HENLEY-ON-THAMES
☎ 01491 / pop 10,513

Set on the banks of the river and studded with elegant stone houses, a few Tudor relics, chichi shops and affluent residents, Henley is a conservative but well-heeled kind of place that bursts into action for its world-famous regatta and festival each year. Outside the summer festivities it's a reasonably pleasant but workaday commuter town with an interesting museum, a scenic setting and a good choice of facilities.

The **tourist office** (☎ 578034; www.visithenley-on -thames.com; The Barn, King's Rd; ⊗ 11am-4.45pm Mon-Sat Mar-Oct, 11am-3.45pm Mon-Sat Nov-Feb) is next to the handsome town hall.

Sights

Life in Henley has always focused on the river, and the impressive **River & Rowing Museum** (☎ 415600; www.rrm.co.uk; Mill Meadows; adult/under 18yr £7/5; ⊗ 10am-5.30pm May-Aug, 10am-5pm Sep-Apr; 🕭) takes a look at the town's relationship with the Thames, the history of rowing, and the wildlife and commerce the river supports. Hands-on activities and interactive displays make it a good spot for children, and the *Wind in the Willows* exhibition brings Kenneth Grahame's stories of Ratty, Mole, Badger and Toad to life.

Walking around Henley you'll come across a wealth of historic buildings, with many Georgian gems lining Hart St, the main drag. You'll also find the imposing **town hall** here, and the 13th-century **St Mary's Church** with its 16th-century tower topped by four octagonal turrets.

Festivals & Events
HENLEY ROYAL REGATTA

The first ever Oxford and Cambridge boat race was held in Henley in 1839 and ever since the cream of English society has descended on this small town each year for a celebration of boating, back-slapping and the beau monde. The five-day **Henley Royal Regatta** (☎ 572153; www.hrr.co.uk) has grown into a major fixture in the social calendar of the upwardly mobile, and is a massive corporate entertainment opportunity. These days hanging out on the lawn swilling champagne and looking rich and beautiful is the main event, and although rowers of the highest calibre compete, most spectators appear to take little interest in what's happening on the water.

The regatta is held in the first week of July, but you'll need contacts in the rowing or corporate worlds to get tickets in the stewards' enclosure. Mere mortals should head for the public enclosure (tickets £10 to £16), where you can lay out your gourmet picnic and hobnob with the best of them.

HENLEY FESTIVAL
In the week following the regatta the town continues its celebrations with the **Henley Festival** (☎ 843404; www.henley-festival.co.uk), a vibrant black-tie affair that features everything from big-name international stars to quirky, alternative acts. Expect anything from opera to rock, jazz, comedy and swing. The main events take place on a floating stage on the Thames and tickets vary in price from £83 for a seat in the grandstand to £25 for a space on the promenade.

Sleeping & Eating
Henley has a good choice of accommodation, especially at the top end, but if you're planning to visit during either festival book well in advance.

Alftrudis (☎ 573099; www.alftrudis.co.uk; 8 Norman Ave; s/d £45/60; P ✗) Set on a quiet leafy street close to the centre of town, this Victorian guesthouse has pretty, period-style rooms at good prices. They're a little twee but not too fussy, and feature ornate beds, swag curtains, subtle florals and high ceilings.

Apple Ash (☎ 574198; www.appleash.com; Woodlands Rd, Harpsden Woods; s/d £50/70; P ✗) Lovingly maintained and beautifully decorated, it's well worth the 2-mile trip from town to stay at this charming Edwardian country house. The spacious rooms retain their period character but also offer modern comfort and style, with pale fabrics and restrained floral touches.

Milsoms (☎ 845789; www.milsomshotel.co.uk; 20 Market Pl; r £95) Set in an 18th-century former bakery, Milsoms offers sleek and stylish rooms, with bespoke artwork, subtle lighting and a muted colour scheme. They can be pretty compact though, so ask for light and airy room 1 for more space. Downstairs, **Loch Fyne** (☎ 845780; mains £8.50-14; ✆ lunch & dinner; ✚) serves its usual impeccably prepared fish dishes in bright surroundings.

our pick **Hotel du Vin** (☎ 848400; www.hotelduvin .com; New St; d £115-395; P ✗ ☐) Set in the former Brakspears Brewery, this upmarket hotel chain scores highly for its blend of industrial chic and top-of-the-line designer sophistication. The spacious rooms and opulent suites are slick and stylish and are matched by a walk-in humidor, incredible billiards rooms, huge wine cellar and a popular bistro (mains £14.50).

Green Olive (☎ 412220; 28 Market Pl; meze £3.95-6.50; ✆ lunch & dinner) Bright, airy and usually buzzing, the Green Olive serves up a menu of more than 40 traditional Greek meze. Portions are generous, so choose carefully for a light lunch or go the whole hog and opt for all your favourites for dinner. There's a lovely garden area at the back for alfresco summer dining.

Henley Bar & Grill (☎ 576126; Bell St; mains £8-11; ✆ lunch & dinner) This contemporary-styled brasserie with high-backed leather chairs, an open fire, grand piano and airy conservatory, features solid fare such as char-grilled tuna and Barbary duck, and a killer Guinness ice cream.

Getting There & Around
Bus X39 links Henley and Oxford (50 minutes, every two hours). Trains to London Paddington take about one hour (£11.40, hourly).

If you fancy seeing the local area from the river, **Hobbs & Son** (☎ 572035; www.hobbs-of-henley. com) runs hour-long afternoon river trips from April to September (adult/under 16 years £5.50/4.50) and hires five-seater rowing boats (£12 per hour) and four-seater motorboats (£20 per hour).

WANTAGE
☎ 01235 / pop 10, 613
Sleepy but handsome Wantage is a medieval market town of sturdy timber-framed buildings, old coaching inns and crooked cottages. The market square is dominated by a statue of Alfred the Great (see p37), who was born here in AD 849, and traders still flog their wares beneath his feet every Wednesday and Saturday. To the west of the square is the beautiful 13th-century church of St Peter & St Paul, with its hammer-beam roof and beautiful corbels. Wantage also provides easy access to the ancient Ridgeway trail (see p163), which is less than 3 miles to the south.

There's a **tourist office** (☎ 760176; www.wantage .com; ◷ 10am-4.30pm Mon-Sat) in the **Vale & Downland Museum** (☎ 771447; www.wantage.com/museum; Church St; adult/under 25yr in full-time education £2.50/1; ◷ 10am-4.30pm Mon-Sat). Set in a converted 16th-century cloth merchant's house, the museum covers local geology and archaeology, as well as everything from King Alfred and Victorian kitchens to the local Williams Formula 1 team.

Sleeping & Eating

Ridgeway YHA Hostel (☎ 0870 770 6064; www.yharidge way.org.uk; Court Hill; dm per adult/under 18yr £15.50/10.95; ◷ Apr–early Sep, Tue-Sat Oct-Mar; ☐) Just 500m from the Ridgeway, this lovely hostel is an ideal base for walkers. Set in a series of converted barns, it has an oak-beamed dining room, excellent views over the Vale, and a choice of family rooms. The hostel is about 2 miles south of Wantage off the A338.

Manor Farm (☎ 763188; www.manorfarm-wantage .co.uk; Silver Lane, West Challow; s/d £40/70; Ⓟ ☒) By far the most atmospheric place to stay in the area, this early-15th-century Queen Anne manor house makes a wonderful base and is incredible value for money. The charming rooms have high ceilings, cast-iron fireplaces, antique furniture and loads of period style.

King Alfred's Head (☎ 765531; 31 Market Pl; mains £6.50-12.50) Recently refurbished with a collection of old church pews, sturdy tables and a gentle colour scheme, this bar and bistro serves a decent menu of loosely Mediterranean food from goats cheese bruschetta to pastas, fish cakes and Thai prawns.

Getting There & Away

Bus X30 runs direct to Oxford (35 minutes) every half-hour, while the slower buses 31, 32 and 33 run roughly hourly through Abingdon and Didcot.

AROUND WANTAGE
Uffington White Horse

One of England's most remarkable and mysterious ancient sites, the **Uffington White Horse** is a stylised image cut into a hillside almost 3000 years ago. No-one is sure why the people of the time went to so much trouble to create the image or what exactly it is supposed to represent. It may be the Celtic horse goddess Epona, a celebration of King Alfred's victory over the Danes, or even an image of the horse ridden by St George when he killed the dragon.

SOMETHING SPECIAL

Crooked Billet (☎ 01491-681048; www .thecrookedbillet.co.uk; Stoke Row; mains £12-20; ◷ lunch & dinner) Hidden down a back lane and surrounded by trees, the Crooked Billet is a 17th-century inn famous as the one-time hideout of highwayman Dick Turpin. Today it is little changed – beer is drawn directly from casks in the cellar and the low beams, flagstone floor and inglenook fireplace are all originals. However, it's the food that really draws the crowds, with local produce being whipped into modern, mouthwatering fare such as chicken baked with goats cheese, warm chorizo salad and puy lentils, or venison with haggis and roast figs in a port and juniper sauce.

Either way, it is an extraordinary figure, measuring 114m long and 49m wide, and is thought to be the oldest chalk figure in Britain. It is best seen from a distance, or from the air, because of the stylised lines of perspective.

Just below the figure is **Dragon Hill** – so called because it is believed that St George slew the dragon here – and above it the grass-covered earthworks of **Uffington Castle**. From the youth hostel, near Wantage, a wonderful 5-mile walk leads along the Ridgeway to the White Horse.

In the nearby village of Uffington you can visit the lovely 13th-century **St Mary's Church**, known locally as the 'Cathedral of the Vale', and the **Uffington Museum** (☎ 01376-820259; www .uffington.net/museum; Broad St; admission free; ◷ 2-5pm Sat & Sun Easter-Oct). The museum is set in the old school room featured in Thomas Hughes' *Tom Brown's Schooldays* and features displays on the author, local history and archaeology.

THE COTSWOLDS

Undeniably beautiful, quintessentially English and beloved by tourists and locals alike, the lush rolling hills and picture-postcard villages of the Cotswolds are one of the country's most popular spots. With glorious honey-coloured villages riddled with beautiful old mansions, thatched cottages, atmospheric churches and rickety almshouses, the region just oozes old-world English charm.

A boom in the medieval wool trade brought the area its wealth and left it with such a glut of beautiful buildings that its place in history is secured for ever more. If you've ever craved exposed beams, dreamed of falling asleep under English rose wallpaper or lusted after a cream tea in mid-afternoon, there's no finer place to fulfil your fantasies. Just be aware that you won't be alone – the Cotswolds can be besieged by tourists and traffic in summer.

Plan to visit the main centres early in the morning or late in the evening, focus your attention on the south or take to the hills on foot or by bike to avoid the worst of the crowds.

Orientation & Information

The limestone hills of the Cotswolds extend across a narrow band of land east of the M5, stretching almost as far as Oxford at their widest point, north to Chipping Campden and south almost as far as Bath. Most of the region lies within Gloucestershire, but parts leak out into Oxfordshire, Wiltshire, Somerset, Warwickshire and Worcestershire. The Cotswolds are protected as an Area of Outstanding Natural Beauty (AONB).

For online information on attractions, accommodation and events:

Cotswolds (www.the-cotswolds.org)
Cotswolds Tourism (www.cotswolds.com)
Oxfordshire Cotswolds (www.oxfordshirecotswolds.org)

Activities

The gentle hills of the Cotswolds are perfect for walking, cycling and riding.

The long-distance **Cotswold Way** (102 miles) gives walkers a wonderful overview of the area. The route meanders from Chipping Campden to Bath, with no major climbs or difficult stretches, and is easily accessible from many points en route if you fancy tackling a shorter section. Ask at local tourist offices for details of day hikes or pick up a copy of one of the many walking guides to the region.

Away from the main roads, the winding lanes of the Cotswolds make fantastic cycling territory, with little traffic, glorious views and gentle gradients. Again, the local tourist offices are invaluable in helping to plot a route.

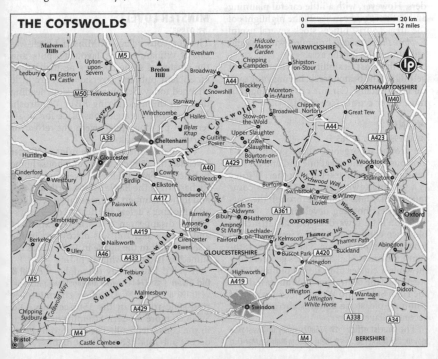

THE COTSWOLDS

A COTTAGE OF YOUR OWN

If you'd like to rent your own Cotswold cottage, try the websites listed here for properties throughout the region:

Campden Cottages (www.campdencottages.co.uk)

Cotswold Cottage Company (www.cotswoldcottage.co.uk)

Cotswold Cottages (www.cotswolds.info/cottages.shtml)

Discover the Cotswolds (www.discoverthecotswolds.net)

Manor Cottages & Cotswold Retreats (www.manorcottages.co.uk)

For more information on companies operating self-guided and guided tours of the region, see the boxed text, p404.

Getting Around

Public transport through the Cotswolds is fairly limited, with bus services running to and from major hubs only, and train services just skimming the northern and southern borders. However, with a little careful planning and patience you can see all the highlights of the area. Tourist offices stock several useful *Explore the Cotswolds* brochures with bus and rail summaries for the area.

For the most flexibility and the option of getting off the beaten track, having your own car is unbeatable. Car hire can be arranged in most major centres (see p782).

WITNEY
☎ 01993 / pop 22,765

Set around a gorgeous village green with a glorious wool church at one end and a 17th-century covered market at the other, Witney is a thriving town firmly on Oxford's commuter belt. Make your way through the traffic and new housing developments though and you'll be rewarded with an attractive old town centre built on the wealth earned from blanket production. The Baroque, 18th-century Blanket Hall dominates genteel High St, while a cluster of beautiful old buildings surrounds the central green. Walk east down the High St to get to Wood Green, an area of stunning old stone cottages surrounding a second village green.

The **tourist office** (☎ 775802; witney.tic@westoxon .gov.uk; 26A Market Sq; ⊙ 9.30am-5.30pm Mon-Sat Mar-Oct,

10am-4.30pm Mon-Sat Nov-Feb) provides information on local attractions, though the only real place of note is **Cogges Manor Farm Museum** (☎ 772602; www.cogges.org; adult/under 16yr £5.40/2.30; ⊙ 10.30am-5.30pm Tue-Fri, noon-5.30pm Sat & Sun Apr-Oct), a 13th-century manor house reconstructed as a working farm.

If you'd like to stay overnight your best bet for a meal and a bed is the **Fleece** (☎ 892270; www.fleecewitney.co.uk; 11 Church Green; s/d £75/85; P ⊗), a contemporary hotel and restaurant on the main village green. The rooms are sleek and stylish, while the spacious brasserie (mains £7.50 to £13.50) offers an ambitious modern menu.

Stagecoach bus 100 runs from Oxford to Witney roughly every 20 minutes Monday to Saturday, hourly on Sunday (30 minutes). **Swanbrook** (www.swanbrook.co.uk) runs three buses Monday to Saturday (one on Sunday) between Cheltenham (£6.50, one hour) and Oxford (30 minutes) via Witney. This service also goes to Gloucester (£6.50, 1½ hours) and serves a number of Cotswold towns along the way, including Northleach, Minster Lovell and Burford.

MINSTER LOVELL
☎ 01993

The gorgeous village of Minster Lovell was one of William Morris' favourite spots, and the cluster of stone cottages nestled beside an ancient pub and riverside mill are little changed today. Set on a gentle slope leading down to the meandering River Windrush, Minster Lovell is a glorious place for an afternoon pit stop, quiet overnight retreat or start to a valley walk.

The main sight here is the ruins of **Minster Lovell Hall**, the 15th-century manor house home to Viscount Francis Lovell. Lovell fought with Richard III at the Battle of Bosworth in 1485, and joined Lambert Simnel's failed rebellion after the king's defeat and death. Lovell's mysterious disappearance was never explained and when a skeleton was discovered inside a secret vault in the house in 1708, it was assumed he had died while in hiding.

If you'd like to stay overnight, the **Mill & Old Swan** (☎ 774441; www.millandoldswan-isc.co.uk; s £50-100, d £60-140; P ▢) offers charming period-style rooms in the 15th-century Old Swan or more modern Scandinavian design in the converted mill. The Old Swan serves decent pub food (£8 to £10) at night.

Swanbrook coaches stop here on the Oxford to Cheltenham run (see opposite). Stagecoach buses 233 and X3 between Witney and Burford stop here 10 times a day, Monday to Saturday (10 minutes each way).

BURFORD

☎ 01993 / pop 1877

Little changed since its glory days at the height of the wool trade, Burford is a stunningly picturesque place slithering down a steep hill to a medieval crossing point on the River Windrush. The main street and the quiet lanes off it are lined with higgledy-piggledy stone cottages, fine Cotswold town houses and the odd Elizabethan or Georgian gem. This incredible array of buildings attracts hoards of visitors, though, and the town can be frustratingly busy in midsummer. Add on a glut of specialist boutiques, tearooms and antique shops peddling flowery china and nostalgia and it can all feel a bit overwhelming.

The helpful **tourist office** (☎ 823558; Sheep St; ☻ 9.30am-5.30pm Mon-Sat Mar-Oct, 10am-4.30pm Mon-Sat Nov-Feb) has several leaflets describing walks in the local area.

Sights & Activities

Burford's main attraction lies in its remarkable buildings, including the 16th-century **Tolsey House** (Toll House; High St; admission free; ☻ 2-5pm Mon-Fri, 11am-5pm Sat & Sun), where the wealthy wool merchants held their meetings. This quaint building perches on sturdy pillars and now houses a small museum on Burford's history.

Off the High St you'll find the town's 14th-century **almshouses** and the gorgeous **Church of St John the Baptist**. The Norman tower here is topped by a 15th-century steeple and inside you'll find a fine fan-vaulted ceiling and medieval screens dividing the chapels.

Younger visitors will enjoy a visit to the excellent **Cotswold Wildlife Park** (☎ 823006; www.cotswoldwildlifepark.co.uk; adult/under 16yr £9/6.50; ☻ 10am-4.30pm Mar-Sep, 10am-3.30pm Oct-Feb), set around a Victorian manor house. The park is home to everything from penguins to white rhinos and giant cats.

If you have the time and fancy getting away from the crowds, it's worth the effort to walk east along the picturesque river path to the untouched and rarely visited village of **Swinbrook** (3 miles), where the beautiful church has some remarkable tombs.

Sleeping & Eating

Burford has a wonderful choice of atmospheric, upmarket hotels but far fewer options at more affordable prices.

Priory (☎ 823249; 35 High St; s £22.50-47.50, d £47.50-60) The only budget beds in town, the standard rooms here are small and functional, while the en suite 'superior' rooms are newer and better but far from spacious. The restaurant serves fairly predictable but decent fare (mains £6 to £8).

Westview House (☎ 824723; www.westview-house.co.uk; 151 The Hill; s/d £45/70; ☒) This lovely old stone cottage has two bright and spacious guest rooms with plenty of period character. The Heritage Room has exposed beams, stone walls and a cast-iron bed, while the Windrush Room has its own private balcony overlooking the garden.

our pick **Lamb Inn** (☎ 823155; www.lambinn-burford .co.uk; Sheep St; r £145-165; ℗) Step back in time with a stay at the Lamb, a 15th-century inn just dripping with character. Expect flagstone floors, low, beamed ceilings, creaking stairs and a charming, laid-back atmosphere downstairs, and luxurious period-style rooms with antique furniture and cosy comfort upstairs.

Jonathan's at the Angel (☎ 822714; www.theangel -uk.com; 14 Witney St; mains £11-16; ☻ lunch & dinner)

SOMETHING SPECIAL

One of the hidden gems of the Cotswolds, the gorgeous village of Great Tew is little changed since medieval times, with the 16th-century **Falkland Arms** (☎ 683653; www.falklandarms.org.uk; Great Tew; r £85-110) sitting right on the village green. Roaring fires, flagstone floors and low beams are only part of its charm – the real joy comes in the local ales, ciders and wines, the traditional clay pipes and snuff still on sale, and the refreshing walk down the road when you need to use the loo. The food (mains £5 to £9) ranges from homemade soups and crusty baguettes to traditional Sunday roasts with all the trimmings, while upstairs the six guest rooms offer four-poster or cast-iron beds and period style. It doesn't get much more genuine than this.

Great Tew is about 4 miles east of Chipping Norton.

Set in a lovely 16th-century coaching inn, this atmospheric brasserie serves up a good range of modern British and European food. Equally good but less formal dining (£7.95) is available at the bar.

For something more informal, the **Cotswold Arms** (☎ 822227; 46 High St; mains £8-14) and the **Old Bull** (☎ 822220; 105 High St; mains £7-15) do a good choice of food.

Getting There & Away

From Oxford, Swanbrook runs three buses a day (one on Sunday) to Burford (45 minutes) via Witney. Stagecoach buses 233 and X3 run between Witney and Burford 10 times a day, Monday to Saturday (20 minutes).

CHIPPING NORTON

☺ 01608 / pop 5688

Largely undiscovered by the tourist hoards, Chipping Norton – or 'Chippy' as it is locally known – is a sleepy but attractive place with a workaday attitude and some lovely buildings. The market square is surrounded by handsome Georgian buildings, stone cottages and old coaching inns and on Church St you'll find a row of beautiful honey-coloured **almshouses** built in the 17th century. Further on is the secluded **Church of St Mary**, a classic example of the Cotswold wool churches, with a magnificent 15th-century perpendicular nave and clerestory. Chippy's most enduring landmark, however, is the arresting **Bliss**

TOP FIVE PUBS FOR SUNDAY LUNCH

- **Crooked Billet** (p396; Stoke Row) Top-notch food, old-world charm and tales of dashing highwaymen.

- **Falkland Arms** (p399; Great Tew) Real ales, clay pipes and snuff behind the bar; it doesn't get more authentic than this.

- **Village Pub** (p406; Barnsley) Honest but gourmet fare in a hideout for the rich and famous.

- **Trout at Tadpole Bridge** (p389; Buckland Marsh) Riverside pub with fine food and a welcome for walkers.

- **Wild Duck Inn** (p406; Ewen) Rustic period character and lashings of contemporary comfort food.

Tweed Mill (now converted to apartments) on the outskirts of town. This monument to the industrial architecture of the 19th century is more like a stately home than a factory and is topped by a domed tower and chimney stack of the Tuscan order. A small, local-history **museum** (☎ 641712; 4 High St; admission £1; ⏲ 2-4pm Tue-Sat Easter-Oct) in the centre of town explains the importance of wool-manufacturing in the area.

For overnight accommodation, **Norten's B&B** (☎ 645060; www.nortens.co.uk; 10 New St; s £45, d £55-65; ☒) offers a range of really lovely contemporary rooms with simple, minimalist design. The downstairs café does a good range of bistro-style food (mains £4 to £7).

Another good bet is **Off the Beaten Track** (☎ 646383; www.offthebeatentrack.uk.com; 18 Horsefair; s/d £45/70) a brasserie and bar with a selection of comfortable, modern guest rooms. The restaurant (mains £8 to £15) serves a modern British menu and is probably the top spot in town for food.

Stagecoach bus 20 runs between Chippy and Oxford roughly every half-hour.

MORETON-IN-MARSH

☎ 01608 / pop 3198

Unassuming Moreton-in-Marsh was once a lovely town but is now a major road axis and is rather spoiled by its incessant traffic problems. However, it's a useful transport hub and still has a clutch of beautiful buildings. On Tuesday the town bursts into life for its weekly market.

Just east of Moreton, **Chastleton House** (NT; ☎ 674255; adult/under 18yr £6.50/3.30; ⏲ 1-5pm Wed-Sat Apr-Sep, 1-4pm Oct) is one of England's finest and most complete Jacobean houses, full of rare tapestries, family portraits and antique furniture. Outside there's a classic Elizabethan topiary garden and, nearby, a lovely 12th-century church.

Pulhams Coaches (☎ 01451-820369; www.pulham scoaches.com) runs eight services daily between Moreton and Cheltenham (one hour, Monday to Saturday). Two Sunday services run from May to September only. All buses go via Stow-on-the-Wold (15 minutes) and Bourton-on-the-Water (20 minutes).

There are trains roughly every hour to Moreton from London Paddington (£27.50, 1½ hours) via Oxford (£9.30, 35 minutes) and on to Worcester (£10.10, 45 minutes) and Hereford (£14.20, 1½ hours).

THE COTSWOLDS OLIMPICKS

The medieval sport of shin-kicking lives on in Chipping Campden, where each year the townspeople gather to compete at the Cotswolds Olimpicks, a traditional country sports day first celebrated in 1612. It is one of the most entertaining and bizarre sporting competitions in England and many of the original events such as welly wanging (throwing), the sack race and climbing a slippery pole are still held. The competition was mentioned in Shakespeare's *Merry Wives of Windsor* and has even been officially sanctioned by the British Olympic Association. It is held annually at the beginning of June.

CHIPPING CAMPDEN

☎ 01386 / pop 1943

The graceful curving main street of Chipping Campden is flanked by a wonderful array of wayward stone cottages, fine terraced houses, ancient inns and historic homes, making it a truly unspoiled gem in an area full of achingly pretty villages. Despite its obvious allure and the presence of chichi boutiques and upmarket shops, the town remains relatively unspoiled by tourist crowds and is a wonderful place to visit.

The helpful **tourist office** (☎ 841206; www.visitchip pingcampden.com; High St; ☽ 10am-5pm Mon-Fri) stocks a town trail guide with some background on the town's most historic buildings. On Wednesday from July to September you can also join a guided tour (1.30pm, tour £2) that leaves from the wonderful 17th-century **Market Hall** with its multiple gables and elaborate timber roof.

At the western end of the High St is the 15th-century **St James's**, one of the great wool churches of the Cotswolds. Built in the perpendicular style, it has a magnificent tower and some wonderful 17th-century monuments. Nearby on Church St is a remarkable row of **almshouses** dating from the 17th century, and the Jacobean lodges and gateways of the now-ruined Campden House. The surviving Court Barn will open as an arts and crafts (see p457) museum in summer 2007, celebrating Campden's connection with CR Ashbee and the Guild of Handicrafts, who moved here in 1902.

About 4 miles northeast of Chipping Campden, **Hidcote Manor Garden** (NT; ☎ 438333;

Hidcote Bartrim; adult/under 18yr £7/3.50; ☽ 10.30am-6pm Sat-Wed late-Mar–Sep) is one of the finest examples of arts and crafts landscaping in Britain.

Sleeping & Eating

Manor Farm (☎ 840390; www.manorfarmbnb.demon .co.uk; s/d £50/60) Set in a beautiful 17th-century farmhouse, this lovely B&B has all the period charm of a Cotswold home, but contemporary style and modern facilities. Along with the exposed oak beams and creaking stairs you'll find king-size beds, power showers and neutral colour schemes.

Eight Bells (☎ 840371; www.eightbellsinn.co.uk; Church St; s £50-65, d £80-115; ✗) The oldest inn in town has had a recent makeover, banished the chintz from its bedrooms and replaced it with sleek contemporary décor that works wonderfully with the period character of this 14th-century inn. The restaurant downstairs serves a British and Continental menu (mains £8.50 to £16) in rustic settings.

our pick **Cotswold House Hotel** (☎ 840330; www .cotswoldhouse.com; The Square; r £140-285; P ✗ ▣) Relax in utter luxury at this chic Regency town house turned boutique hotel. Bespoke furniture, massive beds, Frette linens, cashmere throws, private gardens and hot tubs are the norm here. You can dine in style at Juliana's or take a more informal approach at **Hick's Brasserie** (mains £8-17), a slick operation with an ambitious menu.

Getting There & Around

Between them buses 21 and 22 run almost hourly to Stratford-upon-Avon or Moreton-in-Marsh. Bus 21 also stops in Broadway. There are no Sunday services.

To catch a real glimpse of the countryside, try hiring a bike from **Cotswold Country Cycles** (☎ 438706; Longlands Farm Cottage; per day £12) and discovering the quiet lanes and trails around town.

BROADWAY

☎ 01386 / pop 2496

Quintessentially English, absurdly pretty and little changed since medieval times, Broadway is another stunning Cotswold village firmly on the tourist trail. The graceful golden-hued cottages set at the foot of a steep escarpment have inspired writers, artists and composers in times past, but today it's tearooms, antique shops, boutiques, art galleries and coaches that line the village green.

The **tourist office** (☎ 852937; 1 Cotswold Ct; ⏰ 10am-1pm & 2-5pm Mon-Sat) is in a shopping arcade off the northern end of High St.

Beyond the charm of the village itself there are few specific attractions to visit. If you're feeling energetic the lovely, 12th-century **Church of St Eadburgha** is a signposted 30-minute walk (1 mile) from town. Near here, a more challenging path leads uphill for 2 miles to **Broadway Tower** (☎ 852390; www.broadwaytower.co.uk; adult/under 14yr £3.80/2.30; ⏰ 10.30am-5pm Apr-Oct, 11am-3pm Sat & Sun Nov-Mar), a crenulated, 18th-century Gothic folly on the crest of the escarpment. It has a small William Morris exhibition on one floor and stunning views from the top.

The best of the B&Bs in town is the **Olive Branch Guest House** (☎ 853440; www.theolivebranch-broadway.com; 78 High St; s £40-58, d £68-8; ✗), a lovely 16th-century home with bright, spacious rooms decked out in cosy, country-style fabrics and pine furniture. Another good bet is **Milestone House** (☎ 853432; www.milestone-broadway .co.uk; High St; s/d £45/68; P ✗), a 17th-century coaching inn with exposed beams, an inglenook fireplace and subtle florals.

For food, head for the **Broadway Brasserie** (☎ 858435; 20A High St; mains £7-11), which serves a classic range of brasserie-style food, or sleek and stylish **Russels** (☎ 853555; www.russellsofbroadway .com; 20 High St; mains £9-17; ⏰ lunch & dinner) for more upmarket modern British fare. Russels also has a selection of slick, modern rooms (£105 to £245) with simple, contemporary design, flatscreen TVs and lots of little luxuries.

For a glimpse of the splendour of the medieval **Lygon Arms** (☎ 852255; www.thelygonarms.com; High St, Broadway; mains £9-20) and its barrel-vaulted, oak-panelled Great Hall of a dining room, you could drop in for a modern British meal, or alternatively just order a drink at the bar.

Getting There & Away
Bus 22 goes to Moreton-in-Marsh, Chipping Campden and Stratford (four daily Monday to Saturday, 20 minutes) and bus 606 goes to Cheltenham (four Monday to Saturday, 50 minutes).

AROUND BROADWAY
About 3 miles south of Broadway is **Snowshill Manor** (NT; ☎ 01386-852410; Snowshill; adult/under 18yr £7.30/3, garden only £4/2; ⏰ noon-5pm Wed-Sun mid-Mar–Oct), a wonderful Cotswold mansion once home to the marvellously eccentric Charles

Paget Wade. The house contains Wade's extraordinary collection of craftsmanship and design and includes everything from musical instruments to Victorian perambulators and Japanese armour. Outside, the lovely gardens were designed as an extension of the house, with pools, terraces and wonderful views.

Also worth visiting nearby is the stunning Jacobean mansion **Stanway House** (☎ 01386-584469; www.stanwayfountain.co.uk; Stanway; adult/under 14yr £6/1.50; ⏰ 2-5pm Tue & Thu Jun-Aug, garden only 2-5pm Sat Jul & Aug). Little changed since it was a family home, it contains much of its original furniture and is surrounded by wonderful Baroque water gardens that include the highest gravity fountain in the world.

WINCHCOMBE
☎ 01242 / pop 3682
Capital of the Saxon kingdom of Mercia and one of the most important towns in the Cotswolds until the Middle Ages, Winchcombe is now a sleepy place with the timeless charm of a typical Cotswold town. Beautiful houses line the streets, and the picturesque cottages on Vineyard St and Dents Tce offer quintessential Cotswold views. Fine gargoyles adorn the lovely St Peter's Church and just outside the town are the evocative ruins of Cistercian **Hailes Abbey** (EH; ☎ 01242-602398; adult/under 15yr £3.30/1.70; ⏰ 10am-5pm Easter-Oct), once one of the country's main pilgrimage centres.

The town's main attraction, however, is **Sudeley Castle** (☎ 604357; www.sudeleycastle.co.uk; adult/under 15yr £7.20/4.20; ⏰ 10.30am-5pm Sun-Thu selected weeks Easter-Oct), once a favoured retreat of Tudor and Stuart monarchs. Much of the house is off limits to visitors, but you can get a glimpse of its grand proportions while visiting the exhibitions of costumes, memorabilia and paintings, and the surrounding gardens. To see the private apartments you'll need to join the 'Connoisseur Tours' (Wednesday 11am, 1pm, and 3pm Easter to October, tour £15).

The **tourist office** (☎ 602925; www.winchcombe .co.uk; ⏰ 10am-1pm & 2-4pm Mon-Sat, 10am-4pm Sun Apr-Oct) is located on High St.

Sleeping & Eating
Gower House (☎ 602616; www.cotswolds.info/accommodation/gower-house.htm; 16 North St; s/d £40/53; ✗ P) Two 17th-century cottages have been converted into this lovely B&B close to the centre of town. The simple, uncluttered rooms have pine furniture, plain white bedspreads and plenty of light.

A HIKE TO BELAS KNAP

There's easy access to the Cotswold Way from Winchcombe, and the 2½-mile hike to **Belas Knap** is one of the most scenic short walks in the region. Five-thousand-year-old Belas Knap is the best-preserved Neolithic burial chamber in the country and although visitors are not allowed inside, the views down to Sudeley Castle and across the surrounding countryside are breathtaking.

White Hart Inn (☎ 602359; www.the-white-hart-inn .com; r £65-135; ✗) The individually styled rooms at the White Hart range from simple and contemporary twins to the tartan-bedecked Highland room, the Moroccan boudoir and the four-poster Swedish room. The food is equally eclectic, with light bites at the bar (£5 to £8), pizzas (£6 to £8) in the basement and modern British fare in the main restaurant (mains £14 to £16).

our pick **5 North St** (☎ 604566; 5 North St; 2-course lunch £18.50, 2-course dinner £28-37) Winchcombe's top spot for food is this cosy, unpretentious place that also happens to hold a prestigious Michelin star. The menu is a mix of British ingredients and French flair and promises consistently good food at surprisingly keen rates.

Getting There & Away

Bus 606 runs four times daily (Monday to Saturday) from Winchcombe to Cheltenham (25 minutes), while bus 559 goes once to Broadway (Monday to Saturday, 40 minutes).

STOW-ON-THE-WOLD

☎ 01451 / pop 2074

Stow has long held a strategic place in Cotswold history, standing as it does on the Roman Fosse Way and at the junction of six roads. At its heart is a large market square surrounded by handsome buildings and steep-walled alleyways originally used to funnel the sheep into the fair. Today the sheep have been replaced with tourists and instead of farmers brokering deals the town is full of antique shops, pretentious boutiques, tearooms and delis. It's great if you're on a pit stop from a coach tour, but all a little artificial if you're looking for true Cotswold charm.

The **tourist office** (☎ 831082; Hollis House; ✆ 9.30-5.30pm Mon-Sat) on Market Sq sells discounted tickets to local attractions.

Sleeping & Eating

Stow-on-the-Wold YHA Hostel (☎ 0870 770 6050; www .yha.org.uk; The Square; dm £14.95; ✆ Mar-Sep, Fri & Sat only Nov-Dec; Ⓟ ✗ ⬜) Slap bang on the market square, this hostel is in a wonderful 16th-century town house and has small dorms, a children's play area and a warm welcome for families.

Number 9 (☎ 870333; www.number-nine.info; 9 Park St; s £45, d £55-70; ✗) Centrally located and wonderfully atmospheric, this beautiful B&B has three simple, contemporary-styled rooms with plenty of space, brand-new bathrooms and subtle décor.

Old Butchers (☎ 831700; 7 Park St; mains £11-16; ✆ lunch & dinner) Stow's top spot for dining is this chic brasserie serving up a great selection of modern British cuisine with more than a hint of continental European influence thrown in. Expect grilled marinated quail, roast pork belly and succulent fish all done to perfection.

Eagle & Child (☎ 830670; Digbeth St; mains £9-12; ✆ lunch & dinner) Smart, simple but sophisticated food is served at the Eagle & Child, supposedly England's oldest inn. The décor is all exposed beams and old-world charm, but the menu is decidedly modern, blending traditional English favourites with modern European flair.

Getting There & Away

Bus 55 links Stow with Moreton, Bourton, Northleach and Cirencester eight times daily Monday to Saturday. Bus 801 runs to Cheltenham, Moreton and Bourton four times daily Monday to Friday and nine times on Saturday.

The nearest train stations are 4 miles away at Kingham and Moreton-in-Marsh.

BOURTON-ON-THE-WATER

☎ 01451 / pop 3093

Crass, commercialised and overwhelmed by coach tours, Bourton is an exceptionally beautiful place that has sold its soul to the tourist trade. Not content with its handsome houses and stunningly picturesque low bridges over the trickling River Windrush, the town has turned theme park with a series of 'attractions' including a model railway and village, bird-conservation project, perfume factory, maze and motor museum.

If you're travelling in the high season, visit in the evening, when most of the coaches have left, or wait until the depths of winter, when the village's understated charm is free to reveal itself. One occasion worth battling the crowds for is the annual **water football match** held in the river on the August Bank Holiday Monday. The tradition dates back to the 1800s.

The **tourist office** (☎ 820211; www.bourtoninfo .com; Victoria St; ⏰ 9.30am-5pm Mon-Fri, 9.30am-5.30pm Sat Apr-Oct, 9.30am-4pm Mon-Sat Nov-Mar) can help find accommodation.

If you'd like to stay, **Larks Rise** (☎ 822613; www.larksrisehouse.co.uk; Old Gloucester Rd; r £50-80; ✗) offers beautiful, bright simple rooms with DVD players and complimentary toiletries in a lovely Edwardian house.

For more upmarket accommodation and excellent food, the chic and stylish **Dial House** (☎ 822244; www.dialhousehotel.com; The Chestnuts; r £110-160; ✗) is the only place to go. Luxurious rooms with hand-painted wallpaper, giant beds, silky throws and a wonderful mix of period charm and designer style are on offer. The restaurant (mains lunch £8 to £10, dinner £12 to £18) serves up excellent modern British cuisine.

Buses 801 and P1 operate to Cheltenham, Moreton and Stow up to four times every day Monday to Friday and nine times on Saturday.

THE SLAUGHTERS
☎ 01451

A little over a mile from Bourton and yet half a world away, the Slaughters – Upper and Lower – are some of the Cotswolds' most scenic and unspoiled villages. The names derive from the Old English 'sloughre', meaning 'slough', and despite the camera-wielding crowds that are drawn here, they maintain their unhurried medieval charm.

To see the Slaughters at their best, arrive on foot from Bourton (about 30 minutes; walk) across the fields. Your first sight of the village will be the meandering river that weaves between the glorious buildings, past the 17th-century Lower Slaughter Manor (now a top-notch hotel) to the **old mill** (☎ 820052; www.oldmill-lowerslaughter.com; admission £2; ⏰ 10am-6pm Mar-Oct), which houses a small museum and teashop. From here you can continue for another mile (about 30 minutes' walk) across the fields to Upper Slaughter, with its own fine manor house and glorious cottages.

NORTHLEACH
☎ 01451 / pop 1923

Little visited and under-appreciated, Northleach is a lovely little market town of half-timbered Tudor houses, imposing merchants' stores and late-medieval cottages. There's a wonderful mix of architectural styles clustered around the gorgeous market square and the narrow laneways leading off it, but the highlight of a visit is the **Church of St Peter and St Paul**, a masterpiece of Cotswold perpendicular style. The large traceried stained-glass windows and collection of memorial brasses are unrivalled in the region.

Near the square is Oak House, a 17th-century wool house that contains **Keith Harding's World of Mechanical Music** (☎ 860181; www .mechanicalmusic.co.uk; admission £5; ⏰ 10am-6pm; ♿), a fascinating museum of self-playing musical instruments, where you can hear Rachmaninoff played on a reproducing piano.

Just outside town on the A429, the **Old Prison** now houses a café, information point and a collection of historic agricultural machinery. Further south on the same road is **Chedworth Roman Villa** (NT; ☎ 01242-890256;

THROW AWAY YOUR GUIDEBOOK!

As wonderful as the Cotswolds villages may be, they can be a nightmare of camera-wielding crowds, slow-moving pensioners and chaotic coach parking in the summer months. However, most tourists stick to a well-trodden path and it's easy to get away from the crowds and discover the rarely visited villages lurking in the hills. Stick to the B-roads and visit places like **Guiting Power** near Bourton, **Broadwell** near Stow, **Elkstone** south of Cheltenham, **Blockley** near Chipping Campden, **Great Tew** near Chipping Norton, **Ampney St Mary** and **Ampney Crucis** near Cirencester or **Coln St Aldwyns** and **Hatherop** near Bibury. Or you could see the region on foot by joining a walking tour with companies such as **Cotswold Walking Holidays** (☎ 01242-254353; www.cotswoldwalks.com) or a bike tour with **Cotswold Country Cycles** (☎ 01386-438706; www.cotswoldcountrycycles.com).

Yanworth; adult/under 18yr £5.50/3; ⏰ 10am-5pm Tue-Sun Apr-Oct, 11am-4pm Feb-Mar & Nov), one of the most complete Roman villas in England. Built as a stately home in about AD 120, it contains some wonderful mosaics illustrating the seasons, bathhouses, and, a short walk away, a temple by the River Coln.

For overnight stays try **Prospect Cottage** (☎ 860875; www.prospectcottage.co.uk; West End; s/d £60/75; ✗), an atmospheric 17th-century home with bright simple rooms featuring pine furniture and spacious bathrooms. Alternatively, the **Wheatsheaf** (☎ 860244; www.wsan.co.uk; West End; s £50-60, d £60-80; ✗) has eight excellent-value en suite rooms decked out in slick contemporary style. The restaurant serves a good selection of light lunches (£6 to £8) and a modern British dinner menu (mains £11 to £13).

Getting There & Away
Swanbrook runs three buses Monday to Saturday (one on Sunday) between Cheltenham (30 minutes) and Oxford (one hour) via Northleach.

CIRENCESTER
☎ 01285 / pop 15,861
Affluent, elegant and steeped in history, the charming town of Cirencester is a refreshingly unpretentious place of narrow winding streets and graceful town houses. The lovely market square is surrounded by wonderful 18th-century and Victorian architecture, while the nearby streets showcase a harmonious medley of buildings from various eras.

Under the Romans, Cirencester was second only to London in terms of size and importance and although little of this period remains, you can still see the grassed-over ruins of one of the largest amphitheatres in the country. The medieval wool trade was also good to the town, with wealthy merchants funding the building of a superb perpendicular-style church. Today, Cirencester is the most important town in the southern Cotswolds, and retains an authentic, unaffected air, with the lively Monday and Friday markets as important as the expensive boutiques and trendy delis that line its narrow streets.

Pick up a copy of *Cirencester – A Town Walk* at the **tourist office** (☎ 654180; Corn Hall; ⏰ 9.30am-5.30pm Mon-Sat Apr-Dec, 9.30am 5pm Mon Sat Jan-Mar) for information on historic buildings around town.

Church of St John the Baptist
Standing elegantly on the Market Sq, cathedral-like **St John's** (admission £2 donation; ⏰ 10am-5pm) is one of England's largest parish churches. A superb perpendicular-style tower with wild flying buttresses dominates the exterior, but it is the majestic three-storey south porch that is the real highlight. Built as an office by late-15th-century abbots, it subsequently became the medieval town hall.

Soaring arches, magnificent fan vaulting and a Tudor nave adorn the light-filled interior, where you'll also find a 15th-century painted stone pulpit and memorial brasses recording the matrimonial histories of important wool merchants. The east window contains fine medieval stained glass, while a wall safe displays the **Boleyn Cup**, made for Anne Boleyn, second wife of Henry VIII, in 1535.

Corinium Museum
Modern design, innovative displays and computer reconstructions bring one of Britain's largest collections of Roman artefacts to life at the **Corinium Museum** (☎ 655611; www.cotswolds.gov .uk/museum; Park St; adult/under 16yr £3.50/2; ⏰ 10am-5pm Mon-Sat, 2-5pm Sun). You can dress as a Roman soldier, meet an Anglo-Saxon princess and discover what Cirencester was like during its heyday as a wealthy medieval wool town. Highlights of the Roman collection include the beautiful Hunting Dogs and Four Seasons floor mosaics and a reconstructed Roman kitchen and butcher's shop.

Other Sights
Set in a converted Victorian brewery, the **Brewery Arts Centre** (☎ 657181; www.breweryarts .org.uk; Brewery Ct; admission free; ⏰ 10am-5pm Mon-Fri, 9.30am-5.30pm Sat) is home to 18 resident craft workers and hosts regular exhibitions, workshops and classes.

Also worth visiting is **Cirencester Park** (Cecily Hill; ⏰ 8am-5pm), the Baroque landscaped grounds of the Bathurst Estate. The park features magnificent geometrical landscaping and has a lovely short walk along Broad Ride.

The remains of the **Roman amphitheatre** are on Cotswold Ave.

Sleeping & Eating
Old Brewhouse (☎ 656099; www.theoldbrewhouse.com; 7 London Rd; s £45-50, d £55-65; Ⓟ ✗) Set in a charming 17th-century town house, this lovely B&B has bright, pretty rooms with cast-iron beds

SOMETHING SPECIAL

Set in the picturesque village of Barnsley, **Village Pub** (☎ 01285-740421; www.thevillagepub.co.uk; Barnsley; r £90-125; lunch & dinner; P) is an unpretentious place full of mismatched furniture, oriental rugs and mahogany bookcases. Its real appeal, however, lies in its deceptively simple menu, the true strength of which is only revealed when the sublime food (mains £10 to £16) is delivered to your table. Upstairs, the beautifully furnished rooms all feature Victorian iron bedsteads or oak four-posters, power showers or antique freestanding baths.

If you're after something even more luxurious, nearby sister property **Barnsley House** (☎ 01285-740000, www.barnsleyhouse.com; d £270-475; P X) has justly become a hideout for the rich and famous, with its funky chic rooms and indulgent sophistication.

Barnsley is on the B4425 between Cirencester and Bibury.

and subtle, country-style florals or patchwork quilts. The beautiful garden room even has its own patio.

Leauses (☎ 653643; www.theleauses.co.uk; 101 Victoria Rd; s £45-50, d£55-60; P X) This Victorian house offers a range of calm guestrooms with plenty of period features and modern amenities. Elegant but understated décor, soothing colour schemes and good bathrooms make it a great deal.

Wild Duck Inn (☎ 770310; www.thewildduckinn.co.uk; Ewen; s £70-100, d £95-150; P X) Dripping with period character and romance, the four-poster rooms at this 16th-century inn are a treat. Ranging from full-on period drama to Chinese-influenced simplicity, they are as luxurious as they are comfortable. The rustic restaurant downstairs serves seriously good comfort food (mains £6 to £16). The inn is in the village of Ewen, 3 miles from Cirencester off the A433.

our pick **Jesse's Bistro** (☎ 641497; Blackjack St; mains £7-15; lunch daily & dinner Wed-Sat) Hidden away in a cobbled stableyard with its own fishmonger and cheese shop, Jesse's is a great little place with flagstone floors, wrought-iron chairs and mosaic tables. The modern menu features a selection of great dishes, but the real treat is the fresh fish and meat cooked in the wood-burning oven.

1651 (☎ 658507; Market Pl; mains £11-16; lunch & dinner) Stripped wood floors, red walls and a modern Mediterranean menu make 1651 one of the best dining spots in town. It's a stylish place in the Fleece Hotel and serves dishes such as pan-fried monkfish with leek, braised fennel and tamarind jus.

Getting There & Away

National Express buses run roughly hourly from Cirencester to London (£17, 2½ hours) and to Cheltenham Spa (30 minutes) and Gloucester (one hour). Stagecoach bus 51 also runs to Cheltenham hourly Monday to Saturday (40 minutes). Bus 852 goes to Gloucester four times daily Monday to Saturday.

BIBURY

☎ 01285 / pop 623

Firmly on the tourist trail and thoroughly overexposed, the gorgeous village of Bibury is best seen early in the morning or in the soft golden light of the setting sun. Its impossibly quaint collection of riverside buildings prompted William Morris to describe it as 'the most beautiful village in England', and at a quiet moment it's hard to disagree.

For many visitors Bibury's chief attraction is **Arlington Row**, a stunning sweep of riverside cottages now thought to be the most photographed street in Britain. Originally built as a sheep house in the 14th century, the building was converted into weavers' cottages in the 17th century. Also worth a look is the 17th-century **Arlington Mill**, just a short stroll away across Rack Isle, a wildlife refuge once used to dry cloth.

Few visitors make it past these two sights, but for a glimpse of the real Bibury you should venture into the village proper behind Arlington Row, where you'll find a cluster of stunning cottages and the Saxon **Church of St Mary**. Although much altered since its original construction, many 8th-century features are still visible among the 12th- and 13th-century additions.

If you'd like to experience Bibury after the crowds have dispersed, the riverside **Swan** (☎ 740695; www.swanhotel.co.uk; r £140-220, X) is a 17th-century coaching inn with a selection of classically styled rooms with billowing swag curtains, cute florals and chunky beds.

A good bet for food, the jasmine-clad **New Inn** (☎ 750651, www.new-inn.co.uk; Coln-St-Aldwyns; mains

£8-12), a 16th-century place with the requisite exposed beams, antique atmosphere and has a modern British menu. It also has a series of potently styled rooms (singles/doubles £95/126).

Buses 860, 863, 865, 866 and 869 pass through Bibury en route to Cirencester at least once daily from Monday to Saturday (20 minutes).

LECHLADE-ON-THAMES
☎ 01367 / pop 2415

The sleepy market town of Lechlade is an attractive place nestled on the banks of the Thames. Once an important staging post for goods and passenger traffic, it is now a quiet backwater dominated by the graceful spire of **St Lawrence's Church**. Originally a wool church, it was rededicated to the Spanish saint by Catherine of Aragon.

Just three miles east of Lechlade is the gorgeous Tudor pile **Kelmscott Manor** (☎ 252486; www .kelmscottmanor.co.uk; adult/under 16yr £8.50/4.25; ☺ 11am-5pm Wed Apr-Sep & selected Sat in summer), once the summer home of William Morris, the poet, artist and founder of the Arts and Crafts movement (p457). The house contains many of Morris' personal effects, as well as fabrics and furniture designed by him and his associates.

Set in gardens designed by Harold Peto, **Buscot Park** (NT; ☎ 240786; www.buscot-park.com; admission £7, grounds only £5; ☺ 2-6pm Wed-Fri, grounds only Mon & Tue Apr-Sep & selected weekends) is another worthwhile side trip from Lechlade. This ornate Italianate country house is home to the Faringdon art collection, which includes paintings by Rembrandt, Reynolds, Rubens, Van Dyck and Murillo. The house is 2¾ miles southeast of Lechlade on the Faringdon road.

Bus 77 runs from Lechlade to Cirencester (40 minutes) five times daily from Monday to Saturday.

TETBURY
☎ 01666 / pop 5250

From medieval cottages to Georgian Gothic gems, Tetbury is an unspoilt town of stunning buildings and numerous antique shops. Once a prosperous wool-trading centre, Tetbury has managed to preserve most of its architectural heritage and is well worth a wander. A row of gorgeous medieval weavers' cottages lines the steep hill at **Chipping Steps** and lead up to the **Chipping**, which is surrounded by graceful 17th- and 18th-century town houses. From here, it's a short stroll to Market Sq, where the 17th-century **Market House** stands as if on stilts. Close by, the Georgian Gothic **Church of St Mary the Virgin** has a towering spire and wonderful interior.

Just south of Tetbury is the **National Arboretum** (☎ 880220; www.forestry.gov.uk/westonbirt; adult £5-7.50, under 18yr £1; ☺ 10am-dusk) at Westonbirt. The park boasts a magnificent selection of temperate trees, with some wonderful walks and great colour throughout the year, especially in autumn.

The friendly **tourist office** (☎ 503552; www .tetbury.org; 33 Church St; ☺ 9.30am-4.30pm Mon-Sat Mar-Oct, 9.30am-2.30pm Mon-Sat Nov-Feb) has plenty of information on the town and its history and stocks a trail guide to the arboretum.

Sleeping & Eating
No 65 (☎ 503346; www.number65.co.uk; 65 Long St; s £30, d £50-65; ✗) This unassuming restaurant has a couple of simple, country-style guest rooms on offer and serves up a modern British

---

SOMETHING FOR THE WEEKEND

Kick-start your weekend by checking into the seductively stylish **Cotswold House Hotel** (p401) in Chipping Campden and take a sunset stroll around the village before dining at Juliana's or Hick's Brasserie. First thing the following morning, blow away the cobwebs with a short stroll and magnificent views at **Broadway Tower** (p401) and then head south to **Winchcombe** (p402), where you can loll about the lovely village or take in some history at the Tudor pile **Sudeley Castle** (p402). Stop for lunch at the seriously unpretentious but exceptionally good **5 North St** (p402) before taking the cross-country route to stunning **Lower Slaughter** (p404). If you're feeling sprightly, follow the trail over the rolling hills to Upper Slaughter or alternatively just sit and feed the ducks, before swinging back to Bourton to check into the sumptuous **Dial House** (p403) for an evening of luxury and fine food. On Sunday head east to **Woodstock** to ramble the grounds or the stately rooms of **Blenheim Palace** (p392) and work up an appetite for a hearty traditional lunch at the glorious thatched **Falkland Arms** (see boxed text, p399) in Great Tew.

menu (3-course set menu £26) featuring such delicacies as pistachio and almond rissole with roasted pepper purée.

Ormond's Head (☎ 505690; www.theormond.co.uk; 23 Long St; s £60, d £85-95; ✕ P) You'll find bright, modern rooms with minimalist décor at the Ormond, a good-value place in the centre of town. The modern bar and grill downstairs serve excellent-value food (mains £8 to £15).

Close Hotel (☎ 502272; www.theclose-hotel.com; Long St; s £100, d £120-180; P ✕) This mellow hotel in the centre of town has a selection of classically styled but contemporary rooms with sleigh beds, individual décor and, if you're lucky, a view over the walled garden. The restaurant menu features decent international cuisine (mains £9 to £19).

Blue Zucchini (☎ 505852; 7-9 Church St; dinner mains £11-15; ☿ 10am-11pm Mon-Sat, 10am-4pm Sun) Bright, cheery and usually buzzing, this modern brasserie-bar is as good for a quick read of the paper with a coffee and fresh pastry, as for a lunchtime panini or pizza (£6 to £8) or a strapping evening meal.

Getting There & Away

Bus 29 runs between Tetbury and Stroud (30 minutes) six times daily Monday to Saturday. Bus 620 goes to Bath (1¼ hours) six times daily Monday to Friday and four times on Saturday, stopping at Westonbirt Arboretum en route.

ULEY

☎ 01453 / pop 1100

The lovely little village of Uley, with its quaint village green and jumble of pretty houses, sits below the overgrown remains of the largest Iron Age hill fort in England, **Uley Bury**. Dating from about 300 BC, the fort and its 2-mile perimeter walk provide spectacular views over the Severn Vale. To get there on foot, follow the steep path that runs from the village church. If you're driving, access to the car park is off the B4066 north of the village.

Just east of Uley you'll find the wonderfully romantic **Owlpen Manor** (☎ 860261; www .owlpen.com; adult/under 14yr £5.25/2.25; ☿ 2-5pm Tue, Thu & Sun May-Sep), a Tudor mansion nestled in a wooded valley and surrounded by formal terraced gardens. The house was built between 1450 and 1616 and has a magnificent Tudor **Great Hall**, which contains unique painted

wall hangings. Owlpen suffered 100 years of neglect in the 19th century and was rescued and partially refurbished in 1926 by architect Norman Jewson, a follower of William Morris. The house now contains a rich collection of Arts and Crafts (see p457) furniture and fittings.

Virtually untouched since the mid-1870s, **Woodchester Mansion** (☎ 861541; www.woodchester mansion.org.uk; adult/under 14yr £5/free; ☿ 11am-4pm Sun Easter-Oct, 11am-4pm Sat & Sun Jul-Aug) is an incredible place, abandoned before it was finished, yet incredibly grand and graceful. Doors here lead nowhere, fireplaces are stuck halfway up walls and corridors end at ledges with views of the ground below. The house also features an impressive set of gruesome gargoyles, and is home to a large colony of bats and several resident ghosts. Woodchester Mansion is a mile north of Uley on the B4066.

Bus 20 runs between Uley and Stroud hourly Monday to Saturday (40 minutes).

BERKELEY

☎ 01453 / pop 1865

An astounding relic from medieval times, **Berkeley Castle** (☎ 810332; www.berkeley-castle.com; adult/under 16yr £7.50/4.50, grounds only £4/2; ☿ 11am-4pm Tue-Sat Apr-Sep, 2-5pm Sun Apr-Sep, 2-5pm Sun Oct) has remained virtually untouched since it was built as a sturdy fortress in Norman times. Edward II was imprisoned and then murdered here on the order of his wife Queen Isabella and her lover in 1327, and you can still see the King's Gallery with its cell and dungeon. You can also visit the castle's state rooms, as well as the medieval Great Hall, Picture Gallery and kitchen. Regular jousting events and medieval banquets are held here in summer.

Berkeley is also home to the **Jenner Museum** (☎ 810631; www.jennermuseum.com; adult/under 18yr £3.50/2; ☿ 12.30-5.30pm Tue-Sat, 1-5.30pm Sun Apr-Oct), which honours the life and works of Edward Jenner, country doctor and pioneer of vaccination. The museum is in the beautiful Queen Anne house where the doctor performed the first smallpox vaccination in 1796. To get to the museum on foot, follow the path from the castle through **St Mary's** churchyard.

Bus VL3 runs twice daily between Berkeley and Gloucester. Bus 207 does the same journey once daily. Both services operate Monday to Saturday.

STROUD

☎ 01453 / pop 32,052

Once a thriving centre for the wool industry and home to 150 cloth mills, Stroud is a pleasant town set in a steep-sided river valley surrounded by forested hills. Although only a handful of the handsome old mills are still operating, many others have been converted into apartments or offices and the town itself has become a bohemian enclave littered with fair-trade and wholefood shops, delis, and organic cafés. The picturesque Shambles still holds a market three times weekly and the Tudor town hall is also worth a look. In the centre of town the imposing Subscription Rooms are home to the **tourist office** (☎ 760960; George St; ◷ 10am-5pm Mon-Sat).

Stroud's main attraction for tourists is the diverting **Museum in the Park** (☎ 763394; www.stroud.gov.uk/museum; Stratford Pk; admission free; ◷ 10am-5pm Tue-Fri Apr-Oct, 11am-5pm Sat & Sun Apr-Oct, 10am-4pm Tue-Fri Oct-Mar, 11am-4pm Sat & Sun Oct-Mar) set in an 18th-century mansion surrounded by parkland. The museum tells the history of the town and its cloth-making along with displays of everything from dinosaurs to Victorian toys and the world's first lawnmower.

For food, head for **Woodruffs Organic Café** (☎ 759195; 24 High St; mains £5-8; ◷ 9am-5.30pm Mon-Sat), a small, cheerful place with a wholesome selection of salads, soups and stews, or you could try the **Angel Café** (☎ 767123; 12 Union St; tapas £4-5; ◷ lunch & dinner Thu-Sun), another popular spot serving organic tapas. Just around the corner, slick bar and restaurant **Nine** (☎ 755447; 9 John St; mains £9-13; ◷ 11am-11pm Mon-Thu, 11am-2am Fri & Sat, noon-10.30pm Sun) serves up modern British food in a very trendy environment.

The nicest place to stay is in nearby Nailsworth at the 16th-century **Egypt Mill** (☎ 833449; wwww.egyptmill.com; s £65, d £80-95; ✗ P), where you can fall asleep to the sound of the gurgling weir. The rooms vary quite a bit and it's definitely worth paying the extra tenner for a superior.

Bus 46 runs hourly to Painswick (10 minutes) and Cheltenham (30 minutes), while 93 runs roughly hourly to Gloucester (25 minutes). Both services operate Monday to Saturday. Trains run roughly every 90 minutes to London (£38, 1½ hours), Gloucester (£4, 20 minutes) and Cheltenham (£5.60, 40 minutes).

PAINSWICK

☎ 01452 / pop 1666

Largely untouched, totally unassuming and gloriously uncommercialised, Painswick is a real gem. This gorgeous Cotswold village is a maze of narrow winding streets lined with picture-perfect cottages, handsome stone town houses and medieval inns. Despite its obvious charm, Painswick sees only a trickle of visitors and you can wander the backstreets here and feel genuinely lost in time.

The village centres on **St Mary's Church**, a fine perpendicular wool church surrounded by table-top tombs and 99 clipped yew trees. Legend has it that, should the hundredth yew tree be allowed to grow, the devil would appear and shrivel it. They planted it anyway – to celebrate the millennium – but there's been no sign of the Wicked One.

Sliding downhill beside and behind the church is a series of gorgeous streetscapes. Look out for Bisley St, the original main drag, which was superseded by the now ancient-looking New St in medieval times. Just south of the church, rare iron stocks stand in the street.

The **tourist office** (☎ 813552; Library, Stroud Rd; ◷ 10am-4pm Tue-Fri, 10am-1pm Sat) has information on short walks in the area and the **Cotswold Way**, which runs through the village.

Painswick Rococo Garden

Just a mile north of town, the ostentatious **Painswick Rococo Garden** (☎ 813204; www.rococogarden.co.uk; adult/under 16yr £5/2.50; ◷ 11am-5pm Jan-Oct) is the area's biggest attraction. These flamboyant pleasure gardens were designed by Benjamin Hyett in the 1740s, and have now been restored to their former glory. Winding paths soften the otherwise strict geometrical precision, and bring visitors around the central vegetable garden to the many Gothic follies dotted in the grounds. There's also a children's nature trail and maze.

Sleeping & Eating

Hambutts Mynd (☎ 812352; www.hambuttsmyndguesthouse.co.uk; Edge Rd; s/d £30-36/60; P ✗) Set on the edge of the village with lovely views from the rooms, this converted, early-18th-century corn mill has simple but comfortable rooms with tasteful décor.

Cardynham House (☎ 814006; www.cardynham.co.uk; The Cross; s £50-59 d £69-185; ✗ ▣) The individually decorated rooms at 15th-century Cardynham

House offer four-poster beds, heavy patterned fabrics and buckets of character. Choose the Shaker-style New England room, bright and airy Palm Beach or chintzy Cottage Rose. Downstairs, the **March Hare** (☎ 813452; set menu £24; ❂ 7-10pm Tue-Sat) Thai restaurant is probably the best place to eat in town.

For a light lunch or evening meal, the **Falcon Inn** (☎ 814222; New St; mains £9-13) and the **Royal Oak Inn** (☎ 813129; St Mary's St; mains £8-12) both do decent, if fairly standard, grub.

Getting There & Around

Bus 46 connects Cheltenham (30 minutes) and Stroud (10 minutes) with Painswick hourly Monday to Saturday. Bus 256 connects Painswick to Gloucester twice daily on Wednesday and Saturday.

GLOUCESTERSHIRE

The unhurried charm of Gloucestershire is one of is greatest pleasures, and after the crowds and commercialism of the Cotswolds it's an authentic alternative, with its fair share of mellow stone villages and rustic allure. Here too is the elegant Regency town of Cheltenham with its graceful, tree-lined terraces and upmarket boutiques, and the county capital, Gloucester, with its magnificent Gothic cathedral. Tudor Tewkesbury, to the north, has a gracious Norman abbey and numerous half-timbered houses, while to the west, the historic Forest of Dean is a leafy backwater crisscrossed by numerous trails and littered with vestiges of its mining past.

Information

Much of Gloucestershire falls into the Cotswold district and information on sights, activities, accommodation and transport can be found on www.glos-cotswolds.com.

Activities

The quiet roads, gentle gradients and numerous footpaths in Gloucestershire make it perfect for walking and cycling. Tourist offices can help with route planning and stock numerous guides to the trails.

Compass Holidays (☎ 250642; www.compass-holidays .com; bikes per 2 days/week from £34/64) hires bikes and also offers a bag-drop service (£6) and guided cycling tours of the area.

Getting Around

A host of companies operate bus services in Gloucestershire. Most tourist offices stock local bus timetables or can help with finding connecting services. As always, **Traveline** (☎ 0870 608 2608; www.traveline.org.uk) has details of all routes.

GLOUCESTER

☎ 01452 / pop 123,205

Despite its glorious Norman cathedral and glimmer of medieval character, workaday Gloucester (*glos*-ter) is forever destined to live in the shadow of its more glamorous neighbour. Yet unlike glitzy Cheltenham, it's a refreshingly unpretentious place and between the modern architectural blunders and steak-and-kidney-pie cafés, the city is beginning to transform its fortunes, redeveloping its historic docks into trendy apartments and heaving itself out of financial decline.

Gloucester began life as a Roman settlement for retired soldiers, built its wealth on profits from river trade and its reputation during a period of medieval piety. For a while the good times rolled but as trade shifted to Bristol the city fell into serious decline. In modern times Gloucester prospered on the back of heavy industry and is only today beginning to heal the scars left from this time.

Orientation & Information

The city centre is based on a medieval cruciform pattern, with Northgate, Southgate, Eastgate and Westgate Sts converging on The Cross. The **tourist office** (☎ 396572; 28 Southgate St; ❂ 10am-5pm Mon-Sat Sep-Jun, 11am-3pm Sun Jul & Aug) is in the centre of town and there's an additional **information point** (❂ 10.30am-3.30pm) at Merchant's Quay in the docks.

If you don't mind queuing, **Gloucester Library** (☎ 426973; Brunswick Rd; ❂ 9am-7pm Mon, Tue & Thu, 9am-5.30pm Wed & Fri, 9am-4pm Sat) has free internet access. Otherwise, head for **Surf Scorpio** (☎ 528030; 135 Eastgate St; per hr £1.50; ❂ 9am-9pm Mon-Sat, 10am-9pm Sun).

Sights
GLOUCESTER CATHEDRAL

The main reason to visit Gloucester is to see its magnificent Gothic **cathedral** (☎ 528095; www .gloucestercathedral.org.uk; College Green; suggested donation £3; ❂ 7.30am-6pm), a stunning example of English perpendicular style. Originally the site of a Saxon abbey, a Norman church was

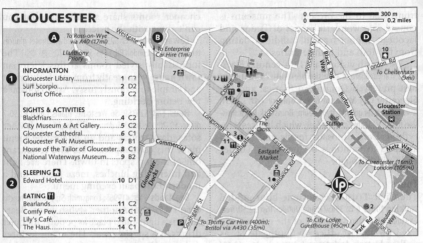

GLOUCESTER

0 — 300 m
0 — 0.2 miles

INFORMATION
Gloucester Library...............1 C2
Surf Scorpio.........................2 D2
Tourist Office.......................3 C2

SIGHTS & ACTIVITIES
Blackfriars...........................4 C2
City Museum & Art Gallery...5 C2
Gloucester Cathedral...........6 C1
Gloucester Folk Museum......7 B1
House of the Tailor of Gloucester..8 C1
National Waterways Museum..9 B2

SLEEPING
Edward Hotel.......................10 D1

EATING
Bearlands............................11 C2
Comfy Pew...........................12 C1
Lily's Café............................13 C1
The Haus.............................14 C1

built here by a group of Benedictine monks in the 12th century and when Edward II was murdered in 1327 the church was chosen as his burial place.

Edward's tomb proved so popular, however, that Gloucester became a centre of pilgrimage and the income generated from the pious pilgrims financed the church's conversion into the magnificent building seen today. Inside, the cathedral skilfully combines the best of Norman and Gothic design, with thick, sturdy columns along the nave creating a sense of gracious solidity, and wonderful Norman arcading draped with beautiful mouldings. From the elaborate 14th-century wooden choir stalls you'll get a good view of the imposing eastern window, one of the largest in England.

To see the window in more detail, head for the **Tribune Gallery**, where you can also see an **exhibition** (admission £2; ☽ 10.30am-4pm Mon-Fri, 10.30am-3pm Sat) on its making. As you walk around the **Whispering Gallery** you'll notice that even the quietest of murmurs reverberates across the wonderfully elaborate lierne vaulting. Beneath the window in the northern ambulatory is Edward II's magnificent tomb and, nearby, the late-15th-century **Lady Chapel**, a glorious patchwork of stained glass.

One of the cathedral's greatest treasures, however, is the exquisite **Great Cloister**. Completed in 1367, it is the first example of fan vaulting in England and is only matched in beauty by Henry VIII's Chapel at Westmin-

ster Abbey. You (or your children) might recognise the cloister from the first two Harry Potter films: it was used in the corridor scenes at Hogwart's School.

For more cathedral insights and a fantastic view of the town you can climb the 225ft **tower** on an hour-long guided **tour** (adult/under 16yr £2.50/1; ☽ tours 2.30pm Wed-Fri, 1.30pm & 2.30pm Sat & Bank Hol). Because of the steep steps it's not recommended for children under 10. Civic Trust volunteers also provide free guided tours of the **cathedral** (☽ 10.30am-3pm Mon-Sat, noon-2pm Sun).

OTHER SIGHTS & ACTIVITIES

A major part of the city's regeneration is taking place at Gloucester Docks, once Britain's largest inland port. Fifteen beautiful Victorian warehouses, many now restored, surround the canal basins and house a series of museums, shops and cafés.

The largest warehouse, Llanthony, is home to the excellent **National Waterways Museum** (☎ 318200; www.nwm.org.uk; adult/under 16yr £6.60/5.25; ☽ 10am-5pm), a hands-on kind of place where you can discover the history of inland waterways. There's a collection of historic boats and plenty of interactive exhibits that are great for children. You can also take a 45-minute **boat trip** (adult/under 16 £4.50/3.50; ☽ tours noon, 1.30 & 2.30pm Apr-Oct) along the canal.

For more local history you should head for the **Gloucester Folk Museum** (☎ 396868; 99-103 Westgate St; admission free; ☽ 10am-5pm Tue-Sat), which examines domestic life, crafts and industries from 1500 to the present. The museum is housed in a wonderful series of Tudor and Jacobean timber-framed buildings dating from the 16th and 17th centuries.

Also worth visiting are 13th-century **Blackfriars** (Ladybellgate St; admission free), one of Britain's best-preserved Dominican friaries, and the **Gloucester City Museum & Art Gallery** (☎ 396131; www.gloucester.gov.uk/citymuseum; Brunswick Rd; admission free; ☾ 10am-5pm Tue-Sat), which houses everything from dinosaur fossils and Roman artefacts to paintings by the artists Turner and Gainsborough.

Tours

The Civic Trust operates one-hour guided **walking tours** (☎ 396572; adult/under 16yr £2.50/free; ☾ tours 11am Mon-Sat Jun-Aug) of the city leaving from the tourist office on Southgate St, as well as **historic dock tours** (adult/under 16yr £2.50/ free; ☾ tours 11am Sat & Sun Jun & Jul) that depart from the information point at Merchant's Quay. On Sunday during August, it also runs **Blackfriars tours** (adult/under 16yr £5.50/free; ☾ tours 3pm). You can also pick up a free Via Sacra self-guided walk brochure from the tourist office. It will guide you on an hour-long walking trail around the city's most historic buildings.

Sleeping & Eating

Gloucester's hotels are a grim lot and you'd be wise to consider staying in Cheltenham instead.

City Lodge Guesthouse (☎ 526380; www.city lodgeguesthouse.co.uk; 72 Weston Rd; s £25-29, d £39-49; P 🖳) This bargain B&B offers basic but clean and comfortable rooms close to the city centre. The décor is pretty nondescript and

cheaper rooms share a bathroom, but you can't argue with the price.

Edward Hotel (☎ 525865; www.edwardhotel-glouces ter.co.uk; 88-92 London Rd; s £45-55, d£60-70; P ☒) The individually styled rooms at this Victorian town house vary greatly from relatively bright and simple to seriously fussy. Ask to look at a few before deciding.

Haus (☎ 525359; 56 Westgate; mains lunch £3.50-dinner £9-20; ☾ lunch & dinner) Slick décor, leather sofas, dark woods and an interesting menu make this contemporary bar and restaurant one of the top spots in town. There are light and interesting lunches, meze (£3.50) and a modern European evening menu.

Bearlands (☎ 419966; Longsmith St; 2-course lunch/ dinner £11.95/19.95) Another stylish joint, Bearlands is a light-filled place as popular for quiet drinks as a special meal. The menu features dishes such as supreme of pheasant with a warm apricot and cinnamon stuffing, and the drinks menu is tailored to suit.

There are plenty of simple cafés around town for lunch:

Lily's Café (☎ 307060; College Ct; mains £5-8) A cosy, country-style place serving a decent range of sandwiches and cakes.

Comfy Pew (☎ 415648; 11 College St; mains £6) A quiet spot by the cathedral serving panini, baguettes and jacket potatoes.

Getting There & Away

National Express has buses roughly every two hours to London (£17, 3½ hours). Bus 94 runs to Cheltenham every 10 minutes (30 minutes), with an express bus X94 cutting the journey to 15 minutes during rush hour. The quickest journey between the two cities is by train (every 20 minutes, 10 minutes).

THE TAILOR OF GLOUCESTER

Beatrix Potter's magical tale of good-hearted mice saving a feverish Gloucester tailor from ruin was inspired by a local legend about real-life tailor John Prichard. Like the tailor in Potter's tale, Prichard had been commissioned to make a coat for the mayor, but left the garment at cutting stage on a Friday night. He returned on Monday to find it finished, save for a single button hole. A note pinned to it read 'No more twist'.

Commercially minded Mr Prichard was soon encouraging people to come in and see where 'waistcoats are made at night by the fairies'. In reality, his two assistants had slept off a Saturday night bender at the workshop and woke to see the faithful heading to the cathedral for mass. Consumed by guilt and hoping to make amends, they had tried to finish the coat but ran out of thread.

The original house that Potter used in her illustrations is at 9 College Ct and is due to reopen as an attraction once funding has been secured.

AROUND GLOUCESTER
Forest of Dean
☎ 01594 / pop 79,982

The steep hills, winding tree-lined roads, lakes and unspoilt vistas of the Forest of Dean make for excellent touring by car, foot or bike. The area, England's first National Forest Park, was formerly a royal hunting ground and a centre of iron and coal mining and its mysterious depths were supposedly the inspiration for JRR Tolkien's setting for *The Lord of the Rings*. The forest covers a 42-sq-mile swathe between Gloucester, Ross-on-Wye and Chepstow and is dotted with trails for walkers and cyclists.

Coleford, the main population centre has good transport connections to Gloucester, making it a convenient base, but it's hard to resist the charm of the magnificent youth hostel near Lydney.

The **tourist office** (☎ 812388; www.visitforestofdean .co.uk; High St, Coleford; ☒ 10am-4pm Mon-Fri, 10am-2pm Sat) stocks walking and cycling guides and also offers a free accommodation booking service. If you've got your own transport, pick up the *Royal Forest Route* and *Heritage Trail* leaflets, which describe tours through the forest and its most significant sights.

SIGHTS & ACTIVITIES
Your first stop should be the **Dean Heritage Centre** (☎ 822170; www.deanheritagemuseum.com; Camp Mill, Soudley; adult/under 16yr £4.50/2.50; ☒ 10am-5.30pm Apr-Sep, 10am-4pm Feb, Mar & Oct), which explains the history of the forest and its free miners from medieval times to the industrial age. There's also a reconstructed forest home, adventure playground and art gallery on site.

If you're travelling with children, **Puzzle Wood** (☎ 833187; adult/under 12yr £3.25/2.25; ☒ 11am-5.30pm Tue-Sun Easter-Sep, 11am-4pm Feb & Oct) is a must. This overgrown pre-Roman, open-cast ore mine has a maze of paths, weird rock formations, tangled vines and eerie passageways and offers a real sense of discovery. Puzzle Wood is 1 mile south of Coleford on the B4228.

Mined for iron ore for more than 4000 years, the **Clearwell Caves** (☎ 832535; www.clear wellcaves.com; adult/under 16yr £4.50/2.80; ☒ 10am-5pm Mar-Oct) are a warren of passageways, caverns and pools that help explain the forest's history of mining. The caves are signposted off the B4228 a mile south of Coleford.

In contrast to the caves, **Hopewell Colliery** (☎ 810706; www.hopewellcoalmine.co.uk; adult/under 14yr £3.50/2.50; ☒ 10am-4pm Easter-Oct) offers un-

derground tours of the mine workings, with miners as guides. The colliery is on the B4226 between Coleford and Cinderford.

In Newland, you can visit the 'Cathedral of the Forest', the 13th-century **All Saints**. The church was restored and partially rebuilt in the 19th century and houses some fine stained-glass windows as well as a unique brass depicting a miner with a *nelly* (tallow candle) in his mouth, a pick in his hand and a *billy* (backpack) on his back.

SLEEPING & EATING
our pick **St Briavels Castle YHA Hostel** (☎ 0870 770 6040; www.yha.org.uk; Lydney; dm £17.90; ℗ ☒) Set in an imposing moated castle once used as King John's hunting lodge, this is your chance to live like a medieval lord for a night. One of the most unique hostels in the country, it's well worth considering whatever your budget. There are lively medieval banquets on Wednesday and Saturday nights in August.

Tan House Farm (☎ 832222; pchamberlain@cix.co.uk; Laundry Lane, Newland; s £25, d £60 64; ℗) Set in a wonderfully imposing former tannery complete with a 16th-century drying barn, this lovely B&B has simple, elegant rooms and tranquil gardens just dripping with character.

Forest House Hotel (☎ 832424; www.forest-house -hotel.co.uk; Cinder Hill, Coleford; s/d £45/65; ℗ ☒) This recently refurbished 18th-century house offers a selection of tastefully furnished rooms with simple décor and good bathrooms. The Bluebell restaurant downstairs is a good bet for modern British food (mains £13 to £19).

Tudor Farmhouse Hotel (☎ 833046; www.tudorfarm house.co.uk; High St, Clearwell; s £65, d £80-130; ☒) For some country-style luxury, this charming 13th-century hotel has a wide variety of rooms featuring exposed stonework, oak beams and tasteful décor. The popular restaurant (mains £15 to £18) is also a good bet for an evening meal.

GETTING THERE & AROUND
From Gloucester, bus 31 runs to Coleford roughly every half-hour (one hour) and there are hourly trains to Lydney (20 minutes). The **Dean Forest Railway** (☎ 843423; www.deanforestrailway .co.uk) runs steam trains from Lydney to Parkend (day ticket adult/under 16 years £8/5) on selected days from March to October.

You can hire bikes (£13 per day), buy maps and get advice on cycling routes at **Pedala-bikeaway** (☎ 860065; www.pedalabikeaway.com; Cannop Valley, nr Coleford).

CHELTENHAM

☎ 01242 / pop 98,875

Riddled with historic buildings and still exuding the gracious air of an 18th-century spa resort, Cheltenham is a cosmopolitan hub at the centre of the rustic Cotswolds. The town grew dramatically after its spa waters were discovered in 1716 and in its heyday rivalled Bath as *the* place for the sick, hypochondriac and merely moneyed to go.

Today its period charms and elegant architecture attract a well-heeled class of resident and the leafy crescents, beautifully proportioned terraces, wrought-iron balconies and expansive parks are kept in top-notch condition. But Cheltenham also has a reputation for partying on a grand scale, with festivals of national importance held throughout the year. There's also a host of fine hotels, restaurants and expensive boutiques, making it a popular base for exploring the region.

History

Cheltenham languished in the obscurity of most Cotswold towns until local pigeons began eating and thriving on the salt crystals from a local spring in the early 18th century. Soon several pumps had been bored, property speculators were throwing up terraced housing and the sick were arriving in droves. By the time George III visited in 1788 the town's fate had been sealed and Cheltenham became the most fashionable holiday destination for England's upper crust. Handel, Samuel Johnson and Jane Austen came here and by the mid-19th century the Victorian neo-Gothic Cheltenham College had sprung up, and soon after came the genteel Cheltenham Ladies' College. The town retained its period glamour and allure and in the 20th century became known as the 'Anglo-Indian's Paradise' as so many Empire-serving, ex-military men retired here. Today, Cheltenham is the most complete Regency town in England, but millions have been spent propping up the quick-buck buildings that the Regency entrepreneurs rushed to erect.

Orientation

Central Cheltenham is fairly compact and easy to get around on foot. The High St runs roughly east–west; south from it is The Promenade, a more elegant shopping area, which extends into Montpellier, the most exclusive area of town. Pittville Park and the old Pump Room are about a mile north of High St.

The bus station is behind The Promenade in the town centre, but the train station is out on a limb to the west; bus D runs to the town centre every 10 minutes.

Information

You'll find all the major banks and the main post office on High St. The **tourist office** (☎ 522878; www.visitcheltenham.info; 77 The Promenade; ☥ 9.30am-5.15pm Mon-Sat) runs a free accommodation booking service, sells event tickets and stocks copies of walking, cycling and driving guides to the Cotswolds. For internet access try **Equals** (☎ 237292; 287 High St; per 30 min £2) or the **Loft** (☎ 539573; 8-9 Henrietta St; per hr £3).

Sights

THE PROMENADE & MONTPELLIER

Famed as one of England's most beautiful streetscapes, The Promenade is a wide, tree-lined boulevard flanked by imposing period buildings. The Municipal Offices, built as private residences in 1825, are among the most striking on this street and face a **statue of Edward Wilson** (1872–1912), a local man who joined Captain Scott's ill-fated second expedition to the South Pole.

Continuing on from here you'll pass the grandiose **Imperial Gardens**, built to service the Imperial Spa (now the Queens Hotel), en route to **Montpellier**, Cheltenham's most fashionable district. Along with the handsome architecture of the area, there's a buzzing collection of bars, restaurants and boutiques. Along Montpellier Walk **caryatids** (draped female figures based on those on the Acropolis in Athens) act as structural supports between the shops, each balancing an elaborately carved cornice on its head.

PITTVILLE PUMP ROOM

Built in 1830 as a centrepiece to a vast estate, the **Pittville Pump Room** (☎ 523852; Pittville Park; admission free; ☥ 10am-4pm Wed-Mon) is Cheltenham's finest Regency building. Originally used as a spa and social centre, it is now used for occasional art exhibitions and summer concerts. You can still take the spa waters here or just explore the remarkable building and vast parklands and lake it overlooks.

ART GALLERY & MUSEUM

Cheltenham's excellent **Art Gallery & Museum** (☎ 237431; www.cheltenhammuseum.org.uk; Clarence St; admission free; ☥ 10am-5.20pm Mon-Sat) is well worth

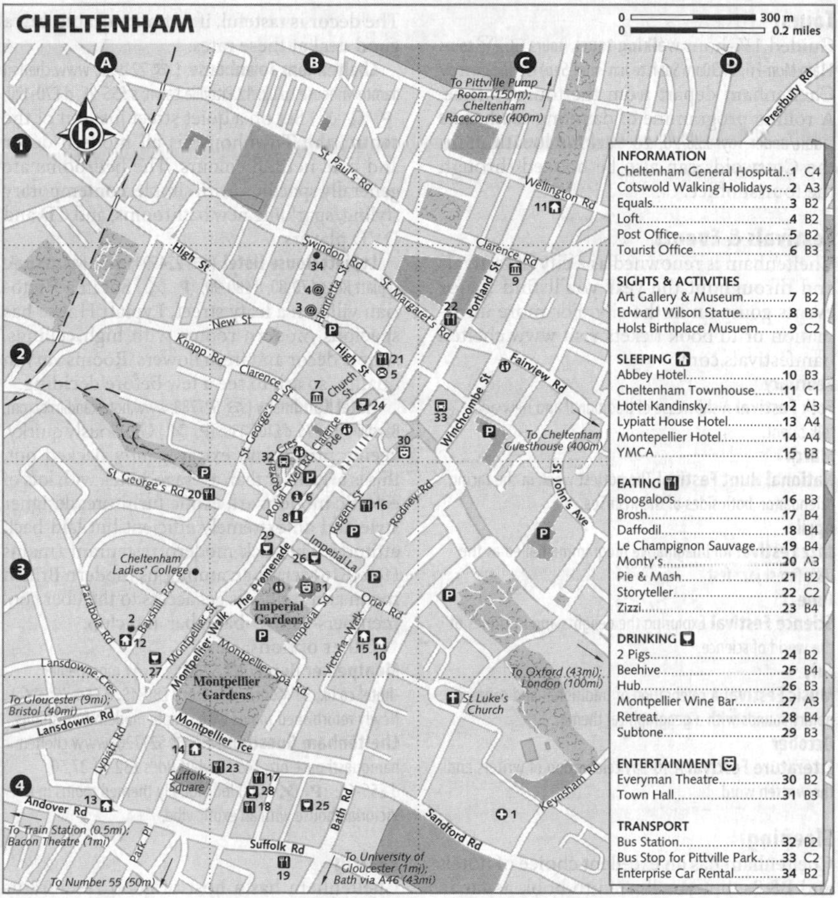
CHELTENHAM
0 300 m
0 0.2 miles
A
B
C
D
1
2
3
4
To Pittville Pump Room (150m); Cheltenham Racecourse (400m)
INFORMATION
Cheltenham General Hospital..1 C4
Cotswold Walking Holidays.....2 A3
Equals.....3 B2
Loft.....4 B2
Post Office.....5 B2
Tourist Office.....6 B3
SIGHTS & ACTIVITIES
Art Gallery & Museum.....7 B2
Edward Wilson Statue.....8 B3
Holst Birthplace Musuem.....9 C2
SLEEPING
Abbey Hotel.....10 B3
Cheltenham Townhouse.....11 C1
Hotel Kandinsky.....12 A3
Lypiatt House Hotel.....13 A4
Montepellier Hotel.....14 A4
YMCA.....15 B3
EATING
Boogaloos.....16 B3
Brosh.....17 B4
Daffodil.....18 B4
Le Champignon Sauvage.....19 B4
Monty's.....20 A3
Pie & Mash.....21 B2
Storyteller.....22 C2
Zizzi.....23 B4
DRINKING
2 Pigs.....24 B2
Beehive.....25 B4
Hub.....26 B3
Montpellier Wine Bar.....27 A3
Retreat.....28 B4
Subtone.....29 B3
ENTERTAINMENT
Everyman Theatre.....30 B2
Town Hall.....31 B3
TRANSPORT
Bus Station.....32 B2
Bus Stop for Pittville Park.....33 C2
Enterprise Car Rental.....34 B2
Prestbury Rd
St Paul's Rd
Wellington Rd
Swindon Rd
Clarence Rd
Portland St
St Margaret's Rd
High St
New St
Henrietta St
Knapp Rd
Clarence St
Church St
Fairview Rd
Winchcombe St
Clarence Pde
St George's Pl
Royal Cres
Royal Well Rd
St George's Rd
Regent St
Rodney Rd
To Cheltenham Guesthouse (400m)
St John's Ave
Imperial La
Cheltenham Ladies' College
The Promenade
Imperial Gardens
Imperial Sq
Oriel Rd
Parabola Rd
Bayshill Rd
Montpellier St
Montpellier Walk
Montpellier Spa Rd
Victoria Walk
Lansdowne Cres
Montpellier Gardens
To Oxford (43mi); London (100mi)
To Gloucester (9mi); Bristol (40mi)
Lansdowne Rd
Montpellier Tce
St Luke's Church
Lypiatt Rd
Suffolk Square
Keynsham Rd
Andover Rd
Bath Rd
To Train Station (0.5mi); Bacon Theatre (1mi)
Sandford Rd
Park Pl
Suffolk Rd
To University of Gloucester (1mi); Bath via A46 (43mi)
To Number 55 (50m)

a visit for its depiction of Cheltenham life through the ages. It also has wonderful displays on William Morris and the Arts and Crafts movement (p457), as well as Dutch and British art, rare Chinese and English ceramics and a section on Edward Wilson's expedition to Antarctica.

HOLST BIRTHPLACE MUSEUM

The composer Gustav Holst was born in Cheltenham in 1874 and his childhood home has been turned into the **Holst Birthplace Museum** (☎ 524846; www.holstmuseum.org.uk; 4 Clarence Rd; adult/under 16yr £2.50/2; ⌚ 10am-4pm Tue-Sat). The rooms are laid out in typical period fashion and feature much Holst memorabilia, including the piano on which most of *The Planets* was composed. You can also visit the Victorian kitchen, which explains what life was like 'below stairs'.

CHELTENHAM RACECOURSE

More famous in some circles for its horse racing than its architecture, Cheltenham's racecourse can attract up to 40,000 punters a day during an event simply known as 'The Festival'. Held in mid-March each year, this is England's premier steeplechase event and is attended by droves of breeders, trainers, riders and race enthusiasts. To experience what all the fuss is about you'll need to buy your **tickets** (☎ 226226; www.cheltenham.co.uk) well in advance.

Visit the **Hall of Fame museum** (☎ 513014; admission free; ⌚ 8.30am-5.30pm Mon-Fri), which charts the history of steeplechasing since 1819.

Tours

Guided 1¼-hour **walking tours** (tours £3; ☺ tours 11am Mon-Fri, 11.30am Sat late Jun–mid-Sep) of Regency Cheltenham depart from the tourist office. A rolling programme of day-long **coach tours** (adult/under 16yr £28/20) to various locations in the Cotswolds can also be booked through the tourist office.

Festivals & Events

Cheltenham is renowned as a city of festivals and throughout the year you'll find major events going on in the city. For more information or to book tickets visit www.cheltenhamfestivals.com.

February
Folk Festival A showcase of traditional and new age folk talent.
March
National Hunt Festival The hottest week in the racing calendar on both sides of the Irish Sea.
April
Jazz Festival An imaginative programme hailed as the UK's finest jazz fest.
June
Science Festival Exploring the delights and intrigues of the world of science.
July
Music Festival A celebration of traditional and contemporary sounds with a geographical theme.
October
Literature Festival A 10-day celebration of writers and the written word.

Sleeping

Cheltenham has an excellent choice of hotels and B&Bs, but you'll need to book as far in advance as possible during the festivals – especially for race week.

YMCA (☎ 524024; www.cheltenhamymca.com; 6 Victoria Walk; dm/s £16.50/25) This elegant building right in the city centre now houses the cheapest beds in town. The four-bed dorms are fairly basic and well worn, but the price includes breakfast and access to the attached fitness centre.

Number 55 (☎ 584915; www.number55.co.uk; 55 Painswick Rd; s £30-40, d £55-70; Ⓟ ⊠ 🖳) Simple, contemporary rooms with white linens and original fireplaces are available at this new B&B just minutes' walk from Montpellier. It's an ideal location and excellent value.

Abbey Hotel (☎ 516053; www.abbeyhotel-cheltenham .com; 14-16 Bath Pde; s/d £40/70; Ⓟ ⊠) Conveniently situated in the centre of town, the Abbey offers good, comfortable rooms in a perfect location.

The décor is tasteful, if not memorable, but a good deal at these rates.

Cheltenham Townhouse (☎ 221922; www.cheltenhamtownhouse.co.uk; 12 Pittville Lawn; s £55-95, d £70-120; Ⓟ 🖳 ♿) Set on a quiet street just out of the centre, the Townhouse is all modern décor and pale neutral colours. The bedrooms are generally spacious, with simple, contemporary styling, sparkling new bathrooms, and CD and DVD players.

Lypiatt House Hotel (☎ 224994; www.lypiatt.co.uk; Lypiatt Rd; s £70-80, d £80-90; Ⓟ ⊠) Set in a Victorian villa on a leafy street, Lypiatt House has spacious modern rooms with high ceilings, simple décor and fresh flowers. Rooms vary in quality, so ask to see a few before deciding.

Hotel Kandinsky (☎ 527788; www.hotelkandinsky.com; Bayshill Rd; s £75, d £105-130; Ⓟ ⊠) Gloriously quirky, keenly priced and extravagantly decked out, this is a 'funkier than average' hotel, with lots of eclectic modern art, exotic furniture, designer style and an extremely efficient but laid-back attitude. The slick modern restaurant (mains £9 to £16) serves an ambitious modern British menu and residents get access to the über cool members-only U-bahn bar and club.

Other options:
Montpellier Hotel (☎ 526009; www.montpellier -hotel.co.uk; 33 Montpellier Tce; s £30-45, d £54-75; ⊠) Newly refurbished rooms with simple modern furnishings.
Cheltenham Guesthouse (☎ 521726; www.cheltenhamguesthouse.biz; 145 Hewlett Rd; s £32.50-37.50, d £55-65; Ⓟ ⊠ 🖳) Individually themed rooms in a Victorian house with an exotic vibe.

Eating

Cheltenham has a host of good restaurants to eat in. Stroll up through Montpellier for a choice of the city's finest.

Boogaloos (☎ 702259; 16 Regent St; mains £5-10; ☺ 8am-5pm Mon-Sat) Chilled out Boogaloos serves up tasty sandwiches, salads and hot lunches in a cosy Georgian town house with warm colours, big sofas and mellow music. Make up your own sandwich or go for pasta, fish cakes or hot dishes such as chicken with mozzarella and basil.

Pie & Mash (☎ 702785; 10 Bennington St; mains £5-10; ☺ dinner Thu, lunch & dinner Fri & Sat) Wholesome to the core, this certified organic restaurant serves up hearty pies, sausages, puddings and flavoured mash designed with meat eaters, vegans, veggies, coeliacs and diabetics in mind. There's even organic beers, wines and champagnes, and live music on Saturday evening.

Storyteller (☎ 250343; 11 North Pl; mains £6-15; 🕑 lunch & dinner) Enduringly popular for its generous proportions, buzzing atmosphere and extensive menu, this place serves up comfort food with an innovative twist. It's got the kind of menu where you'll be spoiled for choice, with inspiration from Mexico to the Mediterranean.

Brosh (☎ 227277; 8 Suffolk Pde; mains £12-18; 🕑 lunch & dinner Wed-Sat) Small, quirky and brave enough to take on the Montpellier big boys, this lovely little place has white walls, dark-wood tables and a menu of interesting Middle Eastern and Mediterranean dishes.

Daffodil (☎ 700055; 18-20 Suffolk Pde; mains £14-19; 🕑 lunch & dinner; 🕭) A Cheltenham institution, this converted Art Deco cinema harks back to the roaring '20s and serves up a top-notch selection of modern English brasserie food with a dollop of French and Mediterranean influences thrown in. Come on a Monday night for live jazz and blues.

Le Champignon Sauvage (☎ 573449; 24-26 Suffolk Rd; set menu 2-/3-course £38/47; 🕑 lunch & dinner; wheelchair access) A shower of Michelin stars, rosettes and foodie awards have been heaped on this unpretentious but oh-so-delectable restaurant for its inspired French cuisine. Go for slow-roast local lamb with liquorice and crushed Jerusalem artichokes, or scallops with pumpkin purée and squid-ink sauce.

Other good options:
Zizzi (☎ 252493; St James's Church, Suffolk Sq; mains £6-9; 🕑 lunch & dinner) Italian chain restaurant set in wonderfully atmospheric former church.

Monty's Brasserie & Seafood Restaurant
(☎ 227678; 41 St George's Rd; mains £11-19; 🕑 lunch & dinner) Contemporary-styled brasserie and seafood restaurant with a good bar menu (£8) for lunch.

Drinking

Beehive (☎ 579443; 1-3 Montpellier Villas; 🕑 noon-11pm Mon-Sat, noon-10.30pm Sun) A traditional boozer with a modern take on quirky cool, this perennially popular pub is a jumble of mismatched furniture, chilled-out clientele and bar-room games. There's a courtyard garden and a surprisingly good restaurant (mains £8 to £12) upstairs .

Hub (☎ 238001; 1A Imperial Lane; admission £2-5; 🕑 9pm-2am Thu-Sat & Mon) This late-night club and music venue has two bars, live bands, top-name guest DJs and a groovy attitude. The music ranges from hip-hop and drum 'n' bass to funk, and pulls in the crowds all weekend.

Subtone (☎ 575925; 117 The Promenade; admission £2-6; 🕑 8pm-late) One of the city's most popular club and music venues, Subtone has three floors of DJs and live music at its basement club and piano bar. Expect everything from jazz and house to funk and rock.

Montpellier Wine Bar (☎ 527774; Bayshill Lodge, Montpellier St; 🕑 10am-11pm) Slick, sophisticated and self-consciously cool, this is where Cheltenham's beautiful people come to hang out, sip wine and dine on modern British food (mains £7 to £14). There's an extensive wine list, cask ales and plenty of people-watching.

Other options:
Retreat (☎ 235436; 10-11 Suffolk Pde; 🕑 noon-11pm Mon-Sat) Trendy bar full of preppie girls and businessmen during the day and a more relaxed crowd by night.

2 Pigs (☎ 07840 763799; Church St; 🕑 7pm-2am) Alternative live music venue featuring anything from hard rock to indie anthems.

Entertainment
THEATRE & MUSIC

The **Everyman Theatre** (☎ 572573; www.everyman theatre.org.uk; Regent St) is Cheltenham's main stage and hosts everything from Elvis impersonators to comedy and panto, while the modern **Bacon Theatre** (☎ 258002; www.bacontheatre.co.uk; Hatherly Rd) showcases touring shows, jazz and ballet. Classical music lovers should look out for concerts at the **Pittville Pump Room** (☎ 523852; Pittville Park), while the **town hall** (☎ 227979; Imperial Sq) offers more mainstream talent as well as hosting many festival events.

Getting There & Away

For information on public transport to and from Cheltenham, pick up a free copy of the handy *Getting There by Public Transport* guide from the tourist office.

BUS

National Express runs buses to London roughly hourly (£17, 3½ hours) and Swanbrook bus 853 goes to Oxford three times daily Monday to Saturday (one on Sunday, £6.50, 1½ hours).

Bus 94 runs to Gloucester every 10 minutes (30 minutes), Monday to Saturday, every 20 minutes on Sunday. Bus 51 goes to Cirencester hourly (40 minutes).

Pulhams bus 801 runs to Moreton (one hour) via Bourton (35 minutes) and Stow (50 minutes) seven times daily Monday to Saturday. Castleways Coaches 606 runs four times daily to Broadway (50 minutes) via Winchcombe (20 minutes), Monday to Saturday.

TRAIN

Cheltenham has trains to London (£50, 2¼ hours), Bristol (£8.10, 50 minutes) and Gloucester (£2.80, 10 minutes) roughly every half-hour, and hourly services to Bath (£12.50, 1¼ hours).

Getting Around

Compass Holidays (☎ 250642; www.compass-holidays.com; bikes per 2 days/week from £34/64) has bicycles for hire at the train station.

TEWKESBURY

☎ 01684 / pop 9978

Crooked half-timbered houses, buckled roof lines and narrow alleyways lined with medieval buildings give Tudor-heavy Tewkesbury a higgledy-piggledy charm. There's also a lovely riverside area with ancient passageways leading up to Church St, where you'll find the town's most glorious building, the magnificent medieval abbey church.

The **tourist office** (☎ 295027; www.tewkesburybc.gov.uk; 64 Barton St; ❍ 9.30am-5pm Mon-Sat, 10-4pm Sun) is housed in a 15th-century timber-framed house, which is also home to a small **museum** displaying finds from Roman and medieval times.

Each year at the end of May Tewkesbury celebrates the Coopers Hill cheese-rolling competition, a 200-year-old tradition that sees locals running, tumbling and sliding down a local hill in pursuit of a seven-pound block of Double Gloucester cheese. For the truly committed there is also an uphill competition.

Tewkesbury Abbey

Magnificent **Tewkesbury Abbey** (☎ 850959; www.tewkesburyabbey.org.uk; suggested donation £2; ❍ 7.30am-6pm) is one of Britain's largest churches, far bigger than many of the country's cathedrals. The Norman abbey, built for the Benedictine monks, was consecrated in 1121 and was one of the last monasteries to be dissolved by Henry VIII. Although many of the monastery buildings were destroyed, the abbey church survived after being bought by the townspeople for the princely sum of £453.

The church has a massive 40m-high tower and some spectacular Norman piers and arches in the nave. The Decorated-style chancel dates from the 14th century, however, and still retains much of its original stained glass. The church also features an organ dating from

1631, which was originally made for Magdalen College, Oxford, and an extensive collection of medieval tombs. The most interesting is that of John Wakeman, the last abbot, who is shown as a vermin-ridden skeleton.

A **visitor centre** (❍ 10am-4pm Mon-Sat), by the gate, houses an exhibition on the abbey's history.

Sleeping & Eating

Ivydene House (☎ 592453; www.ivydenehouse.net; Uckinghall; s/d £35/60; **P**) Slightly out of town but well worth the effort, Ivydene is a real gem, offering gorgeous rooms at excellent rates. On top of the charming but contemporary rooms there are large gardens, a tennis court and log fires to enjoy.

Royal Hop Pole (☎ 293236; www.royalhoppole.co.uk; Church St; s £55-75, d £65-90; **P** ✗) Right in the centre of town and one of the oldest inns around, this imposing half-timbered place offers period-style rooms with exposed beams and frumpy décor. There's a garden leading down to the river, and a restaurant serving a competent modern British menu (mains £10 to £13).

Aubergine (☎ 292703; 73 Church St; mains £7-13; ❍ lunch & dinner) Set in a 15th-century building but decidedly modern inside, this place is a welcome change from Tewkesbury's tearooms. The menu ranges from standard fare to more adventurous dishes such as venison casserole with honey and roast cardamom vegetables.

Getting There & Away

Bus 41 runs to Cheltenham every 15 minutes (hourly on Sunday, 25 minutes) and 71 goes to Gloucester hourly (30 minutes). The nearest train station is at Ashchurch, 1½ miles away.

Around Tewkesbury

For a great short hike with majestic views, head for **Bredon Hill** (961ft), 6 miles northeast of Tewkesbury, where an Iron Age fort sits atop the isolated summit. Along with the impressive fort ramparts, there are Roman earthworks, several ancient standing stones and the curious 18th-century Parson's Folly.

If you've got your own transport, you can climb the hill in about an hour from the lovely village of Overbury. Between them buses 395, 540 and 562 run from Tewkesbury to Bredon six times daily (10 minutes), from where it takes about 1½ hours to get to the top.

The Marches

Perhaps it's the crisp ciders and mellow ales enjoyed after a long day's hill-walking, or the warm glow from eating fine foods fresh from the surrounding fields. Possibly it's the sensation of exploring border villages that seem to have been slumbering since the Middle Ages. Or maybe it's the time spent patiently pondering life as you potter along behind tractors on winding country roads. For whatever reason, the Marches is a beautiful corner of England that imbues a rare sense of peace and perspective.

It wasn't always so tranquil here. For centuries the untamed border with Wales reeled with ferocious fighting for control or independence, and the rippling hills are scattered with castles and ruins that testify to the tumult of times past. Today, however, the unhurried pace of rural life is addictive, and a wonderful balance between Welsh and English cultures has been struck. It's a region where you can be assured of a warm welcome, a wealth of simple country pleasures and a fine time romping around the surging hills and lush farmland by foot, pedal or four wheels.

Seriously beautiful Shropshire is home to enchanting Tudor capital Shrewsbury; a remarkable World Heritage site at Ironbridge Gorge; an epicurean enclave at historic Ludlow; and soul-restoring scenery in the south Shropshire Hills. Further south, sleepy Herefordshire boasts lovely landscapes that uncoil along the canoe-friendly meandering River Wye and fairy-tale black-and-white villages, while Worcestershire has its historic capital, dignified Victorian hill resorts and the dramatic Malvern peaks.

HIGHLIGHTS

- Be awed by the cradle of the Industrial Revolution, **Ironbridge Gorge** (p441)
- See the world through medieval eyes at Hereford's **Mappa Mundi** (p428)
- Feed your inner foodie in gourmet mecca, **Ludlow** (p447)
- Don your hiking boots and roam the lush **Malvern Hills** (p426)
- Get lost amid the black-and-white streets of **Shrewsbury** (p437)
- Meet the king of the bookworms at **Hay-on-Wye** (p431)

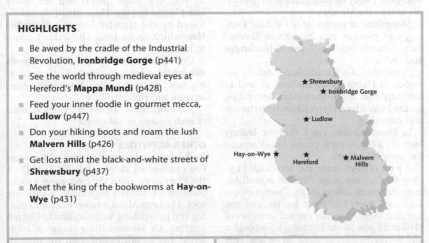

★ Shrewsbury
★ Ironbridge Gorge
★ Ludlow
Hay-on-Wye ★   ★ Hereford   ★ Malvern Hills

■ POPULATION: 1 MILLION   ■ AREA: 2541 SQ MILES

History

This region has seen its share of territorial scuffles and all-out battles for centuries. These conflicts took place between feuding kingdoms along what is today the border separating England and Wales. In the 8th century the Anglo-Saxon king Offa of Mercia built an earthwork barricade along the border to attempt to quell the ongoing tension. It became known as Offa's Dyke, and much of it is still traceable as a very popular walking route today.

In an effort to subdue the Welsh and secure his new kingdom, William the Conqueror set up powerful, feudal barons – called Lords Marcher after the Anglo-Saxon word *mearc*, meaning 'boundary' – along the border, from where they repeatedly raided Wales, taking as much territory as possible under their control.

Activities

The Marches is ripe with beautiful walking and cycling routes, snaking through pastoral idylls, wooded valleys and gentle hills. But not all the action is situated on terra firma – there are ample opportunities for fun in the water and sky too. See the Outdoor Activities chapter (p75) and county-specific Activities sections in this chapter for more information.

CYCLING

There are plenty of good reasons to get saddle-sore in the Marches.

Shropshire in particular is ideal for touring, and you can rent bicycles in Shrewsbury, Church Stretton, Ludlow, Ironbridge and Ledbury.

Areas apt for off-road biking include the woods of Hopton near Ludlow, as well as Eastridge near Shrewsbury. High-level riding on the Long Mynd above Church Stretton is also rewarding.

In Herefordshire, you'll find the **Ledbury Loop** – a 17-mile rural circuit based around the town of Ledbury.

A pack of route maps and notes called *Cycling for Pleasure in the Marches* is available from the tourist offices for £6. Tourist offices also stock many free route leaflets, and you can find them on newly opened stretches of National Cycle Route 45 through Shropshire and Worcestershire through the **National Cycle Network** (www.sustrans.org) or you can download

leaflets from www.shropshire.gov.uk/cycling.nsf.

WALKING

One of many great routes on which to muddy your hiking boots, the glorious **Offa's Dyke** is a 177-mile national trail following an ancient earthen border defence. Running south–north from Chepstow to Prestatyn, it passes through some of the most spectacular scenery in Britain, but it's not for the inexperienced or unfit.

A less taxing option is the gentle 107-mile **Wye Valley Walk**, which follows the course of the River Wye from Chepstow upstream to Rhayader in Wales. Another firm favourite is the beautiful 100-mile **Three Choirs Way** linking the cathedral cities of Hereford, Worcester and Gloucester.

Shorter walks include the famous ridges of Wenlock Edge (p444) and the lovely Long Mynd (p446). These are in turn swallowed by the circular 136-mile **Shropshire Way**, which loops from Shrewsbury south to Ludlow.

One of the loveliest spots of all is the **Malvern Hills** (p426), offering easy paths and breathtaking views on the boundary between Worcestershire and Herefordshire.

For more ideas, see the Activities sections of each county in this chapter.

OTHER ACTIVITIES

Both easy-grade canoeing and white-water fun can be had at Symonds Yat (p434) on the River Wye, while the river gorge's rocky buttresses are also a popular rock climbing spot. The Long Mynd is renowned for its gliding and paragliding, with facilities in Church Stretton. Or for something completely different, tourist offices can point you towards hotspots for mountain-boarding.

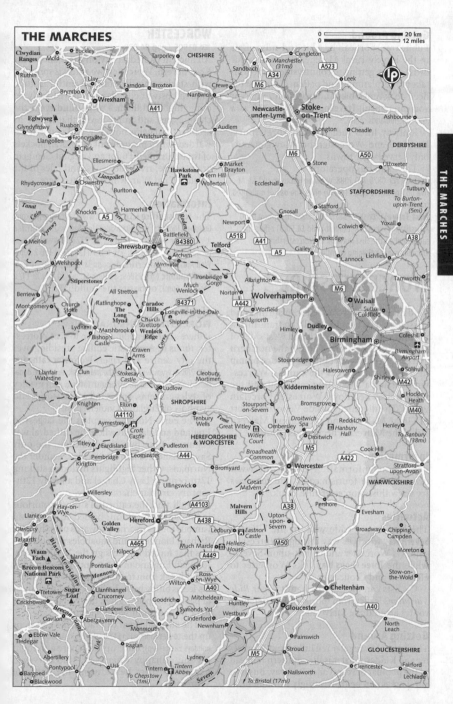

THE MARCHES

Getting Around

Public transport can be a hit-and-miss affair in the largely rural Marches. Without your own wheels, getting to countryside attractions takes time, planning and patience. Tourist offices stock timetables for most rural routes, or you can consult **Traveline** (☎ 0870 608 2608; www.travelinemidlands.co.uk).

Railway lines radiate from Shrewsbury, Hereford and Worcester, but they generally only serve larger towns.

The main bus operators:

Arriva (☎ 0870 120 1088; www.arrivabus.co.uk) An Arriva Go Anywhere ticket (£6.50) gives one day of unlimited travel.

First Travel (☎ 0800 587 7381; www.firstgroup.com) A FirstDay Wyvern ticket (adult/child £4.50/3) offers the same deal on the First network in Worcestershire, Herefordshire and adjoining counties.

WORCESTERSHIRE

Verdant hills honeycombed with springs and crisscrossed by beautiful walking trails thrust up alluringly over the south and west sides of serene Worcestershire. Though the northern and eastern plains offer little to visitors, plump in its regional heart is the capital, Worcester, boasting a fascinating cathedral and the world-renowned Royal Worcester Porcelain works. The dignified hillside Victorian resort of Great Malvern and the rolling Malvern Hills (the Malverns) beckon just south.

Information

For online information check out www.worcestershire-tourism.co.uk and for news try www.thisisworcestershire.co.uk.

Activities

The longest riverside walk in the UK, the **Severn Way** winds its way through Worcestershire via Worcester and Upton-upon-Severn, while the **Three Choirs Way** links Worcester to Hereford and Gloucester.

Cyclists can pick up the handy *Elgar Ride Variations* leaflet from tourist offices detailing routes around the Malverns.

Getting Around

There are a few regular rail links from Worcester and Kidderminster is the southern railhead of the popular Severn Valley Railway. Buses to rural areas can be frustratingly infrequent.

WORCESTER

☎ 01905 / pop 94,029

An ancient cathedral city on the banks of the River Severn, Worcester (*woos*-ter) is sprinkled with stark reminders of its eventful history, though postwar city planners have hardly set out to highlight them. Turn a blind eye to the chain stores and multistoreys that nuzzle its architectural gems however, and you'll be rewarded with a magnificent cathedral, pockets of timber-framed Tudor and elegant Georgian architecture, riverside walks, and tales of the English Civil War, which finished here.

Information

The **tourist office** (☎ 726311; www.visitworcester.com; Guildhall, High St; ◷ 9.30am-5pm Mon-Sat) will organise 1½-hour **walking tours** (☎ 222117; www.worcesterwalks.co.uk; adult £3; ◷ tours 11am Mon-Fri, 2.30pm Wed Apr-Sep). Internet access is available at **Coffee Republic** (☎ 25069; 31 High St; per 20 min/hr £1/3; ◷ 7am-6pm), opposite the Guildhall.

Sights
WORCESTER CATHEDRAL

If there's one overriding reason to visit Worcester, *this* is it. A majestic edifice presiding over the city centre and river, **Worcester Cathedral** (☎ 28854; www.worcestercathedral.org.uk; suggested donation £3; ◷ 7.30am-6pm) amalgamates a rich medley of styles and eras, and is full of the stories and symbols of England's violent past.

The eerie Norman crypt is the largest in England and dates to when the cathedral was begun in 1084 by Saint Wulfstan, the only Saxon bishop to hang on to his see under the Normans. Other highlights include a striking 13th-century Lady Chapel and a lovely 12th-century circular chapterhouse.

You'll find the cathedral's most notorious inhabitant, King John, buried in the choir. Famous for his treachery towards older brother Richard Lionheart, and squabbles with the barons that forced him to sign the Magna Carta, John left England in chaos and in a somewhat fitting break from tradition the stone lion under his feet is biting back. To boost his slim chances of passing the pearly gates, the dying king asked to be buried disguised as a monk.

The strong legged can tackle the 249 steps up the **tower** (admission £1.50; ◷ 10am-4pm Sat & school holidays Easter-Sep); once up top, spare a thought for the unhappy Charles II, who surveyed his troops from here during the Battle of Worcester.

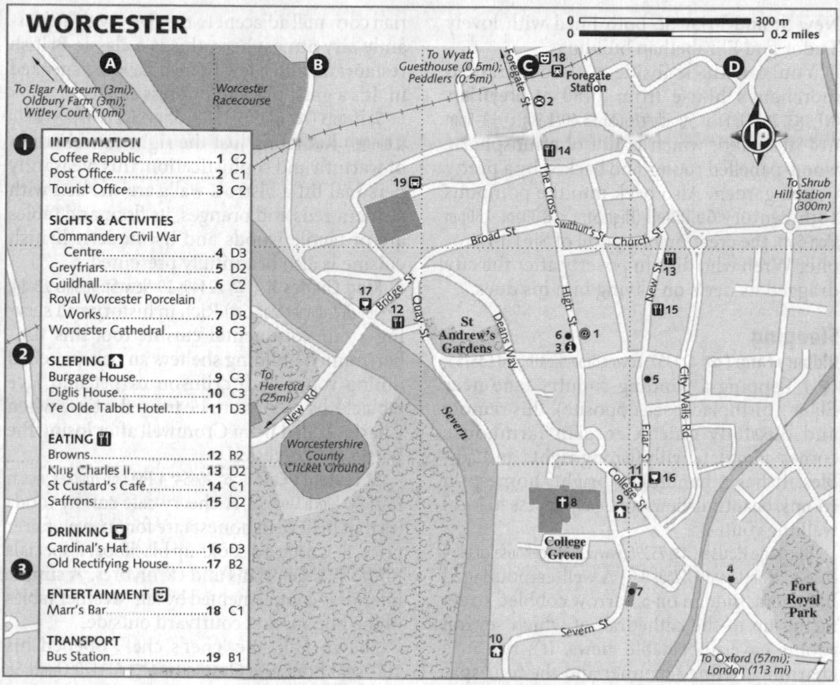

One-hour long **cathedral tours** (adult/child £3/free) run from the gift shop at 11am and 2pm daily Monday to Saturday from April to September. Evensong is a splendid affair; it's held at 5.30pm Monday to Wednesday, Friday and Saturday, and at 4pm Sunday.

COMMANDERY CIVIL WAR CENTRE

Set to reopen after a major overhaul in early 2007, the **Commandery** (☎ 361821; www.worcestercitymuseums.org.uk; adult/child £4/3; 🕑 10am-5pm Mon-Sat) is a splendid Tudor building with a painted chamber containing important frescoes from the 15th century. It also houses exhibits detailing the ins and outs of the Civil War; the city was a key Royalist stronghold until defeat in the 1651 Battle of Worcester.

ROYAL WORCESTER PORCELAIN WORKS

This venerated old-timer of British porcelain manufacture has come a long way since founder Dr John Wall started making ornate bone china as a hobby in 1751. Granted a royal warrant in 1789, the factory still supplies Her Royal Highness (HRH) with some of her preferred crockery, and now runs an entire visitor complex to promote its wares.

Worth visiting even for those that aren't potty about pottery, the **Worcester Porcelain Museum** (☎ 746000; www.worcesterporcelainmuseum.org.uk; Severn St; adult/concession £5/4.25; 🕑 10am-5.30pm Mon-Sat, 11am-5pm Sun) enlivens its exhaustive collection of works with quirky asides detailing everything from the china's use by British Royals to the factory's sidelines in porcelain dentures and 'portable fonts' designed for cholera outbreaks. Entry includes an audio tour.

The enjoyable **Visitor Experience Tour** (adult/concession £5/4.25; 🕑 10am-5.30pm Mon-Sat, 11am-5pm Sun) walks visitors through the porcelain's design and manufacture. Combined tickets for the museum and tour cost £9/8 per adult/child.

You can browse the bewildering array of porcelain goodies in the onsite **shops**, from the daintiest traditional dinnerware to 'Cheeky Mugs' by Naked Chef Jamie Oliver.

HISTORICAL PROPERTIES

For more of Worcester's bulldozer-dodging buildings of old, stroll through the idyllic cathedral-side College Green, then amble down

New St and Friar St, both lined with lovely Tudor and Elizabethan buildings.

You can duck inside a timber-framed merchant's house from 1480 at **Greyfriars** (NT; ☎ 23571; Friar St; adult/child £3.60/1.90; ۞ 1-5pm Wed-Sat Mar-Dec), which is full of atmospheric wood-panelled rooms and backed by a pretty walled garden. Also peek into the pompous 18th-century **Guildhall** (High St; ۞ 8.30am-4.30pm Mon-Sat), the creation of a pupil of Sir Christopher Wren who died in poverty after the city dragged its heels on paying him his dues.

Sleeping

Oldbury Farm (☎ 421357; Lower Broadheath; s/d £35/55; P) Topping a winding country lane near Elgar's birthplace (see opposite), this remote and blissfully quiet Georgian farmhouse comes complete with fishing rights and stables. It has a handful of bright, homespun rooms, beautiful views and easy access to local walking routes.

Burgage House (☎ 25396; www.burgagehouse.co.uk; 4 College Precincts; s/d £35/60; ✕) A well-camouflaged little gem, hidden on a narrow cobbled street facing up to the cathedral, of which several rooms have unbeatable views. It's run in a charming, refined manner and the four spacious and elegantly decorated en suite rooms are up a spiral staircase. Family friendly.

Ye Olde Talbot Hotel (☎ 23573; www.oldenglish .co.uk; Friar St; s/d £65/85; ✕) Attached to a popular bar and bistro bang in the town centre, this thoroughly renovated period inn is pretty good value. Rooms sport rich fabrics, deep colours, modern gadgets and an occasional smattering of antique features. Discounted parking is available nearby.

Diglis House (☎ 353518; www.diglishousehotel .co.uk; Severn St; s/d Fri-Sun from £75/90, Mon-Thu £90/100; P ✕ ♿) This polished 18th-century abode with a lovely terraced garden idyllically set by the river is surprisingly tranquil despite being a short stroll from town and close to a school. For name-droppers, the artist Constable was another visitor here.

Another option:

Wyatt Guesthouse (☎ 26311; wyatt.guest@virgin .net; 40 Barbourne Rd; s/d £32/50; ✕) Victorian house with eight pleasant bedrooms (one for smokers, three for families), half a mile north of the centre.

Eating

Browns (☎ 26263; 24 Quay St; mains £9.50-17, set dinner £33.50; ۞ Tue-Sun) Housed in a converted Victorian corn mill adjacent to the river, with a pleasantly airy atmosphere, this is a classic British restaurant with a few French flavours sneaked in. It's a great place to impress a date.

Saffrons (☎ 610505; 15 New St; meals £13-17; ۞ lunch & dinner) Radiating just the right combination of warmth and sophistication, this pleasantly personal little bistro's walls are washed with strident reds and oranges, its floor and tables are of tactile woods and its modern British cuisine is also beautifully presented.

King Charles II (☎ 22449; 29 New St; mains £8-14; ۞ lunch & dinner Mon-Sat) Rich in history and serving a fair continental cuisine too, this timber-framed building shelters an oak-panelled dining room with crimson carpet and lace tablecloths thought to be from the time when Charles II fled from Cromwell after losing the Battle of Worcester.

St Custard's Café (☎ 26654; 4 The hop market; mains £6-7; ۞ lunch Mon-Sat) A cheery café run by foodies that believe in honest fare for an even fairer price, St Custard's cooks up blackboard specials for both vegetarians and carnivores. A simple interior is complemented by fair-weather tables in the hop market courtyard outside.

Shawn Hill, the 'chef's chef', opened his 100-seat brasserie **Glasshouse** (☎ 611120; Church St; mains £13-18, 2/3 course set lunch £10-14; ۞ daily) in late 2006. Early reviews look promising.

Drinking

Cardinal's Hat (☎ 22066; 31 Friar St) At first glance a traditional old-English pub, split into several snug old-world rooms, this atmospheric Worcester institution now has a decidedly Austrian flavour. It sells Austrian beers in traditional steins and flutes and a choice of Austrian food at lunchtime.

Old Rectifying House (☎ 619622; www.theoldrec .co.uk; North Pde; ۞ noon-1am) This multigabled riverside pile has a laid-back lounge bar over a chic restaurant; a beers, cider and real ales list as long as your arm; bangers-and-mash bar food; and DJs playing chill-out music on weekends.

Entertainment

Marr's Bar (☎ 613336; www.marrsbar.co.uk; 12 Pierpoint St) The best live music venue for miles around, Marr's still has its original sprung dance floors from its days as a dance studio and you can bounce on them to your heart's content most nights thanks to packed listings. Gigs range from hard rock to world music.

If sport is your thing you can catch spring and summer racing at **Worcester Racecourse** (☎ 0870 220 2772; www.worcester-racecourse.co.uk), while the central **Worcestershire County Cricket Ground** (☎ 337921; www.wccc.co.uk) is a lovely spot to cheer on the chaps

Getting There & Around

Worcester has two stations but most trains run to Worcester Foregate (the other is Worcester Shrub Hill). Trains run hourly to London Paddington (£29.90, 2¼ to three hours) and Hereford (£8.40, 43 to 50 minutes).

National Express has several daily coaches to London changing in Birmingham (£18.30, four hours). Bus 44 runs twice-hourly to Great Malvern (30 minutes), bus 364 goes to Upton (30 minutes) hourly, and bus 417 goes to Ledbury (50 minutes, five daily Monday to Saturday).

Bikes can be hired from **Peddlers** (☎ 24238; 46 Barbourne Rd; per day from £8).

AROUND WORCESTER
Elgar Birthplace Museum

Due pomp and circumstance is given to England's greatest classical composer at the **Elgar Museum** (☎ 01905-333224; www.elgarmuseum .org; Lower Broadheath; adult/child £5/2; ☉ 11am-5pm), partly housed in the humble cottage in which he was born in 1857, 3 miles west of Worcester. You can browse through an engrossing collection of the walrus-moustachioed composer's possessions, which range from his gramophone and musical manuscripts to endearing doodlings in the morning paper. Admission includes an audio tour with musical interludes so you can appreciate what all the fuss is really about.

Buses 310, 311 and 312 go from Worcester to Broadheath Common, a short walk from the museum (15 minutes, three times Monday to Saturday).

Witley Court

One of the country's most romantic ruins, **Witley Court** (EH; ☎ 01299-896636; Great Witley; adult/ under 5/5-15yr £5.20/free/2.60; ☉ 10am-5pm Mar-Oct, 10am-4pm Thu-Mon Nov-Feb) was a lavish Italianate mid-19th-century home left to moulder after a disastrous fire in 1937. It now acts as a stunning folly crowning the Victorian splendour of its restored landscaped grounds. The spectacular Perseus and Andromeda fountain is one of Europe's biggest.

Don't miss the glittering gilded-plaster interior at the neighbouring **Great Witley Church** (www.greatwitleychurch.org.uk), the most magnificent Baroque church in England. It's home to paintings by Bellucci and a glorious organ that composer Handel once played.

Bus 758 from Worcester to Tenbury Wells passes eight times daily (55 minutes).

Droitwich Spa & Around

Home to brine springs around 10 times stronger than sea water, Droitwich has been the centre of England's salt industry since the Iron Age. Then in the 19th century the town opened brine baths, transforming itself into a fashionable spa town. Today there are still public baths and several elaborate medieval buildings worth seeing.

Housed in the former brine baths, the **tourist office** doubles as the town's **Heritage Centre** (☎ 01905-774312; Victoria Sq; ☉ 10am-4pm Mon-Sat).

The area's biggest attraction is stately home **Hanbury Hall** (NT; ☎ 01527-821214; School Rd; adult/child £6/3; ☉ 1-5pm Sat-Wed Mar-Oct), 4 miles east of Droitwich Spa. Built in 1701, the house is famed for its painted ceilings and elaborate staircase and stunning grounds.

To Droitwich Spa's west, **Ombersley** is the kind of picture-postcard village you'd like to stick a stamp on and post home for granny. Its magpie black-and-white main road is studded with excellent pubs and eateries that include the wonderful **Venture In** (☎ 01905-620552; Main Rd; 3-course lunch/dinner £21.50/31.50; ☉ lunch & dinner Tue-Sat, lunch Sun), serving modern British cuisine in a supposedly haunted building dating from 1430.

Bus 144 runs to Worcester (25 minutes) every 20 minutes.

Redditch

Now a rather featureless dormitory town to big brother Birmingham, Victorian Redditch once dominated the world's needle trade, and the fascinating and often grisly tale is told in the lively **Forge Mill Needle Museum & Bordesley Abbey Visitor Centre** (☎ 01527-62509; Needle Mill Lane; adult/child £3.80/65p; ☉ 11am-4.30pm Mon-Fri & 2-5pm Sat & Sun Easter-Sep), where the original water-powered machinery still runs on weekends. The museum sits in the riverside grounds of ruined 12th-century Bordesley Abbey.

Bus 350 goes direct to Worcester (55 minutes) three times daily; at other times change in Bromsgrove (15 minutes).

THE MARCHES

GREAT MALVERN

☎ 01684 / pop 35,558

Tumbling picturesquely down the slopes of the gorgeous Malvern Hills, which soar suddenly upwards from the flat plains of Worcestershire, this well-heeled Victorian spa town still seems to exude health and wellbeing courtesy of its lush hill views, wide tree-lined avenues, rosy-cheeked inhabitants, booted hikers and its pure spring waters that bubble up in unexpected places. Today the medicinal waters that first attracted overindulgent Victorians are harnessed for a thriving bottled-water business.

The **tourist office** (☎ 892289; www.malvernhills .gov.uk; 21 Church St; ☉ 10am-5pm) is brimming with walking and cycling information. Guided tours of the town (£3, 1½ hours) leave here at 10.30am on weekends. The **Library** (☎ 566553; Graham Rd; ☉ 9.30am-5.30pm Mon, Fri-Sat & 9.30am-8pm Tue-Thu) has free internet access: bring ID.

In June the town goes music mad in the biannual **Elgar Festival** (☎ 892277; www.elgar-festival .com) to celebrate the life and works of the composer who lived nearby at Malvern Link.

Sights & Activities

MALVERN PRIORY

A treat even for those tired of England's draughty churches, the 11th-century **priory church** (☎ 561020; www.greatmalvernpriory.org.uk; Church St; suggested donation £3; ☉ 9am-6.30pm Apr-Oct, 9am-4.30pm Nov-Mar) is lined by elephantine Norman pillars and shelters an entrancing collection of weird and wonderful 14th-century misericords under the tip-up seats of the monks' stalls. Every one a gem, they depict everything from three rats hanging a cat to the mythological basilisk, and run through domestic labours of the months from the 15th century.

MALVERN MUSEUM OF LOCAL HISTORY

Straddling the pathway in the grand Priory Gatehouse (1470), the **Malvern Museum of Local History** (☎ 567811; adult/child 1.50/50p; ☉ 10.30am-5pm Easter-Oct, except Wed during school term) offers a small but thorough exploration of the things for which Great Malvern is renowned, from hills' geology to Victorian water cures.

MALVERN THEATRES

One of the country's best provincial theatres, **Malvern Theatre** (☎ 892277; www.malvern-theatres.co.uk; Grange Rd) packs in a lively programme of classical music, dance, comedy, drama and cinema.

Occupying a strange parallel universe in a converted Victorian men's lavatory decked out in theatrical Italianate flourishes, the **Theatre of Small Convenience** (☎ 568933; www.wctheatre .co.uk; Edith Walk) is one of the world's smallest theatres, seating just 12 people for acts that range from puppetry to opera.

WALKING

The jack-in-the-box Malvern Hills, which pop dramatically up out of the innocently low Severn plains on the boundary between Worcestershire and Herefordshire, are made up of 18 named peaks; highest of the bunch being Worcester Beacon at 419m. The hills are crisscrossed by more than 100 miles of paths; trail guides (£1.75) are available at the tourist office. More than 70 springs and fountains pouring out the famous medicinal waters are dotted around the hills, and the tourist office has a map guide (£3.95) to all of them.

Sleeping

Como House (☎ 561486; www.comohouse.co.uk; Como Rd; s/d £36/56; ⓟ ☒ ▣ wi-fi only) An explosion of lilac greets you to this handsome Malvern-stone converted schoolhouse. All three tastefully furnished rooms are south facing and the elaborate gardens, complete with a bridged pond and numerous statues, are a stunning feature. The owner picks guests up from the station and drops them at walking points.

Cowleigh Park Farm (☎ 01684-566750; www.cow leighparkfarm.co.uk; Cowleigh Rd; s/d £45/65; ⓟ ☒) This 13th-century timber-framed farmhouse on the far northwestern brink of town is surrounded by countryside and overflows with bonhomie. You'll be greeted by friendly family dogs, and led up to oak-beamed rooms with sloping floors, tasteful furnishings and plentiful home comforts.

Bredon House Hotel (☎ 566990; www.bredonhouse hotel.co.uk; 34 Worcester Rd; s/d from £45/80; ⓟ ▣) A short saunter from the centre, this genteel Victorian B&B has superb views and courteous service. Rooms are decorated in a quirky but tasteful mix of new and old; one room even has a raised bath from which to enjoy the panorama while popping bubbles. Pets and children welcome.

Cottage in the Wood Hotel (☎ 575859; www.cot tageinthewood.co.uk; Holywell Rd, Malvern Wells; s/d from £88/135; ⓟ ☒ ▣) Something of an institution in the Malverns, this is an old-fashioned hotel swaddled by woodland, with sweeping views and a well-respected restaurant with a 600-strong wine list.

Other possibilities:

Malvern Hills YHA (☎ 0870 770 5948; malvern@yha .org.uk; 18 Peachfield Rd, Malvern Wells; dm £10.95; ☺ Easter-Oct) Muddy boots welcome at this 58-bed hostel in an elegant Edwardian building, 1½ miles south.

Copper Beech (☎ 565013; www.copperbeechhouse .co.uk; 32 Avenue Rd; s/d from £43/70; P ✗) Wonderful guesthouse, run by a young family in a dignified late-Victorian house, a 15-minute walk (about 1 mile) from the town centre.

Eating

St Ann's Well Cafe (☎ 560285; St Ann's Well; ☺ lunch Apr-Sep, Sat & Sun only Oct-Mar) The pick of Malvern's doily-and-tea-cosy brigade is in a handsome early-19th-century villa atop a steep 99-step ascent from town. It rewards the climb with great vegetarian and vegan food, wholesome salads and eye-widening cakes, which you can wash down with fresh spring water that bubbles into a carved basin by the door.

Anupam (☎ 573814; 85 Church St; mains £8-11; ☺ lunch & dinner) This stylish Indian restaurant, tucked just off the main road, is so passionate about flavours that it has its own range of blended spices. Walls coated in primary colours, and bubbly service put guests in a cheerful mood, and superb dishes such as *murg-e-nashilee* (chicken with onion and roasted poppy seed) keep them that way.

Priors Croft (☎ 891369; Grange Rd; mains £9-13; ☺ lunch & dinner) This grand lemon-coloured mansion has sprawling terraces facing the theatre and a welcoming neo-Gothic interior. It serves drinks all day, pre-theatre suppers and has a menu that straddles the divide somewhere between pub grub and restaurant food.

Getting There & Around

There are twice-hourly trains to Worcester (12 to 18 minutes) and roughly hourly to Hereford (£5.90, 30 minutes). Trains also go regularly to Ledbury (13 minutes).

National Express runs one bus daily to London (£18.60, four hours) via Worcester (20 minutes). Bus 44 connects Worcester (30 minutes) with Great Malvern hourly.

Handy for walkers, the Malvern Hills Hopper (five daily weekends and Bank Holidays mid-April to October) runs a hop-on hop-off service through the hills to Upton-upon-Severn and Eastnor Castle.

UPTON-UPON-SEVERN
☎ 01684 / pop 1789

A lovely little town with a hodgepodge of Tudor and Georgian buildings lining its narrow meandering streets, Upton makes for a pleasant stop or a visit for the **Oliver Cromwell jazz festival** (☎ 593254; www.uptonjazz.co.uk) at the end of June.

The **tourist office** (☎ 594200; upton.tic@malvernhills .gov.uk; 4 High St; ☺ 10am-5pm Mon-Sat year-round, 10am-4pm Sun Easter-Sep) has details. Walkers and map enthusiasts should head for the **Map Shop** (☎ 593146; www.themapshop.co.uk; 15 High St), which has the best selections in the county.

The town's oldest building, a stunted tower nicknamed the 'Pepperpot' for its round-topped shape, now houses the **Heritage Centre** (☎ 592679; Church St; admission free; ☺ 1.30-4.30pm May-Sep), where displays detail the town's history. Opposite is **Tudor House** (☎ 592447; 16 Church St; adult/concession £1/50p; ☺ 2-5pm Apr-Oct), packed haphazardly with a treasure-trove of local life and history – some decidedly on the quirky side.

Sleeping & Eating

White Lion (☎ 592551; www.whitelionhotel.biz; 21 High St; s/d £70/99; P ✗ ⅋) This charming 16th-century coaching inn, famous for English Civil War connections and its place in Henry Fielding's *History of Tom Jones*, is now known just as well for its richly furnished classic rooms and its romantic oak-beamed and candle-lit restaurant (mains £15 to £19) serving excellent modern British food.

Tiltridge Vineyard (☎ 592906; www.tiltridge.com; Upper Hook Rd; s/d £40/60; P ✗) A homey farmhouse B&B connected to a thriving vineyard 1 mile west of town, Tiltridge offers little luxuries such as quaffing its award-winning tipples on the south-facing terrace, and a cracking breakfast made with freshly laid eggs, local apple juice and homemade jams. The three country-styled rooms are unpretentious, and packed lunches are available.

TOP FIVE PUBS FOR SUNDAY LUNCH

- Riverside Inn (p431; Aymestrey)
- Stagg Inn (p430; Titley)
- Three Crowns Inn (p430; Ullingswick)
- Waterdine Inn (p449; Llanfair Waterdine)
- Frog (p450; Leintwardine)

Getting There & Away

Bus 363 runs between Upton and Worcester (30 minutes) at least nine times daily from Monday to Saturday (less frequently on Sunday).

HEREFORDSHIRE

An oasis of tranquillity, rural Herefordshire is scattered with quintessentially English villages of black-and-white timbered charm, a cherished sense of community and well-developed appreciation of the quiet life. Though it's challenging to get around, the effort is rewarded with bucolic landscapes of lush fields, twisting lanes and more than enough leafy orchards to whet your appetite for the county's famous ciders. The River Wye wiggles provocatively through the county, tempting canoeists from across the country. County capital Hereford hosts the superb medieval Mappa Mundi, and tip-toeing into Wales is renowned kingdom of books, Hay-on-Wye.

Information

For online county-wide information on attractions, accommodation and events:

Visit Heart of England (www.visitheartofengland.com)
Visit Herefordshire (www.visitherefordshire.co.uk)

Activities

Herefordshire is a haven for walkers, with several established long-distance paths meandering through it (see p420). **Offa's Dyke Path** hugs the Welsh border, while the 107-mile **Wye Valley Walk** begins in Chepstow (Wales) and follows the river upstream into Herefordshire. The **Three Choirs Way** is a 100-mile route connecting the cathedrals of Hereford, Worcester and Gloucester, where the music festival of the same name has been celebrated for more than three centuries.

Newest addition to local long-distance tramps is the **Herefordshire Trail** (www.herefordshiretrail.com), a 150-mile circular loop linking Leominster, Ledbury, Ross-on-Wye and Kington.

Getting Around

Busy railway stations with nationwide links can be found at Hereford, Leominster and Ledbury. To plan your way about, pick up a free *Public Transport Map & Guide* from tourist offices and bus stations, or go online through **Hereford Bus** (www.herefordbus.info) and **National Traveline** (☎ 0870 608 2608; www.travelinemidlands.co.uk).

HEREFORD

☎ 01432 / pop 56,353

Home to one of the most extraordinary sights in England, the magnificent medieval Mappa Mundi, the dignified cathedral city of Hereford straddles the River Wye plump in the centre of its county. Known largely for its cattle, cider and connections with the composer Elgar, it has a relatively provincial feel but an increasingly youthful energy fizzles along its riverside and centre.

Orientation & Information

The triangular, pedestrianised High Town is the city's heart, just north of the River Wye. The cathedral is close to the river, while the bus and train stations lie to the northeast, on Commercial Rd.

The **tourist office** (☎ 268430; www.visitherefordshire.co.uk; 1 King St; 9am-5pm Mon-Sat) is opposite the cathedral. **Guided walks** (walks £3; 11am Mon-Sat & 2.30pm Sun May-Sep) start from here. There's free internet access at the **library** (Broad St; 9.30am-7.30pm Tue-Wed & Fri, 9.30am-5.30pm Thu, 9.30am-4pm Sat) in the same building as the Hereford Museum & Art Gallery.

Sights

HEREFORD CATHEDRAL

After the Welsh torched the town's original cathedral, the new **Hereford Cathedral** (☎ 374200; www.herefordcathedral.co.uk; 5 College Cloisters; 7.30am-Evensong) was begun on the same site in the 11th century. The building has evolved into a well-packaged lesson on the entire history of English architecture: the sturdy south transept is Norman but holds a 16th-century triptych; the exquisite north transept with its soaring windows dates from the 13th century; the choir and the tower date from the 14th; while the Victorian influence is visible almost everywhere.

But the cathedral is best known for two ancient treasures housed here. The awe-inspiring 13th-century **Mappa Mundi** (adult/child £4.50/3.50; 10am-4.15pm Mon-Sat & 11am-3.15pm Sun May-Sep, 11am-3.15pm Mon-Sat Oct-Apr) is a large calfskin vellum map intricately painted with the vivid (to modern eyes, wacky) world vision of the era's scholars and an enthralling pictorial encyclopaedia of the times. It is the largest

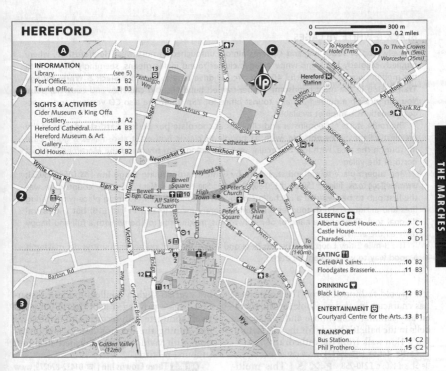

HEREFORD

0	300 m
0	0.2 miles

INFORMATION
Library..............................(see 5)
Post Office..............................**1** B2
Tourist Office..............................**2** B3

SIGHTS & ACTIVITIES
Cider Museum & King Offa
  Distillery..............................**3** A2
Hereford Cathedral..............................**4** B3
Hereford Museum & Art
  Gallery..............................**5** B2
Old House..............................**6** B2

SLEEPING
Alberta Guest House..............................**7** C1
Castle House..............................**8** C3
Charades..............................**9** D1

EATING
Café@All Saints..............................**10** B2
Floodgates Brasserie..............................**11** B3

DRINKING
Black Lion..............................**12** B3

ENTERTAINMENT
Courtyard Centre for the Arts...**13** B1

TRANSPORT
Bus Station..............................**14** C2
Phil Prothero..............................**15** C2

To Hopbine Hotel (1mi)
To Three Crowns Inn (5mi); Worcester (25km)
To Golden Valley (12mi)
To London (140mi)

THE MARCHES

and best-preserved example of this type of cartography anywhere, but more than that it's a bewitching journey through the world as then envisioned, peopled by strange beings with eyes in their chest, roamed by basilisks and mythological monsters. Navigate your way through the barely recognisable mash of continents and you can even find Hereford itself.

The same wing contains the world's largest surviving **chained library**, hooked to its shelves by a cascade of long thin shackles. The unique collection of rare books and manuscripts includes a 1217 copy of the revised Magna Carta and the 8th-century *Hereford Gospels*, although the gospels' fragility means they aren't always on display.

The cathedral comes alive with Evensong at 5.30pm Monday to Saturday and 3.30pm on Sunday, and every three years in August it holds the famous **Three Choirs Festival** (www.3choirs.org) shared with Gloucester and Worcester Cathedrals.

OTHER SIGHTS

Stranded alone amid a sea of bustling shops, the **Old House** (☎ 260694; admission free; ☉ 10am-5pm

Tue-Sat year-round, plus 10am-4pm Sun Apr-Sep) is a wonderfully creaky black-and-white, three-storey wooden house, built in 1621, panelled and furnished in exquisitely carved wood.

The quirky collection at **Hereford Museum & Art Gallery** (☎ 260692; Broad St; admission free; ☉ 10am-5pm Tue-Sat year-round, plus 10am-4pm Sun Apr-Sep) includes everything from 19th-century witches' curses to a two-headed calf. There are hands-on antiquities boxes and dressing-up gear to keep kids engaged.

Don't forget to claim your free samples in the **Cider Museum & King Offa Distillery** (☎ 354207; www.cidermuseum.co.uk; Pomona Pl; adult/child £3/2; ☉ 10am-5pm Tue-Sat Apr-Oct, 11am-3pm Tue-Sat Nov-Mar), which explores cider-making history. Look for the fine costrels (mini barrels) and horn mugs used by agricultural workers to carry and quaff their wages, which were partially paid in cider.

Sleeping

Charades (☎ 269444; www.charadeshereford.co.uk; 34 Southbank Rd; s/d £45/65; P ✗) This fine old Georgian gentleman's residence built around 1860 has five light, cosy rooms with slightly

THE MARCHES

BLACK-&-WHITE VILLAGES

A lovely loop of Tudor England survives almost untouched in northwest Herefordshire, where higgledy-piggledy black-and-white villages cluster round idyllic greens, seemingly oblivious to the modern world. A wonderful 40-mile circular drive here follows the **Black & White Village Trail**, taking in the most handsome timber-framed buildings, old churches and convivial pubs. You can pick up a guide from any tourist office for 75p (there are also CD versions and an accommodations pamphlet available).

The route starts at Leominster and climaxes at chocolate-box perfect **Eardisland**. One of the prettiest villages is **Pembridge**, with its huddle of classic houses; it also makes a good base for touring the area, with lots of circular walks radiating from town and the Mortimer Trail just north of the village.

One superb place to eat and stay close by is the award-winning **Stagg Inn** (☎ 01544-230221; www.thestagg.co.uk; Titley; s £50-60, d £70-90; ☺ closed Sun evening & Mon). This cosy country inn was the first pub to be awarded a Michelin star, and is a wonderfully welcoming place with roaring fires and antiques, stylish touches and contemporary menu (mains £11 to £16) but with a traditional soul. They offer a handful of lovely rooms, making the roll home with a full and happy belly all the easier.

The 3-mile Titley Loop Walk begins here and winds through gorgeous countryside, making it a good way to work up an appetite.

---

frumpy old-fashioned décor. The house itself has character in spades – look for the suspiciously familiar dolls house and old service bells in the hall. It's handy for the bus station, but a 1km walk from the cathedral.

Castle House (☎ 356321; www.castlehse.co.uk; Castle St; s £120, d £210-258; P ☒ ☖) This multi-award-winning and oh-so-refined Georgian town house, once the bishop's residence, is Hereford's best boutique hotel. Rooms have rich fabrics, classic décor with a modern twist, there's a lovely garden and riverside seating, as well as a seriously sophisticated restaurant with an innovative chef.

Other possibilities:

Alberta Guest House (☎ 270313; www.thealbertaguesthouse.co.uk; 7/13 Newtown Rd; s/d £30/50; P ☒) Simple but warm welcome in the town's north.

Hopbine Hotel (☎ 268722; www.hopbine.com; Roman Rd; s/d £35/50; P) Family-run hotel in grassy grounds a mile northeast of town.

Eating

Café@All Saints (☎ 370414; www.cafeatallsaints.co.uk; High St; mains £4.75-6; ☺ lunch) Trade nods with the clergy and sit up among lofty stone arches as you sip fair-trade coffee or wolf down superbly wholesome (mostly vegetarian) lunches in this natty two-level café at the rear of a working church. You can even enjoy a glass of wine – just remember, God's watching.

Floodgates Brasserie (☎ 349000; Left Bank Centre, Bridge St; mains £10-15; ☺ lunch & dinner) This sleek but ever-so-slightly soulless modern restaurant bags a privileged spot overlooking the river, complete with terrace; and if the sun's not shining the interior does a fair imitation, with vivid colours, polished steel and sunburst motifs.

our pick Three Crowns Inn (☎ 01432-820279; www.threecrownsinn.com; Ullingswick; mains £15-20; ☺ lunch & dinner Tue-Sun) Buried deep in the countryside 5 miles northeast of Hereford, this gorgeous 16th-century half-timbered gastropub is worth seeking out for its exquisite organic food, rare-breed meats and homemade cheese. It also has classy rooms (singles/doubles £80/95).

Drinking & Entertainment

Black Lion (☎ 343535; 31 Bridge St) The more real ales and local ciders you imbibe in this traditional pub, the more you may believe the tales of 14 resident ghosts from the site's history as a monastery, an orphanage, a brothel and even a Chinese restaurant – presumably a colourful crew. Ghosts aside, it's one of the friendliest inns in the area and often stages live gigs.

Courtyard Centre for the Arts (☎ 0870 112 2330; www.courtyard.org.uk; Edgar St) This lively arts centre has two venues staging a busy schedule of comedy, theatre, film and poetry.

Getting There & Around

Hire bikes at **Phil Prothero** (☎ 359478; Bastion Mews) for £12 per day.

There are hourly trains to London Paddington (£35, 3¼ hours) via Worcester (£8.40, 45 minutes); and to Birmingham (£11.80, 1½ hours). National Express goes to London (£18.60, 4¼ hours, three daily), Heathrow (£18.60, 3¼ hours, three daily), Gloucester (£5, 1¼ hours, three daily) and Ross-on-Wye (30 minutes, two daily) or Ledbury (25 minutes, two daily).

From the bus station, bus 420 runs every two hours to Worcester (1¼ hours). Bus 38 runs hourly to Ross-on-Wye (40 minutes, six on Sunday), and 476 goes hourly to Ledbury (30 minutes, five on Sunday) – both from the bus station on Commercial Rd.

AROUND HEREFORD
Golden Valley

Nestling at the foot of the Black Mountains, this lush valley is more green than gold, taking its name from the meandering River Dore. It was made famous by children's author CS Lewis of *Narnia* acclaim and the film that sought to portray him, *Shadowlands*. A sprinkling of historical ruins peppers its gently undulating vistas.

For more details or accommodation ideas, see www.golden-valley.co.uk.

Aymestrey & Around

Two miles east of the pocket-sized village of Aymestrey, and beyond all hope of a bus, is castellated country house **Croft Castle** (NT; ☎ 01568-780246; off the B4362; adult/child £5/2.50; ⊙ 1-5pm Wed-Sun Apr-Sep, 1-4.30pm Sat & Sun Mar & Oct), worth the trip if flamboyant 18th-century interiors flick your switch.

our pick **Riverside Inn** (☎ 01568-708440; www.the riversideinn.org; Aymestrey; s/d £40/65; P ✕), in Aymestrey itself, is a classic 16th-century black-and-white coaching inn nudging the gurgling River Lugg. Hop-strewn beams and red lamps mellow the bar and restaurant and it has a handful of cosy bedrooms containing sturdy wooden furniture and rough walls. The modern British menu (mains £11 to £16) uses overwhelmingly local produce, much of it freshly plucked from the inn's own garden. Walkers should note that this place is about midway along the Mortimer Trail and it makes a wonderful stopover or a thirst-quenching pause to indulge in their real local ale.

Aymestrey is on the A4110, 15 miles north of Hereford.

Kilpeck Church

A passionate couple, Disney-esque animals and a famous spread-legged *sheila-na-gig* (Celtic fertility figure) are just some of the extraordinary 12th-century carvings that ring this enchanting gem of a church, buried deep in the Herefordshire countryside in the tiny hamlet of Kilpeck. Astonishingly, the church remains practically unchanged since the 12th century and is well worth the 1-mile trip south of the main A465 road that comes from Hereford. Kilpeck is 9 miles south of Hereford, off the A465.

HAY-ON-WYE
☎ 01497 / pop 1450

Your inner bookworm will wriggle with joy upon discovery of Hay-on-Wye: this tightly knotted little border town is totally given over to the second-hand book trade and is the spiritual home of eagle-eyed collectors, casual browsers and burrowing academics the world over. That said, it's not just for bibliophiles but anyone who enjoys a good riffle through everything from whodunits to Who's Who, Marvel comics to marvellous antique maps.

The town straddles the border with Wales and on 1 April 1977 famously declared itself independent from Britain, kicking up a thunderous media storm that echoed internationally (see boxed text, p433). Every year for a week in May/June the town becomes the centre of the literary universe for the **Hay Festival of Literature** (www.hayfestival.com), which keynote speaker Bill Clinton once dubbed the 'Woodstock of the Mind'.

The **tourist office** (☎ 820144; www.hay-on-wye.co.uk; Oxford Rd; ☷ 10am-1pm & 2-5pm Easter-Oct, 11am-1pm & 2-4pm Nov-Easter) is by the main car park. It has a couple of internet terminals (per 15 minutes 75p).

Activities

Hay sits on the northeastern corner of Brecon Beacons National Park and makes an excellent base to explore western Herefordshire and the Welsh Black Mountains. The **Offa's Dyke** walking route (see p420) passes nearby. The Offa's Dyke Flyer circular minibus runs three times on summer Sundays and Bank Holidays to help you along the way. The tourist office has schedules.

For fun on the River Wye, hire kayaks and Canadian canoes from **Paddles & Pedals** (☎ 820604; www.canoehire.co.uk; 15 Castle St; canoes per half-/full day £22.50/35, kayaks £15/20; ☷ Easter-Oct), which, despite the name, doesn't do bikes. Rental prices include return transport to points along the Wye, depending on which route you're taking.

Shopping

The tourist office and most shops stock the handy pamphlet guide to the town's three dozen bookshops, from 'Murder and Mayhem' to 'Rare Comics and Cards'. Most famous is **Booth's Bookshop** (☎ 820322; www.richardbooth.demon.co.uk; 44 Lion St; ☷ 9am-8pm Mon-Sat, 11.30am-5.30pm Sun Apr-Oct 9am-8pm Mon, Fri & Sat, 11.30am-5.30pm Sun, 9am-5.30pm Tue-Thu Nov-Mar), which supposedly has the highest turnover of second-hand books of any bookshop in the world. A smaller specialist arm is housed in a Jacobean mansion built into the walls of the battered 13th-century town castle.

Sleeping

Don't bet on a bed *anyplace* nearby while the festival is on.

Start (☎ 821391; www.the-start.net; Hay Bridge; s/d £35/60; P ☒) A winner for position, this solitary 18th-century stone cottage stands on the opposite riverbank, affording it a blissful feeling of isolation despite being but a short scenic walk across. Patchwork quilts adorn the pleasant country-style rooms, some with a view of the river, and there are good lock-up and drying facilities for hikers and bikers.

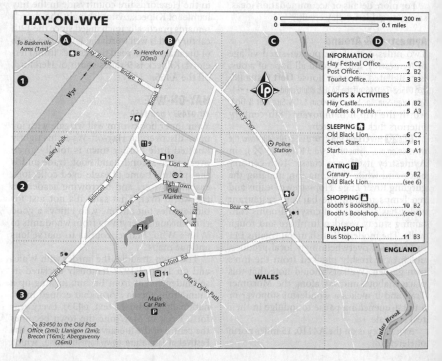

HAY-ON-WYE

0 .... 200 m
0 .... 0.1 miles

To Baskerville Arms (1mi)
Hay Bridge
To Hereford (20mi)
Bridge St
Wye
Broad St
Heol-y-Dwr
Police Station
Lion St
Bailey Walk
The Pavement
High Town Old Market
Belmont Rd
Castle St
Castle La
Bell Bank
Bear St
Lion St
Church St
Oxford Rd
Offa's Dyke Path
Main Car Park P
WALES
ENGLAND
Dulas Brook

To B3450 to the Old Post Office (2mi); Llanigon (2mi); Brecon (16mi); Abergavenny (26mi)

THE MARCHES

KING OF HAY-ON-WYE

King of the world's first book town, Richard Booth opened his first bookshop in Hay in 1961 but was dismayed by the falling fortunes and declining populations of rural areas. Not content to sit back and watch, he hatched a wacky plan to regenerate the town.

By 1977 he had persuaded a clutch of other booksellers to join him and on April Fools' Day of that year declared the border town independent from Britain. The town celebrated with a giant party as Booth was crowned in royal robes, orb and a sceptre made from an old ball cock and copper piping. As weird as the idea was, it had the desired effect and Hay hit the headlines all over the country.

Almost 30 years on, Hay has more bookshops than even the most dedicated bibliophile can handle and a host of thriving local businesses catering to the five million visitors a year. It has also been the inspiration for roughly 20 other international book towns, often in rural areas facing similar decline.

Aspiring lords and ladies can even apply for Hay Peerage, awarded by the king himself. See www.haypeerage.ukhome.net for information.

Seven Stars (☎ 820886; www.theseven-stars.co.uk; 11 Broad St; s/d £40/65; P ✕ ☲) A comely 16th-century house with chunky stone walls, sloping floor and, surprise, a heated indoor swimming pool and sauna! If that's not enough to help ease hikers' aching muscles, this central eight-room guesthouse can arrange massage. The homey rooms are free from airs and graces, and the breakfasts are hearty.

Old Post Office (☎ 820008; www.oldpost-office.co.uk; Llanigon; s £35, d £50-70; P ✕) One for walkers or those with wheels, this gorgeous converted village post office, 2 miles southwest of Hay off the B4350, is worth the extra legwork for its character-rich polished-oak floors, exposed beams, earthy colour scheme and rural Welsh furniture. Breakfasts are vegetarian: no artery-clogging meat feasts here.

Old Black Lion (☎ 820841; www.oldblacklion.co.uk; Lion St; s/d £50/85; P ✕) A succession of blackened oak beams give the low ceilings of this fabulous 17th-century inn the look of an up-turned zebra crossing. The low-lit restaurant is the best in town, while the spacious bedrooms feature thick, richly textured fabrics, darkly impressive antique furniture and show-stealing teddy bears.

Eating

Old Black Lion (☎ 820841; Lion St; mains £12-18; ☯ lunch & dinner) For quality food and atmosphere thick enough to cut with a knife, this famous old inn's candle-lit dining room with hops hanging from its low-beamed ceiling, stripped-pine tables, local ales and a memorable menu including wonderful locally sourced lamb.

Granary (☎ 820790; Broad St; mains £5-10; ☯ 10am-5pm) True to its name, this wholesome café-restaurant is housed in a converted grain-store, complete with rustic stone walls, high loading door and protruding arm. The home-style food features local cheeses, smoked fish, tummy-rumbling cakes and various vegetarian and vegan dishes.

Baskerville Arms (☎ 821609; www.baskervillearms .co.uk; Clyro; mains £7-12; ☯ lunch & dinner) This country hotel, just over a mile northwest of Hay, has a good French chef, welcoming staff and lovely views of the countryside. It lights up a log fire in winter and candles on the tables at night.

Getting There & Away

If you're driving, allow time to cruise, because the countryside is spellbinding.

Bus 39 from Hereford (55 minutes) and from Brecon (45 minutes) runs roughly every two hours Monday to Saturday. At the time of writing, bus 40 had three services on Sunday but may be cancelled in late 2006.

ROSS-ON-WYE
☎ 01989 / pop 10,085

Snoozy little Ross-on-Wye, which perches prettily on a red sandstone bluff over a kink in the River Wye, is a placid place to rest before or after exertions in the beautiful countryside that surrounds it. The town sparks to life in mid-August, when the International Festival brings fireworks, raft races, music and street theatre.

The salmon-pink 17th-century Market House sits atop its weathered sandstone columns in the Market Place. It still shelters

SOMETHING SPECIAL

Penrhos Court (☎ 01544 230720; www.penrhos.co.uk; Kington; 4-course menu £35; P ✗) A cosy over-grown charm exudes from this 13th-century half-timbered farm, which has a few footy field–sized rooms (singles/doubles from £85/110) overlooking tranquil countryside and some boasting terraces. The hotel is so passionate about garden-fresh organic food that it runs residential cookery courses, and everything revolves around the great medieval Cruck Hall dining room, which is thick with oak beams, and graced by chunky wooden furniture, flagstoned floors and a colossal fireplace. Dishes are largely vegetarian, but good enough to convert any carnivore. Advance booking is essential. Kington is about 12 miles north of Hay-on-Wye.

the small market in a motherly fashion. It contains a **Heritage Centre** (☎ 260675; ⓨ 10am-5pm Apr-Oct, 10.30am-4pm Mon-Sat Nov-Mar) with local history displays. The **tourist office** (☎ 562768; tic-ross@herefordshire.gov.uk; Edde Cross St; ⓨ 9am-5pm Mon-Sat) has information on activities and walks.

Sleeping & Eating

Linden House (☎ 565373; www.lindenguesthouse.com; 14 Church St; s/d without bathroom £32/58, with bathroom £45/65; P ✗) Window boxes splash colour across this handsome 17th-century town house B&B. The beautifully furnished rooms are equally vivid, painted with cute stencilling and some sporting exposed beams and brass beds. It's run by a trained hypnotherapist who'll happily offer her services for a good night's sleep.

Bridge House Hotel & Restaurant (☎ 562655; www.bridge-house-hotel.com; Wilton; s/d from £65/96; P ✗) A dignified Georgian country house, a riverside setting a short tumble down from town, and a praised modern British restaurant (mains £12 to £20) dedicated to local produce make this an affable place to linger. Eight classically styled rooms overlook the gardens and river.

Nature's Choice (☎ 763454; www.natures-choice.biz; 17 Broad St; mains £4.50-6; ⓨ 10am-5pm Mon-Wed, 10am-5pm & 6.15-9pm Thu-Sat) This bright little organic café in a Regency-style building has wholesome home-baked and light meals for carnivore, vegetarian and vegan alike. It also offers ecofriendly B&B (singles/doubles £42/60), with cute rooms in pastel shades; breakfast costs extra but it's worth it.

The closest hostel is 6 miles south at Welsh Bicknor (see right).

Drinking

Riverside Inn (☎ 564688; Wye St) This lively pub makes an idyllic base on a summer evening, its outdoor decking adjoining a grassy expanse by the river, where children and dogs scamper at will.

Getting There & Around

Buses 38 and 33 run hourly Monday to Saturday to and from Hereford and Gloucester respectively (40 minutes each way).

You can hire bikes from **Revolutions** (☎ 562 639; 48 Broad St; per day from £10).

AROUND ROSS-ON-WYE
Goodrich

Seeming to sprout organically from its craggy bedrock, **Goodrich Castle** (EH; ☎ 01600-890538; adult/child £4.50/2.30; ⓨ 10am-5pm Apr-Oct, 10am-4pm Thu-Mon Nov-Feb) is an exceptionally complete medieval castle, topped by a superb 12th-century keep that rewards the trek up tight winding staircases with spectacular views. Don't miss clambering around the ramparts or sticking your head into 'Roaring Meg', the squat mortar cannon that breached these mighty walls during the English Civil War.

Welsh Bicknor YHA (☎ 0870 770 6086; welshbicknor@yha.org.uk; dm £13.95; ⓨ Apr-Oct; P ✗) is well worth the steep 1½-mile ascent to reach it from Goodrich village. This former Victorian rectory enjoys glorious views and languishes amid 10 hectares of lovely riverside grounds. The Wye Valley Walk passes the hostel.

Goodrich is 5 miles south of Ross off the A40. Bus 34 stops here every two hours on its way between Ross (15 minutes) and Monmouth (20 minutes).

Symonds Yat
☎ 01600

A remote nook beautifully situated beside the River Wye, Symonds Yat is well worth a visit for water-babies, bird enthusiasts and those fond of a relaxed riverside pint. An ancient hand-hauled ferry (adult/child 80/40p) joins the two separate hill-hugging villages on either bank, usually with a few ducks stowing away in the back. There's an abrupt change of mood in upper Symonds Yat West, which hosts a big, sore-thumb fairground jingling to the sound of pocket change, slot-machines and carousels.

ACTIVITIES

This is prime canoeing and rock-climbing territory and there's good hiking in the nearby Forest of Dean. The **Wyedean Canoe Centre** (☎ 01594-833238; www.wyedean.co.uk) hires out canoes/kayaks from £20/16 for a half-day, £10 for an hour, and also organises multiday kayaking trips, white-water trips, caving and climbing. Note that the river has a strong current and is not suitable for swimming.

From Symonds Yat East, it's a steep but easy walk – at least on a dry day – up 504m to the crown of the region, **Symonds Yat Rock**, which provides tremendous views of the river and valley. You can catch a rare glimpse of the world's fastest creature doing aerial acrobatics here, as peregrine falcons nest in the cliffs opposite.

If that all sounds like too much hard work, **Kingfisher Cruises** (☎ 891063; adult/child £5/3) runs sedate 35-minute gorge cruises from beside the ferry.

SLEEPING & EATING

Garth Cottage (☎ 890364; garthcot@yateast.fsnet.co.uk; Symonds Yat East; d £70; ☼ Apr-Oct; Ⓟ ☒) The pick of accommodation on the east side, this friendly family-run B&B sits demurely by the riverside near the ferry crossing, and is spotlessly maintained. Breakfast is served in the conservatory or on the terrace, both overlooking the water.

Saracen's Head (☎ 890435; www.saracensheadinn .co.uk; Symonds Yat East; mains £5-15; Ⓟ ☒) This black-and-white traditional inn is Symonds Yat's principal focal point, next to the ferry crossing. It has some river-view rooms (singles/doubles from £45/64) sporting pine furniture, and two luxury suites in the boathouse. It's a popular spot to tuck into bar food and restaurant fare while waiting for the moment when the ferryman topples into the river.

Old Court Hotel (☎ 890367; www.oldcourthotel.co.uk; Symonds Yat West; s/d £60, d £80-100; Ⓟ ☒ ☏) This grand 16th-century manor house will give history buffs a kick while also catering to comfort lovers. It's set in lovely gardens, complete with heated pool, and has character-filled rooms with exposed beams and frilly country-cottage décor. Children over 12 are welcome. Old

Court is on the northern entrance to Symonds Yat West, across the river and roughly a mile's walk from the ferry.

GETTING THERE & AWAY

Bus 34 can drop you on the main road 1½ miles from the village. Bikes are available for hire from the Royal Hotel (Symonds Yat East) for £13 per day.

LEDBURY

☎ 01531 / pop 8491

This atmospheric little town is a favourite for day-trippers on account of its dense core of crooked black-and-white streets, which zero in on a delightfully leggy gingerbread-style market house.

The helpful **tourist office** (☎ 636147; tic-ledbury@herefordshire.gov.uk; 3 The Homend; ☼ 10am-5pm Mon-Sat) has details about a lovely 17-mile cycle route called the Ledbury Loop (50p). To get online visit part ice-cream parlour, part internet café **Ice Bytes** (☎ 634700; 38 The Homend; per 15 min £1).

Sights

Ledbury's showpiece is the gorgeous black-and-white **Market House**, a 17th-century, timber-framed structure precariously balanced atop 16 narrow wooden posts supposedly gleaned from the defeated Spanish Armada. From here, wander up the narrow cobbled **Church Lane**, crowded with tilted timber-framed buildings, including the **Painted Room** (☼ 11am-1pm & 2-4pm Mon-Fri Easter-Sep), with jigsaw puzzle 16th-century floral frescoes.

Here too are several small museums, including **Butcher's Row House** (☎ 632942; Church Lane; admission free; ☼ 11am-5pm Easter-Sep), a pocket-sized folk museum stuffed with curios from 19th-century school clothing to an 18th-century communal 'boot' bath that used to be carted from door to door for the poor to scrub in. The **Heritage Centre** (☎ 260692; admission free; ☼ 10.30am-4.30pm Easter-Oct) sits in another half-timbered treasure opposite and has more displays on the town.

At the top of the lane lies the 12th-century church of **St Michael and All Angels**, with a splendid 18th-century spire and tower separate from the church.

Sleeping & Eating

Budget travellers may struggle to find accommodation in Ledbury.

Talbot Hotel (☎ 632963; www.visitledbury.co.uk/tal bot; New St; s/d £38.50/63.50; **P**) A black-and-white late-16th-century coaching inn with a lively little bar and dark oak-panelled restaurant (mains £8 to £15) complete with painstakingly carved overmantle and musket-ball holes, the Talbot also has a handful of simple but quaint floral rooms in what used to be the hay loft. Breakfast costs extra.

Verzons Country Inn (☎ 670381; www.theverzon .co.uk; A438, Trumpet; s £75, d £98-130; **P** ✕ ▢) The ultimate country-chic retreat, 2 miles west of Ledbury, this lovely Georgian farmhouse has undergone a rather debonair makeover without sacrificing its rustic charm. Its 10 rooms are luxuriously appointed in tactile tweeds, seagrass and leather, and the brasserie's classic menu ranges from scrumptious beer-battered cod to delicious duck (mains £10 to £17).

Feathers Hotel (☎ 635266; www.feathers-ledbury .co.uk; High St; s/d from £79.50/110; **P** ✕ ▨) The oldest part of this black-and-white Tudor building, which looms over the main road, has the kind of slanting floorboards, painted beams and rich colours that leave you in no doubt of its age. However, many of the modern rooms lack these charms.

Ceci Paolo (☎ 632976; www.cecipaolo.com; 21 High St; mains £6-7; ☙ lunch) This irresistible food emporium hooks foodies from the moment they wander into its wonderful deli, wine and kitchen shop downstairs, then reels them in with its chic contemporary café above. Daily specials showcase the deli's produce, with everything from manchego cheese to exotic verjuice marinade.

Seven (☎ 631317; jasonkay@btconnect.com; 11 The Homend; mains £9-16; ✕) Black-and-cream timber-framed exterior hides a superb modern bistro, rich in Mediterranean flavours but using mostly local produce. It also has several attractive rooms (singles/doubles £65/85) available.

Getting There & Around
There are roughly hourly trains to Hereford (15 minutes), less often to Great Malvern (11 minutes), Worcester (23 to 27 minutes) and Birmingham (£9.60, 1¼ hours).

Bus 476 runs to Hereford hourly (30 minutes, every two hours on Sunday); bus 132 runs hourly to Gloucester (one hour); and 675 to Great Malvern (30 minutes, every two hours Monday to Saturday).

You can hire mountain bikes at **Saddle Bound Cycles** (☎ 633433; 3 The Southend; per day £10).

AROUND LEDBURY
Eastnor Castle
Built more for fancy than fortification, the extravagant 19th-century medieval-revival folly of **Eastnor Castle** (☎ 01531-633160; www.eastnorcastle .com; adult/child £7/4, grounds only £3/1; ☙ 11am-5pm Sun-Fri Jul & Aug, plus Sun & Bank Hol Apr-Sep) makes you half expect to see a fire-breathing dragon appear or a golden-haired princess lean over its walls. The opulent interior continues the romantic veneer, decorated in Gothic and Italianate features, tapestries and antiques. Even when the castle is closed, its maze, adventure playground and lakeside walks are worth a look. Its beautiful deer park is also stage to the **Big Chill** (☎ 020-7684 2020; www.bigchill.net; ☙ Aug), when campers, musicians, performers and artists round off summer festival season in relaxed fashion.

The castle is just over 2 miles east of Ledbury on the A438. The Malvern Hills Hopper runs here from Upton-upon-Severn and Great Malvern on summer weekends and Bank Holidays.

Much Marcle
While the tiny village of Much Marcle is barely more than a blip on the map, it's home to one of Britain's oldest and most enthralling houses, **Hellens** (☎ 01531-660504; www.hellensmanor .com; adult/child £5/2.50; ☙ tours 2pm, 3pm & 4pm Wed, Thu, Sun & Bank Hol Apr-Sep), a time capsule of British history dating right back to the 11th century. The superb 17th-century interiors echo the gallantry of that age, and there are heirlooms of Ann Boleyn, Mary Tudor, King Charles and more. The descendents of its 13th-century masters still own the house and admit visitors on guided tours only. Outside, the restored Tudor and Jacobean gardens and charming octagonal dovecote are wonderful.

Afterwards, you can celebrate the fact that you're deep in cider country by raising a glass at **Westons Cider Mills** (☎ 01531-660233; www.westons -cider.co.uk; The Bounds; ☙ 9am-4.30pm Mon-Fri, 10am-4pm Sat & Sun), just under a mile west of Hellens over the A449. Henry Weston started dabbling with cider and perry here in the 1870s; soon the local MP got Westons cider put on tap in the parliament bar and the rest is history. **Tours** (adult/child £4/2.50; 1¼ hr) are at 2.30pm Monday to Friday, and include the all-important tasting session.

Bus 459 from Ledbury (40 minutes) goes to Much Marcle once on Thursday, while bus 479 runs on Tuesday and Saturday.

SHROPSHIRE

Jewel in the Marches' crown, the charming county of Shropshire ripples with heather-tickled hills, beautiful moorland and gushing rivers. It's a large pastoral region whose sparse population prizes the good life filled with fine food, health, peace and quiet. The county capital of Shrewsbury is one of England's loveliest Tudor towns, and nestled nearby is the fascinating industrial-heritage site of Iron-bridge Gorge. Peppered with pretty villages, the beautiful southern Shropshire Hills undu-late southwards and make wonderful walking territory. And at the county's base you'll find gourmet hub Ludlow, with its handsome cas-tle and fanaticism for food.

Information

For online county information:
North Shropshire (www.northshropshire.co.uk)
Secret Shropshire (www.secretshropshire.org.uk)
Shropshire Tourism (www.shropshiretourism.info)
Virtual Shropshire (www.virtual-shropshire.co.uk)
Visit South Shropshire (www.visitsouthshropshire .co.uk)

Getting Around

You can hop on handy rail services from Shrewsbury to Church Stretton, Craven Arms and Ludlow. The invaluable *Shropshire Bus & Train Map*, available free from tourist of-fices, shows public transport routes. **Shropshire Hills Shuttle Buses** (www.shropshirehillsshuttles.co.uk) also drops off walkers along popular hiking routes on weekends and Bank Holidays. Call

Traveline (☎ 0870 608 2608; www.traveline.org.uk) with any queries.

SHREWSBURY

☎ 01743 / pop 67,126
It takes just seconds to fall in love with the spaghetti-bowl tangle of medieval streets in the heart of Shropshire's most picturesque town. Time-worn Tudor buildings tilt their ponderous frames over mysterious passage-ways; dusky-red sandstone warms an ancient abbey and castle, and sweeping gardens run down to the River Severn.

Nestled in a horseshoe bend of the river, Shrewsbury was for many centuries a critical defensive point to help keep the Welsh in line. Then in medieval times the town grew fat on the wool trade. It is also the birthplace of Charles Darwin (1809–82), whose theory of evolution left the world reeling.

Orientation

Shrewsbury's near-island status helps preserve the Tudor and Jacobean streetscapes of its centre and protects it from unattractive urban sprawl. The train station is a five-minute walk northeast of the centre and is as far as you'll need to venture.

Information

Royal Shrewsbury Hospital (☎ 261000; Mytton Oak Rd)
Shrewsbury Library (☎ 255300; Castle Gates; ⏳ 9.30am-5pm Mon, Wed, Fri & Sat, 9.30am-8pm Tue & Thu, 1-4pm Sun) Free internet access.
Tourist office (☎ 281200; www.visitshrewsbury.com; Music Hall, The Square; ⏳ 9.30am-5.30pm Mon-Sat, 10am-4pm Sun May-Sep; 10am-5pm Mon-Sat Oct-Apr) Guided walking tours (adult/child £3.50/1.50, 1½ hours) leave the tourist office at 2.30pm from May to September and at 2.30pm Saturday only from November to April.

SOMETHING FOR THE WEEKEND

Kick off your weekend with a night of loved-up escapism and fine food at the pleasantly potty **Hundred House Hotel** (p446). Next morning, nip over to **Ironbridge Gorge** (p441) for a stroll across the world's first iron bridge, then roll down to the beautiful **Long Mynd** (p446) to build up an afternoon appetite on its stunning walking trails. Hold onto your hunger pangs just long enough to put them to good use in the region's gourmet capital, **Ludlow** (p447), where **Hibiscus** (p449) and **Mr Underhill's** (p449) are just two of the superb restaurants to choose between. Sleep off your excesses in the stunning timber-framed **Feathers Hotel** (p449), then on Sunday morning head south for a quick tour through the picture-postcard **black-and-white villages** (p430). For a final fling, linger over an indulgent Sunday lunch at the **Stagg Inn** (p430) and book yourself a trip to the gym on Monday.

THE MARCHES

SHREWSBURY

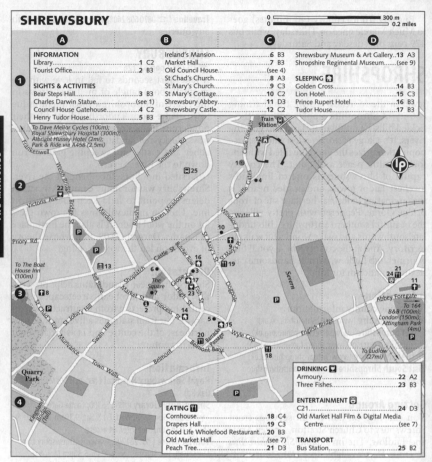

INFORMATION		Ireland's Mansion.................................6 B3	Shrewsbury Museum & Art Gallery..13 A3
Library...............................1 C2		Market Hall...7 B3	Shropshire Regimental Museum.......(see 9)
Tourist Office......................2 B3		Old Council House..........................(see 4)	
		St Chad's Church................................8 A3	SLEEPING
SIGHTS & ACTIVITIES		St Mary's Church................................9 C3	Golden Cross.....................................14 B3
Bear Steps Hall...................3 B3		St Mary's Cottage.............................10 C2	Lion Hotel..15 C3
Charles Darwin Statue.....(see 1)		Shrewsbury Abbey............................11 D3	Prince Rupert Hotel...........................16 B3
Council House Gatehouse...4 C2		Shrewsbury Castle.............................12 C2	Tudor House.......................................17 B3
Henry Tudor House............5 B3			

EATING		DRINKING	
Cornhouse.........................18 C4		Armoury...22 A2	
Drapers Hall......................19 C3		Three Fishes.......................................23 B3	
Good Life Wholefood Restaurant....20 B3		ENTERTAINMENT	
Old Market Hall.............(see 7)		C21...24 D3	
Peach Tree.........................21 D3		Old Market Hall Film & Digital Media	
		Centre..(see 7)	
		TRANSPORT	
		Bus Station...25 B2	

Sights

SHREWSBURY ABBEY

Most famous as a setting for monastic whodunits the *Chronicles of Brother Cadfael* by Ellis Peters, this lovely red-sandstone **abbey** (☎ 232723; www.shrewsburyabbey.com; Abbey Foregate; adult/child £2/1 donation; ☒ 10am-4.30pm Mon-Sat, 11.30am-2.30pm Sun) is what remains of a large Benedictine monastery founded in 1083, its outbuildings mostly lost and its flanks unceremoniously chopped. It's graced by a mix of Norman, Early English and Victorian features and there's an exceptional 14th-century west window of heraldic glass. The abbey is renowned for its fine acoustics and a notice board provides information on upcoming recitals.

SHREWSBURY MUSEUM & ART GALLERY

The stunning timber-framed Tudor merchant's mansion and warehouse in which **Shrewsbury Museum & Art Gallery** (☎ 361196; www .shrewsburymuseums.com; Barker St; admission free; ☒ 10am-4pm Tue-Sat year-round, 10am-5pm Tue-Sat & 10am-4pm Sun Jun-Sep) is housed are as much of an attraction as its exhibits, which range from Roman finds to Darwin's times.

Walking Tour

Start at the tourist office. The mellow-stone building balancing on chunky legs opposite you is Shrewsbury's 16th-century **Market Hall**, hub of the historic wool trade. A few pillars are still dented by rows of holes used to count how many fleeces were sold.

THE MARCHES

One of Shrewsbury's most magnificent black-and-white beauties, the lordly timber-framed **Ireland's Mansion** grabs attention to your left as you step up to High St. Turn right and cross over into the charmingly named and almost claustrophobically narrow **Grope Lane**, with overhanging storeys that seem to close in around you. You'll emerge into atmospheric **Fish Street**, and see some steps leading to the 14th-century **Bear Steps Hall** (10am-4pm), now home to a small exhibition space. On the hall's other side is **Butcher Row**, home to more half-timbered lovelies.

Head another street north for a peek inside medieval **St Mary's Church** (St Mary's St; 11am-4pm Fri-Sun May-Sep), which has one of the highest spires in England and the astonishingly vivid Jesse window of rare mid-14th-century glass.

Pass the tilted 17th-century **St Mary's Cottage** and turn left into Windsor Place, before taking the second right into Castle St. You can't miss the entrance right to terracotta-coloured **Shrewsbury Castle**, which houses the stiff-upper-lip **Shropshire Regimental Museum** (358516; adult/child £2.50/1.25; 10am-5pm Tue-Sat & 10am-4pm Sun-Mon May-Sep, 10am-4pm Wed-Sat Feb-Apr) and has wonderful views.

Back near the entrance is Jacobean-style **Council House Gatehouse**, dating from 1620, and **Old Council House**, where the Council of the Welsh Marches used to meet.

Opposite the castle is the rather ostentatious **library**, with a **statue** of Shrewsbury's most famous son, Charles Darwin. Returning to St Mary's St, follow it into Dogpole and turn right into Wyle Cop, Welsh for 'hilltop'. Henry VII stayed in the seriously overhanging **Henry Tudor House** before the Battle of Bosworth. At the bottom of Wyle Cop is the graceful 18th-century **English Bridge**, which takes you across to **Shrewsbury Abbey**.

If your feet aren't yet aching, double back over the bridge and stroll left along the riverside to enjoy an ice cream in the tumbling gardens of **Quarry Park**, and listen to the cacophonous bells of odd 18th-century round church **St Chad's**, which dominates the park's top.

Sleeping

164 (367750; www.164bedandbreakfast.co.uk; 164 Abbey Foregate; s/d £35/54, with bathroom £45/58; wi-fi only) A breath of fresh air, this B&B eschews chintz and celebrates its lovely 16th-century timber frame, rough walls and lopsided floors with vivid colours, contemporary fabrics and a quirky mix of artwork. And as a cherry on the top, breakfast is served in bed.

Lion Hotel (0870 609 6167; www.corushotels.com /thelion; Wyle Cop; s/d from £60/79, ste from £108;) A cowardly lion presides over the doorway of this grand old coaching inn, which has hosted many a luminary through its 400-year history. Although the three-score standard rooms have a bland style with faded leafy motifs your granny would pick, the suites are the real deal, with bags of character and oodles of antiques.

Tudor House (351735; www.tudorhouseshrewsbury.com; 2 Fish St; s/d from £69/79;) For a more rose-tinted picture of the past, this gloriously creaky medieval building is festooned with floral window boxes and its handful of traditional oak-beamed rooms are turned out in high-shine fabrics, some with spindly metal-framed headboards entwined with flowers. Not all rooms have an en suite.

Prince Rupert Hotel (499955; www.prince-rupert-hotel.co.uk; Butcher Row; s/d £85/105, tudor r £105-175;) King James' grandson Prince Rupert once lived at this oak-panelled hotel. Though most rooms are modern, tapestries, armour and heraldry haphazardly push the theme and a few spectacular 12th-century suites have all the quirky angles and beams you could ask for.

There are plenty more B&Bs huddled around Abbey Foregate.

Other options for bedding down:

Golden Cross (362507; www.goldencrosshotel.co.uk; 14 Princess St; s/d £32.50/47.50) Medieval timber-beamed inn with simple rooms; prices may rise following renovations.

Albright Hussey Hotel (290571; www.albrighthussey.co.uk; Ellesmere Rd; s/d from £65/79;) Romantic manor complete with moat, 2 miles north.

Eating

Old Market Hall (281281; Market Sq; mains £5-7; 10am-late) Hobnob with the local arts brigade in this posh café-bar in the old drapers hall, underneath a stunning timbered roof and styled to combine city chic with cosy rustic touches. As well as speciality teas, soul-restoring coffees and wines, it serves up a range of sandwiches, wraps, and calorific pastries. It's based in a lively film and media centre.

Cornhouse (231991; 59A Wyle Cop; mains £8-14; lunch & dinner) This classy but relaxed wine-bar and restaurant successfully mixes contemporary style with period features from its working corn-house days. Its consistently good British food is served up in the shadow of a superb cast-iron spiral staircase.

Good Life Wholefood Restaurant (☎ 350455; Barracks Passage; mains £3.50-7; ☷ lunch Mon-Sat) Run by a dietician and devotee of good honest vegetarian food, this cute little refuge off Wyle Cop is a great place for hearty and wholesome salads, hot bakes and delicious desserts. Takeaway is available.

Drapers Hall (☎ 344679; St Mary's Pl; mains £12-17.50; ☷ lunch & dinner) The atmosphere is thick with history in this well-fossilised 16th-century hall, fronted by an elegant Elizabethan façade. Dining is divided between dark oak-panelled rooms decked out in sumptuous fabrics and antique screens. The sophisticated Anglo-French menu and connoisseur's wine list are also well worthy of a special occasion.

Peach Tree (☎ 355055; 18-21 Abbey Foregate; mains £8-14; ☷ 9am-midnight) A cosy combination of timber-framed antiquity and comfortable modern style, this café-bar also has streetside seating opposite the abbey and can be relied upon for all-day food and drinks.

Drinking

Armoury (☎ 340525; www.armoury-shrewsbury.co.uk; Victoria Ave; mains £8-14) There's an irresistibly infectious bonhomie to this converted riverside warehouse. Towering bookshelves, old pictures and curios help straddle the divide between posh restaurant and informal pub, while a plethora of blackboard menus invite you to sample wines, guest ales and hearty British dishes.

Three Fishes (☎ 344793; 4 Fish St) The quintessential small English alehouse, with a jolly owner, mellow regulars and hops hanging from the 15th-century beamed ceiling. No music here, just real ales on tap and the refreshing atmosphere of a pub that has long been sending smokers outside.

Boat House Inn (☎ 362965; New St) Summer evenings are well spent in the riverside beer garden of this otherwise unexceptional pub, enjoying a view back over the sprawling Quarry Park and the baby-sized Port Hill Suspension Bridge, opened in 1922.

Entertainment

C21 (☎ 271821; 21 Abbey Foregate; admission after 10pm £3-5; ☷ 8.30pm-3am) A polished city-chic club for

over-25s to indulge in late-night cocktails and dance-floor acrobatics. Also home to Shrewsbury's main lesbigay night on Monday.

For mainstream and arthouse movies in an Elizabethan setting, try the **Old Market Hall Film & Digital Media Centre** (☎ 281281; www.oldmarkethall.co.uk).

Getting There & Around

BIKE
You can hire bikes at **Dave Mellor Cycles** (☎ 366662; www.thecycleshop.co.uk; 9 New St; bikes/tandems per day from £15/25).

BUS
National Express has two direct buses to London (£16.50, 4½ hours) and two more via Birmingham (£16.50, five hours). Bus 96 serves Ironbridge (30 minutes) every second hour Monday to Saturday. Bus 435 travels to Ludlow (1¼ hours) via Church Stretton (45 minutes) eight times daily and bus 553 heads to Bishop's Castle (one hour) 10 times daily.

TRAIN
There are no direct trains connecting Shrewsbury and London – you must change at Wolverhampton (£38.70, 2½ to three hours). There are twice-hourly trains to Ludlow (£7.70, 30 minutes).

Shrewsbury is a popular starting point for two scenic routes into Wales: one loop takes in Shrewsbury, northern Wales and Chester; the other, **Heart of Wales Line** (☎ 0870 9000 772; www.heart-of-wales.co.uk), runs southwest to Swansea (£20, 3¾ hours, four daily).

AROUND SHREWSBURY
Attingham Park
Shropshire's finest stately home is Palladian-style **Attingham Park** (NT; ☎ 01743-708123; house & grounds adult/child £6.50/3.25, grounds only £3.30/1.65; ☷ house 1-5pm Fri-Tue mid-Mar–Oct, grounds 10am-dusk), built in the late 18th century and reminiscent of many a corset-and-lace drama. Behind the high-and-mighty neoclassical façade, you'll find a picture gallery by John Nash, two wings respectively decorated into staunch masculine and oh-so-pretty feminine Regency interiors. The landscaped grounds shelter a herd of deer and pleasant walks along the River Tern.

Attingham Park is 4 miles southeast of Shrewsbury at Atcham. Buses 81 and 96 (18 minutes) run six times Monday to Friday, less frequently on weekends.

Wroxeter Roman City

An engrossing tale of Roman Britain can be traced through the stubby foundations of Viroconium, at **Wroxeter** (EH; ☎ 01743-761330; adult/child £4/2; ☼ 10am-5pm Mar-Oct, 10am-4pm Wed-Sun Nov-Feb). Geophysical work has revealed a Roman city as large as Pompeii underneath the lush surrounding farmland, though for now you'll have to content yourself with exploring the public baths and marketplace. Note the hastily filled-in outdoor swimming pool, optimistically built before the Romans realised their miscalculation of the northern English climes.

Wroxeter is 6 miles southeast of Shrewsbury, off the B4380. Bus 96 stops nearby, and runs six times Monday to Friday, less on weekends.

IRONBRIDGE GORGE

☎ 01952

It can be hard to fully grasp the world-rocking events that took place in this tranquil river gorge as you wind your way through its wooded slopes and sleepy villages. But the Industrial Revolution was dramatically kick-started here in the 18th century. Three generations of the pioneering Darby family set about transforming their industrial processes and in so doing irreversibly changed the world.

The story began quietly in 1709, when Abraham Darby determinedly set about restoring an old furnace to prove it was possible to smelt iron ore with coke. After much trial and error he was proved right, and his breakthrough paved the way for local factories to mass-produce the first iron wheels, rails and steam locomotives. Abraham Darby II's innovative forging process then enabled the production of single beams of iron, allowing Abraham Darby III to stun the world with the very first iron bridge, constructed here in 1779. The bridge remains the valley's showpiece and dominates the main village, a jumble of cottages sliding down the gorge's steep bank.

Now written into history books as the birthplace of the Industrial Revolution, Ironbridge is a World Heritage Site and the Marches' top attraction. Ten very different museums now tell the story in the very buildings where it took place.

Orientation & Information

Driving or cycling can make life easier, as the museums are peppered throughout the long gorge. See p444 for public transport options.

The **tourist office** (☎ 884391; www.visitironbridge .co.uk; Tollhouse; ☼ 10am-5pm) is by the bridge.

Sights & Activities

You can buy a **passport ticket** (adult/child £14/9.50) that allows year-round entry to all of the sites at any of the museums or the tourist office. The museums open from 10am to 5pm unless stated otherwise.

MUSEUM OF THE GORGE

A succinct overview of the site is on offer at the **Museum of the Gorge** (The Wharfage; adult/child £2.50/1.50), making it a good spot to start. Housed in a Gothic warehouse by the river, it's filled with touchscreens, fun exhibits and details of the horrific consequences of pollution and environmental hazards at the cutting edge of industry (Abraham I and III both died at 39). An absorbing video sets the museum in its historical context.

COALBROOKDALE MUSEUM OF IRON & DARBY HOUSES

Coalbrookdale is the gorge's key site, as it was here that trailblazing Abraham Darby first smelted iron ore with coke. You can even peer into the very furnace he used, which sits in a wacky sculpture garden beside the **Museum of Iron** (adult/child £6/4); the museum is in turn set in the site's sprawling iron foundry, where an army of men and boys once churned out heavy-duty iron equipment and later, ever more fancy ironwork castings. The excellent interactive exhibits chart the company's history and showcase some extraordinary creations.

The early industrial settlement that surrounds the site has also happily survived, with workers cottages, chapels, church and graveyard undisturbed. Just up the hill are the beautifully restored 18th-century **Darby Houses** (☎ 433522; adult/child £3.50/2; ☼ Apr-Oct), which housed generations of the industrial big cheeses in gracious but modest Quaker comfort. Rosehill House is furnished with much original furniture and next door, Dale House includes the wood-panelled office in which the third Abraham Darby pored over his bridge designs.

IRON BRIDGE & TOLLHOUSE

The gorge's defining image, this flamboyant arch was the world's first such iron bridge and a triumph of engineering that left contemporaries flabbergasted by its apparent flimsiness. It still impresses visitors more than 225 years

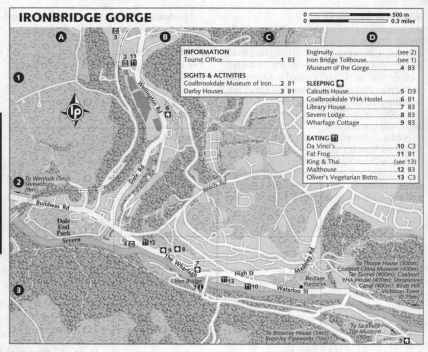

IRONBRIDGE GORGE

0 — 500 m
0 — 0.3 miles

INFORMATION
Tourist Office.....................................1 B3

SIGHTS & ACTIVITIES
Coalbrookdale Museum of Iron.....2 B1
Darby Houses.................................3 B1

Enginuity..(see 2)
Iron Bridge Tollhouse....................(see 1)
Museum of the Gorge....................4 B3

SLEEPING
Calcutts House...............................5 D3
Coalbrookdale YHA Hostel............6 B1
Library House.................................7 B3
Severn Lodge.................................8 B3
Wharfage Cottage.........................9 B3

EATING
Da Vinci's.......................................10 C3
Fat Frog...11 B1
King & Thai...................................(see 13)
Malthouse.....................................12 B3
Oliver's Vegetarian Bistro.............13 C3

on as a fitting symbol of the pioneering success of this remote Shropshire town and of its visionary creator Abraham Darby III's own technological prowess. The **tollhouse** (admission free; ⊗ 10am-5pm) houses a small exhibition on the bridge's history.

BLISTS HILL VICTORIAN TOWN
To immerse yourself in 19th-century Britain, hear the pounding of steam hammers and the clip-clop of horse hooves, or knock a coconut off its stand, head to the vast open-air Victorian theme park, **Blists Hill** (☎ 433522; Legges Way, Madeley; adult/child £9/6; ⊗ 10am-5pm). This ambitious project does a remarkably good job of reconstructing an entire village, encompassing everything from a working foundry to bank and sweet shop. Costumed staff explain displays, craftspeople demonstrate skills, and if it all gets too much you can grab yourself a stiff drink at the Victorian pub.

COALPORT CHINA MUSEUM & TAR TUNNEL
When ironmaking moved elsewhere, Coalport china slowed the region's decline and the restored works now house an absorbing **China Museum** (adult/child £5/3.50) tracing the region's glory days as a manufacturer of elaborate pottery and crockery. Craftspeople demonstrate china-making techniques and two enormous bottle kilns are guaranteed to awe even if the gaudily glazed chinaware leaves you cold.

A short ramble along the canal brings you to the 200-year-old **Tar Tunnel** (adult/child £1.50/1; ⊗ Apr-Sep), dug as a water-supply channel but halted abruptly when natural bitumen unexpectedly started trickling treacle-like from its walls. You can still don a hard hat and stoop in deep enough to see the black stuff ooze.

JACKFIELD TILE MUSEUM
A kaleidoscopic collection of Victorian tiles, faience and ceramics can be found at the **Jackfield Tile Museum** (adult/child £5/3.50), displayed through a series of gas-lit period-style galleries reconstructing lustrous tiled interiors of everything from pubs to churches, tube stations and remarkably fancy toilets. Kids especially love the fairy-tale friezes for children's hospital wards.

BROSELEY PIPEWORKS

Tobacco-smoking was the height of gentlemanly chic in the late 17th and early 18th centuries, and a vast range of clay pipes from short-stemmed 'pipsqueaks' to arm-length 'church wardens' were produced in the **Broseley Pipeworks** (adult/child £3.50/2; 1-5pm mid-May–Sep), once Britain's most prolific pipe manufacturer. The factory finally closed in 1957, but has now reopened for visitors to explore its time-capsule contents, which are largely unchanged since the last worker turned out the lights. It's a mile-long walk to get here, signposted from the bridge.

ENGINUITY

Championing Ironbridge's spirit of brains before brawn, the fabulous interactive design and technology centre **Enginuity** (adult/child £5.50/4) invites you to move a steam engine with the flick of a wrist, X-ray everyday objects, power up a vacuum cleaner with self-generated electricity and basically dive headfirst into a vast range of hands-on, brains-on challenges, games and gadgets that explore design and engineering in modern life. If you have kids with you, allow at least two hours.

Sleeping

Coalport YHA (0870 770 5882; ironbridge@yha.org .uk; High St, Coalport; dm £15.50;) This historic former china factory, a big bluff industrial-looking building mere paces from the China Museum, the canal and close to pleasant countryside walks, now houses an 83-bed hostel. The plain, modern rooms betray little of their long history, however.

Coalbrookdale YHA (0870 770 5882; ironbridge@ yha.org.uk; Paradise Rd, Coalbrookdale; dm £13.95;) The rather imposing former Literary and Scientific Institute, a grand blue-grey building from 1859 sitting high on the hillside behind sturdy iron gates, now houses a comfortable hostel within easy walking distance of the Museum of Iron. It has several en suite family rooms.

Library House (432299; www.libraryhouse.com; 11 Severn Bank; s/d £55/70; wi-fi only) A lovingly restored Georgian library building hugged by vines, nudged by a beautiful garden and elegantly decorated with deep leather sofas, light colours and plentiful frills. There are extra home comforts and welcoming hosts. It's set back from the road on a tiny curving street close to the iron bridge.

Calcutts House (882631; www.calcuttshouse.co.uk; Calcutts Rd; s/d/f from £40/60/85;) This former ironmaster's pad built in the 18th century is tucked away a few strides from the Jackfield Tile Museum. Its traditionally decorated rooms have bags of character, quality furniture and furnishings and are each named after a celebrated former owner of or visitor to the house. It's also family friendly, as testified by a trampoline and goalposts in the garden.

Wharfage Cottage (432721; www.wharfagecottage .co.uk; 17 The Wharfage; s £30, d £40-48, f £55) This higgledy-piggledy little whitewashed cottage, once a sweet manufactory and smithy, has prime position, a pocket-sized garden and pretty country cottage–style rooms with river views.

Other options:

Severn Lodge (432147; www.severnlodge.com; New Rd; s/d £59/72;) Lovely hillside Georgian lodge peering over town, with three elegant rooms.

Thorpe House (586789; www.thorpehousebedan-dbreakfast.co.uk; Coalport; s/d £25/42, d with bathroom £55;) Red-brick Victorian house B&B popular with outdoorsy folk, cyclists, families and fisherfolk.

Eating

Malthouse (433712; www.themalthouseironbridge.com; The Wharfage; mains £9-15; lunch & dinner) Doubly popular for its buzzing atmosphere and huge portions, this former malting house turned vibrant gastropub and jazz bar sits by the riverfront and serves some seriously good traditional dishes. The terrace is a big plus in summer. Stylish contemporary rooms (£63) are also available.

Fat Frog (432240; www.fat-frog.co.uk; Coalbrookdale; mains £10-17; lunch & dinner Mon-Sat, lunch Sun) A quirky French bar-bistro cluttered with toy frogs and showbiz memorabilia, with a rustic candle-lit basement and playing nostalgic music from the ebullient Gallic proprietor's prime. The food is excellent, and as you'd expect, there's a great wine list with plenty of half-bottles.

King & Thai (433913; 33A High St; mains £8-11; dinner) Accessed via an unlikely looking passageway near the bridge, this snug little Thai emporium piles plates high with tongue-tinglingly spicy food untamed for the English market. It's a surprisingly authentic place, with staff busily scurrying between levels and discharging rapid-fire smiles at every turn.

Other spots to consider:

Da Vinci's (432250; 26 High St; mains £11-18; dinner Tue-Sat) Gourmet Italian food served in a classy wood-panelled dining room.

Oliver's Vegetarian Bistro (☎ 433086; 33 High St; mains £8.95; ☺ lunch & dinner) Stylish meat-free food beside the bridge.

Getting There & Away

The nearest train station is 5 miles away at Telford. Bus 96 runs every two hours (Monday to Saturday) between Shrewsbury (40 minutes) and Telford (15 to 20 minutes) via Ironbridge, stopping near the Museum of the Gorge. Bus 39 runs from Much Wenlock (30 minutes, three daily).

Getting Around

The Gorge Connect bus connects nine of the museums every half-hour on weekends and Bank Holidays only. It costs 50p per journey.

Midweek your only options are to walk or hire a bike from **Broseley House** (☎ 882043; www .broseleyhouse.co.uk; 1 The Square, Broseley; per day £10), a mile and a half south of the bridge; booking is advised. You may also like to look into **Tandem Experience** (☎ 0845 60 66 456; www.tandeming.co.uk; tandem per day £50), based at the Coalport YHA; the price includes tuition for tandem riding.

MUCH WENLOCK

☎ 01952 / pop 1959

A spider's web of narrow streets flanked by Tudor, Jacobean and Georgian buildings, an arresting timbered guildhall and the enchanting remains of a 12th-century priory make this little town a big hit with visitors. It can also claim to have jump-started the modern Olympics (see boxed text, opposite).

The **tourist office** (☎ 727679; muchwenlock.tourism@ shropshire-cc.gov.uk; The Square; ☺ 10.30am-1pm & 2-5pm Mon-Sat Apr-Oct, plus Sun Jun-Aug) shares a 19th-century building and opening hours with the local **museum** (admission free).

Sights & Activities

The tourist office provides a 10p map to the town's sights of historical interest, as well as copies of *The Olympian Trail*, a pleasant 1½-mile walking tour of the town exploring the link between the village and the modern Olympics.

Or you can skip straight to the town's highlight, the evocative 12th-century ruins of **Wenlock Priory** (EH; ☎ 727466; adult/child £3.30/1.70; ☺ 10am-5pm May-Jun, 10am-6pm Jul-Aug, 10am-5pm Thu-Mon Apr & Sep-Oct, 10am-4pm Thu-Sun Nov-Feb), surrounded by neatly snipped grounds studded

with kooky topiaries of squirrels and teddy bears. The remains include part of a finely decorated chapterhouse and an unusual carved lavabo. In July and August the ruins make a stunning backdrop for Shakespearean plays.

Sleeping & Eating

The closest hostel is Wilderhope Manor YHA (see below).

Talbot Inn (☎ 727077; www.the-talbot-inn.com; High St; s/d £47.50/70; Ⓟ ☒) Through a flower-dappled archway, this wonderfully atmospheric medieval inn with colossal beams, cavernous fireplaces and good home-style fare (mains £10 to £15) also has six rooms in a converted 18th-century malthouse, with whitewashed walls, exposed beams and wood furniture.

Raven Hotel (☎ 727251; www.ravenhotel.com; Barrow St; s/d £75/110; Ⓟ ☒) Much Wenlock's finest, this 17th-century coaching inn and converted stables has thick oak beams, open fires and rich country-chic styling throughout. The excellent restaurant overlooks a flowery courtyard and serves up classic British and Mediterranean fare (bar food £7 to £13, two-course meal £20.50).

Eden Café (☎ 727555; 44 High St; lunch £4.50-7; ☺ 9.30am-5pm Mon-Sat) This gourmet delicatessen, stocked high with fresh coffees, artisan cheeses, cured meats, organic breads and other goodies, also has a snug café with a woody organic feel, beamed roof and fresh Continental-style food.

Getting There & Away

Bus 436 runs from Shrewsbury (35 minutes) to Bridgnorth (20 minutes) hourly (five on Sunday).

AROUND MUCH WENLOCK
Wenlock Edge

This spectacular limestone escarpment swells up like an immense petrified wave, its ancient oceanic rock rich in fossils and its flanks frothy with woodland. It stretches for 15 miles from Much Wenlock to Craven Arms and makes for wonderful walking and dramatic views. The National Trust (NT) owns much of the ridge, and there are many waymarked trails starting from car parks dotted along the B4371. There are no helpful buses along this route.

For a bite, a beer or a bed en route, the snug 17th-century **Wenlock Edge Inn** (☎ 01746-785678; B4371, Hilltop; s/d £50/70; Ⓟ) is a firm favourite with hikers and locals alike. It's a down-to-earth place with walls of Wenlock stone, low beams and handsome Inglenook fireplace and dishes up hearty sustenance for the road ahead (mains £7 to £9) It also has three rustic rooms available, and showers fed by the well. The pub is about 4½ miles southwest of Much Wenlock on the B4371.

For top-value budget accommodation, ramble out to the remote **Wilderhope Manor YHA** (☎ 0870 770 6090; wilderhope@yha.org.uk; Longville-in-the-Dale; dm £13.95; ☒ Fri-Sat & school holidays; ℗ ☒), a gloriously atmospheric gabled Elizabethan manor, with oak spiral staircases, wood-panelled walls and an impressive dining hall. The hostel is set deep in lush countryside and adjoins a picturesque if pongy farmyard.

You can catch buses from Ludlow and Bridgnorth to Shipton, a half-mile walk from Wilderhope.

BRIDGNORTH & AROUND
☎ 01746 / pop 11,891
Cleaved into two by a dramatic sandstone bluff that tumbles down to the River Severn, Bridgnorth's upper head and lower body are joined by means of the steepest inland railway in Britain, **Bridgnorth Cliff Railway** (☎ 762052; return 80p; ☒ 8am-8pm Mon-Sat & noon-8pm Sun May-Sep, to dusk Oct-Apr), which has been trundling its way up the cliff since 1892. The town also boasts a cute colonnaded mid-17th-century town hall, and two interesting churches.

Bridgnorth is also the northern terminus of the **Severn Valley Railway** (☎ 01299-403816; www.svr.co.uk; adult/child £11.80/5.80; ☒ May-Sep, Sat & Sun Oct-Apr), whose trains chug down the picturesque valley to Kidderminster.

There's something for cyclists here too: a beautiful new 20-mile section of National Cycle Route 45, the **Mercian Way**, runs alongside the Severn Valley Railway from here to the Wyre Forest.

Organic, free-range and fair-trade foods rule the roost in central Bridgnorth's **Cinnamon** (☎ 762944; Waterloo House, Cartway; mains £5-8; ☒ 9am-6pm Mon-Fri, 10am-5pm Sat), a darling vegetarian wholefood café where you can pick between squashy sofas, a quiet library lounge, an airy conservatory-style perch or patio with views over the river.

Getting There & Away
Buses 436 and 437 run from Shrewsbury to Bridgnorth 10 times daily (one hour, five times on Sunday), via Much Wenlock (25 minutes). You can catch the steam train from any of the stations in the Severn Valley.

CHURCH STRETTON & AROUND
☎ 01694 / pop 3841
Cradled in a deep valley between the beautiful Long Mynd and the Caradoc Hills, this scenic if restrained little town is the ideal base from which to venture into the glorious surroundings. It also shelters some interesting old

---

GRANDDADDY OF THE MODERN OLYMPICS

All eyes will be on London when the Olympic Games arrive in 2012, but they will not be the only Olympics taking place in England at that time. The altogether more modest annual games at tiny Much Wenlock were instrumental in the rebirth of their big fat Greek brother.

Local doctor and sports enthusiast William Penny Brookes fused his knowledge of the ancient Olympics and rural British pastimes to launch the Much Wenlock Olympic Games in 1850. Begun as a distraction for the beer-swilling local youth, the games soon pricked the interest of Baron Pierre Coubertin, who visited Much Wenlock in 1890 to see them for himself.

He and Brookes became firm friends, with the shared dream of reviving the ancient Olympics. Coubertin went on to launch the modern Olympics in Athens in 1896; the games featured many of the events he had seen in Much Wenlock (although wheelbarrow racing and chasing a greased pig around town never really caught on). Brookes was invited to the event but he died, aged 86, before the games opened.

The good doctor never really got his share of the Olympic limelight until almost a century later, when International Olympic Committee President Juan Antonio Samaranch visited his grave to 'pay tribute and homage to Dr Brookes, who really was the founder of the Modern Olympic Games'.

The Much Wenlock Olympics are still held every July, with events that range from the triathlon to bowls. You can find details at www.wenlock-olympian-society.org.uk.

buildings, including a 12th-century Norman church most famous for its weather-beaten but still undauntedly exhibitionist *sheila-na-gig* over its north door.

The **tourist office** (☎ 723133; www.churchstretton.co.uk; Church St; ☼ 9.30am-1pm & 2-5pm Mon-Sat), adjoining the library, has abundant walking information as well as free internet access.

Activities
WALKING
Shropshire's most famous mountain, the glorious hogback hill of **Long Mynd** heaves its bulk up above Church Stretton. This is one of the best walking areas in the Marches, dubbed 'Little Switzerland' by the Victorians, who flocked here for its healthy climes and spring waters. The entire area is webbed by walking trails with memorable views.

You could start with the **Carding Mill Valley Trail**, which starts just outside Church Stretton and leads up to the 517m summit of the Long Mynd. This trail can get very busy at weekends and in summer, so you might prefer to pick your own peak or cross the A49 and climb towards the 459m summit of Caer Caradoc.

You can drive part of the way up the Carding Mill Valley, although the NT would rather you took the **Long Mynd shuttle bus** (☼ weekends & Bank Hol only Apr-Oct) from Beaumont Rd or the station.

OTHER ACTIVITIES
The tourist office has maps of local mountain biking circuits and details of riding stables. Daredevils can also look up **Beyond Extreme** (☎ 682640; www.beyondextreme.co.uk; 2 Burway Rd) to organise hill-launch paragliding lessons and tandem flights.

Sleeping
Bridges Long Mynd YHA (☎ 01588-650656; www.yha.org.uk; Ratlinghope; dm £10.95; P ✗) Built as an 18th-century village school, this big stone pile is now one of the country's longest-running YHA hostels. Tucked deep in the Shropshire hills, on the doorstep of the Shropshire Way and walks to Long Mynd and Stiperstones, it houses basic but comfortable dorms. Boulton's bus 551 comes here from Shrewsbury on Tuesday only. On weekends from April to October the Long Mynd shuttle runs hourly to Church Stretton.

Brookfields (☎ 722314; paulangie@brookfields51.fsnet.co.uk; Watling St North; s/d/f from £30/59/65; P ✗) A short stroll east across the A49 from town,

this substantial red-brick Edwardian family home retains much of its period character, has pristine and thoughtfully appointed en suite rooms in muted colours and a terrific breakfast served companionably with other guests around a large dining table.

ourpick Jinlye Guest House (☎ 723243; www.jinlye.co.uk; Castle Hill, All Stretton; s/d £50/70; P ✗ &) The Long Mynd is literally your back garden and sheep your neighbours at this beautifully restored crofter's cottage perched on the hilltop, and graced by old beams, log fires and leaded windows. Bedrooms are bright and elegantly furnished with antiques and butter-wouldn't-melt floral fabrics. Expect a good old-fashioned welcome.

Other options include:

Willowfield (☎ 751471; www.willowfieldguesthouse.co.uk; Lower Wood; s/d £35/70; P ✗) A 17th-century farmhouse in an idyllic isolated location.

Longmynd Hotel (☎ 722244; www.longmynd.co.uk; Cunnery Rd; s/d £65/130; P ✗ 🛒 🖳 wi-fi only) Hilltop pile with airy rooms, stunning vistas, sculpture trail and excellent food.

Eating
Berry's Coffee House (☎ 724452; www.berryscoffeehouse.co.uk; 17 High St; meals £5.50-7; ☼ lunch Wed-Sat) A delightful gossipy café in an 18th-century building with alfresco courtyard just off the main street. Berry's cherishes its organic free-range and fair-trade ethos and proffers wholesome locally sourced dishes, though the halo slips when confronted with scandalous desserts.

Studio (☎ 722672; 59 High St; meals £14-16.50; ☻ dinner only Tue-Sat, lunch Sun) A converted artist's studio, still littered with interesting works, sets the scene for this, the town's best and most intimate restaurant. The award-winning menu jumps confidently between modern British and traditional French food, and uses plenty of local game and fish.

Van Doesburg's Deli (☎ 722867; 3 High St) There are rich pickings for walkers putting together a picnic at this excellent patisserie-delicatessen.

Getting There & Around

There are hourly trains to Shrewsbury (20 minutes) and bus 435, which runs between Shrewsbury (45 minutes) and Ludlow (40 minutes) six times daily, stops here.

You can hire 24-speed mountain bikes with front or full suspension and cheaper, simpler bikes from **Shropshire Hills Bike Hire** (☎ 723302; 6 Castle Hill, All Stretton; bikes per day £10-17.50).

BISHOP'S CASTLE
☎ 01588 / pop 1630

Stress seems an alien concept in this languorous little border town, home to an enchanting medley of renowned breweries, contorted half-timbered buildings, second-hand bookshops and eclectic boutiques that endear it to day-trippers. At the top of High St sits the adorable Georgian **town hall** and delightfully crooked 16th-century **House on Crutches** (☎ 630007; admission free; ☻ 1-5pm Sat & Sun), which also houses the town **museum**.

The pleasingly potty **Old Time** (☎ 638467; www .bishopscastle.co.uk; 29 High St; ☻ 10am-10pm Mon-Sat, 10am-2pm Sun) offers limited tourist information.

Sights & Activities
WALKING

Walk along the **Shropshire Way**, which runs through the town and joins up with **Offa's Dyke Path** to the south; the **Kerry Ridgeway** to the south; or head north and risk the forbidding ridges of the **Stiperstones**, where Satan is said to hold court.

Sleeping & Eating

Poppy House (☎ 638443; www.poppyhouse.co.uk; 20 Market Sq; s/d £45/70) Sweetly stylish rooms with an air of simple elegance, adorned by luxurious red textiles, timber-framed walls and sloping floors, and a complimentary breakfast-in-bed service win this B&B much praise. Poppy motifs colour the reliable restaurant (mains

£5 to £9; open 10am to 5pm and 6.30pm to 11pm) downstairs.

Castle Hotel (☎ 638403; www.thecastlehotelbishop scastle.co.uk; The Square; s/d £40/70; P ☒) Haughtily perched in an elevated square, this handsome 18th-century coaching inn has lovely terraced gardens and six relaxing beamed rooms furnished with antiques and strait-laced floral designs. Room 8 is especially atmospheric. The oak-panelled restaurant (mains £6 to £10) dishes up classic British food.

Other possibilities:

Porch House (☎ 638854; www.theporchhouse.com; High St; d £60-70; P ☐) Gorgeous Elizabethan porch house with chic central rooms.

Old Brick (☎ 638471; www.oldbrick.co.uk; 7 Church St; s/d £35/60; P ☒ ☐ wi-fi only) Staunch 18th-century home. Walkers and cyclists welcome.

Drinking

Three Tuns (☎ 638797; Salop St) One of Shropshire's most famous alehouses is a surprisingly ordinary place but for the fact that it is next door to a Victorian brewery, close enough to smell the roasting malt. Though they're no longer run by the same folk, you can still sample the brewery's best at the Three Tuns bar.

Six Bells Inn (☎ 630144; Church St; mains £7.50-13; ☻ lunch & dinner Tue-Sat, lunch Sun) This historic 17th-century coaching inn buzzes with loyal locals and serves ales from its adjoining brewery on tap. The pub also has a reputation for good ol' English comfort food like Big Nev's bangers made with local ale and Shropshire fidget pie.

Getting There & Away

Buses 552 and 748 run to and from Shrewsbury (one hour) seven times daily.

LUDLOW
☎ 01584 / pop 9548

All those walks in the Shropshire hills may come to naught once you reach the gourmet capital of England's northwest, Ludlow. This town has the twin attractions of being a crucible of culinary excellence, with more Michelin stars per head than anywhere but Paris, and boasting a rich historical core that fans out from its fine Norman castle. Its lovely muddle of narrow streets is flanked by half-timbered Jacobean and elegant Georgian buildings, many hosting independent butchers, bakers, grocers and cheesemongers all vying to whet your appetite. Our advice: book ahead and punch a few extra holes in your belt.

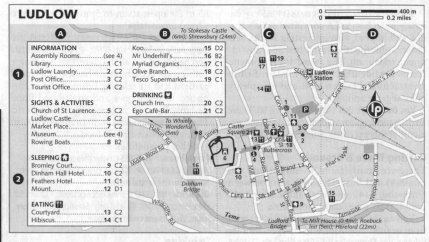

LUDLOW

0 — 400 m
0 — 0.2 miles

A

INFORMATION
Assembly Rooms............(see 4)
Library..................................1 C1
Ludlow Laundry..................2 C2
Post Office...........................3 C2
Tourist Office......................4 C2

SIGHTS & ACTIVITIES
Church of St Laurence.......5 C2
Ludlow Castle......................6 C2
Market Place.......................7 C2
Museum.........................(see 4)
Rowing Boats......................8 B2

SLEEPING
Bromley Court......................9 C2
Dinham Hall Hotel............10 C2
Feathers Hotel..................11 C1
Mount.................................12 D1

EATING
Courtyard...........................13 C2
Hibiscus..............................14 C1

B

To Stokesay Castle
(6mi); Shrewsbury (24mi)

Koo.....................................15 D2
Mr Underhill's....................16 B2
Myriad Organics................17 C1
Olive Branch......................18 C2
Tesco Supermarket..........19 C1

DRINKING
Church Inn..........................20 C2
Ego Café-Bar.....................21 C2

To Wheely
Wonderful
(5mi)

Castle
Square

Buttercross

To Mill House (0.4mi); Roebuck
Inn (5mi); Hereford (22mi)

To Stokesay Castle

Ludlow's helpful **tourist office** (☎ 875053; www
.ludlow.org.uk; Castle St; ☼ 10am-5pm) is in the 19th-
century assembly rooms, now a lively arts
and community centre. There's also a small
back-to-front **museum** (☎ 813666; admission free;
☼ 10.30am-1pm & 2-5pm Easter-Oct) on the town and
surrounding area here.

Internet can be tracked down at the **library**
(☎ 813600; 7/9 Parkway; ☼ 9.30am-5pm Mon-Wed & Sat,
9.30am-7.30pm Fri) and clothes can be washed,
dried and pressed at **Ludlow Laundry** (Tower St;
per bag £4.80; ☼ 9am-6pm Mon-Sat).

Sights & Activities

With seductive delicatessens and distracting
antique dealers around every corner, the best
way to explore Ludlow is to simply surrender
to getting pleasurably lost on foot.

The town's crowning jewel is its splendid
Castle (☎ 873355; www.ludlowcastle.com; Castle Sq; adult/
senior & student/child £4/3.50/2; ☼ 10am-5pm Apr-Sep,
10am-4pm Oct-Mar, 10am-4pm Sat & Sun Jan only), which
snags an ideal defensive location atop a cliff
above the river's elbow. One of a line of fortifications built along the Marches to ward off
the marauding Welsh, it is now a great castle
for hide-and-seek, with myriad nooks, ruined
rooms and mysterious stairwells. The sturdy
Norman keep was built around 1090 and has
wonderful views. The castle was transformed
into a 14th-century palace by the notorious
Roger Mortimer, who was instrumental in the
grisly death of Edward II. The round chapel in
the inner bailey was built in 1120 and is one
of few surviving.

The waymarked 30-mile **Mortimer Trail** to
Kington starts just outside the castle entrance.
The tourist office can provide a free leaflet on en
route services, or a more thorough booklet for
£1.50. Also see www.mortimercountry.co.uk.

Some delightfully cheeky medieval misericords lurk in the choir of **Church of St Laurence**
(☎ 872073; www.stlaurences.org.uk; King St; requested
donation £2; ☼ 10am-5.30pm Apr-Sep, 11am-4pm Oct-
Mar), one of the biggest parish churches in
Britain. These painstakingly carved 'mercy
seats' show scenes of domestic 15th-century
life both pious and profane, including a beer-
swilling chap raiding his barrel.

Guided walks (£2) run from April to October,
leaving the Cannon in Castle Sq at 2.30pm on
Saturday and Sunday. You can also take the
ghost walk (www.shropshireghostwalks.co.uk; adult/child
£3.50/2; ☼ 8pm Fri) from outside the Church Inn
on the Buttercross.

You can also hire **rowing boats** (per 30 min/hr
£3.50/6.50) to splash about on the river below
the castle.

Festivals & Events

Markets are held every Monday, Wednesday,
Friday and Saturday. The town's busy calendar
peaks with the **Ludlow Festival** (☎ 872150; www.lud
lowfestival.co.uk), a fortnight of theatre and music
in June and July that uses the castle as its dramatic backdrop. No surprise that most of the
other events are foodie affairs. The renowned
Ludlow Marches Food & Drink Festival (☎ 873957; www
.foodfestival.co.uk) is one of Britain's best, and takes
place over a long weekend in September.

Sleeping

Mount (☎ 874084; www.themountludlow.co.uk; 61 Gravel Hill; s £30, d £50-60; **P** **X**) Its hillside location secures this attractive Victorian house a glorious sunset view over town and hills, alone worthy of the modest price tag. Walkers and cyclists are well catered to, despite unforgivingly crisp white bed linen and cream carpets, and the welcoming hostess offers lifts from the railway station.

Bromley Court (☎ 876996; www.ludlowhotels.com; 73 Lower Broad St; d £75-110) In Ludlow's heart, these three gorgeous stone-walled Georgian cottages form carefully furnished split-level suites complete with lounge and kitchenette. The balance of period features and modern luxury is spot on. Breakfast is served in a connected cottage, and there's also a communal patio.

Feathers Hotel (☎ 875261; www.feathersatludlow.co.uk; Bull Ring; s/d £75/100; **P**) Three storeys of stunning black-and-white timber-framed façade serve to introduce this famous Jacobean inn. Not all rooms are in the wonderfully atmospheric original building, so make sure you're getting the real McCoy when booking. Newer rooms follow the usual bland template with antique-styled trimmings. The modern restaurant (set lunch/dinner £15/25) is recommended.

Other options include:

Mill House (☎ 872837; www.virtual-shropshire.co.uk /mill; Squirrel Lane, Lower Ledwyche; s/d £25/60; **P** **X**) Converted mill within walking distance of town beside the Shropshire Way.

Dinham Hall Hotel (☎ 876464; www.dinhamhall.co .uk; s £95, d £140-240; **P** **X**) Resplendent 18th-century country manor with superb traditional restaurant.

Eating

If you can afford to splurge on food, this is unquestionably the place to do it. While we've cherry-picked our favourites, you needn't go far for more epicurean delights.

Courtyard (☎ 878080; www.thecourtyard-ludlow.co.uk; 2 Quality Sq; mains £6.50-9; **⊙** lunch) A wholesome affair and antidote to too much extravagance, this staunchly old-fashioned café spills out onto a tranquil courtyard and has a faithful local following for its lightning service, good seasonal food and simple snacks.

Koo (☎ 878462; 127 Old St; 3-course set menu £18.95; **⊙** lunch & dinner Tue-Sat) The simple flower-dotted décor mirrors the crisp clean flavours of this authentic little Japanese cubbyhole, which is both a culinary and a cultural experience to savour. Favourites include sushi, gyoza and during the festival, takeaway bento boxes (£8.50) for impromptu picnics.

Mr Underhill's (☎ 874431; www.mr-underhills.co.uk; Dinham Weir; 6-course set menu £40; **⊙** lunch & dinner Wed-Mon) Ludlow's other Michelin-rated big cheese is set in a converted corn mill that dips its toes in the river. Expect exquisite modern British food, though there's little choice before dessert, so make any dietary requests beforehand. It also offers stylish rooms (singles £100, doubles £115 to £160).

Hibiscus (☎ 872325; www.hibiscusrestaurant.co.uk; 17 Corve St; set lunch/dinner menu £25/45; **⊙** lunch & dinner Tue-Sat) This ground-breaking twice Michelin-starred restaurant serves modern French cuisine with inventive flavour fusions to make your knees go weak. The serious business of eating is conducted within the oak-panelled and exposed brick walls of a 17th-century coach house.

Some other options:

Myriad Organics (☎ 872665; 22 Corve St; **⊙** 8.30am-6pm Mon-Sat) Excellent all-organic deli opposite arch rival supermarket Tesco.

Olive Branch (☎ 874314; 2-4 Old St; mains £5-8; **⊙** 10am-3pm) Healthful and mostly vegetarian lunch stop with seasonal menu.

Roebuck Inn (☎ 711230; Brimfield; mains £9-18; **⊙** lunch & dinner) A 15th-century country inn with excellent food 5 miles south of Ludlow.

SOMETHING SPECIAL

our pick **Waterdine Inn** (☎ 01547-528214; www.waterdine.com; Llanfair Waterdine; s/d with dinner & breakfast £80/160; **P** **X**), a flower-traced 16th-century longhouse, is nestled well and truly in the back of beyond, with the River Teme border with Wales trickling in the back garden the only reminder of an outside world. Expect a warm welcome that's helpful to a fault, and lovely cottage-style rooms with low ceilings, wooden furniture and springy beds. The restaurant also has a just-like-home atmosphere divided between several rooms, while the excellent modern Anglo-French menu (mains £11 to £16) focuses on organic meats and wild game. Llanfair Waterdine is about 12 miles west of Ludlow.

THE MARCHES

SOMETHING SPECIAL

Landlocked Shropshire is famous for its food, but generally not for its fresh fish. But bucking the trend 10 miles west of Ludlow is gastropub the **Frog** (☎ 540298; www.thefrogdining.com; Toddings, Leintwardine; mains £10-17; ☽ lunch & dinner Mon-Sat, lunch only Sun), which receives overnight deliveries of line-caught critters direct from Cornwall for its French chef to work his Michelin-starred magic with. Though cleared of all olde-worlde clutter within, the pub is very much a relaxed family-run affair and on a sunny afternoon, its alfresco decking overlooking the Teen Valley is the place to be.

Drinking

For an atmospheric pint of real ale, traditional hop-strewn pub the **Church Inn** (☎ 872174) is tucked away on narrow Buttercross. For a more contemporary atmosphere, surround yourself with images of Hollywood starlets at **Ego Café-Bar** (☎ 878000; 8 Quality Sq; mains £7-14; ☽ lunch & dinner), which also has secluded courtyard seating and Sunday-afternoon jazz.

Getting There & Around

Trains go twice-hourly to Shrewsbury (£7.70, 30 minutes) and Hereford (£5.90, 24 minutes), and hourly to Church Stretton (16 minutes). Slower buses go to Shrewsbury (bus 435, 1½ hours, eight daily) and to nearby towns.

You can hire bikes from **Wheely Wonderful** (☎ 01568-770755; www.wheelywonderfulcycling.co.uk; Petchfield Farm, Elton; bike/tandem per day £15/28), 5 miles west of Ludlow.

AROUND LUDLOW
Stokesay Castle

The wonky timber-framed tops and stunning Jacobean gatehouse of **Stokesay Castle** (EH; ☎ 01588-672544; adult/under 5/5-15yr £4.80/free/2.40; ☽ 10am-6pm Jun-Aug, 10am-5pm Thu-Mon Mar-May & Sep-Oct, 10am-4pm Fri-Mon Nov-Feb) give this fortified 13th-century manor house a fairy-tale glow that is hard to shake off. Built by Britain's most successful wool merchant, Lawrence of Ludlow, it has changed little since it was completed in 1291 and boasts a cavernous Great Hall, original timber staircase and gabled windows, and an enchanting garden that's hardly been touched since the original owners first pitched their medieval forks.

Stokesay Castle is 7 miles northwest of Ludlow, just off the A49. Bus 435 runs five times daily between Shrewsbury and Ludlow. Alternatively, catch the train to Craven Arms, just over a mile away.

NORTH SHROPSHIRE
Market Drayton to Ellesmere

A patchwork of pretty market towns, verdant countryside and glacial meres make northern Shropshire well worth exploring. With a market dating back 750 years, **Market Drayton** is also famed for its gingerbread and for being home to terrible teen Clive of India, founder of Britain's Indian Empire. The town has a scattering of medieval buildings. The **tourist office** (☎ 653114; marketdrayton.scf@shropshire-cc.gov. uk; 49 Cheshire St; ☽ 9.30am-4pm Mon-Sat) can point you towards sights.

Gardeners will find plenty of inspiration five miles southwest at **Wollerton Old Hall** (☎ 01630-685760; www.wollertonoldhallgarden.com; Wollerton; adult/child £4.50/1; ☽ Fri, Sun & Bank Hol noon-5pm), with its neatly snipped modern knot gardens surrounding a 16th-century house.

Another 4 miles west is the ideal energy-burning spot for kids, **Hawkstone Park & Follies** (☎ 01939-200611; www.hawkstone.co.uk; Weston-under-Redcastle; adult/child £5.95/3.95; ☽ 10am-4pm Mar-Sep, 10am-3pm Oct, 10am-2pm weekends only Jan-Feb), an 18th-century woodland fantasy of spooky rock-hewn caves, cliffs and underground grottos.

Another leap westwards will bring you to the beautiful mere-drizzled countryside around **Ellesmere**. The six glacial lakes surrounding town are ideal for gentle walking, with well-signposted circular routes to guide you.

For a real treat, stay in the small country house hotel **Pen-y-Dyffryn Hotel** (☎ 01691-653700; www.peny.co.uk; Rhydycroesau, Oswestry; s £84, d £106-152; P ☒), where the birdsong outguns any other noise and sheep roam the steep valley sides. Serving award-winning organic food (three-course set menu £32) and offering 12 traditional rooms, the hotel is in a remote Georgian rectory with gorgeous views of the Welsh mountains.

For somewhere still more personable, the lovely 16th-century **Top Farm House** (☎ 01691-682582; www.topfarmknockin.co.uk; Knockin; s/d/f £35/55/60; P ☒) is crisscrossed with an elaborately painted black-and-white timber façade, has just three old-maidish floral rooms and serves the best breakfast around.

THE MARCHES

The Midlands

Forget what the snobs say about the Midlands. Yes, the cities *are* scarred from WWII bombings. Yes, the 1950s' town planning *was* pathologically drab, and there *are* some bleak urban landscapes – what do you expect in the area that gave the world the Industrial Revolution? But the cities are vibrant and brim with influences from a hundred different nations, while the nightlife, restaurants and shopping give that uppity London a run for its money – and a thorough drubbing when it comes to value.

And, in a region known for being built-up, the countryside isn't half pretty. Just a short drive through suburbia or a gentle wend on the canals and you enter a different world. The stunning Peak District may be 'discovered' but it still feels isolated and wild. Charming villages dot the Nottinghamshire and Northamptonshire countryside while stately homes pocket the area, testament to its rich past.

Nowhere is that past more evocative than in the russet crumbling walls of Kenilworth Castle, the magnificent triple spires of Lichfield's cathedral or in Coventry's ruined old church cathedral.

And the Midlands are home to two of the country's best-known attractions: Warwick Castle, one of the finest medieval buildings in England, and Stratford-upon-Avon, a pilgrimage site for Shakespeare-lovers from around the world. Much ado about nothing? Not a chance.

THE MIDLANDS

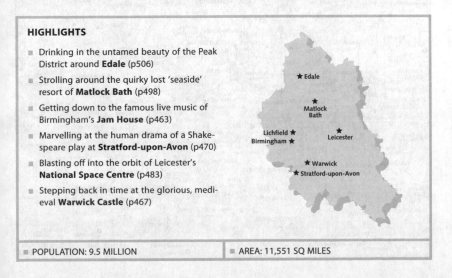

HIGHLIGHTS

- Drinking in the untamed beauty of the Peak District around **Edale** (p506)
- Strolling around the quirky lost 'seaside' resort of **Matlock Bath** (p498)
- Getting down to the famous live music of Birmingham's **Jam House** (p463)
- Marvelling at the human drama of a Shakespeare play at **Stratford-upon-Avon** (p470)
- Blasting off into the orbit of Leicester's **National Space Centre** (p483)
- Stepping back in time at the glorious, medieval **Warwick Castle** (p467)

★ Edale

★ Matlock Bath

Lichfield ★
Birmingham ★

★ Leicester

★ Warwick
★ Stratford-upon-Avon

| POPULATION: 9.5 MILLION | AREA: 11,551 SQ MILES |

Orientation

It is perhaps easiest to orientate yourself here by motorways. The M1 winds north from London, demarking the eastern third of the region (which is bounded to the east by the A1). It runs parallel with a line of the East Midlands' major towns: Bedford, Northampton, Leicester, Derby and Nottingham, in that order. The M40 does the same for the south and west of the region, passing Stratford-upon-Avon and Warwick on its way to the M42 and Birmingham in the centre of the Midlands. Routes spider out from Birmingham: the M6 runs east towards Coventry and the M1, and northwest up towards Wolverhampton, Stafford and Stoke-on-Trent; the M54 splits off at Wolverhampton to head over to Telford and Shrewsbury. The Peak District is midway between the M1 and the M6.

Information

The **Heart of England Tourist Board** (☎ 01905 761100; www.visitheartofengland.com) has centralised tourist information for the region and is a good place to start your planning.

Activities

The Peak District National Park is one of the finest areas in England for walking and cycling; more details are given in the introduction to the Peak District section (p500). It's also home to the start of the Pennine Way national trail, which leads keen walkers for 268 miles through Yorkshire and Northum-

THE MIDLANDS

berland into Scotland. The Pennine Bridle-way starts south of the walking route and is designed for horse riding, off-road cycling as well as walking. About one third of a planned 350-mile route is now open.

But these long-distance epics are the tip of the iceberg; the Peak District is crisscrossed with a vast network of paths for walkers, country lanes for touring cyclists, and tracks and bridleways for mountain bikers – with something for every level of ability. Ideal bases include the villages and towns of Buxton, Matlock Bath, Edale and Castleton, or the national park centre at Fairholmes on the Derwent Reservoirs. Bikes can be hired at Fairholmes and various other points around the Peak District, especially in the areas where old railway lines have been converted into delightful walking and cycling tracks.

In the south of the Midlands region, other good places for walking and cycling include Cannock Chase and, for those who are after more sedate options, the National Forest, an ongoing project to plant 30 million trees across this part of central England. The main centre (called Conkers) is near Ashby-de-la-Zouch in Leicestershire.

Sailors, windsurfers and water-lovers of all levels also flock to Rutland Water, a giant reservoir. It is surrounded by cycling and walking trails if the wet stuff is not your thing.

A canal boat is one of the most fun ways to get active, with the metropolis of Birmingham the unlikely epicentre. Get a group of you on board with bikes, and you can enjoy the canal-side paths by wheel or by foot at your leisure, as you gently chug your way through the country's massive network of artificial waterways; see boxed text, p79 for how to get started.

More information on all the above can be found in the Outdoor Activities chapter, p75.

Getting There & Around

National Express (☎ 08705 808080; www.nationalexpress.com) is the main coach service in the Midlands and throughout the country. Birmingham is a major hub. For regional bus timetables, consult **SCB East Midlands Travel & Leisure** (www.scbeastmidstravel.co.uk). Regional bus services are provided by **Stagecoach** (☎ 01788-535555; Explorer tickets adult/child £6.50/4.50) and **Travel West Midlands** (www.travelwm.co.uk). Make sure you take the right money for the latter as no change is given on any of its services. **Traveline** (☎ 0870 608 2608;

www.travelinemidlands.co.uk) is a comprehensive and impartial guide to transport in the region and beyond.

BIRMINGHAM

☎ 0121 / pop 977,087

Once a drab, grimy urban basket case, England's second-largest city – nicknamed 'Brum' – has spectacularly re-invented itself as a vibrant, cultural hot spot. Huge regeneration projects have breathed life into the industrial landscapes and canals that crisscross the city; now there are more glamorous shops, buzzing pubs and jumping nightclubs than you can shake a bargepole at.

Mind you, it's still no oil painting. The familiar destructive brew of WWII bombs and woeful town planning left a legacy of concrete and ring roads that will probably never fully be disguised. But, no matter: Birmingham is making the most of what it's got. Established cultural and architectural gems dot the city centre and planners keep coming up with ever more innovative architectural makeovers: the striking postindustrial Bullring shopping centre is just the latest. Although the manufacturing industry that defined Birmingham as the 'workhorse of the world' is declining (workers at the Longbridge Rover car factory recently felt the pinch of the moribund UK car industry), the city is well placed to adapt. More self-assured, cool and confident than it has been in many a year, it is hampered by only one thing – its inhabitants' accent, which is consistently voted England's least attractive.

HISTORY

One of the great centres of the Industrial Revolution, Birmingham has been the birthplace of several inventions; it was home to steam pioneers James Watt (1736–1819) and Matthew Boulton (1728–1809) and chemist Joseph Priestley (1733–1804), to name a few. By the mid-19th century, though, the city exemplified much that was bad about industrial development. It wasn't until the mid-1800s, under enlightened mayors such as Joseph Chamberlain (1836–1914), that Birmingham first became a trendsetter in civic regeneration. But WWII air raids and postwar town planners were to undo their good work in large part.

Fortunately, the city's leadership is once again devoting itself to ground-breaking civic

BIRMINGHAM

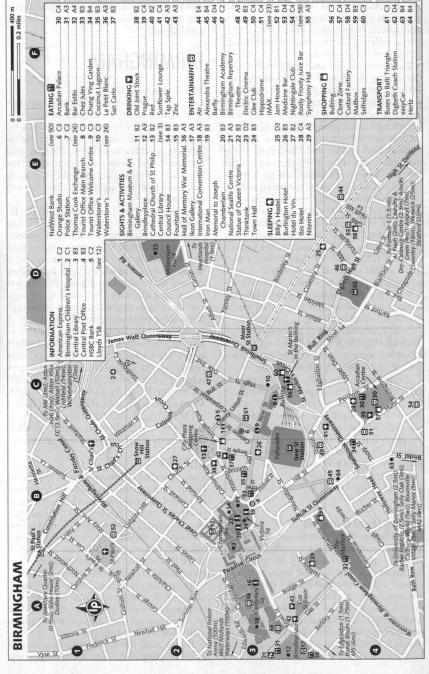

THE MIDLANDS

0   400 m
0   0.2 miles

INFORMATION
American Express.........................1 C2
Birmingham Children's Hospital...2 C1
Central Library............................3 B3
Central Post Office......................4 B3
HSBC Bank.................................5 C2
Lloyds TSB.............................(see 12)

SIGHTS & ACTIVITIES
Birmingham Museum & Art
 Gallery...................................6 C3
Brindleyplace............................7 A3
Cathedral Church of St Philip........8 C3
Central Library......................(see 3)
Council House............................9 B3
Fountain.................................10 C3
Hall of Memory War Memorial...16 A3
Ikon Gallery.............................17 A3
International Convention Centre...18 A3
Iron Man.................................19 B3
Memorial to Joseph
 Chamberlain..........................20 B3
National Sealife Centre...............21 A3
Statue of Queen Victoria............22 B3
Thinktank................................23 D2
Town Hall................................24 B3

SLEEPING
Billy's Hostel.............................25 D3
Burlington Hotel........................26 B3
Hotel du Vin............................27 B2
Ibis Hotel................................28 C4
Nitenite..................................29 A3

NatWest Bank......................(see 50)
Orange Studio............................6 C3
Police Station.......................(see 26)
Thomas Cook Exchange...............8 B3
Tourist Office Main Branch.............9 C3
Tourist Office Welcome Centre.....10 C3
Waterstone's......................(see 26)

EATING
Arcadian Palace........................30 C4
Bank......................................31 A3
Bar Estilo...............................32 A4
Chez Jules.............................33 B3
Chung Ying Garden...................34 B4
Coconut Lagoon.......................35 B3
Le Petit Blanc..........................36 B3
San Carlo...............................37 B3

DRINKING
Old Joint Stock.........................38 B2
Prague...................................39 C4
Red.......................................40 B2
Sunflower Lounge.....................41 C4
Tap Spile................................42 A3
Zinc......................................43 A3

ENTERTAINMENT
Air..44 E4
Alexandra Theatre.....................45 B4
Barfly....................................46 D4
Birmingham Academy.................47 C2
Birmingham Repertory
 Theatre................................48 A3
Electric Cinema.........................49 B3
Glee Club................................50 C4
Hippodrome............................51 C4
IMAX...............................(see 23)
Jam House..............................52 B1
Medicine Bar...........................53 D4
Nightingale Club.......................54 C4
Rooty Frooty Juice Bar..........(see 58)
Symphony Hall.........................55 A3

SHOPPING
Bullring..................................56 C3
Clone Zone.............................57 C4
Custard Factory........................58 D4
Mailbox..................................59 B3
Selfridges...............................60 C3

TRANSPORT
Buses to Balti Triangle................61 C3
Digbeth Coach Station................62 D4
easyCar..................................63 B4
Hertz.....................................64 B4

revitalisation, creating the award-winning Brindleyplace, the Mailbox, Millennium Point and, most recently, the Bullring in formerly grim urban wastelands.

ORIENTATION

The one aspect of Birmingham that's still indisputably a nightmare is driving in it. The endless ring roads, roundabouts and underpasses make it particularly confusing for motorists to navigate. It's wise to park somewhere and explore the city on foot until you get your bearings.

Taking the huge Council House as the centre, to the west is Centenary Sq, the International Convention Centre and Symphony Hall, and the development at Gas St Basin and Brindleyplace.

Southeast of the Council House, most of Birmingham's shops can be found along pedestrianised New St and in the modern City Plaza, Pallasades and Pavilions shopping centres. The Arcadian centre is further south, but still in the centre, and marks the beginning of Chinatown. Between New St station and Digbeth coach station is the Bullring, a sleek, architecturally striking shopping complex (see www.bullring.co.uk).

INFORMATION

Bookshops

Bonds Books (☎ 427 9343; www.bondbooks.co.uk; 97A High St, Harborne) Well-known independent bookstore, about 10 minutes' bus journey from the centre.
Waterstone's High St (☎ 633 4353; 24 High St); New St (☎ 631 4333; 128 New St)

Emergency

Police station (☎ 0845 113 5000; Steelhouse Lane)

Internet Access

Central Library (☎ 303 4511; Chamberlain Sq; ⏰ 9am-8pm Mon-Fri, to 5pm Sat) Internet access is free by reservation.
Orange Studio (☎ 634 2800; www.orangestudio.co.uk; 7 Cannon St; per hr £2; ⏰ 8.30am-6.30pm Mon-Fri, 10am-6.30pm Sat) This hip 'chat café' – an offshoot of a major mobile phone network – also has an upmarket 1st-floor restaurant.

Internet Resources

BBC Birmingham home page (www.bbc.co.uk /birmingham)
Birmingham Museums & Art Gallery (www.bmag .org.uk) Information on most of the city's museums and galleries, including opening hours, admission costs and forthcoming exhibitions.
Birmingham UK (www.birminghamuk.com)
icBirmingham (http://icbirmingham.icnetwork.co.uk) The local newspaper's website.
Birmingham Council (www.birmingham.gov.uk)
Gay Birmingham (www.gaybrum.com) Information for gay visitors.
Travel West Midlands (www.travelwm.co.uk) Travel planning from the main bus company.

Laundry

Laundry & Dry Cleaning Centre (☎ 771 3659; 236 Warwick Rd, Sparkhill)

Left Luggage

New Street Station (☎ 632 6884; Station Forecourt; locker hire per day £5.50; ⏰ 7am-11pm Mon-Sat, 8am-10pm Sun)

Media

Various free magazines fill hotel lobbies, bars and restaurants, providing handy updates on current exhibitions, restaurants, and the hippest bars and night clubs. The pick of the bunch is the fortnightly *What's On* magazine, available for free at some bars and the tourist office.

Medical Services

Birmingham Children's Hospital (☎ 333 9999; Steelhouse Lane)
Heartlands Hospital (☎ 424 3263; Bordesley Green E) Catch bus 15, 17 or 97.

Money

American Express (☎ 644 5555; Bank House, Cherry Union St)
Lloyds TSB (2 Brindleyplace)
HSBC Bank & Thomas Cook Exchange (☎ 643 5057; 130 New St)
NatWest Bank (Arcadian Centre)

Post

Central post office (1 Pinfold St, Victoria Sq; ⏰ 9am-5.30pm Mon-Fri, to 6pm Sat)

Tourist Information

Tourist office (www.birmingham.org.uk) Main branch (☎ 202 5099; The Rotunda, 150 New St; ⏰ 9.30am-5.30pm Mon, Wed-Sat, 10am-5.30pm Tue, 10.30am-4.30pm Sun); Welcome Centre (cnr New St & Corporation St; ⏰ 9am-5pm Mon-Sat, 10am-4pm Sun) The helpful, brochure-stuffed main branch has a wide range of maps and themed leaflets.

THE MIDLANDS

BIRMINGHAM IN...

Two Days

There's no mistaking where Birmingham excels these days: shopping. Feel your cash burn a hole in your pocket as you work through the series of exceptional commercial redevelopments that have rejuvenated the city. Perhaps work from east to west. Take in the quirkily original **Custard Factory** (p463) before heading up to the more mainstream **Bullring** (p463) with its space-age Selfridges building and hundreds of outlets. Dip south to the chic **Mailbox** (p464) and then take the trek up to the historical **Jewellery Quarter** (opposite). Even if the credit has run dry, it is well worth a look. Being a shameless consumer is hungry work, but Brindleyplace has the answer. **Bank** (p462) restaurant is one of the city's slickest places to eat. Then retrace your steps either to the **Jam House** (p463) in the Jewellery Quarter or the Medicine Bar in the Custard Factory – both rocking nights out. Gently does it on day two. Nourish the soul with the free, pre-Raphaelite-studded **Birmingham Museum & Art Gallery** (below). We then recommend a bit of people-watching in Birmingham's historical core around Victoria, Chamberlain and Centenary Squares before you catch a bus or taxi to the famous **Balti Triangle** (p461) to sample the curry dish that was born in Birmingham.

Four Days

Follow the two-day itinerary, but add a **cruise** (p460) along Birmingham's extraordinary canal network. A show at the world-class **Repertory** (p463) should be next on the cards. Next morning, make a pilgrimage to the **Barber Institute** (p458) and **Aston Hall** (p458) to see the region's most outstanding art collections. For a sweet interlude, make your way down to the chocolate paradise of **Cadbury World** (p458) for a seriously sugary experience. In the evening, take in an art-house film at the **Electric** (p463), the oldest working cinema in the country.

One Week

Follow the four-day schedule then use the extra days to visit outlying areas. In the summer, you can take a steam train to Shakespeare's **Stratford-upon-Avon** (p464). More conventional trains head to **Lichfield** (p475), with its marvellous three-spired cathedral, while the **Black Country Living Museum** (p464) in Dudley is also within easy reach for a day or half-day trip. Twenty miles east of Birmingham is Coventry, with Sir Basil Spence's fantastic postwar **St Michael's Cathedral** (p466), which is symbolically joined to the bombed-out old cathedral. Or, for a longer jaunt, escape to the **Peak District** (p500) for three days of long walks and cosy pubs.

DANGERS & ANNOYANCES

What were once the scariest parts of Birmingham – the area around the Bullring, for example – have been transformed by the city's dramatic refurbishments. And the city's vibrant nightlife means there's as much activity on the main streets at 2am as there is at 2pm, although the area around Digbeth bus station has an edge to it. As in most large cities, it's wise to avoid walking alone late at night in unlit areas, particularly if you're a woman.

SIGHTS & ACTIVITIES

Town Centre

The central pedestrians-only Victoria Sq features a giant **fountain** of a bathing woman (nicknamed, amusingly, 'the floozy in the Jacuzzi'), and a drab **statue of Queen Victoria**. It

adjoins Chamberlain Sq, with its **memorial to Joseph Chamberlain**, one of Birmingham's more enlightened mayors. These squares share some eye-catching architecture. The imposing **Council House** forms the northeastern face of the precinct. Its northwestern corner is formed by the modernist **Central Library**, reminiscent of an inverted ziggurat, with the Paradise Forum shop and café complex next to it.

To the south stands the **Town Hall**, opened in 1834, and designed by Joseph Hansom (creator of the hansom cab, forerunner to London's black taxis) to look like the Temple of Castor and Pollux in Rome. For those who won't make it to Gateshead to see Antony Gormley's *Angel of the North* statue (p736), his wingless **Iron Man** (1993), on Victoria Sq, is a step in the same direction.

THE PRE-RAPHAELITES & THE ARTS AND CRAFTS MOVEMENT

The Pre-Raphaelite Brotherhood, in a classic case of artists romanticising the 'good old days' they never experienced, shunned the art of their time in favour of the directness of art prior to the High Renaissance, especially the work preceding that of Raphael. Three young Brits, Dante Gabriel Rossetti, William Holman Hunt and John Everett Millais led the movement in 1848; four others soon joined them. Their work was characterised by almost photographic attention to detail, a combination of hyper-realism and brilliant colours. The themes and methods attracted criticism at the time but ensured the movement's popularity to this day.

Birmingham Museum & Art Gallery (below) has one of the best collections of works by the Pre-Raphaelites. If you get the bug, there are more fine paintings in the **Lady Lever Art Gallery** (p674) at Port Sunlight near Liverpool.

The Arts and Crafts movement followed Pre-Raphaelitism in yearning for a pure, idealised mode. The socialist William Morris, the movement's leading light, was a close friend of Pre-Raphaelite Edward Burne-Jones and projected the same ideals into tapestries, jewellery, stained glass and textile prints, following the principles of medieval guilds, in which the same artists designed and produced the work.

Those passing through Birmingham should stop at Wightwick Manor (p465), an Arts and Crafts masterpiece complete with original William Morris wallpaper and fabrics.

West of the precinct, Centenary Sq is another pedestrian square closed off at the western end by the **International Convention Centre** and the Symphony Hall (p463), and overlooked by the Repertory Theatre. Inside Centenary Sq is the **Hall of Memory War Memorial**, and there are often temporary exhibitions in the square.

The impressive **Birmingham Museum & Art Gallery** (☎ 303 2834; www.bmag.org.uk; Chamberlain Sq; admission free; ☑ 10am-5pm Mon-Thu & Sat, 10.30am-5pm Fri, 12.30-5pm Sun) houses displays of local and natural history, fine archaeology and ethnography exhibits, and a renowned collection of Pre-Raphaelite paintings. Other highlights include a fine porcelain collection, works by Degas, Braque, Renoir and Canaletto. You can sip coffee and nibble cake in the charming Edwardian tearoom.

One of England's smallest cathedrals, the striking **Cathedral Church of St Philip** (☎ 262 1840; Colmore Row; donations requested; ☑ 7am-7pm Mon-Fri, 8.30am-5.30pm Sat & Sun) was constructed in a neo-classical style between 1709 and 1715. The Pre-Raphaelite artist Edward Burne-Jones was responsible for the magnificent stained-glass windows: the *Last Judgement*, which can be seen at the western end, and *Nativity*, *Crucifixion* and *Ascension* at the eastern end.

Gas St, Brindleyplace & the Mailbox

Birmingham sits at the heart of England's canal network (the city actually has more canals than Venice), and visiting narrow-boats can moor in the Gas St Basin right in the heart of the city. Nearby Brindleyplace, a waterfront development of trendy shops, restaurants and bars created during the 1990s, has transformed the area west of Centenary Sq into a buzzing nightlife scene. A similar development to the southeast, the Mailbox, is even more style-conscious, bristling with designer boutiques and smart restaurants.

The **Ikon Gallery** (☎ 248 0708; www.ikon-gallery.co .uk; 1 Oozells Sq, Brindleyplace; admission free; ☑ 11am-6pm Tue-Sun) is a stylishly converted Gothic schoolhouse divided into smallish rooms. It has changing exhibitions of contemporary visual art. The Spanish cuisine dished up in the adjoining café is a great option for refuelling between cultural hot spots – but it will lighten your pockets.

The **National Sealife Centre** (☎ 633 4700; www .sealifeeurope.com; 3A Brindleyplace; adult/child £12.50/8.50; ☑ 10am-4pm Mon-Fri, to 5pm Sat & Sun), a state-of-the-art facility designed by Sir Norman Foster, is the largest inland aquarium in England; it swarms with exotic marine life. There's a sea-horse breeding facility – if you're lucky you might get a rare glimpse of a male sea horse delivering his thousand babies. The otter sanctuary is also a favourite with kids.

Jewellery Quarter

Birmingham has long been a major jewellery production centre, and the Jewellery Quarter is packed with manufacturers and showrooms. The tourist office provides a free booklet *Jewellery Quarter: The Essential Guide*, which includes background information about the industry and details of walking trails around the district.

In the **Museum of the Jewellery Quarter** (☎ 554 3598; 75-79 Vyse St; admission free; ☽ 11.30am-4pm Tue-Sun), the Smith & Pepper jewellery factory is preserved as it was on the day it closed in 1981 – including abandoned tea mugs and Marmite jars – after 80 years of operation. You can explore the long history of jewellery-making in Birmingham and watch demonstrations of the art.

The Jewellery Quarter is about three-quarters of a mile northwest of the centre; catch one of a host of buses (101 is the easiest), or take the metro from Snow Hill or the train from Moor St to Jewellery Quarter station.

Within walking distance of the Jewellery Quarter is **Soho House** (☎ 554 9122; Soho Ave, Handsworth; admission free; ☽ 11.30am-4pm Tue-Sun Apr-Oct), where the industrialist Matthew Boulton lived from 1766 to 1809. It has been painstakingly restored to reflect the styles of Boulton's era, and features displays on the great man's life and associates, including James Watt. Buses 74 and 79 pass nearby, or take the metro to Benson Rd station from Snow Hill.

Outlying Areas

Chocoholics from miles around flock to **Cadbury World** (☎ 0845 450 3599; www.cadburyworld.co.uk; Linden Rd; adult/child £12.50/9.50), which provides a lip-smacking exploration into the history, production and consumption of the ever popular cocoa-based confectionery, seen through the eyes of one of the world's largest chocolate-makers. Kids – and sweet-toothed grown-ups – will love it, but beware of the afternoon sugar-crash! Ride a beanmobile or take a wander down Cocoa Rd, paved with 'talking chocolate splodges'. If you're lucky, you may get to see the finishing touches being put to your favourite chocolate. Book ahead – it's very popular in July and August. Opening hours vary. It's closed for some of December and most of January, but open from 10am to 3pm or 10am to 4pm for most of the rest of the year (phone or check the website for details).

Cadbury World is part of pretty **Bournville Village**, designed for early-20th-century factory workers by the Cadbury family. Large houses, each unique, are set around a green. **Selly Manor** (☎ 472 0199; Maple Rd; adult/child £3/1;

☽ 10am-5pm Tue-Fri year-round, plus 2-5pm Sat & Sun Apr-Sep), dating from 1327 or earlier, was carefully taken apart and reconstructed by George Cadbury – who looks remarkably like Sigmund Freud – in order to save it from destruction. It has 18th-century furnishings and a Tudor garden.

The easiest way to get to Bournville is by train from Birmingham New St (five minutes). You can also get bus 45 or 47. Ask the driver to let you off at Pershore Road.

East of the centre, the Millennium Point development is designed to help people understand science and technology. The focal point is **Thinktank** (☎ 202 2222; www.thinktank.ac; Curzon St; adult/child £6.95/4.95; ☽ 10am-5pm), an ambitious attempt to make science accessible (primarily to kids). Interactive displays cover topics such as the body and medicine, science in everyday life, nature, future technology, and industrial history, as well as an impressive new digital **Planetarium** (admission £1, advance booking required).

A visit to the **Barber Institute** (☎ 414 7333; www.barber.org.uk; admission free; ☽ 10am-5pm Mon-Sat, noon-5pm Sun) is, for art-lovers, a highlight of a trip to Birmingham. The collection takes in Renaissance masterpieces, paintings by old masters such as Rubens and Van Dyck, British greats including Gainsborough, Reynolds and Turner, an array of impressionist pieces and modern classics by the likes of Picasso and Schiele.

The Barber Institute is at the University of Birmingham, 2½ miles south of the city centre. Take the train from New St to University station, or catch bus 61, 62 or 63 from Corporation St.

Aston Hall (☎ 327 0062; Trinity Rd, Aston; admission free; ☽ 11.30am-4pm Tue-Sun Easter-Oct), a mansion built in the extravagant Jacobean style between 1618 and 1635, boasts some impressive friezes, ceilings and tapestries. It also displays some furniture, paintings and textiles from the Birmingham Museum's collection. It's about 3 miles north of the city centre. To get there, take a train to Aston station from New St station.

BRUM NIGHTLIFE WALKING TOUR

Birmingham by night is one of the most buzzing, vibrant metropolises in the UK – no onlooker could call this part of the world drab after a wander through the streets at midnight on a Friday. This tour, about 2 miles, will take

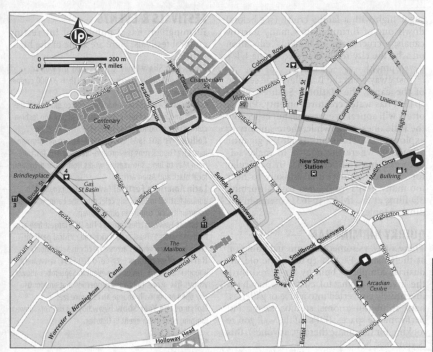

Start Bullring
Finish Prague
Distance 2 miles
Duration two hours or more

you through some of the hippest, most happening and memorable nightspots in town. Put aside two hours if you're pressed for time, otherwise just go with the flow...

Ease yourself into the tour with a shot of caffeine at the balcony café by the space-age Selfridges in the **Bullring** (1; p463). A spot of people-watching later and it's time to hit the road. Weave between the New St late shoppers and branch off to the magnificent **Old Joint Stock** (2; p462) pub where you can share the suits' relief as they spill out of the nearby offices. Skirt by the old Cathedral, ease your way through Victoria Sq then Chamberlain Sq and wander through Centenary Sq, mingling with the theatre fans and concertgoers. In winter, get your skates on at the ice rink, while temporary open-air exhibitions divert passers-by at most times of the year. Hungry yet? Just a little bit further and swanky Brindleyplace has just

the answer with the peerless **Le Petit Blanc** (3; p462). Sit down and let your olfactory senses be pampered. Appetite sated? Now creep out to Broad St. Look right, look left. Quick, dash between the screeching hen and lairy stag parties and duck into the one oasis of sanity in this part of town, the **Tap and Spile** (4; p462). Fine ales on tap in a nooks-and-crannies pub are your reward. Now take the downstairs exit by the canal and stroll south by the water where the new, the flashily revamped Mailbox development looms ahead. Join the city's bright young things in **Bar Estilo** (5; p461). There are plenty of other sleek places to be seen in this well-heeled part of town, which could easily distract you from the final leg of our tour, the Arcadian Centre, chock-a-block with night-time options, including buzzing **Prague** (6; p462). You've got this far, the rest of the night is up to you...

BIRMINGHAM FOR CHILDREN

The most obvious place to keep the kids entertained is Cadbury World (opposite). Partly educational, it should also satisfy any sweet-tooth cravings until Christmas. Ease away the

THE MIDLANDS

sugar high with a family cruise (see below) down one of Birmingham's many narrow canals; a crucial part of the kids' education on why the city really mattered in the UK's development.

Just away from the Brindleyplace section of the canal, the National Sealife Centre (p457) has water creatures aplenty. Playful otters will appeal to everyone, but especially the little ones. Meanwhile, there's plenty to explore at the Thinktank (p458), a gigantic attraction where the goal is to make science exciting and accessible, in particular for children. And you're unlikely to hear too many peeps from them with absorbing 3D films at the IMAX (p463) cinema in the same complex.

QUIRKY BIRMINGHAM

There's always something unusual going on at the Custard Factory (p463). The old industrial complex – built by Sir Alfred Bird, the inventor of instant custard – has been inventively converted into a hive of galleries, bars, exhibition rooms, studios, shops and performance spaces. If it's off the wall you're looking for (aromatic therapy, anyone?), this is your best bet.

Brindleypace's Ikon Gallery (p457) also plays host to unconventional modernist exhibits. Mainstream is not the word – be sure take an open mind. The same is required for the adults-only Birmingham Bizarre Bazaar, held the third Sunday of every month at the Nightingale Club (p462). Entrance is £4.50. For details, check out www.brumbazaar.co.uk or phone ☎ 602 1316. It's for those whose fetishes go well beyond the realm of stiletto-heel shoes.

TOURS

Second City Canal Cruises (☎ 236 9811; www.sec ondcityboats.co.uk; adult/child £3.50/2.50) Hour-long tours leave by arrangement from the Canalside Souvenir Shop in Gas St Basin.

Sherborne Wharf (☎ 455 6163; www.sherbornewharf .co.uk; Sherborne St; 🕙 trips at 11.30am, 1pm, 2.30pm & 4pm daily mid-Apr–Oct, Sat & Sun all year; adult/child £4.50/4) Canal cruises leave from the International Convention Centre quayside.

West Midlands Waterways (☎ 200 7400; www.wat erscape.com; Cambrian House, 2 Canalside; 🕙 9am-5pm Mon-Fri, 10am-5pm Sat & Sun Apr-Oct) Has leaflets, advice on days out by the water and details on how and where to hire canal boats. It's off King Edwards Rd.

FESTIVALS & EVENTS

Birmingham has a number of interesting cultural festivals. Here are some of the highlights.

Crufts Dog Show (www.crufts.org.uk) The world's largest dog show, in March, with more than 20,000 canines on parade.

Gay Pride (www.birminghamgaypride.co.uk) One of the largest and most colourful celebrations of gay and lesbian culture in the country, held in May.

Collide (☎ 303 3984; www.collide-arts.co.uk) Birmingham City Council runs this ground-breaking arts festival, from May to June, showcasing works from up-and-coming local black and Asian artists.

Latin American Festival (www.abslatin.co.uk) This annual festival in June/July celebrates the Latin American community and culture in Birmingham.

Artsfest (www.artsfest.org.uk) The UK's largest free arts festival features visual arts, dance and musical performances in various venues across the city in September.

Heritage Open Days (☎ 0870 240 5251; www.herit ageopendays.org) This unique event in September allows visitors free access to historic properties that are not usually open or normally charge an entrance fee.

Horse of the Year Show (www.hoys.co.uk) Top show-jumping equestrian event in October.

SLEEPING

Central hotels tend to target the business traveller and are usually at the higher end of the price spectrum. They often reduce their rates at the weekend. Check online or ask about specials at the tourist office, which also makes accommodation bookings. Few B&Bs are central, but many are situated within a 3-mile radius of the city centre, especially in Acocks Green (to the southeast) and the area that stretches from Edgbaston to Selly Oak (southwest).

Budget

Billy's Hostel (☎ 0795 1745 102, 0793 014 3439; gdblrmingham@hotmail.co.uk; 58 Coventry St; dm £17; P) It's the only backpackers joint in town, a very basic place a short walk from Digbeth bus station. It's not salubrious, but it seems secure. The welcome is warm enough – and the pub is literally right downstairs.

Formule 1 (☎ 773 9583; www.hotelformule1.com; 3 Bordesley Park Rd, Small Heath Highway; r £24.95; P) Cheap as chips, soulless, modern and clean: this place uses the same formula here as it does elsewhere. Rooms fit up to three people and it's about 20 minutes' walk from the centre.

Midrange

The better midrange options tend to be out of town – character-challenged chains dominate the centre, although they are convenient.

Awentsbury Hotel (☎ 472 1258; www.awentsbury .com; 21 Serpentine Rd, Selly Park; s/d incl breakfast from £42/56; P) The imposing Victorian exterior belies a welcoming B&B in the best English tradition at this house in Selly Park, close to the university. It also boasts a private vintage-car collection and a top-notch cooked breakfast.

Nitenite (☎ 236 9000; www.nitenite.com; 18 Holliday St; r £49.95; P) This unusual place shouldn't be comfortable but somehow is. The rooms are tiny and you get giant plasma TV screens with live Birmingham webcam images instead of windows. Yet the custom-made beds and leather fittings make it seem cosy rather than cramped.

Westbourne Lodge (☎ 429 1003; www.westbourne lodge.co.uk; Fountain Rd; s/d incl breakfast £55/75; P) Removed from the bustle of the city centre, this is still conveniently located just off the main road in southwest Edgbaston. Affable owners take pride in their terrace, a boon in the summer months. White-linen rooms are frilly but not overly so.

Ibis Hotel (☎ 622 6010; fax 622 6020; Arcadian Centre, Ladywell Walk; d £56.95; P) You know exactly what you're getting here: a spotless identikit room with the same wallpaper that you'll get in the same hotel chain in Mozambique. Within the Arcadian Centre by Chinatown, it's in a convenient location for a night out. Parking is £10 per night.

Top End

Burlington Hotel (☎ 643 9191; www.burlingtonhotel.com; Burlington Arcade, 126 New St; s/d Sun-Thu £145/155, Fri & Sat £90/130; P) The venerable old gentleman of Birmingham hotels, the Burlington is lavishly furnished with marble hallways and expensive glass lampshades. Some classic rooms have stand-alone bathtubs. Despite its size (there are 112 rooms), it feels quite personal and the restaurant is a fine option for sophisticated Continental cuisine.

Hotel du Vin (☎ 200 0600; www.hotelduvin.com; Church St; d from £135; P) Elegant, chic... and cher, this is a seriously opulent boutique hotel, converted, bizarrely, from a Victorian eye hospital. Egyptian linen and duck-down duvets characterise the bedrooms. Ask for an inside room overlooking the courtyard.

Manicures, massages and spas are all options for the indulgent. Bookings are advised for its bistro restaurant.

EATING

Birmingham's most famous contribution to cuisine is the balti, a Pakistani dish that has been adopted by curry houses across the country. The heartland is the Birmingham **Balti Triangle** in Sparkbrook, 2 miles south of the centre. Pick up a complete listings leaflet in the tourist office (or see the website www. thebaltiguide.com) and head out on bus 4, 5, 6, 12, 31 or 37 from Corporation St.

Al Frash (☎ 753 3120; www.alfrash.com; 186 Ladypool Rd, Sparkbrook; mains £3-8; 5pm-1am Sun-Thu, to 2am Fri & Sat; P) This is *the* place to experience the legendary Birmingham balti. Don't go for the flourishes – there aren't any. Just go for the massive excellent-value portions, and the good-natured service. If you're getting the bus ask the driver to stop by Ladypool Road.

San Carlo (☎ 633 0251; 4 Temple St; mains £10-16; noon-11pm) With Italian food far better than most mammas ever manage, this slick central restaurant is a magnet for local celebrities – although the service can be on the haughty side.

Chez Jules (☎ 633 4664; 5A Ethel St; mains £8-13, 2-course lunch £7.90; noon-4pm & 5-11pm Mon-Sun, closes Sun evening) French finesse defines the great-tasting dishes served up at this excellent bistro. Burgundy walls, a spacious dining area, long benches – perfect for group dining – and reasonable house wine prices add a certain *je ne sais quoi*.

Bar Estilo (☎ 643 3443; 110-114 Wharfside St; mains £8-13, 2-course set lunch £8; noon-11pm Mon-Sat, to 10.30pm Sun) A rustic chic interior, all terracotta, dimmed lighting and plush sofas, makes this bar/restaurant the venue of choice for the Mailbox smart set. The Mediterranean-influenced menu – the same as in the restaurant's London-based siblings – is reasonable, especially at lunchtime.

Chung Ying Garden (☎ 666 6622; 17 Thorp St; mains £8-14; noon-11pm) Get beyond the occasionally surly service and you'll be hard-pressed to fault the fine Cantonese dishes at this cavernous Chinatown favourite. With 70 varieties of dim sum, the biggest challenge is selecting from the menu!

Coconut Lagoon (☎ 643 3045; 12 Bennetts Hill; mains £10-14; noon-2.30pm & 5.30-11pm) Fusing culinary influences as diverse as Dutch, Portuguese and south Indian, this authentically decorated branch of a regional chain is one of the Midlands' finest curry houses. Try the coconut milk–bathed Kerala chicken stew (£9.75).

Le Petit Blanc (☎ 633 7333; 9 Brindleyplace; mains £10-17; ⏱ noon-2.45pm & 5.30-10.30pm Mon-Fri, noon-11pm Sat, noon-10pm Sun) Seriously stylish brasserie with contemporary French cuisine, this place exhibits all the hallmarks of its owner, français superchef Raymond Blanc. Reservations are recommended.

Arcadian Palace (☎ 622 3283; Unit B109 Arcadian Centre, Pershore St; mains £6-9; ⏱ noon-9.30pm Fri-Wed) Run by a supernice family, this simple, dinky, cafélike Chinese restaurant heaps the portions high and keeps the prices reasonably low. We liked the sizzling satay beef with crispy noodles (£6.80).

Bank (☎ 633 4466; 4 Brindleyplace; 3-course meal £12.50, mains £12-20; ⏱ breakfast, lunch & dinner Mon-Fri, lunch & dinner Sat & Sun; Ⓟ) Huge glass front panels make this swanky restaurant a bit of a culinary goldfish bowl, but most diners don't complain – the sophisticated modern-Brit dishes are quite special.

DRINKING

Chain pubs litter the city centre, especially on the deeply unappealing main Broad St drag. There are, however, more than a few gems if you know where to look.

Tap and Spile (☎ 632 5602; Gas St; ⏱ 11am-11pm Sun-Thu, 11am-4am Fri & Sat) Overlooking the canal, this traditional pub is all hidden alcoves and corners, especially once you move away from the sardine tin that is the top bar. There's a good selection of ales on tap here too.

Old Joint Stock (☎ 200 1892; 4 Temple Row West; ⏱ closes Sun) This vast, high-ceilinged cathedral of beer, a former bank, is marred by service without a smile. But the glittering furnishings and impressive setting, together with some half-decent ales, make it worth a stop.

Sunflower Lounge(☎ 4720138; 76 Smallbrook Queensway; ⏱ noon-11pm Mon-Wed, noon-1am Thu & Fri, 1pm-2am Sat, 5pm-10.30pm Sun) A quirky little mod bar in an unlikely setting by a dual carriageway near the New St rail station, this is a relatively undiscovered little gem favoured by the indie crowd, and with a great alternative soundtrack. Live gigs occur regularly in the tiny underground basement venue.

Prague (☎ 666 7789; 101 Hurst St; ⏱ 11am-11pm Mon-Wed, to 2am Thu-Sat, to midnight Sun) Leather sofas, white-tile floor, glammed-up crowds and a

cool, funk-grooved dance soundtrack make this the bar of choice among discerning Arcadian Centre revellers. Portuguese-inspired dishes are also served.

Red (☎ 643 0194; 3 Temple St; ⏱ noon-8pm Mon & Tue, to midnight Wed & Thu, to 3am Fri & Sat) Over-25s who have been there, done that, and moved away from boisterous Broad St head here for a mellower vibe. It's small, comfy and red all over, with DJs on Friday and Saturday nights.

Zinc (☎ 200 0620; Regency Wharf, Gas St Basin) Übermodern Conran bar-diner with an enticing menu and relaxed jazz and funk soundtrack.

ENTERTAINMENT

Tickets for most Birmingham events can be purchased through the national **TicketWeb** (☎ 08700 600 100; www.ticketweb.co.uk). It is cheaper to book online than on the phone. Also check the listings (see p455) for what's going on.

Nightclubs

Birmingham is throbbing with some of the best nights out in the country. Discover just how rocking the city's after-hours life can be at any of the following:

Medicine Bar (☎ 224 7502; www.factoryclub.co.uk; Custard Factory, Gibb St; ⏱ doors open 10pm) The crew working this joint are too cool for school. But they know only too well they are mixing it in the hippest, most happening nightspot in town with a truly eclectic range of nights, from Asian dub to hip-hop to electro pop. A blast.

Air (☎ 766 8400; www.airbirmingham.com; Heath Mill Lane) Supersleek, chic home to the renowned Godskitchen night (www.godskitchen.com), where some of the country's top DJs whip the crowd into arms-in-the-air delight with trance mixes.

Nightingale Club (☎ 0871 505 5000; Kent St) Birmingham's most established gay nightclub, the Nightingale rocks on three levels, with pop on the bottom floor, and techno rocking the upstairs. Remarkably, after more than three decades of action, it still tops polls as the region's premier gay club and is a known breeding ground for top-name DJs.

Rooty Frooty Juice bar (☎ 224 8458; Custard Factory, Gibb St; ⏱ 10pm-6am) A popular organic vegan/vegetarian restaurant by day, this tiny little place metamorphoses into a kicking, inventive night venue, dropping roots, reggae and dancehall beats. It also features comedy nights.

THE MIDLANDS

Glee Club (☎ 0870 241 5093; www.glee.co.uk; Arcadian Centre; tickets £8-15; ✆ Thu-Sat) One of the city's best-known comedy clubs, this place regularly attracts big-name comedians.

Live Music

Jam House (☎ 200 3030; www.thejamhouse.com; 1 St Paul's Sq; ✆ noon-midnight Mon & Tue, noon-2am Wed-Fri, 6pm-2am Sat) Legendary pianist Jools Holland directs the tunes here, a effortlessly classy live-music bar that features live swing, jazz, R&B and rock and roll, mixed in with the occasional reggae and ska. This is a real treat. Drinks are pricey, but the vibe is worth it. And if you're feeling like a splurge, the global cuisine of the top-floor restaurant hits all the right notes too.

Birmingham Academy (☎ 262 3000; www.birmingham-academy.co.uk; 52-54 Dale End) The best rock and pop venue in town, regularly attracting big name acts such as The Strokes and Primal Scream. Its indie club nights are also a big draw.

Barfly (☎ 633 8311; www.barflyclub.com; 78 Digbeth High St) Recently opened, this place is a grooming stable for up-and-coming indie bands, spawned by the success of a London-based night. It is warming up now – the bands are getting bigger, and the crowds are getting thicker. The entrance is on Milk St.

Symphony Hall (☎ 780 3333; www.symphonyhall .co.uk; Broad St; tickets from £7.50) For classical music, including performances by the City of Birmingham Symphony Orchestra, seek out the ultramodern Symphony Hall, which is known for its superb acoustics. World music and jazz acts also feature.

The giant **National Exhibition Centre Arena** (☎ 767 2937), near Birmingham International Airport, hosts major rock and pop acts, as does its sister venue, the **National Indoor Arena** (☎ 767 2937; King Edwards Rd) behind Brindleyplace.

Theatre & Cinemas

Birmingham Repertory Theatre (☎ 236 4455; www .birmingham-rep.co.uk; Centenary Sq, Broad St) In two venues, the Main House and the more experimental Door, 'the Rep' presents top-notch drama, Noel Coward comedies and plays fresh from London's best theatres.

Hippodrome (☎ 0870 730 1234; www.birmingham hippodrome.co.uk; Hurst St) This is the venue for musical extravaganzas from *Miss Saigon* to *Chitty Chitty Bang Bang*.

Alexandra Theatre (☎ 0870 607 7535; Suffolk St) This established venue stages everything from West End musicals and Broadway hits to opera from Verdi.

Electric Cinema (☎ 643 7879; www.theelectric.co.uk; 47-49 Station St; adult/child £6/4) Projectors have been rolling here for nigh 100 years, making it the oldest working cinema in the UK. It has an interesting art-house line-up.

IMAX (☎ 202 2222; www.imax.ac; Curzon St; adult/child £6.50/4.50) Birmingham's first Imax cinema, with a five-storey screen, is housed in the same building as the Thinktank (p458).

Sport

Villa Park (☎ 327 5353; www.avfc.co.uk; tickets adult/child from £25/15) Aston Villa football club, one of the Midlands' most enduring teams, play in this arena north of the city centre.

Warwickshire County Cricket Club (☎ 446 5506; www.edgbaston.com; County Ground, Edgbaston; tickets from £12) Tickets for international test matches sell out early, but local matches are usually available. The Twenty 20 games are pulsating, even for the uninitiated.

SHOPPING

Custard Factory (☎ 604 7777; www.custardfactory.com; Gibb St, Digbeth) One of the most unique, quirky places to shop in Birmingham, full of original, independent shops. So named because the building was constructed a century ago by custard magnate Sir Alfred Bird, this fantastic, eye-catching development is a memorable place to buy things you never knew you wanted. Funky niche shops are dotted between an arts and media centre; try the Urban Village for some retro-chic clothing and furnishings.

Jewellery Quarter (www.the-quarter.com) The obvious place for unique local shopping in Birmingham. Much of the jewellery manufactured in England comes from this region and there are more than a hundred shops selling traditionally handcrafted gold, silver jewellery, watches and more. The Museum of the Jewellery Quarter (p458) has leaflets detailing notable retail outlets and artisans.

Other options for serious retail therapy: **Bullring** (☎ 632 1500) This hellhole-turned-gleaming mall boasts '26 football pitches worth of shops, boutiques and restaurants'. The Selfridges department store is worth a visit for the architecture alone.

Clone Zone (☎ 666 6640; 84 Hurst St; ✆ 11am-9pm Mon-Sat, noon-7pm Sun) A branch of the world's largest gay retail chain, this place sells sex toys, clothes, accessories and adult novelties.

Mailbox (☎ 632 1000; www.mailboxlife.com; Wharfside St) Chic designer boutiques – Armani, Harvey Nichols – are gathered in the one place for label-hungry fashion victims. They are on various levels in the unlikely setting of a converted mail-sorting factory, along with a raft of swish restaurants and bars.

GETTING THERE & AWAY
Air
Birmingham has a busy **international airport** (☎ 0870 733 5511; www.bhx.co.uk) with flights mainly to European destinations and New York. It's about 8 miles east of the centre of Birmingham.

Bus
Most intercity buses run from dismal Digbeth coach station, which thankfully is due to be knocked down and rebuilt soon. **National Express** (☎ 0870 580 8080, www.nationalexpress.com) runs coaches between Birmingham and destinations around England including London (£14.50 single, 2¾ hours, hourly), Oxford (£10.20 single, 1½ hours, five daily) and Manchester (£11.20 single, 2½ hours, 11 daily). Bus X20 runs to Stratford-upon-Avon hourly on weekdays (1¼ hours) from Birmingham Moor St.

Train
Most of the longer distance trains are operated by Virgin Trains from New St station, beneath the Pallasades shopping centre, including those to and from London (£14.50 value advance single, 1½ hours, every 30 minutes) and Manchester (£9.50 value advance single, 1¾ hours, every 15 minutes). Other services, such as those to Stratford-upon-Avon (£5.40 single, 50 minutes, hourly), run from Snow Hill and Moor St stations.

In July and August, the **Shakespeare Express** steam train (☎ 708 4960; www.vintagetrains.co.uk; standard return £20) operates between Birmingham Snow Hill and Stratford-upon-Avon twice each Sunday. Journeys take one hour.

GETTING AROUND
To/From the Airport
Trains are the easiest option for getting to the airport. They run frequently between New St and Birmingham International station (20 minutes, every 10 minutes). Bus 900 runs to the airport (45 minutes, every

20 minutes) from Moor St Queensway. A **taxi** (☎ 427 8888) from the airport to the centre costs about £20.

Car
easyCar (☎ 0906 333 3333; www.easycar.co.uk; 17 Horse Fair, Birmingham)
Hertz (☎ 0121 782 5158; 7 Suffolk St)

Public Transport
Centro (☎ 200 2700; www.centro.org.uk), the transport authority for the Birmingham and Coventry area, provides general travel advice and a guide to getting around the West Midlands for those with mobility difficulties. The Daytripper ticket (adult/child £4.50/2.80) gives all-day travel on buses and trains after 9.30am; if you need to start earlier, buy a Centrocard (£5.60). Tickets are available from the **Central Travel Information Centre** (New St Station). **Traveline** (☎ 0870 608 2608) has comprehensive travel information.

Local trains operate from Moor St station, which is only a few minutes' walk from New St; follow the red line on the pavement.

Birmingham's tram system, the **Metro** (www.travelmetro.co.uk), runs from Snow Hill to Wolverhampton via the Jewellery Quarter, West Bromwich and Dudley. Fares start at 70p and rise to £2.20 for the full length. A day pass covering both Metro and bus costs £4.25/2.80.

TOA black cabs taxis (☎ 427 8888) are a good, reliable taxi firm.

AROUND BIRMINGHAM

THE BLACK COUNTRY
The industrial region west of Birmingham is known as the Black Country, a 19th-century description given because of the factory and foundry smoke, as well as the exposed coal seams. Now cleaned up, it's still not a tourist hot spot, but is a fascinating stop for anyone interested in how industry shapes a country. Don't mistake the locals for 'brummies'; as anyone round here will tell you, the 'yam yams' (so called because of a Black Country dialect habit of saying 'you am' instead of 'you are') have a very distinct identity of their own.

The extensive, lively **Black Country Living Museum** (☎ 0121-557 9643; www.bclm.co.uk; Tipton Rd, Dudley; adult/child £11/6; ☽ 10am-5pm daily Mar-Oct, 10am-4pm Wed-Sun Nov-Feb) features a coal mine, village and fairground, all restored to how they would have appeared in the industrial heyday of the 19th century. Costumed characters re-create the living conditions of the time. It's entertaining, enlightening and kid-friendly, with a full programme of mine trips, Charlie Chaplin films and opportunities to watch glass-cutters and sweet-makers in action.

Another reason to visit is Walsall's **New Art Gallery** (☎ 01922-654400; Gallery Sq; admission free; ⏰ 10am-5pm Tue-Sat, noon-5pm Sun), home to the eclectic Garman Ryan collection donated to the town by the second wife of renowned sculptor Sir Jacob Epstein. It includes works by Turner, Picasso, Rembrandt, Modigliani and Van Gogh. Trains to Walsall go to and from Birmingham New Street station (25 minutes, hourly). Take the train from Birmingham New St to Tipton, 1 mile from the museum. You can either walk or wait for the 312 bus. A Daytripper ticket will cover the entire bus and train journey.

To get to the museum from Birmingham's city centre by bus, take the 126 from Corporation St and go to Dudley. Again, the 312 will take you the rest of the way to the museum.

Wolverhampton

☎ 01902 pop 236,000

Another town defined largely by its industrial past, Wolverhampton could not be called pretty. But it's a welcoming place and there are a couple of attractions that are worth a look.

For information on the area, visit the **tourist office** (☎ 556110; www.wolverhampton.tic.dial.pipex.com; 18 Queen Sq; ⏰ 9.30am-5pm Mon-Sat Apr-Sep, 9.30am-4pm Mon-Sat Oct-Mar).

Wolverhampton Art Gallery (☎ 552055; Lichfield St; admission free; ⏰ 10am-5pm Mon-Sat) boasts fine collections of pop art and 18th- and 19th-century landscape paintings. The city is also home to **Wightwick Manor** (NT; ☎ 761400; Wightwick Bank; adult/child £6.60/3.30; ⏰ 1.30-5pm Thu, Sat & bank holidays Mar-Dec), an Arts and Crafts masterpiece, complete with original William Morris wallpaper and fabrics, Kempe glass and de Morgan tiling.

The **Civic & Wulfrun Halls** (☎ 552121; www.wolves civic.co.uk; North St) draw fans from all across the West Midlands for rock, pop and alternative music concerts. Check the website for upcoming gigs.

See opposite for details on getting here from Birmingham.

WARWICKSHIRE

Warwickshire got lucky: it could have been just another picturesque English county but history makes it one of the most visited areas outside of London. Shakespeare's birthplace at Stratford-upon-Avon and Warwick's superb castle are the main draws. Other, lesser known attractions can be just as rewarding, however: try the hauntingly atmospheric Kenilworth Castle ruins or visit the cathedrals (yes, plural) that shaped Coventry's history.

Orientation & Information

Warwickshire is roughly kidney shaped, with Coventry sitting between the lobes. Kenilworth, Leamington Spa and Warwick lie in the line running south from Coventry; Stratford-upon-Avon sits on the southern side of the M40 motorway bisecting the lower lobe.

The Shakespeare Country tourism website (www.shakespeare-country.co.uk) has information on the whole region.

Getting Around

The Warwickshire transport site (www.war wickshire.gov.uk/transport) has details of local bus and train services, as well as news on roads. Coventry is a major transport hub, with rail connections to London Euston and Birmingham New St.

A good ticket option is the Chiltern Rover (adult three days £39), which allows return train travel from London Marylebone or Paddington to Stratford-upon-Avon, Warwick or Leamington Spa on three chosen days within a seven-day period. It also includes unlimited travel in areas between, including Oxfordshire and Buckinghamshire, and free travel on Warwickshire's Stagecoach bus network. You can only buy the ticket from London's Marylebone Station.

COVENTRY

☎ 024 / pop 300,848

The city was blitzed so badly in WWII that the Nazis coined a new verb 'Coventrieren', meaning 'to flatten'. Postwar planning doomed Coventry to a nondescript concrete centre apart from the striking new cathedral, which was built alongside the bombed-out shell of the old. There are enough cathedrals to go round here – another even older one was recently excavated. The city also has an interesting industrial history as a prolific car-maker, the product of which can be seen in an absorbing transport museum.

Orientation & Information

Central Coventry is surrounded by a stark concrete ring road; most of the city's sights lie within. The main Pool Meadow bus station is central, while the train station is just outside of the ring road to the south. The **tourist office** (☎ 7622 7264; www.visitcoventry.co.uk; 4 Priory Row; ☻ 9.30am-5.30pm Mon-Fri, 9am-5pm Sat, 10.30am-2.30pm Sun) is on a cobbled street on the approach to the cathedrals.

Sights

The pretty **cathedral quarter** is historically the richest part of the city. The wonderfully evocative **cathedral ruins** of St Michael's Church Cathedral, destroyed by Nazi incendiary bombs in the blitz of 14 November 1940, still stand as a permanent memorial. The 180 steps of its **Gothic spire** can be climbed for some panoramic views. Symbolically adjoining the old cathedral's sandstone walls is the Sir Basil Spence–designed **cathedral** (☎ 7622 7597; www.coventrycathedral.org.uk; Priory Row; suggested donation £3; ☻ 9am-5pm), a modern, almost Gothic, architectural masterpiece. It includes a giant Graham Sutherland tapestry of Christ, glorious stained-glass nave windows (best seen from the altar), and a towering etched glass front. Look out for the Jacob Epstein statue of St Michael's conquest over the devil outside the main entrance. The story of the massive **St Mary's** cathedral, the original Coventry cathedral dismantled following the Reformation, is told in the small but well-presented **Priory Visitor Centre** (☎ 7655 2242; Priory Row; admission free; ☻ 10am-5.30pm Mon-Sat, noon-4pm Sun). In the same area is the **Guildhall** (☎ 7683 3328; Bayley Lane; admission free; ☻ 10am-4pm), one of the country's finest medieval guildhalls, where Mary Queen of Scots was briefly held. Look out for the centuries-old tapestry depicting Henry VI.

Further north, the extensive **Coventry Transport Museum** (☎ 7683 2425; www.transport-museum.com; Hales St; admission free; ☻ 10am-5pm) shows off the city's turbo-charged manufacturing past. It boasts the biggest collection of British-built vehicles in the world, most of them assembled in Coventry. They range from early bicycles to the slightly zippier Thrust SSC, the fastest land vehicle ever.

Sleeping

Ashdowns Guest House (☎ 7622 9280; 12 Regent St; s/d £25/50; P) Quirky, chintzy place nestled in a quiet residential street, seven minutes' walk from the train station. It is run by a welcoming, retired couple, who will give you chapter and verse on their interesting assorted antique clutter if you enquire.

Hylands Hotel (☎ 7650 1600; hylands@bestwestern.co.uk; 153 Warwick Rd; s/d incl breakfast from £56/85; P 🖳) Some rooms here greet you with a faded, musty air; pine bed-frames and park views freshen up others, especially rooms numbered in the 80s. It's less than five minutes from the train station.

Eating & Drinking

Habibi (☎ 7622 0669; 142 Far Gosford St; mains £7-12; ☻ 6pm-midnight Tue-Thu, to 1am Fri & Sat, to midnight Sun) Coventry's only Arabic restaurant is relatively normal downstairs, and like something out of Arabian nights upstairs, all silk cushions, cross-legged diners on the floor. The food is fantastic although expect a wait.

Browns (☎ 7622 1100; Earl St; ☻ closed Sun evening) With a door policy that makes Groucho's look slack, Browns nevertheless is one of the most easy-going, stylish places around. Spacious (you can normally find a seat here) and split on two levels, it also dishes out excellent-value canteen-style meals.

Café bar Inspire (☎ 7655 3355; New Union St; ☻ 11am-4pm Tue, noon-midnight Wed & Thu, 11am-2.30am Fri & Sat) Coventry's Christchurch church was destroyed during World War II, leaving only the spire, which now, slightly sacrilegiously, shelters this bar. This is forgivable as it is very good. It serves an international selection of bottled brews, as well as baguette and salad snacks (from £3.25) throughout the day.

Tin Angel (☎ 7655 9958; Spon St; ☻ closed Mon & Tue) It's a shame Coventry's coolest bar is the size of a sardine tin (although there are expansion plans), but this is the most hip, laid-back place in town. DJs, acoustic music and poetry evenings are just part of the entertainment.

Getting There & Away

Coventry is a convenient transport hub. Trains go south to London Euston (every 20 minutes, one hour 10 minutes) and Bournemouth, and you will rarely have to wait more than 10 minutes for a train to Birmingham. From the main bus station, there is a constant flow of National Express buses to most parts of the country. Bus X17 goes to Kenilworth, Leamington and Warwick (every 20 minutes).

WARWICK

☎ 01926 / pop 25,434

The magnificent turreted castle is the lure for most of the visitors to this quiet county town. It's an awe-inspiring sight – as are the queues in summer. Several other sights are less over-run, but also well worth stopping for. A gentle stroll round the centre reveals well-preserved historic buildings – survivors of a fire in 1694 that destroyed much of the town – as well as absorbing museums and fine riverside views.

Orientation & Information

Warwick is simple to navigate; the A429 runs right through the centre with Westgate at one end and Eastgate at the other. The town centre lies just north of this axis. The castle, which looms over the River Avon, is just south.

The **tourist office** (☎ 492212; www.warwick-uk.co .uk; Court House, Jury St; ☉ 9.30am-4.30pm), near the junction with Castle St, sells the informative *Warwick Town Trail* leaflet (50p).

Sights

WARWICK CASTLE

Incredibly well-preserved medieval **Warwick Castle** (☎ 0870 442 2000; www.warwick-castle.co.uk; adult/ child £15.95/9.95, peak dates £17.95/10.95; ☉ 10am-6pm Apr-Sep, to 5pm Oct-Mar; **P**) is an absolute stunner. Part of the Tussauds Group (hence the eerily lifelike wax inhabitants), it is prone to commercialism and crowds. However, its grandeur, magnificent landscaped gardens, and a palpable sense of history, including displays on influential historical figures such as 'kingmaker' Earl of Warwick Richard Neville, make it a must-see.

Plan on spending a full day if time permits. With waxwork-populated private apartments, superb interiors, ramparts, armour displays, dungeons (with torture chamber), the 'ghost tower' (called Warwick Ghosts 'Alive', entry £2.50), and a 19th-century power-generating mill house, there's more than enough to see.

COLLEGIATE CHURCH OF ST MARY

Originally built in 1123, this magnificent **church** (☎ 492909; Old Sq; suggested donation £2; ☉ 10am-6pm Apr-Oct, to 4.30pm Nov-Mar) has a soaring

THE MIDLANDS

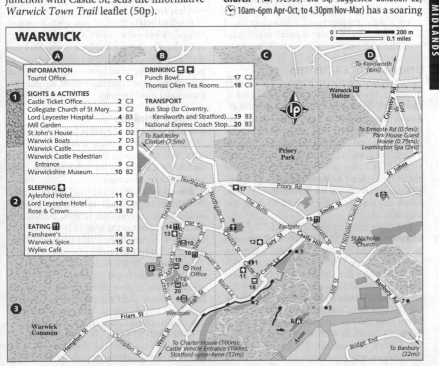

WARWICK

0 .... 200 m
0 .... 0.1 miles

INFORMATION	
Tourist Office..................1 C3	
SIGHTS & ACTIVITIES	
Castle Ticket Office..............2 C3	
Collegiate Church of St Mary.....3 C2	
Lord Leycester Hospital..........4 B3	
Mill Garden....................5 D3	
St John's House................6 D2	
Warwick Boats..................7 D3	
Warwick Castle.................8 C3	
Warwick Castle Pedestrian	
Entrance....................9 C2	
Warwickshire Museum...........10 B2	
SLEEPING	
Aylesford Hotel................11 C3	
Lord Leycester Hotel............12 C2	
Rose & Crown..................13 B2	
EATING	
Fanshawe's.....................14 B2	
Warwick Spice..................15 C3	
Wylies Café....................16 B2	

DRINKING
Punch Bowl.....................17 C2
Thomas Oken Tea Rooms........18 C3
TRANSPORT
Bus Stop (to Coventry,
Kenilworth and Stratford)....19 B3
National Express Coach Stop....20 B3

tower, visible for miles around. Climb it for a spectacular panorama (adult/child £2/50p). It was completed in 1704 after the 1694 Great Fire of Warwick gutted the original along with much of the church. The remarkable Beauchamp Chapel (built 1442–64) survived and the bronze tomb of Richard Beauchamp, earl of Warwick, still graces its centre. Ask one of the knowledgeable guides to point out 'the angel', a ghostly outline barely visible on the wall that was only recently spotted. Don't miss the 12th-century crypt with remnants of a medieval dunking stool, used to drench scolding wives.

LORD LEYCESTER HOSPITAL

At the Westgate end of the town, the road cuts through a sandstone cliff, above which perches the improbably leaning, timber-framed **Lord Leycester Hospital** (☎ 491422; High St; adult/child £4.90/3.90, garden only £2; hospital ☼ 10am-5pm Tue-Sun Apr-Sep, 10am-4pm Tue-Sun Oct-Mar). Despite its name, it was never a hospital. Robert Dudley, earl of Leicester and favourite of Queen Elizabeth I, made it a retirement home for soldiers and their wives in 1571 – and it still is today. It has a beautiful courtyard, a fine chapel and a guildhall. There is also a small regimental museum and a café.

OTHER SIGHTS & ACTIVITIES

For a fragrant perspective of the castle, nosey down to the **Mill Garden** (☎ 492877, 55 Mill St; admission £1; ☼ 9am-6pm Apr-Oct), a wonderful effusion of plants and colours within splashing distance of the weir that powered the castle mill. Money raised from this enchanting little enclave goes to charity. A fine alternative view of the castle is offered actually on the river itself. Head to **Warwick Boats** (☎ 494743; St Nicholas Park; rowing boat hire 30/60min £6/9; ☼ 10am-6.30pm daily Jun-Aug, 10am-6.30pm Sat & Sun Mar-May & Sep-Oct).

Other interesting sights include the **Warwickshire Museum** (☎ 412501; Market Pl; admission free; ☼ 10am-5pm Tue-Sat year-round, plus 11.30am-5pm Sun Apr-Sep), in the 17th-century market building. It displays the Sheldon's Tapestry Map, a woven map of Warwickshire stretching 5m across, which dates from 1647. **St John's House** (☎ 412132; St John's; admission free; ☼ 10am-5pm Tue-Sat year-round, plus 2.30-5pm Sun Apr-Sep) is a striking Jacobean mansion with an antique doll and toy display, reconstructed Victorian rooms and a regimental museum.

Sleeping

The nearest hostel is in Stratford-upon-Avon (see p472). Midrange B&Bs line Emscote Rd, the eastern end of the main road through Warwick toward Leamington Spa.

Park House Guest House (☎ 494359; 17 Emscote Rd; s/d £27.50/45) This is a basic but affordable option in a Gothic-style town house, 5–10 minutes' walk from the centre towards Leamington Spa.

Charter House (☎ 496965; sheila@penon.gotadsl.co.uk; 87-91 West St; s/d incl breakfast from £56/85; ℗) This has six rooms convincingly decorated in medieval period styles. Choose from 10 different types of breakfast. Book early.

Lord Leycester Hotel (☎ 491481; www.lord-leycester .co.uk; 17 Jury St; r £57.50; ℗) Pleasant staff and dated décor define this rambling manor house turned hotel, built in 1726, with small but comfortable rooms.

Rose & Crown (☎ 411117; www.roseandcrownwarwick .co.uk; 30 Market Pl; r incl breakfast £65; ℗ ▯) These modernist, smartly decorated lodgings, all en suite, lie above a chic gastropub. There are only five rooms, so call in advance. Some have wireless Internet access.

Aylesford Hotel (☎ 492799; www.aylesfordhotel.co.uk; 1 High St; s/d incl breakfast £65/80) A classic Georgian town house, the atmospheric Aylesford has well-kept rooms (including some with four-poster beds), a casual bistro and a revamped French restaurant that has reaped the plaudits from local food critics.

Eating & Drinking

Wylies Café (☎ 490448; The Old Iron Yard; scones and tea £3; ☼ 9.30am-5pm Mon-Sat) Hidden down a little side alley, this traditional tearoom is a delightful discovery. It is famous for its homemade cakes and delicious ice cream.

Warwick Spice (☎ 491736; 24 Smith St; mains £4.50-10; ☼ 5.30pm-midnight) Small, relaxed and specialising in Indian and Bangladeshi dishes, this place is regarded as the king of Warwick curry houses. You can claim a 10% discount if you have a ticket to the castle.

Fanshawe's (☎ 410590; 22 Market Pl; mains £11-19; ☼ 6-10pm Mon-Sat) From the rows of fussy flowers to the decorative china plates, this looks like an elderly aunt's living room. One that you don't mind visiting, however – the English cuisine is quite delectable.

Punch Bowl (☎ 403846; 1 The Butts) Guitars dangle from beams over the flagstone floors in this interesting Warwick pub. There are, of course, cask-conditioned ales and it serves reasonable food. Charming in a slightly cluttered way.

Thomas Oken Tea Rooms (☎ 499307; 20 Castle St; ☽ 10am-6pm) Just an arrow's flight away from the castle, this tearoom in a medieval house is pricey and usually packed – but it does have bags of atmosphere.

Getting There & Away

National Express coaches operate from Puckerings Lane on Old Sq. Local bus X17 runs to Coventry (55 minutes). Bus 18 goes to Stratford-upon-Avon (40 minutes, hourly) in one direction, and Leamington Spa (15 minutes) the other. The main bus stops are on Market St.

Trains run to Birmingham (30 minutes, every half-hour), Stratford-upon-Avon (30 minutes, hourly) and London (1½ hours, every 20 minutes).

AROUND WARWICK
Baddesley Clinton

Boasting Elizabethan interiors that have barely changed since the 17th century, **Baddesley Clinton** (NT; ☎ 01564-783294; adult/child £6.80/3.40, grounds only £3.40/1.70; ☽ 1.30-5pm Wed-Sun Mar, Apr, Oct & Nov, 1.30pm-5.30pm Wed-Sun May-Sep) is a small, enchanting 15th-century moated house. Persecuted Catholics took refuge in the home in the 16th century, as three cramped priest-holes show. It also has a murderous history: a priest was killed here after the owner, Nicholas Broom, found his wife in the man of religion's arms.

Baddesley Clinton is 7½ miles northwest of Warwick, just off the A4141. It is a pleasant 25-minute walk from Lapworth train station. Trains run direct from Warwick (15 minutes) and Birmingham (30 minutes).

Compton Verney

The once-ailing neoclassical mansion of **Compton Verney** (☎ 01926-645500; adult/child £6/2; ☽ 10am-5pm Tue-Sun) is reaping the rewards of a multimillion pound overhaul. It now houses an art gallery, which includes a permanent exhibition on British folk art, Neapolitan masterpieces, Germanic medieval art, and bronze artefacts from China. There are regular high-profile exhibitions too. Word has spread quickly – the small galleries quickly get crowded. If it gets too packed, duck out with a picnic hamper to the lovely grounds, land-scaped by Lancelot 'Capability' Brown. Bus 77 runs directly here from Leamington Spa and Stratford-upon-Avon (not on Sundays).

KENILWORTH
☎ 01926 / pop 23,219

One thing stands out in this pleasant, unremarkable pocket of middle England – its stunningly atmospheric ruined castle. With crumbling walls and vivid history, it inspired Walter Scott to use it as a setting for his novel, called...*Kenilworth*.

Information

Contact the **tourist office** (☎ 852595; Library, 11 Smalley Pl; ☽ 9am-7pm Mon & Thu, 9am-5.30pm Tue & Fri, 10.30am-5.30pm Wed, 9.30am-4pm Sat) for local tourist information.

Sights & Activities

Dramatic, red-sandstone **Kenilworth Castle** (EH; ☎ 852078; adult/child £4.90/3.30; ☽ 10am-5pm Mar-May & Sep-Oct, 10am-6pm Jun-Aug, 10am-4pm Nov-Feb) is less visited than its more commercial neighbour in Warwick, but arguably more rewarding. Founded around 1120 and enlarged in the 14th and 16th centuries, powerful men, including John of Gaunt, Simon de Montfort and Robert Dudley (favourite of Elizabeth I), have held sway here. There is now a new exhibition on the relationship between Dudley and the 'Virgin Queen', who visited the castle to tremendous fanfare, in the recently refurbished Leicester's Gatehouse. Following the Civil War siege, the castle's vast lake was drained in 1644, and it fell into disrepair. The audio tour is highly recommended – you almost feel like Elizabeth I is sitting at your side. Various jousting events and performances take place here throughout the year. Call for details.

Jane Austen and King Charles I are among the famous former guests in the 850-year history of **Stoneleigh Abbey** (☎ 858535; www.stoneleighabbey.org; adult/child £6.50/3; ☽ tours 11am, 1pm & 3pm Tue-Thu & Sun Easter-Oct). Founded by Cistercian monks in 1154, it became the home of the wealthy Leigh family in the 16th century. The splendid Palladian west wing, completed in 1726, contains richly detailed plasterwork ceilings and panelled rooms. Don't miss the medieval gatehouse, dating from 1346. The landscaped grounds are fine picnic territory. Stoneleigh is 2 miles east of Kenilworth, off the B4115.

THE MIDLANDS

Sleeping & Eating

Ferndale Guest House (☎ 853214; 45 Priory Rd; s/d incl breakfast £35/57; P 💻) Priory Rd is Kenilworth's B&B central – and this is the pick of the bunch. Its beds and sofas with plumped-up cushions are made to sink into. All are in elegantly furnished – if a little conservative – surrounds.

Castle Laurels Hotel (☎ 856179; www.castlelaurels.co.uk; 22 Castle Rd; s/d incl breakfast £45/75; P 💻) A stately guesthouse (B&B does not seem a posh enough name for it) opposite the castle, where the owners pride themselves on the spotless rooms and the warmth of the welcome. The home-cooked breakfasts (with free-range eggs) are lovely.

Virgins & Castle (☎ 853737; 7 High St; pub food £4-6, mains £9-11) This sprawling, comfortable old pub is a real local favourite, full of nooks and crannies and welcoming staff. It has a decent menu of Filipino specialities.

Clarendon Arms (☎ 852017; 44 Castle Hill; pub food £4-8, dinners £8-13) Right opposite the castle, this atmospheric pub has home-cooked food, a warm ambience and a cosy little beer garden.

Getting There & Away

Bus X17 runs to and from Warwick (20 minutes), Coventry (25 minutes) and Leamington Spa (15 minutes).

STRATFORD-UPON-AVON

☎ 01789 / pop 22,187

Few towns are so dominated by one man's legacy as Stratford is by a certain William Shakespeare, who was born here more than four centuries ago. Prepare to jostle for elbow room with coachloads of tourists in the antique houses associated with England's most famous wordsmith – certainly during summer and on most weekends. But if you choose your time, this pretty, historic market town should definitely be on your 'to visit' list: be sure to take in a play if you're hitting the Shakespeare trail. It is also a handy base for exploring the mighty Warwick and Kenilworth Castles and the picturesque Cotswold countryside.

Orientation

Arriving by coach or train, you'll find yourself within walking distance of the town centre, which is easy to explore on foot. Transport is only really essential for visiting Mary Arden's House.

Information

Cyber Junction (☎ 263400; 28 Greenhill St; 🕑 10am-6pm Mon-Fri, 10.30am-5.30pm Sat; per hr £4) Internet access and game play.

Sparklean Laundrette (☎ 269075; 74 Bull St; 🕑 8am-9pm)

Tourist office (☎ 0870 160 7930; www.shakespeare-country.co.uk; Bridgefoot; 🕑 9am-6pm Mon-Sat, 10.30am-4.30pm Sun Apr-Oct, 9am-5pm Mon-Sat, 10am-3pm Sun Nov-Mar) Helpful, but frantically busy in summer.

Sights & Activities

THE SHAKESPEARE HOUSES

The **Shakespeare Birthplace Trust** (☎ 204016; www.shakespeare.org.uk; adult/child all 5 properties £14/6.50, three in-town houses £11/5.50; 🕑 generally 9am-5pm Mon-Sat, 10am-5pm Sun Jun-Aug, variable at other times) manages five buildings associated with Shakespeare. Three of the houses are central, one is an easy walk away, and the fifth a drive or bike ride out; a combination ticket costs about half as much as the individual admission fees combined. Opening times are complicated and vary during the off season (check the website for details). In summer, enormous crowds pack the small Tudor houses; a visit out of season is much more enjoyable. Note that wheelchair access to the properties is restricted.

The number one Shakespeare attraction, **Shakespeare's Birthplace** (Henley St), has a modern façade on one side, but behind that it's very much 'olde'. It's been a tourist hot spot for three centuries (though there's no conclusive evidence Will was born here). Famous 19th-century visitor-vandals have scratched their names on a window, and the guest book bears the signatures of some big-time literati. Family rooms have been re-created in the style of Shakespeare's time, and there's a 'virtual reality' display downstairs for visitors unable to access the upper areas. Tickets include admission to the adjacent **Shakespeare Exhibition**, where well-devised displays chart the life of Stratford's most famous son.

The wealthy, retired Shakespeare bought a fine home at New Pl on the corner of Chapel St and Chapel Lane. He died there in April 1616 and the house was demolished in 1759. An attractive Elizabethan **knot garden** now occupies part of the grounds. Displays in the adjacent **Nash's House**, where Shakespeare's granddaughter Elizabeth lived, describe the town's history and contain a collection of 17th-century oak furniture and tapestries.

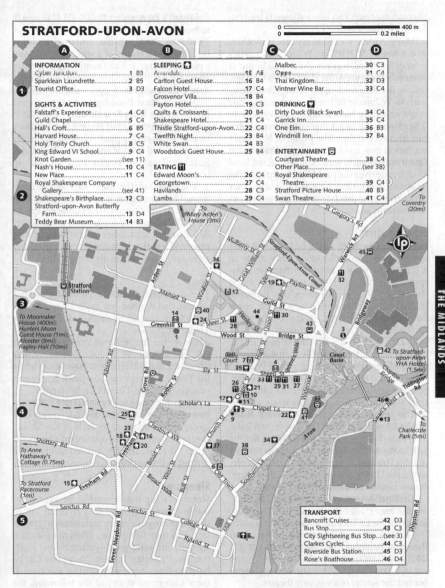

STRATFORD-UPON-AVON

0 — 400 m
0 — 0.2 miles

INFORMATION
Cyber Junction.....................1 D3
Sparklean Laundrette............2 B5
Tourist Office.......................3 D3

SIGHTS & ACTIVITIES
Falstaff's Experience............4 C4
Guild Chapel........................5 C4
Hall's Croft..........................6 B5
Harvard House......................7 C4
Holy Trinity Church...............8 C5
King Edward VI School..........9 C4
Knot Garden....................(see 11)
Nash's House......................10 C4
New Place...........................11 C4
Royal Shakespeare Company
  Gallery.........................(see 41)
Shakespeare's Birthplace......12 C3
Stratford-upon-Avon Butterfly
  Farm.............................13 D4
Teddy Bear Museum............14 B3

SLEEPING
Arundale............................15 A5
Carlton Guest House.............16 B4
Falcon Hotel........................17 C4
Grosvenor Villa....................18 B4
Payton Hotel.......................19 C3
Quilts & Croissants...............20 B4
Shakespeare Hotel................21 C4
Thistle Stratford-upon-Avon...22 C4
Twelfth Night.......................23 B4
White Swan.........................24 B3
Woodstock Guest House........25 B4

EATING
Edward Moon's....................26 C4
Georgetown.........................27 C4
Havilands............................28 C3
Lambs................................29 C4

DRINKING
Dirty Duck (Black Swan).........34 C4
Garrick Inn..........................35 C4
One Elm..............................36 B3
Windmill Inn........................37 B4

Malbec...............................30 C3
Oppo.................................31 C4
Thai Kingdom......................32 D3
Vintner Wine Bar..................33 C4

ENTERTAINMENT
Courtyard Theatre................38 C4
Other Place.....................(see 38)
Royal Shakespeare
  Theatre..........................39 C4
Stratford Picture House.........40 B3
Swan Theatre......................41 C4

TRANSPORT
Bancroft Cruises..................42 D3
Bus Stop............................43 C3
City Sightseeing Bus Stop...(see 3)
Clarkes Cycles.....................44 C3
Riverside Bus Station............45 D3
Rose's Boathouse.................46 D4

To Mary Arden's House (3mi)
To Coventry (20mi)
To Moonraker House (400m); Hunters Moon Guest House (1mi); Alcester (8mi); Ragley Hall (10mi)
To Anne Hathaway's Cottage (0.75mi)
To Stratford Racecourse (1mi)
To Stratford-upon-Avon YHA Hostel (1.5mi)
To Charlecote Park (5mi)

THE MIDLANDS

Shakespeare's daughter Susanna married the eminent doctor John Hall, and their fine Elizabethan town house, **Hall's Croft** (☎ 292107), stands near Holy Trinity Church. The main exhibition offers a fascinating insight into medical practice way back in Shakespeare's time.

Before marrying, Shakespeare's wife lived in Shottery, a mile west of the centre, in a pretty thatched farmhouse now known as **Anne Hathaway's Cottage** (☎ 292100). As well as contemporary furniture there's an orchard and **Shakespeare Tree Garden**, with examples of all the trees mentioned in Shakespeare's plays. A footpath (no bikes allowed) leads to Shottery from Evesham Pl.

Mary Arden was Shakespeare's mother, and a **house** (☎ 293455) at Wilmcote, 3 miles west of Stratford, was her childhood home. If you cycle there via Anne Hathaway's Cottage, follow the Stratford-upon-Avon Canal towpath to Wilmcote rather than retracing your route or riding back along the busy A3400. The easiest way to get there otherwise is on a bus tour (see right). The home of William's mother is now used to house the **Shakespeare Countryside Museum**, with exhibits tracing local country life over the past four centuries. Plan to spend more time here than at the other properties to appreciate its unique collection of rare farm animals.

OTHER SIGHTS

Holy Trinity Church (☎ 266316; Old Town; 🕑 8.30am-6pm Mon-Sat & 12.30-5pm Sun Apr-Oct, 9am-4pm Mon-Sat & 12.30-5pm Sun Nov-Mar; admission to church free, Shakespeare's grave adult/child £1/50p) is thought to be the most visited parish church in England, as Shakespeare lies buried here. It's a lovely building in its own right, situated on the banks of the River Avon. The transepts from the mid-13th century are the oldest part. In the chancel are photocopies of Shakespeare's baptism and burial records, the graves of Will and his wife, and a bust created seven years after Shakespeare's death but before his wife's and thus assumed to be a good likeness.

The exuberantly carved **Harvard House** (☎ 204407; High St; adult/child £2.75/free, free with Shakespeare Houses ticket; 🕑 noon-5pm Wed-Sun Jul-Sep, Wed, Thu, Sat & Sun May, Jun & Sep-Oct) was home to the mother of John Harvard, after whom Harvard University in the USA was named in the 17th century. It now houses a **Museum of British Pewter**.

The **Royal Shakespeare Company Gallery** (☎ 412617; admission free; 🕑 1.30-6.30pm Mon-Sat, 11.15-4.15pm Sun), inside the Swan Theatre, is a small but absorbing display of props, costumes, photos and theatrical paraphernalia. **Theatre tours** (☎ 0870 609 1110; adult/child incl admission to RSC Gallery £5/4; 🕑 times vary, call in advance to check) offer a fascinating glimpse behind the scenes of a working theatre.

The **Stratford-upon-Avon Butterfly Farm** (☎ 299288; www.butterflyfarm.co.uk; Swan's Nest Lane; adult/child £4.95/3.95) is a large greenhouse housing hundreds of species of exotic butterflies in tropical foliage. Other displays, including the creepy 'Arachnoland' scorpion and spider section, are also here.

Falstaff's Experience (☎ 0870 350 2770; www.falstaffsexperience.co.uk; 40 Sheep St; adult/child £5/4; 🕑 10.30am-5.30pm), an old timbered building housing re-creations of a witches' glade and a plague cottage, is like a rambling, stationary ghost train with some history thrown in; mordant kids (and grown-ups) will enjoy it.

Meet the first Paddington Bear to appear on TV at the **Teddy Bear Museum** (☎ 293160; 19 Greenhill St; adult/child £2.95/1.95; 🕑 9.30am-5.30pm), a strangely unsettling place founded by former politician and broadcaster Gyles Brandreth. Smokey Bear and Fozzie Bear are also in residence.

The **Guild Chapel** (cnr Chapel Lane & Church St) dates from 1269, though it was rebuilt in the 15th century. It's not open to the public except for services (10am Wednesday and noon Saturday April to September). Next door is **King Edward VI School**, which Shakespeare probably attended; it was originally the guildhall.

Tours

Two-hour **guided walks** (☎ 292478; adult/child £5/2; 🕑 tours 11am Mon-Wed, 2pm Thu-Sun) depart from Swan fountain just by the Royal Shakespeare Theatre. Chill-seekers can also go to the same group for the **Stratford Town Ghost Walk** (adult/child £5/3; 🕑 7.30pm Mon, Thu & Fri) An alternative **walk** (☎ 292478; adult/child £8/6; 🕑 10.30am Sat) is run by the Royal Shakespeare Company, and leaves outside the Swan Theatre on Waterside.

Open-top buses of **City Sightseeing** (☎ 299123; www.city-sightseeing.com; adult/child £9/4; 🕑 every 15min Apr-Sep, fewer in winter) go to each of the Shakespeare properties. They operate on a jump-on, jump-off basis, and are a convenient way of getting to the out-of-town houses.

Sleeping

Stratford's big hotels tend to be geared towards group travel, so they're often out of the price range of many independent travellers, and they fill up fast. B&Bs are plentiful though, and offer good-quality rooms in attractive Victorian houses. Vacancies can be hard to find, especially during summer. If there's no room at any of the following, the tourist office charges £3 plus 10% deposit to find something.

BUDGET

Stratford-upon-Avon YHA Hostel (☎ 0870 160 7930; stratford@yha.org.uk; Hemmingford House, Alveston; dm incl breakfast members/nonmembers £19.95/22.95; 🅿 🖥)

This four-star youth hostel is situated in a large, 200-year-old mansion 1.5 miles east of the town centre along Tiddington Rd. Buses X17/18/18A operate to Alveston from Bridge St.

Quilts & Croissants (☎ 267629; rooms@quilt-crois sants.demon.co.uk; 33 Evesham Pl; s/d incl breakfast £26/52; **P** ✗) A likeable family welcomes you here. Earth colours abound and the B&B is correspondingly warm and comfortable. The owners are keen theatregoers themselves, and can fill you in on the latest performances. Credit cards not accepted.

Other good budget options:

Stratford Racecourse (☎ 201063; info@ stratfordracecourse.net; Luddington Rd; 2-person pitches £10; ☾ Easter-Sep; **P**) Camp site just off Evesham Rd a mile west of town.

Arrandale (☎ 267112; www.arrandale.netfirms.com; 208 Evesham Rd; d incl breakfast £17-20; **P**) Neatly kept lodgings, 10 minutes' walk from the centre.

Grosvenor Villa (☎ 266192; www.grosvenorvilla.com; 9 Evesham Pl; s/d incl breakfast £23/50; **P**) Staff are very friendly at this chintzy but spotless B&B.

Carlton Guest House (☎ 293548; 22 Evesham Pl; s/d incl breakfast £26/52; **P**) The jolly proprietor has several reasonable en-suite rooms available.

MIDRANGE

Twelfth Night (☎ 414595; www.twelfthnight.co.uk; 13 Evesham Pl; s/d from £36/70; **P** ✗) Now an up-market B&B, with flowery frills and gleaming brass bed frames, this once belonged to Royal Shakespeare Company governors. Breakfast is served on Wedgwood china.

Moonraker House (☎ 268774; www.moonrakerhouse .com; 40 Alcester Rd; s/d incl breakfast from £40/65; **P**) Pristine to the point of fussy, the rooms behind the whitewashed façade of this memorable B&B are frilly, almost feminine affairs. Rooms have an unusual mix of themes – James Bond and Shakespeare. Impeccably attentive owners provide healthy organic and vegetarian options for breakfast.

Other recommended midrange options:

Woodstock Guest House (☎ 299881; woodstockhou se@compuserve.com; 30 Grove Rd; s/d from £35/64; **P**) Comfortable and welcoming with carpets you sink into.

Hunters Moon Guest House (☎ 292888; www.hunter smoonguesthouse.com; 150 Alcester Rd; s/d £35/70; **P** ✗) About 15 minutes' walk out of town with hospitable owners.

Payton Hotel (☎ 266442; www.payton.co.uk; 6 John St; s/d from £64/72; **P**) Fastidiously well-kept, upper-crust Georgian town house in a quiet area of town.

TOP END

White Swan (☎ 297022; www.thewhiteswanstratford .co.uk; Rother St; s/d from £60/80; **P**) All the quaint traits of a centuries-old hotel are here, from carved bed headboards to the atmospherically uneven floors. Rooms do vary. Plump for the oak-panelled delights of the traditional rooms (room 103 is perhaps the most charming) if possible – the standard rooms are quite ordinary.

Falcon Hotel (☎ 279953; info@legacy-hotels.co.uk; Chapel St; s/d £105/125; **P** 🖳) The rooms here veer from fantastically antique with creaky floorboards and angled bed posts at the 16th-century hotel front to anodyne modern rooms in the sprawling recent extension. Special deals are available. Breakfast is £7 to £10 extra.

Shakespeare Hotel (☎ 0870 400 8182; www.theshake speare-hotel.co.uk; Chapel St; s/d £128/138; **P** 🖳) A labyrinth of rooms enchants guests at this classic hotel, the classiest in Stratford by a sonnet. The pick of the rooms are those named after Shakespeare's plays. Some you have to stoop to get into, but with their wooden panelled headboards complemented by luxury bathrooms, they are the perfect base for soaking up the town's rich Elizabethan heritage.

Thistle Stratford-upon-Avon (☎ 294949; stratford.uponavon@thistle.co.uk; Waterside; s/d incl breakfast from £135/165; **P** 🖳) Superbly located across the road from the Swan Theatre, the Thistle overlooks the River Avon and pretty bankside parkland. Brass reading lights brighten the corridors, and the fragrant, comfortable rooms are everything you would expect from a top-end chain. There's a terrace for summer dining. Large discounts are available in low season.

Eating

Shakespearean tourism clearly makes you hungry: there's certainly no shortage of good restaurants. Sheep St is clustered with refined but relaxed eating options, mostly aimed at theatregoers.

Vintner Wine Bar (☎ 297259; 5 Sheep St; mains £9-13; ☾ 10am-10pm Mon-Thu, to 11pm Fri & Sat, to 9.30pm Sun) The most down-to-earth of all the restaurant options on the gourmet Sheep St strip, this place is unpretentious and fun. The menu includes several inventive vegetarian options.

Lambs (☎ 292554; 12 Sheep St; mains £11-18; ☾ noon-2pm Mon-Sun, plus 5-10pm Mon-Sat, 6-9.30pm Sun) From the imposing manor-house door to the aristocratic interior, this courses with effortless

THE MIDLANDS

sophistication. Dishes, such as roasted saddle of lamb (£15.95), are not cheap, but it's the company you are keeping that counts, my dear.

Edward Moon's (☎ 267069; 9 Chapel St; mains £10-14; ☾ lunch & dinner) Inspired by an itinerant cook who loved English food spiced with local ingredients, Moon's is relaxed and distinguished by the entirely glass-panelled front.

Georgetown (☎ 204445; 23 Sheep St; mains £11-15; ☾ noon-2.30pm & 5-11pm) Fresh daisies on each table, chandeliers: there is more than a hint of Raffles at this classy vegetarian-friendly Malaysian restaurant, which blends Indian, Chinese and European culinary influences.

Other recommendations:

Haviland's (☎ 415477; 5 Meer St; cream tea £3.95; ☾ 9am-3.30pm Mon-Fri, to 5pm Sat) 'Full of yummy things' as one local put it. The sandwich range makes perfect picnic fodder.

Thai Kingdom (☎ 261103; 11 Warwick Rd; mains £6-11; ☾ noon-2pm & 6-10.45pm) The dishes are so good they were once ordered as a takeaway by a prince of Thailand…when he was in Thailand!

Oppo (☎ 269980; 13 Sheep St; mains £9-12 ☾ noon-2pm Mon-Sun, plus 5-9.30pm Mon-Thu, 5-11pm Fri & Sat, 6-9.30pm Sun) Global cuisine in elegant surroundings.

Malbec (☎ 269106; 6 Union St; mains £12-19; ☾ noon-2pm Tue-Sat, plus 7-9.30pm Tue-Thu, 6-9.30pm Fri & Sat) Very swish but relaxed with a delicious, á la carte menu and personable service. The whitewashed lower level is particularly atmospheric.

Drinking

Dirty Duck (☎ 297312; Waterside) If you only have one drink in Stratford, come here. It's almost as essential as a trip to the theatre. Officially called the Black Swan, this enchanting alehouse is a favourite postperformance thespian watering hole, and has a roll call of former regulars (Olivier, Attenborough etc) that reads like an actors' *Who's Who*. It's in a very pretty location across from the river. The adjoining restaurant (11am to 10pm) is good value.

Windmill Inn (☎ 297687; Church St) Ale was flowing here at the same time as rhyming couplets flowed from Shakespeare's quill – it's been around a while. Despite its age it's still one of the liveliest places in town.

One Elm (☎ 404919; 1 Guild St) A swanky place with leather seats and sun-tanned clientele, this popular gastropub has a pleasant courtyard and owners who are real foodies – the restaurant dishes are a treat.

Garrick Inn (☎ 292186; 25 High St) Steeped in history and stooping with age, the Garrick boasts 'good victuals and finest ales'.

Entertainment

Royal Shakespeare Company (☎ 0870 609 1110; www.rsc.org.uk; box office inside Royal Shakespeare Theatre; tickets £5-42; ☾ 9.30am-8pm Mon-Sat) Seeing a RSC production is a must. Major stars have trod the boards here and productions are of a very high standard. Performances include the Bard's classics as well as contemporary offerings and take place in the main Royal Shakespeare Theatre, the adjacent Swan Theatre or the nearby Other Place. The main theatre will close for refurbishment in summer 2007. Performances will take place in the striking temporary Courtyard Theatre by the Other Place. Ticket prices depend on the performance and venue, but there are offers for under 25s, students, seniors and other groups, plus discounts for previews. Call or check the website for details – and book ahead for good seats. There are usually a few tickets sold on the day of performance.

Stratford Picture House (☎ 0870 7551 229; www.picturehouse-cinemas.co.uk; Windsor St; adult/child £6/4.50) This cinema, tucked away just off the main drag, shows Hollywood blockbusters as well as art-house films.

Getting There & Away

The train station is a few minutes' walk west of the centre. Chiltern Railways offers direct services to London Marylebone (2¼ hours). Cheap returns (£15) are often available after 11am.

National Express destinations from Stratford's Riverside Bus Station include Birmingham (£6.50, one hour, twice daily), Oxford (£8.30, one hour, daily) and London Victoria (£15.00, 3½ hours, three daily).

In July and August, the **Shakespeare Express steam train** (☎ 0121-708 4960; www.vintagetrains.co.uk; single adult/child £10/5, return £20/10, 1 hr, twice each Sunday) operates between Birmingham Snow Hill and Stratford stations.

Getting Around
BICYCLE

Stratford is small enough to explore on foot, but a bicycle is good for getting out to the surrounding countryside or the rural Shakespeare properties. The canal towpath offers a fine route to Wilmcote.

Clarkes Cycles (☎ 205057; Guild St; per half/full day from £6/10; ☼ 9.15am-5pm Tue-Sat) rents bikes. It's most easily reached down a little alley off Henley St (look out for the old sign saying Pashley Cycles).

BOAT

Punts, canoes and rowing boats are available from **Rose's Boathouse** (☎ 267073; row boats/punts per 1/2hr £3/2) by Clopton Bridge. **Bancroft Cruises** (☎ 269669; www.bancroftcruises.co.uk) runs 45-minute trips (adult/child £4.50/2, daily April to October) leaving from the Holiday Inn hotel pier.

AROUND STRATFORD-UPON-AVON

If you're tired of looking at historic landmarks and greenery from the ground, **Heart of England Balloons** (☎ 01789-488219; www.ukballoons.com; Cross Lanes Farm, Walcote; 1hr flight per person £149), based near Alcester, offers the chance to soar above it all in a hot-air balloon. Alcester is about 8 miles west of Stratford-upon-Avon along the A46.

Charlecote Park

A youthful Shakespeare is said to have poached deer in the grounds of **Charlecote Park** (NT; ☎ 01789-470277; charlecote.park@nationaltrust .org.uk; adult/child £6.90/3.50; ☼ noon-5pm Fri-Tue Mar-Sep, noon-4.30pm Fri-Tue Oct); deer still roam the park, which was skilfully landscaped by Capability Brown. The house, built around 1551, has an interior redesigned in Elizabethan style in the early 19th century; the Victorian kitchen and Tudor gatehouse are particularly interesting. Charlecote is in Wellesbourne, around 5 miles east of Stratford-upon-Avon. Bus 18 runs from Stratford at quarter past every hour.

Ragley Hall

The **family home** (☎ 01789-762090; www.ragleyhall.com; adult/child £7.00/4.50; ☼ 10am-6pm Thu-Sun Apr-Sep) of the Marquess and Marchioness of Hertford is a grand Palladian mansion built between 1679 and 1683, with a later baroque plasterwork ceiling and some good modern paintings. The intriguing South Staircase Hall with its murals and ceiling painting was restored between 1969 and 1983. Youngsters weary of behaving themselves indoors can be turned loose in Ragley Adventure Wood, a forest playground. Taking in a play or concert in the beautiful landscaped gardens is a real summer pleasure – weather permitting. Ragley is 2 miles south-

west of Alcester off the A435/A46, or about 8 miles west of Stratford-upon-Avon.

STAFFORDSHIRE

Staffordshire, in the words of Stoke-born novelist Arnold Bennett, has long been 'unsung by searchers after the extreme' – but if you took that to mean 'boring' you'd be mistaken. Though it's tucked between the urban sprawls of Birmingham and Manchester, the county has a surprising abundance of natural beauty, from rolling Cannock Chase, a magnet for walkers and cyclists, to the prickly spine of the Peak District known as the Roaches. The haunting Gothic might of Lichfield's wonderful cathedral, the wild rides at Alton Towers, and the neoclassical mansion of Shugborough are among the county's other charms.

Orientation

Staffordshire's attractions are spread fairly evenly around the county: Stoke to the northwest; the Peak District and Leek northeast, with Alton Towers just south; Lichfield to the southeast; and Stafford just southwest of the centre.

Information

Staffordshire Tourism (☎ 0870 500 4444; www.staffordshire.gov.uk/tourism) has general information on where to stay and what to do in the county.

Getting There & Around

Central Trains (☎ 0121-654 2040; www.centraltrains .co.uk)
Travel Line (☎ 0870 608 2608)
Virgin Trains (☎ 0845 722 2333; www.virgin.com/trains)

LICHFIELD

☎ 01543 / pop 27,900

This pretty market town is home to one of England's most beautiful cathedrals, a monumental three-spired Gothic masterpiece that is worth the trip alone. It's also been something of a think-tank in its time: famed wit and lexicographer Samuel Johnson was born here, and Erasmus Darwin, Charles' grandfather and a man of note in his own right, lived and studied here for years.

Information

The thinly stretched **tourist office** (☎ 412121; www.visitlichfield.com; Lichfield Garrick, Castle Dyke; ☼ 9am-

6pm Mon-Sat) doubles as the box office for the new Lichfield Garrick theatre.

Sights & Activities
LICHFIELD CATHEDRAL
The magnificent **cathedral** (☎ 306120; requested donation £4; ⏰ 7am-6pm) boasts a fine Gothic west front adorned with exquisitely carved statues of the kings of England from Edgar to Henry I, and the major saints. Approach the blackened façade from town by Minster Pond and you won't be the first to get goose bumps as you look up to the cathedral's hallmark three spires – especially when they are floodlit by night. Most of what you see dates from the various rebuildings of the Norman cathedral between 1200 and 1350.

Inside, there is a superb illuminated manuscript from AD 730, the *Lichfield Gospels*, which is displayed in the beautifully vaulted mid-13th-century chapterhouse, while the Lady Chapel to the east boasts 16th-century Flemish stained glass. Following archaeological work in 2003, a Saxon statue of the Archangel Gabriel was uncovered beneath the nave, attracting a lot of media interest. If restoration work succeeds, it should soon be on display.

There are tours of the cathedral at 2pm Monday to Saturday and 1.30pm Sunday.

A stroll round the tranquil **Cathedral Close**, which is ringed with imposing 17th- and 18th-century houses, is also rewarding.

OTHER SIGHTS & ACTIVITIES
The amateurish but absorbing **Samuel Johnson Birthplace Museum** (☎ 264972; www.lichfield.gov.uk/sj museum; Breadmarket St; admission free; ⏰ 10.30am-4.30pm Apr-Sep, noon-4.30pm Oct-Mar) charts the life of one of the most remarkable figures in the history of the English language. Samuel Johnson, the pioneering lexicographer (dictionary-maker), was born here in 1709 and spent his formative years in this ramshackle, five-floored property that belonged to his bookseller father. Credited with inventing the dictionary, Samuel Johnson was immortalised in the famous biography *The Life of Samuel Johnson*, written by his close friend James Boswell. You can inspect the ground-breaking dictionary using the computer in the bookshop in the lobby.

Grandfather of the more famous Charles, Erasmus Darwin was himself a remarkable autodidact, doctor, inventor, philosopher and poet, influencing the Romantics. The **Erasmus**

Darwin Centre (☎ 306260; Beacon St; adult/child £2.50/2; ⏰ noon-5pm Tue-Sun, last admission 4.15pm), in the house where he lived from 1758 to 1781, commemorates his life with a video, pictures and personal items. Exhibits and displays illustrate his varied work and association with luminaries such as Wedgwood, Boulton and Watt.

The **St Mary's Heritage Centre & Treasury** (☎ 256611; St Mary's Centre, Market Sq; adult/child £3.50/1; ⏰ 10am-5pm) is a nicely presented series of exhibits covering 1300 years of Lichfield history in a former church. Climb the tower (adult/child £2/1) for fine views of the city.

Sleeping
32 Beacon St (☎ 262378; s/d incl breakfast from £28/48) An unmarked gem, this is in a lovely centuries-old town house. The friendly proprietors have furnished the building impeccably, and offer a cracking full English breakfast.

No 8 (☎ 418483; www.ldb.co.uk/accommodation .htm; 8 The Close; s/d incl breakfast from £30/50) The cathedral looms large over No 8 The Close, a comfortable family home that doubles as a B&B. There's no sign outside this listed town house; you should call in advance to make arrangements.

George Hotel (☎ 414822; www.thegeorgelichfield .co.uk; 12-14 Bird St; s/d Mon-Thu from £82/99, Fri-Sun £48/58; ℗ 🖳) A rabbit warren of rooms winds through this 18th-century coaching inn in the heart of the city. Some of the double beds err on the small side, and parts are a bit worn, but The George (now part of the Best Western group) is generally comfortable and convenient.

Eating & Drinking
Tudor of Lichfield (☎ 263951; Bore St; sandwiches £2-3; ⏰ 9am-5.30pm Mon-Sat, 11am-4.30pm Sun) This café trumps all its local rivals in terms of age – the half-timbered building it is in was built in 1510. The signs are still there, with a suit of armour overlooking diners munching their sandwiches. Prepare to be seduced by a mouth-watering chocolate selection around the till.

Chapters Cathedral Coffee Shop (☎ 306125; 19 The Close; sandwiches and salads £4-5; ⏰ 9.30am-4.45pm Mon-Sat, noon-4.45pm Sun) In a charming 18th-century house with a view onto some fine gardens, this café is ideal for a caffeine or snack pit stop, or even a full Sunday lunch (three-courses meal £14.50).

Eastern Eye (☎ 415047; 19 Bird St; mains £6-12; ⏲ 5pm-midnight) This smart Indian restaurant – all chrome lighting, crisp white tablecloths and dark chairs – boasts an award-winning chef who earned a place in the *Guinness Book of World Records* in 2005 for producing the biggest curry ever made (so far).

Chandlers (☎ 416688; Conduit St; 2-/3-course dinner £13/16.50) With gleaming brass fittings, smart cane chairs, a spacious dining area, and refined Mediterranean-style nosh, Chandlers deserves its reputation as one of the poshest places to eat out in town. It is on the 1st floor of the old Corn Exchange.

King's Head (☎ 256822; 21 Bird St) Samuel Johnson described Lichfield folk as 'the most sober, decent people in England' – but that was 250 years ago, and there are pubs aplenty these days. This place should be your first port of call. A traditional olde worlde pub, it has been shaken up by new owners who put on live music on Thursdays and Saturdays. It is Lichfield's most welcoming alehouse.

Getting There & Away

Bus 112 runs to Birmingham, while the 825 serves Stafford (both £2.60 single, 1¼ hours, hourly). The bus station is opposite the central Lichfield City train station, with trains to Birmingham New St station (30 minutes, every 15 minutes). Direct trains to London Euston (from one hour 15 minutes, around eight daily) depart from Lichfield Trent Valley station, about 20 minutes' walk from town.

STOKE-ON-TRENT

☎ 01782 / pop 240,636

Staffordshire's industrial heart, though historically important in pottery production, holds limited appeal to the visitor, except in one department: the porcelain for which the city is famed. For a preview of Stoke, check out Arnold Bennett's memorable descriptions of the area in its industrial heyday in his novel *Anna of the Five Towns* (something of a misnomer as Stoke actually consists of six towns).

Orientation

Stoke-on-Trent is made up of Tunstall (Robbie Williams' hometown), Burslem, Hanley, Stoke, Fenton and Longton, together often called the Potteries. Hanley is the official 'city centre'. Stoke-on-Trent train station is south of Hanley, but buses from outside the main entrance run there in minutes. The bus station is in the centre of Hanley.

Information

Ask at the helpful **tourist office** (☎ 236000; www.visitstoke.co.uk; Victoria Hall, Bagnall St, Hanley; ⏲ 9.15am-5.15pm Mon-Sat), adjacent to the bus station, for a map with the locations of the various showrooms, factory shops and visitor centres.

Sights & Activities

The **Wedgwood Visitor Centre** (☎ 0870 606 1759; www.thewedgwoodvisitorcentre.com; Barlaston; Mon-Fri/ Sat & Sun £8/6; ⏲ 9am-5pm Mon-Fri, 10am-5pm Sat & Sun), set in 200 acres of attractive parkland, offers a fascinating insight into bone-china production. Tours take in an extensive collection of historic pieces, artisans who deftly paint designs onto china while you watch, and best of all, a troupe of Star Wars-esque anthropomorphic robots churning out perfect plates and mugs. Equally interesting are the film and displays on the life of founder Josiah Wedgwood (1730–95). An innovative potter, he was also a driving force behind the construction of England's canal system and the abolition of slavery.

The **Potteries Museum & Art Gallery** (☎ 232323; Bethesda St, Hanley; admission free; ⏲ 10am-5pm Mon-Sat & 2-5pm Sun Mar-Oct, 10am-4pm Mon-Sat & 1-4pm Sun Nov-Feb) covers the history of the Potteries and houses an impressively extensive ceramics display as well as a fine-art collection (Picasso, Degas).

Constructed around Stoke's last remaining bottle kiln, the wonderfully evocative **Gladstone Pottery Museum** (☎ 319232; Uttoxeter Rd, Longton; adult/child £4.95/3.50; ⏲ 10am-5pm) has an authentic working Victorian pottery factory where skilled potters tell visitors about their work. Those of a scatological bent will enjoy the Flushed With Pride exhibition, which charts the story of the toilet from chamber pots and shared privy holes (with smell effects!) to modern hi-tech conveniences. Buses 6 and 6a go to the museum from Hanley.

Sleeping & Eating

Verdon Guest House (☎ 264244; www.verdonguesthouse.co.uk; 44 Charles St, Hanley; s/d from £24/40; Ⓟ) A large, family-run guesthouse near the main bus station in an imposing Victorian building. Rooms are frilly but not flash and the no-nonsense owners are a mine of local travel advice.

The **Ivy House Restaurant** (☎ 0870 606 1759; www
.thewedgwoodvisitorcentre.com; Barlaston; ⏱ 9am-5pm
Mon-Fri, 10am-5pm Sat & Sun) is a large buffet-style
restaurant and café in the Wedgwood Visitor
Centre – all dishes are, of course, served on
fine Wedgwood bone china.

Getting There & Away
National Express coaches run to/from London
(four hours, five daily) and Manchester (1½
hours, eight daily). Trains run to Stafford (20
minutes, every 30 minutes), and hourly to
London (1¾ hours).

AROUND STOKE-ON-TRENT
Biddulph Grange Gardens
These stunning, superbly landscaped Victorian **gardens** (NT; ☎ 01782-517999; adult/child
£5.30/2.60; ⏱ 11.30am-6pm Wed-Sun late Mar-Oct, 11am-
3pm Sat & Sun Nov & Dec) include a Chinese pagoda
garden, an Egyptian courtyard, and Italian
formal gardens: it's an exotic botanical world
tour. A highlight is the Rainbow, a huge bank
of rhododendrons that flower simultaneously
in spring. The gardens are 7 miles north of
Stoke; take bus 6A from Hanley bus station
(40 minutes, every 20 minutes). The gardens
are a short walk from the bus stop.

Little Moreton Hall
England's most spectacular black-and-white
timber-framed house (☎ 01260-272018; adult/
child £5.50/2.80; ⏱ 11.30am-5pm Wed-Sun late Mar-Oct,
11.30am-4pm Sat & Sun Nov-late Dec) dates back to the
16th century; within its over-the-top exterior
there are a series of important wall paintings
and an indefinable sense of romance. Little
Moreton is off the A34 south of Congleton.

Alton Towers
Deservedly England's most popular theme
park, **Alton Towers** (☎ 0870 444 4455; www.altontowers
.com; adult/under 12yr £29.50/19; ⏱ 9.30am-5pm Oct–mid-
Mar, longer hr mid-Mar–Sep) is an absolute must for
white-knuckle fiends. There are more than
100 rides, including the terrifying vertical
drop of the Oblivion, upside-down roller
coasters, log flumes and more. Entry prices
are almost as steep as the rides and are highest
during school holidays.

There's a hotel within the park, but most
visitors opt to stay in nearby villages. The
park's website features a list of accommodation options. Alton itself is an attractive village
with several B&Bs. **Old School House** (☎ 01538-

702151; old_school_house@talk21.com; Castle Hill Rd, Alton;
d incl breakfast £60) is an exceptional guesthouse
in an 1845 listed school building (just over
1 mile from the park) with accommodating
hosts. Much more basic is the **Dimmingsdale
YHA Hostel** (☎ 0870 770 5794; dimmingsdale@yha.org
.uk; Oakamoor; dm members/non-members £11.95/14.95), 2
miles northwest of the park. There are plenty
of good rambles around the hostel too.

Alton Towers is east of Cheadle off the
B5032. Public transport is sketchy, but various train companies offer all-in-one packages from London and other cities; check the
website for current details.

Drayton Manor Park
Southern Staffordshire's answer to Alton
Towers, **Drayton Manor** (☎ 08708 725252; www
.draytonmanor.co.uk; weekday/weekend adult £18.95/20.95,
child £14.95/16.95; ⏱ 10.30am-5pm Easter-Oct, longer hr
May-Sep) is another massive theme park. Rides
include the Apocalypse, a 54m 'stand up'
drop from a tower, and Pandemonium, in
which two rotating gondolas swing with 64
screaming passengers. The park is near junctions 9 and 10 of the M42 on the A4091. Bus
110 leaves from Birmingham Bull St just off
Corporation St and goes to Tamworth, from
where it is another 10 minutes' walk.

LEEK
☎ 01538 / pop 18,768
Gateway to the Staffordshire Moorlands, including the spectacular Roaches, Leek is an
attractive market town that makes a convenient base for visiting the Potteries and the
Peak District.

The **tourist office** (☎ 483741; tourism.smdc@staf
fordshire.gov.uk; 1 Market Pl; ⏱ 9.30am-5pm Mon-Fri, 10am-
4pm Sat) will book rooms for a £3 fee.

St Edward's Church (☎ 388134; Church St; ⏱ 10am-
3pm), completed in 1306, has a beautiful rose
window by William Morris' decorative-arts
makers.

Described by John Betjeman as 'one of the
finest churches in Britain', **All Saints Church**
(☎ 382588; Compton; ⏱ 11am-4pm Wed & Sat) features Morris & Co stained-glass windows
at the eastern end (from designs by Edward
Burne-Jones), and ornate Arts and Crafts
wall-painting.

Brindley Mill (www.brindleymill.net; Mill St; adult/child
£2/1.50; ⏱ 2-5pm Mon-Wed mid-Jul–Aug, 2-5pm Sat & Sun
Easter-Sep) was built in 1752 by canal pioneer
James Brindley. It's been beautifully restored

and once again mills corn; inside is a small museum dedicated to Brindley and the art of millwrighting.

The **Peak Weavers Hotel** (☎ 383729; www.peak weavershotel.co.uk; 21 King St; s/d incl breakfast from £30/60; **P** **□**) is a lovingly restored former mill owner's property (once also a convent). Its bedrooms are light and airy and there is a fine restaurant.

Bus 18 runs to Leek from Hanley (Stoke-on-Trent, 45 minutes).

STAFFORD
☎ 01785 / pop 63,681

The county town of Stafford was once a major crossroads for travellers. It still has a couple of attractions that are worth a look on your way through.

The **tourist office** (☎ 619619; Market St; ☼ 9.30am-5pm Mon-Fri, 10am-4pm Sat) is behind the town hall. Call here for details on the thrills and spills of mountain biking and walking in Cannock Chase.

The **Ancient High House** (☎ 619131; Greengate St; admission free; ☼ 10am-4pm Tue-Sat) is the largest timber-framed town house in the country and has period rooms containing displays on the history of the house since its construction in 1595.

The ruined remains of **Stafford Castle** (☎ 257698; Newport Rd; admission free; visitor centre ☼ 10am-5pm Tue-Sun Apr-Oct, 10am-4pm Nov-Mar), which was built by the Normans, perch romantically on a hilltop with sweeping views. The lovely castle grounds stage plays and historical re-enactments throughout the summer. There's a small visitor centre and a 'medieval herb garden', as well as a network of forested trails for postpicnic wanders. It's about 20 minutes' walk from the town centre.

Bus 101 runs between Stafford and Stoke-on-Trent (1¼ hours, every 30 minutes).

AROUND STAFFORD
Shugborough

The regal, neoclassical mansion of **Shugborough** (☎ 01889-881 388; adult/child £10/7; ☼ 11am-5pm Tue-Sun Mar-Oct) is the ancestral home of renowned photographer Lord Lichfield (there's an exhibition of his work here). Started in 1693 and considerably extended during the 18th and 19th centuries, Shugborough has marvellous state rooms and a fine collection of Louis XV and XVI furniture. The estate is famous for the monuments within its grounds, including a Chinese House, a Doric temple and the Triumphal Arch. It includes the **Staffordshire County Museum**, exploring life 'below stairs' for servants, and a farm.

Shugborough is 6 miles east of Stafford on the A513; bus 825 runs nearby.

NORTHAMPTONSHIRE

Beyond its obvious appeal as a batch of pretty villages and winding country lanes, Northamptonshire has special relevance for fans of George Washington, Princess Diana, footwear and religious eccentrics. Its far-flung attractions also include some historic Saxon churches, honey-coloured historic towns with pretty thatched cottages and stately homes. It's a great region for driving – attractions are interspersed throughout lovely countryside – and, as there's no single tourism blockbuster, you don't have to fight the masses to take in its charms.

Orientation & Information

Northamptonshire is roughly 50 miles long and 20 miles wide, running southwest to northeast. The M1 cuts diagonally across the county just below Northampton, which lies in the middle. Attractions are scattered.

For general (but sketchy) information about the county, check the website www.visitnorthamptonshire.co.uk. Otherwise, visit Northampton's tourist office.

Getting Around

Driving is the way to see the most of the county. Turning a corner on a winding country lane and coming across a sleepy village is one of the joys of the region. All the major car-hire companies have branches in Northampton.

Buses do run to most places of interest from Northampton and other nearby towns, but services can be sporadic; some run only a few times daily, so it's best to check times with the operator.

Stagecoach (www.stagecoachbus.com/northants/)
Traveline (☎ 0870 608 2608)

NORTHAMPTON
☎ 01604 / pop 194,458

Unassuming Northampton is surprisingly steeped in historical significance. In Saxon days it was perhaps the most important city in England, and Mary, Queen of Scots, was executed in nearby Fotheringhay. Nowadays, soulless stretches of shopping precincts blight the centre but the town has some buildings of architectural note, and it's a good base for trips around a remarkably pretty county. It's particularly notable for two other things: shoes (factories here used to protect the feet of half the country) and its hideous 1970s bus station, recently voted one of the ugliest buildings in Britain.

Orientation

The town is centred on Market Sq, with the main pedestrianised shopping route, Abington St, running east from it, where it becomes the Kettering Rd, with its hotels and bars. To the south of Market Sq is the Guildhall and the tourist office. The infamous bus station is to the north.

Information

The helpful **tourist office** (☎ 838800; www.northampton.gov.uk/tourism; The Guildhall, St Giles Sq; ☻ 10am-5pm Mon-Sat) is within the city's town hall.

Sights & Activities

You don't have to be a shoe fetishist to get a kick out of the impressive displays at **Northampton Museum & Art Gallery** (☎ 838111; Guildhall Rd; admission free; ☻ 10am-5pm Mon-Sat, 2-5pm Sun). From Turkish stilted clogs to rawhide sandals, the footwear collection is fantastic, varied and vast. There are also some fine paintings and changing special exhibitions.

St Peter's Church (Marefair) is a marvellous Norman edifice built in 1150 and restored in the 19th century by Gilbert Scott. Beautiful Norman-era carvings still adorn the pillars. For rock nuts: William Smith, known as the father of modern geology, is buried here. The Old Black Lion pub next door has the key to the church, which was being refurbished at the time of research.

The **Church of the Holy Sepulchre** (☎ 754782; ☻ noon-4pm Wed, 2-4pm Sat) is Northampton's oldest building at nine centuries and counting. It is also one of the few surviving round churches in the country. Founded after the first earl of Northampton returned from the Crusades in 1100, it is modelled on its Jerusalem namesake.

Sleeping

Coach House Hotel (☎ 250981; www.thecoachhousenorthampton.com; 10 East Park Pde; s/d incl breakfast from £55/65; P) In an attractive Victorian terrace

façade, this family-run hotel (effectively on the Kettering Rd) has reasonable rooms in a fine location opposite parkland.

Lime Trees Hotel (☎ 632188; www.limetreeshotel.co.uk; 8 Langham Pl; s/d from £85/105; P 🖳) This welcoming Best Western affiliate is in an attractive Georgian property about half a mile north of the centre. It has a pretty courtyard at the back. Rooms err on the small side, but the restaurant beats most of the town's eating options.

Eating & Drinking

Church Restaurant (☎ 603800; 67-83 Bridge St; mains £12-19; ☻ noon-2.30pm Tue-Fri, 6pm-11pm Tue-Sat) This upmarket restaurant is merely the latest incarnation of an historic site; previous uses include hospice, church and even train station. Its French cuisine is a rare example of fine dining in Northampton city centre.

Vineyard (☎ 633978; 7 Derngate; mains £13-17; ☻ noon-2pm Mon-Thu & Sat, 6-10pm Mon-Sat) This light, airy restaurant, specialising in fresh fish, brings in well-heeled businesspeople during the day and even better heeled theatregoers when night falls.

Malt Shovel Tavern (☎ 234212; 121 Bridge St) Despite its slightly desolate position on the outskirts of town opposite the Carlsberg brewery, this real-ale favourite retains the cosy atmosphere of a local pub. It serves 13 different beers, as well as continental bottled beers, and home-cooked food (not Sundays).

Some appealing coffee houses line St Giles St just down from the town hall, including **Dreams Coffee Lounge** (59 St Giles St), which appeals to the caffeine-deprived executive, and **J Lawrence** (37 St Giles St), which has a vast array of gorgeous pastries.

Entertainment

Picturedrome (☎ 230777; www.thepicturedrome.com; 222 Kettering Rd) A little way out of town, this is a breath of fresh air after the humdrum chain pubs of the centre. Gilt-edged mirrors are part of the slick décor, which, along with decent food and an easy-going vibe, attract the more discerning of Northampton's twenty-somethings. There are regular comedy nights, live music and other events.

Royal Theatre (☎ 624811; www.northamptontheatres.com; Guildhall Rd) is managed cooperatively along with Derngate. Following a major refurbishment, they were re-opened in 2006. Derngate is Northampton's arts centre and hosts anything from Bill Wyman to *Madame Butterfly*.

The Royal is an impressive Victorian structure staging local theatre and quality West End productions.

Getting There & Away

Northampton has good rail links with Birmingham (one hour, hourly) and London Euston (one hour, at least every 30 minutes). The train station is about half a mile west of town along Gold St.

National Express coaches run to London (£10.60 single, 2¼ hours, five daily), Nottingham (£10.20, 2½ hours, daily) and Birmingham (£5.70, one hour 40 minutes, two daily). The truly awful Greyfriars bus station is on Lady's Lane, just north of the Grosvenor shopping centre.

AROUND NORTHAMPTON
Althorp

Famous as the final resting place of Diana, Princess of Wales, after her life was tragically cut short in a Paris car crash, **Althorp House** (bookings ☎ 0870 167 9000; www.althorp.com; adult/child £12/6, plus access to upstairs in house £2.50; ☺ 11am-5pm Jul-Aug, last entry 4pm) had an acclaimed collection of art and books before the world's eyes turned upon it. Diana is commemorated in a memorial and museum in the grounds of her ancestral home.

Meanwhile, the slightly forbidding looking 16th-century mansion contains works by Rubens, Gainsborough and Van Dyck. Profits from ticket sales go to the Princess Diana Memorial Fund. The limited number of tickets must be booked by phone or on the web. Althorp should be pronounced *altrup*.

Althorp is off the A428 5.5 miles northwest of Northampton. There are five buses daily (not Sundays) linking Northampton with Althorp, leaving from Greyfriars bus station.

Stoke Bruerne

The Grand Union Canal, the main artery of England's canal network, glides through this pretty waterside village 8 miles south of Northampton. On its banks in a converted corn mill, the engaging **Canal Museum** (☎ 01604-862229; www.thewaterwaystrust.co.uk; adult/child £3.75/3.25; ☺ 10am-5pm daily Apr-Oct, 10am-4pm Tue-Sun Nov-Mar) charts the history of the waterways system and the sometimes harsh way of life for people working on it.

Nowadays, the canals are all about leisure time: you can mess about on boats in sum-

mer on the **Indian Chief** (☎ 01604-862428; ☺ Sun and bank holiday weekends only), run by the Boat Inn (see following). Trips range from 25 minutes (£2.50) to six hours (£14).

If you fancy staying longer (easily done), try **Waterways Cottage** (☎ 01604-863865; www.waterwayscottage.co.uk; Bridge Rd; s/d incl breakfast £40/55), a newly refurbished B&B opposite the Boat Inn run by a polite, welcoming couple. The **Boat Inn** (☎ 01604-862428; www.boatinn.co.uk; mains £5-12) is a charming thatched canalside pub, one of several in the village.

Buses 86 and 87 take a circular route from Northampton's bus station around the local rural villages, calling in at Stoke Bruerne (1¼ hours, five daily Monday to Saturday).

Sulgrave Manor

Built by Lawrence Washington after Henry VIII sold him the property in 1539, **Sulgrave Manor** (☎ 01295-760205; www.sulgravemanor.org.uk; adult/child £5.75/2.50; ☺ 2-5.30pm Tue-Thu, noon-5.30pm Sat & Sun Apr-Oct, last entry 4pm) is a well-preserved Tudor mansion. A certain family descendant named George Washington became the first president of the USA 250 years later, a draw for many overseas visitors. The family lived here for almost 120 years before Colonel John Washington sailed to Virginia in 1656.

Sulgrave Manor is located just off the B4525, 7 miles northeast of Banbury where the nearest train station is. Public transport links are poor; you'll probably need to get a taxi from there.

Brixworth

The main sight here is the ancient **All Saints** (☎ 01604-880286; ☺ usually 10am-6pm Apr-Sep, to 4pm Oct-Mar), one of England's oldest churches. Built in Saxon times, around AD 680, way before the Normans were conquering, it has changed somewhat since it first appeared, but the nave is as it was. It is thought to be based on a Roman basilica plan, and was an early example of effective recycling: disused Roman brickwork was used in its construction. The tower and stair turret were added after 9th-century Viking raids, and the spire was built around 1350. Head to the sheep-inhabited churchyard for an evocative view of the church.

Brixworth is 6 miles north of Northampton off the A508. Bus X7 runs from Northampton (10 minutes, hourly Monday to Saturday, five on Sunday).

Earls Barton

Earls Barton's wonderful place of worship, **All Saints** (☎ 01604-810045; ☺ 10.30am-12.30pm & 2-4pm Mon-Sat Apr-Sep, by appointment Oct-Mar), is notable for its solid Saxon tower with patterns that seem to imitate earlier wooden models. Probably built during the reign of Edgar the Peaceful (r 959–75), it has a 1st-floor door that may have offered access to the tower during Viking raids. Around 1100 the Norman nave was added to the original tower; other features were added in subsequent centuries.

Earls Barton is 8 miles east of Northampton. Bus 45 runs from Northampton (20 minutes, every 20 minutes, seven on Sunday).

Rushton Triangular Lodge

This mysterious **lodge** (EH; ☎ 01536-710761; adult/child £2.40/1.20; ☺ 10am-5pm Thu-Mon Apr-Oct) with esoteric inscriptions shows the power of Sir Thomas Tresham's Catholic faith. He designed a number of buildings in the area (and was imprisoned more than once for expressing his beliefs). With three of everything, from sides to floors to gables, the lodge is in a magical setting among rapeseed fields and is Tresham's enduring symbol of the trinity. It was built at the end of the 16th century.

The lodge is 4 miles northwest of Kettering. Bus 19 from Kettering stops in Desborough, 2 miles away (20 minutes, every 30 minutes Monday to Saturday, every two hours on Sunday). Kettering is 15 miles northeast of Northampton along the A43.

Kirby Hall

Once one of the finest Elizabethan mansions, the 'Jewel of the English Renaissance', **Kirby Hall** (EH; ☎ 01536-203230; adult/child £4.50/2.30; ☺ 10am-5pm Thu-Mon Apr-Jun, 10am-6pm daily Jul-Aug, 10am-5pm Thu-Mon Sep-Oct, 10am 4pm Thu-Mon Nov-Mar) was begun in 1570, and additions were made up to the 19th century. Abandoned and left to fall into disrepair, it's still a remarkable, atmospheric site – it was used as the location for the 1999 film of Jane Austen's *Mansfield Park* – with fine filigree stonework, ravens cawing in the empty halls and peacocks strutting around its restored formal parterre gardens.

Kirby Hall is 4 miles northeast of Corby; Corby is 9 miles north of Kettering along the A43.

Oundle & Fotheringhay

Its streets and squares graced with the honey-coloured Jurassic limestone and Colleyweston slate roofs of 16th- and 17th-century buildings, the village of Oundle is the photogenic face of Northamptonshire. It's also a good base for visiting nearby Fotheringhay, birthplace of Richard III (demonised by the Tudors and Shakespeare) and execution place of Mary, Queen of Scots, in 1587. The castle in which these events took place is now merely a hillock, but Fotheringhay is a charming village with thatched cottages and a pub known for its excellent Italian food, the **Falcon** (☎ 01832-226254; mains £7-15).

Oundle's **tourist office** (☎ 01832-274333; oundletic@east-northamptonshire.gov.uk; 14 West St; ☺ 9am-5pm Mon-Sat, also 1-4pm Sun Easter-Aug) has several leaflets that help visitors explore its picture-postcard streets.

Haunted **Talbot Hotel** (☎ 01832-273621; www.the talbot-oundle.com; New St; s/d £79/99), built in 1626, apparently incorporates an oak staircase brought in from the ruins of nearby Fotheringhay Castle, which Mary descended on the way to her execution. Pleasantly refurbished rooms, all oak beams, and open fires make for a lovely olde-worlde atmosphere. There is also an upmarket restaurant.

Bus X4 runs to Oundle from Northampton (two hours, hourly), and from Peterborough (30 minutes, hourly) in the other direction.

LEICESTERSHIRE & RUTLAND

In typical Midlands fashion, Leicestershire self-deprecatingly plays down its own attractions, yet it boasts several picturesque villages, a rich industrial heritage and a few key historic sites – not to mention magnificent Belvoir Castle. Leicester, meanwhile, is a vibrant multicultural city.

Tiny Rutland was merged with Leicestershire in 1974, but in April 1997 regained its 'independence' as a county. With magnificent Rutland Water and charming settlements, it's a hit with lovers of water sports and quaint villages.

Orientation & Information

Leicestershire and Rutland together look like an upside-down map of Australia. Leicester is virtually bang in the centre of its county, with the M1 motorway running north–south just to the west, dividing the largely industrial towns and National Forest of the west from the more rural east, including Belvoir Castle. To the east of Leicester, Rutland, wedged between four counties, revolves around central Rutland Water.

For general countywide information, contact **Leicestershire Tourism** (☎ 0906 294 1113).

Getting There & Around

Arriva Midlands (www.arrivabus.co.uk) Operates Leicestershire bus services.

Traveline (☎ 0870 608 2608) Latest timetables, bus routes and numbers.

LEICESTER

☎ 0116 / pop 279,923

Filled with the sense of excitement that comes from a mix of cultures and ethnicities, Leicester (*les*-ter) may not be beautiful but it certainly has a lot going on. Around since the Roman times, Leicester had an unwelcome face-lift from the Luftwaffe, while industrial decline hollowed it out and poor urban planning capped off the aesthetic crimes against the city. But Leicester has reinvented itself as a socially and environmentally progressive melting pot with a lot going on. It has a large and vibrant Asian community, with many interesting events staged around religious festivals such as Holi, Diwali and Eid-ul-Fitr.

Orientation

For drivers, Leicester is plagued by a maze of one-way streets and forbidden turns. Although there isn't a ring road as such, the A594 does almost a whole circuit and most attractions flank it or are contained within it.

The centre of the Asian community, Belgrave Rd (the 'Golden Mile') is about a mile northeast of the centre. Castle Park, with many of the historic attractions, lies immediately west of the centre.

Information

Ice Mango (☎ 262 6255; www.icemango.co.uk; 4 Market Pl; per hr £2.20; ☽ 9.30am-6.30pm Mon-Fri, 9am-7pm Sat, noon-5.30pm Sun) Relaxed juice bar with computers for internet access.

Tourist office (☎ 0906 294 1113, calls charged at 25p/min; www.goleicestershire.com; 7-9 Every St; ☽ 9am-5.30pm Mon-Wed & Fri, 10am-5.30pm Thu, 10am-5pm Sat)

Sights

JEWRY WALL & MUSEUMS

All Leicester's **museums** (www.leicestermuseums .ac.uk) are free.

Despite its name, **Jewry Wall** is one of England's largest Roman civil structures and has nothing to do with Judaism. You can wander among excavated remains of the Roman public baths, which date back almost two millennia. Notwithstanding its grim external appearance, the **Jewry Wall Museum** (☎ 225 4971; St Nicholas Circle; ☽ 11am-4.30pm Sat, 1-4.30pm Sun Feb-Nov, & some school holidays) contains wonderful Roman mosaics and frescoes, as well as an interactive exhibition The Making of Leicester, which explains the history of the city with archaeological reconstructions and paintings.

New Walk Museum & Art Gallery (☎ 225 4900; New Walk; ☽ 11am-4pm Mon-Fri, to 4.30pm Sun) is a child-friendly series of displays on space, materials and art. Adults should get something from the surprisingly varied exhibits too, which range from a Siberian mammoth-ivory paperknife to a life-size portrait of local rugby legend Martin Johnson.

Newarke Houses Museum (☎ 225 4980; The Newarke; ☽ 11am-4pm Mon-Fri, to 4.30pm Sun) is housed in two 16th-century buildings. Revolving around the theme 'ordinary people, extraordinary lives', it charts the life of everyday Leicester residents, and includes reconstructed period shops, and exhibitions on well-known local citizens including Thomas Cook, the package-holiday pioneer.

In the late-14th-century **Guildhall** (☎ 253 2569; Guildhall Lane; ☽ 11-4.30pm Mon-Wed & Sat, 1-4pm Sun), which is reputedly the most haunted building in Leicester, you can peer into old police cells and inspect a copy of the last gibbet used to expose the body of an executed murderer.

NATIONAL SPACE CENTRE

This **centre** (☎ 0870 607 7223; www.spacecentre .co.uk; adult/child £11/9; ☽ 10am-5pm Tue-Sun, plus Mon during Leicester school holidays, last entry 3.30pm) is a spectacular and successful attempt to bring space science to us ordinary mortals. Interactive displays cover cosmic myths, the history of astronomy and the development of space travel; in the Space Now! area you can check on the status of all current space missions. Films in the domed Space Theatre (included in the admission price) launch you to the

far reaches of the galaxy, and you can come back down to earth with a coffee in Boosters Café. Don't miss the displays on zero-gravity toilets and the amazing germ-devouring underpants.

The centre is off the A6 about 1.5 miles north of the city centre. Take bus No 54 from Charles St in the centre.

TEMPLES

Materials were shipped in all the way from India to convert a disused church into a **Jain Centre** (☎ 254 3091; www.jaincentre.com; 32 Oxford St; ◷ 2-5pm Mon-Fri, or by prior arrangement). The building is faced with marble, and the temple – the first Jain temple outside the subcontinent and the only one in Europe – boasts a forest

of beautifully carved pillars inside. Jainism evolved in India at around the same time as Buddhism.

Close to the Jewry Wall is the Sikh **Guru Nanak Gurdwara** (☎ 251 7460; 9 Holy Bones; ◷ 1 4pm Thu, 7-8.30pm Sat, 11.30am-1.30pm Sun). There is a small museum, which contains an impressive model of the Golden Temple in Amritsar, India, and a Sikh/Panjabi heritage exhibition.

Festivals & Events

Leicester hosts numerous cultural and religious festivals throughout the year. Contact the tourist office for details.

Comedy festival (☎ 261 6812; www.comedy-festival .co.uk) In February; is the country's longest running comedy festival, drawing big names such as Jack Dee and fresh comic talent.

Caribbean carnival (www.lccarnival.org.uk) In August the city hosts the biggest UK Caribbean carnival outside London's Notting Hill Carnival.

Diwali The Hindu community celebrates this during autumn, and the celebration, the largest of its kind outside India, draws visitors from around the world.

Sleeping

Leicestershire Backpackers Hostel (☎ 267 3107; 157 Wanlip Lane, Birstall; dm incl breakfast per night/week £11/45; P) This odd little place 3 miles north of the centre takes under-28 travellers/students only. Cooking is communal, and the breakfast is basic. Don't expect luxury or personal space here. Take bus 70 from Haymarket station or 125 from St Margaret's station to get there.

Scotia Hotel (☎ 254 9200; 10 Westcotes Dr; s/d incl breakfast from £20/35; P) Staff admit with disarming honesty 'it's not the Hilton' but no matter – rooms are tidy, the people are friendly and it's one of the best-value options in town. It lies just west of Castle Park.

Spindle Lodge (☎ 233 8801; www.spindlelodge.com; 2 West Walk; s/d from £49/67; P ⌨) This charming Victorian town house, now a small family-run hotel, is elegantly furnished, the varnished floors gleam with good care, and the welcome is warm.

Belmont House Hotel (☎ 254 4773; www.belmontho tel.co.uk; De Montfort St; s/d Sun-Thu £110/120, Fri & Sat £70/90; P ⌨) In an elongated Georgian building, this hotel has spotless rooms, although the décor is due a face-lift. It is favoured by executives during the week, with some weekend deals available.

Ramada Hotel (☎ 255 5599; www.ramadajarvis .co.uk; Granby St; s/d Sun-Thu from £115/145, Fri-Sun £41/82; P ⌨ ♿) In a listed Victorian building, the city's top hotel is clinically comfortable. Rates vary according to availability. Get a room set back from the street away from the blare of pubgoers below on weekend nights – unless you're doing the blaring.

Eating

The Golden Mile on Belgrave Rd is located a mile to the north of the centre (take bus 22 from Haymarket bus station) and teems with good Indian and vegetarian restaurants.

Liquid (☎ 261 9086; 5 Guildhall Lane; toasted baguettes £2.30; ⌚ 8.30am-6pm Mon-Sat, plus Sun Dec) Fresh and friendly with enough juices to satisfy anyone's daily vitamin requirements.

Sardaar Restaurant (☎ 299 3300; 30 Narborough Rd; mains £3-8; ⌚ 10am-10pm) Very cheap vegetarian Indian platters are served in this stripped-back diner-style café. Dishes won't do the cholesterol count much good, but the mango *lassi* style drink is to die for. It's west of the centre.

Friends (☎ 266 8809; 41-43 Belgrave Rd; mains £6-12; ⌚ noon-2pm Mon-Sat, dinner daily) Chefs from New Delhi proudly prepare authentic North Indian recipes at this mainstay of the Golden Mile, still going strong after more than two decades.

Case (☎ 251 7675; 4-6 Hotel St; mains £8-18 ⌚ 7-10.30pm Mon-Sat) One of Leicester's finest places to eat out, this is in the unlikely setting of a former suitcase factory. A refined hubbub fills the airy 1st-floor space where exotic influences infuse traditional English recipes. The Champagne Bar downstairs is easier on the wallet.

THE MIDLANDS

Opera House (☎ 223 6666; 10 Guildhall Lane; mains £15-19) Located in a very historical building with a colourful history (it used to be a brothel), this classy Leicester restaurant has an excellent chef. Head downstairs for the intimate, atmospheric underground dining area.

Drinking

Amid the rash of chain pubs in the centre, there are a few places for more discerning drinkers. Some great options are away from downtown. Head to Braunstone Gate, Narborough Rd and Hinckley Rd to experience Leicester's vibrant bar and pub scene at its best.

Globe (☎ 262 9819; 43 Silver St; ☽ Sun-Thu 11am-11pm, 11am-1am Fri & Sat) At last, that rare beast, a traditional old pub (built in 1720) in a city centre where there's no edge to the night-time drinking – just fine draught ales, a warm atmosphere and little alcoves to lose yourself in.

Orange Tree (☎ 223 5256; 99 High St) A laid-back Bohemian crowd mills down to the Orange Tree, wedged between two much less appealing chain pubs. Decked with colourful, modernist paintings, it also has a beer garden that overflows in the summer. Meals are £4 to £7.

Looking Glass (☎ 255 9002; 68-70 Braunstone Gate; ☽ 3.30pm-1am Sun-Thu, to 2am Fri & Sat) If you hadn't sussed it from the name, this is the place to see and be seen on Braunstone Gate. Funky mirror-decked walls, beautiful young things and a basement with decent live acoustic music make this well worth a visit.

O-Bar (☎ 255 8223; 59-61 Braunstone Gate; ☽ 4.30pm-1am Mon-Sat, 3pm-12.30am Sun) A relaxed, unpretentious crowd heads to the colourful, retro-cool of this bar, which gets absolutely packed to the rafters on weekend nights.

Bossa (☎ 255 9551; 110 Granby St; ☽ 11am-10.30pm Mon-Thu, 11am-1am Fri-Sat) Latin rhythms, cheap, tasty snacks (toasties £1.25) and a relaxed, bohemian crowd populate this pint-sized, gay-friendly bar/café.

Entertainment

NIGHTCLUBS

Charlotte (☎ 255 3956; www.thecharlotte.co.uk; 8 Oxford St; ☽ doors open 8pm) Leicester's legendary venue has staged Oasis and the Stone Roses, among others, before they became megastars. With a late licence and club nights, it's grungy, it's lively, it caters for all sorts of musical tastes – and it keeps packing 'em in.

Original Four (☎ 254 1638; 2 King St; admission Sat night £7) Behind a mock-Tudor façade, this place cooks up four floors of diverse beats, from electric tracks to live-music sets. It has seen more popular days but is still one of the best clubbing options in town.

Attik (☎ 222 3800; 15 Free Lane) Small, grungy venue off Halford Lane, Attik hosts drum and bass nights, as well as a string of punk rock, Goth, industrial and guitar-led indie acts.

Po Na Na (☎ 253 8190; 24 Careys Close) An eclectic mix of reggae, electronic, funk and indie somehow works in this popular venue.

De Montfort Hall (☎ 233 3111; www.demontforthall.co.uk; Granville Rd) Bigger bands sometimes play at this hall, southeast of the centre, which also stages everything from cheesy crooners to gospel choirs.

THEATRE & COMEDY

Phoenix Arts Centre (☎ 255 4854; www.phoenix.org.uk; Newarke St) This is Leicester's main venue for art-house films, fringe plays, comedy and dance events.

Other venues for plays include the **Little Theatre** (☎ 255 1302; www.thelittletheatre.net; Dover St); **Haymarket Theatre** (☎ 253 0021; www.lhtheatre.co.uk; 1 Belgrave Gate), which has some innovative theatre; and the **Y** (☎ 255 7066; 7 East St), a theatre and bar attached to the YMCA, hosting concerts, cabaret, poetry and plays.

Getting There & Away

National Express operates from St Margaret's bus station on Gravel St, north of the centre. The express bus JL367 runs to Nottingham (one hour, eight daily Monday to Saturday), while the 310 runs to Coventry (45 minutes, four daily). Other options for Coventry include the X67 (one hour, hourly).

Trains run to London St Pancras (1½ hours, every 30 minutes) and Birmingham (one hour, every 30 minutes).

A tourist jaunt rather than a serious transport option, the classic **Great Central Railway** (☎ 01509-230726; www.gcrailway.co.uk; return tickets £12/8) operates steam locomotives between Leicester North station on Redhill Circle and Loughborough Central. This dual-track railway runs the 8-mile route along which Thomas Cook ran his original package tour in 1841. The trains run daily from May to August and every weekend the rest of the year. Take bus 70 from Haymarket bus station.

Getting Around

Central Leicester is easy to get around on foot. As an alternative to local buses, the open-top bus run by **Discover Leicester** (☎ 299 8888; adult/child under 15yr £6/4, ⌚ on the hour 10am-4pm July Sep) runs a jump-on jump-off bus around the city and up to Belgrave Rd, the Great Central Railway and the National Space Centre with on-board commentary from a local expert. It starts by the Thomas Cook statue outside the main railway station.

AROUND LEICESTER
Bosworth Battlefield

The **Battlefield Visitor Centre** (☎ 01455-290429; admission £3.25; ⌚ 11am-5pm Apr-Oct) features an exhibition about the Battle of Bosworth Field, one of the most important battle sites in England, where Richard III was defeated by the future Henry VII in 1485. This ended the Wars of the Roses; 'a horse, a horse, my kingdom for a horse' was Richard's famous death cry (at least according to William Shakespeare). He may be known as a villain for his supposed role in the murder of the 'princes in the tower', but Leicester has adopted him as something of a folk hero, not the hunchback of Shakespearean spin. The battle is re-enacted annually in August.

The battlefield is 16 miles southwest of Leicester at Sutton Cheny. Bus 153 runs hourly from Leicester to Market Bosworth, 2 miles to the north. **Bosworth Gold Cars** (☎ 01455-291999) taxi firm will take you there if you need a lift.

Ashby-de-la-Zouch

☎ 01530 / pop 12,758

The real draw of Ashby-de-la-Zouch is its **castle** (☎ 413343; adult/child £3.40/1.70; ⌚ 10am-6pm daily Jul-Aug, 10am-5pm Mon & Thu-Sun Apr-Jun & Sep-Oct, 10am-4pm Mon & Thu-Sun Nov-Mar). Built in Norman times and owned by the Zouch family until 1399, it was extended in the 14th and 15th centuries and then reduced to its present picturesquely ruined state in 1648 after the English Civil War. A lively audio guide introduces the characters and details the history. Bring a torch to explore the underground passageway connecting the tower with the kitchen.

For accommodation, contact the **tourist office** (☎ 411767; North St; ⌚ 9.30am-5pm Mon-Fri, to 4pm Sat). Ashby is on the A511 about 15 miles northwest of Leicester. Buses 117 and 118 (218 Sunday) run hourly from St Margaret's bus station in Leicester.

Conkers & the National Forest

The National Forest is an ambitious project to generate sustainable woodland by planting 30 million trees from Leicester through Derbyshire into Staffordshire. Central to the scheme is **Conkers** (☎ 01283-216633; www.visitconkers.com; Rawdon Rd, Moira; adult/child £6.50/4.50; ⌚ 10am-6pm Apr-Sep, to 5pm Oct-Mar), a purpose-built visitor centre with interactive displays on woodland life, biology and the environment. There's lots of touching, smelling and hearing: it's a multisensory experience to captivate children, but it's engaging for all ages.

Conkers is 20 miles northwest of Leicester off the A444.

Belvoir Castle

In the wilds of the county is **Belvoir** (*bee*-ver) **Castle** (☎ 01476-8/0262; www.belvoircastle.com; adult/child £10/5; ⌚ 11am-5pm Tue-Thu, Sat & Sun May-Sep, Sun Apr & Oct), a magnificent baroque and Gothic fantasy rebuilt in the 19th century after suffering serious damage during the English Civil War. It is also home to the duke and duchess of Rutland. Much of the sumptuous interior is open to the public, and collections of weaponry, medals and art (including pieces by Reynolds, Gainsborough and Holbein) are highlights. There are marvellous views across the countryside, and peacocks roam the delightful gardens.

Belvoir is 6 miles west of Grantham, off the A1; Grantham is about 25 miles east of Nottingham along the A52.

RUTLAND

Rutland's motto 'Multum in Parvo' (so much in so little) refers to its status as England's smallest county. Rutland Water, one of the largest reservoirs in Europe, makes it a haven for water-sport lovers, as well as climbers and bird-watchers.

Information

Oakham tourist office (☎ 01572-758441; Catmose St, Oakham ⌚ 10.30am-5pm Mon-Sat, 2-4pm Sun) Housed in the Rutland County Museum.
Rutland Water tourist office (☎ 01572-653026; Sykes Lane, Empingham; ⌚ 10am-5pm Easter-Sep, 10am-4pm Tue-Sat Oct-Mar, shorter hours in winter)

Sights & Activities

In Rutland Water, the **Rutland Belle** (☎ 01572-787630; www.rutlandwatercruises.com; the Harbour, Whitwell Park; adult/child £6/4) offers pleasure cruises every afternoon, May to September.

The **Watersports Centre** (☎ 01780-460154; Whitwell) organises windsurfing, canoeing and sailing and offers tuition. **Rutland Sailing School** (☎ 01780-721999; www.rutlandsailingschool.co.uk; Edith Weston) offers tuition to sailors of all abilities, from catamarans to dinghies.

For bike hire contact **Rutland Water Cycling** (☎ 01780-460705; www.rutlandcycling.co.uk; Whitwell Car Park).

The sleepy county town of **Oakham** has a famous school and **Oakham Castle** (admission free; ☽ 10.30am-1pm & 1.30-5pm Mon-Sat, 2-4pm Sun, shorter hours Nov-Feb), where an impressive Great Hall from a 12th-century Norman structure still stands.

South of Oakham is the village of Lyddington, home to the **Bede House** (EH; ☎ 01572-822438; adult/child £3.30/1.70; ☽ 10am-5pm Thu-Mon Apr-Sep). Originally a wing of the medieval rural palace of the bishops of Lincoln, it was converted into almshouses in 1600. Look out for the beautifully carved cornice in the Great Chamber.

Getting There & Away

Bus 19 runs from Nottingham's Broadmarsh bus station to Oakham (1¼ hours, hourly). Trains run hourly from Leicester, Peterborough and Birmingham.

NOTTINGHAMSHIRE

Nottinghamshire seems to breed good stories: this is the land of the legendary Robin Hood and his merry men, and the home of provocative writer DH Lawrence and decadent bad-boy poet Lord Byron. Even its castles and pubs are draped in myth and mystery. The city of Nottingham is a vibrant hub of business, shopping and clubbing, while the surrounding countryside is dotted with the occasional gem of a stately home.

Orientation & Information

Nottinghamshire is tall and thin, spreading a surprising distance north of Nottingham to finish level with Sheffield. Most of the county's attractions are in the southern half, including Nottingham, with Newstead and Eastwood just north, Sherwood Forest in the centre and Newark-on-Trent and Southwell to the east.

Find countywide information at www.visitnottingham.co.uk.

Getting Around

A journey planner and comprehensive bus, rail, tram and plane information can be found at www.itsnottingham.info. **Sherwood Forester buses** (☎ 0115-977 4268; Ranger ticket adult/child £6/3; ☽ Sun & bank holidays Jun-Aug) go to tourist attractions all over Nottinghamshire; some offer admission discounts if you show the ticket.

NOTTINGHAM

☎ 0115 / pop 266,988

Linked forever to Robin Hood and his merry band of men in Lincoln green, Nottingham today is a dynamic mix of medieval and modern. Amid multistorey car parks and who-cares-what-you-think architectural eyesores, you'll stumble upon a centuries-old landmark that crusaders probably knew – it's that kind of place. Transformed by the riches of the 19th-century lace industry, the city developed into a powerful manufacturing engine-room, churning out Raleigh bikes, the Boots pharmacy empire and cigarettes. Industry has since declined, but the nightlife, culture and shopping most definitely have not. The city boasts fashion designer Paul Smith as one of its own, while the clubs and bars are some of the liveliest in the country. Trent Bridge is a major draw for cricket fans, and the reds of Nottingham Forest football club have an impressive heritage that belies their current form.

Orientation

Like other Midlands cities, Nottingham is enclosed by an inner ring road within which lie most of the attractions, bars and restaurants. The train station is on the southern edge of the centre. There are two bus stations: Victoria bus station is hidden away behind the Victoria shopping centre, just north of the centre, while Broadmarsh bus station is beneath Broadmarsh shopping centre to the south.

Information

Combat Strike (☎ 988 1880; floor 2, The Cornerhouse, Forman St; per hr £3; ☽ 11am-10pm Mon-Thu, to late Fri-Sun) Internet access.

Tourist office (☎ 915 5330; www.visitnottingham .com; 1-4 Smithy Row; ☽ 9am-5.30pm Mon-Fri, 9am-5pm Sat, 10am-4pm Sun) The staff here are very helpful. Ask them about discount combination tickets for major attractions.

Sights & Activities

NOTTINGHAM CASTLE MUSEUM & ART GALLERY

More of a mansion than a castle, the stately building here now has been standing since the 1670s. The last Nottingham Castle was demolished after the English Civil War, while the original was put up by William the Conqueror. The castle **museum** (☎ 915 3700; adult/child £3/1.50; ⊙ 10am-5pm Mar-Oct, 10am-4pm Sat-Thu Nov-Feb) opened in 1878. It vividly sets out Nottingham's history and displays some of the medieval alabaster carvings for which Nottingham was noted. Textiles and costumes peculiar to the city are also on show. Upstairs there's an art gallery with changing exhibitions and some fine permanent pieces (including works by Dante Gabriel Rossetti). There's a stylish café and an excellent shop.

An underground passageway, **Mortimer's Hole** (45min tours £2; ⊙ tours 11am, 2pm & 3pm Mon-Thu, 2pm & 3pm Fri & Sat), leads from the castle to Brewhouse Yard. Roger Mortimer, who arranged Edward II's murder, is said to have been captured by supporters of Edward III who entered via his passage. Ask to see the Sheriff Room (there is still a Sheriff of Nottingham today, a purely symbolic role).

CAVES OF NOTTINGHAM

Nottingham stands on Sherwood sandstone riddled with artificial caves that date back to medieval times. Bizarrely, the entrance to the most fascinating, readily accessible **caves** (☎ 924 1424; www.cityofcaves.com; admission £3.75; ⊙ 10am-5pm Mon-Sat, 11am-5pm Sun) is inside Broadmarsh shopping centre, on the upper level. These contain an air-raid shelter, a medieval underground tannery, several pub cellars and a mock-up of a Victorian slum dwelling.

TALES OF ROBIN HOOD

The **tales** (☎ 948 3284; www.robinhood.uk.com; 30 38 Maid Marian Way; adult/child £8.95/6.95; ⊙ 10am-6pm) is still piggybacking off the popularity of Kevin Costner's *Prince of Thieves* – back in 1991! It's tacky, outdated and overpriced but kids might get a kick out of the actors prancing around in merry men costumes.

WOLLATON HALL

Built in 1588 by Sir Francis Willoughby, land and coal-mine owner, **Wollaton Hall** (☎ 915 3900; Wollaton Park, Derby Rd; admission free Mon-Fri, adult/child Sat & Sun £1.50/1; ⊙ 11am-5pm Apr-Oct, to 4pm Nov-Mar) is a

magnificent example of Elizabethan architecture at its most extravagant. Architect Robert Smythson was also responsible for the equally avant-garde Longleat in Wessex (p316). It was undergoing restoration at the time of research; call to check opening hours. The hall also has a mediocre natural history museum.

The **Industrial Museum** (admission free Mon-Fri, adult/child Sat & Sun £1.50/1; ⊙ 10am-5pm Apr-Oct), in the 18th-century stable block, displays lace-making equipment, Raleigh bicycles, a gigantic 1858 beam engine and oddities such as a locally invented, 1963 video recorder that never got off the ground.

Wollaton Hall is on the western edge of the city, 2.5 miles from the centre; get there on the number 30 bus, which stops right in front (15 minutes). Wollaton Park, surrounding the hall, is a popular picnic spot.

BREWHOUSE YARD MUSEUM

Housed in five 17th-century cottages carved into the cliff below the castle, this engaging **museum** (☎ 915 3600; Castle Blvd; admission Mon-Fri free, Sat & Sun £1.50; ⊙ 10am-4.30pm) re-creates everyday life in Nottingham over the past 300 years with particularly fine reconstructions of traditional shops.

GALLERIES OF JUSTICE

In the impressive Shire Hall building, the well-presented **Galleries of Justice** (☎ 952 0555; www .galleriesofjustice.org.uk; High Pavement; adult/child £7.95/5.95; ⊙ 10am-4pm Tue-Sun Apr-Oct, 10am-3pm Tue-Fri, 11am-4pm Sat & Sun Nov-Mar) takes you through an interactive history of the judicial system. From medieval ordeals by water or hot iron to modern crime detection, 'gaolers' and 'prisoners' guide you through. Careful, you may find yourself sentenced to death in a Victorian courtroom!

Tours

Nottingham Tours (☎ 925 9388; www.nottingham tours.com) Offers a well-respected walking tour of the city, as well as tours of Sherwood Forest and boat trips.
Original Nottingham Ghost Walk (☎ 01773-769300; www.ghost-walks.co.uk; adult/child £4/3; 7pm Sat Jan-Nov) Departs from Ye Olde Salutation Inn (p492) to delve into the city's supernatural past – descend into the medieval caves if you dare...

Festivals & Events

A **Shakespeare Festival** has been held in July each summer for almost a decade at the Nottingham Playhouse (p493). Meanwhile, the

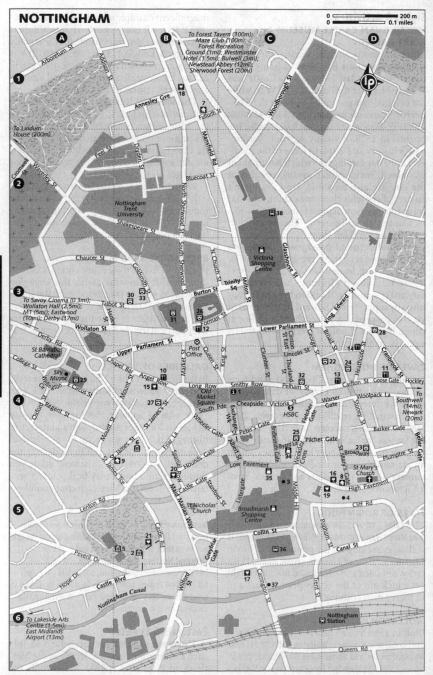

NOTTINGHAM

0 _____ 200 m
0 _____ 0.1 miles

To Forest Tavern (100m);
Maze Club (100m);
Forest Recreation
Ground (1mi); Westminster
Hotel (1.5mi); Bulwell (3mi);
Newstead Abbey (12mi);
Sherwood Forest (20mi)

To Lindum
House (200m)

Nottingham
Trent
University

To Savoy Cinema (0.3mi);
Wollaton Hall (2.5mi);
MT (5mi); Eastwood
(10mi); Derby (17mi)

Victoria
Shopping
Centre

Post
Office

Old
Market
Square

HSBC

St Mary's
Church

St Nicholas'
Church

Broadmarsh
Shopping
Centre

Sky
Mirror

St Barnabas'
Cathedral

Lakeside Arts
Centre (1.5mi);
East Midlands
Airport (13mi)

Nottingham Canal

Nottingham
Station

Nottingham Castle Museum & Art Gallery (p489) plays host to a **Robin Hood Pageant**, in October each year, reliving the times of the local outlaw legend.

The city's famed **Goose Fair** dates back to the Middle Ages. These days it's an outsized funfair that takes place around the beginning of October in the Forest Recreation Ground, a mile north of the city centre.

Sleeping

Igloo Backpackers Hostel (☎ 947 5250; www.igloohostel .co.uk; 110 Mansfield Rd; dm £13.50) Easy-come, easy-go budget travellers' favourite, this basic 36-bed independent hostel is a short walk north of Victoria bus station. The entrance is on Fulforth St. It's always full at weekends so book ahead. Breakfast is extra.

Lindum House (☎ 847 1089; 1 Burns St; s/d £40/50) On the outskirts of the centre in a striking Gothic residence, this is a quirky option and a good one for self-caterers: two of the rooms have adjoining kitchens. Beware of the steep cancellation policy of 72 hours advance notice. It's a 10-minute walk northwest of the centre.

Rutland Square Hotel (☎ 941 1114; rutlandsquare @zoffanyhotels.co.uk; St James St; s/d from £85/120) The rooms at this central business hotel are clean and serviceable, but the overall feel is clinical with little personal touch or charm. But there are good weekend discounts.

Westminster Hotel (☎ 955 5000, 312 Mansfield Rd; s/d £90/100; P ⊠) With a sprawl of rooms throughout a series of converted Victorian terraces, this Best Western-affiliate has good-natured but thinly stretched staff and excellent weekend offers with rooms going for less than half the rack rates.

Lace Market Hotel (☎ 852 3232; www.lacemarketho tel.co.uk; 29-31 High Pavement; s/d £90/115; P ⊠) Nottingham's best place to stay by a country mile, this is a lovely boutique hotel in a beautifully historic, well-heeled pocket of the city centre. It's in an old town house with a slick contemporary interior and young, attentive staff. Check the website for weekend discounts.

Eating

Alley Café (☎ 955 1013; 19 Cannon Court; mains £6-9; ☽ 11am-6pm Mon-Tue, to 11pm Wed-Sat) This pint-sized café bar has created quite a buzz with its excellent, globally inspired vegetarian and vegan dishes, not to mention its funky DJs and tunes. It is hidden down an ancient back alley. Seek it out.

Skinny Sumo (☎ 952 0188; 11-13 Carlton St; sushi platters from £8, lunch menu £6.90; ☽ noon-3pm & 6-11pm Tue-Fri, noon-11pm Sat, noon-3pm & 6-10pm Sun) Frills are sparse, but taste is plenty in this basic, highly regarded white-tiled Japanese café/restaurant with a sushi-bar conveyor belt.

Punchinello (☎ 941 1965; 35 Forman St; mains £8-13; ☽ noon-3pm Mon-Sat, plus 7.30-10pm Mon-Thu, 7.30-10.30pm Fri & Sat) Low-slung beamed ceilings distinguish this established central restaurant, the oldest in town, but it has moved with the times with a hint of the Mediterranean infusing most of its dishes.

Fresh (☎ 924 3336; 15 Goose Gate; dinner mains £9-12; ☽ 8am-late Mon-Fri, 9am-late Sat) The downstairs eatery specialises in wholesome snacks, salads and sandwiches, while the thriving upstairs restaurant fuses culinary influences from such diverse sources as Thailand and the Mediterranean. Beautiful lilies deck the tables and brighten the surroundings.

THE MIDLANDS

Other recommended places:

Broadway Cinema Cafébar (☎ 952 1551; 14-18 Broad St; specials £5.25; ☯ 9am-11pm Mon-Fri, 11am-11pm Sat, noon-10.30pm Sun) Perfect for a prefilm bite, this good-value café has lunchtime baguettes (£4.50) and a cultured crowd.

Squeek (☎ 955 5560; 23-25 Heathcote St; mains £9-12; ☯ 6-11pm Mon-Sat) Fresh flowers adorn the simple wooden tables and inventive vegetarian cuisine should keep even ardent carnivores contented.

Drinking

Ye Olde Trip to Jerusalem (☎ 947 3171; Brewhouse Yard, Castle Rd) Tucked into the cliff below the castle, this fantastically atmospheric alehouse claims to be England's oldest pub; it supposedly slaked the thirst of departing crusaders. The phrase 'nooks and crannies' could have been invented for here. Just when you think there are no more, you'll find another – and there are usually more than enough to accommodate the many tourists who come to sample the brews.

Cock & Hoop (☎ 852 3217; 25 High Pavement) Sophisticated yet easy-going, this cosy, traditional refurbished alehouse in a well-heeled pocket of Nottingham is a most pleasant place for a knees-up.

Bell Inn (☎ 947 5241; 18 Angel Row) Another must for the history buffs, this atmospheric old coaching inn lies at the heart of the shopping district and has warmed the cockles of Nottingham drinkers for hundreds of years.

Ye Olde Salutation Inn (☎ 988 1948; Maid Marian Way) A dual carriageway disguises the centuries-old atmosphere (c 1240) of 'the Sal', as regulars know it. Ask at the bar if you can have a peek at the labyrinth of underground caves spiralling down behind an innocuous-looking door.

Other good places to drink:

Forest Tavern (☎ 947 5650; 257 Mansfield Rd) Recently re-opened, this has a buzzing programme of live music and more types of beer than you could poke a pint glass at. It's just north of the centre.

Fellows, Morton & Clayton (☎ 950 6795; 54 Canal St) This is an excellent brewpub overlooking the revamped canal area of town.

Lincolnshire Poacher (☎ 941 1584; 161-163 Mansfield Rd) This great pub for the beer-drinking connoisseur has ales from Suffolk to Belgium, and boasts eight different types of sausage on its menu. Live bands rock the joint on Sunday nights.

Pitcher & Piano (☎ 958 6081; Unitarian Church, High Pavement; ☯ 11am-midnight Sun-Wed, to 1am Thu, to 2am Fri & Sat) It's a big chain pub in a converted Gothic church. OK, slightly sacrilegious, but this is still one of the most happening places in town.

Entertainment

NIGHTCLUBS

Nightclub fads come and go at breakneck speed in Nottingham. The converted warehouse/nightclubs on Lace Market's Broadway are still a hub, but the beats could soon move on – and there are plenty of great nights elsewhere. Check the local guides for more.

Stealth (☎ 958 0672; www.stealthattack.co.uk; Masonic Pl, Goldsmith St; admission £2-10) The bold new thing on the Nottingham nightclub scene, Stealth has an eclectic music mix, from indie to highly charged dance all-nighters that lure an up-for-it crowd from miles around.

NG1 (☎ 958 8440; www.ng1club.co.uk; 76-80 Lower Parliament St; admission £2-7) Nottingham's very own gay superclub, NG1 is pure, unpretentious hedonistic fun, with two dance floors belting out classic funky house, pop, cheese or indie depending on the night.

Social (☎ 950 5078; 23 Pelham St) Techno/dance-heads make for this sister club of the famous London venue. DJs rock the upstairs dance floor.

Bluu (☎ 950 5359; 5 Broadway; ☯ 11am-midnight Sun-Tue, to 1am Wed & Thu, to 2am Fri & Sat) This part restaurant, part bar, part nightclub offers a swish menu by day (slow braised lamb hotpot £15.50), and a jumping downstairs bar by night, attracting a chic, shirted and high-heeled crowd mostly in their mid-20s.

LIVE MUSIC & COMEDY

Malt Cross (☎ 941 1048; 16 St James St) What a great place! In an old music hall with a colourful history (it was a brothel in a previous incarnation), this has got the best vibe in town. Good live music and decent food are all dished up under the glass arched roof, an architectural treasure in itself.

Rock City (☎ 941 2544; www.rock-city.co.uk; 8 Talbot St) The dance floor jumps here on the popular 'Tuned' student night on Thursdays, and on '80s night every Friday. Big-name pop acts usually head here.

Maze Club (☎ 947 5650; 270 North Sherwood St; ☯ 6pm-midnight Mon, 4pm-midnight Tue-Thu, 4pm-2am Fri & Sat, noon-4pm & 7pm-midnight Sun) Behind the Forest Tavern traditional alehouse, this popular revamped venue puts on live music – mostly of an indie persuasion – almost every night.

Cabaret (☎ 910 0009; www.cabaret-nottingham.com; 22 Fletcher Gate; ☺ from 7pm Fri-Sun) The Sunday comedy night 'Just the Tonic' is justifiably famous, but there's plenty of other stuff going on here too, including the mosh-friendly Friday Rock club.

THEATRE, CINEMAS & CLASSICAL MUSIC
Cineworld cinema (☎ 0871 200 2000; www.ugccinemas .co.uk; Cornerhouse, Forman St) The Cornerhouse mall, opposite the Theatre Royal, is run-of-the-mill but it does house this 15-screen cinema.

Broadway Cinema (☎ 952 6611; www.broadway .org.uk; 14-18 Broad St; adult/concession £5.50/4.20) The Broadway is the city's art-house film centre.

Savoy (☎ 947 5812; 233 Derby Rd) This child-friendly independent cinema west of the city has double seats and has an ice-cream interval during kids' films.

Lakeside Arts Centre (☎ 846 7777; www.lakeside arts.org.uk; DH Lawrence Pavilion, University Park) A multipurpose venue southwest of the city, this centre hosts films, classical music, comedy and dance.

Dedicated theatres include the lower-profile **Arts Theatre** (☎ 947 6096; www.artstheatre.org .uk; George St), which also stages amateur productions, and the **Nottingham Playhouse** (☎ 941 9419; www.nottinghamplayhouse.co.uk; Wellington Circus), a respected venue outside of which sits *Sky Mirror*, a superb Anish Kapoor sculpture. For musicals or established music acts, try the Royal Concert Hall or the Theatre Royal, which share a **booking office** (☎ 989 5555; www .royalcentre-nottingham.co.uk; Theatre Sq) and an imposing building close to the centre.

Shopping
Paul Smith is the local boy made good in the heady environment of the London fashion scene. He's done so well, he has not one, but two upmarket exclusive shops in the city centre. One is on Byard Lane, the other is Willoughby House.

Getting There & Away
Nottingham is well situated for both trains and buses. The train station just to the south of the town centre has frequent – but no fast services – that go to Birmingham (1½ hours), Manchester (two hours) and London (two hours). Coaches are the cheaper option, mostly operating from the dingy confines of Broadmarsh bus station. There are five direct services to Birmingham and around

10 to London. Bus services to outlying villages are regular and reliable too. Services to Southwell, Eastwood and Newark also mostly depart from Broadmarsh bus station. If you're going further, the nearby airport might be your best bet.

Central Trains (☎ 08457 48 49 50; www.centraltrains .co.uk) Links up to Liverpool to the northwest, and as far south as Stansted Airport.

East Midlands Airport (☎ 0871 919 9000; www.not tinghamema.com)

Midland Mainline (☎ 08457 48 49 50; www.midland mainline.com) Serves East Midlands, London, and goes up north too.

Trent Barton (☎ 01773-712265; www.trentbuses. co.uk) Buses depart from Broadmarsh and Victoria bus stations.

Getting Around
For information on buses within Nottingham, call **Nottingham City Transport** (☎ 950 6070; www.nctx.co.uk). The Kangaroo ticket gives you unlimited travel on buses and trams within the city for £2.70.

The city tram system (www.thetram.net; single/all day from £1.20/£2.20) runs to the centre from Hucknall, 7 miles to the north of central Nottingham, through to the town centre and the train station.

Full details on Nottingham transport can be found at the **Nottingham Travelwise Service** (www.itsnottingham.info). You can also pick up a free transport planner and map from the tourist office.

Bunneys Bikes (☎ 947 2713; bike hire per day £8.99; ☺ 9am-5.30pm Mon-Fri, 9.30am-5pm Sat, 11am-3pm Sun; 97 Carrington St) is near the train station.

AROUND NOTTINGHAM
Newstead Abbey
With its attractive gardens, evocative lakeside ruins and notable connections with Romantic poet Lord Byron (1788–1824), whose country pile it was, **Newstead Abbey** (☎ 01623-455900; www.newsteadabbey.org.uk; adult/child £6/3, gardens only £3/1.50; ☺ house noon-5pm Apr-Sep, garden 9am-dusk year-round) is a popular weekend destination for tourists and local families alike. Founded as an Augustinian priory around 1170, it was converted into a home after the dissolution of the monasteries in 1539. Beside the still-imposing façade of the priory church are the remains of the manor. It now houses some interesting Byron memorabilia, from pistols to manuscripts, and you can have a peek at

his old living quarters. Many of the rooms are re-created in convincing period styles.

The house is 12 miles north of Nottingham, off the A60. The Stagecoach bus 233 runs at 23 minutes past the hour from Victoria Bus Station, weekends only. The Sherwood Forester bus runs right there on summer Sundays. Bus 737 runs from Nottingham (25 minutes, every 30 minutes, hourly on Sundays) to the abbey gates, where you will have to walk a mile to the house and gardens.

DH Lawrence Sites

The **DH Lawrence Birthplace Museum** (☎ 01773-717353; 8A Victoria St, Eastwood; admission Mon-Fri free, Sat & Sun £2; ✆ 10am-5pm Apr-Oct, to 4pm Nov-Mar), former home of Nottingham's controversial author (1885–1930), has been reconstructed as it would have been in Lawrence's childhood, with period furnishings. Down the road, the **Durban House Heritage Centre** (☎ 01773-717353; Mansfield Rd; admission £2, or £3.50 for both; ✆ 10am-5pm Apr-Oct, to 4pm Nov-Mar) sheds light on the background to Lawrence's books by re-creating the life of the mining community at the turn of the 20th century.

Eastwood is about 10 miles northwest of the city. Take Trent Barton service 1.

Sherwood Forest Country Park

Don't expect to lose yourself like an outlaw: there are almost more tourists than trees in today's Sherwood Forest, although there are still peaceful spots to be found. The **Sherwood Forest Visitor Centre** (☎ 01623-823 202; www.sherwood-forest.org.uk; admission free, parking £3; ✆ 10am-5.30pm Apr-Oct, to 4.30pm Nov-Mar) houses 'Robyn Hode's Sherwode', a cute but corny exhibition describing the lifestyles of bandits, kings, peasants and friars. One of the major attractions is the Major Oak, which is supposed to have been a hiding place for Mr Hood; these days it's more likely he'd have to hold it up, not hide in it. The **Robin Hood Festival** is a massive medieval re-enactment that takes place here every August.

The **Sherwood Forest YHA Hostel** (☎ 0870 770 6026; sherwood@yha.org.uk; Forest Corner, Edwinstowe; dm member/nonmember £15.50/18.50) is a modern hostel with comfortable dorms just a bugle-horn cry away from the visitor centre.

Sherwood Forester buses run the 20 miles to the park from Nottingham on Sunday. Catch bus 33 from Nottingham Monday to Saturday.

SOUTHWELL
☎ 01636 / pop 6285

Like it fell out of a Jane Austen novel, Southwell is a sleepy market town. **Southwell Minster** (☎ 812649; suggested donation £2; ✆ 8am-7pm May-Sep, to dusk Oct-Apr) is a Gothic cathedral unlike any other in England, its two heavy, square front towers belying the treats within. The nave dates from the 12th century, although there is evidence of an earlier Saxon church floor, itself made with mosaics from a Roman villa. A highlight of the building is the chapterhouse, filled with 13th-century carvings of leaves, pigs, dogs and rabbits. The library is fascinating, with illuminated manuscripts and heavy tomes from the 16th century and earlier.

A visit to **Southwell Workhouse** (NT; ☎ 817250; Upton Rd; adult/child £4.90/2.40; ✆ noon-5pm Thu-Mon Mar-Oct, 11am-5pm Thu-Mon Aug) is a sobering but fascinating experience. An audio guide, narrated by 'inmates' and 'officials', describes the life of paupers in the mid-19th century to good (if grim) effect, despite the fact that most of the rooms are empty.

Bus 100 runs from Nottingham (40 minutes, every 20 minutes, hourly on Sunday) and on to Newark-on-Trent (25 minutes, hourly, every two hours on Sunday).

NEWARK-ON-TRENT
☎ 01636 / pop 25,376

Another market town with a pedigree rich in history, Newark-on-Trent was once a strategically important place. Evidence lies in the ruins of **Newark Castle** (admission to gate £2, grounds free; ✆ until dusk), one of the few places to hold out against Cromwell's men during the Civil War – only for Charles I to order surrender, condemning the building to rapid destruction. An impressive Norman gate remains, part of the structure in which King John died in 1216. Entry to the gate itself is by guided tour only; contact the **tourist office** (☎ 655765; gilstrap@nsdc.info; Gilstrap Centre, Castlegate; ✆ 9am-6pm Apr Sep, to 5pm Oct-Mar) for details. The office also houses a small display on the town's history. Pick up the *Walkabout Tour* leaflet and explore.

The town has a large, cobbled square overlooked by the fine, timber-framed, 14th-century **Olde White Hart Inn** (now a building society) and the **Clinton Arms Hotel** (now a shopping precinct), from where former prime minister Gladstone made his first political speech and where Lord Byron stayed while his first book of poems was published.

Gannets Daycafé (☎ 702066; 35 Castlegate; snacks £2-5) scoops the lunchtime trade with excellent-value snacks, coffee and toffee pudding that's worth getting sticky fingers for. The riverside setting of **Café Bleu** (☎ 610141; 14 Castlegate; mains £11-14; ☯ lunch daily, dinner Mon-Sat) is part of this sophisticated (and pricey) restaurant's charm. Live jazz accompanies diners. In winter, the log fire roars, while in summer the courtyard garden is open.

Buses 90 and 100 run to Nottingham (1¼ hours, hourly, every two hours Sunday). A central train service also leaves from here.

DERBYSHIRE

Without doubt one of the prettiest parts of England, Derbyshire is a winning combination of rolling green hills dotted with lambs and lined with stone fences, beautiful wild moors, remote windswept farms and greystone villages. And, er, Derby.

Part of the county is within the Peak District National Park, and for many visitors the two areas are synonymous – although the park overlaps several other counties, and there are parts of Derbyshire beyond the national park boundary that contain many other attractions. There's the misplaced seaside resort of Matlock Bath, the twisted spire of Chesterfield cathedral, and some wonderful stately homes including dishevelled Calke Abbey and unforgettable Chatsworth.

Derbyshire is one of the most visited counties in England, and justifiably so.

Orientation

Derbyshire's main city, Derby, lies toward the south of this very pretty county, which stretches much taller than it does wide. The north contains some of the prettiest stretches of the Peak District, but south is also blessed with some fine scenery, perhaps most instantly accessible from the pretty market town of Ashbourne. Matlock Bath is almost plumb in the county's centre.

Activities

Outdoor activities in Derbyshire include walking, cycling, rock climbing, caving and paragliding, to name but a few. Many take place inside the Peak District National Park, and are covered under the Activities heading in that section (p501).

Getting There & Around

Derbyshire Wayfarer (☎ 0870 608 2608, Traveline; www.derbysbus.net; day pass adult/family £7.90/12.50) Covers buses and trains throughout the county and beyond (eg to Manchester and Sheffield).

Trent Barton Buses (☎ 01773-712265; www.trent buses.co.uk; day ticket £4) Operates the TransPeak bus service.

DERBY

☎ 01332 / pop 229,407

The Industrial Revolution created a major manufacturing centre out of Derby, which made its name churning out such varied goods as silk, china, railways and Rolls-Royce aircraft engines. Not the prettiest town, it is a useful stepping stone to some lovely Derbyshire countryside. And while you're here you can delve into the history of English engineering, the bone-china industry and sample a pint in a city that residents claim to be the real-ale capital of the UK.

Orientation & Information

Derby has a pedestrianised shopping centre and a small but attractive old-town district. A partly cobbled central thoroughfare called Irongate, with a few good pubs and cafés, leads up to the cathedral.

The helpful **tourist office** (☎ 255802; www.visit derby.co.uk; Market Pl; ☯ 9.30am-5.30pm Mon-Fri, 9am-5pm Sat, 10.30am-2.30pm Sun) is in the main square.

Sights

Derby's grand 18th-century **cathedral** (Queen St; adult/child £5/2.50; ☯ 9.30am-4.30pm Mon-Sat) boasts a 64m-high tower and impressive wrought-iron screens. Large windows enhance the magnificent light interior. Tours run at 10.30am on the second Monday in the month. Don't miss the huge tomb of Bess of Hardwick, one of Derbyshire's most formidable residents in days gone by. For more about her, see Hardwick Hall (p500). Bird-lovers should watch out for peregrines, regularly spotted around the tower.

Next to the River Derwent in a former silk mill (Britain's first 'modern' factory), the **Derby Museum of Industry & History** (☎ 255308; Silk Mill Lane; admission free; ☯ 11am-5pm Mon, 10am-5pm Tue-Sat, 1-4pm Sun & bank holidays) tells the city's manufacturing history; trainspotters will have a field day, while plane buffs should get a buzz out of displays on the development of the Rolls-Royce aero-engine.

The factory of **Royal Crown Derby** (☎ 712841; www.royalcrownderby.co.uk; Osmaston Rd; tours £4.95, 4 daily Mon-Fri, demonstration studio only £2.95/2.75; ☻ 9am-5pm Mon-Sat, 10am-4pm Sun;) turns out some of the finest bone china in England. In the demonstration studio, you'll see workers skilfully making delicate china flowers, using little more than a hat-pin, spoon handle and even a head-lice comb. There's also a shop (watch your elbows).

Sleeping

Crompton Coach House (☎ 365735; www.coachhouse derby.co.uk; 45 Crompton St; s/d incl breakfast £28.50/55) Bright sunny rooms along with cheery hosts in this colourful B&B make this the best option in a city short on choices for the cash-conscious traveller. It lies just south of the central shopping area.

Midland Hotel (☎ 345894; www.midland-derby.co .uk; Midland Rd; s/d £99/117; **P** 🖳) The grand old dame of Derby hotels lies right opposite the train station. Business delegates hobnob in its welcoming and convivial environs during the week. Prices tumble at the weekends. Ask for an interior room away from traffic noise. The hotel restaurant is good and particularly popular for Sunday lunch.

Eating & Drinking

Derby's best pubs are near the train station.

Café B (☎ 368822; Sadler Gate; bagels £2.50; ☻ 8.30am-5pm Mon-Fri, 9am-5.30pm Sat, 11.30am-4.30pm Sun) On the narrow pedestrian street branching out from central Market Place, this place is busy, bright and bustling (to use 'b' words). It's also 'boxlike' and you'll need to scrap for space to munch very tasty bagels.

Ye Olde Dolphin Inn (☎ 267711, Queen St; snacks & meals £3-6) Just by the cathedral, this flag-stone-floored inn boasts a haunted cellar, apparently, while spirits of another sort are served at its snug bars. Reasonable pub grub is also on offer.

Haus (☎ 832926; Jacobean House, mains £9-15; ☻ 6-10pm Tue-Sat) The restaurant of the moment, with excellent European cuisine and a fresh, contemporary look. Book ahead at weekends.

Brunswick Inn (☎ 290677; 1 Railway Tce) This award-winning inn has a warm ambience, all maroon leather upholstery and wood panels, but the real reason to come here is the beers (some made on site), which are a wet dream for real-ale-lovers.

Alexandra Hotel (☎ 293993, 203 Siddals Rd) Just down the road, this austerely decorated hotel also has a range of decent ales on tap.

Victoria Inn (☎ 740091; www.thevicinn.co.uk; 12 Midland Pl) Directly across from the station; has live music gigs – from punk to indie – several nights a week.

Derby Cathedral Centre (☻ 9.30am-4.30pm Mon-Sat) Opposite the cathedral. Staff here pour pots of fair-trade coffee (£1.35) to accompany good-value snacks and cakes.

Getting There & Away

Derby's main bus station is currently closed, with temporary stands in place nearby. TransPeak buses run every two hours between Nottingham and Manchester via Derby, Matlock, Bakewell and Buxton (Derby to Nottingham 30 minutes, Derby to Bakewell one hour). Outgoing services currently leave from stand Y1 on Derwent St just north of the tourist office. From London, there are trains to Derby (two hours, hourly), continuing to Chesterfield, Sheffield and Leeds. There is also a direct service from Birmingham (45 minutes).

AROUND DERBY
Kedleston Hall

Sitting proudly in vast landscaped parkland, the superb neoclassical mansion of **Kedleston Hall** (NT; ☎ 01332-842191; adult/child £6.90/3.30; ☻ noon-4pm Sat-Wed Easter-Oct) is a must for fans of stately homes. The Curzon family has lived here since the 12th century; Sir Nathaniel Curzon tore down an earlier house in 1758 so this stunning masterpiece could be built. Meanwhile, the poor old peasants in Kedleston village had their humble dwellings moved a mile down the road, as they interfered with the view! Ah, the good old days…

Entering the house through a grand portico you reach the breathtaking Marble Hall with its massive alabaster columns and statues of Greek deities. Curved corridors on either side offer splendid views of the park – don't miss the arc of floorboards, specially cut from bending oak boughs. Other highlights include richly decorated bedrooms and a circular saloon with a domed roof, modelled on the Pantheon in Rome. Another great building, Government House in Calcutta (now Raj Bhavan), was modelled on Kedleston Hall, as a later Lord Curzon was viceroy of India around 1900. His collection of oriental artefacts is on show, as is his wife's 'peacock' dress – made of gold and silver thread and weighing 5kg.

If the sun is out, take a walk around the lovingly restored 18th-century-style pleasure gardens.

Kedleston Hall is 5 miles northwest of Derby. By bus, service 109 between Derby and Ashbourne goes within about 1½ miles of Kedleston Hall (20 minutes, seven daily Monday to Saturday, five on Sunday). It leaves from Albert St in Derby, stand B1. On Sundays and bank holidays the bus loops right up to the house.

Calke Abbey

Like an enormous, long-neglected cabinet of wonders, **Calke Abbey** (NT; ☎ 01332-863822; adult/child £6.80/3.40; ⏱ 12.30-4.30pm Sat-Wed Apr-Oct) is not your usual glitzy, wealth-encrusted stately home. Built around 1703, it's been passed down a dynasty of eccentric and reclusive baronets. Very little has changed since about 1880 – it's a mesmerising example of a country house in decline. The result is a ramshackle maze of secret corridors, underground tunnels and rooms crammed with ancient furniture, mounted animal heads, dusty books, stuffed birds and endless piles of bric-a-brac from the last three centuries. Some rooms are in fabulous condition, while others are deliberately untouched, complete with crumbling plaster and mouldy wallpaper. (You exit the house via a long, dark tunnel – a bit more thrilling than one might like, given the state of the buildings.) A stroll round the gardens is a similar time-warp experience – in the potting sheds nothing has changed since about 1930, but it looks like the gardener left only yesterday.

Admission to Calke Abbey house is by timed ticket at busy times. On summer weekends it's wise to phone ahead and check there'll be space. You can enter the gardens and grounds at any time. Calke is 10 miles south of Derby. Visitors coming by car must enter via the village of Ticknall. The Arriva bus 68 from Derby to Swadlincote stops at Ticknall (40 minutes, hourly, change to the 69 in Melbourne) and from there it's a 2-mile walk through the park.

Ashbourne

☎ 01335 / pop 7600

The picturesque little market town of Ashbourne is nestled in a bowl formed by the Derbyshire Dales. It lies at the very southern tip of the Peak District National Park, about 15 miles northwest of Derby. Fine stone terraces line the marketplace and the precariously sloping main street, where visitors flock at weekends, either to recharge after a hike, or simply hang out in the flurry of cafés, pubs and antique shops. (Things get even busier once a year when the game of Shrovetide Football is rigorously pursued; see the boxed text p498.)

The **tourist office** (☎ 343666; Market Pl; ⏱ 9.30am-5pm Apr-Oct, 10am-4pm Mon-Sat Nov-Feb) can provide leaflets or advice on B&Bs in the area.

Of particular interest to walkers and cyclists, Ashbourne is the southern terminus of the **Tissington Trail**, a former railway line and now a wonderful easy-gradient path cutting through fine west Derbyshire countryside. The Tissington Trail takes you north towards Buxton and connects with the High Peak Trail running south towards Matlock Bath; for more details on circular route possibilities see p501). About a mile outside town along Mapleton Lane, **Ashbourne Cycle Hire** (☎ 343156; day's cycle hire £13) is on the Tissington Trail, with a huge stock of bikes and trailers for all ages, and free leaflets showing the route with pubs and teashops along the way.

Ivy-covered **Bramhall's** (☎ 346158; www.bram halls.co.uk; 6 Buxton Rd; s/d £27.50/55) lies just up the road from the main market square. Its fine restaurant is known well beyond Ashbourne and it also has a great little B&B.

The half-timbered **Ashbourne Gingerbread Shop** (☎ 346753; St John's St) takes the biscuit as the best bakery and tearoom in town. It serves some of the gingerbread Ashbourne is famous for. Down-to-earth **Smith's Tavern** (☎ 342264; 36 St John's St) is a cosy, cluttered and popular pub with decent brews and good grub.

Without your own transport, bus is the only way to get to Ashbourne. Numerous services leave from the forecourt of Derby railway station and the trip takes from 40 minutes to just under an hour. Direct buses include the 109 (five services daily Monday to Saturday), and 108 (four per day on Sunday and bank holidays). The One, operated by Trent Barton, leaves from Derby's Albert St, stand B1 (four daily Monday to Saturday).

Dovedale

About 3 miles northwest of Ashbourne the River Dove winds through the steep-sided valley of Dovedale. It's one of the most accessible

---

BIZARRE ENGLAND: SHROVE TUESDAY FOOTBALL

Shrove Tuesday comes before Ash Wednesday, the first day of Lent – the Christian time of fasting – so Shrove Tuesday is the day to use up all your rich and fattening food. This led to the quaint tradition of Pancake Day in England and the flamboyant Mardi Gras festival in other parts of the world.

On Shrove Tuesday, various English towns celebrate with pancake races, but in Ashbourne they go for something much more energetic. Here they play Shrovetide Football, but it's nothing like the football most people are used to. For a start, the goals are 3 miles apart, the 'pitch' is a huge patch of countryside, and the game lasts all afternoon and evening (then starts again the day after). There are two teams, but hundreds of participants, and very few rules indeed. A large leather ball is fought over voraciously as players maul their way through fields and gardens, along the river, and up the main street – where shop windows are specially boarded over for the occasion. Visitors come from far and wide to watch, but only the brave should take part!

---

ways to sample the beauty of Derbyshire, so it can get crowded on summer weekends – especially near the famous Stepping Stones that cross the river – but the crowds thin out as you go further up, and midweek it's a lovely place for a walk.

The quaint *Dovedale Guide* (£1.50), available from Ashbourne's tourist office, has more background and a map showing footpaths. Romantic Victorian travellers went on outings to Dovedale, bestowing fanciful names on the natural features, so today we can admire hills and rocky buttresses called Thorpe Cloud, Dovedale Castle, Lovers' Leap, the Twelve Apostles, Tissington Spires, Reynard's Kitchen and Lion Head Rock. Another early visitor was Izaak Walton, the 17th-century fisherman and author of *The Compleat Angler*. The quaintly elegant **Izaak Walton Hotel** (☎ 01335-350555) at the southern end of Dovedale is named in his honour, and the public bar, pretty garden and scrumptious scones make it well worth a stop for after-walk refreshment.

MATLOCK BATH
☎ 01629 / pop 2202

Charming, tacky and quirky in a uniquely British way, Matlock Bath is like a seaside resort that got lost in landlocked rural Derbyshire. Day-trippers wander down the brash promenade, popping into amusement arcades, an aquarium, Victorian cafés, pubs and the souvenir shops – some with stock that seems left over since Victorian times. The tiny tourist beauty spot lies on the southeastern edge of the Peak District National Park. Bisected by the smooth, twisty A6, the town's buzz becomes a roar (of engines) at the weekend, as hundreds of motorcyclists flock here. If

you're lucky, you may catch the memorable sight of a leather-clad burly biker sipping tea from a bone-china mug.

It sits next to the pleasant town of Matlock, which has little in the way of sights but is a handy gateway to the scenic dales.

Orientation & Information

Matlock Bath is 2 miles south of Matlock. Everything revolves around North Pde and South Pde, a line of seaside-style shops, attractions, pubs and places to eat along one side of the main road through town (the A6), with the murmuring River Derwent and a plush gorge on the other side.

Matlock Bath's **tourist office** (☎ 55082; www .derbyshire.gov.uk; the Pavilion; ☼ 9.30am-5pm daily Mar-Oct, Sat & Sun Nov-Feb) is run by helpful staff armed with reams of leaflets and guidebooks.

Sights & Activities

One of the delights of Matlock Bath is simply strolling along the promenade, munching on chips or candy-floss. For a scenic detour, you can meander across the river to the park on the other side and take one of the steep paths to great cliff-top viewpoints.

At the enthusiast-run **Mining Museum** (☎ 583834; the Pavilion; adult/child £3/2; ☼ 10am-5pm May-Sep, 11am-3pm Nov-Apr) you can clamber through the shafts and tunnels where Derbyshire lead miners once eked out a risky living. Bizarrely, part of the museum was once a dancehall. For £2 extra (child £1), you can go down **Temple Mine** and pan for 'gold'.

For a different view, go to the **Heights of Abraham** (☎ 582365; adult/child £9.50/6.50; ☼ 10am-5pm daily Mar-Oct, Sat & Sun Feb-Mar), which claims to be the Peak District's 'oldest attraction'.

It is an excellent, wholesome family day out, with underground caverns, an adventure playground and woodland nature trails. The price includes a spectacular cable-car ride up from the valley floor.

Near the cable car base, **Whistlestop Centre** (admission free; ☿ 10am-5pm Tue-Sun Apr-Oct, Sat & Sun Nov-Mar), at the old train station, has wildlife and natural garden exhibits, and runs children's activities in the summer.

From the cable-car base, walking trails lead up to viewpoints on top of **High Tor**. You can see down to Matlock Bath and over to **Riber Castle**, a Victorian folly.

Gulliver's Kingdom (☎ 01925-444888; admission £8.99; ☿ usually 10.30am-5pm late May-early Sep, weekends & holidays Oct-Apr) is a theme park for younger kids with the usual favourites: log flume, pirate ship and roller coaster. Under-12s will love it. It includes a nonviolent Punch and Judy show (presumably just with Judy).

A mile south of Matlock Bath is **Masson Mills Working Textile Museum** (☎ 581001; adult/child £2.50/1.50; ☿ 10am-4pm Mon-Fri, 11am-5pm Sat, 11am-4pm Sun), built in 1783 for pioneering industrialist Sir Richard Arkwright. It's still working today, with renovated looms and weaving machines, and the world's largest collection of bobbins bringing over 200 years of textile history to life. It's now cunningly combined with a 'shopping village', including three floors of High St textile and clothing names.

From the beginning of September to October don't miss the **Matlock Illuminations** (Derwent Gardens; admission £3; ☿ evenings from dusk Fri-Sun), with streams of pretty lights, outrageously decorated Venetian boats on the river and fireworks.

Sleeping

Matlock Bath has several B&Bs in the heart of things on North Pde and South Pde, and a few places just out of the centre. There are also more choices in nearby Matlock.

Matlock YHA Hostel (☎ 0870 770 5960; matlock@yha .org.uk; 40 Bank Rd; dm member/nonmember £13.95/16.95) is a basic, big housing block 2 miles from Matlock Bath, with likeable, friendly staff. It is due to close in October 2007.

Sunnybank Guesthouse (☎ 584621; sunward@lineone .net; Clifton Rd; per person from £26; ☖) This lovely, well-kept guesthouse is blessed with bright interiors and fine views from its hillside perch. The comfortable wooden-floored breakfast room has a reassuring lingering scent of marmalade and toast.

Hodgkinson's Hotel & Restaurant (☎ 582170; www .hodgkinsons-hotel.co.uk; 150 South Pde; s/d from £38/70; **P**) You seem to stumble into the 19th century when you enter this brilliantly quirky hotel. From the wooden-handled umbrellas by the door to the bizarrely shaped rooms and antique chairs, it is soaked in Victorian atmosphere and charm. Rooms come with beams and brass bed-knobs.

Temple Hotel (☎ 583911; www.templehotel.co.uk; Temple Wk; s/d £55/92; **P** **X**) The views from this hillside hotel are fantastic – so lovely that poet Lord Byron once felt inspired to etch a poem on the restaurant window. It's been a hotel for four hundred years (and a good chunk of its recent history with the same décor). The rooms are straight from the 1970s but that's part of the charm. Bar meals are available.

Eating & Drinking

North Pde and South Pde are lined end-to-end with cafés, teashops and takeaways, serving chocolate cake, fish and chips, fried chicken, pies, and burgers – hear those arteries scream!

Temple Hotel (☎ 583911; Temple Wk) On the hillside, the bar at this hotel has reasonable pub food and a fine restaurant.

Fishpond (☎ 581000; 204 South Pde) This pub gets a lively, spirited crowd and is surprisingly jumping for a pub in rural Derbyshire. It has some great (and some not-so-great) live music.

Victorian Tea Shop (☎ 583325; 118 North Pde; ☿ 10am-5.30pm Mon-Fri) For the pick of the teahouses, stroll elegantly into this placed all lace curtains, cream cakes and delicate crockery. You may find yourself mingling with bikers with slightly less finesse!

Getting There & Away

The Peak District is extremely well served by public transport, and Matlock is a hub. Buses 213 and 214 go to and from Sheffield (one hour 10 minutes) several times a day. There are hourly buses to and from Derby (1¼ hours) and Chesterfield (35 minutes). There is also a train station. Several trains a day serve Derby (30 minutes). For detailed travel planning information, go to www.der bysbus.net.

AROUND MATLOCK BATH

From just outside Matlock town centre, about 2½ miles from Matlock Bath, steam trains and scenic railcars trundle along **Peak Rail** (☎ 01629-580381; www.peakrail.co.uk; adult/child return £6/3) via stops at Darley Dale to the northern terminus near the village of Rowsley. For train buffs and families, it's a great ride. There are nine services daily Saturday and Sunday, Sunday only November to March, extra weekday services June to September.

From Rowsley train station a riverside path leads to **Caudwell's Mill** (☎ 01629-734374; adult/child £3.50/1.25; ⏲ 10am-5.30pm), a huge, fascinating flour mill, full of working belts, shafts and other machinery – some almost a century old. There's a tearoom here, several craft workers, and a shop selling gifts and flour 'for the discerning housewife'. You can get to Rowsley direct from Matlock by bus; it's on the road to Bakewell.

CHESTERFIELD
☎ 01246 / pop 100,879

This is an unremarkable town with the exception of one famous landmark: the eye-catching crooked spire of **St Mary & All Saints Church** (☎ 206506; admission free, tours adult/child £3.50/1.50; ⏲ 9am-5pm). Dating from 1360, the giant corkscrew spire is 68m high and leans almost 3m southwest. There are various theories why: it probably was due to green timber warping, although some still prefer to believe that the spire was so amazed to hear of a virgin being married in the church that it twisted to see the sight for itself. Tour times vary; call to arrange.

The **tourist office** (☎ 345777; Rykneld Sq; ⏲ 9am-5.30pm Mon-Sat Apr-Oct, 9am-5pm Mon-Sat Nov-Mar) is right opposite the crooked spire in a sleek black building. It's very useful for planning a trip to the Peak District.

The easiest way to get here is by train. Chesterfield is between Nottingham/Derby (20 minutes) and Sheffield (10 minutes), with services about hourly. The station is just east of the centre.

AROUND CHESTERFIELD
Hardwick

If you're weighing up which stately homes to see, **Hardwick Hall** (NT; ☎ 01246-850430; adult/child £7.80/3.90; ⏲ noon-4.30pm Wed, Thu, Sat & Sun Apr-Oct) should be high on your list. It was home to the 16th century's second most powerful woman, Elizabeth, countess of Shrewsbury – known to all as Bess of Hardwick. Unashamedly modelling herself on the era's *most* famous woman – Queen Elizabeth I – Bess gained power and wealth by marrying four times, upwards each time.

When her fourth husband died in 1590, Bess had a huge fortune to play with, and had Hardwick Hall built using the designs of eminent architect Robert Smythson. Glass was a status symbol, so she went all-out on the windows, and a contemporary ditty quipped 'Hardwick Hall – more glass than wall.' Also astounding are the magnificent High Great Chamber and Long Gallery. These and many other rooms and broad stairways are decorated with fabulous large tapestries.

Next door is **Hardwick Old Hall** (EH; adult/child £3.50/1.80, joint ticket £10.60/5.30; ⏲ 11am-6pm Mon, Wed, Thu, Sat & Sun Apr-Sep, to 5pm Mon, Wed, Thu, Sat & Sun Oct), Bess's first house, now a romantic ruin.

Also fascinating are the formal gardens, again virtually unchanged for centuries, and around the hall spreads the great expanse of **Hardwick Park** with short and long walking trails leading across fields and through woods. Ask at the ticket office for details. Just near the south gate is the sandstone **Hardwick Inn** (☎ 01246 850 245; Hardwick Park, Doe Lea), a traditional, historic pub where the menu is far more sophisticated than your average local.

Hardwick Hall is 10 miles southeast of Chesterfield, just off the M1. A special coach, Service 101, runs from Chesterfield train station (Sundays only June to August, Thursdays July to August, tickets £6, with 20% discount at Hardwick), out in the morning, back in the afternoon, giving about three hours at Hardwick. The bus also passes **Stainsby Mill** – a quaint working flour mill dating from 1245 – and ends at **Bolsover Castle**, yet another stately home. For details, contact the Chesterfield tourist office or call **Chesterfield Community Transport** (☎ 01246-209668).

PEAK DISTRICT

The Peak District National Park features some of England's wildest, most beautiful scenery: pretty villages, historic sites, grand houses, fascinating limestone caves and the southernmost hills of the Pennines. Called the Peak not because of the hills, which are quite rounded, but because early British tribe the Picts once lived here, this is one of the country's best-loved national parks (it's the busiest in Europe, and the second busiest in the world after Mt Fuji). But don't be put off by its popularity: escaping the crowds is no problem if you avoid summer weekends, and even then, with a bit of imagination, it's easy to enjoy this wonderful area in relative peace and solitude.

Orientation & Information

The Peak District is principally in Derbyshire but spills into five adjoining counties (including Yorkshire, Staffordshire and Cheshire) and is one of the largest national parks in England. This 555-sq-mile protected area is divided into two distinct zones: the harsher, higher, wilder Dark Peak to the north, characterised by peaty moors and dramatic gritstone cliffs called 'edges'; and the lower, prettier, more pastoral White Peak to the south, with green fields marked by dry-stone walls, and divided by deep dales.

There are tourist offices (those run by the national park are called visitor centres) in Buxton, Bakewell, Castleton, Edale and other locations, all overflowing with maps, guidebooks and leaflets detailing walks, cycle rides and other activities. For general information, the free *Peak District* newspaper and the official park website at www.peakdistrict.org cover transport, activities, local events, guided walks and so on.

Activities

CAVING & CLIMBING

The Peak District limestone is riddled with caves and caverns, including 'showcaves' open to the public in Castleton, Buxton and Matlock Bath (described in each of those sections). For serious caving (or potholing) trips, tourist offices can provide a list of accredited outdoor centres, and if you know what you're doing, Castleton makes a great base.

For guidebooks, gear (to buy or hire) and a mine of local information, contact **Hitch n Hike** (☎ 01433-651013; www.hitchnhike.co.uk; Mytham Bridge, Bamford, Hope Valley, Derbyshire), a specialist caving and outdoor activity shop in Bamford, near Castleton. The website also has more info about caving in the area.

If you'd rather be on top of the rock, the Peak is a popular climbing area, and has long been a training ground for England's top mountaineers. There are multipitch routes on limestone faces such as High Tor, overlooking Matlock Bath, and there's a great range of short climbing routes on the famous gritstone 'edges' of Froggatt, Curbar and Stanage.

CYCLING

The Peak District is a very popular cycling area, especially the White Peak and the parts of Derbyshire south of here around Matlock and Ashbourne, which have a network of quiet lanes, and tracks for mountain bikers. In the Dark Peak there are fewer roads, and they are quite busy with traffic, although there are some good off-road routes. A good place to start any ride is a tourist office; all stock maps, books and leaflets for cyclists and mountain bikers.

In the Dark Peak, Edale is a popular starting point for mountain bikers, and near the Derwent Reservoirs is also good. In the White Peak, all the villages mentioned in this section make good bases for cycle tours.

For easy traffic-free riding, head for the 17.5-mile **High Peak Trail**, a route for cyclists and walkers on the mostly flat track of an old railway. You can join the trail at Cromford, near Matlock Bath, but it starts with a very steep incline, so if you seek easy gradients a better start is Middleton Top, a mile or so north. The trail winds through beautiful hills and farmland to a village called Parsley Hay, and continues on for a few more miles towards Buxton. At Parsley Hay another former-railway-turned-walking-and-cycling-route, the **Tissington Trail**, heads south for 13 miles to Ashbourne. You can go out and back as far as you like, or make it a triangular circuit, following the busy B5053 or (a better choice) the quiet lanes through Bradbourne and Brassington.

The **Pennine Bridleway** is another, more recent addition, and is suitable for horse riders, cyclists and walkers.

There are several cycle-hire centres in the Peak District, including **Derwent Cycle Hire** (☎ 01433-651261), and **Parsley Hay** (☎ 01298-84493) and **Middleton Top** (☎ 01629-823204) for the Tissington and High Peak Trails. Tourist offices have a leaflet detailing all other hire centres, opening times etc. Charges hover around £10 to £15 per day for adults' bikes (deposit and ID required), and kids' bikes and trailers are also available.

WALKING

The Peak District is one of the most popular walking areas in England, crossed by a vast network of footpaths and tracks – especially in the White Peak – and you can easily find a walk of a few miles or longer, depending on your energy and interests. If you want to explore the higher realms of the Dark Peak,

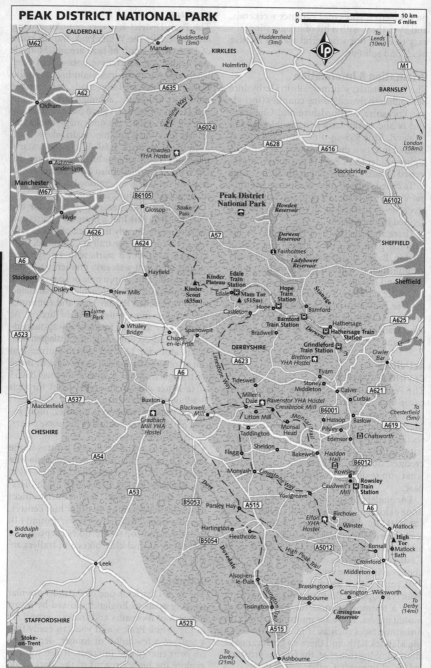

PEAK DISTRICT NATIONAL PARK

which often involves the local art of 'bog trotting', make sure your boots are waterproof and be prepared for wind and rain – even if the sun is shining when you set off.

The Peak's most famous walking trail is the **Pennine Way**, with its southern end at Edale and its northern end over 250 miles away in Scotland. If you don't have a spare three weeks, from Edale you can follow the trail north across wild hills and moors for just a day or two, or even less. An excellent three-day option is to Hebden Bridge, a delightful little town in Yorkshire.

The 46-mile **Limestone Way** winds through the Derbyshire countryside from Castleton to Rocester in Staffordshire on a mix of footpaths, tracks and quiet lanes. The northern section of this route, through the White Peak between Castleton and Matlock, is 26 miles, and hardy folk can do it over a long summer day, but two days is better. The route goes via Miller's Dale, Monyash, Youlgreave and Bonsall, with YHA hostels and B&Bs along the way, and ample pubs and cafés. Tourist offices have a detailed leaflet.

Various shorter walks are described throughout this section. All the villages make good bases for exploring the surrounding area, and Fairholmes at the Derwent Reservoirs is great for getting deep into the hills. The High Peak and Tissington Trails described in the previous Cycling section are equally popular with walkers.

Sleeping

Tourist offices have lists of accommodation for every budget. Perhaps the best budget options are the various camping barns (beds per person from £5) dotted around the Peak. Usually owned by farmers, they can be booked centrally through the **YHA** (☎ 0870 870 8808).

Getting There & Around

The Peak District authorities are trying hard to wean visitors off their cars, and tourist offices stock the excellent *Derbyshire Bus Timetable* (80p) covering local buses and trains. For more details, see (p495).

BUXTON

☎ 01298 / pop 24,112

With its grand Georgian architecture, central crescent, leafy parks, tourists and thermal waters, Buxton invites comparisons to Bath. It's smaller in scale, however, and lodged a little less far up its own backside. While the Romans discovered the natural warm-water springs, the town's heyday was not until the 18th century when 'taking the waters' was highly fashionable. After years of relative obscurity, ambitious restoration projects have put the sparkle back into the town, especially the resurrection of the Opera House, which had fallen into disuse in the 1970s.

Every Tuesday and Saturday, colourful stalls light up Market Pl. The town itself is made for hours of browsing idly and café-crawling.

Situated just outside the border of the Peak District National Park, Buxton is an excellent, picturesque base to get to the northern and western areas.

Orientation & Information

Buxton effectively has two centres: the historical area, with the Crescent, Opera House and Pavilion; and Market Pl, surrounded by pubs and restaurants. There are several banks with ATMs on the Quadrant.

Cyber@Emporium (☎ 214455; 28 High St; 🕑 noon-9pm Mon-Fri, 11am-9pm Sat, 11am-7pm Sun; per hr £3) Internet access.

Post office (Spring Gardens; 🕑 8.30am-6pm Mon-Fri, to 3pm Sat)

Tourist office (☎ 25106; www.peakdistrict-tourism .gov.uk; the Crescent; 🕑 10am-12.30pm & 1.30-4pm Mon-Fri Oct-Mar, 9.30am-5pm Mon-Fri, 10am-4pm Sat & Sun Apr-Sep) Has useful leaflets on walks in the area.

Sights & Activities

Buxton's gorgeously restored **Opera House** (☎ 0845-127 2190; www.buxton-opera.co.uk; Water St) enjoys a full programme of drama, dance, concerts and comedy as well as staging some renowned festivals and events (see p505). Tours (£2) of the auditorium and backstage areas are available at 11am most Saturday mornings.

Next to the Opera House is the **Pavilion**, an impressive palace of glass and cast iron built in 1871, which overlooks the impeccably manicured **Pavilion Gardens**. Skirting the gardens, the grand, pedestrian **Broad Walk** promenade is the perfect place for a gentle evening stroll.

Another impressive Buxton construction, the graceful curved terrace of the **Crescent** – reminiscent of the Royal Crescent in Bath – is waiting its turn for regeneration. A luxury hotel complex is imminent. Just east of here is **Cavendish Arcade**, formerly a thermal bathhouse (you can still see the chair used for lowering

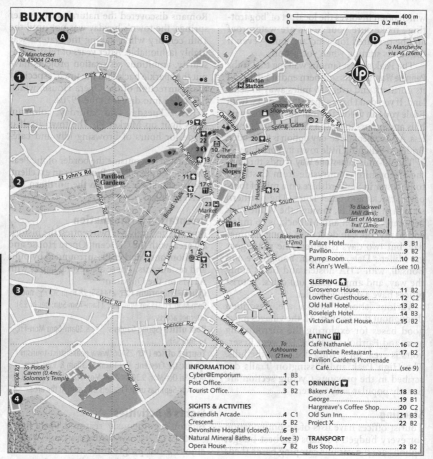

BUXTON

0 _____ 400 m
0 _____ 0.2 miles

Palace Hotel.............................**8**	B1
Pavilion...................................**9**	B2
Pump Room.........................**10**	B2
St Ann's Well......................(see 10)	

SLEEPING 🏠
Grosvenor House.................**11**	B2
Lowther Guesthouse..............**12**	C2
Old Hall Hotel....................**13**	B2
Roseleigh Hotel..................**14**	B3
Victorian Guest House........**15**	B2

EATING 🍴
Café Nathaniel....................**16**	C2
Columbine Restaurant.........**17**	B2
Pavilion Gardens Promenade	
Café...............................(see 9)	

DRINKING 🍷
Bakers Arms........................**18**	B2
George..................................**19**	B1
Hargreave's Coffee Shop......**20**	C2
Old Sun Inn.........................**21**	B3
Project X.............................**22**	B2

TRANSPORT
Bus Stop..............................**23**	B2

INFORMATION
Cyber@Emporium.......................**1**	B3
Post Office..................................**2**	C1
Tourist Office..............................**3**	B2

SIGHTS & ACTIVITIES
Cavendish Arcade........................**4**	C1
Crescent....................................**5**	B2
Devonshire Hospital (closed).......**6**	B1
Natural Mineral Baths.............(see 3)	
Opera House...............................**7**	B2

the infirm into the restorative waters) with several craft and book shops, and a striking coloured-glass ceiling.

On the other side of the Crescent, the tourist office is in the old **Natural Mineral Baths**, where you can still see the source of the mineral water, now Buxton's most famous export. A small display tells the full story.

Across from the tourist office, the **Pump Room**, which dispensed Buxton's spring water for nearly a century, now hosts temporary art exhibitions. Just outside is **St Ann's Well**, a fountain from which Buxton's famous thermal waters still flow – and where a regular procession of tourists queue to fill plastic bottles and slake their thirst with the liquid's 'curative' power.

Opposite the Crescent, a small park called the **Slopes** rises steeply in a series of grassy terraces. From the top there are views over the centre and across to the grand old **Palace Hotel** and the former **Devonshire Hospital**, with its magnificent dome. It is now part of the University of Derby.

Poole's Cavern (☎ 26978; www.poolescavern.co.uk; adult/child £6.20/3.50; ⏰ 10am-5pm Mar-Oct) is a magnificent natural limestone cavern, about a mile from central Buxton. Guides take you deep underground to see an impressive formation of stalactites (the ones that hang down) – including one of England's longest – and distinctive 'poached egg' formation stalagmites.

From the cave car park, a 20-minute walk leads up through Grin Low Wood to **Solomon's**

Temple, a small tower with fine views over the town and surrounding Peak District.

A longer walk is the **Monsal Trail**, beginning 3 miles east of the town, which leads all the way to Bakewell; see p511 for details. **Parsley Cycle Hire** (☎ 84493), at the junction of the High Peak and Tissington Trails, is the nearest place to rent bicycles.

Festivals & Events

All the big events in Buxton revolve around its beautifully restored Opera House.

Four Four Time An annual live-music festival staged in February each year, including a medley of jazz, blues, folk and world music acts.

Buxton Festival (www.buxtonfestival.co.uk) This renowned festival takes place in July and is one of the largest of its kind in the country. As well as opera, literary notables such as Louis de Bernières hold sway.

Buxton Fringe (www.buxtonfringe.com) In the same month, the more contemporary Buxton Fringe is gathering popularity.

International Gilbert & Sullivan Festival (www .gs-festival.co.uk) This very popular festival is held at the end of July/beginning of August.

Sleeping

Buxton is awash with good-value, elegant guesthouses – many dating from Victorian times – that are steeped in atmosphere. You'll find the pick of the bunch located on Broad Walk.

Roseleigh Hotel (☎ 24904; www.roseleighhotel.co.uk; 19 Broad Walk; s/d incl breakfast from £30/64; P X □) This tasteful family-run B&B in a spacious old terraced house gives a delightful panorama from the breakfast room onto the ducks paddling in the picturesque Pavilion Gardens lake. The owners are a welcoming couple, both seasoned travellers, who have given each room a warm, Victorian style.

Victorian Guest House (☎ 78759; www.buxtonvicto rian.co.uk; 3A Broad Walk; r incl breakfast from £40; P) Put on your best airs and graces for this elegant house, which has been lovingly decorated in a well-heeled Victorian style. The home-cooked breakfasts are renowned. Book ahead – its charms are no secret.

Grosvenor House (☎ 72439; grosvenor.buxton@ btopenworld.com; 1 Broad Walk; s/d incl breakfast from £40/60; P □) Affable owners run this tranquil, period-decorated hotel with fine views from the front bedrooms. It's well situated on the corner of Pavilion Gardens.

Lowther Guesthouse (☎ 71479; www.lowtherguest house.co.uk; 7 Hardwick Sq West; d from £54) This typi-cal Derbyshire gritstone house is located on a quiet street just a few moments' walk from Market Place. It is fussily decorated – perfect for frill seekers.

Old Hall Hotel (☎ 22841; www.oldhallhotelbuxton.co .uk; the Square; s/d incl breakfast £65/110) There is a tale to go with every creak of the floorboards at this genial, history-soaked establishment, supposedly the oldest hotel in England. Mary, Queen of Scots, was held here from 1576 to 1578, and the wood-panelled corridors and rooms are as well appointed and elegant as they must have been in her day.

Eating & Drinking

The Market Sq/High St strip spills over with lairy, alco-fuelled revellers on weekend evenings, but there are a few great pubs all the same. Head down to the area around the Opera House for a more laid-back evening. Spring Gardens, an otherwise uninspiring pedestrianised shopping street, has several cheap cafés.

Café Nathaniel (☎ 23969; Market St; mains £7.50-10; 🕙 10am-10pm Mon-Sat, to 3pm Sun) It's worth pitching up early to snare a seat at this relaxed but small café with scrubbed wooden tables and fresh seafood. It has an adjoining linen, lace and antique shop next door.

Columbine Restaurant (☎ 78752; Hall Bank; mains £10-12.50; 🕙 lunch Thu-Sat, dinner 7-11pm Mon & Wed-Sat) Perched on the slope leading down to the Crescent, this excellent understated restaurant is top choice among Buxtonites in the know. Choose from local produce (Derbyshire lamb £12.50) and an extensive vegetarian menu.

Pavilion Gardens Promenade Café (☎ 23114; mains £7-8.50; 🕙 10am-5pm Apr-Sep, to 3pm Oct-Mar) This bustling, touristy and spacious café has full-length leaded windows that offer fine views over the Buxton park.

Old Sun Inn (☎ 23452; 33 High St) The pick of the town's watering holes, and it retains an Edwardian-era ambience. Low ceilings, antique light fittings, flagstone floors and a different crowd in every cranny of this warrenlike alehouse make it *the* place to head for a pint – not to mention the surprisingly sophisticated pub grub.

Bakers Arms (☎ 24404; 26 West Road) Attracts connoisseurs with a fine nose for locally brewed ale; this venerable old gentleman of a pub is regularly in the *Good Beer Guide*.

Project X (☎ 77079; The Old Court House, George St; 🕙 8am-6pm Mon & Tue, to 11pm Wed-Sat, to 10.30pm

Sun) Buxton hipsters head here, where lavender walls and stainless-steel tables mark this wine/cocktail bar of choice.

George (☎ 24711; The Square) Just across the way, a convivial, bohemian crowd at the George sit on a hotchpotch of chairs and lean across big wooden tables to put the world to rights.

Hargreaves Coffee Shop (☎ 26640; Market Pl; ☼ 9am-4.30pm Mon-Sat) Easily the pick of the bunch of the Spring Gardens cafés, on the 1st floor of a renovated Edwardian showroom. It has good cakes served in a room lined with historic china and porcelain.

Getting There & Away

Buxton is well served by public transport. The best place to get the bus is Market Sq, where services go to Derby (twice hourly, 1½ hours), Chesterfield (several daily, 1¼ hours) and Sheffield (65 minutes, every 30 minutes). Trains run hourly to and from Manchester (50 minutes).

AROUND BUXTON
Tideswell

About 8 miles east of Buxton, deep in lovely White Peak countryside, the village of Tideswell makes a good base for walking.

Tideswell's centrepiece is the massive parish church – known as the **Cathedral of the Peak** – which has stood here virtually unchanged for 600 years. Look out for the old box pews, shiplike oak ceiling and huge panels inscribed with the Ten Commandments. For accommodation, **Poppies** (☎ 01298-871083; www.poppiesbandb .co.uk; poptidza@dialstart.net; Bank Sq; s/d from £20.50/41) is frequently recommended by walkers, and with its hearty excellent evening meals, no wonder.

Bus 65 runs about six times per day between Buxton and Calver, via Tideswell, and with connections to Sheffield and Chesterfield.

EDALE
☎ 01433

Time seems to have stood still at this enchanting picture-postcard village. Surrounded by sweeping Peak District countryside at its most majestic, the tiny cluster of imposing stone houses and the parish church are eye-catching in their own right. Ramblers and mountain bikers love it here: Edale lies between the White and Dark Peak areas, and is the southern terminus of the Pennine Way. Its train station makes this seemingly remote enclave very accessible – and highly popular.

Information

All the leaflets, maps and guides you'll need can be found at the recently revamped **tourist office** (☎ 670207; www.edale-valley.co.uk; Grindsbrook; ☼ 10am-5pm), which also includes some updated displays telling the story of the landscape.

Activities

Heading south, a great walk from Edale takes you up to **Hollins Cross**, a point on the ridge that runs south of the valley. From here, you can aim west to the top of spectacular **Mam Tor** and watch the hang-gliders swoop around above. Or go east along the ridge, with great views on both sides, past the cliffs of **Back Tor** to reach Lose Hill (which, naturally, faces Win Hill). Or you can continue south, down to the village of Castleton (p508).

From Edale you can also walk north onto the **Kinder Plateau**, dark and brooding in the mist, gloriously high and open when the sun's out. Weather permitting, a fine circular walk starts by following the Pennine Way through fields to **Upper Booth**, then up a path called Jacobs Ladder and along the southern edge of Kinder, before dropping down to Edale via the steep rocky valley of Grindsbrook Clough, or the ridge of Ringing Roger.

Sleeping

Edale YHA Hostel (☎ 0870 770 5808; edale@yha.org.uk; dm members/nonmembers incl breakfast £16.45/19.45; P ▣) This Spartan hostel is in a large old country house 1.5 miles east of the village centre, with spectacular views across to Back Tor. It's also an activity centre and very popular with youth groups.

Mam Tor House (☎ 670253; www.mamtorhouse.co.uk; Grindsbrook; B&B per person around £22.50; P) Lovely stained-glass windows distinguish this characterful lodging in an Edwardian house right next to the church.

Stonecroft (☎ 670262; www.stonecroftguesthouse .co.uk; Grindsbrook; B&B per person from £32; P) A charming family runs this handsomely fitted-out home, built at the turn of the 1900s in the large stone typical of the area. Vegetarians are well catered for – the organic breakfast is excellent.

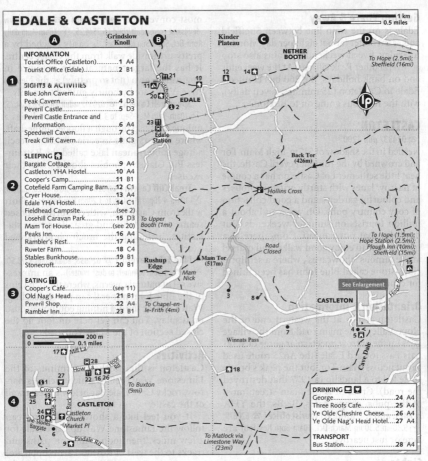

EDALE & CASTLETON

INFORMATION
Tourist Office (Castleton)............1 A4
Tourist Office (Edale)..................2 B1

SIGHTS & ACTIVITIES
Blue John Cavern.......................3 C3
Peak Cavern............................4 D3
Peveril Castle..........................5 D3
Peveril Castle Entrance and
Information...........................6 A4
Speedwell Cavern.......................7 C3
Treak Cliff Cavern......................8 C3

SLEEPING
Bargate Cottage.........................9 A4
Castleton YHA Hostel.................10 A4
Cooper's Camp.........................11 B1
Cotefield Farm Camping Barn....12 C1
Cryer House............................13 A4
Edale YHA Hostel......................14 C1
Fieldhead Campsite...................(see 2)
Losehill Caravan Park.................15 D3
Mam Tor House.......................(see 20)
Peaks Inn...............................16 A4
Rambler's Rest........................17 A4
Ruwter Farm...........................18 C4
Stables Bunkhouse....................19 B1
Stonecroft..............................20 B1

EATING
Cooper's Café.........................(see 11)
Old Nag's Head........................21 B1
Peveril Shop............................22 A4
Rambler Inn............................23 B1

DRINKING
George..................................24 A4
Three Roofs Cafe......................25 A4
Ye Olde Cheshire Cheese......26 A4
Ye Olde Nag's Head Hotel....27 A4

TRANSPORT
Bus Station............................28 A4

THE MIDLANDS

Options abound for campers:

Cooper's Camp (☎ 670372; sites per person £3.50, per car £1.50; **P**) At the far end of the village on a farm. With great views of the surrounding hills, it is a little more rustic, but hot showers run year-round. Caravans are also welcome and there is a shop and post office just by the entrance.

Fieldhead Campsite (☎ 670386; www.fieldhead -campsite.co.uk; sites per person £4.50; **P**) This National Park Authority–owned place, by the tourist office (visitor centre), is the most convenient option. With good facilities, it is also popular with youth groups.

Cotefield Farm Camping Barn (☎ 0870 870 8808; per person £5; **P**) is bookable through the YHA, while **Stables Bunkhouse** (☎ 670235; Ollerbrook Farm; per person £8; **P**), with four beds in each of its four basic rooms, is cheap and welcoming.

Both places are less than a mile east of the village centre.

Eating

Cooper's Café (☎ 670401; Cooper's Camp; ⏰ 8.30am-5pm, closed Tue) To stock up on cholesterol energy for hiking, head to this greasy spoon.

Otherwise, Edale has two walker-friendly pubs, the refurbished **Old Nag's Head** (☎ 670291; Grindsbrook) and the **Rambler Inn** (☎ 670268; Grindsbrook), which also does B&B. Both serve OK pub grub (£5 to £7). The best food is served beneath the beamed ceilings of the **Cheshire Cheese** (☎ 620381; Edale Road; mains £7-10). Around 4 miles from Edale near the neighbouring village of Hope, it has a mud-scraper on hand for dirty boots and is perfect for a posthike pint.

Getting There & Away

Edale is on the train line between Sheffield and Manchester (about eight per day Monday to Friday, five at weekends). Trains also stop at several other Peak villages. At the weekends and on bank holidays, the 260 bus connects Edale to Castleton (25 minutes, seven daily), with the final bus going on to Buxton.

CASTLETON

☎ 01433/ pop 1200

Nestled in the shadow of 517m-high Mam Tor and crowned by the ruins of Peveril Castle, the neat little settlement of Castleton has a couple of narrow lanes with sturdy gritstone houses and colourful gardens, and a good collection of cosy country pubs. Oh yes – and about a million tourists on summer weekends. But don't let that put you off. Come here at a quieter time to enjoy good walks, and marvel at the famous 'showcaves', where a semiprecious stone called Blue John has been mined for centuries.

Orientation & Information

Castleton stands at the western end of the Hope Valley. The main road from the village goes up the narrow, spectacular gorge of Winnats Pass toward Edale (the A625 route used to cut across Mam Tor, but the peak's brittle shale led to a landslip in 1977 that destroyed the road). Cross St is the main street; most of the pubs, shops, cafés, B&Bs, the YHA hostel, and the modern **tourist office** (☎ 620679; ☯ 9.30am-5.30pm March-Oct, 10am-5pm Nov-Feb) are here or just nearby.

Sights

Crowning the hill to the south of Castleton is ruined **Peveril Castle** (EH; ☎ 620613; adult/child £3/1.50; ☯ 10am-6pm daily May-Jul, 10am-7pm Aug, 10am-5pm Sep-Oct, 10am-4pm Thu-Mon Nov-Mar, 10am-5pm daily Apr), well worth the steep walk up from the village. William Peveril, son of William the Conqueror, built it originally, and Henry II added the central keep in 1176. The ruins are wickedly atmospheric, and the setting isn't bad either, with a stunning view over the Hope Valley, straight down to Castleton's medieval street grid and north to Mam Tor and beyond.

The area around Castleton is riddled with underground limestone caves, and four are open to the public. Although mostly natural, they have expanded from extensive lead, silver and Blue John mining over the centuries. The

most convenient, **Peak Cavern** (☎ 620285; www .devilsarse.com; adult/child £6.25/4.25; ☯ 10am-4pm daily April-Oct, Sat & Sun Nov-Mar), is easily reached by a pretty streamside walk from the village centre. It has the largest natural cave entrance in England, known (not so prettily) as the Devil's Arse. Visits are by hourly guided tour only.

Speedwell Cavern (☎ 620512; adult/child £6.75/4.75; ☯ 10am-5pm May-Sep, to 3.30pm Oct-Apr) includes a unique boat trip through a flooded mineshaft, where visitors glide in eerie silence to reach a huge subterranean lake called the Bottomless Pit. Claustrophobics should make their excuses.

Treak Cliff Cavern (☎ 620571; adult/child £6.50/3.50; ☯ 10am-4.20pm Mar-Oct, to 3.20pm Nov-Feb) is a short walk from Castleton, with colourful exposed seams of Blue John and great limestone stalactites, including the much-photographed 'stork'.

Blue John Cavern (☎ 620638; adult/child £7/3.50; ☯ 9.30am-5pm summer; to dusk winter) is an impressive set of natural caverns, where the rich veins of the Blue John mineral can prove dazzling. Watch out for the old mining equipment, also on display. You can get here on foot up the closed section of the Mam Tor road.

Activities

Castleton is the northern terminus of the Limestone Way (p503), which includes narrow, rocky Cave Dale, far below the east wall of the castle.

If you feel like a shorter walk, you can follow the Limestone Way up Cave Dale for a few miles, then loop round on paths and tracks to the west of Rowter Farm (opposite) to meet the Buxton Rd. Go straight (north) on a path crossing fields and another road to eventually reach Mam Nick, where the road to Edale passes through a gap in the ridge. Go up steps here to reach the summit of Mam Tor, for spectacular views along the Hope Valley. (You can also see the fractured remains of the old main road.) The path then aims northwest along the ridge to another gap called Hollins Cross, from where paths and tracks lead back down to Castleton. This 6-mile circuit takes three to four hours.

A shorter option from Castleton is to take the path direct to Hollins Cross, then go to Mam Tor, and return by the same route (about 4 miles, two to three hours). From Hollins Cross, you can extend any walk by dropping down to Edale, or you can walk direct from Castleton to Edale via Hollins Cross. Maps are available at the tourist office, and its *Walks around Castleton* leaflet (30p) has plenty of alternative routes.

Sleeping

Prices listed are peak weekend rates, but almost all Castleton options have good weekday deals.

Castleton YHA Hostel (☎ 0870 770 5758; castle ton@yha.org.uk; Castle St; dm members/nonmembers £13.95/16.95; P ⬚) Rambling, old building with an abundance of rooms, this hostel is a great pit stop with knowledgeable staff who also conduct guided walks. There's a licensed bar too.

Rambler's Rest (☎ 620125; www.ramblersrest-castle ton.co.uk; Mill Bridge; s/d from £25/40; P) Rooms are well appointed and comfortable in this attractively restored 17th-century stone cottage. It has a large en suite room with three or four beds (£22 per person), ideal for small groups or people with kids. Some rooms have shared bathrooms.

Cryer House (☎ 620244; Castle St; s/d £25/50; P ⬚) Affable hosts make this a long-standing favourite. It is blessed with a sweet front garden, distinguished by the climbers trailing up the grey stone exterior, and inviting rooms within.

Bargate Cottage (☎ 620201; www.bargatecottage .co.uk; Market Pl; d £55) The floors within this ancient character soaked gritstone building are gnarled with age, but the quaint bedrooms are bright and welcoming, as are the owners.

Peaks Inn (☎ 620247; www.peaks-inn.co.uk; How Lane; d £80) Wooden floors that positively gleam with varnish are just part of a pleasing fresh look in these high-class rooms. What's more, you don't even have to leave the building to get to the pub, which is just below.

For campers, the nearest place is well-organised **Losehill Caravan Park** (☎ 620636; Hope Rd; per site £6, plus per adult £5.30). **Rowter Farm** (☎ 620271; sites per person £4, ☽ Easter-Sept) is a simple campsite about 1 mile west of Castleton in a stunning location up on the hills. Drivers should approach via Winnats Pass; if you're on foot you can follow paths from Castleton village centre as described in the Activities section earlier.

Eating & Drinking

Ye Olde Nag's Head Hotel (☎ 620248; Cross St; bar meals £7-10) This cosy, traditional local is a 17th-century coaching house, where the conversation gets livelier as the night goes on. The all-you-can-eat carvery lures hungry diners from miles around. Comfy B&B rooms (per person £36), including one with Jacuzzi, are upstairs; get the ones on the top floor with a view and away from the noise.

George (☎ 620238; Castle St; mains around £7) Flagstone floors, and the tankards dangling from the ceiling, give this ageing local a measure of 'olde worlde' charm. But it's very much on the beaten tourist track – and don't expect any earth-shattering cuisine.

Ye Olde Cheshire Cheese (☎ 620330; How Lane; mains £7-9) One-armed bandits are most definitely off limits at this well-known alehouse, where tradition is everything. The home cooking needs a little attention but go for the peaceful, snug atmosphere.

Peveril Shop (☎ 620928; How Lane; ☽ 6.30am-5pm Mon-Sun) Near the bus stop, this place sells food and groceries, and does sandwiches to take away, ideal for a day on the hills or a long bus ride.

For hot drinks, snacks and lunches, teashops abound in Castleton. Most convenient is the **Three Roofs Café** (☎ 620533; The Island; ☽ 10am-5pm Mon-Fri, to 5.30pm Sat-Sun), where muddy boots are welcome. At busy times, this can be packed, so just meander the streets in search of a cream-tea joint with chairs – it's all part of the fun in Castleton.

Getting There & Away

You can get to Castleton from Bakewell on bus 173 (45 minutes, five per day Monday to Friday, three per day at weekends) via Hope and Tideswell. The 68 goes to Buxton at 9am from Monday to Saturday, while the 174 gets all the way to Matlock on Sundays and bank holidays (4.35pm start).

The nearest train station is Hope, about 1 mile east of Hope village (a total of 3 miles east of Castleton) on the line between Sheffield and Manchester. At summer weekends a bus runs between Hope station and Castleton tying in with the trains, although it's not a bad walk in good weather.

DERWENT RESERVOIRS

Toward the north of the Peak District, three huge artificial lakes – Ladybower, Upper Derwent and Howden, known as the Derwent Reservoirs – collect water for nearby cities. Once used as a flying practice area for the famous WWII 'dam busters', this is now prime walking and mountain-biking territory.

The place to head is **Fairholmes**, a national park centre near the Derwent Dam, which has a **tourist office** (☎ 01433-650953), a car park, a snack bar and cycle hire. Numerous walks start here, from gentle strolls along the lakeside to more serious outings on the moors above the valley. For cycling, a lane leads up the west side of Derwent and Howden reservoirs (it's closed to car traffic at weekends), and a dirt track comes down the east side, making a good 12-mile circuit. Challenging off-road routes lead deeper into the hills. The tourist office stocks a very good range of maps and guidebooks.

Fairholmes is 2 miles north of the A57, the main road between Sheffield and Manchester. Stagecoach bus 274 runs to Fairholmes from Sheffield Interchange at 9.15am from Monday to Saturday, and there are three buses on Sundays and bank holidays.

EYAM

☎ 01433 / pop 900

The former lead-mining village of Eyam (ee-em) is a quaint little spot with a morbidly touching history. In 1665 a consignment of cloth from London delivered to a local tailor carried the dreaded Black Death plague. What could have been a widespread disaster remained a localized tragedy thanks to the bravery of the village inhabitants: as the plague spread, the rector, William Mompesson, and his predecessor Thomas Stanley, convinced villagers to quarantine themselves rather than transmit the disease further. Selflessly, they did so; by the time the plague ended in late 1666, it had wiped out whole families, killing around 250 of the village's 800 inhabitants. People in surrounding villages remained relatively unscathed. Even independently of this poignant story, Eyam is well worth a visit; its sloping streets of old cottages backed by rolling green hills form a classic postcard view of the Peak District.

Sights

The **Church of St Lawrence** (☎ 630930; ☯ 9am-6pm Apr-Sep, to 4pm Oct-Mar) dates from Saxon times and carries a moving display on the plague and its devastating effect on the village. Look out for the plague register, recording those who died, name by name, day by day. Perhaps most likely to bring a lump to your throat (although there are several contenders) is the extract from a letter the rector wrote to his children about his wife, Catherine Mompesson, who succumbed to the disease. Her

headstone lies in the churchyard. In the same grounds is an 8th-century **Celtic cross**, one of the finest in England. Before leaving, you could also check your watch against the **sundial** on the church wall.

Around the village, many buildings have information plaques attached; these include the **plague cottages**, where the tailor lived, next to the church.

Eyam Hall (☎ 631976; adult/child £6.25/4; ☯ 10.30am-5pm Wed, Thu & Sun Jun-Aug) is a fine old 17th-century manor house. The courtyard contains a tearoom and numerous craft workshops.

Eyam Museum (☎ 631371; www.eyam.org.uk; Hawkhill Rd; adult/child £1.75/1.25; ☯ 10am-4.30pm Tue-Sun Easter-Oct) has some vivid displays on Eyam's plague experience, as well as putting it into the wider context of the effect of the bubonic plague elsewhere. There are also neat exhibits on geology, Saxon history and the village's time as a lead-mining and silk-weaving centre.

Look out too for the **stocks** on the village green – somewhere handy to leave the kids, perhaps, while you look at the church.

Activities

Eyam makes a great base for **walking** and **cycling** in the surrounding White Peak area. A short walk for starters leads up Water Lane from the village square, then up through fields and a patch of woodland to meet another lane running between Eyam and Grindleford; turn right here and keep going uphill, past another junction to **Mompesson's Well**, where food and other supplies were left during the plague time for Eyam folk by friends from other villages. The Eyam people paid for the goods using coins sterilised in vinegar. You can retrace your steps back down the lane, then take a path which leads directly to the church. This 2-mile circuit takes about 1½ hours at a gentle pace.

Sleeping & Eating

Bretton YHA Hostel (☎ 0870 7705720; bretton@yha .org.uk; Bretton, Hope Valley; dm members/nonmembers £10.95/13.95) If the YHA's full, this basic place is only 1.5 miles away.

Eyam YHA Hostel (☎ 0870 770 5830; eyam@yha.org .uk; Hawkhill Rd; dm members/nonmembers £13.95/16.95) In a fine old Victorian house with a folly, perched up a hill overlooking the village.

Miner's Arms (☎ 630853; Water Lane; s/d £45/75) A grand old pub with beamed ceilings, affable staff, a cosy stone fireplace and reasonable nosh. Comfortable rooms with en-suite bathrooms are just a short climb upstairs for the weary-limbed or the bleary-eyed. Tea- and cake-lovers are well catered for too.

Crown Cottage (☎ 630050, www.crown-cottage .co.uk; Main Rd; d £50) is bright, walker- and cyclist-friendly – and full to the rafters most weekends. Book ahead to be sure of a spot.

Peak Pantry (☎ 631293; cakes & tea £4-5; ☽ 8.30am-5pm Mon-Sat, 10am-5pm Sun) This unpretentious place, on the village square, has a mouth-watering array of slices and coffee.

Eyam Tea Rooms (☎ 631274; fruit cake tea £4.95) Just up the road; is slightly frillier, but does a delicious fruit cake tea where fruit cake and grapes are served with Wensleydale cheese and a pot of coffee.

Getting There & Away

Eyam is 7 miles north of Bakewell and 12 miles east of Buxton. The 175 from Bakewell goes to Eyam (three daily Monday to Saturday, no Sunday service). From Buxton, buses 65 and 66 run about six times per day to and from Chesterfield, stopping at Eyam (40 minutes).

BAKEWELL

☎ 01629 / pop 3,979

After Buxton, this is the largest town in the Peak District (though it's hardly a metropolis). It's not as interesting or picturesque as its posh spa-town neighbour, but it's a useful base for cyclists and walkers. It has a famous pudding (the Bakewell Pudding – it's not a tart you know), a couple of fine country houses within ambling distance and a reputation for traffic trail-backs on summer weekends.

Orientation & Information

The centre of town is Rutland Sq, from where roads radiate to Matlock, Buxton and Sheffield. The helpful **tourist office** (☎ 813227; Bridge St; ☽ 10am-5pm), in the old Market Hall, has racks of leaflets and books about Bakewell and the national park.

Sights & Activities

Bakewell's weekly market is on Monday, when the square behind the tourist office is very lively. Up on the hill above Rutland Sq, **All Saints Church** has some ancient Norman features, and even older Saxon stonework remains, including a tall cross in the churchyard, which sadly has suffered at the hands of time.

Near the church, **Old House Museum** (☎ 813642, Cunningham Pl; adult/child £2.50/1.50; ☽ 11am-4pm Apr-Oct) displays a Tudor loo and, also on a scatological theme, shows how early Peakland houses used to be made with materials including cow dung.

A stroll from Rutland Sq down Bridge St brings you – not surprisingly – to the pretty **medieval bridge** over the River Wye, from where riverside walks lead in both directions. Go upstream through the water meadows, and then along Holme Lane to reach **Holme Bridge**, an ancient stone structure used by Peak District packhorses for centuries.

On the northern edge of Bakewell, a former railway line has been converted to a walking and cycling track called the **Monsal Trail**. From Bakewell you can cycle about 3 miles north and 1 mile south on the old railway itself, and there are numerous other tracks and country lanes nearby. The nearest bike hire is near Buxton (see p505). Walkers on the Monsal Trail follow alternate sections of the old railway and pretty footpaths through fields and beside rivers. From Bakewell, an excellent out-and-back walk (3 miles each way) goes to the dramatic viewpoint at Monsal Head, where a good pub, Stables Bar at the Monsal Head Hotel, provides welcome refreshment. Allow three hours for the round trip.

If you're out for the day, from Monsal Head you can keep following the Monsal Trail northwest towards Buxton. A good point to aim for is Miller's Dale, where viaducts give a spectacular vista across the steep-sided valley (and there's another good café), or you can go all the way to Blackwell Mill (3 miles east of Buxton) – a total distance of about 9 miles – and get a bus back. Alternatively, get a bus to Buxton, and walk back to Bakewell. The tourist offices at Bakewell and Buxton have a *Monsal Trail* leaflet with all the details.

Other walking routes go to the stately homes of Haddon Hall and Chatsworth House (p513). You could take a bus or taxi there and walk back, so you don't muddy the duke's carpet.

Sleeping

Bakewell YHA Hostel (☎ 0870 770 5682; bakwell@yha .org.uk; Fly Hill; dm members/nonmembers £11.95/14.95) This no-frills, modern hostel is just a short walk from the centre of town at the top of a very steep hill. It's set in a quiet residential area; the curfew is 11pm, and there are no

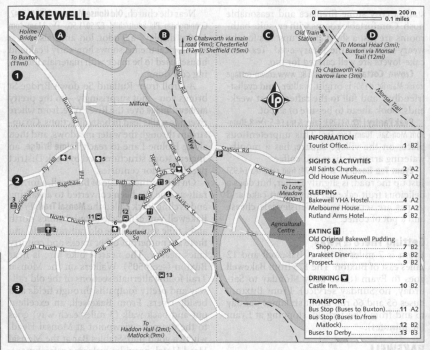

BAKEWELL

INFORMATION	
Tourist Office................................1	B2

SIGHTS & ACTIVITIES	
All Saints Church..........................2	A2
Old House Museum.......................3	A2

SLEEPING	
Bakewell YHA Hostel.....................4	A2
Melbourne House...........................5	A2
Rutland Arms Hotel.......................6	B2

EATING	
Old Original Bakewell Pudding	
Shop.......................................7	B2
Parakeet Diner..............................8	B2
Prospect.......................................9	B2

DRINKING	
Castle Inn...................................10	B2

TRANSPORT	
Bus Stop (Buses to Buxton)........11	A2
Bus Stop (Buses to/from	
Matlock)................................12	B2
Buses to Derby............................13	B3

laundry facilities or internet access. But it's a comfortable, friendly base for walking in the surrounding area. Note: this youth hostel has been earmarked to close down in autumn 2007.

Melbourne House (☎ 815357; Buxton Rd; s/d £35/50; P ☒) Located in a picturesque, listed building dating back more than three centuries, this is an inviting B&B in the very best Peak District tradition. It is situated on the main road leading to Buxton.

Rutland Arms Hotel (☎ 812812; www.rutland armsbakewell.com; The Square; s/d £65/120; P) Aristocratic but slightly careworn, this hotel is the most refined of the Bakewell accommodation options. Get a higher room if traffic noise keeps you up at night. Room 20 has a four-poster bed that costs the same as a normal double.

Eating & Drinking

Bakewell's streets are lined with cute teashops and bakeries, most with 'pudding' in the name, selling the town's eponymous cake. It would be bad manners not to try the local specialty when in town.

Old Original Bakewell Pudding Shop (☎ 812193; The Square) Probably has the best claim for having the original Bakewell Pudding recipe. They come in seriously jumbo sizes here, should you require.

Prospect (☎ 810077; Bath St; mains £13-15; ☺ noon-2pm & 7-8.30pm Tue-Sun) The flavour of the local restaurant scene. It's a smart bistro, with slick presentation, from the dark varnished bar to the serving of specials like belly pork with local black pudding mash (£14.50).

Parakeet Diner (☎ 812349; The Square; haddock & chips £4.70; ☺ 9am-5pm) Has not a frill to be seen, right down to the plastic-backed chairs, but service comes with a smile, it's easy on your wallet and its generous portions help fuel the day's activities.

Castle Inn (☎ 812103; Bridge St) The ivy-draped Castle Inn is one of the better pubs in Bakewell, with four centuries practice in warming the cockles of hamstrung hikers.

Getting There & Away

Buses serve Bakewell from Derby via Matlock (most 90 minutes but there are some faster buses, twice hourly) and Chesterfield (45 minutes, hourly). The TransPeak service goes on to Nottingham (one hour 50 minutes, hourly).

AROUND BAKEWELL
Haddon Hall

You won't be the first to fall under the spell of Haddon Hall (☎ 01629-812855; www.haddonhall.co.uk; adult/child £7.75/4; ☾ noon-4.30pm Sat-Mon Apr & Oct, daily May-Sep), one of the finest medieval houses you'll find anywhere. Film producers have long been aware of its charms. Most recently, the people behind *Pride and Prejudice*, starring Dame Judi Dench and Keira Knightley, chose the magnificent turreted house and its fragrant terraced gardens as their shooting location. The hall dates back to the 12th century, and what you see today dates mainly from the 14th to 16th centuries. Haddon Hall was abandoned in the 18th and 19th centuries, so it escaped the 'modernisation' experienced by many other country houses. Highlights include the Chapel; the Long Gallery, stunningly bathed by natural light; and the vast Banqueting Hall, virtually unchanged since the days of Henry VIII.

The house is 2 miles south of Bakewell on the A6. You can get there on any bus heading for Matlock (every 30 minutes) or walk along the footpath through the fields, mostly on the east side of the river.

Chatsworth

The great stately home, manicured gardens and perfectly landscaped park of Chatsworth together form a major highlight for many visitors to England. The main draw is sumptuous Chatsworth House (☎ 01246-582204; www .chatsworth.org; adult/child £9.75/3.50; ☾ 11am-5.30pm Mar-Dec). Known as the 'Palace of the Peak', this vast edifice has been occupied by the dukes of Devonshire for centuries. The original house

was started in 1551 by the inimitable Bess of Hardwick; a little later came Chatsworth's most famous guest, Mary, Queen of Scots. She was imprisoned here on and off between 1570 and 1581 at the behest of Elizabeth I, under the guard of Bess's fourth husband, the earl of Shrewsbury. The Scots bedrooms (adult/child incl admission to the house £12.40/4.95), nine Regency rooms named after the imprisoned queen, are sometimes open to the public.

The house was extensively altered between 1686 and 1707, and again enlarged and improved in the 1820s; much of what you see dates from these periods. Among the prime attractions are the painted and decorated ceilings, although the 30 or so rooms are all treasure-troves of splendid furniture and magnificent artworks.

The house is surrounded by 25 sq miles of gardens (adult/child £6/2.75), complete with a fountain so high it can be seen when you're miles away in the hills of the Dark Peak. For the kids an adventure playground (admission £4.50) provides hours of fun.

Beyond that is another 400 hectares of parkland, originally landscaped by Capability Brown, open to the public for walking and picnicking.

Chatsworth is 3 miles northeast of Bakewell. If you're driving, it's £1.50 to park. The only direct service from Bakewell runs on a Sunday (215, seven times daily). Virgin Trains runs a bus between Macclesfield, Buxton and Bakewell (two per day) that extends to Chatsworth June through September.

Another option is to walk or cycle from Bakewell. Start out on the quiet lane that leads uphill from the old train station; walkers can take footpaths through Chatsworth park via the mock-Venetian village of Edensor (ensor), and cyclists can pedal via Pilsley.

THE MIDLANDS

Eastern England

Flat in geography but not in atmosphere, the sprawling counties of Cambridgeshire, Suffolk, Norfolk and Lincolnshire unfurl gently eastwards to the sea, forming a barely wrinkled carpet of rich farmland, vast fens, sparkling rivers and lakes. Its fabric is flecked with stunning cathedral cities and medieval village gems, Edwardian seaside resorts and windmills, and of course, one rather famous university.

The region's very smoothness is at turns eerie, mind-expanding, monotonous, and at sunset, an uncluttered canvas for the sublime. So too, it highlights the soaring churches and cathedrals that whisper of the region's once-flourishing wool and weaving industry. What placid hills and valleys there are shelter pretty market towns, slow-flowing rivers and the same bucolic scenes that once inspired painters like Constable and Gainsborough.

Top of every visitor's list is Cambridge, the ancient seat of learning that awes not only for its academia but also for its architecture, atmosphere and all-round beauty. In the same county, Ely and Peterborough boast superb cathedrals, and the Imperial War Museum lets you follow the flight path of WWII bombers. To the east, largely rural Suffolk is littered with implausibly pretty medieval towns, half-timbered inns and a coastline of well-heeled resorts and nature reserves. Rolling north, sleepy Norfolk is riddled with waterways and the glistening Broads beckon boaters from around England. Its tranquil coastline is lined by crisp beaches and wildlife-rich marshes. And still further north, lovely laid-back Lincolnshire is home to a dramatic hilltop capital, softly undulating landscape and a medley of film-friendly towns and mansions.

HIGHLIGHTS

- Gliding a river punt past historic colleges in **Cambridge** (p524)

- Falling in love with the fairy-pink timber-framed houses of **Lavenham** (p543)

- Popping in to see the Queen at **Sandringham House** (p562)

- Climbing the picturesque cobbled streets of **Lincoln** (p563)

- Cruising through the tranquil waterways of the **Norfolk Broads** (p556)

- Picturing yourself in a period drama in historic **Stamford** (p569)

- POPULATION: 2.66 MILLION
- AREA: 19,000 SQ MILES

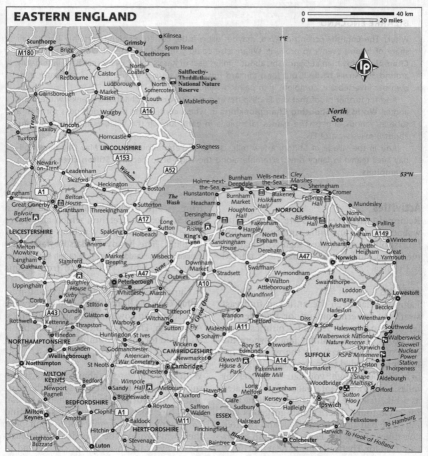

EASTERN ENGLAND

History

East Anglia was a major Saxon kingdom and the treasures unearthed in the Sutton Hoo burial ship (see p541) proved that they enjoyed something of the good life here.

The region's heyday, however, was in the Middle Ages, during the wool and weaving boom. Flemish weavers settled in the area, and the region's long drainage canals, windmills and architecture also illustrate the cultural crossover with the Continental lowlands. Not to mention the grand churches and world-famous university that the new wealth helped to fund.

By the 17th century the emergence of a work-happy urban bourgeoisie coupled with a strong sense of religious duty resulted in the parliamentarianism and Puritanism that would climax in the Civil War. Oliver Cromwell, the uncrowned king of the parliamentarians, was a small-time merchant residing in Ely when he answered God's call to take up arms against the fattened and corrupt monarchy of Charles I.

Eastern England's fortunes waned in the 18th century, however, when the real Industrial Revolution action was taking place up north. The cottage industries of East Anglia dwindled and today crops have replaced sheep as the rural mainstay.

Information

Regional tourist information can be had from the **East of England Tourist Board** (☎ 0870 225 4800; www.visiteastofengland.com).

BIZARRE ENGLAND

What? The English? Eccentric? Well, maybe just a little. Eastern England certainly has its fair share of bizarre events to prove it. Where else could you find the annual **World Snail Racing Championships** than at Congham, about 7 miles east of King's Lynn? Every year here in mid-July around 300 snails battle it out for a tankard full of juicy lettuce leaves. Visitors can enter their own pet invertebrate, complete with painted shell.

And for further proof that the English never quite grow out of childhood pranks, witness the annual **World Pea Shooting Championships** in which contestants blast dried peas through a tube at various targets. The games take place in early July on the Village Green, at Witcham, about 8 miles west of Ely.

And in the village of Stilton, a few miles south of Peterborough, every May Day bank holiday sees teams in fancy dress scramble along the High St to become **Stilton cheese rolling champions**.

Activities

Regional tourist websites are packed with walking, cycling and sailing information, and tourist offices are stacked high with leaflets, maps and guides covering activities offered in the area.

CYCLING

Famously flat, even the unfit can find vast swaths of Eastern England for a gentle potter on two wheels. All four counties boast networks of quiet country lanes, where the biggest natural hazard is the wind sweeping in unimpeded from the coast. When it's behind you though, you can freewheel for miles. Cambridge is internationally celebrated as a bike-friendly city and an excellent base for cycle tours. There's also gorgeous riding to be had along the Suffolk and Norfolk coastlines and in the Fens. Mountain bikers can head for Thetford Forest, near Thetford, while much of the popular on- and off-road Peddars Way (see below) walking route is also open to cyclists.

WALKING

Flat as an open palm, Eastern England is not everybody's idea of classic walking country. But itchy hiking feet can still be well satisfied with gentle rambles through farmland, beside rivers and lakes and along the wildlife-rich coastline.

The well-known **Peddars Way and Norfolk Coast Path** is a six-day, 88-mile national trail from Knettishall Heath near Thetford to Cromer on the coast. The first half trails along an ancient Roman road, then finishes by meandering along the beaches, sea walls, salt marshes and fishing villages of the coast. Day trippers and weekend walkers tend to dip into its coastal stretches, which also cover some of the best bird-watching country in England. The handy **Peddars Wayfarer** (www .nationaltrail.co.uk/peddarsway; ◯ twice daily Mar-Oct) bus service can whisk you to and from points en route.

Curving round further south, the 50-mile **Suffolk Coast and Heaths Path** wanders between Felixstowe and Lowestoft, via Snape Maltings, Aldeburgh, Dunwich and Southwold, but is also good for shorter rambles.

OTHER ACTIVITIES

With wind and water so abundant here, it's no surprise that **sailing** is all the rage on the coast and in the Norfolk Broads, where you can easily hire boats and arrange lessons. Mind you, many people simply opt to phut-phut their way around the Broads in **motorboats** these days. More watery fun can be had in Cambridge, where the daring can try their hand at a spot of **punting**. Alternatively, landlubbers can take advantage of the long, wide and frequently empty beaches of the Norfolk coast by **land-yachting**, a growing sport in the region.

Getting There & Around

Getting about the region on public transport, both rail and coach, is straightforward. **One Anglia** (☎ 0845 600 7245; www.onerailway.com; Anglia Plus Pass 1/3 days in 7 £11/22) offers some handy regional rail passes to explore Norfolk, Suffolk and parts of Cambridgeshire; the one-day pass can be used for unlimited regional travel after 9am, while the three-day pass covers any three separate days over a period of seven days. For train travel in Lincolnshire, **Central**

Trains (www.centraltrains.co.uk) has Day Ranger tickets (£16.50). For public transport information, consult **Traveline** (☎ 0870 608 2608; www .travelineeastanglia.org.uk).

CAMBRIDGESHIRE

It's easy to fall into the trap of thinking Cambridgeshire equals Cambridge, the breathtakingly beautiful city and world-renowned brains trust where a visit feels like plunging into the past and meeting the future rolled into one. And the university rightly tops any agenda to the region. But don't let Cambridge's dazzling attractions blind you to the county's other charms. Anywhere else, the extraordinary cathedrals at Peterborough and Ely would steal the limelight, and the riproaring Imperial War Museum would leave everyone from aeroplane-obsessed kids to their nostalgic grandparents wriggling with anticipation. Flat as an ironing board, the county also offers leisurely cycling through reclaimed fen, lush farmland and across myriad waterways. A nightmare for agoraphobics, the vast open landscapes nonetheless impress with epic sunsets and unsullied horizons.

Getting Around

The region's public transport radiates from Cambridge, which is a mere 55 minute train ride from London. This line continues north through Ely to King's Lynn in Norfolk. From Ely, branch lines run east through Norwich, southeast into Suffolk, and northwest to Peterborough and into Lincolnshire. The useful *Cambridgeshire and Peterborough Passenger Transport Map* is available at all tourist offices

or you can call **Traveline** (☎ 0870 608 2608; www .travelineeastanglia.org.uk).

CAMBRIDGE

☎ 01223 / pop 108,863

Few cities can take the breath away quite like Cambridge. It's not just its tightly packed core of exquisite architecture, or even the mind-boggling mass of brain power that has passed through its world-famous university, but also it's the sensation of drowning in history, tradition and quirky ritual that only seems to deepen the more you discover. But so too there is plentiful opportunity to come up for air, relaxing in the manicured college gardens, punting along the beautiful river 'backs' and roaming the lush water meadows that run out of the city.

And of course Cambridge is no mere repository of history and charm, it is very much a living city; its narrow streets are alive with the click and whirr of cyclists. The river is clogged with red-faced rowers, drifting punts and on occasion floundering freshmen. College porters still potter around in bowler hats, while gowned students wine and dine in cavernous medieval halls. Historic pubs echo with the same equal mix of intellectual banter and rowdy merrymaking that they have for centuries past. And a new generation of designer boutiques, coffee houses and slick nightlife venues is finding its niche in among the intriguing passageways and medieval doorways of the old town.

While you'll find all these qualities and more in 'the other place' (as rival Oxford is referred to here), Cambridge is the more concentrated of England's two great university cities and in our humble opinion, far the prettier.

SOMETHING FOR THE WEEKEND

Start your weekend in style by ensconcing yourself for a night of romance and fine dining at Cambridge's **Hotel Felix** (p533) or snag a river-view room at **Cambridge Garden House** (p533) and venture out for a nightcap at the celebrated pub the **Eagle** (p535). Next morning check out the university colleges, dip into the sublime **King's College Chapel** (p520) and then reward yourself with lunch at swanky **Midsummer House** (p534). In the afternoon, work off your excesses by **punting** (p524) along the backs before bidding farewell to the dreamy spires and breezing east to the **Stour Valley** (p542) and the time-transcending streets of gorgeous **Lavenham** (p543). Install yourself in the spectacular and none-too-frugal **Lavenham Priory** (p543), and explore the town's higgledy piggledy lanes to work up an appetite for steak-and-ale pies at the ancient inn, the **Angel** (p544). On Sunday morning roll west to check out the twin stately homes of **Long Melford** (p542) then east for the picture postcard hamlet of **Kersey** (p544), where you can toast the weekend with a pint and pub lunch at the medieval **Bell Inn** (p550).

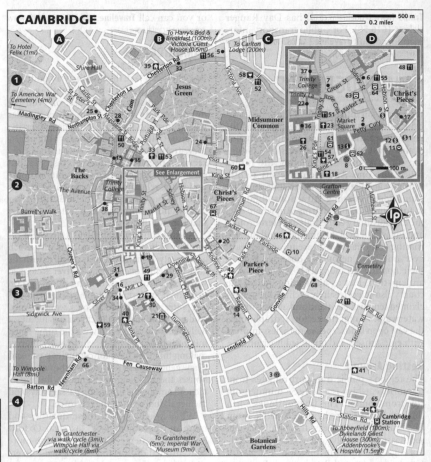

History

The University of Cambridge celebrates its 800th birthday in 2009, and its eventful eight centuries are inextricably linked to the history of England, and even thanks to some of the earth-shaking discoveries made here, also of worldwide import.

First a Roman fort and then a Saxon settlement, Cambridge was little more than a rural backwater until 1209, when the university town of Oxford exploded in a riot between townspeople ('town') and scholars ('gown'), forcing a group of students to quit while their heads were still intact and move to Cambridge to found a new university. The plan was for tutors and students to live together in a community, much as a monastery. This collegiate system, unique to Oxford and Cambridge, came into being gradually, and the first Cambridge college, Peterhouse, was founded in 1284.

More colleges followed from the 14th century, founded by all manner of great and good: royalty, nobility, church figures, statesmen, academics, trade guilds and anyone rich enough to court the prestige that their own institution offered. All the colleges were for men only, until 1869 and 1871, women were finally allowed to study here with the founding of women-only Girton and Newnham Colleges. However, the girls had to wait until 1948 to actually graduate.

The honour roll of famous graduates reads like an international who's who of high achiev-

INFORMATION		
Abbey National Bank	1	D2
Boots	2	D1
Budget Internet Café	3	C4
CB2	4	D2
Cleanomat Dry Cleaners & Laundrette	5	C1
Galloway & Porter	6	D1
Heffers	7	D1
International Telecom Centre	8	D2
Lloyds TSB (bank)	9	D1
Police Station	10	C3
Post Office	11	D2
Thomas Cook	12	D2
Tourist Office	13	D2
Victoria Café	14	C3

SIGHTS & ACTIVITIES		
Bridge of Sighs	15	B2
Cambridge Chauffer Punts	16	B3
Christ's College	17	D1
Church of St Bene't	18	D2
Corpus Christi College	19	B3
Emmanuel College	20	C3
Fitzwilliam Museum	21	B3
Folk Museum	(see 25)	
Gonville & Caius College	22	C1
Great St Mary's Church	23	D1
Jesus College	24	B2

Kettle's Yard	25	A1
King's College Chapel	26	C2
Little St Mary's	27	B3
Magdalene College	28	B1
Pembroke College	29	B3
Peterhouse College	30	B3
Queens' College	31	B3
Riverboat Georgina	32	B1
Round Church	33	B2
Scudamore's	34	B3
St John's College	35	B2
Senate House	36	C1
Trinity College	37	C1
Trinity Hall College	38	A2

SLEEPING		
Arundel House Hotel	39	B1
Cambridge Garden House	40	B3
Cambridge YHA Hostel	41	D4
De Vere University Arms Hotel	42	C3
Regent Hotel	43	C3
Sleeperz	44	D4
Tenison Towers Guest House	45	D4
Warkworth House	46	C2

EATING		
Al Casbah	47	D3
Clowns	48	D1

Fitzbillies	49	B3
Galleria	50	B2
Michaelhouse	51	D1
Midsummer House	52	C1
Pizza Express	53	B2
Rainbow Vegetarian Bistro	54	D2
Tatties	55	D1
Twenty-Two	56	B1

DRINKING		
Eagle	57	D2
Fort St George	58	C1
Granta (and Punt Hire)	59	A3
St Radegund	60	C2

ENTERTAINMENT		
ADC Theatre	(see 53)	
Arts Theatre	61	D2
Corn Exchange	62	D2
Fez	63	D1
Po Na Na Souk Bar	(see 53)	
Twentytwo	64	D1

TRANSPORT		
Cambridge Station Cycles	65	D4
City Cycle Hire	66	A4
Drummer St Bus Station	67	B2
Mike's Bikes	68	C3

ers, and a list of their accomplishments could fill several libraries. The discovery of DNA, theories of gravity and evolution: all by Cambridge students. Since 1904, the university has produced 81 Nobel Prize winners (more than any other institution in the world), 13 British prime ministers, nine archbishops of Canterbury, an immense number of scientists, and a healthy host of poets and other scribblers…and this is but a limited selection. Today the university remains at the top of the research league in British universities, and in the top three worldwide, and international academics have polled it as the top university in the world for science.

Orientation

The colleges and university buildings comprise the centre of the city. The central area, lying in a wide bend of the River Cam, is easy to get around on foot or by bike. The best-known section of the Cam is the Backs, which combines lush river scenery with superb views of six colleges, and King's College Chapel. The other 25 colleges are scattered throughout the city. The bus station is central on Drummer St, but the train station is a 20-minute walk to the south.

Information

BOOKSHOPS

Galloway & Porter (☎ 367876; 30 Sidney St) Remaindered and damaged stock.

Heffers (☎ 568568; 20 Trinity St) Vast temple of academic tomes and lighter reads.

EMERGENCY
Police station (☎ 358966; Parkside)

INTERNET ACCESS
The going rate for internet access is £1 per hour.
Budget Internet Café (☎ 464625; 30 Hills Rd; ☺ 9am-11pm)
CB2 (☎ 508503; 5-7 Norfolk St; ☺ noon-midnight)
International Telecom Centre (☎ 357358; 2 Wheeler St; ☺ 9am-10pm)
Victoria Café (☎ 307272; 86 Regent St; ☺ 8am-10pm)

LAUNDRY
Cleanomat Dry Cleaners & Laundrette
(☎ 464719; 10 Victoria Ave; per wash £2; ☺ 8.30am-9pm)

LEFT LUGGAGE
Cambridge Station Cycles (☎ 307125; Station Bldg, Station Rd; ☺ 7am-8pm Mon-Fri, 9am-5pm Sat, 10am-5pm Sun, 10am-4pm Oct-Mar) Stores left luggage for £3 per day.

MEDICAL SERVICES
Addenbrooke's Hospital (☎ 245151; Hills Rd)
Boots (☎ 350213; 28 Petty Cury)

MONEY
Helpful banks and bureaux de change:
Abbey National (☎ 350495; 60 St Andrew's St)
Lloyds TSB (☎ 0845 072 3333; 3 Sidney St)
Thomas Cook (☎ 543100; 8 St Andrew's St)

POST
Main post office (☎ 323325; 9-11 St Andrew's St)

TOURIST INFORMATION
Tourist office (☎ 0871 266 8006; www.visitcambridge
.org; Wheeler St; ☺ 10am-5.30pm Mon-Fri, 10am-5pm Sat,
11am-4pm Sun Apr-Sep, 10am-5.30pm Mon-Fri, 10am-5pm
Sat Oct-Mar) This large bustling office helps with
maps, accommodation, tours and tickets. A
£2.50 Visitor Card from here will get you
three weeks worth of discounts in restaurants,
attractions and on guided tours.

Sights

CAMBRIDGE UNIVERSITY
Five of the university colleges – King's,
Queen's, Clare, Trinity and St John's – charge
tourists admission. Some other colleges deem
visitors too disruptive and often deny them
entry. Most colleges close to visitors for the
Easter term and all are closed for exams from
mid-May to mid-June. Opening hours vary
year to year, so contact the colleges, the tourist office or the university's **central information
service** (☎ 337733) for updates.

King's College Chapel
In a city crammed with show-stopping architecture, this is *the* show-stealer. Chances are
you will already have seen it on a thousand
postcards, tea towels and choral CDs before
you catch your first glimpse of the grandiose
realty of **King's College Chapel** (☎ 331212; www
.kings.cam.ac.uk/chapel; King's Pde; adult/concession £4.50/3;
☺ during term 9.30am-3.30pm Mon-Sat, 1.15pm-2.30pm
Sun, outside academic terms 9.30am-4pm Mon-Sat, 10am-

5pm Sun), but still it awes. It's one of the most
extraordinary examples of Gothic architecture
in Britain, and was begun in 1446 as an act
of piety by Henry VI and finished by his son
Henry VIII around 1516.

While you can enjoy stunning front and
back views of the chapel from King's Pde and
the river, the real drama is within. Mouths
drop open upon first glimpse of the inspirational **fan-vaulted ceiling**, its intricate tracery
soaring upwards before exploding into a series
of stone fireworks. This vast 80m-long canopy
is the work of John Wastell and is the largest
expanse of fan vaulting in the world.

The chapel's length is also remarkably
light, its sides flanked by lofty **stained-glass
windows** that retain their original glass, rare
survivors of the excesses of the Civil War in
this region. It's said that these windows were
ordered to be spared by Cromwell himself,
who knew of their beauty from his own studies in Cambridge.

The antechapel and the choir are divided
by a superbly carved **wooden screen**, designed
and executed by Peter Stockton for Henry
VIII. The screen bears his master's initials
entwined with those of Anne Boleyn. Look
closely and you may find an angry human
face – possibly Stockton's – amid the elaborate
jungle of mythical beasts and symbolic flowers. Above is the magnificent bat-wing organ,
originally constructed in 1686 though much
altered since.

The thickly carved wooden stalls just beyond
the screen are a stage for the chapel's world-
famous **choir**, whose Festival of the Nine Lessons and Carols on Christmas Eve are beamed
all over the globe. And even the most pagan
heavy-metal fan will get shivers down the spine
during **Evensong** (admission free; ☺ 5.30pm Tue-Sat,
10.30am & 3.30pm Sun mid-Jan–mid-Mar, mid-Apr–mid-Jun,
mid-late Jul, Oct-early Dec, & Dec 24 & 25), in which the

CAMBRIDGE FOR CHILDREN

Consider taking your little bears to meet the original Winnie the Pooh in a manuscript by ex-
alumnus AA Milne at Trinity College's **Wren Library** (see opposite). Or take advantage of myriad
events laid on partly or wholly for kids, including the **Children's Festival** (mid-June), **Pop in the
Park** (mid-July), **Summer Sunday** (mid-July) and the **Children's Marquee** (early August); details
for all these events can be found at www.cambridge-summer.co.uk. Another possibility is to book
them in for a guided walk with **Cambridge Junior Explorers** (☎ 457574; admission £4).

Alternatively, if you're hoping a little of the university's vast reserves of knowledge will rub
off, there are a host of museums on **Downing St**, covering subjects such as geology, archaeology
and anthropology, zoology and the history of science.

sound waves almost seem to mirror and mingle with the extraordinary ceiling.

Beyond the dark-wood choir, light suffuses the **high altar**, which is framed by Rubens' masterpiece *Adoration of the Magi* (1634) and the magnificent east window. An eye-opening **Chapel Exhibition** is in the side chapels left of the altar, and charts the stages and methods of building set against its historical panorama.

Audio tours of the chapel are available for £2, and guided tours can be arranged at the tourist office.

Trinity College

As you walk through the impressive Tudor gateway to **Trinity College** (☎ 338400; www.trin .cam.ac.uk; Trinity St; adult/child £2.20/1.30), first created in 1546, have a look at the statue of the college's founder Henry VIII that adorns it. His left hand holds a golden orb, while his right grips not the original sceptre but a table leg, put there by student pranksters and never replaced. It's a wonderful introduction to one of Cambridge's most venerable colleges, and a reminder of who really rules the roost.

As you enter the **Great Court**, scholastic humour gives way to wonderment, for it is the largest of its kind in the world and drips with history. To the right of the entrance is a small tree, planted in the 1950s and reputed to be a descendant of the apple tree made famous by Trinity alumnus Sir Isaac Newton. Other alumni include Tennyson, Francis Bacon, Lord Byron and at least nine prime ministers, British and international, and a jaw-dropping 31 Nobel Prize winners.

The square is also the scene of the run made famous by the film *Chariots of Fire* – 350m in 43 seconds (the time it takes the clock to strike 12). Although many students attempt it, Harold Abrahams (the hero of the film) never actually did, and the run wasn't even filmed here. If you fancy your chances remember that you'll need Olympian speed to even come close.

The college's vast hall has a dramatic hammer-beam roof and lantern, and beyond this are the dignified cloisters of Nevile's Court and the renowned **Wren Library** (☎ 338400; noon-2pm Mon-Fri, plus during term 10.30am-12.30pm Sat). It contains 55,000 books dated before 1820 and more than 2500 manuscripts, including AA Milne's original *Winnie the Pooh*. Both he (Milne that is, not Winnie) and his son, Christopher Robin, were graduates.

Henry VIII would have been proud to note, too, that his college would eventually come to throw the best party in town, its lavish college May Ball in June.

Gonville & Caius

Known locally as Caius (pronounced 'keys'), this fascinating old **college** (☎ 332400; www.cai .cam.ac.uk; Trinity St) was founded twice, first by a priest called Gonville, in 1348, and then again in 1557 by Dr Caius, a brilliant physician who supposedly spoilt his legacy by insisting the college admit no 'deaf, dumb, deformed, lame, chronic invalids, or Welshmen'! Given his attitude to the disabled then, it's a darn good thing then he wasn't around to deny wheelchair-bound megastar of astrophysics, Stephen Hawking, who is a fellow here.

Of particular interest here are its three gates: Virtue, Humility and Honour. They symbolise the progress of the good student, since the third gate (the *Porta Honoris*, a fabulous domed and sundial-sided confection) leads to the Senate House and thus graduation.

Trinity Hall College

Henry James once wrote of this delightfully diminutive **college** (☎ 332500; www.trinhall.cam .ac.uk; Trinity Lane), 'If I were called upon to mention the prettiest corner of the world, I should draw a thoughtful sigh and point the way to the gardens of Trinity Hall'. Wedged cosily among the great and the famous, but unconnected to better-known Trinity, it was founded in 1350 as a refuge for lawyers and clerics escaping the ravages of the Black Death, thus earning it the nickname of the 'Lawyers' College'. It's home to an unusual 16th-century library, which has original Jacobean reading desks, and books chained to the shelves to prevent theft like 16th-century electronic bar codes. Writer JB Priestley and Hollywood honey Rachel Weisz are among Trinity Hall's graduates.

St John's College

After King's, **St John's** (☎ 338600; www.joh.cam .ac.uk; Trinity St; adult/child £2.50/1.50; 10am-5pm Mon-Fri, 9.30am-5pm Sat & Sun Mar-Oct, Sat & Sun only Nov-Feb) is one of the city's most photogenic colleges, and is also the second biggest after Trinity. Founded in 1511, it sprawls along both banks of the river, joined by the aptly named Bridge of Sighs, a masterpiece of stone tracery that for a moment makes you question whether you're in Cambridge or Venice. Over the bridge and out to the left there are stunning views of the Backs.

Christ's College

Grand old institution **Christ's** (☎ 334900; www .christs.cam.ac.uk; St Andrew's St; ☼ 9am–dusk) celebrated its 500th birthday in 2005 and is worth visiting if only for its gleaming Great Gate emblazoned with heraldic carving of spotty Beaufort yale (antelope-like creatures), Tudor roses and portcullis. Its founder Lady Margaret Beaufort hovers above like a guiding spirit. A stout oak door leads into First Court, which has an unusual circular lawn, magnolias and wisteria creepers. Pressing on through the Second Court there is a gate to the fellows' garden, which contains a mulberry tree under which 17th-century poet John Milton reputedly wrote *Lycidas*. Naturalist Charles Darwin also studied here.

Jesus College

A comical rebus or heraldic pun crowns the main gate of this late 15th-century **college** (☎ 339339; www.jesus.cam.ac.uk; Jesus Lane), which is accessed via a handsome bricked approach nicknamed the 'chimney'. Here you'll see a clutch of red-faced cockerels to represent the 'cock' and a globe to represent the 'all' in the college founder's name, Bishop Alcock. Inside, it's an unusually tranquil place, perhaps because it was once a nunnery before the bishop expelled the nuns for misbehaving. Be sure to visit the stunning chapel, which has a Norman arched gallery from the nunnery building, a 13th-century chancel and Art Nouveau features by Pugin, William Morris (ceilings), Burne-Jones (stained glass) and Madox Brown.

Magdalene College

Originally a Benedictine hostel, this appealing riverside **college** (☎ 332100; www.magd.cam .ac.uk; Magdalene St) was refounded in 1542 by Lord Audley. It has the dubious honour of being the last college to allow women students; when they were finally admitted in 1988, male students wore black armbands and flew the college flag at half-mast. Its greatest asset is the Pepys Library, housing the magnificent collection of books the famous mid-17th-century diarist bequeathed to his old college.

Corpus Christi College

Entry to this illustrious **college** (☎ 338000; www .corpus.cam.ac.uk; Trumpington St) is via the so-called New Court that dates back about 200 years. The door to the chapel here is flanked by two statues; on the right is Matthew Parker, who was college master in 1544 and Archbishop of Canterbury to Elizabeth I. A bright lad, Mr Parker was known for his curiosity; his endless questioning gave us the term 'nosy parker'. Meanwhile monastic atmosphere still oozes from the inner Old Court, which retains its medieval form. Playwright and Shakespeare's contemporary Christopher Marlowe (1564–93), author of *Dr Faustus* and *Tamburlaine*, was a Corpus man – as a plaque, next to a fascinating sundial, bears out. The college library has the finest collection of Anglo-Saxon manuscripts in the world.

Queens' College

This gorgeous **college** (☎ 335511; www.queens.cam .ac.uk; Silver St; adult £1.50) sits elegantly astride the river and takes its name from two queens who founded it in the 15th century. For visitors, the college's main entrance is off Queens' Lane and this is where its two most enchanting medieval courtyards are found: Old Court and especially Cloister Court, unmistakable for its intimate cloisters and matchbox lawn that irresistibly call to mind images of distracted academics in slippers and poets draped in the corners. Here too is the beautiful half-timbered President's Lodge and the tower in which famous Dutch scholar and reformer Erasmus lodged from 1510 to 1514. Old Ras wasn't particularly enamoured of Cambridge: he thought that the wine tasted like vinegar, that the beer was slop and that the place was too expensive, but he did note that the local women were good kissers.

Peterhouse College

The oldest and smallest college, **Peterhouse** (☎ 338200; www.pet.cam.ac.uk; Trumpington St) will leave you wanting to slip it in your handbag to take home. Founded in 1284 by Hugo de Balsham, later Bishop of Ely, it stands just south of **Little St Mary's Church**. The church's unwieldy original name was St Peter's-without-Trumpington-Gate, which gave the college its name. Inside is a memorial to student Godfrey Washington, great-uncle of George. His family coat of arms was the stars and stripes, the inspiration for the US flag. Henry Cavendish, the first person to measure the density of water also studied here. He also calculated the planet's weight: about six billion trillion metric tonnes if you must know.

Much of Peterhouse was rebuilt or added over the years, including the exceptional little chapel built in 1632, but the main hall is bona fide 13th century and beautifully restored.

Emmanuel College

Neither too big nor too small and surprisingly tranquil, this 16th-century **college** (☎ 334200; St Andrew's St) is particularly famous for two things. The first is facing you as you enter its Front Court: the 1677 Wren chapel, cloister and gallery is an architectural gem. And there's a plaque nearby commemorating its other oft-repeated claim to fame, which is that it educated one of America's most famous educators. John Harvard (BA 1632) was a scholar here before he settled in New England and left his money to found his namesake university in the Massachusetts town of Cambridge. His portrait also graces one of the chapel's stained-glass windows – but, as the artist had no likeness of Harvard from which to work, he used the face of Harvard's college contemporary John Milton!

THE BACKS

Ah, the Backs. The place to be on a sunny day, these idyllic parklands line the river behind some of the most famous colleges and eat up camera films with their picture-postcard views of the college walls, graceful bridges, weeping willows and neatly manicured lawns upon which students picnic. There are several interesting bridges, especially the fanciful **Bridge of Sighs** (built in 1831) and the oldest crossing at **Clare College**, built in 1639 and ornamented with decorative balls. Its architect was paid a grand total of 15p for his design and, feeling aggrieved at such a measly fee, it's said he cut a chunk out of one of the balls adorning the balustrade so the bridge would never be complete. Most curious of all is the flimsy looking wooden construction joining the two halves of Queen's College known as the **Mathematical Bridge**, first built in 1749. Don't fall prey to the punt-chauffeur's rose-tinted myths that it was the handiwork of Sir Isaac Newton or originally built without any nails though. Whether it would actually hold without the nuts and bolts we'll leave to the university mathematicians to resolve.

GREAT ST MARY'S CHURCH

Cambridge's staunch university **church** (☎ 741716; Senate House Hill; tower admission adult/child £2/1; ☽ 10am-4pm Mon-Sat, 12.30-4pm Sun, until 5pm Jun-Auq) was built between 1478 and 1519 in the late-Gothic perpendicular style. A quirky fact about the church is that it's home to England's oldest bell-ringing society. If you're fit and fond of a view, climb the 123 steps of the tower past the cacophonous bells for superb vistas of the dreamy spires, albeit marred by wire fencing.

The beautiful classical building directly across King's Pde is the **Senate House**, designed in 1730 by James Gibbs; graduations are held here in summer when gowned and mortar-boarded students parade the streets to pick up those all-important scraps of paper.

ROUND CHURCH

The pop-up-book pretty **Round Church** (☎ 311602; Bridge St; adult/child £1/free; ☽ 1-5pm Sun-Mon, 10am-5pm Tue-Sat) is another of Cambridge's most visited gems and one of only four such structures in England. It was built by the mysterious Knights Templar in 1130 and shelters an unusual circular nave ringed by chunky Norman pillars. It now houses an exhibition on, shows videos about and runs walking tours on Cambridge's Christian heritage.

CHURCH OF ST BENE'T

The oldest structure in the county, the **Saxon tower** of this Franciscan **church** (Bene't St) was built around 1025. The round holes above the belfry windows were designed to offer owls nesting privileges; they were valued as mouse killers. The church also has a Bible that belonged to Thomas Hobson, owner of a nearby livery stable, who told customers they could hire any horse they liked as long as it was the one nearest the door – hence the term 'Hobson's choice', meaning no choice at all.

FITZWILLIAM MUSEUM

Fondly dubbed 'the Fitz' by locals, this colossal neoclassical pile was one of the first public **art museums** (☎ 332900; www.fitzmuseum.cam.ac.uk; Trumpington St; admission free; ☽ 10am-5pm Tue-Sat, noon-5pm Sun) in Britain, built to house the fabulous treasures that the seventh Viscount Fitzwilliam had bequeathed to his old university. Particularly in the entrance hall, this unabashedly over-the-top building sets out to mirror its contents in an ostentatious jumble of styles

---

HOW TO PUNT

Punting looks pretty straightforward but, believe us, it's not. As soon as we dried off and hung our clothes on the line, we thought it was a good idea to offer a couple of tips on how to move the boat and stay dry.

1. Standing at the end of the punt, lift the pole out of the water at the side of the punt.

2. Let the pole slide through your hands to touch the bottom of the river.

3. Tilt the pole forward (that is, in the direction of travel of the punt) and push down to propel the punt forward.

4. Twist the pole to free the end from the mud at the bottom of the river, and let it float up and trail behind the punt. You can then use it as a rudder to steer with.

5. If you've not yet fallen in, raise the pole out of the water and into the vertical position to begin the cycle again.

---

that mixes mosaic with marble, Greek with Egyptian and more. It was begun by George Basevi in 1837, but he did not live to see its completion: while working on Ely Cathedral he stepped back to admire his handiwork, slipped and fell to his death.

The lower galleries are filled with priceless treasures from ancient Egyptian sarcophagi to Greek and Roman art, Chinese ceramics to English glass, and some dazzling illuminated manuscripts. The upper galleries shine with an incandescent collection of paintings by the likes of Leonardo da Vinci, Titian, Rubens, the Impressionists, Gainsborough and Constable, right through to Rembrandt and Picasso.

KETTLE'S YARD

Neither gallery nor museum, this **house** (☎ 352124; www.kettlesyard.co.uk; cnr Northampton & Castle Sts; admission free; ☼ house 2-4pm Tue-Sun, gallery 11.30am-5pm Tue-Sun) nonetheless oozes artistic excellence, with a collection of 20th-century art, furniture, ceramics and glass that would be the envy of many an institution but sit perfectly at ease in a domestic setting. It is the former home of HS 'Jim' Ede, a former assistant keeper at the Tate Gallery in London, who opened his home to young artists, resulting in a beautiful collection by the likes of Miro, Henry Moore, Henri Gaudier-Brzeska and others. There are also exhibits of contemporary art in the modern **gallery** next door.

While here, take a peek in the neighbouring **Folk Museum** (☎ 355159; www.folkmuseum.org.uk; 2/3 Castle St; adult/child £3/1; ☼ 10.30am-5pm Mon-Sat, 2-5pm Sun), a 300-year-old former inn now cluttered with the detritus of centuries of local domesticity.

Activities
PUNTING
Gliding a self-propelled punt along the Backs is a blissful experience once you've got the knack, though it can also be a wobbly-legged and manic challenge to begin. If you wimp out you can always opt for a relaxing chauffeured punt.

Cambridge Chauffer Punts (☎ 354164; www.punting-in-cambridge.co.uk; Silver St; per hr £14, chauffeured £50)

Granta (☎ 301845; Newnham Rd; per hr £10) A pub that hires punts on the side.

Scudamore's (☎ 359750; www.scudamores.com; Silver St; per hr £12, chauffeured £40)

WALKING & CYCLING
For an easy stroll into the countryside, you won't find a prettier route than the 3-mile walk to Grantchester (see p536) following the meandering River Cam and its punters southwest through flower-flecked meadows.

Scooting around town on a bike is easy thanks to the pancake-flat landscape, although the surrounding countryside can get a bit monotonous. The Cambridge tourist office stocks several useful guides including the free *Cambridge Cycle Route Map*.

Tours
City Sightseeing (☎ 0871 666 0000; www.city-sightseeing.com; adult/child £9/4.50; ☼ 10am-4pm) Hop-on hop-off tour buses that run every 20-30 minutes. You can get on or off at 16 points along the route, including the train station, Fitzwilliam Museum, the Round Church and the American Military Cemetery.

Riverboat Georgina (☎ 307694; www.georgina.co.uk; per person £12-23) Two-hour cruises from the river at Jesus Lock. Four-hour cruises may also be available. Prices vary depending on food and refreshments.

(Continued on page 533)

People

Dressing up, Royal Ascot (p174), Ascot racecourse, Berkshire

Cricket scoreboard attendant (p32), Yorkshire

Glastonbury Festival (p284), Glastonbury

Notting Hill Carnival (p133), London

Cities

MARK DAFFEY

Water fountain, Piccadilly Gardens, Manchester (p641)

Bullring shopping complex (p463), Birmingham

ADINA TOVY AMSEL

LAWRENCE WORCESTER

View of St Paul's Cathedral (p120), London

Shaftesbury Ave, London (p91)

Albert Dock (p667), Liverpool

Country

Pastures, the Cotswolds (p396)

Castlerigg Stone Circle (p708), Lake District

Valley of the Rocks (p291), Exmoor
National Park

Signpost, South Downs Way Trail (p180), Sussex

IAN CONNELLAN

DAVID TOMLINSON

River, Grasmere (p697), Lake
District National Park

Cycling (p77), New Forest, Hampshire

IAN CONNELLAN

Coast

Lighthouse, Dover (p198)

Puffins, Farne Islands (p753),
Northumberland

Fishing trawlers, Whitby (p634)

CHRISTOPHER GROENHOUT

Carousel, Brighton (p212)

CHRISTER FREDRIKSSON

Beach, Bournemouth (p294)

Walking path, Land's End (p362), Cornwall

GLENN BEANLAND

Activities

Walking, South West Coast Path (p325), Cornwall

ANDREW MARSHALL & LEANNE WALKER

Horse riding (p80), Hyde Park, London

DOUG MCKINLAY

Yachting (p81), Fowey, Cornwall

WAYNE WA

(Continued from page 524)

Tourist Tracks (☎ 305847; www.tourist-tracks.com)
For those that prefer to wander at their own pace, there are MP3 walking tours of the city. They can be downloaded for £5, mail ordered on CD for £7 or hired with an MP3 player at the tourist office for £6. The pack contains four separate 30-minute tours of the city centre.

Walking tours (☎ 457574; tours@cambridge.gov.uk; ⏱ 1.30pm daily, sometimes with extra tours at 10.30am, 11.30am and 2.30pm depending on season; tickets including entry to King's/St John's Colleges £9/7) The tourist office arranges these, as well as other less frequent tours such as colourful 'Ghost Tours' (adult/concession/child under 7yr £14/12/7) and 'Punt and Pint Tours' (adult/concession/child under 12yr £20/17.50/10). The tourist office has more details; book in advance.

Festivals & Events

Cambridge has a jam-packed schedule of almost continual events from beer festivals to hippie fairs, of which the tourist office has exhaustive listings. One of the biggies is late July's **Folk Festival** (☎ 457521; www.cambridgefolkfestival.co.uk), which has hosted the likes of Elvis Costello to Paul Simon. Two of the biggest events in the college year are the **May Balls** (June) when students glam up and get down after exams, and traditional rowing races, the **Bumps** (☎ 467304; www.cucbc.org), held in March and May, in which college boat clubs compete to collide with the crew in front and supporters line the river or charge along its bank on bikes.

There will also be events marking the university's **800th birthday** in late 2008 and 2009; check with the tourist office for details.

Sleeping
BUDGET

Cambridge YHA (☎ 0870 770 5742, 354601; www.yha.org.uk; 97 Tenison Rd; dm £16.95; ✗ 🖳) The cheapest digs in the city and a position just 600m from the train station make this L-shaped hostel the busiest in the region. Basically sound, the dorms are small, functional and well-worn. Lockers and laundry available. Breakfasts can be a harried affair, however, due to large groups.

Abbeyfield Guesthouse (☎ 246474; www.abbeyfield guesthouse.com; 2 Rustat Rd; s £18-25, d £25-55, tr £45-60, f £60-65; P ✗) Simply furnished soulless house with off-site owners, but close to station and Cambridge's cheapest off-season deal for a private room. Rates exclude breakfast but there's a fridge and eating area.

Carlton Lodge (☎ 367792; www.carltonlodge.co.uk; 245 Chesterton Rd; s/d/tr from £23/56/69; P 🖳 wi-fi only) Provided you don't come expecting luxury or modern furnishings, this homely guesthouse is still great value in an expensive city. Run by a friendly and widely travelled family, it has a mixed bag of comfortably ageing rooms, which come with freeview TV channels. It's a pleasant 10-minute walk to town or a quick bus ride from the hotel's doorstep.

Tenison Towers Guest House (☎ 363924; www.cambridgecitytenisontowers.com; 148 Tenison Rd; s/d £30/55) The aroma of freshly baked muffins greets you at this home-style B&B just 300m from the train station. As well as bubbly personal service, it has a cute little patio, comfortably furnished rooms with hand-sponged walls and yes, muffins on the menu for breakfast.

MIDRANGE

Victoria Guest House (☎ 350086; www.cambridge-accommodation.com; 55-57 Arbury Rd; s from £30, d £48-60, f £70; P ✗ 🖳 wi-fi only) Worth the walk, this delightfully homey semidetached 19th-century property has a yellow- and orange-brick façade and a crenulated front window. It is run by a young family, with beautifully kept contemporary rooms touched with peach and lemon palate, polished-wood floors and original mantelpieces. Children are welcome.

Sleeperz (☎ 304050; www.sleeperz.com; Station Rd; s/tw/d from £39/49/59; P ✗) Sitting amid a lawn of bicycles beside the train station is this converted warehouse with beamed ceiling and iron shutters, housing a one-night-wonder hotel that welcomes tired arrivals late into the night. Its pint-sized rooms squeeze in minuscule en suite, TV and functional futon or cabin-style bunk bed, all spotless but so snug that early-morning stretches may result in bruising. Doubles are larger.

Harry's Bed & Breakfast (☎ 503866; www.welcome toharrys.co.uk; 39 Milton Rd; s £45-56, d £65; P ✗ 🖳 wi-fi only) Originally an Edwardian nursing home, this lively four-room B&B is a gem. Its perennially cheerful host bends over backwards for guests, and the en suite rooms are tastefully decorated in warm colours and modern furnishings. One has a shared toilet, but shower and basin within. Rates include free wi-fi and, joy of joys, free local and national calls.

Warkworth House (☎ 363682; www.warkworthhouse.co.uk; Warkworth Tce; s/d/f from £45/65/85; ✗) Behind the blonde-brick façade and flower-flanked front steps of this Victorian terraced house, just off Parkside, is a long-established and much-loved guesthouse that retains period fireplaces, creaky wood floors, bay windows and a pleasant patio. The comfy rooms have modern pastel-coloured furnishings, and children are welcome.

Arundel House Hotel (☎ 367701; www.arundel househotels.co.uk; 53 Chesterton Rd; s/d/f from £75/95/120; P ⊠) Late 19th-century decorum meets bland 1990s-hotel style in this handsome Victorian terraced building overlooking the Cam, with 103 uniformly pink-Chintz rooms. Other than comfort, the biggest plus are pleasant views across the water and Jesus Green to central Cambridge – a short and extremely pleasant walk away.

Other recommendations:

Dykelands Guest House (☎ 244300; www.dykelands .com; 157 Mowbray Rd; s with bathroom £39, d £45-55, tr £68; P) Comfy modern choice, south of train station.

Regent Hotel (☎ 351470; www.regenthotel.co .uk; 41 Regent St; s/d/tr/f incl continental breakfast £92/99/130/140; ⊠ ▯) Gorgeous boutique hotel.

TOP END

Cambridge Garden House (Moat House; ☎ 259988; www .moathousehotels.com; Granta Pl, Mill Lane; s/d from £134/144; P ⊠ 🐾 ▯ 🐕 ♿) Bagging an enviable riverside spot in the city's heart, the interior of this resort-style hotel far surpasses expectations formed by its ugly modern shell. Design-mag perfect rooms are decorated with suede, leather, dark wood and boldly striped carpets, and even the bathrooms scream style. Best of all are the river-facing pool and the waterside gardens from which to watch punters glide past.

our pick Hotel Felix (☎ 277977; www.hotelfelix .co.uk; Whitehouse Lane, Huntingdon Rd; s/d incl breakfast from £136/168; P ⊠ ▯ ♿) Upper crust yet ultramodern, this luxurious boutique hotel occupies a lovely grey-brick Victorian villa in landscaped grounds a mile from the centre's hustle and bustle. Its 52 rooms embody designer-chic with liberal use of rich natural textures. Its award-winning Graffiti restaurant serves sublime Mediterranean cuisine with a modern twist (mains £13 to £24).

De Vere University Arms Hotel (☎ 351241; www .devere.co.uk; Regent St; d incl breakfast from £159; P ⊠ 🐾 ▯ ♿) Cambridge's most distinguished hotel, this huge early Victorian pile hunkers down beside bustling Parker's Piece as though fondly overseeing his great-great-grandchildren. Its public spaces ooze gentleman's-club atmosphere, its 120 rooms

comfort and elegance. Look out for the enormous, creaky cage-lift from 1927. Parking costs £10.

Eating
BUDGET

Fitzbillies (☎ 352500; www.fitzbillies.com; 52 Trumpington St; ☯ shop 9am-5.30pm, restaurant 9am-9.30pm) Cambridge's oldest bakery, beloved by generations of students for its ultra-sticky buns and quaint wood shopfront, also has a classy music-free restaurant dotted with fresh flowers, perfect for tranquil cream teas or meals.

Tatties (☎ 323399; 11 Sussex St; mains £2-6; ☯ 8.30am-7pm Mon-Sat, 10am-5pm Sun) Fast-in, fast-out fish-tank-style café and budget favourite that whips out baked and stuffed potatoes with innumerable fillings at lightening pace, as well as breakfasts, baguettes, salads and cakes. It gets very busy over lunch.

Clowns (☎ 355711; 54 King St; sandwiches from £2.75; ☯ 8am-midnight) Decorated with children's daubings of clowns, this is a thoroughly laid-back and charmingly personal spot for reading the newspaper, chatting over cappuccino, reasonably priced pasta or gelato, and relaxing on the roof terrace.

our pick Michaelhouse (☎ 309167; Trinity St; mains £3.50-6; ☯ 9.30am-5.30pm Mon-Fri) You can sup fair-trade coffee and nibble focaccia among soaring medieval arches or else take a pew within reach of the altar at this stylishly converted church, which still has a working chancel. The simple lunch menu is mostly vegetarian but also offers wine and beer for when God's back is turned.

MIDRANGE & TOP END

our pick Rainbow Vegetarian Bistro (☎ 321551; 9a King's Pde; mains £8-9; ☯ 10am-10pm Tue-Sat) First-rate vegetarian food and a pious glow emanate from this snug subterranean gem, accessed down a narrow passageway off King's Pde. It's decorated in funky colours and serves up organic dishes with a hint of the exotic, such as scrumptious Latvian potato bake and Indonesian gado gado.

Midsummer House (☎ 369299; www.midsummer house.co.uk; set lunch £20, 3-course dinner £55; ☯ lunch Tue-Sun, dinner Tue-Sat) Cambridge's gastronomic big-hitter, with two Michelin stars to its credit, this sophisticated restaurant is in lovely grey-brick Victorian villa backing onto the river from its namesake common. Its adventurous French Mediterranean menu sends serious foodies weak at the knees. Book well ahead.

Twenty-Two (☎ 351880; www.restaurant22.co.uk; 22 Chesterton Rd; set dinner £24.50; 7-9.45pm Tue-Sat) Discretely disguised amid a row of Victorian terraced housing is this outstanding restaurant, blessed by both its romantic candle-lit ambiance and its wonderful gourmet British and European menu with a commitment to local produce.

Galleria (☎ 362054; www.galleriacambridge.co.uk; 33 Bridge St; 2-course set lunch £6.50, mains £7-14; noon-10pm) This glass-fronted Continental-style brasserie is perfectly perched beside Magdalene Bridge, and has two balconies overlooking the exertions of punters below. It's decorated with metal tracery, plants and colourful prints, and serves good French-influenced food.

Pizza Express (☎ 324033; 7a Jesus Lane; mains £5-8; 11.30am-11.30pm) This Cambridge mainstay is recommended for its surprisingly classy setting, split between an airy marble hall with mirrored walls and a wood-panelled library room, that'll trick you into thinking you're shelling out twice the cash for its good but familiar Italian fare. Live jazz piano often tinkers in the background.

Al Casbah (☎ 579500; 62 Mill Rd; mains £6.50-9; lunch & dinner Mon-Sat, dinner only Sun) This fabric-draped Algerian restaurant has the feel of a nomadic tent and really tasty food is cooked on an indoor barbecue. The cous cous is simply wonderful.

Drinking

Punting and drinking are two of Cambridge students' favourite pastimes, and put the two together and you can really hit the relaxation jackpot or else end up quite literally drinking like a fish. The punting pubs, where rowers hang out and tourists can rent punts, are the best spots to join in on the fun.

Eagle (☎ 505020; Bene't St) Cambridge's most famous pub has loosened the tongues and pickled the grey cells of many an illustrious academic in its day; among them Nobel Prize-winning scientists Crick and Watson, who are thought to have discovered the form of DNA. It's a traditional 16th-century pub with five cluttered cosy rooms, the back one popular with WWII airmen, who left their signatures on the ceiling.

Fort St George (☎ 354327; Midsummer Common) The ideal English summertime pub sandwiched between the grassy expanse of Midsummer Common and the punt-littered River

Cam, and with lots of picnic tables to install yourself at. Dating from the 16th century the fort is said to be the oldest pub on the river, and has a snug crookedly beamed interior to decamp when the sun's gone in.

St Radegund (☎ 311794; 127 King St; 5-11pm Mon-Fri, noon-11pm Sat & Sun) A quirky little one-off pub – the smallest in town – run by an endearing eccentric and pulling a superb selection of unusual real ales St Radegund is hidden behind a bluff exterior and sackcloth curtains; the interior is hung with paraffin lamps and the ceiling burnt with graffiti.

Granta (☎ 505016; Newnham Rd) If the exterior of this picturesque waterside pub, overhanging a pretty mill pond, looks strangely familiar it could be because it's the darling of many a television director. Its terrace sits directly beside the water and when your Dutch courage has been sufficiently fuelled, there are punts for hire alongside.

Entertainment

Pick up a *What's On* events guide from the tourist office or log on to www.cam.ac.uk /whatson.

NIGHTCLUBS

Fez (☎ 519224; www.cambridgefez.com; 15 Market Passage; admission £5-7; 8pm-2am Mon-Sat) The city's top club, popular with town and gown ever since the stone age, Moroccan-themed Fez plays everything from hip hop to Latin funk and scores the cream of visiting DJs. Come early or expect queues.

Po Na Na Souk Bar (☎ 323880; www.ponana.co.uk; 7b Jesus Lane; 8pm-midnight) Sipping your cocktail in the intimate atmosphere of a Moroccan kasbah and nodding along to an eclectic mix of Latin, house and hip hop music, it's easy to understand why this late-night bar has remained a local favourite for a decade. Monday is hip-twisting salsa night.

Twentytwo (☎ 324600; www.twentytwo-cambridge .co.uk; Hobson's Passage, Sidney St; admission £5; 10pm-2am) Tucked down a tight passageway is this funky club kitted out in '70s décor with hallucinogenic carpets baby blue-pink backlights and playing mostly mainstream choons. On Tuesday night, it hosts the city's best-loved gay and lesbian night.

THEATRE

Corn Exchange (☎ 357851; www.cornex.co.uk; Wheeler St) This colossal ex-market building near the tourist office is the city's main centre for arts and entertainment, attracting the top names in pop and rock to ballet.

Arts Theatre (☎ 503333; www.cambridgeartsthea tre.com; 6 St Edward's Passage) Cambridge's biggest bona fide theatre puts on everything from pantomime to drama fresh from London's West End.

ADC (☎ 300085; www.adctheatre.com; Park St) Students' theatre and current home to the university's Foot-lights comedy troupe, which jump-started the careers of scores of England's comedy legends, including John Cleese and Peter Cook.

Getting There & Away
Cambridge is well served by trains, though not so well by bus. Trains run at least every 30 minutes from London's King's Cross and Liverpool St stations (£17.90, 45 minutes to 1¼ hours). There are also three trains per hour to Ely (15 minutes) and hourly connections to Bury St Edmunds (£7.50, 44 minutes) and King's Lynn (£9.30, 48 minutes).

From Drummer St bus station there are hourly buses to Stansted airport (£9.70, 55 minutes), Heathrow (£25, 2½ up to 3¼ hours) and Gatwick (£29, 3¾ hours) airports while a Luton (£12.20, 1½ hours) service runs every two hours.

Buses to Oxford (£6, 3¼ hours) are regular but take a very convoluted route.

Getting Around
BICYCLE
There are few more bike-friendly cities than Cambridge, and joining the ranks of students on their mad dashes to lectures or leisurely rides around town is an experience in itself. No mountain bikes necessary here; most places rent three-speeds.

Cambridge Station Cycles (☎ 307125; www .stationcycles.co.uk; Station Bldg, Station Rd; per half day/day/week £6/8/16) Handily positioned by the station; free map provided.

City Cycle Hire (☎ 365629; www.citycyclehire.com; 61 Newnham Rd; per hour/half-day/day/week from £3/5/8/15)

Mike's Bikes (☎ 312591; 28 Mill Rd; per week/month £12/35) Only long-term rentals.

BUS
A free gas-powered City Shuttle runs around the centre stopping at Emmanuel St every 15 minutes. Four bus lines run around town from Drummer St bus station, including bus 3

from the train station to the town centre. Dayrider passes (£2.70) offer unlimited travel on all buses within Cambridge for one day; Megarider passes (£9.50) are valid for one week. Buy them on board.

CAR
Cambridge's centre is largely pedestrianised. It's best to use the well-signposted Park & Ride car parks (£1.40 to £1.80) on the out-skirts of town. Shuttle buses run to the centre every 10 minutes between 7am and 7pm daily, then twice-hourly until 10pm.

TAXI
For a taxi, phone **A1 Cabco** (☎ 312444) or **Panther** (☎ 715715).

AROUND CAMBRIDGE
Grantchester
Punting, strolling or cycling along the river or through dreamy flower-speckled meadows to this too-cute-to-be-true riverside village of thatched cottages, cosy pubs and chocolate-box pretty gardens is a Cambridge tradition going back over a century.

And once here, it's an absolute joy to flop into a deckchair shaded by apple trees and wolf down cream teas and calorific cakes at the quintessentially English **Orchard tea garden** (☎ 01223-845788; www.orchard-granchester.com; Mill Way; ☺ approx 9.30am-5.30pm), favourite haunt of the Bloomsbury Group (see the boxed text The Bloomsbury Group, p211) and other cultural icons.

Or to indulge in a post-punt pint, the **Red Lion** is a lovely pub near the river, with plenty of nooks and crannies to squirrel yourself away in.

Grantchester is 3 miles southeast of Cam-bridge on the River Granta.

American War Cemetery
Glenn Miller, Joseph Kennedy and 3809 more American servicemen who lost their lives in battle while based in Britain are commemo-rated at this moving **cemetery** (☎ 01954-210350; www.abmc.gov/ca.htm; Madingley; ☺ 8am-5.30pm mid-Apr–Sep, 8am-5pm Oct–mid-Apr), 4 miles west of the city. You can visit the cemetery as part of a City Sightseeing tour (see p524).

Imperial War Museum
The romance of the winged war machine is alive and well at Europe's biggest **aviation**

museum (☎ 835000; www.iwm.org.uk; adult/child under 16yr £13/free; ☺ 10am-6pm mid-Mar–Sep, 10am-4pm Oct–mid-Mar) in Duxford, 9 miles south of Cambridge by the motorway. Almost 200 lovingly waxed aircraft from dive bombers to biplanes, Spitfire to Concorde are housed on this vast airfield, over which grown men scurry as though they just pulled their noses from boyhood *Biggles* books.

This airfield was no idle choice for the museum: it was a frontline fighter station in WWII, and played a crucial role in the pivotal Battle of Britain. It was the home of the famous Dambuster squadron of Lancasters, and today is home to the Royal Air Force's Red Arrows squadron, which performs all kinds of celestial trickery at air shows throughout the world.

Also included is the stunning **American Air Museum** hangar, designed by Norman Foster, which has the largest collection of American civil and military aircraft outside the USA. Look out for the flying fortress Memphis Belle, which flew from here. The museum's legendary **airshows** of modern and vintage planes are some of the best you'll ever see (see the website for dates) and battlefield scenes are displayed in the land-warfare hall, where you can check out WWII tanks and artillery. Kids will enjoy the adventure playground and the flight simulator. And a swanky new Air-Space hangar is also set to open in 2007.

Monday to Saturday, Stagecoach bus C7 runs to Duxford (45 minutes) from Cambridge Drummer St bus station, via the train station every 20 minutes until about 6pm: show your bus ticket and you'll get a reduced rate in the museum. On Sundays and bank holidays, Myalls run services every two hours from 11am to about 5.25pm.

Wimpole Hall

A masterful 18th-century mansion imperiously overseeing 140 hectares of gorgeous landscaped woodland and serpentine lakes, **Wimpole Hall** (NT; ☎ 206000; www.wimpole.org; adult/child £7.50/4, with Home Farm £11/6; ☺ farm 10.30am-5pm Sat-Wed mid-Mar–Oct, also Thu Jul & Aug,11am-4pm Sat & Sun Nov–mid-Mar; hall 1-5pm Sat-Wed mid-Mar–Oct, also Thu Jul & Aug) was the home of Rudyard Kipling's daughter until her death in 1976. The 18th-century model farm next to it preserves and shows rare livestock.

Wimpole Hall is 8 miles south of Cambridge on the A603.

ELY

☎ 01353 / pop 15,102

An easy and rewarding day trip from Cambridge, Ely (ee-lee) is a charming and historic city-town with a dazzling cathedral, scrupulously tidy Georgian and medieval centre and pretty riverside walks running out into the eerie fens around it. It's a thriving place, and while it used to be something of a joke that such a diminutive town could technically rank as a city, these days it's one of the fastest-growing cities in Europe. The odd name harks back to the days when Ely was an island marooned amid the undrained fens, which were inhabited by an abundance of eels that still make it into local cooking pots today.

Information

The **tourist office** (☎ 662062; tic@eastcambs.gov.uk; 29 St Mary's St; ☺ 10am-5.30pm Apr-Oct, 11am-4pm Mon-Fri, 10am-5pm Sat & Sun Nov-Mar) makes accommodation bookings and has maps, and dishes out leaflets on the town's 'Eel Trail' walking tour, studded by modern works of art. Ask here about guided walking tours, including ghostly night-time tours. Banks and ATMs can be found along High St.

Sights
ELY CATHEDRAL

Not only dominating the town but visible across the flat fenland for vast distances, the ghostly silhouette of **Ely Cathedral** (☎ 667735; www.cathedral.ely.anglican.org; adult/concession/child £5.20/4.50/free; ☺ 7am-7pm Easter-Aug, 7.30am-6pm Mon-Sat, 7.30am-5pm Sun Sep-Easter) is locally dubbed the 'Ship of the Fens'.

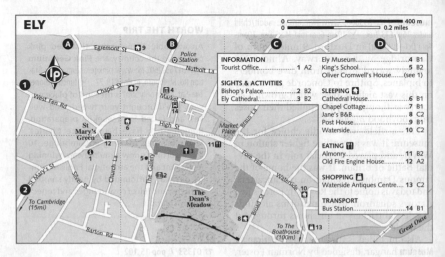

ELY

INFORMATION
Tourist Office.....................................1 A2

SIGHTS & ACTIVITIES
Bishop's Palace...............................2 B2
Ely Cathedral..................................3 B2

Ely Museum.......................................4 B1
King's School....................................5 B2
Oliver Cromwell's House........(see 1)

SLEEPING
Cathedral House...............................6 B1
Chapel Cottage................................7 B1
Jane's B&B..8 C2
Post House.......................................9 B1
Waterside.......................................10 C2

EATING
Almonry..11 B2
Old Fire Engine House.................12 A2

SHOPPING
Waterside Antiques Centre.....13 C2

TRANSPORT
Bus Station....................................14 B1

Walking into the early 12th-century Romanesque nave, you're immediately struck by its clean, uncluttered lines and lofty sense of space. The cathedral is renowned for its entrancing ceilings and the masterly 14th-century octagon and lantern tower, which soar upwards in shimmering colours that are well worthy of a crick in your neck for gazing at them.

The vast 14th-century Lady Chapel is the biggest in England; it's filled with eerily empty niches that once held statues of saints and martyrs. They were hacked out unceremoniously by iconoclasts during the English Civil War. However, the astonishingly delicate tracery and carving remain.

Ely cathedral was a centre of pilgrimage for many centuries thanks to the 7th-century queen of Northumbria, Etheldreda, who founded an abbey here in 673. A colourful character, Ethel shrugged off the fact that she had been twice married in her determination to become a nun. She was canonised shortly after her death.

There are free guided tours of the cathedral, and an octagon and roof tour (£8 including admission).

Near the entrance there's a small but gleaming **stained-glass museum** (☎ 665025; www.stainedglassmuseum.com; adult/child £3.50/2.50) that lets you get eye to eye with saints, misshapen monsters and all manner of domestic barbarity through vivid glasswork from the 14th century onwards.

To lap up a good singsong in splendid surroundings, Choral Sunday service is at 10.30am and Evensong is at 5.30pm Monday to Saturday, 3.45pm on Sunday.

OTHER SIGHTS & ACTIVITIES

Historic sites cluster about the cathedral's toes. Within spitting distance of the tower are both the former **Bishop's Palace**, now used as a nursing home, and **King's School**, which keeps the cathedral supplied with fresh-faced choristers.

A short hop across St Mary's Green is the attractive half-timbered **Oliver Cromwell's House** (☎ 662062; adult/child £3.95/2.70; ☼ 10am-5pm Apr-Oct, 11am-4pm Nov-Mar), where England's warty warmonger lived with his family from 1636 to 1646, when he was the tithe collector of Ely. The house now has Civil War exhibits, portraits, waxworks and echoes with canned commentaries of – among other things – the great man's grisly death, exhumation and posthumous decapitation.

More town history can be explored in **Ely Museum** (☎ 666655; www.elymuseum.org.uk; adult/child £3/free; ☼ 10.30am-5pm Mon-Sat, 1-5pm Sun May-Oct, 10.30am-4pm Wed-Mon Nov-Apr), which is housed in the Old Gaol House complete with prisoners' cells and their scrawled graffiti.

Ely is also a great place for rummaging through antiques, and signs lead down to the river and bargain-hunting heaven **Waterside Antiques Centre** (☎ 667066; The Wharf; ☼ 9.30am-5.30pm Mon-Sat, 11.30am-5pm Sun). From here, charming riverside ambles flank the **Great Ouse**, which brims with activity, from Olympic rowers and riverboats to swans and hungry ducks.

The towpath winds up- and downstream: for a quiet walk, turn left; turn right for the pub and tea garden. If you continue along this path you'll see the Fens stretching to the horizon.

Sleeping

Accommodation is mostly one- or two-room B&Bs so book ahead for your first choice.

our pick **Cathedral House** (☎ 662124; www.cathedralhouse.co.uk; 17 St Mary's St; s/d £45/75; P ⊠) Plenty of love has gone into the restoration of this gorgeous Georgian house, which is choc-a-bloc with fascinating antiques and curios. The individually decorated rooms are graced by original and period features, even in the bathrooms. Add to this a walled garden, converted stables and a central position and you're set.

Waterside (☎ 614329; www.29waterside.org.uk; 29 Waterside; d £60; ⊠) This pocket-sized B&B is in a wonderfully character-rich 18th-century oak-beamed and wooden-floored building near the waterfront. It's furnished with reclaimed pine and has a cute walled garden.

Other recommendations:

Jane's B&B (☎ 667609; 82 Broad St; s/d from £22/44; ⊠) Friendly spot near the station.

Chapel Cottage (☎ 668768; daffmort@talk21.com; 11 Chapel St; s/d £25/50; ⊠) Tiny cottage filled with homely clutter and a friendly dog.

Post House (☎ 667184; www.posthouse-ely.co.uk; 12a Egremont St; s/d from £25/50; P ⊠) Old-fashioned B&B plastered with photos of grandchildren.

Eating

Slippery eels are still a local delicacy dished up in several of the restaurants in Ely.

Almonry (☎ 666360; High St; snacks £1.50-4, lunch £7-9; ☒ 10am-5pm Mon-Sat, 11am-5pm Sun) Also vying for the best-setting award, this traditional teashop cosies up to the cathedral, spilling into attractive gardens, left of the Lady Chapel. Alternatively, you can shelter in its atmospheric 12th-century vaulted undercroft. Meals here are simple, but there's a also a wide range of caffeinated pick-me-ups.

Old Fire Engine House (☎ 662582; St Mary's St; mains about £15.50; ☒ 10.30am-5.30pm & 7.30pm-9pm Mon-Sat, 12.30-5.30pm Sun) Dining at this delightfully homespun restaurant and art gallery feels like eating at a friend's. Backed by beautiful gardens and housing various intimate nooks, it serves classic seasonal and local dishes (with refills on request) and its afternoon cream teas are excellent.

Boathouse (☎ 664388; 5 Annesdale; set lunch £5-10, dinner £25; ☒ lunch & dinner Wed-Sat, lunch Sun) This sleek riverside restaurant dishes up quality British food presented in chic but skimpy portions. It has wonderful patio dining overlooking the water ideal for summer evenings, while the interior is lined by oars and the chefs can be seen at work.

Getting There & Away

Ely is on the A10, 15 miles northeast of Cambridge. Following the Fen Rivers Way (map available from tourist offices), it's a lovely 17-mile towpath walk.

Bus 19 and X12 run every hour from Cambridge's Drummer St bus station (one hour), or in Ely from the bus stop on Market St. Trains are much quicker and more frequent (15 minutes, every 20 minutes). There are also twice hourly trains to Peterborough (£7.40, 35 minutes) and Norwich (£12.20, 55 minutes), and hourly services to King's Lynn (£5.60, 30 minutes).

PETERBOROUGH

☎ 01733 / pop 156,061

The sprawling shopping-mad city of Peterborough is home to a remarkable cathedral that alone justifies it as a day-trippers' destination from Cambridge or London. And while the city's high-gloss shopping malls are unlikely to quicken the pulse of visitors, they do inject a lively buzz into its streets. A scattering of other mildly interesting attractions beef up the town's credentials, but really, see the cathedral and you can leave happy.

Peterborough's bus and train stations are an easy walk west of the city centre. The **tourist office** (☎ 452336; www.visitpeterborough.com; 3-5 Minster Precincts; ☒ 9am-5pm Mon & Wed-Fri, 10am-5pm Tue, 10am-4pm Sat) is in front of the cathedral's west front, and has information on guided walking and ghost tours (adult/child £4/2). It also has information on other attractions in the vicinity, including a steam railway and reconstructed Bronze Age roundhouses at Flag Fen.

Peterborough Cathedral

England may be filled with fine cathedrals boasting ostentatious façades, but few can rival the instant 'wow' factor of Peterborough's unique early-13th-century western front, with its three deep yawning arches and arrow-sharp crests.

Visitors enter the **cathedral** (☎ 355300; www
.peterborough-cathedral.org.uk; requested donation £3;
⊙ 9am-5.15pm Mon-Sat, noon-5pm Sun), which was
founded in 1118, through an odd 14th-
century porch that peeks out between the
cavernous arches like a dog from its ken-
nel. Inside, you'll be immediately struck by
the height of the magnificent three-storeyed
Norman nave and by its lightness, created
by the mellow local stone and fine clerestory
windows. The nave is topped by a breathtaking early-13th-century painted-timber ceiling
that is one of the earliest and most important
of its kind in Europe, and still sports much of
its original diamond-patterned paintwork.

Press on below the Gothic tower, which was
painstakingly reconstructed in the 19th century, to the northern choir aisle and you'll find
the rather plain tombstone of Henry VIII's
first wife, the tragic Catherine of Aragon,
buried here in 1536. Her divorce, engineered
by the king because she could not produce a
male heir, led to the Reformation in England.
Her only child (a daughter) was not even allowed to attend her funeral. Every 29 January
there is a procession in the cathedral to commemorate her death.

Just beyond this is the cathedral's wonderful 15th-century eastern tip, which has superb
fan vaulting thought to be the work of master
mason John Wastell, who worked on King's
College Chapel in Cambridge.

Loop around into the southern aisle, and
you'll find gold lettering marking the spot
where the ill-fated Mary, Queen of Scots was
once buried. On the accession of her son,
James, to the throne, her body was moved to
Westminster Abbey.

Sleeping & Eating

Good central accommodation is thin on
the ground, but **Aaron Park Hotel** (☎ 564849;
aaronparkhotel@yahoo.co.uk; 109 Park Rd; s/d/f £44/59/70;
Ⓟ ☒) is a cosy family-run affair in a characterful Victorian building on a relatively quiet
tree-lined street. It has a variety of en suite
rooms of different sizes and styles.

Alternatively, the **Bull Hotel** (☎ 561364; www
.bull-hotel-peterborough.com; Westgate; s/d £100/112;
Ⓟ ☒ ☐) is a well-equipped and regally furnished inn built from chunky grey stone in
the heart of town and about 200m from the
train station.

Beckets Restaurant (☎ 342310; 2 Minster Precincts;
mains £2.50-8; ⊙ 9.30am-4pm) is a wholesome café

in a loftily restored 14th-century chapel just
within the cathedral grounds, and offers great
value daily specials, as well as snackish baguettes, toasties, soups and more.

Getting There & Away

There are regular trains to London (£22.30, 50
minutes to 1¼ hours), Cambridge (£11.90, 48
minutes) and Ely (£7.40, 35 minutes).

SUFFOLK

You have to pinch yourself to remember that
this charming rural backwater of England was
once an astonishingly rich place that amassed
great wool wealth and operated a string of
busy ports. However, its gentle hills and lush
valleys are filled with reminders of its golden
age, from the magnificent 'wool churches'
(as in paid for by, not made of) that dot the
landscape, to the lavish pargeting (decorative
stucco plasterwork) that adorns its buildings.
The Stour Valley particularly delights with villages that seem freeze-dried since the Middle
Ages, Bury St Edmunds impresses with both
its mighty past and lively present, while the
coast is strung with pretty and poignant seaside resorts increasingly nibbled by the sea.

Information

You can whet your appetite for the region
further through the websites www.visitsuf
folkattractions.co.uk and www.visit-suffolk
.org.uk.

Getting Around

Consult **Suffolk County Tourism** (www.suffolkonboard
.com) or **Traveline** (☎ 0870 608 2608; www.travelineeast
anglia.co.uk) for local transport information.

IPSWICH

☎ 01473 / pop 117,069

Suffolk's county capital was one of the very
first Saxon towns in England, a thriving medieval centre of commerce and a major point
of emigration to America. But while heavy
investment jazzes up its lively waterfront marinas, in its centre beautiful timber-framed
buildings moulder behind scruffy boards and
ugly modern chain stores nudge medieval
churches. The most beautifully preserved
buildings, of which there are several humdingers, are occupied by private enterprises.
That said the town has some beautiful park-

land, a burgeoning cultural scene and great transport connections.

Information & Orientation

The **tourist office** (☎ 258070; www.visit-ipswich .com; tours adult/child £2.50/2; ☒ 9am-5pm Mon-Sat) is in 15th-century St Stephen's Church, off St Stephen's Lane. It organises 90-minute guided tours from May to September at 2.15pm Tuesday and Thursday. In summer there are also walks on Saturday at 11am.

The train station is a 15-minute walk southwest of the tourist office along Princes St and across the roundabout.

Sights

A glorious wedding-cake façade of crisp sugary-white pargeting decorates the front of the 17th-century **Ancient House** (☎ 214144; 40 Buttermarket; ☒ 9am-5.30pm Mon-Sat), its four panels each representing the continents discovered at the time. It's one of the finest examples of the craft you'll see anywhere and crawls with mythological creatures and characters. The building now houses a kitchen outfitters, but you can take a peek at the hammer-beam roof inside. The house is about 50m north of the tourist office.

Set in a lovely rolling park 300m north of town, the multigabled 16th-century **Christchurch Mansion** (☎ 433554; Soane St; admission free; ☒ mansion & gallery 10am-5pm Tue-Sat, 2.30-4.30pm Sun, closes at dusk in winter) is filled with period furniture and works by the likes of Constable and Gainsborough. Outside, look for the statue of a delightfully cantankerous granny – immediately recognisable to Britons as being the creation of local comic strip artist Giles.

Less exciting are the dusty stuffed-and-mounted displays at **Ipswich Museum** (☎ 433551; High St; admission free; ☒ 10am-5pm Tue-Sat), with

---

A COTTAGE OF YOUR OWN

For self-catering country cottages in the area, have a browse through these sites:

Farm Stay Anglia (www.farmstayanglia.co.uk)
Holiday Cottages Cambridge (www .holidaycottagescambridge.co.uk)
Just Suffolk (www.justsuffolk.com)
Lincolnshire Cottages (www.lincolnshire cottages.com)
Suffolk Secrets (www.suffolk-secrets.co.uk)

---

exhibits from natural history to Anglo-Saxon Ipswich.

Ipswich doesn't especially deserve an overnight stay, but contact the tourist office if you need accommodation.

Getting There & Away

There are trains every 20 minutes to London's Liverpool St station (£26.80, 1¼ hours), twice hourly to Norwich (£10.90, 45 minutes) and Bury St Edmunds (£6, 30 to 40 minutes). There are bus services roughly every half-hour to Sudbury Monday to Saturday and less frequently on Sunday. **Ipswich Buses** (☎ 0800 919 390; www.ipswichbuses.co.uk) runs one-hour city sightseeing buses from April to August.

AROUND IPSWICH
Sutton Hoo

Soon after the world was consumed by Tutankhamen fever, England was to discover its own ancient treasure trove. It was right here on this rather lonely rural spot that in 1939 archaeologists uncovered the hull of an enormous Anglo-Saxon ship, in which a king-like individual was interred with a fabulous wealth of Saxon riches. It's thought that this may be the burial site of Raedwald, King of East Anglia.

His exquisitely crafted helmet is now the site's symbol, and you can see a fine replica in the **visitors centre** (NT; ☎ 01394-389714; www .suttonhoo.org; Woodbridge; adult/child £5.50/2.50, discounts for those arriving on foot or bicycle; ☒ 11am-5pm daily Jul-Sep, 11am-5pm Wed-Sun Easter–mid-April & Sep-Oct, Sat & Sun Nov-Easter) along with many of the original finds and a full-scale reconstruction of his ship and burial chamber. The finest treasures, including a warrior's helmet and shield, gold ornaments and Byzantine silver, are displayed in London's British Museum (p119).

There's little other than pimpled burial mounds to see at the site itself, although you may still get an attack of the heebee-geebies recalling that they were also used as a place of execution. For a better appreciation you can always join one of the enlightening one-hour tours (adult/child £2.50/1.50).

Sutton Hoo is 2 miles east of Woodbridge and 6 miles northeast of Ipswich. Bus 73, 71 and 171 together visit Sutton Hoo 10 times per day Monday to Saturday, passing through Woodbridge (10 minutes) en route to Ipswich (40 minutes).

Seckford Hall (☎ 01394-385678; www.seckford.co .uk; Woodbridge; s/d from £85/130; P ⬚ ⬚ ⬚) is one of the best places to stay in the area. It's a commanding 16th-century Elizabethan country mansion just outside Woodbridge with luxuriously appointed rooms, oodles of antiques, a terrific restaurant and an 18-hole golf course next door.

STOUR VALLEY

The River Stour trickles gently through a soft, pastoral landscape that has inspired some of Britain's best-loved painters from Constable to Gainsborough. It's impossibly pretty villages are filled with the timber-framed houses and elegant churches that recall the region's 15th-century weaving boom, when this unlikely valley produced more cloth than anywhere else in England. In the 16th century, however, production gradually shifted elsewhere and the valley reverted to a rural backwater, ignored by the Industrial Revolution and virtually everyone else – bad news for locals, but great for today's visitors as its medieval villages have survived miraculously intact.

Long Melford
☎ 01787 / pop 3675
For such a small and stringy village, self-important Long Melford has a lot to boast of. For starters there are its two fine stately homes and a 2-mile High St that claims to be the longest in England, not to mention the stunning timber-framed buildings and antique shops that line it. Here too is a magnificent church, which presides over a sprawling village green that's totally disproportionate to the village's size.

From outside, the romantic Elizabethan mansion of **Melford Hall** (NT; ☎ 376395; adult/child £5/2.50; ☽ 1.30-5pm Wed-Sun May-Sep, 1.30-5pm Sat & Sun Apr & Oct) seems little changed since it entertained the queen in 1578. Inside, you can imagine her being fussed over in the panelled banqueting hall. There's also much Regency and Victorian finery and a display on Beatrix Potter, who was related to Parker family who owned the house from 1786 to 1960.

There's a noticeably different atmosphere at Long Melford's other red-brick Elizabethan mansion, just up the road and down a tree-lined avenue. **Kentwell Hall** (☎ 310207; www.kentwell.co.uk; adult/child £7.50/4.75, admission varies on event days; ☽ noon-5pm Apr-Sep), is a private home with a wonderfully lived-in feel despite being as full of centuries-old

ghost stories and as much Tudor pomp as you could hope for. It's surrounded by a rectangular moat and there's a Tudor-rose maze and a rare-breeds farm that'll keep the kids happy. Kentwell bristles with bodices and hose from mid-June to mid-July, when several hundred Tudor enthusiasts don traditional attire and recreate a year in the Tudor calendar.

The magnificently pompous **Great Church of the Holy Trinity** (☎ 281836; ☽ 10am-5pm Apr-Sep, 10am-4pm Mar & Oct, 11am-3pm Nov-Feb) nearby is a very stately affair, well worth sticking a nose into if only for its stained-glass windows.

Long Melford is also famed for its **antique shops**, thanks in part to a hit TV series called *Lovejoy* that was shot here. Viewing appointments are required in some.

SLEEPING & EATING
Denmark House (☎ 378798; www.denmarkhousebb.co.uk; Hall St; s/d £33/55; ✗) Situated in the village's heart, this modest-fronted little townhouse B&B is a grade II listed building with a long history, and parts dating back to medieval times. It has cosy beamed rooms with décor your granny would just love.

Black Lion Hotel & Restaurant (☎ 312356; www .blacklionhotel.net; the Green; s/d from £88/120) A gorgeous little 10-room hotel on the village green, the 17th-century Black Lion has individually styled rooms, some with period style and romantic four-posters, and some altogether more quirky such as the zebra-striped family room. It also has a superb restaurant (set menu £28).

Scutcher's Bistro (☎ 310200; www.scutchers.com; Westgate St; mains £14-19; ☽ lunch & dinner Tue-Sat) Renowned throughout the Stour Valley for its exquisite menu of classic and more contemporary British dishes, Scutcher's nonetheless has a wonderfully unpretentious bistro feel, cheerfully painted and wood-beamed. It's just west of the Black Lion.

Several impressive black-and-white timber-framed buildings along the main road also offer eats and accommodation, including the photogenic 15th-century **Bull** (☎ 378494; Hall St; s/d £80/120; mains £8-12).

GETTING THERE & AWAY
Buses leave from the High St outside the post office. There are hourly services Monday to Saturday to Bury St Edmunds (52 minutes) calling at Sudbury (10 minutes). More services also shuttle back and forth to Sudbury (10 minutes) twice hourly during the week.

Sudbury

☎ 01787 / pop 11,933

Birthplace of celebrated portrait and landscape painter Thomas Gainsborough (1727–88) and the model for Charles Dickens fictional town Eatanswill in *The Pickwick Papers* (1836–37), Sudbury is a bustling market town that makes for a pleasant hour or two's wanderings. The town flourished in the Middle Ages on the back of the roaring wool trade, although these days Sudbury's sheep have given way to crops.

The **tourist office** (☎ 881320; sudburytic@babergh .gov.uk; Market Hill; ⏱ 9am-5pm Mon-Fri year-round, plus 10am-4.45pm Sat Apr-Sep, 10am-2.45pm Sat Oct-Mar) dispenses advice from alongside the town hall.

Most visitors come to drop into **Gainsborough's House** (☎ 372958; 46 Gainsborough St; www. gainsborough.org; adult/child £3.50/2.80; ⏱ 10am-5pm Mon-Sat), which houses the largest collection of his work in the world. The newly renovated house and gardens feature a Georgian façade built by Gainsborough's own father, and a mulberry tree that features in some of his son's paintings. Inside, look for his earliest known work, *A Boy and a Girl in a Landscape,* now oddly in two parts, and the exquisite *Lady Tracy* celebrated for its delicate portrayal of drapery. Meanwhile in the parlour is a statue of a horse, the artist's only known sculpture.

Originally home to a wealthy 16th-century merchant, the **Olde Bull Hotel** (☎ 374120; www .theoldebullhotel.co.uk; Church St; s/d from £45/55; P ✗) is a nicely characterful but down-to-earth family-run coaching inn with nine rooms, most of which are treated to wonderful oak-beamed ceilings. Rates exclude breakfast.

GETTING THERE & AWAY

Sudbury has a train station with an hourly service to London (£19.50, 1¼ hours). Bus travel can be trickier. Beestons runs about eight buses daily Monday to Saturday to Ipswich (one hour), but to go elsewhere often involves changing.

Lavenham

☎ 01787 / pop 1738

There's barely a straight line in the whole of topsy-turvy Lavenham, Eastern England's loveliest medieval wool town. Crammed into its centre are around 300 exquisitely preserved buildings that lean and lurch like old folks balancing their old wooden bones against each other. Lavenham reached its peak in the heady

15th-century wool wealth days, after which the town quietly fossilised. So modern day visitors are treated to a remarkably complete medieval town where pretty, pink thatched cottages rub shoulders with timber-framed and pargeted houses that now house curiosity shops, art galleries, quaint tearooms and ancient inns.

The **tourist office** (☎ 248207; lavenhamtic@babergh .gov.uk; Lady St; ⏱ 10am-4.45pm Apr-Oct, 11am-3pm Sat & Sun Mar & Nov) offers guided walks (£3.25) around the village departing at 2.30pm Saturday and 11am and 2.30pm Sunday.

SIGHTS

Many of Lavenham's most enchanting buildings cluster along the High St, Water St and around the Market Pl, which is dominated by the early 16th-century **guildhall** (NT; ☎ 247646; adult/child £3.50/1.50; ⏱ 11am-5pm Apr-Oct, 11am-4pm Sat & Sun Mar, 11am-4pm Thu-Sun Nov-Dec), a superb example of a close-studded, timber-framed building and now a local history museum, with displays on the wool trade and weaving demonstrations on Thursdays.

Also on the Market Pl, the atmospheric 14th-century **Little Hall** (☎ 247179; adult/child £2.50/ free; ⏱ 2-5.30pm Wed, Thu, Sat & Sun Easter-Oct) is another gem, with soft ochre plastering, timber frame and crown-post roof. Once home to a successful wool merchant, it's now a private residence open to the public.

At the village's high southern end rises the soaring steeple of the medieval **Church of St Peter & St Paul** (⏱ 8.30am-5.30pm Apr-Sep, 8.30am-3.30pm Oct-Mar) is a further testament to Lavenham's past prosperity. Built between 1485 and 1525, it is approached by avenues of box hedges.

SLEEPING & EATING

Brett Farm (☎ 248533; www.brettfarm.com; off Water St; s £35/60; P ✗) The budget-minded will do very well at this modern farmhouse bungalow, a very friendly unpretentious place with onsite stables, comfortable spotless rooms with wicker furniture and textured ceilings. It's a short, pleasant walk south of the village. Carriage and bike hire are available.

our pick **Lavenham Priory** (☎ 247404; www.laven hampriory.co.uk; Water St; s/d from £75/95; P ✗) A rare treat, this sumptuously restored 15th-century building was once home to Benedictine monks, then medieval cloth merchants and still perfectly captures its Elizabethan spirit with cavernous fireplaces, leaded windows and exquisite period rooms. Now an upmarket six-room B&B, it must be booked well in advance.

Swan Hotel (☎ 247477; www.theswanatlavenham .co.uk; High St; d £105-235; ⓟ ⊠) A warren of stunning timber-framed 15th-century buildings now shelters one of the region's best-known hotels. Rooms are suitably spectacular affairs, some with immense fireplaces, colossal beams and magnificent four posters. Elsewhere the hotel cultures a gentlefolk's country-club feel. The modern British restaurant in the lofty Great Hall has also won acclaim (set lunch/dinner £20/28.50).

Angel (☎ 247388; www.theangelhotel.com; Market Pl; s/d from £55/80; mains £9-13; ⓟ ⊠) Eating is a deceptively informal affair at this lovely 15th-century inn, which actually serves award-winning modern British cuisine, with lip-smacking steak-and-ale pies the speciality of the house. The Angel also has beautifully appointed country-style rooms.

GETTING THERE & AWAY
Chambers Buses connects Lavenham with Bury St Edmunds (30 minutes) and Sudbury (20 minutes), with an hourly bus (until 6pm Monday to Saturday, no service on Sunday) from Bury St Edmunds to Colchester via Sudbury and Lavenham. There are no direct buses from Cambridge; you must go via Sudbury, also the location of the nearest train station.

Kersey
☎ 01473
Just when you thought a cuter village than Lavenham was impossible, along comes Kersey. This pocket-sized hamlet has just one big-dipper of a road, troughing into a shallow ford (known as the Water Splash) before reappearing on the other side, but it packs in many more than its fair share of handsome timber-framed houses.

Strolling the length of the street takes all of five minutes, after which there is little to do here save snap photos, visit the wonderful potter's studio by the ford or pop in for a pint or pub grub at the 14th-century, oak-timbered **Bell Inn** (☎ 823229).

Kersey is 8 miles southeast of Lavenham off the A1141, though there are no direct buses connecting the two. There are three buses daily to Ipswich (one hour) from Monday to Saturday, two on Sunday.

Hadleigh
☎ 01473 / pop 7239
Though it's hard to envisage now, the quiet country town of Hadleigh was once one of the biggest and busiest wool towns in Eastern England, and hidden just off the High St is a lovely cluster of buildings to prove it.

The town's principal jewel is its handsome three-storeyed 15th-century **guildhall** (☎ 827752; Church St; www.fohg.co.uk; admission free; ☽ 2-5pm Thu & Sun Jun-Sep), timber framed and topped by a splendid crown-post roof. Next door, there are some fabulous original features (including a very stiff oaken door) to appreciate in 12th-century **St Mary's Church**, with its lanky spire and lofty ceiling.

Also beside the church is the high-and-mighty **Deanery Tower**, built in 1495 as a gatehouse to an archbishop's mansion that never actually got built. It's a very fanciful affair, considering it was built by a clergyman, embellished with decorous battlements and machicolation and oriel windows.

Hadleigh is 2 miles southeast of Kersey. There are hourly buses from Ipswich (30 minutes) and Sudbury (35 minutes).

BURY ST EDMUNDS
☎ 01284 / pop 36,218
A new buzz with an old message has settled over the genteel market town of Bury St Edmunds of late. Once home to one of the most powerful monasteries of medieval Europe, the town has just seen the completion of its fine cathedral with a new Gothic lantern tower – a mere 500 years after the present building was begun.

However, Bury has long attracted travellers for its powerful history, atmospheric ruins, handsome Georgian architecture and bustling agricultural markets, still held at Angel Hill on Wednesdays and Saturdays. While others come to the town on a mission to investigate the other reason for its fame: beer. Greene King, the famous Suffolk brewer, is based here with its doors wide open and welcome to thirsty visitors.

History
Bury's slogan 'Shrine of a King, Cradle of the Law' recalls two defining events in its history. The town's namesake St Edmund was the last king of East Anglia, decapitated by the Danes in 855. The martyr's body was reburied here in 903, and began to trot out ghostly miracles

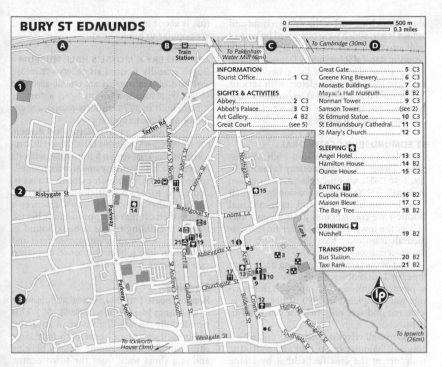

BURY ST EDMUNDS

0 — 500 m
0 — 0.3 miles

To Cambridge (30mi)

To Pakenham
Water Mill (6mi)

INFORMATION
Tourist Office..................... 1 C2

SIGHTS & ACTIVITIES
Abbey................................ 2 C3
Abbot's Palace................... 3 C3
Art Gallery......................... 4 B2
Great Court..................(see 5)

Great Gate......................... 5 C3
Greene King Brewery.......... 6 C3
Monastic Buildings............. 7 C3
Moyse's Hall Museum......... 8 B2
Norman Tower..................... 9 C3
Samson Tower................(see 2)
St Edmund Statue............. 10 C3
St Edmundsbury Cathedral.. 11 C3
St Mary's Church.............. 12 C3

SLEEPING
Angel Hotel....................... 13 C3
Hamilton House................. 14 B2
Ounce House..................... 15 C2

EATING
Cupola House.................... 16 B2
Maison Bleue.................... 17 C3
The Bay Tree..................... 18 B2

DRINKING
Nutshell........................... 19 B2

TRANSPORT
Bus Station....................... 20 B2
Taxi Rank......................... 21 B2

To Ipswich
(26mi)

To Ickworth
House (3mi)

from the grave. His shrine became a centre of pilgrimage and the core of a new Benedictine monastery. At its height the abbey was one of the most famous and wealthy in the country, at least until Henry VIII got his grubby hands on it in 1536, during the dissolution of the monasteries.

'Cradle of the Law' refers to how in 1214 the English barons drew up a petition that would form the basis of the Magna Carta here in the abbey, thus setting the country on the road to a constitutional government.

Orientation & Information

Bury is easily navigated thanks to Abbot Baldwin's original 11th-century grid layout – one of the first in the country. The train station is 900m north of the tourist office, with frequent buses to the centre. The bus station is in the town's heart.

Bury's **tourist office** (☎ 764667; tic@stedsbc.gov.uk; 6 Angel Hill; 🕓 9.30am-5.30pm Mon-Sat, 10am-3pm Sun Easter-Oct, 10am-4pm Mon-Fri, 10am-1pm Sat Nov-Easter) has maps and advice and is also the starting point for guided walking tours (£3) that depart at 2.30pm daily Easter to September.

Audio tours (adult/child £2.50/1.50) of the abbey ruins are also available here.

Sights

ABBEY & PARK

Now a picturesque ruin residing in beautiful gardens behind the cathedral, the once all-powerful **abbey** (admission free; 🕓 dawn-dusk) still impresses despite the townspeople having made off with much of the stone and St Edmund's grave and bones having disappeared long ago.

You enter the park via one of two well-preserved old gates: opposite the tourist office, the staunch mid-14th-century **Great Gate** is intricately decorated but nevertheless ominously defensive, complete with battlements, portcullis and arrow slits. The other entrance sits further up along Angel Hill, where a gargoyle-studded early-12th-century **Norman Tower** looms beside the cathedral.

Just beyond the Great Gate is a peaceful garden where the **Great Court** was once a hive of activity. Just beyond is a dovecote that marks the only remains of the **Abbot's Palace**. The best-conserved remains of this once mighty abbey church are part of the western front and **Samson Tower**, which were borrowed by houses built into them. In front of Samson Tower is a beautiful **statue of St Edmund** by Dame Elisabeth Frink (1976). The rest of the abbey spreads eastward like a ragged skeleton, with various lumps and pillars hinting at its immense size. Just north of the church lie more clustered remains of **monastic buildings**.

ST EDMUNDSBURY CATHEDRAL

Completed in 2005, the 45m-high Millennium Tower of **St Edmundsbury Cathedral** (St James; ☎ 754933; www.stedscathedral.co.uk; requested donation £3; ☉ 7.30am-6pm) is a vision in virginal Lincolnshire limestone, and its traditional Gothic-style construction gives a good idea of how the towers of many other English cathedrals must once have looked fresh from the stonemason's chisel.

Most of the rest of the building dates from the early 16th century, though the eastern end is postwar 20th-century, and the northern side was completed in 1990. It began life as a church and was only made a cathedral in 1914.

The overall effect is light and lofty, with a gorgeous hammer-beam roof and a striking sculpture of the crucified Christ by Dame Elisabeth Frink in the north transept. The impressive entrance porch has a tangible Spanish influence, a tribute to Abbot Anselm (1121–48), who opted against pilgrimage to Santiago de Compostela in favour of building a church dedicated to St James (Santiago in Spanish) right here.

ST MARY'S CHURCH

One of the biggest parish churches in country, **St Mary's** contains the tomb of Mary Tudor (Henry VIII's sister and a one-time queen of France). Built around 1430, it also has a host of somewhat vampirish angels swooping from its roof, and a bell is still rung to mark curfew, as it was in the Middle Ages.

GREENE KING BREWERY

Churning out some of Britain's favourite booze since Victorian times, this famous **brewery** (☎ 714297; www.greeneking.co.uk; Crown St; museum adult/child £2/1, day/evening tours £8/10; ☉ museum 10am-5pm Mon-Sat, noon-4pm Sun, tours noon & 3pm Mon-Fri, 10.30am, 12.30pm & 3pm Sat, 11.30am Sun, 7pm Wed-Fri Easter-Sep) has a museum and runs tours, after which you can appreciate what all the

fuss is about in their brewery tap bar. Tours are popular so book ahead.

ART GALLERY & MOYSE'S HALL MUSEUM

Bury's grandly housed **art gallery** (☎ 762081; www.burystedmundsartgallery.org; Cornhill; adult/child £1/50p; ☉ 10.30am-5pm Tue-Sat) is in a former theatre built in 1774. It hosts temporary exhibitions of contemporary art.

Just across the square, **Moyse's Hall Museum** (☎ 706183; Cornhill; adult/child £2.60/2.10; ☉ 10.30am-4.30pm Mon-Fri, 11am-4pm Sat & Sun) wows with its impressive 12th-century undercroft and tells some particularly gruesome stories in a room dedicated to death, burial and witchcraft. Among other curiosities, you'll discover a mummified cat that was purposefully buried alive in a building's walls, a book bound in the tanned skin of an infamous murderer and an armour-like gibbet that once displayed executed criminals.

Sleeping

Hamilton House (☎ 703022; terrywelsh821@btinternet .co.uk; 4 Nelson Rd; s/d/tr from £25/48/58; ✖) This wonderfully friendly B&B is in an attractive red-brick Edwardian house with four large cheerfully decorated rooms, nearby parking and is a short walk from the town centre. Packed lunches can be arranged on request.

Ounce House (☎ 761779; www.ouncehouse.co.uk; Northgate St; s/d from £65/85; P ✖) There are only a few rooms up for grabs at this dignified Victorian merchant's house, which mixes a personable atmosphere with pristine country-style rooms and the kind of neat 19th-century interior that makes you sit up straight and mind your Ps and Qs at the breakfast table. Request a room overlooking the walled garden.

Angel Hotel (☎ 714000; www.theangel.co.uk; 3 Angel Hill; s/d from £125/135; P ✖ ☐ ☁) Peeking from behind a shaggy mane of vines, this famous old coaching inn has hosted many a dignitary in its long history, including fictional celebrity Mr Pickwick who Dickens wrote enjoyed an 'excellent roast dinner' here. And you can follow his example in the hotel's top-class restaurant (set dinner £25 to £40). Rooms are split between a slick contemporary wing and traditional Georgian building.

Eating

Bay Tree (☎ 700607; 11 St John's St; mains £4.25-9) A cosy and reliable modern café popular with everyone from grannies to suits to young families and serving a varied menu of delicious soups, salads, meat dishes and pies, and even a fair Belgian beers selection.

Maison Bleue (☎ 760623; www.maisonbleu.co.uk; 31 Churchgate St; mains £9-19, set lunch/dinner £14/24; ☻ lunch & dinner Tue-Sat) This superb seafood bistro is justly popular with locals for its imaginative preparations of salmon, skate, monkfish and more. It has crisp white-linen style, chic waiters and colourful marine murals.

Cupola House (☎ 765808; www.the-cupola.com; The Transverse; mains £16-20, bar food £6-8.50) This grand 17th-century apothecary's home is topped by a baroque-style octagonal cupola and rich with historic features. It was recently rescued from a severe state of disrepair and now houses a stylish contemporary restaurant with a meaty menu and relaxed atmosphere.

Drinking

Nutshell (☎ 764867; The Traverse) Recognised by the *Guinness Book of Records* as Britain's smallest, this midget-sized timber-framed pub is an absolute gem and a tourist attraction in its own right. Mind how you knock back a pint here as in the crush you never know who you're going to elbow.

Getting There & Away

Centrally placed, Bury is a convenient point from which to explore western Suffolk. There are three daily National Express buses to London (£12.60, 2½ hours). From Cambridge, Stagecoach No 11 runs buses to Bury (1¼ hours) hourly from Monday to Saturday; the last bus back to Cambridge leaves at 7.30pm.

Trains go to Ipswich (£6, 30 to 40 minutes, two per hour), Ely (£8, 30 minutes, six daily) and hourly to Cambridge (£7.50, 45 minutes), all of which have links to London (£30, two hours).

For taxis call **A1 Cars** (☎ 766777) or try the rank alongside the market.

AROUND BURY ST EDMUNDS
Ickworth House & Park

The puffed-up pomposity of stately home **Ickworth House** (NT; ☎ 735270; adult/child house & park £7/3, park only £3.40/90p; ☻ house 1-5pm Fri-Tue mid-Mar–Oct, park 8am-8pm year-round) is palpable from the minute you catch sight of its immense oval rotunda and wide outspread wings. The building is the whimsical creation of fourth Earl of Bristol and Bishop of Derry, Frederick

Hervey (1730–1803; see the boxed text The Eccentric Earl, p548), and contains fine paintings by Titian, Gainsborough and Velasquez. There's also a lovely Italian garden, parkland bearing the landscaping eye of Lancelot 'Capability' Brown, a deer enclosure and a hide to explore.

You can even imagine yourself a houseguest of the nutty earl thanks to the swanky new **Ickworth Hotel** (☎ 735350; www.ickworthhotel .com; d £180-490; 🅿 ⌧ 🖵 🐾) in the east wing.

Ickworth is 3 miles southwest of Bury on the A143. Burtons bus service 344/5 from Bury train station (15 minutes) to Haverhill can drop you nearby.

Pakenham Water Mill

Corn has been ground for almost a thousand years on the site of Suffolk's last working **watermill** (☎ 01359-230629; www.pakenhamwatermill.co.uk; Mill Rd, Pakenham; adult/child £2.50/1.50; ☻ 2-5.30pm Sat & Sun, 9.30-11.30am Thu Easter-Sep), situated 6 miles northeast of Bury St Edmunds along the A143. The present building is 18th century, and still dutifully pounds out fresh flour and covers visitors with a layer of filmy white powder.

Bus 337 runs hourly from the Bury St Edmunds bus station (22 minutes), Monday to Saturday only.

ALDEBURGH
☎ 01728 / pop 2790

The adorable little fishing village of Aldeburgh paints a rosy picture of a traditional British seaside resort, with ramshackle fishing huts selling fresh-from-the-nets catch, fine restaurants serving the best fish and chips in the southeast, a sweeping shingle beach that is steadily encroaching into the town's heart and a lively cultural scene.

Composer Benjamin Britten and lesser known poet George Crabbe both lived and worked here; Britten founded East Anglia's primary arts and music festival, the **Aldeburgh Festival** (☎ 687110; www.aldeburgh.co.uk), which takes place in June and tops the grand old age of 60 in 2007. Britten's legacy is commemorated by Maggi Hambling's wonderful new *Scallop* sculpture, a short stroll left along the seashore. Its delicate sometimes bird-like, sometimes fan-like interlocking shells invite clambering and crawling by holidaying kids who are only too quick to oblige.

Aldeburgh's other photogenic gem is the intricately carved and timber-framed **Moot**

EASTERN ENGLAND

THE ECCENTRIC EARL

The Hervey family had such a reputation for eccentricity that it was said of them that when 'God created the human race he made men, women and Herveys'. Perhaps the biggest weirdo of them all was the creator of Ickworth House, Frederick, the third son of the third Earl of Bristol. As Bishop of Derry (Ireland) he was renowned not for his piety but for his agnosticism, vanity and oddity: he would force his clergymen to race each other through peat bogs in the middle of the night, sprinkle flour on the floor of his house to catch night-time adulterers, champion the cause of Catholic emancipation (he was, after all, a Protestant bishop) and earn himself the sobriquet of 'wicked prelate' from George III.

Not content with his life in Ireland, in later years Frederick took to travelling around Europe, where he indulged each and every one of his passions: women, wine, art and intrigue. He tried to pass himself off as a spy in France, and for his trouble he was rewarded with a nine-month prison sentence in a Napoleonic gaol. While in Italy, he horrified visiting English aristocrats with his dress sense and manners; he often dressed in military garb and once chucked a bowl of pasta onto a religious procession because he hated the sound of tinkling bells.

Hall (adult £1; ☼ 2.30-4pm May-Sep), which now sits warily beside the approaching seashore when once it sat plump in the town's centre.

Information can be found at the **tourist office** (☎ 453637; atic@suffolkcoastal.gov.uk; 152 High St; ☼ 9am-5.15pm Apr-Oct, 10am-4pm Mon-Sat Nov-Easter).

Walking

A fun way to enjoy the bracing salt air is by following the Suffolk Coast and Heaths Path, passing around half a mile north of Aldeburgh, along the coast for a few miles. Alternatively, from Aldeburgh follow the path inland for a 3-mile walk towards the village of Snape, through some pleasant wooded areas and fields.

Sleeping

Blaxhall YHA (☎ 0870 770 5702; blaxhall@yha.org.uk; Heath Walk; dm £11; ℗) Housed in an old school building that gives it an extra-institutional aura, this hostel nonetheless has small great value dorms. It's situated in good walking, cycling and birding country 6 miles from Aldeburgh, and west of Snape Maltings.

Ocean House (☎ 452094; jbreroh@aol.com; 25 Crag Path; s/d from £60/70, sea-facing r extra £5; ☒) Plump in the middle of the town's shoreline this cosy red-brick Victorian guesthouse has period décor and unimpeded sea views. Unexpected touches include crocheted bedspreads, a rocking horse and the top floor room even has a grand piano! Bikes can be borrowed and there's a table tennis table in the cellar.

White Lion Hotel (☎ 452720; www.whitelion.co.uk; Market Cross Pl; s/d with sea view £90/156, without £78/132; ℗ ☒) Aldeburgh's oldest hotel is a large tra-

ditionally run place overlooking the shingle beach, simple fishing shacks and historic Moot Hall. The building retains some 16th-century features, especially in the oak-panelled restaurant, but has straight-laced rooms.

Also recommended:

Toll House (☎ 453239; www.tollhouse.travelbugged .com; 50 Victoria Rd; s/d £35/65; ℗ ☒) Immaculate Victorian-era B&B on the entrance to town.

Eating

Regatta Restaurant (☎ 452011; www.regattaaldeburgh .com; 171 High St; mains £8.50-13.50; ☼ lunch & dinner Mon-Sat, Wed-Sat Nov-Mar) Good ol' British seaside food is given star treatment at this deceptively informal restaurant, strung with bunting and nautical bits and bobs. The celebrated owner-chef supplements his wonderful local fish dishes with regular gourmet nights.

Café 152 (☎ 454594; www.152aldeburgh.co.uk; 152 High St; mains £10-18; ☼ lunch & dinner) Freshly netted seafood is always the dish of the day in this stylishly minimalist bistro, warmed by fresh flowers, simple wooden furniture and stripped-wood floors. The seasonal menu is creative, ranging from poached skate with vegetable ribbons to crisp anchovy fritter.

AROUND ALDEBURGH

Strung along the coastline north of Aldeburgh are traditional pier-and-prom family-fun seaside resorts like **Lowestoft**, while the down-to-business south is dominated by the busy cargo port **Felixstowe**. However, in between is a poignant trail of serene and little-visited coastal heritage towns that are gradually succumbing to the sea. Most dramatically, the once-thriving village of **Dunwich** is now chopped in half, with all of its 12 churches now collecting seaweed underwater.

The region is a favourite haunt of the binocular-wielding bird-watcher brigade, and **RSPB Minsmere** (☎ 01728-648281; Westleton; adult/child £5/1.50; ☼ 9am-dusk) flickers with airborne activity year-round. Another step south towards Aldeburgh, is the odd early 20th-century 'Tudorbethan' holiday village of **Thorpeness**, which sports idiosyncratic follies, a windmill and a boating lake. Looming just north of Thorpeness is **Sizewell**, a notorious nuclear-power plant topped by a golf-ball shaped tumour.

With public transport lacking you'll need your own wheels, or the will to walk or bike this stretch of peaceful and varied coastline.

Orford

This diminutive village, 6 miles south of Snape Maltings, is worth visiting for the odd polygonal keep of the English Heritage **Orford Castle** (☎ 01394-450472; adult/child £4.50/2.30; ☼ 10am-6pm Apr-Sep, 10am-4pm Thu-Mon Oct-Mar), an innovative 12th-century 18-sided drum design with three square turrets that will enthral the kids.

Once you've got the lay of the land from the castle's lofty battlements, you can advance by ferry towards the nearby spit, which acted as a secret ex-military testing ground, but is now home to the altogether more tranquil nature reserve of **Orford Ness** (NT; ☎ 01394-450057; admission incl ferry crossing £5.90; ☼ 10am-5pm Tue-Sat Jul-Sep, Sat only mid-Apr–Jun & Oct). The largest vegetated shingle spit in Europe, it's home to many rare wading birds, animals and plants. There's a 3-mile path lined with information boards and military installations. Ferries run from Orford Quay: the last ferry departs at 2pm and returns from the reserve at 5pm.

Or to cruise around the sights with a bacon butty in your hand, contact **MV Lady Florence** (☎ 07831-698298; www.lady-florence.co.uk; per person £20). It takes diners on all-inclusive, 2½-hour brunch boat trips (£20 including food) or four-hour lunch or dinner cruises (£12.50 plus food), year-round from Orford Quay.

SOUTHWOLD

☎ 01502 / pop 3858

One of the very prettiest of Eastern England's seaside resorts, Southwold sits atop sturdy cliffs that have largely protected it from the fate of its increasingly subaquatic neighbours. Its reputation as a well-heeled holiday getaway

has earned it the nickname 'Kensington-on-Sea' after the posh district of London, and its gorgeous sandy beach, pebble-walled cottages, cannon-dotted clifftop and rows of beachfront bathing huts are all undeniably picturesque. The occasional whiff of roasting malt is also a reminder that Southwold is home to the **Adnams Brewery** (☎ 727200; www.adnams.co.uk; Adnams Pl, Sole Bay Brewery), so what better excuse to try its creamy ales in one of the town's old coaching inns.

The **tourist office** (☎ 724729; www.visit-southwold .co.uk; 69 High St; ☼ 10am-5pm Mon-Sat, 11am-4pm Sun Apr-Sep, 10.30am-3.30pm Mon-Fri, to 4pm Sat Oct-Mar) can help out with accommodation and information.

Starting inland, the **Church of St Edmund** (Church St; admission free; ☼ 9am-6pm Jun-Aug, to 4pm rest of year) is worth a quick peek for its fabulous medieval screen and 15th-century bloodshot-eyed Jack-o-the-clock, which grumpily overlooks the church's rear. A mere stone's throw away is an old weavers' cottage that now houses the **Southwold Museum** (☎ 726097; www.southwoldmuseum.org; 9-11 Victoria St; admission free; ☼ 10.30am-noon & 2-4pm Aug, 2-4pm Apr Oct), where you can gen up on the explosive 132-ship and 50,000-men Battle of Solebay (1672), fought between the English, French and Dutch fleets just off the coast.

But Southwold's shorefront is really the place to be. Take time to amble along its promenade, admire the squat 19th-century **lighthouse** before ending up at the cute little **pier** (☎ 722105; www.southwoldpier.co.uk), first built in 1899 but recently reconstructed. In among a few cheap-and-cheerful bars, fast-food dispensers and amusements, you'll find a quirky collection of handmade slot machines including a mobility masterclass for zimmerframe-users, and a modern water clock sculpture with a naughty secret revealed every half hour.

Sleeping & Eating

Acton Lodge (☎ 723217; www.southwold.ws/actonlodge; 18 South Green; s/d £40/68; 🅿 ✗) This huge Victorian homestead with a Gothic-style tower sits beside a sprawling green that runs down to the seafront. It's peppered with antiques and has just three colourful rooms with either sea or green views. The Aga-cooked breakfasts are uncommonly healthy with fish options.

Northcliffe Guest House (☎ 724074; www.northcliffe-southwold.co.uk; 20 North Pde; s/d £55/70; ✗) This spacious three-storey Victorian terraced house sits snootily overlooking the sea and pier. It has courteous owners, tasteful décor and lovely rooms variously decorated in pastel shades.

Buchenham Coffee House (☎ 723273; 81 High St; mains £6.60; ☺ lunch) Tucked away in a basement with a low-beamed ceiling, exposed brick and art in the wall cavities, this café serves delicious vegetarian specials such as Tuscan bean crunch and vegetable moussaka.

Crown (☎ 722275; www.adnams.co.uk; 90 High St; fixed lunch/dinner £18.50/29; ☺ lunch & dinner) This special old posting inn has a superb restaurant that changes its meaty seasonal menu daily. It blends well with the wine bar and wood-panelled snugs and serves real ales. It also has a few plush rooms (doubles £120).

Getting There & Away

Bus connections are surprisingly limited: your best bet is to catch one of the hourly services to Lowestoft (45 minutes) or Halesworth train station (30 minutes) and continue from there.

AROUND SOUTHWOLD
Walberswick
☎ 01502

These days it requires an interstellar leap of the imagination to picture the sleepy seaside village of Walberswick as the thriving medieval port that it once was. Nestled behind sandy dunes, it's a tranquil little backwater popular with well-heeled holidaymakers and home to a huddle of fresh fish stalls.

If your timing's right, don't miss the chance to participate in the bizarre **British Open Crabbing Championships** (☎ 722359; www.walberswick .ws/crabbing), held here in July or August, in which contestants compete to capture the heaviest crustacean. Anyone can take part, and competition is fierce with baits a closely guarded secret.

Just south of the village is the largest block of freshwater reedbed in Britain, incorporated into the **Walberswick National Nature Reserve** (☎ 676171; www.english-nature.org.uk) and home to otters, deer and rare butterflies. It's accessed by a web of public footpaths.

Oak beams, open fires and flagstone floors make the 600-year-old **Bell Inn** (☎ 723109; www .blythweb.co.uk/bellinn; mains £8-10; s/d from £70/80, d with sea view £100) your best bet by far for food and bedding. The bar downstairs serves award-winning seafood but also invites hiding behind high wooden settles with a pint and newspaper. The spacious en suite rooms also sport beams and character in spades.

Walberswick is a mile south of Southwold separated by the River Blyth. Pick up the path from Southwold's High St to reach a pedestrian bridge, or catch the summer **ferry** (60p; ☺ 10am-12.30pm & 2-5pm Jun-Sep, 10am-5pm weekends only Easter-May & Oct), which crosses at half-hourly intervals.

NORFOLK

There's an old saying that folks in Norfolk 'have one foot on the land, and one in the sea' although in truth there's a whole watery grey area in between. Seemingly spread by palette knife in a wide coastal arc, Norfolk is drizzled with inland waterways. The idyllic Norfolk Broads beckon for boating holidays. Birdwatchers flock to its marshy nature reserves, and the county's shingly coastline is a largely unspoilt crescent, fringed by pretty flint houses and boats hauling in fresh shellfish. And when you've had enough peace and quiet, you can always head for bustling county town, Norwich; which in addition to castle, cathedral and medieval churches galore has the liveliest pubs, clubs and restaurants around.

Information

Some handy websites include:
Independent Traveller's Norfolk (www.itnorfolk .co.uk)
Norfolk Coast (www.norfolkcoast.co.uk)
Visit Norfolk (www.visitnorfolk.co.uk)
Visit West Norfolk (www.visitwestnorfolk.com)

Activities

Waymarked walking trails include the well-known **Peddars Way and Norfolk Coast Path** national trail (see p516). Other long-distance paths include the **Weavers Way**, a 57-mile trail from Cromer to Great Yarmouth, and the **Angles Way**, which negotiates the valleys of the Rivers Waveney and Little Ouse for 70 miles. Meanwhile the **Wherryman's Way** (www .wherrymansway.net) is a newly launched 35-mile walking and cycling route through the Broads, following the River Yare from Norwich to Great Yarmouth.

For a real challenge, the **Around Norfolk Walk** is a 220-mile circuit that combines most of the above.

Getting Around

There's comprehensive travel advice and timetable information available at **Passenger Transport Norfolk** (www.passengertransport.norfolk.gov.uk) or you can call the national **Traveline** (☎ 0870 608 2608).

NORWICH

☎ 01603 / pop 121,550

Once described as having a pub for every day of the year and a church for every Sunday, vibrant Norwich (pronounced 'norritch') still has both in abundance and plenty more besides. These days the fabulous medieval wool churches that crop up on almost every street corner house everything from cybercafés to a puppet theatre in a heart-warming demonstration of how preservation and innovation can go hand in hand. Choice modern developments and the city's artsy student population further ensure that its steep zigzagging warren of historic streets brim with activity. The city is home to a remarkable Norman keep and a marvellous cathedral, and while the city's economic clout has waned considerably since its medieval heyday, Norfolk's capital is still one of the region's most appealing cities after Cambridge.

History

Though Norwich's history stretches back well over a thousand years, the city's golden age was during the Middle Ages, when it was England's most important city besides London. Edward III encouraged Flemish weavers to settle here in the 14th century, and their arrival helped establish the wool industry that fattened the city and sustained it right through to the 18th century.

Mass immigration from the Low Countries peaked in the troubled 16th century. In 1579 more than a third of the town's citizens were foreigners of a staunch Protestant stock, which proved beneficial during the Civil War when the Protestant parliamentarians caused Norwich little strife.

Orientation

The castle crowns central Norwich, surrounded by a compact medieval street plan. Within the circle of river and city walls, there are scattered more than 30 parish churches and the Anglican cathedral. At the city's heart is its candy-stripe canopied **market** (Market Sq; ⌚ approx 8am-4.30pm), one of the biggest and oldest markets in England, running since 1025. The enormous modern **Forum** building houses the tourist office.

Information

Banks and ATMs can be found around the Market Sq.
Boots (☎ 767970; 19 Castle Mall) Well-stocked pharmacy.
Library (☎ 774774; Forum; ⌚ 9am-8pm Mon-Fri, 9am-5pm Sat, 10.30am-4.30pm Sun) Free internet for those with ID and the patience to fill out a few forms.
Norfolk & Norwich University Hospital (☎ 286286; Colney Lane) Four miles west of the centre.
Norwich Internet Café (All Saints Church, Westlegate; per 20 min £1; ⌚ 10am-4pm Mon-Sat, 12.30-4pm Sun)
Post office (☎ 761635; 84-85 Castle Mall)
Tourist office (☎ 727927; www.visitnorwich.co.uk; ⌚ 9.30am-6pm Mon-Sat & 10.30am-4.30pm Sun Apr-Oct, 9.30am-5.30pm Mon-Sat Nov-Mar) Just inside the Forum on Millennium Plain.

Sights

NORWICH CASTLE MUSEUM & ART GALLERY

A solid sentinel overlooking medieval and modern Norwich from its hilltop perch, this massive Norman **castle keep** (☎ 493636; www.museums.norfolk.gov.uk; castle & museum adult/child £4.30/3.15, art gallery & exhibitions £4.30/3.15, all museum zones £6.30/4.60; ⌚ 10am-5.30pm Mon-Sat, 1-5pm Sun Jun-Sep, to 4.30pm Oct-May) – built in 1160 – ranks highly in the list of best-preserved examples of Anglo-Norman military architecture despite a 19th-century facelift and a gigantic shopping centre grafted to one side.

It's now home to a superb interactive **museum** and an **art gallery** to boot. The museum crams in a wealth of history, including

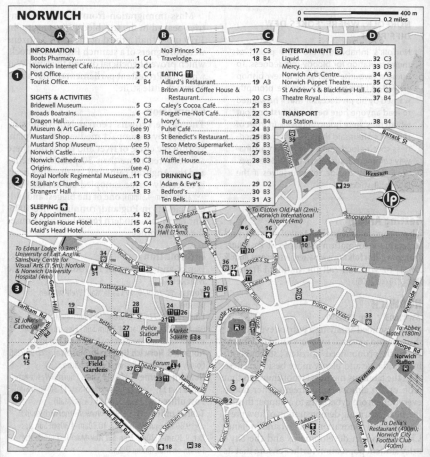

NORWICH

0 _____ 400 m
0 _____ 0.2 miles

INFORMATION	
Boots Pharmacy.........................1	C4
Norwich Internet Café..................2	C4
Post Office..................................3	C4
Tourist Office..............................4	B4

SIGHTS & ACTIVITIES	
Bridewell Museum.......................5	C3
Broads Boatrains.........................6	C2
Dragon Hall................................7	D4
Museum & Art Gallery............(see 9)	
Mustard Shop.............................8	B3
Mustard Shop Museum..........(see 5)	
Norwich Castle...........................9	C3
Norwich Cathedral....................10	C3
Origins................................(see 4)	
Royal Norfolk Regimental Museum..11	C3
St Julian's Church......................12	C4
Strangers' Hall..........................13	B3

SLEEPING	
By Appointment........................14	B2
Georgian House Hotel................15	A4
Maid's Head Hotel.....................16	C2

No3 Princes St...........................17	C3
Travelodge...............................18	B4

EATING	
Adlard's Restaurant...................19	A3
Briton Arms Coffee House &	
Restaurant............................20	C3
Caley's Cocoa Café....................21	B3
Forget-me-Not Café..................22	C3
Ivory's.....................................23	B4
Pulse Café................................24	B3
St Benedict's Restaurant............25	B3
Tesco Metro Supermarket..........26	B3
The Greenhouse........................27	B3
Waffle House............................28	B3

DRINKING	
Adam & Eve's...........................29	D2
Bedford's.................................30	B3
Ten Bells..................................31	A3

ENTERTAINMENT	
Liquid.......................................32	C3
Mercy.......................................33	D3
Norwich Arts Centre..................34	A3
Norwich Puppet Theatre............35	C2
St Andrew's & Blackfriars Hall....36	B3
Theatre Royal...........................37	B4

TRANSPORT	
Bus Station...............................38	B4

---

lively exhibits on Boudicca and the Iceni, the
Anglo-Saxons and Vikings, natural history
displays and even an Egyptian gallery complete with mummies. Every room is enlivened
with plenty of fun for kids, but best of all
is the atmospheric keep itself, which sends
shivers down the spine with graphic displays
on grisly punishments meted out in its days
as a medieval prison. Guided tours also run
around the battlements and dungeons.

Meanwhile the art gallery houses paintings of the acclaimed 19th-century Norwich
School of landscape painting founded by John
Crome and – trust the English – the world's
largest collection of ceramic teapots.

A claustrophobic tunnel from the castle also
emerges into a reconstructed WWI trench at

the **Royal Norfolk Regimental Museum** (☎ 493649;
adult/child £3/1.60; ☼ 10am-4.30pm Mon-Sat), which
details the history of the local regiment since
1830. It has another less dramatic entrance
from the road.

THE FORUM & ORIGINS
The all-glass **Forum** is the most impressive
building to hit Norwich's skyline in decades,
and is home to Norfolk's main library, the
regional BBC and the tourist office. Here
too is family-focused **Origins** (☎ 727920; www
.originsnorwich.co.uk; the Forum; adult/child £5.95/3.95;
☼ 10am-5.15pm Mon-Sat, 11am-4.45pm Sun), a wonderful interactive museum that surrounds
you with film, images and noise in its exploration of 2000 years of regional history. There

are numerous buttons to push and games to play; you can have a go at speaking the original Norfolk dialect (not easy), flooding the Norfolk Fens or simply sit back for story time with weird and wonderful tales of the area's mythology.

ELM HILL

An utterly charming medieval cobbled street of crooked timber beams and doors, intriguing shops and snug cafés, this street is also the centre of the local antique business. From here walk down Wensum St to Tombland, where the market was originally located. Despite its ominous overtones, 'tomb' is an old Norse word for empty, hence space for a market.

NORWICH CATHEDRAL

Focal point of the city, the creamy-coloured Anglican **cathedral** (☎ 218321; suggested donation £4; 7.30am-7pm May-Sep, 7.30am-6pm Oct-Apr) is an undeniably fine spectacle, its barbed spire soaring higher than any in England except Salisbury, while the size of its cloisters is second to none. But there's far more to this cathedral than its impressive scale.

Begun in 1096, it has managed to hang onto its character as a great Anglo-Norman abbey church more than any other English cathedral except Durham. However, the building's most renowned feature came in 1463 when its nave was topped by magnificent Gothic rib-vaulting punctuated with around 1200 sculpted roof bosses depicting bible stories. Together they represent one of the finest achievements of English medieval masonry, although you'll find yourself longing for a telescope to view them in all their finely detailed glory.

Outside the cathedral's eastern end is the grave of WWI heroine Edith Cavell, a Norfolk nurse who was shot by the Germans for helping POWs to escape. The cathedral close also contains handsome houses and the old chapel of King Edward VI School (where English hero Admiral Nelson was educated). Its current students make up the choir, which performs in at least one of the three services held daily.

ST JULIAN'S CHURCH

Tucked away in a tiny alley, this simple **church** (☎ 767380; St Julian's Alley; admission free; 7.30am-5.30pm Apr-Sep, to 4pm Oct-Mar) is a shrine to Julian

of Norwich and has been a centre for pilgrimage for centuries. Writer and mystic Julian (also known as Juliana, 1342–c 1429) wrote down her religious visions in a collection called *The Revelations of Divine Love*, which is unparalleled in English literature for its clarity and depth of perception. Sadly the cell where she wrote the book was torn down in the Reformation, much of the building was reconstructed after WWII.

OTHER MUSEUMS

Though it's more shop than museum, the **Mustard Shop** (☎ 627889; 15 Royal Arcade; admission free; 9.30am-5pm Mon-Sat) tells the 200-year story of Colman's Mustard, a famous local product. It's in the lavish Art Nouveau Royal Arcade shopping arcade.

Nearby is **Bridewell Museum** (☎ 629127; Bridewell Alley; adult/child £3/1.60; 10am-4.30pm Tue-Sat Apr-Oct), housed in a former merchant's house and 14th-century bridewell or 'prison for women, beggars and tramps', and filled with fascinating paraphernalia and reconstructions of Norwich's principal industries right through to a room devoted to the Norwich City football team.

About 250m west of here, along St Andrew's St and Charing Cross is the maze-like early-14th-century townhouse **Strangers' Hall** (☎ 667229; adult/child £3/1.60; 10.30am-4.30pm Wed & Sat), with atmospheric rooms furnished in period styles from Tudor to Victorian. Another remarkable medieval townhouse, this time built by a local businessman and four-times mayor of Norwich, **Dragon Hall** (☎ 663922; www .dragonhall.org; 115-123 King St; adult/child £5/3; 10am-5pm Mon-Sat Apr-Dec) has a stunning crown-post roof and timber-framed great hall from 1430. It's famous for its darling little carved green-and-orange dragon waving flame-like wings and sticking its tongue out amid the timber ceiling beams.

SAINSBURY CENTRE FOR VISUAL ARTS

Reopened in mid-2006 with a swish new wing, the **Sainsbury Centre** (☎ 593199; www.scva .org.uk; admission free; 11am-5pm Tue-Sun, to 8pm Wed) was Norman Foster's first high profile building and is filled with an eclectic collection of works by Picasso, Moore, Degas and Bacon, displayed beside art from Africa, the Pacific and the Americas. It's to the west of the city (a 20-minute bus trip from Castle Meadow).

Tours

City Sightseeing (☎ 0871 666 000; www.city-sightseeing.com; adult/child £8/4; ☉ hourly 10am-4pm Apr-Oct) runs a hop-on hop-off bus service stopping at nine destinations around the city centre including city hall. Or if you prefer to potter about on the river, **Broads Boatrains** (☎ 701701; www.cityboats.co.uk; adult/child £8.50/5.50) runs cruises from Station Quay, off Elm Hill, and rents out self-drive boats.

Sleeping

BUDGET

Norwich has no hostel and scarce budget options. Most of the more affordable B&Bs are outside the ring road, and around the train station.

Abbey Hotel (☎ 612915; 16 Stracey Rd; s/d £24/44, d with bathroom £58; ✗) This Victorian terraced house is one of the best value B&Bs in a row of them up behind the station. It has simple, prim and proper floral rooms and pleasant service.

Norwich Central Travelodge (☎ 0870 191 1797; www.travelodge.co.uk; Queens Rd; r £26-55; ✗) Who cares if it has personality if its new, central and has early-booking online deals in an expensive city? This no-frills addition to the chain is close to the bus station and has pay-and-display parking alongside.

Edmar Lodge (☎ 615599; www.edmarlodge.co.uk; 64 Earlham Rd; s/d from £35/40; ℗ ✗) A big blonde-brick B&B with straightforward rooms and a familial atmosphere is situated in a residential area a 10-minute walk from town.

MIDRANGE & TOP END

Georgian House Hotel (☎ 615655; www.georgian-hotel.co.uk; 32-34 Unthank Rd; s/d from £60/80; ℗ ✗) A rambling, elegant Victorian house opposite the Roman Catholic cathedral, houses this 28-room boutique hotel, which has spacious modern rooms and a tree-filled garden. The restaurant wins much praise for its use of local ecofriendly ingredients.

No3 Princes St (☎ 662692; www.3princes-norwich.co.uk; 3 Princes St; s/d £60/85; ✗) This recently restored handsome red-brick Georgian home in the city's heart has four absolutely beautiful and individually styled en suite rooms, three of which overlook St Andrews opposite, the other with a view of a pretty gravel-filled back courtyard. The continental breakfasts are eaten in your room.

ourpick By Appointment (☎ 630730; 25-29 St George's St; s/d from £70/110; ✗ 🖵) This fabulously theatrical and delightfully eccentric B&B occupies three heavy-beamed 15th-century merchant's houses, also home to a labyrinthine restaurant well-known for its classic English fare. Its antique furniture, creaky charm and superb breakfasts make this one of the best deals around. Book ahead.

Catton Old Hall (☎ 419379; www.catton-hall.co.uk; Lodge Lane, Old Catton; d £70-120; ℗ ✗) This is a splendid early 17th-century gentleman's house with brick-and-flint walls, mullioned windows, oak timbers and plush furnishings 2 miles north of Norwich. Rooms are decorated in flouncy pink frills and floral drapes.

Maid's Head Hotel (☎ 0870 609 6110; www.corushotels.com; Tombland; s/d weeknights £105/125, weekends per person £51; ℗ ✗ 🖵) The stunning black-and-white exterior is the most arresting thing about this 700-year-old coaching inn near the cathedral. There's altogether less personality inside and its 83 modern rooms are comfortable but somewhat soulless.

Eating

BUDGET

Norwich's strong vegetarian scene is a great source of budget value.

ourpick Pulse Café (☎ 765562; Labour in Vain Yard, Guildhall Hill; snacks £2-4, mains £6-7; ☉ 10am-11pm Mon-Sat) You needn't be vegetarian to fall for this funky lounge bar in the old fire station stables, which offers outstanding meat-free fare from enchilada to risotto. Eat in the tranquil courtyard or beside lovely low-arched windows inside. The drinks list is surprisingly lengthy, jumping between wines, organic ciders, beers and fruit liqueurs.

Waffle House (☎ 612790; www.wafflehouse.co.uk; 39 St Giles St; waffles £3-7; ☉ 10am-10pm Mon-Sat, 11am-10pm Sun) Delicious smells encase this small and ever-popular Belgian waffles café, which uses quality organic and free range produce to concoct a long list of sweet and savoury creations. It's very family friendly, but just as beloved by students and professionals.

Greenhouse (☎ 631007; www.greenhousetrust.co.uk; 42-48 Bethel St; snacks & mains £2.95-7; ☉ 10am-5pm Tue-Sat) This simple organic, free-trade, vegetarian, vegan and all-round goody-two-shoes café is a hit with students and has a cute little vine-covered, herb-planted terrace.

Other options:

Forget-me-Not Café (☎ 723411; Redwell St; snacks & mains £2.95-7; ☉ 10am-4pm Mon-Sat) Medieval church turned peaceful, old-school café.

Tesco Metro Supermarket (☎ 0845 677 9501; 5 Guildhall Hill; ⏰ 7am-10pm Mon-Sat, 11am-5pm Sun)

MIDRANGE & TOP END

Adlard's Restaurant (☎ 633522; www.adlards.co.uk; 79 Upper St Giles St; 3-course dinner £35; ⏰ 12.30-10.30pm) This elegant and airy Michelin-starred eatery is the place to splurge on both food and excellent wines. It specialises in modern British cuisine with a French accent and keeps the décor simple and pleasing with wooden floors, large canvasses and large windows.

Briton Arms Coffee House & Restaurant (☎ 623367; 9 Elm Hill; mains £5-10; ⏰ 9.30am-5pm) Romantics and traditionalists should make a beeline to this darling little 15th-century thatched cottage tearoom, overhanging cobbled Elm Hill and snug with wooden beams, rustic wooden benches and a little terraced garden. It serves classic English comfort food as well as good coffee and cakes.

Caley's Cocoa Café (☎ 629364; Guildhall, Market Sq; ⏰ 9am-5pm Mon-Sat) Chocolate-makers Caley's are a Norwich institution, and you'll see why upon visiting their café in the equally confection-like Guildhall's old Court of Record, a handsome oval Georgian courtroom complete with judge's chair. They serve light meals and of course, choccies to make your knees wobble.

St Benedict's Restaurant (☎ 765377; 9 St Benedict's St; mains £6-10; ⏰ lunch & dinner Tue-Sat) A bubbly little brasserie with excellent husband-and-wife chefs at the helm, St Benedict's has an Edwardian frontage, cheerful modern interior and an original modern British menu that includes such quirky desserts as Horlicks ice cream.

Ivory's (☎ 627526; www.assemblyhousenorwich.co.uk; Theatre St; mains £6.50-9; ⏰ lunch & dinner Mon-Sat, lunch Sun) In a grand Georgian building with high ceilings graced by decorative plaster and heavy chandeliers, Ivory's serves traditional British dishes, while a piano tinkers in the background.

Drinking

Adam & Eve's (☎ 667423; Bishopsgate) A 13th-century brew-house built to quench the thirst of cathedral builders, this is now Norwich's oldest-surviving pub, and an adorable little sunken-floored gem. So snug it is that the upper bar barely fits the barmaid, perhaps why the staff have a reputation for grumpiness! Take a pew outside amid the old mangle flowerpots, or keep an eye out for the resident ghost in the character-rich interior.

Ten Bells (☎ 667833; 76 St Benedict's St; ⏰ 5pm-midnight, from noon Sat & Sun) This is this kind of faded 18th-century pub where people feel instantly at ease, calmed by the real ales, mellow red velvet, quirky memorabilia and amused by the red phone booth in the corner. It also fancies itself as an intellectuals' hang-out, with poetry readings and arts-school regulars.

Bedford's (☎ 666869; 1 Old Post Office Yard; ⏰ 11.30am-11pm Mon-Sat) Bedford's main selling point is its wonderfully atmospheric subterranean wine bar beneath a vaulted brick ceiling; it also has a wicked selection of cocktails.

Entertainment

Norwich has a flourishing arts scene and pulsating weekend nightlife. For what's on information from ballet to boozing try www.norwichtonight.com.

NIGHTCLUBS

Nightclubs run from 9pm or 10pm to at least 2am.

Liquid (☎ 611113; www.liquidnightclub.co.uk; Prince of Wales Rd; admission £5; ⏰ Mon, Fri & Sat) True to its name, Liquid is a big molten-themed club filled with warped furniture, lava lamps and bubble projections, and playing everything from retro to R&B.

Mercy (☎ 627666; www.mercinightclub.com; 86 Prince of Wales Rd; ⏰ Tue & Thu-Sat) A former cinema complete with mock-marble entrance and Renaissance inspired décor, Mercy is a massive club with huge projection screens and DJs that favour R&B and club classics.

THEATRE

Once home to Dominican Blackfriars, this spookily Gothic-looking **St Andrew's and Blackfriars' Halls** (☎ 628477; St George's St) now serves as an impressive civic centre where concerts, antique and craft markets, the Music and Arts Festival and even the annual beer festival are held.

Theatre Royal (☎ 630000; www.theatreroyalnorwich.co.uk; Theatre St) features programmes by touring drama, opera and ballet companies. **Norwich Arts Centre** (☎ 660352; www.norwichartscentre.co.uk; St Benedict's St), also in a medieval church, has a wide-ranging programme of alternative drama, concerts, dance, cabaret and jazz. **Norwich Puppet Theatre** (☎ 629921; www.puppettheatre.co.uk; St James,

Whitefriars; adult/child £6/4) set in a cute little repurposed church goes down a treat with small and big kids.

Getting There & Away

National Express runs buses to London (£15.40, three hours, five daily). First Eastern Counties runs hourly buses to King's Lynn (1½ hours) and Cromer (one hour). There are twice-hourly services to Great Yarmouth (40 minutes).

There are twice hourly train services to Ely (£12.20, 56 minutes) and Cambridge (£13.20, 1¼ hours), as well as regular links to Peterborough (£16.30, 1½ hours). Twice hourly trains also go to London Liverpool Street (£35.80, two hours). For city cabs, call **Loyal Taxis** (☎ 619619).

Norwich International Airport (☎ 411923; www.norwichinternational.com) is just 4 miles north of town, and has cheap flights to Europe and several British destinations. Hourly buses go from Norwich's train and bus stations.

If you're driving, the city has six Park & Ride locations (buses £2.80 return).

AROUND NORWICH
Blickling Hall

Despite being a glorious Jacobean house with illustrious roots as far back as 1057, this isolated stately home is best known for a ghost story. In 1437 the house was claimed by the Boleyn family, passed through the generations to Thomas, father of Anne Boleyn. Poor old Anne, of course, made the fatal error of becoming one of King Henry VIII's six wives, and was executed in 1533. It's said that every year on the anniversary of her death a coach drives across Norfolk's 11 bridges and up to the house, drawn by headless horses, driven by headless coachmen and containing the queen with her head on her lap.

Ghosts and ghoulies aside, the current **house** (NT; ☎ 01263-738030; Blickling; adult/child £8/4, garden only £5/2.50; ⏰ house 1-5pm Wed-Sun Apr-Jul, Sep & Oct, & Mon Aug, gardens 10.15am-5.15pm Wed-Sun Easter-Oct, 11am-4pm Thu-Sun rest of year) is a striking sight, surrounded by neatly snipped gardens and inviting parkland. Largely rebuilt for Sir Henry Hobart, James I's chief justice, it's now filled with fine Georgian furniture, pictures and tapestries. There's an impressive Jacobean plaster ceiling in the long gallery.

Blickling Hall is 15 miles north of Norwich. Sanders runs hourly buses here from Norwich bus station from June to August (20 minutes). Aylsham is the nearest train station, 1¾ miles away.

NORFOLK BROADS

Nature lovers, birders, boaties and anyone fond of splashing about in the water will undoubtedly want to linger in the county's most beautiful attraction, the Norfolk Broads. A member of the national park's family, the Broads are a mesh of navigable slow-moving rivers, freshwater lakes, wild water meadows, fens, bogs and saltwater marshes, flourishing nature reserves and bird sanctuaries that together form 125 miles of lock-free waterways.

A boat is by far the best vantage point from which to spy on its myriad birds, butterflies and watery wildlife. The tranquil landscape may not be dramatic in itself, but it is hypnotically peaceful and its very flatness means there's little to shield your binocular vision from the winged and water-bound action taking place on all sides.

The Broads' highest point is at How Hill, just 12m above sea level, which is scattered with many of the picturesque wind pumps first built to drain the marshland and to return water to the rivers.

RECIPE FOR FOOTBALLING SUCCESS?

Football crazy England has seen many an ailing club funded by unlikely fans; Elton John famously rescued Watford from the fourth division, while big-beat DJ Fatboy Slim owns a sizeable stake in his beloved Brighton & Hove Albion. But Norwich City FC, aka the Canaries, have perhaps the most unlikely saviour of them all in England's original celebrity chef and a beacon of light to amateur cooks the county over, Delia Smith. Now the club's majority shareholder, she's dubbed 'Mother Delia' by many fans and delights spectators with outbursts totally at odds with her former kitchen-maam image. And though she's now retired from TV cookery, Delia still deigns to dip into the kitchen at her club's weekend **Delia's restaurant** (☎ 218704; www.deliascanarycatering.com; Norwich City Football Club; 3-course meal £29.50; ⏰ 7pm-late Fri & Sat).

THE BROADS: A NATURAL MANSCAPE

A great deal of head scratching occurred over the years in response to the puzzle of how and why the Norfolk Broads came to exist. Though the rivers were undoubtedly natural, and many thought the lakes were, too – it's hard to believe they're not when you see them – still nobody could quite explain how they were formed.

However, the mystery was solved when records were discovered in the remains of St Benet's Abbey on the River Bure. They revealed that from the 12th century the land was used for peat-cutting. Since the area had little woodland, peat would have been the only reliable source of fuel and around 1040 hectares were dug over about 200 years.

But dig gaping holes in low-lying land and they're bound to spring a leak someday. And sure enough, water gradually seeped through, causing marshes and eventually lakes to develop. The first to be recorded was Ranworth Broad in 1275. Eventually, the increasingly aquatic diggers could dig no more, and the peat-cutting industry died out. In no other area of England has human effort changed the natural landscape so dramatically.

Orientation

The Broads form a triangle, with the Norwich–Cromer road, the Norwich–Lowestoft road and the coastline as the three sides.

Wroxham, on the A1151 from Norwich, and Potter Heigham, on the A1062 from Wroxham, are the main centres. Along the way there are plenty of waterside pubs, villages and market towns where you can stock up on provisions, and stretches of river where you can feel you are the only person around.

Information

Details on scores of conservation centres and bird-watching hides can be found through the **Broads Authority** (☎ 01603-610734; www.broads-authority.gov.uk), including those at Berney Marshes and Breydon Water, Cockshoot Broad, Hickling Broad, Horsey Mere, How Hill, Ranworth, Strumpshaw Fen, Surlingham Church Marsh and Whitlingham. There's more information on Norfolk Broads at www.norfolkbroads.com and the RSPB at www.rspb.org.uk.

Getting Around

You can hire a variety of launches from large cabin cruisers to little craft with outboards for a couple of hours' gentle messing about on the river.

Boating holidays are operated by **Blakes** (☎ 0870 2202 498; www.blakes.co.uk) and **Hoseasons** (☎ 01502-502588; www.hoseasons.co.uk) among others. Depending on boat size, facilities and season, a boat for two to four people costs around £490 to £840 for a week including fuel and insurance.

Meanwhile boat yards around Wroxham and Potter Heigham hire out boats for shorter cruises, from an hour to several days. Look out for the traditional flat-bottomed boats known as wherries. In the height of summer, prices start from £28 for two hours, £39 for four hours and £67 for one day. Prices drop outside summer.

No previous experience is necessary, but remember to stay on the right-hand side of the river, that the rivers are tidal and to stick to the speed limit – you can be prosecuted for speeding.

If you don't feel like piloting your own boat, try **Broads Tours** (www.broads.co.uk; Wroxham ☎ 01603-782207; the Bridge; Potter Heigham (☎ 01692-670711; Broads Haven) which runs 1½-hour pleasure trips (adult/child £6/4.50) from April to September.

GREAT YARMOUTH

☎ 01493 / pop 90,810

A seaside resort for 250 years, Great Yarmouth is frequently dismissed as a one-trick pony, famous for its neon-lit esplanade of jingling amusement arcades and grim greasy spoons, vast beaches and cheek-by-jowl hotels. But the resort also has a calmer old town sheltering a string of museums. So if ice cream, crazy golf, sandy-toed strolls and the odd educational interlude are on your agenda, Great Yarmouth will happily deliver. And while recent years saw it become increasingly run down, new investment is now perking up its fortunes and improving its seafront parade.

The **tourist office** (☎ 846345; www.great-yarmouth.co.uk; 25 Marine Pde; ☼ 9.30am-5.30pm Easter-Sep) is on the seafront and can point you towards the lovely **Weavers Way** (see p550) walking trail, which cuts into the Broads from here.

EASTERN ENGLAND

Most absorbing of Yarmouth's museums is **Time & Tide** (☎ 743930; www.museums.norfolk.gov .uk; Blackfriars Rd; adult/child £5.80/3.70; ☿ 10am-5pm Apr-Oct, 10am-4pm Mon-Fri, noon-4pm Sat & Sun Nov-Mar) in a Victorian herring curing works (with a few lingering smells to prove authenticity). It tackles everything from prehistory to penny arcades and naughty postcards, but dwells on maritime heritage and reconstructs typical 17th-century row houses. There's plenty for kids, from touch screens to taking the wheel of a coastal drifter.

A cluster of other museums surround historic South Quay. The 16th-century **Elizabethan House Museum** (NT; ☎ 855746; 4 South Quay; adult/child £3/1.60; ☿ 10am-5pm Mon-Fri, 1.15-5pm Sat & Sun Apr-Oct) is a fine merchant's house faithfully reconstructed to showcase Tudor and Victorian domestic life and home to the 'Conspiracy Room' where Cromwell and chums decided Charles I must be executed.

Around the corner, the **Tolhouse Museum** (☎ 858900; Tolhouse St; adult/child £3/1.60; ☿ 10am-5pm Mon-Fri, 1.15-5pm Sat & Sun Apr-Oct) is a medieval gaol dating back 700 years; it dwells on macabre inmates, witchcraft, grisly murders, nasty punishments and you can peek inside the spooky cells, all of which make it an instant hit with kids.

The **Norfolk Nelson Museum** (☎ 850698; www .nelson-museum.co.uk; 26 South Quay; adult/child £2.90/1.50; ☿ 10am-5pm Mon-Fri, 1-4pm Sat & Sun Apr-Oct) celebrates the life, times, romances and – in obsessive detail – the death of the one-eyed hero of Trafalgar, who was a regular visitor to Great Yarmouth.

B&Bs are everywhere, especially choc-a-bloc Trafalgar St, and cost from £18 to £35 per person. The worn Edwardian corner-house hostel **Great Yarmouth YHA** (☎ 0870 770 5840; greatyarmouth@yha.org.uk; 2 Sandown Rd; dm £11; ☿ Apr-Oct) is three-quarters of a mile from the train station, near the beach.

There are hourly buses (40 minutes) and trains (32 minutes) to Norwich.

CROMER
☎ 01263

Once a fashionable Victorian coastal resort, this faintly forlorn but still attractive town is perched on a clifftop overlooking the sea. It's famous for its crabs, and has a long sandy beach and scenic coastal walks but there's also a spooky side to Cromer: the nearby village of Shipden was washed into the sea in the 14th century and in stormy weather, locals say, you can still hear its subaquatic church bells ringing. Here too, Arthur Conan Doyle hatched his ghostly plot for *The Hound of the Baskervilles*, after hearing the local legend of Black Shuck, a black canine phantom that roams the shoreline.

Located by the bus station, the **tourist office** (☎ 0871 200 3071; cromertic@north-norfolk.gov.uk; Cadogan Rd; ☿ 10am-5pm late-May–Aug, 10am-4pm Sep–late-May) has a town map, and can direct you to the small town **museum** (☎ 513543; Church St; adult/ child £2.50/1.25; ☿ 10am-5pm Mon-Sat, 2-5pm Sun Apr-Oct, 10am-4pm Mon-Sat Nov-Feb) nearby.

If you need a fix in 17th- and 18th-century finery, **Felbrigg Hall** (NT; ☎ 837444; adult/child £7/3.50; ☿ 1-5pm Sat-Wed end-Mar–Oct) is one of the best stately homes in Norfolk. It incorporates a walled garden and orangery and is 2 miles southwest of Cromer. The **Weavers Way** walk runs through its estate.

The tourist office has lists of accommodation, but our favourite is the superbly situated **Captain's House** (☎ 515434; www.captains-house.co.uk; 5 The Crescent; d £68-76; ℗ ✗) a curvaceous Georgian townhouse overlooking the seafront in the heart of town. There are three freshly decorated rooms and a hearty breakfast of local sausages, homemade jams and biscuits.

Cromer has direct trains to Norwich hourly Monday to Saturday and services every two hours on Sunday (43 minutes).

SHERINGHAM
☎ 01263

Chomping on fresh crab meat is just one of the delights of this traditional little Victorian seaside resort and fishing town. Its shingly shoreline, small fishermen's heritage centre and pretty flint houses make the town worth a stop, but its main attraction is a steam railway, the **Poppy Line** (☎ 820808; www.nnr.co.uk; adult/child £9/5.50), which runs round to Holt and back via a 10-mile route through woodland and villages. If you decide to stay put, there's **Sheringham YHA** (☎ 0870 770 6024; sheringham@yha .org.uk; 1 Cremer's Drift; dm £16.95; ℗ ✗), a modern purpose-built hostel with great facilities and stacks of family beds.

CLEY MARSHES

A bird-watching mecca with over 300 species recorded, Cley Marshes sits between Cromer and Wells. There's a **visitors centre** (☎ 740008; www.norfolkwildlifetrust.org.uk; adult/child £3.75/free;

(✆) 10am-5pm Apr-Oct), built on high ground but the best spot for bird-watching is in the many hides hidden amid the golden reedbeds.

BLAKENEY POINT
☎ 01263

The pretty village of **Blakeney** was once a busy fishing and trading port before its harbour silted up. These days it's a good place to jump aboard boat trips out to a 500-strong colony of common and grey seals that live, bask and breed on nearby Blakeney Point. The hour-long trips (adult/child £7/4) run daily April to October but the best time to come is between June and August when the common seals pup. Companies are split between the town's harbour and nearby Morston. They include:

Beans Boat Trips (☎ 740505; www.beansboattrips.co .uk; Morston)

Bishop's Boats (☎ 740753; www.bishopsboats.co.uk; Blakeney Harbour)

WELLS-NEXT-THE-SEA
☎ 01328 / pop 2451

A fetching little holiday town with a silty harbour set back from the sea, Wells makes for a charming day trip or stopover. While there are few sights, the attractive Georgian streets, flint cottages and curio shops are good to browse and you can bag fresh fish and join the kids gillying (crabbing) on the waterfront.

There's a **tourist office** (☎ 710885; www.wells guide.com; Staithe St; (✆) 10am-5pm Mon-Sat, 10am-4pm Sun Mar–mid-Jul, Sep & Oct; 9.30am-6pm Mon-Sat, 9.30am-5pm Sun mid-Jul–Aug) on hand for inquiries and accommodation lists. One agreeable distraction is to catch the **narrow-gauge steam train** (☎ 711630; www.wellswalsinghamrailway.co.uk; adult/child return £7/5.50; duration 30 min, 3-5 departures daily Apr-Oct) that chuffs 5 miles to **Little Walsingham**, where

there are shrines and a ruined abbey that have drawn pilgrims since medieval times.

Wells YHA Hostel (☎ 0870 770 6084; wellsnorfolk@yha .org.uk; Church Plains; dm £13.95; (P) (✖) (&)) is a superb little 32-bed hostel with mostly family-sized rooms and is housed in an ornately gabled early 20th-century church hall.

Another option is **Glebe Barn** (☎ 711809; 7a Glebe Rd; d £44; (P) (✖)), a hospitable B&B in a converted 18th-century storehouse just 200m from the harbour, with just three rooms that are themed around the sea, Art Nouveau and the theatre. It's run by keen walkers and has a sheltered gravel courtyard.

The Coast Hopper bus goes through Wells approximately every two hours on its way between Hunstanton (45 minutes) and Sheringham (40 minutes).

AROUND WELLS-NEXT-THE-SEA
Holkham Hall

The high-and-mighty stately home of **Holkham Hall** (☎ 710227; www.holkham.co.uk; adult/child 6.50/3.25; (✆) noon-5pm Sun-Thu Easter & May-Sep) is an extraordinarily grand Palladian mansion set in a vast deer park designed by Capability Brown. There's also a separate **Bygones Museum** (adult/ child £5/2.50 or combined ticket £10/5; (✆) same as hall) of local folklore and domestic paraphernalia, though you're better off roaming the beautiful park, which is open year-round, or discovering the pristine white-gold sands of nearby Holkham Bay beach.

The hall is 2 miles from Wells.

Burnham Deepdale
☎ 01485

In-the-know backpackers and walkers flock to this lovely coastal spot, with its tiny twin villages of Burnham Deepdale and Brancaster

---

RURAL ROMANTICS

While much of the world goes dewy eyed or faintly cynical on Valentine's Day, visit Norfolk on 14 February and you'd be forgiven for thinking it's a county of veritable Cupids. There are scores of centuries-old valentine traditions to get hearts a-fluttering here. Bags filled with love tokens would be given away left right and centre and children would be just as much a part of the action, getting up before dawn to sing valentine rhymes and beg for sweets. It was also common for valentine gifts to be of greater value than Christmas goodies.

But perhaps the most famous Norfolk ritual involves a mysterious character called Jack Valentine, a kind of loved-up February Father Christmas also known as Old Father or Mother Valentine, who deposits a doorstep gift, rattles on the door and then promptly disappears into thin air. And it seems Jack is just as busy as ever today; it has been known for whole streets to wake up and find valentine's treats stuck to their doors.

Staithe strung along a rural road. Stroked by the beautiful Norfolk Coastal Path, surrounded by beaches and reedy marshes alive with birdlife, crisscrossed by cycling routes and a base for a whole host of water sports from kitesurfing to kayaking to sailing, Burnham Deepdale is also home to one of the country's best backpacker hostels, around which activities pool.

The hostel operates a superb **tourist office** (☎ 210256; www.deepdalefarm.co.uk ⊗ 10am-4pm Apr-Sep, closed Tue-Wed Oct-Mar), which is flush with information on the surrounding area, and can help arrange accommodation and a variety of tours. It also has internet access (per 30 minutes/hour £1/1.50). For more information on the area, go to www.itnorfolk.co.uk and www.brancasterstaithe.co.uk.

Anywhere else it might seem odd to have campers poking their heads out of Native American-style tepees, but at ecofriendly backpackers haven and hostel **ourpick Deepdale Farm** (☎ 210256; www.deepdalefarm.co.uk; camping per adult/child £6.50/3, dm Sun-Thu/Fri-Sat £10.50/12.50, tepees for 2 £60, 6 £75-90; Ⓟ Ⓧ ▣) it's just part of a wonderful experience. The set-up includes small and stylish en suite dorms in converted 17th-century stables, camping space, a coffee shop, laundry, barbecue facilities, lounges and picnic tables. Bike hire is also available. Tepees come with faux fur mattresses, fuel for the iron chiminea and a lantern.

Just west of the hostel is gastro-pub extraordinaire the **White Horse** (☎ 210262; www.whitehorse brancaster.co.uk; mains £5-9; d Sun-Thu/Fri-Sat Apr-Oct £120/140, Nov-Mar £90/140; ⊗ lunch & dinner; Ⓟ Ⓧ Ⓖ ▣ wi-fi only), which has award-winning platters of fresh fish and shellfish, a cosy bar, plus a conservatory and sun deck with lovely views overlooking the tidal marsh. It also has upscale rooms, some with terraces, others with telescopes for bird-watching over the marshes.

Meanwhile, whitewashed, pebble-fronted pub the **Jolly Sailors** (☎ 210314; www.jollysailors.co.uk) makes a great spot to toast your day's exertions; it boasts an adjacent brewery, creamy real ales and a livelier atmosphere than the White Horse. It's on the main road about 800m west of the hostel.

The Coast Hopper bus stops outside Deepdale Farm hourly in summer on its run between Sheringham (1¼ hours) and Hunstanton (23 minutes); it also goes less frequently to King's Lynn (one hour). Ask at the tourist office for timetables.

KING'S LYNN

☎ 01553 / pop 34,565

Long labelled as 'the Warehouse on the Wash,' the medieval port town of King's Lynn was once so busy with waterborne traders that it was said you could cross from one side of the River Great Ouse to the other by simply stepping from boat to boat. Staunchly pious citizens and wild-and-woolly sailors would mingle in its cobbled streets, and fishing fleets would rub woodwork with trading vessels and even New World explorers. Something of the salty port-town tang can still be felt in old King's Lynn, though the petite modern-day port barely passes as a shadow of its former self.

Orientation

Old King's Lynn huddles along the eastern bank of the river. The train station is on its eastern side, while unexciting modern King's Lynn and the bus station are between them. Three markets still take place weekly on Tuesday, Friday and Saturday. The biggest is the Tuesday market, held in the unimaginatively named Tuesday Market Pl, while the others are conducted in front of St Margaret's Church.

Information

Banks and ATMs can be found around Tuesday Market Pl.

Post office (☎ 692185; Baxter's Plain)

Tourist office (☎ 763044; kings-lynn.tic@west-norfolk.gov.uk; ⊗ 10am-5pm Mon-Sat, noon-5pm Sun Apr-Sep, 10.30am-3.30pm Mon-Sat, noon-3pm Sun Oct-Mar) In the Custom House (Purfleet Quay). It organises guided walks on historic Lynn (adult/concession/child £3/2.50/1, Apr-Oct, duration 1½-2 hr).

Sights

Oddities worth seeking out at grand **St Margaret's Church** include two extraordinarily elaborate Flemish brasses etched with vivid details of a peacock feast, strange dragon-like beasts and a mythical wild man. Outside by the west door there are also flood-level marks – 1976 was the highest, but the 1953 flood claimed more lives. Also remarkable is the 17th-century moon dial, which tells the tide, not the time and sports a cute dragon-head pointer and man-in-the-moon face.

Another important historical landmark to tick off is the nearby 15th-century **St Margaret's House**, once the warehouse or 'steelyard' of the

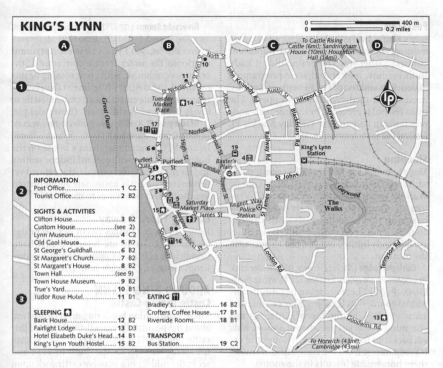

KING'S LYNN

0 ____ 400 m
0 ____ 0.2 miles

To Castle Rising
Castle (6mi); Sandringham
House (10mi); Houghton
Hall (14mi)

INFORMATION
Post Office.............................1 C2
Tourist Office..........................2 B2

SIGHTS & ACTIVITIES
Clifton House..........................3 B2
Custom House.....................(see 2)
Lynn Museum..........................4 C2
Old Gaol House.......................5 R7
St George's Guildhall...............6 B2
St Margaret's Church...............7 B2
St Margaret's House................8 B2
Town Hall............................(see 9)
Town House Museum...............9 B2
True's Yard............................10 B1
Tudor Rose Hotel...................11 B1

SLEEPING
Bank House..........................12 B2
Fairlight Lodge......................13 D3
Hotel Elizabeth Duke's Head....14 B1
King's Lynn Youth Hostel.........15 B2

EATING
Bradley's..............................16 B2
Crofters Coffee House.............17 B1
Riverside Rooms....................18 B1

TRANSPORT
Bus Station...........................19 C2

EASTERN ENGLAND

Hanseatic League (the Northern European merchants' group). Across Queen St is the chequer-boarded flint-and-brick **town hall**, dating back to 1421.

Next door the petite **Town House Museum** (☎ 773450; 46 Queen St; adult/child £2.80/1.60; ⏰ 10am-5pm Mon-Sat May-Sep, 10am-4pm Mon-Sat Oct-Apr) has exhibits on the town from the Middle Ages up to the 1950s; quirkier exhibits include an outdoor privy and basket made from an unfortunate armadillo.

Just around the corner, you can explore the old cells then gawp at the town's priceless civic treasures in the **Old Gaol House** (☎ 774297; adult/child £2.70/1.95; ⏰ 10am-5pm Mon-Sat Easter-Oct, 10am-4pm Tue-Sat Nov-Easter); its pride and joy is the breathtaking 650-year-old King John Cup, exquisitely decorated with scenes of hunting and hawking.

Sauntering back along Queen St, look for **Clifton House**, with its barley-sugar columns and strange merchant's watchtower. Near the market square is **Purfleet Quay**, in its heyday the principal harbour. The odd boxy building with the lantern tower is the 17th-century **Custom House**, which houses the tourist office. Outside is a statue of **Captain George Vancouver**

(1757–98), a local boy who charted 5000 miles of the northwest coast of the Americas; his family worked in the Custom House.

A short hop north again is the biggest 15th-century guildhall in England. **St George's Guildhall** has been variously incarnated as a warehouse, courthouse and armoury (during the Civil War), and now contains art galleries, a theatre and eateries. Then topping King St is the roomy **Tuesday Market Pl**, flanked by handsome old buildings and still host to weekly markets.

On St Nicholas St is the **Tudor Rose Hotel**, a late-15th-century house with its original main door. North of here, on the corner of St Ann's St, is **True's Yard**, where the two remaining cottages of the 19th-century fishing community that used to be here have been restored and now house a **museum** (☎ 770479; www.truesyard .co.uk; North St; adult/child £2.50/1; ⏰ 10am-4pm Tue-Sat) detailing the life of a shellfish fisherman around 1850.

The newly revamped **Lynn Museum** (☎ 775001; Market St) is set to fully reopen in 2007, and to display the famous Bronze Age timber circle dubbed 'Seahenge'.

Festivals

July's **King's Lynn Festival** (☎ 767557; www.kingslynn festival.org.uk) is East Anglia's most important cultural gathering. The brainchild of Lady Ruth Fermoy, it offers a diverse programme of concerts and recitals of all kinds of 'serious' music, from medieval ballads to opera. The main festival is preceded by the free rock-and-pop festie in and around Tuesday Market Pl, **Festival Too** (www.festivaltoo.co.uk).

Sleeping

King's Lynn YHA (☎ 0870 770 5902; kingslynn@yha.org .uk; Thoresby College, College Lane; dm £11.95; ☽ Easter-Oct by advance booking & varied times rest of year; ☒) Visitors are warned to watch their heads on low beams in this beautiful early 16th-century courtyard hostel on the quayside. Its facilities are relatively limited but you can't argue with the location.

Fairlight Lodge (☎ 762234; www.fairlightlodge.co.uk; 79 Goodwins Rd; s/d without bathroom £27/43, with bathroom £32/49; P ☒) There are seven beautifully furnished country-style rooms, four en suite and some overlooking the pretty garden, at this charming Victorian guesthouse a short walk via parkland from the centre. Thoughtful extras separate it from the competition, among them homemade biscuits in the rooms.

ourpick **Bank House** (☎ 660492; www.thebankhouse .co.uk; Kings Staithe Sq; d from £75; P ☒) This outstanding B&B has ticks in all the right boxes: history, location, atmosphere, comfort and welcome. On the waterfront near the tourist office, it's an 18th-century former bank and is now an elegantly furnished townhouse with five hotel-standard rooms, mixing original features and modern furnishings.

Hotel Elizabeth Duke's Head (☎ 0870 116 2720; www.elizabethhotels.co.uk; Tuesday Market Pl; s/d from £80/90; P ☒) A fine old salmon-pink Georgian institution, the Duke's Head lords it up over the Tuesday Market Pl. It has classy parlour sitting rooms and six dozen busily decorated rooms that your granny would approve of.

Eating

Crofters Coffee House (☎ 773134; 27 King St; snacks £3.75-7; ☽ 9.30am-5pm Mon-Sat) This long brick-vaulted undercroft, once used as a civil-war gunpowder store and now a low-lit café, scores top marks for atmosphere and serves light lunches, sandwiches, soups, salads, hot drinks and cakes. It's in the guildhall arts centre.

Riverside Rooms (☎ 773134; www.riversiderestaurant .com; King St; lunch £6.95-13.95, dinner £8.95-18; ☽ lunch & dinner Mon-Sat; ☒) Lynn's classiest restaurant overlooks the water from a converted 15th-century warehouse, with crisscrossing beams overhead and elegant white-linen tables below. It serves upscale cuisine from crab omelette to lovely beef-and-Boddingtons (bitter ale) pie.

Bradley's (☎ 819888; www.bradleysbytheriver.co.uk; 10 South Quay; 3-course lunch £14.95; ☽ lunch & dinner) In an old Georgian merchant's house on the historic quayside with elegant indoor seating and river-facing tables outside, this refined yet relaxed restaurant is passionate about matching the perfect fine wines to its dishes.

Getting There & Away

King's Lynn is 43 miles north of Cambridge on the A10. There are hourly trains from Cambridge (£9.30, 48 minutes) and London Kings Cross (£25.50, 1¾ hours).

AROUND KING'S LYNN
Castle Rising Castle

There's something bordering on ecclesiastical about the beautifully embellished keep of this **castle** (EH; ☎ 631330; adult/child £3.85/2.20; ☽ 10am-6pm Apr-Oct, 10am-4pm Nov-Mar), built in 1138 and set in the middle of a massive earthwork upon which pheasants scurry about like guards. So extravagant is the stonework that it's no surprise to learn that it shares stonemasons with some of Eastern England's finest cathedrals. It was once the home of Queen Isabella, who (allegedly) arranged the gruesome murder of her husband, Edward II.

It's well worth the trip 4 miles south of King's Lynn. Bus 41 runs here (13 minutes) hourly from King's Lynn bus station.

Sandringham House

Royalists and those bemused by the English sovereigns will have plenty to mull over at this, the Queen's country **estate** (☎ 612908; www.sandringhamestate.co.uk; adult/child £8/5, gardens & museum only £5.50/3.50; ☽ 11am-4.45pm mid-Apr–Oct unless royal family is in residence) set in 25 hectares of landscaped gardens and lakes, and open to the hoi polloi when the court is not at home.

Queen Victoria bought the estate in 1862 for her son, the Prince of Wales (later Edward VII), but he promptly had it overhauled in the style later named Edwardian. Half of the surrounding 8000 hectares is leased to farm tenants (a royal living doesn't pay for itself, you know), while the rest is managed by the Crown Estate as forestry.

Visitors can shuffle around the house's ground floor rooms, regularly used by the royal family, then head out to the old stables, which house a flag-waving **museum** filled with diverse royal memorabilia. The vintage royal car collection is simply superb. It includes the very first royal motor from 1900, darling electrical toy cars driven by various princes when they were but knee high and the buggy in which the recently deceased Queen Mother (who had a famously soft spot for the horses) would bounce around race tracks in. For another oddity, look for the pet cemetery just outside the museum.

There are guided tours of the gardens on Friday and Saturday at 11am and 2pm. The **shop** is also worthy of a visit if only to browse the organic goodies produced on the sprawling estate, from bramble or walnut liqueurs to rare-breed pork bangers.

First Eastern Counties bus 411 or Coastliner run here from King's Lynn bus station (22 minutes), 10 miles to the southwest.

Houghton Hall

Built for Britain's first de facto Prime Minister Sir Robert Walpole in 1730, pompous Palladian-style **Houghton Hall** (☎ 01485-528569; www .houghtonhall.com; adult/child £7/3; ⊙ 1.30-5pm Wed, Thu & Sun Easter-Sep) is worth seeing for the ornate staterooms alone; you could build another half-dozen houses with the amount of swirling decorative plasterwork here. Six hundred deer roam the surrounding parkland and there's an obsessive model soldiers exhibit with over 20,000 of the little guys.

It's 14 miles northeast of King's Lynn but beyond the reach of buses; if you're without your own wheels catch a cab from King's Lynn for about £12. Try **Ken's Taxis** (☎ 01553-766166).

LINCOLNSHIRE

A steady stream of movie makers searching for ready-made period sets find their quarry in the stunning stately homes and time-capsule towns of rural Lincolnshire. This sparsely populated corner of Eastern England has a reputation of being flat, plain and proper, although on closer inspection it's re-markably varied and uncommonly friendly.

County capital, Lincoln, is the perfect place to start, with a stunning Gothic cathedral, Tudor streetscapes and a dramatic hilltop location.

The gently rippling hills of the Lincolnshire Wolds smooth down to eastern marshlands and sandy coast, and the dyke-scored Lincolnshire Fens flat-iron the southeast. While flamboyant medieval wool-wealth churches, red-roofed stone houses and windmills grace many towns, here too you'll find arms-in-the-air beach resort Skegness and rich wildlife reserves where the loudest din is birdsong.

Information

South West Lincs (www.southwestlincs.com)
Visit Lincolnshire (www.visitlincolnshire.com)
Visit the Fens (www.visitthefens.co.uk)

Activities

To follow in the footsteps of history, the 140-mile **Viking Way** trails from the Humber Bridge through the Lincolnshire Wolds to Oakham in Leicestershire.

It can be more rewarding to explore by bike, however. Wheels can be hired in Lincoln, and leaflets on county cycle trails are available at tourist offices.

Getting There & Away

Other than a speedy rail link between Grantham and London, Lincolnshire isn't the easiest county to get to and around. You're better off on the buses to reach Stamford and Lincoln, and don't be surprised if you have to change services en route.

Getting Around

For regional travel information, contact **Traveline** (☎ 0870 608 2608; www.travelineeastmidlands.org.uk) or consult the travel pages of the **Lincolnshire County Council** (www.lincolnshire.gov.uk) website. Useful bus operators include **Lincs Interconnect** (☎ 0845 234 3344; www.lincsinterconnect.com) and **Lincolnshire Roadcar** (www.roadcar.co.uk).

LINCOLN

☎ 01522 / pop 85,595
An undervisited delight, Lincoln's tightly knotted core of cobbled streets and majestic medieval architecture is enough to leave visitors breathless, albeit as much for its thigh-pumping slopes as the superb stonework and timber-framed treasures to be found there. Uptown Lincoln is crowned by an extraordinary hill-topping cathedral, an unusual

Norman castle and compact Tudor streets, although the town then tumbles down the hillside losing charm and picking up modern pace as it goes. At the hill's base, the university breathes life into a waterfront quarter where bars are positioned to watch boats come and go. While there's little to keep you for a longer stay, Lincoln has a welcoming aura and enough cultural clout in its centre to keep you very happy for a day or two at a stretch.

History

With a hill that affords views for miles around and a river for swift sea access, it's hardly surprising that Lincoln's defensive location has been exploited by invading forces for the last 2000 years. The Romans set up camp soon after arriving in Britain and in the 11th century the Normans speedily constructed a castle after their invasion. The city yo-yoed between Royalist and Parliamentarian forces during the Civil War, and the warfare theme continued into the 20th century, when Lincoln's heavy engineering industry spawned the world's first tank, which saw action in WWI.

Orientation

The cathedral stands imperiously on top of the hill in the old city, with the castle and other attractions clustered nearby. Three-quarters of a mile downhill is the new town, and the bus and train stations. Joining the two is the appositely named Steep Hill, and believe us, they're not kidding. Even locals stop to catch their breath.

Information

Several banks and ATMs sit on the High St. Check www.lincolntoday.co.uk and www .lincoln.gov.uk for events listings.

Abbey Washeteria (☎ 530272; 197 Monks Rd; per load £3; ☺ 9am-6pm Mon-Sat, 9am-4pm Sun) Self-service laundrette.

County hospital (☎ 512512; off Greetwell Rd)

Post office (☎ 526031; 90 Bailgate)

Sun Internet Café (36 Portland St; ☺ 11am-7pm Mon-Sat)

Tourist office (tourism@lincoln.gov.uk; www.visit lincolnshire.com) Main branch (☎ 873213; 9 Castle Hill; ☺ 9.30am-6pm Mon-Sat & 10.30am-4.30pm Sun Jul-Sep, 9.30am-5.30pm Mon-Thu Oct-Jun); Cornhill branch (☎ 873256; 21 the Cornhill; ☺ 9.30am-5.30pm Mon-Sat, 11am-3pm Sun Jul-Sep, 9.30am-5pm Mon-Sat Oct-Jun)

Sights

The tourist office sells the Lincoln Time Travel Pass, which gives access to several heritage sites, including the castle, cathedral and Bishop's Palace for single/family £9.99/20 and lasts three/seven days.

LINCOLN CATHEDRAL

All kinds of marvels and mischief can be found in the county's top attraction, **Lincoln cathedral** (☎ 544544; www.lincolncathedral.com; adult/under 16yr £4/1; ☺ 7.15am-8pm Mon-Sat, 7.15am-6pm Sun Jun-Aug, 7.15am-6pm Mon-Sat, 7.15am-5pm Sun Sep-May). This soaring edifice has three great towers that dominate the city, one of which is the third highest in England at 81m, but it's claimed that until a storm in 1547 its spire was a jaw-dropping 160m high, topping even the great pyramids of Giza.

An eye-stretching façade carved with gargoyles, kings, dragons and hunters leers over the Great West Door. There are some fabulous but grisly friezes being steadily restored by stonemasons here, including maniacal devils jabbing sinners into the jaws of hell. On closer inspection you'll spot that the façade is divided into two eras; the lower of which is from the Norman cathedral toppled in an earthquake in 1185, and the rest dates to the building's 12th- and 13th-century reconstruction by Bishop Hugh of Avalon (St Hugh). The saint himself tops a pinnacle on one side of the West Front, and his counterpart on the other side is a swineherd who devoted his meagre lifesavings to the cathedral's reconstruction.

Inside the lofty nave, there's a chunky black-marble font from the 11th century, ringed with fearsome mythological beasts. Two awesome stained-glass rose windows face each other at either end of the transepts. The unique Dean's Eye still contains glass from the 13th century, while the 14th-century Bishop's Eye has some truly exquisite carved stone-leaf tracery.

Up in the central tower, the veteran Victorian bell Great Tom still swings its ponderous 2m, 270kg bulk to sound the hours. Just beyond the tower, the elaborate choir screen is studded with grotesque characters, including a stonemason sticking out his tongue just to the left of the door.

St Hugh's Choir itself is topped by some quirky vaulting dubbed the 'crazy vault' for its odd angles, while the superbly carved and canopied stalls below are a classic example

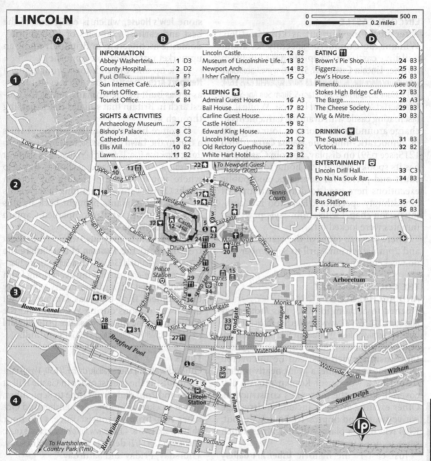

LINCOLN

INFORMATION	Lincoln Castle................12 B2	**EATING** 🍴
Abbey Washerteria..........1 D3	Museum of Lincolnshire Life..13 B2	Brown's Pie Shop..............24 B3
County Hospital..............2 D2	Newport Arch................14 B2	Figgerz.....................25 B3
Post Office..................3 B2	Usher Gallery................15 C3	Jew's House.................26 B3
Sun Internet Café............4 B4		Pimento.....................(see 30)
Tourist Office................5 B2	**SLEEPING** 🛏	Stokes High Bridge Café.......27 B3
Tourist Office................6 B4	Admiral Guest House..........16 A3	The Barge...................28 A3
	Bail House..................17 B3	The Cheese Society...........29 B3
SIGHTS & ACTIVITIES	Carline Guest House..........18 A2	Wig & Mitre.................30 B3
Archaeology Museum..........7 C3	Castle Hotel.................19 B2	
Bishop's Palace..............8 C3	Edward King House...........20 C3	**DRINKING** 🍷
Cathedral....................9 C2	Lincoln Hotel................21 C2	The Square Sail..............31 B3
Ellis Mill...................10 B2	Old Rectory Guesthouse.......22 B2	Victoria.....................32 B2
Lawn.......................11 B2	White Hart Hotel............23 B2	
		ENTERTAINMENT 🎭
		Lincoln Drill Hall............33 C3
		Po Na Na Souk Bar...........34 B3
		TRANSPORT
		Bus Station.................35 C4
		F & J Cycles................36 B3

of medieval craftsmanship. Just beyond this, the Angel Choir is graced by 28 angels carved high up the walls. It was built as a shrine to St Hugh but modern pilgrims are mostly preoccupied with hunting for the famous Lincoln Imp, a lovably roguish little horned character that is now the city's emblem. Various fun legends surround the imp, but we like the one that the mischievous creature was caught chatting up one of the carved angels and was promptly turned to stone.

One last stop before leaving, take a peek at the cathedral's round Chapterhouse, where the climax of *The Da Vinci Code* film was shot in 2005.

There are one-hour tours at least twice a day plus less frequent tours of the tower.

Evensong takes place daily except Wednesday at 5.15pm (3.45pm on Sunday), and Eucharist is sung at 9.30am on Sunday.

BISHOPS' PALACE

Beside the cathedral are the ravaged but still imposing ruins of the 12th-century **Bishops' Palace** (EH; ☎ 527468; adult/child £3.70/1.90; ☾ 10am-6pm daily Jul-Aug, 10am-5pm Apr-Jun & Sep-Oct, 10am-4pm Thu-Mon Nov-Mar), which was gutted by parliamentary forces during the Civil War. In its day it was the power base of medieval England's largest diocese, and highlights of scrambling around its remaining walls include a barrel-vaulted undercroft and walled terrace garden with wonderful panoramas of the town below.

EASTERN ENGLAND

LINCOLN CASTLE

After installing himself as king in 1066, William the Conqueror speedily set about building castles to keep his new kingdom in line. **Lincoln Castle** (☎ 511068; www.lincolnshire .gov.uk/lincolncastle; adult/child £3.80/2.50, event days £6/4; 9.30am-5.30pm Mon-Sat, 11am-5.30pm Sun Apr-Sep, to 4pm daily Oct-Mar) was one of his first. While it's a fascinating castle with dramatic battlements to charge around and one of only four originals of democratic-milestone **Magna Carta** (dated 1215; see p39) on display, Lincoln Castle also has its spooky side. It was home to the city's court and prison for centuries, and public executions here used to draw thousands of bloodthirsty spectators. Here too is a chilling prison chapel with coffin-style pews that inmates were locked into.

There are free tours of the castle at 11am and 2pm daily from April to September and on weekends in winter.

THE COLLECTION: ART AND ARCHAEOLOGY

Opened to acclaim in 2005, this **Archaeology Museum** (☎ 550990; www.thecollection.lincoln.museum; Danes Tce; admission free; 10am-5pm) aims to inspire budding Indiana Joneses, underlining how Lincolnshire's rich past can be uncovered by anyone at any time, a point neatly underscored by a wonderful Roman mosaic discovered during the museum's construction. Other exciting artefacts include an Iron Age votive sword and impressive 7m log dugout. Kids will have a blast with the games, touch screens, dress up and more.

Just east is the historic **Usher Art Gallery** (☎ 527980; Lindum Rd; admission free; 10am-5pm Tue-Sat, 1-5pm Sun), which now belongs to the same complex but sits separately in a grand mansion amid parkland. It dwells on the paintings and drawings of Peter de Wint (1784–1849) but also has works by JMW Turner, LS Lowry and others. The museum is also temporary home to bits and bobs belonging to Lincolnshire-born poet Alfred Lord Tennyson (1809–92), but you'll need to be accompanied to a back room to see them.

OTHER SIGHTS

The whole length of **Steep Hill** is a delight to explore (at least until the climb back up), crowded with black-and-white Tudor beauties and curious antiquarian bookshops. Of particular note, however, is the Romanesque stone **Jew's House**, which is easily one of the best and earliest examples of 12th-century domestic architecture in Britain. It's now an upmarket restaurant (see opposite).

Back up and through town, rough-edged **Newport Arch** (Bailgate) dates back even further as it was built by the Romans, and is the oldest arch in Britain that still has traffic passing through it.

If you're barmy about botany don't miss a trip to the **Lawn** (☎ 568080; www.thelawninlincoln .co.uk; admission free; Union Rd; 10am-5pm; shorter hr Nov-Feb), a former lunatic asylum – but also where you'll find the steamy Sir Joseph Banks Conservatory, containing descendants of some of the plants brought back by this Lincoln explorer who accompanied Captain Cook to Australia.

History buffs may also make the short trek north to the **Museum of Lincolnshire Life** (☎ 528448; adult/child £3/2; 10am-5pm May-Oct, 10am-5pm Mon-Sat Nov-Apr), displaying everything from a reconstructed Edwardian nursery to an early tank named 'flirt' that was famous for all the wrong reasons during WWI. Round the corner from the museum is cute little **Ellis Mill** (☎ 528448; Mill Rd; adult/child £1/0.50) windmill.

Tours

Guided **walking tours** (adult/child £3/1.50, 1½ hr) run from outside the tourist office in Castle Hill at 11am and 2pm daily from June to September, and at weekends in June, September and October. Also from the tourist office, a 1¼-hour **ghost walk** (☎ 874056; www.lincolnhistorywalks.co.uk; adult/under 12yr £4/2) departs at 7pm Wednesday, Thursday, Friday and Saturday.

Horse-drawn tours (£25) also run around the city from Castle Hill in summer. Down below the centre on Brayford Wharf several boats offer one-hour summer **boat trips** (adult/child £5/3; 10.30am-4pm) along Fossdyke Canal and the River Witham.

Sleeping

BUDGET

Hartsholme Country Park (☎ 873578; hartsholmecp@ lincoln.gov.uk; Skellingthorpe Rd; tent sites £6-14; Mar-Oct) A stand-out camping ground next to a sprawling nature reserve, filled lovely lakes, woods and meadows. It's 3 miles southwest of the train station. Take the regular daytime SB6 or evening 66A bus towards Birchwood Estate from Lincoln bus station; alight at Swanpool (15 minutes).

Old Rectory Guesthouse (☎ 514774; 19 Newport; s/d from £25/46; P ☒) This attractive red-brick Edwardian building, which while well-kept and charmingly run by its motherly host, clearly hasn't been updated much since the last century. But far from minding, you'll find that adds to the homely character.

Admiral Guest House (☎ 544467; nicola.major1@ntlworld.com; 16-18 Nelson St; s/d £25/40, f £50-60; P) Things are kept simple at this nautically themed B&B just off Carholme Rd, one of several in the area. The straightforward rooms are all en suite and smokers can puff away in their rooms.

MIDRANGE

Edward King House (☎ 528778; www.ekhs.org.uk; The Old Palace, Minster Yard; per person £30; P ☒) This one's different. It's a Christian-run pilgrim's house in the former home to Bishops of Lincoln, alongside the historic palace ruins. Accommodation is on the basic, budget side with no en suite or double beds but it's unusually tranquil, and the location makes it unique. Always call ahead.

Carline Guest House (☎ 530422; www.carlineguesthouse.co.uk; 1-3 Carline Rd; s/d £35/50; P ☒) Occupying a refined Edwardian house, this 12-room place has rather plushly decorated en suite rooms for such a modestly priced guesthouse, and each is quite different in character.

Newport Guest House (☎ 528590; www.newportguesthouse.co.uk; 26-28 Newport; s/d/f £35/52/70; P ☒) Brightly coloured, fresh-feeling rooms with contemporary style and plenty of space, plus a filling Lincolnshire breakfast are the winning qualities of this cheerful and efficiently run guesthouse just outside the city's historic core.

ourpick Bail House (☎ 520883; www.bailhouse.co.uk; 34 Bailgate; s/d from £64.50/79, d superior £139-165; P ☒ ☲ ☐ wi-fi only) Stone walls, worn flagstones, Mediterranean-style gardens and one room with an extraordinary medieval timber-vaulted ceiling are only a few of the charms of this lovingly restored townhouse in central Lincoln. There's even a heated outdoor swimming pool for fair-weather days.

Castle Hotel (☎ 538801; www.castlehotel.net; Westgate; s/d from £70/90; P ☒) A hefty red-brick former school from the Victorian era, this privately owned hotel looks up towards the castle battlements. It has personable and attentive staff, a mixed bunch of rooms with sober if fussy furnishings and good facilities.

TOP END

White Hart Hotel (☎ 526222; www.whitehart-lincoln.co.uk; Bailgate; s/d £75/100; P ☒ ☐ wi-fi only) You can't get more central or venerable than Lincoln's grand dame of hotels, neatly sandwiched between castle and cathedral, and with a history of hostelry here dating back 600 years. It has four dozen luxurious country-casual rooms, a few with partial views of the cathedral façade.

Lincoln Hotel (☎ 520348; www.thelincolnhotel.com; Eastgate; d £80-150; P ☒ ☲ ☐ wi-fi only) This pristine retro-chic hotel shrugs off its blockish exterior and lays on sleek modern rooms with funky lights in unexpected places, stars on the doors, clean lines and bright colours. In a disorientating juxtaposition, it lies opposite the ancient cathedral's backside, of which front-facing rooms have simply unbeatable views.

Eating

Stokes High Bridge Café (☎ 513825; 207 High St; ☯ 9am-5pm Mon-Sat) This delightfully precarious-looking 16th-century half-timbered building on the bridge over the River Witham houses a traditional teashop, and is also the perfect place to people-gaze on the busy shopping street below. Lunches are available.

Pimento (☎ 544880; 27 Steep Hill; mains £4-7; ☯ 10am-5pm) This split-level parlour café is a must for tea and coffee connoisseurs and also sells good-value dishes using local ingredients and delicious Lincolnshire plum bread. The front room has a big roasting machine, making it the warmest spot to be. And with 40 exotic brews the drinks menu resembles a cocktail list. Haiti voodoo-comet coffee anyone?

Brown's Pie Shop (☎ 527330; 33 Steep Hill; pies £8-12; ☯ lunch & dinner) Rustic-chic in a nutshell, this popular pie shop serves Lincolnshire's speciality pies in lovely brick-vaulted cellars with candle-lit tables and bare-wood floors. The local wild-rabbit pie is terrific and the stout pie popular.

Wig & Mitre (☎ 535190; www.wigandmitre.com; 30 Steep Hill; mains £11-20; ☯ 8am-midnight) Civilised pub-restaurant the Wig has been steadily upgrading its menu for three decades and now considers itself an upscale eatery despite retaining the mellow cosiness of an old-world watering hole. No music will disturb your meal here, and the candle-lit evening meals are good for romantic liaisons.

our pick Jew's House (☎ 524851; Steep Hill; set lunch/dinner £12/27; ⏲ lunch & dinner Tue-Sun) Pass through the ancient round-arched doorway of this 12th-century stone house and you'll immediately know you're in for a treat. This ancient house, an attraction in its own right, is flush with antiques and oil paintings, and its award-winning Anglo-French cuisine will not disappoint. Dress smart and book ahead.

Some more options:

Cheese Society (☎ 511003; 1 St Martins Lane; ⏲ 10am-4.30pm Mon-Sat) Café-deli that sends aficionados of fermented foodstuffs straight to the moon.

Barge (☎ 511448; Brayford Wharf; mains £7-15; ⏲ 11am-11pm) Salty-dog floating seafood restaurant.

Figgerz (☎ 576277; 1 Newland; mains takeaway/eat-in £3/4.50; ⏲ 8am-3pm Mon-Sat) Local organic fare for sensible prices.

Drinking

Victoria (☎ 536048; 6 Union Rd) A serious beer-drinker's pub with a pleasant patio looking up at the castle's western walls, Victoria has a huge selection of guest brews, cask ales, thick stouts and superb ciders and preserves a mellow historic ambience undisturbed by sports or flashy lights. The pub runs two beer festivals a year.

Square Sail (☎ 559920; Brayford Wharf; ⏲ noon-1am Mon-Sat, to 10.30pm Sun) Student-friendly clubs, pubs and bars cluster along the regenerated Brayford Wharf beside the university, and while none are rich in character, there's an agreeable buzz that spills onto the waterside walk outside. It's the place to be on summer evenings.

Entertainment

Po Na Na Souk Bar (☎ 525828; 280-281 High St; ⏲ 10pm-3am Mon-Sat) Every night is different at this Moroccan-themed chain club, which alternately rocks to the sounds of indie, rock, R&B and house music, with some high-profile international guest DJs to get the party started. It has some kaleidoscopic cocktails, and there are hookah pipes in the chill-out room.

Lincoln Drill Hall (☎ 873894; www.lincolndrillhall .com; Free School Lane) The city's premier venue for music, theatre and comedy.

Getting There & Away

Lincoln is 142 miles from London, 94 miles from Cambridge and 81 miles from York.

National Express runs a direct service between Lincoln and London (£21, 4¾ hours)

daily. Buses also run daily from Lincoln to Birmingham (£13, three hours).

Getting to and from Lincoln usually involves changing trains. There are hourly links to Boston (£8.40, 1¼ hours) and Skegness (£11.50, two hours); change at Sleaford. There are also hourly trains to Cambridge (£24.50, 2½ hours); change at Peterborough or Ely. Links to Grantham (£7.50, 1½ hours) run twice hourly.

Getting Around
BICYCLE

F&J Cycles (☎ 545311; 41 Hungate; ⏲ 9am-5.30pm Mon-Sat) rents a few secondhand bikes for £6 to £8 per day and up to £40 per week.

BUS

Regular buses link the lower town bus and train stations with the uptown cathedral area. To avoid the climb up Steep Hill, a 'Walk and Ride' electric bus also runs every 20 minutes during the day from outside the House of Fraser store on High St to Castle Sq (90p, five minutes).

GRANTHAM
☎ 01476 / pop 34,592

Those that recall the colourful 12-year reign of Britain's first female prime minister, Margaret Thatcher, will find a fine model of her vision for Britain in the pleasing red-brick town of her birth. Baroness Thatcher first came into the world above her father's grocery shop at 2 North Pde, now a chiropractor's clinic with a modest plaque to signify its former inhabitant. Sir Isaac Newton was also born and raised in the vicinity, and his statue stands erect in front of the guildhall; as yet conspicuously unaccompanied by a statue of Maggie.

The **tourist office** (☎ 406166; granthamtic@south kesteven.gov.uk; St Peter's Hill; ⏲ 9.30am-4.30pm Mon-Fri, 9.30am-1pm Sat) is in the guildhall complex.

Until a commemorative statue is erected, the Iron Lady must content herself with her latex puppet from the hit 1980s political satire *Spitting Image* (see the boxed text Puppet Politicians, opposite) in the town's **museum** (☎ 568783; St Peter's Hill; admission free; ⏲ 10am-5pm Mon-Sat). Here too is one of her famous handbags and spangled gowns, as well as displays on Sir Isaac Newton and another of Grantham's trailblazing women, Edith Smith, who became Britain's first policewoman in 1914.

PUPPET POLITICIANS

England's incisive political satire is notorious for being almost as vicious as its tabloid press, and many would point the finger at a controversial but iconic series that ran here from 1984 to 1996 as being where it all got a little bit nasty. *Spitting Image* was a satirical puppet show that crudely caricatured public figures, who were voiced by a modern day who's who of British impressionists many of whom went on to lampoon politicians in their own shows. At its height *Spitting Image* was deemed so subversive that it was banned from showing in the run up to a general election. And while politicians were hammered by the show, they recognised that to be on it was to be somebody, so many more secretly craved their own puppet persona.

The most recognisable and enduring of all its latex stars was then British Prime Minister Margaret Thatcher, who was portrayed as a tyrannical man-woman who wore suits and used urinals. Her latex likeness now leers from behind glass in Grantham's museum while the town of her birth still awaits a genuine statue of its Iron Lady.

The part 13th- part 16th-century parish church of **St Wulfram's** (9am-4pm Apr-Sep, 9am-12.30pm Oct-Mar) is easily tracked down thanks to its needle-sharp 85m spire. It has an interesting crypt chapel and hidden up a steep stairwell is a rare 16th-century chained library where a young Isaac Newton once pored over his studies.

One of several favoured sets for ruffle-and-lace English period dramas in the region, the Restoration country-mansion **Belton House** (NT; ☎ 566116; A607; adult/child under 16yr £8/4.50, grounds only £6/3.50; 12.30-5pm Wed-Sun Apr-Oct) sits sedately amid a 400-hectare park 3 miles northeast of Grantham. Built in 1688 for Sir John Brownlow, it shelters some astonishingly ornate woodcarvings attributed to the master Dutch carver Grinling Gibbons. In the beautiful gardens is a sundial made famous in Helen Cresswell's children's classic *Moondial*. Bus 609 (15 minutes) runs here from near Grantham's train station.

Sleeping & Eating

Red House (☎ 579869; www.red-house.com; 74 North Pde; s/d £27/55; P X) This handsome Georgian townhouse near Maggie's birthplace has large, spick-and-span rooms, three with en suite, three without. The welcome is very friendly, beauty treatments are available and some rooms even boast a fridge and microwave.

Angel & Royal Hotel (☎ 565816; www.angelandroyal .co.uk; High St; s/d from £80/100; P X) This veteran coaching inn claims to be England's oldest, with no less than seven kings of England purportedly having stayed here since 1200. Its 29 rooms are each individually decorated, beds occupied by a teddy bear, quaint floral patterns and copious olde-Englishe charm. The

beautiful period-styled King's Dining Room is open for fine dining at weekends.

Beehive (☎ 404554; Castlegate) This famous old pub is best known not for its drinks or ambiance but for its sign – a real beehive full of live South African bees! Buzzing around since 1830, it's one of the oldest bee populations in the world. Cheap lunches and drinks are available.

Getting There & Away

Grantham is 25 miles south of Lincoln. Interconnect bus 1 runs hourly between the two Monday to Saturday and four times on Sunday (one hour 10 minutes). Bus K17 (three daily Monday to Saturday) runs to Stamford (1½ hours), as does National Express (£5.70, 30 minutes).

You'll need to change at Newark to get to Lincoln by train (£7.50, 1½ hours, two per hour). Direct trains run from London King's Cross to Grantham (£25, 1¼ hours) hourly throughout the day.

STAMFORD

☎ 01780 / pop 19,525

Come rain or shine, this elegant town seems bathed in a warm glow thanks to the beautiful honey-coloured Lincolnshire limestone with which it's built. Sloping gently up from the River Welland and a sprawling waterside park, its winding streets overflow with fine medieval and Georgian buildings. And if you feel as though you're walking through a period drama, there's a reason: Stamford has been used as a set for more drama productions than you can shake a clapperboard at.

The **tourist office** (☎ 755611; stamfordtic@south kesteven.gov.uk; 27 St Mary's St; 9.30am-5pm Mon-Sat

EASTERN ENGLAND

year-round, & 10am-4pm Sun Apr-Oct) is in the Stamford Arts Centre, and helps with accommodation. They can also arrange guided town walks (£3.50) and chauffeured punt trips.

The **Stamford Museum** (☎ 766317; Broad St; admission free; ☉ 10am-5pm Mon-Sat year-round, & 1-4pm Sun Apr-Sep) has a muddle of displays on the town's history, including models of circus-performing midget Charles Stratton (aka Tom Thumb) and local heavyweight Daniel Lambert (see the boxed text A Tale of Little & Large, opposite).

Sleeping & Eating

Stamford Lodge (☎ 482932; www.stamfordlodge.co.uk; 66 Scotgate; s/d £45/65) This former bakehouse sits in a lovely row of 18th-century Georgian buildings and has exposed stone walls and sloping ceilings. Rooms are sprucely decorated with modern furnishings and facilities and small en suites. The friendly hostess is keen to help out, and breakfasts are excellent. There's pay-and-display parking across the road.

our pick **George** (☎ 750750; www.georgehotelofstamford.com; 71 St Martin's St; s/d from £78/115, superior d £185; P ⊠ ⬜) Recognised by a gallows sign across the road, welcoming travellers but warning of highwaymen, this wonderful riverside hotel likes to call itself 'England's greatest coaching inn', and with some justification. Parts of it date back a thousand years and its long history is reflected in its 47 luxurious rooms, each of which has its own unique character and flair, décor and price tag. The oak-panelled restaurant serves classy British and international cuisine.

Meadows (☎ 762739; www.themeadowsrestaurant.co.uk; 1-2 Castle Pl; mains £8-14; ☉ lunch & dinner Tue-Sun) This lovely semiformal restaurant in a 17th-century stone building serves traditional English dishes from sea bass to good ol' Lincolnshire sausages. It has a terrace at the back overlooking the meadows.

Other recommendations:

Dolphin Guest House (☎ 757515; mik@mikdolphin.demon.co.uk; 12 East St; r £25-60; P ⊠) Bland modernish rooms but central.

No86 Casterton Road (☎ 754734; 86 Casterton Rd; s/d £25/50; P ⊠) Three-bedroom bungalow, a 10-minute walk from town.

Getting There & Away

Stamford is 46 miles from Lincoln and 21 miles south of Grantham.

National Express serves Stamford once daily from London (£12.80, 2¾ hours) via Lincoln (£8.30, 1½ hours). Kimes operates three buses daily Monday to Saturday between Stamford and Grantham (1½ hours). National Express also runs two buses daily (£5.70, 30 minutes). Delaine Buses run to Peterborough (one hour, hourly).

There are hourly trains to Cambridge (£15.80, 1¼ hours) and Ely (£11.80, 55 minutes). Trains to Norwich (£19.60, 2¼ hours) usually involve changing at Ely or Peterborough.

AROUND STAMFORD
Burghley House

This staggeringly ostentatious **Elizabethan palace** (☎ 752451; www.burghley.co.uk; adult/child incl sculpture garden £9/4; ☉ 11am-5pm Sat-Thu Apr-Oct) was built to awe and still does a darn good job of it. Situated just a mile south of Stamford, Burghley (bur-lee) is the home of the Cecil family and was built by Queen Elizabeth's adviser William Cecil. These days it's a regular star of the silver screen, with hit films like *The Da Vinci Code* and *Pride and Prejudice* just some of the productions utilising its showy interior as a dramatic stage.

Its roof bristles with cupolas, pavilions, belvederes and chimneys, and every inch of its 18 magnificent staterooms seems drenched with lavish finery. Hundreds of masterpieces from Gainsborough to Brueghel hang from the walls, while other rooms skip the frames and are splashed with wonderful 17th-century Italian

---

WORTH THE TRIP

Possibly the world's smallest Michelin-starred eatery, **Harry's Place** (☎ 01476-561780; 17 High St, Great Gonerby; mains £32; ☉ lunch & dinner Tue-Sat) squeezes in just 10 people, and fills them up so well that it can be hard to squeeze out again. The restaurant is run personally by its celebrated husband-and-wife owners, and is set in their own Georgian residence giving it the feel of an intimate dinner party. The limited menu is seriously good, with strong French influence and the very best ingredients.

Harry's Place is 2 miles northwest of Grantham. You'll need to book well ahead to get in here, and warn them if you're vegetarian.

A TALE OF LITTLE & LARGE

Stamford guides are fond of telling the story of the unfortunate Daniel Lambert, who was born a healthy baby in 1770, but who soon began to tip the scales at ever more alarming totals. Despite just eating one meal per day, he ballooned to an astounding 336kg and was hailed by contemporaries as 'the most corpulent man of whom authentic record exists'. When the reluctant celebrity died here in 1809 a wall of his house had to be taken down for the coffin to exit, and 20 pallbearers were needed to heave it to the graveyard. Then adding insult to injury, after Lambert's death his suits were displayed in a local pub where the mischievous dwarf Charles Stratton (1838–83), otherwise known as 'General Tom Thumb', would cause hilarity by disappearing up the suit's armholes.

---

murals overflowing with muscles, mammaries and mythology. Most impressive is the Heaven Room, which writhes with floor-to-ceiling gods and goddesses disporting among the columns; on the flip side, there's the nearby stairway to Hell, which depicts Satan as a giant cat-eyed uterus devouring the world. Other highlights include cavernous Tudor kitchens decorated with turtle skulls left over from the master's soup and an exhibit detailing the career of David Cecil, the Lord Burghley who was an Olympic athlete and part-inspiration for the film *Chariots of Fire*.

Meanwhile the landscaped deer park outside is now home to a splendid **sculpture garden** with organic-looking contemporary works sprinkled sympathetically and often humorously throughout the grounds.

The house is a pleasant 15-minute walk through the park from Stamford train station. The internationally famous **Burghley Horse Trials** take place here in early September.

BOSTON

☎ 01205 / pop 35,124

It was from this major medieval port that the Pilgrim Fathers – the first white settlers of the US – began their break for the freedom of the New World in 1607. These religious separatists suffered persecution and imprisonment, yet when word of their success made it back here, a crowd of locals followed them across the Atlantic to found a namesake town in the new colony of Massachusetts. Lying near the mouth of the River Witham, in the bay known as The Wash, the town is now a mere blip on the map in comparison to its US namesake, but it has hung onto much of its medieval appearance, timber-framed Tudor buildings and labyrinthine street grid with two main streets flanking the river and linked by footbridges.

The **tourist office** (☎ 356656; ticboston@boston.gov .uk; Market Pl; ☽ 9am-5pm Mon-Sat year-round) is under the Assembly Rooms on Market Pl.

Sights & Activities

In keeping with the town's high-flying status in medieval times, the early 14th-century **St Botolph's Church** (☎ 362864; church free, tower adult/under 18yr £2.50/1; ☽ 9am-4.30pm Mon-Sat, btwn services Sun) has a showy 88m-high tower, fondly dubbed the Boston Stump for its square tip as its fenland base was not firm enough to support a thin spire. Puff your way up the 365 steps on a clear day and you'll see to Lincoln, 32 miles away. Downstairs there's a 17th-century **pulpit** from which fiery vicar John Cotton delivered five-hour catechisms in the 1630s, and convinced his parishioners to emigrate in the footsteps of the Pilgrim Fathers.

You can see the very cells in which the Pilgrim Fathers were imprisoned in the 14th-century **guildhall** (☎ 365954; South St; adult/child £1.25/free; ☽ 10am-5pm Mon-Sat & 1.30-5pm Sun May-Sep), now a visitors centre with multimedia eulogies on their struggles. The museum will reopen from renovations in mid-2007.

About 800m northeast of Market Pl is the fully functional five-sailed **Maud Foster Windmill** (☎ 352188; adult/child £2.50/1.50; ☽ 11am-5pm Wed-Sun Jul-Aug, Wed, Sat & Sun only Sep-Jun), built in 1819 and the tallest working windmill in the country with no less than seven floors that creak and tremble with its flour-grinding exertions. It's well worth the walk, just don't wear black or you'll come out grey.

Sleeping & Eating

Palethorpe House (☎ 359000; 138 Spilsby Rd; s/d £50/70; [P] [X] [☐]) This delightful vine-covered Victorian villa has just two beautifully refurbished en suite rooms complete with living room, and it's situated a 10-minute walk from Boston's

THE FENS

One of England's most melancholy landscapes, the manmade Fens were once strange and deso-late marshlands that stretched from Cambridge north to The Wash and beyond into Lincolnshire. Amid the wilderness lived isolated pockets of people who survived by fishing and farming scraps of land among a maze of waterways. Though Romans and land-hungry medieval monasteries dabbled with building flood banks to exploit the fertile land, it took the 17th-century arrival of Dutch engineer Sir Cornelius Vermuyden to begin the wholesale draining of the Fens. Not that the scheme proved easy or unopposed – unhappy Fen folk were known to diligently dig the dykes during the day, then sneak back at night when their landlords weren't looking and fill in their hard work! However, with the aid of wind and later steam pumps, the flat, open plains with their rich, black soil were created. Now an eerie windswept but strangely mesmerising landscape, the region has inspired a wealth of literature, including Graham Swift's excellent novel *Waterland*.

As the world's weather pattern changes and the sea level rises, however, the Fens are beginning to disappear underwater again. It's estimated that by the year 2030 up to 400,000 hectares could be lost. To find out more on the past and future of the Fens, visit **Fenscape Discovery Centre** (☎ 761161; www.fenscape.org; A151 at A16; admission free) near Spalding, Lincolnshire, or appreciate its wildlife at **Wicken Fen National Nature Reserve** (☎ 01353-720274; Lode Lane, Wicken; adult/child £4.50/2; ☽ dawn-dusk), 8 miles south of Ely.

centre. It only serves continental breakfasts during the week.

Maud's Tea Rooms (☎ 352188; Maud Foster Windmill, Willoughby Rd; mains £5-8; ☽ 11am-5pm Wed-Sun Jul-Aug, Wed, Sat & Sun only Sep-Jun) A quaint teashop with a difference, Maud's is set in its namesake tower windmill, and serves a wealth of cakes baked the old-fashioned way with organic flour whisked straight from the millstone. It also offers filling lunches that include Lincoln-shire cheeses, local sausages and vegetarian options.

Getting There & Away

Interconnect 5 buses run hourly between Lin-coln and Boston (1½ hours), or you can take the train from Lincoln, changing at Sleaford (£8.40, 1¼ hours).

SKEGNESS
☎ 01754 / pop 16,806

Famous for its saccharine candy-floss fun, vast bucket-and-spade beaches and a seafront parade drowning in greasy fish-and-chip shops, bleeping and flashing penny arcades and kiss-me-quick hats, 'Skeggy' is a classic English seaside resort where many thousands of Britons descend each year to do brave impressions of sunbathing, inhale ice cream, fly kites and hit the town for nightly disco, bingo or cheesy cabaret. But the resort also works to keep fresh generations of punters rolling in, and its newer attractions include an orphaned seal pup sanctuary, facilities

for windsurfing and kitesurfing and a fancy new skate park.

Cheap and cheerful B&Bs are just about everywhere and start at just £18 per person, but the **tourist office** (☎ 899887; www.funcoast.co.uk; Grand Pde; ☽ 9.30am-5pm Apr-Oct, 9.30am-4.30pm Mon-Fri Nov-Mar) is also happy to help you find digs. It sits opposite the **Embassy Centre** (☎ 768333; www .embassytheatre.co.uk), the mothership of Skeggy's cabaret scene and the place to watch your favourite Abba tribute band. From July to Sep-tember, this stretch of beach suffuses the night sky with light pollution as 25,000 glowing light bulbs ignite the **Skegness Illuminations**.

Skegness is simple to reach by public trans-port. Interconnect 7 buses depart hourly from Boston (1¼ hours) Monday to Saturday. From Lincoln, the Interconnect 6 buses run hourly Monday to Saturday and five times on Sunday (1¾ hours).

There are trains at least hourly Monday to Saturday and nine on Sunday between Skeg-ness and Boston (32 minutes).

LOUTH
☎ 01507 / pop 15,930

A bustling market town of narrow lanes lined with Georgian and Victorian architecture, Louth straddles the River Lud between the Wolds to the west and the marshes of the Lin-colnshire coast. The town is cleaved into two hemispheres, as the zero longitude line splits the town; it is marked by a plaque in Eastgate and sculptures dot the line as part of the Louth

Art Trail. Louth's other claim to fame is that it was the scene of a dramatic if short-lived revolt against Henry VIII in 1536.

The **tourist office** (☎ 609289; louthinfo@e-lindsey .gov.uk; New Market Hall, off Cornmarket; ☟ 9am-5pm Mon-Sat, to 4.30pm Oct-Easter) has maps and can help find accommodation.

While mustering the strength to climb Louth's main attraction – the tallest parish church spire in England – pop into **Louth Museum** (☎ 601211; www.louthmuseum.co.uk; 4 Broadbank; adult/child £2/1.20; ☟ 10am-4pm Tue-Sat Apr-Oct) to see its reproduction of an enormous panorama of Louth, which was painted from the top of the church's tower in the 19th century and makes a fascinating comparison to today's view.

With that image burnt into your retina, head for the spire itself. The part medieval, part Tudor **St James' Church** (☟ 10.30am-4pm Easter-Christmas) was described by Sir John Betjemen as 'one of the last great medieval Gothic masterpieces' and is propped up by dramatic buttresses and fortified by battlements. Inside, take a good look down the nave and you'll see that the left row of pillars – which are older than their opposite twins – are lurching off balance. Strange to think that the famous New World adventurer Captain John Smith (yes, the one in *Pocahontas*) once worshiped here. A long elbow-scraping climb up to the tower (£1) is rewarded by views better still than you'd hoped.

Louth's most elegant street is Georgian Westgate, which runs from beside the church. Opposite the mid-17th-century **church precincts** at No 47 is Westgate Pl. Sneak through its archway and you'll find an impossibly cute row of terraced houses, one of which bears a plaque commemorating Tennyson's four-year residence here.

Sleeping & Eating

our pick Priory (☎ 602930; www.theprioryhotel.com; 149 Eastgate; s/d/f from £45/60/110; P ☒) Half-castle, half-house but never a priory, this glorious whitewashed Gothic-style building from 1818 is set in sprawling gardens complete with folly and lake. The formidable task of its upkeep has been taken on by a passionate young family, and the rooms have beautiful period-style furnishings. Dinner is available most nights, and children are very welcome.

Getting There & Away

Louth is 23 miles northeast of Lincoln, from where bus 10 runs every two hours (one hour).

AROUND LOUTH
Saltfleetby-Theddlethorpe National Nature Reserve

Birdsong rings from all around you in the grassy dunes and orchid-speckled marshes of Saltfleetby-Theddlethorpe, one of the Fens most attractive **nature reserves** (☎ 01507-338611; www.english-nature.org.uk; admission free; ☟ dawn-dusk). Ten miles east of Louth along the B1200, the reserve is best appreciated in early summer, when the yellow and mauve marsh orchids bloom. Although in spring and autumn, migratory wildfowl flock to the reserve. Crisscrossing the whole area are dozens of short and long trails to keep your feet dry as you negotiate the myriad lagoons.

You'll need your own transport to get here. At the end of the B1200, turn right onto the A1031 and follow the signs.

Yorkshire

Yorkshire is England's most interesting region. A bold statement, no doubt, but they'd expect nothing less in God's Own Country, as Yorkshire folk half-jokingly refer to where they're from, a place so bloody huge that it's divided into four separate counties: South Yorkshire, West Yorkshire, North Yorkshire and the East Riding of Yorkshire. The last of these is the only geographical hangover from the far-off days of the Danelaw, the 9th-century Viking-governed region that roughly covered the same territory when the notion of 'England' as we know it didn't even exist.

So what is it about this place that's so heaven-blessed? Well, the landscapes for one: from the dark moors and brooding hills that roll their way to the dramatic cliffs of the coast, Yorkshire has been walked on, climbed over, cycled through and written about for centuries.

Secondly, there's the sheer breadth of history and place. In Yorkshire you can explore virtually every facet of the English experience – past and present – from the Middle Ages to today, in abbeys, castles, historic houses, medieval cities, industrial centres and urban playgrounds.

But the most compelling argument for Yorkshire's greatness is the people themselves, the English epitome – and stereotype – of 'them up north'. Proud, industrious, hard-living and terribly opinionated about all subjects great and small, Yorkshire folk can be tough nuts to crack but they're a warm and welcoming bunch that don't stand on ceremony and dispel all notions of the English as cool and distant.

HIGHLIGHTS

- Winding your way through the narrow streets and exploring **York's** (p609) awe-inspiring cathedral and fabulous museums
- Finding your inner Heathcliff and Cathy amid the green valleys and high moors of the **Yorkshire Dales** (p594)
- Lolling in **Leeds** (p582): shopping, eating, drinking, dancing…and more shopping
- Exploring the depths of **Whitby** (p634), a favourite with sea dogs, sun-lovers and lackeys of Dracula, the Prince of Darkness
- Riding the length of the **Settle–Carlisle Line** (p599) and getting some scenery by steam engine
- Going underground: the dark side of mining at the **National Coal Mining Museum for England** (p590) near Wakefield

- POPULATION: 4.96 MILLION
- AREA: 5958 SQ MILES

YORKSHIRE

Information

Yorkshire Tourist Board (☎ 01904 707070; www.yorkshi-revisitor.com; 312 Tadcaster Rd, York YO24 1GS) has plenty of general leaflets and brochures. For more detailed information, contact the local tourist offices listed throughout this chapter.

Activities

Within Yorkshire are high peaks, wild hills, tranquil valleys, farmland, moorland and a stupendous coastline. With this fantastic selection, not surprisingly, it's a great place for outdoor activities.

CYCLING

Cycling is a great way to see Yorkshire; there's a vast network of country lanes, although the most scenic areas are also attractive to car drivers, so even some minor roads can be busy at weekends. Options include:

North York Moors Off-road bikers can avail themselves of the networks of bridle paths, former railways and disused mining tracks now turned over to two-wheel use.

Whitby to Scarborough A traffic-free route that includes a disused railway line, and an effortless way to tour this rugged coastline.

White Rose Cycle Route A 120-mile cruise from Hull to York to Middlesbrough, via the rolling Yorkshire Wolds and the dramatic edge of the North York Moors, and a traffic-free section on the old railway between Selby and York. It is part of the National Cycle Network (p78).

Yorkshire Dales Great cycling in the quieter areas in the north around Swaledale and Wensleydale, and the west around Dentdale. The areas just outside the park, like Nidderdale, are also good. Also an excellent network of old 'drove roads' (formerly used for driving cattle to market) which wind across lonely hillsides, and tie in neatly with the narrow country lanes in the valleys.

WALKING

For shorter walks and rambles, the best area is the **Yorkshire Dales**, with a great selection of hard and easy walks through scenic valleys or over wild hilltops, with even a few peaks thrown in for good measure. The **Yorkshire Wolds** hold hidden delights, while the quiet valleys and dramatic coasts of the **North York Moors** also have many good opportunities, although the broad ridges of the high moors can be a bit featureless and less attractive for keen walkers.

For general information get the *Walk Yorkshire* brochure from tourist offices or see www.walkyorkshire.com. All tourist offices stock a mountain of leaflets (free or up to £1.50) on local walks, and sell more detailed guidebooks and maps. At train stations and tourist offices, it's worth looking out for leaflets produced by companies such as Northern Spirit, detailing walks from train stations. Some tie in with train times, so you can walk one way and ride back.

Long-distance Walks

Cleveland Way A venerable moor-and-coast classic (details in the North York Moors section, p629).

Coast to Coast Walk England's No 1 walk, 190 miles across northern England eastwards from the Lake District, crossing the Yorkshire Dales and North York Moors. Doing the Yorkshire section would take a week to 10 days and offers some of the finest walking of its kind in England.

Dales Way Charming and not-too-strenuous amble from the Yorkshire Dales to the Lake District (details in the Yorkshire Dales section, p594).

Pennine Way The Yorkshire section of England's most famous walk starts on day two and runs for over 100 miles, via Hebden Bridge, Malham, Horton-in-Ribblesdale and Hawes, passing near Haworth and Skipton.

Wolds Way Beautiful but oft-overlooked walk that winds through the most scenic part of eastern Yorkshire (see p603).

Getting There & Around

Yorkshire covers a large part of northern England, and a vast range of landscapes. From the Pennine Hills on the western side of the region (separating Yorkshire from age-old rival Lancashire), you can travel through the green valleys of the Yorkshire Dales, across the plains of the Vale of York and the rolling hills of the North York Moors and Yorkshire Wolds, to finally end at the dramatic east coast.

The major north–south transport routes – the M1 and A1 motorways and the main London to Edinburgh railway line – run through the middle of Yorkshire following the flat lands between the Pennines and the Moors, and serving the key cities of Sheffield, Leeds and York.

Yorkshire's main gateway cities by road and rail are Sheffield in the far south, Leeds for the west and York for the centre and north. If you're coming by sea from northern Europe, Hull (in the East Riding) is the region's main port. More specific details for each area are given under Getting There & Away in the separate sections throughout this chapter. For inquiries, the national **Traveline** (☎ 0870 608 2608) covers buses and trains all over Yorkshire.

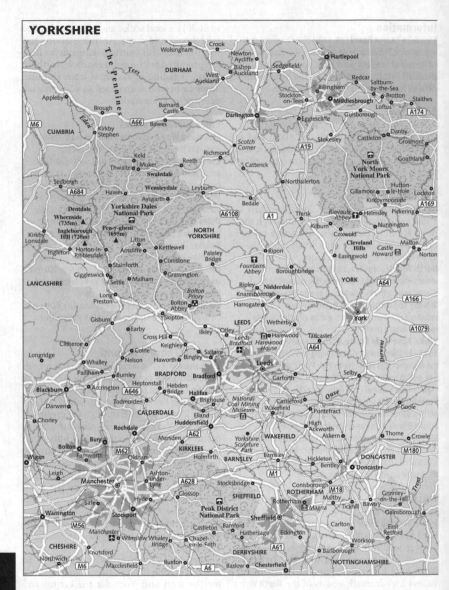

YORKSHIRE

BOAT

Details on passenger ferries to Hull from northern Europe are given in the main Transport chapter (see p781).

BUS

Long-distances buses and coaches run by **National Express** (☎ 08705 808080) regularly service most cities and large towns in Yorkshire from London, the south of England, the Midlands and Scotland. More details are given under Getting There & Away in the individual town and city sections.

Bus transport around Yorkshire is frequent and efficient, especially between major towns. Services are more sporadic in the national

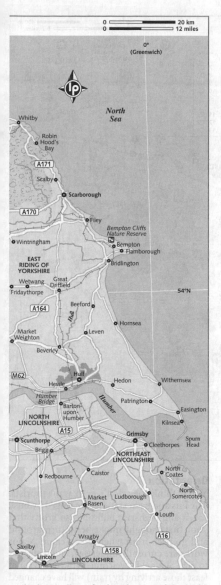

parks but still perfectly adequate for reaching most places, particularly in the summer months (June to September).

TRAIN

The main line between London and Edinburgh runs through Yorkshire with at least 10 services per day, via York and Doncaster –

where you might change to reach other places in Yorkshire. There are also direct services between the major towns and cities of Yorkshire and other northern cities like Manchester and Newcastle. One of England's most famous and scenic railways is the Settle–Carlisle Line (SCL), which crosses the Yorkshire Dales via a spectacular series of tunnels and viaducts. Trains start/end in Leeds, and Carlisle is a good stop on the way to Scotland (see p599). Call or check out **National Rail Enquiries** (☎ 08457 484950; www.nationalrail.co.uk) for timetable details.

SOUTH YORKSHIRE

When you think of South Yorkshire, you generally think of Sheffield, a city famous for its steel, especially the kind you use to cut and hold your dinner. This steel was forged, shaped and cooled in the city's mills, which were in turn fuelled by the coal mined in the outlying pits – a most productive arrangement.

That particular industrial idyll may have been consigned to history's dustbin some time ago, but the hulking reminders of the irrepressible Victorian Age remain, and not just in the mills or pits, some of which have been turned into enthralling museums of the past or brilliantly converted into art galleries and exhibitions spaces, but in the grand civic buildings that crown Sheffield's city centre – fitting testaments to the untrammelled ambitions of their 19th-century patrons.

And, just to prove that it's not all about the grey charms of urbanity, Sheffield's western outskirts brush up against the Peak District National Park, and the city serves as a handy gateway between the south and the north of England.

SHEFFIELD
☎ 0114 / pop 640,720

Like most of northern England's cities, Sheffield has grabbed the opportunities presented by urban renewal with both hands and has worked hard to reinvent itself as something other than the city famous for steel and snooker. The steel industry is long since gone – although the 'Sheffield Steel' stamp on locally made cutlery has quite the touch of boutique class about it – and snooker is only worth talking about for a couple of weeks a

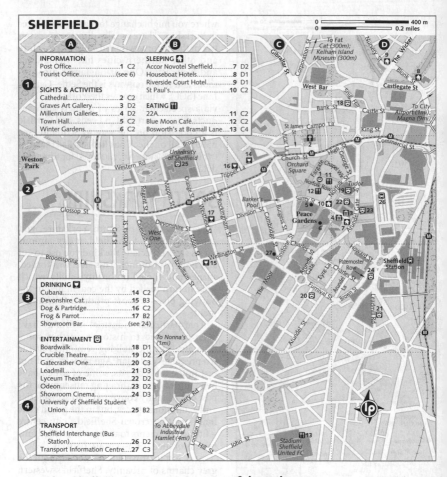

SHEFFIELD

INFORMATION
Post Office.....................1 C2
Tourist Office.................(see 6)

SIGHTS & ACTIVITIES
Cathedral........................2 C2
Graves Art Gallery..........3 D2
Millennium Galleries.......4 D2
Town Hall.......................5 C2
Winter Gardens..............6 C2

SLEEPING
Accor Novotel Sheffield........7 D2
Houseboat Hotels................8 D1
Riverside Court Hotel...........9 D1
St Paul's..........................10 C2

EATING
22A................................11 C2
Blue Moon Café................12 C2
Bosworth's at Bramall Lane....13 C4

DRINKING
Cubana..........................14 C2
Devonshire Cat................15 B3
Dog & Partridge...............16 C2
Frog & Parrot..................17 B2
Showroom Bar................(see 24)

ENTERTAINMENT
Boardwalk......................18 D1
Crucible Theatre..............19 D2
Gatecrasher One..............20 C3
Leadmill........................21 D3
Lyceum Theatre...............22 D2
Odeon...........................23 D2
Showroom Cinema...........24 D3
University of Sheffield Student
  Union..........................25 B2

TRANSPORT
Sheffield Interchange (Bus
  Station)........................26 D2
Transport Information Centre....27 C3

year, when Sheffield plays host to the still immensely popular World Championships in late March and early April.

There are smart hotels and interesting galleries all over the town centre (which has been cleaned up and made rather attractive), some excellent restaurants and, inevitably, enough good bars to justify a rampant nightlife for the thousands of young people attending university here. Indeed, the real spark for the city's rebirth was lit by a younger generation, both home-grown and imported: theirs is the vision that is leading the city's transformation, and in their spare time they're indulging in Sheffield's long-standing reputation as a top spot for music. Ever heard of the Arctic Monkeys?

Orientation

You'd think they don't even want tourists. The bus and train stations are ringed by busy roads and high-rise buildings so grotty that your first thought might be to turn around and go back from whence you came. Major works are currently underway, and if all goes to plan Sheffield's welcome to the world (or at least those arriving by train) will have changed for the better by the time you read this.

The most interesting bits, however, are just beyond them, in a central area around Church St, Tudor Sq, Fargate and a square called Barker's Pool. Just west Division St and Devonshire St have hip clothes and record shops, popular restaurants and trendy bars. A block north is West St, also pretty trendy.

Information
Check your email for free at the **Central Library** (☎ 273 4711; Surrey St; ⏱ 10am-8pm Mon, 9.30am-5.30pm Tue & Thu-Sat, 9.30am-5pm Wed). The **post office** (Norfolk Row; ⏱ 8.30am-5.30pm Mon-Fri, to 3pm Sat) is just off Fargate, and the **tourist office** (www.sheffield.gov.uk; Winter Gardens; ⏱ 9.30am-4pm Mon-Sat) – more of an info point than an actual office – is little more than a desk in the Winter Gardens.

Sights & Activities
Pride of place goes to the **Winter Gardens** (admission free; ⏱ 8am-6pm), a wonderfully ambitious public space with glass roof, exotic plants and soaring wood-clad arches. The 21st-century architecture contrasts sharply with the Victorian **town hall** next door, and is further enhanced by the nearby **Peace Gardens** – complete with fountains, sculptures and lawns of lunching office workers whenever there's a bit of sun.

Sheffield's cultural revival is spearheaded by the **Millennium Galleries** (☎ 278 2600; www .sheffieldgalleries.org.uk; Arundel Gate; admission free, special exhibitions £4; ⏱ 8am-5pm Mon-Sat, 11am-5pm Sun). Displays cover Sheffield steel and metalworking, contemporary art, craft and design, and an eclectic collection established and inspired by Victorian artist, writer, critic and philosopher John Ruskin.

Nearby, **Graves Art Gallery** (☎ 278 2600; Surrey St; admission free; ⏱ 10am-5pm Mon-Sat) has a neat and accessible display of British and European modern art; the big names represented include Cézanne, Gaugin, Miró, Klee and Picasso.

The **cathedral** on Church St has wonderful stained glass (ancient and modern), a memorial to the crew of the HMS *Sheffield* lost during the Falklands conflict and the grave of the earl of Shrewsbury, famous for being the jailer of Mary Queen of Scots and husband to Bess of Hardwick (see p500).

Sheffield's prodigious industrial heritage is the subject of the excellent **Kelham Island Museum** (☎ 272 2106; www.simt.co.uk; Alma St; adult/child £4/3; ⏱ 10am-4pm Mon-Thu, 11am-4.45pm Sun). The most impressive display is the 12,000-horse-power steam engine (the size of a house) that is powered up twice a day. It's just north of the centre.

For a view of steel from an earlier era, go to **Abbeydale Industrial Hamlet** (☎ 236 7731; adult/child £3/2; ⏱ 10am-4pm Mon-Thu, 11am-4.45pm Sun mid-Apr–Oct). It's 4 miles southwest of the centre on

the A621 (towards the Peak District) and well worth a stop. In the days before factories, metalworking was a cottage industry, just like wool or cotton. These rare (and restored) houses and machines take you right back to that era.

Sleeping
Most of the central options cater primarily to the business traveller, which makes for cheaper weekend rates; there are, alas, no budget options in the city centre.

MIDRANGE
Riverside Court Hotel (☎ 273 1962; www.riversidecourt .co.uk; 4 Nursery St; s/d/tr from £37/47/65) The riverside location and its relative proximity to the city centre make this hotel a pretty good choice if you don't want to get stung for a midweek business rate; the rooms are fairly bland but utterly inoffensive.

Accor Novotel Sheffield (☎ 278 1781; www.accorho tels.com; 50 Arundel Gate; r £58-112) The French hotel chain has brought its own modern take on the midrange business hotel to town with some success: extremely central, well-appointed and utterly contemporary, this hotel is surprisingly stylish.

Houseboat Hotels (☎ 232 6556; www.houseboatho tels.com; Victoria Quays, Wharfe St; d/q from £65/86) For a little watery luxury, kick off your shoes and relax on board your very own houseboat, which comes with its own self-catering kitchen and patio area. Available for groups of two or four only; guests are also entitled to use the gym facilities across the road at the Hilton.

TOP END
St Paul's (☎ 0870 122 6585; www.macdonaldhotels.co.uk; 119 Norfolk St; r £85-145; P ⃟) Sheffield's top spot is this brand-new hotel with all the trimmings, a superb central location and great big windows so you can stare down onto the Winter Gardens and the cathedral.

Eating
For a wide range of city centre options, you can't go wrong on Division St, Devonshire St, West St and Glossop Rd. There are cafés, takeaways, pubs and bars doing food, and a wide range of restaurants.

BUDGET
22A (☎ 276 7462; 22A Norfolk Row; wraps about £4; ⏱ 8am-5pm Mon-Thu, to 7pm Fri & Sat) Probably our

---

YORKSHIRE DINING

You simply can't visit Yorkshire without indulging in a meal of local treats. Fish fans will relish the thought of succulent fish and chips in Whitby, while red-blooded carnivores can rest easy: roast beef and Yorkshire pudding, with a light spread of horseradish sauce, is an absolute must (veggies are excused). Follow it with a Fat Rascal – a traditional teacake with currants and candied orange peel. To round it off, cut yourself a chunk of Wensleydale – one of England's best cheeses. What do you wash it all down with? A pint of Yorkshire bitter, of course – although make sure that it's pulled from a hand pump.

---

favourite café in town; does a mean wrap – hummus and roasted veggie the current choice – and serves it with a decent cup of java. Perfect ingredients for a spot of people-watching. Nice music, nice people, nice place.

Blue Moon Café (☎ 276 3443; 2 St James St; mains £5-6; ☺ 8am-8pm Mon-Sat) Tasty veggie creations, soups and other good-for-you dishes, all served with the ubiquitous salad, in a very pleasant atmosphere – perfect for a spot of Saturday afternoon lounging.

MIDRANGE

Runaway Girl (☎ 270 6160; 111 Arundel St; mains £6-10; ☺ lunch & dinner Tue-Fri, dinner only Mon & Sat) The lunchtime crowd love this French bistro in the heart of the city centre for its tasty and affordable menu – as well as the free wi-fi access and lounge-around atmosphere that sees the students linger long after the suits have gone back to work.

Nonna's (☎ 268 6166; 537 Ecclesall Rd; mains £10-15; ☺ lunch & dinner) Authentic Italian cuisine straight from nana's kitchen is the overpowering draw for the city's groove brigade, who flock to this south-of-the-centre restaurant in their droves, and so should you: the food is so good that the shortish taxi ride is well worth it.

TOP END

Bosworth's at Bramall Lane (☎ 292 2777; Sheffield United Football Club, Bramall La; mains £10-25; ☺ dinner Tue-Sat except match days, lunch Sun) Fine dining at a football ground? Top local chef (and lifelong

Blades' fan) Jamie Bosworth thinks it's a good fit, and so far so very good: his new venture has generated rave reviews for its excellent modern British cuisine.

Drinking

Sheffield, a buzzing student town in Yorkshire = a really, really good night out. A pretty straightforward formula, really. Virtually every bar does pub grub until about 7pm.

Fat Cat (☎ 249 4801; 23 Alma St) One of Sheffield's finest pubs, the Fat Cat serves a wide range of real ales (some brewed on the premises) in a wonderfully unreconstructed interior. There are three bars (one nonsmoking), good pub grub, a roaring fire in winter and – in the men's toilets – a fascinating exhibit on local sanitation. It's next door to the Kelham Island Museum.

Frog & Parrot (Division St) Home to the world's strongest beer, the 12%-strong 'Roger & Out', unsuspecting ale-heads saunter in looking to down the equivalent of a pint of fortified wine. Which is precisely why they only serve this particular brew in half-pint glasses – so that you have more than a 50/50 chance of walking out under your own steam. This no-frills popular pub also serves a range of less challenging beers.

Dog & Partridge (☎ 249 0888; 55 Trippett Lane) A no-nonsense Irish pub with a warren of cosy rooms, a fireplace to warm those places beer won't get to and traditional music in the evenings. It's a little bit of the Auld Sod in Sheffield.

Devonshire Cat (49 Wellington St) A beer-lover's haven, this modern bar looks a bit bland, but one look at the wide selection of top-notch beers from around England and the world will explain its enduring popularity.

Cubana (☎ 276 0475; 34 Trippet Lane) Sheffield goes Latino at this top-class bar that is about as authentic as you're ever likely to find so far from Havana. It's tiny, the mojitos are great and the soundtrack is wonderful.

Showroom Bar (7 Paternoster Row) Originally aimed at film fans, this terrific bar with its arty, hip clientele is one of the best night-time destinations in town. The ambience is good, and so is the food, but the service is horribly slow. Out of term-time the slothful moonlighting students go home and real bar-staff pour the drinks. Sunday afternoons have live jazz. Nice.

Entertainment

Sheffield has a good selection of nightclubs, a couple of top-notch theatres, and venues that attract big names in music – both classical and popular. The weekly *Sheffield Telegraph* (75p, every Friday) has the lowdown on Sheffield's entertainment scene, as does the freebie *Exposed*, available most everywhere.

LIVE MUSIC

Boardwalk (☎ 279 9090; www.theboardwalk live.co.uk; 39 Snig Hill) This is an institution, and excellent for live music: local bands, old rockers, up-and-coming stars, world music, the obscure, the novel and the downright weird – they all play here. No real music fan should miss checking what's on.

Leadmill (☎ 275 4500; www.leadmill.co.uk; 6-7 Leadmill Rd) Every touring band has played the dark and dingy Leadmill on the way up (or on the way down), and it remains the best place in town to hear live rock and alternative music. There are club nights, but they're cheesy rubbish.

NIGHTCLUBS

Gatecrasher One (☎ 279 6777; www.neverstandstill.com; 112 Arundel St; admission £4-8) Sheffield's premier nightclub has abandoned its techno roots in favour of floor-friendly house, crowd pleasers and other safe bets, but it's still immensely popular. Saturdays feature a rotation of big name DJs from all over.

University of Sheffield Student Union (☎ 222 8500; Western Bank) A varied and generally good schedule of rock gigs and club nights – including appearances by some pretty class DJ names – make this a good spot to spend a night, not to mention the cheap lager.

THEATRE & CINEMAS

The Crucible and Lyceum theatres on Tudor Sq share the same **box office** (☎ 249 6000). Both are home to excellent regional drama, and the Crucible's respected resident director draws in the big names; the Crucible is also home to the annual snooker world championships.

Showroom Cinema (☎ 275 7727; Paternoster Row) This is the largest independent cinema in England, with a great mix of art-house, off-beat and not-quite-mainstream films on four screens.

For everything else, there's the **Odeon** (☎ 272 3981; Arundel Gate).

Getting There & Away

For all travel-related info in Sheffield and South Yorkshire, call ☎ 01709 515151.

BUS

The bus station – called the Interchange – is just east of the centre, about 100m north of the train station. National Express services link Sheffield with most major centres in the north; there are frequent buses linking Sheffield with the Peak District via Leeds (£4.50, 1¼ hours, hourly) and London (£14.50, four hours, eight daily).

TRAIN

Sheffield is served by trains from all directions: Leeds (£6.60, 30 minutes, hourly); London St Pancras (£69.50, 2½ hours, around 10 daily) via Derby or Nottingham; Manchester airport (£16.70, 70 minutes); Manchester Piccadilly (£12.20, one hour); and York (£12.70, 80 minutes).

Getting Around

Buses run every 10 minutes during the day (Monday to Saturday). Sheffield also boasts a modern Supertram that trundles through the city centre.

For a day of sightseeing, a South Yorkshire Peak Explorer pass (adult/concession £6.75/4) is valid for one day on all of the buses, trams and trains of South Yorkshire and north Derbyshire. Buy passes on your first bus, or at the helpful **transport information centre** (◷ 9am-5pm Mon-Sat) just off Pinstone St.

AROUND SHEFFIELD

Northeast of Sheffield, just off the M1 motorway near Rotherham, it's well worth aiming for **Magna** (☎ 01709 720002; www.visitmagna.co.uk; Sheffield Rd, Rotherham; adult/child Apr-Oct £9.95/7.95, Nov-Mar £9/7; ◷ 10am-5pm). An unashamed celebration of heavy industry and high technology, this science adventure centre is split into four main themes: earth, air, fire and water. You can stand in a tornado (or try to), mess around with kid-sized JCB mechanical diggers, see a video of steel being forged or blast away with water cannons. The hourly Big Melt in the main hall – where the original arc furnace is part of a massive light and sound show – is especially effective. It advertises as fun for the whole family, but it's mostly for the kids.

YORKSHIRE

From Sheffield, take bus 69 (20 minutes; every 15 minutes Monday to Saturday, hourly Sunday) towards Rotherham. It'll drop you at the door.

WEST YORKSHIRE

Think West Yorkshire and you'll probably come up with textiles. You're not far wrong, for that tough and unforgiving industry drove the county's economy and defined much of the landscape for centuries. But that's all in the past, and West Yorkshire's *other* identity – the softer, prettier one – has seen the transformation of a once hard-bitten area into quite the picture postcard. They may have gone a little soft round these parts, but don't say it out loud, for it wouldn't do in this no-nonsense, down-to-earth part of the world to suggest that West Yorkshire folk didn't eat nails for breakfast.

Leeds and Bradford are the perfect case in point. Two adjoining cities so big that they've virtually become one, yet each maintains a distinct identity. Bradford is a tough old place, industrious and not overly concerned with how it looks, whereas its near neighbour can't get enough of the mirror and works overtime to ensure that it's as gorgeous as it can be for the world to enjoy.

Beyond the cities, West Yorkshire is all about a landscape of bleak moorland separated by deep valleys dotted with old mill towns and villages. The relics of the wool and cloth industries are still in evidence, in the rows of weavers' cottages and workers' houses built along ridges overlooking the towering chimneys of the mills in the valleys – landscapes so vividly described by the Brontë sisters, West Yorkshire's most renowned literary export and biggest tourist draw.

Activities
CYCLING
West Yorkshire isn't great cycling country; many roads are too urban in flavour, and the hills are darned steep too. The National Cycle Network (see p78) in West Yorkshire includes the short but traffic-free Leeds to Shipley route, which mostly follows a canalside path, passing Saltaire and on to Bradford.

WALKING
The valleys and moors of West Yorkshire make good walking country, although the South Pennines (as this area's called) is wedged between the Peak District and the Yorkshire Dales, and has to defer to these areas in terms of sheer quality. The tourist offices all have leaflets and guidebooks on local walks, or see the main sections on the towns mentioned here, for more ideas. Hebden Bridge and especially Haworth make ideal bases for circular walks, with several long and short options.

The **Haworth to Hebden Bridge Path** is a popular trail that passes through quiet farmland and scenic wooded valleys.

The Pennine Way (p575), England's longest trail, follows the watershed through the area, and some good walks are possible following it for just a day or two.

Getting There & Around
The Metro is West Yorkshire's highly efficient train and bus network, centred on Leeds and Bradford – which are also the main gateways to the county. For transport details call **Metroline** (☎ 0113-245 7676; www.wymetro.com) or the national **Traveline** (☎ 0870 608 2608). The excellent Day Rover (£3.80 for train or bus, £4.50 train and bus) tickets are good for travel on buses and trains after 9.30am on weekdays and all day at weekends. There's a thicket of additional Rovers covering buses and/or trains, plus heaps of useful Metro maps and timetables, all available at tourist offices.

LEEDS
☎ 0113 / pop 715,402
Leeds struts across England's urban stage like John Travolta in *Saturday Night Fever*, oozing the confidence that befits the favourite child of the New Urban Revolution, that unassailable force that has turned punch-drunk postindustrial cities into visions of the future. And the future round these parts is all about retail. For Leeds is the 'Knightsbridge of the North', the shopping mecca whose counter is just getting longer. Its heart is lined with busy pedestrianised streets, packed with shops, restaurants, upstanding Victorian edifices and stunning arcades. From cutting-edge couture to contemporary cuisine, Leeds will serve it to you on a plate…or in a stylishly designed bag. And when you're through for the day, the night awaits, full of pubs, clubs and more restaurants to keep you fed and fuelled for more.

LEEDS

0 ——— 400 m
0 ——— 0.2 miles

A · **B** · **C** · **D**

INFORMATION
Central Library..............................1 B3
Gateway to Yorkshire Tourist
Office...2 B4
Leeds General Infirmary...............3 A3
Post Office..................................4 B4
Waterstone's...............................5 B3

SIGHTS & ACTIVITIES
City Art Gallery............................6 B3
Henry Moore Institute..................7 B3
Royal Armouries...........................8 D5
St John's Church..........................9 C3

SLEEPING
42 The Calls..........................(see 22)
City Centre Hotel.......................10 C3
Golden Lion Hotel.....................11 C5
Jury's Inn..................................12 D5
Malmaison................................13 C5
Quebecs...................................14 B4
Radisson SAS.............................15 B3

EATING
Akbar.......................................16 C3
Anthony's.................................17 C4
Anthony's at Flannel's.................18 C4
Arts Café..................................19 C4
Babycream................................20 B3
Bibi's Criterion..........................21 B5
Brasserie Forty4........................22 D4
Fourth Floor Café................(see 48)
Little Tokyo...............................23 C4
No 3 York Place.........................24 A4
Norman....................................25 C4
Tampopo..................................26 B3

DRINKING
Adelphi....................................27 C5
Baby Jupiter..............................28 A4
Babycream.........................(see 20)
Bar Fibre..................................29 C4
Dr Wu's....................................30 C4
Duck & Drake............................31 D4
Elbow Room..............................32 C5

Guildford..................................33 B3
Milo...34 C4
MPV...35 C4
Sandinista.................................36 C3
Whitelocks................................37 C4

ENTERTAINMENT
City Varieties............................38 C4
Fruit Cupboard..........................39 C5
Grand Theatre & Opera House....40 C3
HiFi Club...................................41 C4
Mission.....................................42 C5
Vue Cinema...............................43 B3
Warehouse................................44 A4
West Yorkshire Playhouse...........45 D4
Wire...46 C4

SHOPPING
Corn Exchange...........................47 C4
Harvey Nichols..........................48 C4
Kirkgate Market.........................49 C4
Victoria Quarter.........................50 C4

TRANSPORT
Central Bus Station....................51 D4

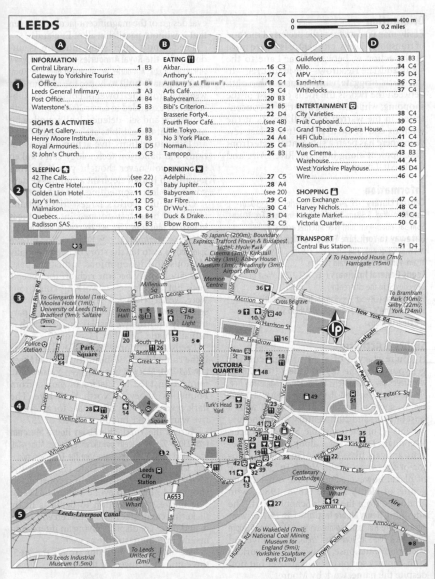

Underpinning Leeds' remarkable ability to turn a profit from hedonism is the ubiquitous northern grit, that stubborn fortitude that has overcome the demise of the city's textile industry and seen it become the country's second-most important financial centre after London. They might like to party around here, but they're tough as old boots, too.

Some critics (OK, us) feel that Leeds is a little light in terms of nonretail attractions compared to its neighbours in Manchester and York, but the city is in the midst of a huge transformation and that may all have changed by the time you read this. In the meantime, besides its own draws, Leeds is an excellent base for excursions to Haworth, Hebden Bridge and Bradford.

YORKSHIRE

Orientation

Easily managed on foot (the preferred method of transport), Leeds' city centre is where most of the action is, between Boar Lane to the south and The Headrow – the main drag – to the north. Briggate, which runs north–south between the two, is the focus of most of the shopping, while the best nightlife is concentrated in the warren of small streets at the western end of Boar Lane. In the last few years there has been a substantial waterfront development along both the River Aire and the Leeds-Liverpool Canal.

Information

Central Library (☎ 247 8274; Calverley St; ☽ 9am-8pm Mon-Wed, 9.30am-5.30pm Thu, 9am-5pm Fri, 10am-5pm Sat, noon-4pm Sun) Free internet access.
Gateway to Yorkshire Tourist Office (☎ 242 5242; www.leeds.gov.uk; The Arcade; ☽ 9am-5.30pm Mon-Sat, 10am-4pm Sun) In the train station.
Leeds General Infirmary (☎ 243 2799) West of Calverley St in the city centre.
Post office (City Sq; ☽ 9am-5.30pm Mon-Sat)
Waterstone's (☎ 244 4588; 97 Albion St) Has a good selection of maps.

Sights & Activities

If you're starved of a bit of high culture, get yourself to the **City Art Gallery** (☎ 247 8248; www.leeds.gov.uk/artgallery; The Headrow; admission free; ☽ 10am-5pm Mon-Tue & Thu-Sat, 10am-8pm Wed, 1-5pm Sun) as soon as possible. It is packed with a host of 19th- and 20th-century British heavyweights – Turner, Constable, Stanley Spencer, Wyndham Lewis et al – along with more recent arrivals like Antony Gormley, sculptor of the *Angel of the North* (p736). Pride of place, however, goes to the outstanding genius of Henry Moore (1898–1986), who graduated from the Leeds School of Art. The adjoining **Henry Moore Institute** (☎ 246 7467; www.henry-moore-fdn.co.uk; admission free; ☽ 10am-5.30pm Mon, Tue & Thu-Sun, 10am-9pm Wed), in a converted Victorian warehouse, showcases the work of 20th-century sculptors from all over but not, despite the name, work by Moore.

Tucked away off northern Briggate is the redundant but lovingly nurtured **St John's Church** (☎ 244 1689; ☽ 9.30am-5.30pm Tue-Sat), a one-off masterpiece consecrated in 1634 – the first in the north of England following the Reformation. The gorgeous (and original) oak box pews are certainly eye-catching, but they're only a temporary distraction from the intricate medieval design of the magnificent Jacobean screen that is without parallel in all of England.

Leeds' most interesting museum is undoubtedly the **Royal Armouries** (☎ 220 1940; www.armouries.org.uk; Armouries Dr; admission free; ☽ 10am-5pm), originally built to house the armour and weapons from the Tower of London but subsequently expanded to cover 3000 years' worth of fighting and self-defence. It all sounds a bit macho, but the exhibits are as varied as they are fascinating: films, live-action demonstrations and hands-on technology can awaken interests you never thought you had, from jousting to Indian elephant armour. We dare you not to learn something. Catch bus 95.

One of the world's largest 'dark satanic mills' has been transformed into the **Leeds Industrial Museum** (☎ 263 7861; www.leeds.gov.uk/armleymills; adult/child £3/1; ☽ 10am-5pm Tue-Sat, noon-5pm Sun) so as to tell the story of Leeds' equally glorious and ignominious industrial past. The city literally became rich off the sheep's back but at some cost: working conditions were, well, Dickensian. Apart from the usual selection of working machinery, there's a particularly informative display on how cloth is actually made. Take bus 14, 66 or 67.

Leeds' most impressive medieval structure is the ruined-but-still-beautiful **Kirkstall Abbey** (☎ 263 7861; Abbey Rd; admission free; ☽ dawn-dusk), founded in 1152 by Cistercian monks from Fountains Abbey in North Yorkshire. The dark, severe Norman ruins make for an evocative wander. Take bus 50, 733, 737 or 757.

Across the road, the **Abbey House Museum** (☎ 230 5492; www.leeds.gov.uk/abbeyhouse; Abbey Rd; adult/child £3.50/1.50; ☽ 10am-5pm Tue-Fri & Sun, noon-5pm Sat), once the Great Gate House to the abbey, contains meticulously reconstructed shops and houses to evoke Victorian Leeds. The impressive attention to detail is lit by flickering candlelike light. Children will enjoy it, and there are displays giving an interesting insight into monastic life as well.

The abbey and museum are off the A65, three miles northwest of the centre.

Festivals & Events

The August Bank Holiday (the last weekend) sees 50,000-plus music fans converge on Bramham Park, 10 miles outside the city centre, for the **Leeds Festival** (☎ 0870 060 3775; www.leedsfestival.com), one of England's biggest rock music extravaganzas, spread across four separate stages.

Sleeping

There are no budget options in the city centre and the midrange choices are between absolute fleapits and the odd chain hotel. If you don't want to spend money, you're forced to head for the 'burbs, where there are plenty of decent B&Bs and smallish hotels.

MIDRANGE

City Centre Hotel (☎ 242 9019; www.citycentrehotelleeds. co.uk; 51A New Briggate; s/d from £45/59) A pretty ramshackle place with pea-sized bathrooms gets our vote – only just – for its central location, which makes it a good option if you're looking for somewhere to crash after a late night.

Golden Lion Hotel (☎ 243 6454; www.thegoldenlion-leeds.co.uk; 2 Lower Briggate; r £59; P) Leeds' oldest hotel got a much-needed makeover and can now compete with the rest. The rooms are tidy and modern, if a little small, but the central location is second-to-none.

Jury's Inn (☎ 283 8800; www.jurysdoyle.com; Bowman La, Brewery Pl; r £59-69; P &) The successful Irish hotel chain has another hit with its Leeds hotel; large, functional rooms, plenty of personal charm and few complaints. If you're walking, just cross the Centenary footbridge from the city centre.

There are a couple of decent hotels about a mile northwest of the city centre near the university on Woodsley Rd; it's five minutes by taxi or catch bus 63 from Stand S10 at the train station. The **Glengarth Hotel** (☎ 245 7940; fax 216 8033; 162 Woodsley Rd; s/d from £25/36) is a converted family home with a dozen or so tiny rooms that are nevertheless quite comfortable; just down the street, the **Moorlea Hotel** (☎ 243 2653; www.moorleahotel.co.uk; 146 Woodsley Rd; s/d from £32/44) is a family-friendly hotel with larger, slightly more comfortable rooms.

The other midrange alternatives are around Headingley – home of the famous cricket ground and a pretty residential part of town. They include the very friendly **Boundary Express** (☎ /fax 274 7700; 42 Cardigan Rd; s d with/without bathroom £55/42) and **Trafford House & Budapest Hotel** (☎ 275 2034; fax 274 2422; 16-18 Cardigan Rd; s/d/tr from £32/49/70), both with rooms full of cricket memorabilia. The latter has rooms with good views of the cricket ground; three have balconies.

TOP END

Radisson SAS (☎ 236 6000; www.leeds.radissonsas.com; The Light, Cookridge St; r £90-175; P &) The newest bit of luxury to hit Leeds is the extraordinary conversion of the listed former HQ of the Leeds Permanent Building Society. The standard rooms are anything but, and you have a choice of three styles: hi tech, Art Deco and Italian. The public areas are truly elegant and the location is superb.

Malmaison (☎ 398 1000; www.malmaison.com; Sovereign St; s/d/ste £99/140/295) Self-consciously stylish, this typical Malmaison property has a fabulous waterfront location and all of the trademark touches: huge comfy beds, sexy lighting and all the latest designer gear. The entrance is actually on Swinegate, but Sovereign St just sounds classier.

Quebecs (☎ 244 8989; www.theetoncollection.com; 9 Quebec St; s/d/ste from £150/160/235) Victorian grace at its opulent best is the theme of our favourite hotel in town, a brilliant conversion of the former Victorian Leeds and County Liberal Club. The elaborate wood panelling and stunning heraldic stained-glass windows in the public areas are matched by the contemporary but equally luxurious design of the bedrooms. Two of the deluxe suites – the cutely named Sherbert and Liquorice suites – have dramatic spiral staircases.

42 The Calls (☎ 244 0099; www.42thecalls.co.uk; 42 The Calls; r £150-395) This snazzy boutique hotel in what was once a 19th-century grain mill is a big hit with the trendy business crowd, who love its sharp, polished lines and designer aesthetic. The smaller studio rooms are pretty compact indeed. Breakfast is not included; it'll cost you an extra £10.95. In for a penny, in for a pound? Sunday night rates start at £85.

Eating

Eating well is never a problem; the choice is getting better all the time and the quality just keeps going up.

BUDGET

Akbar (☎ 245 6566; 15 Eastgate; mains £4-6; ☾ dinner only) The naan served at this exceptionally popular Indian restaurant are absolutely massive, and that's just one of many reasons to tuck into some of England's favourite cuisine at this particular spot.

Arts Café (☎ 243 8243; www.artscafebar.co.uk; 42 Call Lane; lunch mains about £5, dinner mains about £8; ☾ lunch & dinner, to 2am Fri & Sat) Local art on the walls and a Bohemian vibe throughout make this a popular place for quiet reflection, a chat and a really good cup of coffee to wash down the excellent food – how about some monkfish lasagne?

Norman (☎ 234 3988; 36 Call Lane; mains £5-8; ☺ lunch & dinner) The tasty Japanese noodle menu at one of the city's best bars is the reason to come here before nightfall; this place is as stylish by day as it is popular by night.

Tampopo (☎ 245 1816; 15 South Pde; mains £6-8; ☺ lunch & dinner Mon-Sat, lunch Sun) Masters of the art of conveyor-belt cuisine, Tampopo gets 'em in and out in virtually record time; between coming and going, diners tuck into tantalising noodle and rice dishes from Southeast Asia.

MIDRANGE

Little Tokyo (☎ 243 9090; 24 Central Rd; mains about £6.95-13.95; ☺ lunch & dinner Mon-Sat) Fans of genuine Japanese food should go no further than this superb restaurant, which serves a wide array of sushi and sashimi (including half-portions) and Bento box – those handy divided trays that serve the Japanese equivalent of a four-course meal.

Bibi's Criterion (☎ 243 0905; Criterion Pl, Swinegate; mains £8-15; ☺ lunch & dinner Mon-Fri, dinner Sat & Sun) The mamma of Leeds' Italian eateries looks increasingly like Donnatella Versace dresses – lots of bling and shine – but with age comes experience and the nosh remains the best Italian in town.

Babycream (☎ 08000 277171; 153-155 The Headrow; mains £10-19; ☺ lunch & dinner) Cool drips off the white walls and onto the white leather furniture, where you and your party are gathered to share, fondue-style, in a platter of delicacies from around the globe. As you eat, the background music makes you tap your feet, and before you know it you've settled in for the day and moved on to cocktails. It's the Cream experience, and it's pretty good...

Anthony's at Flannel's (☎ 242 8732; Flannel's, 68-78 Vicar Lane; afternoon tea £10.75; ☺ 9am-6pm Tue-Sat, 11am-5pm Sun) The brasserie brother of the award-winning (and much more expensive) Anthony's (right), this 3rd-floor cafe features much of Anthony's style stuffed into the excellent sandwiches, salads and luxurious afternoon tea.

Fourth Floor Café (☎ 204 8000; Harvey Nichols, 107-111 Briggate; mains from £11; ☺ 10am-6pm Mon-Wed & Fri, 9am-10pm Thu & Sat, noon-5pm Sun) A department store with a fancy restaurant? It could only be Harvey Nicks. It's called a café, but don't be fooled: the nosh here is the best of British, even if the portions would only satisfy the models in their catalogue.

TOP END

If you want to splurge, Leeds has a handful of restaurants that are worth every last penny.

Brasserie Forty4 (☎ 343232; 44 The Calls; mains about £12; ☺ lunch & dinner Mon-Fri, dinner Sat) This top spot serves Modern British cuisine, which is pretty much anything Brits who like food would eat. The wide-ranging menu is sure to satisfy virtually every taste, although we're not at all convinced about the chintzy décor – leaf and leopard skin do not a good combination make.

No 3 York Place (☎ 245 9922; www.no3yorkplace.co.uk; 3 York Pl; mains £13.95-23.95; ☺ lunch & dinner Mon-Fri, dinner Sat) Any debate over which is the best restaurant in town will feature this superb French eatery, with its regularly changing menu of Gallic delicacies with an English bent – how about roast of lamb with Savoy cabbage, olive mash and a Niçoise sauce?

Anthony's (☎ 245 5922; www.anthonysrestaurant.co.uk; 19 Boar Lane; mains £22-27; ☺ lunch & dinner Tue-Sat) Probably the most talked about restaurant in town, Anthony's serves superb British cuisine to a clientele so eager that they'll think nothing of booking a month in advance. If you go at any other time except Saturday evening, you'll get away with making your reservations a day or so earlier.

Drinking

Leeds is justifiably renowned for its terrific selection of pubs and bars. The glammed-up hordes of party animals crawl the clusters of venues around Boar Lane and Call Lane, where bars are opening all the time. Most bars open till 2am; they turn into clubs after 11pm or midnight, with an admission charge of £2 to £4, up to £6 at weekends. The more traditional pubs keep regular hours.

PUBS

Duck & Drake (☎ 246 5806; 43 Kirkgate) High ceilings, obligatory pub characters, real ales and regular, free live music – mostly jazz.

Whitelocks (☎ 245 3950; Turk's Head Yard) Great beer and good, old-fashioned décor in a very popular traditional pub dating from 1715. In summer, the crowds spill out into the courtyard.

Other recommendations:

Adelphi (☎ 245 6377; 3-5 Hunslet Rd) Built in 1898 and hardly changed since.

Guildford (☎ 244 9204; 115 The Headrow) An attractive Art Deco classic.

BARS

Babycream (☎ 08000 277171; www.babycream.co.uk; 153-155 The Headrow) The Scouse gurus of groove hit Leeds with a stylish bang – hardly surprising that one of the brand names of new-millennium cool should be so popular with virtually everyone.

Dr Wu's (☎ 242 7629; 35 Call Lane) Small and chock-full of black leather seats, this grungy bar would slot comfortably into New York's East Village, and don't the punters just know it. The vibe is studied cool and the DJs play a suitable blend of eclectic (but always alternative) sounds.

Baby Jupiter (☎ 242 1202; 11 York Pl) A retro gem with lots of purple velvet, hanging fishbowls and a very funky soundtrack, this was – at the time of writing – the 'in' place with those who make it their business to define what 'in' actually is.

Sandinista (☎ 305 0372; www.sandinistaleeds.co.uk; 5/5A Cross Belgrave St) Our favourite bar in town has a Latin look but a unifying theme, attracting virtually everyone with its mixed bag of music and unpretentious atmosphere. If you're not too fussed about looking glam, this is the spot for you.

Japanic (☎ 244 9550; 19 Queen Sq) Take a traditional English pub and combine it with a modern, hi-tech karaoke bar and you get Japanic, where students flock to share a £5 bottle of sake, knock back a few ales and take to the microphone. What's not to like? It's just north of the centre.

Bar Fibre (☎ 200888; www.barfibre.com; 168 Lower Briggate) Leeds' most popular gay bar, which spills out onto the cleverly named Queen's Court, is where the beautiful congregate to congratulate themselves on being so lucky.

Other tips for a tipple:

Elbow Room (☎ 245 7011; www.theelbowroom.co.uk; 64 Call Lane) Pop art, purple pool tables and laid-back music.

Milo (☎ 245 7101; 10 Call Lane) Great bar for eclectic music, from reggae to electronica. Ricky from the Kaiser Chiefs used to work here!

MPV (☎ 243 9486; 5-8 Church St, Kirkgate) Four bright-red, huge Portakabins with glass fronts make this the wackiest bar in northern England.

Entertainment

In order to make sense of the ever-evolving scene, get your hands on the monthly *Leeds Guide* (£1.70; www.leedsguide.co.uk) or *Absolute Leeds* (£1.50; www.absoluteleeds.co.uk).

NIGHTCLUBS

The tremendous Leeds club scene attracts people from miles around. In true northern tradition, people brave the cold wearing next to nothing, even in winter, which is a spectacle in itself. Clubs charge a variety of admission prices, ranging from as little as £1 on a slow weeknight to £10 or more on Saturday.

HiFi Club (☎ 242 7353; www.thehificlub.co.uk; 2 Central Rd) This intimate club is a good break from the hardcore sound of four to the floor: if it's Tamla Motown or the percussive beats of dance-floor jazz that shake your booty, this is the spot for you.

Fruit Cupboard (☎ 244 3168; www.leedsclubscene .com; 50-52 Call Lane) Hip-hop, R & B and other urban beats make up the menu at this compact club known by some as 'Fight Cupboard' – but alco-fuelled trouble is a potential feature most everywhere.

Wire (☎ 234 0980; 2-8 Call Lane) The best of the new openings, this super basement club throbs to the sound of virtually everything, from rock and roll to drum 'n' bass. If you're serious about music, queue up and get down.

Mission (☎ 0870 122 0114; www.clubmission.com; 8-13 Heaton's Ct) A massive club that redefines the term 'up-for-it'. Thursday night is gay go-go dancers at the appositely named Homo.

Also check out **Warehouse** (☎ 246 8287; 19-21 Somers St), home to the gay bootie-shaker **Speed Queen** (www.speedqueen.co.uk; ☽ 10pm-4am Sat).

THEATRE & CINEMAS

Culture vultures will find plenty to keep them entertained in Leeds.

City Varieties (☎ 243 0808; www.cityvarieties.co.uk; Swan St) This old-fashioned music hall features anything from clairvoyants to country music.

West Yorkshire Playhouse (☎ 213 7700; www .wyplayhouse.com; Quarry Hill Mount) The Playhouse has a reputation for excellent live drama.

Hyde Park Picture House (☎ 275 2045; www.leeds .gov.uk/hydepark; Brudenell Rd) This Edwardian cinema shows a meaty range of art-house and mainstream choices. Take bus 56 or 63 from the city centre.

The **Grand Theatre & Opera House** (☎ 222 6222; www.leeds.gov.uk/grandtheatre; 46 New Briggate) hosts musicals, plays and opera, including performances by acclaimed **Opera North** (☎ 244 5326; www.operanorth.co.uk).

Otherwise, for mainstream new releases, there's the **Vue Cinema** (☎ 0871 224 0240; 22 The

Light, The Headrow) on the second floor of The Light entertainment complex.

SPORT

Leeds United Football Club (☎ 226 1000; www.leeds united.com; Elland Rd) Supporters know all about pain: relegation from the Premiership in 2004 to the relative wilderness of the Championship was bad enough, but in 2006 they lost out to Watford in a promotion play-off. Loyal fans had no option but to wait another year, but they continue to pack the Elland Rd stadium in their masses. Take bus 51, 52 or 54 from Kirkgate Market.

Headingley has been hosting cricket matches since 1890. It is still used for test matches and is the home ground of the **Yorkshire County Cricket Club** (☎ tickets 278 7394; www .yorkshireccc.org.uk; test match from £28.50). Take bus 74 or 75 from Infirmary St.

Shopping

Leeds' city centre has so many shopping arcades that they all seem to blend into one giant mall. Most of them are unremarkable, but the designer-ridden **Victoria Quarter** (☎ 245 5333) is worth visiting for aesthetic reasons alone. A handful of mosaic-paved, stained-glass roofed Victorian arcades have been beautifully restored (check out the County Arcade). Here, the biggest name is undoubtedly **Harvey Nichols** (☎ 204 8000; 107-111 Briggate), which has its usual selection of upmarket clothes.

Kirkgate Market (☎ 214 5162; ✆ 9am-5pm Mon-Sat, to 1pm Wed, open-air market Thu-Tue) Closer to earth, this market, once home of Marks, who later joined Spencer, sells fresh produce and cheap goods.

Corn Exchange (☎ 234 0363; Vicar La; ✆ 9am-6pm) The circular Corn Exchange, built in 1865 to house the grain trade, has a wonderful wrought, armadillolike lid, and is the place to come for one-off clothes, eclectic jewellery or records.

Getting There & Away

AIR

Eight miles north of the city via the A65, **Leeds-Bradford airport** (☎ 250 9696) offers domestic and charter flights, plus international flights to a few major European cities. The Airlink 757 (£1.80, 45 minutes) operates every 30 minutes between the airport and the bus station and train station. A taxi costs about £17.

BUS

National Express (☎ 0870 580 8080; www.nationalex press.com) serves most major cities, including hourly services from London (£19.20, 4¼ hours) and half-hourly services from Manchester (£7.80, one hour).

Yorkshire Coastliner (☎ 01653 692556; www.york shirecoastliner.co.uk; Coastliner Freedom Ticket adult per day £11) has useful services linking Leeds, York, Castle Howard, Goathland and Whitby (840, 842 and X40), York and Scarborough (843, 845 and X45).

TRAIN

Leeds City Station has hourly services from London King's Cross (£84, 2½ hours), Sheffield (£7.15, 45 minutes), Manchester (£12.70, one hour) and York (£8.80, 30 minutes).

Leeds is also the starting point for services on the famous Settle–Carlisle Line. For more details see p599.

Getting Around

Metro buses go from the Central Bus Station and on or near City Sq. The various Day Rover passes (see p582) covering trains and/or buses are good for reaching Bradford, Haworth and Hebden Bridge.

AROUND LEEDS

A day out from Leeds opens up a fascinating range of options: stately splendour at Harewood, dust and darkness at the National Coal Mining Museum, or technology and poppadoms at Bradford, to name but a few. Places are listed roughly in order of distance from Leeds, first to the west and north, then to the south.

Bradford

☎ 01274 / pop 293,717

Their suburbs are so close that they've virtually merged into one sprawling urban conurbation, but Bradford remains far removed from its much more glamorous neighbour, Leeds. Or so they would have you believe in Leeds. But even Bradford is getting a facial: much of the dour city centre is scheduled for a revamp which, according to town planners, will see it recast as an urban park with its very own lake in front of city hall. It sounds so promising, and a far cry from the kind of 'ugliness that could not only be tolerated but often enjoyed,' as the city's favourite son, the cantankerous JB Priestley (1894–1984), once described it.

Thanks to its role as a major player in the wool trade, Bradford attracted large numbers of Bangladeshis and Pakistanis throughout the 20th century, who – despite occasional racial tensions – have helped reinvigorate the city and give it new energy. A high point of the year is the colourful Mela (see below).

SIGHTS
The top sight for any visit to Bradford is the **National Museum of Photography, Film & Television** (NMPFT; ☎ 202030; www.nmpft.org.uk; admission free, special events & cinemas adult/child £5/3.30, IMAX adult/child £6.50/4.30; ⏰ 10am-6pm Tue-Sun). Five exhibit-packed floors in this impressive, glass-fronted building tell the story of the recorded visual image from 19th-century cameras and early animation to digital technology and the psychology of advertising. There's lots of hands-on stuff too; you can film yourself in a bedroom scene or play at being a TV newsreader. The IMAX screen shows the usual combination of in-your-face nature films and space documentaries.

The oft-overlooked **SDC Colour Museum** (☎ 390955; www.sdc.org.uk; Providence St; adult/child £2/1.50; ⏰ 10am-4pm Tue-Sat), run by the Society of Dyers and Colourists, is a little gem, just a 10-minute walk from the centre. It tells the story of Bradford's wool-dying trade, and has a fascinating section on how our eyes perceive colour, including a display contrasting the visual sense of different species (what's blue to you isn't blue to Fido).

Bradford Industrial Museum (☎ 435900; www.bradfordmuseums.org; Moorside Rd, Eccleshill; admission free; ⏰ 10am-5pm Tue-Sat, noon-5pm Sun), 3 miles out of the centre, gives a hint of what a Yorkshire textile spinning mill was like at the peak of the Industrial Revolution. Other exhibits include various steam engines (sometimes working), transport from the last 100 years, and a horse-drawn tram to give a quick 'step back in history' round the car park.

FESTIVALS & EVENTS
The excellent **Bradford Mela** (www.bradfordfestival.com) is a two-day celebration (from the Sanskrit word 'to meet') of Asian music, dance, arts, crafts and food. It's held in mid-June.

EATING
Bradford is famous for its curries, so if you're still here in the evening, don't miss trying one of the city's hundred or so restaurants. A great help is the **Bradford Curry Guide** (http://website.lineone.net/~bradfordcurryguide), which sorts the rogan josh from the rubbish nosh.

Kashmir (☎ 726513; 27 Morley St; mains £4-5; ⏰ evenings to 3am) Bradford's oldest curry house has top tucker, served with no frills or booze (it's BYO). Whatever you do, go for a table upstairs, as the soul-destroying, windowless basement has all the character of a public toilet. It's just around the corner from the NMPFT.

GETTING THERE & AWAY
Bradford is on the Metro train line from Leeds, with very frequent services every day.

Saltaire
A Victorian-era landmark, Saltaire was a model industrial village built in 1851 by philanthropic wool-baron and teetotaller Titus Salt. Overlooking the rows of neat honey-coloured cottages was the largest factory in the world at that time. Heating, ventilation and good lighting were high on Titus Salt's list of priorities, but there was no way on earth this sober humanitarian was going to give his workers somewhere to indulge in the demon drink, so the town had no pub.

The factory is now **Salt's Mill** (☎ 01274 531163; www.saltsmill.org.uk; admission free; ⏰ 10am-5.30pm Mon-Fri, 10am-6pm Sat & Sun), a splendidly bright and airy cathedral-like building where the main draw is a permanent exhibition of work by local boy David Hockney (1937–). There are also shops of books and crafts, and a café.

Saltaire's **tourist office** (☎ 01274 774993; www.visitsaltaire.com; 2 Victoria Rd; ⏰ 10am-5pm) has maps of the village and runs hour-long guided walks (adult/child £3/2) of the town throughout the year.

Saltaire is 9 miles west of Leeds centre, and 3 miles north of Bradford centre (effectively an outer suburb of Bradford). It's easily reached by Metro rail from both.

Harewood
There's only one reason to stop in Harewood, a tiny hamlet about 7 miles north of Leeds, and that is to visit the great park, sumptuous gardens and mighty edifice of **Harewood House** (☎ 0113-218 1010; www.harewood.org; admission £12.50, Sun & bank holidays £14.50; ⏰ grounds 10am-6pm, house 11am-4.30pm Feb- mid Nov, house & grounds 10am-4pm mid-Nov–Jan). As an outing from Leeds you can easily fill a day here, and if you're heading

for Harrogate, stopping off is highly recommended.

A classic example of a stately English pile, the house was built between 1759 and 1772 by the era's designer superstars, a team assembled by John Carr (who designed the exterior). Lancelot 'Capability' Brown laid out the grounds, Thomas Chippendale supplied the furniture (the largest commission he ever received, costing the unheard of amount of £10,000), Robert Adams designed the interior, and Italy was raided to create an appropriate art collection. The superb terrace was added 100 years later by yet another top name, Sir Charles Barry – he of the Houses of Parliament.

Many locals come to Harewood just to relax or saunter through the grounds, without even thinking of going inside the house. Hours of entertainment can be had in the **Bird Garden**, with many colourful species including penguins (feeding time at 2pm is a highlight), and there's also a boating lake, café and adventure playground. For more activity, there's a network of walking trails around the lake or through the parkland.

From Leeds, use bus 36 (20 minutes; at least half-hourly Monday to Saturday, hourly on Sunday) which continues to Harrogate. Visitors coming by bus get half-price admission too (so hang on to your ticket). From the main gate, it's a 2-mile walk through the grounds to the house and gardens. At busy times there's a free shuttle service.

National Coal Mining Museum

For close to three centuries, West and South Yorkshire was synonymous with coal production; the collieries shaped and scarred the landscape, while entire villages grew up around the pits, each male inhabitant and their descendants destined to spend their working lives underground. The industry came to a shuddering close in the 1980s, but the imprint of coal is still very much in evidence, even if there's only a handful of collieries left. One of these, at Claphouse, is now the **National Coal Mining Museum for England** (☎ 01924 848806; www.ncm.org.uk; Overton, near Wakefield; admission free; ⏰ 10am-5pm, last tour 3.15pm), a superb testament to the inner workings of the coal mine.

Highlight of a visit is the tour underground; complete with helmet and head-torch you ride in a 'cage' almost 150m down, then follow passages all the way to the coal seam where mas-

sive drilling machines now stand idle. Former miners now work as guides, and explain the details – sometimes with a suitably authentic and almost impenetrable mix of local dialect (known in Yorkshire as Tyke) and technical terminology.

Up on top, there are modern audiovisual displays, some fascinating memorabilia (including sketches by Henry Moore), plus exhibits about trade unions, strikes and the wider mining communities – only slightly over-romantic in parts. You can also stroll round the pit-pony stables (with their equine inhabitants also now retired) or the slightly eerie bathhouse, totally unchanged since the miners scrubbed off the coal dust and emptied their lockers for the last time. There are also longer nature trails in the surrounding fields and woods.

The museum is about 10 miles south of Leeds, on the A642, which drivers can reach from the M1. By public transport, take a train from Leeds to Wakefield (15 minutes, at least hourly), and then bus 232 towards Huddersfield can drop you outside the museum (25 minutes, hourly).

Yorkshire Sculpture Park

One of England's most impressive collections of sculpture is housed within the formidable 18th-century estate of Bretton Park, 500-odd acres of lawns, fields and trees dotted with statues and abstract work. The **sculpture park** (☎ 01924 830302; www.ysp.co.uk; Bretton, near Wakefield; admission free; ⏰ 10am-6pm Apr-Sep, to 5pm Oct-Mar) features the work of dozens of sculptors both national and international, but the main focus is on the work of local kids Henry Moore and Barbara Hepworth (1903–75), who was born in nearby Wakefield. The setting is especially good for Moore's work, as the artist was hugely influenced by the outdoors and preferred his art to be sited in the landscape rather than indoors. Your wish is their command, Henry. Of the other sculptors exhibited, make sure not to miss the work of Scot Ronald Rae, who carves wonderful animals *in* (not out of) blocks of granite; you can see them along the Access Sculpture Trail. The Longside Gallery, reached by shuttle bus or a gentle 2km walk through the park, houses temporary exhibitions from the Arts Council's own collection.

The park is 12 miles south of Leeds and 18 miles north of Sheffield, just west of the M1 motorway, making it a cinch to get to for drivers. If you're on public transport, take a train from Leeds to Wakefield (15 minutes, at least hourly), or from Sheffield to Barnsley (20 minutes, at least hourly); then Bus X41 runs between Wakefield and Barnsley via Bretton Park (30 minutes, hourly Monday to Saturday). Bus 231 (hourly on Sunday) from Wakefield goes to Bretton Park then continues on to the National Coal Mining Museum (opposite).

HEBDEN BRIDGE

☎ 01422 / pop 4086

Yorkshire's funkiest little town is a former mill town that refused to go gently into that good night with the dying of industry's light; it raged a bit and then turned itself into an attractive little tourist trap with a slightly off-centre reputation. Besides the honest-to-God Yorkshire folk who have lived here for years, the town is home to university academics, die-hard hippies and a substantial gay community – all of which explains the inordinate number of craft shops, organic cafés and second-hand bookstores.

Above the town is the much older village of **Heptonstall**, its narrow cobbled street lined with 500-year-old cottages and the ruins of a beautiful 13th-century church. But it is the churchyard of the newer St Thomas' Church that draws the curious visitors, for here is buried the poet Sylvia Plath (1932–63), wife of another famous rhymer, Ted Hughes (1930–98), who was born in these parts.

Plath's grave lists her full name as 'Sylvia Plath Hughes', with the 'Hughes' in bronze: this is because it had been repeatedly chiselled off by Plath lovers who believe that Hughes' adultery with Assia Wevill provoked Sylvia's suicide (Wevill later also committed suicide) and so leading church authorities to ensure that the name couldn't be removed.

The **Hebden Bridge Visitor & Canal Centre** (☎ 843 831; www.calderdale.gov.uk; Butlers Wharf, New Rd; ⊙ 9.30am-5.30pm Mon-Fri, 10.30am-5pm Sat & Sun mid-Mar–mid-Oct, 10am-5pm Mon-Fri, 10.30am-4.15pm Sat & Sun rest of year) has a good stock of maps and leaflets on local walks, including saunters in **Hardcastle Crags**, two unspoilt wooded valleys run by the National Trust (NT), 1.5 miles northwest of town off the A6033. There are streams and waterfalls, and numerous walking trails, some of which link to the Pennine Way, and another that takes you all the way to Haworth.

Sleeping & Eating

Pennine Camp & Caravan Site (☎ 842287; High Greenwood House, Heptonstall; sites £6) Basically just a large, sloping field with a block of facilities in a converted barn, this camp site about three miles northwest of town is reached on the lane that runs through Heptonstall. It's just off the footpath between Hebden Bridge and Haworth, near Hardcastle Crags, and the Pennine Way runs nearby too, so it's popular with walkers.

Mankinholes YHA Hostel (☎ 0870 770 5952; www.yha .org.uk; Todmorden; dm £12.50) A converted 17th-century manor house 4 miles southwest of Hebden Bridge, this hostel has limited facilities (no TV room) but it is very popular with walkers; the Pennine Way is only half a mile from here.

White Lion Hotel (☎ 842197; www.whitelionhotel .net; Bridge Gate; s/d from £46/60) The choicest accommodation in town is this large 400-year-old coaching inn smack in the middle of it; the rooms in the converted coach house are that little bit more comfortable than the ones in the main house. Downstairs is a popular pub and a pretty good restaurant (mains £6 to £11) with a standard pub grub menu.

Crown Fisheries (☎ 842599; 8 Crown St; mains about £4; ⊙ 10am-6.30pm) A terrific chipper that serves up a great supper (fish, chips, bread and butter and tea), and also does takeaways.

Getting There & Away

Hebden Bridge is on the Leeds–Manchester Victoria Metro train line (45 minutes, services about every 30 minutes Monday to Saturday, hourly on Sunday). Get off at Todmorden for the Mankinholes YHA Hostel.

HAWORTH

☎ 01535 / pop 6078

It seems that only Shakespeare himself is held in higher esteem and affection than the beloved Brontë sisters Emily, Anne and Charlotte, at least judging from the sheer numbers who trudge up the hill from the station to pay homage to them in the handsome parsonage where a handful of literary classics were born, including *Jane Eyre* and *Wuthering Heights*.

Not surprisingly, the whole place is given over to Brontë-linked tourism, but even without the literary associations Haworth is worth a trip, although you'll be hard pushed not to be overwhelmed by the cottage industry that has grown up around the Brontës and their wonderful creations.

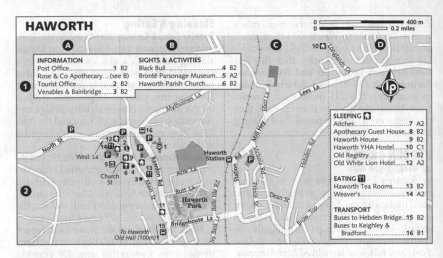

HAWORTH

INFORMATION
Post Office...................1 B2
Rose & Co Apothecary....(see 8)
Tourist Office................2 B2
Venables & Bainbridge.....3 B2

SIGHTS & ACTIVITIES
Black Bull.................................4 B2
Brontë Parsonage Museum...5 A2
Haworth Parish Church........6 B2

SLEEPING
Aitches.............................7 A2
Apothecary Guest House..8 B2
Haworth House.................9 B2
Haworth YHA Hostel.......10 C1
Old Registry...................11 B2
Old White Lion Hotel.....12 A2

EATING
Haworth Tea Rooms.......13 B2
Weaver's........................14 A2

TRANSPORT
Buses to Hebden Bridge..15 B2
Buses to Keighley &
      Bradford...................16 B1

Information

The **tourist office** (☎ 642329; www.haworth-village.org
.uk; 2-4 West Lane; ⊙ 9am-5.30pm Apr-Sep, to 5pm Oct-Mar)
has an excellent supply of information on the
village, the surrounding area and, of course,
the Brontës. Another good source of information is www.brontecountry.co.uk.

Main St is lined with cafés, tearooms, pubs
and shops selling everything imaginable (and
more) bearing the Brontë name. Handy stops
might include: the **post office** (Rawdon Rd; ⊙ 9am-
5.30pm Mon-Fri, to 12.30pm Sat); **Venables & Bainbridge**
(Main St), selling used books, including many
vintage Brontë volumes; and **Rose & Co Apothecary** (84 Main St), the beautifully restored drug-
gist so favoured by Branwell Brontë.

Sights

Your first stop should be **Haworth Parish Church**
(admission free), a lovely old place of worship,
built in the late 19th century, on the site of
the 'old' church that the Brontë sisters knew,
which was demolished in 1879. In the surrounding churchyard, gravestones are covered
in moss, or thrust to one side by growing trees,
which gives the whole place a tremendous
feeling of age.

Set in a pretty garden overlooking the
church and graveyard, the **Brontë Parsonage
Museum** (☎ 642323; www.bronte.info; admission £5;
⊙ 10am-5.30pm Apr-Sep, 11am-5pm Oct-Mar) is where
the Brontë family lived from 1820. Rooms
are meticulously furnished and decorated,
exactly as they were in the Brontë era, with
many personal possessions on display. There's

also a neat and informative exhibition, which
includes the fascinating miniature books the
Brontës wrote as children.

Activities

Haworth is surrounded by the moors of the
South Pennines – immediately familiar to
Brontë fans – and the tourist office has leaflets
on local **walks** to endless Brontë features. A
6.5-mile favourite leads to Top Withins, a ruined farm thought to have inspired *Wuthering
Heights*, even though a plaque clearly states
that the farmhouse bore no resemblance to
the one Emily wrote about. Other walks can be
worked around the **Brontë Way**, a longer route
linking Bradford and Colne via Haworth.
Alternatively, the Pennine Way runs west of
Haworth and can be followed south to Hebden Bridge. There's also a direct walking route
between Haworth and Hebden Bridge, via the
scenic valleys of Hardcastle Crags.

Sleeping & Eating

Virtually every second house on Main St does
B&B; they're mostly indistinguishable from
each other but some are just that little bit
cuter. There are a couple of good restaurants
in town and many of the B&Bs also have small
cafés that are good for a spot of tourist lunch
– mediocre servings of local dishes and nice
safe bets like sandwiches.

Haworth House (☎ 643374; www.hazelhurst.fsbusi
ness.co.uk; 6 Church St; s/d from £20/40) Almost attached
to the church, this place has spacious rooms
with New Age décor; the smaller, budget

BAD LUCK BRONTËS

The Rev Patrick Brontë, his wife Maria and six children moved to Haworth Parsonage in 1820. On 15 September 1821 Maria died of cancer, after which her unmarried sister Elizabeth Branwell arrived from Penzance to help raise the children. Three years later, the eldest girl, Maria, was sent home from school on account of ill-health and died in May 1825, aged 11. A few weeks later, her younger sister Elizabeth arrived home sick from the same school and died, aged 10, on June 15. (Years later, Charlotte immortalised the school as the infamous Lowood in *Jane Eyre*.)

The double tragedy led the good reverend to keep his remaining family close to him, and for the next few years the children were home-schooled in a highly creative environment. The children conjured up mythical heroes and countries, and produced miniature homemade books. It was an auspicious start, at least for the three girls, Charlotte, Emily and Anne; the lone boy, Branwell, was more of a painter but he lacked his sisters' drive and discipline. After a short stint as a professional artist, he ended up spending most of his days in the Black Bull pub, drunk and stoned on laudanum obtained across the street at Rose & Co Apothecary. While the three sisters were setting the London literary world alight with the publication of three superb novels – *Jane Eyre, Wuthering Heights* and *Agnes Grey* – in one extraordinary year (1847), Branwell was fading quickly, and he died of tuberculosis on 24 September 1848. The family was devastated, but things quickly got worse. Emily contracted a cold at the funeral that also developed into tuberculosis; she never left the house again and died on 19 December. Anne, who had also been sick, was next: Charlotte took her to Scarborough to seek a sea cure but she died on 28 May 1849.

The remaining family never recovered. Despite her growing fame, Charlotte struggled with depression and never quite adapted to her high position in literary society. Despite her misgivings, however, she eventually married, but she too died, in the early stages of pregnancy, on 31 March 1855. All things considered, it's hardly surprising that poor old Patrick Brontë spent the remaining years of his life going increasingly insane.

rooms are pretty cramped. Breakfast (£2.50 to £3.50) is served in the room.

Aitches (☎ 642501; www.aitches.co.uk; 11 West Lane; s/d from £35/50; ✉) A very classy Victorian stone bungalow with four beautiful rooms, each with wrought-iron beds and handsome furnishings. There's a residents' restaurant on the premises; a three-course meal will cost £15.

Old Registry (☎ 646503; www.theoldregistryhaworth. co.uk; 2-4 Main St; r £57-85) This is a favourite place in town, a stylishly rustic (or rustically stylish) hotel where each of the carefully themed rooms has a four-poster bed: the Blue Heaven room is just that – at least for fans of Laura Ashley's delphinium blue. We're just that little bit dramatic, so we loved the Stage Room, complete with theatrical memorabilia.

Weaver's (☎ 643822; 15 West Lane; bar suppers £5-12, 3-course meal £20-26; ✉ Tue-Sat) Smart and stylish, with simply the best food in town and a menu featuring local specialities. Get there early to try the tasty two-course bar 'sampler' menu (£12.95).

Other options:

Apothecary Guest House (☎ 643642; www.theapoth ecaryguesthouse.co.uk; 86 Main St; s/d £25/45) Oak beams

and narrow, slanted passageways lead to smallish rooms with chintzy wallpaper.

Haworth Old Hall (☎ 642709; Sun St; snacks £3, salads £6, mains £6-10) A highly rated inn, with decent food, wine and beer, all served in convivial surroundings. The steak-and-ale pie is a classic. If you want to linger longer, two comfortable doubles cost £50.

Haworth Tea Rooms (68 Main St; lunch mains £6-10, dinner mains £7-12) A selection of healthy options including baked spuds and veggie nachos.

Haworth YHA Hostel (☎ 0870 770 5858; www.yha .org.uk; Longlands Dr; dm £13.95; ✉ Feb-Nov, Fri & Sat only Nov-Jan) A big old house with plenty of facilities, including a games room, lounge, cycle store and laundry. It's on the northeastern edge of town, off Lees Lane.

Old White Lion Hotel (☎ 642313; www.oldwhite lionhotel.com; West Lane; s/d from £52/72) Pub-style accommodation – comfortable if not spectacular – above an oak-panelled bar and highly rated restaurant (mains £10 to £13).

Getting There & Away

From Leeds, the easiest approach to Haworth is via Keighley, which is on the Metro train network. Bus 500 runs between Keighley and Haworth (15 minutes, six daily), and also serves Todmorden and Hebden Bridge.

STEAM ENGINES & RAILWAY CHILDREN

Haworth is on the **Keighley & Worth Valley Railway** (KWVR; ☎ 645214; www.kwvr.co .uk; adult/child single £8/4, adult/child Day Rover £12/6), which runs steam and classic diesel engines between Keighley and Oxenhope. It was here, in 1969, that the classic movie *The Railway Children* was shot; Mr Perks was stationmaster at Oakworth, where the Edwardian look has been meticulously maintained. Trains operate around hourly at weekends all year; in holiday periods they run hourly every day.

However, the most interesting way to get to Haworth from Keighley is via the Keighley & Worth Valley Railway (see boxed text, above).

YORKSHIRE DALES NATIONAL PARK

Sitting snugly between the brooding North York Moors to the east and the dramatic Lake District to the west are the Yorkshire Dales (from the Viking word *dalr*, meaning 'valleys'), a marvellous area of high hills and moors, cut through by rugged stone walls and spotted with extravagant houses and the faded, spectral grandeur of monastic ruins.

Thankfully, nature's feast has been protected as a national park since the 1950s, assuring its status as a walker's and cyclist's wonderland. But the fabulous scenery attracts plenty of four-wheeled visitors, making the roads very crowded, especially during the summer. If you can't avoid busy summer weekends, try to come by bus or train, and even then it's well worth getting off the beaten track.

Orientation & Information

The 683-sq-mile Yorkshire Dales National Park divides into two parts: in the north, two main valleys run west to east – broad expansive Wensleydale (home of the famous cheese) and narrow secretive Swaledale. In the south, the main valleys – Ribblesdale, Malhamdale, Littondale and Wharfedale – all run north–south and are the most popular areas for tourists.

The main Dales gateways are Skipton in the south, and Richmond in the northeast. Good bases in the park itself include Settle, Grassington and Hawes. All have excellent tourist offices (some are called park visitor centres), stocking a mountain of local guidebooks and maps, and providing accommodation details.

To the northwest and west, the towns of Kirkby Stephen and Kirkby Lonsdale can also make handy jumping-off points, although both these spots are outside the national park boundary, and actually in the county of Cumbria (despite definite Dales affiliations).

The *Visitor* newspaper, available from tourist offices, lists local events and walks guided by park rangers, as well as many places to stay and eat. The official park website at www.yorkshiredales.org.uk is similarly useful.

Activities

CYCLING

Other than on busy summer weekends, this is excellent cycling country. Most roads follow the rivers along the bottom of the Dales so, although there are still some steep climbs, there's also plenty on the flat. Tourist offices stock maps and leaflets with suggested routes (on-road and off-road) for a day or longer.

Just one example is the **Yorkshire Dales Cycle Way**, an energetic and exhilarating 130-mile loop, taking in the best of the park. Skipton is a convenient start, from where you ride up Wharfedale, then steeply over Fleatmoss to Hawes. From here turn east along Wensleydale to Aysgarth, then north over the wild hills to Reeth. The roads are steep but the scenery is breathtaking. Follow Swaledale westwards, through remote Keld and down to the market town of Kirkby Stephen. Then it's south to Sedbergh, and up beautiful Dentdale to pop out at Ribblehead. It's plain sailing now, through Horton-in-Ribblesdale to Stainforth, one more climb over to Malham, and finally back to Skipton for tea and medals.

WALKING

The Yorkshire Dales has a vast footpath network, with options for everything from easy strolls to challenging hikes; we suggest a few options throughout this section. Look out at tourist offices for leaflets on organised walks from train stations, notably on the Settle–Carlisle Line. Serious walkers should equip

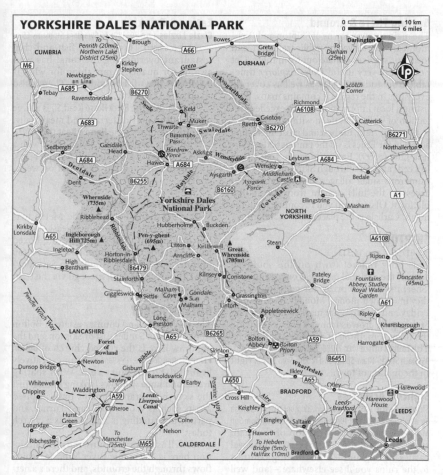

YORKSHIRE DALES NATIONAL PARK

themselves with *OS Outdoor Leisure Maps Nos 2, 10* and *30*.

Two of England's most famous long-distance routes cross the Dales. The Pennine Way goes through the rugged western half of the park. If you haven't got the three weeks required to cover all 259 miles, a few days in the Dales, between Malham and Hawes for example, will repay the effort. The Coast to Coast Walk (a 190-mile classic; p575) goes through lovely Swaledale in the northern Dales. Following the route for a few days is highly recommended; see p601.

Another long-distance possibility is the Dales Way, which begins in Ilkley, follows the River Wharfe through the heart of the Dales, and finishes at Bowness-on-Windermere in the Lake District. If you start at Grassington, it's an easy five-day 60-mile journey. A handy companion is *Dales Way Route Guide* by Arthur Gemmell and Colin Speakman (1996, £5.99), mostly strip maps at 1:25,000 in scale, available at most bookshops.

Sleeping

There are many villages in and around the park with a good range of hotels, B&Bs, hostels and camp sites. Most rural pubs also do B&B. Walkers and hardy outdoor types can take advantage of camping barns. Usually owned by farmers, booking is organised centrally through the **YHA** (☎ 0870 870 8808). For details, tourist offices have a *Camping Barns in England* leaflet.

YORKSHIRE

Getting There & Around

The main gateway towns of Skipton and Richmond are well served by public transport, and local bus services radiate out from there. Get hold of the very useful *Dales Explorer* timetable from tourist offices; as well as covering every bus in the region it contains maps, B&B listings, local information and an excellent selection of walks that tie in with bus services.

Going by train, the best and most interesting access to the Dales is via the famous Settle–Carlisle Line (p599). From the south, trains start in Leeds and pass through Skipton, Settle, and numerous small villages, offering unrivalled access to the hills straight from the station platform. Of course, if you're coming from the north, Carlisle is the place to get on board.

SKIPTON

☎ 01756 / pop 14,313

This busy market town on the southern edge of the national park was once known as 'Sheeptown' – no prizes for guessing where they made their money. Monday, Wednesday, Friday and Saturday are market days on High St, bringing crowds from all over and giving the town something of a festive atmosphere. The **tourist office** (☎ 792809; www.skiptononline.co.uk; 35 Coach St; ⊗ 10am-5pm Mon-Fri, 9am-5pm Sat) is right in the middle of town.

Sights & Activities

Skipton Castle (☎ 792442; www.skiptoncastle.co.uk; High St; admission £5.40; ⊗ 10am-6pm Mon-Sat, noon-6pm Sun Mar-Sep, to 4pm Oct-Feb), at the top of the main street, is one of the best-preserved medieval castles in England – a fascinating contrast to the ruins you'll see elsewhere – and well worth a visit.

If you fancy a cruise on the Leeds–Liverpool Canal that runs through the middle of town, **Pennine Boat Trips** (☎ 790829; www.canaltrips. co.uk; adult/child £5/2.50) has daily hour-long trips departing from April to October; call for the departure times.

Sleeping

There's a strip of B&Bs just outside the centre on Keighley Rd. All those between Nos 46 and 57 are worth trying.

Carlton House (☎ 700921; www.carltonhouse.rapidial .co.uk; 46 Keighley Rd; s/d from £25/45) A handsome house with five pretty, comfortable rooms – no frills but lots of floral prints. The house is deservedly popular on account of the friendly welcome.

Eating & Drinking

Bizzie Lizzies (☎ 793189; 36 Swadford St; mains £5-6; ⊗ lunch & dinner) This modern fish-and-chip restaurant overlooking the canal has won awards for quality, a rare thing for what is essentially deep-fried goodness. There's also an attached takeaway.

Of the pubs, the **Black Horse** (Coach St) is a large place with an outside terrace and meals daily, but our favourite is the **Narrow Boat** (☎ 797922; 38 Victoria St), a traditionally styled place with a great selection of local ales and foreign beers, friendly service and bar food (not on weekends).

Getting There & Away

Skipton is the last stop on the Metro network from Leeds (40 minutes, at least hourly). For heading into the Dales, see the boxed text p599. For Grassington, take bus 72 (30 minutes, six per day Monday to Saturday) or 67 (hourly, Sunday); most go via the train station.

BOLTON ABBEY

The tiny village and country estate of Bolton Abbey is about 5 miles east of Skipton, and the big draw here is the ruined church of **Bolton Priory** (admission free; ⊗ 9am-dusk), an evocatively beautiful 12th-century ruin. With soaring arches and huge windows looking frail against the sky, these grand remains have inspired artists such as Wordsworth and Turner, and part of the building is still used as a church today.

As well as the priory ruins, the main attraction here is the scenic River Wharfe, which flows through the grounds, and there's a network of footpaths and walking trails beside the river and through the surrounding area. It's very popular with families (part of the riverbank looks like a beach at weekends), and you can buy teas and ice creams in the Cavendish Pavilion, a short walk from the priory. Other highlights include the stepping stones (with a large gap between two stones in the middle of the river, frequently forcing faint-hearted walkers to turn around and use the bridge) and The Strid, a narrow, wooded, picturesque gorge just upstream from the pavilion.

The shop and information centre in the village has leaflets (free) with walking maps and more details or you can check www. boltonabbey.com.

As country house hotels go, the **Devonshire Arms Hotel** (☎ 01756-718111; www.thedevonshirearms .co.uk; s/d £160/220), owned by the dukes of Devonshire, is actually like staying in one of their homes. The decoration of each bedroom was undertaken by the duchess herself, and while her tastes might not be everyone's cup of tea, there's just no arguing with the quality and beauty of the furnishings; almost all of them were permanently borrowed from another of their properties, Chatsworth in Derbyshire.

There are half-hourly buses from Skipton and Grassington Monday to Saturday; on Sunday there is only an hourly service from Skipton.

GRASSINGTON
☎ 01756 / pop 1120

The perfect base for south Dales jaunts, Grassington's handsome Georgian centre teems with walkers and visitors throughout the summer months, soaking up an atmosphere that – despite the odd touch of faux rustication – is as attractive and traditional as you'll find in these parts. It is 6 miles north of Skipton.

The **tourist office** (☎ 752774; ☉ 9.30am-5pm Apr-Oct, shorter hours Nov-Mar) is at the big car park on the edge of town. There's a good stock of maps and guides, and a nice little display that puts the surrounding scenery in context.

Sleeping & Eating
There are several B&Bs along and just off Main St.

Devonshire Fell (☎ 718111; www.devonshirefell .co.uk; Burnsall; s/d from £75/125) The sister property to Bolton Abbey's Devonshire Arms Hotel (above), this one-time gentleman's club for mill owners offers a substantially different aesthetic; here, the style is distinctly contemporary, with beautiful modern furnishings crafted by local experts. It's more like a big city boutique hotel than a rustic country property.

Ashfield House (☎ 752584; www.ashfieldhouse.co.uk; Summers Fold; r from £85; ☉ Feb-Nov only) A secluded 17th-century country house behind a walled garden with exposed stone walls, open fireplaces and an all-round cosy feel. It's just off the main square.

Dales Kitchen (☎ 753208; 51 Main St; mains about £5.50; ☉ 9am-6pm) Classic Yorkshire munchies – rarebits, local sausage and, of course, Wensleydale – in a lovely tearoom in the middle of town.

Getting There & Away
To reach Grassington, see opposite). For onward travels the 72 bus continues up the valley to the nearby villages of Kettlewell and Buckden.

AROUND GRASSINGTON
North of Grassington, narrow roads lead up the beautiful valley of Wharfedale. Drivers take the road on the west side of the river; if you're cycling, take the quieter east-side option. If you're walking, follow the charming stretch of the Dales Way long-distance footpath through a classic Yorkshire Dales landscape of lush meadows surrounded by dry-stone walls, with traditional field barns dotting the hillsides.

About 7 and 11 miles respectively from Grassington, the villages of **Kettlewell** and **Buckden** make good places to aim for, between them offering a good choice of camp sites, B&Bs, teashops and pubs (all doing food and accommodation). Favourite hostelries include the **Blue Bell Inn** (☎ 01756 760230; www.bluebellinn .co.uk) and the **Racehorses** (☎ 01756 760233), which has a nice riverside garden, in Kettlewell, and the **Buck Inn** (☎ 01756 760228) in Buckden. A few miles beyond Buckden, in the tiny settlement of **Hubberholme**, is the **George Inn** (☎ 01756 760223; www.thegeorge-inn.co.uk; r £60-70), also worth a stop.

Another option is a triangular route taking in Kettlewell, Buckden and the village of **Litton** in the little valley of Littondale, to the west of Wharfedale, where the **Queens Arms** (☎ 01756 770208) is another fine historical inn.

Check at Grassington tourist office about the local buses that trundle up and down Wharfedale daily in the summer months (weekends in winter) – ideal for bringing home weary walkers.

MALHAM
☎ 01729 / pop 120

At the northern end of the quiet and beautiful valley of Malhamdale, this small, traditional village is probably the most visited place in the valley, not only for its charm but also for the natural wonders nearby – all easily reached by foot.

The excellent **tourist office** (☎ 830363; malham@ytbtic.co.uk; ☉ 10am-5pm daily Apr-Oct, Fri-Sun Nov-Mar) has the usual wealth of information, local walks leaflets, maps and guidebooks.

Activities

The 5-mile **Malham Landscape Trail** (the tourist office has details) takes in **Malham Cove**, a huge rock amphitheatre that was once a waterfall to rival Niagara, and **Gordale Scar**, a deep lime-stone canyon with scenic cascades and the remains of an Iron Age settlement.

For something longer, you can follow vari-ous paths eastwards through remote farmland for anything between 6 miles and 11 miles to reach Grassington, or head west on a great 6-mile hike over the hills to Settle. An even better option is a two-day hike between Grass-ington and Settle via Malham.

The long-distance Pennine Way passes right through Malham, and you can go north or south for as many days as you like. A day's walk away is Horton-in-Ribblesdale (right).

Sleeping & Eating

Malham YHA Hostel (☎ 0870 770 5946; www.yha.org.uk; dm £13.95; ◷ mid-Feb–Nov, Fri & Sat only Dec–mid-Feb) In the village centre is this purpose-built hostel; the facilities are top-notch and young children are well catered for.

Beck Hall (☎ 830332; www.beckhallmalham.com; s/d from £23/48) This rambling 17th-century country house on the edge of the village is a favourite place to stay; of the 11 different rooms, we recommend the Green Room, with its old-style furnishings and four-poster bed. There's a rustling stream flowing through the garden and a nice tearoom (snacks about £4).

SETTLE

☎ 01729 / pop 3621

The largish town of Settle is far too bustling to be really homely and quaint, but it retains enough of its traditional character to make it a worthwhile stop. Narrow cobbled streets lined with shops and decent pubs lead out from the central market square, which still sees stalls and traders every Tuesday. Access from the main A65 to the east is easy, and there are plenty of accommodation options.

The **tourist office** (☎ 825192; settle@ytbtic.co.uk; Town Hall; ◷ 9.30am–5pm) has maps and guide-books, and an excellent range of local walks leaflets (free).

Sleeping & Eating

Stainforth YHA Hostel (☎ 0870 770 5946; www.yha.org.uk; dm £13.95) A three-star hostel in an old Geor-gian country house with excellent facilities, including a shop, TV lounge, laundry, BBQ

areas and a restaurant as well as a self-catering kitchen It is two miles north of Settle on the B6479 to Horton-in-Ribblesdale.

Golden Lion Hotel (☎ 822203; www.goldenlionhotel .net; Duke St; s/d with bathroom £41/72, without £34/60) This handsome 17th-century coaching inn has 12 warm and comfortable rooms, an old-style pub and a pleasant restaurant that is one of the most popular in town (lunch mains about £7, evening £9 to £13).

Around Market Place are several cafés, including the excellent **Shambles** (☎ 822652; fish & chip supper £6.25) and – in reference to the old Yorkshire saying that 'you don't bring now't into the world and you take now't out' – **Ye Olde Naked Man** (☎ 823230) formerly an under-takers and now a bakery with cakes, snacks and ice cream.

Getting There & Away

The easiest way to get here is by train. From the south, trains from Leeds or Skipton head-ing for Carlisle (see the boxed text, opposite) stop at the station near the town centre; those heading for Morecambe (on the west coast) stop at Giggleswick, about 1.5 miles outside town.

AROUND SETTLE
Horton-in-Ribblesdale

☎ 01729 / pop 558

A favourite with walkers, cyclists and cavers, the little village of Horton is 5 miles north of Settle. Everything centres on the **Pen-y-ghent Cafe** (☎ 860333; ◷ 9am–6pm Mon & Wed–Fri, 8am–6pm Sat & Sun), which serves up filling meals, homemade cakes and pint mugs of tea. The friendly owners sell maps, guidebooks and walking gear, and the café acts as the village **tourist office** (horton@ytbtic.co.uk). Walkers on a long hike should avail themselves of the 'safety service', whereby they can register in and out. There's also a **post office shop** for groceries and takeaways.

SLEEPING & EATING

Horton is popular, so your best bet is to book your accommodation in advance.

Golden Lion (☎ 860206; www.goldenlionhotel.co.uk; dm/s/d £9/27.50/55) Popular with walkers, the Golden Lion is a lively pub with dorms and basic private rooms upstairs, and three public bars downstairs where you can tuck into a bit of grub and wash it down with a pint of hand-pumped ale. It also does evening meals (three courses £10) and makes packed lunches (£4.95). Breakfast (£6.50) is not included.

Crown Hotel (☎ 860209; www.crown-hotel.co.uk; s/d from £28.50/54) Another popular rest stop with walkers, the Crown has a variety of basic rooms (with slightly over-the-top floral patterns) and a cosy bar that serves a range of meals.

Other options:

Dub-Cote Farm Camping Barn (☎ 860238; www .threepeaksbarn.co.uk; dm £9.50) A basic-but-lovely 17th-century stone barn half a mile southeast of the village, well equipped with self-catering facilities (BYO sleeping bag and pillow case).

Knoll (☎ 860283; s/d £28/48; ✹ Mar-Oct only) A handsome house near the village centre with the Pennine Way on its doorstep.

The Three Peaks

The countryside north of Settle is dominated by the Three Peaks – Whernside (735m), Ingleborough (723m) and Pen-y-ghent (694m) – and the summits are linked by a long circular route that has been a classic walk for many years. The traditional start is the Pen-y-ghent Cafe in Horton-in-Ribblesdale and walkers try to complete the whole 25-mile route in under 12 hours. Others knock it off in six hours or less. You can also do just a section of the walk – for instance walking from Horton as far as Ribblehead, and returning by train – which is highly recommended.

HAWES

☎ 01969 / pop 700

Hawes – from the Saxon word *haus* (mountain pass) – is busy, not especially pretty but very useful: right at the heart of Wensleydale, it's the best base for exploring the northern Yorkshire Dales. The main street and the narrow lanes off it are lined with old-style shops, some small supermarkets, banks with ATMs, outdoor shops, half a dozen pubs, even more cafés, a couple of smart restaurants, some basic fish-and-chip takeaways, endless craft and pottery studios, a laundrette and a post office…pretty much everything you'll need.

There's also the **Wensleydale Creamery Visitor Centre** (☎ 667664; www.wensleydale.co.uk; admission £2.50; ✹ 9.30am-5pm Mon-Sat, 10am-4.30pm Sun),

---

THE SETTLE–CARLISLE LINE

The Settle–Carlisle Line (SCL), built between 1869 and 1875, is one of the great engineering achievements of the Victorian era and a very scenic ride to boot. The railway's construction was a Herculean task: 5000 navvies armed with picks and shovels built 325 bridges, 21 viaducts and blasted 14 tunnels in Dickensian conditions that defy the imagination – nearly 200 of them died on the job.

The line was part of the national rail network until 1983, but the public outcry upon its announced closure ensured that it remained open; today it is a huge tourist attraction (as well as a working railway).

The Journey

Trains run between Leeds and Carlisle via Settle about eight times a day. The first section of the journey from Leeds is along the Aire Valley, stopping at **Keighley**, where the Keighley & Worth Valley Railway branches off to **Haworth** (p591), **Skipton** – gateway to the southern Dales – and **Settle**. The train chugs up the valley beside the River Ribble, through **Horton-in-Ribblesdale**, across the spectacular Ribblehead Viaduct and then through Blea Moor Tunnel, popping out at **Dent** station, one of the highest in the country.

Upwards and onwards to its highest point (356m) at Ais Gill, before leaving the Dales behind and trundling down to **Kirkby Stephen**. The last halts are **Appleby** then **Langwathby,** just northwest of Penrith (a jumping-off point for the Lake District), then the train finally pulls into **Carlisle**.

The Nuts & Bolts

The entire journey takes two hours and 40 minutes and costs £35 return. Various hop-on hop-off passes for one or three days are also available. You can pick up a free SCL timetable – which includes a colour map of the line and brief details about places of interest – from most Yorkshire stations; for more information, contact **National Rail Enquiries** (☎ 08457 484950) or click on to www.settle-carlisle.co.uk or www.settle-carlisle-railway.org.uk.

THREE PEAKS CHALLENGE

Fancy a gruelling test of your endurance? Why not join the fell-runners on the last Sunday in April to complete the Three Peaks Challenge – not the more famous climb of the three highest peaks in England, Scotland and Wales, but Yorkshire's very own: in 2006, Rob Jebb won his sixth in a row. Cyclists have their chance to race like lunatics in the last week of September, racing over 38 miles and climbing 1524m. Only cyclocross bikes are allowed – mountain bikes are a big no-no. For entry forms, contact **British Cycling** (www.britishcycling.org.uk).

---

devoted to the production of Wallace and Gromit's favourite powdery-white cheese, but watching guys shovel tons of cheese around is only marginally interesting. You can taste it in the museum and then buy it in the shop, which is free to enter. There are daily tours of the creamery every day at 10am, which also include a video called 'From Cow to Customer'.

The **tourist office** (☎ 667450; hawes@ytbtic.co.uk; ☷ 10am-5pm) shares the Old Station building with the **Dales Countryside Museum** (adult/child £3/free), a beautifully presented social history of the area. There's still an old train in the yard too.

About 1.5 miles north of town is Hawes' other attraction, **Hardraw Force**, the highest above-ground waterfall in the country. For most of the year it's little more than a trickle on the rocks and not really worth the £1 'toll' you pay at the Green Dragon pub to walk up to it.

Sleeping & Eating

Bainbridge Ings Caravan & Camp Site (☎ 667354; www.bainbridge-ings.co.uk; car & 2 adults/hikers & cyclists £9.50/3.50) Pitches are around the edges of stonewalled fields located around a spacious farmhouse about half a mile east of town. Gas, milk and eggs are sold on site.

Hawes YHA Hostel (☎ 0870 770 5854; www.yha.org.uk; Town Head; dm £13.95) A modern place on the western edge of town, at the junction of the main A684 (Aysgarth Rd) and B6255.

Laburnum House (☎ 667717; www.stayatlaburnumhouse.co.uk; The Holme; s/d from £23/45) A quaint cottage in the centre, with a busy tearoom and terrace downstairs serving tea and scones

(£3), hearty sandwiches (£3 to £5) and meals (£8 to £10). The rooms are decorated in various shades of blue.

Green Dragon Inn (☎ 667392; www.greendragonhardraw.co.uk; Hardraw; s/d with breakfast £28/49 without from £22/40) About 1.5 miles north of town is this 'famous' inn where you pay the fee for the nearby waterfall. It's terrific, with unspectacular but thoroughly comfortable rooms, good beer, home-cooked food (mains about £6) and live bands at weekends.

Cocketts (☎ 667312; www.cocketts.co.uk; Market Pl; d from £58) The most stylish place in town is a handsome 17th-century stone house with eight pretty, delightful rooms decorated in traditional style, two with four-poster beds. Two-/three-course meals in the restaurant are £17/19.

There are plenty of pubs, including the **Fountain** (☎ 667206; Market Pl; bar food about £6). The traditional **White Hart** (Market Pl; pub grub about £8) is also good for a pint or a bar meal.

Getting There & Away

Hawes is a public transportation nightmare. From Northallerton, buses 156/157 run to Hawes (two hours, four Monday to Friday) via Leyburn, where you can connect with transport to/from Richmond. On Sunday (March to October) there are buses to Hawes from Manchester (X43) via Skipton and Grassington, and from Leeds (803). Between Hawes and the Lake District, bus 112 runs to/from Kendal (1½ hours, twice daily), very early in the morning and late in the evening, with a few extra services on some other weekdays. The tourist office can advise on other bus services aimed at visitors.

RICHMOND
☎ 01748 / pop 8178

If Richmond was at the heart of the English tourist trail, you'd probably have to jostle for position with busloads of tourists and film crews, for this is surely one of England's most handsome market towns. Radiating from the busy, cobbled market square are streets and alleyways (cobbled, naturally) lined with elegant Georgian buildings and photogenic stone cottages; between the gaps you can catch glimpses of the surrounding hills and dales. And if you want that panoramic view of the whole lot, climb the rocky outcrop overlooking the rushing River Swale and clamber about the ruins of the massive castle.

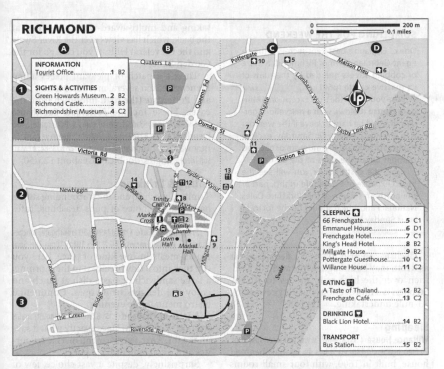

RICHMOND

0 ────── 200 m
0 ────── 0.1 miles

INFORMATION	
Tourist Office.................1	B2

SIGHTS & ACTIVITIES	
Green Howards Museum..2	B2
Richmond Castle.............3	B3
Richmondshire Museum....4	C2

SLEEPING	
66 Frenchgate.........................5	C1
Emmanuel House......................6	D1
Frenchgate Hotel....................7	C1
King's Head Hotel....................8	B2
Millgate House........................9	B2
Pottergate Guesthouse..........10	C1
Willance House......................11	C2

EATING	
A Taste of Thailand..............12	B2
Frenchgate Café..................13	C2

DRINKING	
Black Lion Hotel..................14	B2

TRANSPORT	
Bus Station........................15	B2

Orientation & Information

Richmond is east of the Yorkshire Dales National Park but makes a good gateway for the northern area. Centre of everything is Trinity Church Sq (with market day on Saturday). Just north of here, the **tourist office** (☎ 850252; www.richmond.org.uk; Friary Gardens, Victoria Rd; ☺ 9.30am-5.30pm Apr-Oct, to 4.30pm Nov-Mar) has the usual maps and guides, plus several leaflets (around 80p) showing walks in town and the surrounding countryside.

Sights

Top of the pile is the impressive heap that's left of **Richmond Castle** (EH; ☎ 822493; admission £3.60; ☺ 10am-6pm Apr-Sep, to 4pm Oct-Mar), founded in 1070 and one of the first castles in England since Roman times to be built of stone. It's had many uses through the years, including a stint as a prison for conscientious objectors during WWI (there's a small and sobering exhibition about their part in the castle's history). The best part of a visit is the view from the top of the remarkably well-preserved 30m-high tower; you can look down on the market place or over the surrounding hills.

Veterans and military buffs will enjoy the three floors of the **Green Howards Museum** (☎ 822133; www.greenhowards.org.uk; Trinity Church Sq; adult/child £3/2; ☺ 9.30am-4.30pm Mon-Sat, 2-4.30pm Sun mid-May–Sep, 9.30am-4.30pm Mon-Sat Oct, 10am-4.30pm Mon-Fri Feb-Mar & Nov), which pays tribute to the famous Yorkshire regiment.

In a different vein, the **Richmondshire Museum** (☎ 825611; Ryder's Wynd; adult/child £2/1; ☺ 10.30am-4.30pm Easter-Oct) is a delightful little gem, with very informative staff and local history exhibits including an early Yorkshire cave-dweller, James Herriot's surgery, and informative displays on lead mining, which forever altered the Swaledale landscape a century ago.

Activities

West from Richmond walkers can follow paths along the River Swale, upstream and downstream from the town. A longer option is along the north side of Swaledale, following the famous long-distance Coast to Coast walk (p575) all the way to Reeth. For a grand day out, take the first bus from Richmond to Reeth then walk back; the tourist office has route and bus time details.

YORKSHIRE

SOMETHING FOR THE WEEKEND

One of England's best-kept secrets is the elegant Georgian town of Richmond, a maze of cobbled streets guarded by the ruins of its massive **castle** (p601).

Base yourself in the truly exceptional **Millgate House** (below), with a marvellous garden that will be hard to leave if the weather is in any way clement. On Saturday, explore the town itself, take in a museum or two and clamber about the ruins of the castle.

From the castle tower you will see the broad expanse of **Swaledale** (right), part of the northern section of the Yorkshire Dales National Park, which should be the focus of your Sunday activities.

Cyclists can also follow Swaledale: as far as Reeth may be enough, while a trip to Keld, then over the high wild moors to Kirkby Stephen is a more serious but very rewarding 33-mile undertaking.

Sleeping

Willance House (☎ 824467; www.willancehouse.com; 24 Frenchgate; s/d £30/55) This is an oak-beamed house, built in 1600, with four small rooms full of cutesy character (lots of floral prints and pillows) and one four-poster.

Frenchgate Hotel (☎ 822087; www.frenchgatehotel .com; 59-61 Frenchgate; s/d from £58/98; **P**) Eight immaculate bedrooms occupy the upper floors of this converted Georgian town house, now an elegant boutique guesthouse. One of the bedrooms has a beautiful canopied bed, which fits somewhat snugly into the room (the others are equally compact). Downstairs there's a hospitable lounge with oak beams and an open fire.

King's Head Hotel (☎ 850220; www.kingsheadrich mond.co.uk; Market Pl; s/d £80/112) Right on Market Pl, Richmond's fanciest hotel was once described by the painter Turner as 'the finest in Richmondshire'. That was a long time ago. It's still pretty fancy though; each of the traditionally furnished 30 bedrooms have wrought-iron or hardwood beds and plenty of comfort.

our pick Millgate House (☎ 823571; www.millgate house.com; Market Pl; r £85-95; **P** **☐**) Behind the unassuming green door and plaque is the unexpected pleasure of one of the nicest guesthouses in England. While the house itself is wonderful, it is overshadowed by the breath-

taking and multi-award-winning garden at the back, which has views over the River Swale and the Cleveland Hills. If you can, go for the Garden Suite.

There's a batch of pleasant places along Frenchgate, and several more on Maison Dieu and Pottergate (the road into town from the east). These include **Pottergate Guesthouse** (☎ 823826; gary53uk@hotmail.com; 4 Pottergate), **66 Frenchgate** (☎ 823421; paul@66french.freeserve.co.uk; 66 Frenchgate) and **Emmanuel House** (☎ 823584; 41 Maison Dieu). Singles/doubles cost about £25/50.

Eating & Drinking

Trinity Church Sq and the surrounding streets have a huge choice of pubs, teashops, cafés and takeaways.

Frenchgate Café (☎ 824949; 29 Frenchgate; lunches about £5, evening mains £7-12; ☒ 10am-10pm Tue-Sun) An all-meals-in-one kind of place, here you can tuck into a tidy breakfast in the morning, a large sandwich or pasta dish at lunch and enjoy the delights of its quasi-Continental bistro menu in the evening.

A Taste of Thailand (☎ 829696; 15 King St; mains about £10; ☒ dinner only) Does exactly what it says on the tin. An extensive menu of Thai favourites and a convenient BYO policy.

Surprisingly, despite a vast choice, few of the pubs in Richmond are up to much. After extensive research, the best we found was the **Black Lion Hotel** (☎ 823121; Finkle St), with cosy bars, low beams, good beer and food (bar food £5, mains in restaurant about £9.50), plus B&B.

Getting There & Away

From Darlington (on the railway between London and Edinburgh) it's easy to reach Richmond on bus 34 (30 minutes, hourly, four on Sunday). All buses stop in Trinity Church Sq.

SWALEDALE

The quietest and least-visited of the Dales lies just west of Richmond and is all the better for the lack of attention. The wild and rugged beauty of the valley is in sharp contrast to the softer, greener places further south, and it's difficult to imagine that only a century ago this was a major lead-mining area. When the price of ore fell in the 19th century, many people left Swaledale for good. Some went to England's burgeoning industrial cities, and others emigrated – especially to Wisconsin in the USA – leaving Swaledale almost empty, a legacy that remains today, with just a few small lonely villages scattered along its length.

Reeth

☎ 01748 / pop 730

In the heart of Swaledale is the pretty village of Reeth – a great base for exploring Swaledale, with shops, cafés and some good pubs dotted around a large sloping green (Friday is market day). There's a **tourist office** (☎ 884059; reeth@ytbtic.co.uk), and to understand Swaledale's fascinating history, the dusty little **Swaledale Folk Museum** (☎ 884373; admission £1.50; ⏱ 10.30am-5pm Thu-Sun Easter-Oct) is well worth a look.

There are many B&B options; one excellent choice is the **Arkleside Hotel** (☎ 884200; www.arklesidehotel.co.uk; s/d from £55/92), made up of a converted row of old cottages just by the green.

EAST RIDING OF YORKSHIRE

Its Viking roots still present in the name, the East Riding of Yorkshire (from Old Danish *Thriding*, or third) was one of three administrative regions of the Danelaw created in the 9th century – west and north ridings are now the slightly less evocative West and North Yorkshire.

The county's beating heart is the tough old sea dog of Hull, a no-nonsense port that goes about its business with little fuss between the broad horizons of the Rivers Humber and Hull.

The expanse of the River Humber, with its soaring, powerful bridge, flows to meet the sea by a flat, deserted coast and the strange protuberance of Spurn Head. Further north up the coast, there are some classic, small seaside settlements: Bridlington and the rather-more-restrained Filey, and beyond that the drama of the Flamborough cliffs and Bempton Cliffs Nature Reserve. Inland, the respite from the largely flat and nondescript drained marshland comes with the Yorkshire Wolds, an area of gently rolling chalky hills between Hull, York and the coast. In between them and Hull is the county's most attractive town, Beverley, with lots of 18th-century character, and an enormous medieval religious and cultural legacy.

Activities

The Yorkshire Wolds are ideal for gentle walks and cycle tours. Whether you're on two feet or two wheels, the town of Beverley makes a good base, and the northern Wolds can also be easily reached from York.

The area's main long-distance walk is the 80-mile Wolds Way. This national trail starts at Hessle, a riverside town 4 miles west of Hull, close to the Humber Bridge, and leads northwards through farmland, hills and quiet villages, to end at the tip of Filey Brigg, a peninsula on the east coast just north of the town of Filey. Billed as 'Yorkshire's best-kept secret', it takes five days, and is an excellent beginners' walk, as the landscape is not high and conditions not too strenuous.

The Cleveland Way (p629) also ends at Filey, and for a shorter walk in bracing sea air you can follow the Cleveland Way along a scenic stretch of coast northwards from Filey to Scarborough.

Getting There & Around

Hull is easily reached by rail from Leeds, York, Beverley, Filey and Scarborough, and is also the hub for regional bus services. There's a useful website at www.gettingaround.eastriding.gov.uk.

HULL

☎ 01482 / pop 301,416

Tough, uncompromising Hull is a curmudgeonly English seaport with a proud seafaring tradition and a hard-bitten attitude to all things in life, perhaps the inevitable consequence of growing up amid salt and sweat. But there is life beyond the port, and while you may get the impression that Hull remains determinedly unaffected by the exotic trade that has passed through its docks, a quick tour of the city's cultural offerings should convince you otherwise. But not too much, for this is still a northern port, and with the marked exception of the almost lunatic nightlife, Hull balks at all indulgences: its full and proper name – Kingston-upon-Hull – seems like an unnecessary extravagance when plain old Hull will do, and it seems apt that jaundiced, rueful poet Philip Larkin (1922–85) presided over its university library for many years.

Orientation & Information

The Old Town of Hull, which retains a sense of the prosperous Victorian era, is bounded by

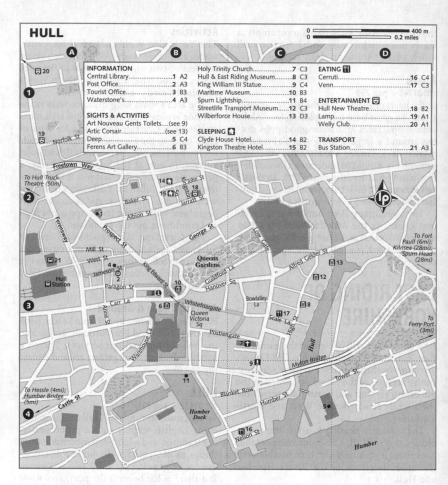

HULL

INFORMATION
Central Library...................1 A2
Post Office.........................2 A3
Tourist Office.....................3 B3
Waterstone's......................4 A3

SIGHTS & ACTIVITIES
Art Nouveau Gents Toilets....(see 9)
Artic Corsair...................(see 13)
Deep..................................5 C4
Ferens Art Gallery..............6 B3

Holy Trinity Church...............7 C3
Hull & East Riding Museum......8 C3
King William III Statue............9 C4
Maritime Museum................10 B3
Spurn Lightship...................11 B4
Streetlife Transport Museum...12 C3
Wilberforce House................13 D3

SLEEPING
Clyde House Hotel................14 B2
Kingston Theatre Hotel..........15 B2

EATING
Cerruti..............................16 C4
Venn................................17 C3

ENTERTAINMENT
Hull New Theatre................18 B2
Lamp...............................19 A1
Welly Club........................20 A1

TRANSPORT
Bus Station........................21 A3

Ferensway and Freetown Way and the Rivers Humber and Hull. Perched on the waterfront overlooking the Humber is the city's main attraction, a huge aquarium called The Deep. It's all walkable.

Central library (☎ 223344; Albion St) For Internet access.

Post office (57 Jameson St; 🕑 9am-5.30pm Mon-Sat)

Tourist office (☎ 223559; www.hullcc.gov.uk; 1 Paragon St; 🕑 10am-5pm Mon-Sat, 11am-3pm Sun)

Waterstone's (☎ 580234; 19-21 Jameson St) Best bookshop.

Sights
THE DEEP

The colossal, angled monolith that is the **Deep** (☎ 381000; www.thedeep.co.uk; Tower St; adult/child £8/6;

🕑 10am-6pm, last entry 5pm) stands at the edge of the port, with great views across the Humber. Inside it's just as dramatic, as echoing commentaries and computer-generated interactives run you through the formation of the seas, and onwards. The largest aquarium contains 2.5 million litres of water (and 87 tonnes of salt) and even has a glass lift. To get a good view of the tank's seven different types of sharks, eels, rays and other watery dwellers, it's best (if more pedestrian) to take the stairs, as the lift ride is over no sooner than you start it. And it's rare you see a pod full of people zoom through a tank.

OTHER SIGHTS

Hull has a remarkable collection of city-run **museums** (☎ 613902; www.hullcc.gov.uk/museums;

🕙 10am-5pm Mon-Sat, 1.30-4.30pm Sun). All share the same phone number and opening hours and are free unless otherwise stated.

The serene **Ferens Art Gallery** (Queen Victoria Sq), built in 1927, has a decent collection that includes works by Stanley Spencer and Peter Blake.

The dusty-feeling but interesting **Maritime Museum**, in the former dock offices (1871), celebrates Hull's long maritime traditions, and includes some daunting whale skeletons.

The well-preserved High St has some eclectic museums. The **Streetlife Transport Museum** has re-created 1930s streets, all sorts of historic vehicles to get on and off, and a pleasant garden. Next door, attractive, Georgian **Wilberforce House** (1639) was the birthplace in 1759 of the antislavery crusader William Wilberforce. It covers the history of slavery and the campaign against it – a major renovation saw its closure through 2006 but it should have reopened early in 2007. Behind it is the **Arctic Corsair**; tours demonstrate the hardships of trawling in the Arctic Circle.

The **Hull & East Riding Museum** traces local history from Roman times to the present, with new Anglo-Saxon, medieval and geology galleries.

At the heart of the Old Town, **Holy Trinity Church** (☎ 324835; Market Pl; 🕙 11am-2pm Tue-Fri Oct-Mar, 11am-3pm Mon-Fri, 9.30am-noon Sat Apr-Sep, services Sun year-round) is a magnificent 15th-century building with a striking central tower, and a long, tall, unified interior worthy of a cathedral. It features huge areas of windows, built to keep the weight of the walls down as the soil here is unstable.

Moving to some more prosaic architectural treasures, southeast of the church are some famous rare **Art Nouveau gents toilets** (Market Pl) that have been relieving the pressure since 1902. The nearby **King William III Statue** (Market Pl) was erected in 1734 in honour of William of Orange, who besides being king also has the distinction of introducing England to gin, which he brought from his native Holland. The statue's proximity to the toilet is pure coincidence.

Built in 1927, the **Spurn Lightship** is now anchored in the marina. It once provided guidance for ships navigating the notorious Humber estuary.

Around 6 miles east of the centre, along the A1033, **Fort Paull** (☎ 893339; www.fortpaull.com; adult/child £4.50/3; 🕙 10am-6pm Apr-Oct, 11am-4pm Nov-Mar) is a grand, lavishly restored fort. The 1860s structure, with its underground labyrinths, is interesting, while stilted waxworks and warlike stuff document the fort's history from the AD 910 Viking landing onwards.

Activities

The tourist office sells a brochure called *The Seven Seas Fish Pavement Trail* (60p), a delightful, historic self-guided tour of the Old Town, following fish shapes embedded in the pavement. Kids love it. Adults might prefer the *Hull Ale Trail* (60p), which needs no explanation.

Festivals

Hull Literature Festival (www.humbermouth.org.uk) A two-week celebration of the written word in the second half of June; a fitting tribute to Hull's rich literary heritage: besides Larkin, poets Andrew Marvell, Stevie Smith and playwrights Alan Plater and John Godber all hail from here.
Hull Jazz Festival (www.hulljazzfestival.co.uk) Sees a week-long, impressive line-up of great jazz in the first week in July.
Hull Fair (☎ 300300) The second week in October sees the town taken over by Europe's largest travelling funfair, with 250 different attractions including all kinds of stalls selling everything from palm reading to candy floss and all manner of rides, from the gentle, traditional kind to more modern white-knucklers.

Sleeping & Eating

Good accommodation options are pretty thin on the ground – most of them are made up of business-oriented hotels and mediocre guesthouses. The tourist office will help book accommodation for free.

Clyde House Hotel (☎ 214981; www.clydehousehotel.co.uk; 13 John St; s/d £30/50) Next to leafy Kingston Sq, this is one of the best B&B options near the Old Town. The rooms are nothing fancy, but they're very tidy and comfortable.

Kingston Theatre Hotel (☎ 225828; www.kingstontheatrehotel.com; 1-2 Kingston Sq; s/d/ste from £40/55/90) This 19th-century building is a privately owned hotel in a quiet part of the centre. The rooms are perfectly charming if not quite memorable; upgrade to a suite if you're looking for a little leg room.

Venn (☎ 224004; www.vennrestaurant.co.uk; 21 Scale Lane; brasserie mains £7-10, restaurant mains £18-24; 🕙 Tue-Sat) Modern British cuisine in all its cool, posh guises hits Hull and – guess what? – sticks nicely. This trendy brasserie serves fancy sandwiches, pizzas and salads, while the more upmarket upstairs restaurant goes to town with dishes like leg and saddle of local rabbit with Parma ham…gorgeous.

Cerruti (☎ 328501; 10 Nelson St; mains about £13; ☽ lunch Mon-Fri, dinner Mon-Sat) Hull's best Italian restaurant is an attractive spot that specialises – unsurprisingly – in seafood.

Entertainment

Come nightfall – especially at weekends – Hull gets raucous and often rowdy. What else did you expect from sea dogs in a seaport? Groups of dangerously underdressed kids party like tomorrow didn't matter. If you're that pissed, it wouldn't.

Welly Club (☎ 326131, 221676; 105-107 Beverley Rd; admission free-£5; ☽ to 2am, closed Wed & Sun) Best known these days for its devotion to trance and drum 'n' bass, this is the place to go if you like your beats hard and extremely fast.

Lamp (☎ 326131; 2 Norfolk St) One of the more modern watering holes in town, with DJs, cocktails, a plush atmosphere and all the other devices to attract the beautiful kids.

Hull Truck Theatre (☎ 323638; www.hulltruck.co.uk; Spring St) Home to acclaimed down-to-earth playwright John Godber, it presents vibrant drama, comedy and Sunday jazz. It's just northwest of the Old Town.

Hull New Theatre (☎ 226655; Kingston Sq) A traditional regional theatre hosting popular drama, concerts and musicals.

Getting There & Away

The bus station is on Ferensway, just north of the train station. National Express has buses to/from London (£21.50, 5¾ hours, two daily) and Manchester (£12.75, 4¼ hours, one daily). Both National Express and Bus X46 run frequently to/from York (£6.25, 1¾ hours). Local services also leave from here.

The train station is west of Queen Victoria Sq, in the town centre. Hull has good rail links north and south, and west to York (£13.50, 1¼ hours, hourly) and Leeds (£13.10, one hour, hourly).

The ferry port is 3 miles east of the centre at King George Dock. A bus to/from the train station connects with the ferries. For details of departures, see p781.

AROUND HULL
Humber Bridge

The graceful, concrete-and-metal Humber Bridge swoops 1410m across the broad river – the world's third-longest single-suspension

bridge – seemingly hung by fine threads. It has linked Yorkshire and Lincolnshire since 1981, opening up what was an often-overlooked corner of the country.

Near the base of the bridge on the north side is a small park with nature trails that run from the parking area all the way down to the riverbank. The park can be reached from the bridge access roads. The park is also home to the **Humber Bridge tourist office** (☎ 01482 640852; ☽ 9am-5pm Mon-Fri, 9am-6pm Sat & Sun May-Sep, 10am-3pm Nov-Feb, 9am-4pm Mar, Apr & Oct). It handles information requests for all of the East Riding of Yorkshire and the Wolds Way and has a display documenting the construction of the bridge.

The bridge is a mile west of the small riverside town of **Hessle**, about 4 miles west of Hull and effectively an outer suburb. Buses 66, 67 and 68 run regularly from Hull's centre (30 minutes) to Hessle, and this is also a stop for local trains on the line from Hull to Leeds, Doncaster and Sheffield.

Spurn Head

A narrow, hooked sandbank dangling off the coast on the north side of the Humber estuary, **Spurn Head** (admission per car £3.50) has a long military history and is an important nature reserve.

In 1804 gun batteries were built to meet the expected French; in following decades the fortifications were greatly expanded to meet various threats. By WWII there were guns of all sizes mounted in heavy concrete emplacements. After the war, the odds of some enemy force arriving in assault boats faded and the guns were removed, although remnants of the many concrete emplacements and roadways survive.

A benefit of the years of military use is that Spurn Head was spared commercial development. Today it is made up of large rolling sand dunes covered with various sea grasses. Most of the land is now part of the **Spurn National Nature Reserve**.

There are two tourist offices. One has a café and is at the end of the B1445 in **Kilnsea**, the last village on the mainland. Called the **Blue Bell Tea Room** (☎ 01964 650139; ☽ 11am-4.30pm Jul-Sep, 11am-5pm Sat & Sun Sep-Jun), it is close to the beach, and allows free camping on its grassy land. The other is run by the **Yorkshire Wildlife Trust** (☽ 10am-5pm Sat & Sun) and is a mile further south along the Spurn Head access road.

The single-track road to the point is 2.5 miles long. There are many good walks, and at the tip of the head you can see the spurting tides of the Humber as well as the busy shuttle boats used by the pilots of the many passing freighters.

Back in Kilnsea, along the B1445, the **Crown & Anchor** (☎ 01964-650276; mains £6-9) is a fine pub with good food, and a dramatic, isolated, waterside location. Singles/doubles are £32/48.

Public transport to Kilnsea and Spurn Head is nonexistent. It's about 28 miles east of Hull. The flat roads are good for bikes.

BEVERLEY

☎ 01482 / pop 29,110

Handsome, unspoilt Beverley is one of the most attractive of Yorkshire towns largely on account of its magnificent minster – a rival to any cathedral in England – and the tangle of streets that lie beneath it, each brimming with exquisite Georgian and Victorian buildings.

Orientation & Information

Beverley is small and easily walked to from either the train or bus stations. There's a large market in the main square on Saturday.

Beverley Bookshop (☎ 0800 616394; 16 Butcher Row)

Post office (Register Sq; 9am-5.30pm Mon-Fri, to 12.30pm Sat)

Library (☎ 885355; Champney Rd; 9.30am-5pm Mon & Wed, 9.30am-7pm Tue, Thu & Fri, 9am-1pm Sat) Internet access and a small art gallery with changing exhibitions.

Tourist office (☎ 391672; www.visiteastyorkshire.com; 34 Butcher Row; 9.30am-5.15pm Mon-Fri, 10am-4.45pm Sat, also 10am-2pm Sun Jun-Aug only)

Sights

The third church to be built on this site (the first was constructed during the 7th century), **Beverley Minster** (☎ 868540; www.beverleyminster.org; admission by donation; 9am-5.30pm Mon-Sat May-Aug, 9am-5pm Sep-Oct & Mar-Apr, 9am-4pm Nov-Feb, also noon-4pm Sun year-round) dates from 1220, but construction continued for two centuries, spanning the Early English, Decorated and Perpendicular periods. Hailed for its unity of forms, the church has a magnificent Gothic perpendicular west front (1390–1420).

Inside, the nave is strikingly high. Extraordinary medieval faces and demons peer down from every possible vantage point, while expressive stone musicians play silent instruments. Note particularly the 10th-century *fridstol* (Old English for 'peace chair') which gave sanctuary to anyone escaping the law; the fruit- and angel-laden Gothic canopy of the Percy Tomb; the 68 medieval misericords (the largest collection in the country) and the late Norman font (c 1170).

There's an interesting display showing the history of the minster and town. Check out the rebuilt treadwheel crane, where workers ground around like hapless hamsters to lift the huge loads necessary to build such medieval structures.

Doomed to play second fiddle to the mother church, **St Mary's** (☎ 865709; admission free; 9.15am-noon & 1.30-5pm Mon-Fri, 10am-5.30pm Sat, 2-5pm Sun Apr-Sep, 2-4.15pm Oct-Mar) is a glorious church, built in stages between 1120 and 1530. In the North Choir Aisle look out for a carving (c 1330) thought to have inspired Lewis Carroll's White Rabbit. The West Front is considered one of England's finest (early 15th century).

Sleeping & Eating

Friary YHA Hostel (☎ 0870 770 5696; www.yha.org.uk; Friar's Lane; dm £11.95; Mon-Sat Easter-end Oct) Here's your chance to stay in a beautiful, restored 14th-century Dominican friary mentioned in Chaucer's *The Canterbury Tales*. This place might just have the best setting in town, only 100m southeast of the minster.

Number One (☎ 862752; http://numberone-bedandbreakfast-beverley.co.uk; 1 Woodlands; s/d from £25/50) Three very comfortable rooms in a friendly, welcoming house packed with pictures, books and bric-a-brac just west of the town centre.

Eastgate Guest House (☎ 868464; 7 Eastgate; s/d with bathroom £41/53, without from £27/42) This relatively central B&B is highly recommended for sheer friendliness and relaxed atmosphere more than for the floral, simple rooms.

Swallow Beverley Arms (☎ 869241; www.swallowhotels.com; North Bar Within; s/d from £56/92) Beverley's top spot is a very elegant Georgian coaching house with all the trimmings, a handsome combination of old-world style and contemporary comfort.

White Horse Inn (☎ 861973; 22 Hengate; mains £7-9; lunch & dinner) Also known as Nellie's, this lovely, dimly lit place has rambling rooms, open fires and tables outside. There's regular live music and poetry.

Cerutti 2 (☎ 866700; Station Sq; mains £10-19; dinner Mon-Sat) The only restaurant of note in town is unusually positioned inside the old waiting

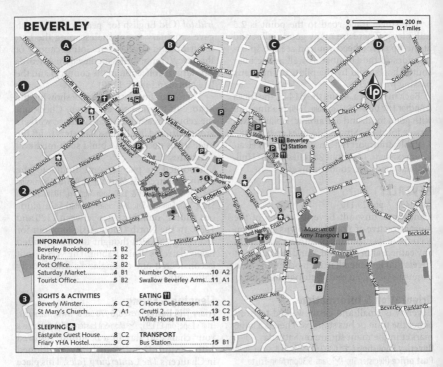

BEVERLEY

INFORMATION
Beverley Bookshop...........**1** B2
Library..................................**2** B2
Post Office........................**3** B2
Saturday Market..............**4** B1
Tourist Office..................**5** B2

Number One....................**10** A2
Swallow Beverley Arms...**11** A1

SIGHTS & ACTIVITIES
Beverly Minster...............**6** C2
St Mary's Church.............**7** A1

EATING
C Horse Delicatessen......**12** C2
Cerutti 2............................**13** C2
White Horse Inn..............**14** B1

SLEEPING
Eastgate Guest House....**8** C2
Friary YHA Hostel............**9** C2

TRANSPORT
Bus Station.......................**15** B1

room of the train station. Italian dishes of all kinds are on offer, without the seafood leanings of its sister restaurant in Hull. Attached is the 'C' Horse Delicatessen, perfect for takeaway meals.

Getting There & Away
The train station lies east of the town centre. The bus station is north on Sow Hill.

Bus X46/X47 links Beverley with York (70 minutes, hourly). There are frequent services to Hull (buses 121, 122, 246 and X46/X47, 30 minutes).

There are regular trains to/from Scarborough via Filey (£11.90, 1½ hours). Trains to/from Hull (20 minutes) run at least hourly.

Details on boats to Hull from northern Europe are given in the main Transport chapter, p781.

BRIDLINGTON
☎ 01262 / pop 33,589
The little town of Bridlington presents a roll call of the English seaside's usual suspects, with all the tawdry charm that such diversions involve. The promenade has a small funfair, candy floss, arcades, all-day breakfasts, palmists, lager specials and often windswept people. There's a long, attractive sandy beach.

The **tourist office** (☎ 673474; 25 Prince St; ⏱ 9.30am-5.30pm Mon-Sat, 11am-3pm Sun) is near the north beach and has short-term parking at the front. It can book a vast array of rooms.

Bridlington is on the line from Hull to Scarborough with frequent trains to the former (45 minutes) and the latter (45 minutes).

AROUND BRIDLINGTON
As well as seaside towns, the coast of the East Riding of Yorkshire has long unpeopled stretches, and fine blustery cliff tops.

Bempton Cliffs Nature Reserve
The Royal Society for the Protection of Birds' **nature reserve** (☎ 01262-851179; pedestrian/car free/£3.50; visitor centre ⏱ 10am-5pm Mar-Nov, 10am-5pm Sat & Sun Dec & Feb) is a delightful place for nontwitchers too. Around 3 miles of paths (open at all times) skirt the top of the imposing chalk cliffs, which are home to more than 200,000 nesting sea birds – the largest

colony in England – every spring and summer. There are many other feathered residents in place the rest of the year as well. The species flapping about include gannets, auks, guillemots, razorbills, kittiwakes and ever-popular puffins.

There is a good visitor centre with a small snack bar set back from the cliffs. Binoculars can be rented for £3 and there are usually volunteers on hand to provide guidance.

The reserve is a well-marked 1.25 miles from the village of Bempton and the B1229. By public transport, take one of the frequent trains on the Hull–Scarborough line and then walk.

Flamborough

The small village of Flamborough is 3 miles east of Bridlington. Fine views soar out from the milk-coloured cliffs at Flamborough Head, 2 miles east of the village.

Seabirds (☎ 01262-850242; Tower St; mains £6-11; ☻ lunch & dinner) is a classic country pub with several rooms, open fires and a beer garden. The real-ale selection is good and the seafood lunches and dinners excellent.

NORTH YORKSHIRE

The largest of Yorkshire's four counties is also the most beautiful, if only because unlike the rest of northern England, mills and mines are nowhere to be found. Blissfully free of the landmarks of the Industrial Revolution, North Yorkshire has, since the Middle Ages, always been about sheep and the woolly wealth that they produced.

Instead of smoke-bellowing factories and labour-abusing mills and mines, the manmade monuments that dot the landscape round these parts are of the magnificent variety: the great houses and rich abbeys that sit ruined or otherwise in glorious isolation from the rest of the world are a reminder that there was lots of money to be made off the sheep's back. Indeed, much of North Yorkshire's untamed, untouched quality is preserved within the confines of the county's two superb national parks – the Yorkshire Dales (p594) and North York Moors (p628).

But North Yorkshire's biggest attraction is urban. Sure, the genteel spa town of Harrogate and the blowsy, dramatically situated resorts of Scarborough and Whitby have many fans, but literally nothing compares to the unparal-

leled splendour of York, northern England's most visited town.

Activities

The best walking and cycling is in the Yorkshire Dales (p594) and the North York Moors (p629).

Getting There & Around

The main gateway town is York and a web of buses and trains connect places in North Yorkshire. More specific details on the Yorkshire Dales and the North York Moors are given in those sections. For countywide information, call the national **Traveline** (☎ 0870 608 2608). There are various Explorer passes, and individual bus and train companies also offer their own saver schemes, so it's always worth asking for advice on the best deal when you buy your ticket.

YORK

☎ 01904 / pop 137,505

York is the kind of place that makes you wish – if only for an instant – that the Industrial Revolution never happened, and reminds us of a world before the machines. A city of extraordinary cultural and historical wealth, its medieval spider's web of narrow streets is enclosed by a magnificent circuit of 13th-century walls. At its heart lies the immense, awe-inspiring minster, one of the most beautiful Gothic cathedrals in the world. The city's long history and rich heritage is woven into virtually every brick and beam; modern, tourist-oriented York – with its myriad museums, restaurants, cafés and traditional pubs – is a carefully maintained heir to that heritage.

Orientation

Compact and eminently walkable, York has five major landmarks to take note of: the wall enclosing the small city centre; the minster at the northern corner; Clifford's Tower at the southern end; the River Ouse that cuts the centre in two; and the train station to the west. Just to avoid the inevitable confusion, remember that round these parts *gate* means street and *bar* means gate.

Information

American Express (Amex; ☎ 676501; 6 Stonegate; ☻ 9am-5.30pm Mon-Fri, 9am-5pm Sat) With foreign exchange service.

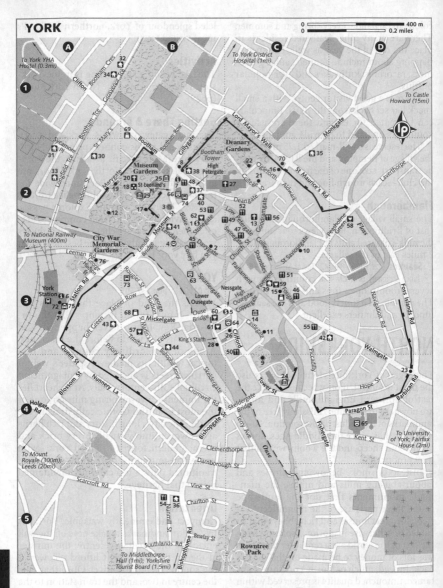

YORK

Borders (☎ 653300; 1-5 Davygate; ☺ 9am-9pm Mon-Sat, 11am-5pm Sun) Well-stocked bookshop.

City Library (☎ 552815; Museum St; ☺ 9am-8pm Mon-Wed & Fri, to 5.30pm Thu, to 4pm Sat; per 30min £1) Internet access.

Post office (22 Lendal; ☺ 8.30am-5.30pm Mon & Tue, 9am-5.30pm Wed-Sat).

This is York (www.thisisyork.co.uk)

Thomas Cook (☎ 653626; 4 Nessgate) A travel agent offering a full service.

Tourist Office (☎ 550099; www.visityork.org; De Grey Rooms, Exhibition Sq; ☺ 9am-6pm Mon-Sat, 10am-5pm Sun Apr-Sep, 9am-5pm Mon-Sat, 10am-4pm Sun Oct-Mar) There's another branch at the train station.

York District Hospital (☎ 631313; Wiggington Rd) A mile north of the centre.

Sights

YORK MINSTER

Get your camera ready. Make sure your neck muscles are loose and relaxed. Prepare to be bowled over. England's largest medieval cathedral and Yorkshire's most important historic building is the simply awesome **minster** (☎ 624426; www.yorkminster.org; adult/child/concession £5/free/4, undercroft £4/2/3, minster & undercroft £7/5/5; ⏰ 9am-5pm Mon-Sat, noon-3.45pm Sun Apr-Oct, 9.30am-5pm Mon-Sat, noon-3.45pm Sun Nov-Mar, undercroft, treasury & crypt 9.30am-5pm Mon-Sat, noon-5pm Sun Sep-Jun, to 5.30pm Jul & Aug) that dominates the city. Seat of the archbishop of York, the primate of England, it is second in importance only to Canterbury, home of the primate of *all* England (the two titles were given to settle a debate over whether York or Canterbury was the true centre of the church in England), but that's where Canterbury's superiority ends, for this is without doubt one of the world's most beautiful Gothic buildings. If this is the only cathedral you visit in England, you'll still walk away satisfied – so long as you have the patience to deal with the constant flow of school groups and organised tours that will invariably clog up your viewfinder.

The first church on the site was a wooden chapel built for Paulinus' baptism of King Edwin on Easter Day 627; its site is marked in the crypt. With deliberate symbolism, the church was built on the site of a Roman basilica, a vast central assembly hall; parts can be seen in the foundations. A stone church was started but fell into disrepair after Edwin's death. St Wilfred built the next church but this was destroyed during William the Conqueror's brutal suppression of the north. The first Norman church was built in stages to 1080; you can see surviving fragments in the foundations and crypt.

The present building, built mainly from 1220 to 1480, manages to represent all the major stages of Gothic architectural development. The transepts were built in Early English style between 1220 and 1255; the octagonal chapter house was built between 1275 and 1290 in the Decorated style; the nave from 1291 to 1340; and the west towers, west front and central, or lantern, tower were built in Perpendicular style from 1470 to 1472.

You enter from the south transept, which was badly damaged by fire in 1984 but has now been fully restored. To your right is the 15th-century **choir screen** depicting the 15 kings from William 1 to Henry VI. Facing you is the magnificent **Five Sisters Window**, with five

YORK: FROM THE BEGINNING

York – or the marshy area that preceded the first settlement – has been coveted by pretty much everyone that has ever set foot on this island. In the beginning there were the Brigantines, a local tribe that minded their own business. In AD 71 the Romans – who were spectacularly successful at minding everyone else's business – built their first garrison here for the troops fighting the poor old Brigantines. They called it Erboracum, and in time a civilian settlement prospered around what became a large fort. Hadrian used it as the base for his northern campaign, while Constantine the Great was proclaimed emperor here in AD 306 after the death of his father. After the collapse of the Roman Empire, the town was taken by the Anglo-Saxons who renamed it Eoforwic and made it the capital of the independent kingdom of Northumbria.

Enter the Christians. In 625 a Roman priest, Paulinus, arrived and managed to convert King Edwin and all his nobles. Two years later, they built the first wooden church; for most of the next century the city was a major centre of learning, attracting students from all over Europe.

The student party lasted until 866, when the next wave of invaders arrived. This time it was those marauding Vikings, who chucked everybody out and gave the town a more tongue-friendly name, Jorvik. It was to be their capital for the next 100 years, and during that time they put a rest to their pillaging ways and turned the city into an important trading port.

The next arrival was King Eadred of Wessex, who drove out the last Viking ruler in 954 and reunited Danelaw with the south, but trouble quickly followed. In 1066 King Harold II managed to fend off a Norwegian invasion-rebellion at Stamford Bridge, east of York, but his turn came at the hands of William the Conqueror a few months later at the Battle of Hastings.

Willie exercised his own brand of tough love in York. After his two wooden castles were captured by an Anglo-Scandinavian army, he torched the whole city (and Durham) and the surrounding countryside so that the rebels knew who was boss – the 'harrying of the north'. The Normans then set about rebuilding the city, including a new minster. From that moment, everything in York was rosy – except for a blip in 1137 when the whole city caught fire – and over the next 300 years it prospered through royal patronage, textiles, trade and the church.

No sooner did the church finally get built, though, than the city went into full recession. In the 15th century Hull took over as the region's main port and the textile industry moved elsewhere. Henry VIII's inability to keep a wife and the ensuing brouhaha with the church that resulted in the Reformation also hit York pretty hard. Henry did establish a branch of the King's Council here to help govern the north, and this contributed to the city's recovery under Elizabeth I and James I.

The council was abolished during Charles I's reign, but the king established his court here during the Civil War, which drew the devastating attentions of the Parliamentarians. They besieged the rabidly promonarchist York for three months in 1644, but by a fortunate accident of history their leader was a local chap called Sir Thomas Fairfax, who prevented his troops from setting York alight, thereby preserving the city and the minster.

Not much happened after that. Throughout the 18th century the city was a fashionable social centre dominated by the aristocracy, who were drawn by its culture and new racecourse. When the railway was built in 1839 thousands of people were employed in the new industries that sprung up around it, such as confectionary. These industries went into decline in the latter half of the 20th century, but by then a new invader was asking for directions at the city gates, armed only with a guidebook.

lancets over 15m high. This is the minster's oldest complete window; most of its tangle of glass dates from around 1250. Just beyond it to the right is the 13th-century **chapter house**, a fine example of the Decorated style. Sinuous stonework surrounds a wonderful uninterrupted space. There are more than 200 expressive carved heads and figures.

Back in the main church, you should notice the unusually wide and tall nave, the aisles (to the sides) of which are roofed in stone in contrast to the central roof, which is wood painted to look like stone. On both sides of the nave are painted stone shields of the nobles who met Edward II at a parliament in York. Also note the **dragon's head** projecting from the gallery – it's a crane believed to have been used to lift a font cover. There are several fine **windows** dating from the early 14th century, but the most dominating is the **Great West Window**, from 1338, with beautiful stone tracery.

Beyond the screen and the choir is the **lady chapel** and, behind it, the **high altar**, which is dominated by the huge **Great East Window** (1405). At 23.7m by 9.4m – roughly the size of a tennis court – it is the world's largest medieval stained-glass window and the cathedral's single most important treasure. Needless to say, its epic size matches the epic theme depicted within: the beginning and end of the world as described in Genesis and the Book of Revelations.

The minster's heart is dominated by the awesome **central tower** (adult/child £3.50/2; ⏰ every 30min 10am-5pm Mon-Sat, noon-5pm Sun Apr-Jun & Sep-Oct, to 6.30pm Jul-Aug, to 30min before dusk Nov-Mar), which is well worth climbing for the unparalleled views of York. You'll have to tackle a fairly claustrophobic climb of 275 steps and, most probably, a queue of people with cameras in hand. Access to the tower is near the entrance in the south transept, which is dominated by the exquisite **Rose Window** commemorating the union of the royal houses of Lancaster and York, through the marriage of Henry VII and Elizabeth of York, which ended the Wars of the Roses and began the Tudor dynasty (see p40).

Another set of stairs in the south transept leads down to the **undercroft**, where you'll also find the **treasury** and the **crypt**. These should on no account be missed. In 1967 the foundations were excavated when the central tower threatened to collapse; while engineers worked frantically to save the building, archaeologists uncovered Roman and Norman ruins that attest to the site's ancient history – one of the most extraordinary finds is a Roman culvert, still carrying water to the Ouse. The treasury houses 11th-century artefacts, including relics from the graves of medieval archbishops. The crypt contains fragments from the Norman cathedral, including the font showing King Edwin's baptism that also marks the site of Paulinus' original wooden chapel.

AROUND THE MINSTER

Owned by the minster since the 15th century, **St William's College** (☎ 637134; College St) is an attractive half-timbered Tudor building with elegant oriel windows built for the minster's chantry priests.

The **Treasurer's House** (NT; ☎ 624247; Minster Yard; admission £5, house & basement £7; ⏰ 11am-4.30pm Sat-Thu Apr-Oct) was home to the minster's medieval treasurers. Substantially rebuilt in the 17th and 18th centuries, the 13 rooms house a fine collection of furniture and supply a good insight into 18th-century life. The house is also the setting for one of the city's most enduring ghost stories: during the 1950s, a plumber working in the basement swore he saw a band of Roman soldiers walking *through* the walls; his story remains popular if unproven – but you can explore the cellar to find out.

CITY WALLS

You can get onto the walls, built in the 13th century, via steps by **Bootham Bar** (on the site of a Roman gate) and follow them clockwise to Monk Bar, a walk offering particularly beautiful views of the minster. There are oodles more access points including off Station Rd and Monk Bar.

Monk Bar is the best-preserved medieval gate, with a small **Richard III Museum** (☎ 634191; www.richardiiimuseum.co.uk; admission £2.50; ⏰ 9am-5pm Mar-Oct, 9.30am-4pm Nov-Feb) upstairs. The museum sets out the case of the murdered 'Princes in the Tower' and invites visitors to judge whether their uncle, Richard III, killed them (see Dark Deeds In The Tower, p40 and also the boxed text, The Wars of the Roses, p39).

Walmgate Bar is England's only city gate with an intact barbican (an extended gateway to ward off uninvited guests), and was built during the reign of Edward III.

MERCHANT ADVENTURERS' HALL

Built between 1357 and 1361, the outstanding **Merchant Adventurers' Hall** (☎ 654818; Fossgate; admission £2; ⏰ 9am-5pm Mon-Sat, 9am-3.30pm Fri & Sat, noon-4pm Sun Apr-Sep, 9.30am-3.30pm Mon-Sat Oct-Mar) is one of the most handsome timber-framed buildings in Europe. This stunning building testifies to the power of the medieval guilds, which controlled all foreign trade into and out of York until 1830 – a handy little monopoly.

JORVIK

Interactive bells-and-whistles exhibits aimed at 'bringing history to life' usually result in the opposite, but the much-trumpeted **Jorvik** (☎ 543403; www.vikingjorvik.com; Coppergate; adult/child £7.20/5.10, Jorvik & Dig £11/8.30; ⏰ 10am-6pm Apr-Oct, to

5pm Nov-Mar), the most visited attraction in town besides the minster, manages to convey the essence of the Viking settlement with admirable success. It's a smells-and-all reconstruction of the settlement unearthed in this area during excavations in the late 1970s, brought to you courtesy of a 'time-car' monorail that transports you through 9th-century Jorvik. If you listen closely you will hear snippets of a language derived from modern Icelandic, but the vague smell of something putrescent is all-embracing. While the fibreglass figures don't really appear all that believable and some of the 'you will now go back in time' malarkey is just that, you still come away with a pretty good idea of what it must have been like to have been a Viking. Thanks but no thanks.

It is a bit of fun (for kids at least) and the staff in the ubiquitous shop go to great lengths to answer questions with great enthusiasm. To cut the queue time considerably, book your tickets online – it only costs £1 more.

DIG
York's newest attraction, run by the folks who brought you Jorvik, is **Dig** (☎ 543403; www.viking jorvik.com; St Saviour's Church, St Saviourgate; adult/child £5.50/5, Dig & Jorvik £11/8.30; ⏰ 10am-5pm), which is pretty much self explanatory. This time, you're an 'archaeological detective', unearthing the 'secrets' of York's distant past as well as discovering something of the archaeologist's world – what they do, how they do it and that kind of thing. Much more hands-on than Jorvik, it is plenty of fun and a little bit educational too.

CLIFFORD'S TOWER
There's precious little left of York Castle except for this evocative stone **tower** (EH; ☎ 646940; admission £2.30; ⏰ 10am-6pm Apr-Sep, to 5pm Oct, to 4pm Nov-Mar), a highly unusual figure-eight design built into the castle's keep after the original

one was destroyed in 1190 during anti-Jewish riots. An angry mob forced 150 Jews to be locked inside the tower, but it wasn't enough, and the hapless victims took their own lives rather than be killed. There's not much to see inside but the views over the city are excellent.

YORK CASTLE MUSEUM
Near Clifford's Tower, this excellent **museum** (☎ 653611; adult/child £6.50/5, with Yorkshire Museum £9.50/5; ⏰ 9.30am-5pm) contains displays of everyday life, with reconstructed domestic interiors, and a less-than-homely prison cell where you can try out the condemned man's bed – in this case Dick Turpin's. There's a bewildering array of evocative everyday objects from the past 400 years, gathered together by a certain Dr Kirk from the 1920s onwards for fear that the items would become obsolete and disappear completely. He wasn't far wrong, which makes this place all the more interesting.

NATIONAL RAILWAY MUSEUM
Most railway museums are the sole preserve of lone men with dog-eared notebooks and grandfathers looking to bond with their grandchildren. While there's no shortage of either here, this **museum** (☎ 621261; www.nrm .org.uk; Leeman Rd; admission free; ⏰ 10am-6pm) stands apart on account of its sheer size and incredible collection. Trainspotters and nostalgics will salivate at the massive gathering of engines and carriages from the past, but the attractions for regular folk are the gleaming carriages of the royal trains used by Queen Victoria and Edward VII; the speed-record-breaking *Mallard* (a mighty 2 miles a minute in 1938, still a record for a steam train); and a Series 'O' Japanese bullet train (1964–86), which you can sit in – it is a testament to the speed of technology that the train now appears a tad dated. Just next to it is a **simulator** (£3), which allows you to travel from London to Brighton in real time at supersonic speed – the journey takes four minutes. You can also wander around a vast annexe including the restoration workshops. Allow two hours to do the museum justice.

The museum is slightly out of the way (about 400m west of the train station), so if you don't fancy the walk, you can ride the road train (adult/child £2/1) that runs every 30 minutes from noon to 5pm between the minster and the museum.

OTHER SIGHTS

The **Museum Gardens** (dawn-dusk) make a peaceful four-hectare city-centre oasis. Assorted picturesque ruins and buildings include the **Museum Gardens Lodge** (Victorian Gothic Revival), dating from 1874, and a 19th-century working **observatory**. The **Multangular Tower** was the western tower of the Roman garrison's defensive wall. The small Roman stones at the bottom have been built up with 13th-century additions.

The classical **Yorkshire Museum** (629745; adult/child £5.50/2.50, with York Castle Museum £9.50/5; 10am-5pm) is linked with the Castle Museum (opposite) and has some interesting Roman, Anglo-Saxon, Viking and medieval exhibits and good temporary exhibitions.

The ruins of **St Mary's Abbey** (founded 1089) date from 1270 to 1294. The ruined **Gatehall** was its main entrance, providing access from the abbey to the river. The adjacent **Hospitium** dates from the 14th century, although the timber-framed upper storey is a much-restored survivor from the 15th century; it was used as the abbey guesthouse. **St Mary's Lodge** was built around 1470 to provide VIP accommodation.

St Olave's Church (9am-5pm Mon-Fri) dates from the 15th century, but there has been a church dedicated to Norway's patron saint here since at least 1050.

Adjacent to Museum Gardens on Exhibition Sq is the 19th-century **York City Art Gallery** (551861; Exhibition Sq; admission free; 10am-5pm), which includes works by Reynolds, Nash, Boudin and LS Lowry.

Back inside the walls, the wonky lines inside **Holy Trinity** (613451; Goodramgate; 10am-5pm Tue-Sat May-Sep, 10am-4pm Oct-Apr) almost induce seasickness. The church was started in the 13th century and added to over the next 200 years. Rare 17th- to 18th-century box pews surround a two-tier pulpit.

If 18th-century Georgian houses are for you, then a visit to **Fairfax House** (655543; www .fairfaxhouse.co.uk; Castlegate; adult/child £5/free; 11am-4.30pm Mon-Thu & Sat, 1.30-5pm Sun, guided tours 11am & 2pm Fri) should be on your itinerary. This exquisitely restored property was designed by John Carr (of Harewood House fame; see p589) and features the best example of rococo stucco work to be found in the north of England.

North of here, the quaintly cobbled **Shambles** (www.yorkshambles.com), complete with overhanging Tudor buildings, hints at what a medieval street might have looked like if it was overrun with people told they have to buy something silly and superfluous and be back on the tour bus in 15 minutes. It takes its name from the Saxon word *shamel*, meaning 'slaughterhouse'.

York Dungeon (632599; www.thedungeons.com; 12 Clifford St; adult/child £11.45/8.45; 10.30am-5pm Apr-Sep, 11am-4pm Nov-Jan, 10.30am-4.30pm Oct & Feb-Mar) is a series of exultantly gruesome and markedly overpriced historical reconstructions. For the especially hardened there's a lovely bit on the plague.

Tours

There's a bewildering array of tours on offer, from historic walking tours to a host of ever-competitive night-time ghost tours – pretty popular in what is reputed to be England's most haunted city. For starters, check the tourist office's own website for walking itineraries (www.visityork.org/explore).

BOAT

YorkBoat (628324; www.yorkboat.co.uk; Lendal Bridge; 1hr cruises adult/child £6.50/3.30, ghost cruises adult/child £7.50/4) Runs one-hour Ouse cruises from Lendal Bridge at 10.30am, noon, 1.30pm and 3pm February to November. The obligatory ghost cruise runs nightly at 6.30pm in high season (April to October) from King's Staith (behind the fire station).

BUS

York Citysightseeing (655585; www.city-sightseeing.com; day tickets adult/child £8.50/4; 9am-5pm Apr-Oct) Two hop-on hop-off services calling at all the main sights; buses leave every 15 minutes from Exhibition Sq outside the main tourist office.

WALKING

Association of Voluntary Guides (640780; www .york.touristguides.btinternet.co.uk; tours 10.15am, also 2.15pm Apr-Sep & 6.45pm Jun-Aug) Free two-hour walking tours of the city from Exhibition Sq in front of York City Art Gallery.

Breadcrumbs Trail (610676; www.endpapers .co.uk; Collage Corner, 2 Norman Ct; book £9.95) Explore York by following the Hansel-and-Gretel-type trails laid out in the book – a novel and excellent way to keep the kids entertained. The book is available from bookshops and El Piano restaurant (see p617)

Complete York Tour (706643) A walk around the city and the minster that can be adapted to your preferences. Call for details.

Ghost Hunt of York (608700; www.ghosthunt .co.uk; adult/child £5/4; tours 7.30pm) Award-winning and highly entertaining 75-minute tour beginning at the Shambles.

Original Ghost Walk of York (☎ 01759 373090; adult/child £4/2.50; ☯ tours 8pm) Ghouls and ghosts courtesy of a well-established group departing from the King's Arms pub by Ouse Bridge.

Roam'in Tours of York (☎ 07931 668935; www .roamintours.co.uk) History and specialist tours (adult/child £4/2) or you can take its DIY audio tour (£4.50).

Yorkwalk (☎ 622303; www.yorkwalk.co.uk; adult/child £5/2) Offers a series of two-hour themed walks on an ever-growing list of themes, from the classics – Roman York, the snickelways (alleys) and City Walls – to specialised walks on chocolates and sweets, women in York, secret York and the inevitable graveyard, coffin and plague tour. Walks depart from Museum Gardens Gate on Museum St.

Festivals & Events

For a week in mid-February, York is invaded by Vikings once again as part of the **Jorvik Viking Festival** (☎ 643211; www.vikingjorvik.com; Coppergate), which features battle re-enactments, themed walks, markets and other bits of Nordic fun.

Sleeping

Beds are tough to find midsummer, even at the spiked prices of the high season. The tourist office's efficient accommodation booking service charges £4, which might be the best four quid you spend in town.

Needless to say, prices go up the closer to the city centre you are. However, there are plenty of decent B&Bs on the streets north and south of Bootham, the northwest continuation of High Petergate; Grosvenor Tce, a handsome street along the railway tracks, is particularly full of them. Southwest of the town centre, there are B&Bs clustered around Scarcroft Rd, Southlands Rd and Bishopthorpe Rd.

BUDGET

York Backpackers (☎ 627720; www.yorkbackpack ers.co.uk; 88-90 Micklegate; dm/d from £14/34; ☐) In a Grade I Georgian building that was once home to the High Sheriff of Yorkshire, this large, well-equipped hostel has all the usual facilities as well as Internet access and a residents-only bar that serves cheap beer until 1am.

York Youth Hotel (☎ 625904; www.yorkyouthhotel .demon.co.uk; 11 Bishophill Senior; dm £14-18, s/d £30/50; ☐) Offering the cheapest single rooms within the city walls, this is a good option for travel-

lers who are on a budget but still want to stay close to the action.

York YHA Hostel (☎ 0870 770 6102/3; www.yha.org .uk; Water End, Clifton; dm £18.50) Once the Rowntree (Quaker confectioners) mansion, this handsome Victorian house in its own grounds is almost entirely self-contained – there's even a bar on the property. Most of the rooms are four-bed dorms. It's about a mile northwest of the tourist office; turn left into Bootham, which becomes Clifton (the A19), then left into Water End. There's a riverside footpath from Lendal Bridge, but it's ill lit so avoid it after dark. Alternatively, take Bus 2 from Museum St.

Fairfax House (☎ 434784; www.york.ac.uk; 99 Heslington Rd; s/d £26.50/52; ☯ Jun-Sep only) Part of the University of York, this ivy-clad building offers accommodation in standard, well-equipped rooms, but only outside of term. It is 2 miles southeast of the city. Take bus 4.

MIDRANGE

Dairy Guesthouse (☎ 639367; www.dairyguesthouse .co.uk; 3 Scarcroft Rd; s/d £35/60; ℗) A wonderful Victorian home that has retained many of its original features, including pine doors, stained glass, and cast-iron fireplaces, but the real treat is the flower- and plant-filled courtyard, off of which are the cottage-style rooms. The name comes from the time when it served as a town dairy.

Brontë House (☎ 621066; www.bronte-guesthouse .com; 22 Grosvenor Tce; s/d from £36/64) Five wonderful en suite rooms all decorated completely differently: particularly good is the double with a carved, 19th-century sleigh bed, William Morris wallpaper and assorted bits and bobs from another era.

23 St Mary's (☎ 622738; www.23stmarys.co.uk; 23 St Mary's; s £36-45, d £60-80; ℗) A smart and stately town house with handsome en suite rooms; some have hand-painted furniture for that country look, while others are decorated with antiques, lace and a bit of chintz.

Golden Fleece (☎ 625171; www.goldenfleeceyork.com; 16 Pavement; s/d from £40/80) Four distinctive rooms (including the Shambles Room, with views over York's most famous street) that are said to be haunted. We've yet to see a ghost, but we liked what we did see: nice furnishings, comfortable beds and great hospitality.

Arnot House (☎ 641966; www.arnothouseyork.co.uk; 17 Grosvenor Tce; r £60-70; ℗) With four exquisitely appointed rooms (if you're a fan of Victorian floral patterns and gee-gaws), Arnot House is especially popular with older guests who appreciate the old-fashioned look.

Four High Petergate (☎ 658516; www.fourhighpeter gate.co.uk; 4 High Petergate; s/d £65/100) This stunning 18th-century house next to Bootham Bar has been converted into a gorgeous boutique hotel. Indonesian teak furniture, crisp white linen, flat-screen TV and DVD player are standard in all 14 bedrooms, even if the standard single and doubles are substantially more compact than the superior rooms (£110 to £125). Highly recommended for its class and location. The bistro next door is also excellent.

Guy Fawkes (☎ 671001; www.theguyfawkeshotel.com; 25 High Petergate; r £90-120) Directly opposite the minster is this comfortable new hotel, the premises of which include a cottage that is reputed to be the birthplace of Guy Fawkes himself. We're not convinced, but the cottage is now the handsomest room in the building, complete with a four-poster and lots of red velvet.

Other options:

Briar Lea Guest House (☎ 635061; www.briarlea .co.uk; 8 Longfield Tce; s/d from £26/52) Clean, simple rooms and a friendly welcome in a house just off Bootham.

Alcuin Lodge (☎ 632222; alcuinlodge@aol.com; 15 Sycamore Pl; d from £30) Pretty doubles in a cluttered Victorian house.

City Guesthouse (☎ 622483; www.cityguesthouse .co.uk; 68 Monkgate; s/d from £37/64; P) Very tidy house with meticulously arranged furniture and bric-a-brac; vegetarians catered for.

St Denys Hotel (☎ 622207; www.stdenyshotel.co.uk; St Denys Rd; s/d from £45/65) Slightly worn but still comfortable rooms. Good location inside the city walls.

TOP END

Judges Lodging Hotel (☎ 638733; www.judgeslodg ings.com; 9 Lendal; s/d from £85/120) An elegant and excellent choice for central accommodation, this fine Georgian mansion has very tasteful rooms – despite one with a Queen Mother theme – in what was once the private home of an assizes judge.

Dean Court Hotel (☎ 625082; www.deancourt-york .co.uk; Duncombe Pl; s/d from £95/125) With a commanding position directly across from the minster (you'll only get a church view from the superior rooms), this fine hotel has large, comfortable rooms, although we'd have to put a question mark next to some of the chintzy, pseudo-Georgian décor.

Mount Royale (☎ 628856; www.mountroyale.co.uk; The Mount; r from £107; P) A grand, William IV listed building converted into a superb luxury hotel, complete with a solarium, beauty spa and outdoor heated tub and swimming pool. The rooms in the main house are gorgeous, but the best of the lot are the open-plan garden suites, reached via a corridor of tropical fruit trees and bougainvillea.

Middlethorpe Hall (☎ 641241; www.middlethorpe .com; Bishopsthorpe Rd; s £115-150, d £150-475; P) York's top spot is this breathtaking 17th-century country house set in 20 acres of parkland that was once the home of diarist Lady Mary Wortley Montagu. The rooms are spread between the main house, the restored courtyard buildings and three cottage suites. Although we preferred the grandeur of the rooms in the main house, every room is beautifully decorated with original antiques and oil paintings carefully collected so as to best reflect the period. The magnificent grounds include a white and walled garden and a small lake; guests are invited to use the facilities of the attached spa. Bus 11 stops outside.

Eating

Eating well in York is not a problem – there are plenty of fine options throughout the centre; many of the city's pubs also do grub – they're listed in the Drinking section.

BUDGET

Café Concerto (☎ 610478; 21 High Petergate; cakes £2-3, starters £5-8, mains £12.50-13.95; 10am-10pm) 'Music for your mouth' is the theme of this lovely café facing the minster. The walls are papered with sheet music, but it's the delicious food that makes the most noise – the chicken and avocado sandwich is sensational.

Betty's (☎ 659142; St Helen's Sq; sandwiches about £4.50, cream tea £6.50; 9am-9pm) Afternoon tea, old-school style, in a Yorkshire institution. Hardly surprising that most of the people in the fast-moving queue are of the older generations. Still, it's a bit of class, especially after 6pm, when the pianist adds colour to the proceedings.

El Piano (☎ 610676; www.elpiano.co.uk; 15 Grape Lane; mains £6; 10am-1am Mon-Sat, noon-midnight Sun) A vegetarian haven, this colourful, Hispanic-style spot has a lovely café downstairs and three themed rooms upstairs: check out the Moroccan room, complete with floor cushions.

MIDRANGE

Siam House (☎ 624677; 63a Goodramgate; mains £7-10; ☺ lunch & dinner Mon-Sat, dinner Sun) Delicious, authentic Thai food in about as authentic an atmosphere as you could muster up 6000km from Bangkok. The early bird, three-course special (£10.95) is an absolute steal.

Melton's Too (☎ 629222; 25 Walmgate; mains £8-12; ☺ lunch & dinner) A very comfortable, booth-lined restaurant that does modern Brit cuisine like Yorkshire sirloin steak as well as a host of salads and sandwiches. It's the slightly scruffier younger brother to Melton's (below).

La Vecchia Scuola (☎ 644600; 62 Low Petergate; mains £8-15; ☺ lunch & dinner) Housed in the former York College for Girls, the faux elegant dining room – complete with self-playing grand piano – is straight out of *Growing Up Gotti*, but there's nothing fake about the food: authentic Italian cuisine served in suitably snooty style by proper Italian waiters.

Fiesta Mexicana (☎ 610243; 14 Clifford St; burritos £9.95; ☺ dinner) Chimichangas, tostadas and burritos served in a relentlessy happy atmosphere. Students and party groups on the rip add to the fiesta; it's not subtle or subdued, but when is Mexican food ever so?

Buzz Bar (☎ 640222; 20-24 Swinegate; bento boxes £12-14; ☺ lunch & dinner) It was the owners' dream to open a Japanese restaurant-cum-trendy bar, and while the delicious bento box meals are worth the struggle with the chopsticks, this place kind of falls between two stools, so it's neither restaurant nor bar.

Little Betty's (☎ 622865; 46 Stonegate; afternoon tea £12.75; ☺ 10am-5.30pm) Betty's younger sister is more demure, less frequented, but just as good; you go upstairs and back in time to what feels like the interwar years – it's possible to spot a couple of Agatha Christie lookalikes. The afternoon tea would feed a small village.

TOP END

Melton's (☎ 634341; 7 Scarcroft Rd; mains £14-20; ☺ lunch & dinner Tue-Sat, dinner only Mon, lunch only Sun) Foodies come from far and wide to dine in one of Yorkshire's best restaurants. It tends to specialise in fish dishes but doesn't go far wrong with practically everything else, from Yorkshire beef to the asparagus risotto with pinenuts and herbs. There's an excellent lunch and early dinner set menu (£17).

Blue Bicycle (☎ 673990; 34 Fossgate; mains £15-24; ☺ lunch & dinner) Once upon a time, this building was a well-frequented brothel; these days it serves up a different kind of fare to an equally enthusiastic crowd. French food at its finest, served in a romantic, candlelit room, makes for a top-notch dining experience.

J Baker's (☎ 622688; 7 Fossgate; 2-/3-course meal £18.95/24.50; ☺ lunch & dinner) Superstar chef Jeff Baker left Leeds' Pool Court and his Michelin star to pursue his own vision of Modern British cuisine here. The defiantly traditional menu offers classics like ox tongue, egg 'n' chips and steaks – these days, it's all about being one of the lads, so long as Messrs Michelin are paying close attention.

Drinking

With only a couple of exceptions, the best drinking holes in town are older, traditional pubs. In recent years, the area around Ousegate and Micklegate has gone from moribund to mental, especially at weekends.

Ackhorne (☎ 671421; 9 St Martin's Lane) Tucked away from beery, sloppy Micklegate, this locals' inn is as comfortable as old slippers. Some of the old guys here look like they've morphed with the place. There's a pleasant beer garden at the back.

Black Swan (☎ 686911; Peasholme Green) A classic black-and-white Tudor building where you'll find decent beer, friendly people and live jazz on Sundays. Nice.

Blue Bell (☎ 654904; 53 Fossgate) A tiny, tiny pub with décor dating from 1798 and a surprisingly contemporary crowd (read: lots of young people).

Capital (☎ 639971; 1A Lower Ousegate) Trendy Casa was bought out in 2006 and remodelled so that it's newest incarnation is even trendier: lots of glass, plenty of beautiful people and great views over the River Ouse.

King's Arms (☎ 659435; King's Staith; lunch about £6) York's best-known pub is a creaky place with a fabulous riverside location – hence its enduring popularity. A perfect spot for a summer's evening.

Ye Olde Starre (☎ 623063; 40 Stonegate) Licensed since 1644, this is a bit of a tourist trap, but an altogether excellent pub that is popular with locals. It was used as a morgue by the Roundheads, but the atmosphere's improved since then. It has decent ales and a heated outdoor patio overlooked by the minster.

Entertainment

There are a couple of good theatres in York, a fairly interesting cinema, but as far as clubs are concerned, forget it: historic York is best enjoyed without them.

York Theatre Royal (☎ 623568; St Leonard's Pl) Stages well-regarded productions of theatre, opera and dance.

York Barbican Centre (☎ 656688; Barbican Rd) Big-name concerts in a partly pyramidal, modern building.

City Screen (☎ 541144; www.picturehouses.co.uk; 13-17 Coney St) Mainstream and art-house films.

Grand Opera House (☎ 671818; Clifford St) Despite its name puts on a wide range of productions.

Shopping

Coney St and its adjoining streets are the hub of York shopping, but the real treat for visitors are the second-hand and antiquarian bookshops, mostly clustered in two main areas, Micklegate and Fossgate.

Worm Holes Bookshop (☎ 620011; www.worm-holes .co.uk; 20 Bootham) Our favourite of York's dusty bookshops, with a decent and far-reaching selection of old and new titles.

Ken Spellman Booksellers (☎ 624414; 70 Micklegate) This fine shop has been selling rare, antiquarian and second-hand books since 1910.

Fossgate Books (☎ 641389; 36 Fossgate) Cheap paperbacks and unusual books.

Getting There & Away

BUS

The very useful **York Travel Bus Info Centre** (☎ 551400; 20 George Hudson St; ◷ 8.30am-5pm Mon-Fri) has complete schedule information and sells local and regional tickets. All local and regional buses stop along Rougier St, off Station Rd inside the city walls on the western side of Lendal Bridge.

National Express coaches also stop here as well as outside the train station. Tickets can be bought at the tourist offices. There are services to London (£24.50, 5¼ hours, four daily), Birmingham (£23, three hours, one daily) and Edinburgh (£30.50, 5½ hours, one daily).

CAR & MOTORCYCLE

You won't need a car around the city, but it comes in handy for exploring the surrounding area. Rental options include: **Europcar** (☎ 656161), by platform 1 in the train station, which also rents bicycles and stores luggage (£5); and **Hertz** (☎ 612586) near platform 3 in the train station.

TOP FIVE PUBS FOR A PROPER PINT

- Fat Cat (p580; Sheffield)
- Duck & Drake (p586; Leeds)
- Hales (p625; Harrogate)
- Ye Olde Starre (opposite; York)
- Star Inn (p631; Harome near Helmsley)

TRAIN

York train station is a stunning masterpiece of Victorian engineering. It also has plenty of arrivals and departures: Birmingham (£35, 2½ hours); Edinburgh (£65, 2½ hours, hourly); Leeds (£8.80, 50 minutes, hourly); London's King's Cross (£85, two hours, hourly); Manchester (£16.80, 1½ hours, six daily); and Scarborough (£10.30, 45 minutes).

Trains also go via Peterborough (£44.50, 1¾ hours, every 30 minutes) for Cambridge and East Anglia.

Getting Around

York is easily walked on foot. You're never really more than 20 minutes from any of the major sights or areas.

BICYCLE

The Bus Info Centre has a useful free map showing York's bike routes. If you're energetic you could pedal out to Castle Howard (15 miles), Helmsley and Rievaulx Abbey (12 miles) and Thirsk (another 12 miles), and then catch a train back to York. There's also a section of the Trans-Pennine-Trail cycle path from Bishopthorpe in York to Selby (15 miles) along the old railway line. The tourist offices have maps.

Two hire places are: **Bob Trotter** (☎ 622868; 13 Lord Mayor's Walk; rental per day £10), outside Monk Bar; and **Europcar** (☎ 656161; rental per day from £12), by platform 1 in the train station.

BUS

The local bus service is provided by **First York** (☎ 622992), which sells a day pass (£2.20) valid on all of its local buses – although you'll hardly need it if you're sticking close to town. The Bus Info Centre (left) has service details.

CAR & MOTORCYCLE

York gets as congested as most English cities in summer and parking in the centre can be

YORKSHIRE

expensive (up to £9 for a day); but most guesthouses and hotels have access to parking.

TAXI

Station Taxis (☎ 623332) has a kiosk outside the train station.

AROUND YORK

Castle Howard

Stately homes may be two a penny in England, but you'll have to try pretty damn hard to find one as breathtakingly stunning as **Castle Howard** (☎ 01653-648333; www.castlehoward.co.uk; adult/child house & grounds £9.50/6.50, grounds £7/6.50; ⏲ house 11am-4.30pm, grounds 10am-4.30pm mid-Mar–Oct), a work of supreme theatrical grandeur and audacity set in the rolling Howardian Hills with wandering peacocks on its terraces. This is one of the world's most beautiful buildings, and instantly recognisable for its starring role in *Brideshead Revisited* – which has done its popularity no end of good since the TV series first aired in the early 1980s.

When the earl of Carlisle hired his mate Sir John Vanbrugh in 1699 to design his new home, he was hiring a bloke who had no formal training and was best known as a playwright; luckily Vanbrugh hired Nicholas Hawksmoor, who had worked for Christopher Wren, as his clerk of works – not only would Hawksmoor have a big part to play in the house's design but the two would later do wonders with Blenheim Palace (p392).

If you can, try to visit on a weekday, when it's easier to find the space to appreciate this hedonistic marriage of art, architecture, landscaping and natural beauty. Wandering about the grounds, views open up over the hills, Vanbrugh's playful Temple of the Four Winds and Hawksmoor's stately mausoleum, but the great baroque house with its magnificent central cupola is an irresistible visual magnet. Inside, it is full of treasures, such as the chapel's Pre-Raphaelite stained glass.

Castle Howard is 15 miles northeast of York, 4 miles off the A64. It can be reached by several tours from York. Check with the tourist office for up-to-date schedules. Yorkshire Coastliner bus 840 (40 minutes from York, one daily) links Leeds, York, Castle Howard, Pickering and Whitby. The Coastliner Freedom ticket (adult £11) is good for unlimited rides all day; buy tickets on the bus.

THIRSK

☎ 01845 / pop 9099

Monday and Saturday are market days in handsome Thirsk, which has been trading on its tidy, attractive streets and cobbled square since the Middle Ages. Thirsk's brisk business was always helped by its key position on two medieval trading routes: the old drove road between Scotland and York, and the route linking the Yorkshire Dales with the coast. That's all in the past, though: today, the town is all about the legacy of James Herriot, the wry Yorkshire vet adored by millions of fans of *All Creatures Great and Small.*

Thirsk does a good job as the real-life Darrowby of the books and TV series, and it should, as the real-life Herriot was in fact local vet Alf Wight, whose house and surgery has been dipped in 1940s aspic and turned into the incredibly popular **World of James Herriot** (☎ 524234; www.worldofjamesherriot.org; 23 Kirkgate; adult/child £4.99/3.50; ⏲ 10am-5pm Apr-Oct, 11am-4pm Nov-Mar), an excellent museum full of Wight artefacts, a video documentary of his life and a re-creation of the TV show sets. It's all quite well done and you'll be in the company of true fans, many of whom have that look of pilgrimage on their faces.

Almost directly across the street is the less-frequented **Thirsk Museum** (☎ 527707; www.thirskmuseum.org; 14-16 Kirkgate; admission £1.50; ⏲ 10am-4pm Mon-Wed, Fri & Sat), which manages to cram a collection of items from Neolithic times to the Herriot era into a tiny house where Thomas Lord (of Lord's Cricket Ground fame) was born in 1755.

Thirsk's **tourist office** (☎ 522755; thirsk@ytbtic.co.uk; 49 Market Pl; ⏲ 10am-5pm Easter-Oct, 11am-4pm Nov-Easter) is on the main square.

Sleeping & Eating

The tourist office books B&Bs and has an accommodation list.

Three Tuns Hotel (☎ 523124; www.the-three-tuns-thirsk.co.uk; Market Pl; s/d from £50/70) A fairly imposing 18th-century coaching inn best known as having hosted the Wordsworths on their honeymoon in 1802. The bedrooms have changed somewhat since then, and today offer comfortable if unspectacular accommodation. Restaurant mains from £7.

Crab Manor (☎ 577286; www.crabandlobster.co.uk; Dishforth Rd, Asenby; r £150-200) Here's your chance to stay in the world's most famous hotel rooms – without the effort of getting there. From

Raffles of Singapore to the Waldorf Astoria in New York, this quirky hotel re-creates them...of a fashion. The spirit and fabrics are all there, but the sizes and views don't quite conform. No arguments about the fish restaurant, though (mains £11 to £18). It's 4 miles southwest of Thirsk along the A168 to Ripon.

Getting There & Away

There are frequent daily buses from York (45 minutes).

Thirsk is well served by trains on the line between York and Middlesbrough. However, the train station is a mile west of town and the only way to cover that distance is on foot or by **taxi** (☎ 522473).

RIPON

☎ 01765 / pop 16,468

Small town, huge cathedral: Ripon – all winding streets and a broad, symmetrical marketplace lined with Georgian houses – is mostly about its elegant church, but tourists seem quite taken by the Ripon Hornblower, who 'sets the watch' every evening at 9pm by the central obelisk in a tradition that supposedly dates back to 886, when Alfred the Great gave the locals a horn to sound the changing of the guard. Much more interesting goings-on occur on Thursdays, when the busy market takes place.

The **tourist office** (☎ 604625; Minster Rd; ☯ 10am-1pm & 1.30-5.30pm Mon-Sat, 1-4pm Sun) is near the cathedral and has information on local walks, and will book accommodation.

Ripon Cathedral (☎ 602072; www.riponcathedral.org.uk; suggested donation £3, treasury £1; ☯ 7.30am-6.30pm, Evensong 5.30pm) is well worth exploring. The first church on this site was built in 660 by St Wilfred, and its rough, humble crypt lies intact beneath today's soaring edifice. Above ground, the building dates from the 11th century, with its noble and harmonious Early English west front clocking in at 1220. Medieval additions have resulted in the medley of Gothic styles throughout, culminating in the rebuilding of the central tower – work that was never completed. It was not until 1836 that this impressive parish church got cathedral status. Look out for the fantastical creatures decorating the animated medieval misericords, believed to have inspired Lewis Carroll – his father was canon here (1852–68).

Until 1888 Ripon was responsible for its own peacekeeping, and this has resulted in a grand array of punishing attractions. **Law & Order Museums** (☎ 690799; www.riponmuseums.co.uk; 7-day combined ticket adult/child £5/free; ☯ 1-4pm Apr-Sep, 11am-4pm Oct-Mar) combine the **Courthouse Museum**, a 19th-century courthouse (recognisable from sappy TV series *Heartbeat*), the **Prison & Police Museum**, which includes the medieval punishment yard and the clammy cells where no-good Victorians ended up, and the **Workhouse Museum**, which shows the grim treatment of poor vagrants from the 19th century to WWII.

Bus 36 comes from Leeds via Harrogate every 20 minutes.

AROUND RIPON

Sheltered in the secluded valley of the River Skell are two of Yorkshire's most beautiful attractions and an absolute must on your northern itinerary. The strangely obsessive and beautiful formal **Studley Royal water gardens** were built in the 19th century so as to enhance the extensive ruins of the 12th-century **Fountains Abbey** (NT; ☎ 01765-608888; www.fountainsabbey.org.uk; abbey, hall & garden £6.50; ☯ 10am-5pm Mar-Oct, to 4pm Nov-Feb). Together they create a breathtaking picture of pastoral elegance and tranquillity that have made them the most visited of all the National Trust's pay-in properties and Yorkshire's only World Heritage Site.

After falling out with the Benedictines of York in 1132, a band of rebel monks came here to what was then a desolate and unyielding patch of land to found their own monastery. Struggling to make it on their own, they were formally adopted by the Cistercians in 1135: by the middle of the 13th century the new abbey had become the most successful Cistercian venture in the country. It was during this time that most of today's ruins were built, including the church's nave and transepts, outlying buildings and the church's eastern end (the tower was added in the late 15th century).

After the dissolution (p40) the estate was sold into private hands and between 1598 and 1611 Fountains Hall was built with stone from the abbey ruins. The hall and ruins were united with the Studley Royal Estate in 1768.

The main house of Studley Royal burnt down in 1946 but the superb landscaping, with its serene artificial lakes, survives hardly changed from the 18th century. Studley Royal was owned by John Aislabie (once Chancellor of the Exchequer), who dedicated his life to creating the park after a financial scandal saw him expelled from parliament.

Fountains Abbey is 4 miles west of Ripon off the B6265. The **deer park** (admission free, car park £2) opens during daylight hours. **St Mary's Church** (1-5pm Apr-Sep) features occasional concerts. There are free one-hour guided tours (11am and 2.30pm April to October and 3.30pm April to September, garden 2pm April to October).

Public transport is limited to summer Sunday services; call for details of any buses that might be running.

HARROGATE

 01423 / pop 85,128
The doyenne of the Victorian spa town, prim, pretty Harrogate has long been associated with a certain kind of old-fashioned Englishness, the kind that seems to be the preserve of retired army chaps and formidable dowagers who, inevitably, will always vote Conservative. They come to Harrogate to enjoy the formidable flower shows and gardens that fill the town with an almost unparalleled array of colour, especially in spring and autumn, when the floral displays are at their height. It is truly fitting that the town's most famous visitor was Agatha Christie, who fled here incognito in 1926 to escape her broken marriage.

Yet this picture of Victoriana redux is not quite complete. While it's undoubtedly true that Harrogate remains a firm favourite of visitors in their golden years, the New Britain makeover has left its mark in the host of smart new hotels and trendy eateries that dot the town, catering to the boom in Harrogate's newest trade, conferences. All those dynamic young guns have to eat and sleep somewhere...

Orientation & Information

Harrogate is almost surrounded by gardens including the 80-hectare Stray in the south. The mostly pedestrianised shopping streets, Oxford and Cambridge Sts, are lined with smart shops and the **post office** (11 Cambridge Rd; 9am-5.30pm Mon-Sat). The **tourist office** (537300; www.harrogate.gov.uk/tourism; Crescent Rd; 9am-6pm Mon-Sat, 10am-1pm Sun Apr-Sep, 9am-5pm Mon-Fri, 9am-4pm Sat Oct-Mar) is in the Royal Baths Assembly Rooms; staff can give information

about free historical walking tours offered daily from Easter to October.

Sights & Activities

THE WATERS
Take the plunge into the waters and the past in the fabulously tiled **Turkish Baths** (556746; www .harrogate.co.uk/turkishbaths; Tue/Sat & Sun to 5pm/all other times £10/15/13; 9am-9pm) in the Royal Baths Assembly Rooms. The mock Moorish facility is gloriously Victorian and offers a range of watery delights – steam rooms, saunas, and so on. A visit should last at least two hours.

There's a complicated schedule of opening hours that are at turns single sex and mixed pairs – call or look online for more details. You can prebook a range of reasonably priced massages and other therapies.

Just around the corner is the ornate **Royal Pump Room Museum** (556188; Crown Pl; admission £2.80; 10am-5pm Mon-Sat, 2-5pm Sun Apr-Oct, 10am-4pm Mon-Sat, 2-4pm Sun Nov-Mar), built in 1842 over the most famous of the sulphur springs. It gives an insight into how the phenomenon created the town and the illustrious visitors that it attracted, and there's a chance to tuck into some stinky spa water.

MERCER ART GALLERY
Another surviving spa building, the Promenade Room, is now home to this elegant **gallery** (556188; Swan Rd; admission free; 10am-5pm Tue-Sat, 2-5pm Sun), a stately space that hosts constantly changing exhibitions of visual art; one of the highlights of 2007 was the retrospective of the work of artist William Powell Frith (1819–1909).

GARDENS
A huge green thumbs-up to Harrogate's gardeners; the town has some of the most beautiful public gardens you'll ever see. The quintessentially English **Valley Gardens** are overlooked by the vast, ornate, glass-domed **Sun Pavilion**, built in 1933. The nearby bandstand houses concerts on Sunday afternoons from June to August. Flower-fanatics should make for the **Harlow Carr Botanical Gardens** (565418; www.rhs.org.uk; Crag Lane, Beckwithshaw; adult/child £6/1.60; 9.30am-6pm, dusk if earlier), the northern showpiece of the Royal Horticultural Society. The gardens are 1.5 miles southwest of town. To get here, take the B6162 Otley Rd or walk through the Pine Woods southwest of the Valley Gardens.

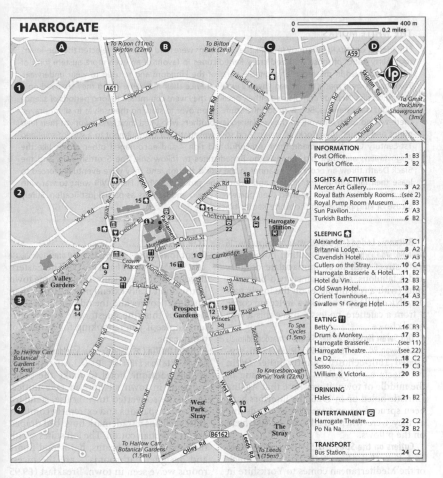

HARROGATE

0 — 400 m
0 — 0.2 miles

To Ripon (11mi);
Skipton (22mi)

To Bilton
Park (2mi)

To Great
Yorkshire
Showground
(3mi)

To Harlow Carr
Botanical
Gardens
(1.5mi)

To Spa
Cycles
(1.5mi)

To Knaresborough
(8mi); York (22mi)

To Harlow Carr
Botanical Gardens
(1.5mi)

To Leeds
(15mi)

INFORMATION
Post Office.................................1 B3
Tourist Office............................2 B2

SIGHTS & ACTIVITIES
Mercer Art Gallery.....................3 A2
Royal Bath Assembly Rooms....(see 2)
Royal Pump Room Museum.......4 B3
Sun Pavilion.............................5 A3
Turkish Baths...........................6 B2

SLEEPING
Alexander.................................7 C1
Britannia Lodge........................8 A2
Cavendish Hotel........................9 A3
Cutlers on the Stray.................10 C4
Harrogate Brasserie & Hotel.....11 B3
Hotel du Vin............................12 B3
Old Swan Hotel.......................13 B2
Orient Townhouse....................14 A3
Swallow St George Hotel..........15 B2

EATING
Betty's...................................16 B3
Drum & Monkey......................17 B3
Harrogate Brasserie...............(see 11)
Harrogate Theatre..................(see 22)
Le D2.....................................18 C2
Sasso....................................19 C3
William & Victoria...................20 B3

DRINKING
Hales....................................21 B2

ENTERTAINMENT
Harrogate Theatre..................22 C2
Po Na Na...............................23 B2

TRANSPORT
Bus Station...........................24 C2

The **West Park Stray** is another fine garden and park, south of the centre.

Festivals & Events

The year's main event is the immense **Spring Flower Show** (☎ 0870 758 3333; www.flowershow.org.uk; admission £11-14), held in late April, followed in late September by the **Autumn Flower Show** (admission £11). Both take place at the Great Yorkshire Showground.

If fancy shrubs aren't your thing, there's a lot more fun to be had at the **Great Yorkshire Show** (☎ 541000; www.greatyorkshireshow.org; adult/child £18/8), a three-day exhibition staged in mid-July by the Yorkshire Agricultural Society (also held at the showground). It's a real treat, with all manner of farm critters competing

for prizes and last year's losers served up in a variety of ways.

Sleeping

BUDGET

Bilton Park (☎ 863121; biltonpark@tcsmail.net; Village Farm, Bilton; tent sites £11; ☼ Apr-Oct) A convenient camp site 2 miles north of town. Take bus 201, 203 or 204 from the bus station.

MIDRANGE

Swallow St George Hotel (☎ 561431; www.swallow-hotels.com; 1 Ripon Rd; s/d £49/85; Ⓟ Ⓢ) Big Edwardian building across from the tourist office with spacious albeit slightly characterless rooms. There's a health club and indoor pool.

THE WHITE MONKS

Founded at Cîteaux in Burgundy in 1098, the Cistercians were hard-core. They rejected the free-lovin', toga-party antics of those wild and crazy Benedictines in favour of an even more austere form of living: they lived in the most inhospitable parts of the kingdom and refused to wear underwear. Their habits were made of undyed sheep's wool – hence their nickname – and they survived on a starvation diet. Nobody complained either, because they were committed to long periods of silence and eight daily services. But, with so much time given over to starving themselves in silent prayer, there was no room for work so they ordained lay brothers who tilled their lands, worked their lead mines and tended their flocks of sheep. And so it was that their commitment to a superdisciplined 1st-century Christianity made them powerful and rich – and encouraged other orders like the Augustinians and their old nemesis the Benedictines to follow suit. The Scottish Wars and the Black Death threw an economic spanner in the works though, and they were eventually forced to lease their lands to tenant farmers and live off the proceeds. When Henry VIII went to war with the monasteries in 1536, he used their perceived greed and laziness as partial justification. Surely a case of king pot calling the white kettles black?

Britannia Lodge (☎ 508482; www.britlodge.co.uk; 16 Swan Rd; s/d £55/85; P) A beautiful home on a leafy street with three immaculate doubles and a fabulous, self-contained two-bedroom suite (with a real fireplace) on the lovely garden. Nice little touches like a welcome coffee – from a cafetière, no less – make this a very good choice.

Old Swan Hotel (☎ 500055; www.macdonaldhotels .co.uk; Swan Rd; s/d from £69/90; P &) An ivy-coated 18th-century country hotel set in two hectares of gardens – smack, bang in the middle of town. It was here that Agatha Christie holed up in 1926; the interiors have been spruced up and are now as handsome as they were when Agatha rested her head on the pillows.

Cutlers on the Stray (☎ 524471; www.cutlers-web .co.uk; 19 West Park; d from £85; P &) A little touch of the Mediterranean comes to Yorkshire in the shape of this stylish boutique hotel and brasserie inside a converted coaching inn. Yellows, creams and reds are used to great effect in the rooms, which are thoroughly modern in design. Some rooms even have Stray views.

Other options:

Alexander (☎ 503348; thealexander@amserve.net; 88 Franklin Rd; s/d £30/60; P) Handsome Victorian mansion with immaculate, unstintingly floral rooms.

Cavendish Hotel (☎ 509637; 3 Valley Dr; s/d from £38/57, 4-poster £75) Comfortable rooms with a touch of flounce, the best of which overlook the Valley Gardens.

Harrogate Brasserie & Hotel (☎ 505041; www .brasserie.co.uk; 28-30 Cheltenham Pde; s/d from £52.50/85) Has 14 stylish rooms, an excellent restaurant and frequent live jazz.

TOP END

Orient Townhouse (☎ 565818; www.orienttownhouse .com; 51 Valley Drive; s/d from £105/130) The Eastern flavours of this particularly handsome town house don't really extend much further than the duvet covers and the odd bit of decoration, but this fine guesthouse is an excellent choice if you're looking for a touch of pampering.

Hotel Du Vin (☎ 856800; www.hotelduvin.com; Prospect Pl; r/ste from £105/150; P ▣) An extremely stylish boutique hotel to make the other lodgings in town sit up and take notice. Inside the converted town house, standard rooms are spacious and extremely comfortable; each has a trademark huge bed draped in soft Egyptian cotton. The loft suites – with their exposed oak beams, hardwood floors and designer bathrooms – are the nicest rooms we've seen in town. Breakfast (£9.95 to £13.50) is not included. The Sunday to Thursday rate is about £20 cheaper than on the weekend.

Eating
BUDGET

Harrogate Theatre (Oxford St; sandwiches about £5; ☽ 10am-6pm Mon-Sat) A grand old café that's popular at lunchtime.

Betty's (☎ 502746; www.bettysandtaylors.co.uk; 1 Parliament St; mains around £7.50; ☽ 9am-9pm) A classic tearoom dating from 1919, founded by a Swiss immigrant confectioner who got on a wrong train, ended up in Yorkshire and decided to stay. It heaves with scone groupies (tea and scones about £5). A pianist tinkles among the teacups from 6pm.

MIDRANGE

Le D2 (☎ 502700; 7 Bower Rd; mains £6-9; ❤ lunch & dinner Tue-Sat) Mediterranean colours and red-and-white tablecloths are often a substitute for proper food, but they're merely the backdrop for a genuinely good menu at this smart brasserie. The fresh bread rolls and salads are terrific.

Sasso (☎ 508838; 8-10 Princes Sq; lunch menu £8, mains £8-15; ❤ lunch & dinner Tue-Sat, dinner Mon) A top-class basement trattoria where homemade pasta is served in a variety of traditional and authentic ways, along with a host of Italian specialties.

Drum & Monkey (☎ 502650; 5 Montpellier Gardens; mains £8-12; ❤ lunch & dinner Mon-Sat) Our favourite restaurant in town serves up mouthwatering seafood dishes to an enthusiastic and loyal clientele.

William & Victoria (☎ 506883; 6 Cold Bath Rd; mains £8-16; ❤ Mon-Fri lunch, Mon-Sat dinner) A dark and cosy, wood-lined wine bar that serves traditional British food.

Harrogate Brasserie (☎ 505041; 30 Cheltenham Pde; 2-course meal £15.95; ❤ dinner) There's more than a hint of New Orleans at this friendly, popular brasserie serving up some pretty good French cuisine. Photos of jazz greats adorn the red walls to complement the regular live performances.

Drinking

Hales (☎ 725571; 1-3 Crescent Rd) Have a decent pint of ale or some filling pub grub by flickering gaslight at this traditional pub.

Entertainment

Po Na Na (☎ 509758; 2 Kings Rd; free before 11pm; ❤ 10pm-2am Wed-Sat) Harrogate's only half-decent late bar-club, with a none-too outlandish soundtrack of funky stuff, from cheesy '70s disco to contemporary House.

Harrogate Theatre (☎ 502116; www.harrogatethe atre.com; Oxford St) Drama, comedy and music staged in Art Deco surroundings.

Getting There & Away

Trains serve Harrogate from Leeds (50 minutes, about half-hourly) and York (45 minutes, 10 to 12 daily).

National Express bus 561 runs from Leeds (50 minutes, six daily). Bus 383 comes from Ripon (25 minutes, four daily). Buses 36 and 36A also run regularly between Ripon, Harrogate and Leeds.

SCARBOROUGH

☎ 01723 / pop 57,649

At first glance, Yorkshire's favourite seaside resort stands up quite well. It has a spectacular setting above two beautiful white-sand bays; it is graced by a host of handsome buildings built at various times during the reigns of Edward, Victoria and the four Georges; and is topped by the romantic hulk of a castle. It sounds inviting, but once you're on the waterfront the seaside kitsch overwhelms what is left of Scarborough's more genteel side: neon-lit amusement arcades and casinos draw punters away from the donkey rides and tacky souvenir stands.

The town might have remained forever in medieval obscurity were it not for the announcement in 1620 that the waters were medicinal, making it one of the first places in England to popularise sea bathing. From the mid-18th century it was a successful seaside resort; it is the vestiges of that era that are most interesting about Scarborough today. Its renowned theatre is the base of England's popular playwright, Alan Ayckbourn, whose plays always premier here.

Orientation

Modern suburbs sprawl west of the town centre, which is above the old town and the South Bay. The town is on a plateau above the beaches; cliff lifts, steep streets and footpaths provide the links. The Victorian development to the south is separated from the town centre by a steep valley, which has been landscaped and is crossed by high bridges.

The main shopping street, Westborough, has a dramatic view of the castle rising in the distance. The North Bay is home to all the tawdry seashore amusements; the South Bay is more genteel. The old town lies between St Mary's Church, the castle and the Old Harbour.

Information

Laundrette (☎ 375763; 48 North Marine Rd)

Post office (11-15 Aberdeen Walk; ❤ 9am-5.30pm Mon-Fri, to 12.30pm Sat)

Scarborough Library (☎ 383400; Vernon Rd; ❤ 9.30am-5.30pm Mon-Fri, 9.30am-noon Sat; per 30min £1) For internet use.

Tourist office (☎ 383637; www.discoveryorkshirecoast .com; Brunswick Shopping Centre, Unit 15A, Westborough; ❤ 9.30am-5.30pm Mon-Sat, 11am-5pm Sun Apr-Oct, 10am-4.30pm Mon-Sat Nov-Mar)

Waterstone's (☎ 500414; 97-98 Westborough) For books and magazines.

SCARBOROUGH

0 — 500 m
0 — 0.3 miles

INFORMATION
Laundrette..........................1 B2
Post Office..........................2 B3
Scarborough Library...........3 B3
Tourist Office......................4 B3
Waterstone's.......................5 B3

SIGHTS & ACTIVITIES
Church of St Martin-on-the-Hill..6 B4
Rotunda Museum..................7 B3
Scarborough Castle...............8 D2
Sea Life Centre & Marine
   Sanctuary..........................9 A1
Secret Spot Surf Shop...........10 B3
St Mary's Church...................11 C2

SLEEPING
Argo Hotel...........................12 B1
Crown Hotel.........................13 B4
Interludes.............................14 C2
Red Lea Hotel.......................15 C4
Royal Hotel..........................16 C3
Windmill Hotel......................17 A3

EATING
Bonnet..................................18 B3
Golden Grid..........................19 C2
Lanterna................................20 C2

DRINKING
Indigo Alley..........................21 B2
Tap & Spile...........................22 A4

ENTERTAINMENT
Stephen Joseph Theatre...23 B3

Sights & Activities

Scarborough is not exclusively about bingo, buckets and burgers – there are a number of sights to distract you from the beach and its goings-on.

Battered **Scarborough Castle** (EH; ☎ 3/2451; admission £3.50; ☺ 10am-6pm Apr-Sep, 10am-4pm Thu-Mon Nov-Mar) has excellent views across the bays and the town. There's been some kind of fortification here for nearly 2500 years, but the current structure dates from the 12th century. Legend has it that Richard III loved the views so much his ghost just keeps coming back. More corporeal beings can get to it via a 13th-century barbican.

Below the castle is **St Mary's Church** (☎ 500541; Castle Rd; ☺ 10am-4pm Mon-Fri, 1-4pm Sun May-Sep),

dating from 1180 and rebuilt in the 15th and 17th centuries, with some interesting 14th-century chapels. Anne Brontë is buried in the churchyard.

Of all the family-oriented attractions on the bays, the best of the lot is the **Sea Life Centre & Marine Sanctuary** (☎ 376125; www.sealife.co.uk; Scalby Mills; adult/child £10.95/8.95; ☺ 10am-6pm) overlooking North Bay. Here you can explore the Jurassic seas, coral reefs and the newest addition, Turtle Reef, all about the shelled creatures. The rescue work done with woebegone seals is quite uplifting.

The Pre-Raphaelite, high Victorian interior of the **Church of St Martin-on-the-Hill** (☎ 360437; Albion Rd; ☺ 7.30am-5.30pm) was worked on by Burne-Jones, Morris, Maddox Brown and Rossetti.

YORKSHIRE

The **Rotunda Museum** (☎ 374839; Vernon Rd) traces local matters from prehistory to the present, but is currently closed for a major renovation.

There are some decent waves out in the North Sea. The friendly **Secret Spot Surf Shop** (☎ 500467; www.secretspot.co.uk; 4 Pavilion Tce) can advise on conditions, recommend places for lessons and rent all manner of gear. The best time for waves is September to May.

See p635 for more information about the 20-mile Whitby–Scarborough Coastal Cycle Trail.

Sleeping
If something stays still long enough in town, it'll offer B&B; competition is intense and it's difficult to choose between places. In such a tough market, multinight stay special offers are two a penny, which means that single-night rates are the highest of all.

BUDGET
Scalby Close Caravan Park (☎ 366212; www.scalby closepark.co.uk; Burniston Rd; sites £12-15; ꙮ Easter-Oct) A small park about 2 miles north of town with plenty of pitches for vans and tents as well as five fixed holiday caravans for rent (£140 to £325 per week). The park has all the usual facilities. Take bus 12 or 21.

Scarborough YHA Hostel (☎ 0870 7706022; www .yha.org.uk; Burniston Rd; dm £13.95; ꙮ Apr-Aug) This simply idyllic hostel in a converted water mill from around 1600 has comfortable four- and six-bed dorms as well as a lounge, self-catering kitchen and laundry. It is two miles north of town along the A166 to Whitby. Take bus 3, 12 or 21.

Argo Hotel (☎ 375745; 134 North Marine Rd; s/d £17/34) Pleasant, small, floral rooms overlooking the cricket ground; it's especially popular with pensioners, who get a special discount in the off season.

MIDRANGE
Interludes (☎ 360513; www.interludeshotel.co.uk; 32 Princess St; s/d from £29/51; P) Owners Ian and Bob have a flair for the theatrical, and have brought it to bear with incredible success on this lovely, gay-friendly Georgian home plastered with old theatrical posters, prints and other thespian mementos. The individually decorated rooms are given to colourful flights of fancy that can't but put a smile on your face. Children, alas, are not welcome.

Windmill Hotel (☎ 372735; www.windmill-hotel.co.uk; Mill St; s/d from £30/60; P) A beautifully converted 18th-century mill in the middle of town offers tight-fitting but comfortable doubles around a cobbled courtyard – the upstairs rooms have a small veranda.

Royal Hotel (☎ 364333; www.englishrosehotels .co.uk; St Nicholas St; s/d from £40/80) Scarborough's most famous hotel has a lavish Regency interior, grand staircase for Shirley Bassey–style entrances, and smart rooms, some with sea views. The perfectly comfortable but characterless rooms just don't compare with the grandeur of the public spaces.

Red Lea Hotel (☎ 362431; www.redleahotel.co.uk; Prince of Wales Tce; s/d £41/82; P 🏊) An elegant terrace of six Georgian houses makes up this popular choice, which has large rooms rich in velvet drapes, lush carpets and king-size beds. Downstairs is a heated, kidney-shaped swimming pool and, next door, a small leisure centre with sauna, sunbeds and a gym.

TOP END
Crown Hotel (☎ 373491; www.scarboroughhotel.com; Esplanade; s/d from £60/110; P 🏊) This grand old hotel opened its nearly regal doors in 1845 and has been going strong ever since, changing constantly with the times. It looks fancy and Victorian, but inside it's just another comfortable business-style hotel. Rooms with sea views cost £10 extra.

Wrea Head Country House Hotel (☎ 378211; www .englishrosehotels.co.uk; Barmoor La, Scalby; s/d £75/130) This fabulous country house about 2 miles north of the centre is straight out of *Remains of the Day*. The 20 individually styled bedrooms have canopied, four-poster beds, plush fabrics and delicate furnishings, while the leather couches in the bookcased, wood-heavy lounges seem fit for important discussions over cigars and expensive brandy.

Eating
Bonnet (☎ 361033; 38-40 Huntriss Row; mains from £5; ꙮ café 9am-5.30pm, restaurant dinner Fri & Sat) An excellent tearoom, open since 1880, with delicious cakes, a serene courtyard, and adjoining shop selling handmade chocolates.

Golden Grid (☎ 360922; 4 Sandside; cod from £6; ꙮ lunch & dinner Apr-Oct, to 5pm Nov-Mar) Who ever said fish and chips can't be eaten with dignity hasn't eaten in Golden Grid, which has been doling them out since 1883. It's bright and traditional, with starched white tablecloths.

Lanterna (☎ 363616; 33 Queen St; mains £12-18; ✦ dinner Mon-Sat) A snug Italian spot that specialises in fresh local seafood as well as favourites from the Old Boot; it's the place to go for that special night out in Scarborough.

Drinking
Indigo Alley (☎ 375823; North Marine Rd) A small, welcoming pub with a good range of beers. Regular live jazz and blues and Monday theatre in a limpet-sized curtained-off space.

Tap & Spile (☎ 363837; 94 Falsgrave Rd) This relaxed pub has a few rooms and a good selection of Yorkshire ales.

Entertainment
Stephen Joseph Theatre (☎ 370541; www.sjt.uk.com; Westborough; tickets about £13) Stages a good range of drama. Renowned chronicler of middle-class mores Alan Ayckbourn premieres his plays here.

Getting There & Away
Reasonably frequent Scarborough & District buses (No 128) go along the A170 from Pickering (one hour) and Helmsley (1½ hours). They leave from Westborough.

There are regular buses, 93 and 93A (via Robin Hood's Bay), from Whitby (one hour). Bus 843 arrives from Leeds (£14.20, eight to 12 daily) via York (£11).

There are regular trains from Hull (£11.25, one hour 20 minutes, hourly), Leeds (£18, one hour 20 minutes, six to eight daily) and York (£13, 45 minutes, hourly).

Getting Around
Victorian funicular lifts slope up and down Scarborough's steep cliffs to the beach daily from February till the end of October. Local buses leave from the western end of Westborough and outside the train station.

For a taxi call ☎ 361009; £4.50 should get you to most places in town.

FILEY
☎ 01723 / pop 6468
The quietest beach town is Filey, a former fishing village that looks upon its brasher neighbours in Bridlington and Scarborough with a vaguely superior air. It is an important walking centre; it is the hub for the Cleveland Way (opposite), and the Wolds Way (p575) finishes here, at the dramatic coastal outcrop of Filey Brigg. Five miles of sandy beach offer

ample scope for paddling weary feet. Murray St is lined with shops and links the train and bus stations to the beach.

Filey's **tourist office** (☎ 518000; www.discover yorkshirecoast.com; John St; ☎ 10am-6pm May-Sep, 10am-12.30pm & 1-4.30pm Oct-Apr) is well appointed and helpful, booking local accommodation.

Filey is served by trains on the line between Hull and Bridlington to the south and Scarborough to the north (every two hours). The bare-bones station is about a mile west of the beach. The town is 7 miles south of Scarborough on the A165. Buses 120 and 121 come from Scarborough (30 minutes, hourly).

NORTH YORK MOORS NATIONAL PARK

Wild, windswept and oh so interesting, the North York Moors – much of them protected by the boundaries of a national park – exist in isolated splendour; lonely, heather-clad hilltops staring down on steeply cut valleys and across to some of the most spectacular views you'll see in the north of England. The ridge-top roads and high open moors afford terrific views of the dramatic countryside – where you will spot an isolated farm or village or come across the odd castle and ruined abbey – while to the east the moors suddenly give way to an even more dramatic coastline of sheer cliffs, sheltered bays and long sandy beaches.

If you visit anytime between July and early September you will be met by the explosive bloom of heather, all bright pinks and mauve. Outside the flowering season, the colours are broody browns and purples – in vivid contrast to the deep greens of the Dales – giving the park its characteristic moody appearance.

Orientation & Information
The park covers 553 sq miles, with hills and steep escarpments forming the northern and western boundaries, and the eastern limit marked by the North Sea coast. The southern border runs roughly parallel to the A170 Thirsk–Scarborough road, and the main gateway towns are Helmsley and Pickering in the south, and Whitby in the northeast – all with good tourist offices. The national park also

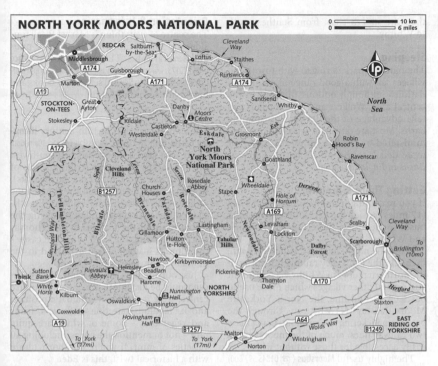

NORTH YORK MOORS NATIONAL PARK

runs tourist offices (called visitor centres) at Sutton Bank, Danby and Robin Hood's Bay. Although outside the park, Scarborough is another good gateway.

The national park produces the very useful *Moors & Coast* visitor guide (60p), available at tourist offices, hotels etc, with information on things to see and do and an accommodation listing. The park website at www.moors.uk.net is even more comprehensive.

Activities

Several ideas for short walks and rides (from a few hours to all day) are suggested in this section, and tourist offices stock an excellent range of walking leaflets (around 60p to 75p), as well as more comprehensive walking and cycling guidebooks.

CYCLING

Once you've puffed up the escarpment, the North York Moors make fine cycling country, with ideal quiet lanes through the valleys and scenic roads over the hills. There's also a great selection of tracks and former railways for mountain bikes.

WALKING

There are over 1400 miles of walking paths and tracks crisscrossing the moors. The best walking opportunities are along the western escarpment and the cliff tops on the coast. The green and tranquil valleys are also ideal for a spot of relaxed rambling, although, for avid walkers, the broad ridges and rolling high ground of the moors can be a bit featureless after a few hours and for that reason this area is not as popular as the Yorkshire Dales or the Lake District – a plus if you're looking for peace and quiet.

For long-distance walks, the famous Coast to Coast walk (p575) strides across the park, and the Cleveland Way covers three sides of the moors' outer rim on its 109-mile, nine-day route from Helmsley to Filey, through a wonderful landscape of escarpments and coastline.

The Cook Country Walk, named for explorer Captain Cook, who was born and raised in this area, links several monuments commemorating his life. This 40-mile, three-day route follows the flanks of the Cleveland Hills from Marton (near Middlesbrough),

YORKSHIRE

then the superb coast from Staithes south to Whitby.

Sleeping

The national park is ringed with towns and villages, all with a good range of accommodation – although options thin out in the central area. Walkers and outdoor fans can take advantage of the network of camping barns. Most are on farms, with bookings administered by the YHA (☎ 0870 870 8808). For more details tourist offices have a *Camping Barns in England* leaflet.

Getting There & Around

If you're coming from the south, from York (17 miles outside the park) there are regular buses to Helmsley, Pickering, Scarborough and Whitby.

From the north, head for Middlesbrough, then take the Esk Valley railway line through the northern moors to Whitby via Grosmont and several other villages which make useful bases. A second line, the North Yorkshire Moors Railway (NYMR), runs through the park from Pickering to Grosmont. Using these two railway lines, much of the moors area is easily accessible for those without wheels.

The highly useful **Moorsbus** (☎ 01845 597 000) operates on Sunday from May to October, daily from mid-July to early September, and is ideal for reaching out-of-the-way spots. Pick up a timetable and route map from tourist offices. A standard Moorsbus day pass costs £3, and for £12.50 the pass covers you on the Esk Valley and NYMR trains too – a good deal if you plan to really make a day of it. Family tickets and one-off fares for short journeys are also available.

Call the national **Traveline** (☎ 0870 608 2608) for all public bus and train information.

HELMSLEY

☎ 01439 / pop 1620

Beneath the watchful gaze of a sturdy Norman castle, Helmsley is a classic North Yorkshire market town, a handsome old place full of old houses, historic coaching inns and – inevitably – a cobbled square where Friday is market day. Nearby are the dreamlike ruins of Rievaulx Abbey and there are a fistful of decent walks in the area. All told, you could do far worse than base yourself here to explore this gorgeous southwest corner of the moors.

Orientation & Information

The centre of everything is Market Pl; all four sides are lined with twee shops, cosy pubs and several cafés. The helpful **tourist office** (☎ 770173; www.ryedale.gov.uk; ⏲ 9.30am-5.30pm Mar-Oct, 10am-4pm Fri-Sun Nov-Feb) sells maps, books and helps with accommodation.

Sights

The impressive ruins of 12th-century **Helmsley Castle** (EH; ☎ 770442; admission £4; ⏲ 10am-6pm Apr-Oct, 10am-4pm Thu-Mon Nov-Mar), just southwest of the Market Pl, have a striking series of deep ditches and banks (aka earthworks), to which later rulers added the thick stone walls and defensive towers – only one toothshaped tower survives today following the dismantling of the fortress by Sir Thomas Fairfax following the Civil War. The castle's tumultuous history is well explained in the newish visitor centre.

Just outside the castle, **Helmsley Walled Garden** would be just another plant and produce centre, were it not for its dramatic position and its fabulous selection of flowers, fruits and vegetables – some of which are quite rare – not to mention the herbs, including 40 varieties of mint. If you're into horticulture with a historical twist, this is Eden.

South of the castle stretches the superb landscape of **Duncombe Park** with the grand stately home of **Duncombe Park House** (☎ 770213; www.duncombepark.com; house & grounds £6.50, park only £3.50; ⏲ house by guided tour only, every 30min 12.30-3.30pm, gardens 11am-5.30pm Sun-Thu late Apr-Oct) at its heart. From the house and formal gardens, wide grassy walkways and terraces lead through woodland to mock-classical temples, while longer walking trails are set out in the parkland – now protected as a nature reserve. The house, ticket office and information centre are 1.5 miles south of town, an easy walk through the park. You could easily spend a day here.

Activities

Of the numerous walks in Duncombe Park, the 3.5-mile route to Rievaulx Abbey is the real star. The tourist office can provide route leaflets, and advise on buses if you don't want to walk both ways. This route is also the overture to the Cleveland Way (p629). Cycling to Rievaulx Abbey is also possible, but the roads are quite busy; a better option for cyclists is the network of quiet (and relatively flat) country lanes east of Helmsley.

Sleeping

Wrens of Rydale (☎ 771260; www.wrensofryedale.fsnet .co.uk; Gale Lane, Nawton; car & 2 adults/hikers £10/8.50) Three acres of pristine parkland divided into sections for tents and caravans. This excellent camp site is 3 miles east of Helmsley, just south of Deadlam.

Helmsley YHA Hostel (☎ 0870 770 5860; www.yha .org.uk; Carlton Lane; dm £13.95) This purpose-built hostel just outside the centre is a bit like an ordinary suburban home; its location at the start of the Cleveland Way means that it's virtually always full so book in advance.

There are a number of old coaching inns on Market Pl that offer B&B, half-decent grub and a pint (or more) of hand-pumped real ale. The **Feathers Hotel** (☎ 770275; www.feathersho telhelmsley.co.uk; Market Pl; s/d from £44/80) has four-poster beds in some rooms and historical trimmings throughout, with mains for £8 to £11, while for something a lot plusher, head for the **Feversham Arms** (☎ 770766; www .fevershamarms.com; s/d £130/140; P 🐾), with mains for £16 to £23, which even has its own pool.

Eating & Drinking

Star Inn (☎ 770397; www.thestarharome.co.uk; Harome; mains £10-17; 🕑 lunch & dinner Tue-Sat) This thatched cottage pub is like hitting the rustic gastro-jackpot. In the middle is the kind of pub you could happily get slowly sloshed in, but the only thing to tear you away is the Michelin-starred feast that awaits you in the dining room. Each dish is a delicious rendering of some local favourite with a flight of fancy to make it really special: how about Nawton-bred middle white pig casserole with baked apples, black pudding and sage and Somerset brandy cream? You won't want to leave, and the good news is you don't have to: the adjacent lodge has eight magnificent bedrooms, each decorated in classic but luxurious country style (rooms £130 to £210). If we could, we'd live here. It's about 2 miles south of town just off the A170.

Royal Oak (Market Pl) The liveliest of the town's pubs, with good beer and bar meals.

Getting There & Away

All buses stop in the Market Pl. From York to Helmsley, take bus 31, 31A or 31X (three daily Monday to Saturday, 1½ hours). Between Helmsley and Scarborough, bus 128 (£6.40, hourly, 1½ hours; four on Sunday) goes via Pickering.

AROUND HELMSLEY
Rievaulx

The moors' most visited attraction is the famous remains of **Rievaulx Abbey** (EH; ☎ 01439-798228; admission £4.20; 🕑 10am-6pm Apr-Sep, to 5pm Thu-Mon Oct, to 4pm Thu-Mon Nov-Mar), about 3 miles west of Helmsley in the small eponymous village. Rievaulx (ree-voh) is everything a ruin should be: battered enough by the passage of time to give a venerable air, but with enough beautiful stonework, soaring pillars and graceful arches remaining so you can imagine how it looked in its 13th-century heyday.

The site is quite simply idyllic – a secluded, wooded valley overlooking fields and the River Rye – with a view pretty much as it was 900 years ago, when Cistercian monks first arrived. And it seems they enjoyed the scenery just as much as we do today: one abbot, St Aelred, famously described the abbey's surroundings as 'everywhere peace, everywhere serenity, and a marvellous freedom from the tumult of the world.' If only he'd known how enduring his words would be. Ponder his words over a picnic. Or a spot of contemplation. Or both.

Near the abbey, **Rievaulx Terrace & Temples** (NT; ☎ 01439-798340; admission £4; 🕑 10.30am-6pm Apr-Sep, to 5pm Oct-Nov) is a wooded escarpment once part of extensive Duncombe Park (opposite). In the 1750s landscape-gardening fashion favoured a natural or Gothic look, and many aristocrats had mock ruins built in their parks. The Duncombe family went one better, as their lands contained a medieval ruin – Rievaulx Abbey – and the half-mile-long grassy terrace was built, with classical-style temples at each end, so lords and ladies could stroll effortlessly in the 'wilderness' and admire the ruins in the valley below. Today, we can do the same, with views over Ryedale and the Hambleton Hills forming a perfect backdrop.

A visit to these two historic sites makes a great day out from Helmsley, but note that there's no direct access between the abbey and the terrace. Their entrance gates are about a mile apart and easily reached along a lane – steeply uphill if you're going from the abbey to the terrace.

Sutton Bank

Sutton Bank is a dramatically steep escarpment 8 miles west of Helmsley. If you're driving, this may be your entry to the North York Moors. And what an entry. The road climbs steeply up, with magnificent views westwards across to the Pennines and Yorkshire Dales. At the top, there's a **tourist office** (☎ 01845 597426; 🕙 10am-5pm Apr-Oct, 11am-4pm Nov, Dec & Mar, 11am-4pm Sat & Sun Jan & Feb) with exhibitions about the moors, books and maps for sale, and handy leaflets on short walks to nearby viewpoints. If you don't have your own wheels, the Moorsbus service M3 links Sutton Bank with Helmsley, from where all other parts of the park can be reached.

Coxwold
☎ 01347 / pop 190

Coxwold is an immaculate village of golden stone with a serene sense of symmetry, nestling in beautiful countryside about 7 miles southwest of Helmsley. It may be in the north but it shouts middle England (it even *sounds* like Cotswold), and Yorkshire accents are pretty scarce hereabouts.

Apart from the quiet picture-postcard beauty of the place, the main attraction is the 15th-century **Shandy Hall** (☎ 868465; admission gardens/house £4.50/2.50; 🕙 house 2-4.30pm Wed, 2.30-4.30pm Sun May-Sep, gardens 11am-4.30pm May-Sep), home to ebullient eccentric Laurence Sterne (1713–68), author of *Tristram Shandy*. The house is full of 'Sterneana', with lots of information on this entertaining character who was seemingly the first to use the expression 'sick as a horse'.

Nearby is **Byland Abbey** (EH; ☎ 868614; admission £3; 🕙 10am-5pm Jul, 10am-5pm Thu-Mon Apr-Jun & Sep), the elegant remains of a fine Cistercian creation, now a series of lofty arches surrounded by open green slopes.

A decent option for a good night's sleep is the **Coxwold Schoolhouse B&B** (☎ 868077; www .coxwoldyorkshire.com; s/d £30/50). For a bite to eat, try the **Fauconberg Arms** (☎ 868214; Main St; mains £10-15), a cosy local in the heart of the village with a fine Continental-style menu in its elegant restaurant.

HUTTON-LE-HOLE
☎ 01751 / pop 210

A contender for best-looking village in Yorkshire, Hutton-le-Hole may sound odd but it's actually a wonderful collection of gorgeous stone cottages centred on a village green, an undulating grassy expanse with a stream creating a small valley that divides the village in two. The dips and hollows on the green might give the village its name – it was once called

simply Hutton Hole, but posh wannabe Victorians added the Frenchified 'le', which the locals defiantly pronounce 'lee'. Its popularity as an understated tourist destination has twee-ified the place somewhat, but it's lovely for a stroll and a streamside picnic.

The **tourist office** (☎ 417367; 🕙 10am-5.30pm mid-Mar–early Nov) has leaflets on walks in the area, including a 5-mile circuit to the nearby village of Lastingham.

Attached to the tourist office is the largely open-air **Ryedale Folk Museum** (☎ 417367; www .ryedalefolkmuseum.co.uk; adult/child £4.50/3; 🕙 10am-dusk Mar-Oct, to 5.30pm Nov-Feb), a constantly expanding collection of North York Moors buildings from different eras, including a medieval manor house, simple farmers' houses, a blacksmith's forge and a row of 1930s village shops. Demonstrations and displays throughout the season give a pretty fascinating insight into local life as it was in the past.

The **Daffodil Walk** is a 2½-mile circular walk following the banks of the River Dove. As the name suggests, the main draws are the daffs, usually at their best in the last couple of weeks in April.

Sleeping & Eating

Hutton-le-Hole has a small choice of places to stay in the village itself, and the tourist office can help with more suggestions if you want B&B on a farm in the surrounding countryside.

Burnley House (☎ 417548; www.burnleyhouse.co.uk; d from £65) This elegant Georgian home offers comfortable B&B, a hearty breakfast and a separate four-poster bedroom (off the main house) that sounds luxurious but is far too small for such a huge bed!

Crown (bar meals £7-11) The village pub, this is a straightforward spot that's popular with locals and visitors.

The main street also boasts a handful of teashops, all offering drinks, snacks and lunches.

Getting There & Away

Hutton-le-Hole is 2.5 miles north of the main A170 road, about equidistant from the market towns of Helmsley and Pickering. Moorsbus services (p630) through Hutton-le-Hole include the M3 between Helmsley and Danby (seven per day) and the M1 and M2 between Pickering and Danby (eight per day). Outside times when the Moorsbus runs, you'll need your own transport to get here. Alternatively catch bus 128 along the A170, get off at the junction east of Kirkbymoorside and walk the 2.5 miles up the lane to Hutton-le-Hole.

PICKERING
☎ 01751 / pop 6616

The lively market town of Pickering has its charms – most notably the Norman castle and the fabulous North Yorkshire Moors Railway, for which Pickering serves as a terminus – but it is too big and bustling to keep you in thrall. It is, however, a handy staging post from which to explore the eastern moors.

The **tourist office** (☎ 473791; www.ryedale.gov.uk; The Ropery; ☽ 9.30am-5.30pm Mon-Sat, 9.30am-4pm Sun Mar-Oct, 10am-4pm Mon-Sat Nov-Feb) has the usual details as well as all NYMR-related info.

Sights & Activities
Pickering Castle (EH; ☎ 474989; admission £3; ☽ 10am-6pm Apr-Sep, 10am-4pm Thu-Mon Oct) is a lot like the castles we drew as kids: thick stone outer walls circling the keep, and the lot perched atop a high motte (mound) with great views of the surrounding countryside. Founded by

William the Conqueror, it was added to and altered by later kings.

The privately owned **North Yorkshire Moors Railway** (NYMR; www.northyorkshiremoorsrailway.com, www.nymr.demon.co.uk; ☎ Pickering Station 472508, recorded timetable 473535) runs for 18 miles through beautiful countryside to the village of Grosmont. Lovingly restored steam locos pull period carriages, resplendent in polished brass and bright paintwork, and the railway appeals to train buffs and day-trippers alike. For visitors without wheels, it's excellent for reaching out-of-the-way spots. Even more useful, Grosmont is also on the main railway line between Middlesbrough and Whitby, which opens up yet more possibilities for walking or sightseeing.

Sleeping & Eating
White Swan Hotel (☎ 472288; www.white-swan.co.uk; Market Pl; s/d from £89/129) The top spot in town successfully combines a smart pub, a superb restaurant serving local dishes with a continental twist (mains £9 to £15) and a luxurious little boutique hotel all in one. Nine new rooms in the converted coach house up the

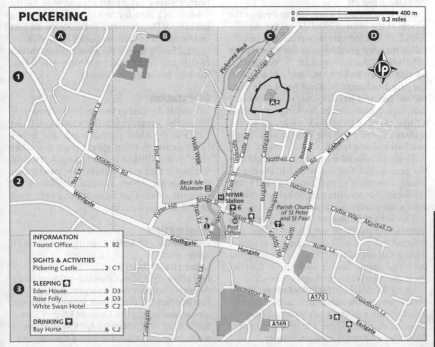

PICKERING

0   400 m
0   0.2 miles

INFORMATION
Tourist Office.................1 B2

SIGHTS & ACTIVITIES
Pickering Castle.............2 C1

SLEEPING 🏠
Eden House.................3 D3
Rose Folly...................4 D3
White Swan Hotel........5 C2

DRINKING 🍺
Bay Horse....................6 C2

YORKSHIRE

ante with LCD flat-screen TVs and other stylish paraphernalia to add to the luxury found elsewhere.

There's a strip of similar B&Bs on tree-lined Eastgate (which becomes the A170 to/from Scarborough). Decent options include **Eden House** (☎ 472289; www.edenhousebandb.co.uk; 120 Eastgate; s/d from £26/52), a pretty house with cottage-style décor, and flower- and plant-clad **Rose Folly** (☎ 475067; www.rosefolly.freeserve.co.uk; 112 Eastgate; s/d £28/52), with lovely rooms and a beautiful breakfast conservatory.

There are several cafés and teashops on Market Pl, and for drinks of another sort the **Bay Horse** (Market Pl) is a good no-nonsense pub.

Getting There & Away

Bus 128 between Helmsley (40 minutes) and Scarborough (50 minutes) runs hourly via Pickering. Yorkshire Coastliner services (840, 842 and X40) run to/from York (£9.10, hourly, 70 minutes).

For train details, see p633.

DANBY

☎ 01287 / pop 290

Danby is an isolated stone village deep in the moors at the head of Eskdale, where the surrounding countryside is particularly beautiful. It makes a good base, as the **Moors Centre** (☎ 01439-772737; www.moors.uk.net; ☒ 10am-5pm Apr-Oct, 11am-4pm Nov-Dec & Mar, 11am-4pm Sat & Sun Jan-Feb), the park headquarters, is just half a mile from the village, and has displays, information, a café, an accommodation-booking service and a huge range of local guidebooks, maps and leaflets as well as all the information you'll need on walking routes.

There are several short circular walks from the centre, but first on your list should be Danby Beacon; it's a stiff 2 miles uphill to the northeast, but the stunning 360-degree views across the moors sweeten the sweat.

The **Duke of Wellington** (☎ 660351; www.danby-dukeofwellington.co.uk; s/d from £34/65), a fine traditional pub – used as a recruitment centre during the Napoleonic Wars – serves good beer and meals (mains about £7); upstairs there are nine well-appointed rooms.

Using the delightful **Esk Valley Railway** (☎ 0845 748 4950; www.eskvalleyrailway.co.uk), access is easy: Whitby is 20 minutes east; Middlesbrough is 45 minutes west. There are four departures Monday to Saturday, two on Sunday.

WHITBY

☎ 01947 / pop 13,594

When it comes to a bit of classy charm, Whitby blows all of northern England's coastal resorts out of the water. The narrow medieval streets are lined with restaurants, pubs and cute little shops, and everything more or less leads down to the handsome harbour, where colourful fishing boats move in and out during the day. Keeping a watchful eye over the whole scene is the ruined and utterly atmospheric abbey atop one of the cliffs that hems the town.

Whitby wouldn't be a coastal resort without the requisite amusements and pleasure arcades, but unlike other resorts they are merely a part of the overall aesthetic rather than the overwhelming, defining feature. In spite of them, Whitby manages to retain much of its 18th-century character, when the town's most famous (adopted) son, James Cook, was making his first forays to sea on his way towards becoming one of the best-known explorers in history.

Besides the caravan of ordinary sun worshippers and beachcombers that flood the town throughout the summer months, Whitby is popular with good-time girls and boys, retirees, hikers, bikers and even Goths – who flock here for two festivals honouring the king of the vampires: Bram Stoker set part of *Dracula* here (see the boxed text, p636).

And finally there's the all-important matter of fish and chips, and in Whitby you'll find the best in the *whole* country.

Orientation

Whitby is divided in two by the harbour and River Esk estuary. On the east bank (East Cliff) is the older part of town; the newer (19th-century) town grew up on the other side, West Cliff. An intriguing feature of Whitby is that many streets have two names. For example, Abbey Tce and Hudson St are opposite sides of the same street, as are West St and The Esplanade.

Information

Java Café-Bar (☎ 820832; 2 Flowergate; per 20 min £1) Internet access.
Laundrette (72 Church St)
Post office (☒ 8.30am-5.30pm Mon-Sat) Across from the tourist office inside the Co-op supermarket.
Tourist office (☎ 602674; www.discoveryorkshirecoast .com, www.visitwhitby.com; Langborne Rd; ☒ 9.30am-6pm May-Sep, 10am-4.30pm Oct-Apr) A wealth of information on the town and the surrounding moors and coast.

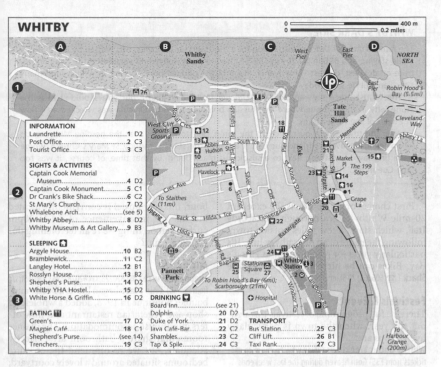

WHITBY

0   400 m
0   0.2 miles

INFORMATION	
Laundrette....................................1	D2
Post Office...................................2	C3
Tourist Office..............................3	C3

SIGHTS & ACTIVITIES	
Captain Cook Memorial	
Museum....................................4	D2
Captain Cook Monument..........5	C1
Dr Crank's Bike Shack................6	C2
St Mary's Church.........................7	D2
Whalebone Arch.....................(see 5)	
Whitby Abbey............................8	D2
Whitby Museum & Art Gallery....9	B3

SLEEPING	
Argyle House...........................10	B2
Bramblewick...........................11	C2
Langley Hotel..........................12	B1
Rosslyn House.........................13	B2
Shepherd's Purse.....................14	D2
Whitby YHA Hostel..................15	D2
White Horse & Griffin...............16	D2

EATING	
Green's....................................17	D2
Magpie Café............................18	C1
Shepherd's Purse.................(see 14)	
Trenchers................................19	C3

DRINKING	
Board Inn...........................(see 21)	
Dolphin..................................20	D2
Duke of York..........................21	D2
Java Café-Bar.........................22	C2
Shambles................................23	C2
Tap & Spile............................24	C3

TRANSPORT	
Bus Station.............................25	C3
Cliff Lift.................................26	B1
Taxi Rank...............................27	C3

Sights

There are ruins, and then there's **Whitby Abbey** (EH; ☎ 603568; admission £4.20; ⏰ 10am-6pm Apr-Sep, 10am-4pm Thu-Mon Oct-Mar). Dominating the town, in a simply stunning location, this ancient holy place dates from the 11th to 14th centuries, with huge solid pillars, soaring arches and gaping windows made all the more dramatic with the North Sea sky behind. Nearby, **St Mary's Church** (⏰ 10am-5pm Apr-Oct, to 4pm Nov-Mar) has an atmospheric interior full of skewed and tilting galleries and box pews. You reach the abbey and the church via the famous 199 steps up the cliff side. Take time out to catch your breath and admire the fantastic view.

Cook-related links are a big deal in Whitby, but the best place to find out about the famous seafarer is at the **Captain Cook Memorial Museum** (☎ 601900; www.cookmuseumwhitby.co.uk; Grape Lane; adult/child £3.50/2.50; ⏰ 9.45am-5pm Apr-Oct, 11am-3pm Sat & Sun Mar), a house once occupied by the ship-owner to whom Cook was apprenticed. Highlights include Cook's own maps and writings, etchings from the South Seas and a wonderful model of the *Endeavour*, with all the crew and stores laid out for inspection.

At the top of the cliff near East Tce, the **Captain Cook Monument** shows the great man looking out to sea, usually with a seagull perched on his head. Nearby is the **Whalebone Arch** (it's just that), remembering Whitby's days as a whaling port.

South of here, in a park overlooking the town, is the wonderfully eclectic **Whitby Museum & Art Gallery** (☎ 602908; Pannett Park; adult/child £3/1, art gallery admission free; ⏰ 9.30am-5.30pm Mon-Sat, 2-5pm Sun May-Sep, 10am-1pm Tue, 10am-4pm Wed-Sat, 2-4pm Sun Oct-Apr), with fossils, Cook memorabilia, ships in bottles and weird stuff like an amputated hand and an invention for weather forecasting using live leeches. The gallery contains work by the Staithes group of artists.

Activities

Although it's hardly tranquil, a walk up the main road to the new bridge high above the Esk is worth it for great views. For something a bit longer, the 5.5-mile cliff-top walk south to Robin Hood's Bay is a real treat (allow three hours). Or head north for 11 miles to reach Staithes (five hours). A bus from Middlesbrough will get you home again (see p637).

WHITBY'S DARK SIDE

The famous story of *Dracula*, inspiration for a thousand lurid movies, was written by Bram Stoker while staying at a B&B in Whitby in 1897. Although most Hollywood versions of the tale concentrate on deepest, darkest Transylvania, much of the original book was set in Whitby, and many sites can still be seen today.

The tourist office sells an excellent *Dracula Trail* leaflet (80p), but you shouldn't miss the stone jetty in the harbour, where the Russian boat chartered by Dracula was wrecked as it flew in ahead of the huge storm.

After the town sites, you can climb the same 199 stone steps that the heroine Mina ran up when trying to save her friend Lucy. At the top of the steps is moody St Mary's Church, where Mina first saw Lucy sitting next to a suspicious black being. By that time, of course, it was too late. Cue music. The End.

First choice for a bike ride is the excellent 20-mile Whitby to Scarborough **Coastal Cycle Trail**, which starts a few miles outside town, following the route of an old railway line. It's particularly good for reaching Robin Hood's Bay. Bikes can be hired from **Dr Crank's Bike Shack** (☎ 606661; 20 Skinner St).

Festivals & Events

There's a full programme of festivals throughout the year, when the town is particularly lively. Tops are:

Whitby Gothic Weekends (www.wgw.topmum.co.uk; tickets from £35) Goth heaven during the last weekends of April and October; anyone in town not wearing black or false fangs is a weirdo.

Moor & Coast Festival (www.moorandcoast.co.uk; tickets £35) A traditional folk festival of music, dance and dubious Celtic art over the May Bank Holiday.

Musicport Festival (www.musicport.fsnet.co.uk; tickets £82.50) A weekend-long world music festival in mid-October.

Sleeping

Most of the B&Bs are concentrated on West Cliff around Hudson St; if a place isn't offering B&B, chances are it's derelict. Accommodation can be tough to find at festival times; it's wise to book ahead.

BUDGET

Whitby YHA Hostel (☎ 0870 770 6089; www.yha.org.uk; Church Lane; dm £11.95; ☺ Apr-Aug, Mon-Sat Sep-Oct, Fri & Sat Nov & Jan-Mar) With an unbeatable position next to the abbey on East Cliff overlooking the town, this hostel doesn't have to try too hard, and it doesn't. You'll have to book well in advance to get your body into one of the basic bunks.

Harbour Grange (☎ 600817; www.whitbybackpackers. co.uk; Spital Bridge; dm £12) Overlooking the har-

bour, this tidy hostel is conveniently located but has the inconvenience of an 11.30pm curfew – good thing we're all teetotalling do-gooders, right?

MIDRANGE

Shepherd's Purse (☎ 820228; fax 820287; 95 Church St; s/d from £25/40) This place began life as a beads-and-baubles boutique in 1973, added a wholefood shop and vegetarian restaurant and now offers guesthouse accommodation. The plainer rooms that share a bathroom are perfectly adequate, but we recommend the en suite bedrooms situated around a lovely courtyard; each has a handsome brass or four-poster bed and nice pine furniture.

White Horse & Griffin (☎ 604857; www.white horseandgriffin.co.uk; 87 Church St; s/d from £35/60) Walk through the suitably olde-worlde frontage of this handsome 18th-century coaching inn and discover a boutique hotel with individually designed, superstylish rooms that have managed to mix the best of tradition (antique panelling, restored period furniture, real flame fires) with the kind of sleek, contemporary lines and modern comforts you'd expect from a top-class guesthouse.

Langley Hotel (☎ 604250; www.langleyhotel.com; 16 Royal Cres; s/d £35/66; Ⓟ) The whiff of Victorian splendour may have faded somewhat, but the panoramic views from West Cliff are as good as ever. The rooms are tidy and neat, if a little cramped.

Other options:

Rosslyn House (☎ 604086; rosslyn_gh@btconnect .com; 11 Abbey Tce; s/d £24/48)

Argyle House (☎ 602733; www.argyle-house.co.uk; 18 Hudson St; s/d £25/48)

Bramblewick (☎ 604 504; www.bramblewick.co.uk; 3 Havelock Pl; s/d from £25/50; Ⓟ)

Eating & Drinking

For many visitors, Whitby cuisine extends no further than a fish-and-chip supper (served with peas, bread and tea), obtainable most everywhere for between £4 and £5 but preferably at the world's most famous chipper. If you want to keep your cholesterol in check, there are a few other options.

Shepherd's Purse (☎ 820228; 95 Church St; mains about £7) A veggie place behind a wholefood shop with the same name, with a great range of healthy, interesting snacks and meals, and a very nice courtyard.

Magpie Café (☎ 602058; 14 Pier Rd; mains £7-10; ☒ lunch & dinner) The world's best fish and chips, or so the reputation would have it. They are bloody delicious, but the one downer is that the world and his wife knows about this place, and summertime queues can be off-putting.

Trenchers (☎ 603212; New Quay Rd; mains £7-10; ☒ lunch & dinner) Excellent fish and chips minus the reputation, Trenchers is your best bet if you want to avoid the queues. Don't be put off by the modern look.

Greens (☎ 600284; www.greensofwhitby.com; 13 Bridge St; mains £14-22; ☒ lunch & dinner Fri-Sun, dinner Mon-Thu) The fanciest restaurant in town does wonderful things with fish, caught fresh and delivered from the harbour: the filets of turbot are sensational. There are meat dishes on the menu, but the menu's real strength is seafood.

Many pubs also serve food, including, of course, fish and chips or crab sandwiches, all

for about £5 to £7. A good first choice is the popular **Duke of York** (Church St) at the bottom of the 199 steps, with plentiful food and a classic Whitby atmosphere, while next door the smaller **Board Inn** (Church St) is another place with views, good beer and seafood. The **Dolphin** (Bridge St) has tables inside or out on the pavement, while the **Shambles** (Market Pl) is modern and spacious with huge picture windows overlooking the harbour. The **Tap & Spile** (☎ 603937; New Quay Rd) is a straightforward place with good local rock and folk bands.

Getting There & Away

Whitby is 230 miles from London and 45 miles from York.

Buses 93 and 93A run to/from Scarborough (one hour, hourly), and to Middlesbrough (about hourly), with fewer services on Sunday. Yorkshire Coastliner (buses 840 and X40) runs between Whitby and Leeds (£9.20, three hours, seven per day) via Pickering and York.

If you're coming from the north, you can get to Whitby by train along the Esk Valley line from Middlesbrough (£10.70, 1½ hours, four per day). From the south, it's easier to get a train from York to Scarborough, then a bus from Scarborough to Whitby.

Getting Around

Whitby is a compact place and those 199 steps help burn off the fish and chips. But if you need one, there's a taxi rank near the tourist office. The west cliff is also accessible via a lift (75p), which perishes the thought of clambering up the steep roads.

AROUND WHITBY
Robin Hood's Bay

Just 6 miles south of Whitby, Robin Hood's Bay has a lot more to do with smugglers than the Sherwood Forest hero, but this picturesque haven is well worth a visit, although like so many places it's very busy on summer weekends.

A single main street called New Rd winds through the old part of town, dropping steeply down from the cliff top to the sea. (There's compulsory parking at the top – don't even think about driving down as there's hardly room to turn at the bottom.) Off New Rd there's a honeycomb of cobbled alleys, secret passages and impossibly small houses. There are gift shops, teashops and a trail of pubs (it

---

CAPTAIN COOK – WHITBY'S FAMOUS (ADOPTED) SON

Although he wasn't actually born in Whitby, the town has adopted the famous explorer Captain James Cook, and since the first tourists got off the train in Victorian times, local entrepreneurs have mercilessly cashed in on his memory, as endless 'Endeavour Cafés' and 'Captain Cook Chip Shops' testify.

Still, Whitby played a key role in Cook's eventual success as a world-famous explorer, in that the design of the ships used for his voyages of discovery – including the famous *Endeavour* – were based on the design of Whitby 'cats', unique flat-bottomed ships carrying coal from Newcastle to London that the young Cook served his apprenticeship on from 1746 to 1755, when he eventually joined the Navy.

YORKSHIRE

might be safer to start from the bottom and work your way up), many with seats outside, so this is an excellent place to just sit and watch the world go by.

Among the pubs, our favourite for ambience is the old **Dolphin** (☎ 01947 880337; King St); the **Victoria Hotel** (☎ 01947 880205; Station Rd) has the best beer and good food; and the **Bay Hotel** (☎ 01947-880278; The Dock) is notable for being the end of the famous Coast to Coast Walk (p575). Some pubs do B&B and there are several other accommodation options – the tourist office in Whitby can advise.

It's eminently possible to walk or cycle here from Whitby. Also, buses 93 and 93A run hourly between Whitby and Scarborough via Robin Hood's Bay – the bus stop is at the top of the hill, in the new part of town.

Staithes

Tucked beneath high cliffs and running back along the steep banks of a river, the small fishing town of Staithes seems to hide from the modern world, focusing still on its centuries-old battle with the sea. It's a lot less touristy than Robin Hood's Bay: the houses are less prettified, you can see fishermen's jackets drying on lines, and seagulls the size of vultures swoop down the narrow alleys that lead off the main street.

The town's claim to fame is that explorer James Cook worked as a grocer here when a boy. Legend says that fishermen's tales of the high seas, and bad treatment by his master, led him to steal a shilling and run away to Whitby. The rest of the tale is told in great detail in the fascinating and lovingly maintained **Captain Cook & Staithes Heritage Centre** (admission £3; ☉ 10am-5.30pm), packed to the gunwales with nautical relics.

Staithes is located 11 miles from Whitby. To get here, the buses on the Whitby-to-Middlesbrough run can drop you at the top of the hill. If you're feeling fit, walking one way and bussing the other makes for a great day out.

Northwest England

Welcome to the northwest, the once-mighty heartland of industrial England and a generous slice of urban heaven. Sounds like an oxymoron, right? What could possibly be so alluring about jam-packed conurbations and the heaving hulks of the industrial past? In this part of the world, plenty. Crammed into relatively tight confines are a couple of the most exciting cities in England, a picture-postcard town whose rich layers of history are revealed in its multitiered architecture and the most eye-popping, stomach-turning roller coaster we've ever been dizzy on. Oh, and the birthplace of the world's best-ever band, bar none. Life, music, history and hedonism. And for those eager for a bit of respite from the concrete pawprint of humankind, there's some of the most beautiful countryside in England. All this from a region that once changed the world.

That's right, the northwest was the very place where the Industrial Revolution was born and raised into the overwhelming force of capitalism; where, in Manchester, the world's first modern city was conceived; and where the endless possibilities of the Age of Reason were put through their original paces. Ancient Rome would have been proud of the accomplishment.

These days, however, the northwest is all about looking forward, about being the region that leaves its imprint on the 21st century in the way that it has for the last couple of centuries. A tall order, no doubt, but the region knows a thing or two about mighty achievements, urban redesign and bloody good music: look and listen for yourself.

HIGHLIGHTS

- Exploring the stunning **Imperial War Museum** (p647) in Manchester
- Walking in Roman footsteps around **Chester's city walls** (p657)
- Getting queasy on the rollercoasters at Blackpool's **Pleasure Beach** (p675)
- Exploring the **Isle of Man** (p680) – not just for tax-dodgers and petrol-heads
- Catching the **ferry across the Mersey** (p668): hum the song while enjoying the best views of Liverpool
- Experiencing the simply marvellous **World Museum Liverpool** (p666)

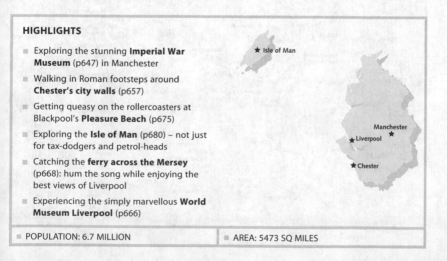

- POPULATION: 6.7 MILLION
- AREA: 5473 SQ MILES

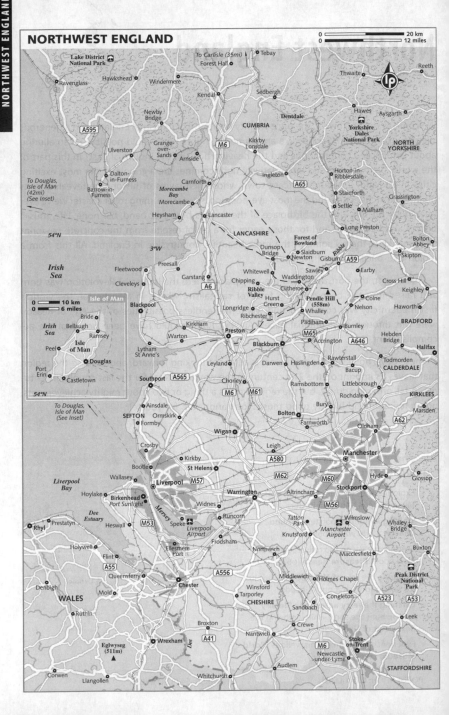

NORTHWEST ENGLAND

0 — 20 km
0 — 12 miles

Information

Discover England's Northwest (www.visitnorthwest.com) is the centralised tourist authority that covers the whole of the northwest.

Activities

The northwest is predominantly an urban area, and there are few walking and cycling options. One main exception is the Ribble Valley, which has plenty of good walks including the 70-mile **Ribble Way**, and is also well covered by the northern loop of the **Lancashire Cycle Way**.

The Isle of Man has top-notch walking and cycling opportunities. Regional tourism websites contain walking and cycling information, and tourist offices all stock free leaflets plus maps and guides (usually £1 to £5) that cover walking, cycling and other activities.

Getting Around

The towns and cities covered in this chapter are all within easy reach of each other, and are well linked by public transport. The two main cities, Manchester and Liverpool, are only 34 miles apart and are linked by hourly bus and train services. Chester is only 18 miles south of Liverpool, but is also easily accessible from Manchester by train or via the M56 motorway. Blackpool is 50 miles to the north of both cities, and is also well connected. Try the following for transport information:

Greater Manchester Passenger Transport Authority (www.gmpte.com) For extensive info on Manchester and its environs.

Merseytravel (☎ 236 7676; www.merseytravel.gov.uk) Taking care of all travel in Merseyside.

National Express (☎ 08705 808080; www.national express.com) Extensive coach services in the northwest; Manchester and Liverpool are major hubs.

MANCHESTER

☎ 0161 / pop 394,270

London has decided to give up the job of capital and go into quiet retirement. When everyone north of Leicester is done cheering, England looks around for a substitute and after some consideration the nation turns to... Sorry Birmingham, but it can be only Manchester, the uncrowned capital of the north and a city embracing change like few others in Europe.

Manchester knows all about improbable scenarios and has never shied away from responsibility. After all, this was the city that gave birth to capitalism and the Industrial Revolution, so what's a little self-inflating urban redesign to a burgh that knows a thing or two about altering the history of the world?

The change and influence of the last decade and a half has been nearly as dramatic. It began with a musical revolution, was interrupted by a bomb and has climaxed in the transformation of Manchester into a modern metropolis that has embraced 21st-century style and technology like no other in England. The envy of any urban centre in Europe, it is surely indicative of more than just northern one-upmanship over London and the south that Manchester looks to Barcelona as its main rival and inspiration.

Not only does Manchester have a wealth of fascinating museums that reflect its unique role in the pioneering developments of the Industrial Age, but it has managed to weave the mementos of its past with a forward-looking, ambitious programme of urban development that has already offered a vision of what the future might hold.

The future, according to Manchester, is to ensure that form follows function, and that cities are first and foremost human dwellings. Testament to this belief is the remarkable life on show at street level, from the trendy bars and boutiques of the bohemian Northern Quarter to the loud-and-proud attitude of the Gay Village and the chic, self-possessed stylings of the Castlefield area. Spend enough time here and you too will be infected with the palpable confidence of a city that knows it's onto a good thing.

HISTORY

Canals and steam-powered cotton mills were how Manchester was transformed from a small disease-infested provincial town into a very big disease-infested industrial city. It all happened in the 1760s – with the opening of the Bridgewater Canal between Manchester and the coal mines at Worsley in 1763, and with Richard Arkwright patenting his super cotton mill in 1769. Thereafter, Manchester and the world would never be the same again. When the canal was extended to Liverpool and the open sea in 1776, Manchester – now dubbed 'Cottonopolis' – kicked into high gear and took off on the coal-fuelled, steam-powered gravy train.

THE WARS OF THE ROSES

The Wars of the Roses was nothing more than a protracted quarrel between two factions, the House of Lancaster (whose symbol was a red rose) and the House of York (represented by a white rose), over who would rule England.

It began with the Lancastrian Henry VI (r 1422–61 and 1470–71), who was terrific as a patron of culture and learning, but totally inept as a ruler, and prone to bouts of insanity. During the worst of these episodes he had to hand over power to Richard, Duke of York, who served as protector but acted as king. Henry may have been nutty, however, his wife Margaret of Anjou was anything but, and in 1460 she put an end to Richard's political ambitions by raising an army to defeat and kill him at the Battle of Wakefield. Round one to Lancaster.

Next it was the turn of Richard's son Edward. In 1461 he avenged his father's defeat by inflicting a defeat of his own on Henry and Margaret, declaring himself Edward IV (r 1461–70 and 1471–83) as a result. One all.

But Edward's victory owed much to the political machinations of Richard Neville, Earl of Warwick – appropriately nicknamed 'the kingmaker' – but the throne proved an amnesiac and in time Eddie forgot his friends. In 1470 Warwick jumped ship and sided with the Lancastrians. Edward was exiled and Henry, Margaret and Warwick were all smiles. Half-time and the score was two–one to Lancaster.

Edward came back strongly a year later. He first defeated and killed Warwick at the Battle of Barnet before crushing Henry and Margaret at Tewkesbury. Henry was executed in the Tower of London and Margaret ransomed back to France, where she died in poverty. Just to make sure, Edward also killed their son.

The Yorkists were back in the game, and Edward proved to be a good and popular king. When he died in 1483 (apparently worn out by his sexual excesses), power passed to his brother Richard, who was to rule as regent until Edward's 12-year-old son came of age. Two months after the king's death, Richard arranged for the 'disappearance' of his nephew and he was crowned Richard III. The Yorkists, however, had scored a goal of their own: when rumours of Dickie's dastardly deed became known, he became as popular as a bad smell. In 1485, the Lancastrians, led by the young Henry Tudor, defeated Richard at the Battle of Bosworth, leaving the fallen king to offer his kingdom in exchange for a horse. Final result: victory to Lancaster.

The coronation of Henry VII, and his subsequent marriage to Edward IV's daughter Elizabeth, put an end to the fighting and ushered in the Tudor dynasty, but it didn't end the rivalry.

The two sides may not be fighting with swords and lances, but one of the great enmities in English football today exists between Lancashire's Manchester United – who wear red – and Yorkshire's Leeds United, who wear all-white.

There was plenty of gravy to go around, but the good burghers of 19th-century Manchester made sure that the vast majority of the city's swollen citizenry (with a population of 90,000 in 1801, and 100 years later, two million) who produced most of it never got their hands on any of it. Their reward was life in a new kind of urban settlement: the industrial slum. Working conditions were scarcely better: impossibly long hours, child labour, work-related accidents and fatalities were commonplace. Mark Twain commented that he would like to live here because the 'transition between Manchester and Death would be unnoticeable'. So much for Victorian values.

The wheels started to come off toward the end of the 19th-century. The USA had begun to flex its own industrial muscles and was taking over a sizeable chunk of the textile trade; production in Manchester's mills began to slow and then it stopped altogether. By WWII there was hardly enough cotton produced in the city to make a tablecloth. In 1996 an IRA bomb wrecked a chunk of the city centre, but from the wreckage sprung the glass-and-chrome revolution so much in evidence today.

ORIENTATION

Shoe power and the excellent Metrolink tram are the only things you'll need to get around the compact city centre. All public transport converges at Piccadilly Gardens, a few blocks southeast of the cathedral. Directly north is the on-the-up boho Northern

MANCHESTER IN...

Two Days

You'll be frustrated you're not staying longer, but we'll do our best to help. After you've explored the glorious trophies of the Industrial Age around **Albert Sq** (p646), hop on a tram and get down to Salford Quays and its trio of top attractions: the **Imperial War Museum North** (p647), the **Lowry** (p648) and then the **Manchester United Museum** (p648). If you'd rather eat glass than set foot in or give money to Man U plc, skip across town to visit Manchester City's ground at the **City of Manchester Stadium** (p655). Pick a restaurant – **Yang Sing** (p652) will do to kick off the evening – then find a bar and round the night off in a club. The next day, head toward **Castlefield Urban Heritage Park** (p647) before indulging in a spot of retail therapy around the **Millennium Quarter** (p655), breaking up the spendfest with a visit to **Urbis** (p646). Venture east and go alternative in the boutiques and offbeat shops of the **Northern Quarter** (p655).

Four Days

Follow the two-day itinerary and also tackle some of the city's lesser-known museums – the **People's History Museum** (p647), **Chetham's Library** (p646) and the **Manchester Jewish Museum** (p647). Head south towards the university and tackle the **Manchester Museum** (p648) and **Whitworth Art Gallery** (p649). If the weather is decent, visit the **Godlee Observatory** (p648) before examining the riches of the **Manchester Art Gallery** (p646).

Quarter, with its offbeat boutiques, hip cafés and fabulous record shops. A few blocks southeast is the Gay Village, centred on Canal St and, just next to it, Chinatown, basically a bunch of restaurants clustered around Portland St.

Southwest of the city centre is Castlefield and Deansgate Locks, a supertrendy development that has successfully converted the 19th-century canalside industrial infrastructure into a groovy weekend playground for the city's fine young things. Further west again – and accessible via Metrolink – are the recently developed Salford Quays, home to the fab Lowry complex and the Imperial War Museum North. Not far away is Old Trafford football stadium, where Manchester United's global stars earn their fabulous keep.

For information on getting around, see p656.

INFORMATION

Bookshops

Cornerhouse (☎ 200 1514; www.cornerhouse.org; 70 Oxford St) Art and film books, specialist magazines and kitschy cards.

Waterstone's Deansgate (☎ 832 1992); St Anne's Sq (☎ 837 3000)

Emergency

Ambulance (☎ 436 3999)

Police station (☎ 872 5050; Bootle St)

Rape Crisis Centre (☎ 273 4500)

Samaritans (☎ 236 8000)

Internet Access

Central Library (☎ 234 1982; St Peter's Sq; per 30 min £1; ⏲ internet access 1-6pm Mon-Sat)

easyInternetcafé (8-10 Exchange St; per 30 min £1; ⏲ 8am-10pm Mon-Fri, 9am-9pm Sat-Sun)

Internet Resources

City Life (www.manchestereveningnews.co.uk) The city's evening paper in electronic form.

Mad For It (www.madforit.com) Restaurants, bars, clubs and other night-time activities using the Manchester clarion call: are you mad for it?

Manchester City Council (www.manchester.gov.uk) The council's official website.

Manchester Online (www.manchesteronline.co.uk)

Real Manchester (www.realmanchester.com) Online guide to nightlife.

Virtual Manchester (www.manchester.com)

Visit Manchester (www.visitmanchester.com) The official website for Greater Manchester.

Medical Services

Cameolord Chemist (☎ 236 1445; St Peter's Sq; ⏲ 10am-10pm)

Manchester Royal Infirmary (☎ 276 1234; Oxford Rd)

Post

Post office (Brazennose St; ⏲ 9am-5.30pm Mon-Fri)

MANCHESTER

A

INFORMATION
Cameolord Chemist..................1 F4
Central Library.....................(see 10)
Cornerhouse.............................2 F5
Early Years & Play.................3 D4
easyInternetcafé....................4 E2
Police Station..........................5 E3
Post Office...............................6 E3
Tourist Office...........................7 F3
Waterstone's............................8 E2
Waterstone's............................9 E2

SIGHTS & ACTIVITIES
Central Library......................10 E4
Chetham's Library & School
   of Music...........................11 F1
Godlee Observatory...........(see 29)
John Rylands Library...........12 E3
Manchester Art Gallery.......13 F3
Museum of Science &
   Industry............................14 C4
People's History Museum....15 D3
Town Hall.............................16 E3
Urbis....................................17 F1

SLEEPING
Castlefield............................18 C4
Great John Street Hotel.......19 C4
Hatters.................................20 H2
Jury's Inn.............................21 E5
Midland................................22 E4
Ox.....................................(see 38)
Palace Hotel.........................23 F5
Premier Travel Inn................24 E4
Premier Travel Inn................25 F4
Radisson Edwardian.............26 E3
Rembrandt Hotel...................27 G4
Rossetti................................28 H3
UMIST..................................29 G4
YHA Manchester...................30 C5

EATING
Café And...............................31 G2
Earth Café.............................32 G2
Eighth Day............................33 G6
El Rincón del Rafa.................34 D4

B

Le Petit Blanc........................35 E3
Love Saves the Day..............36 G2
Market Restaurant................37 G1
Ox...38 C4
Tampopo...............................39 E3
Yang Sing..............................40 F4

DRINKING
Bar Centro.............................41 H2
Britons Protection..................42 E5
Dukes 92...............................43 C5
Kro 2.....................................44 G6
Lass O'Gowrie.......................45 G5
Mr Thomas' Chop House......46 E3
Old Wellington Inn................47 E1
Peveril of the Peak...............48 E5
Rain......................................49 E5
Socio Rehab..........................50 G2
Temple of Convenience........51 F5

ENTERTAINMENT
Band on the Wall...................52 H1
Bridgewater Hall...................53 E5
Club V...................................54 E3
Cornerhouse......................(see 2)
Filmworks.............................55 F1
G-Mex Exhibition Centre.....56 E4
Green Room...........................57 F5
Library Theatre...................(see 10)
Manchester Cathedral...........58 E1
Manchester
   Opera House......................59 D3
Manchester Roadhouse.........60 H3
Music Box..............................61 F5
Royal Exchange.....................62 E2
South....................................63 E3

SHOPPING
Affleck's Palace.....................64 G2
Harvey Nichols.......................65 E2
Oxfam Original......................66 G2

TRANSPORT
Bus Station............................67 G3
Coach Station........................68 G4
Travelshop.............................69 G3

To Salford Quays;
Lowry & Imperial
War Museum
North (1mi)

CASTLEFIELD

To Old Trafford; Lancashire County
Cricket Club; Manchester Backpackers
Hostel; Old Trafford Lodge; Smiths Museum;
Salford Boys Club; Manchester Gay Centre
(2mi); Airport (12mi)

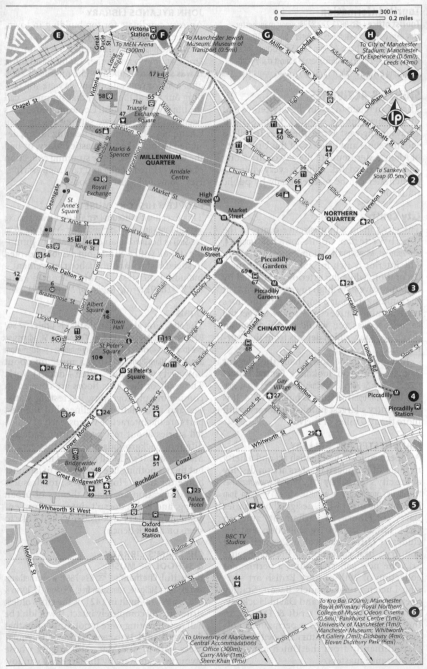

Tourist Information

Tourist office (☎ 0871 222 8223; www.manchester
.gov.uk; Town Hall Extension, St Peter's Sq; ☒ 10am-
5.30pm Mon-Sat, 10am-4.30pm Sun) Sells tickets for all
sorts of guided walks, which operate almost daily year-
round and cost adult/child £5/3.

SIGHTS & ACTIVITIES

There's so much to see in the city centre and
in the surrounding suburbs, from Salford
Quays to the west across the River Irwell, to
the museums and galleries of the University
of Manchester, south of the city centre along
and off Oxford Rd. Almost everywhere in
Manchester can be reached easily by public
transport.

City Centre

The city's main administrative centre is the
superb Victorian Gothic **town hall** (tours £4;
☒ 2pm Sat, Mar-Sep) that dominates Albert Sq.
The interior is rich in sculpture and ornate
decoration, while the exterior is crowned by
an impressive 85m-high tower. You can visit
the building on your own, but as it's the city's
main administrative centre you won't get the
same access as you would get by doing an
organised tour, which departs from the tourist office.

Just behind the town hall, the elegant
Roman Pantheon lookalike **Central Library**
(☎ 234 1900; St Peter's Sq; admission free; ☒ 10am-8pm
Mon-Thu, 10am-6pm Fri & Sat) was built in 1934. It is
the country's largest municipal library, with
more than 20 miles of shelves.

MANCHESTER ART GALLERY

A superb collection of British art and a hefty
number of European masters are on display
at the city's top **gallery** (☎ 235 8888; www.manches
tergalleries.org; Mosley St; admission free; ☒ 10am-5pm
Tue-Sun). The older wing, designed by Charles
Barry (of Houses of Parliament fame) in
1834, has an impressive collection that includes 37 Turner watercolours, as well as the
country's best collection of Pre-Raphaelite
art. The new gallery features a permanent
collection of 20th-century British art starring Lucien Freud, Francis Bacon, Stanley
Spencer, Henry Moore and David Hockney.
Finally, the Gallery of Craft & Design, in
the Athenaeum, houses a permanent collection of pre-17th-century art, with works
predominantly from the Dutch and early
Renaissance masters.

JOHN RYLANDS LIBRARY

An easy candidate for top building in town,
this marvellous Victorian Gothic **library** (☎ 834
5343; 35 Deansgate) was one hell of a way for Rylands' widow to remember her husband John.
It was slated to reopen by the middle of 2006
after a major renovation, but we were still tapping our feet at the end of that summer - call
the library for the latest. Come on, people! It's
been too long since we set foot inside Basil
Champneys' breathtaking Reading Room, designed to look like a monastic library, or had
the chance to gawk at the stunning collection
of early printed books and rare manuscripts.
Hey, some folks just *love* books!

PEOPLE'S HISTORY MUSEUM

This excellent **museum** (☎ 839 6061; www.phm.org
.uk; Left Bank, Bridge St; admission free; ☒ 11am-4.30pm
Tue-Sun) is housed in an old Edwardian pumping station with well laid-out exhibits devoted
to social history and the labour movement –
including the desk at which Thomas Paine
(1737–1809) wrote *Rights of Man* (1791).

URBIS

The stunning glass triangle that is **Urbis** (☎ 907
9099; www.urbis.org.uk; City Park, Corporation St; admission
free to levels 2-4, charge for temporary exhibits; ☒ 10am-6pm
Sun-Wed, 10am-8pm Thu-Sat) is a museum about
how a city works and – often – doesn't work.
The walls of the three floors are covered in
compelling photographs, interesting statistics and informative timelines, but the best
parts are the interactive videos, each of which
tell stories about real people from radically
different backgrounds and how they fare in
Manchester. It's all well and good to theorise,
but there's nothing like a real story to hammer
home the truth. Homelessness, rootlessness
and dislocation are major themes of urban
living, and Urbis doesn't shy away from encouraging visitors to consider what it's like to
sleep on a park bench.

CHETHAM'S LIBRARY
& SCHOOL OF MUSIC

Beautiful **Chetham's** (☎ 834 7861; www.chethams
.org.uk; Long Millgate; admission free; ☒ 9am-12.30pm &
1.30-4pm Mon-Fri), built in 1421, is the city's oldest
structure still completely intact. It wouldn't be
half as interesting were it not for the fact that
during the mid-19th century two of its regular
users were Messrs Marx and Engels, whose
favourite seats were by the large bay window

MORE MUSEUMS

If you can't get enough of annotated exhibits, Manchester has a number of other museums worth checking out.

The **Manchester Jewish Museum** (☎ 834 9879; www.manchesterjewishmuseum.com; 190 Cheetham Hill Rd; adult/child £2.50/1.75; ☷ 10.30am-4pm Mon-Thu, to 5pm Sun), in a Moorish-style former synagogue, tells the story of the city's Jewish community in fascinating detail, including the story of Polish refugee Michael Marks, who opened his first shop with partner Tom Spencer at 20 Cheetham Hill Rd in 1894. From Piccadilly Gardens, take bus 59, 89, 135 & 167.

Nearby, the wonderful **Museum of Transport** (☎ 205 2122; www.gmts.co.uk; Boyle St, Cheetham Hill; admission £4/2; ☷ 10am-5pm Wed, Sat & Sun) is packed with old buses, fire engines and lorries built in the last 100 years.

The **Pankhurst Centre** (☎ 273 5673; www.pankhurstcentre.org.uk; 60-62 Nelson St; admission free; ☷ 10am-5pm Mon-Fri) is the converted childhood home of Emmeline Pankhurst (1858–1928), a leading light of the British suffragette movement. It has displays on her remarkable life and political struggles.

---

in the main reading room. The library is the only part of the building that is open to visitors, as the rest of it is a national school for young musicians.

Castlefield Urban Heritage Park

The heart of 19th-century industrial Manchester, a landscape of enormous, weather-stained brick buildings and rusting cast-iron relics of canals, viaducts, bridges, warehouses and market buildings, Castlefield has been successfully transformed into an interesting heritage park. Aside from the huge science museum, the big draw here is the Castlefield Basin. The Bridgewater Canal runs through it; in summertime thousands of people amble about the place and patronise its fine pubs and trendy restaurants.

MUSEUM OF SCIENCE & INDUSTRY

The city's largest **museum** (☎ 832 1830; www.msim .org.uk; Liverpool Rd; admission free, charge for special exhibitions; ☷ 10am-5pm) comprises 2.8 hectares spread about two huge Victorian warehouses and the world's oldest passenger railway terminal. If there's anything you want to know about the Industrial (and postindustrial) Revolution and Manchester's key role in it, you'll find it among the collection of steam engines and locomotives, factory machinery from the mills, and the excellent exhibition telling the story of Manchester from the sewers up.

With more than a dozen permanent exhibits, you could spend a whole day poking about the place, testing early electric shock machines here and trying out a printing press there. A unifying theme – besides the fact that

science and industry were pretty handy to the development of society – is that Manchester and Mancunians had a key role to play: did you know that Manchester was home to the world's first computer, a giant contraption called 'the baby', in 1948, or that the world's first submarine was built to the designs of local curate the Rev George Garrett in 1880? Nope, neither did we.

Salford Quays

It seems that no 21st-century urban plan is complete without a docklands development; in Manchester's case the docks in question are the Salford Quays, west of the city centre along the Ship Canal. Three major attractions draw in the punters, and a shopping centre makes sure they have outlets to spend their money. It's a cinch to get there from the city centre via Metrolink (£1.80); for the Imperial War Museum North and the Lowry look for the Harbour City stop.

IMPERIAL WAR MUSEUM NORTH

War museums generally appeal to those with a fascination for military hardware and battle strategy (toy soldiers optional), but Daniel Libeskind's visually stunning **Imperial War Museum North** (☎ 836 4000; www.iwm.org.uk/north; Trafford Wharf Rd; admission free; ☷ 10am-6pm Mar-Oct, 10am-5pm Nov-Feb) takes a radically different approach. War is hell, it tells us, but it's a hell we revisit with tragic regularity.

The exhibits cover the main conflicts of the 20th century through a broad selection of displays, but the really effective bit comes every half hour when the entire exhibition hall goes dark and one of three 15-minute films (*Children and War, Why War?* or *Weapons of War*) is projected throughout. Visitors are encouraged to walk around the darkened room so as to get the most out of the sensory bombardment.

Although the audiovisuals and displays are quite compelling, the extraordinary aluminium-clad building itself is a huge part of the attraction, and the exhibition spaces are genuinely breathtaking. Libeskind designed three distinct structures, or shards, that represent the three main theatres of war: air, land and sea.

LOWRY

Directly across the canal from the war museum is a futuristic ship in permanent dock. No, not really, but the **Lowry** (☎ 876 2020; www.thelowry.com; Pier 8, Salford Quays; ☷ 11am-8pm Tue-Fri, 10am-8pm Sat, 11am-6pm Sun-Mon) looks a bit like one. It caused quite a stir when it opened in 2000, but has proved an unqualified success, attracting more than a million visitors a year.

The complex is named after one of England's favourite artists, LS Lowry, who is mostly noted for his industrial landscapes and impressions of northern towns. The Lowry contains more than 300 of his paintings and drawings. It also encapsulates two theatres (see p655), galleries, shops, restaurants and bars.

OLD TRAFFORD (MANCHESTER UNITED MUSEUM & TOUR)

Here's a paradox: the world's most famous and supported football club, beloved of fans from Bangkok to Buenos Aires, is the most hated club in England and has a smaller fan base in Manchester than its far less successful cross-town rivals, Manchester City. United fans snigger and dismiss this as small-minded jealousy, while treating the **Old Trafford stadium** (Sir Matt Busby Way; www.manutd.com; ☷ 9.30am-5pm) like holy ground and the stars that play there like minor deities. Such arrogance is enough to turn the rest of us into ABUs (Anyone But United) and cheer the fact that it's been a few years since Fergie's boys have won a championship (even though Chelsea's dominance is just as irritating, heralding the arrival of ABCs).

But there's no denying that a visit to the stadium is one of the more memorable things

you'll do here. We strongly recommend that you take the **tour** (☎ 0870 442 1994; adult/child £9/6; ☷ every 10 min, 9.40am-4.30pm except match days), which includes a seat in the stands, a stop in the changing rooms, a peek at the players' lounge (from which the manager is banned unless invited by the players) and a walk down the tunnel to the pitchside dugout, which is as close to ecstasy as many of the club's fans will ever get. It's pretty impressive stuff. The **museum** (adult/child £5.50/3.75; ☷ 9.30am-5pm), which is part of the tour but can be visited independently, has a comprehensive history of the club and a state-of-the-art call-up system so you can view your favourite goals.

University of Manchester

About a mile south of the city, the University of Manchester is one of England's most extraordinary institutions, and not just because it is a top-class university with a remarkable academic pedigree and a great place to party. It is also home to a world-class museum and a superb art gallery.

MANCHESTER MUSEUM

If you're into natural history and social science, this extraordinary **museum** (☎ 275 2634; www.museum.man.ac.uk; University of Manchester, Oxford Rd; admission free; ☷ 10am-5pm Mon-Sat, 11am-4pm Sun) is the place for you. It has galleries devoted to archaeology, archery, botany, ethnology, geology, numismatics, Oriental studies and zoology. The real treat here, though, is the Egyptology section and its collection of mummies. One particularly interesting section is devoted to the work of Dr Richard Neave, who has rebuilt faces of people who have been dead for more than 3000 years; his pioneering techniques are now used in criminal forensics.

Take bus 11, 16, 41 or 42 from Piccadilly Gardens or bus 47, 190 or 191 from Victoria station.

WHITWORTH ART GALLERY
Manchester's second most important **art gallery** (☎ 275 7450; www.manchester.ac.uk/whitworth; University of Manchester, Oxford Rd; admission free, guided tours £2; ◷ 10am-5pm Mon-Sat, 2-5pm Sun) has a wonderful collection of British watercolours. It also houses the best selection of historic textiles outside London and a number of galleries devoted to the work of artists from Dürer and Rembrandt to Lucien Freud and David Hockney.

All this high art aside, you may find that the most interesting part of the gallery is the group of rooms dedicated to wallpaper – proof that bland pastels and horrible flowery patterns are not the final word in home decoration.

MANCHESTER FOR CHILDREN
Urbis (p646) is always full of kids who find the interactive displays quite engaging, and the **Castlefield Urban Heritage Park** (p647) is the perfect all-day destination, offering a host of different activities and exhibits suited to younger visitors. Here, too, the canalside parks and walkways are pleasantly distracting. Manchester United's ground **Old Trafford** (opposite) is always popular with fans, who are getting younger and younger (the kids seem to lose interest in Manchester City when

they ask 'but what have they won?'). The **Imperial War Museum North** (p647) is designed to engage the interest of kids barely into double figures, despite its war-based themes not being a bunch of laughs.

City Life Kids (£1), available at the tourist office and all bookshops in the city, is a comprehensive guide to virtually every aspect of family-oriented Manchester.

If you're looking for some free time away from the kids, **Early Years & Play** (☎ 234 7117; Overseas House, Quay St) is a city-centre crèche.

QUIRKY MANCHESTER
You don't have to work too hard to find oddity in Manchester: spend enough time on Piccadilly Circus and you'll know what we mean. However, for a different (and altogether fabulous) view of the city, climb to the parapet of the **Godlee Observatory** (see the boxed text The Sky's the Limit, opposite), a place virtually nobody goes to. It's a far cry from the alternative circus that is **Affleck's Palace** (p655), where in order to go unnoticed it's best if you look like Marilyn Manson or a really scruffy Kurt Cobain.

When you're done, you'll have to unwind with a pint in the **Temple of Convenience** (p652), a tiny basement pub with a terrific atmosphere located in…a former public toilet.

FESTIVALS & EVENTS
Manchester Irish Festival (www.manchesterirish festival.co.uk) Manchester's huge Irish community goes bonkers for a week in mid-March.
Futuresonic (www.futuresonic.com) Superb electronic music and media arts festival that takes place in various venues over a week in July.

GAY & LESBIAN MANCHESTER
The city's gay scene is unsurpassed outside London, and caters to every taste. The useful *Gay & Lesbian Village Guide,* available from the tourist office, lists numerous gay bars, clubs, galleries and groups. It also runs the **Lesbian & Gay Heritage Trail** (£5; ◷ 3pm first Sun of month), a 90-minute walking tour of the city's pink links, some of which date back to the early 1800s. For other information, check with the **Manchester Gay Centre** (☎ 274 3814; Sydney St, Salford) and the **Lesbian & Gay Foundation** (☎ 235 8035; www.lgf.org.uk; ◷ 4-10pm). The city's best pink website is www.visitgaymanchester.co.uk.

At the heart of it all is the Gay Village, centred on gorgeous Canal St. Here you will find bars, clubs, restaurants and hotels that cater almost exclusively to the pink pound.

The country's biggest gay and lesbian arts festival, **Queer Up North** (☎ 833 2288; www.queerup north.com), takes place every two years – the next in spring 2007. **Manchester Pride** (☎ 0870 166 0434; www.manchesterpride.com) is a 10-day festival in the middle of August each year and attracts over 500,000 people.

Manchester Pride (☎ 0871 230 2624; www.manches terpride.com) One of England's biggest celebrations of gay, bisexual and transgender life, held in late August.

SLEEPING

Although Manchester's hotels cater primarily to the business traveller – who can be trusted to provide the steadiest flow of business – the city's reputation as a capital of cool has seen the standards of style go up, and Manchester is now awash with all manner of designer digs. Remember that during the football season (August to May), rooms can be almost impossible to find if Manchester United is playing at home. If you are having difficulty finding a bed, the tourist office's accommodation service (£3) can help.

City Centre
BUDGET
University of Manchester/University of Manchester Institute of Science & Technology (UMIST) (☎ 275 2888; Central Accommodations Office, Precinct Centre, Oxford Rd; dm/d from £11/26; ✆ Jun-Sep) With more than 9000 beds in a variety of rooms, from traditional residence halls to smart, modern flats spread throughout the campuses and suburbs, the university does a roaring summer trade. Call the office (9am to 5pm Monday to Friday) for details and bookings.

Hatters (☎ 236 9500; www.hattersgroup.com; 50 Newton St; dm/s/d/tr from £15.50/27.50/50/68; ℗ ▯ ♿) The old-style lift and porcelain sinks are the only leftovers of this former milliner's factory, now one of the best hostels in town, with location to boot. Smack in the heart of the Northern Quarter, you won't have to go far to get the best of alternative Manchester.

YHA Manchester (☎ 839 9960; www.yha.org.uk; Potato Wharf; dm £20.95 incl breakfast; ℗ ▯ ♿) This purpose-built canalside hostel in the Castlefield area is one of the best in the country. It's a top-class option with four- and six-bed dorms, all en suite, as well as a host of good facilities.

MIDRANGE
Castlefield (☎ 832 7073; www.castlefield-hotel.co.uk; 3 Liverpool Rd; s/d from £45/80; ℗ ♞) This is another successful warehouse conversion that has resulted in a thoroughly modern business hotel overlooking the canal basin. It has spacious, comfortable rooms and excellent amenities, including a fitness centre and pool that are free to guests.

Ox (☎ 839 7740; www.theox.co.uk; 71 Liverpool Rd; r £50) Not quite your traditional B&B (breakfast is extra), but an excellent choice nonetheless: nine ox-blood-red rooms with tidy amenities above a fine gastro-pub (see p652) in the heart of Castlefield. It's the best deal in town for the location.

Palace Hotel (☎ 288 1111; www.principal-hotels.com; Oxford St; r from £80) An elegant refurbishment of one of Manchester's most magnificent Victorian palaces has resulted in a pretty special boutique hotel, combining the grandeur of the public areas with the modern look of the bedrooms.

Other options worth considering:

Jury's Inn (☎ 953 8888; www.jurysdoyle.com; 56 Great Bridgewater St; r from £48; ♿) Comfortable Irish chain hotel a few doors down from the Bridgewater Hall.

Premier Travel Inn (☎ 0870 990 6444; www.premier travelinn.com; r from £58; ♿) G-Mex (Bishopsgate, 11 Lower Mosley St); Portland St (The Circus, 112 Portland St) Two convenient city-centre locations for this tidy chain.

Rembrandt Hotel (☎ 236 1311; www.rembrandt manchester.com; 33 Sackville St; s/d/tr from £35/40/45) *Grande dame* of the Gay Village; spartan rooms but a very friendly welcome.

TOP END
Midland (☎ 236 3333; www.themidland.co.uk; Peter St; r from £88; ▯ ♞) There could hardly have been a more suitably sumptuous setting for Mr Rolls to shake hands with Mr Royce than the lobby of this extraordinary Edwardian hotel just near the G-Mex Exhibition Centre. The luxury is everywhere, although some of the rich fabrics and faux Edwardiana are a little OTT for what is essentially a business hotel.

Radisson Edwardian (☎ 835 9929; www.radisson edwardian.com/manchester; Peter St; r from £100; ℗ ♞ ♿) The Free Trade Hall saw it all, from Emmeline Pankhurst's suffragette campaign to the Sex Pistols' legendary 1976 gig. Today, those rabble-rousing noisemakers wouldn't be allowed to set foot in the door of what is now a sumptuous five-star hotel, all minimalist Zen and luxury; unless of course they were *famous* rabble-rousing noisemakers, and then they would probably be headed straight for one of the four penthouse suites, one of which is named after Bob Dylan, who went electric at the Free Trade Hall in 1965.

Rossetti (☎ 247 7744; www.aliashotels.com; 107 Piccadilly St; r from £110; ▯) So long stevedore, hello Steven Dorff: this converted textile factory is now one of the city's coolest hotels. A favourite with show-biz celebs, it's a very stylish blend of original fittings and features, with hip art and contemporary design. The loft-style bedrooms feature Moltini designer furniture from Italy, Monsoon showers and stacks of Aqua Sulis toiletries. If you want to go all out, go for one of the self-contained suites (£265). The supercool, jeans-wearing staff appear casual, but the service is anything but. Breakfast is extra (£12.95).

Great John Street Hotel (☎ 831 210; www.greatjohn street.co.uk; Great John St; r £235-450; 🖳 💻 🐾) Elegant, designer luxury? Present. Fabulous rooms with all the usual delights (Egyptian cotton sheets, fabulous toiletries, free-standing baths and lots of high-tech electronics)? Present. A butler to run your bath in the grandest rooms? Present. It's all pretty swanky in Manchester's newest boutique hotel, a converted schoolhouse (ah, now we get it) just across the street from Granada TV studios. A rare treat: the rooftop garden has a hot tub and views of the *Coronation Street* set. Now that's something you don't see every day.

Salford Quays
MIDRANGE
Old Trafford Lodge (☎ 874 3333; www.lccc.co.uk; Talbot Rd; d Mon-Fri £59, d Sat & Sun £88) Cricket fans will salivate at the thought of watching a first-class match from the comfort of their bedroom balcony; for the rest of us, this is a pretty good business hotel with decent amenities.

TOP END
Lowry (☎ 827 4000; www.rfhotels.com; 50 Dearman's Pl, Chapel Wharf; s/d from £85/130) Simply dripping with designer luxury and five-star comfort, Manchester's top hotel has fabulous rooms with enormous beds, ergonomically designed furniture, walk-in wardrobes, and bathrooms finished in Italian porcelain tiles and glass mosaic. You can soothe yourself with a skin-brightening treatment or an aromatherapy head massage at the health spa.

Other Areas
BUDGET
Manchester Backpackers' Hostel (☎ 865 9296; 64 Cromwell Rd; dm £17) A very pleasant private hostel in Stretford, 2 miles south of the city centre, with cooking facilities, a TV lounge and some doubles. It's a cinch to get to from the city centre via Metrolink (Stretford stop).

TOP END
Eleven Didsbury Park (☎ 448 7711; www.elevendids burypark.com; 11 Didsbury Pk, Didsbury; r £145-250) Tucked away in fashionably bohemian Didsbury, this utterly wonderful boutique hotel is as romantic and stylish a place as you'll find in the city. Avoid, if you can, the smaller doubles. Although it's about 5 miles south of the city centre, it's reached easily by train from Piccadilly (to East Didsbury station).

EATING
Only London can outdo Manchester for the choice of cafés and restaurants. There's literally something for every palate, from the ubiquitous-but-excellent selections in Chinatown to Wilmslow Rd (the extension of Oxford St/ Rd), aka the Curry Mile, with its unsurpassed concentration of Indian and Pakistani eateries. Organic is the order of the day throughout the Northern Quarter (where you will also find some excellent veggie spots), while the city's fancy fare is spread pretty much all over. Many bars and pubs also do food. Below is but a small starter course.

BUDGET
Café And (☎ 834 1136; 74-76 High St; 🕙 9am-7pm Mon-Fri, 10am-7pm Sat, noon-5pm Sun) A trendy café, hip record store, contemporary art gallery and retro furniture shop all in one, this is your one stop for everything you might possibly need in the Northern Quarter. The toasties and wraps are delicious, but it's the excellent organic soups that kept us coming back for more. Sandwiches are £3.

Eighth Day (☎ 273 4878; 111 Oxford Rd; mains around £4; 🕙 9.30am-5pm Mon-Sat) New and most definitely improved after a major cleanup, this environment-friendly hang-out is a favourite with students and sells everything to make you feel good about your place in the world, from fair-trade teas to homeopathic remedies. The vegetarian- and vegan-friendly menu is substantial.

Love Saves the Day (☎ 832 0777; Tib St) The Northern Quarter's most popular café is a New York–style deli, small supermarket and sit-down eatery in one large, airy room. Everybody comes here – from crusties to corporate types – to sit around over a spot of lunch and discuss the day's goings-on. A wonderful spot. The house salad is £5.

Earth Café (☎ 834 1996; www.earthcafe.co.uk; 16-20 Turner St; chef's special £5.40; 🕙 10am-5pm Tue-Sat) Below the Manchester Buddhist Centre, this gourmet vegetarian café is working hard toward becoming the first 100% organic spot in town. The chef's special – a main dish, side and two salad portions – is generally excellent and always filling.

MIDRANGE

Tampopo (☎ 819 1966; 16 Albert Sq; mains from £7; ☺ lunch & dinner) Fast and furiously efficient, you'll be in and out of this Asian fusion canteen-style restaurant before you can learn the difference between the various *goreng* (fried dishes). The food is uniformly excellent and well worth the 30-second wait.

Shere Khan (☎ 256 2624; 52 Wilmslow Rd; mains around £7; ☺ lunch & dinner Sun-Fri) Of the almost impossible selection of curry houses along the Curry Mile, we recommend this place above all others for its plush setting, unfailingly good cuisine, polite, friendly service and for the fact that its sauces can be found stocked in supermarkets all over the country.

Ox (☎ 839 7740; www.theox.co.uk; 71 Liverpool Rd; mains £9-12; ☺ lunch & dinner) Manchester's only gastropub has elevated boozer-dining to a whole new level and earned plenty of kudos in the process. The Brit *nouvelle cuisine* – how about an oven-roasted T-bone steak with tempura onion rings, beefsteak tomatoes and Portobello mushrooms – is complemented by an almost exclusively Australian wine list.

El Rincón del Rafa (☎ 839 8819; Longworth St; mains £9-13; ☺ lunch & dinner) Descend the steps into this basement restaurant and find yourself in a little corner of Spain, complete with mouthwatering tapas, posters depicting bullfighting and the kind of buzz more in keeping with Madrid than Manchester. It's always packed so book ahead.

Le Petit Blanc (☎ 832 1000; www.lepetitblanc.co.uk; 55 King St; mains £9-18; ☺ lunch & dinner Mon-Sat) Top chef Raymond Blanc brings his winning formula of French cuisine with world influences (Asian primarily, but lots of English touches) to Manchester with some style and plenty of success.

Market Restaurant (☎ 834 3743; www.market-restaurant.com; 104 High St; mains £10-14; ☺ lunch & dinner Wed-Fri, dinner Sat) Excellent British cuisine is on the menu at this Northern Quarter restaurant – and it changes every month or so to take account of the season's best. It ain't especially pretty, but it's very good.

TOP END

Yang Sing (☎ 236 2200; 34 Princess St; mains £9-16; ☺ lunch & dinner) A serious contender for best Chinese restaurant in England, Yang Sing attracts diners from all over with its exceptional Cantonese cuisine. From a dim-sum lunch to a full evening banquet the food is superb, and the waiters will patiently explain the intricacies of each item to punters who can barely pronounce the dishes' names.

DRINKING

There's every kind of drinking hole in Manchester, from the really grungy ones that smell but have plenty of character, to the ones that were designed by a team of architects but have the atmosphere of a freezer…and vice versa. Every neighbourhood in town has its favourites; below we list a mere handful.

Bars

Bar Centro (☎ 835 2863; 72-74 Tib St; mains £5-8) A Northern Quarter stalwart, very popular with the bohemian crowd precisely because it doesn't try to be. Great beer, nice staff and a better-than-average bar menu make this one of the choice spots in the area.

Kro Bar (☎ 274 3100; www.kro.co.uk; 325 Oxford Rd) The ice-cool hand of Scandinavian design is all over this terrific bar in the middle of student-land. An excellent bar menu packs the punters in at lunch while DJs keep it going at night until closing. Sandwiches are £2.50.

Kro 2 (☎ 236 1048; Oxford House, Oxford Rd), Kro Bar's younger brother, is next to the BBC closer to the city, but it's not quite as classy as the original.

Ra!n (☎ 235 6500; 80 Great Bridgewater St) A rival to Dukes 92 (opposite) for best outdoor drinking, indoors Ra!n is both trendy new-style bar and old-fashioned boozer. Whatever your mood, you'll find the right ambience in this former umbrella factory.

Socio Rehab (☎ 757 3422; Edge St) Tiny, supercool and boasting one of the best cocktail menus in town, this terrific bar is the kind that will make you think you're onto a really good secret. You kind of are.

Temple of Convenience (☎ 288 9834; Great Bridgewater St) This tiny basement bar with a capacity of about 30 has a great jukebox and a fine selection of spirits, all crammed into a converted public toilet. Hardly your bog-standard pub.

Pubs

Lass O'Gowrie (☎ 273 6932; 36 Charles St; mains around £6) A Victorian classic off Princess St that brews its own beer in the basement. It's a favourite

---

TOP FIVE PUBS FOR A PINT

- Philharmonic (p671; Liverpool)
- Temple of Convenience (opposite; Manchester)
- Britons Protection (below; Manchester)
- Albion (p660; Chester)
- Hannah's (p671; Liverpool)

---

with students, old-timers and a clique of BBC employees who work just across the street in the Beeb's Manchester HQ. It also does good-value bar meals.

Britons Protection (☎ 236 5895; 50 Great Bridgewater St; mains around £7) Whisky – 200 different kinds of it – is the beverage of choice at this liver-threatening, proper English pub that also does Tudor-style meals (boar, venison and the like). An old-fashioned boozer, no fancy stuff.

Dukes 92 (☎ 839 8646; 2 Castle St) Castlefield's best pub, housed in converted stables that once belonged to the duke of Bridgewater, has comfy, deep sofas inside and plenty of seating outside, overlooking lock 92 of the Rochdale Canal – hence the name. If it's sunny, there's no better spot to enjoy a pint of ale.

Other decent boozers include:

Mr Thomas' Chop House (☎ 832 2245; 52 Cross St; mains around £10) An old-style boozer that is very popular for a pint as well as food.

Old Wellington Inn (☎ 830 1440; 4 Cathedral Gates) One of the oldest buildings in the city and a lovely spot for a pint of genuine ale.

Peveril of the Peak (☎ 236 6364; 127 Great Bridgewater St) An unpretentious pub with wonderful Victorian glazed tilework outside.

ENTERTAINMENT
Nightclubs

Manchester has been 'up for it' for so long that talk of Madchester and the drug-fuelled halcyon days of the 1990s is so jaded that it smacks of a kind of euphoric recall at best. Yet the city has a terrific club scene and Manchester remains at the vanguard of the culture of the dance floor. There's a forever-changing mixture of club nights, so check the *Manchester Evening News* for details of what's on. These are our favourites

Music Box (☎ 236 9971; www.themusicbox.info; 65 Oxford St; admission £6-12; ✆ Wed-Sat) Deep in Jilly's

Rockworld complex you'll find our favourite club in town and – judging by the queues – almost everyone else's, too. The punters come for the superb monthly club nights, such as Mr Scruff's Keep it Unreal, as well as a host of terrific one offs.

Club V (☎ 834 9975; 111 Deansgate; admission £5; ✆ Fri & Sat) White leather sofas and club nights with names like Angel Deelite and Venus don't always augur well if you're looking for some really good music, but this little basement club defies all expectations with its devotion to garage and funky house.

Sankey's Soap (☎ 661 9085; www.tribalgathering .co.uk; Beehive Mill, Jersey St, Ancoats; admission free-£10; ✆ Fri & Sat) With regulars like Danny Tenaglia, Sasha, and Layo & Bushwacka in the box, hard-core clubbers are in good hands when they trek out to the middle of Ancoats. Techno, breakbeats, tribal and progressive house.

South (☎ 831 7756; www.south-club.co.uk; 4A South King St; admission £5-6; ✆ Fri & Sat) An excellent basement club to kick off the weekend: Friday night is Rock'n'Roll Bar, featuring everything from Ibrahim Ferrer to Northern Soul; and Saturday is Disco Rescue, which is more of the same eclectic mix of alternative and dance.

Cinemas

Cornerhouse (☎ 228 2463; www.cornerhouse.org; 70 Oxford St) Your only destination for good art house releases; also has a gallery, bookshop and café.

Filmworks (☎ 0870 010 2030; www.thefilmworks.co.uk; Printworks, Exchange Sq) Ultramodern 20-screen complex in the middle of the Printworks centre; there's also an IMAX theatre.

Odeon Cinema (☎ 0870 505 0007; www.odeon.co.uk; 1 Oxford Rd) Chain cinema that shows only mainstream releases on its seven screens.

Theatre

Green Room (☎ 236 1677; 54 Whitworth St W) The premiere fringe venue in town.

Manchester Opera House (☎ 242 2509; www .manchestertheatres.co.uk; Quay St) West End shows and lavish musicals make up the bulk of the programme.

Library Theatre (☎ 236 7110; Central Library, St Peter's Sq) Old plays and new work in a small theatre beneath the Central Library.

Royal Exchange (☎ 833 9833; St Anne's Sq) Interesting contemporary plays are standard at this magnificent, modern theatre-in-the-round.

NORTHWEST ENGLAND

Live Music

ROCK MUSIC

Band on the Wall (☎ 834 1786; www.bandonthewall.org; 25 Swan St) A top-notch venue that hosts everything from rock to world music, with splashes of jazz, blues and folk thrown in for good measure.

G-Mex Exhibition Centre (☎ 834 2700; www.gmex-micc.co.uk) A mid-size venue that hosts rock con-

certs by not-quite-supersuccessful bands as well as exhibitions and indoor sporting events.

Manchester Roadhouse (☎ 228 1789; www.theroad houselive.co.uk; 8-10 Newton St) Local bands are put through their paces in front of what is usually an enthusiastic crowd.

MEN Arena (☎ 950 5000; Great Ducie St) Giant arena that hosts large-scale rock concerts (as

---

THE MADCHESTER SOUND

It is often claimed that Manchester is the engine room of British pop. If this is indeed the case, then the chief engineer was TV presenter and music impresario Tony Wilson, founder of Factory Records. This is the label that in 1983 released New Order's ground-breaking 'Blue Monday', to this day the best-selling 12" in British history, which successfully fused the guitar-driven sound of punk with a pulsating dance beat.

When the money started pouring in, Wilson took the next, all-important step: he opened his own nightclub that would provide a platform for local bands to perform. The Haçienda opened its doors with plenty of fanfare but just wouldn't take off. Things started to turn around when the club embraced a brand new sound coming out of Chicago and Detroit: house. DJs Mike Pickering, Graeme Park and Jon Da Silva were the music's most important apostles, and when ecstasy hit the scene late in the decade, it seemed that every kid in town was 'mad for it'.

Heavily influenced by these new arrivals, the city's guitar bands took notice and began shaping their sounds to suit the clubbers' needs. The most successful was the Stone Roses, who in 1989 released 'Fools Gold', a pulsating hit with the rapid shuffle of James Brown's 'Funky Drummer' and a druggie guitar sound that drove dancers wild. Around the same time, Happy Mondays, fronted by the laddish Shaun Ryder and the wacked-out Bez (whose only job was to lead the dancing from the stage), hit the scene with the infectious 'Hallelujah'. The other big anthems of the day were 'The One I Love' by the Charlatans, 'Voodoo Ray' by A Guy Called Gerald, and 'Pacific' by 808 State – all by local bands and producers. The party known as Madchester was officially opened.

The party ended in 1992. Overdanced and overdrugged, the city woke up with a terrible hangover. The Haçienda went bust, Shaun Ryder's legendary drug intake stymied his musical creativity and the Stone Roses withdrew in a haze of postparty depression. The latter were not to be heard of again until 1994 when they released *Second Coming*, which just couldn't match their eponymous debut album. They lasted another two years before breaking up. The fertile crossover scene, which had seen clubbers go mad at rock gigs and rock bands play the kind of dance sounds that kept the floor thumping until the early hours, virtually disappeared and the two genres withdrew into a more familiar isolation.

The next five years saw the rise of Manchester's most successful band, Oasis, whose *(What's the Story) Morning Glory* hit the shelves in 1995, selling more copies than all of the Manchester bands that preceded them. Despite their success and the in-your-face posturing of the Gallagher brothers, they were doomed to a limited run because they relied too much on the chord structures and infectious melodic lines created by the Beatles 25 years earlier. They're still going, but their one-time claim of being the most famous band in the world is sadly out of date.

Today, there is no such thing as Madchester. Eager to transcend the clichés that their success engendered, most of the city's musical talents refuse to be labelled as having any particular sound: jazzy house giant Mr Scruff (whose excellent Keep it Unreal nights are yours for the dancing at Music Box; see p653), for instance, doesn't sound anything like the folksy guitar style of About a Boy or the funky hip-hop beats of Rae & Christian.

Madchester is legendary precisely because it is no more, but it was a lot of fun. If you missed the party, you can get a terrific sense of what it was like by watching Michael Winterbottom's *24-Hour Party People* (2002), which captures the hedonism, extravagance and genius of Madchester's cast of characters, particularly Tony Wilson, played with uncanny accuracy by Steve Coogan.

well as being the home of the city's ice-hockey and basketball teams).

CLASSICAL MUSIC

Bridgewater Hall (☎ 907 9000; www.bridgewater-hall .co.uk; Lower Mosley St) The world-renowned Hallé Orchestra has its home at this enormous and impressive concert hall, which hosts up to 250 concerts and events a year, with a widespread programme that includes opera, folk music, children's shows, comedy and contemporary music.

Lowry (☎ 876 2000; www.thelowry.com; Pier 8, Salford Quays) Two theatres – the 1750-capacity Lyric and 460-capacity Quays – host a diverse range of performances, from dance to comedy.

Manchester Cathedral (☎ 833 2220; Victoria St) Hosts a summer season of concerts by the Cantata Choir and ensemble groups.

Royal Northern College of Music (☎ 907 5555; www .rncm.ac.uk; 124 Oxford Rd) Presents a full programme of extremely high-quality classical music and other contemporary offerings.

Sport

For most people, Manchester plus sport equals football, and football means Manchester United. That may be true everywhere else (which is why United are covered in the Sights & Activities section, p648) but not here in Manchester. Like all good northerners, most Mancunians are more comfortable supporting the scrappy underdog with the huge heart rather than the well-oiled football machine.

MANCHESTER CITY

Manchester's best-loved team is the perennial underachiever, Manchester City. In 2003 the team moved to the spanking-new **City of Manchester Stadium** (Sportcity, Rowsley St), where you can enjoy the **Manchester City Experience** (☎ 0870 062 1894; www.mcfc.co.uk; adult/child £8.75/4.75; ☑ 9.30am-4.30pm Mon-Sat, 11am-3pm Sun), a tour of the ground, dressing rooms and museum before the inevitable steer into the kit shop. Tours must be booked in advance.

LANCASHIRE COUNTY CRICKET CLUB

Cricket is a big deal here, and the **Lancashire club** (☎ 282 4000; Warwick Rd), founded in 1816 as the Aurora before changing its name in 1864, is one of the most beloved of all England's county teams, despite not having won the county championship since 1930. The re-

---

---

ally big match in Lancashire's calendar is the Roses match against Yorkshire, but if you're not around for that one, the other games in the county season (admission £10 to £15) are a great day out. The season runs throughout the summer.

International test matches, recently starring local hero Andrew 'Freddie' Flintoff, are also played here occasionally.

SHOPPING

The huge selection of shops here will send a shopper's pulse into orbit; every taste and budget is catered for.

Millennium Quarter

The area around New Cathedral St, Exchange Sq and the impressive Triangle shopping arcade is the hot new shopping district, full of chichi boutiques and the king of all department stores, **Harvey Nichols** (☎ 828 8888; 21 New Cathedral St).

Northern Quarter

Rag-trade wholesalers have given way to independent retailers stocking all manner of hip urban wear, retro fashions and other left-of-centre threads. At the heart of it all is **Affleck's Palace** (Oldham St), a four-storey warehouse full of outlets that Manchester's teenage goths and the rest of the gloomerati have turned into a social day out. The rest of the neighbourhood is full of great shops, including the marvellous **Oxfam Original** (☎ 839 3160; Unit 8, Smithfield Bldg, Oldham St), which has terrific retro gear from the 1960s and '70s.

West End

Everything needs a catchy name, so the traditionally upmarket shopping area around St Anne's Sq, King St and Bridge St – full of attractive boutiques for designers, both home grown and international – is now called the West End.

GETTING THERE & AWAY

Air
Manchester Airport (☎ 489 3000; www.manchester air port.co.uk) is the largest airport outside London, served by 17 locations throughout Britain.

Bus
National Express (☎ 08705 808080; www.national express.com) serves most major cities almost hourly from Chorlton St coach station in the city centre. Destinations include Liverpool (£5.80, 1¼ hours, hourly), Leeds (£7.80, one hour, hourly) and London (£21, 4¾ hours, hourly).

Train
Manchester Piccadilly is the main station for trains to and from the rest of the country, although Victoria station serves Halifax and Bradford. The two stations are linked by Metrolink. Trains head to Blackpool (£11.75, 1¼ hours, half-hourly), Liverpool Lime St (£8.30, 45 minutes, half-hourly), Newcastle (£40.70, three hours, six daily) and London (£101, three hours, seven daily).

GETTING AROUND

To/From the Airport
The airport is 12 miles south of the city. A train to or from Victoria station costs £3.40, and a coach £3.

Public Transport
The excellent public transport system can be used with a variety of **Day saver tickets** (bus £3.50, bus & train £4.50, bus & Metrolink £5, train & Metrolink £5.50, bus, train & Metrolink £7). For inquiries about local transport, including night buses, contact **Travelshop** (☎ 228 7811; www.gmpte.com; 9 Portland St, Piccadilly Gardens; ☻ 8am-8pm).

BUS
Centreline bus 4 provides a free service around the heart of Manchester every 10 minutes. Pick up a route map from the tourist office. Most local buses start from Piccadilly Gardens.

METROLINK
There are frequent **Metrolink** (☎ 205 2000; www .metrolink.co.uk) trams between Victoria and Piccadilly train stations and G-Mex (for Castlefield) as well as further afield to Salford Quays. Buy your tickets from the platform machine.

TRAIN
Castlefield is served by Deansgate station with rail links to Piccadilly, Oxford Rd and Salford stations.

CHESHIRE

The favourite county of residence for the soccerati millionaires of Manchester and Liverpool, largely agricultural Cheshire is a very black-and-white kind of place – if you focus on the genuine half-timbered Tudor farmhouses and the Friesian cows that graze in the fields around them. It's a little bit of ye olde Englande, which is probably why so many footballers choose to live in the mansions and monstrosities behind the top-grade security gates: nothing gives the illusion of good taste like a bit of bling and tradition. For the rest of us, however, handsome, gentle Cheshire is mostly about Chester.

CHESTER
☎ 01244 / pop 80,130

Marvellous Chester is one of English history's greatest gifts to the contemporary visitor. Its red-sandstone wall giftwraps a tidy collection of Tudor and Victorian buildings originally built during Roman times when it was Castra Devana, the largest Roman fortress in Britain.

It's hard to believe it today, but throughout the Middle Ages Chester made its money as the most important port in the northwest, but the River Dee silted up over time and Chester fell behind Liverpool in importance.

Besides its obvious elegance and grace, Chester ekes out a fairly substantial living as a major retail centre and tourist hot spot: visitors come, see and shop.

Orientation
Most places of interest are inside the walls where the Roman street pattern is relatively intact. From the Cross (the stone pillar which marks the town centre), four roads fan out to the four principal gates.

Information
Cheshire Constabulary (☎ 350000; Castle Esplanade)
Chester Royal Infirmary (☎ 365000; St Martin's Way)
Chester Visitors' Centre (☎ 351609; www.visit chester.com; Vicar's Lane; ☻ 9.30am-5.30pm Mon-Sat & 10am-4pm Sun May-Oct, 10am-5pm Mon-Sat Nov-Apr)

i-station (☎ 401680; Rufus Ct; net access per 30 min £1)
Post office (2 St John St; ☺ 9am-5.30pm Mon-Sat)
Tourist office (☎ 402111; www.chester.gov.uk;
Northgate St; ☺ 9am-5.30pm Mon-Sat & 10am-4pm Sun
May-Oct, 10am-5pm Mon-Sat Nov-Apr)

Sights & Activities

CITY WALLS

A good way to get a sense of Chester's unique
character is to walk the 2-mile circuit along
the walls that surround the historic centre.
Originally built by the Romans around AD
70, the walls were altered substantially over
the following centuries but have retained their
current position since around 1200. The tourist office's *Walk Around Chester Walls* leaflet
(£1.50) is an excellent companion guide.

Of the many features along the walls, the
most eye-catching is the prominent **Eastgate**,
where you can see the most famous **clock** in
England after London's Big Ben, built for
Queen Victoria's Diamond Jubilee in 1897.

At the southeastern corner of the walls are
the **wishing steps**, added in 1785; local legend
claims that if you can run up and down these
uneven steps while holding your breath your
wish will come true. We question the verac-
ity of this claim because our wish was not to
twist an ankle.

Just inside Southgate, known here as **Bridge-
gate** (as it's at the northern end of the Old Dee
Bridge), is the 1664 **Bear & Billet** pub, Chester's
oldest timber-framed building and once a
tollgate into the city.

THE ROWS

Chester's other great draw is the **Rows**, a series
of two-level galleried arcades along the four
streets that fan out in each direction from
the central Cross. The architecture is a handsome mix of Victorian and Tudor (original
and mock) buildings that house a fantastic
collection of individually owned shops. The
origin of the Rows is a little unclear, but it
is believed that as the Roman walls slowly
crumbled, medieval traders built their shops
against the resulting rubble banks, while later
arrivals built theirs on top.

OTHER SIGHTS & ACTIVITIES

The **cathedral** (☎ 324756; Northgate St; www.chester
cathedral.com; adult/child £4/1.50; ☺ 9am-5pm Mon-Sat,
1-5pm Sun) was a Benedictine abbey built on the
remains of an earlier Saxon church dedicated
to St Werburgh, patron saint of Chester. The
abbey was closed in 1540 as part of Henry VIII's
dissolution frenzy, but was reconsecrated as
a cathedral the following year. Although the
cathedral itself was given a substantial Victorian face-lift, the 12th-century cloister and
its surrounding buildings are essentially un
altered and retain much of the structure from
the early monastic years. There are 1¼-hour
guided tours (free; ☺ 9.30am-4pm Mon-Sat) to really
get to grips with the building and its history.

The excellent **Grosvenor Museum** (☎ 402008;
Grosvenor St; admission free; ☺ 10.30am-5pm Mon-Sat,
2-5pm Sun) is the place to go if you want to study
Chester's rich and varied history, beginning
with a comprehensive collection of Roman
tombstones, the largest display in the country.
At the back of the museum is a preserved
Georgian house, complete with kitchen, drawing room, bedroom and bathroom.

The **Dewa Roman Experience** (☎ 343407; www
.dewaromanexperience.co.uk; Pierpoint Lane; admission
£4.25; ☺ 9am-5pm), just off Bridge St, takes you
through a reconstructed Roman street with
the aim of showing you what Roman life
was like.

Chester's most complete set of genuine
Roman remains is opposite the visitors centre,
outside the city walls. Here you'll find what's
left of the **Roman amphitheatre** (admission free);
once an arena that seated 7000 spectators
(making it the country's largest), now it's little
more than steps buried in grass.

Adjacent to the amphitheatre is **St John the
Baptist Church** (Vicar's Lane; ☺ 9.15am-6pm), built
on the site of an older Saxon church in 1075.
It started out as a cathedral of Mercia before
being rebuilt by the Normans. The eastern
end of the church, abandoned in 1581 when
St John's became a parish, now lies in peaceful
ruin and includes the remains of a Norman
choir and medieval chapels.

Steps at the back of the church lead down to
the riverside promenade known as the **Groves**.
Here you can hire different kinds of **boats** (per
hr £6-8; ☺ 9am-6pm Apr-Sep) with pedals, oars or

A BIT OF CHARISMA

Buy the new **Charisma Card** (www.chester
charisma.com; £5.99), available from the tourist offices or online, to get 20% discount
at more than 200 restaurants, shops and
visitor attractions.

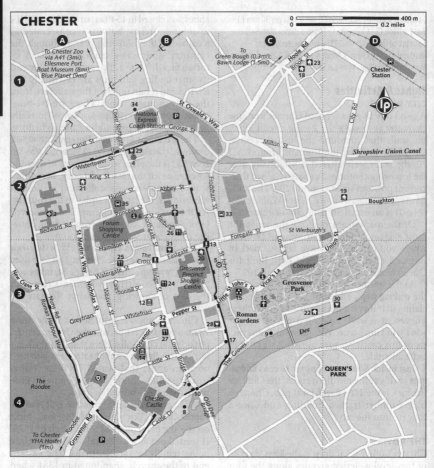

CHESTER

small engines. This is also the departure point for river cruises (see below).

Tours

City Sightseeing Chester (☎ 347452; www.city-sight seeing.com; adult/child £8/3; every 15-30 min Apr-Oct, weekends only Mar) offers open-top bus tours of the city, picking up from the tourist office and Chester Visitors' Centre and the visitor centre.

You can also take a cruise along the Dee; contact **Bithell Boats** (☎ 325394; www.showboats ofchester.co.uk) for details of its 30-minute and hour-long cruises up and down the Dee, including a foray into the gorgeous Eaton Estate, home of the duke and duchess of Westminster. All departures are from the

riverside along the Groves and cost from £6 to £13.50.

The tourist office and Chester Visitors' Centre offer a broad range of walking tours departing from both centres. Each tour lasts between 1½ and two hours.

Ghosthunter Trail (adult/child £4.50/3.50; ⏰ 7.30pm Thu-Sat Jun-Oct, Sat only Nov-May) The ubiquitous ghost tour, looking for things that go bump in the night.

History Hunter (adult/child £4/3; ⏰ 10.15am) Two thousand years of Chester history.

Roman Soldier Patrols (adult/child £4.50/3.50; ⏰ 1.45pm Thu-Sat Jun-Aug) This tour of Fortress Deva is led by Caius Julius Quartus; perfect if you've kids in tow.

Secret Chester (adult/child £4.50/3.50; ⏰ 2pm Tue, Thu, Sat & Sun May-Oct) Exactly what it says on the tin.

Festivals & Events

Held from mid-July to early August, the three-week **Summer Music Festival** (☎ 320700; www.chesterfestivals.co.uk) is a season highlight, featuring performances by all manner of stars both big and small. The **Chester Jazz Festival** (☎ 340005; www.chesterjazz.com; admission free-£10) is a two-week showcase from late August to early September.

Sleeping

If you're visiting between Easter and September, you'd better book early if you want to avoid going overbudget or settling for far less than you bargained for. Except for a handful of options – including the city's best – most of the accommodation is outside the city walls but within easy walking distance of the centre. Hoole Rd, a 10- to 15-minute walk from the centre and leading beyond the railway tracks to the M53/M56, is lined with budget to midrange B&Bs.

BUDGET

Chester Backpackers (☎ 400185; www.chesterbackpackers.co.uk; 67 Boughton; dm from £13) Comfortable dorm rooms with nice pine beds in a typically Tudor white-and-black building. It's just a short walk from the city walls and there's also a pleasant garden.

Chester YHA Hostel (☎ 0870 770 5762; www.yha.org.uk; 40 Hough Green; dm £17.50) Located in an elegant Victorian home about a mile from the city centre, this hostel has a variety of dorms that sleep from two to 10 people; there's also a cafeteria, a kitchen and a shop on the premises.

Brook St near the train station has a couple of good-value B&Bs from around £22 per person. The friendly and accommodating **Ormonde** (☎ 328816; 126 Brook St) and the comfortable **Aplas Guest House** (☎ 312401; 106 Brook St) are both less than five minutes' walk from the train station.

MIDRANGE

Grove Villa (☎ 349713; 18 The Groves; s/d from £30/48) You won't find a more tranquil spot in town than this wonderfully positioned Victorian home overlooking the Dee. The rooms have antique beds and great river views.

Bawn Lodge (☎ 324971; www.bawnlodge.co.uk; 10 Hoole Rd; s/d from £40/50) Spotless rooms with plenty of colour make this charming guesthouse a very pleasant option. It's like staying with a favourite relative: no fuss but plenty of friendliness (and a delicious breakfast). In high season, the rates are double.

Chester Townhouse (☎ 350021; 23 King St; s/d £45/70; Ⓟ) Five beautifully decorated rooms in a handsome 17th-century house within the city walls make for a terrific option – you're close to the action and you'll sleep in relative luxury.

TOP END

⛯ **Green Bough** (☎ 326241; www.greenbough.co.uk; 60 Hoole Rd; r from £150) The epitome of the boutique hotel, this exclusive Victorian town house won England Tourism's 'Best Small Hotel of the Year' award for 2006 – and a worthy winner it was too. The individually styled rooms are dressed in the best Italian fabrics and wall coverings, superb antique furniture and period cast-iron and wooden beds, including a handful of elegant four-posters. Modern touches include plasma-screen TVs, ministereos and a range of fancy toiletries.

Chester Grosvenor Hotel & Spa (☎ 324024; www.chestergrosvenor.com; 58 Eastgate St; s/d/ste from £120/190/380; Ⓟ ✕ ⌨) The best hotel in town with the best location. The huge, sprawling rooms have exquisite period furnishings and all mod cons; the spa (which is open to non-residents) offers a range of body treatments, including Reiki, Lastone therapy, Indian head massage and four-handed massage. There's also Arkle, a Michelin-starred restaurant downstairs (see below).

Eating

There's no shortage of places to eat, but the quality of the fare is often barely above tourist-menu standard. Some pubs do great grub (see below).

Boulevard de la Bastille (Bridge St; sandwiches £3, meals £5-7; 9am-6pm) Our favourite café in town is also one of the most handsome: a very French place on the top tier of the Rows that is perfect for a *café au lait* and *pain au chocolat*.

Katie's Tea Rooms (400322; 38 Watergate St; 9am-5pm Tue-Sat) This stone-walled tearoom located inside a historic building is the place to go for a light lunch. Tea & scones cost £3.40. After 5pm it turns into MD's Restaurant, a continental eatery with a pretty tasty menu. The restaurant is open for dinner from Tuesday to Saturday, and a two-course meal will set you back around £11.

Living Room (0870 442 2805; 13 St Werburgh St; mains £9-11; 11am-late) It's a chain all right, but a very pleasing and popular one at that. The Chester version is spread over three floors, which include the Dining Room and the Study private bar. It's behind the cathedral.

Ruan Orchid (400661; 14 Lower Bridge St; mains £10-14; lunch & dinner) Every conceivable Thai dish and concoction of curry is available at this lovely, intimate restaurant.

Arkle (895618; www.chestergrosvenor.com; Chester Grosvenor Hotel & Spa, 58 Eastgate St; 3-course dinners £55; dinner Tue-Sat only) Named after the famous Irish champion racehorse, Simon Radley's Arkle serves up a sumptuous feast of French-inspired classics such as tranche of monkfish with air-dried ham and braised turbot with baby squid. It's elegant (gentlemen in jackets, please), sophisticated and has a Michelin star to prove it.

Drinking

Falcon (314555; Lower Bridge St; mains from £4.95) This is an old-fashioned boozer with a lovely atmosphere; the surprisingly adventurous menu offers up dishes such as Jamaican peppered beef or spicy Italian sausage casserole. Great for both a pint and a bite.

Albion (340345; 4 Albion St; mains £8-10) No children, no music, and no machines or big screens (but plenty of Union Jacks). This 'family hostile' Edwardian classic pub is a throwback to a time when ale-drinking still had its own *rituals* – another word for ingrained prejudices. Still, this is one of the finest pubs in northwest England precisely because it doggedly refuses to modernise.

Other good pubs include the **Boat House** (The Groves), with great views overlooking the river, and the **Boot Inn** (Eastgate St), where 14 Roundheads were killed. **Alexander's Jazz Theatre** (340005; Rufus Ct; admission £3-10, free before 10pm) is a combination wine bar, coffee bar and tapas bar.

Sport

HORSE RACING

Chester's ancient and very beautiful racetrack is the **Roodee** (304600; www.chester-races.co.uk; May-Sep), on the western side of the walls, which has been hosting races since the 16th century. Highlights of the summer flat season include the two-day July Festival and the August equivalent.

Getting There & Away

BUS

The coach station for **National Express** (08705 808080; www.nationalexpress.com) is just north of the city inside the ring road. Destinations include Birmingham (£10.20, 2½ hours, four daily), Liverpool (£6.20, one hour, three daily), London (£21, 5½ hours, three daily) and Manchester (£5.70, 1¼ hours, three daily).

For information on local bus services, ring the **Cheshire Bus Line** (602666). Local buses leave from the Town Hall Bus Exchange. On Sundays and bank holidays a **Sunday adventurer ticket** (adult/child £3.50/2.50) gives you unlimited travel in Cheshire.

TRAIN

The train station is a 15-minute walk from the city centre via Foregate St and City Rd, or Brook St. City-Rail Link buses are free for people with rail tickets, and operate between the station and Bus Stop A on Frodsham St. Trains travel to Liverpool (£4, 40 minutes, hourly), London Euston (£56.20, three hours, hourly) and Manchester (£10.30, one hour, hourly).

Getting Around

Much of the city centre is closed to traffic from 10.30am to 4.30pm, so a car is likely to be a hindrance. Anyway, the city is easy to walk around and most places of interest are close to the wall.

City buses depart from the **Town Hall Bus Exchange** (☎ 602666).

Davies Bros Cycles (☎ 371341; 5 Delamere St) has mountain bikes for hire at £13 per day.

AROUND CHESTER
Chester Zoo

The largest of its kind in the country, **Chester Zoo** (☎ 380280; www.chesterzoo.org.uk; adult/child £14.50/10.50; 🕙 10am-dusk, last admission 4pm Mon-Fri, 5pm Sat & Sun Apr-Oct & 3pm Mon-Fri & 4pm Sat & Sun Nov-Mar) is about as pleasant a place as caged animals in artificial renditions of their natural habitats could ever expect to live. It's so big that there's even a **monorail** (adult/child £2/1.50) and a **waterbus** (adult/child £2/1.50) to get around on. The zoo is on the A41, 3 miles north of Chester's city centre. Buses 11C and 12C (£2.50 return, every 15 minutes Monday to Saturday, half-hourly Sunday) run between the town hall and the zoo.

Blue Planet Aquarium

Things aren't done by halves around Chester: you'll also find the country's largest aquarium, **Blue Planet** (☎ 0151-357 8804; www.blueplanetaquarium .com; adult/child £9.95/7.50; 🕙 10am-5pm Mon-Fri, 10am-6pm Sat & Sun), home to 10 different kinds of shark able to be viewed from a 70m-long moving walkway that lets you eye them up close. It's 9 miles north of Chester at junction 10 of the M53 to Liverpool. Buses 1 and 4 run there every half-hour from the Town Hall Bus Exchange in Chester.

Ellesmere Port Boat Museum

Near the aquarium, on the Shropshire Union Canal about 8 miles north of Chester, is the superb **Ellesmere Port Boat Museum** (☎ 0151-355 5017; www.boatmuseum.org.uk; South Pier Rd; admission £7.10; 🕙 10am-5pm Apr-Oct, 11am-4pm Sat-Wed Nov-Mar), which has a large collection of canal boats as well as indoor exhibits. Take Bus 4 from the Town Hall Bus Exchange in Chester, or it's a 10-minute walk from Ellesmere Port train station.

KNUTSFORD

☎ 01565 / pop 12,660

Fascinating Knutsford would be a typical lowland English market town if it wasn't for the eccentric philanthropy of Richard Watt (1842–1913), a millionaire glove manufacturer with his own personal vision of Mediterranean architecture. The weird and wonderful build-

ings that he commissioned for the town make it one of the most interesting places in Cheshire.

Although Watt's influence was certainly greater, Knutsford makes the biggest deal of its links with Elizabeth Cleghorn Gaskell (1810–65), who spent her childhood here and used the town as the model for *Cranford* (1853), her most noteworthy novel.

The **tourist office** (☎ 632611; Toft Rd; 🕙 9am-5pm Mon-Fri, 9am-1pm Sat) is in the council offices opposite the train station.

The **Knutsford Heritage Centre** (☎ 650506; 90A King St; admission free; 🕙 1.30-4pm Mon-Fri, noon-4pm Sat, 2-4.30pm Sun) is a reconstructed former smithy that has plenty of information on Gaskell, including the *Cranford Walk Around Knutsford* (£1), a leaflet about her local haunts. The most interesting displays, though, are on Watt and his quirky contributions to English architecture.

You can see the best of these along King St, which is a fine example of the splendidly haphazard harmony of English urban architecture. See in particular the **King's Coffee House** (meant to lure the men from the pubs) and the **Ruskin Reading Room** (Drury Lane).

The eye-catching **Gaskell Memorial Tower** incorporates the swanky **Belle Epoque Brasserie** (☎ 633060; www.thebelleepoque.com; 60 King St; mains £9-14; lunch & dinner Mon-Sat), a *fin-de-siècle* style restaurant that Oscar Wilde would look perfectly at home in. Upstairs are seven gorgeous rooms priced from £80, each styled in accordance with the overall late-19th-century theme of the building.

Getting There & Away

Knutsford is 15 miles southwest of Manchester and is on the Manchester–Chester train line (Chester £8.20, 45 minutes, hourly; Manchester £4.20, 30 minutes, hourly). The train station is on Adams Hill, at the southern end of King St.

AROUND KNUTSFORD

The southern end of King St in Knutsford marks the entrance to the 400-hectare **Tatton Park** (NT; ☎ 01625-534400; www.tattonpark.org .uk; admission free, individual attractions adult/child £3.50/2 🕙 10am-7pm). At the heart is a Regency **mansion** (🕙 1-5pm Tue-Sun Mar-Oct) and a wonderful Tudor **Old Hall** (🕙 noon-4pm Sat & Sun Apr-Oct), a 1930s-style **working farm** (🕙 noon-5pm Tue-Sun Mar-Oct, Sat & Sun Nov-Feb) and a series of superb Victorian **gardens** (🕙 10am-6pm Tue-Sun Apr-Sep, 11am-4pm Oct-Mar). The **Discovery Saver Ticket** (adult/child £5/3) allows you

---

ROYAL MAY DAY

Since 1864 Knutsford has liked to go a bit wild on Royal May Day. The main festivities take place on the Heath, a large area of common land, and include Morris dancing, brass bands and a pageant of historical characters from fiction and fact. Perhaps the most interesting tradition is that of 'sanding', whereby the streets are covered in colourful messages written in sand. Legend has it that the Danish King Knut, while crossing the marsh between Over and Nether Knutsford, scrawled a message in the sand wishing happiness to a young couple who were on the way to their wedding. The custom is also practised on weddings and feast days.

---

entry to any two attractions. Car admission to the park costs £4.

On Sundays bus X2 links Tatton Park with Chester (one hour). At other times you'll need your own wheels.

NANTWICH

☎ 01270 / pop 13,450

Cheshire's second-best example of black-and-white Tudor architecture after Chester is the elegant town of Nantwich. After a devastating fire in 1583, the town was rebuilt thanks to a nationwide appeal by Elizabeth I, who deemed the town's salt production so important that she had to intercede to help. The queen personally donated £1000, and her generosity is proudly commemorated with a plaque on the appositely named **Queen's Aid House** (High St), itself a striking Tudor building.

The rest of the largely pedestrianised centre has plenty of fine examples of the black-and-white style, although it's a wonder how so many of them stay standing, such is their off-kilter shape and design.

Very few buildings survived the fire; the most important of those that did is the 14th-century **Church of St Mary** (☎ 625268; 9am-5pm), a fine example of medieval architecture.

Apart from salt, the town grew up around the production of cheese and leather, and all three are depicted in the **Nantwich Museum** (☎ 627104; Pillory St; admission free; 10am-4.30pm Mon-Sat Apr-Sep, Tue-Sat Oct-Mar).

The helpful **tourist office** (☎ 610983; fax 610880; Church Walk; 9.30am-5pm Mon-Fri, 10am-4pm Sat, 11am-3pm Sun) is near the main square.

Sleeping & Eating

Crown Hotel (☎ 625283; www.crownhotelnantwich.com; High St; s/d from £64/78) There is barely a straight line in the place, but this gorgeous Tudor halftimbered hotel is easily top choice in town. The ground-floor Casa Italiana restaurant is a decent and popular spot that has every possible Italian dish on its menu, with mains priced from £9 to £13.

Pillory House & Coffee Shop (☎ 623524; Pillory St) An old-style tearoom that serves sandwiches (£3 to £4) and inexpensive hot dishes – perfect for that quick lunch.

Getting There & Away

The **bus station** (Beam St) is 300m north of the tourist office; there is an hourly bus from Chester (one hour).

To get to Manchester, Chester or Liverpool, you'll have to change trains in Crewe (15 minutes, half hourly). The train station is about half a mile south of the centre.

LIVERPOOL

☎ 0151 / pop 469, 020

Dogged, determined and for many decades down-at-heel, Liverpool just refused to go down. When unfancied Liverpool FC overcame a 3–0 half-time deficit to win the 2005 European Champions' League final, it transcended the much narrower boundaries of football and was quickly adopted by this passionate, football-mad city as the latest – and most poetic – expression of Scouse defiance in the face of all the odds.

Most people are familiar with the concept of home-town pride, but in Liverpool they're just that little bit more in love with the city. They'll slag it off all right – slagging has always been an Olympic sport around here – but it's a critique born of a deep pride that these days is extremely well placed.

Liverpool will be European Capital of Culture in 2008, and the city has spent the last few years getting ready for the ball. Handsome old buildings have had facials and brand-new ones shine spotlessly on the skyline. The once boarded-up warehouses of the city centre have been transformed into new shops, cafés and fancy apartments.

Impressive stuff, no doubt, but it's the culture on offer that really has us buzzing. The city's store of superb museums and top-class art galleries – all free – have put paid to the scurrilous rumour that Liverpool peaked with the Beatles: in 2004 the whole of the waterfront and docks was declared a Unesco World Heritage Site because there are more listed buildings here than in any other city in England except London. And then, of course, the nightlife: as rich and varied as you'd expect from a good northern city.

HISTORY

Liverpool grew wealthy on the back of the triangular trading of slaves, raw materials and finished goods. From 1700 ships carried cotton goods and hardware from Liverpool to West Africa, where they were exchanged for slaves, who in turn were carried to the West Indies and Virginia, where they were exchanged for sugar, rum, tobacco and raw cotton.

As a great port, the city drew thousands of Irish and Scottish immigrants, and its Celtic influences are still apparent. However, between 1830 and 1930 nine million emigrants – mainly English, Scots and Irish, but also Swedes, Norwegians and Russian Jews – sailed from here for the New World.

The start of WWII led to a resurgence of Liverpool's importance. More than one million American GIs disembarked here before D-Day and the port was, once again, hugely important as the western gateway for transatlantic supplies. The GIs brought with them the latest American records, and Liverpool was thus the first European port of call for the new rhythm and blues that would eventually become rock'n'roll. Within 20 years, the Mersey Beat was *the* sound of British pop and four mop-topped Scousers had formed a skiffle band…

ORIENTATION

Liverpool is a cinch to get around. The main attractions are Albert Dock, west of the city centre, and the trendy Ropewalks area, south of Hanover St and west of the two cathedrals. Lime St station, the bus station, the tourist office and the Cavern Quarter – a mecca for Beatles fans – lie just to the north.

The tourist office and many of the city's hotels have an excellent map with all of the city's attractions clearly outlined.

INFORMATION
Bookshops
Waterstone's (☎ 708 6861; 14-16 Bold St)

Emergencies
Merseyside police headquarters (☎ 709 6010; Canning Pl) Opposite Albert Dock.

Internet Access
CaféLatte.net (☎ 709 9683; 4 S Hunter St; per 30 min £1; ☼ 9am-6pm)
Planet Electra (☎ 708 0303; 36 London Rd; per 30 min £1; ☼ 9am-5pm)

SOMETHING FOR THE WEEKEND

Let's get a little greedy and do a two-for-one weekend: separated by the spine of the Pennines and historic rivalries of nearly epic proportions, Liverpool and Manchester are only 37 miles apart. Spend the first night in Liverpool – check in to the **Hope Street Hotel** (p669) to really do it in style. It's Friday night, so dinner downstairs in the **London Carriage Works** (p670) or down the street at **Alma de Cuba** (p671), should be followed by a pint in the **Philharmonic** (p671) or a spot of dancing at one of the many clubs in and around Ropewalks. Saturday is all about the museums of the city centre and Albert Dock, which should leave you plenty of time to make your train to Manchester.

Claim your room at Manchester's **Great John Street Hotel** (p651) – yup, we're still stylin', but if you're looking for something a little more demure, the **Ox** (p650) offers affordable cool. Then do a little window shopping before grabbing a bite. Pick a bar, any bar, and keep going: there's an unhealthy choice of clubs if you're not that keen on a Sunday morning start.

You have your choice of things to visit, but we recommend **Urbis** (p646) and the **Imperial War Museum North** (p647) for a mere taste of the city's cool culture.

But, if dreams could come true, this would be our ideal way to spend the weekend: we'd have tickets to see Liverpool play (and beat) Chelsea on Saturday afternoon at **Anfield** (p673), while Sunday afternoon would see us make the trek to **Old Trafford** (p648) to see United struggle to get a draw against Manchester City in the derby. Ah, to sleep, perchance to dream…

LIVERPOOL

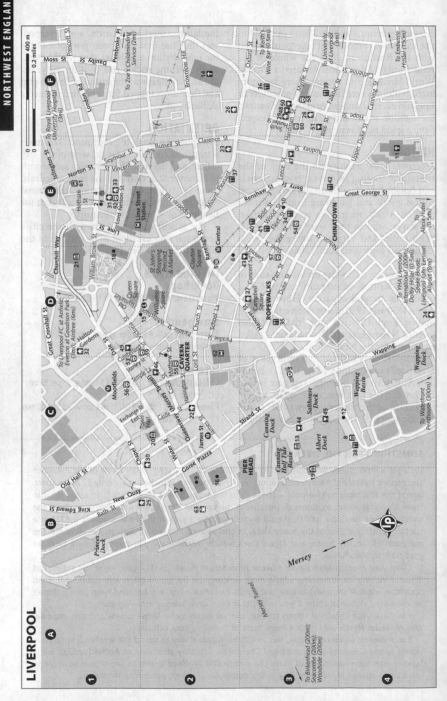

Internet Resources

08 Place (www.liverpool08.com) The capital of culture.

Clubs in Liverpool (www.clubsinliverpool.co.uk)
Everything you need to know about what goes on when the sun goes down.

Mersey Guide (www.merseyguide.co.uk) Guide to the Greater Mersey area.

Merseyside Today (www.merseysidetoday.co.uk) Guide to the city and surrounding area.

Tourist office (www.visitliverpool.com)

Medical Services

Mars Pharmacy (☎ 709 5271; 68 London Rd) Open until 10pm every night.

Royal Liverpool University Hospital (☎ 706 2000; Prescot St)

Post

Post office (Ranelagh St; ☼ 9am-5.30pm Mon-Sat)

Tourist Information

The tourist office has three branches in the city. It also has an **accommodation hotline** (☎ 0845 601 1125).

08 Place tourist office (☎ 233 2008; Whitechapel; ☼ 9am-8pm Mon-Sat & 11am-4pm Sun Apr-Sep, 9am-6pm Mon-Sat & 11am-4pm Sun Oct-Mar) The main branch of the tourist office.

Albert Dock tourist office (☎ 478 4599; Merseyside Maritime Museum; ☼ 10am-6pm)

SIGHTS

The wonderful Albert Dock is the city's biggest tourist draw and the key to understanding the city's history, but the city centre is where you'll find most of Liverpool's real day-to-day life.

City Centre
ST GEORGE'S HALL

Arguably Liverpool's most impressive building, **St George's Hall** (☎ 707 2391; www.stgeorgeshall .com) was built in 1854 and is the first European offering of neoclassical architecture. Curiously, it was built as law courts *and* a concert hall – presumably a judge could pass sentence and then relax to a string quartet. Tours (£4.50) of the newly renovated hall are run in conjunction with the tourist office; check for times.

WALKER ART GALLERY

Touted as the 'National Gallery of the North', the city's foremost **gallery** (☎ 478 4199; www.liver poolmuseums.org.uk/walker; William Brown St; admission free; ☼ 10am-5pm Mon-Sat, noon-5pm Sun) is Liverpool's answer to sneering critics who question the city's cultural credentials in the lead-up to 2008. The history of art from the 14th to the 20th centuries is covered in exquisite detail; strong suits are Pre-Raphaelite art, modern British art, and sculpture.

LIVERPOOL IN...

Two Days

Head to the waterfront and explore the Albert Dock museums – the **Tate** (opposite) and **Merseyside Maritime Museum** (opposite) – before paying tribute to the Fab Four at the **Beatles Story** (opposite). Keep to the Beatles theme and head north toward the Cavern Quarter around Mathew St. Round off your evening with dinner at **London Carriage Works** (p670), a pint at the marvellous **Philharmonic** (p671) and wrap yourself in the crisp linen sheets of the **Hope Street Hotel** (p669). Night hawks can tear it up in the bars and clubs of the hip **Ropewalks** area (p672). The next day, explore the city's two **cathedrals** (below) and check out the twin delights of the **World Museum Liverpool** (below) and the **Walker Art Gallery** (p665).

Four Days

Follow the two-day itinerary but add in a **Yellow Duckmarine tour** (p668) to experience the docks from the water. Make a couple of pilgrimages to suit your interests: visit **Mendips** (p671) and **20 Forthlin Rd** (p671), the childhood homes of John Lennon and Paul McCartney, respectively; or walk on holy ground at **Anfield** (p673), home of Liverpool Football Club. Race junkies can head out to the visitor centre at **Aintree racecourse** (p673), home of England's most beloved race, the Grand National.

WORLD MUSEUM LIVERPOOL

Natural history, science and technology are the themes of this sprawling **museum** (☎ 478 4399; www.liverpoolmuseums.org.uk/wml; William Brown St; admission free; ⏰ 10am-5pm), whose exhibits range from birds of prey to space exploration. It also includes the country's only free planetarium. This vastly entertaining and educational museum is divided into four major sections: the Human World, one of the top anthropological collections in the country; the Natural World, which includes a new aquarium as well as live insect colonies; Earth, a geological treasure trove; and Space & Time, which includes the planetarium. Highly recommended.

NATIONAL CONSERVATION CENTRE

Ever wonder how art actually gets restored? Find out at this terrific **conservation centre** (☎ 478 4999; www.liverpoolmuseums.org.uk/conservation; Whitechapel; admission free; ⏰ 10am-5pm) housed in a converted railway goods depot. Handheld audio wands help tell the story, but the real fun is actually attempting a restoration technique with your own hands. Sadly, our trembling paws weren't allowed near anything of value – that was left to the real experts, whose skills are pretty amazing.

FACT

Proof that Ropewalks isn't all about booze and bars, this **media centre** (☎ 707 4450; www.fact.co.uk; 88 Wood St; ⏰ galleries 11am-6pm Tue-Wed, 11am-8pm Thu-Sat & noon-5pm Sun, cinemas noon-10pm) – whose acronym stands for Foundation for Art & Creative Technology – is all about film and new media such as digital art. Two galleries feature constantly changing exhibitions and three screens show the latest art-house releases – although we've noticed that the odd mainstream release has crept into the schedule, proof that financial pressures often override creative intent. There's also a bar and café.

WESTERN APPROACHES MUSEUM

The **Combined Headquarters of the Western Approaches** (☎ 227 2008; 1 Rumford St; adult/child £4.75/3.45; ⏰ 10.30am-4.30pm Mon-Thu & Sat Mar-Oct), the secret command centre for the Battle of the Atlantic, was abandoned at the end of the war with virtually everything left intact. You can get a good glimpse of the labyrinthine nerve centre of Allied operations.

THE CATHEDRALS

The city's two cathedrals are separated by the length of Hope St. At the northern end, the Roman Catholic **Metropolitan Cathedral of Christ the King** (☎ 709 9222; off Mt Pleasant; ⏰ 8am-6pm Mon-Sat, 8am-5pm Sun Oct-Mar) was completed in 1967 according to the design of Sir Frederick Gibberd and after the original plans by Sir Edwin Lutyens, whose crypt is inside. It's a mightily impressive modern building that looks like a soaring concrete tepee, hence its nickname, Paddy's Wigwam.

At Hope St's southern end stands the neo-Gothic **Liverpool Cathedral** (☎ 709 6271; www.liverpool cathedral.org.uk; Hope St; voluntary donation £3; ☺ 8am-6pm), the life work of Sir Giles Gilbert Scott (1880–1960), whose other contributions to the world were the red telephone box, and the power station in London that is now home to the Tate Modern. Size is a big deal here: this is the largest church in England and the largest Anglican cathedral in the world. The central bell is the world's third-largest (with the world's highest and heaviest peal), while the organ, with its 9765 pipes, is probably the world's largest operational model. Construction on a new visitor centre was underway throughout 2006, but should be open in early 2007.

There are terrific views of Liverpool from the top of the 101m **tower** (admission £4.25; ☺ 11am-3pm Mon-Sat).

Albert Dock

Liverpool's biggest tourist attraction is **Albert Dock** (☎ 708 8854; www.albertdock.com; admission free), 2¾ hectares of water ringed by a colonnade of enormous cast-iron columns and impressive five-storey warehouses that make up the country's largest collection of protected buildings, and now a World Heritage Site. A fabulous development programme has really brought the dock to life; here you'll find several outstanding museums and an extension of London's Tate Gallery, as well as a couple of top-class restaurants and bars.

MERSEYSIDE MARITIME MUSEUM

The story of one of the world's great ports is the theme of this excellent **museum** (☎ 478 4499; www.liverpoolmuseums.org.uk/maritime; Albert Dock; admission free; ☺ 10am-5pm) and believe us, it's a graphic and compelling page-turner. One of the many great exhibits is Emigration to a New World, which tells the story of nine million emigrants and their efforts to get to North America and Australia; the walk-through model of a typical ship shows just how tough conditions on board really were. But the real highlight is the Transatlantic Slavery exhibit, which pulls no punches in its portrayal of the shameful trade that made Liverpool rich and left us with the scourge of modern racism. This is heady stuff, and should on no account be missed.

TATE LIVERPOOL

Touted as the home of modern art in the north, this **gallery** (☎ 702 7400; www.tate.org.uk/liverpool; Al-bert Dock; admission free, special exhibitions adult/child £4/3; ☺ 10am-5.50pm Jun-Aug, Tue-Sun only Sep-May) features a substantial check-list of 20th-century artists across its four floors as well as touring exhibitions from the mother ship on London's Bankside. But it's all a little sparse, with none of the energy we'd expect from the world-famous Tate.

BEATLES STORY

Liverpool's most popular **museum** (☎ 709 1963; www.beatlesstory.com; Albert Dock; adult/child £8.99/5.99; ☺ 10am-6pm) won't illuminate any dark, juicy corners in the turbulent history of the world's most famous foursome – there's ne'er a mention of internal discord, drugs, Yoko Ono or the Frog Song – but there's plenty of genuine memorabilia to keep a Beatles fan happy. Particularly impressive is the full-size replica Cavern Club (which was actually tiny) and the Abbey Road studio where the lads recorded their first singles, while George Harrison's crappy first guitar (now worth half a million quid) should inspire budding, penniless musicians to keep the faith. The museum is also the departure point for the Magical Mystery and Yellow Duckmarine tours (see p668).

North of Albert Dock

The area to the north of Albert Dock is known as **Pier Head**, after a stone pier built in the 1760s. This is still the departure point for ferries across the River Mersey (see p674), and was, for millions of migrants, their final contact with European soil.

Today this area is dominated by a trio of Edwardian buildings known as the 'Three Graces', dating from the days when Liverpool's star was still ascending. The southernmost, with the dome mimicking St Paul's Cathedral, is the **Port of Liverpool Building**, completed in 1907. Next to it is the **Cunard Building**, in the style of an Italian palazzo, once HQ to the Cunard Steamship Line. Finally, the **Royal Liver Building** (pronounced lie-ver) was opened in 1911 as the head office of the Royal Liver Friendly Society. It's crowned by Liverpool's symbol, the famous 5.5m copper Liver Bird.

LIVERPOOL FOR CHILDREN

The museums on Albert Dock are extremely popular with kids, especially the **Merseyside Maritime Museum** (left) – which has a couple of boats for kids to mess about on – and the **Beatles Story** (above). **Yellow Duckmarine Tours** (below) are a sure-fire winner, as is the **National Conservation Centre** (p666), which gets everyone involved in the drama of restoration. Slightly older (and very old) kids – especially those into football – will enjoy the tour of Liverpool FC's **Anfield stadium** (p673) as it means getting your feet on the sacred turf.

Need a break from the tots? Drop them off at **Zoe's Childminding Service** (☎ 228 2685; 15 Woodbourne Rd), about 2 miles east of the city centre.

QUIRKY LIVERPOOL

When a working public toilet is a tourist attraction, you know you have something special, and the men's loo at the **Philharmonic** (p671) is just that. The **Yellow Duckmarine Tour** (below), an amphibious exploration of Albert Dock, is a bit silly but the guides are hilarious, and the **ferry across the Mersey** (below) is something special – the tired commuters will give you more than a stare if you sing the song too loudly. The **Grand National Experience** (p673) at Aintree is proof that the English really do love their horses, and the concerts at the **Philharmonic Hall** (p673) often throw up something completely different and avant-garde instead of the Beethoven concerto you might expect.

TOURS

Liverpool Beatles Tour (☎ 281 7738; www.beatles tours.co.uk; from adult £18) Your own personalised tour of every bit of minutiae associated with the Beatles, from cradle to grave. Tour lengths range from the two-hour Helter Skelter excursion to A Day in the Life, by the end of which you'll presumably be convinced you were actually in the band. Pick-ups are arranged upon booking.

Magical Mystery Tour (☎ 709 3285; www.cavern -liverpool.co.uk; £12.95; ⏰ 2.30pm year-round, plus noon Sat Jul-Aug) This two-hour tour takes in all Beatles-related landmarks – their birthplaces, childhood homes, schools and places such as Penny Lane and Strawberry Field – before finishing up in the Cavern Club (which isn't the original). Departs from outside the Beatles Story on Albert Dock.

River Explorer Cruise (☎ 639 0609; www.mersey ferries.co.uk; adult/child return £4.95/2.75; ⏰ hourly 10am-3pm Mon-Fri, 10am-5pm Sat & Sun) Do as Gerry & the Pacemakers wanted and take a ferry 'cross the Mersey, exploring the bay and all its attractions as you go. Departs from Pier Head.

Yellow Duckmarine Tour (☎ 708 7799; www.theyel lowduckmarine.co.uk; adult/child/family £11.95/9.95/34; ⏰ from 11am) Take to the dock waters in a WWII amphibious vehicle after a quickie tour of the city centre's main points of interest. It's not especially educational, but it is a bit of fun. Departs from Albert Dock, near the Beatles Story.

FESTIVALS & EVENTS

Aintree Festival (☎ 522 2929; www.aintree.co.uk) A three-day race meeting culminating in the world-famous Grand National steeplechase held on the first Saturday in April.

Africa Oye (www.africaoye.com) A free festival celebrating African music and culture in mid-June.

Liverpool Comedy Festival (☎ 0870 787 1866; www .liverpoolcomedyfestival.co.uk) A fortnight of comedy, both local and international, in venues throughout the city. Usually kicks off in mid-July.

Merseyside International Street Festival (www .brouhaha.uk.com) A three-week extravaganza of world culture beginning in mid-July and featuring indoor and outdoor performances by artists and musicians from pretty much everywhere.

Eclectica Music Festival (☎ 01744-755150; www .visitsthelens.com) A new free festival of folk, alternative and roots music in St Helen's town centre over one day in mid-August.

Creamfields (☎ 0208-969 4477; www.cream.co.uk) Alfresco dance-fest that brings some of the world's best DJs and dance acts together during the last weekend in August. It takes place at the Daresbury Estate near Halton, Cheshire.

Mathew St Festival (☎ 239 9091; www.mathew streetfestival.com) The world's biggest tribute to the Beatles features six days of music, a convention and a memorabilia auction during the last week of August.

SLEEPING

As Liverpool's cultural scene heats up, so do its hotels. Stylish new arrivals and business chains have muscled in on the traditional stalwarts and forced them to buck up or close down, with the result that while the choice has improved dramatically, you'll end up paying for the privilege. Beds are extremely tough to find when Liverpool FC are playing at home (it's less of a problem with Everton) and during the Beatles convention in the last week of August.

City Centre
BUDGET

Embassie Hostel (☎ 707 1089; www.embassie.com; 1 Falkner Sq; dm £14.50) Until 1986, this lovely Georgian house was the Venezuelan consulate; it has since been converted into a decent hostel that serves free tea, coffee and toast at all times. There's also a TV lounge, a games room and a self-catering kitchen.

International Inn (☎ 709 8135; www.internationalinn .co.uk; 4 S Hunter St; dm/d £18/40) A superb converted warehouse in the middle of uni-land: en suite, heated rooms with tidy wooden beds and bunks accommodate from two to 10 people. Facilities include a lounge, baggage storage, laundry and 24-hour front desk. The staff are terrific and CaféLatte.net (see p663) internet café is next door.

MIDRANGE

Aachen Hotel (☎ 709 3477; www.aachenhotel.co.uk; 89-91 Mt Pleasant; s/d from £32/50) A perennial favourite is this funky listed-building with a mix of rooms both shared or en suite. The décor is strictly late '70s to early '80s – lots of flower patterns and crazy colour schemes – but it's all part of the welcoming, offbeat atmosphere.

Alicia Hotel (☎ 727 4411; www.feathers.uk.com; 3 Aigburth Dr, Sefton Park; r £55) Once a wealthy cotton merchant's home, Alicia is a sister hotel to the more central Feathers, but it's a far more handsome place. Most of the rooms have extra luxuries, such as CD players and PlayStations. There's also a nice park on the grounds.

Feathers Hotel (☎ 709 9655; www.feathers.uk.com; 119-125 Mt Pleasant; s/d from £52.50/75) A better choice than most of the similar-priced chain hotels, this rambling place spreads itself across a terrace of Georgian houses close to the Metropolitan Cathedral. The rooms are all comfortable (except for the wardrobe-size singles at the top of the building) and all feature nice touches such as full-package satellite TV. The all-you-can-eat buffet breakfast is a welcome morning treat.

Other midrange options in town:

Hanover Hotel (☎ 709 6223; www.hanover.hotel.co .uk; 62 Hanover St; s/d from £40/60) Older breed of hotel-over-a-pub, with decent if unspectacular rooms.

Lord Nelson Hotel (☎ 709 5161; Hotham St; s/d from £35/50) Modern rooms and contemporary style in the middle of town.

TOP END

Liverpool Racquet Club (☎ 236 6676; www.racquetclub .org.uk; Hargreaves Bldg, 5 Chapel St; r £110) Eight individually styled rooms with influences that range from French country house to Japanese minimalist chic (often in the same room). This boutique hotel is one of the most elegant choices in town. Antique beds, sumptuous Frette linen, free-standing baths and exclusive toiletries are all teasers to a pretty classy stay.

62 Castle St (☎ 702 7898; www.62castlest.com; 62 Castle St; s/d £145/175; P 🖳) As exclusive a boutique hotel as you'll find anywhere, this wonderful new property successfully blends the traditional Victorian features of the building with a sexy, contemporary style. The 20 fabulously different suites come with plasma screen TVs, drench showers and Elemis toiletries as standard.

our pick Hope Street Hotel (☎ 709 3000; www.hope streethotel.co.uk; 40 Hope St; r/ste from £140/205) Luxurious Liverpool's pre-eminent flag-waver is this stunning boutique hotel on the city's most elegant street. The building's original features – heavy wooden beams, cast-iron columns and plenty of exposed brickwork – have been incorporated into a contemporary design inspired by the style of a 16th-century Venetian palazzo. King-size beds draped in Egyptian cotton, oak floors with underfloor heating, LCD wide-screen TVs (with DVD players) and sleek modern bathrooms replete with a range of REN bath and beauty products are but the most obvious touches of class at this supremely cool address. Breakfast, taken in the marvellous London Carriage Works (p670), is not included.

APARTMENT LUXURY

If you want to live it up in self-catering style, you can opt for a luxury apartment along the waterfront or in the heart of town. Apartments are available on a per-night basis; the price includes gas and electricity.

Trafalgar Warehouse Apartments (☎ 07715 118419; Trafalgar Warehouse, 17-19 Lord Nelson St; from £85) Beautiful converted warehouses with solid wood floors, Jacuzzis and all the trimmings, close to Lime St Station.

Premier Apartments (☎ 487 7440; www.premierapartments.com; 23 Hatton Gdns; from £70) Award-winning apartments with interiors designed by Irish fashion star, John Rocha.

Waterfront Penthouse (☎ 01695 727 877; www.stayinginliverpool.com; Clippers Quay; from £100) One luxury pad with sensational views and all the trimmings.

Around Albert Dock

BUDGET

YHA Liverpool International (☎ 0870 770 5924; www
.yha.org.uk; 25 Tabley St; dm £20.95) It may look like
an Eastern European apartment complex,
but this award-winning hostel, adorned with
Beatles memorabilia, is one of the most comfortable you'll find anywhere in the country.
The en suite dorms even have heated towel
rails, and rates include breakfast.

MIDRANGE

Campanile Hotel (☎ 709 8104; fax 709 8725; cnr Wapping
& Chaloner Sts; r £46.50; **P**) Functional, motel-style
rooms in a purpose-built hotel next to Albert
Dock. Great location and perfect for families –
children under 12 stay for free.

Dolby Hotel (☎ 708 7272; www.dolbyhotels.co.uk;
36-42 Chaloner St; r from £45) Well-run hotel with
good-sized, well-equipped rooms aimed to
rival some of the more renowned budget
chains. The Dolby does a great job and we
applaud it for it.

TOP END

Crowne Plaza Liverpool (☎ 243 8000; www.cpliver
pool.com; St Nicholas Pl, Princes Dock, Pier Head; r from £90;
P **≋**) The paragon of the modern and luxurious business hotel, the Crowne Plaza has a
marvellous waterfront location and plenty of
facilities including a health club and swimming pool.

EATING

Liverpool's dining scene is getting better all
the time. There are plenty of choices in Ropewalks, along Hardman St and Hope St, along
Nelson St in the heart of Chinatown or slightly
further afield in Lark Lane, near to Sefton
Park, which is packed with restaurants.

City Centre

BUDGET

Everyman Bistro (☎ 708 9545; 13 Hope St; mains £4-
7; ☯ noon-2am Mon-Fri, 11am-2am Sat, 7-10.30pm Sun)
Out-of-work actors and other creative types
on a budget make this great café-restaurant
beneath the Everyman Theatre their second
home – with good reason. Great tucker and
a terrific atmosphere.

Quynny's Quisine (☎ 708 7757; 45A Bold St; mains £5-
7; ☯ 9.30am-9pm) Refried beans, plantains, salads
and other Caribbean goodies are hearty and
genuine at this basement restaurant. Going
underground isn't normally ideal for dining, but in this case it just ensures that fewer
people crowd the place and there's more room
for you.

Kimo's (☎ 709 2355; 61 Mt Pleasant; meals around
£6; ☯ lunch & dinner) A student favourite, this
excellent café serves a good mix, depending
on your mood: perhaps some cous cous or
an authentic kebab for that ethnic kick, or
the local fave club sandwich, which Komo's
claims is the best you'll eat anywhere?

MIDRANGE

Keith's Wine Bar (☎ 728 7688; 107 Lark Lane; mains
around £5; ☯ 11am-11pm) Friendly, bohemian and
mostly vegetarian hang-out with a sensational
wine cellar that is the favourite resting place of
the city's alternative-lifestyle crowd.

Tea Factory (☎ 708 7008; 79 Wood St; mains £7-12;
☯ 11am-late) Who knew that cod'n'chips could
be so…cool? The wide-ranging menu covers
all bases from typical Brit to funky finger food
such as international tapas, but it's the room,
darling, that makes this place so popular. Rock
stars and the impossibly beautiful have found
a home here.

Quarter (☎ 707 1965; 7 Falkner St; mains £8-13;
☯ lunch & dinner) A gorgeous little wine bar and
bistro with outdoor seating for that elusive
summer's day. It's perfect for a lunchtime
plate of pasta or just a coffee and a slice of
mouthwatering cake.

Yuet Ben (☎ 709 5772; 1 Upper Duke St; mains £9-13;
☯ 5-11pm Tue-Sun) When it comes to the best
Chinese food in town, you won't hear too
many dissenting voices: Yuet Ben's Beijing
cuisine usually comes out tops. The veggie
banquet could bring round even the most
avid carnivore. Get a seat by the window to
eat in the shadow of Europe's largest Chinese gate.

TOP END

London Carriage Works (☎ 705 2222; www.tlcw.co.uk;
40 Hope St; 2-/3-course meals £35/45; ☯ 8am-10pm Mon-
Sat, 8am-8pm Sun) Liverpool's dining revolution
is being led by Paul Askew's award-winning
restaurant. Its foot soldiers are the fashionistas, socceristas and other members of the
style brigade who share the large, open space
that is the dining room – actually more of a
bright glass box divided only by a series of
sculpted glass shards – and indulge themselves in the marvellous, eclectic ethnic menu,
which reveals influences from every corner
of the world.

Alma de Cuba (☎ 709 7097; www.alma-de-cuba.com; St Peter's Church, Seel St; mains £15-24; ☯ lunch & dinner) This extraordinary new venture has seen the transformation of a Polish church into a Miami-style Cuban extravaganza, a bar and restaurant where you can feast on a suckling pig (the menu heavily favours meat) or clink a perfectly made *mojito* cocktail at the long bar. ¡Salud!

Colin's Bridewell (☎ 707 8003; Campbell Sq; lunch mains £8-11, dinner mains £15-21; ☯ noon-11pm) Top-notch British nosh *avec un* continental twist served in a converted police station – the booths are in the old cells; if prison food were this good, the crime rate would soar. It isn't as trendy as some of the city's newer offerings, but those on the inside love it.

Around Albert Dock

Pan-American Club (☎ 709 7097; Britannia Pavilion, Albert Dock; mains £12-22) A truly beautiful warehouse conversion has created this top-class restaurant and bar, easily one of the best dining addresses in town. Fancy steak dinners and other American classics can be washed down with drinks from the Champagne Lounge.

DRINKING

A recent survey has put Merseyside at the top of the All-England drinking league. It's official: Scousers love boozing. Health officials may be in despair, but Liverpool has pubs and bars to suit every taste imaginable. Most of the party action takes place in and around Rope-walks, the heart of which is Concert Sq. Unless specified, all the bars included here open until 2am Monday to Saturday, although most have a nominal entry charge after 11pm.

City Centre

Baa Bar (☎ 707 0610; 43-45 Fleet St) One of the first and still the best of Liverpool's style bars, Baa is packed most nights and remains a favourite watering hole with anyone looking for a good night out; the patio is perfect during the longer summer evenings.

Hannah's (☎ 708 5959; 2 Leece St) One of the top student bars in town. Try to land yourself a table on the outdoor patio, which is covered in the event of rain. Staying open late, a friendly, easy-going crowd and some pretty decent music make this one of the better places to get drunk in.

Magnet (☎ 709 6969; 39 Hardman St) Red leather booths, plenty of velvet and a suitably seedy New York–dive atmosphere where Iggy Pop or Tom Waits would feel right at home. The upstairs bar is very cool but totally chilled out, while downstairs the dancefloor shakes to the best music in town, spun by up-and-comers and supported with guest slots by some of England's most established DJ names.

Philharmonic (☎ 707 2837; 36 Hope St; ☯ closes 11.30pm) This extraordinary bar, designed by the shipwrights who built the *Lusitania*, is one of the most beautiful bars in all of

---

DOING THE BEATLES TO DEATH

Between March 1961 and August 1963, the Beatles played a staggering 275 gigs in a club on Mathew St called the Cavern, which was essentially a basement with a stage and a sound system. They shared the stage with other local bands who helped define the Mersey Beat, but it was John, Paul, George and Ringo who emerged into the sunlight of superstardom, unparalleled success and crass marketing.

Forty years later, the club is gone, the band has long broken up and two of its members are dead, but the phenomenon lives on and is still the biggest tourist magnet in town. The Cavern Quarter – basically a small warren of streets around Mathew St – has been transformed to cash in on the band's seemingly unending earning power: the Rubber Soul Oyster Bar, the From Me to You shop and the Lucy in the Sky With Diamonds café should give you an idea of what to expect. For decent memorabilia, check out the **Beatles Shop** (www.thebeatleshop.co.uk; 31 Mathew St).

True fans will undoubtedly want to visit the National Trust–owned **Mendips**, the home where John lived with his Aunt Mimi from 1945 to 1963, and **20 Forthlin Rd**, the rather plain terraced home where Paul grew up; you can only do so by prebooked **tour** (☎ 427 7231; adult/child £12/free; ☯ 10.30am & 11.20am Wed-Sun, Easter-Oct) from outside the National Conservation Centre. Visitors to Speke Hall (see p675) can also visit both from there.

If you'd rather do it yourself, the tourist offices also stock the *Discover Lennon's Liverpool* guide and map, and *Robin Jones' Beatles Liverpool*.

GAY & LESBIAN LIVERPOOL

There's no discernible gay quarter in Liverpool, with most of the gay-friendly clubs and bars spread about Dale St and Victoria St in Ropewalks. **G-Bar** (☎ 255 1148; 1-7 Eberle St), in a small lane off Dale St behind Metrolink, is the city's premier gay bar, even though it attracts a mixed crowd. The **Curzon** (☎ 236 5160; 8 Temple Lane) is what one might euphemistically term a man's bar, with lots of hairy, tough-looking guys getting to know each other. For something a little less provocative, the **Masquerade Bar** (☎ 236 7786; 10 Cumberland St) attracts a real mix of gays, lesbians and bis looking for a few laughs and a sing-song.

Many clubs host gay nights, but **Babystorm** (☎ 07845 298863; 12 Stanley St), a relatively new club and bar aimed primarily at the lesbian and bi community, has really taken off; it is a good rival to **Superstar Boudoir** (22-24 Stanley St) as the best gay club in town. Also worth checking out are the gay nights at **Garlands** (see below). For online listings, check out www.realliverpool.com.

England. The interior is resplendent with etched and stained glass, wrought iron, mosaics and ceramic tiling – and if you think that's good, just wait until you see inside the marble men's toilets, the only heritage-listed lav in the country.

Ye Cracke (☎ 709 4171; 13 Rice St; ☽ closes 11.30pm) Discreet and dilapidated, this atmospheric boozer is a favourite with pensioners and bohemians from the nearby college of art; in the early '60s these included John and Cynthia Lennon.

Albert Dock

Blue Bar (☎ 709 7097; Edward Pavilion) You don't need a premiership contract to guarantee entry anymore, which means that mere mortals can finally enjoy the relaxed ambience of this elegant waterside lounge. So where have all the footballers gone? Downstairs, to the far more glam Baby Blue, a private members' bar.

Baby Cream (☎ 702 5823; www.babycream.co.uk; Atlantic Pavilion) This supertrendy bar, run by the same crowd that created Liverpool's now-defunct-but-still-legendary Cream nightclub, is gorgeous and pretentious in almost equal measure. One pretty cool feature, though, is Creamselector – a set of touch screens where you can make your own compilation CD from a databank of more than 4000 tracks (for a price) – it's like taking a piece of the famous nightclub home with you.

ENTERTAINMENT

The schedule is pretty full these days, whether it's excellent fringe theatre, a performance by the superb Philharmonic or an all-day rock concert. And then there's the constant backbeat provided by the city's club scene, which

pulses and throbs to the wee hours, six nights out of seven. For all information, consult the *Liverpool Echo*.

Nightclubs

Most of the city's clubs are concentrated in Ropewalks, where they compete for customers with a ton of late-night bars; considering the number of punters in the area on a Friday or Saturday night, we're guessing there's plenty of business for everyone. Most clubs open at 11pm and turf everyone out by 3am.

Barfly (☎ 0870 907 0999; 90 Seel St; admission £3-11; ☽ Mon-Sat) This converted theatre is home to our favourite club in town. The fortnightly Saturday Chibuku Shake Shake (www .chibuku.com) is one of the best club nights in all of England, led by a mix of superb DJs including Yousef (formerly of Cream) and superstars such as Dmitri from Paris and Gilles Peterson. The music ranges from hip-hop to deep house – if you're in town, get in line. Other nights feature a superb mixed bag of music, from trash to techno.

Garlands (☎ 236 2307; www.garlandsonline.co.uk; 8-10 Eberle St; admission £6-10; ☽ Fri-Sun) House in all sounds and guises rules the roost at this banging club, whose punters were extolled by *Mixmag* magazine as one of the best crowds in England.

Nation (☎ 709 1693; 40 Slater St/Wolstenholme Sq; admission £4-13) It looks like an air-raid shelter, but it's the big-name DJs dropping the bombs at the city's premier dance club, formerly the home of Cream. These days, it also hosts live bands as well as pumping techno nights.

Theatre

Most of Liverpool's theatres feature a mixed bag of revues, musicals and stage successes that are as easy on the eye as they are on the mind, but there is also more interesting work on offer.

Everyman Theatre (☎ 709 4776; 13 Hope St) This is one of England's most famous repertory theatres and an avid supporter of local talent, which has included the likes of Alan Bleasdale.

Unity Theatre (☎ 709 4988; Hope Pl) Fringe theatre for those keen on the unusual and challenging. There's also a great bar on the premises.

Live Music

ROCK MUSIC

Academy (☎ 794 6868; Liverpool University, 11-13 Hotham St) This is the best venue to see touring major bands.

Cavern Club (☎ 236 1965; 8-10 Mathew St) 'The world's most famous club' is not the original basement venue where the Fab Four began their careers, but it's a fairly faithful reconstruction. There's usually a good selection of local bands, and look out for all-day gigs.

CLASSICAL MUSIC

Philharmonic Hall (☎ 709 3789; Hope St) One of Liverpool's most beautiful buildings, the Art Deco Phil is home to the city's main classical orchestra, but it also stages the work of avant-garde musicians such as John Cage and Nick Cave.

Sport

Liverpool's two football teams – the reds of Liverpool FC and the blues of Everton – are pretty much the alpha and omega of sporting interest in the city. There is no other city in England where the fortunes of its football clubs are so inextricably linked with those of its inhabitants. Yet Liverpool is also home to the Grand National – the world's most famous steeplechase event – that is run in the first weekend in April at Aintree, north of the city (see the boxed text, below).

LIVERPOOL FC

Doff o' the cap to Evertonians and Beatle-maniacs, but no single institution represents the Mersey spirit and strong sense of identity more powerfully than **Liverpool FC** (☎ 263 9199, ticket office 220 2345; www.liverpoolfc.tv; Anfield Rd), England's most successful football club. Virtually unbeatable for much of the 1970s and '80s, they haven't won the league championship since 1990, but in 2005 they became European champions for the fifth time and followed it with an FA Cup in 2006. Led by Spanish manager Rafa Benitez and captained by local boy and legend Steven Gerrard, things are looking seriously good once more for the Reds.

The club's home is the marvellous Anfield, but plans are afoot to relocate to a new 60,000-capacity stadium a stone's throw away in Stanley Park before 2010. The experience of a live match is a memorable one, especially the sound of 40,000 fans singing 'You'll Never Walk Alone', but tickets are pretty tricky to come by. You may have to settle for a **tour** (☎ 260 6677; with museum adult/child £9/5.50; ◷ every

---

THE GRAND NATIONAL

England loves the gee-gees, but never more so than on the first Saturday in April when 40-odd veteran stalwarts of the jumps line up at Aintree to race across 4½ miles and over the most difficult fences in world racing. Since the first running of the Grand National in 1839 – won by the appositely named Lottery – the country has taken the race to heart. There's hardly a household that doesn't tune in, betting slips nervously in hand.

The race has captured the national imagination because its protagonists aren't the pedigreed racing machines that line up for the season's other big fixtures, the Derby and the Gold Cup: they're ageing bruisers full of the oh-so-English qualities of grit and derring-do, which they need in abundance to get over tough jumps like the Chair, Canal Turn and Becher's Brook, named after a Captain Becher who fell into it in 1839 and later commented that he had no idea water could taste so awful without whisky in it.

You can book **tickets** (☎ 522 2929; www.aintree.co.uk) for the Grand National, or visit the **Grand National Experience** (☎ 523 2600; adult/child with tour £7/4, without tour £3/2), a visitor centre that includes a race simulator – those jumps are very steep indeed. We recommend the racecourse tour, which takes in the stableyard and the grave of three-time winner Red Rum, the most loved of all Grand National winners.

couple of hours except match days) that includes the home dressing room, a walk down the famous tunnel and a seat in the dugout, or simply a visit to the museum (admission £5), which features plenty of memorabilia – as well as those five European Cups.

EVERTON FC

Liverpool's 'other' team are the blues of Everton FC (☎ 330 2400, ticket office 330 2300; www.evertonfc .com; Goodison Park), who may not have their rivals' winning pedigree but they're just as popular locally.

Tours (☎ 330 2277; adult/child £8.50/5; ☽ 11am & 2pm Sun-Wed & Fri) of Goodison Park run throughout the year except on the Friday before home matches.

GETTING THERE & AWAY
Air

With the clever tagline of 'Above Us Only Sky', Liverpool John Lennon Airport (☎ 0870 750 8484; www.liverpooljohnlennonairport.co.uk) serves a variety of international destinations including Amsterdam, Barcelona, Dublin and Paris, as well as destinations in the UK (Belfast, London and the Isle of Man).

Bus

The National Express Coach Station (☎ 08705 808080; Norton St) is situated 300m north of Lime St station. There are services to/from most major towns, including Manchester (£5.80, 1¼ hours, hourly), London (£22, five to six hours, seven daily), Birmingham (£10.20, 2¾ hours, five daily) and Newcastle (£18.40, 6½ hours, three daily).

Train

Liverpool's main station is Lime St. It has hourly services to almost everywhere, including Chester (£4, 40 minutes), London (£56.50, three hours), Manchester (£8.30, 45 minutes) and Wigan (£4.15, 50 minutes).

GETTING AROUND
To/From the Airport

The airport is 8 miles south of the centre. Arriva Airlink (£1.50; ☽ 6am-11pm) buses 80A and 180 depart from Paradise St station and Airportxpress 500 (£2; ☽ 5.15am-12.15am) buses from outside Lime St station. Buses from both stations take half an hour and run every 20 minutes. A taxi to the city centre should cost no more than £14.

Boat

The famous cross-Mersey ferry (adult/child £1.35/1.05) for Woodside and Seacombe departs from Pier Head Ferry Terminal, next to the Liver Building to the north of Albert Dock.

Car

You won't have much use for a car in Liverpool, and it'll end up costing you plenty in car-park fees. If you must drive, there are parking meters around the city and a number of open and sheltered car parks. Car break-ins are a major problem, so leave absolutely nothing of value in the car.

Public Transport

Local public transport is coordinated by Merseytravel (☎ 236 7676; www.merseytravel.gov.uk). Highly recommended is the Saveaway ticket (adult/child £3.70/1.90), which allows for one day's off-peak travel on all bus, train and ferry services throughout Merseyside. Tickets are available at shops and post offices throughout the city. Paradise St bus station is in the city centre.

MERSEYRAIL

Merseyrail (☎ 702 2071; www.merseyrail.org) is an extensive suburban rail service linking Liverpool with the Greater Merseyside area. There are four stops in the city centre: Lime St, Central (handy for Ropewalks), James St (close to Albert Dock) and Moorfields (for the Western Approaches Museum).

Taxi

Mersey Cabs (☎ 298 2222) operates tourist taxi services and has some cabs adapted for disabled visitors.

AROUND LIVERPOOL

PORT SUNLIGHT

Southwest of Liverpool across the River Mersey on the Wirral Peninsula, Port Sunlight is a picturesque 19th-century village created by the philanthropic Lever family to house workers in its soap factory. The main reason to come here is the wonderful Lady Lever Art Gallery (☎ 478 4136; www.liverpoolmuseums.org.uk/ladylever; off Greendale Rd; admission free; ☽ 10am-5pm) where you can see some of the greatest works of the Pre- Raphaelite Brotherhood, as well as some fine Wedgwood pottery.

Take the Merseyrail to Bebington on the Wirral line; the gallery is a five-minute walk from the station; alternatively, bus 51 from Woodside will get you there.

SPEKE

A marvellous example of a black-and-white half-timbered hall can be visited at **Speke Hall** (NT; ☎ 427 7231; www.spekehall.org.uk; admission £6.50; ☺ 1-5.30pm Wed-Sun Apr-Oct, 1-4.30pm Sat & Sun Nov-Mar), six miles south of Liverpool in the plain suburb of Speke. It contains several priest's holes where 16th-century Roman Catholic priests could hide when they were forbidden to hold Masses. Any airport bus from Paradise St will drop you within a half mile of the entrance. Speke Hall can also be combined with a National Trust 1½-hour **tour** (☎ 486 4006; with Speke Hall adult/child £12/free) to the childhood homes of both Lennon and McCartney (see the boxed text Doing the Beatles to Death, p671) – you can book at Speke Hall or at the tourist offices in Liverpool.

LANCASHIRE

Industrious, isolated Lancashire has a touch of everything, from mighty Manchester in the south – so big that it's administered separately (and given its own section in this chapter) – to the Ribble Valley in the north, a gentle and beautiful warm-up for the Lake District beyond its northern border. Just north of the Ribble Valley is the handsome Georgian county town of Lancaster and, to the west, the ever-popular Blackpool, empress of the tacky, traditional English seaside resorts.

BLACKPOOL

☎ 01253 / pop 142,290

The queen bee of England's fun-by-the-sea-type resorts is unquestionably Blackpool. It's unashamedly bold and brazen in its efforts to cement its position as the country's second-most visited town after London. Tacky, trashy and, in recent years, a little bit tawdry, Blackpool doesn't care because 16 million people don't either.

Blackpool works so well because it has mastered the time-tested, traditional British holiday-by-the-sea formula with high-tech, 21st-century amusements that will thrill even the most cynical observer. Basically, a holiday here is all about pure, unadulterated fun.

The town is famous for its tower, its three piers, its Pleasure Beach and its Illuminations, a successful ploy to extend the brief summer holiday season. From early September to early November, 5 miles of The Promenade are illuminated with thousands of electric and neon lights.

Orientation & Information

Blackpool is surprisingly spread out, but can still be managed easily without a car; trams run the entire 7-mile length of the seafront Promenade.

Tourist office (www.visitblackpool.com) Clifton St (☎ 478222; 1 Clifton St; ☺ 9am-5pm Mon-Sat); Central Promenade (☎ 403223; ☺ 9.15am-5pm Mon-Sat, 10.15am-4.15pm Sun Apr-Sep)

Sights
PLEASURE BEACH

The main reason for Blackpool's immense popularity is the simply fantastic **Pleasure Beach** (☎ 0870 444 5566; www.blackpoolpleasurebeach.com; admission free; ☺ from 10am Apr-early Nov), a 16-hectare collection of more than 145 different rides that attracts some 7 million visitors annually. As amusement parks go, this is the best you'll find anywhere in Europe.

The park's major rides include the Big One, the tallest and fastest roller coaster in Europe, reaching a top speed of 85mph before hitting a near-vertical descent of 75m; the Ice Blast, which delivers you up a 65m steel tower before returning to earth at 80mph; and, new in 2004, Bling, where riders are brought 40m into the air and then spun 360° at 60mph – it's the perfect way to shift the contents of your stomach.

The hi-tech, modern rides draw the biggest queues, but spare a moment to check out the marvellous collection of old-style wooden roller coasters, known as 'woodies'. You can see the world's first Big Dipper (1923), but be sure to have a go on the Grand National (1935), whose carriages trundle along a 1½-mile track in an experience that is typically Blackpool – complete with riders waving their hands (despite the sombre-toned announcement not to).

Rides are divided into categories and you can buy tickets for individual categories or for a mixture of them all. An unlimited ticket to all rides costs £29 for one day, £43 for two.

There are no set times for closing; it depends how busy it is.

OTHER SIGHTS

Blackpool's most recognisable landmark is the 150m-high **Blackpool Tower** (☎ 622242; www.the blackpooltower.co.uk; adult/child £12.95/8.95; ☺ 10am-6pm), built in 1894. Inside is a vast entertainment complex that should keep the kids happy, including a dinosaur ride, Europe's largest indoor jungle gym and a Moorish circus.

The highlight is the magnificent rococo **ballroom** (☺ 10am-6pm Mon-Fri & Sun, to 11pm Sat), with extraordinary sculptured and gilded plasterwork, murals, chandeliers and couples gliding across the beautifully polished wooden floor to the melodramatic tones of a huge Wurlitzer organ.

Across from Pleasure Beach is **Sandcastle Waterworld** (☎ 343602; adult/child £10.50/8.50; ☺ from 10am daily May-Oct, Sat & Sun only Nov-Feb), an indoor water complex complete with its own rides. Forget the beach – this is the most pleasant place to have a swim.

Of the three Victorian piers, the most famous – and the longest – is the **North Pier**, built in 1862 and opened a year later charging a penny admission. Today admission to its plethora of assorted rides and attractions is free.

Near the Central Pier is the state-of-the-art **Sealife Centre** (☎ 622445; New Bonny St; adult/child £8.95/6; ☺ 10am-8pm), which features 2½m-long sharks and a giant octopus.

Sleeping

With more than 2500 hotels, B&Bs and self-catering units, Blackpool knows how to put visitors up for the night. Even so, it is worth booking ahead during the Illuminations. If you want to stay close to the waterfront, prepare for a noisy, boisterous night; accommodation along Albert and Hornby Rds, 300m back from the sea, is that little bit quieter. The tourist offices will assist you in finding a bed.

Big Blue Hotel (☎ 0845 367 3333; www.bigbluehotel .uk.com; Blackpool Pleasure Beach; s/d/ste from £65/75/149; P) Cool, minimalist and very much a look into Blackpool's future, this hotel caters to 21st-century demands: smartly kitted-out rooms come with DVD players and computer games, while its location at the southern entrance to Pleasure Beach should ensure that everyone has something to do.

Number One (☎ 343901; www.numberoneblackpool .com; 1 St Lukes Rd; s/d from £70/120; P) Far fancier than anything else around, this stunning boutique guesthouse is all luxury and contempo-rary style. Everything exudes a kind of discreet elegance, from the dark-wood furniture and high-end mod cons to the top-notch break-fast. It's on a quiet road just set back from the South Promenade near Pleasure Beach.

Other options you can try:

Dutchman (☎ 404812; www.dutchmanhotel.com; 269 The Promenade; s/d from £25/50) Harsh blue neon out the front invites you into a self-styled party hotel.

New President Hotel (☎ 624460; www.thepresident hotel.co.uk; 320-324 North Promenade; s/d from £49/69; P) Newly renovated with 65 comfortable rooms. Also serves meals priced from £7 to £9.

Ruskin Hotel (☎ 624063; www.ruskinhotel.com; Albert Rd; s/d £45/80) Victorian-style hotel at the prom end of Albert Rd, near Blackpool Tower.

Eating

Forget gourmet meals – the Blackpool experience is all about stuffing your face with burgers, doughnuts and fish and chips. Most people eat at their hotels where roast and three vegetables often costs just £5 a head.

There are a few restaurants around Talbot Sq (near the tourist office) on Queen St, Talbot Rd and Clifton St. The most interesting possibility is the Afro-Caribbean **Lagoonda** (☎ 293837; 37 Queen St; mains £8-10), a friendly, no-nonsense eatery that serves up colourful (and often spicy) dishes with a tropical flavour.

Getting There & Away

BUS

The central coach station is on Talbot Rd, near the town centre. Destinations include Liverpool (£7.80, 1½ hours, one daily), London (£25, 6½ hours, five daily) and Manchester (£6.20, 1¾ hours, five daily).

TRAIN

The main train station is Blackpool North, about five blocks east of the North Pier on Talbot Rd. There is a direct service from Manchester (£11.75, 1¼ hours, half-hourly) and Liverpool (£12.60, 1½ hours, seven daily), but most other arrivals change in Preston (£5.65, 30 minutes, half-hourly).

Getting Around

A host of travel-card options for trams and buses ranging from one day to a week are available at the tourist offices and most news-agents. With more than 14,000 car-parking spaces in Blackpool, you'll have no problem parking.

LANCASTER

☎ 01524 / pop 45,960

Lined with handsome Georgian buildings, Lancaster does a good job of representing Lancashire as its county seat and, for our purposes, as a decent stopover on the way to the Ribble Valley. Folks have done business here since Roman times, none more successfully than during the 18th century, when Lancaster was an important port in the slave trade.

Information

Post office (85 Market St; ⏱ 9am-5.30pm Mon-Fri, 9am-12.30pm Sat)

Tourist office (☎ 841656; www.citycoastcountryside .co.uk; 29 Castle Hill; ⏱ 9am-5pm Mon-Sat)

Sights

LANCASTER CASTLE & PRIORY

Lancaster's imposing **castle** (☎ 64998; www .lancastercastle.com; admission £5; ⏱ 10am-5pm) was originally built in 1150. Later additions include the **Well Tower**, more commonly known as the Witches' Tower because it was used to incarcerate the accused of the famous Pendle Witches Trial of 1612, and the impressive twin-towered **gatehouse**, both of which were added in the 14th century. Most of what you see today, however, dates from the 18th and 19th centuries, when the castle was substantially altered to suit its new, and still current, role as a prison. Consequently, you can only visit the castle as part of a 45-minute **guided tour** (⏱ every 30 min, 10.30am-4pm), but you do get

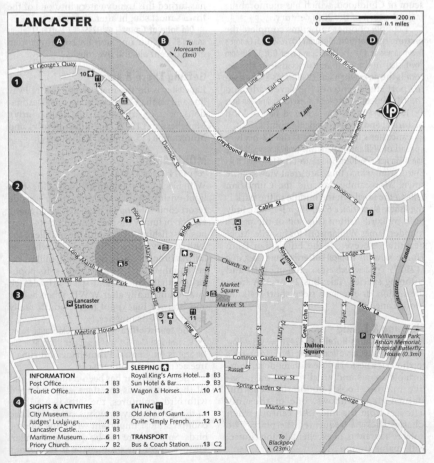

LANCASTER

INFORMATION	
Post Office	1 B3
Tourist Office	2 B3

SIGHTS & ACTIVITIES	
City Museum	3 B3
Judges' Lodgings	4 B3
Lancaster Castle	5 B3
Maritime Museum	6 B1
Priory Church	7 B2

SLEEPING	
Royal King's Arms Hotel	8 B3
Sun Hotel & Bar	9 B3
Wagon & Horses	10 A1

EATING	
Old John of Gaunt	11 B3
Quite Simply French	12 A1

TRANSPORT	
Bus & Coach Station	13 C2

NORTHWEST ENGLAND

a chance to experience what it was like to be locked up in the dungeon.

Immediately next to the castle is the equally fine **priory church** (☎ 65338; admission free; ⏰ 9.30am-5pm), founded in 1094 but extensively remodelled in the Middle Ages.

OTHER SIGHTS

The steps between the castle and the church lead down to the 17th-century **Judges' Lodgings** (☎ 32808; admission £3; ⏰ 10.30am-1pm & 2-5pm Mon-Fri & 2-5pm Sat Jul-Sep, 2-5pm Mon-Sat Oct-Jun). Once the home of witch-hunter Thomas Covell (he who 'caught' the poor Pendle women), it is now home to a Museum of Furnishings by master builders Gillows of Lancaster (whose work graces the Houses of Parliament) and a Museum of Childhood, which has memorabilia from the turn of the 20th century.

A couple of other museums complete the picture: the **Maritime Museum** (☎ 64637; St George's Quay; admission £3; ⏰ 11am-5pm Easter-Oct, 12.30-4pm Nov-Easter), in the 18th-century Custom House, recalls the days when Lancaster was a flourishing port at the centre of the slave trade; and the **City Museum** (☎ 64637; Market Sq; admission free; ⏰ 10am-5pm Mon-Sat) has a mixed bag of local historical and archaeological exhibits.

Lancaster's highest point is the 22-hectare spread of **Williamson Park** (www.williamsonpark.com; admission free; ⏰ 10am-5pm Easter-Oct, 11am-4pm Nov-Easter), from which there are great views of the town, Morecambe Bay and the Cumbrian fells to the north. In the middle of the park is the **Ashton Memorial**, a 67m-high Baroque folly built by Lord Ashton (the son of the park's founder, James Williamson) for his wife. More beautiful, however, is the Edwardian Palm House, now the **Tropical Butterfly House** (adult/child £4.25/2.75; ⏰ same hours as park), full of exotic and stunning species. Take bus 25 or 25A from the station, or else it's a steep short walk up Moor Lane.

Sleeping & Eating

Royal King's Arms Hotel (☎ 32451; www.swallow-hotels.com; Market St; s/d from £55/80; P) Lancaster's top hotel is a period house with modern, comfortable rooms and an all-round business-like interior. Look out for the beautiful stained-glass windows, one of the only leftovers from the mid-19th century when Charles Dickens frequented the place. The hotel restaurant is an excellent dining choice, with mains around £11.

Sun Hotel & Bar (☎ 66006; www.thesunhotelandbar .co.uk; 63 Church St; s/d from £40/60; P) An excellent hotel in a 300-year-old building with a rustic, old world look that stops at the bedroom door; a recent renovation has resulted in eight pretty snazzy sleeping quarters. The pub downstairs is one of the best in town and a top spot for a bit of grub; there are three different menus to choose from, with meals from £8 to £15.

Wagon & Horses (☎ 846094; 27 St George's Quay; s/d £32/45) A pleasant pub near the Maritime Museum with five comfortable rooms upstairs; only one is en suite, but all have river views.

Quite Simply French (☎ 843199; 27A St George's Quay; mains £9-14; ⏰ dinner Mon-Fri, lunch & dinner Sat-Sun) A little bit of contemporary French cuisine – as well as Lancaster's only lobster tank – has turned this trendy eatery into one of the town's most sought after dining spots.

Old John of Gaunt (☎ 32358; 53 Market St; mains around £5-6) Your one stop for traditional pub grub, decent ale and live music.

Getting There & Away

Lancaster is on the main west-coast railway line and on the Cumbrian coast line. Destinations include Carlisle (£21, one hour, hourly), Manchester (£12.20, one hour, hourly) and Morecambe (15 minutes, half-hourly).

MORECAMBE
☎ 01524 / pop 49,570

With Blackpool grabbing so much of the spotlight, visitors to Lancashire's *other* seaside resort come looking for a quieter, less frenetic version of fun by the sea. A minding-its-own-business fishing village until the middle of the 19th century, Morecambe exploded when the railway brought trains packed with mill workers and their families to its shores. Its popularity with the bucket-and-spade brigades fell away dramatically after WWII, when bolder and brasher Blackpool to the south really began to flex its muscles.

The **tourist office** (☎ 582808; Old Station Bldgs; ⏰ 9.30am-5pm Mon-Sat year-round plus 10am-4pm Sun Jun-Sep) is on Central Promenade and runs a free accommodation service.

The old harbour has been refurbished and all that remains is the **stone jetty.** Adorned with bird sculptures, the jetty is a tribute to the glorious bay, which is considered the country's most important wintering site for birds. Sunsets here can be quite spectacular. Further down the promenade is the town's most famous statue: Graham Ibbeson's tribute to Ernie Bartholomew, better known as Eric Morecambe, one half of comic duo Morecambe and Wise.

Trains run half-hourly from Lancaster (15 minutes), only 5 miles to the west.

RIBBLE VALLEY

Lancashire's most attractive landscapes lie trapped between the brash tackiness of Blackpool to the west and the sprawling urban conurbations of Preston and Blackburn to the south.

The northern half of the valley is dominated by the sparsely populated moorland of the Forest of Bowland, which is a fantastic place for walks, while the southern half features rolling hills, attractive market towns and ruins, with the River Ribble flowing between them.

Walking & Cycling

The **Ribble Way**, a 70-mile footpath that follows the River Ribble from its source to the estuary, is one of the more popular walks in the area and passes through Clitheroe. For online information check out www.lancashireshillcountry.co.uk.

The valley is also well covered by the northern loop of the **Lancashire Cycle Way**; for more information about routes, safety and so on contact the **Blazing Saddles Mountain Club** (☎ 01442-844435; www.blazingsaddles.co.uk).

The tourist office in Clitheroe (below) has three useful publications: *Bowlands by Bike* (free), *Mountain Bike Ribble Valley Circular Routes* (£2) and *Mountain Bike Rides in Gisburn Forest* (£1.50).

Clitheroe

☎ 01200 / population 14,700

The Ribble Valley's largest market town is best known for its impressive **Norman keep** (admission free; ⌚ dawn-dusk), built in the 12th century and now, sadly, standing empty; there are great views of the river valley below. The extensive grounds are home to the mildly interesting **castle museum** (☎ 424635; adult/child £2/50p; ⌚ 11am-5pm daily May-Sep, Sat-Wed only Oct-Dec & Feb-Apr, closed Jan).

The **tourist office** (☎ 425566; www.ribblevalley.gov.uk; 14 Market Place; ⌚ 9am-5pm Mon-Sat, 10am-4pm Sun) has information on the town and surrounding area. **Pedal Power** (☎ 422066; Waddington Rd) has bikes for rent.

Decent accommodation options include the **Swan & Royal Hotel** (☎ 423130; www.swanandroyal.co.uk; 26 Castle St; s/d from £32.50/50), a family-run, half-timbered hotel with six rooms; and the **Brooklyn Guesthouse** (☎ 428268; 32 Pimlico Rd; s/d from £27/50), a handsome Georgian house with comfy flower-print rooms. **Halpenny's of Clitheroe** (☎ 424478; Old Toll House, 1-5 Parson Lane; mains around £6) is a traditional teashop that serves sandwiches and dishes such as Lancashire hotpot.

Pendle Hill

The area's top attraction is Pendle Hill (558m), made famous in 1612 as the stomping ground of the Pendle Witches, 10 women who allegedly practiced all kinds of malefic doings until they were convicted on the sole testimony of a child and hanged. The tourist authority makes a big deal of the mythology surrounding the unfortunate women, and every Halloween a pseudomystical ceremony is performed here to commemorate their 'activities'.

If that isn't enough, the hill is also renowned as the spot where George Fox had a vision in 1652 that led him to found the Quakers. Whatever your thoughts on witchcraft and religious visions, the hill, a couple of miles east of Clitheroe, is a great spot to walk to.

Forest of Bowland

☎ 01200

This vast, grouse-ridden moorland is somewhat of a misnomer. The use of 'forest' is a throwback to an earlier definition, when it served as a royal hunting ground. Today it is an Area of Outstanding Natural Beauty (AONB), which makes for good walking and cycling. The **Pendle Witch Way**, a 45-mile walk from Pendle Hill to northeast of Lancaster, cuts right through the area, and the **Lancashire Cycle Way** runs along the eastern border. The forest's main town is Slaidburn, about 9 miles north of Clitheroe on the B6478.

Other villages worth exploring are Newton, Whitewell and Dunsop Bridge.

SLEEPING & EATING

The popular **YHA Youth Hostel** (☎ 0870 770 6034; www.yha.org.uk; King's House, Slaidburn; dm £11.95; ⌚ Apr-Oct), a converted 17th-century village inn, was refurbished to a high standard in 2003. It is especially popular with walkers and cyclists.

More luxurious accommodation is limited. In Slaidburn, the wonderful 13th-century **Hark** to Bounty Inn (☎ 446246; www.harktobounty.co.uk; s/d £32.50/65) has atmospheric rooms with exposed oak beams. An excellent restaurant downstairs specialises in homemade herb breads, and has three-course meals for £16.95.

Elsewhere, the stunning **Inn at Whitewell** (☎ 448222; fax 448298; Whitewell Village; s/d from £80/112) is a remarkable place set amid 1½ hectares of grounds. Once the home of Bowland's forest keeper, it is now a superb guesthouse with a wonderfully eccentric feel. The gorgeous rooms have antique furniture, peat fires and Victorian clawfoot baths. The restaurant (mains £10 to £16) specialises in traditional English game dishes.

Getting There & Around

Clitheroe is served by regular buses from Preston and Blackburn as well as hourly by train from Manchester (£7, 75 mins) and Preston (£5.80, 50 minutes). Once there, you're better off if you have your own transport, as there is only a Sunday bus service between Clitheroe and the rest of the valley villages.

ISLE OF MAN

Mainlanders have long suspected the Isle of Man (Ellan Vannin in Manx) of being an odd place, full of weird island folk and their quirky ways. As 'evidence' they'll point to the island's reputation as a tax haven for wealthy Brits and its summer season of Tourist Trophy (TT) motorbike racing, which every May and June attracts around 50,000 petrol heads. Hardly case closed.

Chances are that those same mainlanders have never actually seen the lush valleys, barren hills and rugged coastlines of what is a surprisingly beautiful island. Perfect for walking, cycling, driving or just relaxing, this is a place that doggedly refuses to sell itself down the river of crass commercialism and mass tourism. Needless to say, if you want a slice of silence, be sure to avoid the TT races, which turn the place into a high-rev bike fest.

Home to the world's oldest continuous parliament, the Isle of Man enjoys special status in Britain, and its annual parliamentary ceremony honours the thousand year history of the Tynwald (a Scandinavian word meaning 'meeting field'). Douglas, the capital, is a run-down relic of Victorian tourism with

fading B&Bs. The tailless Manx cat and the four-horned Loghtan sheep are unique to the Isle.

Orientation & Information

Situated in the Irish Sea, equidistant from Liverpool, Dublin and Belfast, the Isle of Man is about 33 miles long by 13 miles wide. Ferries arrive at Douglas, the port and main town on the southeast coast. Flights come in to Ronaldsway airport, 10 miles south of Douglas. Most of the island's historic sites are operated by Manx Heritage, which offers free admission to National Trust or English Heritage members. Unless otherwise indicated, **Manx Heritage** (MH; ☎ 648000; www.gov.im/mnh) sites are open 10am to 5pm daily, Easter to October. The Manx Heritage **4 Site Pass** (adult/child £10/5) grants you entry into four of the island's heritage attractions; pick it up at any of the tourist offices.

Walking & Cycling

There are plenty of walking trails. Ordnance Survey (OS) Landranger Map 95 (£6.49) covers the whole island, while the free *Walks on the Isle of Man* is available from the tourist office in Douglas. The **Millennium Way** is a walking path that runs the length of the island amid some spectacular scenery. The most demanding of all the island's walks is the 95-mile **Raad ny Foillan** (Road of the Gull), a well-marked path that makes a complete circuit of the island and normally takes about five days to complete. The **Isle of Man Walking Festival** (www.isleofmanwalking.com) takes place over five days in June. It only kicked off in 2004, but it has already proven a favourite with walkers from all over Britain.

There are six designated off-road cycling tracks on the island, each with varying ranges of difficulty.

The island is also home to the **International Cycling Week Festival**, which takes place in mid-July. It's a pretty serious affair, attracting top cyclists from around the world as well as enthusiastic Sunday racers. Check with the tourist office in Douglas for details.

DOUGLAS

☎ 01624 / pop 22,200

All roads lead to Douglas, which is a bit of a shame, as the town isn't all that endearing. Still, it has the best of the island's hotels and restaurants – as well as the bulk of the

ISLE OF MAN

finance houses frequented so regularly by tax-allergic Brits. The **tourist office** (☎ 686766; www.visitisleofman.com; Sea Terminal Bldg; ⊙ 9.15am-7pm daily May-Sep, 9am-5pm daily Apr & Oct, 9am-5.30pm Mon-Fri & 9am-12.30pm Sat Nov-Mar) makes accommodation bookings for free.

The **Manx Museum** (MH; admission free; ⊙ 10am-5pm Mon-Sat) gives an introduction to everything from the island's prehistoric past to the latest TT race winners.

Sleeping & Eating

The seafront promenade is crammed with B&Bs. Unless you booked back in the 1990s, however, there's little chance of finding accommodation during TT week and the weeks each side of it. The tourist office's camping information sheet lists sites all around the island.

Admiral House (☎ 629551; www.admiralhouse.com; Loch Promenade; s/d £50/80; P) Newly refurbished to a high standard of comfort, this elegant guesthouse overlooks the harbour near the ferry port. The 23 spotless and modern rooms are a cheerful alternative to the worn look of a lot of other seafront B&Bs. In the basement, the smart Ciapelli's is a top-notch Italian restaurant that is probably the best eatery in town, serving mains for around £9 to £12.

Sefton Hotel (☎ 645500; www.seftonhotel.co.im; Harris Promenade; s/d from £80/90; P ⊠) Douglas' best hotel is an upmarket oasis with its own indoor water garden and rooms that range from plain and comfy to elegant and very luxurious. The rooms overlooking the water garden are superb, even better than the ones with sea views. You save up to 10% if you book online.

Claremont (☎ 698800; www.sleepwellhotels.com; 18-19 Loch Promenade; d/ste £105/140; P ⌨) The last word in contemporary business style in Douglas, the Claremont has very bright, airy rooms with all the latest gizmos – DVD players, internet connections and fancy TVs – as well as beautiful limestone bathrooms. The executive rooms have terrific harbour views.

Spill the Beans (☎ 614167; 1 Market Hill; snacks £2-4; ☺ 9.30am-6pm Mon-Sat) The most pleasant coffee shop in Douglas delivers proper caffeine kicks as well as cakes, buns and other sweet snacks.

Tanroagan (☎ 472411; 9 Ridgeway St; mains £9-15; ☺ lunch & dinner Mon-Fri, dinner only Sat) The place for all things from the sea, this elegant eatery is the trendiest place in Douglas, serving fresh fish straight off the boats, given the merest of continental twists or just a spell on the hot grill. Reservations are recommended.

There are a few good pubs around, including the trendy **Bar George** (☎ 617799; St George's Chambers, 3 Hill St) and the originally named **Rover's Return** (☎ 676459; 11 Church St), specialising in the local brew, Bushy Ales.

AROUND DOUGLAS

You can follow the TT course up and over the mountain or wind around the coast. The mountain route goes close to the summit of **Snaefell** (621m), the island's highest point. It's an easy walk up to the summit, or take the electric tram from Laxey on the coast.

On the edge of Ramsey is the **Grove Rural Life Museum** (MH; admission £3; ☺ 10am-5pm Apr-Oct). The church in the small village of **Maughold** is on the site of an ancient monastery; a small shelter houses quite a good selection of stone crosses and ancient inscriptions.

It's no exaggeration to describe the **Lady Isabella Laxey Wheel** (MH; admission £3), built in 1854 to pump water from a mine, as a 'great' wheel; it measures 22m across and can draw 1140L of water per minute from a depth of 550m. It is named after the wife of the then lieutenant-governor and is the largest wheel of its kind in the world. The wheel-headed cross at **Lonan Old Church** is the island's most impressive early Christian cross.

CASTLETOWN & AROUND

At the southern end of the island is Castletown, a quiet harbour town that was originally the capital of the Isle of Man. The town is dominated by the impressive 13th-century **Castle Rushen** (MH; admission £4.25). The flag tower affords fine views of the town and coast. There's also a small **Nautical Museum** (MH; admission £3) displaying, among other things, its pride and joy, *Peggy*, a boat built in 1791 and still housed in its original boathouse. There is a school dating back to 1570 in **St Mary's church** (MH; admission free) behind the castle.

Between Castletown and Cregneash, the Iron Age hillfort at **Chapel Hill** encloses a Viking ship burial site.

On the southern tip of the island, the **Cregneash Village Folk Museum** (MH; admission £3) recalls traditional Manx rural life. The **Calf of Man**, the small island just off Cregneash, is a bird sanctuary. **Calf Island Cruises** (☎ 832339; adult/child £10/5; ☺ 10.15am, 11.30am & 1.30pm Apr-Oct weather permitting) run between Port Erin and the island.

Port Erin, another Victorian seaside resort, plays host to the small **Railway Museum** (admission £1; ☺ 9.30am-5.30pm daily Apr-Oct) depicting the history of steam railway on the island.

Port Erin has a good range of accommodation, as does Port St Mary, across the headland and linked by steam train.

The splendid Victorian-style **Aaron House** (☎ 835702; www.aaronhouse.co.uk; The Promenade, Port St Mary; s/d from £35/70) is a B&B that has fussed over every detail, from the gorgeous brass beds and claw-foot baths to the old-fashioned photographs on the walls; it's like stepping back in time, minus the inconvenience of cold and discomfort. The sea views are sensational.

PEEL & AROUND

The west coast's most appealing town, Peel has a fine sandy beach, but its real attraction is the 11th-century **Peel Castle** (MH; admission £3), stunningly positioned atop St Patrick's Island and joined to Peel by a causeway.

The excellent **House of Mannanan** (MH; admission £5; ☺ 10am-5pm year round) museum uses interactive displays to explain Manx history and its seafaring traditions. A combined ticket for both the castle and museum costs £7.

Three miles east of Peel is **Tynwald Hill** at St John's, where the annual parliamentary ceremony takes place on 5 July.

Peel has several B&Bs, including the **Fernleigh Hotel** (☎ 842435; www.isleofman.com/accommodation

/fernleigh; Marine Pde; r per person from £21; ⏰ Feb-Nov), which has 12 decent bedrooms; prices include breakfast. For a better-than-average bite, head for the **Creek Inn** (☎ 842216; jeanmcaleer@manx.net; East Quay; mains around £8), opposite the House of Manannan, which serves Manx queenies (scallops served with white cheese sauce) and has self-catering rooms from £35.

GETTING THERE & AWAY
Air
Ronaldsway Airport (☎ 01624-821600; www.iom-airport.com; Ballasalla) is 10 miles south of Douglas near Castletown. Buses link the airport with Douglas every 30 minutes between 7am and 11pm; a taxi should cost you no more than £18. Airline contacts:

Aer Arann (☎ 0800 587 23 24; www.aerarann.com) From London Luton and Dublin.

British Airways (☎ 0870 850 9850; www.britishairways.com) From London Gatwick, Luton and Manchester.

British Northwest Airlines (☎ 0800 083 7783; www.flybnwa.co.uk) From Blackpool.

Eastern Airways (☎ 01652-681099; www.easternairways.com) From Leeds-Bradford, Bristol, Birmingham and East Midlands.

Emerald Airways (☎ 0870 850 5400; www.flyjem.com) From Liverpool.

EuroManx Airlines (☎ 0870 787 7879; www.euromanx.com) From Belfast, Liverpool, London City and Manchester.

Flybe (☎ 0871 700 0535; www.flybe.com) From Birmingham.

Loganair (☎ 0870 850 9850; www.loganair.com) From Glasgow Prestwick; linked with British Airways.

Boat
Isle of Man Steam Packet (☎ 0870 552 3523; www.steam-packet.com; foot passenger single/return £15/30, car & 2 passengers return £138) is a car ferry and high-speed catamaran service from Liverpool and Heysham to Douglas. There is also a summer service to Dublin (three hours, mid-April to mid-September).

GETTING AROUND
The island has a comprehensive bus service; the tourist office in Douglas has timetables and sells tickets. It also sells the **Island Explorer** (1-day adult/child £10/5, 3-day £20/10), which gives you free transport for the apposite period on all public transport, including the tram to Snaefell and Douglas' horse-trams.

Bikes can be hired from **Eurocycles** (☎ 624909; 8A Victoria Rd; per day £14-18; ⏰ Mon-Sat).

Petrol heads will love the scenic, sweeping bends that make for some exciting driving – and the fact that outside of Douglas town there's no speed limit. Naturally, the most popular drive is along the TT route. Car-hire operators have desks at the airport, and charge from £30 per day.

The 19th-century electric and steam **rail services** (☎ 01624-663366; ⏰ Easter-Sep) are a thoroughly satisfying way of getting from A to B:

Douglas–Castletown–Port Erin Steam Train (£8.40 return)

Douglas–Laxey–Ramsey Electric Tramway (£5.20 return)

Laxey–Summit Snaefell Mountain Railway (£7.40 return)

Cumbria & the Lakes

Cumbria is where rural England unexpectedly takes a walk on the wild side. Crammed into the northwest corner of the country, hard against the border with Scotland, the region's restless landscape was sculpted by glaciers during the last ice age, and weathered into its present form by several millennia of Atlantic winds, Arctic ice and British rain. Riven by sweeping valleys, pockmarked by slate-capped fells and crisscrossed by drystone walls, it's a place that's packed with more natural drama and rich history than almost anywhere else in England.

Though modern Cumbria is a relatively young county, formed in 1974 from the old districts of Cumberland and Westmorland, its history stretches back much further. Stone Age tribes, pagan druids, Viking settlers and Roman legionaries have all left their own mark on the landscape, and for much of the Middle Ages this was a region characterised by conflict, ominously dubbed 'the Debatable Lands' and regularly plundered by Scottish raiders known as Border Reivers. Evidence of its martial past is clear to see in the many fortresses dotted around the region, from the tumbledown keeps of Penrith and Kendal to the massive castle at Carlisle.

But these days Cumbria is better known for its natural charms than its warlike ways. Ever since the arrival of the railway at Windermere in the mid-19th century, people have been flocking here to explore the region's breathtaking mountain walks, glittering lakes and hilltop trails for themselves. The region continues to attract some 14 million visitors every year, most of whom head straight for the Central Lakes; but it's worth taking the time to explore the lesser-known areas of Cumbria too, from the rolling fields and quiet farms of the Eden valley to the sparkling sands and historic ports around the county's coastline.

HIGHLIGHTS

- Tackling some of the Lake District's classic peaks, including **Helvellyn** (p712) and **Scaféll Pike** (p704)

- Drinking in the dramatic views from the **Langdale Valley** (p702)

- Gazing out at the English frontier from the walls of **Carlisle Castle** (p719)

- Exploring the literary landmarks of **Brantwood** (p701) and **Rydal Mount** (p697)

- Taking a leisurely cruise on the lakes of **Windermere** (p688) or **Derwent Water** (p706)

- Pondering Britain's mysterious past at **Castlerigg Stone Circle** (p708)

- ★ Carlisle
- Derwent Water ★ ★ Castlerigg Stone Circle
- ★ Helvellyn
- Scaféll Pike ★ ★ ★ Rydal Mount Langdale
- Brantwood ★ ★ Windermere

- POPULATION: 487,607
- AREA: 2629 SQ MILES

Activities

CYCLING

Cycling is popular in Cumbria, although you'll need sturdy legs to negotiate the region's hills. Mountain biking and downhilling on the fells is fantastic, but you'll need nerves of steel on the more challenging routes. Cycle-hire shops are dotted all over Cumbria, and tourist offices stock a useful Cumbria cycling map showing all the best traffic-free routes.

The Cumbrian section of the 140-mile **Sea to Sea Cycle Route** (C2C; www.c2c-guide.co.uk) begins in Whitehaven and passes through the northern Lake District en route to the North Pennines and Newcastle. For something more challenging, there's the 259-mile circular **Cumbria Cycle Way** (www.golakes.co.uk/map/walks.asp) around Ulverston, Keswick and Carlisle.

WALKING

Many people visit the Lakes solely for its spectacular hiking. The region is covered by a network of footpaths and walking trails, ranging from low-level rambles to full-blown mountain ascents. There are lots of guidebooks available detailing walking routes (see boxed text, p687), sold at tourist offices and bookshops. The classic tome is Alfred Wainwright's hand-drawn, seven-volume set detailing all of Cumbria's main peaks, *A Pictorial Guide to the Lakeland Fells*; the original versions are great for inspiration but need to be read alongside a modern map. Now published by Frances Lincoln, Wainwright's books are currently being updated and rewritten volume by volume, and 'bagging' some of Wainwright's fells remains a rite of passage for many serious walkers.

Wainwright also dreamt up one of northern England's classic walks, the **Coast to Coast** (www.golakes.co.uk/map/walks.asp), which cuts west to east from St Bees to Robin Hood's Bay in North Yorkshire, a distance of 191 miles. The Cumbrian section passes through Honister Pass, Grasmere, Patterdale, Kirkby Stephen and Shap en route to the Yorkshire Dales, a five- to seven-day hike of 82 miles.

Door-to-door baggage services can be useful if you don't want to lug your pack along the whole route. Contact **Coast to Coast Packhorse** (☎ 017683-71689; www.cumbria.com/packhorse), **Sherpa Van** (☎ 020-8569 4101; www.sherpavan.com) or **Brigantes Baggage Couriers** (☎ 01729-830463; www .pikedaw.freeserve.co.uk/walks).

OTHER ACTIVITIES

Cumbria is a haven for adrenaline-fuelled activities ranging from rock-climbing, orienteering and quad biking to the traditional sport of fell running, and newer variants such as ghyll scrambling (a cross between coasteering and river canyoning).

Sailing, kayaking and windsurfing are obviously popular too, especially around Windermere, Derwent Water and Coniston.

Check out www.lakedistrictoutdoors.co.uk, which also publishes a useful brochure available from tourist offices.

Tours

Tailor-made holidays and specialist tours are provided by many companies.

Contours (☎ 017684-80451; www.contours.co.uk) Well-organised walking-holiday provider with a selection of self-guided Cumbrian packages.

Cloudberry Holidays (☎ 01539-733522; www.cloud berry.co.uk; Kendal) Specialist company that provides hiking trips for the YHA.

High Points (☎ 015395-30386; www.highpoints.co.uk; Newby Bridge) Outdoors centre specialising in hill-walking, orienteering, climbing, ghyll scrambling and canoeing.

Knobbly Stick (☎ 01539-737576; www.knobblystick .com; Kendal) Small walking-holiday company with routes through Ullswater, Wasdale, Kendal and the Eastern Lakes.

Mountain Goat (Map p690; ☎ 015394-45161; www .mountain-goat.com; Victoria St, Windermere) Half- and full-day minibus tours (£18.95 to £29.95) of sights across the Lake District.

River Deep Mountain High (☎ 015395-31116; www .rdmh.co.uk; Haverthwaite) Multi-activity company offering archery, climbing, sailing and cycling tours.

Summitreks (☎ 015394-41212; www.summitreks .co.uk; Coniston) Long-established activity company and outdoors-equipment provider.

Getting There & Away

There's a direct rail link from Manchester Airport via Preston and Lancaster to Barrow-in-Furness (2½ hours) and Windermere (2¼ hours). To both Windermere and Carlisle, coaches from London take about 6½ hours, trains 3½ hours.

Getting Around

Traveline (☎ 0870 608 2608; www.traveline-cumbria .co.uk) provides travel information. Tourist offices stock the free *Getting Around Cumbria* booklet, with timetables for buses, trains and ferries.

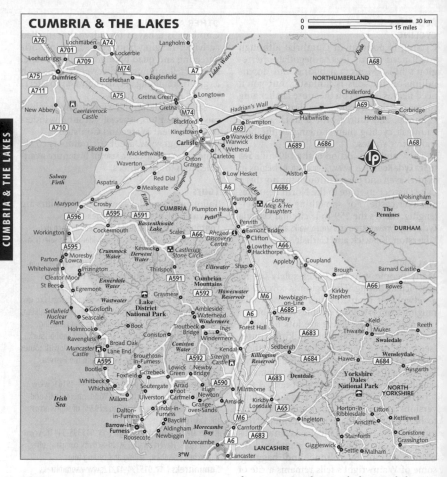

CUMBRIA & THE LAKES

BOAT

Windermere, Coniston Water, Ullswater and Derwent Water all offer ferry services, providing time-saving links for walkers. The **Cross-Lakes Shuttle** (☎ 015394-45161) runs shuttle boats and minibuses between Windermere, Esthwaite Water, Grizedale and Coniston Water; cyclists and hikers are welcome. See the Windermere & Bowness, Coniston and Keswick sections for details.

BUS

The main operator is **Stagecoach** (www.stage coachbus.com). The Explorer ticket (1/4/7 days £8.50/19/26.50), available on the bus, gives unlimited travel on services in Cumbria. There are also Dayrider tickets to various

districts in Cumbria, including Carlisle, Barrow and the West, East and Central Lakes.

Stagecoach operates several useful cross-county buses, including bus 555/556, (Lakes-Link) between Lancaster and Carlisle, which stops at all the main towns; bus 505 (Coniston Rambler), linking Kendal, Windermere, Ambleside and Coniston; and the X4/X5 from Penrith to Workington via Troutbeck, Keswick, and Cockermouth.

The free *Lakesrider* booklet has comprehensive timetables.

CAR

The park authorities are very keen to cut the amount of traffic that clogs up the region, especially on summer weekends, and it's entirely

---

TOP FIVE LAKE DISTRICT BOOKS

- *A Pictorial Guide to the Lakeland Fells* (Frances Lincoln Ltd) – Alfred Wainwright's seven-volume series is the classic walking guide (though you'll need a modern map too)
- *Collin's Lakeland Fellranger* (Collins) – The modern-day successor to Wainwright's guides, impeccably researched by author Mark Richards
- *Pathfinder Guides* (Ordnance Survey, Jarrold) – Another excellent walking series with extracts from Ordnance Survey (OS) maps
- *A Walk Round the Lakes* (Orion) – An entertaining guide to the history of the Lakes by Hunter Davies
- *A Complete Guide to the Lakes* (Frances Lincoln Ltd) – Wordsworth wrote the first travel guide to the Lake District in 1810, and it's still a descriptive read (even if it is a little out of date)

---

possible to get around the Lakes without a car, thanks to the extensive bus network and the main rail link to Windermere. Parking can be a real headache during busy periods anyway, so you might well be thankful you left the car at home.

TRAIN

Aside from the Cumbrian Coast Line and the branch line from Oxenholme to Windermere, there are several steam railways. If you fancy a ride on a steam train, try the Ravenglass & Eskdale Railway (p716) or the Ambleside/Bowness to Haverthwaite Steam Railway (p690).

*Oh there is blessing in this gentle breeze
That blows from the green fields and
from the clouds
And from the sky: it beats against my
cheek,
And seems half-conscious of the joy it
gives.*

William Wordsworth
from The Prelude (1805)

LAKE DISTRICT

For sheer scenic splendour, few places in England can measure up to the outlandishly beautiful Lake District, where Wordsworth, Coleridge and their Romantic compatriots famously sought their poetic muse in the 19th century. The landscape of the Lakes is as breathtaking as any you'll find in Switzerland or the French Alps – a sweeping panorama of humpbacked mountains, razorblade crags and scree-covered hillsides, strewn with mountainous tarns and some of the largest

natural lakes anywhere in England. With such a wealth of natural riches, it's hardly surprising that the Lake District is one of the country's favourite places for savouring the great outdoors, but there's much more to this region than fine views – it's also packed with history and culture, from the abandoned slate mines around Honister and the ruined abbey of Furness to the literary landmarks of Dove Cottage and Rydal Mount, both former homes of one William Wordsworth.

Orientation

The Lake District is shaped in a rough star formation, with valleys, ridges and lakes radiating out from the high ground at its centre. The main bases are Keswick in the north and Windermere and Bowness in the south. Ambleside and Coniston are less hectic alternatives. Windermere is the biggest, busiest lake. Ullswater, Coniston and Derwent Water lakes have a speed restriction of 10mph, and powerboats are banned on Grasmere, Crummock Water and Buttermere. Wastwater is the wildest and least accessible valley.

Information

The region's network of tourist offices stocks mountains of information on accommodation and exploring the Lake District, whether by bus or bike, or on foot. The branches in Windermere and Keswick are the most efficient, or there's a flagship **visitor centre** (☎ 015394-46601; www.lake-district.gov.uk) at Brockhole, on the A591 near Windermere. Some of the smaller centres (eg Hawkshead and Grasmere) were closed during recent cutbacks, much to the chagrin of local businesses. Most tourist offices will book accommodation for a charge of £3.

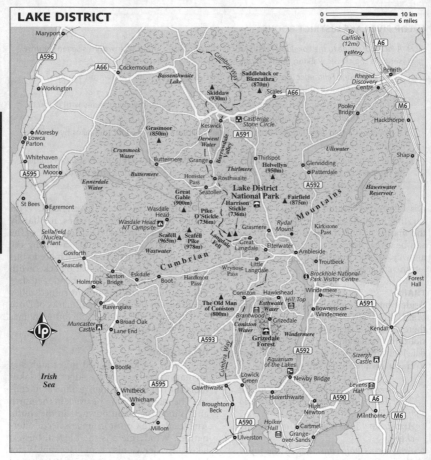

LAKE DISTRICT

CUMBRIA & THE LAKES

Hostels & Camping Barns

There's a fantastic selection of over 30 YHA hostels in the Lake District, including some of the organisation's flagship sites. The main point for information is **Ambleside YHA** (☎ 0870 770 5672, ambleside@yha.org.uk). Bookings for most of the area's hostels can be made direct via phone, email or the YHA reservations website (www.yhabooking.org.uk). The YHA provides a useful shuttle bus around the eight main hostels, and offers free pick-up from Windermere train station – contact Ambleside YHA for details and bookings.

Camping barns – sometimes called 'stone tents' – are run by both the National Park Authority and the YHA, costing from £6 per person per night; you need all the usual camp-ing gear apart from a tent. Contact **Lakeland Camping Barns** (☎ 01946-758198; www.lakelandcamp ingbarns.co.uk) for more information.

WINDERMERE & BOWNESS

☎ 015394 / pop 8203

Framed by fells and encircled by a wooded shoreline, Lake Windermere is the larg-est natural lake in England, stretching in a silvery north–south line all the way from Ambleside to Newby Bridge for a distance of some 10½ miles. Ever since the arrival of the steam railway in 1847 – something that was passionately opposed by William Wordsworth – Windermere has served as the main gateway to the Lake District, and it remains one of the region's busiest spots.

The town itself is split into two main areas – Windermere town, 1½ miles uphill from the lake, and Bowness-on-Windermere, from where cruise boats have been chugging across the waters of the lake since the early 19th century.

Orientation

Windermere town is where you'll find the most restaurants and B&Bs, as well as the main train and bus station. The main road leads 1½ miles downhill to Bowness, which is packed with tearooms, ice-cream shops and boat companies selling tickets for cross-lake cruises.

Information

Brockhole National Park Visitor Centre (☎ 46601; www.lake-district.gov.uk; ☒ 10am-5pm late Mar-Oct) Flagship visitor centre 3 miles north of Windermere on the A591.

Library (☎ 62400; Broad St; ☒ 9am-7pm Mon, 9am-5pm Tue, Thu & Fri, 9am-1pm Sat, closed Wed) Internet access.

Post office (21 Crescent Rd; ☒ 9am-5.30pm Mon-Sat)

Tourist offices Bowness-On-Windermere (☎ 42895; bownesstic@lake-district.gov.uk; Glebe Rd; ☒ 9.30am-5.30pm Easter-Oct, 10am-4pm Fri-Sun Nov-Mar); Windermere (☎ 46499; windermeretic@southlakeland.gov.uk; Victoria St; internet access per 10 mins £1; ☒ 9am-5.30pm Mon-Sat, 9.30am-5.30pm Sun Apr-Oct, hours vary in winter)

Sights

Blackwell Arts & Crafts House (☎ 46139; www.blackwell.org.uk; admission £5.45; ☒ 10.30am-5pm Apr-Oct, 10am-4pm Feb-Mar, Nov-Dec) is one of the finest examples of the Arts and Crafts movement, distinguished by its simple, elegant architecture and sense of space. The house was designed by Mackay Hugh Baillie Scott in the 19th century for a wealthy brewer, and contains many of his trademark designs, including Delft tiles and some gorgeous 18th-century oak panelling. A collection of antiques and furniture from the Arts and Crafts movement is also on display.

The **Windermere Steamboat Museum** (☎ 45565; www.steamboat.co.uk; Rayrigg Rd; admission £3.50; ☒ 10am-5pm July–mid-Sep, 10.30am-4.30pm Apr-June, 10.30am-4.30pm mid-Sep–Nov) will delight closet steamboat Willies, with a marvellous collection of vessels including Beatrix Potter's rowing boat and the *Esperance*, which doubled as Captain Flint's houseboat in the BBC adaptation of *Swallows and Amazons*. The museum offers lake trips on vintage boats (£5.50) from July to September.

Tucked away off Lake Road, the **World of Beatrix Potter** (☎ 88444; www.hop-skip-jump.com; adult/child £6/3; ☒ 10am-5.30pm Apr-Sep, 10am-4.30pm Oct-Mar) is always packed with Beatrix Potter enthusiasts of all ages, as well as an astonishing number of camera-toting Japanese tourists. Various scenes from Potter's books are brought to life inside, including Peter Rabbit's garden and Mr McGregor's greenhouse, and there's a shop with enough Potter-themed memorabilia to satisfy even the most ardent fan.

Aquarium of the Lakes (☎ 015395-30153; www.aquariumofthelakes.co.uk; Lakeside, Newby Bridge; admission £7; ☒ 9am-6pm Apr-Oct, 9am-5pm Nov-Mar) is at the lake's southern end and recreates over 30 freshwater habitats, including an underwater tunnel through Windermere's lakebed, complete with pike, Arctic char and diving ducks. As usual, though, the mischievous otters steal the show. The best way to arrive is by boat from Bowness or Ambleside (see below), or there are regular buses to Newby Bridge, a mile away from the aquarium.

Activities
BOAT TRIPS

Somewhat bizarrely, Lake Windermere is officially a public highway – giving it the same status as a main road or an intercity motorway – and in the early 19th century cargo ships carrying coal, lumber, copper and slate were a common sight on its waters. The first steam passenger ferry was launched on the lake in 1845, just two years before the railway arrived in town, and lake cruises quickly became one of the town's most popular pastimes (and biggest earners).

Windermere's boating heritage continues to this day thanks to **Windermere Lake Cruises** (☎ 015395-31188; www.windermere-lakecruises.co.uk), which offers trips on both modern launches and a couple of period beauties dating back to the 1930s. Regular colour-coded cruises depart from Bowness Pier. The Yellow Cruise runs to Lakeside and back (£7.60 return, hourly), while the Red Cruise runs to Ambleside (£5.50 return, half-hourly). The Blue Cruise offers a leisurely 45-minute cruise around the lake's shoreline and bays (£5.50 return, half-hourly). There are also launch services to Brockhole, Waterhead, Fell Foot and Ferry Landing, from where a shuttle bus departs to Beatrix Potter's cottage at Hill Top (p701) and to xHawkshead (p699) in summer. A Freedom of the

CUMBRIA & THE LAKES

Book accomm

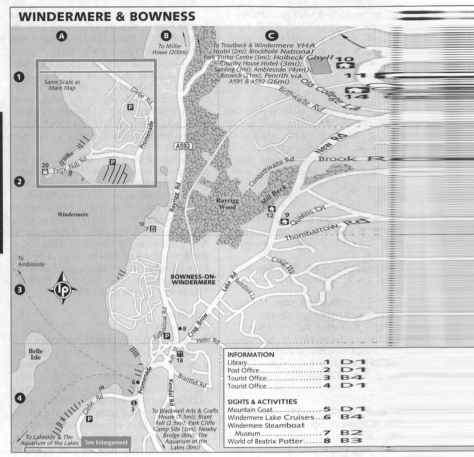

WINDERMERE & BOWNESS

To Miller
Howe (200m)

To Troutbeck & Windermere YHA
Hostel (2mi); Brockhole National
Park Visitor Centre (3mi); Holbeck Ghyll
Country House Hotel (3mi);
Samling (3mi); Ambleside (4mi);
Keswick (21mi); Penrith via
A591 & A592 (26mi)

Same Scale as
Main Map

Glebe Rd

Promenade

A592

Ferry Nab Rd

Old College La

Birthwaite Rd

New Rd

Brook Rd

Combirthwaite Rd

Rayrigg Rd

Windermere

Rayrigg
Wood

Mill Beck

Queens Dr

Thornbarrow Rd

To
Ambleside

BOWNESS-ON-
WINDERMERE

Lake Rd

Belsfield La

Craig Wk

Belle
Isle

Fallbarrow Rd

Crag Brow

Helm Rd

Ash St

Promenade

Kendal Rd

Brantfell Rd

Glebe Rd

To Blackwell Arts & Crafts
House (1.5mi); Brant
Fell (2.5mi); Park Cliffe
Camp Site (3mi); Newby
Bridge (8mi); The
Aquarium of the
Lakes (8mi)

To Lakeside & The
Aquarium of the Lakes

See Enlargement

INFORMATION
Library	1	D1
Post Office	2	D1
Tourist Office	3	B4
Tourist Office	4	D1

SIGHTS & ACTIVITIES
Mountain Goat	5	D1
Windermere Lake Cruises	6	B4
Windermere Steamboat Museum	7	B2
World of Beatrix Potter	8	B3

Lakes ticket allows unlimited cruises (1/3 days, £13.25/24).

Joint tickets tie in with the **Ambleside/Bowness to Haverthwaite Steam Railway** (☎ 015395-31594; return from Bowness £12, from Ambleside £16.50; Apr-Oct) and the **Aquarium of the Lakes** (return ferry & aquarium from Bowness £13.10, from Ambleside £18.75).

You can hire open- and closed-top boats (£14/16) from beside the tourist office on Bowness Pier.

Sleeping
BUDGET
Lake District Backpackers Lodge (☎ 46374; www .lakedistrictbackpackers.co.uk; High St; dm £13.50;) A cramped, basic and rather spartan backpackers, squeezed into a converted slate-roofed

house near the train
walking tours can be
Windermere YHA Host
.org.uk; Bridge Lane, Troutb
Nov, book ahead at other ti
whitewashed hostel st
grounds and offers ro
well as a handy dryin
and a well-stocked s
the station, and offe
phone ahead.
Park Cliffe camp site (
Birks Rd; sites per tent £18)
with all the mod con
It's midway between
Bridge, off the A592;
off, about half a mile

CUMBRIA & THE LAKES

MIDRANGE

Archway (☎ 45613; www.communiken.com/archway; 13 College Rd; d £40-48; ✗) A much-recommended Windermere favourite, located inside a solid grey-stone terraced house along College Rd. The rooms are comfy and understated, with nary a floral pattern in sight, but the real draw here is the gargantuan breakfast of dry-cured bacon, Manx kippers and homemade pancakes.

Applegarth Hotel (☎ 43206; www.applegarthhotel.co.uk; s/d from £40/60; P ✗) Formerly the home of the Victorian industrial magnate John Riggs, this grand manor house certainly shows signs of the splendour of yesteryear. Light streams through stained-glass windows into the wood-panelled foyer, and the house is full of polished period furniture and original cornicing; though the rooms aren't all as impressive, they're still a cut above the B&B norm.

Coach House (☎ 44494; www.lakedistrictbandb.com; Lake Rd; d £54-74; P ✗) An extraordinary little B&B decorated with real flair and imagination – forget flowery bedspreads and magnolia walls, here it's all citrus colours, fairy pinks and duck-egg blues offset by chequerboard floors and cast-iron beds. Some people might find it a little too minimal for their tastes, but if you're looking for something a little out of the ordinary, this funky little gem certainly won't disappoint.

21 The Lakes (☎ 45052; www.21thelakes.co.uk; Lake Rd; d midweek from £70, weekends £110; P ✗) This newly opened boutique B&B is streets ahead of the other hotels around Windermere. Various rooms around the detached townhouse have been converted in their own unique style, from super-frilly four-poster suites to a futuristic beauty that comes with widescreen TV, abstract art and a groovy floating bed.

Waverley (☎ 45026; www.waverleyhotel.com; College Rd; d £76-92; P ✗) Just along the road from Applegarth, this traditional hotel is almost drowned by ivy and creepers in summer, and offers simple, sunny-coloured bedrooms (some of which are rather on the snug side).

TOP END

Holbeck Ghyll Country House Hotel (☎ 32375; www.holbeckghyll.com; Holbeck Lane; s/d £135/190-370) At the more traditional end of the scale sits the ever-so slightly stuffy Holbeck Ghyll, once an aristocratic hunting lodge, and now a favourite Lakeland country retreat. The rooms are big, posh and old-fashioned, mixing Laura Ashley wallpapers with matching furniture and the odd brass chandelier.

our pick Samling (☎ 31922; www.thesamling.com; Dove Nest; r weekdays £195-395, weekends £225-425; P ✗) The venue of choice for A-list celebrities taking a break in the Lakes, this utterly bewitching country-house hotel pulls no punches in terms of luxury, sophistication and style. Set on 67 acres of impeccably kept grounds, the bedrooms at the Samling are all decadent with a capital D, ranging from antique-heavy attic suites to a split-level cottage with mezzanine bedroom and an outdoor Jacuzzi. It's quite rightly a favourite with hotel guides and fashion magazines, and if your budget can bear the damage, it's worth the expense.

Eating

Lighthouse (☎ 88260; Main Rd; mains £8-20; ✗ breakfast, lunch & dinner) A buzzy continental café-restaurant split over three floors. It covers practically all bases, from breakfasts of cappuccino and cinnamon waffles through to sophisticated suppers of fell-bred lamb and sirloin steak.

Kwela's (☎ 44954; 4 High St; mains £11-17; ✗ dinner Tue-Sun) African flavours underpin the menu of this unusual new restaurant, offering intriguing dishes such as moorish skewers and South African *bobotie* (curried lamb with almonds) in an atmospheric dining area filled with canvas chairs and a sackcloth ceiling.

Porthole (☎ 42793; 2 Ash St; mains £11-25; ✗ dinner Wed-Mon) An old hand on the Windermere dining scene, this friendly restaurant specialises in fish and seafood, served at small tables in the hugger-mugger dining room accompanied by a great selection of vintage wines.

Jericho's (☎ 42522; Birch St; mains from £16; ✗ dinner Tue-Sun) The atmosphere at Jericho's might be a little outmoded, but the food's thoroughly up to date, with a menu that ranges from shellfish risotto to pan-seared seabass. The small open-plan kitchen lets you watch the chefs at work.

Getting There & Away
BUS

National Express coaches run from London (£29, eight to nine hours, three times daily), sometimes travelling via Lancaster or Birmingham.

Bus 555/556 travels from Lancaster (1½ hours) via Kendal (30 minutes) to Windermere, before continuing to Ambleside (20 minutes), Grasmere (30 minutes) and Keswick

---

WORTH THE TRIP

Drunken Duck Inn (☎ 36347; www.drunkenduckinn.co.uk; Barngates, Ambleside; mains £15-23; r weekdays £90-185, weekends £115-220; **P** ⊠) This much-fêted place is a gorgeous cross between a traditional Lakeland inn and a thoroughly modern gastropub. The heart of the Drunken Duck, unsurprisingly, is the main bar, where contemporary leather chairs sit happily alongside stuffed stags' heads and period posters, and a huge ale blackboard is chalked up behind the slate-topped bar. The award-winning country restaurant offers a menu stuffed with bold and inventive dishes – pigeon marinated in liquorice, perhaps, or venison with chestnut polenta – and the upstairs rooms are all delightful, packed with special little touches such as Roberts radios, unusual prints and bespoke fabrics.

(50 minutes). There are 10 to 12 buses daily Monday to Saturday, with five direct buses on Sunday.

Bus 505 travels from Windermere to Coniston (40 minutes, eight daily Monday to Saturday, six on Sunday) via Ambleside.

The open-topped, half-hourly 599 bus links Grasmere, Ambleside, Brockhole, Windermere, Bowness and Kendal.

TRAIN

Windermere is on the branch line from Oxenholme (30 minutes, hourly), near Kendal, which connects with London Euston (£106.50, 3½ hours, eight to 10 times daily Monday to Saturday, four on Sunday) to Glasgow or Edinburgh.

AROUND BOWNESS
Troutbeck
☎ 015394

The hilltop hamlet of Troutbeck consists of little more than an old post office, a few crumbling barns and a knot of cob-walled cottages tucked away along the main road through the village. The main reason to visit is **Townend** (NT; ☎ 32628; admission £3.60; ☯ Wed-Sun Mar-Oct), a beautifully preserved Lakeland farmhouse that was built for a wealthy yeoman in the 17th century and has been owned by the Browne family for just under 400 years. The house still contains books, papers and a collection of old farming tools, as well as some original wooden furniture carved by the family.

The **Mortal Man** (☎ 33193; www.themortalman .co.uk; s/d £65/90) is the village's oldest pub, perched in a commanding spot overlooking the Troutbeck Valley. Real ale and hearty pub lunches are served either in the main bar or on the fellview terrace on sunny days; upstairs there are twelve pleasant, rather faded rooms.

Four miles north of the village is the dramatic Kirkstone Pass, which cuts through the fells before winding down towards Lake Windermere.

Bus 517 stops outside the Queen's Head pub on its way from Patterdale to Windermere (12 minutes, three times daily in July and August, weekends only September to June).

KENDAL
☎ 01539 / pop 27,545

The sturdy, grey-slate town of Kendal is practically synonymous with its super-sweet mintcake, a peppermint-flavoured bar that sustained Edmund Hillary and Tensing Norgay on their ascent of Everest in 1953, and still finds its way into the backpacks of many seasoned walkers in the Lake District. During the Middle Ages, Kendal was renowned as a centre for the cloth and wool trades, and the town remains the main commercial centre in the southern Lakes, with some excellent museums and one of the best arts complexes in the county.

Information

Kendal Laundrette (☎ 733754; Blackhall Rd; ☯ 8am-6pm Mon-Fri, 8am-5pm Sat & Sun)

Library (☎ 773520; Stricklandgate; Internet access per hr £2; ☯ 9.30am-5.30pm Mon & Tue, 9.30am-7pm Wed & Fri, 9.30am-1pm Thu, 9am-4pm Sat, noon-4pm Sun)

Post office (75 Stricklandgate; ☯ 9am-5.30pm Mon-Fri, 9am-12.30pm Sat)

Tourist office (☎ 725758; kendaltic@southlakeland .gov.uk; Highgate; ☯ 9am-5pm Mon-Sat Nov-Easter, 10am-4pm Sun Easter-Oct) Inside the town hall.

Sights

Kendal Museum (☎ 721374; www.kendalmuseum.org .uk; Station Rd; admission £2.70; ☯ 10.30am-5.30pm Mon-Sat Apr-Oct, 10.30am-4pm Mon-Sat Feb-Mar & Nov-Dec) was founded in 1796 by a local natural history enthusiast, William Todhunter. Housed in a former wool warehouse, the museum displays local archaeological finds and explores the history of Kendal Castle. There's also a large natural history section, with lots of fossils and spooky stuffed animals. Alfred Wainwright, of *Pictorial Guide* fame, was honorary curator from 1945 to 1974; his former office has been reconstructed inside the museum, with many original Wainwright drawings and a collection of his possessions (including his rucksack, walking jacket and well-chewed pipe).

The **Abbot Hall Art Gallery** (☎ 722464; www.abbothall.org.uk; admission £4.75; ☒ 10.30am-5pm Mon-Sat Apr-Oct, 10.30am-4pm Mon-Sat Nov-Mar) has one of the best arts collections in the northwest, with a strong focus on 18th- and 19th-century portraits and Lakeland landscapes. Highlights include a gallery of 40 drawings and watercolours by John Ruskin (see p701), a fine array of portraits by local artist George Romney and a couple of canvases by JMW Turner.

The **Museum of Lakeland Life** (☎ 722464; www.lakelandmuseum.org.uk; admission £3.75; ☒ 10.30am-5pm Mon-Sat Apr-Oct, 10.30am-4pm Mon-Sat Nov-Mar) is opposite the Abbot Hall Art Gallery. This atmospheric museum retraces the region's past using reconstructed buildings, including an Edwardian street scene, and exhibits on local industries such as spinning, mining and bobbin-making. One room recreates the study of Arthur Ransome, author of *Swallows and Amazons*.

It's worth visiting the 13th-century ruins of **Kendal Castle**, once owned by the family of Katherine Parr, Henry VIII's sixth wife, who was probably born here in 1512. **Castle Howe** – the remains of a Norman motte and bailey – is to the west. At the lower end of town, the 12th-century **parish church** boasts five impressive aisles and several family chapels.

Sleeping

Kendal YHA (☎ 0870 7705893; kendal@yha.org.uk; 118 Highgate; dm £17.50; ☒ Easter-Oct by advance booking; ☐) A decent hostel inside a whitewashed house along the main street through Kendal, handily located for the Brewery Arts Centre. It's only available by advance booking, so phone ahead to make sure it's open.

Lyndhurst Guest House (☎ 723819; www.lyndhurst-kendal.co.uk; 8 South Rd; s/tw/d from £25/50/52; ☒) Another reliable and welcoming B&B within

easy reach of central Kendal, offering eight fluffy rooms decorated in shades of cream and peach.

Highgate Hotel (☎ 724229; www.highgatehotel.co.uk; 128 Highgate; s/d £39/58; ☒ ☒) Right in the middle of town, this black-and-white 18th-century townhouse was built for Kendal's first doctor, but inside it's been thoroughly modernised. The B&B bedrooms come with the usual selection of pine furniture, pale walls and bracket-balanced TVs, but there's not much period character around.

Heaves Hotel (☎ 560396; www.heaveshotel.co.uk; Heaves; s/d from £40/60; ☒ ☒) For something altogether grander, head for this glorious family-run mansion, set on over 10 acres of private grounds and woodland a few miles south of Kendal. It's a classic country house hotel, all gleaming antiques, huge fireplaces and polished mirrors; the traditionally decorated rooms are large and comfortable, and several boast four-poster beds and views across the rolling parkland.

Beech House (☎ 720385; www.beechhouse-kendal.co.uk; 40 Greenside; s £45-75, d £70-90; ☒ ☒) This wonderful B&B is the best option in central Kendal, with a fab range of bedrooms kitted out in natural fabrics, tasteful tones and plasma-screen TVs. The deluxe rooms are worth the extra expense, with small sofa areas and honesty fridges stocked up with booze and cold drinks.

Eating
CAFÉS

Waterside Wholefoods (☎ 729743; Kent View, Waterside; lunches £4-8; ☒ 8.30am-4.30pm Mon-Sat) Great vegetarian food served by the river, with a selection of sandwiches, chillies, soups and quiches, a mouth-watering range of homemade cakes and organic teas to follow.

1657 Chocolate House (☎ 740702; www.thechocolatehouse.co.uk; 54 Branthwaite Brow; lunches £2-6) This Kendal tearoom is a chocoholic's dream come true. Handmade chocolates, toothache-inducing sweets and umpteen varieties of Kendal mintcake are sold on the ground floor; upstairs the lacy café serves ploughman's lunches, cream teas and speciality chocolate drinks – try the orange-tinted Scurvy Knave or the Queen's Corsage, flavoured with violet.

RESTAURANTS

New Moon (☎ 729254; 129 Highgate; mains £9-15; ☒ lunch & dinner Tues-Sat) This fresh, inviting restaurant is the top place to eat in town, serving classic French and modern British food in a bright, contemporary dining room filled with razor-edge tables and stripped wood.

Eclectic (☎ 736184; 36 Kirkland; mains £10-16; ◷ Tue-Sat) Eclectic by name, eclectic by nature; this three-floored café-venue-bar has something of a split personality, with a funky beer and wine bar on the ground floor, a fusion restaurant on the first floor and a private party room on the top level.

Green Room & Vats Bar (◷ from 10am Mon-Sat; pizzas from £8, mains £8-14) The café-bar at the Brewery Arts Centre serves drinks, wraps and sandwiches during the day, and a more upmarket evening menu featuring crispy pizzas and hearty mains such as Grizedale venison and vegetable tian.

Drinking

Mint (☎ 734473; 48/50 Highgate; ◷ to 2am Fri & Sat) Sleek and very chic, this designer bar oozes urban style, from its deep chocolate-coloured sofas to its shiny chrome fixtures and pared-back décor. There's free internet access and an early-evening happy hour, but the real club action kicks in at weekends.

For more traditional drinking, try **Burgundy's Wine Bar** (Lowther St), the traditional **Olde Fleece** (Highgate) or the **Ring O' Bells** (Kirkland Ave), which stands on consecrated ground.

Entertainment

Brewery Arts Centre (☎ 725133; Highgate; www .breweryarts.co.uk) As its name suggests, this former brewery is now the best arts centre in the Lakes, with a brace of cinemas and regular programmes of theatre, dance and live music.

Getting There & Around

BUS

The most useful bus is the 555/556, which stops at Kendal, Windermere, Ambleside, Grasmere and Keswick (10 to 12 daily). There are two daily return buses from Kendal to Coniston (bus 505; 1¼ hours) via Windermere, Hawkshead and Ambleside. Bus X35 travels along the coast to Grange, Newby Bridge, Ulverston and Barrow (hourly Monday to Saturday, three times on Sunday).

TRAIN

Kendal station is on the branch line to Windermere (15 minutes) from Oxenholme, 2 miles

south of town, with hourly trains from Carlisle (£14.80, one hour) and London Euston (£107, four hours).

AROUND KENDAL
Sizergh Castle

South of Kendal is **Sizergh Castle** (☎ 560070; admission £6.20, gardens only £4; ◷ gardens 12.30-5.30pm, castle 1.30-5.30pm Sun-Thu Apr-Oct), home of the Strickland family for over 700 years. The castle is particularly renowned for its collection of antiques, portraits and fine furniture, collected by various members of the family over the centuries, and for its elegant Elizabethan interior. The lavish wood panelling of the Inlaid Chamber was sold to London's Victoria & Albert Museum during hard times, and later returned after 100 years.

Sizergh Castle is 3½ miles south of Kendal along the A590. Bus 555/556 from Grasmere, Ambleside, Windermere and Kendal runs past the castle every hour from Monday to Saturday.

Levens Hall

Two miles further south is **Levens Hall** (☎ 560321; www.levenshall.co.uk; house & gardens £9, gardens only £6; ◷ gardens 10am-5pm, house noon-5pm Sun-Thu Apr–mid-Oct), another impressive Elizabethan manor built around a mid-13th-century *pele* tower. The beautifully kept house is renowned for its fine Jacobean furniture and antique-filled rooms, as well as its historical connections to both Nelson and the Duke of Wellington. It's also famous for its 17th-century topiary garden, which looks like something out of *Alice in Wonderland*, and for its many ghosts – the spirits of Levens Hall include a grey lady, a black dog and a pink lady dressed in a printed dress and a mobcap.

Levens Hall is 5 miles south of Kendal along the A6. Bus 555/556 from Grasmere, Ambleside, Windermere and Kendal stops near the hall roughly every hour.

AMBLESIDE
☎ 015394 / pop 3560

Standing at the northern end of Lake Windermere and backed by an impressive panorama of grey-green fells, the small town of Ambleside is a bustling hub for the region's hikers and trekkers, with more outdoors shops per square foot than almost anywhere else in the Lakes. Victorian villas and slate-fronted houses line the main street all the way to the

SOMETHING FOR THE WEEKEND

Kick your weekend off in style with a night at the swish Waterhead Hotel (p696) in Ambleside, or the more old-fashioned Grey Friar Lodge Hotel (p696). Catch an evening meal at the fabulous Lucy's On A Plate (p696) or the upmarket Glass House (p696) before catching a late-night feature at Zeffirelli's Cinema (p697).

On Saturday it's time for some sightseeing; head for Wordsworth's former houses at Dove Cottage (p697) and Rydal Mount (p697), and grab lunch at the Jumble Room (p699). In the afternoon it's over to Keswick, with stop-offs for a visit to Castlerigg Stone Circle (p708) and an early-evening cruise on Derwent Water (p706), before checking in to the Keswick Country House Hotel (p709).

On Sunday take a leisurely drive into the beautiful Borrowdale valley, with a hearty lunch at the Yew Tree Restaurant (p711) or the historic Fish Hotel (p712) in Buttermere, followed by a brisk walk around Crummock Water to Scale Force, the tallest waterfall in the Lake District.

central square, where you can stock up with new boots, emergency raingear or that all-important industrial-strength sleeping bag before setting out for one of the many walking trails nearby.

Information

Laundromat (☎ 32231; Kelsick Rd; ☺ 10am-6pm)
Library (☎ 32507; Kelsick Rd; internet access per hr £3; ☺ 10am-5pm Mon, Wed & Thu, 10am-7pm Tue & Fri)
Post office (☎ 33267; Market Pl; ☺ 9am-5pm Mon-Fri, 9am-12.30pm Sat)
Tourist office (☎ 32582; www.amblesidetic@southlakeland.gov.uk; Market Cross; ☺ 9am-5pm)

Sights

There's not a great deal to see in Ambleside, although the **Armitt Museum** (☎ 31212; www.armitt.com; Rydal Rd; adult £2.50; ☺ 10am-5pm) is worth a look for its collection of exhibits on the history of the town and several famous Lakeland characters – some of its more unusual artefacts include a lock of John Ruskin's hair, Dorothy Wordsworth's scarf and a gallery of photos by the local photographer Herbert Bell.

The town makes an excellent base for many well-known Lakeland walks. One of the most popular trails is the easy-going woodland stroll up to **Stock Ghyll Force**, a 60ft waterfall plunging into a narrow canyon. For something more strenuous, you could try the hour-long ascent to the top of **Wansfell**, followed by a two-hour return trip via **Jenkins Crag**, with views across to Coniston and the Langdale Pikes. Serious hikers are spoilt for choice – several classic circuits start from Ambleside, including the 10-mile **Fairfield Horseshoe** via Nab Scar, Heron Pike, Fairfield and Dove Crag.

Activities

The brand-new **Low Wood Watersports & Activity Centre** (☎ 39441; watersports@elhmail.co.uk) offers all kinds of ways to get out on the lake, including rowing boats (one/four hours £6/18), kayaks and canoes (two/four hours £10/15), wayfarer sailing boats (two/four hours £30/45) and outboard motor boats (one/four hours £10/33). It also offers sailing, water-skiing and wakeboarding tuition and a climbing wall (£3 per climb).

Ambleside is also on the **Windermere Lake Cruises** route (see p689).

Sleeping

BUDGET

Low Wray (☎ 32810; www.lowwraycampsite.co.uk; sites per adult/car/tent £4.50/3/5; ☺ Easter-Oct) One of three National Trust (NT) camp sites in the Lake District, in a great woody location 3 miles south of Ambleside on the western shore of Windermere.

Ambleside Backpackers (☎ 32340; www.english lakesbackpackers.co.uk; dm £15; P ☒ ☐) This independent hostel offers 72 beds in a converted Lakeland cottage, but the bunk beds are packed in exceedingly tight; thankfully, there's more space to be found in the wood-floored lounge and the huge industrial kitchen.

Ambleside YHA Hostel (☎ 0870-770 5672; ambleside@yha.org.uk; Windermere Rd; dm £19.95; P ☒ ☐) A fantastically organised YHA hostel directly beside the lake, 1 mile south of Ambleside town. It's the centre for many YHA activities and caters for just about every whim, from walking to water sports – though it's very popular and can get a little crowded on busy weekends.

MIDRANGE

Compston House Hotel (☎ 32305; www.compstonhouse
.co.uk; Compston Rd; d from £48; ✗) This imaginative
place is as American as apple pie, run by an
anglicised New York couple who still know
how to give guests the full Stateside welcome.
All the rooms are named after US states, from
flowery Hawaii to maritime Maine (complete
with Cape Cod bedspread), and the breakfast
features authentic American pancakes doused
in maple syrup.

Gables (☎ 34734; www.thegables-ambleside.co.uk;
Church Walk; r £59-90; ✗) In a grand half-timbered
house near St Mary's Church, this is one of
Ambleside's most impressive places to stay.
From the neat lobby filled with rattan chairs
and willow arrangements, the winding stairs
lead to a choice of rooms furnished with
beige carpets, simple curtains and plain pine
furniture.

Easedale Lodge (☎ 32112; www.easedaleambleside
.co.uk; Compston Rd; d £60-80; ✗) On the corner of
Compston Rd, this excellent B&B makes a
great-value base. All the tasteful bedrooms
have crisp white bed linen, country prints and
the odd characterful extra, but it's worth holding out for a fell-view room if you can.

Lakes Lodge (☎ 33240; www.lakeslodge.co.uk; Lake
Rd; r from £90; ✗ 💻) If you're looking for something different from a standard-issue B&B,
this swanky little gem is just the ticket. There's
no sign of any HP sauce or lacy doilies here –
retro chairs, purple walls and laminate floors
adorn the breakfast area, while the low-key
bedrooms feature big white beds, in-room
DVD players and super-minimal décor.

TOP END

Grey Friar Lodge Hotel (☎ 33158; www.cumbria-hotels
.co.uk; Clappersgate; d £56-116; P ✗) A charming
Victorian-era vicarage tucked away in secluded gardens in the hamlet of Clappersgate,
near Ambleside. The period architecture of the
house, with its gabled exterior and chimney-
topped slate roof, is matched by the splendid
olde-worlde rooms, most of which have four-
posters and fell views.

Waterhead Hotel (☎ 08458-504503; waterhead@
elhmail.co.uk; d weekdays £156-210, weekends £170-230;
P ✗) Down by the lakeshore, this beautifully
refurbished hotel has been given the full boutique makeover. The designer décor simply
screams good taste, from the brown leather
chairs, pale pine floors and canvas art in the
lobby through to the stripped-back bedrooms,

all named after a local waterfall and equipped
with a matching photo print.

Eating

our pick **Lucy's on a Plate** (☎ 31191; www.lucyso
fambleside.co.uk; Church St; lunch £5-9, dinner £15-21;
☯ 10am-9pm) This fantastic little gastronomic
emporium is an Ambleside institution. Lucy's started life as a specialist grocery, selling everything from farm-fresh fruit and veg
to homemade chutneys and locally sourced
meats, but these days the deli has expanded
into this gorgeous down-home restaurant
next door. Everything about Lucy's is deliberately laid-back and informal, from the
homely wooden tables to the mix-and-match
crockery. The all-day menu is crammed with
quirkily named dishes such as fruity porker,
fell-walker filler and blushing cod – as well as
a daily missal from Lucy, detailing whatever
happens to be on her mind that day – and if
you're setting out for the fells, the grocery
will happily pack you up a walker's picnic
stuffed with sandwiches, Cumbrian cheeses
and perhaps a bottled ale or two for when you
reach the summit. If you only eat out once in
Cumbria, make sure it's here.

Lucy 4 (☎ 34666; 2 St Mary's Lane; tapas £4-8; ☯ 5-
11pm Mon-Sat, 5-10.30pm Sun) If you just can't get
enough of Lucy's, then head across the road
to her new split-level wine bar and brasserie,
decorated in characteristically eclectic style
with plenty of rustic wood, local stonework
and a vaguely Spanish vibe. Expect a huge
wine list, plenty of world beers and a 'socially
interactive' tapas menu.

Zeffirelli's (☎ 33845; Compston Rd; pizza £5.50-7.45;
☯ lunch & dinner) Inventive pizzas and pasta
served in a light, lively dining room with its
own glazed 'waterfall'. Zeff's also runs an
upstairs jazz club and the town's cinema;
the 'Double Feature' menu (£15.95) includes
cinema tickets and a two-course meal.

Glass House (☎ 32137; Rydal Rd; lunch £6-14, dinner
£11-18; ☯ lunch & dinner) Famous for being featured in gastronomic meltdown on Gordon
Ramsay's *Kitchen Nightmares* TV programme,
the Glass House has since risen from the
ashes and reinvented itself as one of Ambleside's top restaurants. The varied menu mixes
Mediterranean flavours with the best of local
produce, and the smart dining room is housed
inside a converted 16th-century watermill,
complete with original millwheels, cogs and
machinery.

Priest Hole (☎ 33332; Church St; mains £10-16; ☺ lunch Wed-Sun, dinner daily) Next door to the Royal Oak pub inside the old Kelsick Hall, this spicily shaded restaurant has a melting-pot menu of Italian, French, Spanish and Cumbrian cuisine, where Blencathra venison sits alongside Prosciutto ham and manchego cheese.

Apple Pie (☎ 33679; Rydal Rd; lunches £3-8) A sunny café serving sandwiches, jacket potatoes and lots of homemade cakes, including homemade apple pie smothered with vanilla ice cream.

Pippins (☎ 31338; 10 Lake Rd; lunches £4-10) Reliable café serving full English breakfasts, jacket potatoes, and sandwiches.

Drinking & Entertainment

Royal Oak (☎ 33382; Market Pl) This old white-washed inn is the best pub in Ambleside, with hearty pub mains, good ales and a busy outside terrace.

Zeffirelli's Cinema (☎ 33100; Compston Rd) A two-screen cinema next to Zeffirelli's Restaurant, with extra screens in a converted church down the road.

Shopping

Compston Rd has enough equipment shops to launch an assault on Everest, with branches of **Rohan** (☎ 32946) and **Gaymer Sports** (☎ 33305) on Market Cross. **Black's** (☎ 33197; 42 Compston Rd) is a favourite with hikers, and the **Climber's Shop** (☎ 32297; Compston Rd) specialises in rock-climbing gear.

Getting There & Around

Bus 555 (and bus 599 from April to September) regularly travels from Grasmere (20 minutes), to Windermere (15 minutes) and Kendal (45 minutes).

From April to October, bus 505 runs from Coniston (35 minutes, 12 daily Monday to Saturday, six on Sunday), and from Kendal (30 minutes, twice daily) via Windermere.

Ghyllside Cycles (☎ 33592; The Slack) and **Bike Treks** (☎ 31505; Compston Rd) hire mountain bikes from £14 per day.

AROUND AMBLESIDE
Rydal Mount

Though tiny Dove Cottage (right) gets all the plaudits (and most of the visitors), for a real glimpse into Wordsworth's life, head for **Rydal Mount** (☎ 33002; www.rydalmount.co.uk; admission £5, gardens only £2.50; ☺ 9.30am-5pm Mar-Oct, 10am-4pm Wed-Mon Nov & Feb), which is still owned and run by the poet's descendants.

Wordsworth arrived in 1813 with his growing family in tow, and lived here until his death in 1850. In contrast to the pokey charm of Dove Cottage, Rydal Mount still feels like a family home. The house is packed with original furniture, manuscripts and possessions, including Wordsworth's pen, inkstand and picnic box, and his favourite pair of ice skates; you can also wander around the book-lined sitting room, Wordsworth's bedroom and his top-floor study, with views across the fells and Lake Windermere. But perhaps the most revealing insight into the poet's character lies outside, in the hectare of gardens around the main house. Wordsworth often said that if he hadn't been a poet he would have been a landscape gardener, and most of the formal terraces and winding pathways around Rydal Mount were laid out according to his designs. Below the house is **Dora's Field**, which Wordsworth planted with daffodils in memory of his eldest daughter, who died of tuberculosis in 1847.

The house is 1½ miles northwest of Ambleside, off the A591. Bus 555 (and bus 599 from April to October), between Grasmere, Ambleside, Windermere and Kendal, stops at the end of the drive.

GRASMERE
☎ 015394 / pop 1458

Nestled at the base of a broad valley dotted with oak woods and peaceful fields, and overlooked by the domed peaks of Helm Crag and Steel Fell, the little village of Grasmere is one of the prettiest in the Central Lakes. Wordsworth lived at nearby Dove Cottage for nine years and occasionally taught at the village school, which is now a famous gingerbread shop; he's buried under the yew trees of St Oswald's churchyard with his wife Mary and beloved sister Dorothy. Sadly, the Wordsworth connections have their drawbacks; the village is very much on the coach-tour trail, and is practically overrun with day-trippers in summer.

Wordsworth penned some of his greatest poems at **Dove Cottage** (☎ 35544; www.wordsworth .org.uk; adult £5.95; ☺ 9.30am-5.30pm). The building served as an inn called *The Hope and Olive* until 1793; Wordsworth and his sister Dorothy moved in six years later, to be joined in 1802 by William's new wife Mary and the

---

THE LITERARY LAKES

The most famous literary figure of the Lake District is undoubtedly William Wordsworth, who sought inspiration around the region's mountain peaks and lakeshores and also penned one of the first holiday guides (*A Complete Guide to the Lakes*, published in 1810). The Lake District is littered with places associated with the great poet; you can visit his boyhood home in Cockermouth (p705), his boarding school in Hawkshead (opposite), and his former homes at Dove Cottage (p697) and Rydal Mount (p697), as well as his grave in St Oswald's churchyard (p697). Other Romantic figures to have lived and worked in the Lakes include Samuel Taylor Coleridge, the former Poet Laureate Robert Southey and the opium-eating Thomas De Quincey, who lived at Dove Cottage once Wordsworth had departed for Rydal Mount.

The Victorian art critic and social campaigner John Ruskin moved to Coniston in 1872, and over the next 20 years constructed one of the country's great estates at Brantwood (p701). His work is on display at the Ruskin Museum (p701), the Armitt Museum (p695) and the Abbot Hall Gallery (p693).

London-born Beatrix Potter first visited the Lakes on family holidays. She self-published her debut story, *The Tale of Peter Rabbit*, after being turned down by six publishers. The anthropomorphic tales of talking rabbits and house-proud hedgehogs quickly found worldwide success; the proceeds financed the purchase of Hill Top Farm (p701) in Near Sawrey. Later in life she became a passionate sheep farmer and an unlikely property magnate. Her original paintings are displayed at the Beatrix Potter Gallery (p700) and some early drawings are on display at Ambleside's Armitt Museum.

Leeds-born Arthur Ransome spent his boyhood summers by Coniston Water. After a summer teaching friends' children to sail, he was inspired to write the *Swallows and Amazons* series; Peel Island on Coniston served as the model for Wild Cat Island in his famous tale. A room at the **Museum of Lakeland Life** (p693) is dedicated to Ransome.

---

three eldest Wordsworth children – John, Dora and Thomas – who were born in 1803, 1804 and 1806. Covered with climbing roses and illuminated by tiny latticed windows, it's a fascinating and atmospheric place to visit, although it can get very busy. An entertaining half-hour guided tour is included in the admission price, and entry is managed by timed tickets to avoid overcrowding.

Next door, the new **Wordsworth Museum** houses a fascinating collection of letters, portraits and manuscripts relating to the Romantic movement.

Sleeping

BUDGET

Thorney How YHA Hostel (dm £13; ☼ Apr-Oct) This lovely little hostel has a real claim to fame – it was the first one purchased by the YHA, way back in 1931. The small stone house is popular with families and walkers, as it's very quiet and handily situated on the C2C route. Contact Butharlyp How YHA Hostel for bookings.

Butharlyp How YHA Hostel (☎ 0870 7705836; grasmere@yha.org.uk; dm £15.50; ☼ daily Feb-Nov, weekends Dec-Jan; P ⌨) Just to the north of Gras-

mere off Easedale Rd, this converted Victorian house has lots of modern rooms, a café and internet access; staff can arrange guided walks and activity trips.

Grasmere Hostel (☎ 35055; www.grasmerehostel .co.uk; Broadrayne Farm; dm £15.50) A great little independent hostel just off the A591 near the Traveller's Rest pub, boasting a 'Nordic sauna' and a luxurious lounge lit by skylights and a round picture window. Bus 555 stops at the end of the road on request.

MIDRANGE & TOP END

How Foot Lodge (☎ 35366; www.howfoot.co.uk; Town End; d £64; P ✗) Owned by the Wordsworth Trust, this mid-19th-century villa is just a stone's throw from Dove Cottage, and offers four light, flowery rooms including one with a private sun lounge. The décor's a smidgen chintzy, but it's excellent value for money.

Grasmere Hotel (☎ 35277; www.grasmerehotel .co.uk; Broadgate; d £70-110; P ✗) An imposing three-storey Victorian mansion, perched on the banks of the River Rothay, and recently overhauled in seriously grand style. Carved wooden beds, tasteful prints and expensive soft furnishings characterise every room, and downstairs there's a posh vaulted-roof restaurant decked out with padded chairs and sparkling chandeliers, which has recently bagged a brace of AA rosettes.

Lake View Country House (☎ 35384; Lake View Drive; www.lakeviewgrasmere.com; d £77-99; P X) This stone-fronted house has the best view of any hotel in Grasmere, overlooking private gardens all the way to the lakeshore. The four rooms are all individually styled, with a couple of country beauties with private lounges and whirlpool baths – ideal after a long day's slog on the fells.

White Moss House (☎ 35295; www.whitemoss.com; Rydal Water; d £170-188, cottage £218pp; P X) This pricey pile trades heavily on its Wordsworth ties – William bought it for his son Willie, and often stayed here – but it's a lovely place to stay in its own right, with plenty of rambling rooms filled with period trinkets, well-worn armchairs and burnished furniture, and a detached cottage with lake views.

Eating

Rowan Tree (☎ 435528; Stocks Lane; mains £3-10, pizzas £6-9; ☯ lunch & dinner) This peach-coloured riverside café does a mean cream tea by day, with a more extensive menu of pizzas, fish and veggie-friendly mains by night.

Miller Howe Café (☎ 35234; Red Lion Sq; mains £6-10; ☯ breakfast & lunch) This chrome-edged café makes a welcome change from the more traditional tearooms around Grasmere, with a nice line in frothy coffees and morning pastries, and Cumbrian specials such as Cum-

---

WORTH THE TRIP

Lancrigg (☎ 35317; www.lancrigg.co.uk; Easedale; r £140-210; P X) This vegetarian-only country house hotel is an utter gem, tucked away in private grounds half a mile from Grasmere. Formerly the home of surgeon and Arctic adventurer John Richardson, and once a favourite meeting place for the Lakeland poets, the stately house contains a jumble of character-filled rooms, ranging from a four-poster room equipped with Turkish rugs and mahogany furniture to a huge suite in Richardson's old library, complete with plasterwork ceiling, lace-draped bed and freestanding bath. Stunning fell views and a swish vegetarian restaurant are the icing on the cake.

---

berland sausage and boozy beef-and-ale pie for lunch.

Travellers Rest Inn (☎ 35604; www.lakedistrictinns .co.uk; mains from £8-14; d weekdays £84, weekends £104; P X) This sturdy 16th-century pub on the A591 road from Grasmere has all the trappings of a quintessential Lakeland inn, including slate-fronted fireplaces, oak-beamed ceilings and a bevy of real ales.

Jumble Room (☎ 35188; Langdale Rd; mains £11-20; ☯ lunch & dinner Wed-Sun) Hidden away on the edge of the village, this boho bistro recently scooped a top national award from Les Routiers, and it's hard not to be swept up in the sheer energy and enthusiasm of the place. Letter-print tablecloths, porcelain knick-knacks and spotty seats are packed into the tiny dining room, and the menu wanders at will from England to the Far East.

Sarah Nelson's Gingerbread Shop (☎ 35428; www .grasmeregingerbread.co.uk; Church Stile; 6 pieces of gingerbread £5.25; ☯ 9.15am-5.30pm Mon-Sat) It's practically impossible to visit Grasmere without picking up something sweet and sticky from this classic cake shop, where the ladies still dress in frilly pinnies and the gingerbread has been made to the same recipe since 1854.

Getting There & Away

The hourly 555 bus runs from Windermere to Grasmere (15 minutes), via Ambleside, Rydal Church and Dove Cottage. The open-top 599 runs from Kendal via Windermere and Bowness (one hour, five daily April to October).

HAWKSHEAD

☎ 015394 / pop 1640

Lakeland villages don't come much more picturesque than Hawkshead, with its delightful huddle of cobbled streets, whitewashed pubs, arched alleys and rickety cottages. It's hardly changed since the days when Wordsworth arrived here to attend the village school, and was once a bustling centre for the local wool trade; until the 12th century, the village was owned by the monastery at Furness Abbey (p715). Cars are banned in the village centre throughout the year; sadly, the same can't be said for tourist traffic.

You can almost imagine a young Wordsworth gazing out of the windows of the **Hawkshead Old Grammar School** (admission £2; ☯ 10.30am-12.30pm & 1.30-5.30pm Apr-Oct), which the young poet attended from 1779 to 1787 with his younger brother, John. Here Wordsworth

CUMBRIA & THE LAKES

would have studied the traditional classical curriculum (especially Latin and Greek), as well as mathematics, science and contemporary literature – he began writing his first poetry at the age of 14 while at Hawkshead. The ground-floor classroom still contains much of its original furniture (including a desk in which naughty young William carved his name) and upstairs you can visit the headmaster's study and a small exhibition on the history of the school.

The **Beatrix Potter Gallery** (NT; ☎ 36355; Red Lion Sq; admission £3.60; ☯ 10.30am-4.30pm Sat-Wed Apr-Oct, open all week in Oct) contains lots of original illustrations from her children's books, with an annually changing exhibition drawn from the National Trust's Beatrix Potter collection. The museum is housed in the old offices of Beatrix's husband, solicitor William Heelis. Entry is by timed ticket.

Sleeping & Eating

Croft Camping & Caravanning (☎ 36374; www.hawkshead -croft.com; North Lonsdale Rd; sites per tent £13-15.25; ☯ mid-Mar–mid-Nov) A sheltered and well-equipped camp site just east of the town centre.

Hawkshead YHA Hostel (☎ 0870 770 5856; hawkshead@yha.org.uk; dm £13.95; ☐) A beautiful hostel in a fine Regency house with its original staircase crowned by an ornate cupola. It's about a mile south on the road to Newby Bridge; the cross-lakes shuttle and bus 505/506 both pass nearby.

Ann Tyson's Cottage (☎ 36405; www.anntysons.co .uk; Wordsworth St; s £45, d £58-66; ✕) For the full Wordsworth experience, you could stay in the house in which he lodged with his brother John while attending Hawkshead School. The old cob-walled cottage is tucked away down one of Hawkshead's narrow lanes; the rooms are on the cosy side, but very atmospheric, and the dining room still has its original slate fireplace and wood beams, decorated with traditional copper kettles.

Ivy House Hotel (☎ 36204; www.ivyhousehotel.com; Main St; d lodge £70, main house £80; P ✕) A Grade II–listed Georgian house in British racing green, with six plush rooms in the main house and five more in the detached lodge behind. All are decorated in classic country style, with plenty of painted china, soft cushions and antique clocks.

Red Lion (☎ 36213; www.redlionhawkshead.co.uk; mains £6-15; d £70-80; ✕) This beautiful 15th-century coaching inn is the town's oldest

pub – look out for the carved medieval figurines just underneath the eaves. The main bar serves up local dishes such as Cumberland sausage in Yorkshire pudding and steak and Hawkshead bitter pie, and there are pleasant, unfussy B&B rooms upstairs.

There are plenty of tearooms and cafés in Hawkshead – try **Buttercups** (☎ 36490; lunches £3-8; ☯ breakfast & lunch), on the first floor of the old Hawkshead Institute, which does a daily 'special sandwich' and a great value tea and cake combo.

Nearby, the **Hawkshead Relish Company** (☎ 36614; www.hawksheadrelish.com) makes award-winning chutneys, relishes and preserves, including the fantastically named BHM (Bloomin' Hot Mustard).

Getting There & Away

Hawkshead is linked with Windermere, Ambleside and Coniston by bus 505 (12 daily April to October). The **Cross-Lakes Shuttle** (☎ 015394-45161) climbs to Hill Top (10 minutes, nine daily April to September, weekends only October) before connecting with Windermere cruise boats from Ferry House; a couple of daily buses also travel to Grizedale (15 minutes).

AROUND HAWKSHEAD
Grizedale Forest

Stretching out across the hills between Coniston Water and Esthwaite Water is Grizedale Forest, a dense woodland of oak, larch and pine; its name derives from the Old Norse for wild boar. Wandering through Grizedale today, it's hard to believe the forest has been mostly replanted by the Forestry Commission over the last hundred years; by the 19th century, the original woodland had almost disappeared thanks to the local logging industry.

Since 1977 artists have been fashioning outdoor sculptures in the forest, and there are now more than 90 scattered throughout the park, including a wooden xylophone, a wave of carved ferns and a huge 'man of the forest' that would put Treebeard to shame.

Even without its eccentric furniture, Grizedale Forest makes a great destination for walking and mountain biking. Bikes can be hired from **Grizedale Mountain Bike Hire** (☎ 01229-860369; www.grizedalemountainbikes.co.uk; half-/full-day £14/24; ☯ 9am-5pm Mar-Oct, Sat & Sun Nov-Feb), at the visitor centre, to tackle the 40 miles of marked cycle trails.

Grizedale Visitors Centre (☎ 01229-860010; www
.grizedale.org; ⏰ 10am-5pm Easter-Oct, 11am-4pm Nov-
Easter) provides information on trails and sells
a guide to the forest sculptures (£3). There's
also a small café where you can refuel.

The **Cross-Lakes Shuttle** (☎ 015394-45161) runs
from Hawkshead to Grizedale (two daily April
to September, weekends only October).

Hill Top

Beatrix Potter wrote many of her best-known
stories in this picture-postcard **farmhouse** (NT;
☎ 36269; adult £5.10; ⏰ 10.30am-4.30pm Sat-Wed Apr-
Oct) surrounded by a flower-filled garden and
vegetable patch in the quiet village of Near
Sawrey. If you're a Potter fan, you might
well recognise the house already – it was
used in many of her tales, including the
Samuel Whiskers stories. Tickets are sold for
set times; expect long queues during school
holidays.

The house is 2 miles south of Hawkshead;
bus 505 (15 minutes, hourly) travels through
the village, or you can catch the Cross-Lakes
Shuttle (from Hawkshead, nine daily).

CONISTON

☎ 015394 / pop 1948

Above the tranquil surface of Coniston Water,
with its gliding steam yachts and quiet boats,
looms the craggy, pockmarked peak known as
the Old Man of Coniston (801m). The nearby
village grew up around the copper-mining
industry; these days, there are just a few sleepy
streets, with two fine pubs and some tourist
shops, making Coniston an excellent place for
relaxing by the quiet lakeside.

Coniston is best known for the world-
record speed attempts made on the lake by
Sir Malcolm Campbell and his son, Donald,
between the 1930s and 1960s. Tragically, after
smashing the record several times, Donald
was killed during an attempt in 1967, when his
futuristic jet boat *Bluebird* flipped at around
320mph. The boat and its pilot were found in
2001. Campbell was buried in the cemetery
near St Andrew's church.

Information

Summitreks (☎ 41212; www.summitreks.co.uk; 14
Yewdale Rd) Arranges outdoor activities and hires out
walking gear, as well as kayaks and canoes (£16/23 per
day).
Tourist office (☎ 41533; www.conistontic.org;
Coniston Car & Coach Park; ⏰ 9.30am-5.30pm) Run by

local volunteers since its closure by the NPA. Also sells the
Coniston Loyalty Card (£2), which offers local discounts.
Village Pantry (☎ 41155; Yewtree Rd; internet access
per 30min £2)

Ruskin Museum

This fine town **museum** (☎ 41164; www.ruskinmu
seum.com; admission £4.25; ⏰ 10am-5.30pm Mar-Nov) explores Coniston's history, touching on copper
mining, Arthur Ransome and the Campbell
story – the museum's newest acquisition is
the tailfin of the fated *Bluebird* boat, recovered
in 2001. There's also a large section on John
Ruskin, with displays of his writings, watercolours and sketchbooks.

Brantwood

John Ruskin bought the **country estate** (☎ 41396;
www.brantwood.org.uk; admission £5.50; ⏰ 11am-5.30pm
mid-Mar–mid-Nov, 11am-4.30pm Wed-Sun mid-Nov–mid-
Mar) in 1871 and spent the next 20 years
expanding and modifying the house and
grounds, in pursuit of his concept of 'organic
architecture'. The end result is undoubtedly
the finest country estate in the Lake District,
incorporating the lavish mansion and 250
acres of landscaped gardens and woodland
that tumble all the way down to the lakeshore.
The house is full of original furniture, paintings and *objets d'art*, and there's an excellent
café, the **Jumping Jenny** (☎ 41715; lunches £4-8),
which makes a glorious spot for afternoon
tea. Both of the Coniston launches (see below)
stop at Brantwood.

Activities

BOAT TRIPS

Rescued from dereliction by the NT, the steam
yacht **Gondola** (☎ 63850; adult £5.90; ⏰ five daily
Apr-Oct), described by the *Illustrated London
News* as 'a perfect combination of the Venetian gondola and the English steam yacht',
was launched on Coniston Water in 1859.
The luxurious saloons have been completely
refurbished, and the boat runs like clockwork
between Brantwood and Coniston Pier.

The more modern **Coniston Launch** (☎ 36216;
www.conistonlaunch.co.uk) offers various cruises on
the lake. The Northern cruise (return £5)
calls at the Waterhead Hotel, Torver and
Brantwood, while the Southern cruise (£7.40)
sails to the jetties at Torver, Park a Mor, Lake
Bank, Sunny Bank and Brantwood. You can
break your journey and walk to the next jetty.
There are also special cruises exploring the

Campbells on Coniston and the Swallows and Amazons story, as well as a twilight trip (bring your own wine).

The **Coniston Boating Centre** (☎ 41366; Coniston Jetty) hires out rowing boats (£8 per hour), motor boats (£16), canoes (two hours for £15) and dinghies (two hours for £35).

WALKING

The popular climb to the summit of the **Old Man** (7½ miles, four to five hours) starts at St Andrew's Church in Coniston. On a clear day the views stretch to the Cumbrian coast and Windermere. Another walk from St Andrew's Church climbs through picturesque countryside to **Tarn Hows**, an artificial lake backed by woods and mountains. Allow 2½ to three hours for the 5-mile walk. The tourist office has leaflets on both walks.

Sleeping

Coniston Hall Camp Site (☎ 41223; sites from £11; ☼ Easter-Oct) This lovely lakeside camp site unsurprisingly gets very busy, so book ahead.

Holly How YHA Hostel (☎ 0870 779 5770; conistonhh@yha.org.uk; Far End; dm £11.80; ☼ weekends and school holidays) The closest hostel to town is inside an old slate house, right on the main walking trail up to the Old Man; all the accommodation is in dorms with four to 10 beds. It's friendly and efficient, if a little bland; bikes can be hired on site.

Coppermines YHA Hostel (☎ 0870 770 5772; dm £11.95; ☼ Easter-Oct) This old mine manager's house is a couple of miles into the mountains along an unpaved road. The facilities are pretty basic – a kitchen, common room and showers is about all the luxury you'll get – but it makes a good base for hikers looking to get an early start.

Sun Hotel (☎ 41248; www.thesunconiston.com; s £35-50, d £70-80; P ✗) Coniston's most historic inn is this grand gabled affair, commanding the best views across the lake from the hillside just above town. Most of the ten bedrooms have lake outlooks, but the real attraction is the fantastic 16th-century pub next door, with its original stone floor, timber pillars and range fireplace. There are lots of photos of the Bluebird expedition around, too – Donald Campbell had his headquarters here during his fateful campaign. The hotel has a restaurant (mains £8.50 to £16).

Old Rectory Hotel (☎ 41353; www.theoldrectory hotel.com; Torver; r £60-74; ✗) Frilly, frippy rooms

inside a former vicarage surrounded by rolling fields. It's cosy and welcoming, and the owners will make sure you stock up with a gutbusting Cumbrian breakfast.

Wheelgate Country Guest House (☎ 41418; www .wheelgate.co.uk; Little Arrow; r £68-78; ✗) The pastel rooms at this old whitewashed farmhouse are all named after local lakes; the nicest is Buttermere, with a mauve-canopied four-poster bed and wicker chairs, but Derwent is also worth a look, with its oak beams, low ceiling and hefty wooden furniture.

Eating

Black Bull (☎ 41335; www.conistonbrewery.com; Yewdale Rd; lunch £4-6, dinner £8-14) This creaky coaching inn has welcomed many famous guests over the years (including Coleridge, de Quincey and Donald Campbell), but it's best known for its home-brewed Bluebird Bitter and Old Man Ale.

Harry's (☎ 41389; 4 Yewdale Rd; lunches £6, dinner £8-12; ☼ all day) A lively wine bar and bistro with a decent menu of all-day breakfasts, doorstop sandwiches and evening mains, and plenty of deep sofas to sprawl out on after a day's hike.

Bluebird Café (☎ 41649; Lake Rd; lunches £4-6; ☼ breakfast & lunch) This busy café is right by the main Coniston jetty, and makes an ideal spot for a quick sandwich or a slice of cake before hopping onto the cross-lake launch.

Getting There & Around

From April to October, Bus 505 runs from Windermere (50 minutes, eight daily Monday to Saturday, six on Sunday) via Ambleside; it also runs from Kendal (1¼ hours, two daily Monday to Saturday).

The Ruskin Explorer ticket includes travel on the 505 Coniston Rambler between Windermere, a return ticket on the Coniston launch and entrance to Brantwood. It's available from bus drivers and the tourist office.

LANGDALE
☎ 015394

Surrounded on all sides by towering peaks, saw-tooth ridges and scree-strewn slopes, the Langdale Valley is one of the most dramatic sights in the Lake District. The main road snakes past Elterwater into the valley of Great Langdale, the starting point for some of the region's classic trails – including the trail into the Langdale Pikes past Harrison Stickle (736m) and Pike o' Stickle (709m), and the spectacular ascent of Crinkle Crags (819m). An ancient packhorse trail leads through Little Langdale over Wrynose and Hardknott Passes to the coast, passing a ruined Roman fort en route.

Elterwater

Ringed by trees and rolling fields, the small, charming lake of Elterwater derives its name from the Old Norse for 'swan', after the colonies of whooper swans that migrate to its shores every winter. The nearby village later made its living from farming, quarrying and lacemaking; these days it's a popular walking centre, occupying a stunning spot on the Cumbria Way.

The **Elterwater YHA Hostel** (☎ 0870 7705816; elterwater@yha.org.uk; dm £11.95; ☑ Easter-Oct; ☐) is another fine YHA hostel just a stone's throw from the lake, with plenty of double rooms dotted around the old converted farmhouse.

An opulent Victorian mansion halfway between Grasmere and Elterwater, **Langdale YHA Hostel** (☎ 0870 7705816; langdale@yha.org.uk; High Close, Loughrigg; dm £12; ☑ Mar-Oct; P ☐) certainly looks impressive, but the rooms are pretty par for the course – plain, functional and a little bland.

The classic Lakeland **Britannia Inn** (☎ 37210; www.britinn.net; lunch £8, dinner £12; P ☒), much loved by weary hill-walkers and locals alike, stands opposite the famous maple tree on the village green. Local ales are downed in the two hugger-mugger bars, and there's a sophisticated restaurant that's always packed for Sunday lunch.

Eltermere Country House Hotel (☎ 37207; www .eltermere.co.uk; d £90-110; P ☒) is a beautiful country house retreat with fifteen pleasant, modernised rooms, some of which have traditional trappings left over from the days when this was an 18th-century meeting hall. The hotel specialises in themed holidays, ranging from watercolour workshops to photography masterclasses.

Great Langdale

This tiny hamlet is in the heart of Langdale hiking country, with various footpaths leading into the Langdale Pikes, and a couple of fine old inns in which to fortify yourself for the climb ahead.

The **Stickle Barn** (☎ 37356; Great Langdale) is a popular walker's pub tucked at the foot of the Langdale Pikes in a converted barn. As you'd expect it specialises in generous hiking food: Hungarian goulash, sausage and mash and nourishing soup are all on the menu. There's

a basic bunkhouse, with breakfast served in the main inn.

A well-run National Trust camp site, **Great Langdale Camp Site** (☎ 37668; langdalecamp@ nationaltrust.org.uk; sites per car/adult £3/4.50) is about 1 mile up the valley.

You couldn't ask for a more welcome sight at the end of a long trek than the famous **Old Dungeon Ghyll Hotel** (☎ 37272; www.odg.co.uk; d £96-100; P ☒), backed by soaring fells and built from sturdy Lakeland stone. It's been the favourite getaway for many well-known climbers and walkers over the years, and continues to pull in the punters thanks to its reassuringly old-fashioned ambience and its timeless walker's bar (with the requisite oak beams, real ale and roaring fire, of course). The rooms are showing their age in places, but with views like this, do you really care?

For something more modern but still with some Lakeland character, the ivy-clad **New Dungeon Ghyll Hotel** (☎ 37213; www.dungeon-ghyll .co.uk; d £90-104; P ☒) is the perfect choice. Outside it's all stone chimneys and grey slate; inside it's a thoroughly current country hotel, offering spacious rooms with all the mod-cons and a fine-dining restaurant serving local game, meat and fish.

Little Langdale

Separated from Great Langdale by Lingmoor Fell (459m), Little Langdale is a quiet village on the road to Wrynose Pass. There are many little-known walks nearby, and at the head of the valley is the **Three Shire Stone**, marking the traditional meeting point of Cumberland, Westmoreland and Lancashire.

The only place to stay locally is the **Three Shires Inn** (☎ 37215; www.threeshiresinn.co.uk; dinner £22.50; d £93-99; P ☒), ideally placed for walkers on the popular route to Lingmoor Fell via Blea Tarn.

Getting There & Away

Bus 516 (the Langdale Rambler, six daily, five on Sunday) is the only scheduled bus service to the valley, with stops at Ambleside, Elterwater, Skelwith Bridge and the Old Dungeon Ghyll in Great Langdale.

ESKDALE

The Lake District certainly has its fair share of stunning roads, but perhaps the most breathtaking of all is the route from Little Langdale to Eskdale. The snaking, switchback road winds through barren fells and U-shaped valleys all the way to the Cumbrian coast, passing through Wrynose and Hardknott Passes en route. Perched above Eskdale are the ruins of **Hardknott Roman Fort**, which once guarded the hilltop road; you can still make out the outer walls, the commandant's house and a couple of corner towers, as well as the old parade ground.

Nearby, the shoebox-sized village of **Boot** is huddled in the shadow of Scaféll Pike (978m), England's highest mountain. It's the closest settlement to Dalegarth station – the other end of the Ravenglass–Eskdale line (p716) – and makes a good walking base, far from the Lakeland crowds.

Recently awarded top prizes by the gentle-folk from Camra and Les Routiers, the **Boot Inn** (☎ 0845 130 6224; www.bootinn.co.uk; Boot; mains £7-10; r £70; P) is another hiker's haven for stout food and even stouter ale. Tuck into a massive 10oz gammon steak or a crusty chicken-and-leek pie by the glowing fire, or break your expedition with a good night's sleep in the snug rooms upstairs.

Eskdale YHA Hostel (☎ 0870 7705824; eskdale@yha. org.uk; Boot; dm £11.95; Easter-Oct) is a purpose-built hostel mainly set up for hikers and families, and for overnighters on the Raven-glass railway. The rooms are clean, large and modern, and there's a good TV lounge where you can swap stories with your fellow walkers.

Just east of Boot, the **Woolpack Inn** (☎ 019467-23230; s £40-47.50, d £55-75; P) is a slate-roofed pub that has two 'baas' split between walkers and normal drinkers (ie with no muddy boots or wet clothes). The upstairs bedrooms are fairly basic and could do with a lick of paint; the cheaper ones aren't ensuite.

Getting There & Away
Apart from the Ravenglass steam railway and Shanks' pony, there's no public transport to Eskdale.

WASDALE
☎ 019467
Seen on a chill, mist-shrouded winter's day, there's something inescapably sinister about the inky black lake of Wastwater, the deepest in England (79m). Perhaps it's the brooding crown of mountains that frames the lake's shores, or the shattered slopes of scree that tumble into its waters from the surrounding

hilltops. More likely it's simply that this is still one of the wildest locations in the Lakes, a little-visited area that's home to just a few houses and a single sturdy inn, all of which are dwarfed by the majestic peaks of nearby Scaféll Pike and Great Gable. It's a world away from the hustle and buzz of Lake Winder-mere, which makes Wastwater a favourite spot for walkers looking to experience the Lake District's more untamed side.

The **Barn Door Shop** (☎ 26384) sells maps and guides and oversees the Wasdale website (www.wasdaleweb.com).

Sleeping
Wasdale Head Campsite (☎ 26220; www.wasdalecamp site.org.uk; sites per car/tent £3/4.50) The NT's third Lakeland camp site is perhaps the pick of the bunch, nestled in a fantastic spot beneath the Scaféll Range.

Wast Water YHA Hostel (☎ 0870 770 6082; wast water@yha.org.uk; Wasdale Hall; dm £11.95; year-round by advance booking) This lakeside hostel is a real beauty, a half-timbered 19th-century man-sion that still boasts many of its original Gothic features. Accommodation is mostly in four- to eight-bed dorms, with a small library, convivial lounge and decent-sized kitchen, but it's the fantastic location that's the real draw.

Wasdale Head Inn (☎ 26229; www.wasdale.com; d £48-98; P) Renowned as the spiritual home of British rock-climbing, this wonderful inn has everything the discerning hillwalker could possibly wish for: cosy rooms with big, soft beds; a homely restaurant decorated with old mountaineering photos; and a firelit bar where you can rest those weary bones and down a few muscle-soothing drams.

Bridge Inn (☎ 26221; www.santonbridgeinn.com; s £55-58, d £60-75) In the small settlement of San-ton Bridge, 2½ miles southwest of Wastwater, this whitewashed country inn offers decent food and rooms, and plays host to the World's Biggest Liar Competition each November (see the boxed text Fibbing & Face Pulling, opposite).

Lingmell House (☎ 26261; www.lingmellhouse.co.uk; d £60; P) B&Bs don't get much more secluded than this stark granite house, perched at the end of the only single-track road into the valley. The rooms are suitably sparse – don't expect many creature comforts, or even too much furniture – but you can't fault the stun-ning views.

FIBBING & FACE PULLING

Cumbrians are well known for their propensity for telling tall tales, but Will Ritson, a 19th-century landlord at the Wasdale Head Inn, took the tradition to an entirely different level. Will was known throughout the region for his outlandish stories; one of his most famous tales concerned a Wasdale turnip that was so large that local residents burrowed into it for their Sunday lunch, and later used it as a shelter for their sheep. He also claimed to own a cross between a foxhound and a golden eagle that could leap over drystone walls. In honour of Will's mendacious tradition, the Bridge Inn at Santon Bridge holds the World's Biggest Liar competition every November; Cumbrian dialect is allowed, but lawyers and politicians are barred from entering.

Alternatively, you could head for the World Gurning Competition, held in mid-September in Egremont, near St Bees. To gurn is to pull an ugly face; the challenge is believed to stem from the 12th century, when the lord of the manor handed out sour crabapples to his workers. Locally born Anne Wood won the trophy 24 years running till she was finally beaten in 2001.

Getting There & Away

The only public transport to Wastwater is the **Wasdale Taxibus** (☎ 019467-25308), which runs between Gosforth and Wasdale Head on Thursday, Saturday and Sunday – ring to book a seat.

COCKERMOUTH

☎ 01900 / pop 8270

Just outside the northern boundary of the Lake District National Park lies the market town of Cockermouth, which stands at the meeting point of the River Derwent and River Cocker. It might lack the dramatic backdrop of some of the better known Lakeland towns to the south, but Cockermouth is well worth a visit – culture vultures can visit Wordsworth's boyhood home, while ale aficionados can stop off for a tour at the Jenning's Brewery, Cumbria's largest beer maker. It's also an ideal base for exploring Borrowdale and Buttermere.

Information

Library (☎ 325990; Main St; internet access per 30 min £1; ☯ 9.15am-7pm Mon & Wed, 9.15am-5pm Tue & Fri, 9.15am-12.30pm Thu, 9.15am-1pm Sat)

Post office (South St; ☯ 8am-6pm Mon-Sat) Inside the Lowther Went shopping centre.

Tourist office (☎ 822634; email@cockermouth-tic. fsnet.co.uk; ☯ 9.30am-4.30pm Mon-Sat Apr-Jun & Oct, 9.30am-4pm Jan-Mar, Nov & Dec) Located inside the town hall.

Sights

Cockermouth boasts not one but two famous sons. The notorious Fletcher Christian, lead mutineer on the *Bounty*, was born just outside Cockermouth in 1764, but the town is better known as the birthplace of the ubiquitous

William Wordsworth, who arrived at **Wordsworth House** (NT; ☎ 824805; Main St; admission £4.70; ☯ 11am-4.30pm Tues Sat Mar-Oct, plus Mon July-Aug) in 1770. This smart Georgian mansion was built in around 1745 and leased to Wordsworth's father John, who was an estate agent for the wealthy landowner Sir James Lowther. Now operated by the National Trust, the house has been painstakingly restored based on family accounts from the Wordsworth archive; highlights include the flagstoned kitchen, the grand 1st-floor drawing room and the beautiful walled garden, immortalised in Wordsworth's epic biographical poem *The Prelude*.

For something less cerebral, head for **Jenning's Brewery** (☎ 821011; www.jenningsbrewery.co.uk; admission £4.95), which has been churning out ales and bitters on this site since 1874. There are over 90 Jennings pubs across Cumbria serving their traditionally brewed ales, and it's now possible to take a tour of the factory to see how the stuff is made. Tours last around two hours and include a tasting session in the Old Cooperage bar – choices include the malty Dark Mild, the light, hoppy Cumberland Ale and the extravagantly named Sneck Lifter.

Just down the street from Wordsworth House is the **Museum of Printing** (☎ 824984; Main St; admission £2.50; ☯ 10am-4pm Mon-Sat), crammed with exotic presses and equipment. If nothing else, it's certainly a lesson in how easy computers have made things.

Castlegate House Gallery (☎ 822149; www.castle gatehouse.co.uk; ☯ 10.30am-5pm Fri, Sat & Mon, 2.30-4.30pm Sun), opposite Cockermouth Castle, exhibits local artists' work in Georgian surroundings, and modern sculpture in its walled garden. The castle itself dates from the 12th century and is now a private residence.

Sleeping

Cockermouth YHA Hostel (☎ 0870 770 5768; cocker mouth@yha.org.uk; Double Mills; dm £10.95; ◎ Apr-Oct) This cramped and basic hostel has three large dorms housed in a 17th-century water mill on the southern edge of town. From Main St follow Station St, then turn left into Fern Bank Rd; look out for the signs.

Croft House (☎ 827533; www.croft-guesthouse.com; 6/8 Challoner St; s £36, d £47-55; P ☒) A superb designer B&B in a lemon-yellow Georgian townhouse that brings metropolitan style to sleepy Cockermouth. Laminate floors, contemporary furniture and Middle Eastern touches enliven the excellent rooms, and there's a daily-changing breakfast menu packed with veggie options and continental tastes.

Graysonside (☎ 822531; www.graysonside.co.uk; Lorton Rd; s/d £40/60 P ☒ 🖳) Fine, tasteful B&B rooms decorated in muted colours are available at this secluded former farmhouse a mile south of Cockermouth. There's also a camp site and a selection of cosy self-catering cottages.

Old Vicarage (☎ 828253; www.bridekirkhouse.co.uk; Bridekirk; d £58; P ☒) Plenty of olde-worlde elegance is on display at this lovely family-owned rectory, which stands in tree-clad gardens in the small village of Bridekirk, a mile from Cockermouth. Varnished tables, antique dressers and old chests of drawers are sprinkled around the sweet rooms, and a couple even boast antique French beds.

Eating & Drinking

our pick **Quince & Medlar** (☎ 823579; 13 Castlegate; www.quinceandmedlar.co.uk; mains £13.55; ◎ dinner Tue-Sat) Britain's best vegetarian restaurant is probably the last thing you'd expect to find in rural Cockermouth, but that's exactly what you've got at the Quince & Medlar – winner of numerous gastronomic awards, and still a favourite with Cumbria's culinary cogniscenti. Rich red carpets, polished wood and padded chairs decorate the main dining room, conjuring an atmosphere that's rather reminiscent of a Westminster gentleman's club; but the menu is in a class all of its own, offering inventive delights such as spinach and Wensleydale gateau, or a nutty bundle of hazelnuts garnished with crushed summer roots, with handmade chocs and coffee to finish.

Cockatoo (☎ 826205; 16 Market Pl; mains £2-6; ◎ lunch Wed-Mon, dinner Mon & Wed-Sat) This ex-cellent little diner is far from your average chippy. Traditional cod and chips are certainly on the menu, but there are plenty more esoteric choices too – you can even choose rice instead of chips, and wash it down with a bottle of decent wine.

Front Room (☎ 826655; Market Pl; mains £7-10; ◎ dinner Thu-Sun) Sunflower-yellow walls and plate-glass windows add to the bright continental ambience of this popular bistro, where you'll find dishes such as baked halloumi and aubergine bake supplemented by a comprehensive chalkboard of daily specials.

Bitter End (☎ 828993; Kirkgate) This delightful flower-covered pub also doubles as the smallest brewery in Cumbria, with a selection of real ales brewed in the time-honoured way using barley, wheat, hops and Cumbrian spring water (our favourite is the lipsmacking Cuddy Lugs).

Getting There & Away

The X4/X5 bus travels from Workington via Cockermouth before travelling on to Keswick (one hour), Troutbeck (1¼ hours) and Penrith (1¾ hours). There are 16 daily buses Monday to Saturday, and six on Sunday.

KESWICK

☎ 017687 / pop 4958

Standing at the head of the island-studded, tree-lined lake of Derwent Water, the grey slate town of Keswick is the busiest tourist centre in the Northern Lakes, and a humming hub for outdoor activities of all descriptions, ranging from fell walking to watersports. Several classic walking trails wind their way across the surrounding hilltops, including the long-distance Cumbria Way and the hilltop climbs to Catbells and Castle Crag, which makes Keswick a popular walking base; it's also famous as the place where graphite was discovered in the early 16th century, and for inventing the humble lead pencil.

Information

Keswick Laundrette (☎ 75448; Main St; ◎ 7.30am-7pm)

Post office (☎ 72269; 48 Main St; ◎ 9am-5.30pm Mon-Fri, 9am-12.30pm Sat)

Tourist office (☎ 72645; www.keswick.org; Moot Hall; Market Pl; ◎ 9.30am-5.30pm Apr-Oct, 9.30am-4.30pm Nov-Mar) Sells discounted launch tickets.

U-Compute (☎ 72269; 48 Main St; ◎ 9am-5.30pm; per hr £3) Internet access, located above the post office.

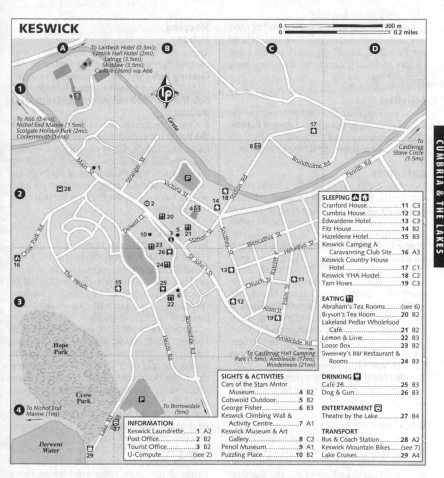

KESWICK

0   300 m
0   0.2 miles

To Lairbeck Hotel (0.3mi);
Lyzzick Hall Hotel (2mi);
Latrigg (3.5mi);
Skiddaw (3.5mi);
Carlisle (36mi) via A66

To A66 (0.4mi);
Nichol End Marine (1.5mi);
Scotgate Holiday Park (2mi);
Cockermouth (14mi)

To
Castlerigg
Stone Circle
(1.5mi)

Brundholme Rd

Penrith Rd

Greta

Main St

Stranger St

Victoria St

Station Rd

Derwent Ct

Crow Park Rd

The Heads

Station St

Southey St

Blencathra St

Helvellyn St

St John's St

Church St

Ratcliff Pl

Eskin St

Acorn St

Borrowdale Rd

Heads Rd

Ambleside Rd

Lake Rd

To Castlerigg Hall Camping
Park (1.5mi); Ambleside (17mi);
Windermere (21mi)

Hope
Park

Crow
Park

To Nichol End
Marine (1mi)

To Borrowdale
(5mi)

Derwent
Water

SLEEPING 🏠 🏡
Cranford House................11 C3
Cumbria House................12 C3
Edwardene Hotel.............13 C3
Fitz House.......................14 B2
Hazeldene Hotel.............15 B3
Keswick Camping &
    Caravanning Club Site.....16 A3
Keswick Country House
    Hotel.........................17 C1
Keswick YHA Hostel........18 C2
Tarn Hows.....................19 C3

EATING 🍴
Abraham's Tea Rooms.........(see 6)
Bryson's Tea Room............20 B2
Lakeland Pedlar Wholefood
    Café..........................21 B2
Lemon & Lime.................22 B3
Loose Box......................23 B2
Sweeney's Bar Restaurant &
    Rooms.......................24 B3

DRINKING 🍸
Café 26.........................25 B3
Dog & Gun....................26 B3

ENTERTAINMENT 🎭
Theatre by the Lake..........27 B4

TRANSPORT
Bus & Coach Station..........28 A2
Keswick Mountain Bikes......(see 7)
Lake Cruises...................29 A4

SIGHTS & ACTIVITIES
Cars of the Stars Motor
    Museum.......................4 B2
Cotswold Outdoor..............5 B2
George Fisher....................6 B3
Keswick Climbing Wall &
    Activity Centre..............7 A1
Keswick Museum & Art
    Gallery........................8 C2
Pencil Museum..................9 A1
Puzzling Place..................10 B2

INFORMATION
Keswick Laundrette......1 A2
Post Office....................2 B2
Tourist Office................3 B2
U-Compute................(see 2)

Sights

Out on the northwestern edge of town is the old Cumberland pencil factory, home to the curious **Pencil Museum** (☎ 73626; www.pencils.co.uk; Southy Works; admission £3; 🕙 9.30am-4pm). The pencil was first mass-produced in Keswick, and the museum explores its history through a variety of odd exhibits; the main draws are a reconstruction of the Seathwaite graphite mine and the world's largest pencil, measuring an impressive 8m from point to tip.

The **Cars of the Stars Motor Museum** (☎ 73757; www.carsofthestars.com; Standish St; admission £4; 🕙 10am-5pm) is a must-see for motorheads. Its fleet of celebrity vehicles includes Chitty Chitty Bang Bang, Herbie the Love Bug, a Batmobile, KITT from *Knightrider*, the

A-Team van and the Delorean from *Back to the Future*, as well as a huge collection of Bond cars.

Keswick Museum & Art Gallery (☎ 73263; Station Rd; admission free; 🕙 10am-4pm Tues-Sat Apr-Oct) has remained largely unchanged since its opening in 1898. It's still decorated in typically austere Victorian style, with plenty of glass cases and dusty exhibits including a pennyfarthing bike, a 'geological piano' and a 500-year-old cat.

If you're a fan of brainteasers, the **Puzzling Place** (☎ 75102; www.puzzlingplace.co.uk; Museum Pl; adult/child £3/2.50; 🕙 10am-6pm) is a real treat, with a maze of rooms crammed with holograms, optical illusions and a truly befuddling anti-gravity gallery.

Keswick Climbing Wall & Activity Centre (☎ 72000; www.keswickclimbingwall.co.uk; 10am-9pm), behind the Pencil Museum, organises outdoor activities including canoeing, abseiling, rock climbing and cycling.

Activities

There are lots of outdoors shops around town, including a huge branch of **Cotswold Outdoor** (☎ 81030; 16 Main St) and the traditionalists' favourite, **George Fisher** (☎ 72178; 2 Borrowdale Rd).

BOAT TRIPS

Derwent Water has an excellent boat service run by the **Keswick Launch Company** (☎ 72263; www.keswick-launch.co.uk), calling at seven landing stages around the lake: Ashness Gate, Lodore Falls, High Brandlehow, Low Brandlehow, Hawse End, Nichol End and back to Keswick. Boats leave every hour, clockwise and anticlockwise (return £6.50, 50 minutes); single fares to each jetty are also available. There are six daily boats from March to November, with a couple of extra afternoon sailings in high summer. There's also an evening cruise at 7.30pm in summer, which includes a free glass of wine (£7.50, one hour, May to September). There are only two daily sailings from November to March.

Nichol End Marine (☎ 73082; Nichol End; 9am-5pm) hires out kayaks, windsurfers, rowboats and motor-boats.

WALKING

There are plenty of walks in the Keswick area. An old railway path (part of the C2C cycle trail) leads up to Lattrigg Fell; other popular routes travel to Walla Crag, Castle Crag and Skiddaw. The tourist office has booklets on many local walks, and organises a daily ramble that leaves from the main office at 10.15am (£8).

> **WORTH THE TRIP**
>
> A mile east of Keswick stands Castlerigg Stone Circle, a group of 48 stones between 3000 and 4000 years old, set on a hilltop surrounded by a brooding amphitheatre of mountains. The purpose of the circle is uncertain (current opinion is divided between a Bronze Age meeting place and a celestial timepiece), but one thing's for certain – those prehistoric builders certainly knew a good site when they saw one.

Sleeping

BUDGET

There are some excellent local camp sites around Keswick, including **Castlerigg Hall Camping Park** (☎ 74499; www.castlerigg.co.uk; sites £13.50-15.50) and **Keswick Camping & Caravanning Club Site** (☎ 72392; Crow Park Rd; sites £14-18) near the lake.

One of the best hostels in the Lakes, **Keswick YHA Hostel** (☎ 0870-770 5894; keswick@yha.org.uk; Station Rd; dm £17.50; ☒ ☐) is recently refurbished and perched in a glorious spot overlooking the river and Fitz Park. Most of the beds are in small, modern dorms, some of which have private balconies above the river for that extra touch of class.

MIDRANGE

Tarn Hows (☎ 73217; www.tarnhows.co.uk; 3-5 Eskin St; s £29.50, d £59-64) Arguably the best of the B&Bs around Eskin St, the impressive Tarn Hows prides itself on its upmarket rooms, all of which are distinguished by a touch of baroque splendour – expect rich fabrics, wrought-iron bedsteads and plush quilts.

Cumbria House (☎ 73171; www.cumbriahouse.co.uk; 1 Derwent Water Pl; r £50-60; ☒) This fine Georgian townhouse B&B has several warm-coloured bedrooms split over several floors, including three top-floor rooms that combine into a single suite. The massive breakfast has been voted the best in northwest England, and the house is admirably eco-friendly – it's carbon neutral and champions fair trade. The owners also organise guided walks.

Hazeldene Hotel (☎ 72106; www.hazeldene-hotel.co.uk; The Heads; d £70-80, suite £90; ☒) One of a string of imposing villas overlooking Hope Park, with lots of excellent-value rooms finished in shades of lavender, turquoise and cream, as well as a glorious 'Dene Suite' with its own stone fireplace and sweeping views across the fells.

Lairbeck Hotel (☎ 73373; Vicarage Hill; www.lairbeckhotel-keswick.co.uk; d £94-123; P ☒) Ticking grandfather clocks, Oriental rugs and faded period photos sum up the atmosphere at this charmingly outmoded country hotel, where you half expect some waistcoated gents to stroll out of the smoking room chugging on their Meerschaum pipes. Heavy curtains, dark-wood furniture and cast-iron beds are dotted around the spacious rooms, all of which continue the unmistakably Victorian vibe.

CUMBRIA & THE LAKES

Other reliable and good value choices include the following:

Cranford House (☎ 71017; www.cranfordhouse.co .uk; s £23, d £50-60; ✗) Family-run guesthouse with a refreshing absence of doilies and floral wallpaper.

Edwardene Hotel (☎ 73586; 26 Southey St; www.ed wardenehotel.com, s £33, d £68-72; ✗) Snug rooms in an end-of-terrace Victorian house.

Fitz House (☎ 74488; www.fitzhouse.co.uk; 47 Brundolme Tce; r £40-50; ✗) Lovely B&B with views across Fitz Park and a private guest conservatory.

TOP END

Keswick Country House Hotel (☎ 0845-458 4333; www .thekeswickhotel.co.uk; Station Rd; s/d £104/124; P ✗) For a little more luxury head for this turret-topped, turn-of-the-century pile just above town, which stands in four acres of grassy grounds and boasts an elegant selection of executive-style rooms – the best are the junior suites, with private sitting areas, king-size beds and those all-important fell views.

Lyzzick Hall Hotel (☎ 72277; www.lyzzickhall.co.uk; Underskiddaw; r £108; P ✗ ☎) Settings just don't get any better than at this fabulously situated hotel, huddled on the slopes of Skiddaw a couple of miles from Keswick. The plain rooms are unfussy, simply furnished and boast the kind of jaw-dropping Lakeland view you'd normally pay through the nose for; added extras include a heated pool and Jacuzzi, a country restaurant and a panoramic patio terrace that's out of this world.

Eating

CAFÉS

Lakeland Pedlar Wholefood Café (☎ 74492; www.lake landpedlar.co.uk; Hendersons Yard; mains £3-8; ☺ 9am-5pm) This homely wholefood café-cum-bike shop is one of Keswick's best kept secrets, dishing out generous portions of home-made soups, chunky sandwiches, Tex-Mex mains and crumbly cakes. If you feel the need to work off some calories, bikes are available for hire upstairs.

Bryson's Tea Room (☎ 72257; 42 Main St; cakes £2-5) Perhaps the most famous bakery in the Lakes, renowned for its traditional fruitcakes, Battenburgs and chocolate sponges.

Abraham's Tea Rooms (☎ 72178; 2 Borrowdale Rd; mains around £5) Take a break from your boot shopping in the attic café at George Fisher.

RESTAURANTS

Lemon & Lime (☎ 73088; 31 Lake Rd; mains £6-14; ☺ lunch & dinner) This global bistro takes a mix-and-match approach to its wide-ranging cuisine – for starters you might choose falafels, spring rolls or *yakitori* (grilled chicken), with Malaysian noodles, Thai curry or chicken schnitzel to follow.

Loose Box (☎ 772003; Kings Arms Courtyard; pizzas £6-8) The best pizzas in town are dished up at this small Italian diner, attached to the Kings Arms.

Sweeney's Bar Restaurant & Rooms (☎ 772990; 18-20 Lake Rd; mains £7-12) This sophisticated wine brasserie–bar is the perfect marriage between modern style and classic Cumbrian cooking. Enjoy a pre-dinner drink on one of the deep-brown leather sofas before tucking into a plate of Cumberland sausage or steamed fish in the airy dining room.

Drinking

Café 26 (☎ 80863; 26 Lake Rd) Knightsbridge comes to Keswick at this groovy wine bar, decked out with leather bench seats, burgundy paintwork and plenty of velour cushions. Oenophiles will appreciate the extensive wine list, and if you enjoy yourself just a little *too* much, there are several contemporary rooms above the bar.

Dog & Gun (☎ 73463; 2 Lake Rd; mains around £6) With its low ceilings, tobacco-tinted walls and wooden booths, this old Keswick boozer makes a fine place for a swift pint and a plate of nosh.

Entertainment

The Lake District's only repertory theatre company, **Theatre by the Lake** (☎ 74411; www .theatrebythelake.com; Lakeside) stages new and classic drama in its lakeside venue on the shores of Derwent Water.

Getting There & Away

The ever-reliable bus 555/556 (the Lakes-Link) connects Keswick with Ambleside (40 minutes), Windermere (50 minutes) and Kendal (1½ hours), 10 times daily (including Sundays).

The hourly X4/X5 travels from Penrith to Workington via Keswick (17 daily Monday to Saturday, six on Sunday).

Getting Around

Off-road bikes can be hired from **Keswick Mountain Bikes** (☎ 75202; 1 Daleston Crt) and from **Keswick Climbing Wall & Activity Centre** (☎ 72000; www.keswickclimbingwall.co.uk) for £15 to £17 per day.

CUMBRIA & THE LAKES

BORROWDALE & BUTTERMERE VALLEYS

☎ 017687

Hemmed in by wooded fells, flat fields and pointy granite peaks, and sprinkled with the kind of remote farmhouses and sturdy cottages that grace many a Lakeland postcard, the valleys of Borrowdale and Buttermere are many people's idea of the quintessential Lake District landscape. Separated by the old Honister Pass – once the county's main slate-mining area – these twin valleys are hugely popular with walkers and hikers, with a network of walking trails and easy access to some of the region's highest peaks.

Borrowdale stretches for 6 miles from the western edge of Derwent Water to Honister Pass. Buttermere runs northwest from Honister Pass along the shores of Buttermere Lake and Crummock Water towards Cockermouth.

Borrowdale

The main B5289 road tracks the edge of Derwent Water into the heart of the Borrowdale valley, dotted with small copses and rickety barns, and overlooked by the impressive peaks of Scaféll and Scaféll Pike.

Derwent Water YHA Hostel (☎ 0870-770 5792; derwentwater@yha.org.uk; Barrow House; dm £13.95; ❉ Feb-Nov, weekends Nov-Jan; P ▣) This lakeside mansion 2 miles south of Keswick once belonged to the local aristocrat Joseph Pocklington. It's now perhaps the poshest hostel in the entire Lake District, with huge rooms, children's playgrounds, a great TV lounge and even a man-made waterfall.

Borrowdale to Rosthwaite

A couple of miles south of Borrowdale is the small village of **Grange**. Nearby, the valley winds into the jagged ravine known as the **Jaws of Borrowdale**, a famous hiking spot with world-renowned views, especially from the 300m **Castle Crag**. From here, the road winds round into **Rosthwaithe**, a rural hamlet scattered with stone cottages, slate-roofed farmhouses and a couple of country hotels.

Sleeping & Eating

Borrowdale YHA Hostel (☎ 0870-770 5706; borrowdale@yha.org.uk; Longthwaite; dm £15.50; ❉ Feb-Dec) A little way up the valley is this excellent purpose-built, timber-clad hostel that specialises in walking trips and outdoor activities.

Yew Tree Farm (☎ 77675; www.borrowdaleherdwick .co.uk; d from £60; ✗) There are only three rooms at this whitewashed farmhouse in Rosthwaite, and they're all a bit heavy on the flowery décor, but the traditional oak-beamed, low-ceilinged atmosphere is lovely and the farm-cooked breakfast is huge. The owners also run the Flock-in Tea Room across the road, which sells delicious home-baked cakes, flapjacks and scones.

Scaféll Hotel (☎ 77208; www.scafell.co.uk; d from £97; P ✗) This unpretentious Lakeland inn is slightly more affordable than its upmarket neighbours, and still boasts the same magnificent Borrowdale views. It's a popular overnight stop for walkers, thanks to its unfussy rooms, inexpensive restaurant and the wonderful Riverside Bar – the village's only pub.

Borrowdale Gates Hotel (☎ 77204; www.borrowdale-gates.com; Grange; mains £16-22; d £134-180; P ✗) This seriously swish country mansion was built as a private residence in the mid-19th-century, and has now been converted into the finest hotel in the valley. The unusual P-shaped layout means all the rooms have slightly different views (ranging from pleasant to utterly awe-inspiring), but they're all cosily finished with antique chairs, heavy bedspreads and luxurious curtains.

Hazel Bank Country House (☎ 77248; www.hazelbankhotel.co.uk; r £158-178; P ✗) Another fine rural retreat built for a wealthy businessman in 1850, this award-winning stone-fronted hotel is accessed via its own humpbacked bridge and stands in spectacular private gardens. As you'd expect for the elevated pricetag, the ambience is one of understated English luxury – silver trays, ruffled curtains and aristocratic furniture abound, and the service is first-class.

Seatoller

The last stop before Honister Pass, Seatoller was originally a settlement for workers employed in the local slate quarries. These days, it's still a remote village, with just a few houses, a homely restaurant and a character-filled hotel.

The delightful 17th-century **Seatoller House** (☎ 77218; www.seatollerhouse.co.uk; s/d £52/104; P ✗) nestled at the foot of Honister Pass is a charming refuge from the buzz and bustle of the outside world. None of the small rooms have TVs. All are named after local wildlife and are different in size and layout – Osprey is tucked in under the roof beams, while Owl boasts views across to Glaramara. Downstairs there's a fine slate-floored tearoom and a lovely lounge with its original Victorian tiled hearth.

The rural **Yew Tree Restaurant** (☎ 77634; mains £8-15; ☺ lunch Tue-Sun) is the ideal pit-stop before tackling the hair-raising Honister road, with a light lunch menu of ploughman's sandwiches and country pies, as well as a more sophisticated à la carte menu serving locally sourced fish, meat and fowl. Our tip? Try the Rum Nicky (a sticky tart made with rum, ginger and dates).

Honister Pass

This bleak, wind-battered mountain pass into Buttermere was once the most productive quarrying area in the Lake District, and still continues to produce much of the region's distinctive grey-green Westmorland slate. Claustrophobes should steer well clear of the tours of the **Honister Slate Mine** (☎ 017687-77230; www.honister-slate-mine.co.uk; tours £8.50; ☺ tours 10.30am, 12.30pm & 3.30pm Mar-Oct), and settle for buying a few slate souvenirs at the on-site shop instead.

Thanks to a couple of remote hostels, Honister makes a great base for an early-morning hike. A track to Great Gable starts nearby, and there are sweeping views from the top across the smoky, black-grey landscape, down into Buttermere valley. Bus 77/77A stops here from May to October.

Black Sail YHA (☎ 07711-108450; Ennerdale, Cleator; dm £11.95; ☺ Easter to Oct, Nov-Mar by advance booking) is a fantastically isolated shepherd's bothy (cottage) 2½ miles west of Honister Pass and only accessible on foot.

Right beside the Honister mine at the summit of the pass is **Honister House YHA** (☎ 0870 770 5870; Seatoller; dm £11.95; ☺ Easter-Oct, weekends Nov), a basic hostel that offers functional dorms in grey concrete buildings once used by mineworkers.

Buttermere

From Honister Pass the main road plunges down into the bowl-shaped Buttermere valley, skirting along the lakeshore all the way to Buttermere village, 4 miles from Honister and 9 miles from Keswick. From here, the B5289 cuts north along the eastern shore of Crummock Water.

Buttermere YHA Hostel (☎ 0870 7705736; buttermere@yha.org.uk; dm £17.50) is another spectacularly situated hostel in a slate-stone house above Buttermere Lake, with views of Red Pike and High Stile.

Apart from the Fish Hotel (see the boxed text The Maid of Buttermere, p712), the only accommodation in Buttermere is at the luxurious **Bridge Hotel** (☎ 70252; www.bridge-hotel.com; r incl dinner £130-190; ℗ ☒), which has a choice of standard rooms and some seriously lavish suites, complete with hill-view balconies and antique furniture.

GETTING THERE & AWAY

Bus 79 (the Borrowdale Rambler) provides a regular service (at least hourly) from Keswick bus station to Seatoller, with eight buses on Sunday.

From Easter to October bus 77/77A – the Honister Rambler – makes the round trip from Keswick to Buttermere via Borrowdale and the Honister Pass four times daily. The Honister Dayrider pass costs £6.

ULLSWATER & AROUND
☎ 017684

Stretching in a glassy arc for 7½ miles between Pooley Bridge in the north and Glenridding and Patterdale in the south, the tranquil lake of Ullswater is the second-largest in the Lakes after Windermere, and was one of Wordsworth's favourites. During an afternoon walk along the wooded shores of Ullswater with his sister Dorothy, William was inspired to write the work for which he is perhaps best remembered – the so-called 'Daffodils' poem, which begins with the immortal refrain, 'I wandered lonely as a cloud...' It's still a beautiful and inspiring place, where quaint steamers chug along the lake against a backdrop of majestic hills and woodland groves, and although the western edge gets busy in summer, you can usually escape the traffic along the eastern side.

Ullswater 'Steamers' (☎ 82229; www.ullswater -steamers.co.uk; adult return £7.40-10.30) ply the lake from Pooley Bridge to Glenridding via Howtown. The first paddle steamers were launched on Ullswater in 1859 but the current vessels, Lady (in operation since 1887) and Raven (since 1889), have been converted to conventional power. A new steamer, the Lady Dorothy, has recently been brought over from Guernsey and was to be launched in September 2006.

Pooley Bridge

elevation 301m

The busy village of Pooley Bridge stands at the northern edge of Ullswater along a pebble-strewn shoreline, and serves as the main base for visitors to the lake, with a couple of pleasant pubs and shops, and a jetty for the Ullswater cruise boats.

Park Foot Camping (☎ 86309; www.parkfootullswater .co.uk; Howtown Rd; sites £10-21) is nestled on the edge of Ullswater, 1 mile south of Pooley Bridge. Alternatively, try **Hillcroft Park** (☎ 486363; Roe Head Lane; sites from £10), a little closer to the village.

Pooley Bridge Inn (☎ 86215; www.pooleybridgeinn .co.uk; d £65-90; P ✗) This comfy inn has a whiff of Alsatian atmosphere thanks to its hanging baskets, whitewashed exterior and wooden balconies. The rooms are pleasant and attractively rustic, with the odd brass horseshoe or watercolour print to cheer up the décor; first-floor bedrooms all have private balconies.

The **Sharrow Bay Country House Hotel** (☎ 86301; www.sharrow-bay.com; d from £350) is a Lakeland legend, standing in a fabulous position at the edge of Ullswater and surrounded by 12 acres of private woods and gardens. The pamper factor is off the scale – gilt-edged mirrors, chaise-longues and canopied beds feature in every room; there's a nationally renowned, Michelin-starred restaurant; and just in case you're arriving in your own chopper, there's a private helipad reserved for guests' use.

For something rather less lavish, there's always the homely **Sun Inn** (☎ 486205; mains £5-12) with the usual range of ales and a beautiful beer garden.

Glenridding & Patterdale

elevation 253m

The neighbouring villages of Glenridding and Patterdale are 7 miles south from Pooley Bridge. Glenridding is little more than a cluster of cottages and tearooms straggling along the main road, and is best known as a base for tackling the challenging ascent of Helvellyn (949m), the second-highest peak in the Lakes, which looms ominously above the village. There are also lots of tranquil low-level walks nearby, and a couple of places where you can hire boats and explore the lake at your own pace.

Ullswater Information Centre (☎ 82414; glenrid dingtic@lake-district.gov.uk; Beckside car park; ☻ 9am-5.30pm Apr-Oct) has plenty of tips on accommodation and local hikes.

SLEEPING

Helvellyn YHA Hostel (☎ 0870-770 5862; helvellyn@yha .org.uk; Greenside; dm £11.95; ☻ Easter-Oct, phone ahead at other times) This high-altitude hostel is perched 274m above Glenridding along a rough mountain track, and is mainly used by walkers setting out for Helvellyn; guided walks to the summit can be arranged through the hostel staff.

Mosscrag (☎ 82500; www.mosscrag.co.uk; s £40, d £56-70; P ✗) A reliable B&B near the banks of Glenridding Beck, offering pleasant rooms in peaceful shades of white and peach.

Glenridding Hotel (☎ 82228; www.bw-glenrid dinghotel.co.uk; d £120-130; P ✗ ☎) This totally modernised hotel is owned by the Best Western chain, so the standard rooms are a little bland and anonymous; for something with a

---

THE MAID OF BUTTERMERE

The **Fish Hotel** (☎ 70253; www.fish-hotel.co.uk; 2-night minimum stay d £144; P ✗) in Buttermere is famous as the home of the legendary beauty Mary Robinson, the so-called 'Maid of Buttermere'. A visiting hiker by the name of Joseph Palmer was the first to spy this 18th-century glamourpuss during a brief stopover at the inn in 1792; he later wrote about her in his book *A Fortnight's Ramble in the Lake District*. Soon visitors were trekking from all across the Lakes to see if Mary's beauty lived up to its reputation – Wordsworth was suitably impressed, devoting several lines to her in *The Prelude*, although the rakish Coleridge was apparently rather underwhelmed. Mary later became notorious for being duped by the notorious conman John Hatfield, who passed himself off as an army colonel and an MP in order to win her hand in marriage; within a year Hatfield had been exposed as a bankrupt and a bigamist, arrested by the Bow Street Runners in Swansea, and sentenced to death by hanging. Despite her terribly public embarrassment, Mary soldiered on and later married again, this time to a more reliable local type from Caldbeck; together they ran the inn until Mary's death in 1837. The local author Melvyn Bragg used the tale as the basis for his novel *The Maid Of Buttermere*.

little more character, you can pay extra for one of the feature rooms, which come with luxurious extras such as four-poster beds and duo baths.

Inn on the Lake (☎ 82444; www.innonthelakeullswa ter.co.uk; d £128-184; P ✗ ☐) Huge, extravagant rooms, regal quilts, bubbling Jacuzzis and palatial beds sum up this lakeside beauty, by far the best hotel anywhere near Ullswater. The bedrooms offer a choice of mountain or lake views, and you'll be more than happy with either.

Traveller's Rest (☎ 82298; mains from £6) An unpretentious pub with a couple of friendly bars and a small outside patio beside the fells. Hikers looking to refuel should opt for the ridiculously generous 'Traveller's Mixed Grill'.

Getting There & Around

Bus 108 runs from Penrith to Patterdale and stops at Pooley Bridge and Glenridding (five daily Monday to Saturday). Bus 517 runs from Bowness Pier to Glenridding (three daily late-July to September, weekends only from the end of March to July).

CUMBRIAN COAST

Most visitors never make the trek out to the Cumbrian coast, and with such a wealth of spectacular sights to discover around the Central Lakes, it's not really surprising. But they're missing out on one of the county's hidden gems – a sweeping panorama of gentle fields, coastal trails and sandy bays, dotted with some of Cumbria's oldest and most historic towns. The Edwardian holiday resort of Grange-over-Sands and the medieval village of Cartmel are both within easy reach of Morecambe Bay, on the county's southern coast, while on the western coast you'll find the Roman settlement of Ravenglass – starting point for the classic L'aal Ratty steam railway – and the ancient port of Whitehaven, as well as the controversial nuclear reprocessing plant at Sellafield.

Getting Around

The Cumbrian Coast railway line loops 120 miles from Carlisle to Lancaster (both on the main line between London and Glasgow). Trains operate hourly, and a single ticket costs £21.

GRANGE-OVER-SANDS

☎ 015395 / pop 4034

During the 19th century the seaside town of Grange-over-Sands, standing on the edge of Morecambe Bay, was one of the most popular resorts in the northwest of England. Traces of its Edwardian heyday are still clear to see: grand holiday villas and several huge hotels line its hilly streets, and the glorious seafront promenade is dotted with formal terraces and tranquil landscaped gardens, tailor-made for an invigorating afternoon stroll. But the English gentry have long since moved on to pastures new, and Grange is better known these days as a favourite seaside retreat for members of the blue-rinse brigade.

The crossing over Morecambe Bay was once the main route to the Lakes from the south of England. It's still possible to walk across the flats at low tide, but only with the official Queen's guide (a role established in 1536), as the crossing is fraught with unpredictable tides and quicksand – even experienced local fishermen have been known to lose carts, horses and tractors. The 8-mile crossing takes around 3½ hours – contact the Grange tourist office for details.

Information

Library (☎ 32749; Grange Fell Rd; ◷ 9am-5pm Mon-Fri, 9.30am-12.30pm Sat)

Post office (☎ 34713; Main St; ◷ 9am-5pm Mon-Fri, 9am-12.30pm Sat)

Tourist office (☎ 34026; grangetic@southlakeland.gov .uk; Victoria Hall, Main St; ◷ 10am-5pm Easter-Oct)

Sleeping & Eating

Lymehurst Hotel (☎ 33076; www.lymehurst.co.uk; Kents Bank Rd; s £35-38, d £74-90; P ✗) There are several B&Bs along Kents Bank Rd, but this large townhouse is the pick of the bunch, with a maze of faded rooms scattered over several floors, connected together by a circuitous staircase.

Somerset House (☎ 32631; www.somersethouse-cum bria.co.uk; Kents Bank Rd; s £35, d £56-60; P ✗) The next best option is this small, colourful guesthouse, with eight ensuite rooms filled with china trinkets and cheery quilts.

Graythwaite Manor (☎ 32001; www.graythwaite manor.co.uk; Fernhill Rd; s/d £65.50/116; P ✗) This beautiful manor house is packed with period detail and makes a splendidly ostentatious place to stay. Carved wood panels, leather-backed chairs and an ornate fireplace adorn the grand sitting room, and the old-fashioned feel is carried through into the upstairs rooms, most of which have views over Morecambe Bay.

Hazelmere Cafe (☎ 32972; 1-2 Yewbarrow Tce; sandwiches £4-6, mains £6-9; ☺ 10am-5pm summer, 10am-4.30pm winter) This delightful café doubles as the town's top bakery, and offers Cumbrian delicacies such as potted Morecambe Bay shrimps, wild rabbit pie and Kendal crumbly cheese toasties. Try a slice of lemon-curd tart or fruitcake before you leave.

Getting There & Away

Both the train station and bus stop are just downhill from the tourist office.

Bus X35 from Kendal stops at Grange (30 minutes, hourly) on its way to Ulverston (one hour).

Grange is on the Cumbrian Coast Line, with frequent connections to Lancaster (30 minutes, hourly) and Carlisle (£24.50, 1½ hours, hourly).

AROUND GRANGE
Cartmel
☎ 015395 / pop 1798

Tucked away in the countryside above Grange, the tiny village of Cartmel is known for three things – its beautiful 12th-century priory, its miniature racecourse and its world-famous sticky toffee pudding, which is produced at the **Cartmel Village Shop** (☎ 36201; www.stickytoffee pudding.co.uk; The Square; ☺ 9am-5pm Mon-Sat, 10am-4.30pm Sun) and sold all over Cumbria.

The heart of the village is the medieval market square, from where a winding lane leads around to **Cartmel Priory** (☎ 36261; ☺ 9am-5.30pm May-Oct, 9am-3.30pm Nov-Apr), one of the few priories to escape demolition during the dissolution of the monasteries under Henry VIII. Light pours in through the glorious 15th-century **east window**, illuminating the many tombs set into the flagstoned floor; look out for the engravings of skulls and hourglasses, intended to remind the pious of their own inescapable mortality.

SLEEPING & EATING

Prior's Yeat (☎ 35178; priorsyeat@hotmail.com; Aynsome Rd; s/d £29/58; P ⊠) The only B&B worth recommending in Cartmel proper is this brick-built Edwardian house on the edge of the village, offering four ensuite rooms with just the faintest trace of flounce.

Cavendish Arms (☎ 36240; www.thecavendisharms .co.uk; mains £6-14; s/d £40/55) Just inside the gateway off the square, this venerable coaching inn has been whetting Cartmel's whistle for several centuries, and it's still the village's finest pub. Superior pub food and pints of ale are served in the bar or at tables on the streetside patio; the upstairs rooms are rather stark but not bad for the price.

Aynsome Manor Hotel (☎ 36016; www.aynsome manorhotel.co.uk; s/d £92/162; P ⊠) A fine detached manor house set in pastoral countryside just outside Grange, offering pink-tinged, lacy-edged rooms that are comfortable, if a little on the expensive side.

our pick **L'Enclume** (☎ 36362; lenclume.co.uk; Cavendish St; lunch 2/3 courses £18/25, dinner menu £65; r from £170) For the full-blown fine-dining experience, few places in Cumbria can compare to this stunning designer restaurant nestled in the shadow of Cartmel Priory. The décor is minimal, the service is impeccable and the cooking is about as good as you'll get anywhere in England; traditional dishes are reinvented with a wilfully avant-garde twist, so you might need some guidance to negotiate the extraordinary menu (unless you're already au fait with dishes such as 'foie gras from cubism to realism'). The same imaginative flair seeps into the upstairs rooms, where Toile de Jouy wallpaper and grand antiques meet the stripped-back 21st century.

GETTING THERE & AWAY

Bus 532 runs from Grange to Cartmel (30 minutes, four daily).

Holker Hall & Lakeland Motor Museum

Set in stately gardens, **Holker Hall** (☎ 58328; www .holker-hall.co.uk; admission house & grounds £8.80, grounds only £5.70; ☺ house 10.30am-4.30pm Sun-Fri, grounds 10am-6pm Mar-Oct) dates from the 16th century but is mainly a Gothic Victorian creation, furnished with stately drapery and grand woodcarving. There's a deer park, and the stables house the **Lakeland Motor Museum** (admission £6; ☺ 10.30am-4.45pm), with truckloads of classic cars, as well as a replica of Donald Campbell's *Bluebird* (see p701).

ULVERSTON
☎ 01229 / pop 11254

It's far from the prettiest town along the Cumbrian coastline, but Ulverston's rather drab, workmanlike appearance derives from its history as an industrial centre for leather, copper and iron ore. On a wet winter's day it can be a dispiriting place to visit, but in the summer months the streets come alive with market stalls, and the town is packed with walkers setting out for the Cumbria Way, which has its official starting point in Ulverston.

Information

Library (☎ 894151; Kings Rd; internet access per 30 min £1)

Tourist office (☎ 587120; ulverstontic@southlakeland .gov.uk; County Sq; ☒ 9am-5pm Mon-Sat)

Sights

If you're an aficionado of the silent era, then you'll already know Ulverston's main claim to fame: Stan Laurel, the spindlier half of Laurel and Hardy, was born here in 1890. The **Laurel & Hardy Museum** (☎ 582292; 4c Upper Brook St; admission £2.50; ☒ 10am-4.30pm Feb-Dec) has floor-to-ceiling memorabilia and shows some of their cinematic creations too.

The tower on top of Hoad Hill commemorates local hero Sir John Barrow (1764–1848), explorer and author of *Mutiny of the Bounty* (1831). The tiny 16th-century **yeoman's cottage** (☎ 585788; admission free; ☒ 11am-4pm Sat, noon-4pm Sun) where he was born is usually open to the public at weekends.

Sleeping

Walkers Hostel (☎ 585588; www.walkershostel.co.uk; Oubas Hill; dm £14) As its name suggests, this eco-friendly hostel is mainly aimed towards walkers, but it's a great budget base even if you're not hitting the trail. An evening meal is available for an extra £8. The hostel is 10 minutes' walk from town on the A590 to Kendal.

St Mary's Mount Manor House (☎ 849005; www .stmarysmount.co.uk; Belmont; s £35, d £45-75; P ☒) Brass beds, half-tester canopies and original fireplaces distinguish the rooms at this slate-roofed manor house on the hill above town.

Virginia House (☎ 584844; www.ulverstonhotels.com; 24 Queen St; s £35-50, d £55-60; ☒) This centrally positioned guesthouse has a smattering of antiques and Victorian knick-knacks dotted around its dining room and foyer, but most of its bedrooms are exactly what you'd expect from a British B&B.

Lonsdale House Hotel (☎ 581260; www.lonsdale househotel.co.uk; 11 Daltongate; s/d £55/85; P ☒) A smart, welcoming B&B with 20 bright rooms furnished with sunny checks, pine furniture and tasteful table lamps; four rooms have a Jacuzzi hidden away in the bathroom, and

four-poster beds for that little bit of nocturnal class.

Eating & Drinking

Hot Mango Café (☎ 584866; 27 King St; lunch £5-8; ☒ breakfast & lunch Tue-Sat) Don't expect jacket potatoes and soggy sandwiches at this fiery-coloured café – here the menu's crammed with tangy dishes such as saddleback pork burgers and 'camembert in a box'.

King's (☎ 588947; 15-17 Queen St; mains £5-11; ☒ lunch Mon-Sat) Knock back a beer or try a technicolour cocktail at this cool café-bar just down the road from Laurel's. Burgers, club sandwiches and nachos are on the lunchtime menu, too.

Laurel's Bistro (☎ 583961; 13 Queen St; set menu £9.95; ☒ dinner) Despite the name, the Laurel & Hardy memorabilia is kept to a bare minimum at this excellent little bistro, where country standards such as noisettes of pork, braised beef and steamed trout all feature on the fantastic value set-menu.

Getting There & Away

Regular trains from Carlisle (£27.50, two hours) and Lancaster (£6, 40 minutes) stop at Ulverston station, five minutes' walk south of the centre. To reach Cartmel by bus, you have to change at Grange (eight daily Monday to Saturday).

AROUND ULVERSTON
Conishead Priory

Two miles south of Ulverston is **Conishead Priory** (☎ 584029; www.manjushri.org.uk; admission free, tours £2.50; ☒ 2-5pm Sat & Sun Easter-Oct), one of the largest Manjushri Buddhist Centres in the UK. The Victorian Gothic manor houses a 24 sq metre Buddhist temple and some of the largest Buddhist statues in Europe; tours begin at 2.30pm and 3.45pm, and meditation retreats are available if you're bitten by the Buddhist bug.

Bus 11 makes regular trips from Ulverston to Barrow-in-Furness via the priory (12 daily Monday to Saturday).

Furness Abbey

The rosy ruins of **Furness Abbey** (EH; ☎ 823420; admission £3.40; ☒ 10am-6pm Apr-Sep, 10am-5pm Oct; 10am-4pm Wed-Sun Nov-Mar) are 1½ miles north of Barrow-in-Furness and 8½ miles from Ulverston. Founded in the 12th century by Savignac monks, and later merged with the

Cistercian order, the abbey became one of the most powerful in the north of England, but finally met an ignominious end in 1537 during the dissolution. The bell-tower and part of the north and south transepts are still standing, and the atmospheric ruins are scattered with carved arches and elegant vaulting, hinting at the abbey's former grandeur.

An audio guide is included in the admission price. The small museum contains a collection of stone carvings, including two rare 13th-century effigies of armoured knights.

Bus 6 or 6A from Ulverston to Barrow-in-Furness passes by the abbey.

RAVENGLASS & AROUND

It's difficult to imagine the tiny village of Ravenglass, a quiet cluster of seaside houses 27 miles north of Barrow, as an important Roman port. The Romans were drawn to its sheltered harbour, but all that remains of their substantial fort are the walls of a 4th-century **bath house**, half a mile from the train station down a signposted track.

Ravenglass is more familiar to steam enthusiasts as the home of the **Ravenglass & Eskdale Railway** (☎ 01229-717171; www.ravenglass-railway.co.uk; adult £9), affectionately known as La'al Ratty, and originally built in 1875 to carry iron ore. The miniature trains chug along a beautiful 7-mile track into Eskdale and the foothills of the Lake District mountains. A Wainwright booklet called *Walks from Ratty* (£1.50) is available from the station shop, and there's an interesting **museum** exploring the history of the railway beside the car park.

A mile south of Ravenglass is **Muncaster Castle** (☎ 01229-717614; www.muncaster.co.uk; gardens £6.50, castle £2.50; ✹ gardens 10.30am-6pm/dusk, castle noon-5pm Sun-Fri), home to the Pennington family for some 800 years. The castle was built around the original 14th-century *pele* tower, but its most famous features date from the 19th century: highlights include the elegant dining room, an imposing great hall and an extraordinary octagonal library. It's also renowned for its ghosts, especially that of Tom Fool, once a court jester at the castle. The surrounding gardens also contain an impressive ornamental maze and an owl centre.

Five miles from Ravenglass is **Sellafield**, Britain's largest nuclear reprocessing plant. Long a source of controversy due to its proximity to the Lake District National Park, Sellafield is still a huge local employer, though

it's scheduled to be decommissioned over the next decade. In the meantime, the **visitor centre** (☎ 019467-27027; www.sellafield.com; admission free; ✹ 10am-6pm Apr-Oct, 10am-4pm Nov-Mar) houses a huge-scale interactive exhibition called Sparkling Reaction, which does its level best to bring out nuclear power's more entertaining side.

Ravenglass is on the Cumbrian Coast Line, with frequent links north and south along the coast. Bus 6 from Whitehaven stops at Ravenglass and terminates at Muncaster (70 minutes, five daily). Bus X6 travels the same route on Sunday (four daily).

WHITEHAVEN
☎ 01946 / pop 22622

The large harbour at Whitehaven was once the third-largest port in England, and officially made its fortune exporting local coal and iron ore, though the town was also a mover and shaker in the slave trade. Following the decline of the coal and iron industries, many of the town's buildings fell into disrepair, but a recent facelift has spruced up the marina, and its pastel-painted Georgian houses fairly gleam along the waterfront. Whitehaven hosts a bi-annual maritime festival.

The main **tourist office** (☎ 852939; tic@copelandbc .gov.uk; Market Pl; ✹ 9.30am-5pm Mon-Sat Apr-Oct, 10am-4.30pm Nov-Mar) is near the town centre. There's another small branch in the Beacon.

The **Beacon** (☎ 592302; www.thebeacon-whitehaven .co.uk; West Strand; admission £4.50; ✹ 10am-5.30pm Tue-Sun Apr-Oct, 10am-4.30pm Nov-Mar) sets out to explore Whitehaven's shipshape heritage, with displays on smuggling, sailing and the sugar, rum and slave trades, as well as an interactive gallery where you can try your hand at being a TV weather forecaster.

Whitehaven's dark spirit comes alive at the tacky **Rum Story** (☎ 592933; www.rumstory.co.uk; Lowther St; admission £4.95; ✹ 10am-5pm Apr-Sep, 10am-4pm Wed Sun Oct-Mar), housed in an 18th-century liquor warehouse. It probably won't be of much interest unless you're a fan of fibreglass models and dodgy interactive exhibits – the most interesting time to visit is after dark, when there's a nightly ghost tour. Ask at the ticket office for details.

Sleeping & Eating

Corkickle Guest House (☎ 692073; 1 Corkickle; s/d from £30/45; ✗) This pale-cream townhouse stands at the end of a delightful Regency ter-

CUMBRIA & THE LAKES

race near Corkickle train station, and offers quaint rooms as well as a lovely lounge for guests' use.

Glenfield Guest House (☎ 691911; www.glenfield -whitehaven.co.uk; s/d £35/55; P ✗) A Victorian house decorated with bay windows and red-brick surrounds, set in the heart of Whitehaven's conservation area. The six rooms are finished in light colours and pretty wallpapers, and all have private bathrooms.

Moresby Hall (☎ 696317; www.moresbyhall.co.uk; Moresby; s £45-65, d £70-90; P ✗) Ever fancied staying in a stately home? Then this ornate Grade I–listed mansion house is for you. While not all the bedrooms quite live up to the impressive standard set by the house itself, most are very comfortable and great for the price – the very best have freestanding baths, hydromassage showers and extravagant beds, so make sure you see a few before you make your choice.

Zest (☎ 66981; 8 West Strand; ☾ breakfast, lunch & dinner) Right beside the harbour, this citrus-coloured café-bar has all the trappings of a contemporary eatery (globe lights, chrome tables and funky colours) and a lively menu to match, ranging from gourmet burgers to seafood and salad wraps. There's a more up-market branch on Low Rd that's welcomed several famous guests, including none other than Tony and Cherie Blair.

Getting There & Away

Whitehaven is on the Cumbrian Coast Line with hourly trains in each direction. Bus 6/X6 travels to Ravenglass (one hour, four daily).

NORTH & EAST CUMBRIA

Many visitors speed through the northern and eastern reaches of Cumbria in a headlong dash for the Central Lakes, and if you're arriving by road or rail, chances are you'll skip this region altogether. But that's a shame, as this is an area that's well worth exploring in its own right – a bleakly beautiful landscape of isolated farms, barren heaths and solid hilltop towns, cut through by the Roman-built barrier of Hadrian's Wall.

CARLISLE
☎ 01228 / pop 70,409

Flung out on the very edge of England, on the border of the Debatable Lands, the fortress city of Carlisle is certainly no stranger to conflict: throughout its 2000-year history it's been the site of more sieges, skirmishes and sackings than almost anywhere else in the country.

The city's massive castle still stands as a reminder of its tempestuous past, but somehow its crenellated battlements, turrets and stout walls have managed to survive the centuries relatively intact. Carlisle is also home to Cumbria's only cathedral, built from the same rosy red sandstone that characterises the castle and many of the city's houses; during the 18th and 19th centuries, Carlisle became a bustling hub of the Industrial Revolution, and many of its neat red-brick terraces grew up to house the huge numbers of workers needed to keep the factories and mills running. These days, most of the heavy industries have moved on, and Carlisle is better known for its lively nightlife and busy shops, and as a handy base for exploring the Eden Valley and the Northern Lakes.

History
A Celtic camp or *caer* (preserved in the name of Carlisle) provided an early military station for the Romans. After the construction of Hadrian's Wall, Carlisle became the Romans' administrative centre in the northwest. Following centuries of intermittent conflict between Picts, Saxons and Viking raiders, the Normans seized Carlisle from the Scots in 1092, and William Rufus began construction of the castle and town walls.

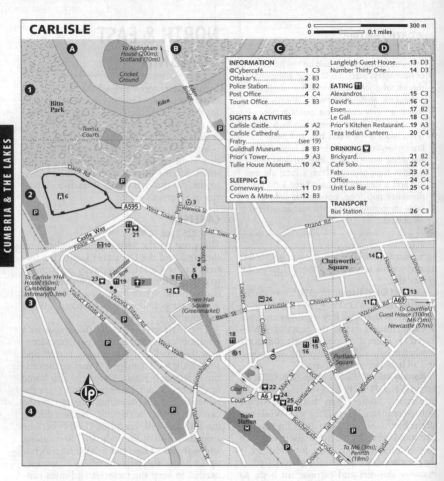

CARLISLE

INFORMATION
@Cybercafé......................1 C3
Ottakar's...........................2 B3
Police Station..................3 B2
Post Office........................4 C4
Tourist Office...................5 B3

SIGHTS & ACTIVITIES
Carlisle Castle..................6 A2
Carlisle Cathedral............7 B3
Fratry.............................(see 19)
Guildhall Museum...........8 B3
Prior's Tower....................9 A3
Tullie House Museum.....10 A2

SLEEPING
Cornerways....................11 D3
Crown & Mitre...............12 B3

Langleigh Guest House.......13 D3
Number Thirty One............14 D3

EATING
Alexandros......................15 C3
David's.............................16 C3
Essen...............................17 B2
Le Gall.............................18 C3
Prior's Kitchen Restaurant..19 A3
Teza Indian Canteen........20 C4

DRINKING
Brickyard.........................21 B2
Café Solo.........................22 C4
Fats..................................23 A3
Office...............................24 C4
Unit Lux Bar.....................25 C4

TRANSPORT
Bus Station......................26 C3

The English continued to develop Carlisle as a military stronghold throughout the Middle Ages, constructing the city walls, citadels and the great gates. During the Civil War, Royalist Carlisle was an important strategic base; the city was eventually taken, battered and starving, by the Roundhead Scottish army after a nine-month siege.

Peace only came to Carlisle with the Restoration. The city's future as an industrial centre was sealed with the arrival of the railways and the first cotton mills during the Industrial Revolution.

Orientation

From the M6, the main routes into town are London Rd and Warwick Rd. The train sta-

tion is south of the city centre, a 10-minute walk from Town Hall Sq (also known as Greenmarket) and the tourist office. The bus station is on Lonsdale St, about 250m east. Most of the town's B&Bs are dotted along Victoria Pl and Warwick Rd.

Information

@Cybercafé (☎ 512308; www.atcybercafe.co.uk; 8-10 Devonshire St; ☽ 10am-10pm Mon-Sun; per hr £3)
Cumberland Infirmary (☎ 523444; Newtown Rd) Half a mile west of the city centre.
Ottakar's (☎ 542300; 66 Scotch St; 9am-5.30pm Mon-Sat, 10am-4pm Sun) Large chain bookshop stocking new titles and local books.
Police station (☎ 528191) Just north of Town Hall Sq off Scotch St.

Post office (20-34 Warwick Rd)
Tourist office (☎ 625600; www.historic-carlisle.org.uk; Greenmarket; internet access per 15min £1; ☻ 9.30am-5pm Mon-Sat, 10.30am-4pm Sun) Offers a free accommodation-booking service for independent travellers.

Sights & Activities

CARLISLE CASTLE

English Heritage's brooding, rust-red **Carlisle Castle** (☎ 591922; admission £4.10; ☻ 9.30am-5pm Apr-Sep, 10am-4pm Oct-Mar) was built on the site of Celtic and Roman fortresses. The Norman keep was built in 1092 by William Rufus, and Mary Queen of Scots was briefly imprisoned here in 1568 after losing the Scottish throne. A maze of passages and chambers winds around the castle, and there are great views from the ramparts – you can even see some stones in the dungeon that prisoners licked to keep themselves hydrated. The castle also houses the Kings Own Royal Border Regiment Museum, which explores the history of Cumbria's Infantry Regiment. There are daily castle tours (£1.50) from April to September.

CARLISLE CATHEDRAL

The city's red sandstone **cathedral** (☎ 548151; donation £2; ☻ 7.30am-6.15pm Mon-Sat, 7.45am-5pm Sun) was originally constructed as a priory church in 1122. During the 1644–45 siege by Parliamentarian troops, two-thirds of the nave was torn down to help repair the city wall and castle. Serious restoration didn't begin until 1853, but a surprising amount survives, including the east window and part of the original Norman nave.

Features include the fine 14th-century east window, the 15th-century misericords, the lovely Brougham Triptych in the north transept, and some ornate choir carvings.

Surrounding the cathedral are other priory relics, including the 16th-century **Fratry** (see p720) and the **Prior's Tower**.

TULLIE HOUSE MUSEUM

This excellent **museum** (☎ 534781; Castle St; www .tulliehouse.co.uk; admission £5.20; ☻ 10am-5pm Mon-Sat & 11am-5pm Sun July-Aug, 10am-5pm Mon-Sat, noon-5pm Sun Apr-June & Sep-Oct, 10-4pm Mon-Sat, 12-4pm Sun Nov-Mar) brings Carlisle's history to life with exhibitions exploring the foundation of the city, life under Roman rule and the development of modern Carlisle. Highlights include an impressive reconstruction of Hadrian's Wall, and a lively audiovisual display on the Border Reivers.

The museum has a particularly good collection of local archaeology, including a Bronze Age spear-mould, a Saxon sword and several artefacts recovered from local Viking burial sites. There are also some good displays on fossils and minerals, as well as an impressive array of 18th- to 20th-century artwork including several pre-Raphaelite masterpieces.

GUILDHALL MUSEUM

This tiny **museum** (☎ 532781; Greenmarket; admission free; ☻ noon-4.30pm Tue-Sun Apr-Oct) is housed in a 15th-century townhouse that was later used by Carlisle's trade guilds. The various exhibits dotted around its wonky floors include a ceremonial mace, the city's stocks and an intriguing section of exposed wall showing the building's traditional wattle-and-daub construction.

Tours

Open Book Visitor Guiding (☎ 670578; www.grea tguidedtours.co.uk) offers tours of Carlisle and the surrounding area from April to September, including visits to Carlisle Castle and Hadrian's Wall.

Sleeping

BUDGET

Carlisle YHA Hostel (☎ 0870-770 5752; dee. carruthers@unn.ac.uk; Bridge Lane; dm £17.50; ☻ Jul-Sep) The old Theakston Brewery has been converted into student digs for the university; rooms are usually available during the summer holidays.

Courtfield Guest House (☎ 522767; mdawes@ courtfieldhouse.fsnet.co.uk; 169 Warwick Rd; s/d from £25/50; ✗) Another fine red-brick house in the guesthouse-heavy area around Warwick Rd, distinguished by its great-value rooms and friendly owners.

Cornerways (☎ 521733; www.cornerwaysguesthouse .co.uk; 107 Warwick Rd; s/d from £30/50; Ⓟ ✗) This Grade II–listed corner house still boasts its original Victorian tiled hallway and much of its original cornicing; the rooms are simple and inviting, with smart quilted bedspreads and pine furniture, although not all are en-suite.

MIDRANGE & TOP END

Langleigh Guest House (☎ 530440; www.langleigh house.co.uk; 6 Howard Pl; s/d £30/60; Ⓟ ✗) Victorian grandeur is the watchword at this beautifully appointed B&B, which positively brims with polished furniture, leather armchairs, oil paintings and gilt mirrors, and a range of variable rooms positioned around its meandering staircase. More rooms are offered in a second townhouse along the street.

Aldingham House (☎ 522554; www.aldinghamhouse .co.uk; 1 Eden Mount; s/d £50/75; ℗ ☒ ⌨) Just north of the city centre across the River Eden, this lovely, luxurious B&B has three individually decorated bedrooms, selectively splashed in checks, spots and stripes and furnished with rich fabrics and muted lighting. The sumptuous breakfast includes Loch Fyne kippers, crumpets and fresh smoothies.

Number Thirty One (☎ 597080; www.number31 .freeservers.com; 31 Howard Pl; s/d from £60/85; ℗ ☒) An utterly ravishing B&B-cum-boutique hotel, with three bedrooms furnished with invention, wit and idiosyncratic style. Each room has its own cute character, ranging from an Oriental den to a cool blue boudoir, and the house is crammed with brassy antiques, period photos and Victorian ephemera. Why can't all B&Bs be like this?

Crown & Mitre (☎ 525491; www.crownandmitre-hotel -carlisle.com; English St; s £84, tw £100-115; ℗ ☒ ☙) This stately red-brick pile occupies a commanding spot overlooking the main market square, and in its heyday must have offered a taste of true Edwardian splendour. These days it's been totally modernised in standard chain-hotel style, so the rooms are efficient and well equipped but inescapably dull.

Eating

Alexandros (☎ 592227; 68 Warwick Rd; meze £3-6, mains £9-14; ☾ dinner Mon-Sat) A lively Greek restaurant serving up huge, authentic plates of meze, seared chicken kebabs and grilled octopus.

Prior's Kitchen Restaurant (☎ 543251; lunches £4-6; ☾ 9.45am-3pm or 4pm Mon-Sat) Housed in the former Fratry (monks' dining room) beside the cathedral, this reliable little tearoom is a good spot for cheap sandwiches, jacket spuds and afternoon tea.

Le Gall (☎ 818388; 7 Devonshire St; mains £5-8; ☾ lunch & dinner) Don't let the name fool you – this buzzy little bistro doesn't just do Franco-flavoured cuisine. The eclectic menu takes in flavours from practically everywhere, so you should be able to find something to take your fancy, whether it's an Italian panini or a Mexican fajita.

Essen (☎ 536336; 6-8 Fisher St; mains from £6; ☾ lunch & dinner) This groovy new bar-diner is the newest entry on Carlisle's culinary scene, split over two floors and decked out in spare, contemporary style. There's a light lunch menu or a more extensive evening menu offering mainly fish, chicken and fusion flavours.

Teza Indian Canteen (☎ 525111; 4a English Gate Plaza; mains £8-12; ☾ lunch & dinner Mon-Sat) The good old Indian comes crashing into the 20th century at this utterly contemporary restaurant. Forget flock wallpaper, fish-tanks and piped sitars – here it's all about clean lines, industrial styling and wireframe chairs, with a menu of Indian standards supplemented by 'contemporary mains' such as *narangi nu* duck, marinated in cloves and orange juice.

David's (☎ 523578; 62 Warwick Rd; mains £10-18; ☾ lunch & dinner Tue-Sat) Arguably Carlisle's top table, this refined French-British restaurant offers a carefully composed menu of *haute cuisine* dishes such as roast venison and monkfish in parma ham.

Drinking

Loads of designer bars and drinking holes have sprung up around the newly renovated Botchergate area, so head there if you're after some after-dark action.

Office (☎ 404303; Botchergate) Sleek and chic, this is one of the favourite hang-outs for Carlisle's hip set. Kitted out in urban style with cube lights, razor-sharp tables and a massive industrial bar, breakbeat, hip-hop and soul spin on the turntables.

Unit Lux Bar (☎ 514823; Botchergate) Just along the street from Office, this is another achingly trendy bar with the requisite flat-screen TVs, retro seats and deep leather sofas.

Fats (☎ 511774; 48 Abbey St; ☾ 11am-11pm) Hidden away near the cathedral, this swish open-plan bar is another fine place for a night on the tiles, with a huge menu of 'classic' and 'bespoke' cocktails.

Café Solo (☎ 631600; 1 Botchergate) For something rather less exclusive, this corner coffee bar has a vaguely Spanish vibe and serves great coffee by day, and cool Sol beers by night.

Brickyard (☎ 512220; 14 Fisher St) Carlisle's main venue for gigs and live music, housed in the former Memorial Hall.

Getting There & Away
BUS

Carlisle is Cumbria's main transport hub. Direct National Express buses travel to London (£30.50, six hours, two direct daily, with extra buses via Preston and Birmingham), Glasgow (£15.60, two hours, 13 daily) and Manchester (£22, three hours, six daily).

Local buses include bus 554 to Keswick (one hour, three daily), where you can catch the 555 LakesLink into the central Lake District. The 104 bus operates to Penrith (40 minutes, hourly Monday to Saturday, nine on Sunday), and Bus AD122 (the Hadrian's Wall bus; six daily late May to late September) connects Hexham and Carlisle.

TRAIN

Regular trains operate from London Euston (£111, four hours, nine to 12 daily).

Carlisle is the terminus for the following five scenic railways (call ☎ 08457 484950 for timetable details and information on Day Ranger passes):

Cumbrian Coast Line This follows the coastline to Lancaster (£21, 3½ hours), with beautiful views over the Irish Sea.

Glasgow–Carlisle Line The main route to Glasgow passes through spectacular Scottish landscape (£30.50, 1½ hours).

Lakes Line This line branches off the main north–south line at Oxenholme near Kendal for Windermere (£17.50, 1½ hours).

Settle–Carlisle Line Cuts southeast across the Yorkshire Dales (£14.45, 1½ hours).

Tyne Valley Line Follows Hadrian's Wall to Newcastle-upon-Tyne (£10.60, 1½ hours).

Getting Around

To book a taxi, call **Radio Taxis** (☎ 527575), **Citadel Station Taxis** (☎ 523971) or **County Cabs** (☎ 596789).

PENRITH

☎ 01768 / pop 14,966

Nestled at the head of the lush Eden Valley, the sturdy red-brick market town of Penrith was once the capital of Cumbria, and it's still an important commercial centre, with a bustling high street and a network of colonnaded arcades packed with outdoors shops, cafés, tearooms and traditional grocery stores. All roads in Penrith lead to the main market square, dominated by an ornate 19th-century clock tower built in memory of local notable Philip Musgrave; high above the town stands Beacon Fell, where beacons have been lit in times of emergency since the days of Henry VIII, and where sentries were once posted to warn of border raids.

Information

Library (☎ 242100; St Andrew's Churchyard; ⏳ Mon-Sat)

Tourist office (☎ 867466; pen.tic@eden.gov.uk; Middlegate; ⏳ 9.30am-5pm Mon-Sat, 1-4.45pm Sun) Also houses a small town museum.

Sights

The plundered ruins of **Penrith Castle** (⏳ 7.30am-9pm Easter-Oct, 7.30am-4.30pm Oct-Easter) occupy a park opposite the station. The 14th-century castle was built by William Strickland (later Bishop of Carlisle and Archbishop of Canterbury) to resist Scottish raids, one of which razed the town in 1345. The castle was later expanded by Richard, Duke of Gloucester – better known as Richard III – but fell into disrepair in the 16th century.

Penrith's name derives from an old Celtic word meaning 'red fell', and most of the town's buildings are built from the same rust-red sandstone, including the 18th-century **St Andrew's Church**. A legendary giant (the 'rightful king of all Cumbria') is said to be buried in the churchyard, but the stone pillars that supposedly mark his grave are actually the weathered remains of Celtic crosses.

Sleeping

Penrith's best B&Bs stand side by side along Portland Pl.

Hornby Hall (☎ 891114; www.hornbyhall.co.uk; Brougham; s £30, tw £50-76, d £80; P ✗) Three miles south of Penrith in the hamlet of Brougham, this amber-stoned 16th-century mansion house still has a stunning assortment of medieval and Victorian features, including a huge dining hall, a massive cast-iron cooking range and a spiral stone staircase that dates from the days of Columbus. The rooms are quaint, sunny and delightfully simple, and a slap-up dinner is available on request.

Brandelhow (☎ 864470; www.brandelhowguesthouse .co.uk; 1 Portland Pl; s £30, d/tw £60; ✗) Just a few rooms are on offer at this dignified townhouse at the head of Portland Pl, and all are furnished in fairly typical style with lashings of pine and magnolia paint, as well as the odd antique rocking chair and wrought-iron bed. Tea and homemade cake greets guests on their arrival – try the bootle gingerbread.

Brooklands (☎ 863395; www.brooklandsguesthouse .com; 2 Portland Pl; s £30-35 d £60-70; ✗) Behind the characteristic red-brick exterior of this three-floored Victorian residence you'll discover an enticing array of top-drawer rooms; some feature huge pine four-posters and scarlet fabric bedspreads, while others opt for more modest tints of cream and apple-green. Best of all, though, is the flashy, fluffy-pillowed suite, which comes with brass bedstead and wall-mounted plasma TV.

George Hotel (☎ 862696; www.georgehotelpenrith .co.uk; Devonshire St; s £55-71, d £96-156; P ✗) Smack bang in the middle of town is Penrith's most venerable hotel, a historic coaching inn built in Penrith brick and furnished in upmarket style. Pelmeted drapes, rich country furnishings and thick carpets find their way into every room, although they lack that all-important personal touch.

Eating

No 15 Café Bar (☎ 867453; 15 Victoria Rd; lunches £6-8; ☺ daily) Fifteen reasons to visit this café-bar-gallery are chalked up on the blackboard behind the counter, but you won't need much persuasion. It's Penrith's best place for lunch, cakes and coffee, with a light-filled dining room and a gallery annexe displaying local photography and artwork; lunchtime mains range from turkey and cranberry burgers to homemade soups.

George Hotel (☎ 862696; Devonshire St; mains from £11; ☺ lunch & dinner) For a sit-down meal in Penrith, you can't do much better than the good old George, which has been feeding hungry wayfarers for well over two centuries. Country dishes are very much the mainstays here, served up in a semi-formal dining room embellished with candles, country prints and Victorian frosted glass.

ourpick Yanwath Gate Inn (☎ 862886; Yanwath; mains £14-19) Two miles south of Penrith, and affectionately known to locals as the Yat, this wonderful 17th-century inn has scooped up a clutch of national pub awards for its imaginative cooking and creative use of local produce – Fellbred lamb, organic guinea fowl and Bessyback trout all feature on the varied menu, and the traditional Cumbrian interior is crammed with oak-beamed, stone-walled character.

Getting There & Away

BUS

The bus station is northeast of the centre, off Sandgate. Bus 104 runs between Penrith and Carlisle (45 minutes, 16 daily Monday to Saturday, nine on Sunday).

Bus X4/X5 connects Penrith to the Lakes and the Cumbrian coast hourly Monday to Saturday and six times on Sunday, calling at Keswick and Cockermouth before terminating at Workington.

TRAIN

Penrith has frequent connections to Carlisle (£6.40, 20 minutes, hourly) and Lancaster (£11.50, 50 to 60 minutes, hourly).

AROUND PENRITH
Rheged Discovery Centre

Cunningly disguised as a Lakeland hill 2 miles west of Penrith, **Rheged** (☎ 01768-686000; www.rheged.com; 1 film or attraction £5.95; ☺ 10am-6pm) houses a large-screen Imax cinema and the Helly Hansen National Mountaineering Exhibition. The cinema shows five Imax films covering the Amazonian rainforest, the Grand Canyon, Mount Everest and Shackleton's Antarctic explorations; rather less impressive is *Rheged*, a ropey time-travel film that follows its central character from the days of King Arthur through to the Romantic era. Current and classic films are also shown on the big screen.

The mountaineering exhibition includes memorabilia, photographs and archive film, as well as a collection of artefacts belonging to George Mallory (the British mountaineer who died climbing Everest in 1924).

The frequent X4/X5 bus between Penrith and Workington stops at the centre.

ALSTON
☎ 01434 / pop 2181

Surrounded on every side by the bleak hilltops of the North Pennines, isolated Alston's main claim to fame is its elevation: at around 305m above sea level, it's thought to be the highest market town in England (despite no longer having a market). With its steep cobbled main street and sturdy stone buildings, it's long been a favourite with directors looking for that classic northern backdrop, and was recently used in TV adaptations of *Jane Eyre* and *Oliver Twist*.

The narrow-gauge **South Tynedale Railway** (☎ 381696, talking timetable 382828; www.strps.org.uk; adult return £5) puffs from Alston to Kirkhaugh, along a route that originally operated from 1852 to 1976. It's a picturesque, high-level journey, following the River Tyne northwards; there and back takes one hour.

WORTH THE TRIP

The third-largest prehistoric stone circle in England, Long Meg and Her Daughters is a ring of 59 stones, 6 miles northeast of Penrith. Local legend maintains that the circle was once a coven of witches, zapped into stone by a local wizard. The circle is said to be uncountable (if anyone manages twice the spell will be lifted) and a terrible fate awaits anyone who disturbs the stones. Just outside the circle stands Long Meg herself, a 12ft red sandstone pillar decorated with faint spiral traces – another local legend says that the stone would run with blood if it were ever damaged.

The circle is about 6 miles northeast of Penrith, along a minor road about ¾ mile north of Little Salkeld, just off the A686.

The **tourist office** (☎ 382244; alston.tic@eden.gov.uk; Town Hall; ☑ 10am-5.30pm Mon-Sat & 10am-4pm Sun Apr-Oct) is just south of the town square.

Sleeping & Eating

Alston YHA Hostel (☎ 0870 770 5668; The Firs; dm £11.95; ☑ Easter-Oct) There are only three dorms at this modern hostel overlooking the South Tyne Valley, and they fill up fast with walkers and cyclists on the C2C route, so book ahead.

Lowbyer Manor (☎ 381230; www.lowbyer.com; Alston; s/d £33/66; ☒) The rooms at this Georgian manor house might be a little old-fashioned, but the mismatched furniture and occasionally tired décor is livened up by patchwork quilts and the odd colourful cushion. The best rooms have valley views and period trappings, so ask to see a few before you choose.

Nenthall Country House Hotel (☎ 381584; www.nenthallcountryhousehotel.co.uk; d £35-70; P ☒) Stay in truly regal style at this former country retreat of a well-heeled mine-owner, 2 miles east of Alston. A selection of rooms are scattered around the huge multi-winged building, the best of which are furnished in period style with huge mirrors, flouncy pelmets and soft sofas – pick of the bunch is the lavish five-room tower suite, with views across the landscaped grounds and enough space to swing a Cumbrian cow.

Angel Inn (☎ 381363; Front St) The town's oldest inn is still the best choice for fortifying pub food, especially Alston's trademark sausage accompanied by creamy mash and a pint of warm bitter.

Getting There & Away

Bus 888 runs between Newcastle and Keswick via Alston and Penrith once daily. Bus 680 runs from Nenthead to Carlisle via Alston (three daily Monday to Saturday).

Northeast England

Perched atop of England, along the border with Scotland, the northeast has always been frontier country – its people passionate, independent and generally isolated from the rest of the island below. You only need take a glance at the vast, almost epic countryside to get a sense of its brooding, menacing beauty – from the wind-lashed stretch of coast through the heather-carpeted Cheviot Hills and on into the wilderness of Northumberland National Park before arriving at the feet of the dark slopes of the North Pennines. Beyond them is Scotland, the other actor in an 800-year-old historical drama of war, bloodshed and conquest: no wonder the folks up here have a reputation for being hardy.

It's been tough round these parts since prehistory, and it's taken an almost superhuman effort to leave a mark on this indomitable landscape. The Romans were successful; their legacy is the magnificent Hadrian's Wall, which served as their empire's northern frontier for nearly 300 years. The Normans weren't half bad either: they dotted the landscape with more castles and, in Durham, built one of the world's most beautiful cathedrals. Against their splendid backdrops, these marvellous constructions serve only to reinforce an impression of a landscape that hasn't changed much since the region was part of the ancient kingdom of Northumbria.

If you look closely, however, you will see that the landscape is run through with dark, menacing scars: dotted throughout are the rusting hulks of an industry that drove this region for nearly 700 years. Mining is all but defunct now, yet the cities it built are still very much alive, none more so than Newcastle, the biggest in the region and one of the most dynamic urban centres in England.

NORTHEAST ENGLAND

HIGHLIGHTS

- Gettin' doon in toon with a bottle of dog, aka taking on **Newcastle's wild nightlife** (p734)
- Walking like a Roman – hiking along the stunning **Hadrian's Wall** (p746)
- Castle-spotting along the blustery white-sand beaches of **Northumberland** (p750)
- Exploring Durham's industrial history at the **Beamish Open Air Museum** (p741)
- Going Norman in **Durham** (p737), whose cathedral is a spectacular World Heritage Site
- Hiking to the top of the **Cheviot** (p761) in Northumberland National Park

★ Northumberland

Northumberland National Park ★

★ Hadrian's Wall

Newcastle-upon-Tyne ★

Durham ★

■ POPULATION: 2.5 MILLION | ■ AREA: 3320 SQ MILES

Orientation & Information

The Pennine hills are the dominant geological feature, forming a north–south spine that divides the region from Cumbria and Lancashire in the west and provides the source of major rivers such as the Tees and the Tyne.

The major transport routes are east of this spine, from Durham northwards to Newcastle and Edinburgh. Newcastle is an important ferry port for Scandinavia (see p735 for details). There's a northeast region website at www.thenortheast.com.

Activities

With the rugged moors of the Pennines and stunning seascape of the Northumberland coast, there's some good walking and cycling in this region. The scenery is beautiful in a wild and untouched way – quite different from the picture-postcard landscape of areas such as Devon or the Cotswolds. If you're out in the open, be prepared for wind and rain at any time of year. But when the sun shines, you can't go wrong. More details on walking and cycling are given in the Outdoor Activities chapter (p75), and suggestions for shorter routes are given throughout this chapter. Regional tourism websites all contain walking and cycling information, and tourist information centres (TICs; referred to throughout this book simply as tourist offices) all stock free leaflets plus maps and guides (usually £1 to £5) covering walking, cycling and other activities.

CYCLING

There are some excellent cycling routes in this part of the world. A longtime favourite is the **Coast & Castles Cycle Route**, which runs south–north along the glorious Northumberland coast between Newcastle-upon-Tyne and Berwick-upon-Tweed, before swinging inland into Scotland to finish at Edinburgh. (This route is part of the National Cycle Network – see the boxed text, p78) Of course you can also do it north–south, or just do the northeast England section. The coast is exposed, though, so check the weather and try to time your ride so that the wind is behind you.

The 140-mile **Sea to Sea Cycle Route** (C2C; www .c2c-guide.co.uk) runs across northern England from Whitehaven or Workington on the Cumbrian coast, through the northern part of the Lake District, and then over the wild hills

of the North Pennines to finish at Newcastle-upon-Tyne or Sunderland. This popular route is fast becoming a classic, and most people go west–east to take advantage of prevailing winds. You'll need five days to complete the whole route; the northeast England section, from Penrith (in Cumbria) to the east coast is a good three-day trip. If you wanted to cut the urban sections, Penrith to Consett is perfect in a weekend. The C2C is aimed at road bikes, but there are several optional off-road sections.

The other option is the brand-new **Hadrian's Cycleway** (www.cycleroutes.org.uk), a 172-mile route opened in July 2006 that runs from South Shields in Tyneside, west along the wall and down to Ravenglass (p716) in Cumbria.

The newish **Wheels to the Wild** is a 70-mile circular cycle route that explores the dales of the North Pennines. From Wolsingham, it weaves a paved route through Weardale, Allendale and Teesdale on mostly quiet country lanes.

For dedicated off-road riding, good places to aim for in northeast England include Kielder Forest in Northumberland and Hamsterley Forest in County Durham, which both have a network of sylvan tracks and options for all abilities.

WALKING

The North Pennines are billed as 'England's last wilderness', and if you like to walk in quiet and fairly remote areas, these hills – along with the Cheviots further north – are the best in England. Long routes through this area include the famous **Pennine Way**, which keeps mainly to the high ground as it crosses the region between the Yorkshire Dales and the Scottish border, but also goes through sections of river valley and some tedious patches of plantation. The whole route is over 250 miles, but the 70-mile section between Bowes and Hadrian's Wall would be a fine four-day taster. If you prefer to go walking just for the day, good bases for circular walks include the towns of Alston (p722) and Middleton-in-Teesdale (p743).

Elsewhere in the area, the great Roman ruin of **Hadrian's Wall** is an ideal focus for walking. There's a huge range of easy loops taking in forts and other historical highlights. A very popular walk is the long-distance route from end to end, providing good options for anything from one to four days (see p747).

NORTHEAST ENGLAND

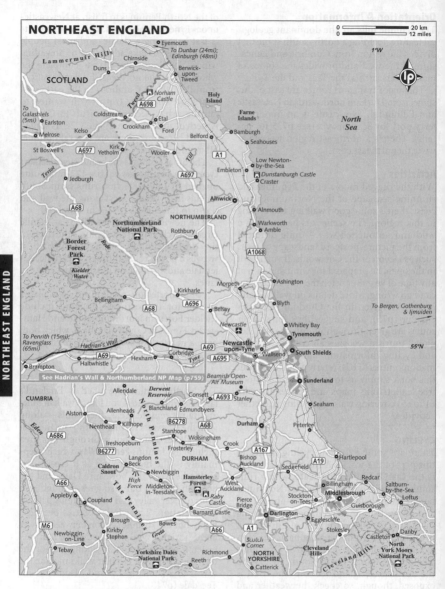

NORTHEAST ENGLAND

The Northumberland coast has endless miles of open beaches, and little in the way of resort towns (the frequently misty weather has seen to that), so walkers can often enjoy this wild, windswept shore in virtual solitude. One of the finest walks is between the villages of Craster and Bamburgh via Dunstanburgh, which includes two of the area's most spectacular castles.

Getting There & Around

BUS

Bus transport around the region can be difficult, particularly around the more remote parts of Northumbria in the west. Call ☎ 0870 608 2608 for information on connections, timetables and prices.

Several one-day Explorer tickets are available; always ask if one might be appropriate. The Explorer North East (adult/child £5.75/4.75), available on buses, covers from Berwick down to Scarborough, and allows unlimited travel for one day, as well as numerous admission discounts.

TRAIN

The main lines run north to Edinburgh via Durham, Newcastle and Berwick, and west to Carlisle roughly following Hadrian's Wall. Travelling to/from the south, it may be necessary to make connections at Leeds. Phone ☎ 0845 748 4950 for all train inquiries.

There are numerous Rover tickets for single-day travel and longer periods, so ask if one might be worthwhile. For example, the North Country Rover (adult/child £61.50/30.75) allows unlimited travel throughout the north (not including Northumberland) any four days out of eight.

NEWCASTLE-UPON-TYNE

☎ 0191 / pop 189,870

For the uninitiated, Newcastle is all about coal and industry – the lifeblood of modern civilisation but not that interesting for tourists. First things first: get rid of all those notions. You won't find a trace of coal dust anywhere and what little industry there is left is safely confined to the suburbs not mentioned anywhere in these pages. These days, Newcastle is superstylin', a cool urban centre that knows all about how to take care of itself and anyone else who comes to visit.

Yet, thankfully, Newcastle has built this new reputation as a hipster capital on a set of deep-rooted traditions and mores embodied by the city's greatest strength: the locals. Geordies (see the boxed text, right) are a fiercely independent bunch, tied together by history, adversity and that impenetrable dialect, the closest language to 1500-year-old Anglo-Saxon left in England. They are also proud, hard-working and indefatigably positive – perhaps their greatest quality considering how tough life has been.

Their city is a reflection of all those characteristics. Raised and subsequently abandoned by coal and steel, Newcastle has matured into an elegant city of some grace and culture, exemplified not just by its excellent new art galleries and magnificent concert hall, but by its growing number of fine restaurants, choice hotels and interesting bars. It's not just about the Tyne bridges – although the eclectic, cluttered array of Newcastle's most recognisable feature is pretty impressive.

As is the city's great draw. A night out on the town is the alpha and omega of so many visits to the city, and the energy you'll find is so irrepressible that it borders on the irresponsible – how can they wear so little when it's so bloody cold?

ORIENTATION

The River Tyne marks the boundary between Newcastle to the north and Gateshead to the south; it is also one of the focal points for visitors to the city. Newcastle's attractive Victorian centre – which the local council has called Grainger Town to the uncertain shrugs of the locals – is only a short, uphill walk from the river. Between the river and the centre is Central Station (train). The coach station is on Gallowgate, while local and regional buses leave from Eldon Square and Haymarket bus stations. Jesmond is north of the city centre, and easily reached by bus or with the excellent Metro underground system.

The Tyne's southern bank – home to the impressive Baltic gallery and stunning Sage – is as far into Gateshead as you'll likely need to venture.

WHY A GEORDIE?

Truth is, no one really knows for sure, not even the Geordies themselves. The most attractive explanation, at least here, is that the name was coined to disparage the townspeople who chose to side with the German Protestant George I against the 'Old Pretender', the Catholic James Stuart, during the Jacobite Rebellion of 1715. But a whole other school contends that the origins are a little less dramatic, and stem from Northumberland miners opting to use a lamp pioneered by George 'Geordie' Stephenson over one invented by Sir Humphrey Davy.

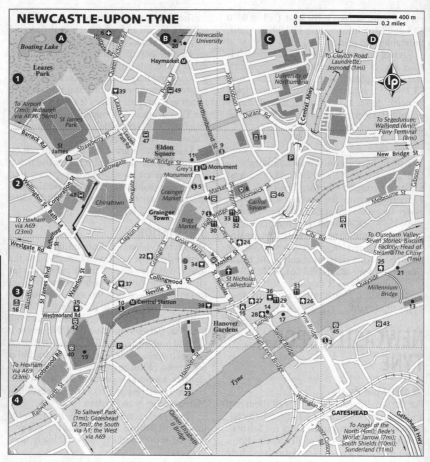

NEWCASTLE-UPON-TYNE

Maps

All tourist offices have handy, free tearaway maps of Newcastle and Gateshead. The Ordnance Survey's *Mini-Map* (£1.50) is a handy foldaway pocket map of Newcastle, but not Gateshead.

The **Newcastle Map Centre** (☎ 261 5622; www .newtraveller.com; 1st fl, 55 Grey St) supplies copious maps and guides.

INFORMATION
Bookshops

Blackwell's Bookshop (☎ 232 6421; 141 Percy St) A comprehensive range of titles.
Waterstone's (☎ 261 6140; 104 Grey St) There's another branch, also near Monument Metro, but this one is particularly finely housed.

Emergency

Police station (☎ 214 6555; cnr Pilgrim & Market Sts)

Internet Access

Internet Exchange (☎ 221 1746; Newcastle City Library, Princess Sq; 9am-7.45pm Mon-Sat, noon-3.45pm Sun; 30 mins £1)

Laundry

Clayton Road Laundrette (☎ 281 5055; 4 Clayton Rd, Jesmond)

Medical Services

Newcastle General Hospital (☎ 273 8811; Westgate Rd) Half a mile northwest of the city centre, off Queen Victoria St.

Money

Thomas Cook (☎ 219 8000; 6 Northumberland St) Has a bureau de change; it's just east of Monument.

Post

Main post office (35 Mosley St; ☺ 9am-5.30pm Mon-Fri, to 12.30pm Sat) In the city centre.

Tourist Information

Gateshead Quays Visitor Centre (☎ 478 4222; St Mary's Church, Oakwellgate; ☺ 9am-5pm Mon-Fri, 11am-5pm Sat & Sun) Information on Gateshead's attractions.

Tourist offices Grainger St (☎ 277 8000; www.visit-newcastlegateshead.com; 132 Grainger St; ☺ 9.30am-5.30pm Mon-Wed, Fri & Sat, to 7.30pm Thu year-round, plus 10am-4pm Sun Jun-Sep); Guildhall (☎ 277 8000; ☺ 11am-6pm Mon-Fri, 9am-6pm Sat, 9am-4pm Sun); Airport (☎ 214 4422). All offices listed here provide a booking service (☎ 277 8042) as well as other assorted tourist sundries.

SIGHTS
Quayside

Newcastle's most recognisable attractions are the seven bridges that span the Tyne and some of the striking buildings that line it. Along Quayside, on the river's northern side, is a handsome boardwalk that makes for a pleasant stroll during the day but really comes to life at night, when the bars, clubs and restaurants that line it are full to bursting. A really great way of experiencing the river and its sights is by cruise (see Tours, p732).

TYNE BRIDGES

The most famous view in Newcastle is the cluster of Tyne bridges, and the most famous of these is the **Tyne Bridge** (1925–28), built at about the same time as (and very reminiscent of) Australia's Sydney Harbour Bridge. The quaint little **Swing Bridge** pivots in the middle to let ships through. Nearby, **High Level Bridge**, designed by Robert Stephenson, was the world's first road and railway bridge (1849). The most recent addition is the multiple award winning **Millennium Bridge** (aka Blinking Bridge; 2002), which opens like an eyelid to let ships pass.

OTHER SIGHTS

The Tyne's northern bank was the hub of commercial Newcastle in the 16th century. On Sandhill is **Bessie Surtee's House** (☎ 261 1585; 41-44 Sandhill; admission free; ☺ 10am-4pm Mon-Fri), a combination of two 16th- and 17th-century merchant houses – all dark wood and sloping angles. Three rooms are open to the public. The daughter of a wealthy banker, feisty Bessie annoyed Daddy by falling in love with John Scott (1751–1838), a pauper. It all ended in smiles because John went on to become Lord Chancellor. Today it is run in conjunction with English Heritage (EH; for details see p776).

Just across the street is the rounded **Guildhall**, built in 1658. It now houses a branch of the tourist office.

City Centre

Newcastle's Victorian centre, a compact area bordered roughly by Grainger St to the west and Pilgrim St to the east, is supremely elegant and one of the most compelling examples of urban rejuvenation in England. At the heart of it is the supremely handsome Grey St, lined with fine classical buildings – undoubtedly one of the country's finest thoroughfares.

LIFE SCIENCE CENTRE

This excellent **science village** (☎ 243 8210; www .lifesciencecentre.org.uk; Scotswood Rd; adult/child £7.50/4.95; ☼ 10am-6pm Mon-Sat, 11am-6pm Sun, last admission 4pm), part of the sober-minded International Centre for Life (a complex of institutes devoted to the study of genetic science), is one of the more interesting attractions in town. Through a series of hands-on exhibits and the latest technology you (or your kids) can discover the incredible secrets of life. The highlight is the Motion Ride, a motion simulator that, among other things, lets you 'feel' what it's like to score a goal at St James' Park and bungee jump from the Tyne Bridge. There's lots of thought-provoking arcade-style games, and if the information sometimes gets lost on the way, never mind, kids will love it.

LAING ART GALLERY

The exceptional collection at the **Laing** (☎ 232 7734; www.twmuseums.org.uk; New Bridge St; admission free; ☼ 10am-5pm Mon-Sat, 2-5pm Sun) includes works by Kitaj, Frank Auerbach, Henry Moore and an important collection of paintings by John Martin (1789–1854), a Northumberland-born artist.

Outside the gallery is Thomas Heatherwick's famous **Blue Carpet** (2002) with shimmering blue tiles made from crushed glass and resin.

DISCOVERY MUSEUM

Newcastle's rich history is uncovered through a fascinating series of exhibits at this excellent **museum** (☎ 232 6789; www.twmuseums.org.uk; Blandford Sq; admission free; ☼ 10am-5pm Mon-Sat, 2-5pm Sun). The exhibits, spread across three floors of the former Co-operative Wholesale Society building, surround the mightily impressive 30m-long *Turbinia*, the fastest ship in the world in 1897. The different sections are all worth a look; our favourites were the self-explanatory Story of the Tyne and the interactive Science Maze.

CASTLE GARTH KEEP

The 'New Castle' that gave its name to the city has been largely swallowed up by the railway station, leaving only the square Norman **keep** (adult/child £1.50/50p; ☼ 9.30am-5.30pm Apr-Sep, to 4.30pm Oct-Mar) as one of the few remaining fragments. It has a fine chevron-covered chapel

NORTHEAST ENGLAND

NEWCASTLE IN...

Two Days

Newcastle is all about Quayside, where you'll find the famous **Tyne bridges** (p729) and the remaining bits of 17th-century Newcastle, including **Bessie Surtee's House** (p729). A good walk is to cross the Millennium Bridge into Gateshead and check out **Baltic** (opposite) and the **Sage** (p735). Wander back across the bridge and hop on a Quayside Q2 bus out to the Ouseburn Valley to visit the **Biscuit Factory** (opposite) and (if you're with the kids) **Seven Stories** (opposite).

Back in the elegant Victorian centre, visit the **Laing Art Gallery** (above) and the **Life Science Centre** (above). Stop off in **Blake's Coffee House** (p733) for a pick-me-up. Work your way up to the **Trent House Soul Bar** (p734) and find that song you-love-but-haven't-heard-in-years on the incredible jukebox. And just keep going; everyone else is, so why shouldn't you?

The next day, if your head can take it, take the bus south through Gateshead to the **Angel of the North statue** (p736). Unfortunately, there's not much else going on here, so you'll have to head back into town. In the afternoon, take the Metro to Haymarket and explore the **museums** (opposite) at Newcastle University.

Four Days

Follow the two-day itinerary and add a side-trip to **Bede's World** (opposite) in the eastern suburb of Jarrow. In the afternoon, take a three-hour **sightseeing tour** (p732) along the Tyne. The next day, head for the Roman fort at **Segedunum** (p736), at the start of Hadrian's Wall. All the while, be sure to fuel your efforts; **Blackie Boy** (p734), a pub in the centre of town, is another great choice.

and great views across the Tyne bridges from its rooftop.

Ouseburn Valley

About a mile east of the city centre is the **Ouseburn Valley**, the 19th-century industrial heartland of Newcastle and now one of the city's hippest districts. Pubs, bars, restaurants and clubs now occupy the once-derelict Victorian mills and warehouses. To get there, jump onto the yellow Quayside Q2 bus that runs a loop through the valley from the city centre.

THE BISCUIT FACTORY

No prizes for guessing what this brand-new public **art gallery** (☎ 261 1103; www.thebiscuitfactory.com; Stoddart St; admission free; ⏰ 10am-8pm Tue-Sat, 11am-5pm Sun) used to be. What it is now, though, is the country's biggest art shop, where you can peruse and buy work by artists from near and far in a variety of mediums, including painting, sculpture, glassware and furniture. Prices are thoroughly democratic, ranging from £20 to £25,000, but even if you don't buy, the art is excellent and there's a top-class restaurant upstairs.

SEVEN STORIES – THE CENTRE FOR CHILDREN'S BOOKS

A marvellous conversion of a handsome Victorian mill has resulted in **Seven Stories** (☎ 0845-271 0777; www.sevenstories.org.uk; 30 Lime St; adult/child £5/4; ⏰ 10am-5pm Mon-Wed & Fri-Sat, to 6pm Thu, 11am-5pm Sun), a very hands-on museum dedicated to the wondrous world of children's literature. Across the seven floors you'll find original manuscripts, a growing collection of artwork from the 1930s onwards and a constantly changing programme of exhibitions, activities and events designed to encourage the AA Milnes of the new millennium.

University Museums

Just north of the city, Newcastle University's rich array of museums and galleries are set to be transformed by the opening of the **Great North Museum** (www.greatnorthmuseum.org) sometime in 2009. It will combine the natural-history and archaeological collections of the Shefton and Hancock museums, the Museum of Antiquities and the Hatton Gallery.

The small but well-stocked **Shefton Museum of Greek Art & Archaeology** (☎ 222 8996; www.ncl.ac.uk /shefton-museum; Armstrong Bldg; admission free; ⏰ 10am-4pm Mon-Fri) will remain open until 2008, as will

---

---

the excellent **Museum of Antiquities** (☎ 222 7849; The Quadrangle; admission free; ⏰ 10am-5pm Mon-Sat), on the main university courtyard, where you can explore the history of Hadrian's Wall and all things Roman. The large spiders, iguanas and creepy stuffed birds of the **Hancock Museum** (☎ 222 6765; www.twmuseums.org.uk; Barras Bridge; admission £2.50; ⏰ 10am-5pm Mon-Sat, 2-5pm Sun) will not be seen again until the new museum's opening, but the well-known **Hatton Gallery** (☎ 222 6057; www.ncl.ac.uk/hatton; The Quadrangle; admission free; ⏰ 10am-5.30pm Mon-Fri, to 4.30pm Sat), with its permanent collection of West African art, will be part of the new project but will neither close nor move. Take the Metro to Haymarket.

Gateshead

You probably didn't realise that that bit of Newcastle south of the Tyne is the 'town' of Gateshead, but local authorities are going to great lengths to put it right, even promoting the whole kit-and-caboodle-on-Tyne as 'NewcastleGateshead'. A bit clumsy, but we get the point. To date, the ambitious programme of development has seen the transformation of the southern banks of the Tyne, but there's as yet little to make you travel further afield than the water's edge.

BALTIC – THE CENTRE FOR CONTEMPORARY ART

Once a huge, dirty, yellow grain store overlooking the Tyne, **Baltic** (☎ 478 1810; www.baltic mill.com; admission free; ⏰ 10am-6pm Mon-Tue & Thu-Sun, to 8pm Wed) is now a huge, dirty, yellow art gallery to rival London's Tate Modern. Unlike the Tate, there are no permanent exhibitions here, but the constantly rotating shows feature the work and installations of some of contemporary art's biggest show stoppers. The complex has artists-in-residence, a performance space, a cinema, a bar, a spectacular rooftop restaurant (you'll need to book) and a ground-floor restaurant with riverside tables. There's also a viewing box for a fine Tyne vista.

NEWCASTLE FOR CHILDREN

Newcastle is friendly, full stop. Although at first glance the bonhomie mightn't seem to extend past buying rounds in the pub, on closer inspection there's plenty to keep the young 'uns entertained.

The new and utterly wonderful **Seven Stories** (p731) is the perfect destination for any kid who has an imagination, while closer to the centre the **Life Science Centre** (p730) and the **Discovery Museum** (p730) are brilliant and should keep the kids busy for the guts of a day.

The most popular park in town is **Leazes Park**, just north of St James Park, which has a rowing lake, but the nicest of all is **Saltwell Park** (dawn-dusk), an elegant Victorian space behind Gateshead College and easily accessible by bus 53 and 54 from the Gateshead Interchange. Pedestrians can get in through entrances on East Park Rd, West Rd, Saltwell Rd South, Saltwell View and Joicey Rd.

QUIRKY NEWCASTLE

Take in the David Lynch vibe at **Blackie Boy** (p734), where it's not all it appears to be. Pop your coins into the world's best jukebox at the **Trent House Soul Bar** (p734) for the stomping sound of Northern Soul and pretend that James Blunt had stayed in the army. Buy some art at the **Biscuit Factory** (p731) before checking out the gig list at the **Head of Steam@The Cluny** (p735). Take a rowing boat onto the lake at **Leazes Park** (above) – watch out for those fishing rods. Cross one of the **Tyne bridges** (p729) on foot.

TOURS

There are a handful of tour options:
River Tyne Cruises (296 6740/1; www.tyneleisure line.co.uk; adult/child £12/7; noon Sat-Sun May-early Sep) Three-hour river cruises departing from Quayside pier at Millennium Bridge, opposite Baltic.
Tom Keating Tours (488 5115; www.tomkeating .co.uk) Expert, tailor-made tours of the city by a well-

respected blue-badge guide. Tours of surrounding region also available.
Walking Tours (adult/child £3/2; 2pm Wed & Sat Jun & Sep, Mon-Sat Jul-Aug) 1½-hour walking tours of the main sites of interest, run by and departing from the Grainger St branch of the tourist office.

SLEEPING

Although the number of city-centre options is on the increase, they are still generally restricted to the chain variety – either budget or business – that caters conveniently to the party people and business folk that make up the majority of Newcastle's overnight guests. Most of the other accommodations are in the handsome northern suburb of Jesmond, where the forces of gentrification and student power fight it out for territory; Jesmond's main drag, Osborne Rd, is lined with all kinds of bed types as well as bars and restaurants – making it a strong rival with the city centre for the late-night party. As the city is a major business destination, weekend arrivals will find that most places drop their prices for Friday and Saturday nights.

City Centre

With only one exception, the closer you get to the river, the more you'll be required to fork out.

BUDGET

Albatross Inn! (233 1330; www.albatrossnewcastle .com; 51 Grainger St; dm/d from £16.50/22.50;) Finally a hostel in the city centre! It's brand new, clean and fully equipped with decent-sized dorms, a self-catering kitchen, top-notch bathroom facilities, CCTV, electronic key cards and an internet station. There's even a small car park.

MIDRANGE

Premier Lodge (0870 990 6530; www.premierlodge .com; Quayside; r from £28) With a superb location in the old Exchange Building, this budget chain is right in the heart of the action. If you're here for the party, you shouldn't care that your room has about as much flavour as day-old chewing gum – if all goes according to plan, you won't be spending much time here anyway!

TOP END

Greystreethotel (230 6777; www.greystreethotel.com; 2-12 Grey St; d/ste £135/175;) A bit of designer

class along the classiest street in the city centre
has been long overdue: the rooms are gorgeous if a tad poky, all cluttered up with flatscreen TVs, big beds and handsome modern
furnishings.

Malmaison (☎ 245 5000; www.malmaison.com; Quayside; d £119-140, ste £225-350; **P**) The affectedly
stylish Malmaison touch has been applied
to this former warehouse with considerable
success, although they could pull the brake
on the quasi-poetic publicity. Big beds, sleek
lighting and designer furniture flesh out the
Rooms of Many Pillows.

Waterside Hotel (☎ 230 0111; www.watersidehotel
.com; 48-52 Sandhill, Quayside; s/d £65/80) The rooms
are a tad small, but they're among the most
elegant in town: lavish furnishings and heavy
velvet drapes in a heritage-listed building. The
location is excellent.

Other good options in the high-end business hotel model:

Copthorne (☎ 222 0333; www.millenniumhotels.com;
The Close, Quayside; r £110-185; **P** 🖵 wi-fi 🐾) Superb
waterside location.

Vermont (☎ 233 1010; www.vermont-hotel.com; Castle
Garth; r £110-200; **P** 🖵 wi-fi) Mid-1930s Manhattan
with new-millennium facilities.

Jesmond

The bulk of Newcastle's budget and midrange accommodation is concentrated in the
northeastern suburb of Jesmond, mainly on
Osborne Rd. There are literally dozens of
hotels and B&Bs along this street; here we
recommend our favourites.

Catch the Metro to Jesmond or West Jesmond, or bus 80 from near Central Station, or
bus 30, 30B, 31B or 36 from Westgate Rd.

BUDGET

Newcastle YHA Hostel (☎ 0870 770 5972; www.yha.org
.uk; 107 Jesmond Rd; dm from £13.95; ☉ end Jan–end Dec)
This nice, rambling place has small dorms that
are generally full, so book in advance. It's close
to the Jesmond Metro stop.

MIDRANGE

Adelphi Hotel (☎ 281 3109; 63 Fern Ave; s/d £39.50/60)
Just off Osborne Rd, this attractive hotel has
nice floral rooms that are clean and very
neat – a rare thing around here for this price
range.

Gresham Hotel (☎ 281 6325; www.gresham-hotel
.com; 92 Osborne Rd; s/d from £50/70) Plenty of colours
light up the rooms at this pleasant hotel attached to the trendy Bar Bacca; it's extremely
popular with weekend visitors who swear by
the attentive-but-informal service.

Whites Hotel (☎ 281 5126; www.whiteshotel.com;
38-42 Osborne Rd; s/d £45/75) First impressions don't
promise a great deal, as the public areas are
a bit tatty, but don't let that put you off;
the bedrooms at this fine hotel are all uniformly modern and the service is positively
first rate.

TOP END

our pick **Jesmond Dene House** (☎ 212 3000; www
.jesmonddenehouse.co.uk; Jesmond Dene Rd; s £115, d £145-
195, ste £225-270; **P**) As elegant a hotel as you'll
find anywhere, this exquisite property is the
perfect marriage between traditional styles
and modern luxury. The large, gorgeous
bedrooms are furnished in a modern interpretation of the Arts and Crafts style and are
bedecked with all manner of technological
goodies (flat-screen digital TVs, digital radios,
wi-fi) and wonderful bathrooms complete
with underfloor heating.

EATING

The Geordie palate is pretty refined these
days and there are a host of fine dining options in all price categories that make their
mark. Conversely, if all you're looking for is
stomach-lining crappy fast-food and dodgy
ethnic cuisine, well there's plenty of that
as well.

City Centre

BUDGET

Blake's Coffee House (☎ 261 5463; 53 Grey St; breakfast
£2-3.95, sandwiches £3; ☉ 9am-6pm) There is nowhere better than this high-ceilinged café
for a Sunday-morning cure on any day of the
week. It's friendly, relaxed and serves up the
biggest selection of coffees in town, from the
gentle push of a Colombian blend to the toxic
shove of Old Brown Java. We love it.

MIDRANGE

Big Mussel (☎ 232 1057; www.bigmussel.co.uk; 15 The
Side; mains £6-12; ☉ lunch & dinner) Mussels and
other shellfish – all served with chips – are
a very popular choice at this informal diner.
There are pasta and vegetarian options as well,
and students get 15% off everything. There's
another branch (☎ 261 8927) on Leazes Park
Rd, close to St James' Park, that does a roaring
trade on match days.

Paradiso Café Bar (☎ 221 1240; 1 Market Lane; mains £8-12; ✋ lunch & dinner Mon-Sat, to 7pm Sun) Hidden away in a small alley off Pilgrim St is one of the city's most popular spots. Good food, a mellow atmosphere and a fabulous little balcony for alfresco action keeps this place full almost all the time.

TOP END

Café 21 (☎ 222 0755; 19-21 Queen St; mains £13-17; ✋ lunch & dinner Mon-Sat) Simple but hardly plain, this elegant restaurant – all white tablecloths and smart seating – offers new interpretations of England's culinary backbone: pork and cabbage, liver and onions and a sensational Angus beef and chips.

Secco Ristorante Salentino (☎ 230 0444; 86 Pilgrim St; mains £17-22; ✋ lunch & dinner) Top-notch food from Salento in the Italian heel of Puglia makes this place an easy contender for best Italian restaurant in town. Some punters have been disappointed with the slowish service, which, for the price, should probably be a little snappier.

Jesmond
MIDRANGE

Pizzeria Francesca (☎ 281 6586; 134 Manor House Rd, Jesmond; mains £4-12; ✋ lunch & dinner Mon-Sat) This is how all Italian restaurants should be like: chaotic, noisy, friendly, packed cheek-to-jowl and absolutely worth making the effort for. Excitable, happy waiters and huge portions of pizza and pasta keep them queuing at the door – get in line and wait because you can't book in advance.

TOP END

Jesmond Dene House (☎ 212 3000; www.jesmonddene house.co.uk; Jesmond Dene Rd; mains £18-22) Chef Terry Laybourne is the architect of an exquisite menu heavily influenced by the northeast – venison from County Durham, oysters from Lindisfarne and the freshest herbs plucked straight from the garden. The result is a gourmet delight and one of the best dining experiences in the city.

DRINKING

Hey, guess what? Geordies love a good night out! Whether it's the scantily clad brash and brazen draining coloured cocktails in and around the bars of Bigg Market or the more sophisticated punter sipping the same in the hotspots along Quayside and Mosley St, there are few cities that pursue the art of the bevvy with the same untrammelled fervour. And if you're looking for a spit 'n' sawdust kind of place to enjoy a traditional ale, well there are plenty of those too.

We daren't even begin to list the pubs and bars in town, but here's a handful to start with. Get a bottle of dog and get doon.

Blackie Boy (11 Groat Market) At first glance, this darkened old boozer looks like any old traditional pub. Look closer. The overly red lighting. The single bookcase. The large leather armchair that is rarely occupied. The signage on the toilets: 'Dick' and 'Fanny'. This place could have featured in *Twin Peaks*, which is why it's so damn popular with everyone.

Crown Posada (31 The Side) An unspoilt, real-ale pub that is a favourite with more seasoned drinkers, be they the after-work or instead-of-work crowd.

Forth (Pink Lane) It's in the heart of the gay district, but this great old pub draws all kinds with its mix of music, chat and unpretentious atmosphere.

Tokyo (17 Westgate Rd) Tokyo has a suitably darkened atmosphere for what the cognoscenti consider the best cocktail bar in town, but we loved the upstairs garden bar where you can drink, smoke and chat with a view.

our pick Trent House Soul Bar (1-2 Leazes Lane) The wall has a simple message: 'Drink Beer. Be Sincere.' This simply unique place is the best bar in town because it is all about an ethos rather than a look. Totally relaxed and utterly devoid of pretentiousness, it is an old-school boozer that out-cools every other bar because it isn't trying to. And because it has the best jukebox in all of England – you could spend years listening to the extraordinary collection of songs it contains. It is run by the same folks behind the superb **World Headquarters** (see opposite).

TOP FIVE PUBS FOR A PINT

- Trent House Soul Bar (above; Newcastle)
- Allenheads Inn (p746; Allen Valley)
- Ship Inn (p753; Low-Newton-by-the-Sea, Embleton Bay)
- Ye Old Cross (p752; Alnwick)
- Ship (p755; Holy Island)

NORTHEAST ENGLAND

ENTERTAINMENT

Are you up for it? You'd better be, because Newcastle's nightlife doesn't mess about. There is nightlife beyond the club scene – you'll just have to wade through a sea of staggering, glassy-eyed clubbers to get to it. For current listings go online to www.the-crackmagazine.com. Club admissions range from £4 to £15.

Live Music

Head of Steam@The Cluny (☎ 230 4474; www.head ofsteam.co.uk; 36 Lime St, Ouseburn Valley) This is one of the best spots in town to hear live music, attracting all kinds of performers, from experimental prog heads to up-and-coming pop goddesses. Touring acts and local talent fill the bill every night of the week. Take the Metro to Byker.

Sage Gateshead (☎ 443 4666; www.thesagegateshead .org; Gateshead Quays) Norman Foster's magnificent chrome-and-glass horizontal bottle is not just worth gaping at and wandering about in – it is also a superb venue to hear live music, from folk to classical orchestras. It is the home of the Northern Sinfonia and Folkworks.

Nightclubs

Digital (☎ 261 9755; www.yourfutureisdigital.com; Times Sq) The newest of Newcastle's megaclubs is this two-floored danceteria with one of the best sound systems we've ever heard. Our favourite night is Thursday's Stonelove (£4), a journey through 40 years of alternative rock and funk. Saturday's Shindig (£10 before 11pm, £12 after) is all about four to the floor.

Foundation (☎ 261 8985; www.foundation-club.com; 57-59 Melbourne St) This warehouse-style club features a massive sound system, fantastic lighting rig and regular guest slots of heavyweight DJs from all over. If you want a night of hard-core clubbing, this is the place for you.

Tuxedo Princess (☎ 477 8899; Hillgate Quay) A rite of passage for all Geordies, 'the Boat' is like dancing on the cross-Channel ferry. It's cheesy, sloppy and full of drunken teenagers holding down vomit while spinning on the revolving dance floor. Sounds crap, but it's still packed.

World Headquarters (☎ 261 7007; www.trenthouse .com; Curtis Mayfield House, Carliol Sq) Dedicated to the genius of black music in all its guises – funk, rare groove, dance-floor jazz, northern soul, genuine R&B, lush disco, proper house and reggae – this fabulous club is strictly for true

believers, and judging from the numbers, there are thousands of them.

Theatre

Theatre Royal (☎ 232 2061; www.theatre-royal-newcas tle.co.uk; 100 Grey St) The winter home of the Royal Shakespeare Company is full of Victorian splendour and has an excellent programme of drama.

Sport

Newcastle United Football Club (☎ 201 8400; official www.nufc.co.uk, unofficial www.nufc.com; St James' Park, Strawberry Pl) is more than just a football team: it is the collective expression of Geordie hope and pride as well as the release for decades of economic, social and sporting frustration. Its fabulous ground, St James' Park (☎ box office 261 1571) is always packed. Match tickets go on public sale about two weeks before a game or you can try the stadium on the day, but there's no chance for big matches, such as those against arch-rivals Sunderland.

GETTING THERE & AWAY
Air

Newcastle International Airport (☎ 286 0966; www .newcastleairport.com) is 7 miles north of the city off the A696. It has direct services to Aberdeen, London, Cardiff, Dublin, Belfast, Oslo, Amsterdam, Paris, Prague, Brussels and a number of destinations in Spain.

Boat

Norway's **Fjord Line** (☎ 296 1313; www.fjordline.co.uk) operates ferries between Newcastle, Stavanger and Bergen. **DFDS Seaways** (☎ 0870 533 3000; www .dfdsseaways.co.uk) operates ferries to Newcastle

NORTHEAST ENGLAND

NORTHEAST ENGLAND

from Kristiansand in Norway, the Swedish port of Gothenburg and the Dutch port of Ijmuiden, near Amsterdam. For online ferry bookings, check out www.newcastleferry.co.uk.

Bus

National Express buses arrive and depart from the Gallowgate coach station. You can get to most anywhere, including London (£27.50, seven hours, six daily) and Manchester (£16.60, five hours, six daily). For Berwick-upon-Tweed (two hours, five daily) take bus 505, 515 or 525 from Haymarket bus station.

Local and regional buses leave from Haymarket or Eldon Square bus stations. For local buses around the northeast, don't forget the excellent-value Explorer North East ticket, valid on most services for £6.50.

Train

Newcastle is on the main rail line between London and Edinburgh. Services go to Alnmouth (for connections to Alnwick; £6.20, 20 minutes, four daily), Berwick (£15.30, 45 minutes, every two hours), Edinburgh (£39, 1½ hours, half-hourly), London King's Cross (£105.50, three hours, half-hourly) and York (£21.30, 45 minutes, every 20 minutes). There's also the scenic Tyne Valley Line west to Carlisle. See p747 for details.

GETTING AROUND
To/From the Airport & Ferry Terminal

The airport is linked to town by the Metro (£3, 20 minutes, every 15 minutes).

Bus 327 links the ferry (at Tyne Commission Quay, 8½ miles east), Central Station and Jesmond Rd. It leaves the train station 2½ hours and 1¼ hours before each sailing.

There's a taxi rank at the terminal; it costs about £15 to the city centre.

Car

Driving around Newcastle isn't fun thanks to the web of roads, bridges and one-way systems, but there are plenty of car parks.

Public Transport

There's a large bus network, but the best means of getting around is the excellent underground Metro, with fares from 55p. There are also several saver passes. The tourist office can supply you with route plans for the bus and Metro networks.

The **DaySaver** (£4.20, £3.40 after 9am) gives unlimited Metro travel for one day, and the **DayRover** (adult/child £5/2.50) gives unlimited travel on all modes of transport in Tyne & Wear for one day.

Taxi

On weekend nights taxis can be rare; try **Noda Taxis** (☎ 222 1888), which has a kiosk outside the entrance to Central Station.

AROUND NEWCASTLE

ANGEL OF THE NORTH

The world's most frequently viewed work of art is this extraordinary 200-tonne, rust-coloured human frame with wings (aka the Gateshead Flasher) towering over the A1 (M) about 5 miles south of Newcastle – if you're driving, you just can't miss it. At 20m high and with a wingspan wider than a Boeing 767, Antony Gormley's most successful work is the country's largest sculpture. Buses 723 and 724 from Eldon Square, or 21, 21A and 21B from Pilgrim St, will take you there.

SEGEDUNUM

The last strong post of Hadrian's Wall was the fort of **Segedunum** (☎ 295 5757; www.twmuseums .org.uk; adult/concession/child £3.95/2.25/free; ☑ 9.30am-5.30pm Apr-Aug, 10am-5pm Sep, 10am-3.30pm Nov-Mar) 4 miles east of Newcastle at Wallsend. Beneath the 35m tower, which you can climb for some terrific views, is an absorbing site that includes a reconstructed Roman bathhouse (with steaming pools and frescoes) and a fascinating museum that gives visitors a well-rounded picture of life during Roman times.

Take the Metro to Wallsend.

COUNTY DURHAM

Picturesque, peaceful villages and unspoilt market towns dot the lonely, rabbit-inhabited North Pennine and the gentle ochre hills of Teesdale. At the heart of it all is County Durham's simply exquisite capital, one of England's most visited towns and an absolute must on your northern itinerary.

Ironically, this pastoral image, so resonant of its rich medieval history, has only come back to life in recent years; for most of the last three centuries the county was given over almost entirely to the mining of coal, and the countryside is punctuated with the relics of that once all-important industry, now slowly being reclaimed by nature. A brutal and dangerous business, coal mining was the lifeblood of entire communities and its sudden end in 1984 by the stroke of a Conservative pen has left some purposeless towns and an evocatively scarred landscape.

Durham has had a turbulent history, though it pales in comparison with its troublesome northern neighbour. To keep the Scots and local Saxon tribes quiet, William the Conqueror created the title of prince bishop in 1081 and gave them vice-regal power over an area known as the Palatinate of Durham, which became almost a separate country. It raised its own armies, collected taxes and administered a separate legal system that – incredibly – wasn't fully incorporated into the greater English structure until 1971.

Getting Around
The Explorer North East ticket (see opposite) is valid on many services in the county.

DURHAM
☎ 0191 / pop 42,940
The best way to arrive in Durham is by early-morning train on a clear day. As you emerge from the train station, look across the River Wear to the hilltop peninsula, and you'll see the main reason for coming in all its resplendent glory. England's most beautiful Romanesque cathedral, a masterpiece of Norman architecture, rates pretty high on our brilliant Britain list. Consider the setting: a huge castle, the aforementioned cathedral and, surrounding them both, a cobweb of cobbled streets usually full of upper-crust students attending Durham's other big pull, the university. It's all so...English.

OK, so the university may not have the hallowed prestige of Oxbridge – it was only founded in 1832 – but its terrific academic reputation and competitive rowing team make the disappointment of not getting into Oxford or Cambridge that bit easier to bear.

Once you've visited the cathedral, there's little else to do save walk the old town streets and find new spots from which to view Durham's main attraction. We recommend that you visit as a day trip from Newcastle unless you're planning some in-depth exploration

of the surrounding county, in which case Durham is a tidy base.

Orientation
Market Place, the tourist office, castle and cathedral are all on the peninsula surrounded by the River Wear. The train and bus stations are to the west, on the other side of the river. Using the cathedral as your landmark, you can't really go wrong. The main sites are within easy walking distance of each other.

Information
Post office (Silver St; ☼ 9am-5.30pm Mon-Sat)
Public library (Millennium Pl; ☼ 9.30am-5pm Mon-Sat) The only place in town to check email.
Thomas Cook (☎ 382 6600; 24-25 Market Pl) Near the tourist office.
Tourist Office (☎ 384 3720; www.durhamtourism. co.uk; 2 Millennium Pl; ☼ 9.30am-5.30pm Mon-Sat, 10am-4pm Sun) In the Gala complex, which includes a theatre and cinema.
Waterstone's (☎ 383 1488; 69 Saddler St) A good selection of books.

Sights
DURHAM CATHEDRAL
Durham's most famous building – and the main reason for visiting unless someone you know is at university here – has earned superlative praise for so long that to add more would be redundant; how can you do better than the 19th-century novelist Nathaniel Hawthorne, who wrote fawningly: 'I never saw so lovely a magnificent a scene, nor (being content with this) do I care to see better.' Let's not go nuts here. No building is *that* beautiful, but the definitive structure of the Anglo-Norman Romanesque style is still pretty amazing. We would definitely put it in our top-church-in-England list – as do many others, including Unesco, who declared it a World Heritage Site in 1986.

The **cathedral** (☎ 386 4266; www.durhamcathedral .co.uk; donation requested; ☼ 9.30am-8pm mid-Jun–Aug, 9.30am-6.15pm Mon-Sat & 12.30-5pm Sun Sep–mid-Jun, private prayer & services only 7.30-9.30am Mon-Sat, 7.45am-12.30pm Sun year-round) is enormous and has a pretty fortified look; this is due to the fact that although it may have been built to pay tribute to God and to house the holy bones of St Cuthbert, it also needed to withstand any potential attack by the pesky Scots and Northumberland tribes who weren't too thrilled by the arrival of the Normans a few

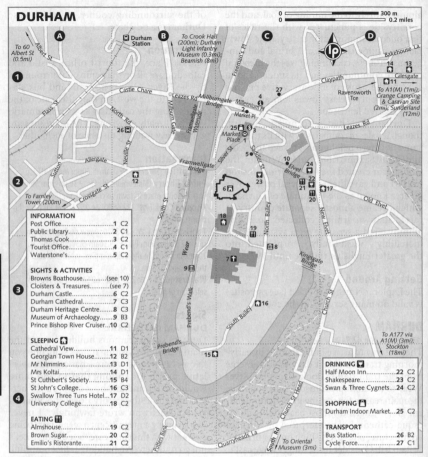

NORTHEAST ENGLAND

years before. Times have changed, but the cathedral remains an overwhelming presence, and modern-day visitors will hardly fail to be impressed by its visual impact.

The interior is genuinely spectacular. The superb nave is dominated by massive, powerful piers – every second one round, with an equal height and circumference of 6.6m, and carved with geometric designs. Durham was the first European cathedral to be roofed with stone-ribbed vaulting, which upheld the heavy stone roof and made it possible to build pointed transverse arches – the first in England, and a great architectural achievement. The central tower dates from 1262, but was damaged in a fire caused by lightning in 1429, and was unsatisfactorily patched up until it was entirely rebuilt in 1470. The western towers were added in 1217–26.

Built in 1175 and renovated 300 years later, the **Galilee Chapel** is one of the most beautiful parts. The northern side's **paintings** are rare surviving examples of 12th-century wall painting and are thought to feature Sts Cuthbert and Oswald. The chapel also contains the **Venerable Bede's tomb**. Bede was an 8th-century Northumbrian monk, a great historian and polymath whose work *The Ecclesiastical History of the English People* is still the prime source of information on the development of early Christian Britain. Among other things, he introduced the numbering of years from the birth of Jesus. He was first buried at Jarrow (p731), but in

1022 a miscreant monk stole his remains and brought them here.

The **Bishop's Throne**, built over the tomb of Bishop Thomas Hatfield, dates from the mid-14th century. Hatfield's effigy is the only one to have survived another turbulent time: the Reformation. The **high altar** is separated from **St Cuthbert's tomb** by the beautiful stone **Neville Screen**, made around 1372–80. Until the Reformation, the screen included 107 statues of saints.

The cathedral has worthwhile **guided tours** (adult/student/child £3.50/2.50/free; 10.30am, 11.30am & 2.30pm Mon & Sat). Evensong is at 5.15pm from Tuesday to Saturday (Evening Prayer on Monday) and at 3.30pm on Sunday.

There's a splendid view from the top of the **tower** (adult/child £3/1.50; 10am-4pm Mon-Sat mid-Apr–Sep, to 3pm Oct-Mar), but you've got to climb 325 steps to enjoy it.

Cloisters & Treasures

The monastic buildings are centred on the cloisters, which were heavily rebuilt in 1828. The west door to the cloisters is famous for its 12th-century ironwork. On the western side is the **Monks' Dormitory** (adult/child £1/30p; 10am-3.30pm Mon Sat, plus 12.30-3.15pm Sun Apr-Sep), now a library of 30,000 books and displaying Anglo-Saxon carved stones, with a vaulted undercroft that houses the Treasures and a restaurant. There is also an **audiovisual display** (adult/child £1/30p; 10am-3pm Mon-Sat Apr-Nov) on the building of the cathedral and the life of St Cuthbert.

The **Treasures** (adult/child £2.50/70p; 10am-4.30pm Mon-Sat, 2-4.30pm Sun) refer to the relics of St Cuthbert, but besides his cross and coffin, there's very little here related to the saint. The collection is made up mostly of religious paraphernalia from later centuries.

DURHAM CASTLE

Built as a standard motte-and-bailey fort in 1072, **Durham Castle** (374 3800; www.durhamcastle .com; adult/concession £5/3.50; tours only, on the hour 10am-12.30pm & 2-4pm Jun-Oct, 2-4pm Mon, Wed, Sat & Sun Nov-May) was the prince bishops' home until 1837, when it became the first college of the new university. It remains a university hall, and you can stay here (see p740).

The castle has been much altered over the centuries, as each successive prince bishop sought to put his particular imprimatur on the place, but heavy restoration and reconstruction were necessary anyway as the castle is built of soft stone on soft ground. Highlights of the 45-minute tour include the groaning 17th-century Black Staircase, the 16th-century chapel and the beautifully preserved Norman chapel (1080).

OTHER SIGHTS

Near the cathedral, in what was the St Mary-le-Bow Church, is the **Durham Heritage Centre** (386 8719; St Mary le Bow, North Bailey; admission £1.50; 2pm-4.30pm Jun, 11am-4.30pm Jul-Sep, 11am-4.30pm Sat & Sun Apr, May & Oct), with a pretty crowded collection of displays on Durham's history from the Middle Ages to mining. It's all suitably grim, especially the reconstructed prison cells.

Durham and its environs have other museums that may be of interest, including the small **Museum of Archaeology** (334 1823; Old Fulling Mill, The Banks; admission £1; 11am-4pm Apr-Oct, 11.30am-3.30pm Fri-Mon Nov-Mar), located in a converted riverside mill building; and the **Oriental Museum** (334 5694; Elvet Hill; admission £1.50; 10am-5pm Mon-Fri, noon-5pm Sat & Sun), 3 miles south of the city centre in the university campus. It has a good collection that ranges from fine Egyptian artefacts to a monster of a Chinese bed. Take bus 5 or 6.

Crook Hall (384 8028; www.crookhallgardens.co.uk; Sidegate; adult/child £4.50/4; 1-5pm Fri-Mon Easter, Sun May & Sep, Sun-Fri Jun-Aug) is a medieval hall with 1.6 hectares of charming small gardens, about 200m north of the city centre.

Finally, if you really can't get enough of war and the uniforms people wear to fight them, you won't want to miss the **Durham Light Infantry (DLI) Museum** (384 2214; Aykley Heads; admission £2.50; 10am-4pm), 500m northwest of town. The history of Durham's County Regiment and its part in various wars from 1758 to 1968 is brought to life through anecdotes and poignant artefacts; there's a small art gallery with changing exhibitions.

Activities
BOATING

The **Prince Bishop River Cruiser** (386 9525; Elvet Bridge; adult £4.50; 2pm & 3pm Jun-Sep) offers one-hour cruises.

You can hire a rowing boat from **Browns Boathouse** (386 3779; per hr per person £3), below Elvet Bridge.

WALKING

There are superb views back to the cathedral and castle from the riverbanks; walk around the bend between Elvet and Framwellgate Bridges, or hire a boat at Elvet Bridge.

Guided walks (adult/child £3/free; ☺ 2pm Wed, Sat & Sun May-Sep) of 1½ hours leave from Millennium Place – contact the tourist office for details.

Ghost walks (☎ 386 1500; adult/child £3/1; ☺ 6.30pm Mon Jun-Sep, 8.30pm Jul & Aug) lasting 1½ hours also drift around town.

Sleeping

It's all about a cathedral view round these parts. But when you consider that it's visible from pretty much everywhere, it's quality, not quantity, that counts. The tourist office makes local bookings free of charge, which is a good thing considering that Durham is always busy with visitors: graduation week in late June results in accommodation gridlock.

Cathedral View (☎ 386 9566; www.cathedralview .com; 212 Gilesgate; s/d from £60/75) This plain-fronted Georgian house has no sign, but inside it does exactly what it says on the tin. Six large rooms decorated with lots of cushions and coordinated bed linen and window dressings make up the numbers, but it's the three at the back that are worth the fuss: the views of the cathedral are superb. A small breakfast terrace with the same splendid vista is an added touch of real class.

Farnley Tower (☎ 375 0011; www.farnley-tower.co.uk; The Avenue; s/d from £55/75; Ⓟ ✖) A beautiful Victorian stone building that looks more like a small manor house than a family-run B&B, this place has 13 large rooms, none better than the superior rooms, which are not just spacious but have excellent views of the cathedral and castle. The service is impeccable.

Georgian Town House (☎ /fax 386 8070; 10-11 Crossgate St; s/d from £60/80) A listed building smack in the middle of town, this B&B has large, airy rooms decorated in the true spirit of Laura Ashley: elaborate stencilling, plenty of pillows and fancy window dressings. It's close to the cathedral, so the rooms facing it have great views. There is also a small garden with flowers and a rockery.

60 Albert St (☎ 386 0608; www.sixtyalbertstreet.co.uk; s/d from £50/70; Ⓟ) This tiny place has only three rooms – each stylishly restored with painted, cast-iron beds – which makes for truly attentive, individual service. The breakfast room is a Victorian showcase, with original antiques, polished wood floors and a beautiful fireplace.

Swallow Three Tuns Hotel (☎ 386 4326; www.swallowhotels.com; New Elvet; s/d from £52/102) A converted 16th-century coaching inn, the Three Tuns has plenty of olde-worlde feel – in the low-hanging ceilings, creaking passageways and heavy wooden beams throughout – until you get to the bedrooms, which are comfortable, modern and, well, a little bland. The rooms in the older section are larger than those in the new wing.

A couple of small, similarly priced B&Bs on Gilesgate may not offer much in the way of décor, size or cathedral view, but are worth a try if you're stuck:

Mrs Koltai (☎ 386 2026; 10 Gilesgate; s/d £25/42)

Mr Nimmins (☎ 384 6485; www.nimmins.co.uk; 14 Gilesgate; s/d £24/44)

Eating

Cheap eats aren't a problem in Durham thanks to the students, but quality is a little thin on the ground. Some pubs do good bar food; see Drinking (opposite).

Almshouse (☎ 386 1054; Palace Green; dishes £4-7; ☺ 9am-5pm) Fancy imaginative and satisfying snacks (how about spicy beef with red-bean casserole and rice?) served in a genuine 17th-century house right on Palace Green? It's a

---

UNIVERSITY ACCOMMODATION

Several colleges rent their rooms during the holidays (Easter and July to September). The rooms are generally modern and comfortable, like most contemporary student halls. Phone ☎ 374 7360 or click on www.dur.ac.uk/conferences/tourism for more information.

St John's College (☎ 334 3877; 3 South Bailey; s/d £25.50/48) This college is right next to the cathedral; none of the rooms are en suite.

St Cuthbert's Society (☎ 374 3364; 12 South Bailey; s/d £24/45) A few doors down from St John's, with similar student-style rooms.

University College (☎ 374 3863; s/d with bathroom £36/66, without bathroom £25/45) Smack on the Palace Green, this has the best location. Some rooms are available year-round, such as the bishop's suite (per person £85), decked out with 17th-century tapestries.

shame about the interior, which has been restored to look like any old museum café.

Brown Sugar (☎ 454 2242; New Elvet; dishes £5-7.50; ☑ 7.30am-11pm Mon-Sat, 9am-10.30pm Sun) This trendy coffee shop-cum-bar is a favourite with university students, who fold into the oversize leather couches, nibble on a ciabatta sandwich (no ordinary bread here, mate) and talk about how much study they should be doing. A perfect hang-out.

Emilio's Ristorante (☎ 384 0096; 96 Elvet Bridge; pizza or pasta from £6.95; ☑ lunch & dinner Mon-Sat, dinner only Sun) Durham's top spot for pizza, pasta and other Italian staples has a wonderful location overlooking the Wear. Try the *malfatti al forno*, a kind of oven-baked ravioli filled with ricotta cheese and spinach.

Drinking

Durham may be a big student town, but most students seem to take the whole study thing really seriously, because the nightlife here isn't as boisterous as you might expect from a university town. There is, however, a fistful of lovely old bars. The tourist office has a bimonthly *What's On* guide.

Half Moon Inn (New Elvet) Sports fans love this old-style bar for its devotion to the mixed pleasures of Sky Sports; we like it for its wonderful collection of whiskies and ales. There's a summer beer garden if you want to avoid the whoops and hollers of the armchair jocks.

Shakespeare (63 Saddler St) As authentic a traditional bar as you're likely to find in these parts, this is the perfect local's boozer, complete with nicotine-stained walls, cosy snugs and a small corner TV to show the racing. Needless to say, the selection of beers and spirits is terrific. Not surprisingly, students love it too.

Swan & Three Cygnets (☎ 384 0242; Elvet Bridge) This high-ceilinged riverside pub with courtyard tables overlooks the river. It also serves some pretty good food (mains around £8.50) – usually fancy versions of standard bar fare like bangers and mash.

Shopping

It's less about what you might buy and more about the place itself, but the Victorian **Durham Indoor Market** (☎ 384 6153; ☑ 9am-6pm Mon-Sat) is worth a browse, if only for the motley collection of wares on sale, from fruit and veg to garden gnomes.

Getting There & Away

BUS

The bus station is west of the river on North Rd. All National Express buses arrive here, while bus 352 links Newcastle and Blackpool via Durham, Barnard Castle, Raby Castle and Kirkby Stephen. Destinations include Edinburgh (£21.50, four hours, one daily), Leeds (£13.80, 2½ hours, four daily) and London (£27.50, 6½ hours, four daily). There are three daily National Express buses to Newcastle (£2.50, 30 minutes); bus 21 provides a half-hourly service but takes twice as long because it makes plenty of stops along the way.

TRAIN

There are services at least hourly to London (£105.50, three hours), Newcastle (£4.60 single, 20 minutes) and York (£20.60, one hour).

Getting Around

Pratt's Taxis (☎ 386 0700) charges a minimum of £2.40. **Cycle Force** (☎ 384 0319; 29 Claypath) charges £10/17 per half-/full day for mountain-bike hire.

AROUND DURHAM
Beamish Open-Air Museum

County Durham's greatest attraction is **Beamish** (☎ 0191-370 4000; www.beamish.org.uk; admission Nov-Mar £6, Apr-Oct adult/child £16/10; ☑ 10am-5pm Apr-Oct, to 4pm Tue-Thu, Sat & Sun Nov-Mar, last entry 3pm year-round), a living, breathing, working museum that offers a fabulous, warts-and-all portrait of industrial life in the northeast during the 19th and 20th centuries. Instructive and lots of fun to boot, this huge museum spread over 121 hectares will appeal to all ages.

You can go underground, explore mine heads, a working farm, a school, a dentist and a pub, and marvel at how every cramped pit cottage seemed to find room for a piano. Don't miss a ride behind an 1815 Steam Elephant locomotive or a replica of Stephenson's Locomotion No 1.

Allow at least three hours to do the place justice. Many elements (such as the railway) aren't open in the winter – call for details.

Beamish is about 8 miles northwest of Durham; it's signposted from the A1(M) – take the A693 west at junction 63. Buses 709 from Newcastle (50 minutes, hourly) and 720 from Durham (30 minutes, hourly) operate to the museum.

NORTHEAST ENGLAND

BARNARD CASTLE

☎ 01833 / pop 6720

Barnard Castle, or just plain Barney, is anything but: a thoroughly charming market town packed with atmospheric pubs and antique shops, with a daunting ruined castle at its edge and an extraordinary French chateau on its outskirts. If you can drag yourself away, it is also a terrific base for exploring Teesdale and the North Pennines.

Staff at the **tourist office** (☎ 690909; tourism@ teesdale.gov.uk; Woodleigh, Flatts Rd; ⏱ 9.30am-5.30pm Easter-Oct, 11am-4pm Mon-Sat Nov-Mar) handle visitor inquiries.

Sights

THE CASTLE

Once one of northern England's largest castles, **Barnard Castle** (EH; ☎ 638212; www.english-heri tage.org.uk; admission £3.40; ⏱ 10am-6pm Easter-Sep, to 4pm Oct, Thu-Mon only Nov-Mar) was partly dismantled during the 16th century, but its huge bulk, on a cliff above the Tees, still manages to cover more than two very impressive hectares. Founded by Guy de Bailleul and rebuilt around 1150, its occupants spent their time suppressing the locals and fighting off the Scots – on their days off they sat around enjoying the wonderful views of the river.

BOWES MUSEUM

The 19th-century industrialist and art fanatic John Bowes didn't do things by halves, so when he commissioned French architect Jules Pellechet to build a new museum to show off his terrific collection, the result was this extraordinary, Louvre-inspired French chateau 1.5 miles west of town. Opened in 1892, the **Bowes Museum** (☎ 690606; www.bowesmuseum.org.uk; adult/child £7/free; ⏱ 11am-5pm) could give the V&A a run for its money, with lavish furniture and paintings by Canaletto, El Greco and Goya. The museum's most beloved exhibit, however, is the marvellous mechanical silver swan, which operates at 12.30pm and 3.30pm.

Sleeping & Eating

Greta House (☎ 631193; www.gretahouse.co.uk; 89 Galgate; s/d £28.50/55) This lovely Victorian home stands out for the little touches that show that extra bit of class – fluffy bathrobes, face cloths and posh toiletries. What really did it for us though was the stay-in service: a tray of lovely homemade sandwiches and a superb cheeseboard to nibble at from the comfort of bed.

Marwood House (☎ 637493; www.kilgarriff.demon .co.uk; 98 Galgate; s/d £27/48) Another handsome Victorian property with tastefully appointed rooms (the owner's tapestries feature in the décor and her homemade biscuits sit on a tray), Marwood House's standout feature is the small fitness room in the basement, complete with a sauna that fits up to four people.

Old Well Inn (☎ 690130; www.oldwellinn.co.uk; 21 The Bank; s/d from £34.50/79) You won't find larger bedrooms in town than at this old coaching inn, which makes it an excellent option for families – it even takes pets. It has a reputation for excellent, filling pub grub, although the service is somewhat lacklustre at times.

Getting There & Away

Bus 352 runs daily between Newcastle and Blackpool via Durham, Bishop Auckland, Barnard Castle, Raby Castle and Kirkby Stephen.

AROUND BARNARD CASTLE

The ransacked, spectral ruins of **Egglestone Abbey** (⏱ dawn-dusk), dating from the 1190s, overlook a lovely bend of the Tees. You can envisage the abbey's one-time grandeur despite the gaunt remains. They're a pleasant mile-long walk south of Barnard Castle.

About 7 miles northeast of town is the sprawling, romantic **Raby Castle** (☎ 660202; www .rabycastle.com; admission £7; ⏱ castle 1-5pm, grounds 11am-5.30pm Sun-Fri Jun-Aug, Wed & Sun May & Sep), a stronghold of the Catholic Neville family until it engaged in some ill-judged plotting (the 'Rising of the North') against the oh-so Protestant Queen Elizabeth in 1569. Most of the interior dates from the 18th and 19th centuries, but the exterior remains true to the original design, built around a courtyard and surrounded by a moat. There are beautiful formal gardens and a deer park. Buses 8 and 352 zip between Barnard Castle and Raby (20 minutes, eight daily).

BISHOP AUCKLAND

☎ 01388 / pop 24,770

The name's a giveaway, but this friendly market town 11 miles southwest of Durham has been the country residence of the bishops of Durham since the 12th century and their official home for over 100 years. The castle is just next to the large, attractive market square; leading off it are small-town streets lined with high-street shops and a sense that anything exciting is happening elsewhere.

The **tourist office** (☎ 604922; Market Pl; ☼ 10am-5pm Mon-Fri, 9am-4pm Sat year-round, plus 1-4pm Sun Apr-Sep) is in the town hall on Market Pl.

The imposing gates of **Auckland Castle** (☎ 601627; www.auckland-castle.co.uk; adult/child £4/free; ☼ 2-5pm Sun-Mon Easter-Jul & Sep, plus Wed Aug), just off Market Pl behind the town hall, lead to the official home of the bishop of Durham. It's palatial – each successive bishop extended the building. Underneath the spiky Restoration Gothic exterior, the buildings are mainly medieval. The outstanding attraction of the castle is the striking 17th-century chapel, which thrusts up into the sky. It has a remarkable partially 12th-century interior, converted from the former great hall. Admission is by guided tour only.

Around the castle is a hilly and wooded 324-hectare **deer park** (admission free; ☼ 7am-sunset) with an 18th-century deer shelter.

AROUND BISHOP AUCKLAND

One and a half miles north of Bishop Auckland is **Binchester Roman Fort** (☎ 663089; www.durham.gov.uk/binchester; admission £2; ☼ excavations 11am-5pm Easter-Sep), or Vinovia as it was originally called. The fort, first built in wood around AD 80 and rebuilt in stone early in the 2nd century, was the largest in County Durham, covering 4 hectares. Excavations show the remains of Dere St, the main high road from York to Hadrian's Wall, and the best-preserved example of a heating system in the country – part of the commandant's private bath suite. Findings from the site are displayed at the Bowes Museum in Barnard Castle (opposite).

The stones of the abandoned Binchester Fort were often reused, and Roman inscriptions can be spotted in the walls of the hauntingly beautiful **Escomb Church** (☎ 602861; admission free; ☼ 9am-8pm Apr-Sep, to 4pm Oct-Mar). The church dates from the 7th century – it's one of only three complete surviving Saxon churches in Britain. It's a whitewashed cell, striking and moving in its simplicity, incongruously encircled by a 20th-century cul-de-sac. If no-one's about, collect the keys from a hook outside a nearby house. Escomb is 3 miles west of Bishop Auckland (bus 86, 87 or 87A; 15 per day Monday to Saturday, 10 on Sunday).

Bus 352 running from Newcastle to Blackpool passes through Bishop Auckland (daily March to November, Saturday and Sunday

December to February), as does bus X85 from Durham to Kendal (one on Saturday June to September).

You need to change at Darlington for regular trains to Bishop Auckland.

NORTH PENNINES

The North Pennines stretch from western Durham to just short of Hadrian's Wall in the north. In the south is Teesdale, the gently undulating valley of the River Tees; to the north is the much wilder Weardale, carved through by the River Wear. Both dales are marked by ancient quarries and mines – industries that date back to Roman times. The wilds of the North Pennines are also home to the picturesque Derwent and Allen Valleys, north of Weardale.

For online info, check out www.northpennines.org.uk.

TEESDALE
☎ 01833

From the confluence of the Rivers Greta and Tees to Caldron Snout at the source of the Tees, Teesdale is filled with woods, scattered unspoilt villages, rivers, waterfalls and sinuous moorland. There are huge numbers of rabbits bounding about, as if competing for a role in *Watership Down*. The Pennine Way snakes along the dale.

Middleton-in-Teesdale

This tranquil, pretty village of white and stone houses among soft green hills was from 1753 a 'company town', the entire kit and caboodle being the property of the London Lead Company, a Quaker concern. The upshot was that the lead miners worked the same hours in the same appalling conditions as everyone else, but couldn't benefit from a Sunday pint to let off steam.

For information on local walks, go to the **tourist office** (☎ 641001; ☼ 10am-1pm & 2-5pm Apr-Oct, 10am-4pm Nov-Mar).

Middleton to Langdon Beck

As you travel up the valley past Middleton towards Langdon Beck, you'll find **Bowlees Visitor Centre** (☎ 622292; ☼ 10.30am-5pm Apr-Oct, 10.30am-4pm Sat & Sun Nov-Feb) 3 miles on, with plenty of walking and wildlife leaflets and a small natural-history display. A number

NORTHEAST ENGLAND

of easy-going trails spread out from here, including one to the tumbling rapids of **Low Force**, a number of metre-high steps along a scenic stretch of river. One mile further on is the much more compelling **High Force** (adult/child £1.50/1, car park £2), England's largest waterfall – 21m of almighty roar that shatters the general tranquillity of the surroundings. It's a sight best appreciated after a rainfall, when the torrent is really powerful.

The B6277 leaves the River Tees at High Force and continues up to **Langdon Beck**, where the scenery quickly turns from green rounded hills to the lonely landscape of the North Pennines, dotted with small chapels. You can either continue on the B6277 over the Pennines to Alston and Cumbria or turn right and take a minor road over the moors to St John's Chapel in Weardale.

Bus 73 connects Middleton and Langdon Beck, via Bowlees and High Force, at least once a day Tuesday, Wednesday, Friday and Saturday. Buses 75 and 76 serve Middleton from Barnard Castle several times daily.

Sleeping & Eating

Brunswick House (☎ 640393; www.brunswickhouse .net; 55 Market Pl, Middleton-in-Teesdale; s/d £45/54) This pretty Georgian house has a floral, fluffy theme: nice quilted duvets and big pillows with flowers all over them. Everything else is painted white.

High Force Hotel & Brewery (☎ 622222; www.high forcehotel.com; Forest-in-Teesdale; s/d £35/70) This former hunting lodge by the High Force waterfall is best known for the award-winning beers brewed on the premises: Teesdale Bitter, Forest XB and Cauldron Snout – at 5.6% it has a kick like a mule. Upstairs are six decent enough bedrooms, while the bar also serves food.

Langdon Beck YHA Hostel (☎ 0870 770 5910; www .yha.org.uk; Forest-in-Teesdale; dm £11.95; ☽ Mon-Sat Apr-Sep, Fri & Sat Nov, Tue-Sat early Feb-Mar, Sep-Oct) Walkers on the Pennine Way are avid fans of this hostel between High Force and Langdon Beck. The hostel is also a good base for short walks into the dales and the Pennines, in particular to Cow Green Reservoir, the source of the Tees.

WEARDALE
☎ 01388

Sheltered by the Pennines, Weardale was once the hunting ground of the prince bishops, but for most of the 19th century it was primarily a lead-mining centre, which has left the rust-

and olive-coloured patchwork moors pitted with mining scars. Don't be put off, however, as there are a handful of splendid walks in the surrounding countryside.

Stanhope & Ireshopburn

Peaceful Stanhope is a honey-coloured town with a cobbled marketplace – a good base for windswept walks across the moors. Its interesting church is Norman at the base, but mostly dates from the 12th century.

The **tourist office** (☎ 527650; www.durhamdalescen tre.co.uk; Market Pl; ☽ 10am-5pm Apr-Oct, to 4pm Nov-Mar) has lots of information on walks in the area, and there's a small tearoom.

In **Ireshopeburn**, 8 miles west of Stanhope, the **Weardale Museum** (☎ 537417; www.weardale museum.co.uk; adult/child £1.50/50p; ☽ 2-5pm Wed-Sun May-Jul & Sep, daily Aug) allows a glimpse into local history, including a spotless lead-mining family kitchen and information on preacher John Wesley. It's next to **High House Chapel**, a Methodist chapel (1760) that was one of Wesley's old stomping grounds.

SLEEPING & EATING

Redlodge Guest House (☎ 527851; www.redlodgegh .co.uk; 2 Redlodge Cottages, Market Pl, Stanhope; s/d £25/50) This friendly B&B is in a stone house originally built in 1850 as part of Stanhope Castle. The three bedrooms are perfectly adequate, but they fill up quickly as the town is the last stop on the C2C route before cyclists push on to Sunderland. The single room is not en suite.

Queen's Head (☎ 528160; 89 Front St, Stanhope; mains £5-8) This handsome pub in the middle of Stanhope is a good spot for hearty pub grub.

Killhope

At the top of the valley, about 13 miles from Stanhope, is a salutary example of just how bleak miners' lives really were. In the **Killhope Lead Mining Centre** (☎ 537505; www.durham. gov.uk/killhope; adult/child £4.50/1.70, with mine trip £6/3; ☽ 10.30am-5pm Apr-Oct), the blackened machinery of the old works is dominated by an imposing 10m-high water wheel that drove a crushing mechanism.

In one of those unfortunate linguistic ironies, 'hope' actually means 'side valley', but once you get a look inside the place you'll understand the miners' black humour about the name. An absorbing exhibition explains what life was like: poor pay, poorer living conditions and the constant threat of the 'Black Spit' (coal dust in the lungs) that killed so many of its sufferers. The most poignant records are those of the washer boys – children employed in freezing, backbreaking work. The mine closed in 1910 but you can visit its atmospheric underground network as it was in 1878, on an hour-long guided tour; wear warm clothes.

It's possible to buy a combined ticket for the mine and the South Tynedale Railway (p722). From the mining centre it's another 7 miles up over the highest main road in England (617m) and the North Pennines and down into Alston.

Bus 101 makes the regular trip up the valley from Bishop Auckland to Stanhope (10 daily). If you ring ahead, it will go on to Killhope mid-morning and pick you up in the afternoon. Call **Wearhead Motor Services** (☎ 01388-528235) to arrange the service.

DERWENT VALLEY

Pretty Blanchland and Edmundbyers, two small, remote villages, are south of the denim expanse of the **Derwent Reservoir**, surrounded by wild moorland and forests. The 3.5-mile-long reservoir has been here since 1967, and the county border separating Durham and Northumberland runs right through it. The valley's a good spot for walking and cycling, as well as sailing, which can be arranged through the **Derwent Reservoir Sailing Club** (☎ 01434-675258).

Nestling among trees, and surrounded by wild mauve and mustard moors, **Blanchland** is an unexpected surprise. It's a charming, golden-stoned grouping of small cottages arranged around an L-shaped square, framed by a medieval gateway. The village was named after the white cassocks of local monks – there was a Premonstratensian abbey here from the 12th century. Around 1721 the prince bishop of the time, Lord Crewe, seeing the village and abbey falling into disrepair, bequeathed the buildings to trustees on the condition that they be protected and looked after.

Another inviting, quiet village, **Edmundbyers** is 4 miles east of Blanchland on the B6306 along the southern edge of Derwent Reservoir.

Edmundbyers is 12 miles north of Stanhope and 10 miles south of Hexham on the B6306. Bus 773 runs from Consett to Townfield via Blanchland and Edmundbyers three times a day, Monday to Saturday.

Sleeping & Eating
Edmundbyers YHA Hostel (☎ 0870 770 5810; www .yha.org.uk; Low House, Edmundbyers; dm £11.95; ☑ daily Jul-Aug, Wed-Sun Apr-Jun & Sep-Oct) This beautiful hostel is in a converted 17th-century former inn. The hostel helps to serve walkers in the area and cyclists on the C2C route.

Lord Crewe Arms Hotel (☎ 01434-675251; Blanchland; s/d £85/120) This glorious hotel was built as the abbot's lodge. It's mainly 17th-century building, with a 12th-century crypt that makes a cosy bar. If you're looking for a bit of atmosphere – open fires, hidden corners, tall windows and superb food (lunch £6 to £11, 4-course dinner £32) – you won't find better, but there have been criticisms of the service, which can be a little brusque.

ALLEN VALLEY
The Allen Valley is in the heart of the North Pennines, with individual, remote villages huddled high up, surrounded by bumpy hills and heather- and gorse-covered moors. It's fantastic walking country, speckled with the legacy of the lead-mining industry.

Tiny **Allendale** is a hamlet around a big open square. The quiet rural community hots up on New Year's Eve when the distinctly pagan and magical 'Tar Barrels' ceremony is performed (see the boxed text Flaming Allendale, below). It's 7 miles from Hexham on the B6295.

Four miles further south towards the Wear Valley is England's highest village, **Allenheads**,

---

FLAMING ALLENDALE

Thought to be Viking or pagan in origin, the Baal Fire (aka Tar Barrels) on New Year's Eve – a procession of flaming whisky barrels through Allendale – has certainly been taking place for centuries. The 45 barrels are filled with tar and carried on the heads of a team of 'guisers' with blackened or painted faces – this hot and hereditary honour gets passed from generation to generation. The mesmerising procession, accompanied by pounding music, leads to a pile of branches, where the guisers chuck the scorching barrels to fire up an enormous pyre at midnight, doing their best not to set themselves alight.

nestled at the head of Allen Valley. It really just consists of a few houses and a marvellously eccentric hotel. There's a small **heritage centre** (☎ 685395; admission £1; ◷ 9am-5pm Apr-Oct) with some displays on the history of the village and surrounding area and access to a blacksmith's cottage, and a small nature walk.

Bus 688 runs up and down the Allen Valley from Hexham to Allenheads (stopping at Allendale town; 25 minutes, 11 daily).

An attraction in its own right, **Allenheads Inn** (☎ 685200; www.theallenheadsinn.co.uk; Allenheads; s/d £28/50), an 18th-century low-beamed pub, has a quite extraordinary and bizarre collection of assorted bric-a-brac and ephemera, from mounted stag heads to Queen Mum plates. It's a friendly, creaky place to stay, and serves up hearty, tasty food (mains around £7) as well.

HADRIAN'S WALL

What exactly have the Romans ever done for us? The aqueducts. Law and order. And this enormous wall, built between AD 122 and 128 to keep 'us' (Romans, subdued Anglo-Saxons) in and 'them' (hairy barbarians from Scotland) out. Or so the story goes. Hadrian's Wall, named in honour of the emperor that ordered it built, was Rome's single greatest engineering project, a spectacular 73-mile testament to ambition and the practical Roman mind. Even today, almost 2000 years after the first stone was laid, the sections that are still standing remain an awe-inspiring sight, proof that when the Romans wanted something done, they just knuckled down and did it.

It wasn't easy. When completed, the mammoth structure ran across the narrow neck of the island, from Solway Firth in the west almost to the mouth of the Tyne in the east. The section from Newcastle to the River Irthing was built of stone, and turf blocks were used on the section to Solway – roughly 3m thick and 4.5m high. A 3m-deep, 9m-wide ditch and mound were excavated immediately in front (except where there were natural defences). Every Roman mile (1.62 miles; even in measurement the Romans outdid us) there was a gateway guarded by a small fort (milecastle) and between each milecastle were two observation turrets. Milecastles are numbered right across the country, starting with Milecastle 0 at Wallsend and ending with Milecastle 80 at Bowness-on-Solway.

Between each was a series of turrets, tagged alphabetically, so Milecastle 39 (a good one) was followed by Turret 39B, Turret 37B and then Milecastle 40.

A series of forts were developed as bases some distance south (and may predate the wall), and 16 lie astride it. The prime remaining forts on the wall are Cilurnum (Chesters), Vercovicium (Housesteads) and Banna (Birdoswald). The best forts behind the wall are Corstopitum at Corbridge, and Vindolanda, north of Bardon Mill.

History

Emperor Hadrian didn't order the wall built because he was afraid of northern invasion. Truth is no part of the wall was impenetrable – a concentrated attack at any single point would have surely breached it – but was meant to mark the border as though to say that the Roman Empire would extend no further. By drawing a physical boundary, the Romans were also tightening their grip on the population to the south – for the first time in history, passports were issued to citizens of the empire, marking them out not just as citizens but, more importantly, as taxpayers.

But all good things come to an end. It's likely that around 409, as the Roman administration collapsed, the frontier garrisons ceased receiving Roman pay. The communities had to then rely on their own resources, gradually becoming reabsorbed into the war-band culture of the native Britons – for some generations soldiers had been recruited locally in any case.

Orientation

Hadrian's Wall crosses beautiful, varied landscape. Starting in the lowlands of the Solway coast, it crosses the lush hills east of Carlisle to the bleak, windy ridge of basalt rock known as Whin Sill overlooking Northumberland National Park, and ends in the urban sprawl of Newcastle. The most spectacular section lies between Brampton and Corbridge.

Carlisle, in the west, and Newcastle, in the east, are good starting points, but Brampton, Haltwhistle, Hexham and Corbridge all make good bases.

The B6318 follows the course of the wall from the outskirts of Newcastle to Birdoswald; from Birdoswald to Carlisle it pays to have a detailed map. The main A69 road and the railway line follow 3 or 4 miles to the south. This section follows the wall from east to west.

Information

Carlisle and Newcastle tourist offices are good places to start gathering information, but there are also tourist offices in Hexham, Haltwhistle, Corbridge and Brampton. The **Northumberland National Park Visitor Centre** (☎ 01434-344396; Once Brewed; ◷ 10am-5pm mid-Mar–May, Sep & Oct, 9.30am–6pm Jun–Aug) is off the B6318. There's a **Hadrian's Wall information line** (☎ 01434-322002; www.hadrians-wall.org) too. May sees a spring festival, with lots of re-creations of Roman life along the wall (contact tourist offices for details).

Walking & Cycling

The newish **Hadrian's Wall Path** is an 84-mile National Trail that runs the length of the wall from Wallsend in the east to Bowness-on-Solway in the west. The entire route should take about seven days on foot, giving plenty of time to explore the rich archaeological heritage along the way. Anthony Burton's *Hadrian's Wall Path – National Trail Guide* (Aurum Press, £12.99) available at most bookshops and tourist offices in the region, is good for history, archaeology and the like, while the *Essential Guide to Hadrian's Wall Path National Trail* (Countryside Agency; £3.95) is a guide to everyday facilities and services along the walk.

If you're planning to cycle along the wall, tourist offices sell the *Hadrian's Wall Country Cycle Map* (£3); you'll be cycling along part of Hadrian's Cycleway (see p725).

Getting There & Around

BUS

The AD 122 Hadrian's Wall bus (get it? three hours, six daily June to September) is a hail-and-ride guided service that runs between Hexham (the 9.15am service starts in Wallsend) and Bowness-on-Solway. Bus 185 covers the route the rest of the year (Monday to Saturday only).

West of Hexham the wall runs parallel to the A69, which connects Carlisle and Newcastle. Bus 685 runs along the A69 hourly, passing near the youth hostels and 2 to 3 miles south of the main sites throughout the year.

The **Hadrian's Wall Rover** (adult/child 1-day £6.50/4.50, 3-day £13/9) is available from the driver or the tourist offices, where you can also get timetables.

TRAIN

The railway line between Newcastle and Carlisle (Tyne Valley Line) has stations at Cor-bridge, Hexham, Haydon Bridge, Bardon Mill, Haltwhistle and Brampton. This service runs daily, but not all trains stop at all stations.

CORBRIDGE
☎ 01434 / pop 2800

The mellow commuter town of Corbridge is a handsome spot above a green-banked curve in the Tyne, its shady, cobbled streets lined with old-fashioned shops. Folks have lived here since Saxon times when there was a substantial monastery, while many of the buildings feature stones nicked from nearby Corstopitum.

The **tourist office** (☎ 632815; www.thisiscorbridge .co.uk; Hill St; ◷ 10am-6pm Mon-Sat & 1-5pm Sun mid-May–Sep, 10am-5pm Mon-Sat Easter–mid-May & Oct) is part of the library.

Corbridge Roman Site & Museum

What's left of the Roman garrison town of **Corstopitum** (EH; ☎ 632349; admission £3.80, incl museum; ◷ 10am-6pm Apr-Sep, to 4pm Oct, Sat & Sun only Nov-Mar) lies about a half a mile west of Market Place on Dere St, once the main road from York to Scotland. It is the oldest fortified site in the area, predating the wall itself by some 40 years, when it was used by troops launching retaliation raids into Scotland. Most of what you see here, though, dates from around AD 200, when the fort had developed into a civilian settlement and was the main base along the wall.

You get a sense of the domestic heart of the town from the visible remains, and the Corbridge Museum displays Roman sculpture and carvings, including the amazing 3rd-century Corbridge Lion.

HADRIAN'S WALL CIRCULAR WALK

Starting at Once Brewed National Park Centre, this walk takes in the most complete stretch of Hadrian's Wall. The walk is 7.5 miles long and takes approximately 4½ hours. The wall follows the natural barrier created by steep dramatic cliffs, and the views north are stunning. Some parts of the wall are so well preserved that they have featured in films. You might recognise Milecastle 39, which acted Kevin Costner off the screen in *Robin Hood – Prince of Thieves*. The trail returns to the YHA hostel across swaths of farmland. The centre has a good map.

Sleeping & Eating

Riverside Guesthouse (☎ 632942; www.theriverside guesthouse.co.uk; Main St; s/d with bath from £42/62, without bath from £32/50; **P**)) An excellent guesthouse in the middle of town, Riverside has large, comfortable rooms and unfussy, friendly service. It's especially popular with walkers.

Errington Arms (☎ 672250; Stagshaw, B6318 off A68 roundabout; mains £8-13; ☽ 11am-11pm Mon-Sat, noon-3pm Sun) About three miles north of town is this marvellous 18th-century stone pub where delicious food is served up in suitably atmospheric surroundings. From the mouthwatering ploughman's lunch to more intricate delicacies like loin of lamb with mushroom and chive risotto, it won't disappoint; you can wash it all down with a pint of real ale.

Valley Restaurant (☎ 633434; www.valleyrestaurants .co.uk; Station Rd; mains £9-14; ☽ dinner Mon-Sat) This fine Indian restaurant in a lovely building above the station supplies a unique service as well as delicious food. A group of 10 or more diners from Newcastle can catch the 'Passage to India' train to Corbridge accompanied by a waiter, who will supply snacks and phone ahead to have the meal ready when the train arrives!

Getting There & Away

Bus 685 between Newcastle and Carlisle comes through Corbridge, as does the half-hourly bus 602 from Newcastle to Hexham, where you can connect with the Hadrian's Wall bus AD 122. Corbridge is also on the Newcastle–Carlisle railway line.

HEXHAM

☎ 01434 / pop 10,690

Long famed for its fine Augustinian abbey, handsome Hexham was awarded Country Life's Best Market Town award for 2005, a fitting tribute to this bustling town interlinked with cobbled alleyways. It is the most substantial of the wall towns, with more restaurants, hotels and high-street shops than anywhere between Newcastle and Carlisle. The **tourist office** (☎ 652220; www.hadrianswallcountry.org; Wentworth Car Park; ☽ 9am-6pm Mon-Sat, 10am-5pm Sun mid-May–Oct, 10am-5pm Mon-Sat Oct–mid-May) is northeast of the town centre.

Sights

Stately **Hexham Abbey** (☎ 602031; ☽ 9.30am-7pm May-Sep, to 5pm Oct-Apr) is a marvellous example of early English architecture. Inside, look out for the Saxon crypt, the only surviving element

of St Wilifrid's Church, built with inscribed stones from Corstopitum in 674.

The **Old Gaol** (☎ 652349; adult/child £3.50/2; ☽ 10am-4.30pm Apr-Oct, Mon, Tue & Sat Oct–mid-Nov), completed in 1333 as England's first purpose-built prison, was recently revamped and all four floors can be visited in all their gruesome glory. The history of the Border Reivers – a group of clans who fought, kidnapped, blackmailed and killed each other in an effort to exercise control over a lawless tract of land along the Anglo-Scottish border throughout the 16th century – is also retold, along with tales of the punishments handed out in the prison.

Sleeping & Eating

Acomb YHA Hostel (☎ 0870 770 5664; www.yha.org.uk; Main St; dm £9.50; ☽ Easter-Oct) Simple accommodation – basic bunks and functional bathrooms – is on offer in this converted stable on the edge of Acomb village, 2.5 miles north of Hexham and 2 miles south of the wall. Hexham can be reached by frequent bus 745 and 880 services, or by train.

West Close House (☎ 603307; Hextol Tce; s/d from £22/48; ✗ **P**)) This immaculate 1920s house, in a leafy cul-de-sac off Allendale Rd (the B6305) and surrounded by a beautiful garden, is highly recommended for its friendliness and comfort.

There are several bakeries on Fore St and, if you turn left into the quaintly named Priest-popple near the bus station, you'll find a selection of restaurants.

Dipton Mill (☎ 606577; Dipton Mill Rd; mains around £6-10) For sheer atmosphere, you can't beat this superb country pub 2 miles out on the road to Blanchland, among woodland and by a river. It offers sought-after ploughman's lunches and real ale, not to mention a terrific selection of whiskies.

Getting There & Away

Bus 685 between Newcastle and Carlisle comes through Hexham hourly. The AD 122 and the winter-service bus 185 connect with other towns along the wall, and the town is on the Newcastle–Carlisle railway line (hourly).

CHESTERS ROMAN FORT & MUSEUM

The best-preserved remains of a Roman cavalry fort in England are at **Chesters** (EH; ☎ 01434-681379; admission £3.80; ☽ 9.30am-6pm Apr-Sep, 10am-4pm Oct-Mar), set among idyllic green woods and

WORTH THE EFFORT

Langley Castle (☎ 688888; www.langleycastle.com; s £99.50, d £118-184, tr £240) This 14th-century castle in 4 hectares of woodland is the real deal minus the medieval privations. Live like one of the many nobles associated with the castle's history in one of the grand rooms, with pointy four-poster beds and window seats set in 2m-thick walls. Top of the heap is the fabulous Radcliffe Room, with a sunken circular bath and a sauna – modern guests are better off than the room's namesake, Sir Edward, who bought the Langley Estate in 1631 and pronounced himself the top aristocrat in Northumberland. The rooms in the recently converted gate lodge also have canopied beds but aren't nearly as grand. It's off the A686 (the road for Alston), which is off the A69 just before Haydon Bridge.

meadows and originally constructed to house a unit of troops from Asturias in northern Spain. They include part of a bridge (beautifully constructed and best appreciated from the eastern bank) across the River North Tyne, four well-preserved gatehouses, an extraordinary bathhouse and an underfloor heating system. The museum has a large collection of Roman sculpture. Take bus 880 or 882 from Hexham; it is also on the route of Hadrian's Wall bus AD 122.

HALTWHISTLE

☎ 01434 / pop 3810

It's one of the more important debates in contemporary Britain: where exactly is the centre of the country? The residents of Haltwhistle, basically one long street just north of the A69, claim that they're the ones. But then so do the folks in Dunsop Bridge, 71 miles to the south. Will we ever know the truth? In the meantime, Haltwhistle is the spot to get some cash and load up on gear and groceries. Thursday is market day.

The **tourist office** (☎ 322002; 9.30am-1pm & 2-5.30pm Mon-Sat, 1-5pm Sun May-Sep, 9.30am-noon & 1-3.30pm Mon-Tue & Thu-Sat Oct-Apr) is in the train station.

Ashcroft (☎ 320213; www.ashcroftguesthouse.co.uk; Lanty's Lonnen; s/d from £34/68) is a marvellous Edwardian home surrounded by beautifully manicured, layered lawns and gardens from which there are stunning views (also enjoyed from the breakfast room). The owners like their flowers so much they decorated most of the house accordingly. Highly recommended.

Bus 685 comes from Newcastle (1½ hours) and Carlisle (45 minutes) 12 times daily. Hadrian's Wall bus AD 122 (June to September) or 185 (October to May) connects Haltwhistle with other places along the wall. Bus 681 heads south to Alston (55 minutes, three daily Monday to Saturday). The town is also on the Newcastle–Carlisle railway line (hourly).

AROUND HALTWHISTLE

Vindolanda Roman Fort & Museum

The extensive site of **Vindolanda** (☎ 01434-344277; www.vindolanda.com; admission £4.95, with Roman Army Museum £7.50; 10am-6pm Apr-Sep, to 5pm Feb-Mar & Oct-Nov) offers a fascinating glimpse into the daily life of a Roman garrison town. The time-capsule museum displays leather sandals, signature Roman toothbrush-flourish helmet decorations, and countless writing tablets such as a student's marked work ('sloppy'), and a parent's note with a present of socks and underpants (things haven't changed – in this climate you can never have too many).

The museum is just one part of this large, extensively excavated site, which includes impressive parts of the fort and town (excavations continue) and reconstructed turrets and temple.

It's 1.5 miles north of Bardon Mill between the A69 and B6318 and a mile from Once Brewed.

Housesteads Roman Fort & Museum

The wall's most dramatic site – and the best-preserved Roman fort in the whole country – is at **Housesteads** (EH; ☎ 01434-344363; admission £3.80; 10am-6pm Apr-Sep, to 4pm Oct-Mar). From here, high on a ridge and covering 2 hectares, you can survey the moors of Northumberland National Park, and the snaking wall, with a sense of awe at the landscape and the aura of the Roman lookouts.

The substantial foundations bring fort life alive. The remains include an impressive hospital, granaries with a carefully worked-out ventilation system and barrack blocks. Most memorable are the spectacularly situated communal flushable latrines, which summon up Romans at their most mundane.

Housesteads is 2.5 miles north of Bardon Mill on the B6318, and about 3 miles from Once Brewed. It's popular, so try to visit outside summer weekends, or late in the day when the site will be quiet and indescribably eerie.

Other Sights

One mile northwest of Greenhead near Walltown Crags, the kid-pleasing **Roman Army Museum** (☎ 016977-47485; www.vindolanda.com; admission £3.95, with Vindolanda £7.50; ⏰ 10am-6pm Apr-Sep, to 5pm Feb-Mar & Oct-Nov) provides lots of colourful background detail to wall life, such as how far soldiers had to march per day and whether they could marry.

Ok, so *technically* it's in Cumbria (we won't tell if you don't), but the remains of the once-formidable **Birdoswald Roman Fort** (EH; ☎ 016977-47602; admission £3.80; ⏰ 10am-5.30pm Mar-Oct), on an escarpment overlooking the beautiful Irthing Gorge, were part of the wall and so merit inclusion in this chapter on logical grounds. They're on a minor road off the B6318, about 3 miles west of Greenhead; a fine stretch of wall extends from here to Harrow Scar Milecastle. About half a mile away, across the impressive river footbridge, is another good bit of wall, ending in two turrets and the meticulous structure of the **Willowford Bridge abutment**.

Still in Cumbria, about 3 miles further west along the A69, are the peaceful raspberry-coloured ruins of **Lanercost Priory** (EH; ☎ 016977-3030; admission £2.70; ⏰ 10am-6pm Apr-Sep, to 4pm Thu-Mon Oct), founded in 1166 by Augustinian canons. Ransacked several times, after the dissolution it became a private house and a priory church was created from the Early English nave. The church contains some beautiful Pre-Raphaelite stained glass. The AD 122 bus can drop you at the gate.

Sleeping

Once Brewed YHA Hostel (☎ 0870 7705980; www.yha .org.uk; Military Rd, Bardon Mill; dm £13.95; ⏰ year-round) This modern and well-equipped hostel is central for visiting both Housesteads Fort, 3 miles away, and Vindolanda, 1 mile away. Bus 685 (from Hexham or Haltwhistle train stations) will drop you at Henshaw, 2 miles south, or you could leave the train at Bardon Mill 2.5 miles southeast. The Hadrian's Wall bus can drop you at the door from June to September.

Greenhead YHA Hostel (☎ 016977-47401; www .yha.org.uk; dm £11.95; ⏰ Jul-Aug, call to check other times) A converted Methodist chapel by a trickling stream and a pleasant garden, 3 miles west of Haltwhistle. The hostel is served by bus AD 122 or 685.

Birdoswald YHA Hostel (☎ 0870 7706124; www .yha.org.uk; dm £15.50; ⏰ Easter-Oct, call to check other times) This farmhouse within the grounds of the Birdoswald complex has recently been converted into a hostel with basic facilities, including a self-service kitchen and laundry. The price includes a visit to the fort.

Holmhead Guest House (☎ 016977-47402; www .bandbhadrianswall.com; Thirlwall Castle Farm, Greenhead; dm/s/d £10/43/66) Four fairly compact rooms are available in this lovely remote old cottage; most of the space is taken up by the big beds. All the rooms have a shower rather than a bath. A barn was recently converted into a large dorm room, perfect for budget walkers and cyclists. It's about half a mile north of Greenhead.

NORTHUMBERLAND

It's difficult to imagine that there would be such a thing as 'undiscovered' country in a place so populated, so thoroughly modern, as England. But Northumberland is it: utterly wild and stunningly beautiful, with ne'er a trace of Man save the fortified houses and friendly villages that speckle the rugged interior, itself protected by the boundaries of a huge national park. Along the magnificent and pale sweeping coast to the east are long, stunning beaches bookmarked by dramatic wind-worn castles and tiny islands offshore that really do have an air of magic about them. To the west is Kielder Water, an astoundingly huge yet secluded lake, with land on all sides enveloped by forest. The most strikingly evocative part of Hadrian's Wall slices through the south.

History

Northumberland takes its name from the Anglo-Saxon kingdom of Northumbria (north of the River Humber). For centuries it served as the battleground for the struggle between north and south. After the arrival of the Normans in the 11th century, large numbers of castles and *peles* (fortified buildings) were built and hundreds of these remain. All

---

SOMETHING FOR THE WEEKEND

Northumberland's historic ducal town of Alnwick is the perfect choice for a getaway weekend and the **White Swan Hotel** (p752) in the middle of town is the perfect base. On Saturday, visit the **castle** and its spectacular **garden** (below) – but don't miss the market, which has been running since the early 13th century. Also not to be missed is a pilgrimage to **Barter Books** (p752), arguably the best bookshop in the country and a browser's dream. Round off the evening with a pint in **Ye Old Cross** (p752).

Sunday should be about exploring the surrounding area. **Warkworth Castle** (p752) is only a few miles away, while further on up the coast (only six miles from Alnwick) is the little sea village of **Craster** (p752), famous for its kippers. A short walk from here is **Dunstanburgh Castle** (p753) and **Embleton Bay** (p753), a wonderfully idyllic spot that reveals the best of Northumberland's windswept coastline.

---

this turmoil made life a tad unsettled till the 18th century brought calm. Today the land's turbulent history has echoes all around the sparsely populated countryside.

Getting Around

The excellent *Northumberland Public Transport Guide* (£1.60) is available from local tourist offices. Transport options are good, with a train line running along the coast from Newcastle to Berwick and on to Edinburgh.

ALNWICK

☎ 01665 / pop 7770

Northumberland's historic ducal town, Alnwick (no tongue gymnastics: just say 'annick') is an elegant maze of narrow cobbled streets spread out beneath the watchful gaze of a colossal medieval castle. Not only will you find England's most perfect bookshop, but also the most visited attraction in the northeast at Alnwick Garden.

The castle is on the northern side of town and overlooks the River Aln. The **tourist office** (☎ 510665; www.alnwick.gov.uk; 2 The Shambles; ☑ 9am-5pm Mon-Sat, 10am-4pm Sun) is by the marketplace, in a handsome building that was once a butcher's shop.

There has been a market in Alnwick for over 800 years. Market days are Thursday and Saturday, with a farmers market on the last Friday of the month.

Sights

ALNWICK CASTLE & GARDEN

The outwardly imposing **Alnwick Castle** (☎ 510 777; www.alnwickcastle.com; adult/concession/child £8.50/7.50/free; ☑ 10am-6pm Apr-Oct), ancestral home of the Duke of Northumberland and a favourite set for filmmakers, has changed little

since the 14th century. The interior is sumptuous and extravagant; the six rooms open to the public – staterooms, dining room, guard chamber and library – have an incredible display of Italian paintings, including Titian's *Ecce Homo* and many Canalettos.

The castle is set in parklands designed by Lancelot 'Capability' Brown. The woodland walk offers some great aspects of the castle, or for a view looking up the River Aln, take the B1340 towards the coast.

As spectacular a bit of green-thumb artistry as you'll see anywhere in England, **Alnwick Garden** (☎ 510777; www.alnwickgarden.com; adult/concession/child £8/7.50/free; ☑ 10am-7pm Jun-Sep, to 6pm Apr-May & Oct, to 4pm Nov-Jan, to 5pm Feb-Mar) is one of the northeast's great success stories. Since the project began in 2000, the 4.8-hectare walled garden has been transformed from a derelict site into a spectacle that easily exceeds the grandeur of the castle's 19th-century gardens, a series of magnificent green spaces surrounding the breathtaking Grand Cascade – 120 separate jets spurting over 31,822L of water down 30-odd weirs for everyone to marvel at and kids to splash around in.

Other gardens include the Franco-Italian–influenced Ornamental Garden (with more than 15,000 plants) and the Rose Garden, with its pergola-lined paths and lots and lots of roses. It's an ongoing project: new gardens are being added all the time and 2006 saw the opening of a new visitor centre.

Festivals

The yearly **Alnwick Fair** is a costumed re-enactment of an original medieval *fayre*. It features arts and crafts stalls, hog roasts, street theatre and the ubiquitous Dunking of the Wenches (in icy cold water): surely no fair is complete

NORTHEAST ENGLAND

TOP FIVE CASTLES

- Chillingham Castle (p762; Wooler)
- Warkworth Castle (right; Warkworth)
- Bamburgh Castle (p754; Bamburgh)
- Dunstanburgh Castle (p753; Embleton Bay)
- Lindisfarne Castle (p755; Holy Island)

---

without it? Festivities kick off the last Sunday in June.

Sleeping & Eating

White Swan Hotel (☎ 602109; fax 510400; Bondgate Within; s/d from £59/118; P) Alnwick's top address is this 300-year-old coaching inn right in the heart of town. Its rooms are all of a pretty good standard, but this spot stands out for its dining room, which has elaborate original panelling, ceiling and stained-glass windows filched from the *Olympic*, sister ship to the *Titanic*.

A row of handsome Georgian houses along Bondgate Without offers several worthwhile options that all charge around £28 per person, including **Lindisfarne Guest House** (☎ 603430; 6 Bondgate Without) and the **Teapot** (☎ 604473; 8 Bondgate Without), which has the largest teapot collection in town.

A number of atmospheric pubs do a good line in traditional food. The **Market Tavern** (☎ 602759; 7 Fenkle St; stottie £5.50), near Market Sq, is the place to go for a traditional giant beef stottie (bread roll), while **Ye Old Cross** (☎ 602735; Narrowgate; mains £6) is good for a drink and is known as 'Bottles', after the dusty bottles in the window: 150 years ago the owner collapsed and died while trying to move them and no-one's dared attempt it since.

Shopping

One of the country's largest secondhand bookshops is the magnificent, sprawling **Barter Books** (☎ 604888; www.barterbooks.co.uk; Alnwick Station; ☼ 9am-7pm), housed in a Victorian railway station with coal fires, velvet ottomans and reading (once waiting) rooms. You could spend days in here.

Getting There & Away

There are regular buses from Newcastle (501, 505 and 518; one hour, 28 per day Monday to Saturday, 18 on Sunday). Bus 518 has 10 to 14 daily services to the attractive towns of

Warkworth (25 minutes) and Alnmouth (15 minutes), which has the nearest train station. Buses 505 and 525 come from Berwick (45 minutes, 13 daily Monday to Saturday). The **Arriva Day Pass** (adult/child £5/4) is good value.

WARKWORTH
☎ 01665

Biscuit-coloured Warkworth is little more than a cluster of houses around a loop in the River Coquet, but it makes for an impressive sight, especially if you arrive on the A1068 from Alnwick, when the village literally unfolds before you to reveal the craggy ruin of the enormous 14th-century castle.

A 'worm-eaten hold of ragged stone', **Warkworth Castle** (EH; ☎ 711423; adult £3.40; ☼ 10am-5pm Apr-Sep, to 4pm Oct, Sat-Mon only Nov-Mar) features in Shakespeare's *Henry IV* Parts I and II and will not disappoint modern visitors. Yes, it is still pretty worm-eaten and ragged, but it crowns an imposing site, high above the gentle, twisting river. The film *Elizabeth* (1998), starring Cate Blanchett, was filmed here.

Tiny, mystical, 14th-century **Warkworth Hermitage** (EH; admission £2.30; ☼ 11am-5pm Wed & Sun Apr-Sep), carved into the rock, is a few hundred yards upriver. Follow the signs along the path, then take possibly the world's shortest ferry ride. It's a lovely stretch of water and you can hire a **rowing boat** (adult/child per 45 min £3/2.50; ☼ Sat & Sun May-Sep).

Fourteen huge, country-style bedrooms sit above a cosy bar at the **Sun Hotel** (☎ 711259; www.rytonpark-sun.co.uk; 6 Castle Tce; s/d from £49/75, £75/104 with dinner; P), and an elegant restaurant serves local dishes given the French treatment. There are excellent views of both the castle and the river.

Right in the centre of the village, the **Greenhouse** (☎ 712322; 21 Dial Pl; mains £7-13; ☼ lunch & dinner Mon & Wed-Sat, lunch only Sun) is a café-bistro that serves great coffee, cakes and more substantial fish and meat dishes on large pine tables.

Bus 518 links Newcastle (1½ hours, hourly), Warkworth, Alnmouth and Alnwick. There's a train station on the main east-coast line, about 1.5 miles west of town.

CRASTER
☎ 01665

Sandy, salty Craster is a small sheltered fishing village about 6 miles north of Alnwick that is famous for its kippers. In the early 20th century, 2500 herring were smoked here *daily*; these days, it's mostly cigarettes that are smoked, but the kippers they do produce are excellent.

The place to buy them is **Robson & Sons** (☎ 576223; 2 for around £8.50), which has been stoking oak-sawdust fires since 1865. For fish facts and other info, call into the **tourist office** (☎ 576007; Quarry Car Park, ☒ 9.30am-5.30pm Apr-Oct, to 4.30pm Sat & Sun Nov-Mar).

You can also sample the day's catch – crab and kipper pâté are particularly good – and contemplate the splendid views at the **Jolly Fisherman** (☎ 576218; sandwiches £3-5).

Bus 401 or 501 from Alnwick calls at Craster (30 minutes, around five daily). A pay-and-display car park is the only place in Craster where it's possible to park your car.

Dunstanburgh Castle

A dramatic one-mile walk along the coast from Craster is the only path to the striking, weather-beaten ruins of yet another atmospheric **castle** (EH; ☎ 576231; admission £2.70; ☒ 10am-5pm Apr-Sep, to 4pm Oct-Mar, Thu-Mon only Nov-Mar). The haunting sight of the ruins, high on a basalt outcrop famous for its sea birds, can be seen for miles along this exhilarating stretch of shoreline.

Dunstanburgh was once one of the largest border castles. Its construction began in 1314, it was strengthened during the Wars of the Roses, but then left to rot. Only parts of the original wall and gatehouse keep are still standing; it was already a ruin by 1550, so it's a tribute to its builders that so much is left today.

You can also reach the castle on foot from Embleton.

EMBLETON BAY

From Dunstanburgh, beautiful Embleton Bay, a pale wide arc of sand, stretches around to the endearing, sloping village of **Embleton**. The village has the seaside **Dunstanburgh Castle Golf Club** (☎ 01665-576562; www.dunstanburghcastlegc.co.uk), first laid out in 1900, and a cluster of houses. Bus 401 or 501 from Alnwick calls here too.

Past Embleton, the broad vanilla-coloured strand curves around to end at **Low-Newton-by-the-Sea**, a tiny whitewashed, National Trust-preserved village with a fine pub. Behind the bay is a path leading to the **Newton Pool Nature Reserve**, an important spot for breeding and migrating birds such as black-headed gulls and grasshopper warblers. There are a couple of hides where you can peer out at

them. You can continue walking along the headland beyond Low Newton, where you'll find **Football Hole**, a delightful hidden beach between headlands.

Sleeping & Eating

Sportsman (☎ 01665-576588; www.sportsmanhotel.co.uk; Embleton; s/d from £34/68) This large, relaxed place set up from the bay has a wide deck out the front and a spacious, plain wooden bar that serves top nosh. Upstairs are 12 beautifully appointed rooms – nine of which look over the bay and golf course – but all have solid-oak beds and handsome pine furniture. Three rooms have shared facilities.

Ship Inn (☎ 576262; Low-Newton-by-the-Sea; mains £9, bar food £4-8) Our favourite pub in all of Embleton Bay is this wonderfully traditional ale house with a large open yard for fine weather, although it would take a real dose of sunshine to tear yourself away from the cosy interior. The menu puts a particular emphasis on local produce, so you can choose from local lobster (caught 50m away), Craster kippers or perhaps a good ploughman's lunch made with cheddar from a local dairy.

Blink Bonny (☎ 01665-576595; Christon Bank; mains £6-8) Named after a famous racehorse, this typical stone country pub is a cut above the average. A huge open fireplace, oak panelling everywhere and a menu that puts a heavy accent on seafood (the lobster is particularly recommended), plus traditional music at weekends – what more could you want?

FARNE ISLANDS

One of England's most incredible sea-bird conventions is to be found on a rocky archipelago of islands about three miles offshore from the undistinguished fishing village of **Seahouses**. There's a **tourist office** (☎ 01655-720884; Seafield Rd; ☒ 10am-5pm Apr-Oct) near the harbour in Seahouses and a **National Trust Shop** (☎ 01665-721099; 16 Main St; ☒ 10am-5pm Apr-Oct) for all island-specific information.

The best time to visit the **Farne Islands** (NT; ☎ 01665-720651; admission £5.20, £4.20 Apr & Aug-Sep; ☒ 10.30am-6pm Apr & Aug-Sep, Inner Farne also 1.30-5pm May-Jul, Staple also 10.30am-1.30pm May-Jul) is during breeding season (roughly May to July), when you can see feeding chicks of 20 species of sea bird, including puffin, kittiwake, Arctic tern, eider duck, cormorant and gull. This is a quite extraordinary experience, for there are few places in the world where you can get so close to nesting sea birds. The islands are also home to England's only colony of grey seals.

To protect the islands from environmental damage, only two are accessible to the public: Inner Farne and Staple Island. Inner Farne is the more interesting of the two, as it is also the site of a tiny chapel (1370, restored 1848) to the memory of St Cuthbert, who lived here for a spell and died here in 687.

Getting There & Away

There are various tours, from 1½-hour cruises to all-day specials, and they get going from 10am April to October. Crossings can be rough, and may be impossible in bad weather. Some of the boats have no proper cabin, so make sure you've got warm, waterproof clothing if there's a chance of rain. Also recommended is an old hat – those birds sure can ruin a head of hair!

Of the operators from the dock in Seahouses, **Billy Shiel** (☎ 01665-720308; www.farne-islands.com; 3hr tour adult/child £12/8, all-day tour with landing £25/15) is recommended – he even got an MBE for his troubles.

BAMBURGH
☎ 01668

Bamburgh is all about the castle, a massive, imposing structure high up on a basalt crag and visible for miles around. The village itself – a tidy fist of houses around a pleasant green – isn't half bad, but it's really just about the castle, a solid contender for England's best.

Bamburgh Castle (☎ 214515; www.bamburghcastle.com; adult/child £6/2.50; ♡ 11am-5pm mid-Mar–Oct) is built around a powerful Norman keep and played a key role in the border wars. It was restored in the 19th century by the great industrialist Lord Armstrong, who also turned his passion to Cragside (p760) and was the owner of Jesmond Dene House in Newcastle (p733). The great halls within are still home to the Armstrong family. It's just inland from long open stretches of empty white-sand beach, ideal for blustery walks.

The **Grace Darling Museum** (☎ 214465; by donation £1.50; ♡ 10am-5pm) has displays on Bamburgh's most famous resident, lighthouse keepers in general and the small boats they rescued people in. Grace was a local lass who rowed out to the grounded, flailing SS *Forfarshire* in 1838 and saved its crew in the middle of a dreadful storm. She became the plucky heroine of her time – a real Victorian icon.

Sleeping & Eating

Bamburgh Hall (☎ 214230; cresswell@farming.co.uk; r £80; ℗) This magnificent farmhouse built in 1697 has only one room, but we highly recommend it for the sheer pleasure of the views, right down to the sea, and the huge breakfast, served in the very dining room where the Jacobite officers met during the rebellion of 1715.

Victoria Hotel (☎ 214431; www.victoriahotel.net; Front St; s/d from £50/100; ℗) Overlooking the village green is this handsome hotel with bedrooms decorated with quality antiques and – in the superior rooms – handcrafted four-posters. Here you'll also find the best restaurant in town, with a surprisingly adventurous menu (mains £12 to £14) where, for instance, chorizo is preferred over Cumberland sausage.

ourpick Waren House Hotel (☎ 214581; www.warenhousehotel.co.uk; Waren Mill; d/ste £137/184) This most romantic of getaway hotels presents a delicious dilemma: whether to spend more time enjoying the superb setting, overlooking Budle Bay and Holy Island to the east and the Cheviot Hills to the west, or to lock yourself indoors and lose yourself in the luxurious trappings (try the three-course dinner, £27) of this magnificent house. The hotel is in the small hamlet of Waren Mill, 2 miles northwest of Bamburgh along the B1340.

Greenhouse (☎ 214513; www.thegreenhouseguesthouse.co.uk; 5-6 Front St; r from £65; ℗) With four large, modern rooms with power showers and a mix of views (rooms 1 and 2 overlooking the front are best), this is a decent option, although they are loath to sell a room as a single during the summer.

The **Copper Kettle** (☎ 214361; 22 Front St; afternoon tea £4-6) is a gift shop with a pleasant tea room; you can stock up for a picnic at the **Pantry** (☎ 214455; 13 Front St; sandwiches £2-4).

Getting There & Away

Bus 501 runs from Newcastle (2¼ hours, two daily Monday to Saturday, one Sunday) stopping at Alnwick and Seahouses. Bus 401 or 501 from Alnwick (four to six daily) takes one hour.

HOLY ISLAND (LINDISFARNE)
☎ 01289

'A strange and mystical island,' a local might whisper solemnly in your ear, suggesting even the possibility of magic. Holy Island is often referred to as an unearthly place, and while a lot of this talk is just that (and a little bit of bring 'em-in tourist bluster), there *is* something almost other-worldly about this small island (it's only 2 sq miles). It's tricky to get to, as it's connected to the mainland by a narrow, glinting causeway that only appears at low tide. It's also fiercely desolate and isolated, barely any different from when St Aidan came to what was then known as Lindisfarne to found a monastery in 635. As you cross the empty flats to get here, it's not difficult to imagine the marauding Vikings that repeatedly sacked the settlement between 793 and 875, when the monks finally took the hint and left. They carried with them the illuminated *Lindisfarne Gospels* (now in the British Library in London) and the miraculously preserved body of St Cuthbert, who lived here for a couple of years but preferred the hermit's life on Inner Farne. A priory was re established in the 11th century but didn't survive the dissolution in 1537.

It is this strange mix of magic and menace that attracts the pious and the curious; during summer weekends the tiny fishing village, built around the red-sandstone remains of the medieval priory, swarms with visitors. The island's peculiar isolation is best appreciated midweek or preferably out of season, when the wind-lashed, marram-covered dunes offer the same bleak existence as that taken on by St Aidan and his band of hardy monks.

Whatever you do, pay attention to the crossing-time information, available at tourist offices and on notice boards throughout the area. Every year there is a handful of go-it-alone fools who are caught midway by the incoming tide and have to abandon their cars.

Sights

Lindisfarne Priory (EH; ☎ 389200; admission £3.70; ⊙ 9.30am-5pm Apr-Oct, to 4pm Oct & Feb-Mar, 10am-2pm Sat-Mon Nov-Jan) consists of elaborate red and grey ruins and the later 13th-century St Mary the Virgin Church. The recently refurbished museum next to these displays the remains of the first monastery and tells the story of the monastic community before and after the dissolution.

Twenty pages of the luminescent *Lindisfarne Gospels* are on view electronically at the **Lindisfarne Heritage Centre** (☎ 389004; www .holy-island.info; Marygate; adult/child £3/free; ⊙ 10am-5pm Apr-Oct, according to tides Nov-Mar), which also has displays on the locality.

Also in the village is **St Aidan's Winery** (☎ 389230), where you can buy the sickly sweet Lindisfarne Mead, cleverly foisted upon unsuspecting pundits as an age-old aphrodisiac.

Half a mile from the village stands the tiny, storybook **Lindisfarne Castle** (NT; ☎ 389244; adult £4; ⊙ 10.30-3pm or noon-4.30pm Tue-Sun Apr-Oct), built in 1550, and extended and converted by Sir Edwin Lutyens from 1902 to 1910 for Mr Hudson, the owner of *Country Life* magazine. You can imagine some decadent parties have graced its alluring rooms – Jay Gatsby would have been proud. Its opening times may be extended depending on the tide. A **shuttle bus** (☎ 389236) runs here from the car park.

Sleeping & Eating

It's possible to stay on the island, but you'll need to book in advance.

Open Gate (☎ 389222; theopengate@theopengate .ndo.co.uk; Marygate; s/d £32/54) This spacious Elizabethan stone farmhouse with comfortable rooms caters primarily to those looking for a contemplative experience – you're not as much charged a room rate as 'encouraged' to give the listed price as a donation. There is a small chapel in the basement and a room full of books on Celtic spirituality, and there are organised retreats throughout the year.

Ship (☎ 389311; www.theshipinn-holyisland.co.uk; Marygate; s/d/tr £52/68/90) Three exceptionally comfortable rooms – one with a four-poster – sit above an 18th-century public house known here as the Tavern. There's good local seafood in the bar.

Getting There & Around

Holy Island can be reached by bus 477 from Berwick (Wednesday and Saturday only, Monday to Saturday July and August). People taking cars across are requested to park in one of the signposted car parks (£5 per day). The sea covers the causeway and cuts the island off from the mainland for about five hours each day. Tide times are listed at tourist offices, in local papers and at each side of the crossing.

BERWICK-UPON-TWEED
☎ 01289 / pop 12,870

This salt-crusted fortress town is England's northernmost city and the holder of two unique honours: it is the most fought-over settlement in European history (between

1174 and 1482 it changed hands 14 times between the Scots and the English) and its football team, Berwick Rangers, are the only English team to play in the Scottish League – albeit at the low-level 3rd division in 2006–7.

Although it has been firmly English since the 15th century, it retains its own peculiar identity, as though the vagaries of its seesaw history have forced it to look inwards and not trust anyone but its own – you need only walk its massive ramparts, built during Elizabethan times and still virtually complete, to understand the town's insularity.

Orientation & Information

The fortified town of Berwick is on the northern side of the Tweed; the three bridges link with the uninteresting suburbs of Tweedmouth, Spittal and Eastcliffe.

The **tourist office** (☎ 330733; www.berwick-upon -tweed.gov.uk; 106 Marygate; ⏰ 10am-6pm Easter-Jun, to 5pm Jul-Sep, to 4pm Mon-Sat Oct-Easter) is helpful. Access the internet at **Berwick Backpackers** (☎ 331481; 56-58 Bridge St; per 20 mins £2).

Sights & Activities

Berwick's superb **walls** (EH; admission free) were begun in 1558 to reinforce an earlier set built during the reign of Edward II. They represented state-of-the-art military technology of the day and were designed both to house artillery (in arrowhead-shaped bastions) and to withstand it (the walls are low and massively thick, but it's still a long way to fall).

You can walk almost the entire length of the walls, a circuit of about a mile. It's a must, with wonderful, wide-open views. Only a small fragment remains of the once mighty **border castle**, by the train station. The tourist office has a brochure describing the main sights.

Designed by Nicholas Hawksmoor, **Berwick Barracks** (EH; ☎ 304493; The Parade; admission £3.30; ⏰ 10am-5pm Apr-Oct, to 4pm Nov-Mar) are the oldest purpose-built barracks (1717) in Britain and now houses the By Beat of Drum Museum, chronicling the history of British soldiery from 1660 to 1900.

The original gaol cells in the upper floor of the town hall (1750–61) have been preserved to house the **Cell Block Museum** (☎ 330900; Marygate; admission £2; ⏰ tours 10.30am & 2pm Mon-Fri Apr-Oct), devoted to crime and punishment, with tours taking in the public rooms, museum, gaol and belfry.

Recommended are the one-hour **guided walks** (adult/child £3.50/free; ⏰ 10am, 11.15am, 12.30pm & 2pm Mon-Fri Apr-Oct) starting from the tourist office.

Sleeping

There are plenty of B&Bs around the town, most of which offer fairly basic but comfortable rooms; the tourist office can assist in finding one.

Berwick Backpackers (☎ 331481; www.berwickback packers.co.uk; 56-58 Bridge St; dm/s/d from £12/14.95/34) This excellent hostel, basically a series of rooms in the outhouses of a Georgian home

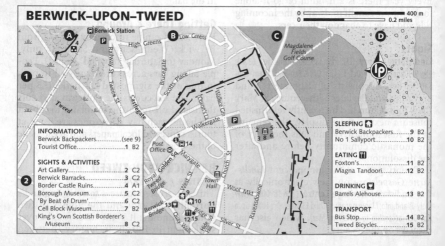

BERWICK–UPON–TWEED

0 — 400 m
0 — 0.2 miles

INFORMATION
Berwick Backpackers..............(see 9)
Tourist Office.........................1 B2

SIGHTS & ACTIVITIES
Art Gallery............................2 C2
Berwick Barracks....................3 C2
Border Castle Ruins.................4 A1
Borough Museum....................5 C2
'By Beat of Drum'...................6 C2
Cell Block Museum..................7 C2
King's Own Scottish Borderer's
    Museum.............................8 C2

SLEEPING
Berwick Backpackers.........9 B2
No 1 Sallyport.................10 B2

EATING
Foxton's........................11 B2
Magna Tandoori..............12 B2

DRINKING
Barrels Alehouse.............13 B2

TRANSPORT
Bus Stop.......................14 B2
Tweed Bicycles...............15 B2

around a central courtyard, has one large comfortable dorm, a single and two doubles, all en suite. It also has internet access. Highly recommended.

our pick No 1 Sallyport (☎ 308827; www.1sallyport -bedandbreakfast.com; 1 Sallyport, off Bridge St; r £90–140) Not just the best in town, but one of the best B&Bs in England, No 1 Sallyport has only five suites – each carefully appointed to fit the theme. The Manhattan Loft, crammed into the attic, makes the minimalist most of the confined space; the Lowry Room is a country-style Georgian classic; the Smuggler's Suite has a separate sitting room complete with widescreen TV, DVD players and plenty of space to lounge around in. Two new rooms were added in 2005: the executive Madison Suite and the super-fancy Tiffany Suite.

Eating & Drinking

Good dining is a little thin on the ground, but there are a few exceptions.

Foxton's (☎ 303939; 26 Hide Hill; mains £8-12; ☯ lunch & dinner Mon-Sat) This decent brasserie-style restaurant has continental dishes to complement the local fare, which means there's something for everyone.

Magna Tandoori (☎ 302736; 39 Bridge St; mains £6-12; ☯ lunch & dinner Mon-Sat, dinner only Sun) There's nothing much in this handsome Georgian room to suggest an Indian restaurant, but the huge menu, chock-full of dishes, makes this the best of its kind in town.

Barrels Alehouse (☎ 308013; 56 Bridge St) Elvis and Muhammad Ali grace the walls of this fine pub, where you'll also find real ale and vintage Space Invaders. There's regular live music in the atmospherically dingy basement bar.

Getting There & Away
BUS
Buses stop on Golden Sq (where Marygate becomes Castlegate); there are good links from Berwick into the Scottish Borders; there are buses west to Coldstream, Kelso and Galashiels. Buses 505, 515 and 525 go to Newcastle (2¼ hours, five daily) via Alnwick. Bus 253 goes to Edinburgh (two hours, six daily Monday to Saturday, two Sunday) via Dunbar.

TRAIN
Berwick is almost exactly halfway between Edinburgh (£16, 50 minutes) and Newcastle (£15.30, 50 minutes) on the main east-coast London–Edinburgh line. Half-hourly trains between Edinburgh and Newcastle stop in Berwick.

Getting Around
The town centre is compact and walkable; if you're feeling lazy try **Berwick Taxis** (☎ 307771), **Tweed Bicycles** (☎ 331476; 17a Bridge St) hires out mountain bikes for £18 a day.

AROUND BERWICK-UPON-TWEED
Norham Castle
Six and a half miles southwest of Berwick on a minor road off the A698 are the pinkish ruins of **Norham Castle** (EH; ☎ 01289-382329; admission £2; ☯ 10am-6pm Apr-Sep). An imposing, battered keep (in use from the 12th to the 16th centuries) rises high on rocks above the green tiling of fields and a swerving bend in the River Tweed. It was originally built by the prince bishops of Durham in 1160 to guard a crossing on the river.

Bus 23 regularly passes Norham Castle from Berwick train station on its way to Kelso in Scotland (seven daily Monday to Saturday).

Etal & Ford
The pretty villages of Etal and Ford are part of a 23.45-sq-mile working rural estate set between the coast and the Cheviots, a lush and ordered landscape that belies its ferocious, bloody history.

Etal (*eet*-le) perches at the estate's northern end, and its main attraction is the roofless 14th-century **castle** (EH; ☎ 01890-820332; admission £3.40; ☯ 11am-4pm Apr-Oct). It was captured by the Scots just before the ferocious Battle of Flodden (p758), and has a striking border-warfare exhibition. It is 12 miles south of Berwick on the B6354.

About 1.5 miles southeast of here is **Ford**, where you can visit the extraordinary **Lady Waterford Hall** (☎ 01890-820524; admission £2; ☯ 10.30am-12.30pm & 1.30pm-5.30pm Apr-Oct, other times by appointment), a fine Victorian schoolhouse decorated with biblical murals and pictures by Louisa Anna, Marchioness of Waterford. The imposing 14th-century **Ford Castle** is closed to the public.

If you're travelling with kids, we recommend a spin on the toy-town **Heatherslaw Light Railway** (☎ 01890-820244; adult/child £5.50/3.50; hourly 11am-3pm Apr-Oct, to 4.30pm mid-Jul–Aug), which chugs from the Heatherslaw Corn Mill (about halfway between the two villages) to Etal Castle. The 3.5-mile return journey follows the river through pretty countryside.

SLEEPING & EATING

Estate House (☎ 01890-820668; www.theestatehouse .supanet.com; Ford; s/d £28/56) This fine house near Lady Waterford Hall has three lovely bedrooms (all with handsome brass beds) overlooking a colourful, mature garden. An excellent choice – the owners have a plethora of local information.

Black Bull (☎ 01890-820200; Etal) This white-washed, popular place is Northumberland's only thatched pub. It serves great pub food and pours a variety of well-kept ales.

GETTING THERE & AWAY

Bus 267 between Berwick and Wooler stops at both Etal and Ford (six daily, Monday to Saturday).

Crookham & Around

Unless you're a Scot or a historian, chances are you won't have heard of the Battle of Flodden, but this encounter between the Scots and the English in 1517 – which left the English victorious and the Scots to count 10,000 dead – was a watershed in the centuries-old scrap between the two. A monument 'to the brave of both nations', which surmounts an innocuous hill overlooking the battlefield, is the only memorial to the thousands used as arrow fodder.

SLEEPING & EATING

our pick Coach House (☎ 01890-820293; www.coach housecrookham.com; Crookham; r £30-55) This is an exquisite guesthouse spread about a 17th-century cottage, an old smithy and other outbuildings. There is a variety of rooms, from the traditional (with rare chestnut beams and country-style furniture) to contemporary layouts flavoured with Mediterranean and Indian touches. The food (dinner £19.50), beginning with an organic breakfast, is absolutely delicious and the equal of any restaurant around.

GETTING THERE & AWAY

The battlefield is 1.5 miles west of Crookham, on a minor road off the A697; Crookham itself is 3 miles west of Ford. Bus 710, which runs between Newcastle and Kelso serves these parts (two daily Monday to Friday).

NORTHUMBERLAND NATIONAL PARK

Welcome to the last great English wilderness: 398 sq miles of natural wonderland spread about the soft swells of the Cheviot Hills, the spiky moors of autumn-coloured heather and gorse, and the endless acres of forest guarding the deep, colossal Kielder Water. Even the negligible human influence – even today, there are only about 2000 inhabitants here – has been benevolent: the finest sections of Hadrian's Wall run along the park's southern edge and the landscape is dotted with prehistoric remains and fortified houses – the thick-walled *peles* were the only solid buildings built here until the mid-18th century.

Orientation & Information

The park runs from Hadrian's Wall in the south, takes in the Simonside Hills in the east and runs into the Cheviot Hills along the Scottish border. There are few roads.

For information, contact the **Northumberland National Park** (☎ 01434-605555; www.northumberland-na tional-park.org.uk; Eastburn, South Park, Hexham). Besides the tourist offices mentioned in this section, there are relevant offices in **Once Brewed** (☎ 01434-344396; ◷ 10am-5pm mid-Mar–May, Sep & Oct, 9.30am-6pm Jun-Aug) as well as **Ingram** (☎ 01665-578890; ingram@nnpa.org .uk; ◷ 10am-5pm Easter-Oct). All the tourist offices handle accommodation bookings.

Walking & Cycling

The most popular stretch of the **Hadrian's Wall Path** (p747) is between Sewingshields and Greenhead in the south of the park.

There are many fine walks into the Cheviots, frequently passing by prehistoric remnants; contact the Ingram, Wooler and Rothbury tourist offices for information.

Though at times strenuous, cycling in the park is a pleasure; the roads are good and the traffic is light here. There's off-road cycling in Border Forest Park.

Getting There & Around

Public transport options are limited, aside from buses on the A69. See the Hadrian's Wall section (p746) for access to the south. Bus 808 (55 minutes, two daily Monday to Saturday) runs between Otterburn and Newcastle. Postbus 815 and bus 880 (45 minutes, eight daily Monday to

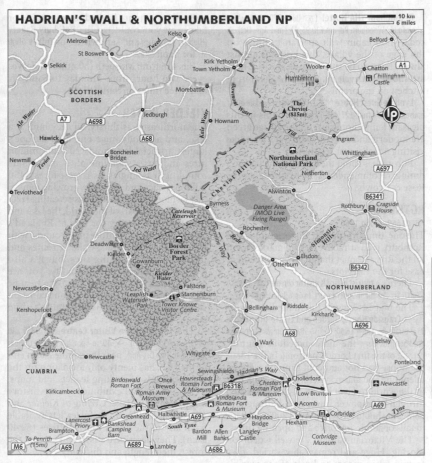

HADRIAN'S WALL & NORTHUMBERLAND NP

Saturday, three on Sunday) run between Hexham and Bellingham. National Express No 383 (three hours, one daily, £15) goes from Newcastle to Edinburgh via Otterburn, Byrness (by request), Jedburgh, Melrose and Galashiels.

BELLINGHAM
☎ 01434

The small, remote village of Bellingham (bellin-*jum*) is a pleasant enough spot on the banks of the Tyne, surrounded by beautiful, deserted countryside on all sides. It is an excellent base from which to kick off your exploration of the park.

The **tourist office** (☎ 220616; Main St; 9.30am-1pm & 2-5pm Mon-Sat, 1-5pm Sun Apr-Oct, 2-5pm Mon-Sat Nov-Mar) handles visitor inquiries.

There's not a lot to see here save the 12th-century **St Cuthbert's Church**, unique because it retains its original stone roof, and **Cuddy's Well**, outside the churchyard wall, which is alleged to have healing powers on account of its blessing by the saint.

The **Hareshaw Linn Walk** passes through a wooded valley and over six bridges, leading to a 9m-high waterfall 2.5 miles north of Bellingham (*linn* is an Old English name for waterfall).

Sleeping & Eating

Bellingham is on the Pennine Way; book ahead for accommodation in summer. Most of the B&Bs are clustered around the village green.

Bellingham YHA Hostel (☎ 0870 770 5694; www .yha.org.uk; Woodburn Rd; dm £10.95; ☷ mid-Apr–Oct) A cedarwood cabin with spartan facilities on the edge of the village, this hostel is almost always busy, so be sure to book ahead. There are showers, a cycle store and a self-catering kitchen on the premises.

Lyndale Guest House (☎ 220361; www.lyndale guest house.co.uk; s/d from £22/44) The bedrooms in this pleasant family home just off the village green are modern and extremely tidy; it's a bit like visiting a really neat relative.

Pub grub is about the extent of the village's dining; recommended is the Black Bull or the Rose & Crown.

ROTHBURY

☎ 01669 / pop 1960

The one-time prosperous Victorian resort of Rothbury is an attractive, restful market town on the River Coquet that makes a convenient base for the Cheviots.

There's a **tourist office & visitor centre** (☎ 620887; Church St; ☷ 10am-5pm Apr-Oct, to 6pm Jun-Aug).

The biggest draw in the immediate vicinity is **Cragside House, Garden and Estate** (NT; ☎ 620 333; estate & garden £6.50; ☷ 10.30am-7pm & 11am-4pm Wed-Sun Nov-Dec), the quite incredible country retreat of the first Lord Armstrong. In the 1880s the house had hot and cold running water, a telephone and alarm system, and was the first in the world to be lit by electricity, generated through hydropower. It was closed throughout 2006 but should reopen in April 2007 – call for details of admission price and opening times.

The Victorian gardens are well worth exploring. Huge and remarkably varied, they feature lakes, moors and one of the world's largest rock gardens. Visit in May to see myriad rhododendrons.

The estate is 1 mile north of town on the B6341; there is no public transport to the front gates from Rothbury – try **Rothbury Motors** (☎ 620516) if you need a taxi.

High St is a good area to look for a place to stay

Beamed ceilings, stone fireplaces and canopied four-poster beds make **Katerina's Guest House** (☎ 602334; Sun Buildings, High St; www.katerinas guesthouse.co.uk; s/d from £40/64) one of the nicer options in town, even though the rooms are a little small.

Other similarly priced options include **Alexander House** (☎ 621463; s/d £38/55) and the **Haven** (☎ 620577; Back Crofts; s/d £32/54), up on a hill.

Food options are limited to pub grub. For takeaway you could try the **Rothbury Bakery** (High St) for pies and sandwiches or **Tully's** (High St) for flapjacks.

Bus 416 from Morpeth (30 minutes) leaves every two hours from Monday to Saturday and three times on Sunday.

KIELDER WATER

The northeast was thirsty, so they built it a lake, and a bloody huge one it is: Europe's largest artificial lake holds 200,000 million litres and has a shoreline of 27 miles. Surrounding it is England's largest forest, 150 million spruce and pine trees growing in nice, tidy fashion. Besides being busy creating H_2O and O_2 for this part of the world, the lake and forest are the setting for one of England's largest outdoor-adventure playgrounds, with water parks, cycle trails, walking routes and plenty of bird-watching sites, but it's also a great place to escape humanity: you are often as much as 10 miles from the nearest village. In summer, however, your constant companion will be the insistent midge: bring strong repellent.

The **Tower Knowe Visitor Centre** (☎ 0870 240 3549; www.kielder.org; ☷ 10am-5pm Jun & Sep, to 6pm Jul-Aug, to 4pm Oct-Apr), near the southeastern end of the lake, has plenty of information on the area, with lots of walking leaflets and maps, a café and a small exhibition on the history of the valley and lake. *Cycling at Kielder* and *Walking at Kielder* are useful leaflets available from any of the area's tourist offices (£2.40 each). They describe trails in and around the forest, their length and difficulty.

Sights & Activities

Most of the lake's activities are focused on **Leaplish Waterside Park** (☎ 0870-240 3549), located a few miles northwest of Tower Knowe. It is a purpose-built complex with a heated outdoor pool, sauna, fishing and other water sports as well as restaurants, cafés and accommodation.

The **Birds of Prey Centre** (☎ 01434-250400; www .discoverit.co.uk/falconry; admission £4.50; ☷ 10.30am-5pm Mar-Oct) is also located here, with owls, falcons and hawks flapping about; the birds are flown twice daily from April to September.

The **Osprey** (☎ 01434-250312; 4 per day Easter-Oct, adult/child £6/4) is a small cruiser that navigates the lake and is the best way to get a sense of its huge size.

At the lake's northern end, 6 miles on from Leaplish and 3 miles from the Scottish border, is the sleepy village of **Kielder**.

Kielder Castle (☎ 01434-250209; admission free; ☽ 10am-5pm Apr-Oct, to 6pm Aug, 11am-4pm Sat & Sun Nov-Dec) was built in 1775 as a hunting lodge by the Duke of Northumberland. It now houses a Forestry Enterprise Information centre – with countless maps and leaflets.

Sleeping & Eating

Leaplish Waterside Park (☎ 0870 240 3549; camp site per person £6, cabin £55, Reiver's Rest dm/d £16/34; ☽ Apr-Oct) The water park offers three distinct types of accommodation. The small campsite (12 pitches) is set among trees; the Reiver's Rest (formerly a fishing lodge) has en-suite doubles and two dorms that all share a kitchen and a laundry, while the fully self-contained log cabins offer a bit of waterside luxury, complete with TVs and videos. The catch is that the cabins can only be rented for a minimum of three nights.

Kielder YHA Hostel (☎ 0870 770 5898; www.yha.org .uk; Butteryhaugh, Kielder Village; dm £13.95; ☽ Apr-Oct) This well-equipped, activities-based hostel on the lake's northern shore has small dorms and a couple of four-bed rooms (£16 per person).

Gowanburn (☎ 01434-250254; s/d £28/50) Probably the most remote B&B in England is Mrs Scott's fabulous spot on the eastern side of the lake at Gowanburn, accessible by a narrow road from Kielder village. The iron-grey lake spreads out before the house, the welcome is warm and the breakfast fantastic.

Falstone Tea Rooms (☎ 01434-240459; Old School House, Falstone) This place has filling all-day breakfasts for around £4.

Getting There & Around

From Newcastle, bus 714 – the 'Kielder Bus' (1½ hours) – goes directly to Kielder on Sundays and bank holidays, May to October. The bus leaves in the morning, turns into a shuttle between the various lake attractions and returns in the afternoon. Bus 814 (one hour, two daily Monday to Friday in term time) arrives from Otterburn, calling at Bellingham, Stannersburn, Falstone, Tower Knowe Information Centre and Leaplish; the bus begins in Bellingham from June to September (Tuesday and Friday only). **Postbus 815** (☎ 01452-333447) runs between Hexham train station and Kielder (two daily Monday to

Friday, one Saturday) on a similar route along the lake and makes a detour to Gowanburn and Deadwater in the morning.

Kielder Bikes (☎ 01434-250392; Castle Hill; bike hire adult/child £20/12; ☽ 10am-6pm Easter-Sep) is opposite Kielder Castle. If no-one's around, there's an excellent long-distance doorbell.

WOOLER
☎ 01668 / pop 1860

The harmonious, stone-terraced town of Wooler owes its sense of unified design to a devastating fire in 1863, which resulted in an almost complete reconstruction. It is an excellent spot to catch your breath in, especially as it is surrounded by some excellent forays into the nearby Cheviots (including a clamber to the top of The Cheviot, at 815m the highest peak in the range) and is the midway point for the 65-mile St Cuthbert's Way, which runs from Melrose in Scotland to Holy Island on the coast.

The **tourist office** (☎ 282123; www.wooler.org.uk; Cheviot Centre, 12 Padgepool Pl; ☽ 10am-5pm Mon-Sat, to 4pm Sun Jul-Aug, to 4pm Apr-Oct, to 5pm Mon-Sat Jul-Aug, Sat & Sun only Nov-Mar) is a mine of information on walks in the hills.

Walking

A popular walk from Wooler bus station takes in **Humbleton Hill**, the site of an Iron Age hill fort and the location of yet another battle (1402) between the Scots and the English. It's immortalised in the *Ballad of Chevy Chase* (no, not *that* Chevy Chase) and Shakespeare's *Henry IV*. There are great views of the wild Cheviot Hills to the south and plains to the north, merging into the horizon. The well-posted 4-mile trail returns to Wooler. It takes approximately two hours.

A more arduous hike leads to the top of the **Cheviot**, 6 miles southeast. The top is barren and wild, but on a clear day you can see the castle at Bamburgh and as far out as Holy Island. It takes around four hours to reach the top from Wooler. Check with the tourist office for information before setting out.

Sleeping & Eating

Black Bull (☎ 281309; 2 High St; mains around £8; s/d from £30/48) A 17th-century coaching inn that has retained much of its traditional character, this is probably the best option in town; it also does decent pub grub.

Tilldale House (☎ 281450; tilldalehouse@freezone .co.uk; 34-40 High St; s/d from £26/50) This place has comfortable, spacious rooms that work on the aesthetic premise that you can never have enough of a floral print.

Wooler YHA Hostel (☎ 0870 770 6100; www.yha.org .uk; 30 Cheviot St; dm £11.95; ☺ Mon-Sat Apr-Jun, Tue-Sat Sep, Fri & Sat Mar) This 46-bed hostel has all the normal amenities.

Getting There & Around

Wooler has good bus connections to the major towns in Northumberland. Bus 464 comes from Berwick (50 minutes, five a day Monday to Saturday) and 470 (six a day Monday to Saturday) or 473 (eight a day Monday to Saturday) come from Alnwick. Bus 710 makes the journey from Newcastle (1½ hours, Wednesday and Saturday).

Cycle hire is available at **Haugh Head Garage** (☎ 01668-281316; per day from £15) in Haugh Head, 1 mile south of Wooler on the A697.

AROUND WOOLER
Chillingham Castle

One of England's most interesting medieval castles, **Chillingham** (☎ 01668-215359; www.chillingham -castle.com; admission £6; ☺ 1-5pm Sun-Fri Easter-Sep) is steeped in history, warfare, torture and ghosts: it is said to be one of the country's most haunted places, with ghostly clientele ranging from a phantom funeral to Lady Mary Berkeley in search of her errant husband.

The current owner, Sir Humphrey Wakefield, has gone to great lengths to restore the castle to its eccentric, noble best. This followed a 50-year fallow period when the Grey family (into which Sir Humphrey married) abandoned it, despite having owned it since 1245, because they couldn't afford the upkeep.

Well done, Sir H. Today's visitor is in for a real treat, from the extravagant medieval staterooms that have hosted a handful of kings in their day to the stone-flagged banquet halls, where many a turkey leg must surely have been hurled to the happy hounds. Belowground, Sir Humphrey has gleefully restored the grisly torture chambers, which have a polished rack and the none-too-happy face of an Iron Maiden. There's also a museum with a fantastically jumbled collection of objects – it's like stepping into the attic of a compulsive and well-travelled hoarder.

In 1220, 148 hectares of land were enclosed to protect the herd of **Chillingham Wild Cattle** (☎ 01668-215250; www.chillingham-wildcattle.org.uk; adult/child £4.50/1.50; ☺ park 10am-noon & 2-5pm Mon & Wed-Sat, 2-5pm Sun Apr-Oct) from borderland raiders; this fierce breed is now the world's purest. They were difficult to steal, as they cannot herd and apparently make good guard animals. Around 40 to 60 make up the total population of these wild white cattle (a reserve herd is kept in a remote place in Scotland, in case of emergencies).

It's possible to stay at the medieval fortress in the seven apartments designed for guests, where the likes of Henry III and Edward I once snoozed. Prices vary depending on the luxury of the apartment; the **Grey Apartment** (£78) is the most expensive – it has a dining table to seat 12, or there's the **Tower Apartment** (£52), in the Northwest Tower. All of the apartments are self-catering.

Chillingham is 6 miles southeast of Wooler. Bus 470 running between Alnwick and Wooler (six daily Monday to Saturday) stops at Chillingham.

Directory

CONTENTS

Country-wide practical information is given in this chapter. For details on specific areas, flip to the relevant regional chapter.

ACCOMMODATION

Accommodation in England is as varied as the sights you visit, and – whatever your budget – is likely to be your main expense. From hip hotels and grand castles to tiny cottages and basic barns, the wide choice is all part of the attraction.

B&Bs & Guesthouses

The B&B ('bed and breakfast') is a great British institution. Basically, you get a room in somebody's house, and at smaller places you'll really feel part of the family. Larger B&Bs may have four or five rooms and more facilities.

'Guesthouse' is sometimes just another name for a B&B, although they can be larger, with higher rates.

In country areas, your B&B might be in a village or isolated farm; in cities it's usually a suburban house. Wherever, facilities usually reflect price – for around £15 to £20 per person you get a simple bedroom and share the bathroom. For around £25 you get extras like TV or 'hospitality tray' (kettle, cups, tea, coffee) and a private bathroom – either down the hall or en suite.

B&B prices are usually quoted per person, based on two people sharing a room. Solo travellers have to search for single rooms and pay a 20% to 50% premium. Some B&Bs simply won't take single people (unless you pay the full double-room price), especially in summer.

Here are some further B&B tips:

- Advance reservations are always preferred at B&Bs, and are essential during popular periods. Many require a minimum two nights at weekends.
- Many B&Bs are nonsmoking or only allow smoking in the lounge.
- Rates may rise at busy times and differ from those quoted in this book.
- If a B&B is full, owners may recommend another place nearby (possibly a private house taking occasional guests, not in tourist listings).
- In cities, some B&Bs are for long-term residents or people on welfare; they don't take passing tourists.
- In country areas, most B&Bs cater for walkers and cyclists, but some don't, so let them know if you'll be turning up with dirty boots or wheels.

BOOK ACCOMMODATION ONLINE

For more accommodation reviews and recommendations by Lonely Planet authors, check out the online booking service at www.lonelyplanet.com. You'll find the true, insider lowdown on the best places to stay. Reviews are thorough and independent. Best of all, you can book online.

PRACTICALITIES

- Be ready for a bizarre mix of metric and imperial measures in England; for example, petrol is sold by the litre, but road sign distances are given in miles.

- Use plugs with three flat pins to connect appliances to the 220V (50Hz AC) power supply.

- Read up on current events in the *Sun* or *Mirror* tabloids, or get a more incisive view in the (from right to left, politically) *Telegraph, Times, Independent* or *Guardian* quality papers.

- Relish the satire, then cringe at tales of corruption, in weekly no-frills mag *Private Eye*.

- Turn on the TV and watch some of the finest programmes in the world from the multi-channel BBC, closely followed by boundary-pushing Channel 4.

- Tune into BBC radio for a wide range of shows, and no adverts. Half the households in England have digital radio and TV, but for those still on analogue, the wavelengths are BBC Radio 1 (98.8MHz FM); Radio 2 (88-92MHz FM); BBC Radio 3 (91.3 MHz FM); Radio 4 (93.5MHz FM). For content details see p57. The *Today* show on Radio 4 (mornings to 9am) is a national institution, the aural equivalent of browsing through the papers then personally grilling the politicians.

- National commercial stations include Virgin Radio (1215Hz MW) and pleasantly nonhighbrow classical specialist Classic FM (100-102MHz FM). Both also on digital, along with about 30 other stations.

- If you're still using tapes, the video format used in England is VHS PAL (not compatible with NTSC or SECAM).

- Some places reduce rates for longer stays (two or three nights).
- Most B&Bs serve enormous breakfasts; some also offer packed lunches (around £3) and evening meals (around £10).
- If you're in a hurry, B&Bs may give discounts for not having breakfast (possibly saving £5), but this is unusual. Bed-only rates are more common at ferry ports.
- If you're on a flexible itinerary and haven't booked in advance, most towns have a main drag or area where the B&Bs congregate; those with spare rooms hang up a 'Vacancies' sign.
- When booking, check where your B&B actually is. In country areas, postal addresses include the nearest town, which may be 20 miles away – important if you're walking! For those on foot, some B&B owners will pick you up by car for a small charge.

Bunkhouses & Camping Barns

A bunkhouse is a simple place to stay, handy for walkers, cyclists or anyone on a budget in the countryside. They usually have a communal sleeping area and bathroom, heating and cooking stoves, but you provide the sleeping bag and possibly cooking gear. Most charge £7.50 to £10 per person per night.

Camping barns are even more basic: they're usually converted farm buildings, providing shelter for walkers and visitors to country areas. They have sleeping platforms, a cooking area, and basic toilets outside. Take everything you'd need to camp except the tent. Charges are around £4 per person.

Most bunkhouses and camping barns are privately owned, but the **Youth Hostels Association** (www.yha.org.uk) handles information and reservations on their behalf. Other bunkhouses and camping barns are listed in the guidebook and website for **Independent Hostels** (www.independenthostelguide.co.uk). For more details see the Accommodation Contacts boxed text, p766.

Camping

The opportunities for camping in England are numerous – great if you're on a tight budget or simply enjoy fresh air and the great outdoors. In rural areas, camping grounds (called camp sites in England) range from farmers' fields with a tap and a basic toilet, costing around £2 per night, to smarter affairs with hot showers and many other facilities, charging £5 or more per person. For an idea of just how smart some can be, we recommend *Cool Camping, England* by Jonathan Knight, a coffee-table book in the Hip Hotels tradition listing 40 exceptional camp sites, and proving that sleeping under canvas doesn't need to be damp and uncomfortable any more.

Hostels

There are two types of hostel in England: those run by the Youth Hostels Association (YHA), and independent hostels. You'll find them in rural areas, towns and cities, and they're aimed at all types of traveller – whether you're a long-distance walker or touring by car – and you don't have to be young or single to use them.

YHA HOSTELS

Many years ago, YHA hostels had a reputation for austerity, but today they're a great option for budget travellers. Some are purpose-built, but many are in cottages, country houses and even castles – often in wonderful locations. Facilities include showers, drying room, lounge and an equipped self-catering kitchen. Sleeping is in dormitories, but many hostels also have twin or four-bed family rooms, some with private bathroom.

To stay, you must join the YHA (£16 per year; £10 for under-26s) or another Hostelling International (HI) organisation. Charges vary – small hostels cost around £10, larger hostels with more facilities are £13 to £19. London's excellent YHA hostels cost around £25. Students, under-26s and over-60s get discounts. If you're not a YHA member you pay around £3 extra per night.

Most hostels offer meals and charge about £4 for breakfast and packed lunches, and around £6 for good three-course dinners. Hostels tend to have complicated opening times and days, especially out of the tourist

season, so check these before turning up. Smaller rural hostels may close from 10am to 5pm. Reservations are usually possible, and you can often pay in advance by credit card.

INDEPENDENT HOSTELS

England's independent hostels and backpacker hostels offer a great welcome. In rural areas, some are little more than simple bunkhouses (charging around £5), while others are almost up to B&B standard, charging £15 or more.

In cities, backpacker hostels are perfect for young budget travellers. Most are open 24/7, with a lively atmosphere, good range of rooms (doubles or dorms), bar, café, internet and laundry. Prices are around £15 for a dorm bed, or £20 to £35 for a bed in a private room.

Hotels

A hotel in England can be a simple place with a few rooms or a huge country house with fancy facilities, grand staircases, acres of grounds and the requisite row of stag-heads on the wall. Charges vary as much as quality and atmosphere, with singles/doubles costing £30/40 to £100/150 or beyond. More money doesn't always mean a better hotel though – whatever your budget, some are excellent value while others overcharge.

If all you want is a place to put your head down, and you're unconcerned about style or ambience, chain hotels (often along motorways and busy roads) can offer bargains. For example, **Travelodge** (www.travelodge.co.uk) offers

---

DECISIONS, DECISIONS

To help you choose where to stay, most sleeping sections throughout this book are divided into three price bands:

- Budget – under £20 per person per night
- Midrange – £20 to £50
- Top end – over £50

The exception is accommodation in London, where 'budget' in this book means up to £80 per person per night, midrange is £80 to £150, and top end is over £150.

Likewise, our definitions in eating sections throughout this book are broken up as follows:

- Budget – up to £10 per person for a meal
- Midrange – £10 to £20
- Top end – £20

Again, London is the exception, where 'budget' is under £15, midrange is £15 to £40 and top end is over £40.

rooms at variable prices based on demand; on a quiet night in November twin-bed rooms with private bathroom start at around £15, and at the height of the tourist season you'll pay up to £45. Other chains include **Hotel Formule 1** (www.hotelformule1.com), with rooms from £25.

In London and other cities you can find similar places – motorway-style, in the centre of town – that can be very good value, although totally lacking in atmosphere. These include **Premier Travel Inn** (www.premiertravelinn .com) and **EasyHotels** (www.easyhotels.com), the latter with no-frills airline-style rates and rooms.

Pubs & Inns

As well as selling drinks, many pubs and inns offer lodging and breakfast, particularly in country areas. Staying in a pub can be good fun – you're automatically at the centre of the community – although accommodation varies enormously, from stylish suites to threadbare rooms aimed at (and last used by) 1950s commercial salesmen. Expect to pay around £15 per person at the cheap end, and around £30 for something better. A major advantage for solo tourists is that pubs are more likely to have single rooms.

If a pub does B&B, it normally does evening meals, served in the bar or adjoining restaurant. Breakfast may also be served in the bar the next morning – not always enhanced by the smell of stale beer and ashtrays.

For more information on pubs, see p89.

Rental Accommodation

If you want to slow down and get to know a place better, renting for a week or two can be ideal. Choose from neat town apartments, quaint old houses or converted farms (although always called 'cottages'), all with bedrooms, bathroom, lounge and equipped kitchen.

At busy times (especially July and August) you'll need to book ahead, and cottages for four people cost from around £200 to £300 per week. At quieter times, £150 to £180 is more usual, and you may be able to rent for a long weekend. There are numerous cottage booking agencies with brochures and websites; Stilwell's (see the Accommodation Contacts boxed text, below) is a great place to start.

ACCOMMODATION CONTACTS

Locally focused accommodation websites (eg Where to Stay Wessex, Reservations London) are listed in the individual regional chapters. For a country-wide view an excellent first stop for a wide range of options is **Stilwell's** (www.stilwell.co.uk), a huge user-friendly database of accommodation for independent tourists, listing holiday cottages, B&Bs, hotels, camp sites and hostels. Stillwell's is not an agency – once you've found what you want, you deal with the cottage or B&B owner direct. From the website you can also order a hard-copy colour holiday cottage brochure.

Other good agencies include **Hoseasons Country Cottages** (☎ 01502-502588; www.hoseasons .co.uk) and **Bed & Breakfast Nationwide** (www.bedandbreakfastnationwide.com), both with websites and colour brochures.

Recommended guidebooks include the annually published *Good Hotel Guide* and the *Which? Good Bed & Breakfast Guide*. Both are genuinely independent – hotels have to be good, they can't pay to get in. These books are available in good bookshops, from online bookstores, and the *Which?* guide direct from www.which.co.uk.

For details on hostels, contact the **YHA** (☎ 0870 770 6113; 01629-592708; www.yha.org.uk). The YHA website also has information about bunkhouses, camping barns and YHA camp sites – even places where you can rent a tipi. The **Independent Hostel Guide** (www.independenthostelguide.co.uk) covers hundreds of hostels in England and beyond, and is by far the best listing available. It's also available as a handy annually updated book (£4.95) at hostels or direct from the website.

If you're planning to camp extensively, or tour England in a camper van (motor home) it's well worth joining the friendly and well-organised **Camping & Caravanning Club** (☎ 0845 130 7631; www.campingandcaravanningclub.co.uk), which owns almost 100 camp sites and lists thousands more in the excellent and invaluable *Big Sites Book* (free to members). Annual membership costs £30 and includes discounted rates on club sites and various other services – including insurance and special rates for cars on ferries.

University Accommodation

Many universities offer student accommodation to visitors during July and August vacations. You usually get a functional single bedroom with private bathroom, and self-catering flats are also available. Prices range from £10 to £30 per person.

ACTIVITIES

Walking and cycling are the most popular activities for travellers to England. For information on these activities and other things to do during your visit, see p75.

BUSINESS HOURS
Shops, Banks & Offices

Monday to Friday, most offices, businesses, shops, banks and post offices operate from 9am to 5pm (possibly 5.30pm or 6pm in cities). On Saturdays, shops keep the same hours, while Sunday shopping hours are around 11am to 4pm. London and large cities have 24-hour convenience stores. In smaller towns, shops tend to close at weekends and for lunch (normally 1pm to 2pm), and in country areas on Wednesday or Thursday afternoon too. In cities and large towns, there's usually 'late-night' shopping on Thursday – up to about 7pm or 8pm.

Museums & Sights

When it comes to sightseeing, large museums and major places of interest are usually open every day. Some smaller places will open just five or six days per week, usually including Saturday and Sunday, but may be closed on Monday and/or Tuesday. Much depends on the time of year too; places of interest will open daily in high season, but may open just at weekends (or keep shorter hours) in quieter periods.

Restaurants & Cafés

Restaurants in England open either for lunch (about noon to 3pm) and dinner (about 7pm to 10pm in smaller towns, up to 11pm or midnight in cities), or they might open for either lunch or dinner only – depending on the location. Restaurants are usually open every day of the week, although some may close on Sunday evening, or all day Monday.

Cafés and teashops also vary according to location. In towns and cities, cafés may open from 7am, providing breakfast for people on their way to work. Others stay open until 5pm or 6pm. In country areas, cafés and teashops will open in time for lunch, and may stay open until 7pm or later in the summer, catering to tourists leaving stately homes or hikers down from the hill.

Throughout this book, we indicate if restaurants and cafés are open for lunch or dinner or both, but precise opening times and days are given only if they differ markedly from the pattern outlined here.

In winter months in country areas, café and restaurant hours will be cut back, while some places may close completely from October to Easter.

Pubs, Bars & Clubs

Pubs in towns and country areas usually open daily from 11am to 11pm Sunday to Thursday, sometimes to midnight Friday and Saturday. Most open all day, although some may shut from 3pm to 6pm. Throughout this book, we don't list pub opening and closing times unless they vary significantly from these hours.

In cities, some pubs open until midnight or later, but it's mostly bars and clubs that have taken advantage of new licensing laws ('the provision of late-night refreshment', as

---

SOMETHING FOR THE WEEKEND?

England has a beguiling selection of hotels and cottages, and throughout this book we list many that stand out above the crowd. To widen the choice still further, and maybe discover a gem for yourself, contact the **Landmark Trust** (☎ 01628-825925; www.landmarktrust.org.uk), an architectural charity that rents historic buildings; your options include medieval castles, Napoleonic forts and 18th-century follies.

Another option is **Distinctly Different** (www.distinctlydifferent.co.uk), specialising in unusual, bizarre or even vaguely risqué accommodation. Can't sleep at night? How about a former funeral parlour? Need to spice up your romance? Then go for the converted brothel or the 'proudly phallic' lighthouse. Feeling brave? We have just the haunted inn for you.

Back safely down to earth with the final option. The **National Trust** (NT; www.nationaltrust.org .uk) has over 300 holiday cottages and 80 B&Bs, many on the land of NT-managed stately homes and working farms, in some of the finest locations in the country.

---

it's officially and charmingly called) to stay open to 1am, 2am or later. As every place is different, we list opening hours for bars and clubs.

CHILDREN

Who'd have 'em? No, really, travel with children can be fun, and kids are a great excuse if you secretly yearn to visit railway museums or ride the scariest roller coaster in the country.

Many national parks and resort towns organise activities for children, especially in the school holiday periods (see p772), and local tourist offices are another great source of information on kid-friendly attractions. To help you further we've also included boxed texts in the big-city sections.

Some hotels welcome kids (with their parents) and provide cots, toys and babysitting services, while others prefer to maintain an adult atmosphere, so you need to check this in advance. Likewise restaurants: some will have crayons and highchairs, and not mind if the menu ends up on the floor; others firmly say 'no children after 6pm'. Pubs and bars ban under-18s, unless they're specifically 'family-friendly' places – and many are, especially those serving food.

On the sticky topic of dealing with nappies while travelling, most museums and historical attractions have very good baby-changing facilities (cue old joke: I swapped mine for a nice souvenir), as do smart department stores. Elsewhere, you will find facilities in motorway service stations and city-centre toilets – although the latter can sometimes be a bit on the grimy side.

Breastfeeding in public remains mildly controversial, but if done modestly is usually considered OK. For more advice see www .babygoes2.com – it's packed with tips, advice and encouragement for parents on the move.

CLIMATE CHARTS

England's changeable weather is discussed on p21. These charts give details for specific regions.

CUSTOMS

The UK has a two-tier customs system – one for goods bought in another EU country where taxes and duties have already been paid, and the other for goods bought duty-free outside the EU. Below is a summary of the rules; for more details see www.hmce.gov.uk or go to the Customs Allowances section at www.visitbritain.com.

Duty Free

If you bring duty-free goods from *outside* the EU, the limits include 200 cigarettes, 2L of still wine, plus 1L of spirits or another 2L of wine, 60cc of perfume, and other duty-free goods (including beer) to the value of £145.

Tax & Duty Paid

There is no limit to the goods you can bring from *within* the EU (if taxes have been paid), but customs officials use the following guidelines to distinguish personal use from commercial imports: 3000 cigarettes, 200 cigars, 10L of spirits, 20L of fortified wine, 90L of wine and 110L of beer – still enough to have one hell of a party.

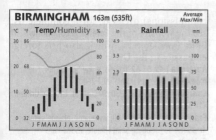

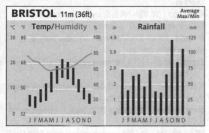

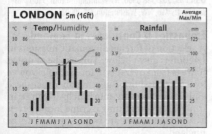

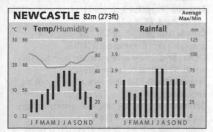

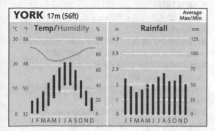

DANGERS & ANNOYANCES

England is a remarkably safe country, considering the wealth disparities you'll see in many areas, but crime is certainly not unknown in London and other cities, so you should take care – especially at night. When travelling by tube, tram or urban train service, choose a carriage containing lots of other people. It's also best to avoid some deserted suburban tube stations at night; a bus or taxi can be a safer choice.

As well as licensed taxis and minicabs (see p784 for the difference), unlicensed minicabs – essentially just a bloke with a car earning money on the side – operate in large cities, but these are worth avoiding unless you know what you're doing. Annoyances include driving round in circles, then charging an enormous fare. Dangers include driving to a remote location then robbery or rape. To avoid this, use a metered taxi or phone a reputable minicab company and get an up-front quote for the ride. London and other big cities have websites and central phone lines to help you find a licensed cab; details are in the relevant chapters of this book.

On the main streets of big cities, mugging or bag-snatching is rare, but money and important documents are best kept out of sight and out of reach rather than in a handbag or shoulder bag. Pickpockets operate in crowded public places such as tube stations or bars (bags and jackets hanging on chair-backs are popular targets), so make sure your stuff is safe here too.

In large hotels, don't leave valuables lying around the room; put them in your bag or use the safe if there is one. There's no harm in doing the same at city B&Bs too, although in rural areas there's far less risk. In hostels with shared dorms, especially in the independent/backpacker hostels in cities and large towns, you should keep your stuff packed away and carry valuables with you. Many hostels provide lockers, but you need your own padlock.

If you're driving, remove luggage from the car when parking overnight in cities and towns. The same applies even in some apparently safe rural locations. While you're out walking in the countryside, someone may well be walking off with your belongings. Where possible, look for secure parking areas near tourist offices.

DIRECTORY

DISABLED TRAVELLERS

If you happen to be in a wheelchair, use crutches or just find moving about a bit tricky, you'll find England a mixed bag. All new buildings have wheelchair access, and even hotels in grand old country houses often have modern lifts, ramps and other facilities added, although smaller B&Bs and guesthouses are often harder to adapt, so you'll have less choice here. In the same way, you might find a fine restaurant with ramps and excellent wheelchair-access loo, but tables 10in apart.

When getting around in cities, new buses have low floors for easy access, but few have conductors who can lend a hand when you're getting on or off, and this 'disabled friendly' development seems to have absolved the rest of the travelling public from offering assistance as well. Many taxis take wheelchairs, or just have more room in the back, so that might be a better way to go.

For long-distance travel, coaches present problems if you can't walk, but staff will help where possible (see the 'Why chose us?' section of www.nationalexpress.com). On trains there's usually more room and better facilities, and usually station staff around; just have a word and they'll be happy to help.

Useful organisations and websites include the following:

All Go Here (www.allgohere.com) Comprehensive info on hotels and travel.

Disability UK (www.disabilityuk.com) Excellent resource, includes details of shop mobility schemes.

Good Access Guide (www.goodaccessguide.co.uk) The name says it all.

Holiday Care Service (☎ 0845 124 9971; www.holidaycare.org.uk) Publisher of numerous booklets on UK travel.

Royal Association for Disability & Rehabilitation (RADAR; ☎ 020-7250 3222; www.radar.org.uk) Published titles include *Holidays in Britain and Ireland*.

DISCOUNT CARDS

There's no specific discount card available for visitors to England, although travel cards (see p782) are discounted for younger and older people. Membership of the YHA (see p765) can get you discounts in bookshops and outdoor gear shops, and on some public transport.

EMBASSIES & CONSULATES
British Embassies & Consulates

Below is a selection of Britain's diplomatic missions (embassies, consulates and high commissions) overseas; for a complete list, see the website of the **Foreign & Commonwealth Office** (www.fco.gov.uk), which also lists foreign embassies in the UK.

Australia (☎ 02-6270 6666; www.britaus.net; Commonwealth Ave, Yarralumla, ACT 2600)

Canada (☎ 613-237 1530; 80 Elgin St, Ottawa, Ontario K1P 5K7)

France (☎ 01 44 51 31 00; www.amb-grandebretagne.fr; 35 rue du Faubourg Saint Honoré, 75383 Paris Cedex 8)

Germany (☎ 030-204 570; www.britischebotschaft.de; Wilhelmstrasse 70, 10117 Berlin)

Ireland (☎ 01-205 3700; www.britishembassy.ie; 29 Merrion Rd, Ballsbridge, Dublin 4)

Japan (☎ 03-5211 1100; www.uknow.or.jp; 1 Ichiban-cho, Chiyoda-ku, Tokyo 102-8381)

Netherlands (☎ 070-427 0427; www.britain.nl; Lange Voorhout 10, 2514 ED The Hague)

New Zealand (☎ 04-924 2888; www.britain.org.nz; 44 Hill St, Wellington 1)

USA (☎ 202-588 6500; www.britainusa.com; 3100 Massachusetts Ave, NW, Washington, DC 20008)

Embassies & Consulates in England

A selection of foreign diplomatic missions in London is given below. This will be of use to tourists from overseas if, for example, you've lost your passport. But remember that these embassies won't be much help if you're in trouble for committing a crime locally; even as a foreigner, you are bound by the laws of England.

Australia (Map pp102-3; ☎ 020-7379 4334; www.australia.org.uk; Strand, WC2B 4LA)

Canada (Map pp102-3; ☎ 020-7258 6600; www.canada.org.uk; 1 Grosvenor Sq, W1X 0AB)

China (☎ 020-7299 4049; www.chinese-embassy.org.uk; 49–51 Portland Pl, London W1B 4JL)

France (☎ 020-7073 1000; www.ambafrance-uk.org; 58 Knightsbridge, SW1 7JT)

Germany (☎ 020-7824 1300; www.german-embassy.org.uk; 23 Belgrave Sq, SW1X 8PX)

Ireland (Map pp102-3; ☎ 020-7235 2171; 17 Grosvenor Pl, SW1X 7HR)

Japan (☎ 020-7465 6500; www.uk.emb-japan.go.jp; 101 Piccadilly, W1J 7JT)

Netherlands (☎ 020-7590 3200; www.netherlands-embassy.org.uk; 38 Hyde Park Gate, SW7 5DP)

New Zealand (☎ 020-7930 8422; www.nzembassy.com/uk; 80 Haymarket, SW1Y 4TQ)

Poland (☎ 0870 774 2700; polishembassy.org.uk; 47 Portland Pl, London W1B 1HQ)

USA (Map pp102-3; ☎ 020-7499 9000; www.usembassy.org.uk; 24 Grosvenor Sq, W1A 1AE)

FESTIVALS & EVENTS

Countless festivals and events are held around the country all year. Below is a selection of biggies that are worth tying in with your travels, and some of the smaller (and, frankly, more bizarre) events that are also worth trying to catch. In addition, many towns and villages have annual fairs or fetes, and many of these are listed in the regional chapters.

JANUARY
New Year Celebrations (1 January, city centres nationwide) Get drunk and kiss strangers as the bells chime midnight.

FEBRUARY
Jorvik Viking Festival (mid-February, York) Horned helmets galore, plus mock invaders and Viking longship races. See p616.

Shrovetide Football (Shrove Tuesday, Ashbourne, Derbyshire) It's football, Jim, but not as we know it: day-long match, 3-mile pitch, hundreds of players, very few rules. See p498.

MARCH
University Boat Race (late March/early April; London) Traditional rowing contest on the River Thames, between Oxford and Cambridge University teams.

Crufts Dog Show (early/mid-March; Birmingham) Highlight of the canine year. Top dogs abound.

APRIL
Grand National (first Saturday in April, Aintree, Liverpool) The most famous horse race of them all, with notoriously high jumps.

Cheltenham Jazz Festival (late April/early May, Cheltenham) One of the largest jazz gatherings in the country; big names, up-and-comings, concerts and funky club-dance evenings. See p416.

MAY
Obby Oss celebrations (1 May, Padstow, Devon) Ancient fertility festival, now an excuse for dressing up, pinching behinds and general good times. See p372.

FA Cup Final (early May, Wembley Stadium, London) Gripping end to venerable football tournament.

Brighton Festival (Brighton) Lively and innovative three-week arts feast. See p216.

Bath International Music Festival (mid-May to early June, Bath) Top-class classical music and opera, plus jazz and world music, with art-full Fringe attached. See p265.

Chelsea Flower Show (late May, London) Blooming marvellous.

Cheese Rolling (late May, Gloucestershire) A simple concept, centuries old: a big lump of cheese is rolled down a very steep hill, chased by hundreds of locals. The winner keeps the cheese. Losers may have broken legs.

Glyndebourne (end of May to August, Lewes, Sussex) World-class opera in country-house gardens.

JUNE
Beating Retreat (early June, London) Military bands march down Whitehall.

Derby Week (early June, Epsom, Surrey) Horse racing and people-watching.

Aldeburgh Festival (all June, Aldeburgh, Suffolk) Classical music at the spiritual home of Benjamin Britten – England's best 20th century composer. See p547.

Cotswold Olimpicks (early June, Chipping Camden) Since 1612 the locals have competed in events like shin-kicking, sack-racing and climbing the slippery pole. See p401.

Trooping the Colour (mid-June, London) Whitehall again; bearskins and pageantry for the Queen's birthday parade.

Royal Ascot (mid-June, Ascot, Berkshire) More horse racing, more people-watching, plus some outrageous hats. See p54.

Mela (mid-June, Bradford, Yorkshire) Multicultural festival with South Asian focus – music, dance food and more. One of the largest events of its kind in Britain.

Isle of Wight Festival (mid-June, Isle of Wight) Successful revival of the 1960s rip-roaring hippy happening. See p240.

Wimbledon – Lawn Tennis Championships (late June, London) Two weeks of rapid-fire returns.

Glastonbury Festival (late June, Pilton, Somerset) Huge open-air musical happening, with hippy roots. See p284.

Henley Royal Regatta (late June/early July, Henley-on-Thames, Oxfordshire) Premier rowing and social event. No hippies here. See p394.

Pride (June/July, London) Formerly **Mardi Gras and Pride in the Park**, and occasionally EuroPride – England's major gay and lesbian festival.

JULY
Hampton Court Palace International Flower Show (early July, London) Does exactly what it says on the tin.

Buxton Festival (July, Buxton, Derbyshire) Relaxed and eclectic mix of opera, music and literature over a few weeks in July. See p505.

Cowes Week (late July, Isle of Wight) Yachting spectacular.

International Flying Display (late July, Farnborough, Surrey) World's largest aeroplane show.

Cambridge Folk Festival (late July, Cambridge) A long-standing favourite, with artists from the realms of roots, world, blues, acoustic, American hillbilly and 1960s pop – as well as top folk names.

Womad (late July, Reading, Berkshire) Global gathering of frontier-crossing world and roots music; laid-back and family-friendly.

DIRECTORY

York Early Music Festival (late July, York) Travel back in time, with medieval choirs and concerts.

Truck (late July, Abingdon, Oxfordshire) A low-key, off-beat, anti-corporate music festival – and jolly good fun indeed.

Eden Sessions (July/August, Eden Project, Cornwall) The famous biomes are transformed into the county's most spectacular live music venue.

AUGUST

Three Choirs Festival (early August) Britain's premier, and the world's oldest, choral festival, held once every three years at the cathedrals of Gloucester, Hereford or Worcester.

Sidmouth Folk Festival (early August, Sidmouth, Devon) A week of traditional music, workshops, concerts, ceilidhs and barn dances.

Whitby Folk Week (mid-/late August, Whitby, Yorkshire) More traditional music and dance. Grab your partner, or sit and listen to the band.

Notting Hill Carnival (late August, London) Spectacular multicultural feast, Caribbean style.

Reading Festival (late August, Reading, Berkshire) Three-day rock, pop and dance extravaganza. A true original but now with a major corporate feel.

Leeds Festival (late August, Leeds, Yorkshire) Dubbed the 'Reading of the North', and pretty much the same type of thing.

V Festival (mid-August, Staffordshire & Chelmsford, Essex) More rock and pop, if you just can't get enough.

Big Chill (late August, Herefordshire) Recover from summer's excesses; an eclectic and relaxed mix of live music, club events, DJs, multimedia and visual art.

OCTOBER

Horse of the Year Show (early October; Birmingham) Top show-jumping event. No long faces here.

NOVEMBER

Guy Fawkes Day (5 November) Bonfires and fireworks around the country.

DECEMBER

New Year Celebrations (31 December) That's another year gone! Get ready for midnight – see January.

FOOD

For a flavour of England's cuisine, see the Food & Drink chapter (p83). Most eating sections are divided into three price bands: budget (less than £10), midrange (£10 to £20) and top end (more than £20). London is the exception, where 'budget' is less than £15, midrange is £15 to £40 and top end is more than £40.

GAY & LESBIAN TRAVELLERS

England is a generally tolerant place for gays and lesbians. London, Manchester and Brighton have flourishing gay scenes, and in other sizable cities (even some small towns) you'll find communities not entirely in the closet. That said, you'll still find pockets of homophobic hostility in some areas too.

For info, listings and contacts, see monthly magazines (and websites) **Gay Times** (www.gay times.co.uk) and **Diva** (www.divamag.co.uk), or the twice-monthly newspaper **Pink Paper** (www .pinkpaper.com). In the capital, a useful source of information is the **London Lesbian & Gay Switchboard** (☎ 020-7837 7324; www.llgs.org.uk; ☺ 24hr); there are similar services in cities and regions across the country. See also the boxes of specific information in the sections on major cities throughout this book.

HOLIDAYS

In England and Wales, most businesses and banks close on official public holidays (hence the quaint term 'bank holiday').

New Year's Day 1 January
Easter (Good Friday to Easter Monday inclusive) March/April
May Day First Monday in May
Spring Bank Holiday Last Monday in May
Summer Bank Holiday Last Monday in August
Christmas Day 25 December
Boxing Day 26 December

If a public holiday falls on a weekend, the nearest Monday is usually taken instead.

On public holidays, some small museums and places of interest close, but larger attractions specifically gear up and have their busiest times, although nearly everything closes on Christmas Day. Generally speaking, if a place closes on Sunday, it'll probably be shut on bank holidays as well.

As well as attractions, virtually everything shops, banks, offices – is closed on Christmas Day, although pubs are open at lunchtime. There's usually no public transport on Christmas Day, and a very restricted service on Boxing Day.

Following is a rough list of the main school holidays:

Easter Holiday Week before and week after Easter
Summer Holiday Third week of July to first week of September
Christmas Holiday Mid-December to first week of January.

There are also three week-long 'half-term' school holidays – usually late February (or early March), late May and late October. At school-holiday times, especially in the summer, roads and resorts get busy, and prices go up.

INSURANCE

Travel insurance is highly recommended for all overseas visitors to England; for details about health insurance, see p787. Car insurance is covered on p782.

INTERNET ACCESS

Places with internet access are reasonably common in England, but you won't find them on every corner. Internet cafés in bigger cities charge around £1 per hour; out in the sticks you can pay up to £5 per hour. Public libraries often have free access, but only for 30-minute slots.

If you're planning to use your laptop to get online, your connection cable may not fit in English sockets, although adaptors are easy to buy at electrical stores in airports or city centres.

An increasing number of hotels, hostels and coffeeshops (even some trains) have wi-fi access, charging anything from nothing to £5 per hour. Throughout this book, we use an 'internet' icon to show if a place has PCs for public use, and the word 'wi-fi' if it has…you guessed it…wi-fi.

LEGAL MATTERS
Driving Crimes & Transport Fines

Drink-driving is a serious offence. See the Transport chapter for more information and

---

LEGAL AGE
The age of consent in England is 16 (gay and straight). You can also get married at 16 (with permission from parents), but you'll have to wait two years for the toast – you must be over 18 to buy alcohol. Over-16s may buy cigarettes, so you can have a celebratory smoke instead.
You usually have to be 18 to enter a pub or bar, although the rules are different if you have a meal. Some bars and clubs are over-21 only, so you won't see many highchairs – although there may be a lot of school uniforms around.

---

details about speed limits (p783) and parking rules (p783).

On buses and trains (including the London Underground), people without a valid ticket for their journey may be fined – usually around £20 – on the spot.

Drugs

Illegal drugs are widely available, especially in clubs. All the usual dangers apply and there have been much-publicised deaths associated with ecstasy. The government reclassified cannabis in 2002: possession remains a criminal offence, but the punishment for carrying a small amount is usually a warning. Dealers face far stiffer penalties, as do people caught with any other 'recreational' drugs.

MAPS

For a map of the whole country, a road atlas is handy – especially if you're travelling by car. The main publishers are Ordnance Survey (OS) and Automobile Association (AA), with atlases in all sizes and scales. If you plan to use minor roads, you'll need a scale of about 1:200,000 (3 miles to 1in). Most road atlases cost £7 to £10 and are updated annually, which means old editions are sold off every January – look for bargains at motorway service stations.

For greater detail, the OS *Landrangers* (1:50,000) are ideal for walking and cycling. OS *Explorer* maps (1:25,000) are even better for walking in lowland areas, but can sometimes be hard to read in complex mountain landscapes. Your best choice here is the excellent specialist series produced for ramblers, walkers, mountaineers and other outdoor types by **Harvey Maps** (www .harveymaps.co.uk), covering upland areas and national parks, plus routes for hikers and bikers.

MONEY

The currency of England (and Britain) is the pound sterling. Paper money comes in £5, £10, £20 and £50 denominations, although £50s can be difficult to change because fakes circulate. Other currencies are not accepted if you're buying goods and services, except for a few places in southern England, which take Euros. A guide to exchange rates is given on the inside front cover, and there are some pointers on costs on p21.

DIRECTORY

ATMs

Debit or credit cards are perfect companions – the best invention for travellers since the backpack. You can use them in most shops, and withdraw cash from ATMs (often called 'cash machines') – which are easy to find in cities and even small towns. But ATMs aren't fail-safe, and it's a major headache if your only card gets swallowed, so take a back-up.

Credit Cards

Visa, MasterCard and AmEx credit cards are widely accepted in England, and are good for larger hotels, flights, long-distance travel, car hire etc. Smaller businesses, such as pubs or B&Bs, often only take cash or cheque.

Since early 2006, nearly all credit and debit cards use the 'chip & pin' system; instead of signing, you enter a PIN (personal identification number). If you're from overseas, and your card isn't 'chip & pin' enabled, you can sign in the usual way.

Moneychangers

Finding a place to change your money (cash or travellers cheques) into pounds is never a problem in cities, where banks and bureaus compete for business. Be careful using bureaus, however; some offer poor rates or levy outrageous commissions. You can also change money at some post offices – very handy in country areas, and rates are fair.

Tipping & Bargaining

In restaurants you're expected to leave around a 10% tip, but at smarter restaurants in larger cities waiters can get a bit sniffy if the tip isn't nearer 12% or even 15%. Either way, it's important to remember that you're not obliged to tip if the service or food was unsatisfactory (even if it's been added to your bill as a 'service charge'). At smarter cafés and teashops with table service around 10% is fine. If you're paying with a credit or debit card, and you want to add the tip to the bill, it's worth asking the waiting staff if they'll actually receive it. Some prefer to receive tips in cash.

Taxi drivers also expect tips (about 10%, or rounded up to the nearest pound), especially in London. It's less usual to tip minicab drivers. Toilet attendants (if you see them loitering) may get tipped around 50p.

In pubs, when you order drinks at the bar, or order and pay for food at the bar, tips are not expected. If you order food at the table

and your meal is brought to you, then a tip may be appropriate – if the food and service have been good, of course.

Bargaining is rare, although it's occasionally encountered at markets. It's fine to ask if there are student discounts on items such as theatre tickets, books or outdoor equipment.

Travellers Cheques

Travellers cheques (TCs) offer protection from theft, so are safer than wads of cash, but are rarely used in England, as credit/debit cards and ATMs have become the method of choice for most people. If you do prefer TCs, note that they are rarely accepted for purchases (except at large hotels), so for cash you'll still need to go to a bank or bureau.

POST

Although queues in main post offices can be long, the Royal Mail delivers a good service. Within the UK, first-class letters cost 32p and usually takes one day; 2nd-class (23p) takes up to three days. Letters by airmail cost 44p to EU countries and 72p to the rest of the world (up to 20g). Postcards are 50p. For details on all prices, see www.postoffice.co.uk.

TELEPHONE

England's iconic red phone boxes can still be seen in city streets and especially in conservation areas, although many have been replaced by soulless glass cubicles. With the advent of mobile phones (cellphones), many phone booths have been removed and not replaced at all. Either way, public phones accept coins, and usually credit/debit cards. The minimum charge is 20p.

Area codes in Britain do not have a standard format and vary in length, which can be confusing for foreigners (and Brits). For example ☎ 020 for London, ☎ 029 for Cardiff, ☎ 0161 for Manchester, ☎ 0113 for Leeds, ☎ 01629 for Matlock, ☎ 015394 for Ambleside, followed as usual by the individual number. In this book, most area codes are listed at the start of each city/area section. For clarity, where area codes and individual numbers are listed together, they're separated by a hyphen.

As well as the geographical area codes, other 'codes' include: ☎ 0500 or ☎ 0800 for free calls and ☎ 0845 for calls at local rate, wherever you're dialling from within the UK. Numbers starting with ☎ 087 are charged at national-call rate, while numbers starting with

089 or 09 are premium rate, and should be specified by the company using the number (ie in their advertising literature), so you know the cost before you call. (These codes and numbers are not separated by hyphen as you always have to dial the whole number.) Note that many numbers starting with 08 or 09 do not work if you're calling from outside the UK, or if they do you'll be charged for a full international call – and then some.

Codes for mobile phones usually start with 07 – more expensive than calling a land line.

International Calls

To call outside the UK dial 00, then the country code (1 for USA, 61 for Australia), the area code (you usually drop the initial zero) and the number. For country codes, see the inside front cover of this book.

Direct-dialled calls to most overseas countries can be made from most public telephones, and it's usually cheaper between 8pm and 8am Monday to Friday and at weekends. You can usually save money by buying a phonecard (usually denominated £5, £10 or £20) with a PIN that you use from any phone by dialling an access number (you don't insert it into the machine). There are dozens of cards, usually available from city newsagents, with rates of the various companies often vividly displayed.

To make reverse-charge (collect) calls, dial 155 for the international operator. It's an expensive option, but what the hell – the other person is paying!

To call England from abroad, dial your country's international access code, then 44 (the UK's country code), then the area code (dropping the first 0) and the phone number.

Most internet cafés now have skype or some other sort of internet telephony system, so you can make international calls for the price of your time on line.

Local & National Calls

Local calls (within 35 miles) are cheaper than national calls. All calls are cheaper from 6pm to 8am Monday to Friday, and from midnight Friday to midnight Sunday. From private phones, rates vary between telecom providers. From BT public phones the weekday rate is about 5p per minute; evenings and weekends it's about 1p per minute.

For the operator, call 100. For directory inquiries, a host of agencies compete for your business and charge from 10p to 40p; numbers include 118 192, 118 118, 118 500 and 118 811.

Mobile Phones

Around 50 million people in the UK have mobile phones, and thus the ability to tell their loved ones they're on the train. The terse medium of SMS is a national passion, with a billion text messages sent monthly.

Phones in the UK use GSM 900/1800, which is compatible with Europe and Australia but not with North America or Japan (although phones that work globally are increasingly common).

Even if your phone works in the UK, because it's registered overseas a call to someone just up the road will be routed internationally and charged accordingly. An option is to buy a local SIM card (around £30), which includes a UK number, and use that in your own handset (as long as your phone isn't locked by your home network).

A second option is to buy a pay-as-you-go phone (from around £50); to stay in credit, you buy 'top-up' cards at newsagents. A third option is to rent a phone – see p95.

TIME

Wherever you are in the world, time is measured in relation to Greenwich Mean Time (GMT, or Universal Time Coordinated, UTC as it's more accurately called), so a highlight for many visitors to London is a trip to Greenwich and its famous line dividing the western and eastern hemispheres.

To give you an idea, if it is noon in London, it is 4am on the same day in San Francisco, 7am in New York and 10pm in Sydney. British summer time (BST) is Britain's daylight saving; one hour ahead of GMT from late March to late October.

TOURIST INFORMATION

Before leaving home, check the comprehensive and wide-ranging websites **VisitBritain** (www.visitbritain.com) and **VisitEngland** (www.visiteng land.com), covering all the angles of national tourism, with links to numerous other sites. Details about local and regional websites and tourist organisations are also given at the start of each main chapter throughout this book.

DIRECTORY

Tourist Offices Abroad

VisitBritain's main overseas offices are listed below. Those in other countries are listed on www.visitbritain.com. Offices with a physical address can deal with walk-in visitors; for the others it's phone or email only. As well as information, they can help with discount travel cards, often available only if you book before arrival in England.

Australia (☎ 02-9021 4400; www.visitbritain.com/au; 15 Blue St, North Sydney, NSW 2060)
Canada (☎ 1 888 847 4885; www.visitbritain.com/ca)
France (☎ 01 58 36 50 50; www.visitbritain.com/fr)
Germany (☎ 01801-46 86 42; www.visitbritain.com/de; Hackescher Markt 1, 10178 Berlin)
Ireland (☎ 01-670 8000; www.visitbritain.com/ie; 22-24 Newmount House, Lower Mount St, Dublin 2)
Japan (☎ 03-5562 2550; www.visitbritain.com/jp; 1F Akasaka Twin Tower, Minato-ku, Tokyo 107-0052)
Netherlands (☎ 020-689 0002; www.visitbritain.com/nl)
New Zealand (☎ 0800 700741; www.visitbritain.com/nz)
USA (☎ 800 462 2748; www.visitbritain.com/us; 551 Fifth Ave, New York, NY 10176)

Local Tourist Offices

All English cities and towns (and some villages) have a tourist information centre (TIC). Some TICs are run by national parks and often have small exhibits about the area. You'll also see visitor welcome centres, visitor information centres or visitor information points, often run by chambers of commerce or civic trusts; for ease of use we've called all these places 'tourist

offices' in this book. Whatever the name, these places have helpful staff, books and maps for sale, leaflets to give away and loads of advice on things to see or do. They can also assist with booking accommodation. Most tourist offices keep regular business hours; in quiet areas they close from October to March, while in popular areas they open daily year-round.

Look out too for tourist information points – usually a rack of leaflets about local attractions set up in a post office or shop in a village not big enough to have its own full-on tourist office.

For a list of all tourist offices around Britain see www.visitmap.info/tic.

VISAS

If you're a European Economic Area (EEA) national, you don't need a visa to visit England (you can also work here freely). Citizens of Australia, Canada, New Zealand, South Africa and the USA are given leave to enter England at their point of arrival for up to six months, but are prohibited from working. (If you intend to seek work, see opposite.)

English immigration authorities are tough, and if they suspect you're coming to England for more than a holiday, you may need to prove that you have funds to support yourself, details of any hotels or local tours booked, or personal letters from people you'll be visiting. Having a return ticket helps too.

Visa and entry regulations are always subject to change, so it's vital to check with your

---

HISTORY TIPS

For many visitors, a highlight of a journey through England is visiting the numerous castles and other historic sites that pepper the country. Membership of the National Trust (NT) and English Heritage (EH) gives you free entry to many properties, reciprocal arrangements with other heritage organisations (in Wales, Scotland and beyond), maps, information handbooks and so on. You can join at the first NT or EH site you visit. If you are a member of a similar organisation in your own country, this may get you free or discounted entry at NT and EH sites in England.

National Trust (☎ 0870 458 4000; www.nationaltrust.org.uk) protects hundreds of historic buildings (normally around £5 to enter) plus vast tracts of land with scenic importance. Membership costs £40 per year (£18 for under-26s, and £55 to £73 for families), reduced by about 25% if you pay by direct debit. Alternatively, a NT touring pass gives free entry to NT properties for seven or 14 days (£17/22 per person); families and couples get cheaper rates.

English Heritage (☎ 0870 333 1181; www.english-heritage.org.uk) is a state-funded organisation, responsible for the upkeep of numerous historic sites. Some are free, while others cost £1.50 to £6. Annual membership costs £38/65 per adult/couple (£26/42 for seniors). Alternatively, an Overseas Visitors Pass allows free entry to most major EH sites for seven/14 days for £18/22 per person (with cheaper rates for couples and families).

We have included the relevant acronym (NT or EH) in the information brackets after properties listed throughout this book.

TRACE THE ANCESTORS

If you're a visitor with ancestors who once lived in England, your trip could be a good chance to find out more about (or simply find) long-lost relatives. Here are a few guidelines to get you started.

The **Family Records Centre** (☎ 0845 603 7788; www.familyrecords.gov.uk; 1 Myddelton St, London EC1R 1UW), a helpful department of the Public Records Office (PRO), is familiar with the needs of ancestor-hunters and has publications (available by post) outlining the process. You'll need a passport as ID to see original records, although documents referring to individuals are closed for 100 years to safeguard confidentiality.

The **Association of Genealogists & Researchers in Archives** (www.agra.org.uk) lists professional researchers. For a fee they can search for ancestors or living relatives on your behalf.

---

local British embassy, high commission or consulate before leaving home. For more information, check www.ukvisas.gov.uk.

WEIGHTS & MEASURES

England is in transition when it comes to weights and measures, as it has been for the last 20 years – and probably will be for 20 more. Most people still use imperial units of inches, feet, yards and miles, although mountain heights on maps are given in metres only.

For weight, many people use pounds and ounces, even though since January 2000 goods in shops must be measured in kilograms. And nobody knows their weight in pounds (like Americans) or kilograms (like the rest of the world); Brits weigh themselves in stones, an archaic unit of 14 pounds.

When it comes to volume, things are even worse: most liquids are sold in litres or half-litres, except milk and beer, which come in pints. Garages sell petrol priced in pence per litre, but measure car performance in miles per gallon. Great, isn't it?

In this book we have reflected this wacky system of mixed measurements. Heights are given in metres (m) and distances in miles. For conversion tables, see the inside front cover.

WOMEN TRAVELLERS

The occasional wolf whistle from a building site or groper on the London Underground aside, solo women will find England fairly enlightened. There's nothing to stop women going into pubs alone, for example – although you may feel conspicuous in a few places. Restaurants may assume you're waiting for a date unless you specify a table for one, but once you've clarified, it's no big deal.

The contraceptive pill is available free on prescription in England, as is the morning-after pill (also on sale at chemists). Most big towns have a Well Woman Clinic that can advise on general health issues; find its address in the local phone book.

Safety is not a major issue, although commonsense caution should be observed in big cities, especially at night. Hitching is always unwise. See p769 for advice on travel by minicab. Should the worst happen, most cities and towns have a rape crisis centre, where information or counselling is free and confidential; see www.rapecrisis.org.uk for details.

WORK

Nationals of most European countries don't need a permit to work in England, but everyone else does. If you're a non-European and this is the main purpose of your visit, you must be sponsored by an English company.

Exceptions include Commonwealth citizens with a UK-born parent; a Certificate of Entitlement to the Right of Abode allows you to live and work in England free of immigration control. If one of your grandparents was born in the UK you may be eligible for an Ancestry Employment Certificate allowing full-time work for up to four years.

Commonwealth citizens under 31 without UK ancestry are allowed to take temporary work during their holiday, but need a Working Holiday Entry Certificate – which must be obtained in advance and is valid for four years. You're not allowed to engage in business, pursue a career (evidently serving in bars doesn't count) or work as a professional athlete or entertainer. Au pair placements are generally permitted.

Useful websites include www.working intheuk.gov.uk (the official government site); www.bunac.org (advice on six-month work permits for students from the USA); and www.workingholidayguru.com (aimed mainly at Australians coming to Europe).

Transport

CONTENTS

GETTING THERE & AWAY

London is an international transport hub, so you can easily fly to England from just about anywhere in the world. In recent years, the massive growth of budget ('no-frills') airlines has increased the number of routes – and reduced fares – between England and cities in Ireland or mainland Europe.

Your other main option for travel between England and mainland Europe is ferry, either port-to-port or combined with a long-distance bus trip – although journeys can be long and savings not huge compared with budget airfares. International trains are much more comfortable, and the Channel Tunnel allows direct services between England, France and Belgium.

Getting from England to Scotland and Wales is easy. The bus and train systems are fully integrated and in most cases you won't even know you've crossed the border. Passports are not required – although some Scots and Welsh may think they should be!

Flights, tours and rail tickets can be booked online by accessing www.lonelyplanet.com/travel_services.

DEPARTURE TAX

Flights within the UK and to EU destinations attract a £10 departure tax. For other international flights from the UK you pay £20. This is usually included in the ticket price.

THINGS CHANGE...

The information in this chapter is particularly vulnerable to change. Check directly with the airline or a travel agent to make sure you understand how a fare (and ticket you may buy) works and be aware of the security requirements for international travel. Shop carefully. The details given in this chapter should be regarded as pointers and are not a substitute for your own careful, up-to-date research.

AIR
Airports

London's Heathrow and Gatwick are the two main airports for international flights. Also near London, Luton and Stanstead airports deal largely with charter and budget European flights, while London City Airport specialises in business flights. For more details on getting between the London airports and central London, see p159.

Some planes on transatlantic and European routes zip direct to major regional airports like Manchester, while smaller regional airports such as Southampton and Birmingham are served by scheduled and charter flights to/from continental Europe and Ireland.

HEATHROW

Some 15 miles west of central London, **Heathrow** (LHR; ☎ 0870 000 0123; www.heathrowairport.com) is the world's busiest airport, often chaotic and crowded, with four terminals (plus a fifth under construction and a sixth mooted).

If you're leaving England via Heathrow, make certain you know which terminal your flight is departing from, and allow plenty of time to stand in queues for security checks or get lost in the labyrinth of shops and soulless eateries.

GATWICK

Smaller than Heathrow, but increasingly busy, **Gatwick** (LGW; ☎ 0870 000 2468; www.gatwickairport .com) is 30 miles south of central London, and served by scheduled, charter and budget airlines.

STANSTED

London's third-busiest airport, **Stansted** (STN; ☎ 0870 000 0303; www.stanstedairport.com) is 35 miles northeast of central London, and used mainly by charter and budget airlines – making it one of Europe's fastest-growing airports.

LUTON

Some 35 miles north of central London, **Luton** (LTN; ☎ 01582-405100; www.london-luton.co.uk) is the main base of low-cost airline EasyJet, and also serves charter flights.

LONDON CITY

About 6 miles east of central London in Docklands, **London City Airport** (LCY; ☎ 020-7646 0088; www.londoncityairport.com) has flights to/from mainland Europe, Ireland and other UK airports.

Airlines

Most of the world's major airlines have services to/from England, including the following (with their UK contact and reservation phone numbers):

Aer Lingus (EI; ☎ 0845 084 4444; www.aerlingus.com)
Air Canada (AC; ☎ 0871 220 1111; www.aircanada.ca)
Air France (AF; ☎ 0845 359 1000; www.airfrance.com)
Air New Zealand (NZ; ☎ 0800 028 4149; www.air newzealand.co.nz)
Alitalia (AZ; ☎ 0870 544 8259; www.alitalia.com)
American Airlines (AA; ☎ 08457 789 789; www .americanairlines.com)
BMI-British Midland (BD; ☎ 0870 607 0555; www .flybmi.com)
British Airways (BA; ☎ 0870 850 9850; www.ba.com)
Cathay Pacific (CX; ☎ 020 8834 8888; www.cathay pacific.com)
Continental Airlines (CO; ☎ 0845 607 6760; www .continental.com)
Delta Air Lines (DL; ☎ 0800 414767; www.delta.com)
Emirates (EK; ☎ 0870 243 2222; www.emirates.com)
Iberia (IB; ☎ 0845 850 9000; www.iberia.com)
KLM-Royal Dutch Airlines (KL; ☎ 08705 074 074; www.klm.com)
Lufthansa Airlines (LH; ☎ 08708 377 747; www .lufthansa.com)
Qantas Airways (QF; ☎ 08457 747 767; www.qantas .com.au)
Scandinavian Airlines (SK; ☎ 0870 607 2772; www .scandinavian.net)
Singapore Airlines (SQ; ☎ 0870 608 8886; www .singaporeair.com)

TRANSPORT

CLIMATE CHANGE & TRAVEL

Climate change is a serious threat to the ecosystems that humans rely upon, and air travel is the fastest-growing contributor to the problem. Lonely Planet regards travel, overall, as a global benefit, but believes we all have a responsibility to limit our personal impact on global warming.

Flying & Climate Change

Pretty much every form of motor transport generates CO_2 (the main cause of human-induced climate change) but planes are far and away the worst offenders, not just because of the sheer distances they allow us to travel, but because they release greenhouse gases high into the atmosphere. The statistics are frightening: two people taking a return flight between Europe and the US will contribute as much to climate change as an average household's gas and electricity consumption over a whole year.

Carbon Offset Schemes

Climatecare.org and other websites use 'carbon calculators' that allow travellers to offset the greenhouse gases they are responsible for with contributions to energy-saving projects and other climate-friendly initiatives in the developing world – including projects in India, Honduras, Kazakhstan and Uganda.

Lonely Planet, together with Rough Guides and other concerned partners in the travel industry, supports the carbon offset scheme run by climatecare.org. Lonely Planet offsets all of its staff and author travel.

For more information check out our website: www.lonelyplanet.com.

South African Airways (SA; ☎ 0870 747 1111; www .flysaa.com)
United Airlines (UA; ☎ 08458 444 777; www.united .com)
Virgin Atlantic (VS; 0870 380 2007; www.virgin-atlan tic.com)

Budget airlines flying between England and other European countries can offer real bargains. Fares vary according to demand, and are best bought online. The only downside is that some no-frills airlines land at minor airports a considerable distance from the centre of the city they claim to serve. The main players are the following:

EasyJet (U2; ☎ 0870 600 0000; www.easyjet.com)
Ryanair (FR; ☎ 0871 246 0000; www.ryanair.com)
Virgin Express (TV; ☎ 0870 730 1134; www.virgin -express.com)

To save trawling several sites, services such as www.skyscanner.com and www.lowcostair lines.org have information on many scheduled airlines.

Charter flights are another option. You can buy seat-only deals on the planes that carry tourists between, for example, England and numerous Mediterranean resorts. Contact high-street travel agencies, or specialist websites such as www.flightline.co.uk and www .cheapflights.co.uk.

Tickets
You can purchase your airline ticket from a travel agency (in person, by telephone or on the internet), or direct from the airline (the best deals are often available online only). Whichever, it always pays to shop around. Internet travel agencies such as www.trav elocity.com and www.expedia.com work well if you're doing a straightforward trip, but for anything even slightly complex there's no substitute for a real-live travel agent who knows the system, the options, the special deals and so on.

The best place to start your search for agencies or airlines is the travel section of a weekend newspaper. Scan the advertisements, phone a few numbers, check a few websites, build up an idea of options, then take it from there. Remember, you usually get what you pay for: cheaper flights may leave at unsociable hours or include several stopovers. For quick and comfortable journeys, you have to fork out more cash.

Australia & New Zealand
The route to England from the southern hemisphere is a very popular one, with a wide range of fares from about AUD$1500 to AUD$3000 return. From New Zealand it's often best to go via Australia. Round-the-world (RTW) tickets can sometimes work out cheaper than a straightforward return. Major agencies include the following:

AUSTRALIA
Flight Centre (☎ 133 133; www.flightcentre.com.au)
STA Travel (☎ 1300 733 035; www.statravel.com.au)

NEW ZEALAND
Flight Centre (☎ 0800 243544; www.flightcentre .co.nz)
STA Travel (☎ 0508 782 872; www.statravel.co.nz)

Canada & the USA
There is a continuous price war on the world's busiest transcontinental route. Return fares from the East Coast to London range from US$300 to US$600. From the West Coast, fares are about US$100 higher. Major agencies include the following:

CANADA
Flight Centre (☎ 1888-967 5355; www.flightcentre.ca)
Travel CUTS (☎ 866 246 9762; www.travelcuts.com)

USA
Flight Centre (☎ 1866-WORLD 51; www.flightcentre .us)
STA Travel (☎ 800 781 4040; www.statravel.com)

LAND
Bus
You can easily get between England and numerous cities in Ireland or mainland Europe via long-distance bus. The international bus network **Eurolines** (www.eurolines.com) connects a huge number of destinations; the website has links to bus operators in each country, and gives contact details of local offices. In England, you can book Euroline tickets on the phone or at the website of **National Express** (☎ 08705 808080; www.nationalexpress.com), and at many travel agencies.

Bus travel may be slower and less comfortable than going by train, but it's usually cheaper, especially if you're under 25 or over 60. Some sample single fares (and approximate journey times): London to/from Amsterdam €40 (12 hours); Barcelona €125

(24 hours); Dublin €30 (12 hours). Frequent special offers (called 'fun fares') can bring these prices way down, but it's still worth checking the budget airlines. You may pay a similar fare and knock a large chunk off the journey time.

Train
CHANNEL TUNNEL SERVICES
The Channel Tunnel makes direct train travel between England and continental Europe a fast and enjoyable option. High-speed **Eurostar** (☎ 08705 186 186; www.eurostar.com) passenger services hurtle at least 10 times daily between London and Paris (three hours), and London and Brussels (2½ hours), via Ashford and Calais. A new high-speed rail link on the English side will be completed in 2007 and slice another 30 minutes off the journey.

You can buy tickets from travel agencies, major train stations or direct from Eurostar. The normal single fare between London and Paris/Brussels is around £150, but advance deals can drop to around £70 return, or less. Seniors and under-25s get reductions. Bicycles must be in a bike bag.

If you've got a car, your other option is **Eurotunnel** (☎ 08705 353535; www.eurotunnel.com). You drive to Folkestone in England or Calais in France, drive onto a train, go through the tunnel, and drive off at the other end. The trains run about four times hourly from 6am to 10pm, then hourly. Loading and unloading is one hour; the journey takes 35 minutes. You can book in advance direct with Eurotunnel or pay on the spot (cash or credit card). The standard cost for a car (and passengers) is around £200 return, but cheaper promotional fares often bring the cost down to nearer £100.

TRAIN & FERRY CONNECTIONS
As well as Eurostar, many 'normal' trains run between England and mainland Europe. You buy a direct ticket, but get off the train at the port, walk onto a ferry, then get another train on the other side. Routes include Amsterdam to London (via Hook of Holland and Harwich); and Paris to London (via Calais and Dover). Standard single fares for all these journeys are about £50, but cheaper deals are usually available.

Travelling between Ireland and England, the main train-ferry-train route is Dublin to London, via Dun Laoghaire and Holyhead. From southern Ireland, ferries sail between

Rosslare and Fishguard or Pembroke (Wales), with train connections on either side.

SEA
The main ferry routes between England and Ireland include Holyhead to Dun Laoghaire. Between England and mainland Europe ferry routes include Dover to Calais (France), Harwich to Hook of Holland (Netherlands), Hull to Zeebrugge (Belgium) and Rotterdam (Netherlands), Portsmouth to Santander or Bilbao (Spain), and Newcastle to Bergen (Norway) or Gothenberg (Sweden). There are many more.

Competition from Eurotunnel and budget airlines has forced ferry operators to offer constant discounted fares, although options vary massively according to time of day or year. The best cross-channel bargains are return fares – often much cheaper than two singles; sometimes cheaper than *one* single! If you're a foot passenger, or cycling, you've got more flexibility. If you're driving a car, planning ahead is worthwhile: as well as the usual variants (time of year etc), fares depend on the size of car and the number of passengers. On longer ferry trips, the fare might include a cabin.

Main ferry operators (and their UK contact numbers) include the following:

Brittany Ferries (☎ 08703 665 333; www.brittany -ferries.com)

DFDS Seaways (☎ 08702 520 524; www.dfds.co.uk)

Hoverspeed (☎ 0870 240 8070; www.hoverspeed .co.uk)

Irish Ferries (☎ 08705 171717; www.irishferries.com)

P&O Ferries (☎ 08705 202020; www.poferries.com)

Speedferries (☎ 0870 220 0570; www.speedferries .com)

Stena Line (☎ 08705 707070; www.stenaline.com)

Transmanche (☎ 0800 917 1201; www.transmanche ferries.com)

Another option is www.ferrybooker.com, an online agency covering all sea-ferry routes, plus Eurotunnel.

GETTING AROUND

For getting around England by public transport, your main options are train and long-distance bus (called coach in England). Services between major towns and cities are generally good, although expensive compared with other European countries. Delays are

TRANSPORT

frequent too, especially on the rail network, but these tend to afflict commuters rather than visitors: if your journey from London to Bath runs 30 minutes late, what's the problem? You're on holiday!

As long as you have time, using a mix of train, coach, local bus, the odd taxi, walking and occasionally hiring a bike, you can get almost anywhere without having to drive. You'll certainly see more of the countryside than you might slogging along grey motorways, and in the serene knowledge that you're doing less environmental damage. Having said that, in some rural areas the bus services can be patchy, so a car can often be handy for reaching out-of-the-way spots.

Traveline (☎ 0870 608 2608; www.traveline.org.uk) is a very useful information service covering bus, coach, taxi and train services nationwide (although some areas are better represented than others), with numerous links to help plan your journey. By phone, you get transferred automatically to an advisor in the region you're phoning from; for details on another part of the country you may have to be transferred to another assistant.

AIR

England's domestic air companies include British Airways, BMI, BMI Baby, EasyJet and Ryanair, but flights around the country aren't really necessary for tourists unless you're really pushed for time. Even if you're going from one end of the country to the other (eg London to Newcastle, or Manchester to Newquay) trains compare favourably with planes, once airport down-time is factored in. On fares, you might get a bargain air fare, but with advance planning trains can be cheaper.

BICYCLE

England is a compact country, and getting around by bicycle is perfectly feasible – and a great way to really see the country – if you've got time to spare. For more ideas see p77.

BUS & COACH

If you're on a tight budget, long-distance buses are nearly always the cheapest way to get around, although they're also the slowest – sometimes by a considerable margin.

In England, long-distance express buses are called coaches, and in many towns there are separate bus and coach stations. Make sure you go to the right place!

National Express (☎ 08705 808080; www.national express.com) is the main operator, with a wide network and frequent services between main centres. Fares are very reasonable (eg London to York around £20, with special-offer 'fun fares' as low as £1).

Also offering fares from £1 is **Megabus** (www .megabus.com), operating a budget airline-style service between about 20 destinations around the country. Go at a quiet time, book early, and your ticket will be very cheap. Book later, for a busy time and…you get the picture.

For information about short-distance and local bus services see p784.

Bus Passes & Discounts

National Express offers NX2 discount passes to full-time students and under-26s. They cost £10, and get you 30% off standard adult fares. Proof and a passport photo are required. People over 60, families and disabled travellers also get discounts.

For touring the country, National Express also offers Brit Xplorer passes, which allow unlimited travel for seven days (£79), 14 days (£139) and 28 days (£219). You don't need to book journeys in advance with this pass; if the coach has a spare seat – you can take it. This deal is only available to non-Brits though.

CAR & MOTORCYCLE

Travelling by private car or motorbike you can be independent and flexible, and reach remote places. For solo budget travellers a downside of car travel is the expense, and in cities you'll need superhuman skills to negotiate heaving traffic, plus deep pockets for parking charges. But if there's two of you (or more), car travel can work out cheaper than public transport.

Motorways and main A-roads are dual carriageways and deliver you quickly from one end of the country to another. Lesser A-roads, B-roads and minor roads are much more scenic and fun, especially in northern England, as you wind through the countryside from village to village – ideal for car or motorcycle touring. You can't travel fast, but you won't care.

Petrol and diesel cost around 95p per litre, although fuel prices rise as you get away from cities and large towns.

Hire

Compared to many countries (especially the USA), hire rates are expensive in England; you should expect to pay around £250 per week for a small car (unlimited mileage). Rates rise at busy times and drop at quiet times (especially at EasyRentacar, where you also get better rates for advance reservations, and special offers can drop to £3 per day). Some main players:

Avis (☎ 08700 100 287; www.avis.co.uk)
Budget (☎ 08701 565656; www.budget.com)
EasyRentacar (☎ 0906 333 3333; www.easycar.com)
Europcar (☎ 0870 607 5000; www.europcar.co.uk)
Hertz (☎ 0870 844 8844; www.hertz.co.uk)
National (☎ 0870 400 4502; www.nationalcar.com)
Sixt (☎ 08701 567567; www.e-sixt.co.uk)
Thrifty (☎ 01494-751600; www.thrifty.co.uk)

Many international websites have separate web pages for customers in different countries, and the prices for a car in England on, say, the UK web pages can be cheaper or more expensive than the same car on the USA or Australia web pages. The moral is – you have to surf a lot of sites to find the best deals.

Your other option is to use an internet search engine to find small local car-hire companies in England who can undercut the big boys. Generally those in cities are cheaper than in rural areas. See under Getting Around in the main city sections for more details, or see a rental-broker site such as **UK Car Hire** (www.uk-carhire.net).

Another option is to hire a motorhome or campervan. It's more expensive than hiring a car but it does help you save on accommodation costs, and gives almost unlimited freedom. Sites to check include www.coolcampervans.com, www.wildhorizon.co.uk and www.justgo.uk.com.

Motoring Organisations

Large motoring organisations include the **Automobile Association** (☎ 0800 085 2721; www.theaa.com) and the **Royal Automobile Club** (☎ 0800 731 7090; www.rac.co.uk); annual membership starts at around £35, including 24-hour roadside breakdown assistance. A greener alternative is the **Environmental Transport Association** (☎ 0800 212 810; www.eta.co.uk); it provides all the usual services (breakdown assistance, roadside rescue, vehicle inspections etc) but *doesn't* campaign for more roads.

Parking

England is small, and people love their cars, so there's often not enough parking space to go round. Many cities have short-stay and long-stay car parks; the latter are cheaper though maybe less convenient. 'Park and Ride' systems allow you to park on the edge of the city then ride to the centre on regular buses provided for an all-in-one price.

Yellow lines (single or double) along the edge of the road indicate restrictions. Find the nearby sign that spells out when you can and can't park. In London and other big cities, traffic wardens operate with efficiency; if you park on the yellow lines at the wrong time, your car will be clamped or towed away, and it'll cost you £100 or more to get driving again. In some cities there are also red lines, which mean no stopping at all. Ever.

Purchase

If you're planning a long tour around England you may want to buy a vehicle. You can find a banger for £300, and a reasonable car for around £1000. If you want a campervan, expect to pay at least £2000 for something reliable. For more ideas and prices, pick up *Autotrader* magazine, or look at www.autotrader.co.uk.

To be on the road, all cars require the following:

- third party insurance – shop around, but expect to pay at least £300
- a registration form ('log book') – signed by both the buyer and seller
- a 'tax disc' – £90/160 for six/12 months (less for small engines)
- a Ministry of Transport (MOT) safety certificate – for cars over three years old (valid for one year).

It saves loads of hassle to buy a vehicle with a valid MOT certificate and tax disc; both remain with the car through change of ownership. Third-party insurance goes with the driver rather than the car, so you'll still have to arrange this.

Road Rules

A foreign driving licence is valid in England for up to 12 months. If you plan to bring a car from Europe, it's illegal to drive without (at least) third-party insurance. Some other important rules:

- drive on the left (!)
- wear fitted seat belts in cars
- wear crash helmets on motorcycles
- give way to your right at junctions and roundabouts

- always use the left-side lane on motorways and dual-carriageways, unless overtaking (although so many people ignore this rule, you'd think it didn't exist)
- don't use a mobile phone while driving unless it's fully hands-free (another rule frequently flouted).

Speed limits are 30mph (48km/h) in built-up areas, 60mph (96km/h) on main roads and 70mph (112km/h) on motorways and dual carriageways. Drinking and driving is taken very seriously; you're allowed a blood-alcohol level of 80mg/100mL and campaigners want it reduced to 50mg/100mL.

All drivers should read the *Highway Code*. It's often stocked by tourist offices, and it's available online at www.roads.dft.gov.uk /roadsafety (and, incidentally, often around number seven in national nonfiction bestseller tables).

HITCHING

Hitching is not as common as it used to be in England, maybe because more people have cars, maybe because few drivers give lifts any more. It's perfectly possible, however, if you don't mind long waits, although travellers should understand that they're taking a small but potentially serious risk, and we don't recommend it. If you decide to go by thumb, note that it's illegal to hitch on motorways; you must use approach roads or service stations.

LOCAL TRANSPORT

English cities usually have good local public-transport systems, although buses are often run by a confusing number of separate companies. The larger cities have tram and underground rail services too. Tourist offices can provide information, and more details are given in the city sections throughout this book.

Bus

All cities have good local bus networks year-round, and in rural areas popular with tourists (especially national parks) there are frequent bus services from Easter to September. Elsewhere in the countryside, bus timetables are designed to serve schools and industry, so there can be few midday and weekend services (and they may stop running in school holidays), or buses may link local villages to a market town on only one day each week.

It's always worth double-checking at a tourist office before planning your day's activities around a bus that you later find out only runs on Thursdays.

BUS PASSES

If you're taking a few local bus rides in a day of energetic sightseeing, ask about day-passes (with names like Day Rover, Wayfarer or Explorer), which will be cheaper than buying several single tickets. If you plan to linger longer in one area, three-day passes are a great bargain. Often they can be bought on your first bus, and may include local rail services. Passes are mentioned in the regional chapters, and it's always worth asking ticket clerks or bus drivers about your options.

POSTBUS

A postbus is a van on usual mail service that also carries passengers. Postbuses operate in rural areas (and some of the most scenic and remote parts of the country), and are especially useful for walkers and backpackers. For information and timetables contact **Royal Mail Postbus** (☎ 08457 740 740; www.royalmail .com/postbus).

Taxi

There are two main sorts of taxi in England: the famous black cabs (some carry advertising livery in other colours these days) that have meters and can be hailed in the street; and minicabs that can only be called by phone. In London and other big cities, taxis cost £2 to £3 per mile. In rural areas, it's about half this, which means when it's Sunday and you find that the next bus out of the charming town you've just hiked to is on Monday, a taxi can keep you moving. If you call **National Cabline** (☎ 0800 123444) from a landline phone, the service will pinpoint your location and transfer you to an approved local company.

See p769 for information about the dangers of using unlicensed minicabs.

TRAIN

For long-distance travel around England, trains are generally faster and more comfortable than coaches but can be more expensive, although with discount tickets they're competitive – and often take you through beautiful countryside. In the 1990s, rail travel had a bad reputation for delays and cancellations. By 2006, the situation had improved markedly, with around 85% of trains running on (or pretty close to) schedule – and the journeys that are delayed or cancelled mostly impact commuters rather than long-distance leisure travellers.

About 20 different companies operate train services in Britain (for example, First Great Western runs from London to Bath, GNER runs London to Leeds), while Network Rail operates track and stations. For passengers this system can be confusing, but information and ticket-buying services are increasingly centralised.

Your first stop should be **National Rail Enquiries** (☎ 08457 48 49 50; www.nationalrail.co.uk), the nationwide timetable and fare information service. The site also advertises special offers, and has real-time links to station departure boards, so you can see if your train is on time (or not). Once you've found the journey you need, links take you to the relevant train operator or to two centralised ticketing services (www.thetrainline.com and www.Qjump .co.uk) to buy the ticket. These websites can be confusing at first (you always have to state an approximate preferred time and day of travel, even if you don't mind *when* you go), but with a little delving around they can offer some real bargains.

You can also buy train tickets on the spot at stations, which is fine for short journeys, but discount tickets for longer trips are usually not available here and must be bought in advance by phone or online.

Classes

There are two classes of rail travel: first and standard. First class costs around 50% more than standard and, except on very crowded trains, is not really worth it. However, at weekends some train operators offer 'upgrades': for an extra £10 to £15 on top of your standard class fare you can enjoy more comfort and leg room.

Costs & Reservations

For short journeys (under about 50 miles), it's usually best to buy tickets on the spot at rail stations. You may get a choice of express or stopping service – the latter is obviously slower, but can be cheaper, and may take you through charming countryside or grotty suburbs.

For longer journeys, on-the-spot fares are always available, but tickets are much cheaper

if bought in advance. (Essentially, the earlier you book, the cheaper it gets.) Advance purchase usually gets you a reserved seat too. The cheapest fares are nonrefundable though, so if you miss your train you'll have to buy a new ticket.

If you have to change trains, or use two or more train operators, you still buy one ticket – valid for the whole of your journey. The main railcards are also accepted by all operators.

If you buy by phone or website, you can have the ticket posted to you (UK addresses only), or collect it at the originating station on the day of travel, either at the ticket desk (get there with time to spare, as queues can be long) or via automatic machines.

For short or long trips, fares are usually cheaper outside 'peak' travel times ('peak' is when everyone else is trying to get to/from work). It's worth avoiding Fridays and Sundays too, as fares are higher on these busy days.

The main fare types are 'open', 'saver' and 'advance', although there are sometimes variations within these main categories (eg 'super-saver' or 'extra-advance') – and just to keep you on your toes, the different train companies sometimes use different brand names for these products (eg 'sunshine-saver' or 'capital-advance'). The main features of each type are outlined below (with the varying prices of London to York tickets given by way of example).

If you're making a return journey (ie coming back on the same route), open return fares are usually just under double the single fare, while saver returns are often just a few pounds more than saver singles. Advance return fares are sometimes hard to find, as an increasing number of train operators have followed the lead set by low-cost airlines and offer advance single fares only. This gives you more flexibility and can turn up some amazing bargains, with two advance singles easily undercutting the saver return price.

Open Available on the spot or in advance. Travel any time; valid for a month. London–York single/return £83/167.

Saver Available on the spot or in advance. Day of outward travel is fixed, but you can change the time. Changing the day of travel costs £5. Return any day/time. Valid for one month. Some restrictions apply (eg no peak travel). London York single/return £71/77

Advance Available in advance only, up to 6pm the day before travel. Valid only on a specified date and time. The

TRANSPORT

BIKES ON TRAINS

Bicycles can be taken on most long-distance train journeys for £1 to £3, but space limitations and ridiculously complicated advance-booking regulations often makes this difficult. It really seems as if the train operators don't want customers, although with persistence you can usually get where you want, especially if you don't travel at peak times. Start with **National Rail Enquiries** (☎ 08457 48 49 50; www.nationalrail.co.uk) and have a big cup of coffee or stress-reliever handy.

On local trains, outside peak times, and shorter trips in rural areas there's generally much less trouble; bikes can be taken free of charge on a first-come-first-served basis. Even so, there may be space limits.

A final warning: when railways are being repaired, cancelled trains are replaced by buses – and they won't take bikes.

earlier you buy, the cheaper the ticket – especially if you travel outside peak times. Non refundable. Singles from £10 to £30.

Children under five travel free on trains; those aged between five and 15 pay half price, except on tickets already heavily discounted. Seniors also get discounts, but again not on already heavily discounted fares.

Train Passes

Local train passes usually cover rail networks around a city (many include bus travel too), and are mentioned in the individual city sections throughout this book.

If you're staying in England for a while, passes known as 'railcards' are available. They cost around £20 (valid for one year, available from major stations) and get you a 33% discount on most train fares. On the Family and Network cards, children get a 60% discount, and the fee is easily repaid in a couple of journeys. Proof of age and a passport photo may be required. For full details see www .railcard.co.uk.

Family Railcard Covers up to four adults and four children travelling together.

Senior Railcard For anyone over 60.

Young Person's Railcard You must be 16 to 25, or a full-time UK student.

A Disabled Person's Railcard costs £14. You can get an application from stations or from the railcard website. Call ☎ 0191-281 8103 for more details.

If you're concentrating your travels on southeast England (eg London to Dover, Weymouth, Cambridge or Oxford) a Network Card covers up to four adults travel-

ling together outside peak times. For details see p163.

For country-wide travel, BritRail Passes are good value, but they're only for visitors from overseas and not available in England. They must be bought in your country of origin from a specialist travel agency. There are many Brit-Rail variants, each available in three different versions: for England only; for the whole of Britain (England, Wales and Scotland); and for the UK and Ireland. Below is an outline of the main options, quoting adult prices. Children's passes are usually half price (or free with some adult passes), and seniors get discounts too. For about 30% extra you can upgrade to first class. Other deals include a rail pass combined with the use of a hire car, or travel in Britain combined with one Eurostar journey. For more details see www.britrail.com.

BritRail England Consecutive Unlimited travel on all trains in England for four, eight, 15, 22 or 30 days, for US$175/250/375/475/560. Anyone getting their money's worth out of the last pass should earn some sort of endurance award.

BritRail England Flexipass Now you don't have to get on a train every day to get full value. Your options are four days of unlimited travel in England within a 60-day period for US$220, eight in 60 days for US$320, or 15 in 60 days for US$480.

If you don't (or can't) buy a BritRail pass, an All Line Rover (£375/565 for seven/14 days) gives unlimited travel anywhere on the national rail network and can be purchased in England, by anyone. Of the other international passes, Eurail cards are not accepted in England, and InterRail cards are only valid if bought in another mainland European country.

Health Dr Caroline Evans

CONTENTS

England is a healthy place to travel, and the National Health Service (NHS) provides an excellent service, free on the point of delivery, which – although Brits may complain – is better than most other countries offer. Across the country, hygiene standards are high (despite what your nose tells you on a crowded tube train) and there are no unusual diseases to worry about. Your biggest risks will be from overdoing activities – physical, chemical or other.

BEFORE YOU GO

No immunisations are mandatory for visiting England.

European Economic Area (EEA) nationals can obtain free emergency treatment in England on presentation of a European Health Insurance Card (EHIC) – which has replaced the old E111 form – validated in their home country.

Reciprocal arrangements between the UK and some other countries around the world (including Australia) allow their residents to receive free emergency medical treatment and subsidised dental care at hospitals, general practitioners (GPs) and dentists. For details, see the Department of Health's website: www.doh.gov.uk, then follow links to 'Policy & Guidance', 'International' and 'Overseas Visitors'.

Regardless of nationality, anyone will receive free emergency treatment at accident and emergency departments of NHS hospitals. Travel insurance, however, is advisable as it offers greater flexibility over where and how you're treated, and covers expenses for emergency repatriation.

Chemists and pharmacies can advise on minor ailments such as sore throats and earaches. In large cities, there's always at least one chemist open 24 hours.

Internet Resources

Lonely Planet's website (www.lonelyplanet.com) has links to the World Health Organization (WHO) and the US Centers for Disease Control & Prevention. Other good sites include the following:

www.who.int/ith WHO International Travel and Health.
www.ageconcern.org.uk Advice on travel for the elderly.
www.mariestopes.org.uk Women's health and contraception.
www.fco.gov.uk/travel For Brits going abroad, but useful for incomers.
www.mdtravelhealth.com Worldwide recommendations, updated daily.

IN TRANSIT
Deep Vein Thrombosis (DVT)

Deep Vein Thrombosis (DVT) refers to blood clots that form in the legs during plane flights, chiefly because of prolonged immobility. The longer the flight, the greater the risk. The chief symptom is swelling or pain in the foot, ankle or calf. When a blood clot travels to the lungs, it may cause chest pain and breathing difficulties.

To prevent DVT on long flights you should walk about the cabin, contract and release leg muscles while sitting, drink plenty of fluids and avoid alcohol.

Jet Lag

To avoid jet lag (common when crossing more than five time zones), try drinking plenty of nonalcoholic fluids and eating light meals. Upon arrival, get exposure to natural sunlight and readjust your schedule (for meals, sleep and so on) as soon as possible.

NATIONAL HEALTH WEBSITES

If you're visiting England from overseas, it's a good idea to consult your government's travel health website before departure. Try the following:

Australia (www.dfat.gov.au/travel)
Canada (www.travelhealth.gc.ca)
USA (www.cdc.gov/travel/)

HEALTH

IN ENGLAND
Sunburn
In summer in England, even when there's cloud cover, it's possible to get sunburnt quickly – especially if you're on water. Use sunscreen, wear a hat and cover up with a shirt and trousers.

Water
Tap water in England is always safe unless there's a sign to the contrary (eg on trains). Don't drink straight from streams in the countryside – you never know what's upstream.

Women's Health
Emotional stress, exhaustion and travel through time zones can contribute to an upset in the menstrual pattern. If using oral contraceptives, remember some antibiotics, diarrhoea and vomiting can stop them from working.

If you're already pregnant, travel is usually possible, but you should always consult your doctor. The most risky times for travel are the first 12 weeks of pregnancy and after 30 weeks.

Glossary

agister – someone paid to care for stock

aka – also known as

almshouse – accommodation for the aged or needy

bailey – outermost wall of a castle

bairn – baby (northern England)

banger – old, cheap car (colloquial)

bangers – sausages (colloquial)

bap – bun

bar – gate (York, and some other northern cities)

barbican – extended gateway in a castle designed to make entry difficult for unwanted guests

beck – stream (northern England)

bent – not altogether legal (slang)

bevvied – drunk (colloquial)

bevvy – drink (originally from northern England)

bill – restaurant check

billion – the British billion is a million million (unlike the American billion – a thousand million)

bitter – ale; a type of beer

black pudding – type of sausage made from dried blood and other ingredients

blatherskite – boastful or talkative person (northern England)

bloke – man

bodge job – poor-quality repair

bonnet (of car) – hood

boot (of car) – trunk

bridleway – path that can be used by walkers, horse riders and cyclists

Brummie – native of Birmingham

bum – backside (not tramp, layabout etc)

bus – local bus; see also *coach*

BYO – bring your own

caff – abbreviated form of café

cairn – pile of stones marking path, junction or peak

canny – good, great, wise (northern England)

capital – head of column

cenotaph – monument, memorial to person/s whose remains lie elsewhere

cheers – goodbye; thanks; also a drinking toast

chemist – pharmacist

chine – valley-like fissure leading to the sea (southern England)

chips – sliced, deep-fried potatoes, eaten hot (what Americans call 'fries')

circus – junction of several streets, usually circular

clunch – chalk (used in connection with chalk walls in building)

coach – long-distance bus

coaching inn – inn along a stagecoach route where horses were changed in the days before trains and motor transport

coasteering – adventurous activity that involves making your way around a rocky coastline by climbing, scrambling, jumping or swimming

cob – mixture of mud and straw for building

cot – small bed for a baby ('crib' to Americans)

couchette – sleeping berth in a train or ferry

courgette – green vegetable ('zucchini' to Americans)

court – courtyard

crack – good conversation, or good times (anglicised version of Gaelic 'craic')

cream tea – cup of tea and a scone loaded with jam and cream

crisps – thinly sliced and salted pieces of potato eaten cold

croft – plot of land with adjoining house worked by the occupiers

dear – expensive

DIY – do-it-yourself, ie home improvements

dolmen – chartered tomb

donkey engine – small (sometimes portable) engine to drive machinery

dosh – money, wealth

dough – money

downs – rolling upland, characterised by lack of trees

dram – whisky measure

duvet – quilt replacing sheets and blankets ('doona' to Australians)

EH – English Heritage

en-suite room – hotel room with private attached bathroom (ie shower, basin and toilet)

Essex – derogatory adjective (as in 'Essex girl'), meaning showy/tarty

EU – European Union

evensong – daily evening service (Church of England)

fag – cigarette; also boring task

fagged – exhausted

fanny – female genitals, not backside

fell race – tough running race through hills or moors

fen – drained or marshy low-lying flat land

fiver – five-pound note

flat – apartment

flip-flops – plastic sandals with a single strap over toes ('thongs' to Australians)
footpath – path through countryside and between houses, not beside a road (that's called a 'pavement')

gaffer – boss or foreman
gate – street (York, and some other northern cities)
ginnel – alleyway (Yorkshire)
graft – work (not corruption)
grand – one thousand
greasy spoon – cheap café
grockle – tourist
gutted – very disappointed
guv, guvner – from governor, a respectful term of address for owner or boss; can sometimes be used ironically

hart – deer
hammered – drunk
HI – Hostelling International (organisation)
hire – rent
hosepipe – garden hose
hotel – accommodation with food and bar, not always open to passing trade
Huguenots – French Protestants

inn – pub with accommodation

jam – fruit conserve often spread on bread
jelly – sweet desert of flavoured gelatine
jumper – woollen item of clothing worn on torso ('sweater' to Americans)

kippers – salted and smoked fish, traditionally herring
kirk – church (northern England)

lager lout – see *yob*
lass – young woman (northern England)
ley – clearing
lift – machine for carrying people up and down in large buildings ('elevator' to Americans)
lock – part of a canal or river that can be closed off and the water levels changed to raise or lower boats
lolly – money; can also mean candy on a stick (possibly frozen)
lorry – truck
love – term of address, not necessarily to someone likeable

machair – grass- and wildflower-covered sand dunes
mad – insane, not angry
manky – low quality, rotten, mouldy
Martello tower – small, circular tower used for coastal defence
mate – friend of any gender; also term of address, usually male-to-male

midge – mosquito-like insect
motorway – major road linking cities (equivalent to 'interstate' or 'freeway')
motte – mound on which a castle was built

naff – inferior, in poor taste
nappies – worn by babies before they're toilet trained ('diapers' to Americans)
neeps – turnips (northern England)
NT – National Trust
NYMR – North Yorkshire Moors Railway

oast house – building containing a kiln for drying hops
off-license ('offie') – carry-out alcoholic drinks shop
OS – Ordnance Survey
owlers – smugglers

p (pronounced 'pee') – pence (ie 2p is 'two p' not 'two pence' or 'tuppence')
pargeting – decorative stucco plasterwork
pele – fortified house
pint – beer (as in 'let me buy you a pint')
Pimms – popular English spirit mixed with lemonade, mint and fresh fruit
piscina – basin for priests to wash their hands
pissed – drunk (not angry)
pissed off – angry
pitch – playing field
ponce – ostentatious or effeminate male; also to borrow (usually permanently)
pop – fizzy drink (northern England)
postbus – minibus delivering the mail, also carrying passengers
provost – mayor
punter – customer

quid – pound

ramble – short easy walk
rebud – heraldic device suggesting the name of its owner
reiver – warrior (historic term – northern England)
return ticket – round-trip ticket
roll-up – roll-your-own cigarette
RSPB – Royal Society for the Protection of Birds
RSPCA – Royal Society for the Prevention of Cruelty to Animals
rubber – eraser; also (and less commonly) condom
rubbish bin – what Americans call a 'garbage can'
rugger – rugby union

sarnie – sandwich (northern England)
sarsen – boulder, a geological remnant usually found in chalky areas (sometimes used in Neolithic constructions eg Stonehenge and Avebury)
sett – tartan pattern

shag – have sex (slang); also a tough or tiring task (colloquial)

shagged – tired

sheila-na-gig – Celtic fertility symbol of a woman with exaggerated genitalia, often seen carved in stone on churches and castles. Rare in England, found mainly in the Marches, along the border with Wales.

shout – to buy a group of people drinks, usually reciprocated

shut – partially covered passage

single ticket – one-way ticket

sixth-form college – further-education college

Sloane Ranger – wealthy, superficial but well-connected young person

snicket – alleyway (York)

snog – long, drawn-out kiss (not just a peck on the cheek)

spondulicks – money

SSSI – Site of Special Scientific Interest

stone – unit of weight equivalent to 14lb or 6.35kg

subway – underpass (for pedestrians)

sweets – what Americans call 'candy' and Australians call 'lollies'

ta – thanks

tatties – potatoes

thwaite – clearing in a forest (northern England)

TIC – Tourist Information Centre

ton – one hundred (slang)

tor – pointed hill (Celtic)

torch – flashlight

Tory – Conservative (political party)

towpath – path running beside a river or canal, where horses once towed barges

trainers – running/tennis shoes

traveller – nomadic person (traditional and New Age hippy types)

tron – public weighbridge

twit – foolish (sometimes annoying) person

twitcher – obsessive birdwatcher

twitten – passage, small lane

tube – London's underground railway system (colloquial term)

Underground – London's underground railway system

VAT – value-added tax, levied on most goods and services, currently 17.5%

verderer – officer upholding law and order in the royal forests

wanker – stupid/worthless person (offensive slang)

wide boy – ostentatious go-getter, usually on the make

wolds – open, rolling countryside

YHA – Youth Hostels Association

yob – hooligan

GLOSSARY OF RELIGIOUS ARCHITECTURE

abbey – monastery of monks or nuns

aisle – passageway or open space along either side of a church's *nave*

ambulatory – processional *aisle* at the east end of a cathedral, behind the altar

apse – semicircular or rectangular area for clergy, traditionally at the east end of the church

baptistry – separate area of a church used for baptisms

barrel vault – semicircular arched roof

boss – covering for the meeting point of the ribs in a *vaulted* roof

brass – memorial common in medieval churches consisting of a brass plate set into the floor or a tomb

buttress – vertical support for a wall; see also *flying buttress*

campanile – free-standing belfry or bell tower

chancel – eastern end of the church, usually reserved for choir and clergy

chantry – *chapel* established by a donor for use in their name after death

chapel – small, more private shrine or area of worship off the main body of the church

chapel of ease – *chapel* built for those who lived too far away from the parish church

chapter house – building in a cathedral *close* where the dean meets with the chapter; clergy who run the cathedral

chevet – *chapels* radiating out in a semicircular sweep

choir – area in the church where the choir is seated

clearstory – see *clerestory*

clerestory – a wall of windows above a church's *triforium*

cloister – covered walkway linking the church with adjacent monastic buildings

close – buildings grouped around a cathedral

collegiate – church with a chapter of canons and prebendaries, but not a cathedral

corbel – stone or wooden projection from a wall supporting a beam or arch

crossing – intersection of the *nave* and *transepts* in a church

flying buttress – supporting *buttress* in the form of one side of an open arch

font – basin used for baptisms, usually towards the west end of a church, often in a separate *baptistry*

frater – common or dining room in a medieval monastery

lady chapel – *chapel*, usually at the east end of a cathedral, dedicated to the Virgin Mary

lancet – pointed window in Early English style

lierne vault – *vault* containing many tertiary ribs

minster – church connected to a monastery
misericord – hinged choir seat with a bracket (often elaborately carved) that can be leant against

nave – main body of the church at the western end, where the congregation gather

presbytery – eastern area of the *chancel* beyond the choir, where the clergy operate
precincts – see *close*
priory – religious house governed by a prior
pulpit – raised box where the priest gives sermons

quire – medieval term for *choir*

refectory – monastic dining room
reredos – literally 'behind the back'; backdrop to an altar
rood – archaic word for cross (in churches)

rood screen – screen carrying a *rood* or crucifix, which separates the *nave* from the *chancel*

squint – angled opening in a wall or pillar to allow a view of a church's altar

transepts – north–south projections from a church's *nave*, which is often added later than the original construction. It gives the church a cruciform (cross-shaped plan).
triforium – internal wall passage above a church's arcade and below the *clerestory*; behind the triforium is the 'blind' space above the side *aisle*

undercroft – vaulted underground room or cellar

vault – roof with arched ribs, usually in a decorative pattern; see also *barrel vault* and *lierne vault*
vestry – robing room, where the parson/priest keeps his robes and puts them on

Behind the Scenes

THIS BOOK

This 4th edition of England was researched by David Else (coordinating author), Jolyon Attwooll, Charlotte Beech, Oliver Berry, Laetitia Clapton, Fionn Davenport and Etain O'Carroll. The 3rd edition was also researched by Becky Ohlsen, Martin Hughes and Sam Martin. This guidebook was commissioned in Lonely Planet's London office and produced by the following:

Commissioning Editor Clifton Wilkinson, Sam Trafford
Coordinating Editor Justin Flynn
Coordinating Cartographer Joshua Geoghegan
Coordinating Layout Designer Jacqueline McLeod
Managing Editor Melanie Dankel
Managing Cartographer Mark Griffiths
Assisting Editors Brooke Clark, Kate Cody, Adrienne Costanzo, Kate Daly, Kim Hutchins, Charlotte Orr, Susan Patterson, Helen Yeates
Assisting Cartographers David Connolly, Diana Duggan, Tony Fankhauser, Andrew Smith
Assisting Layout Designers Wibowo Rusli
Cover Designer Mary Nelson Parker
Project Manager Rachel Imeson

Thanks to Trent Paton, Dr Caroline Evans, Jacqui Saunders, Jim Hsu, Celia Wood, Sally Darmody, Paul Piaia, Lyahna Spencer

THANKS
DAVID ELSE

As always, massive appreciation goes to my wife Corinne, for not minding when I lock myself away for 12 hours at a time, and for bringing coffee when it gets nearer 16 hours. Thanks also to the co-authors of this book; my name goes down as coordinating author, but I couldn't have done it without Laetitia, Charlie, Fionn, Oliver, Etain and Jolyon. Thanks also to the various Arts, Music, Sport and Literature specialists who helped me get my facts straight: Heather Dickson, Sam Trafford, Lydia Cook, Roy Thompson, Sarah Johnstone, Tom Masters, Tom Cook, Tom Parkinson and Tom Hall (surely putting us over the legal Tom quota?). And finally, thanks to my commissioning editors in London – Sam Trafford, Michala Green, Cliff Wilkinson – and to all the friendly faces in the editorial, cartography, layout and design departments at LP Melbourne who helped bring this book to final fruition.

JOLYON ATTWOOLL

I was delighted to get the chance to update the Midlands chapter – thanks to Sam Trafford for letting me have a go. My family in Coventry gave their usual solid back-up and support. Special mention should go to my dad, whose enthusiasm for the area and its history has been infectious. Friends who have kept me company on the way include Alex Boughton, Ruth Gleeson in Birmingham, Paul Deacon (a big help with Stratford), Simon Sheridan and Julie Whiteman, as well as my very entertaining flat-mates Olly Ford and Manel Heredero. Thanks also to all the people who helped me in the tourist offices, especially Robert Scoffings who brightened a snowy Sunday in Nottingham. David Else, Cliff Wilkinson and Mark Griffiths have all dealt with my queries with good humoured efficiency.

CHARLOTTE BEECH

Hearty thanks go to Sam Trafford for first involving me in this book, and to David Else and Clifton

---

THE LONELY PLANET STORY

The story begins with a classic travel adventure: Tony and Maureen Wheeler's 1972 journey across Europe and Asia to Australia. There was no useful information about the overland trail then, so Tony and Maureen published the first Lonely Planet guidebook to meet a growing need.

From a kitchen table, Lonely Planet has grown to become the largest independent travel publisher in the world, with offices in Melbourne (Australia), Oakland (USA) and London (UK). Today Lonely Planet guidebooks cover the globe. There is an ever-growing list of books and information in a variety of media. Some things haven't changed. The main aim is still to make it possible for adventurous ers to get out there – to explore and better understand the world.

At Lonely Planet we believe ers can make a positive contribution to the countries they visit – if they respect their host communities and spend their money wisely. Every year 5% of company profit is donated to charities around the world.

Wilkinson for their support in seeing it through. Gratitude also goes to my various visitors and co-conspirators on the road, especially husband Alex, company through Cambridgeshire Maryanne, extra pair of eyes John and also para Gilma, *por todos los almuerzos y consejitos sabios*. Invaluable tips and advice were offered by Ruth Toulson in Cambridge, Vicqui Stuart Jones in Southend, Jake Collins in Brighton and a multitude of excellent tourist offices throughout the Marches, Eastern England and Southeast Coast.

OLIVER BERRY

A tip of the hat to everyone who helped me out on the roads of Britain this time round. Top of the list as always is Susie Berry, who made it all possible, and to Jenks, the other half of the Ark who made sure things stayed on an even keel. Thanks also to the Hobo, o-region, Twinkletoes, Jonathan Ives, Mr Butler, Mr S. Stevens, and to David Else, Sam Trafford and Clifton Wilkinson, and to Mark Griffiths and everyone on the map team over in Melbourne.

LAETITIA CLAPTON

Thanks to the many helpful staff in the tourist offices, to the lovely British people I met along the way, to the Lonely Planet London office for their many suggestions, to Sam Trafford for commissioning me and to Michala Green, David Else and Clifton Wilkinson for ongoing support. Huge thanks to the very busy Jimmy Carr for the interesting and entertaining interview. Thanks also to Aaron Lamb, Sarah Tay, Peter Morris, Lisa Oliver and Paula Hardy. Finally thanks to Nathan, for always being there.

FIONN DAVENPORT

As always, getting the work done is a community effort. In Leeds, thanks so much to Amanda Warburton, who opened plenty of doors in Yorkshire;

thanks also to Kay Hyde, who made York such a pleasurable trip. A big thank you to the Newcastle-Gateshead tourist office, who explained a bunch of things to me, not least the importance of putting Newcastle and Gateshead into one word; cheers to the folks at Lancashire Tourism who took such good care of me; and, as always, a debt to everyone in Liverpool who made my stay such a comfortable one. Thanks to David Else for piloting this ship so expertly and, finally, thanks to everyone in the London office – Cliff, I promise I'll devote myself to the joys of the industrial northeast.

ETAIN O'CARROLL

Once again I have to offer my huge thanks to all the ladies in the tourist offices across my region who patiently answered endless questions and provided me with truckloads of brochures and flyers. Thanks too to Geddy McCormack for the low down on Henley, to Will Swainson and his lovely wife for the inside deal on eating out in Cheltenham, to Mark for numerous dinners out while attempting to sample every Oxford restaurant, and to David Else for holding the show together when we all got very confused. Thanks to Sam, Michala and Cliff at LP for providing a remarkably smooth commissioning and editorial process and to Mark Griffiths in Melbourne for giving me the electronic go ahead.

OUR READERS

Many thanks to the travellers who used the last edition and wrote to us with helpful hints, useful advice and interesting anecdotes:

Damian Adcock, Richard Allen, Trygve Anderson, Catherine Angus, Marilyn Atamian, Don Bacon, Robin Baggot, Susanna Baird, Joel Barnett, Astrid Bergner, Rosemary Blockley, Jason Brack, Robert Braiden, Michael Brant, Vanessa Brierley, Zoe Brigley, Jerome

SEND US YOUR FEEDBACK

We love to hear from travellers – your comments keep us on our toes and help make our books better. Our well-travelled team reads every word on what you loved or loathed about this book. Although we cannot reply individually to postal submissions, we always guarantee that your feedback goes straight to the appropriate authors, in time for the next edition. Each person who sends us information is thanked in the next edition – and the most useful submissions are rewarded with a free book.

To send us your updates – and find out about Lonely Planet events, newsletters and travel news – visit our award-winning website: **www.lonelyplanet.com/contact**.

Note: we may edit, reproduce and incorporate your comments in Lonely Planet products such as guidebooks, websites and digital products, so let us know if you don't want your comments reproduced or your name acknowledged. For a copy of our privacy policy visit www.lonelyplanet.com/privacy.

Brown, Virginia Buehler, Tony Cahill, Ricky Chaggar, Natalie Cohen, Rowan Crawford, Alan Dangerfield, John Davys, Dorothy Espe, Mike Ferguson, Anneliese Frank, Geer Furtjes, Tapan Ganguli, Lewis Goulding, Anna Guttman, Stuart Hall, Sandra Herms, Lora Hish, June Janh, Magnus Jánssón, Patrick Jones, Alex Julyan, Andrew Kwok, Jamie Leveille, Cathy Lowne, Catherine Macfarlane, Robert Maguire, Ash Mather, Trevor Mazzucchelli, Ashley Mead, Paul Mitchell, Caroline Molenaar, Menendez Monica, David Mulhall, Scott Murdoch, Christopher Neal, Boonsin Ng, Paul O'Dwyer, Anthony Oldfield, Xavier Panades, Mr & Mrs Pearce, Manuela Pichler, Timothy Pollington, William Ponissi, Peter Reed, Arthur Riedel, Valentina Riva, Dean Sabella, Martin Scheitz, Eric Schluessel, Greg Schuurman, Andi Scott, Michaela Scott, Nichola Scott, Ernie Searle, Martin Shortall, Rob Smallwood, James Stacey, Steve Tandy, Nienke Ten, Susanne Ueberhuber, John & Elizabeth Venn, P Williamson, Andrew Young

ACKNOWLEDGMENTS

Many thanks to the following for the use of their content:

London Underground Map © Transport for London 2006

The Central London Bus Map and Tourist Attractions Map © Transport for London 2006

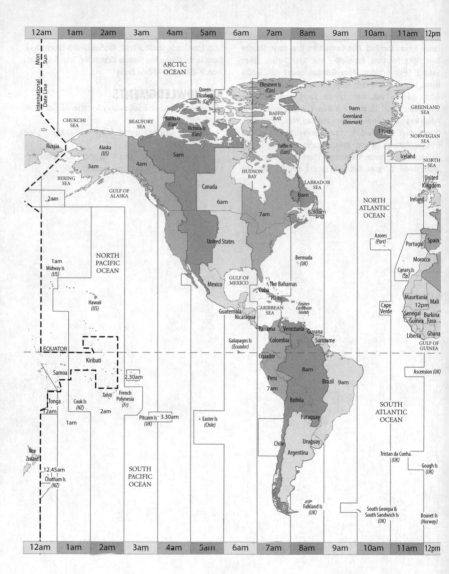

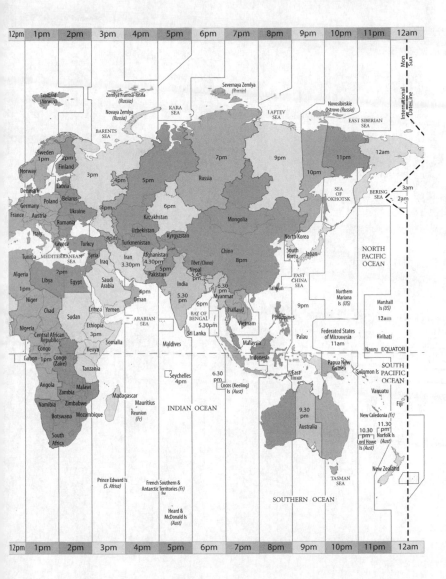

Index

000 Map pages
000 Photograph pages

000 Map pages
000 Photograph pages

820

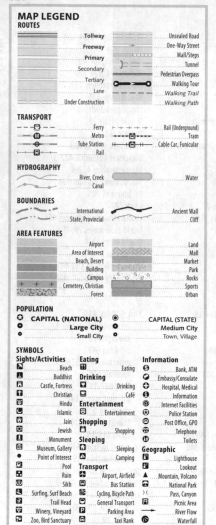

MAP LEGEND

ROUTES

Tollway		Unsealed Road
Freeway		One-Way Street
Primary		Mall/Steps
Secondary		Tunnel
Tertiary		Pedestrian Overpass
Lane		Walking Tour
Under Construction		Walking Trail
		Walking Path

TRANSPORT

Ferry		Rail (Underground)
Metro		Tram
Tube Station		Cable Car, Funicular
Rail		

HYDROGRAPHY

River, Creek		Water
Canal		

BOUNDARIES

International		Ancient Wall
State, Provincial		Cliff

AREA FEATURES

Airport		Land
Area of Interest		Mall
Beach, Desert		Market
Building		Park
Campus		Rocks
Cemetery, Christian		Sports
Forest		Urban

POPULATION

✪ CAPITAL (NATIONAL)	◉ CAPITAL (STATE)
● Large City	● Medium City
● Small City	● Town, Village

SYMBOLS

Sights/Activities
- Beach
- Buddhist
- Castle, Fortress
- Christian
- Hindu
- Islamic
- Jain
- Jewish
- Monument
- Museum, Gallery
- Point of Interest
- Pool
- Ruin
- Sikh
- Surfing, Surf Beach
- Trail Head
- Winery, Vineyard
- Zoo, Bird Sanctuary

Eating
- Eating

Drinking
- Drinking
- Café

Entertainment
- Entertainment

Shopping
- Shopping

Sleeping
- Sleeping
- Camping

Transport
- Airport, Airfield
- Bus Station
- Cycling, Bicycle Path
- General Transport
- Parking Area
- Taxi Rank

Information
- Bank, ATM
- Embassy/Consulate
- Hospital, Medical
- Information
- Internet Facilities
- Police Station
- Post Office, GPO
- Telephone
- Toilets

Geographic
- Lighthouse
- Lookout
- Mountain, Volcano
- National Park
- Pass, Canyon
- Picnic Area
- River Flow
- Waterfall

LONELY PLANET OFFICES

Australia
Head Office
Locked Bag 1, Footscray, Victoria 3011
☎ 03 8379 8000, fax 03 8379 8111
talk2us@lonelyplanet.com.au

USA
150 Linden St, Oakland, CA 94607
☎ 510 893 8555, toll free 800 275 8555
fax 510 893 8572
info@lonelyplanet.com

UK
72–82 Rosebery Ave,
Clerkenwell, London EC1R 4RW
☎ 020 7841 9000, fax 020 7841 9001
go@lonelyplanet.co.uk

Published by Lonely Planet Publications Pty Ltd
ABN 36 005 607 983

© Lonely Planet Publications Pty Ltd 2007

© photographers as indicated 2007

Printed through The Bookmaker International Ltd
Printed in China

Although the authors and Lonely Planet have taken all reasonable care in preparing this book, we make no warranty about the accuracy or completeness of its content and, to the maximum extent permitted, disclaim all liability arising from its use.

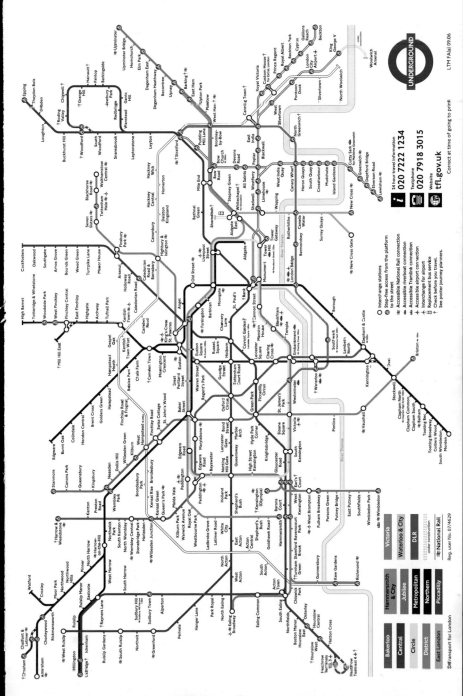

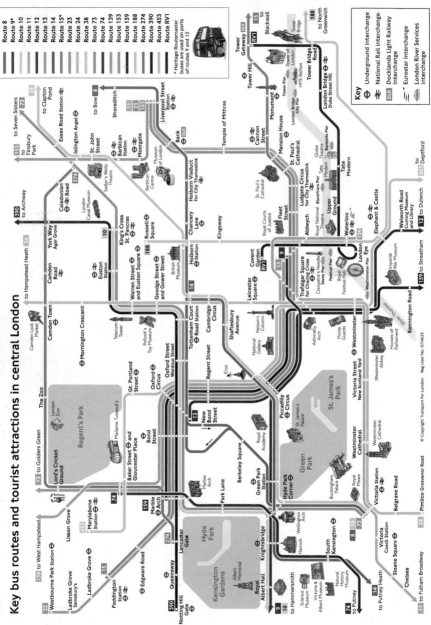

Key bus routes and tourist attractions in central London

Key
- Route 8
- Route 9*
- Route 10
- Route 11
- Route 12
- Route 13
- Route 14
- Route 15*
- Route 23
- Route 24
- Route 38
- Route 73
- Route 74
- Route 139
- Route 153
- Route 159
- Route 188
- Route 274
- Route 390
- Route 453
- Route RV1

*Heritage Routemaster buses are used on parts of routes 9 and 15

Key
- ⊖ Underground interchange
- ≥ National Rail interchange
- DLR Docklands Light Railway interchange
- 🚆 Eurostar interchange
- 🚢 London River Services interchange

© Copyright Transport for London Reg User No 07/4629